Evolution, Genes, and Behavior

ATKINSON & HILGARD'S
INTRODUCTION
TO PSYCHOLOGY

Fourteenth Edition

Edward E. Smith
University of Michigan

Susan Nolen-Hoeksema
University of Michigan

Barbara L. Fredrickson
University of Michigan

Geoffrey R. Loftus
University of Washington

Daryl J. Bem, Contributor
Cornell University

Stephen Maren, Contributor
University of Michigan

THOMSON
™
WADSWORTH

Australia • Canada • Mexico • Singapore • Spain
United Kingdom • United States

THOMSON
WADSWORTH

Publisher: Vicki Knight
Psychology Editor: Marianne Taflinger
Development Editor: Kate Barnes
Assistant Editor: Jennifer Wilkinson
Editorial Assistant: Nicole Root
Technology Project Manager: Darin Derstine
Marketing Manager: Lori Grebe
Marketing Assistant: Laurel Anderson
Advertising Project Manager: Brian Chaffee
Project Manager, Editorial Production: Teri Hyde
Print/Media Buyer: Kris Waller
Permissions Editor: Joohee Lee
Production Service: Graphic World Publishing Services

Text Designer: Jeanne Calabrese
Art Editor: Lisa Torri
Photo Researcher: Meyer's Photo-Art
Copy Editor: Joy Matkowski
Illustrator: Rolin Graphics
Cover Designer: Cheryl Carrington
Cover Image: © 2002 Artists Rights Society (ARS), New York / ADAGP, Paris
Cover Printer: CTPS
Compositor: Graphic World, Inc.
Printer: CTPS

Printed in China
6 7 8 9 09 08 07

For more information about our products, contact us at:
Thomson Learning Academic Resource Center
1-800-423-0563
For permission to use material from this text, contact us by:
Phone: 1-800-730-2214   **Fax:** 1-800-730-2215
Web: http://www.thomsonrights.com

Library of Congress Control Number: 2002110772

Student Edition: ISBN-13: 978-0-15-505069-3
Student Edition: ISBN-10: 0-15-505069-9
Instructor's Edition: ISBN-13: 978-0-534-56804-7
Instructor's Edition: ISBN-10: 0-534-56804-1

Wadsworth/Thomson Learning
10 Davis Drive
Belmont, CA 94002-3098
USA

Asia
Thomson Learning
5 Shenton Way #01-01
UIC Building
Singapore 068808

Australia
Nelson Thomson Learning
102 Dodds Street
South Melbourne, Victoria 3205
Australia

Canada
Nelson Thomson Learning
1120 Birchmount Road
Toronto, Ontario M1K 5G4
Canada

Europe/Middle East/Africa
Thomson Learning
High Holborn House
50/51 Bedford Row
London WC1R 4LR
United Kingdom

Latin America
Thomson Learning
Seneca, 53
Colonia Polanco
11560 Mexico D.F.
Mexico

Spain
Paraninfo Thomson Learning
Calle/Magallanes, 25
28015 Madrid, Spain

PREFACE

The 14th edition of *Atkinson & Hilgard's Introduction to Psychology* marks a new era in this classic introductory psychology textbook. The long-standing authors of the book, Smith, Bem, and Nolen-Hoeksema, are joined by three new authors, Barbara L. Fredrickson and Stephen Maren of the University of Michigan and Geoffrey Loftus of the University of Washington. Fredrickson, Maren, and Loftus bring a fresh new perspective to the text, although they are certainly not new to psychology—all are internationally respected researchers and teachers. Our author team now includes experts who span the broad range of our field, from biological psychology, cognition, and perception to social and personality psychology, and from normal development to psychopathology. All of the authors are award-winning researchers who provide authoritative evaluations of the major issues and findings in psychology.

THE CLASSIC AND THE CONTEMPORARY

The classic studies that are the foundation of psychology are critical for students to understand and appreciate. We continue to cover these studies, emphasizing their impact on the field and on our daily lives. A tremendous amount of innovative work is being done in contemporary psychology, however. In the 14th edition, we cover the most promising new work in psychology, including developments in cognitive neuroscience and research on the brain and behavior, creative applications of basic research in sensation and perception, the "new wave" of research on emotion, genetic and evolutionary theories of personality, critical findings on the origins and treatment of psychopathology, and social psychological perspectives on culture. The result is a comprehensive and exciting overview of the best of the old and the best of the new in psychology.

BIOLOGY, EVOLUTION, AND CULTURE

Three themes are woven throughout this edition of *Introduction to Psychology:* biology, evolution, and culture. Our emphasis on biological bases of behavior is retained from previous editions, but we have expanded our coverage of biologically oriented research in several chapters as well. For example, we have added information on the genetics of temperament in Chapter 3 and on the genetics of personality in Chapter 13, and updated biological models of motives in Chapter 10. We added a section on the biology of posttraumatic stress disorder in Chapter 14, and expanded and updated coverage of research on biological approaches to mental disorders in Chapters 15 and 16. Throughout the book, a new feature called **The Neural Basis of Behavior** is designed to make the biological foundations of behavior more evident.

We have also increased our coverage of evolutionary perspectives in psychology. For example, we added sections on evolutionary psychology to Chapters 1 and 2. We highlighted the evolutionary significance of emotion in Chapter 11 and added a section on evolutionary psychology theories of personality in Chapter 13.

A third emphasis throughout the book is on culture and diversity. For example, in Chapter 6, we discuss cultural variation in alcohol-use disorders. In Chapters 12 and 13, we highlight evidence of cultural bias in tests of intelligence and personality. In Chapters 14 and 15, we discuss differences across cultures in rates of posttraumatic stress and other mental disorders. In Chapter 16, we discuss sociocultural approaches to treatment for mental disorders, and culturally specific treatments. In Chapter 18, we focus on the recent work on culture and social cognition.

MAJOR CONTENT CHANGES

The 14th edition has been extensively revised, with updates to all major sections, reorganization of several chapters, and additions of key new material. Some of the substantive changes in this edition include the following:

CHAPTER 1: THE NATURE OF PSYCHOLOGY

- New examples of how psychology research influences policy are used to help students understand the importance of psychological research. For example, the opening vignette discusses whether a popular reading promotion program is in fact "psychologically correct."
- The coverage of the historical roots of psychology has been completely revised to emphasize connections with modern movements in psychology. For example, a new section entitled "The Subjectivist Perspective," provides strong ties to contemporary social, personality, and cultural psychology.
- A new Cutting-Edge Research feature entitled "21st-Century Psychology" highlights developments in interdisciplinary approaches such as cognitive neuroscience, evolutionary psychology, cultural psychology, affective and social cognitive neuroscience, and positive psychology.
- A new section on "Literature Reviews" explains the logic of meta-analyses, which are mentioned frequently throughout the textbook.

CHAPTER 2: BIOLOGICAL FOUNDATIONS OF PSYCHOLOGY

- An opening vignette has been added to illustrate the linkage between complex psychological traits (i.e., personality) and the brain as revealed by the case of Phineas Gage.
- A section concerning evolution of behavior illustrates the operation of natural selection in the context of a behavioral trait (e.g., male aggression).

CHAPTER 3: PSYCHOLOGICAL DEVELOPMENT

- The new opening vignette illustrates the variability in both children's rate of development and parents' expectations for their development.

- A section on new research in cognitive development on children's theory of mind has been added.
- A new Cutting-Edge Research feature highlights the effects of massage therapy on the development of at-risk babies.
- Information on the genetic influences on temperament has been added.
- The coverage of adolescent development has been expanded and updated and now includes a discussion of ethnic identity development among minority youth.

CHAPTER 4: SENSORY PROCESSES

- A new introduction helps students understand the impact of research on sensation on everyday life.
- The section on sensitivity has been revised and expanded to describe more completely (a) the nature of light and (b) psychophysical procedures (the classical Stevens' power law has been added, described, and illustrated).
- A section on the signal-detection theory has been added.
- The importance of metamers in the development of trichromacy theory has been stressed.

CHAPTER 5: PERCEPTION

- The introduction is entirely changed to (a) motivate the study of perception (via the "The Tent and the Bear" story), and (b) provide an ecological perspective of what perception is used for.
- The new Cutting-Edge Research feature describes research on the use of virtual reality to diminish severe pain.
- Attention—which has been greatly expanded and connected to the Chapter 4 material—is now given its own section, thus providing a framework for viewing the remainder of the chapter. The sections on eye movements have also been expanded.
- A section on "The Binding Problem: Preattentive and Attentive Processes" has been added to the "Recognition" section.
- A section on abstraction has been added.
- The discussion of perceptual constancies has been expanded and the "Illusions" section has been integrated into it.

Chapter 6: Consciousness

- A new chapter opening vignette highlights everyday experiences of dissociation or loss of consciousness.
- Cultural and gender issues in alcohol abuse and dependence are now discussed. New coverage includes the effects of acculturation on drinking behavior among Mexican-Americans. In addition, explanations are given for men's greater consumption of alcohol compared to women.
- Research and statistics on drug abuse have been updated.
- A new Cutting-Edge Research feature focuses on the genetics of smoking.

Chapter 7: Learning and Conditioning

- To illustrate basic principles in learning, an opening vignette about how to teach someone a new trick has been added.
- A new section on inhibitory conditioning is now included.
- A new section on neural mechanisms of learning and conditioning has been added.

Chapter 8: Memory

- The chapter now begins with a true-life story about the importance of understanding memory for making correct decisions in the criminal-justice system.
- The chapter is reorganized such that the traditional trichotomization of memory into sensory store, short-term store, and long-term store is clarified and emphasized. The historical roots in the Atkinson-Shiffrin theory are described.
- The relation between sensory store, attention, and short-term store is now described. In addition, classic experiments involving partial-report and temporal-integration are described.
- The section on constructive memory has been entirely reconceived to incorporate the importance of research on eyewitness testimony within the legal system.

Chapter 9: Language and Thought

- A new discussion of the neural basis of language has been included.
- A new Cutting-Edge Research feature highlights decision making and the brain.

- The coverage of syntax, prototypes, the universality of prototypes and categorization have been thoroughly updated and expanded.

Chapter 10: Motivation

- "Wanting Versus Liking," a new Cutting-Edge Research feature, highlights the work by Berridge and colleagues, which separates the brain systems for "wanting" and "liking."
- A new section on the objectification theory provides a detailed psychological explanation of how thin ideal media images can affect rates of eating disorders and other gender-related differences in mental health.
- The prelude to the Seeing Both Sides debate has been reframed to highlight how each perspective takes a different stand on nature and/or nurture, reprising on a theme of Chapter 1.

Chapter 11: Emotion

- The chapter has been reorganized and a new discussion distinguishes emotions from moods.
- The discussion of cognitive appraisal has been updated by including new experimental research that supports the causal role of appraisal in emotion experiences. Coverage of nonconscious appraisal and the neurobiology of appraisals has also been updated.
- New sections on subjective experiences and thought-action tendencies emphasize the evolutionary significance of the latter.
- The new work on positive emotions has been highlighted throughout the chapter and in the Cutting-Edge Research feature.
- Updated discussions of effects of emotions on evaluations and judgment include new, paradigm-shifting work, the communicative function of facial expressions, and the facial feedback hypothesis.
- New sections about emotion regulation and gender and cultural differences in emotion have been added.
- Updated coverage of aggression now includes brain dysfunction associated with impulsive aggression, and a new meta-analysis on the impact of violent video games.

Chapter 12: Intelligence

- The chapter has been reorganized to focus only on intelligence, with material on personality assessment moved to Chapter 13.

- A new section on cultural issues in the assessment of intelligence discusses possible biases in intelligence tests that result in apparently lower scores among nonmajority people.
- Controversies concerning cultural issues in theories of intelligence are now included.

CHAPTER 13: PERSONALITY

- The coverage of personality assessment has been moved to this chapter.
- A new section on evolutionary theories of personality has been added.
- The discussion of defense mechanisms is now included in the section about Freudian theory.
- Coverage of projective tests has been expanded to include new data on cultural bias.
- A new section on the research on the genetics of personality has been added.
- A new Cutting-Edge Research feature addresses the notion of "changing your personality with a pill" (e.g., with Prozac).

CHAPTER 14: STRESS, HEALTH, AND COPING

- Cultural issues are now discussed more thoroughly throughout the chapter. For example, in the discussion of posttraumatic stress disorder (PTSD), we added data on differential rates by ethnic group and an expanded section on Bosnian refugees as sufferers of PTSD.
- A section on the biology of PTSD has been added.
- Coverage of the relationship between stress and immune functioning has been expanded.
- A new Cutting-Edge Research feature discusses religion and health.

CHAPTER 15: PSYCHOLOGICAL DISORDERS

- The new chapter opening vignette introduces students to psychological disorders by presenting a case study that focuses on a man with obsessive-compulsive disorder.
- A new Cutting-Edge Research feature focuses on the biology of suicide.
- Neuroimaging studies of anxiety disorders, mood disorders, and schizophrenia are highlighted in these respective sections.

- The discussion of "defining abnormality" now emphasizes cultural norms as important in defining abnormality.
- The section on anxiety disorders now includes *ataque de nervios,* an anxiety-like syndrome seen mostly in Latino cultures.
- The section on schizophrenia now discusses cross-cultural differences in the manifestations and prognosis of schizophrenia.

CHAPTER 16: TREATMENT OF PSYCHOLOGICAL DISORDERS

- A new opening vignette describes a man with schizophrenia and various types of treatment he and his family have found helpful.
- The introduction now includes a discussion of ancient Chinese perspectives on mental illness.
- Descriptions of medications used to treat disorders have been greatly updated.
- The new Cutting-Edge Research feature focuses on herbal treatments for mental disorders.
- The chapter has been reorganized to include a new section that provides coverage of culturally specific treatments of psychological disorders.

CHAPTER 17: SOCIAL INFLUENCE

- The new opening section introduces the "power of situations," which is then used as a running theme throughout the chapter.
- The sections on social facilitation, deindividuation, bystander effects, and conformity have been extensively revised and updated.
- The new Cutting-Edge Research feature discusses pluralistic ignorance and college drinking.
- A reorganized and revised discussion of the Milgram obedience studies now includes a new subsection on rapidly emerging situations as an explanation for obedience. The section on ideological justification has also been updated to include mention of Islamic extremists and Jonestown followers, in addition to Nazi Germany and U.S. military personnel.
- A new section, "Self-Justification," covers classic work on the cognitive dissonance theory and the self-perception theory in one place.
- "Institutional Norms," another new section, reframes the classic Stanford Prison Experiment in broader terms and includes a new discussion of how

the lessons of the Stanford Prison Experiment apply to contemporary U.S. prison policies.

- The discussion of groupthink has been updated to reflect new theories that tie poor group decisions to social identity maintenance and group norms, and highlight the benefits of group diversity.

CHAPTER 18: SOCIAL COGNITION

- The new chapter opening vignette focuses on dual-process models (a.k.a. "two modes of thinking, automatic and controlled"), a focus that is woven throughout the chapter.
- A focus on several nonintuitive studies from the late 1990s, and increased coverage on race and gender stereotypes, are now included in the new section on automatic stereotype activation.
- A new section on stereotypes and inferences presents classic studies by Asch (1946) and Kelley (1950). These studies clearly show how stereotypes and advance reputations color inferences and impression formation and make connections to more recent research on inferences made about women and African Americans.
- A substantial revision of the section on self-fulfilling prophecies includes new evidence that demonstrates that self-fulfilling prophecies can occur automatically and unconsciously and a new discussion of two competing explanations for self-fulfilling prophecies of the self.
- Sections on individuation and efforts to control prejudice and stereotypes have been added.
- New sections on love and self-expansion, as well as transference effects on liking, were added to the discussion of interpersonal attraction.
- The new Cutting-Edge Research feature on culture and cognition centers around new theoretical and empirical advances by Nisbett and colleagues.

PEDAGOGY TO INSURE STUDENT SUCCESS

In the 14th edition, we have added new pedagogical features to assist students in learning the material. Our new **Concept Review Tables** provide quick overviews of the key concepts in a tabular format. The new **Interim Summaries** summarize the main points of each major section.

Critical Thinking Questions are now placed at the end of each major section to challenge students to synthesize and expand upon the material they have just read. In addition, the 14th edition continues to have important pedagogical features that were present in earlier editions. **Chapter Outlines** provide students with an overview of the main topics that will be discussed. **In-text definitions** of core concepts identify the most important concepts in each section and highlight the definition of that concept when it is first introduced. Detailed **Chapter Summaries** review the primary points made across the entire chapter. The Interim Summaries and Chapter Summaries help students synthesize and retain the key information from the chapter (Reder & Anderson, 1980).

FEATURES RETAINED AND IMPROVED

Popular features from previous editions have been retained and improved in the 14th edition. **Seeing Both Sides** (formerly titled Contemporary Voices in Psychology) spotlights important debates within psychology with competing essays from internationally recognized leaders in psychology. This feature introduces students to different ways of approaching significant questions in psychology—a lesson in critical thinking skills—and helps them understand what issues are not yet decided. For example, in Chapter 3, Judith Rich Harris, controversial author of *The Nurture Assumption*, and Jerome Kagan, influential developmental psychologist, debate the influence of parents on children's development. In Chapter 8, Elizabeth Loftus and Kathy Pezdek address the contentious debate on recovered memories. In Chapter 17, Madeline Heilman and Faye Crosby use basic research in social psychology to debate the value of affirmative action programs.

Cutting-Edge Research (formerly Frontiers of Psychological Research) highlights new and innovative theories in psychology, or applications of psychological research to contemporary problems. The issues addressed in the Cutting-Edge Research features are new in most chapters of the 14th edition. Students will be fascinated by the new directions psychological research is taking, and the ways psychological research can be used to address important social issues. Some examples include "Distraction Via Virtual Reality Diminishes Severe Pain" (Chapter 5), "The Biology of Suicide"

(Chapter 15), and "Pluralistic Ignorance and College Drinking" (Chapter 17).

COMPLETE TECHNOLOGY INTEGRATION

PSYCH ODYSSEY 1.5

- With every adoption, professors will have the opportunity to include Psych Odyssey 1.5, a 2-disk CD-ROM, free with every new student copy. The CD-ROM features animations, video clips, interactive exercises, and quizzing designed to provide an engaging, multimedia introduction to psychology.
- To help students get the most out of their Psych Odyssey CD-ROM, content tie-ins are provided at the end of every chapter.

PSYK.TREK 2.0

- 2.0, the latest version of Psyk.trek is available separately as a bundle option. Each CD-ROM module provides a multimedia presentation for teaching each topic, mixing real-time video, photographs, and animated graphics with voice-overs, music, and interactive demonstrations of concepts. Students will also benefit from the *Interactive Study Guide,* concept checks, simulations and a multimedia glossary.
- Content tie-ins to Psyk.trek 2.0 are provided at the end of every chapter to help students navigate their CD-ROM.

INFOTRAC

- With every new copy, students will also receive a free 4-month subscription to InfoTrac College Edition, Thomson Learning's exclusive online library. To further their study of psychology, this subscription will provide students access to hundreds of relevant articles and allow them to write up-to-date quick reaction research papers.
- To help students utilize their InfoTrac subscription, suggested search terms are provided at the end of every chapter as well as in the Cutting-Edge Research feature that appears in every chapter.

WEB RESOURCES

- Relevant websites have been hand-picked for interest and appropriateness. These sites are provided at the end of every chapter and can also be accessed via direct link on the book-specific website at http://psychology.wadsworth.com/atkinson14e.
- On the book-specific website, students can also get their bearings with the detailed chapter outline, test their knowledge with interactive quizzing, and access an electronic version of the comprehensive glossary.

CAREFULLY DEVELOPED RESOURCES FOR STUDENTS AND FACULTY ALIKE

Available to qualified adopters. Please consult your local sales representative for details.

Instructor's Manual & Unit Mastery Guide (0-15-505076-1) by Amy Goldring of the University of California and John Carlson of the University of Hawaii

- Resource Integration Guide
- Introduction & Information on the Unit Mastery Program
- Each chapter includes the following:
  - Chapter outline
  - Notable quotes
  - Chapter terms
  - Approximately 5 lecture ideas with suggestions for further reading (print and websites)
  - Student involvers—approximately 10 essay questions
  - Student involvers—approximately 10 activities and discussion questions
  - Student involvers—approximately 3 class activities and assignments with suggested websites.
  - New! Student involvers—2 critical thinking questions per each major sub-category within the chapter.
  - Film suggestions
  - CR-ROM integration (Psych Odyssey and Psyk.trek) with 1 activity and/or writing assignment per CD-ROM.
  - Exercises built around InfoTrac search terms.
  - Five annotated websites.

- Six Unit Mastery quizzes, each with approximately 10 multiple-choice test items.

Study Guide and Unit Mastery Program (0-15-505124-5) by John Carlson of the University of Hawaii

- Introduction and information on the Unit Mastery Program
- Each chapter contains:
  - Learning objectives
  - Fill-in-the-blanks: covers important names from each major subcategory in the chapter. Main text page references supplied with the questions.
  - Ideas & Concepts: short-answer questions for each major subcategory in the chapter. Main text page references supplied with the questions. Asterisked items deal with main points of the text.
  - Essay Questions
  - Two sample quizzes. Each with approximately 10 multiple-choice test items.
- Answers for all chapters are found at the back of the Study Guide.

Test Bank (0-15-505952-1) by Jay Bean of Vassar College

- Approximately 165 multiple-choice items per chapter
  - Each item lists the correct answer, topic covered, difficulty level, type (factual or conceptual), and an asterisk if the item is new to this edition.
  - 10 questions per chapter will revolve around content found on Psych Odyssey and Psyk.trek (5 questions per CD).
  - 15 questions per chapter will be available on our website as an on-line quiz. These items will be identified in the test bank by the notation "WWW."
  - 15 questions per chapter will be pulled from the Study Guide and placed within the Test Bank. These items will be identified in the test bank by the notation "SG."
- Approximately 5 essay test items per chapter
- Also available in ExamView (0-15-505070-2)

WebTutor Advantage on Blackboard (0-534-56796-7) and WebCT (0-15-505094-X)

- Learning Objectives
- Chapter Summary
- Chapter Outlines
- Glossary
- Learning Games: crossword puzzles, concentration, etc.

- Fill-in-the-blank test items
- Multiple-Choice test items
- Discussion Questions
- Discussion Questions
- CD-ROM notation and overview
- InfoTrac College Edition keyword search terms and exercises
- Internet Activities
- Video clips with introductions and two critical thinking questions
- Simulations
- For WebTutor Advantage Plus—E*Book file of complete text

WebTutor Advantage Plus (E*Book) on Blackboard (0-534-56797-5) and WebCT (0-534-56798-3)

- Contains all of the items mentioned above, as well as the entire text in electronic form.

Multimedia Manager for Introductory Psychology (0-15-505100-8)

- Chapter by chapter lecture outlines in Microsoft PowerPoint.
- Within each chapter's lecture outline, you will find integrated art from the text, CNN video clips, and animations.

ACKNOWLEDGMENTS

We wish first to acknowledge the passing of Ernest ("Jack") Hilgard, founder of this book, who died in 2001. Jack Hilgard's first edition of *Introduction to Psychology*, published in 1953, established it as the gold standard in introductory textbooks. He wrote a comprehensive and authoritative review of the field of psychology in a style that was appealing and comprehendible to students. The subsequent authors of his book have always striven to maintain the rigorous standards that Hilgard set for the book. Jack Hilgard remained a productive and creative researcher throughout his career, and a scholar and true gentleman to his last days. We are honored to carry on his work as authors of this book.

Edward Smith wishes to acknowledge his graduate school mentors, Paul Fitts and Arthur Melon. Susan Nolen-Hoeksema acknowledges Martin Seligman and several senior faculty colleagues at Stanford University and University of Michigan, particularly Albert Bandura and Eleanor Maccoby, for their mentorship over the last

20 years. Barbara Fredrickson wishes to acknowledge former mentors Neil Lutsky, Robert Levenson, as well as the psychology faculty at Stanford University and the faculty of the 1989–1992 NIMH postdoctoral program on Emotions Research for their indelible influences on her intellectual growth. Geoffrey Loftus wishes to acknowledge former author of this textbook, and his former research advisor, Richard Atkinson, as well as his postdoctoral sponsor, George Sperling, for their invaluable contributions to his scientific and intellectual development.

We are grateful to the following people at Wadsworth for their critical work on the 14th edition: Marianne Taflinger, Senior Editor; Kate Barnes, Developmental Editor; Jennifer Wilkinson, Senior Assistant Editor; Darin Derstine, Technology Project Manager; Nicole Root, Editorial Assistant; Lori Grebe, Marketing Manager; Laurel Anderson, Marketing Assistant; and Teri Hyde, Project Editor.

We would also like to thank the instructors who provided pre-revision and manuscript reviews for the 14th edition:

Jeff Baker, The University of Texas Medical Branch

Ted A. Barker, Okaloosa-Walton Community College

AG Beese, University of Leeds

Charles Behling, University of Michigan

Rose Capdevila, University College Northampton

Daniel Cervone, University of Illinois at Chicago

Edward Deci, University of Rochester

G. William Domhoff, University of California, Santa Cruz

Karl Gegenfurtner, Justin-Liebig-Universitat

Carla Grayson, University of Michigan

Sandra Grossmann, Clackamas Community College

Charla Hall, Southeastern Oklahoma State University

David T. Hall, Baton Rouge Community College

Andrew Hill, University of Leeds

Stefan Hofmann, Boston University

Addie Johnson, Utrecht University

Richard Keefe, Scottsdale Community College

Cantey Land, Vassar College

Professor David Leiser, Ben-gurion University of the Negev

Emma Lou Linn, St. Edward's University

Daniel Lord, University of Alaska, Anchorage

Traci Mann, University of California, Los Angeles

Douglas Matheson, University of the Pacific

Erin Rasmussen, College of Charleston

Mark Reinitz, University of Puget Sound

Alex Rothman, University of Minnesota

Tony Shelton, Liverpool John Moores University

C.R. Snyder, University of Kansas

Lance Workman, University of Glamorgan

We would also like to recognize the following instructors who contributed to previous editions through insightful manuscript reviews and telephone discussions: James Ackil, Western Illinois University; Cynthia Allen, Westchester Community College; Eileen Astor-Stetson, Bloomsburg University; Gordon D. Atlas, Alfred University; Raymond R. Baird, University of Texas, San Antonio; N. Jay Bean, Vassar College; John B. Best, Eastern Illinois University; Randolph Blake, Vanderbilt University; Terry Blumenthal, Wake Forest University; Richard W. Bowen, Loyola University; Thomas Brothen, University of Minnesota; James P. Buchanan, University of Scranton; James F. Calhoun, University of Georgia; Charles S. Carver, University of Miami; Avshalom Caspi, University of Wisconsin; Janice Chapman, Bossier Parrish Community College; Paul Chara, Loras College; Stephen Clark, Vassar College; Stanley Coren, University of British Columbia; Richard Eglfaer, Sam Houston State University; Gilles Einstein, Furman University; Judith Erickson, University of Minnesota; G. William Farthing, University of Maine; Mary Ann Fischer, Indiana University Northwest; Barbara L. Fredrickson, Duke University; William Rick Fry, Youngstown State University; Richard Gist, Johnson County Community College; W. B. Perry Goodwin, Santa Clara University; Bill Graziano, Texas A&M University; Paul Greene, Iona College; Elizabeth Hillstrom, Wheaton College; David Holmes, University of Kansas; William L. Hoover, Suffolk County Community College; Ralph Hupka, California State University; Fred A. Johnson, University of the District of Columbia; Wesley P. Jordan, St. Mary's College of Maryland; Grace Kannady, Kansas City Kansas Community College; Richard A. Kasschau, University of Houston; Charles Ksir, University of Wyoming; Joan Lauer, Indiana University/Purdue University; Elissa M. Lewis, Southwest Missouri State University; Marc A. Lindberg, Marshall University; Emma

CONTENTS

CUTTING-EDGE RESEARCH

SEEING BOTH SIDES

Continued

Artville/Getty Images

THE NATURE OF PSYCHOLOGY

1

Reading opens the door to education and advancement. What's the best way to encourage kids to read? One national chain of pizza restaurants believes it has the answer: Reward kids for reading. Kids' teachers set monthly reading goals—in terms of books or pages read—and give them Pizza Award Certificates when they reach the goals. The kid who brings a certificate to a local participating restaurant gets a free pizza. Parents and teachers say the program works—it gets their kids to read more. Through this program, for nearly 20 years kids have been earning pizza for reading across the United States. Perhaps you or one of your siblings got a free meal this way.

But is this program PC? Is it "psychologically correct"? Let's see what the research says. You might already be aware of one of the fundamental tenets of learning theory: **When a reward follows a behavior, that behavior is strength-**

ened. In Chapter 7 you'll see that this powerful influence of rewards is termed the **law of effect.**[1] When kids are rewarded with pizzas for reading, they read more. Seems like a great success, right?

Consider other outcomes—like how kids feel about reading and whether they continue to read once the pizza program ends. Dozens of psychology experiments, many conducted in school classrooms, have addressed these questions. In one classic experiment (Greene, Sternberg, & Lepper, 1976),[2] psychologists had teachers introduce several new math games to their students and then for 2 weeks simply observe how much time kids spent playing them. In the 3rd week, kids in some classrooms were rewarded for playing these same math games, and kids in other classrooms were not. As expected, the rewards increased the amount of time kids played the math games; the law of effect held. But what happened several weeks later, when the rewards were discontinued? The kids who had

received rewards suddenly lost interest in the math games and spent hardly any time on them. By contrast, those who were never rewarded continued to play the math games regularly.

This experiment demonstrates how rewards sometimes backfire and undermine kids' intrinsic interest in activities like reading and math. When people see that their behavior is caused by some external, situational factor—like a free pizza—they discount any internal, personal factors—like their own enjoyment of the activity. So when kids ask themselves why they read, they'll say it's for the pizza. And when there's no more pizza to be had, they'll see no particular reason to read. Even though they enjoyed reading, the rewards loomed larger. This undermining influence of rewards is the **overjustification effect**—going overboard and **explaining one's own behavior with too much emphasis on salient situational causes and not enough emphasis on personal causes.**

---

[1]Throughout this book you will find core concepts printed in **bold type** and their definitions provided nearby in blue type. A list of these core concepts is also provided at the end of each chapter as a study aid.

[2]Throughout this book you will also find references, cited by author and date, that document or expand the statements made here. Detailed publishing information on these studies appears in the reference list at the end of the book.

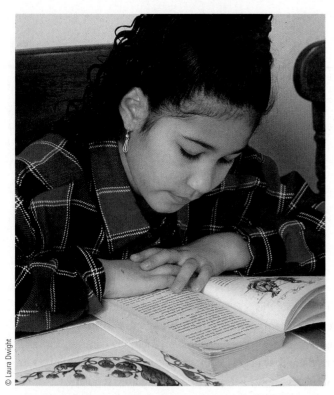
© Laura Dwight

Getting kids to read for external reasons—like for free pizzas—can lead them to discount the contribution of any internal reasons for reading—like their own interest. This overjustification effect explains why rewarding desired behaviors sometimes backfires.

You might be thinking that grades in college are also rewards for learning. Do they backfire in the same way as receiving pizza for reading? Not exactly. One important difference is that the grade you get in a college course depends on how well you perform. Research has shown that performance-contingent rewards are less likely to undermine interest—and at times can even increase interest—because they tell you that you are good at an activity (Tang & Hall, 1995). Even so, a focus on grades can sometimes overshadow the sheer interest you might have in a subject. It's useful to remind yourself that two reasons to study course work can exist side by side: to get a good grade and to enjoy the material. It can be "both-and," not "either-or."

Luckily, most students find psychology fascinating. We do, too, and we do our best to convey this fascination to you in the pages of this book. Psychology interests people because it asks questions that touch virtually every aspect of our lives: How does the way your parents raised you affect the way you'll raise your own children? What is the best treatment for drug dependency? Can a man care for an infant as capably as a woman can? Can you remember a traumatic experience in more detail under hypnosis? How should a nuclear power plant be designed to minimize human error? What effects does prolonged stress have on the immune system? Is psy-

chotherapy more effective than drugs in treating depression? Psychologists are conducting research to find answers to these and many other questions.

Psychology also affects our lives through its influence on laws and public policy. Psychological theories and research have influenced laws dealing with discrimination, capital punishment, courtroom practices, pornography, sexual behavior, and personal responsibility for actions. For example, so-called lie-detector tests are not admissible evidence in U.S. courts because psychological research has shown them to be unacceptably inaccurate.

Because psychology affects so many aspects of our lives, even people who do not intend to specialize in it need to know something about this dynamic field. An introductory course in psychology should give you a better understanding of why people think, feel, and act as they do, as well as insights into your own attitudes and reactions.

This course will also help you evaluate the many claims made in the name of psychology. Everyone has seen newspaper headlines like these:

- New Form of Psychotherapy Facilitates Recovery of Repressed Memories
- Anxiety Controlled by Self-Regulation of Brain Waves
- Proof of Mental Telepathy Found
- Babies Learn Speech Sounds While Snoozing
- Emotional Stability Closely Related to Family Size
- Sweet Drink May Boost Exam Performance
- Transcendental Meditation Extends Life Expectancy
- Appearance Concerns Take Mental Toll

How can we decide whether to believe these claims? You need to know two things to evaluate the validity of psychological claims. First, you need to know what psychological facts are already firmly established. If the new claim is not compatible with those facts, you should be cautious. Second, you need to have the knowledge to determine whether the arguments that support the new claim meet the standards of scientific evidence. If they do not, again you have reason for skepticism. This book aims to meet both needs. First, it reviews the current state of knowledge in psychology. It presents the most important findings in the field so that you know the established facts. Second, it examines the nature of research—how a psychologist designs a research program that can provide strong evidence for or against a hypothesis—so that you know the kind of evidence needed to back up a new claim.

In this chapter, we begin by considering the kinds of topics that are studied in psychology. After a brief review of psychology's historical origins, we discuss the perspectives that psychologists adopt in investigating these topics. Then we describe the research methods of psychological investigation, including the ethical guidelines that have been proposed for such research.

THE SCOPE OF PSYCHOLOGY

Psychology can be defined as the scientific study of behavior and mental processes. An astonishing variety of topics fit this definition, as can be seen in the brief examples presented next. (All of these topics are discussed in more detail at various points in this book.)

BRAIN DAMAGE AND FACE RECOGNITION It is no surprise that when people suffer brain damage, their behavior is affected. What is surprising is that damage in a specific part of the brain may change a person's behavior in one way but not in any other ways. In some cases, for example, people are unable to recognize familiar faces as a result of damage to a particular region on the right side of the brain—yet they can do just about everything else normally, a condition called **prosopagnosia**. A famous example of this condition was described by neurologist Oliver Sacks (1985) in his book *The Man Who Mistook His Wife for a Hat*. In another case, a man with prosopagnosia complained to a waiter that someone was staring at him, only to be informed that he was looking in a mirror! Such cases tell us a lot about the way the normal brain works. They indicate that some psychological functions—like face recognition—are localized in particular parts of the brain.

ATTRIBUTING TRAITS TO PEOPLE Suppose that in a crowded department store a person soliciting for a charity approaches a customer and implores her to make a contribution. The woman writes a $50 check to the charity. Would you think the woman was generous, or would you think she had been pressured into making the donation because so many people were watching her? Experiments designed to study situations like this have shown that most people consider the woman generous, even though the situational pressures were so great that just about everybody would behave similarly. When explaining the behavior of others, people tend to overestimate the causal effect of personality traits and underestimate those of situational factors—a mistake social psychologists call the **fundamental attribution error** (see Figure 1-1). If we contrast the fundamental attribution error with the overjustification effect (discussed in the context of earning pizzas for reading), we begin to see some important distinctions between how we judge others and how we judge ourselves. When making sense of our own behavior, we often overestimate—not underestimate—situational causes.

CHILDHOOD AMNESIA Most adults can recall events from their early years, but only back to a certain point. Almost no one can accurately recall events from the first 3 years of life, a phenomenon called **childhood amnesia**.

■ Figure 1-1
Trait Attribution
In deciding whether another person's substantial donation to charity is caused by the giver's traits or by the situation, we are biased toward believing that a trait was the critical factor. This illustrates the fundamental attribution error.

Consider a significant event like the birth of a sibling. If the birth occurred after you were 3 years old, you may have some memory of it. But if the birth occurred before age 3, you probably remember very little about it, if anything at all (see Figure 1-2). Childhood amnesia is partic-

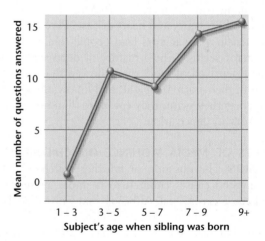

■ Figure 1-2
Recall of an Early Memory
In an experiment on childhood amnesia, college-age participants were asked 20 questions about the events surrounding the birth of a younger sibling. The average number of questions answered is plotted as a function of the participant's age when the sibling was born. If the birth occurred before the participant's 4th year of life, no participant could recall a thing about it; if the birth occurred after that, recall increased with the participant's age at the time of the event. (K. Sheingold and Y. J. Tenney (1982) "Recall of An Early Memory adapted from "Memory for a Salient Childhood Event" from U. Neisser (ed.) *Memory Observed: Remembering in Natural Context,* copyright © 1982 by W. H. Freeman & Company. Adapted by permission of the publisher.)

Psychologists are interested in what causes people to eat too much. Among the possible causes they have studied are genetic factors and environmental influences, such as a tendency to overeat in the presence of certain stimuli.

ularly striking because our first 3 years are so rich in experience: We develop from helpless newborns to crawling, babbling infants to walking, talking children. But these remarkable transitions leave few traces in our memories.

OBESITY More than a quarter of U.S. adults are **obese;** their weight is 30% or more above the level that would be appropriate for their body structure and height. Obesity is dangerous. It increases vulnerability to diabetes, high blood pressure, and heart disease. Psychologists are interested in what factors lead people to eat too much. One factor seems to be a history of deprivation. If rats are first deprived of food, then allowed to eat until they return to their normal weight, and finally allowed to eat as much as they want, they eat more than rats that have no history of deprivation.

EFFECTS OF MEDIA VIOLENCE ON CHILDREN'S AGGRESSION The question of whether watching violence on television causes children to be more aggressive has long been controversial. Although many observers believe that televised violence affects children's behavior, others suggest that watching violence has a **cathartic effect.** It may actually reduce aggression by allowing children to express it vicariously and "get it out of their system." But research evidence does not support the cathartic effect view. In one experiment, one group of children watched violent cartoons while another group watched nonviolent cartoons for the same amount of time. Children who watched violent cartoons became more aggressive in their interactions with peers, but the children who viewed nonviolent cartoons showed no change in aggressive behavior. These effects can persist over time: The more violent programs a boy watches at age 9, the more aggressive he is likely to be at age 19 (see Figure 1-3).

Psychological studies provide evidence that violent television programming may have harmful effects on young viewers.

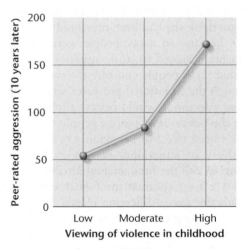

❙ Figure 1-3
The Relationship Between Childhood Viewing of Violent Television and Adult Aggression
A classic study shows that preference for viewing violent TV programs by boys at age 9 is related to aggressive behavior as rated by peers at age 19. (L. Eron, et al. (1972) "Does Television Violence Cause Aggression?" *American Psychologist, 27*:253-262. Copyright © 1972 by The American Psychological Association. Adapted by permission.)

The ancient Greek philosopher Socrates posed fundamental questions about mental life. Many of these questions are as important today as they were in Socrates' time.

THE HISTORICAL ORIGINS OF PSYCHOLOGY

The roots of psychology can be traced to the great philosophers of ancient Greece. The most famous of them, Socrates, Plato, and Aristotle, posed fundamental questions about mental life: What is consciousness? Are people inherently rational or irrational? Is there really such a thing as free choice? These questions, and many similar ones, are as important today as they were thousands of years ago. They deal with the nature of the mind and mental processes, which are the key elements of the cognitive perspective in psychology.

Other psychological questions deal with the nature of the body and human behavior, and they have an equally long history. Hippocrates, often called the "father of medicine," lived around the same time as Socrates. He was deeply interested in **physiology, the study of the functions of the living organism and its parts.** He made many important observations about how the brain controls various organs of the body. These observations set the stage for what became the biological perspective in psychology.

NATURE-NURTURE DEBATE

One of the earliest debates about human psychology is still raging today. This **nature-nurture debate** centers on the question of whether human capabilities are inborn or acquired through experience. The **nature view** holds that human beings enter the world with an inborn store of knowledge and understanding of reality. Early philosophers believed that this knowledge and understanding could be accessed through careful reasoning and introspection. In the 17th century, Descartes supported the nature view by arguing that some ideas (such as God, the self, geometric axioms, perfection, and infinity) are innate. Descartes is also notable for his conception of the body as a machine that can be studied much as other machines are studied. This is the root of modern information-processing perspectives on the mind, discussed later in this chapter.

The **nurture view** holds that knowledge is acquired through experiences and interactions with the world. Although some of the early Greek philosophers had this opinion, it is most strongly associated with the 17th-century English philosopher John Locke. According to Locke, at birth the human mind is a **tabula rasa,** a blank slate on which experience "writes" knowledge and understanding as the individual matures. This perspective gave birth to **associationist psychology**. Associationists denied that there were inborn ideas or capabilities. Instead, they argued that the mind is filled with ideas that enter by way of the senses and then become associated through principles such as similarity and contrast. Current research on memory and learning is related to early association theory.

The classic nature-nurture debate has become much more nuanced in recent decades. Although some psychologists still argue that human thought and behavior result primarily from biology or primarily from experience, most psychologists take a more integrated approach. They acknowledge that biological processes (such as heredity or processes in the brain) affect thoughts, feelings, and behavior, but say that experience leaves its mark, too. So the current question is not whether nature *or* nurture shapes human psychology but rather how nature *and* nurture combine to do so. The nature-nurture issue comes up at numerous points in later chapters.

THE BEGINNINGS OF SCIENTIFIC PSYCHOLOGY

Although philosophers and scholars continued to be interested in the functioning of both the mind and the body through the centuries, scientific psychology is usually considered to have begun in the late 19th century, when Wilhelm Wundt established the first psychological laboratory at the University of Leipzig in Germany in 1879. The impetus for the establishment of Wundt's lab was the belief that mind and behavior, like planets or chemicals or human organs, could be the subject of scientific analysis. Wundt's own research was concerned primarily with the senses, especially vision, but he and his coworkers also studied attention, emotion, and memory.

Wundt relied on introspection to study mental processes. **Introspection** refers to observing and recording the nature of one's own perceptions, thoughts, and feelings. Examples of introspections include people's reports of how heavy they perceive an object to be and how bright a flash of light seems to be. The introspective method was inherited from philosophy, but Wundt added a new dimension to the concept. Pure self-observation was not sufficient; it had to be supplemented by experiments. Wundt's experiments systematically varied some physical dimension of a stimulus, such as its intensity, and used the introspective method to determine how these physical changes modified the participant's conscious experience of the stimulus.

The reliance on introspection, particularly for very rapid mental events, proved unworkable. Even after extensive training, different people produced very different introspections about simple sensory experiences, and

Wilhelm Wundt established the first psychological laboratory at the University of Leipzig. Here he is shown (third from left) in the laboratory with his associates.

few conclusions could be drawn from these differences. As a result, introspection is not a central part of the current cognitive perspective. And, as we will see, some psychologists' reactions to introspection played a role in the development of other modern perspectives.

STRUCTURALISM AND FUNCTIONALISM

During the 19th century, chemistry and physics made great advances by analyzing complex compounds (molecules) into their elements (atoms). These successes encouraged psychologists to look for the mental elements that combined to create more complex experiences. Just as chemists analyzed water into hydrogen and oxygen, perhaps psychologists could analyze the taste of lemonade (perception) into elements such as sweet, bitter, and cold (sensations). The leading proponent of this approach in the United States was E. B. Titchener, a Cornell University psychologist who had been trained by Wundt. Titchener introduced the term **structuralism**—the analysis of mental structures—to describe this branch of psychology.

But some psychologists opposed the purely analytic nature of structuralism. William James, a distinguished psychologist at Harvard University, felt that analyzing the elements of consciousness was less important than understanding its fluid, personal nature. His approach was named **functionalism**, studying how the mind works to enable an organism to adapt to and function in its environment.

Nineteenth-century psychologists' interest in adaptation stemmed from the publication of Charles Darwin's theory of evolution. Some argued that consciousness had evolved only because it served some purpose in guiding the individual's activities. To find out how an organism adapts to its environment, functionalists said that psychologists must observe actual behavior. However, both structuralists and functionalists still regarded psychology as the science of conscious experience.

BEHAVIORISM

Structuralism and functionalism played important roles in the early development of 20th-century psychology. Because each viewpoint provided a systematic approach to the field, they were considered competing schools of psychology. By 1920, however, both were being displaced by three newer schools: behaviorism, Gestalt psychology, and psychoanalysis.

Of the three, behaviorism had the greatest influence on scientific psychology in North America. Its founder, John B. Watson, reacted against the view that conscious experience was the province of psychology. Watson made no assertions about consciousness when he studied the behavior of animals and infants. He decided not only that animal psychology and child psychology could stand on their own as sciences but also that they set a pattern that adult psychology might follow.

For psychology to be a science, Watson believed, psychological data must be open to public inspection like the data of any other science. Behavior is public; consciousness is private. Science should deal only with public facts. Because psychologists were growing impatient with introspection, the new behaviorism caught on rapidly, and many younger psychologists in the United States called themselves "behaviorists." (The Russian physiologist Ivan Pavlov's research on the conditioned response was regarded as an important area of behavioral research, but it was Watson who was responsible for behaviorism's widespread influence.)

Watson, and others ascribing to **behaviorism,** argued that nearly all **behavior is a result of conditioning and the environment shapes behavior by reinforcing specific habits.** For example, giving children cookies to stop them from whining reinforces (rewards) the habit of whining. The conditioned response was viewed as the smallest unit of behavior, from which more complicated behaviors could be created. All types of complex behavior patterns coming from special training or education were regarded as nothing more than an interlinked fabric of conditioned responses.

Behaviorists tended to discuss psychological phenomena in terms of stimuli and responses, giving rise to the term *stimulus-response (S-R) psychology*. Note, however, that S-R psychology itself is not a theory or perspective but a set of terms that can be used to communicate psychological information. S-R terminology is still sometimes used in psychology today.

William James, John B. Watson, and Sigmund Freud were key figures in the early history of psychology. James developed the approach known as functionalism, Watson was the founder of behaviorism, and Freud originated the theory and method of psychoanalysis.

█ Figure 1-4
A Gestalt Image
When we look at the three angles of an equilateral triangle, we see a single large triangle rather than three small angles.

GESTALT PSYCHOLOGY

About 1912, at the same time that behaviorism was catching on in the United States, Gestalt psychology was appearing in Germany. **Gestalt** is a German word meaning "form" or "configuration," which referred to the approach taken by Max Wertheimer and his colleagues Kurt Koffka and Wolfgang Köhler, all of whom eventually emigrated to the United States.

The Gestalt psychologists' primary interest was perception, and they believed that perceptual experiences depend on the patterns formed by stimuli and on the organization of experience. What we actually see is related to the background against which an object appears, as well as to other aspects of the overall pattern of stimulation (see Chapter 5). The whole is different from the sum of its parts, because the whole depends on the relationships among the parts. For example, when we look at Figure 1-4, we see it as a single large triangle—as a single form or Gestalt—rather than as three small angles.

Among the key interests of Gestalt psychologists were the perception of motion, how people judge size, and the appearance of colors under changes in illumination. These interests led them to a number of perception-centered interpretations of learning, memory, and problem solving that helped lay the groundwork for current research in cognitive psychology.

The Gestalt psychologists also influenced key founders of modern social psychology—including Kurt Lewin, Solomon Asch, and Fritz Heider—who expanded on Gestalt principles to understand interpersonal phenomena (Jones, 1998). For instance, Asch (1946) extended the Gestalt notion that people see wholes rather than isolated parts from the simple case of object perception to the more complex case of person perception

(Taylor, 1998). Plus, they saw the process of imposing meaning and structure on incoming stimuli as automatic and outside conscious awareness, a Gestalt view that continues to infuse contemporary research on social cognition to this day (see Chapter 18; Moskowitz, Skurnik, & Galinsky, 1999).

PSYCHOANALYSIS

Psychoanalysis is both a theory of personality and a method of psychotherapy originated by Sigmund Freud around the turn of the 20th century.

At the center of Freud's theory is the concept of the **unconscious**—the thoughts, attitudes, impulses, wishes, motivations, and emotions of which we are unaware. Freud believed that childhood's unacceptable (forbidden or punished) wishes are driven out of conscious awareness and become part of the unconscious, where they continue to influence our thoughts, feelings, and actions. Unconscious thoughts are expressed in dreams, slips of the tongue, and physical mannerisms. During therapy with patients, Freud used the method of **free association,** in which the patient was instructed to say whatever comes to mind as a way of bringing unconscious wishes into awareness. The analysis of dreams served the same purpose.

In classical Freudian theory, the motivations behind unconscious wishes almost always involved sex or aggression. For this reason, Freud's theory was not widely accepted when it was first proposed. Contemporary psychologists do not accept Freud's theory in its entirety, but they tend to agree that people's ideas, goals, and motives can at times operate outside conscious awareness.

LATER DEVELOPMENTS IN 20TH-CENTURY PSYCHOLOGY

Despite the important contributions of Gestalt psychology and psychoanalysis, until World War II psychology was dominated by behaviorism, particularly in the United States. After the war, interest in psychology increased. Sophisticated instruments and electronic equipment became available, and a wider range of problems could be examined. It became evident that earlier theoretical approaches were too restrictive.

This viewpoint was strengthened by the development of computers in the 1950s. Computers were able to perform tasks—such as playing chess and proving mathematical theorems—that previously could be done only by human beings. They offered psychologists a powerful tool for theorizing about psychological processes. In a series of papers published in the late 1950s, Herbert Simon (who was later awarded a Nobel prize) and his colleagues described how psychological phenomena could be simulated with a computer. Many psychological issues were recast in terms of **information-processing models,** which viewed human beings as processors of information and provided a more dynamic approach to psychology than behaviorism. Similarly, the information-processing approach made it possible to formulate some of the ideas of Gestalt psychology and psychoanalysis more precisely. Earlier ideas about the nature of the mind could be expressed in concrete terms and checked against actual data. For example, we can think of the operation of memory as analogous to the way a computer stores and retrieves information. Just as a computer can transfer information from temporary storage in its internal memory chips (RAM) to more permanent storage on the hard drive, so, too, our working memory can act as a way station to long-term memory (Atkinson & Shiffrin, 1971a; Raaijmakers & Shiffrin, 1992).

Another important influence on psychology in the 1950s was the development of modern linguistics. Linguists began to theorize about the mental structures required to comprehend and speak a language. A pioneer in this area was Noam Chomsky, whose book *Syntactic Structures,* published in 1957, stimulated the first significant psychological analyses of language and the emergence of the field of psycholinguistics.

At the same time, important advances were occurring in neuropsychology. Discoveries about the brain and nervous system revealed clear relationships between neurological events and mental processes. In recent decades, advances in biomedical technology have enabled rapid progress in research on these relationships. In 1981 Roger Sperry was awarded a Nobel prize for demonstrating the links between specific regions of the brain and particular thought and behavioral processes, which we discuss in Chapter 2.

The development of information-processing models, psycholinguistics, and neuropsychology has produced an approach to psychology that is highly cognitive in orientation. Although its principal concern is the scientific analysis of mental processes and structures, cognitive psychology is not exclusively concerned with thought and knowledge. As illustrated throughout this book, this approach has been expanded to many other areas of psychology, including perception, motivation, emotion, clinical psychology, personality, and social psychology.

In sum, during the 20th century the focus of psychology came full circle. After rejecting conscious experience as ill-suited to scientific investigation and turning to the study of overt, observable behavior, psychologists are once again theorizing about covert aspects of the mind, this time with new and more powerful tools.

◆ Interim Summary

- The roots of psychology can be traced to the 4th and 5th centuries B.C. One of the earliest debates about human psychology focused on the question of whether human capabilities are inborn or acquired through experience (the nature-nurture debate).

- Scientific psychology was born in the late 19th century with the idea that mind and behavior could be the subject of scientific analysis. The first experimental laboratory in psychology was established by Wilhelm Wundt at the University of Leipzig in 1879.

- Among the early "schools" of psychology in the 20th century were structuralism, functionalism, behaviorism, Gestalt psychology, and psychoanalysis.

- Later developments in 20th-century psychology included information-processing theory, psycholinguistics, and neuropsychology.

◆ Critical Thinking Questions

1. What assumptions about human nature underlie the various historical approaches to psychology?

2. Considering these underlying assumptions, which of the historical approaches are compatible with one another? Which are incompatible?

CONTEMPORARY PSYCHOLOGICAL PERSPECTIVES

What is a **psychological perspective**? Basically, it is an approach, a way of looking at topics within psychology. Any topic in psychology can be approached from different perspectives. Indeed, this is true of any action a person takes. Suppose that, following an insult, you punch someone in the face. From a biological perspective, we can describe this act as involving certain brain areas and as the firing of nerves that activate the muscles that move your arm. From a behavioral perspective, we can describe the act without reference to anything within your body; rather, the insult is a stimulus to which you respond by punching, a learned response that has been rewarded in the past. A cognitive perspective on this action would focus on the mental processes involved in producing the behavior, and we might explain your punch in terms of your goals and plans: Your goal is to defend your honor, and aggressive

▌ Figure 1-5
Perspectives in Psychology
The analysis of psychological phenomena can be approached from several perspectives. Each offers a somewhat different account of why individuals act as they do, and each can make a contribution to our conception of the total person. The Greek letter *psi* (ψ) is sometimes used as an abbreviation for *psychology*.

By imaging the human brain during psychological tasks, researchers learn which brain structures underlie the targeted phenomena. Here we see a 3-dimensional representation of the human brain while listening to speech obtained through functional MRI (magnetic resonance imaging). Red indicates the greatest areas of activation, whereas yellow indicates areas of moderate activation. The neural activity is located in Wernicke's area of the brain. This approach illustrates a biological perspective on psychology.

behavior is part of your plan for achieving that goal. From a psychoanalytic perspective, your action could be described as an expression of an unconscious aggressive instinct. And finally, from a subjectivist perspective, your aggressive act can be understood as a reaction to interpreting the person's utterance as a personal insult.

Despite the many possible ways to describe any psychological act, these five perspectives represent the major approaches to the contemporary study of psychology (see Figure 1-5). Because these five perspectives are discussed throughout the book, here we provide only a brief description of some main points for each of them. Keep in mind that these approaches need not be mutually exclusive; rather, they may focus on different aspects of the same complex phenomenon. In fact, understanding many psychological topics requires an **eclectic approach** that spans multiple perspectives.

The Neural Basis of Behavior

THE BIOLOGICAL PERSPECTIVE

The human brain contains well over 10 billion nerve cells and an almost infinite number of interconnections between them. It may be the most complex structure in the universe. In principle, all psychological events can be related to the activity of the brain and nervous system. The biological approach to the study of human beings and other species attempts to relate overt behavior

to electrical and chemical events taking place inside the body. Research from the **biological perspective** seeks to specify the neurobiological processes that underlie behavior and mental processes. The biological approach to depression, for example, tries to understand this disorder in terms of abnormal changes in levels of neurotransmitters, which are chemicals produced in the brain that make communication between nerve cells possible.

We can use one of the problems described earlier to illustrate this perspective. The study of face recognition in patients with brain damage indicates that particular regions of the brain are specialized for face recognition. The human brain is divided into right and left hemispheres, and the regions devoted to face recognition seem to be located mainly in the right hemisphere. There is considerable hemispheric specialization in humans. In most right-handed people, for example, the left hemisphere is specialized for understanding language, and the right hemisphere is specialized for interpreting spatial relations.

The biological perspective has also assisted in the study of memory. It emphasizes the importance of certain brain structures, including the hippocampus, which is involved in consolidating memories. Childhood amnesia may be partly due to an immature hippocampus, a structure that is not fully developed until a year or two after birth. ▌

THE BEHAVIORAL PERSPECTIVE

As described in our brief review of the history of psychology, the **behavioral perspective** focuses on observable stimuli and responses and regards nearly all behavior as a result of conditioning and reinforcement. For example, a behavioral analysis of your social life might focus on which people you interact with (the social stimuli), the kinds of responses you make to them (rewarding, punishing, or neutral), the kinds of responses they in turn make to you (rewarding, punishing, or neutral), and how the responses sustain or disrupt the interaction.

We can use our sample problems to further illustrate this approach. With regard to obesity, some people may overeat (a specific response) only in the presence of specific stimuli (such as watching television), and learning to avoid these stimuli is part of many weight-control programs. With regard to aggression, children are more likely to express aggressive responses, such as hitting another child, when such responses are rewarded (the other child withdraws) than when their responses are punished (the other child counterattacks).

Historically, the strict behavioral approach did not consider the individual's mental processes at all, and even contemporary behaviorists usually do not conjecture about the mental processes that intervene between the stimulus and the response. Nevertheless, psychologists other than strict behaviorists often record what people say about their conscious experiences (a verbal self-report) and draw inferences about their mental activity

from these subjective data. Although few psychologists today would define themselves as strict behaviorists, many modern developments in psychology have evolved from the work of the earlier behaviorists (Skinner, 1981).

THE COGNITIVE PERSPECTIVE

The contemporary cognitive perspective is in part a return to the cognitive roots of psychology and in part a reaction to the narrowness of behaviorism, which tended to neglect complex human activities like reasoning, planning, decision making, and communication. Like the 19th-century version, the contemporary **cognitive perspective** is concerned with mental processes such as perceiving, remembering, reasoning, deciding, and problem solving. Unlike the 19th-century version, however, the contemporary cognitive approach is not based on introspection. Instead, it assumes that (1) only by studying

If the aggressive child has her way and the other child yields the swing, the aggressive behavior will be rewarded and the child will be more likely to behave aggressively in the future. This exemplifies a behavioral perspective on psychology.

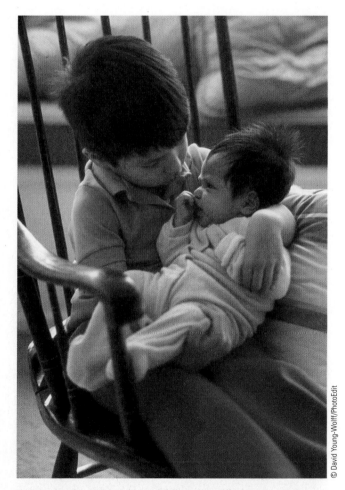

Events that happen early in childhood usually are not remembered. This little boy probably will not remember the events surrounding the birth of his baby brother. An explanation that illustrates the cognitive perspective on psychology emphasizes the important role that language plays in organizing memories.

mental processes can we fully understand what organisms do, and (2) we can study mental processes in an objective fashion by focusing on specific behaviors (just as behaviorists do) but interpreting them in terms of underlying mental processes. In making these interpretations, cognitive psychologists have often relied on an analogy between the mind and a computer. Incoming information is processed in various ways: It is selected, compared and combined with other information already in memory, transformed, rearranged, and so on.

Consider the phenomenon of childhood amnesia described at the beginning of the chapter. Perhaps we cannot remember events from the first few years of life because of a major developmental change in the way we organize our experience in memory. Such changes may be particularly pronounced at about age 3, when our language abilities increase immensely, and language offers us a new way of organizing our memories.

The Psychoanalytic Perspective

Sigmund Freud developed the psychoanalytic conception of human behavior in Europe at about the same time behaviorism was evolving in the United States. In some respects, psychoanalysis was a blend of the 19th-century versions of cognition and physiology. In particular, Freud combined cognitive notions of consciousness, perception, and memory with ideas about biologically based instincts to forge a bold new theory of human behavior.

The basic assumption of the **psychoanalytic perspective** is that behavior stems from unconscious processes, meaning beliefs, fears, and desires that a person is unaware of but that nonetheless influence behavior. Freud believed that many of the impulses that are forbidden or punished by parents and society during childhood are derived from innate instincts. Because each of us is born with these impulses, they exert a pervasive influence that must be dealt with in some manner. Forbidding them merely forces them

In this painting by M. Morales, a dream conveys unconscious desires. This illustrates the psychoanalytic perspective on psychology.

out of awareness into the unconscious. They do not disappear, however. They may manifest themselves as emotional problems and symptoms of mental illness or as socially approved behavior such as artistic and literary activity. For example, if you feel a lot of anger toward your father but you cannot afford to alienate him, your anger may become unconscious, perhaps expressed in a dream about him being hurt in an atrocious accident.

Freud believed that we are driven by the same basic instincts as animals (primarily sex and aggression) and that we are continually struggling against a society that stresses the control of these impulses. The psychoanalytic perspective suggests new ways of looking at some of the problems described at the beginning of the chapter. For example, Freud claimed that aggressive behavior stems from an innate instinct. Although this proposal is not widely accepted in human psychology, it is in agreement with the views of some biologists and psychologists who study aggression in animals.

THE SUBJECTIVIST PERSPECTIVE

The **subjectivist perspective** contends that human behavior is a function of the perceived world, not the objective world. Like the cognitive approach, the subjectivist perspective drew from the Gestalt tradition and reacted against the narrowness of behaviorism. Although allied with cognitive psychology, subjectivism has been most pervasive within social and personality psychology. To understand human social behavior, this view holds, we must grasp the person's own "definition of the situation," which is expected to vary by culture, personal history, and current motivational state. This perspective, then, is the most open to cultural and individual differences and to the effects of motivation and emotion.

In one sense, the idea that people actively construct their own subjective realities calls for introspective methods. Even so, subjectivists do not rely exclusively on subjective self-reports because they also assume that people fail to see their subjective realities as personal constructions. This **naïve realism** refers to people's tendency to take their constructed, subjective realities to be faithful renderings of an objective world. Therefore, a subjectivist approach also involves systematic observation of judgments and behaviors. A subjectivist perspective is illustrated by a classic early study that found that people reliably overestimate the physical size of valuable coins, more so than for coins of lower value. This tendency is exaggerated among poor children (Bruner & Goodman, 1947; note that coins in general probably seemed much more valuable in the 1940s!).

Consider again the problem of trait attribution. The study of how people make sense of other people's actions—

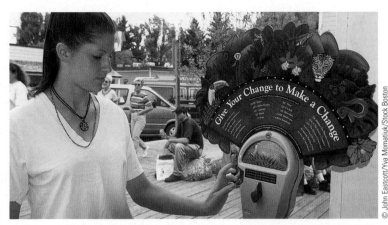

Is this woman generous? Westerners have a strong tendency to say, "Yes, she is," making a trait attribution for her behavior. An emphasis on how people perceive and interpret their social world characterizes the subjectivist perspective.

in the example mentioned earlier, donating $50 to charity—emerged from a subjectivist emphasis on how situations are defined by the people in them (Heider, 1958). One contemporary explanation for the pervasive tendency to attribute other people's actions to their personality traits suggests that, because Western cultures have long emphasized personal agency, Westerners often fail to see the influence of situations (Nisbett, Peng, Choi, & Norenzayan, 2001; see Chapter 18). Likewise, a subjectivist view of the link between media violence and aggression suggests that habitual consumption of violent media instills and strengthens aggressive schemas and scripts, which are later used to define subsequent interpersonal encounters (Anderson & Bushman, 2001).

CONCEPT REVIEW TABLE
Five Perspectives Within Psychology

Biological Perspective	An orientation toward understanding the neurobiological processes that underlie behavior and mental processes.
Behavioral Perspective	An orientation toward understanding observable behavior in terms of conditioning and reinforcement.
Cognitive Perspective	An orientation toward understanding mental processes such as perceiving, remembering, reasoning, deciding, and problem solving and their relationship to behavior.
Psychoanalytic Perspective	An orientation toward understanding behavior in terms of unconscious motives stemming from sexual and aggressive impulses.
Subjectivist Perspective	An orientation toward understanding behavior and mental processes in terms of the subjective realities people actively construct.

RELATIONSHIPS BETWEEN PSYCHOLOGICAL AND BIOLOGICAL PERSPECTIVES

The behaviorist, cognitive, psychoanalytic, and subjectivist perspectives all rely on concepts that are purely psychological (such as perception, the unconscious, and attributions). Although these perspectives sometimes offer different explanations for the same phenomenon, those explanations are always psychological in nature. The biological perspective is different. In addition to using psychological concepts, it employs concepts (such as neurotransmitters and hormones) drawn from physiology and other branches of biology.

There is a way, though, in which the biological perspective makes direct contact with the psychological perspectives. Biologically oriented researchers attempt to explain psychological concepts and principles in terms of their biological counterparts. For example, researchers might attempt to explain the normal ability to recognize faces solely in terms of neurons and their interconnections in a certain region of the brain. Such attempts are termed **reductionism** because they involve reducing psychological notions to biological ones. Throughout this book, we present examples of successful reductionism—situations in which what was once understood at only the psychological level is now understood at least in part at the biological level.

If reductionism can be successful, why bother with psychological explanations at all? Is psychology just something to do until the biologists figure everything out? The answer is clearly no.

First, psychological findings, concepts, and principles direct biological researchers in their work. Given that the brain contains billions of brain cells and countless interconnections between these cells, biological researchers cannot hope to find something of interest by arbitrarily selecting some brain cells to study. Rather, they must have a way of directing their efforts to relevant groups of brain cells. Psychological findings can supply this direction. For example, psychological research indicates that our ability to discriminate among spoken words and our ability to discriminate among spatial positions obey different principles. So, biological psychologists might look in different regions of the brain for the neural basis of these two kinds of discrimination capacities (the left hemisphere for word discrimination and the right hemisphere for spatial-position discrimination). As another example, if psychological research indicates that learning a motor skill is a slow

process that is hard to undo, biological psychologists can direct their attention to brain processes that are relatively slow but permanently alter connections between neurons (Churchland & Sejnowski, 1988).

Second, our biology always acts in concert with our past circumstances and current environment. For example, obesity can be the result of (1) a genetic predisposition to gain weight (a biological factor), (2) learning bad eating habits (a psychological factor), or (3) a reaction to cultural pressures toward extreme thinness (a sociocultural factor). The biologist can seek to understand the first factor, but it is still up to the psychologist to explore and explain the past experiences and current circumstances that influence a person's eating habits.

Nevertheless, the push for reductionism goes on at an ever-increasing rate. For many topics in psychology, we now have both psychological explanations and knowledge about how the relevant psychological concepts are implemented or executed in the brain (for example, what particular parts of the brain are involved and how they are interconnected). This kind of biological knowledge typically falls short of total reductionism, but it is still very important. Memory researchers, for example, have long distinguished between working memory and long-term memory (which are psychological notions), but now they also know something about how these two kinds of memory are actually coded differently in the brain. So, for many of the topics discussed in this book, we review what is known at the biological level as well as at the psychological level.

Indeed, a central theme of this book—and of contemporary psychology in general—is that psychological phenomena can be understood at both the psychological and biological levels. The biological analysis shows us how the psychological notions can be implemented in the brain. Both levels of analysis are clearly needed (although for some topics, including many dealing with social interactions, biological analyses have only just begun). ▮

MAJOR SUBFIELDS OF PSYCHOLOGY

So far, we have gained a general understanding of the nature of psychology by looking at its topics and perspectives. We can further our understanding by looking at what different kinds of psychologists do and at emerging fields of emphasis in 21st-century psychology (see the Cutting Edge Research feature).

About half the people who have advanced degrees in psychology work in colleges and universities. In addition to teaching, they may devote much of their time to research or counseling. Other psychologists work in schools, hospitals or clinics, research institutes, government agencies, or business and industry. Still others are in private practice and offer their services to the public for a fee. We now turn to a brief description of some of the subfields of psychology.

BIOLOGICAL PSYCHOLOGY Biological psychologists (also referred to as physiological psychologists) look for the relationship between biological processes and behavior.

EXPERIMENTAL PSYCHOLOGY Experimental psychologists usually conduct research from a behaviorist or cognitive perspective and use experimental methods to study how people (and other animals) react to sensory stimuli, perceive the world, learn and remember, reason, and respond emotionally.

DEVELOPMENTAL PSYCHOLOGY Developmental psychologists are concerned with human development and the factors that shape behavior from birth to old age. They might study a specific ability, such as how language develops in children, or a particular period of life, such as infancy.

SOCIAL AND PERSONALITY PSYCHOLOGY These two subfields overlap. **Social psychologists** are interested in how people perceive and interpret their social world and how their beliefs, emotions, and behaviors are influenced by the real or imagined presence of others. They are also concerned with the behavior of groups and with social relationships between and among people. **Personality psychologists** study the thoughts, emotions, and behaviors that define an individual's personal style of interacting with the world. Accordingly, they are interested in differences between individuals, and they also attempt to synthesize all the psychological processes into an integrated account of the total person.

CLINICAL AND COUNSELING PSYCHOLOGY Clinical **psychologists** are the largest group of psychologists. They apply psychological principles to the diagnosis and treatment of emotional and behavioral problems, including mental illness, drug addiction, and marital and family conflict. **Counseling psychologists** perform many of the same functions as clinical psychologists, although they often deal with less serious problems. They frequently work with high school or university students.

SCHOOL AND EDUCATIONAL PSYCHOLOGY Because serious emotional problems often make their first appearance in the early grades, many elementary schools employ psychologists whose training combines courses in child development, education, and clinical psychology. These **school psychologists** work with children to evaluate learning and emotional problems. In contrast, **educational psychologists** are specialists in learning and teaching. They may work in schools, but more often they

work in a university's school of education, where they do research on teaching methods and help train teachers.

ORGANIZATIONAL AND ENGINEERING PSYCHOLOGY **Organizational psychologists** (sometimes called *industrial psychologists*) typically work for a company. They are concerned with selecting people who are most suitable for particular jobs or designing structures that facilitate collaboration and teamwork. **Engineering psychologists** (sometimes called human factors engineers) try to improve the relationship between people and machines. For instance, they improve human-machine interaction by designing machines with the most efficient placement of gauges and controls, which leads to better performance, safety, and comfort.

◆ Interim Summary

- The study of psychology can be approached from several perspectives. Five contemporary perspectives are the biological perspective, the behavioral perspective, the cognitive perspective, the psychoanalytic perspective, and the subjectivist perspective.

- The biological perspective differs from the other perspectives in that its principles are partly drawn from biology. Biological researchers often attempt to explain psychological principles in terms of biological ones; this is known as reductionism.

- Among the major subfields of psychology are biological psychology, experimental psychology, developmental psychology, social and personality psychology, clinical and counseling psychology, school and educational psychology, and organizational and engineering psychology.

- Many new areas of inquiry, including cognitive neuroscience (as well as affective neuroscience and social cognitive neuroscience), evolutionary psychology, cultural psychology, and positive psychology, span traditional subfields and disciplines.

◆ Critical Thinking Questions

1. Consider the question, "What are the determinants of an individual's sexual orientation?" How would the different perspectives outlined in this chapter approach this question?

2. Many of the new approaches to 21st-century psychology (described in the Cutting-Edge Research box) integrate divergent perspectives or fill prior gaps in the field. What other new advances might be on the horizon in 21st-century psychology? That is, what other opportunities for integrating perspectives and filling gaps do you predict?

Increasingly, psychologists span multiple subfields in their research and also stretch beyond psychology to forge collaborations with researchers in other disciplines. These cross-area and interdisciplinary approaches have gained considerable momentum at the start of the 21st century and promise to be very important in the next few decades. Of particular interest are cognitive neuroscience, evolutionary psychology, cultural psychology, and positive psychology. Here we briefly describe each of these approaches, with examples of the kinds of research being done in each field.

COGNITIVE NEUROSCIENCE

Cognitive neuroscience focuses on cognitive processes and relies heavily on the methods and findings of neuroscience (the branch of biology that deals with the brain and nervous system). In essence, **cognitive neuroscience** attempts to learn how mental activities are executed in the brain. The key idea is that cognitive psychology provides hypotheses about specific cognitive capacities—such as recognizing faces—and neuroscience supplies proposals about how these specific functions might be executed in the brain.

What is particularly distinctive about cognitive neuroscience is its reliance on new techniques for studying the brains of normal participants (as opposed to

brain-damaged ones) while they are performing a cognitive task. These neuro-imaging or brain-scanning techniques create visual images of a brain in action, with an indication of which regions of the brain show the most neural activity during a particular task. An example is the study of how people remember information for brief or long periods. When people are asked to remember information for a few seconds, neuroimaging results show increases in neural activity in regions in the front of the brain. When they are asked to remember information for a long period, there is increased activity in an entirely different region, one closer to the middle of the brain. Thus, different mechanisms seem to be used for the short-term and long-term storage of information (Smith & Jonides, 1994; Squire, Knowlton, & Musen, 1993).

The connection between psychology and neuroscience is not limited to cognitive psychology. Psychologists have also initiated **affective neuroscience** (Panksepp, 1998) to discover how emotional phenomena are executed in the brain, as well as **social cognitive neuroscience** (Ochsner & Lieberman, 2001) to discover how stereotyping, attitudes, person perception, and self-knowledge are executed in the brain.

EVOLUTIONARY PSYCHOLOGY

Evolutionary psychology is concerned with the biological origins of psychological mechanisms. In addition to psychology and biology, the other disciplines involved in this approach include anthropology and psychiatry. The key idea behind evolutionary psychology is that, like

biological mechanisms, psychological mechanisms must have evolved over millions of years through a process of natural selection. As such, **evolutionary psychology** holds that psychological mechanisms have a genetic basis and in the past increased our ancestors' chances of surviving and reproducing. To illustrate, consider a liking for sweets. Such a preference can be thought of as a psychological mechanism, and it has a genetic basis. Moreover, we have this preference because it increased our ancestors' chances of survival: The fruit that tasted the sweetest had the highest nutritional value, so by eating it they increased the chances of continued survival of the relevant genes (Symons, 1992).

An evolutionary perspective can affect the study of psychological issues in several ways. Certain topics are of particular importance because of their link to survival or successful reproduction. Such topics include how we select our mates and how we think and behave when experiencing particular emotions (Buss, 1991). An evolutionary perspective can also provide new insights into familiar topics. Concerning obesity, we noted earlier that a history of deprivation can lead to overeating in the future. Evolutionary psychology provides an interpretation of this puzzling phenomenon. Until comparatively recently in human history, people experienced deprivation only when food was scarce. An adaptive mechanism for dealing with scarcity is overeating when food is available. So, evolution may have favored individuals with a tendency to overeat following deprivation.

HOW PSYCHOLOGICAL RESEARCH IS DONE

Now that we have some idea of the topics psychologists study and their perspectives, we can consider the research strategies they use to investigate them. In general, doing research involves two steps: (1) generating a scientific hypothesis and (2) testing that hypothesis.

GENERATING HYPOTHESES

The first step in any research project is to generate a **hypothesis**—a statement that can be tested—about the topic of interest. Regarding childhood amnesia, for example, we might generate the hypothesis that people can retrieve more memories of their early life if they are back in the same place where the incidents originally occurred. How does a researcher arrive at such a hypothe-

CULTURAL PSYCHOLOGY

Scientific psychology in the West has often assumed that people in all cultures have exactly the same psychological processes. Increasingly, this assumption is being challenged by proponents of cultural psychology, an interdisciplinary movement of psychologists, anthropologists, sociologists, and other social scientists. **Cultural psychology** is concerned with how the culture in which an individual lives—its traditions, language, and worldview—influences that person's mental representations and psychological processes.

Here is an example. In the West—North America and much of western and northern Europe—we think of ourselves as separate and autonomous agents with unique abilities and traits. In contrast, many cultures in the East—including those of India, China, and Japan—emphasize the interrelationships among people rather than their individuality. Moreover, Easterners tend to pay more attention to social situations than Westerners do. These differences lead Easterners to explain the behavior of another person differently than do Westerners. Rather than explaining a piece of behavior solely in terms of a person's traits, Easterners also explain it in terms of the social situation in which it occurred (Nisbett et al., 2001). This has profound implications for trait attribution, one of the sample problems discussed at the beginning of the chapter. These differences between East and West in explaining behavior can also have educational implications. Because of their emphasis on collectivism rather than individualism, Asian students tend to study together more than American students. Such group study may be a useful technique, and it may be part of the reason why Asian students outperform their American counterparts in math. In addition, when an American student is having difficulty in math, both the student and the teacher tend to attribute the difficulty to the student's individual abilities. When a comparable case arises in a Japanese school, student and teacher are more likely to look to the situation—the student-teacher interaction in the instructional context—for an explanation of the poor performance (Stevenson, Lee, & Graham, 1993).

POSITIVE PSYCHOLOGY

After World War II, psychology—especially clinical psychology—became a science devoted to healing. It adopted a disease model of human functioning from the medical sciences and aimed to cure pathologies. Although this focus produced tremendous advances in the field's understanding and treatment of mental illness (see Chapters 15 and 16), it had little to say about what makes life worth living. **Positive psychology** emerged to balance the field's sophisticated scientific understanding of mental illness with an equally sophisticated scientific understanding of human flourishing (Seligman, 2002). Although positive psychology shares with the earlier humanistic psychology a concern with people's development toward their full potential, it departs from humanistic psychology by relying heavily on empirical methods.

Positive psychology targets psychological phenomena at levels ranging from the study of positive subjective experiences, such as happiness and optimism, to the study of positive personality traits, such as courage and wisdom, and the study of positive institutions—social structures that might cultivate civility and responsible citizenship (Seligman & Csikszentmihalyi, 2000). An example that combines the first two levels of analysis comes from current research on positive emotions (see Chapter 11). Unlike negative emotions, which narrow people's ideas about action (e.g., fight or flight), positive emotions have been found to broaden people's mindsets, encouraging them to discover novel lines of thought or action. Joy, for instance, creates the urge to play, and interest creates the urge to explore. A key incidental outcome of these broadened mindsets is an increase in personal resources: As individuals discover new ideas and actions, they build physical, intellectual, social, and psychological resources. Empirical studies support this new broaden-and-build theory of positive emotions, showing that—through their effects on broadened thinking—positive emotions fuel growth-positive personality traits such as resilience and optimism (Fredrickson, 2001). The take-home message for positive psychology is that positive emotions are worth cultivating, not just as end states in themselves but also as a means of triggering upward spirals toward psychological growth and flourishing.

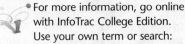 For more information, go online with InfoTrac College Edition. Use your own term or search:

- Affective neuroscience
- Positive psychology

---

sis? There is no single answer. An astute observer of naturally occurring situations may have an advantage in coming up with hypotheses. For example, you might have noticed that you can remember more about your high school years when you are back home, which could generate such a hypothesis. It also helps to be very familiar with the relevant scientific literature—previously published books and articles about the topic of interest.

The most important source for scientific hypotheses, however, is often a scientific **theory,** an interrelated set of propositions about a particular phenomenon. For example, one theory of sexual motivation (discussed in Chapter 10) proposes a genetic predisposition toward heterosexuality or homosexuality. This leads to the testable scientific hypothesis that pairs of identical twins—who have identical genes—should be more likely to have the same sexual orientation than pairs of fraternal twins, who share only about half their genes. A competing theory emphasizes childhood events as the source of an individual's sexual orientation and generates a competing set of hypotheses that can also be tested. As we will see throughout this book, testing hypotheses derived from competing theories is one of the most powerful ways of advancing scientific knowledge.

The term **scientific** means that the research methods used to collect the data are (1) unbiased (do not favor one hypothesis over another) and (2) reliable (other qualified people can repeat the observations and obtain the same results). The methods considered in this section have these two characteristics. Although some are better suited to certain perspectives than to others, each method can be used with each perspective.

EXPERIMENTS

The most powerful scientific method is the experiment. **Experiments** provide the strongest tests of hypotheses about cause and effect. The investigator carefully controls conditions—often in a laboratory—and takes measurements in order to discover the causal relationships among variables. A **variable** is something that can occur with different values (see Concept Review Table). For example, an experiment might explore whether amount of sleep causes memory changes (does recall of childhood events decrease with lack of sleep?). If an experiment shows that memory performance changes systematically with hours of sleep, an orderly causal relationship between these two variables has been found.

The ability to exercise precise control over a variable distinguishes the experimental method from other methods of scientific observation. For example, if the hypothesis is that individuals will perform better on a math problem if they are offered more money for a good performance, the experimenter might randomly assign participants to one of three conditions: One group is told that they will be paid $10 if they perform well, the second group is promised $5, and the third group is not offered any money. The experimenter then measures and compares the performance of all three groups to see if, in fact, more money (the hypothesized cause) produces better performance (the hypothesized effect).

In this experiment, the amount of money offered is the independent variable because it is a variable that is independent of what the participant does. In fact, the **independent variable** is under the complete control of the experimenter, who creates it and controls its variation. In an experiment, the independent variable represents the hypothesized "cause." The hypothesized "effect" in an experiment is the **dependent variable** because it is hypothesized to depend on the value of the independent

variable. In this experiment, the dependent variable is performance on the math problems. The experimenter manipulates the independent variable and observes the dependent variable to learn the outcome of the experiment. The dependent variable is almost always some measure of the participants' behavior. The phrase "is a function of" is often used to express the dependence of one variable on another. For this experiment, we could say that the participants' performance on the math problems is a function of the amount of money offered. The groups that are paid money would be the **experimental groups,** or groups in which the hypothesized cause is present. The group that was not paid would be the **control group,** the group in which the hypothesized cause is absent. In general, a control group serves as a baseline against which experimental groups can be compared.

One important feature of the experiment just described is random assignment of participants to groups or conditions. **Random assignment** means that each participant has an equal probability of being placed in any group. Without random assignment, the experimenter cannot be certain that something other than the independent variable might have produced the results. For example, an experimenter should never let participants choose which group they would like to be in. Although most participants might choose to be in the highest-paid group, those who are made nervous by pressure might choose to be in a "casual" group that was not paid. In any case, the problem is that the groups would now contain different kinds of people, and the differences in their personalities, rather than the amount of money offered, might cause one group to do better than another. Or suppose that an experimenter runs all the paid groups first and runs the no-payment control group afterward. This introduces a host of potential problems. Perhaps performance varies as a function of the time of day (morning, afternoon, or evening); maybe those who participate later in the experiment are closer in time to their final exams than earlier participants. In addition to these uncontrolled variables, many others of which the experimenter is unaware might bias the results. All such problems are resolved by randomly assigning participants to conditions. Only with random assignment can we be certain that all extraneous variables—such as participant personality, time of day, or time of semester—are evenly represented across conditions and therefore unlikely to introduce bias. Random assignment is one of the most important ingredients of an experiment.

The experimental method can be used outside the laboratory as well. For example, in research on obesity, the effects of different methods of weight control can be investigated by trying these methods on separate but similar groups of obese individuals. The experimental method is a matter of logic, not location. Still, most experiments take place in laboratories, chiefly because a laboratory setting allows measuring behavior more precisely and controlling the variables more completely. And again, it is often random assignment that is at issue: If two obesity clinics use different methods and achieve different results, we cannot conclude with confidence that the different methods are responsible because the clinics might attract different kinds of people to their programs or have different staff cultures and expectations.

The experiments described so far examine the effect of one independent variable on one dependent variable. Limiting an investigation to only one independent variable, however, is too restrictive for some problems. **Multivariate experiments**—experiments manipulating several independent variables at once—are common in psychological research. In the hypothetical study in which participants were offered different amounts of money for solving math problems, the experimenter might also vary the level of difficulty of the problems. Now there would be six groups of participants, each combining one of three different amounts of money with one of two levels of difficulty (easy versus difficult).

MEASUREMENT Psychologists using the experimental method often have to make statements about amounts or quantities. Sometimes variables can be measured by physical means, such as hours of sleep deprivation or dosage of a drug. At other times, variables have to be scaled in a manner that places them in some sort of order. In rating a patient's feelings of aggression, for example, a psychotherapist might use a 5-point scale ranging from *never* through *rarely*, *sometimes*, and *often* to *always*. For purposes of precise communication, experiments require some form of **measurement**, a system for assigning numbers to variables.

Experiments usually involve making measurements on many participants, not just one. The results therefore are data in the form of a set of numbers that can be summarized and interpreted. To accomplish this task, the experimenter needs to use **statistics**, the discipline that deals with sampling data from a population of individuals and then drawing inferences about the population from those data. Statistics plays an important role not only in experimental research but in other methods as well.[3] The most common statistic is the **mean**, which is simply the technical term for an arithmetic average, the sum of a set of scores divided by the number of scores in the set. In studies with one experimental group and one control group, there are two means to be compared: a mean for the scores of the participants in the experimental group and a mean for the scores of the participants in the control group. The difference between these two means is, of course, what interests the experimenters. If the difference between the means is large, it can be accepted at face value. But what if the difference is small?

CONCEPT REVIEW TABLE
Terminology of Experimental Research

Hypothesis	A statement about cause and effect that can be tested.
Experiment	A well-controlled test of a hypothesis about cause and effect.
Variable	Something that can occur with different values and can be measured.
Independent variable	A variable that represents the hypothesized "cause" that is precisely controlled by the experimenter and independent of what the participant does.
Dependent variable	A variable that represents the hypothesized "effect" whose values ultimately depend on the value of the independent variable.
Experimental group	A group in which the hypothesized cause is present.
Control group	A group in which the hypothesized cause is absent.
Random assignment	A system for assigning participants to experimental and control groups so that each participant has an equal chance of being assigned to any group.
Measurement	A system for assigning numbers to different values of variables.
Statistics	Mathematical techniques for determining the certainty with which a sample of data can be used to draw generalizations or inferences.

What if the measures used are subject to error? What if a few extreme cases are producing the difference? Statisticians have solved these problems by developing tests for determining the significance of a difference. A psychologist who says that the difference between the experimental group and the control group is **statistically significant** means that a statistical test has been applied to the data and the observed difference is unlikely to have arisen by chance or because of a few extreme cases.

CORRELATION

Not all problems can be easily studied by using the experimental method. In many situations the investigator has no control over which participants go in which conditions. For example, if we want to test the hypothesis that anorexic people are more sensitive to changes in taste than normal-weight people, we cannot select a group of normal-weight participants and require half of

[3]This discussion is designed to introduce the experimental tools of measurement and statistics. A more thorough discussion is provided in the Appendix.

them to become anorexic! Rather, we select people who are already anorexic or already of normal weight and see if they also differ in taste sensitivity. More generally, we can use the correlational method to determine whether some variable that is not under our control is associated—or correlated—with another variable of interest.

In the example just given, there were only two values of the weight variable: anorexic and normal. It is more common to have many values of each variable and to determine the degree to which values on one variable are related to values on another. This is done by using a descriptive statistic called the **correlation coefficient,** an estimate of the degree to which two variables are related. The correlation coefficient, symbolized by r, is expressed as a number between -1.00 and $+1.00$. A perfect relationship—which is rare—is indicated by 1.00 ($+1.00$ if the relationship is positive and -1.00 if the relationship is negative). No relationship at all is indicated by a correlation close to zero. As r goes from 0 to $+1.00$ (or from 0 to -1.00), the strength of the relationship increases.

A correlation can be either $+$ or $-$. The sign of the correlation indicates whether the two variables are **positively correlated,** meaning that the values of the two variables either increase together or decrease together, or **negatively correlated,** meaning that as the value of one variable increases, the value of the other decreases. Suppose that the number of times a student is absent from class correlates $-.40$ with the final course grade (the more absences, the lower the grade). On the other hand, the correlation between the number of classes attended and the course grade would be $+ 40$. The strength of the relationship is the same, but the sign indicates whether we are looking at classes missed or classes attended.[4]

To get a clearer picture of a correlation coefficient, consider the hypothetical study presented in Figure 1-6. As shown in Figure 1-6a, the study involves patients with brain damage leading to problems in face recognition (prosopagnosia). What is of interest is whether the degree of deficit, or error, in face recognition increases with the amount of brain tissue that is damaged. Each point on the graph in Figure 1-6a represents the percentage of errors made by one patient on a test of face recognition. For example, a patient who had only 10% brain damage made 15% errors on the face-recognition test, but a patient who had 55% brain damage made 75% errors. If errors in face recognition *always* increased along with the amount of brain damage, the points in the graph would consistently increase in moving from left to right; if the points had all fallen on the diagonal line in the figure, the correlation would have been $r = 1.0$—a perfect correlation. A couple of points fall on either side of the line,

though, so the correlation is about .90. Such a high correlation indicates a very strong relationship between amount of the brain damage and errors in face recognition. In Figure 1-6a, the correlation is positive because more errors are associated with more brain damage.

If, instead of focusing on errors, we plot the percentage of correct responses on the face recognition test, we end up with the diagram in Figure 1-6b. Now the correlation is negative—about $-.90$—because *fewer* correct responses are associated with *more* brain damage. The diagonal line in Figure 1-6b is simply the inverse of the one in Figure 1-6a.

Finally, consider the diagram in Figure 1-6c. Here we have graphed errors on the face recognition test as a function of the patients' height. Of course, there is no reason to expect a relationship between height and face recognition, and the graph shows that there is none. The points neither consistently increase nor consistently decrease in moving from left to right but rather bounce around a horizontal line. The correlation is 0.

In psychological research, a correlation coefficient of .60 or more is considered quite high. Correlations in the range from .20 to .60 are of practical and theoretical value and are useful in making predictions. Correlations between 0 and .20 must be judged with caution and are only minimally useful in making predictions.

TESTS The familiar use of the correlational method involves tests that measure aptitudes, achievement, or other psychological traits, such as the test of face recognition just discussed. A **test** presents a uniform situation to a group of people who vary in a particular trait (such as brain damage, math ability, manual dexterity, or aggression). The variation in scores on the test can be correlated with variations on another variable. For example, people's scores on a test of math ability can be correlated with their subsequent grades in a college math course. If the correlation is high, then the test score may be used to determine which of a new group of students should be placed in advanced sections of the course.

CORRELATION AND CAUSATION There is an important distinction between experimental and correlational studies. In a typical experimental study, one variable (the independent variable) is systematically manipulated to determine its causal effect on some other variable (the dependent variable). Such cause-and-effect relationships cannot be inferred from correlational studies.

For instance, studies have shown that the more TV violence a young boy watches, the more aggressive he is. But does watching violent TV cause the aggression, or do more aggressive boys choose to watch more violent TV? If all we have is a correlation, we cannot say which variable is cause and which is effect. (As noted earlier in

[4]The numerical method for calculating a correlation coefficient is described in the Appendix.

a) Positive correlation

The patients are ordered along the horizontal axis with respect to the amount of brain damage, with the patient represented by the leftmost point having the least brain damage (10%) and the patient represented by the rightmost point having the most brain damage (55%). Each point on the graph represents a single patient's score on a test of face recognition. The correlation is a positive .90.

b) Negative correlation

The same data are depicted, but we now focus on the percentage of correct responses (rather than errors). Now the correlation is a negative .90.

c) Zero correlation

The patients' performance on the face recognition test is graphed as a function of their height. Now the correlation is 0.

▌ **Figure 1-6**
Scatter Diagrams Illustrating Correlations
These hypothesized data are based on 10 patients, all of whom have some damage in regions of the brain known to be involved in face recognition.

the chapter, however, other studies do demonstrate a causal relationship between watching violent TV and behaving aggressively. Experimenters had control over the independent variable and used random assignment of participants to conditions.)

Two variables can also be correlated when neither is the cause of the other. For example, many years before careful medical experiments demonstrated that cigarette smoking causes cancer, a correlation between smoking and lung cancer was shown. That is, it was already known that people who smoked were more likely to contract cancer. But—as the tobacco companies rushed to point out—this correlation left open the possibility that some third cause was responsible. For example, if people who live in smoggy urban areas are more likely to smoke than people who live in rural areas with cleaner air, then air pollution rather than smoking could cause higher cancer rates in smokers.

In short, when two variables are correlated, variation in one of them may possibly be the cause of varia-

tion in the other. Indeed, correlation is a prerequisite for causation. But, without further experiments, no such conclusion is justified from correlational studies, because correlation does not necessarily imply causation.

OBSERVATION

DIRECT OBSERVATION In the early stages of research, the most efficient way of making progress toward an explanation may be **direct observation**—to simply observe the phenomenon under study as it occurs naturally. Careful observation of animal and human behavior is the starting point for a great deal of research in psychology. For example, observation of primates in their native environment may tell us things about their social organization that will help in later laboratory investigations. Video recordings of newborn babies reveal details of their activity shortly after birth and the types of stimuli to which they respond. However, investigators observing

Field studies can often tell us more about social behavior than experimental studies can. Professor Shirley Strum has been observing the same troop of baboons in Kenya for more than 20 years, identifying individual animals, and making daily recordings of their behaviors and social interactions. Her data have provided remarkable information about the mental abilities of baboons and the role of friendships in their social system.

naturally occurring behavior must be trained to observe and record events accurately so that their own biases do not influence what they report.

Observational methods may be used in a laboratory if the problem being studied is partly biological. For example, in their classic study of the physiological aspects of human sexuality, William Masters and Virginia Johnson (1966) developed techniques for directly observing sexual responses in the laboratory. The data included (1) observations of behavior, (2) recordings of physiological changes, and (3) responses to questions about the participants' sensations before, during, and after sexual stimulation. Although the researchers agreed that human sexuality has many dimensions besides the biological one, their observations of the anatomical and physiological aspects of sexual response have been very helpful in understanding the nature of human sexuality, as well as in solving sexual problems.

THE SURVEY METHOD Some problems that are difficult to study by direct observation may be studied by indirect observation through the use of questionnaires or interviews. Rather than observe people engaging in a particular behavior, such as exercising regularly, researchers using the **survey method** simply ask people if they engage in the behavior of interest. The survey method is more open to bias than direct observation, however. Of particular concern are **social desirability effects,** which occur when some people try to present themselves in a favorable light (for example, by saying that they exercise more than they actually do). Still, the survey method has produced many impor-

tant results. For example, before Masters and Johnson conducted their research on the human sexual response, most of the available information on how people behave sexually (as opposed to how laws, religion, or society said they should behave) came from extensive surveys conducted by Alfred Kinsey and his associates 20 years earlier. Information from thousands of interviews was analyzed, resulting in the publication of two pioneering works: *Sexual Behavior in the Human Male* (Kinsey, Pomeroy, & Martin, 1948) and *Sexual Behavior in the Human Female* (Kinsey, Pomeroy, Martin, & Gebhard, 1953).

Surveys have also been used to discover people's political opinions, product preferences, health care needs, and so on. The Gallup poll and the U.S. census are probably the most familiar surveys. An adequate survey requires presenting a carefully pretested questionnaire to a sample of people who have been selected by methods designed to ensure that they are representative of the larger population being studied.

CASE HISTORIES Still another form of indirect observation is to obtain a **case history,** which is a partial biography of a particular individual. This involves asking people to recall relevant experiences from their past. For example, if the research is concerned with the childhood antecedents of adult depression, the researcher might begin by asking questions about earlier life events. These case histories are biographies designed for scientific use, and they are important sources of data for psychologists who are studying individuals.

A major limitation of case histories is that they rely on a person's memories and reconstructions of earlier events, which are frequently distorted or incomplete. Sometimes other data can be used to corroborate information obtained in a case history. For example, written records, such as death certificates, can be used to check on specific dates, or relatives of the person being interviewed can be asked to report their own memories of the relevant events. Even so, their limitations make case histories less useful for testing a theory or hypothesis than for suggesting hypotheses that can then be tested in more rigorous ways or checked with a larger sample of participants. In this way, scientists use the case history in much the same way that a therapist or physician might when trying to formulate a diagnosis and treatment for a particular individual.

LITERATURE REVIEWS

One final way in which psychological research is done is by conducting literature reviews. A **literature review** is a scholarly summary of the existing body of research on a given topic. Because the field of psychology grows at a fast pace, an up-to-date literature review is an indispensable tool for assessing patterns within the accumulating scientific evidence for a particular psychological hypothesis or theory.

Literature reviews come in two forms. One form is a **narrative review,** in which authors use words to describe studies previously conducted and discuss the strength of the available psychological evidence. College students enrolled in upper-level psychology courses often write narrative reviews of a chosen topic for term papers. Another type of review, which has become increasingly popular, is a **meta-analysis,** in which authors use statistical techniques to combine and draw conclusions about studies previously conducted. In any given experiment, as we have seen, participants are treated as "cases," with each participant contributing his or her own unique data, which are then summarized statistically. In a meta-analysis, by contrast, individual studies are treated as "cases," with each study contributing its own unique summary data, which are then further summarized at a higher—or *meta*—level of analysis. As you might imagine, meta-analyses have the potential to be more systematic and evenhanded than narrative reviews. Throughout this book, we often rely on meta-analyses to describe the state of the evidence for psychological theories and hypotheses.

ETHICS OF PSYCHOLOGICAL RESEARCH

Because psychologists study living beings, they need to be sensitive to ethical issues that can arise in the conduct of research. Accordingly, the American Psychological Association (APA) and its counterparts in Canada and Great Britain have established guidelines for the treatment of both human participants and animal subjects (American Psychological Association, 1990). In the United States, federal regulations require any institution that conducts federally funded research to establish an internal review board, which reviews proposed studies to ensure that participants will be treated properly.

RESEARCH WITH HUMANS The first principle governing the ethical treatment of human participants is **minimal risk.** In most cases, the risks anticipated in the research should be no greater than those ordinarily encountered in daily life. Obviously, a person should not be exposed to physical harm or injury, but deciding how much psychological stress is ethically justified in a research project is not always so clear-cut. In everyday life, of course, people may be impolite, lie, or make other people anxious. Under what circumstances is it ethically justifiable for a researcher to treat a participant in such ways to meet the goals of a research project? These are the kinds of questions that review boards consider on a case-by-case basis.

The second principle governing the ethical treatment of human participants is **informed consent.** Par-

Survey researchers ask individuals or, as in this case, a mother and son about their attitudes and behavior. For survey results to be valid, the respondents must be representative of the larger population being studied.

ticipants must be told ahead of time about any aspects of the study that could influence their willingness to cooperate and, after this disclosure, they must enter the study voluntarily and be permitted to withdraw from it at any time they desire without penalty. Like the principle of minimal risk, informed consent is not always easy to implement. In particular, informed consent is sometimes at odds with another common requirement of research: that participants be unaware of the hypotheses being tested in a study. If a researcher plans to compare participants who learn lists of familiar words with participants who learn lists of unfamiliar words, no ethical problem arises by simply telling participants ahead of time that they will be learning lists of words: They do not need to know how the words vary from one participant to another. Nor are any serious ethical issues raised if participants are given a surprise quiz they did not expect. But what if the researcher wants to compare participants who learn words while in a neutral mood with participants who learn words while they are angry or embarrassed? Clearly the research would not yield valid conclusions if participants had to be told ahead of time that they would be intentionally angered (by being treated rudely) or embarrassed (by being led to believe that they had accidentally broken a piece of equipment). Accordingly, the guidelines specify that if such a study is permitted to proceed at all, participants must be debriefed about it as soon as possible afterwards. During **debriefing,** the reasons for keeping them in ignorance—or deceiving them—about the procedures must be explained, and any residual emotional reactions must be dealt with so that participants leave with their dignity intact and their appreciation for the research enhanced. The review board must be convinced that the debriefing procedures are adequate to this task.

Are We Naturally Selfish?

WE ARE NATURALLY SELFISH
George C. Williams, State University of New York, Stony Brook

Yes we are selfish, in a special biological sense, but an important one that should be borne in mind in discussing human affairs, ethical philosophy, and related topics (Williams, 1996: Chs. 3 & 9). We are selfish in the special way that our genes demand. They are maximally selfish because, if they were not, they would not exist. The genes that get passed on through many generations are those that are best at getting themselves passed on. To do this they must be better than any alternatives at making bodies, human or otherwise, that transmit genes more profusely than other members of their population. Individuals can win this genetic contest mainly by surviving to maturity and then competing successfully for the resources (food, nest sites, mates, etc.) needed for their own reproduction.

In this sense we are necessarily selfish, but this need not imply that we are never expected to be unselfish in the sense in which this term is normally understood. Individuals can and often do assist others in gaining resources and avoiding losses or dangers. For a biological understanding of such behavior, the important observations lie in the circumstances in which the apparent benevolence occurs. The most obvious example of helpful behavior is that performed by parents for their own offspring. Its obvious explanation is that parents would not successfully transmit their genes if they did not help their own young in special ways: mammalian mothers must nurse their babies; birds must bring food to their nestlings; a plant must pack an optimum quantity of nutrients into each

of its seeds. Yet this kind of provisioning is never a generalized helpfulness of adults toward young. There are always mechanisms at work by which parents can usually identify their own offspring and confine their helpfulness to them alone.

If all reproduction is sexual and mates are seldom closely related to each other, each offspring has half of each parent's genes. From a parent's perspective, a son or daughter is genetically half as important as itself, and an offspring's reproduction is half as important as its own, for getting genes transmitted. Yet the same kind of partial genetic identity is true of all relatives, not just offspring. It may serve the genetic selfishness of an individual to behave helpfully toward relatives in general, not merely offspring. Such behavior arises from what is termed kin selection, natural selection for the adaptive use of cues that indicate degrees and probabilities of relationship. To whatever extent there is evidence of genealogical connections, an individual is expected to favor relatives over nonrelatives and close relatives (parents, offspring, siblings) over more distant ones.

A male bird whose mate laid eggs in his nest can be favored in evolution if he incubates the eggs and feeds the later hatchlings. But what about possible cuckoldry? Can he really be sure that his mate was not inseminated by a neighboring male so that one or more of those eggs are not actually his own offspring? Extra-pair mating by female birds, with or without consent, does happen in many species. Males in such

species are especially watchful of their mates' behavior and diligent in chasing rival males from their territories. It is expected that males, in species in which an average of 10% of the eggs are fertilized by rivals, will be less conscientious toward their nestlings than in species in which cuckoldry never happens.

Kin selection is one factor that causes what looks like unselfish behavior. Reciprocation between unrelated individuals, with immediate or likely future profit to each participant, is another. So is that which is caused by the selfish deception or manipulation of another's kin-selected or other altruistic or cooperative instincts. Female birds, like males, cannot be certain that nestlings are their own, because egg dumping (Sayler, 1992), the laying of an egg in another bird's nest while its owner is briefly away feeding, happens in many species. One female gains genetically by exploiting the parental instincts of another. The species in which deception and manipulation are most extensively developed is our own, by virtue of our language capability. Henry V, according to Shakespeare, addressed his army as "We band of brothers." Feminist leaders speak of the "sisterhood." Deception and manipulation of others' emotions can, of course, be for either a worthy or an unworthy cause.

George C. Williams

Are We Naturally Selfish?

WE ARE NOT NATURALLY SELFISH
Frans B. M. de Waal, Emory University

"How selfish soever man may be supposed, there are evidently some principles in his nature, which interest him in the fortune of others, and render their happiness necessary to him, though he derives nothing from it, except the pleasure of seeing it."
Adam Smith, 1759

When Lenny Skutnik dove into the icy Potomac in Washington, DC, in 1982, to rescue a plane-crash victim, or when Dutch civilians sheltered Jewish families during World War II, life-threatening risks were taken on behalf of complete strangers. Similarly, Binti Jua, a lowland gorilla at Chicago's Brookfield Zoo, rescued an unconscious boy who had fallen into her enclosure, following a chain of actions no one had taught her.

Such examples make a deep impression mainly because they benefit members of our own species. But in my work on the evolution of empathy and morality, I have found evidence so rich of animals caring for one another and respond-

An adult male chimpanzee, defeated in a fight with a rival, screams while being comforted by a juvenile with an embrace. Such "consolations" have as yet not been reported for other animals. The behavior seems a form of empathy without tangible benefit to the performer.

ing to each other's distress that I am convinced that survival depends not only on strength in combat but also at times on cooperation and kindness (de Waal, 1996). For example, it is common among chimpanzees that a bystander approaches the victim of an attack to gently wrap an arm around his or her shoulder.

Despite these caring tendencies, humans and other animals are routinely depicted by biologists as complete egoists. The reason is theoretical: all behavior is supposed to have evolved to serve the actor's own interests. It is logical to assume that genes that fail to benefit their carrier are at a disadvantage in the process of natural selection. But is it correct to call an animal selfish simply because its behavior evolved for its own good?

The process by which a behavior came to exist over millions of years of evolution is irrelevant when considering why an animal here and now acts in a particular way. Animals only see the immediate consequences of their actions, and even those are not always clear to them. We may think that a spider builds a web to catch flies, but this is true only at the functional level. There is no evidence that spiders have any idea what webs are for. In other words, a behavior's purpose says nothing about its underlying motives.

Only recently has the concept of "selfishness" been robbed of its vernacular meaning and applied outside the psychological domain. Even though the term is now seen by some as synonymous with self-serving, selfishness implies the intention to serve oneself, hence knowledge of what one stands to gain from a particular behavior. A vine may serve its own interests by overgrowing a tree, but since plants lack intentions and knowledge, they cannot be selfish except in a meaningless, metaphorical sense. For the same reason, it is impossible for genes to be selfish.

Charles Darwin never confused adaptation with individual goals, and endorsed altruistic motives. In this he was inspired by Adam Smith, the moral philosopher and father of economics. It says a great deal about the distinction between self-serving actions and selfish motives that Smith, known for his emphasis on self-interest as the guiding principle of economics, also wrote about the universal human capacity of sympathy.

The origins of this inclination are no mystery. All species that rely on cooperation show group loyalty and helping tendencies. These tendencies evolved in the context of a close-knit social life in which they benefited relatives and companions able to repay the favor. The impulse to help was, therefore, never totally without survival value to the ones showing the impulse. But the impulse became divorced from the consequences that shaped its evolution, permitting its expression even when payoffs were unlikely, such as when strangers were the beneficiaries.

To call all behavior selfish is like describing all life on earth as converted sun energy. Both statements have some general value but offer little help in explaining the diversity we see around us. Some animals survive through ruthless competition, others through mutual aid. A framework that fails to distinguish the contrasting mind-sets involved may be of use to the evolutionary biologist: It has no place in psychology.

A third principle of ethical research is the **right to privacy.** Information about a person acquired during a study must be kept confidential and not made available to others without the research participant's consent. A common practice is to separate the names and other information used to identify participants from the data collected in the study. The data are then identified only by code or case numbers. In that way, no one other than the experimenter has access to how any particular participant responded. Another common practice is to report only aggregated data—for example, data averaged across all participants in the same group or condition. This further protects the privacy of individual research participants.

Even if all of these ethical conditions are met, the researcher must still weigh the costs of the study—not the economic costs but the costs in human terms—against the potential benefits. Is it really necessary to conduct a study in which participants will be deceived or embarrassed? Only if the researcher and the review board are reasonably certain that the study can uncover worthwhile information—either practical or theoretical—can the research proceed.

RESEARCH WITH ANIMALS Another area in which ethical standards must be observed is research with animals. About 7% of psychological studies employ animals, 95% of which are rats, mice, and birds. Psychologists conduct research with animals for two main reasons. One is that animal behavior can itself be interesting and worthy of study. A second is that animal systems can provide models of human systems, and so research on animals can produce knowledge that might be impossible or unethical to obtain from humans. Animal research has in fact played a pivotal role in understanding and treating psychological problems such as anxiety, stress, aggression, depression, drug abuse, eating disorders, hypertension, and Alzheimer's disease (Carroll & Overmier, 2001). Although debate continues about whether and what kind of research with animals is ethical, in the United States most psychologists (80%) and most psychology majors (72%) support the use of animals in research (Plous, 1996a, 1996b). Amid this wide support, concerns remain about the small subset of animal studies that involve painful or harmful procedures. To address these concerns, both federal and APA guidelines require that any painful or harmful procedures imposed on animals must be thoroughly justified in terms of the knowledge to be gained from the study. APA guidelines also underscore that researchers have a moral obligation to treat animals humanely and to minimize their pain and suffering. Specific rules about the living conditions and maintenance of laboratory animals govern how this moral obligation is to be met.

Aside from these specific guidelines, a central principle of research ethics is that those who participate in psychology studies should be considered full partners in the research enterprise. Some of the research discussed in this text was conducted before the ethical guidelines just described were formulated and would not be permitted by most review boards today.

◆ Interim Summary

- Doing psychological research involves generating a hypothesis and then testing it by using a scientific method. Core concepts necessary for understanding psychology experiments include independent and dependent variables, experimental and control groups, random assignment, and measurement and statistics.

- When experiments are not feasible, the correlational method may be used to determine whether one naturally occurring variable is associated with another. The degree of association between two variables is measured by the correlation coefficient, r, which can be positive (up to $+1.00$) or negative (down to -1.00), depending on whether one variable increases with another $(+)$ or one variable decreases as the other increases $(-)$.

- Another way of conducting research is to use the observational method, either through direct observation, indirect survey methods, or case histories.

- A final way of conducting research is by literature review, either narrative reviews or statistical meta-analyses.

- The basic ethical principles governing the ethical treatment of human participants are minimal risk, informed consent, and the right to privacy. Any painful or harmful procedures imposed upon animals must be thoroughly justified in terms of the knowledge to be gained from the study.

◆ Critical Thinking Questions

1. Figure 1-3 displays the results of a classic study showing that preference for viewing violent TV programs by boys at age 9 is related to aggressive behavior at age 19. Why does this study fail to demonstrate that watching violence on TV makes boys more aggressive? What kind of evidence would be needed to make such an argument?

2. Suppose a researcher finds a correlation of $+.50$ between symptoms of disordered eating and a preoccupation with physical appearance. What can the researcher conclude? What might explain the observed relationship? Can you formulate a hypothesis about cause and effect? How could you test that hypothesis?

CHAPTER SUMMARY

1. Psychology is the scientific study of behavior and mental processes.

2. The roots of psychology can be traced to the 4th and 5th centuries B.C. The Greek philosophers Socrates, Plato, and Aristotle posed fundamental questions about the mind, and Hippocrates, the "father of medicine," made many important observations about how the brain controlled other organs. One of the earliest debates about human psychology focused on the question of whether human capabilities are inborn (the nature view) or acquired through experience (the nurture view).

3. Scientific psychology was born in the late 19th century with the idea that mind and behavior could be the subject of scientific analysis. The first experimental laboratory in psychology was established by Wilhelm Wundt at the University of Leipzig in 1879.

4. Among the early "schools" of psychology in the 20th century were structuralism (the analysis of mental structures), functionalism (studying how the mind works so that an organism can adapt to and function in its environment), behaviorism (the study of behavior without reference to consciousness), Gestalt psychology (which focuses on the patterns formed by stimuli and on the organization of experience), and psychoanalysis (which emphasizes the role of unconscious processes in personality development and motivation).

5. Later developments in 20th-century psychology included information-processing theory, psycholinguistics, and neuropsychology.

6. The study of psychology can be approached from several perspectives. The biological perspective relates actions to events taking place inside the body, particularly the brain and nervous system. The behavioral perspective considers only external activities that can be observed and measured. The cognitive perspective is concerned with mental processes, such as perceiving, remembering, reasoning, deciding, and problem solving, and with relating these processes to behavior. The psychoanalytic perspective emphasizes unconscious motives stemming from sexual and aggressive impulses. The subjectivist perspective focuses on how people actively construct and interpret their social worlds, which is expected to vary by culture, personal history, and current motivational state. A particular topic often can be analyzed from more than one of these perspectives.

7. The biological perspective differs from the other viewpoints in that its principles are partly drawn from biology. Often, biological researchers attempt to explain psychological principles in terms of biological ones; this is known as reductionism. Behavioral phe-

nomena are increasingly being understood at both the biological and psychological levels.

8. Among the major subfields of psychology are biological psychology, experimental psychology, developmental psychology, social and personality psychology, clinical and counseling psychology, school and educational psychology, and industrial and engineering psychology. Many new areas of inquiry gaining momentum in 21st-century psychology span traditional subfields and disciplines. These new areas include cognitive neuroscience (as well as affective and social cognitive neuroscience), evolutionary psychology, cultural psychology, and positive psychology.

9. Doing psychological research involves generating a hypothesis and then testing it by using a scientific method. When applicable, the experimental method is preferred because it seeks to control all variables except the ones being studied and can thus test hypotheses about cause and effect. The independent variable is the one that is manipulated by the experimenter; the dependent variable (usually some measure of the participant's behavior) is the one being studied to determine whether it is affected by changes in the independent variable. In a simple experimental design, the experimenter manipulates one independent variable and observes its effect on one dependent variable. An essential element of experimental design is the random assignment of participants to experimental and control groups.

10. In many experiments the independent variable is something that is either present or absent. The simplest experimental design includes an experimental group (with the hypothesized cause present for one group of participants) and a control group (with the hypothesized cause absent for another group of participants). If the manipulation of the independent variable results in a statistically significant difference in the dependent variable between the experimental and control groups, we know that the experimental condition had a reliable effect, and the difference is not due to chance factors or a few extreme cases.

11. In situations in which experiments are not feasible, the correlational method may be used. This method determines whether a naturally occurring difference is associated with another difference of interest. The degree of correlation between two variables is measured by the correlation coefficient, r, a number between -1.00 and $+1.00$. The absence of any relationship is indicated by 0; a perfect relationship is indicated by 1. As r goes from 0 to 1, the strength of the relationship increases. The correlation coefficient can be positive or negative,

depending on whether one variable increases with another (+) or one variable decreases as the other increases (−).

12. Another way of conducting research is to use the observational method, in which one observes the phenomenon of interest. Researchers must be trained to observe and record behavior accurately. Phenomena that are difficult to observe directly may be observed indirectly by means of surveys (questionnaires and interviews) or by reconstructing a case history.

13. The basic ethical principles governing the ethical treatment of human participants are minimal risk, informed consent, and the right to privacy. Any painful or harmful procedures imposed upon animals must be thoroughly justified in terms of the knowledge to be gained from the study.

CORE CONCEPTS

law of effect
overjustification effect
psychology
prosopagnosia
fundamental attribution error
childhood amnesia
obese
cathartic effect
physiology
nature-nurture debate
nature view
nurture view
tabula rasa
associationist psychology
introspection
structuralism
functionalism
behaviorism
Gestalt
psychoanalysis
unconscious
free association
information-processing model
psychological perspective
eclectic approach
biological perspective
behavioral perspective

cognitive perspective
psychoanalytic perspective
subjectivist perspective
naïve realism
reductionism
biological psychologists
experimental psychologists
developmental psychologists
social psychologists
personality psychologists
clinical psychologists
counseling psychologists
school psychologists
educational psychologists
organizational psychologists
engineering psychologists
cognitive neuroscience
affective neuroscience
social cognitive neuroscience
evolutionary psychology
cultural psychology
positive psychology
hypothesis
theory
scientific
experiments
variable

independent variable
dependent variable
experimental group
control group
random assignment
multivariate experiments
measurement
statistics
mean
statistically significant
correlation coefficient
positively correlated
negatively correlated
test
direct observation
survey method
social desirability effects
case history
literature review
narrative review
meta-analysis
minimal risk
informed consent
debriefing
right to privacy

WEB RESOURCES

http://psychology.wadsworth.com/
atkinson14e

Take a quiz, try the activities and exercises, and explore web links.

http://elvers.stjoe.udayton.edu/history/welcome.htm

This History of Psychology website gives you access to information about important psychologists throughout history, provides a host of web links, and even has a trivia section. Do you know who left human bone dust in the drill presses in the mechanical workshops of the Hungarian Post Office while doing research on the inner ear? Find out here!

http://www.apa.org/science/infostu.html

This site—provided by the American Psychological Association—offers you access to the wide variety of opportunities available for psychology students.

http://www.apa.org/ethics/code.html

If you are concerned about the ethics of psychology, search through this detailed site to learn more about the principles of psychologists and their code of conduct.

 InfoTrac Online Library
http://www.infotrac-college.com/
wadsworth

Use InfoTrac College Edition to find popular and scientific articles using the search terms below or your own relevant terms.
- Cognitive Psychology
- Ethnopsychology
- Genetic Psychology
- History of Psychology
- Positive Psychology
- Psychoanalysis

CD-ROM LINKS

 Psych Odyssey

Check out CD Chapter 1, What Is Psychology?
A. Psychological Perspectives: The 1850s and Beyond
B. Fields Within Psychology
See also CD Chapter 2, Research Methods
A. Research Methods in Psychology

 Psyk.trek 2.0

Check out CD Unit 1, History and Methods
1a Psychology's Timeline
1b The Experimental Method
1d Statistics: Correlation
1e How To Do Library Research

BIOLOGICAL FOUNDATIONS OF PSYCHOLOGY

CHAPTER OUTLINE

In 1848, a gentle and thoughtful man named Phineas Gage experienced a horrible accident that left him a shadow of his former self. Gage was a 25-year-old foreman for the Rutland and Burlington Railroad in New England. He and his crew were using explosives to clear a path through a rock wall for a new railway. As Gage prepared to blast a section of rock, he accidentally dropped his tamping iron onto the rock. The force of the iron striking the rock caused the blasting powder to ignite, and the explosion hurled the iron spike, which measured more than a meter in length, directly through Gage's head. The spike entered Gage's left cheek, passed behind his left eye, and exited his skull and brain from the top of his head. The bloodied spike was found several meters away covered with bits of Gage's brain.

Amazingly, Gage survived this horrific trauma. His crew carried him back to his hotel, and a local physician cleaned and dressed his head wound. During his treatment, Gage was lucid and conversed with his friends. Although his bleeding was severe, it stopped 2 days after the accident, and Gage's condition appeared to stabilize. Then he developed a "fungus" on the brain and slipped into a semicomatose state. He languished, nearly mute, for more than a month. Miraculously, his condition began to improve, and Gage ultimately recovered enough strength to return home.

But Gage was "no longer Gage" (Harlow, 1868). The kind and generally reserved man was now boisterous and impulsive. One of the most marked changes in his personality was his indulgence in the grossest of profanity. He was unrestrained and had lost all of his former social graces. Not surprisingly, he was unemployable. He became an itinerant of sorts and tried to gain employment on a new railroad project in Chile. After 8 years in South America and still carrying the spike that took stole his former self, he returned to California, where he died of epilepsy in 1860. Despite the horror of Gage's accident, it taught us a great deal about the emergence of complex psychological processes from the brain (Damasio, Grabowski, Frank, Galaburda, & Damasio, 1994). Indeed, as we will see in this chapter, virtually all aspects of behavior and mental functioning can be better understood with some knowledge of the underlying biological processes. To start, let's consider the cellular foundations of the nervous system.

NEURONS, THE BUILDING BLOCKS OF THE NERVOUS SYSTEM

The basic unit of the nervous system is the **neuron,** a specialized cell that transmits neural impulses or messages to other neurons, glands, and muscles. Neurons hold the secrets of how the brain works and, in turn, the nature of human consciousness. We know the role they play in the transmission of nerve impulses, and we know how some neural circuits work, but we are just beginning to unravel their more complex functioning in memory, emotion, and thought.

The many types of neurons in the nervous system differ markedly in size and appearance, but they all have certain common characteristics (see Figure 2-1). Projecting from the cell body, or soma, are a number of short branches called **dendrites** (from the Greek word *dendron,* meaning "tree"), which receive neural impulses from adjacent neurons. The **axon** is a slender tube that extends from the soma and transmits these messages to other neurons (or to muscles and glands). At its end, the axon divides into a number of tiny branches that end in small swellings called *synaptic terminals.*

The terminal button does not actually touch the adjacent neuron. There is a slight gap between the terminal button and the cell body or dendrites of the receiving neuron. This junction is called a **synapse,** and the gap itself is called the *synaptic gap.* When a neural impulse travels down the axon and arrives at the terminal buttons, it triggers the secretion of a **neurotransmitter,** a chemical that diffuses across the synaptic gap and stimulates the next neuron, thereby transmitting the impulse from one neuron to the next. The axons from a great many neurons form synapses on the dendrites and cell body of a single neuron (see Figure 2-2).

Although all neurons have these general features, they vary greatly in size and shape (see Figure 2-3). A neuron in the spinal cord may have an axon 3 to 4 feet long, running from the end of the spine to the muscles of the big toe; a neuron in the brain may cover only a few thousandths of an inch.

Neurons are classified into three categories, depending on their general function. *Sensory neurons* transmit impulses received by receptors to the central nervous system. The receptors are specialized cells in the sense or-

▌ Figure 2-1
Schematic Diagram of a Neuron
Arrows indicate the direction of the nerve impulse. Some axons are branched; the branches are called *collaterals.* The axons of many neurons are covered with an insulating myelin sheath that helps increase the speed of the nerve impulse. (Adapted from *Human Anatomy* by Anthony J. Gaudin and Kenneth C. Jones. Copyright © 1988 by Anthony J. Gaudin and Kenneth C. Jones. Reprinted by permission of the authors.)

▌ Figure 2-2
Synapses at the Cell Body of a Neuron
Many different axons, each of which branches repeatedly, synapse on the dendrites and cell body of a single neuron. Each branch of an axon ends in a swelling, called a *synaptic terminal,* that contains neurotransmitters. When released, neurotransmitters transmit the nerve impulse across the synapse to the dendrites or cell body of the receiving cell.

Neuron from retina of eye

Dendrite

Cell body

Axon

Neuron from cortex of brain

Dendrite

Cell body

Axon

Neuron from spinal cord

Dendrite

Cell body

Axon

Neuron from olfactory area of brain

Dendrite

Cell body

Axon

❚ Figure 2-3
Shapes and Relative Sizes of Neurons
The axon of a spinal cord neuron (not shown in its entirety in the figure) may be several feet long.

gans, muscles, skin, and joints that detect physical or chemical changes and translate these events into impulses that travel along the sensory neurons. *Motor neurons* carry outgoing signals from the brain or spinal cord to muscles and glands. *Interneurons* receive the signals from the sensory neurons and send impulses to other interneurons or to motor neurons. Interneurons are found only in the brain, eyes, and spinal cord.

A **nerve** is a bundle of elongated axons belonging to hundreds or thousands of neurons. A single nerve may contain axons from both sensory and motor neurons. The cell bodies of neurons are generally grouped together throughout the nervous system. In the brain and spinal cord, a group of cell bodies of neurons is referred to as a **nucleus** (plural: *nuclei*). A group of neuronal cell bodies found outside the brain and spinal cord is called a **ganglion** (plural: *ganglia*).

In addition to neurons, the nervous system has a large number of nonneural cells, called **glial cells,** that are interspersed among—and often surround—neurons. Glial cells outnumber neurons by 9 to 1 and take up more than half the volume of the brain. The name *glia,* derived from the Greek word for "glue," suggests one of their functions—namely, to hold neurons in place. In addition, they provide nutrients to the neurons and appear to "keep house" in the brain by gathering and packaging up waste products and gobbling up dead neurons

and foreign substances, thereby maintaining the signaling capacity of neurons (Haydon, 2001). In this way, the glial cells act to support neurons as the trainer on a football team keeps the players hydrated during a game.

ACTION POTENTIALS

Information moves along a neuron in the form of a neural impulse called an **action potential**—an electrochemical impulse that travels from the cell body down to the end of the axon. Each action potential is the result of movements by electrically charged molecules, known as *ions,* in and out of the neuron. The key to understanding the generation of the action potential lies in appreciating that neurons are normally very selective about what ions can flow in and out of the cell. That is, the cell membrane of the neuron is *semipermeable,* which means that some ions can pass through the cell membrane easily and others are not allowed to pass through except when special passageways in the membrane are open. These passageways, called **ion channels,** are doughnut-shaped protein molecules that form pores across the cell membrane (see Figure 2-4). These proteins regulate the flow of ions such as sodium (Na^+), potassium (K^+), calcium (Ca^{++}), and chloride (Cl^-) in and out of the neuron. Each ion channel is selective, permitting only one type of ion to flow through it when it is open.

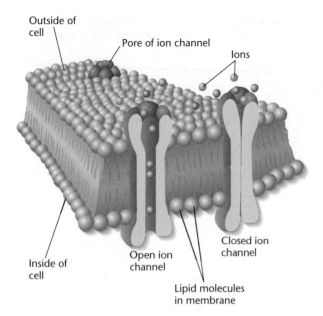

Outside of cell

Pore of ion channel

Ions

Inside of cell

Open ion channel

Closed ion channel

Lipid molecules in membrane

▌ Figure 2-4
Ion Channels
Chemicals such as sodium, potassium, calcium, and chloride pass through the cell membrane via doughnut-shaped protein molecules called *ion channels.*

When a neuron is not generating an action potential, it is referred to as a *resting neuron.* At rest, the cell membrane is not permeable to Na$^+$ ions, and these ions are found at a high concentration outside the neuron. In contrast, the membrane is permeable to K$^+$ ions, which tend to concentrate inside the neuron. In a resting neuron, separate protein structures, called *ion pumps,* help to maintain this uneven distribution of ions across the cell membrane by pumping them into or out of the cell. For example, the ion pumps transport Na$^+$ out of the neuron whenever it leaks into the neuron and transports K$^+$ back into the neuron whenever it gets out. In this way the resting neuron maintains high concentrations of Na$^+$ outside the cell and low concentrations inside it. The overall effect of these ion channels and pumps is to electrically polarize the cell membrane of the resting neuron, making the inside of the neuron more negative than the outside. The electrical potential of a neuron at rest is termed the **resting membrane potential** and ranges from -50 to -100 millivolts. The resting membrane potential of a neuron is similar to the charge held by a battery; both neurons and batteries use electrochemical gradients to store energy. The battery's energy is used to power electronic devices such as portable radios, whereas a neuron's energy is used to power action potentials.

When the neuron is stimulated by an excitatory input, the voltage difference across the cell membrane is reduced. This process is called *depolarization,* and it is caused by the action of neurotransmitter on dendritic receptors. If the depolarization is large enough, voltage-sensing Na$^+$ channels located on the axon open briefly, and Na$^+$ ions flood into the cell. Sodium floods into the cell because opposite charges attract one another; sodium is positively charged, and the inside of the cell is negatively charged. Now the inside of that area of the axon becomes positive relative to the outside. Neighboring Na$^+$ channels sense the voltage drop and open, causing the adjacent area of the axon to depolarize. This process of depolarization, repeating itself down the length of the axon, is an action potential. As the action potential travels down the axon, the Na$^+$ channels close behind it, and the various ion pumps are activated to quickly restore the cell membrane to its resting state (see Figure 2-5). The importance of Na$^+$ channels is shown by the effect of local anesthetic agents such as novocaine and Xylocaine, which are routinely used to numb the mouth during dental procedures. These agents prevent Na$^+$ channels from opening, thus stopping the action potential and preventing sensory signals from reaching the brain (Catterall, 2000).

The speed of the action potential as it travels down the axon can vary from about 2 to 200 miles per hour, depending on the diameter of the axon; larger ones generally are faster. The speed can also be affected by whether the axon is covered with a *myelin sheath.* This sheath consists of specialized glial cells that wrap themselves around the axon, one after another, with small gaps between them (refer back to Figure 2-1). These tiny gaps are called *nodes of Ranvier.* The insulation provided by the myelin sheath allows for **saltatory conduction,** in which the nerve impulse jumps from one node of Ranvier to the next. This greatly increases the speed of transmission of the action potential down the axon. (*Saltatory* comes from the Latin word *saltare,* which means "to leap." In saltatory conduction, the action potential leaps from one node of Ranvier to another.) The myelin sheath is particularly prevalent where rapid transmission of the action potential is critical—for example, along axons that stimulate skeletal muscles. In *multiple sclerosis,* a disorder in which symptoms first become evident between the ages of 16 and 30, the immune system attacks and destroys the body's own myelin sheaths, producing severe motor nerve dysfunction.

Synaptic Transmission

The synaptic junction between neurons is extremely important because neurons transfer signals there. A single neuron fires an action potential when the stimulation

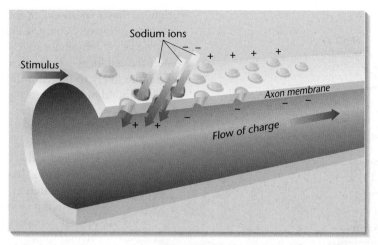

a) During an action potential, sodium gates in the neuron membrane open and sodium ions enter the axon, bringing a positive charge with them.

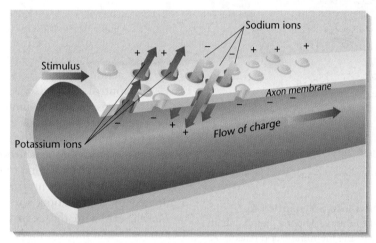

b) After an action potential occurs at one point along the axon, the sodium gates close at that point and open at the next point along the axon. When the sodium gates close, potassium gates open and potassium ions flow out of the axon, carrying a positive charge with them.

▌ Figure 2-5
Action Potential (Modified from Starr & Taggart, 1989)

reaching it via multiple synapses exceeds a certain threshold. The neuron fires an action potential in a single, brief pulse and then becomes inactive for a few thousandths of a second. The size of the action potential is constant and cannot be triggered by a stimulus unless it reaches the threshold level. Thus, in response to any given synaptic input, a neuron either fires an action potential or it does not, and if it fires an action potential, the potential is always the same size. This is referred to as the *all-or-none principle* of neural action. You can think of neuronal action potentials as the binary signals

(0's and 1's) computers use to implement software instructions. Neurons are either firing an action potential (1) or not (0). Once initiated, the action potential travels down the axon to its many axon terminals.

As mentioned earlier, neurons do not connect directly at a synapse, and the signal must travel across a slight gap (see Figure 2-6). When an action potential moves down the axon and arrives at the synaptic terminals, it stimulates *synaptic vesicles* in the terminals. The synaptic vesicles are small spherical structures that contain neurotransmitters. When they are stimulated, they

Figure 2-6
Release of Neurotransmitters Into a Synaptic Gap
The neurotransmitter is carried to the presynaptic membrane in synaptic vesicles, which fuse with the membrane and release their contents into the synaptic gap. The neurotransmitters diffuse across the gap and combine with receptor molecules in the postsynaptic membrane. (Adapted from *Search for the Human Mind* by Robert Sternberg. Copyright © 1994 by Harcourt Brace & Company, reproduced by permission of the publisher.)

(that is, they *hyperpolarize* the cell membrane), either by allowing positively charged ions, such as K^+, to leave the neuron or by letting negatively charged ions, such as Cl^-, enter the cell. In short, the excitatory effect makes the neuron more likely to fire, and the inhibitory effect decreases the likelihood of firing. Any particular neuron may receive neurotransmitters from many thousands of synapses with other neurons. Some of these neurons release excitatory neurotransmitters, and others release inhibitory neurotransmitters. Depending on their pattern of firing, different axons release their neurotransmitter substances at different times. If—at a particular moment and at a particular place on the cell membrane—the excitatory effects on the receiving neuron become larger than the inhibitory effects, depolarization occurs, and the neuron fires an all-or-none action potential.

Once a neurotransmitter substance is released and diffuses across the synaptic gap, its action must be very brief to maintain precise control. For some neurotransmitters, the synapse is almost immediately cleared by **reuptake**, reabsorption of the neurotransmitter by the synaptic terminals from which it was released. Reuptake cuts off the action of the neurotransmitter and spares the axon terminals from having to manufacture more of the substance. For other neurotransmitters, the effect is terminated by **degradation**, the reaction of enzymes in a synaptic gap with the neurotransmitter to break it up chemically and make it inactive.

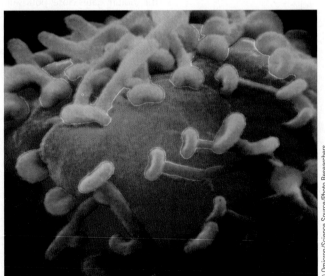

An electron micrograph of a neuron densely packed with synapses.

discharge the neurotransmitters into the synapse. The neurotransmitters diffuse from the sending or presynaptic neuron across the synaptic gap and bind to **receptors**, which are proteins lodged in the dendritic membrane of the receiving or postsynaptic neuron.

The neurotransmitter and the receptor site fit together like the pieces of a jigsaw puzzle or a key and its lock. This lock-and-key action causes a direct change in the permeability of ion channels in the receiving neuron. Some neurotransmitters have an *excitatory effect* that allows positively charged ions, such as Na^+, to enter, which depolarizes the receiving neuron and makes the inside of the cell more positive than the outside. Other neurotransmitters are *inhibitory.* They make the inside of the receiving neuron more negative than the outside

◆ Interim Summary

- The basic unit of the nervous system is the neuron.
- Neurons receive chemical signals on branches called *dendrites* and transmit electrochemical potentials down a tubelike extension called the *axon*.
- Chemical neurotransmitters are released at synapses and carry messages between two neurons. Neurotransmitters exert their action by binding to receptor proteins.
- When a neuron is depolarized enough, it generates an all-or-none action potential. This action potential moves down the axon and initiates the release of neurotransmitter at the terminal buttons.

◆ Critical Thinking Questions

1. Only about a tenth of the cells in your brain are neurons (the rest are glial cells). Does this mean that you use only 10% of your brain when you think? What else might this fact mean?

2. Local anesthetics, such as those dentists use, work by blocking Na^+ gates in the neurons near the point of injection. Of course, dentists and physicians typically inject them in a part of the body near the source of pain. What do you think such a drug would do if it was injected into the brain? Would it still block pain and touch but nothing else, or would its effect be different?

NEUROTRANSMITTERS

More than 70 different neurotransmitters have been identified, and others surely will be discovered. Some neurotransmitters can bind to more than one type of receptor and cause different effects on different types of receptors. For example, the neurotransmitter glutamate can activate at least 10 types of receptor molecules, enabling neurons to respond in distinct ways to this same neurotransmitter (Madden, 2002). Certain neurotransmitters are excitatory at some sites and inhibitory at other sites because two types of receptor molecules are involved. In this chapter we obviously cannot discuss all of the neurotransmitters in the nervous system. Instead, we will focus on a few that influence behavior.

ACETYLCHOLINE Acetylcholine is present at many synapses throughout the nervous system. It is usually excitatory, but it can also be inhibitory, depending on the type of receptor molecule in the membrane of the receiving neuron. Acetylcholine is particularly prevalent in an area of the forebrain called the *hippocampus*, which plays a key role in the formation of new memories (Eichenbaum, 2000). This neurotransmitter plays a prominent role in Alzheimer's disease, a devastating disorder that affects many older people by causing impairment of memory and other cognitive functions. Neurons in the forebrain that produce acetylcholine tend to degenerate in Alzheimer's patients, who then produce less acetylcholine. The less acetylcholine is produced, the more serious the memory loss.

Acetylcholine is also released at every synapse where a neuron terminates at a skeletal muscle fiber. The acetylcholine is directed onto small structures called *end plates* on the muscle cells. The end plates are covered with receptor molecules that, when activated by acetylcholine, trigger a molecular linkage inside the muscle cells that causes them to contract. Certain drugs that affect acetylcholine can produce muscle paralysis. For example, botulinum toxin, which forms from bacteria in improperly canned foods, blocks the release of acetylcholine at nerve-muscle synapses and can cause death by paralyzing the muscles used in breathing. Some nerve gases developed for warfare, as well as many pesticides, cause paralysis by destroying the enzyme that degrades acetylcholine once the neuron has fired. When the degradation process fails, there is an uncontrolled buildup of acetylcholine in the nervous system, and normal synaptic transmission becomes impossible.

NOREPINEPHRINE Norepinephrine is a neurotransmitter in the *monoamine* class. It is produced mainly by neurons in the brainstem. Cocaine and amphetamines prolong the action of norepinephrine by slowing down its reuptake. Because of this delay, the receiving neurons are activated for a longer period, which causes these drugs' stimulating psychological effects. In contrast, lithium speeds up the reuptake of norepinephrine, causing a person's mood level to be depressed. Any drug that causes norepinephrine to increase or decrease in the brain is correlated with an increase or decrease in the individual's mood level.

DOPAMINE Dopamine, also a monoamine, is chemically very similar to norepinephrine. Release of dopamine in certain areas of the brain produces intense feelings of pleasure, and current research is investigating the role of dopamine in the development of addictions. Too much dopamine in some areas of the brain may cause schizophrenia, and too little in other areas may lead to Parkinson's disease. Drugs used to treat schizophrenia, such as chlorpromazine or clozapine, block the receptors for dopamine. In contrast, L-dopa, a drug commonly prescribed to treat Parkinson's disease, increases dopamine in the brain.

SEROTONIN Serotonin is another monoamine. Like norepinephrine, serotonin plays an important role in mood regulation. For example, low levels of serotonin have been associated with feelings of depression. Serotonin reuptake inhibitors are antidepressants that increase serotonin levels in the brain by blocking its uptake by neurons. Prozac, Zoloft, and Paxil, drugs that are commonly prescribed to treat depression, are serotonin reuptake inhibitors. Because serotonin is also important in the regulation of sleep and appetite, it is also used to treat the eating disorder bulimia. Interestingly, the hallucinogenic drug lysergic acid diethylamide (LSD) induces its effects by binding to serotonin receptors in the brain.

GLUTAMATE The excitatory neurotransmitter glutamate, an amino acid, is present in more neurons of the central nervous system than any other transmitter. Glutamate is excitatory because it depolarizes neurons upon which it is released. Of the three or more subtypes of glutamate receptors, one in particular, the NMDA receptor, is thought to affect learning and memory. It is named for the chemical (N-methyl-D-aspartate) that is used to detect it. Neurons in the hippocampus (an area near the center of the brain) are particularly rich in NMDA receptors, and this area seems to be critical in the formation of new memories (Eichenbaum, 2000; see Chapter 7). Disruptions in glutamate neurotransmission have been implicated in schizophrenia.

GABA Another prominent amino acid neurotransmitter is gamma-aminobutyric acid (GABA). This substance is a major inhibitory transmitter; in fact, most synapses in the brain use GABA. The drug picrotoxin, which blocks GABA receptors, produces convulsions because muscle movement cannot be controlled by the brain without GABA's inhibiting influence. The tranquilizing effects of certain antianxiety drugs, the benzodiazepines, are a result of GABA's inhibitory action (see Chapter 15).

The functions of these neurotransmitters are summarized in the Concept Review Table.

◆ Interim Summary

- The most important neurotransmitters include acetylcholine, norepinephrine, dopamine, serotonin, gamma-aminobutyric acid (GABA), and glutamate.
- Neurotransmitters have either excitatory or inhibitory effects on neurons, depending on the type of postsynaptic receptor they bind.

◆ Critical Thinking Questions

1. There are several different neurotransmitter systems in the brain. Why do you think there is such neurochemical diversity?

2. What are some of the advantages provided by chemical signaling in the brain? What are some of the disadvantages?

CONCEPT REVIEW TABLE
Neurotransmitters and Their Functions

Neurotransmitter	Function
Acetylcholine	Involved in memory and attention; decreases associated with Alzheimer's disease. Also transmits signals between nerve and muscle.
Norepinephrine	Increased by psychostimulants. Low levels contribute to depression.
Dopamine	Mediates the effects of natural rewards (food and sex, for example) and drugs of abuse.
Serotonin	Important in mood and social behavior. Drugs that alleviate depression and anxiety increase serotonin levels in synapse.
Glutamate	Major excitatory neurotransmitter in brain. Involved in learning and memory.
GABA	Major inhibitory neurotransmitter in brain. Drugs that alleviate anxiety enhance activity of GABA.

THE ORGANIZATION OF THE NERVOUS SYSTEM
DIVISIONS OF THE NERVOUS SYSTEM

All parts of the nervous system are interrelated, but it is typically considered to have two major divisions (see Figure 2-7). The **central nervous system** includes all the neurons in the brain and spinal cord. The **peripheral nervous system** is the nerves connecting the brain and spinal cord to other parts of the body. The peripheral nervous system is further divided into the **somatic system**, which carries messages to and from the sense receptors, mus-

▌Figure 2-7
The Organization of the Nervous System

cles, and the surface of the body, and the **autonomic system,** which connects with the internal organs and glands.

The *sensory nerves* of the somatic system transmit information about external stimulation from the skin, muscles, and joints to the central nervous system. That is how we become aware of pain, pressure, and temperature variations. The *motor nerves* of the somatic system carry impulses from the central nervous system to the muscles, where they initiate action. All the muscles we use in voluntary movements, as well as involuntary adjustments in posture and balance, are controlled by these nerves. The nerves of the autonomic system run to and from the internal organs, regulating processes such as respiration, heart rate, and digestion. The autonomic system and its major role in emotion are discussed later in the chapter.

Most of the nerve fibers connecting various parts of the body to the brain are gathered in the *spinal cord,* where the bony spinal vertebrae protect them. The spinal cord is remarkably compact—barely the diameter of your little finger. Some of the simplest stimulus-response reflexes are carried out at the spinal cord level. One example is the knee jerk. When the knee tendon is tapped, the attached muscle stretches, and a signal from sensory cells embedded in the muscle is transmitted through sensory neurons to the spinal cord. There the sensory neurons synapse directly with motor neurons. They transmit impulses back to the same muscle, causing it to contract and the leg to extend. Although this response can occur solely in the spinal cord without any input from the brain, it can also be influenced by messages from higher nervous centers. For example, if you grip your hands just before your knee is tapped, then the extension movement will be exaggerated. And if you imagine that your knee cannot move just before the doctor taps the tendon, then you can inhibit the reflex.

THE ORGANIZATION OF THE BRAIN

There are a number of ways to conceptualize the brain. The approach in Figure 2-8a divides the brain into three regions based on location: (1) the **hindbrain,** which includes all the structures located in the hind, or posterior, part of the brain, closest to the spinal cord; (2) the **midbrain,** located in front of the hindbrain, is near the middle of the brain; and (3) the **forebrain,** which includes the structures located in the front, or anterior, part of the brain. The Canadian investigator Paul MacLean proposed a framework for organizing the brain that is based on the function of the brain structures rather than on their location (MacLean, 1973). According to MacLean, we can think of the human brain as three concentric layers: (1) the **central core,** which regulates our most primitive behaviors, (2) the **limbic system,** which controls our emotions, and (3) the **cerebrum,** which regulates our higher intellectual processes. Figure 2-8b shows how these layers fit together. We will use MacLean's organizational framework as we discuss structures in the brain and their functions.

THE CENTRAL CORE

The central core, also known as the *brainstem,* controls involuntary behaviors such as coughing, sneezing, and gagging and "primitive" behaviors that are under voluntary control, such as breathing, vomiting, sleeping, eating, drinking, temperature regulation, and sexual behavior. The brainstem includes all the structures in the hindbrain and midbrain and two structures in the forebrain, the hypothalamus and the thalamus. This means that the central core of the brain stretches from the hindbrain to the forebrain. This chapter discusses five brainstem structures—the medulla, the cerebellum, the thalamus, the hypothalamus, and the reticular formation—that regulate the most important primitive behaviors necessary for survival. The table in Figure 2-8d lists the functions of these five structures, as well as the functions of the cerebral cortex, the corpus callosum, the hippocampus, and the amygdala.

The first slight enlargement of the spinal cord as it enters the skull is the **medulla,** a narrow structure that controls breathing and some reflexes that help maintain upright posture. Also at this point, the major nerve tracts coming up from the spinal cord cross over so that the right side of the brain is connected to the left side of the body, and the left side of the brain is connected to the right side of the body.

THE CEREBELLUM Attached to the rear of the brainstem slightly above the medulla is a convoluted structure called the **cerebellum,** which is concerned primarily with the coordination of movement. Specific movements may

a) Locational organization of the brain

The midbrain is located in the middle of the brain

The forebrain includes structures located in the anterior part of the brain

The hindbrain includes all structures located in the posterior part of the brain

b) Functional organization of the human brain

The central core and limbic system are shown in their entirety, but the left cerebral hemisphere has been removed. The cerebellum of the central core controls balance and muscular coordination; the thalamus serves as a switchboard for messages coming from the sense organs; the hypothalamus (not shown but located below the thalamus) regulates endocrine activity and life-maintaining processes such as metabolism and temperature control. The limbic system is concerned with actions that satisfy basic needs, and with emotion. The cerebral cortex (an outer layer of cells covering the cerebrum) is the center of higher mental processes, where sensations are registered, voluntary actions initiated, decisions made, and plans formulated.

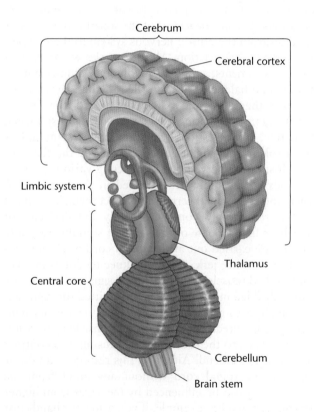

▌**Figure 2-8**
(a) **Locational Organization of the Brain.** Organization of the major brain divisions.
(b) **Functional Organization of the Human Brain.** The human brain is composed of three functional divisions: the central core, the limbic system, and the cerebrum.

c) The human brain

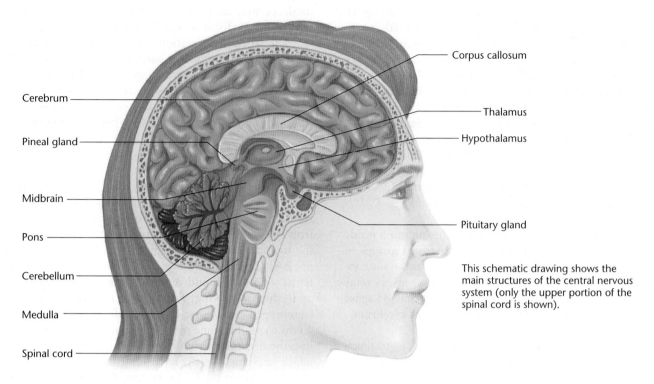

Corpus callosum

Cerebrum

Thalamus

Pineal gland

Hypothalamus

Midbrain

Pons

Cerebellum

Pituitary gland

Medulla

Spinal cord

This schematic drawing shows the main structures of the central nervous system (only the upper portion of the spinal cord is shown).

d) Parts of the human brain

Structure	Function
Cerebral cortex	The cortical areas include the primary motor area, the primary somatosensory area, the primary visual area, the primary auditory area, and the association areas.
Corpus callosum	Connects the two hemispheres of the cerebrum.
Hippocampus	Plays a special role in memory, particularly for episodes.
Amygdala	Involved in mediating emotion, especially fear.
Thalamus	Directs incoming information from the sense receptors to the cerebrum; helps control sleep and wakefulness.
Hypothalamus	Mediates eating, drinking, and sexual behavior; regulates endocrine activity and maintains homeostasis; has a part in emotion and response to stress.
Cerebellum	Concerned with the coordination of movement and motor learning.
Reticular formation	Plays a role in controlling arousal and in ability to focus attention on particular stimuli.
Medulla	Controls breathing and some reflexes that help the organism maintain an upright posture.

❚ **Figure 2-8, cont'd**
(c) **The Human Brain.** Midsagittal view of the human brain, illustrating the major brain divisions. (d) **Functions of the Brain.** A tabular review of the major brain structures and their functions.

be initiated at higher levels, but the coordination of those movements depends on the cerebellum. Damage to the cerebellum results in jerky, uncoordinated movements. In addition to coordinating movement, the cerebellum is important for learning new motor responses (Thompson & Krupa, 1994; see Chapter 7).

Direct neural connections between the cerebellum and frontal parts of the brain are involved in language, planning, and reasoning (Middleton & Strick, 1994). These connecting circuits are much larger in human beings than in monkeys and other animals. This and other evidence suggest that the cerebellum may play a role in the control and coordination of higher mental functions as well as in the coordination of movements.

THE THALAMUS Located just above the midbrain inside the cerebral hemispheres are two egg-shaped groups of nerve cell nuclei, the **thalamus.** It is important in the control of sleep and wakefulness and acts as a sensory relay station, directing incoming information from the sense receptors (such as vision and hearing) to the cerebrum.

THE HYPOTHALAMUS The **hypothalamus** is a much smaller structure located just below the thalamus. Centers in the hypothalamus regulate eating, drinking, and sexual behavior. The hypothalamus also regulates endocrine activity and maintains **homeostasis,** the process that maintains the normal level of functioning that is characteristic of a healthy organism, such as normal body temperature, heart rate, and blood pressure. When an organism is under stress, homeostasis is disturbed, and processes are set into motion to correct the disequilibrium. For example, if we are too warm, we perspire, and if we are too cool, we shiver. Both processes tend to restore normal temperature and are controlled by the hypothalamus.

The hypothalamus also has an important role in the sensation of emotions and in our response to stress-producing situations. Mild electrical stimulation of certain areas in the hypothalamus produces feelings of pleasure; stimulation of adjacent regions produces unpleasant sensations. Through its influence on the pituitary gland, which lies just below it (see Figure 2-8), the hypothalamus controls the endocrine system and thus the production of hormones. This control is particularly important in emergencies, when the body must mobilize a complex set of physiological processes (known as the "fight-or-flight" response). The hypothalamus has been described as the brain's stress center in recognition of this function.

THE RETICULAR FORMATION A network of neural circuits that extends from the lower brainstem up to the thalamus, traversing some of the other central core structures, is called the **reticular formation.** This network of neurons acts to control arousal. When an electric current of a certain voltage is sent through electrodes implanted in the reticular formation of a cat or dog, the animal goes to sleep; stimulation by a current with a more rapidly changing waveform awakens the sleeping animal.

The reticular formation also plays a role in our ability to focus attention on particular stimuli. All of the sense receptors have nerve fibers that feed into the reticular system, which appears to act as a filter. It allows some sensory messages to pass to the cerebral cortex (that is, to conscious awareness) while blocking others.

THE LIMBIC SYSTEM

Around the central core of the brain and closely interconnected with the hypothalamus is the limbic system, a set of structures that appear to impose additional controls over some of the instinctive behaviors regulated by the hypothalamus and the brainstem (refer back to Figure 2-8). Animals that have only rudimentary limbic systems, such as fish and reptiles, carry out activities such as feeding, attacking, fleeing, and mating by means of stereotyped behaviors. In mammals, the limbic system seems to inhibit some of these instinctive patterns and allow the organism to be more flexible and better able to adapt to changes in the environment.

One part of the limbic system, the **hippocampus,** has a special role in memory. This role was discovered in people who had the structure surgically removed to treat their epilepsy in the 1950s. Upon recovery from such an operation, patients readily recognize old friends and recall earlier experiences, and they can read and perform skills learned earlier in life. However, they have little, if any, recall of events that occurred during the year before the operation, and they cannot remember events occurring after the operation. For example, they do not recognize a new person with whom they may have spent many hours earlier in the day. They can do the same jigsaw puzzle week after week without remembering having done it before, and they can read the same newspaper over and over without remembering the contents (Squire & Kandel, 2000).

The limbic system is also involved in emotional behavior. The **amygdala,** an almond-shaped structure deep within the brain, is critical in emotions such as fear (Maren, 2001). For example, monkeys with damage to the amygdala exhibit marked reduction in fear (Klüver & Bucy, 1937). Humans with such damage are unable to recognize facial expressions of fear or learn new fear responses (Bechara et al., 1995).

Describing the brain in terms of three concentric structures—the central core, the limbic system, and the cerebrum (discussed in the next section)—must not lead us to think of these structures as independent. They are analogous to a network of interrelated computers. Each has specialized functions, but they must work together to produce the most effective result. Similarly, the analysis of information coming from the senses requires one

Parietal lobe · Central fissure · Frontal lobe

Occipital lobe · Temporal lobe · Lateral fissure · Insula (embedded under the surface)

a) Lateral view

Left hemisphere · Right hemisphere

Frontal lobe

Longitudinal fissure

Central fissure

Parietal lobe

Occipital lobe

b) Superior view

Cortex

Subcortical tissue — Fissure

c) Tranverse section through the cerebral cortex. Note the distinction between the more superficial gray matter (shown in dark pink) and the deeper white matter.

Parietal lobe

Occipital lobe · Frontal lobe

Cerebellum · Temporal lobe

d) Photograph of human brain

▌Figure 2-9
Occipital Lobe
Each cerebral hemisphere has several large lobes separated by fissures. In addition to these externally visible lobes, a large internal fold of cortex, called the *insula,* lies deep in the lateral fissure. (Adapted from *Human Anatomy* by Anthony J. Gaudin and Kenneth C. Jones. Copyright © 1988 by Anthony J. Gaudin and Kenneth C. Jones. Reprinted by permission of the authors.)

kind of computation and decision process (for which the cerebrum is well adapted), which differs from the kind required for controlling a reflexive sequence of activities (the limbic system). Finer adjustments of the muscles (as in writing or playing a musical instrument) require another kind of control system, which is provided by the primary motor area on the cortex in the forebrain. All these activities are organized into an integrated system that keeps the organism functioning smoothly.

THE CEREBRUM

The cerebrum is more highly developed in humans than in any other organism. The outer layer of the cerebrum is called the **cerebral cortex** (or simply *cortex*) from the Latin word for "bark." The cortex of a preserved brain appears gray because it is largely nerve cell bodies and unmyelinated fibers—hence the term *gray matter.* The in-

side of the cerebrum, beneath the cortex, is mostly myelinated axons and appears white (also called *white matter*).

Each of the sensory systems sends information to specific areas of the cortex. Motor responses, or movements of body parts, are controlled by one area of the cortex. The rest of the cortex, which is neither sensory nor motor, consists of *association areas.* These areas occupy the largest portion of the human cortex and are concerned with memory, thought, and language.

The cerebrum is composed of two **hemispheres** on the left and right sides of the brain that are connected by the corpus callosum. They are basically symmetrical, with a deep division between them running from front to rear. We therefore refer to the right and left hemispheres. Each hemisphere is divided into four **lobes**—frontal, parietal, occipital, and temporal—large regions of the cerebral cortex that perform diverse functions (see Figure 2-9). The frontal lobe is separated from the parietal

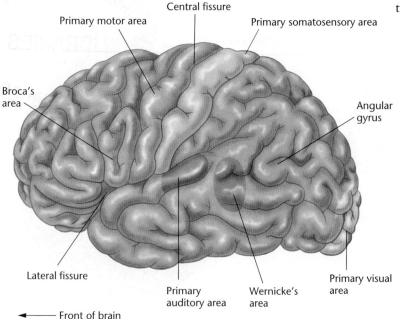

Central fissure

Primary motor area

Primary somatosensory area

Broca's area

Angular gyrus

Lateral fissure

Primary auditory area

Wernicke's area

Primary visual area

◄———— Front of brain

▌**Figure 2-10**
Specialization of Function in the Left Cortex
A major part of the cortex is involved in generating movements and analyzing sensory inputs. These areas (which include motor, somatosensory, visual, auditory, and olfactory areas) are present on both sides of the brain. Other functions are located on only one side of the brain. For example, Broca's area and Wernicke's area are involved in the production and understanding of language, and the angular gyrus helps in matching the visual form of a word with its auditory form; these functions exist only on the left side of the human brain.

lobe by the *central sulcus,* a groove that runs from near the top of the head sideways to the ears. The division between the parietal lobe and the occipital lobe is less clear-cut. For our purposes, we can say that the parietal lobe is at the top of the brain behind the central sulcus and that the occipital lobe is at the rear of the brain. A deep fissure at the side of the brain, the lateral sulcus, sets off the temporal lobe.

THE PRIMARY MOTOR AREA The *primary motor area,* just in front of the central fissure, controls voluntary movements of the body (see Figure 2-10). Electrical stimulation at certain spots on the motor cortex causes specific parts of the body to move. When these same spots on the motor cortex are injured, movement is impaired. The body is represented on the motor cortex in approximately upside-down form. For example, movements of the toes are controlled from an area near the top of the head, but tongue and mouth movements are controlled from near the bottom of the motor area. Movements on

the right side of the body are governed by the motor cortex of the left hemisphere; the right hemisphere governs movements on the left side.

THE PRIMARY SOMATOSENSORY AREA
In the parietal lobe, separated from the motor area by the central sulcus, lies an area that, when stimulated electrically, produces a sensory experience somewhere on the opposite side of the body. Stimulation here feels as though a part of the body is being touched or moved. This is called the *primary somatosensory area* (body-sense area). Heat, cold, touch, pain, and the sense of body movement are represented here.

Most of the nerve fibers in the pathways that radiate to and from the somatosensory and motor areas cross to the opposite side of the body. Sensory impulses from the right side of the body go to the left somatosensory cortex, for example, and the muscles of the right foot and hand are controlled by the left motor cortex.

In general, the amount of somatosensory area associated with a particular part of the body is related to its sensitivity and use. For example, among four-footed mammals, the dog has only a small amount of cortical tissue representing its forepaws, whereas the raccoon—which makes extensive use of its forepaws in exploring and manipulating its environment—has a much larger cortical area to control its forepaws, including regions for separate fingers. The rat, which learns a great deal about its environment by means of its sensitive whiskers, has a separate cortical area for each whisker.

THE PRIMARY VISUAL AREA At the back of each occipital lobe in the cortex is the *primary visual area.* Figure 2-11 shows the optic nerve fibers and neural pathways leading from each eye to the visual cortex. Notice that some of the optic fibers from the right eye go to the right cerebral hemisphere, whereas others cross over at a junction called the *optic chiasm* and go to the opposite hemisphere; the same arrangement holds true for the left eye. Specifically, fibers from the right sides of both eyes go to the right hemisphere of the brain, and fibers from the left sides of both eyes go to the left hemisphere. This fact is sometimes helpful in pinpointing the location of a brain tumor or other abnormalities. For example, damage to the visual area of the left hemisphere produces blind fields in the left sides of both eyes, causing a loss of vision to the right side of the environment.

▌Figure 2-11
Visual Pathways
Nerve fibers from the inner, or nasal, half of the retina cross over at the optic chiasm and go to opposite sides of the brain. Thus, stimuli falling on the right side of each retina are transmitted to the right hemisphere, and stimuli falling on the left side of each retina are transmitted to the left hemisphere.
(Adapted from *Human Anatomy* by Anthony J. Gaudin and Kenneth C. Jones. Copyright © 1988 by Anthony J. Gaudin and Kenneth C. Jones. Reprinted by permission of the authors.)

THE PRIMARY AUDITORY AREA The *primary auditory area,* located on the surface of the temporal lobe at the side of each hemisphere, is involved in the analysis of complex auditory signals—particularly the temporal patterning of sound, as in human speech. Both ears are represented in the auditory areas on both sides of the cortex, but connections to the contralateral (opposite) side are stronger. The right ear sends information to both the right and left primary auditory areas, but it sends more information to the auditory area on the left side of the brain. The opposite is true of the left ear.

ASSOCIATION AREAS As mentioned earlier, the areas of the cerebral cortex that are not directly concerned with sensory or motor processes are *association areas.* The *frontal association areas* (the parts of the frontal lobes in front of the motor area) appear to play an important role in the memory processes required for problem solving (Miller & Cohen, 2001). In monkeys, for example, damage to the frontal lobes destroys their ability to solve a delayed-response problem. In this kind of problem, food is placed in one of two cups while the monkey watches, the cups are covered with identical objects, and an opaque screen is placed between the monkey and the cups. After a specified period, the screen is removed and the monkey is allowed to choose one of the cups. Normal monkeys can remember the correct cup after several minutes, but monkeys with frontal lobe damage cannot solve the problem if the delay is more than a few seconds. Normal monkeys have neurons in the frontal lobe that fire action potentials during the delay, which possibly mediates memory of an event (Goldman-Rakic, 1996).

The *posterior association areas* are located near primary sensory areas and appear to consist of subareas that each serve a particular sense. For example, the lower portion of the temporal lobe is related to visual perception. Lesions (that is, brain damage) in this area cause deficiencies in the ability to recognize and discriminate between different forms. A lesion here does not decrease visual acuity, as would a lesion in the primary visual area of the occipital lobe; the individual can "see" the form and trace its outline but not identify the shape or distinguish it from a different form (Gallant, Shuop, & Mazer, 2000; Goodglass & Butters, 1988).

PICTURES OF THE LIVING BRAIN

Sophisticated computer methods that have become feasible only recently can obtain detailed pictures of the living human brain without causing the patient distress or damage. Before these techniques were perfected, the precise location and identification of most types of brain injury could be determined only by exploratory neurosurgery, a complicated neurological diagnosis, or an autopsy after the patient's death.

One such technique is *computerized axial tomography* (CAT or CT). In this procedure a narrow X-ray beam is sent through the patient's head, and the amount of radiation that gets through is measured. The revolutionary aspect of this technique was that measurements can be made on hundreds of thousands of different orientations (or axes) through the head. These measurements are fed into a computer to construct a cross-sectional picture of the brain that can be photographed or displayed on a monitor. The cross-sectional "slice" (*tomo* is an ancient Greek word meaning "slice" or "cut") can be shown at any level and angle desired.

A newer and even more powerful technique is **magnetic resonance imaging** (MRI), in which scanners use strong magnetic fields, radio-frequency pulses, and computers to compose an image. In this procedure the patient lies in a doughnut-shaped tunnel surrounded by a large magnet that generates a powerful magnetic field. When a selected part of the body is placed in a strong magnetic field and exposed to a certain radio-frequency pulse, the tissues emit a signal that can be measured. As with the CT scanner, hundreds of thousands of measurements can be made and then manipulated by a computer to produce a two-dimensional image of the part of the body under study. Scientists usually call this technique

Growing a New Brain

The picture painted of neuroanatomy in this chapter suggests that the nervous system is a static, hard-wired system, much like your television set. But is neuroanatomy so immutable? Recent studies suggest that it is not. Indeed, the brain appears to be a highly dynamic system capable of enormous plasticity during development and as a result of experience in adults. Perhaps the most exciting new finding is that not only do synapses grow and retract during learning but also new neurons appear to be born in the adult brain after a variety of experiences.

New neurons? That's right. In mammals, the birth of most neurons, called *neurogenesis,* occurs early in embryological development while the fetus is still in the uterus. These immature neurons migrate throughout the developing brain, looking for an address that tells them where they will spend the rest of their lives. When they get to that address, each neuron settles down and differentiates into one of the many shapes and sizes illustrated in Figure 2-3. In most cases, these neurons lose their capacity for cell division once they mature into a differentiated neuron. In other words, once cells are born and migrate, they are not replaced by new generations of cells later in life.

However, recent results have questioned the long-held view that the adult brain is incapable of producing new generations of neurons. In one recent study, investigators injected rats with a compound called BRDU that labels newly born neurons. After injecting the rats, they trained the animals in a classical conditioning task that requires the hippocampus. They found that rats that underwent training in the conditioning task exhibited a significant increase in the number of labeled neurons in the hippocampus (Gould, Beylin, Tanapat, Reeves, & Shors, 1999). Interestingly, training in a similar conditioning task that does not require the hippocampus was not associated with the birth of new neurons in the hippocampus. More re-

cently, these investigators have found that drugs that block hippocampal neurogenesis impair trace eyeblink conditioning (Shors et al., 2001). Collectively, these studies suggest not only that learning is associated with the birth of new neurons in the brain but also that neurogenesis may itself be essential for learning to occur. Interestingly, not only complicated learning tasks induce the birth of new hippocampal neurons. Investigators at the Salk Institute have found that simply giving animals an opportunity to exercise increases the number of newly born hippocampal neurons (van Praag, Kempermann, & Gage, 1999). These neurons develop and behave just like adult neurons (van Praag et al., 2002). So, not only does your daily jog keep you trim—it fuels your brain's potential for learning. So, go ahead, treat your brain and run a few miles today!

 For more information, go online with InfoTrac College Edition. Use your own term or search:

- Neuroanatomy
- Nervous system regeneration
- Exercise and the brain

"nuclear magnetic resonance" because it measures variations in the energy level of hydrogen atom nuclei caused by the radio-frequency pulses. However, many physicians leave out *nuclear* because the public may perceive it as referring to nuclear radiation.

MRI offers greater precision than CT in the diagnosis of diseases of the brain and spinal cord. For example, an MRI cross-section of the brain shows features characteristic of multiple sclerosis that are not detected by a CT scanner. Diagnosis of this disease previously required hospitalization and injection of a dye into the canal around the spinal cord. MRI is also useful in detecting abnormalities in the spinal cord and at the base of the brain, such as herniated disks, tumors, and birth malformations.

In addition to the anatomical details of the brain that CT and MRI provide, it is often desirable to assess neural activity levels at different locations in the brain. A computer-based scanning procedure called *positron emission tomography* (PET) provides this information.

This technique depends on the fact that every cell in the body requires energy to conduct metabolic processes. In the brain, neurons use glucose (obtained from the bloodstream) as their principal source of energy. A small amount of a weakly radioactive tracer compound can be mixed with glucose so that each molecule of glucose has a tiny speck of radioactivity (that is, a *label*) attached to it. If this mixture is injected into the bloodstream, after a few minutes the brain cells begin to use the radiolabeled glucose in the same way that they use regular glucose. The PET scan is essentially a highly sensitive detector of radioactivity. The neurons that are most active require the most glucose and are therefore the most radioactive. The PET scan measures the amount of radioactivity and sends the information to a computer that draws a cross-sectional picture of the brain, with different colors representing different levels of neural activity. The measurement of radioactivity is based on the emission of positrons, which are positively

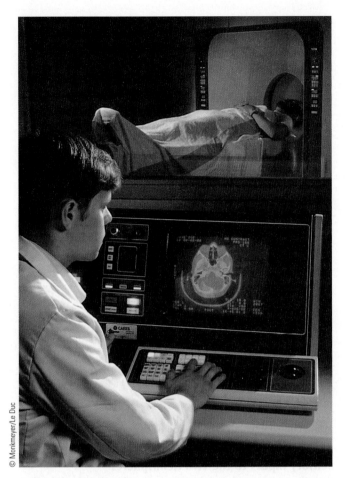

A technician administering a magnetic resonance imaging procedure. An image of the patient's brain appears on the computer screen.

charged particles—hence the term "positron emission tomography."

Brain problems such as epilepsy, blood clots, and brain tumors can be identified with this technique. PET scans comparing the brains of people with schizophrenia with those of normal individuals have shown differences in metabolic levels in certain cortical areas (Schultz et al., 2002). The PET scan has also been used to investigate the brain areas that are activated during higher mental functions such as listening to music, doing mathematics, or speaking, with the objective of identifying the brain structures involved (Posner, 1993).

CT, MRI, and PET are proving to be valuable tools for studying the relationship between the brain and behavior. They are an example of how progress in one field of science forges ahead because of technical developments in another (Pechura & Martin, 1991; Raichle, 1994). For example, PET scans can be used to study differences in neural activity between the two cerebral hemispheres. These hemispheric differences in activity are known as *brain asymmetries*.

ASYMMETRIES IN THE BRAIN

At first glance, the two halves of the brain look like mirror images. But when brains are measured during autopsies, the left hemisphere is almost always larger than the right hemisphere. The right hemisphere also contains many long neural fibers that connect widely separated areas of the brain, whereas the left hemisphere has many shorter fibers that provide large numbers of interconnections within a limited area (Hellige, 1993).

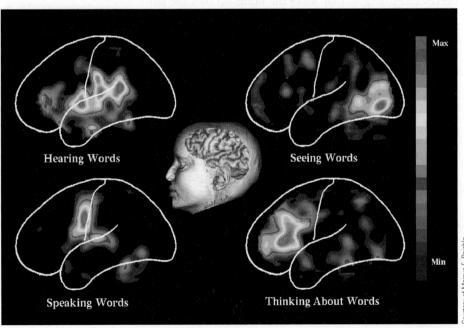

PET scans in a human subject illustrating that different areas of the brain are involved in different modes of word processing.

As early as 1861, the French physician Paul Broca examined the brain of a deceased patient who had suffered speech loss. He found damage in an area of the left hemisphere just above the lateral sulcus in the frontal lobe. This region, now known as *Broca's area* (refer back to Figure 2-10), is involved in speech production. Destruction of the equivalent region in the right hemisphere usually does not result in speech impairment. The areas involved in understanding speech and being able to write and understand written words are also usually located in the left hemisphere. A stroke that damages the left hemisphere is more likely to produce language impairment than one with damage confined to the right hemisphere. Not all people have left-hemisphere speech centers; some left-handed individuals have right-hemisphere speech centers.

Although the left hemisphere's role in language has been known for some time, only recently has it been possible to investigate what each hemisphere can do on its own. In a normal individual, the brain functions as an integrated whole. Information in one hemisphere is immediately transferred to the other via a broad band of connecting nerve fibers, the *corpus callosum*. This connecting bridge is a problem in some forms of epilepsy because a seizure starting in one hemisphere may cross over and trigger a massive discharge of neurons in the other hemisphere. To try to prevent such generalized seizures, neurosurgeons have surgically severed the corpus callosum in individuals with severe epilepsy. These split-brain patients have yielded important insights into the functions of the left and right hemispheres.

SPLIT-BRAIN RESEARCH We have seen that the motor nerves cross over as they leave the brain, so that the left cerebral hemisphere controls the right side of the body, and the right hemisphere controls the left. We noted also that the speech production area (Broca's area) is located in the left hemisphere. Consider also that when the eyes are fixated directly ahead, images to the left of the fixation point go through both eyes to the right side of the brain, and images to the right of the fixation point go to the left side of the brain (see Figure 2-12). Each hemisphere therefore has a view of the half of the visual field in which "its" hand normally functions; for example, the left hemisphere sees the right hand in the right visual field. In the normal brain, stimuli entering one hemisphere are rapidly communicated to the other, and the brain functions as a unit. Now, given these three facts about the brain, let us take a look at what happens when the corpus callosum is severed—leaving a split brain—and the two hemispheres cannot communicate with each other.

Roger Sperry, who pioneered work in this field, was awarded the Nobel Prize in 1981. In one of Sperry's test situations, a person who has undergone split-brain

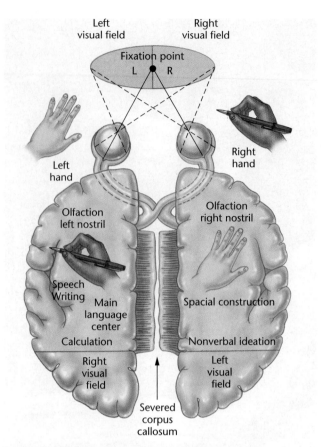

▌Figure 2-12
Sensory Inputs to the Two Hemispheres
With the eyes fixated straight ahead, stimuli to the left of the fixation point go to the right cerebral hemisphere, and stimuli to the right go to the left hemisphere. The left hemisphere controls movements of the right hand, and the right hemisphere controls the left hand. Hearing is largely crossed in its input, but some sound representation goes to the hemisphere on the same side as the ear that registered it. The left hemisphere controls written and spoken language and mathematical calculations. The right hemisphere can understand only simple language; its main ability seems to involve spatial construction and pattern sense.
(Reprinted from *Neuropsychologia*, Volume 9, by R. D. Nebes and W. Sperry, p. 247. Copyright © 1971, with kind permission of Elsevier Science Ltd., the Boulevard Langford Lane, Kiddington, Oxford, OX5 1DX, UK.)

surgery is seated in front of a screen that hides his hands from view (see Figure 2-13a). His gaze is fixed on a spot at the center of the screen. The word *nut* is flashed on the left side of the screen for a tenth of a second. Remember that this visual signal goes to the right side of the brain, which controls the left side of the body. With his left hand, the person can easily pick up a nut from a pile of objects hidden from view. But he cannot tell the experimenter what word flashed on the screen because speech is controlled by the left hemisphere and the visual image of "nut" was not transmitted to that hemisphere. When questioned, he seems unaware of what his left hand is

a) A split-brain patient correctly retrieves an object by touch with the left hand when its name is flashed to the right hemisphere, but he cannot name the object or describe what he has done.

b) The word "hatband" is flashed so that "hat" goes to the right cerebral hemisphere and "band" goes to the left hemisphere. The patient reports that he sees the word "band" but has no idea what kind of band.

c) A list of common objects (including "book" and "cup") is initially shown to both hemispheres. One word from the list ("book") is then projected to the right hemisphere. When given the command to do so, the left hand begins writing the word "book," but when questioned, the patient does not know what his left hand has written and guesses "cup."

❚ **Figure 2-13**
Testing the Abilities of the Two Hemispheres

doing. Because the sensory input from the left hand goes to the right hemisphere, the left hemisphere receives no information about what the left hand is feeling or doing. All information is fed back to the right hemisphere, which received the original visual input of the word *nut*.

In this experiment the word must be flashed on the screen for no more than a tenth of a second. If it remains longer, the person's eyes move, and the word is also projected to the left hemisphere. When people can move their eyes freely, information goes to both cerebral hemispheres; this is one reason why the deficiencies caused by severing the corpus callosum are not readily apparent in a person's daily activities.

Further experiments demonstrate that a split-brain patient can communicate through speech only what is going on in the left hemisphere. Figure 2-13b shows another test situation. The word *hatband* was flashed on the screen so that *hat* went to the right hemisphere and *band* to the left. When asked what word he saw, the person replied, *band*. When asked what kind of band, he made all sorts of guesses—"rubber band," "rock band," "band of robbers," and so forth—and said "hatband" only by chance. Tests with other compound words (such as *keycase* and *suitcase*) have shown similar results. What the right hemisphere perceives is not transferred to the conscious awareness of the left hemisphere. With the corpus callosum severed, each hemisphere seems oblivious to the experiences of the other.

If split-brain patients are blindfolded and a familiar object (such as a comb, toothbrush, or keycase) is placed in the left hand, they appear to know what it is and can demonstrate its use by appropriate gestures. But they cannot express this knowledge in speech. If asked what is going on while they are manipulating the object, they have no idea as long as any sensory input from the object to the left (speaking) hemisphere is blocked. But if the patient's right hand inadvertently touches the object or the object makes a characteristic sound (like the jingling of a keycase), the speaking hemisphere immediately gives the correct answer.

Although the right hemisphere cannot produce speech, it does have some linguistic capabilities. It recognized the meaning of the word *nut* in our first example, and it can produce writing. In the experiment illustrated in Figure 2-13c, split-brain patients are first shown a list of common objects, such as a cup, a knife, a book, and a glass. This list is displayed long enough for the words to be projected to both hemispheres. Next, the list is removed, and one of the words (for example, *book*) is flashed briefly on the left side of the screen so that it goes to the right hemisphere. When patients are asked to write what they saw, the left hand begins writing the word *book*. If asked what the left hand has written, they have no idea and guess any of the words on the original list. They know that they have written something because they feel the writing movements through their body. But because there is no communication between the right hemisphere that saw and wrote the word and the left hemisphere that controls speech, they cannot tell you what they wrote

(Sperry, 1968, 1970; see also Gazzaniga, 1985; Hellige, 1990).

HEMISPHERIC SPECIALIZATION Studies with split-brain patients indicate that the two hemispheres function differently. The left hemisphere governs our ability to express ourselves in language. It can perform complicated logical activities and is skilled in mathematical computations. The right hemisphere can comprehend only very simple language. It can, for example, respond to simple nouns by selecting objects such as a nut or a comb, but it cannot comprehend more abstract linguistic forms. If it is presented with simple commands like "wink," "nod," "shake head," or "smile," it seldom responds.

The right hemisphere, however, has a highly developed spatial and pattern sense. It is superior to the left hemisphere in constructing geometric and perspective drawings. It can assemble colored blocks to match a complex design much more effectively than the left hemisphere can. When split-brain patients are asked to use the right hand to assemble blocks to match a design shown in a picture, they make numerous mistakes. Sometimes they have trouble keeping the left hand from automatically correcting the right hand's mistakes.

Studies with normal individuals tend to confirm the different specializations of the two hemispheres. For example, verbal information (such as words or nonsense syllables) can be identified faster and more accurately when flashed briefly to the left hemisphere (that is, in the right visual field) than to the right hemisphere. In contrast, identification of faces, facial expressions of emotion, line slopes, or dot locations occurs more

Studies with split-brain patients have shown that the two hemispheres specialize in different aspects of mental functioning. The right hemisphere, for example, is superior in constructing geometric and perspective drawings, leading to the belief that artists have a highly developed "right brain."

quickly when these are flashed to the right hemisphere (Hellige, 1990). Also, studies using electroencephalograms (EEGs) indicate that electrical activity from the left hemisphere increases during a verbal task, whereas during a spatial task, electrical activity increases in the right hemisphere (Kosslyn, 1988; Springer & Deutsch, 1989).

This discussion does not mean that the two hemispheres work independently. Just the opposite is true. The hemispheres differ in their specializations, but they continually integrate their activities. It is this interaction that enables mental processes that are greater than and different from each hemisphere's special contribution. As one researcher describes it,

> These differences are seen in the contrasting contributions each hemisphere makes to all cognitive activities. When a person reads a story, the right hemisphere may play a special role in decoding visual information, maintaining an integrated story structure, appreciating humor and emotional content, deriving meaning from past associations and understanding metaphor. At the same time, the left hemisphere plays a special role in understanding syntax, translating written words into their phonetic representations and deriving meaning from complex relations among word concepts and syntax. But there is no activity in which only one hemisphere is involved or to which only one hemisphere makes a contribution. (Levy, 1985, p. 44)

LANGUAGE AND THE BRAIN

Much of our information about brain mechanisms for language comes from observations of patients with brain damage. The damage may be due to tumors, penetrating head wounds, or the rupture of blood vessels. The term **aphasia** is used to describe language deficits caused by brain damage.

As discussed earlier, Broca observed that damage to a specific area on the side of the left frontal lobe was linked to a speech disorder called *expressive aphasia*. People with damage to Broca's area have difficulty enunciating words correctly and speak in a slow, labored way. Their speech often makes sense, but it includes only key words. Nouns are generally expressed in the singular, and adjectives, adverbs, articles, and conjunctions are likely to be omitted. However, these individuals have no difficulty understanding either spoken or written language.

In 1874 a German investigator, Carl Wernicke, reported that damage to another site in the cortex—also in the left hemisphere but in the temporal lobe—is linked to a language disorder called *receptive aphasia*. People with damage in this location, known as *Wernicke's area*, are unable to comprehend words: They can hear words, but they do not know their meaning. They can produce strings of words without difficulty and with proper articulation, but they make errors in usage and their speech tends to be meaningless.

Analyzing defects, Wernicke developed a model to explain how the brain functions in producing and understanding language. Although his model is more than 100 years old, its general features still appear to be correct. Norman Geschwind built on these ideas in developing a theory that has come to be known as the Wernicke-Geschwind model (Geschwind, 1979). According to this model, Broca's area stores articulatory codes, which specify the sequence of muscle actions required to pronounce a word. When these codes are transmitted to the motor area, they activate the muscles of the lips, tongue, and larynx in the proper sequence and produce a spoken word. Wernicke's area, by contrast, is where auditory codes and the meanings of words are stored. For a word to be spoken, its auditory code must be activated in Wernicke's area and transmitted to Broca's area, where it activates the corresponding articulatory code. In turn, the articulatory code is transmitted to the motor area to activate the muscles that produce the spoken word.

To understand a word spoken by someone else, it must be transmitted from the auditory area to Wernicke's area. There the spoken form of the word is matched with its auditory code, which in turn activates the word's meaning. When a written word is presented, it is first registered in the visual area and then relayed to the angular gyrus, which associates the visual form of the word with its auditory code in Wernicke's area; once the word's auditory code has been found, so has its meaning. Thus, the meanings of words are stored along with their acoustical codes in Wernicke's area. Broca's area stores articulatory codes, and the angular gyrus matches the written form of a word to its auditory code. Neither of these areas, however, stores information about word meaning. The meaning of a word is retrieved only when its acoustical code is activated in Wernicke's area.

The Wernicke-Geschwind model explains many of the language deficits aphasics show. Damage that is limited to Broca's area disrupts speech production but has less effect on the comprehension of spoken or written language. Damage to Wernicke's area disrupts all aspects of language comprehension, but the person can still articulate words properly (even though the output is meaningless) because Broca's area is intact. The model also correctly predicts that individuals with damage in the angular gyrus are not able to read but have no difficulty speaking or comprehending speech. Finally, if damage is restricted to the auditory area, a person can read and speak normally but cannot comprehend speech.

THE AUTONOMIC NERVOUS SYSTEM

We noted earlier that the peripheral nervous system has two divisions. The somatic system controls the skeletal muscles and receives information from the skin, muscles, and various sensory receptors. The autonomic system controls the glands and the smooth muscles, including the heart, the blood vessels, and the lining of the stomach and intestines. These muscles are called "smooth" because that is how they look under a microscope. (Skeletal muscles, in contrast, have a striped appearance.) The autonomic nervous system derives its name from the fact that many of the activities it controls, such as digestion and circulation, are autonomous, or self-regulating, and continue even when a person is asleep or unconscious.

The autonomic nervous system has two divisions, sympathetic and parasympathetic, whose actions are often antagonistic. The **sympathetic nervous system** typically is active during times of intense arousal, and the **parasympathetic nervous system** is associated with rest. Figure 2-14 shows the contrasting effects of the two systems on various organs. For example, the parasympathetic system constricts the pupil of the eye, stimulates the flow of saliva, and slows the heart rate; the sympathetic system has the opposite effect in each case. The balance between these two systems maintains the normal state of the body (somewhere between extreme excitement and vegetative placidity).

The sympathetic division tends to act as a unit. During emotional excitement, it simultaneously speeds up the heart, dilates the arteries of the skeletal muscles and heart, constricts the arteries of the skin and digestive organs, and causes perspiration. It also activates certain endocrine glands to secrete hormones that further increase arousal.

Unlike the sympathetic system, the parasympathetic division tends to affect one organ at a time. It is dominant during periods of quiescence, participates in digestion, and, in general, maintains the functions that conserve and protect bodily resources. For example, a decreased heart rate and slowed breathing, which are maintained by the parasympathetic nervous system, require far less energy than a fast heartbeat and rapid breathing, which are by-products of activation of the sympathetic nervous system.

Although the sympathetic and parasympathetic systems are usually antagonistic, there are some exceptions. The sympathetic system is dominant during fear and excitement, for example, but a not-uncommon parasympathetic response to fear is involuntary discharge of the bladder or bowels. Another example is the complete sex act in the male, which requires erection (parasympathetic), followed by ejaculation (sympathetic).

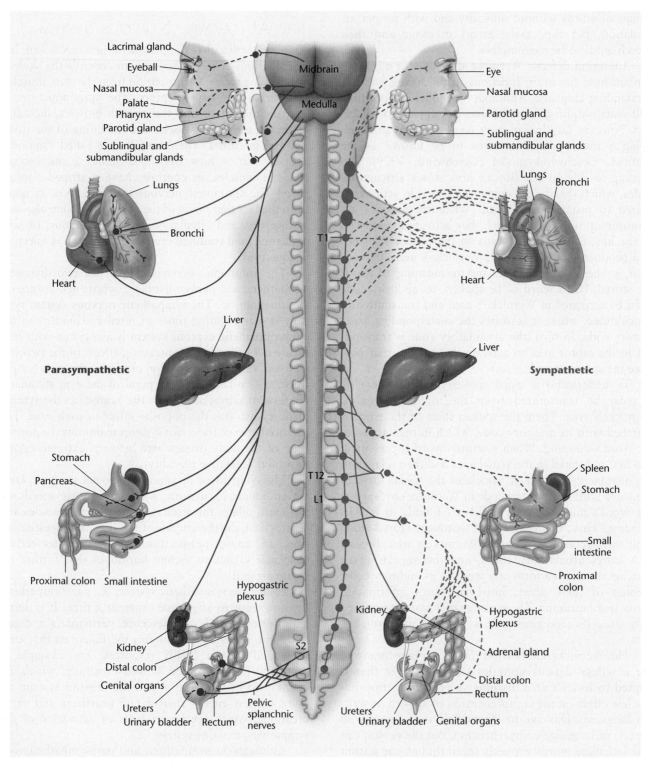

▌ Figure 2-14

Motor Fibers of the Autonomic Nervous System

In this diagram, the sympathetic division is indicated in blue and the parasympathetic division in red. Solid lines indicate preganglionic fibers, and dashed lines indicate postganglionic fibers. Neurons of the sympathetic division originate in the thoracic and lumbar regions of the spinal cord and form synaptic junctions with ganglia lying just outside the cord. Neurons of the parasympathetic division exit from the medulla region of the brainstem and from the lower (sacral) end of the spinal cord; they connect with ganglia near the organs stimulated. Most internal organs are innervated by both divisions, which function in opposition to each other.

◆ Interim Summary

- The nervous system is divided into the central nervous system (the brain and spinal cord) and the peripheral nervous system (the nerves connecting the brain and spinal cord to other parts of the body). Subdivisions of the peripheral nervous system are the somatic system (which carries messages to and from the sense receptors, muscles, and the surface of the body) and the autonomic system (which connects with the internal organs and glands).

- The human brain is composed of three functional divisions: the central core, the limbic system, and the cerebrum. The central core mediates basic autonomic functions, the limbic system is involved in emotion, motivation, and memory, and the cerebrum is responsible for planning and decision making.

- Severing the corpus callosum (the band of nerve fibers connecting the two cerebral hemispheres) causes significant differences in the functioning of the two hemispheres. The left hemisphere is skilled in language and mathematical abilities. The right hemisphere can understand some language but cannot communicate through speech; it has a highly developed spatial and pattern sense.

- The autonomic nervous system consists of the sympathetic and parasympathetic divisions. The sympathetic division is active during excitement, and the parasympathetic system is dominant during quiescence.

◆ Critical Thinking Questions

1. Why is your brain symmetrical (meaning that the left and right sides look alike)? You have a left and right motor cortex, a left and right hippocampus, a left and right cerebellum, and so on. In each case, the left side is a mirror image of the right side (just as, for example, your left eye is a mirror image of your right eye). Can you think of any reason why your brain is symmetrical in this way?

2. In split-brain patients, whose corpus callosum has been cut, the left and right sides of the brain seem to work independently after the operation. For example, a word shown to one side may be read and responded to without the other side knowing what the word was. Does such a person have two minds, each capable of knowing different things, or does the patient still have only one mind?

THE ENDOCRINE SYSTEM

We can think of the nervous system as controlling the fast-changing activities of the body by directly activating muscles and glands. (*Glands* are organs located throughout the body that secrete special substances, such as sweat, milk, or a particular hormone.) The endocrine system acts more slowly, indirectly affecting the activities of cell groups throughout the body. It does so by means of **hormones,** chemicals secreted by the endocrine glands into the bloodstream and transported to other parts of the body, where they have specific effects on cells that recognize their message (see Figure 2-15). Hormones act

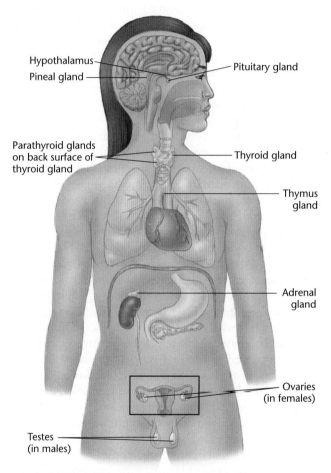

Hypothalamus
Pineal gland
Pituitary gland
Parathyroid glands on back surface of thyroid gland
Thyroid gland
Thymus gland
Adrenal gland
Ovaries (in females)
Testes (in males)

❚ Figure 2-15
Some of the Endocrine Glands
Hormones secreted by the endocrine glands are as essential as the nervous system to the integration of the organism's activity. The two systems differ, however, in the speed with which they can act. A nerve impulse can travel through the organism in a few hundredths of a second. Seconds, or even minutes, may be required for an endocrine gland to produce an effect. The hormone, once released, must travel to its target site via the bloodstream—a much slower process.

in various ways on cells of different types. Each target cell is equipped with receptors that recognize only the hormone molecules that act on that cell. The receptors pull those molecules out of the bloodstream and into the cell. Some endocrine glands are activated by the nervous system, and others are activated by changes in the internal chemical state of the body.

One of the major endocrine glands is the *pituitary*. This gland is partly an outgrowth of the brain and lies just below the hypothalamus (refer back to Figure 2-8c). The pituitary has been called the "master gland" because it produces the most different hormones and controls the secretion activity of other endocrine glands. One of the pituitary hormones, growth hormone, has the crucial job of controlling the body's growth. Dwarfism is caused by too little of this hormone, and gigantism is caused by too much of it. Other hormones released by the pituitary trigger the action of other endocrine glands, such as the thyroid, the sex glands, and the outer layer of the adrenal gland. Courtship, mating, and reproductive behavior in many animals are based on a complex interaction between nervous system activity and the influence of the pituitary on the sex glands.

The relationship between the pituitary gland and the hypothalamus illustrates the complex interactions. In response to stress (fear, anxiety, pain, emotional events, and so forth), certain neurons in the hypothalamus secrete corticotropin-releasing factor (CRF), which is carried to the pituitary through a channel-like structure. CRF stimulates the pituitary to release adrenocorticotropic hormone (ACTH), the body's major stress hormone. ACTH, in turn, is carried by the bloodstream to the adrenal glands and other organs, causing the release of some 30 hormones, each of which plays a role in the body's adjustment to emergency situations. For example, the cellular demand for glucose increases in a state of emergency, and cortisol, an adrenal hormone that is released under stress, promotes liberation of glucose from fat stores in the body. Interestingly, cortisol has effects on cognitive function as well. At low levels, it enhances memory, but at high levels it causes memory impairments and neuronal death.

The adrenal glands play an important role in determining a person's mood, energy level, and ability to cope with stress. The inner core of the adrenal gland secretes epinephrine and norepinephrine (also known as adrenaline and noradrenaline). Epinephrine prepares the organism for an emergency. In conjunction with the sympathetic division of the autonomic nervous system, it affects the smooth muscles and sweat glands. It also constricts the blood vessels in the stomach and intestines and makes the heart beat faster. Norepinephrine also prepares the organism for emergency action. It stimulates the pituitary to release a hormone that acts on the outer layer of the adrenal glands; this hormone, in turn, stimulates the liver to increase the blood sugar level to give the body the energy required for quick action.

The hormones of the endocrine system and the neurotransmitters of neurons perform similar functions: They both carry messages between cells. A neurotransmitter carries messages between adjacent neurons, and its effects are highly localized. In contrast, a hormone may travel a long distance through the body and act in various ways on many different types of cells. Despite these differences, some of these chemical messengers serve both functions. Epinephrine and norepinephrine, for example, act as neurotransmitters when they are released by neurons and as hormones when they are released by the adrenal gland.

◆ Interim Summary

- The endocrine glands secrete hormones into the bloodstream that travel through the body, acting in various ways on cells of different types.

- The pituitary gland controls the secretion activity of other endocrine glands.

◆ Critical Thinking Questions

1. When hormones are released into the bloodstream, they can reach every cell in the body. How then do hormones exert selective actions on certain bodily tissues? Can you think of analogies with synaptic transmission in the brain?

2. During winter, your furnace heats the air inside your house, and the thermostat detects when the indoor air temperature reaches the level you set. How might this principle be used in the endocrine system to maintain levels of hormones in the bloodstream? What master gland might serve as the endocrine system's "thermostat"?

EVOLUTION, GENES, AND BEHAVIOR

To fully understand the biological foundations of psychology, we need to know something about evolutionary and genetic influences as well as biological structures and processes. All biological organisms have evolved over millions of years, and environmental factors have played an important role in shaping the organization and function of their nervous systems. *Natural selection*, the process described by Charles Darwin to account for evolutionary change, plays an essential role in shaping both behavior and brain. The field of **behavior genetics** combines the methods of genetics and psychology to study the inheritance of behavioral characteristics (Plomin, Owen, & McGuffin, 1994). We know that many *physical* characteristics—height, bone structure, hair and eye color, and the like—are inherited. Behavioral geneticists are interested in the degree to which *psychological* characteristics, including mental ability, temperament, and emotional stability, are transmitted from parent to offspring (Bouchard, 1984, 1995). Researchers led by Robert Plomin of London's Institute of Psychiatry have identified chromosomal markers that contribute to intelligence (Fisher et al., 1999). However, such findings are not conclusive. As we will see in this section, environmental conditions have a lot to do with the way a particular genetic factor is expressed in an individual as he or she matures.

EVOLUTION OF BEHAVIOR

Any examination of behavior must include not only *proximate* causes of the behavior, such as the firing of spinal motor neurons that drives the knee jerk reflex, but also *ultimate* causes. Ultimate causes of behavior explain behavior in its evolutionary context. Whereas proximate causes explain "how" a behavior is generated, ultimate causes help us to understand "why" a behavior exists in the first place—that is, why it evolved by natural selection.

Consider, for example, male aggression (see Seeing Both Sides later in this chapter). In both humans and other mammals, males are typically more aggressive than females (Buss & Shackelford, 1997), particularly in same-sex social interactions. In mammals whose sexual reproduction is seasonally regulated, intermale aggression is particularly pronounced during the breeding season. In red deer and elephant seals, for example, males attempt to control small groups of females ("harems") for mating and behave aggressively toward other males that attempt to mate with these females.

The proximate causes of aggressive behavior are reasonably well understood. For example, circulating levels of the gonadal steroid, testosterone, are correlated with aggressive behavior, and damage to subcortical brain structures can reduce or potentiate aggressive behavior in animals. Recent evidence indicates serotonin is important in aggressive behavior (Nelson & Chiavegatto, 2001), and olfactory cues, at least in rodents, appear to mediate male aggression (Stowers, Holy, Meister, Dulac, & Koenteges, 2002). Moreover, social context powerfully modulates the nature and pattern of aggressive behavior. During the breeding season, male red deer and elephant seals display to and attack other males that approach them but do not attack sexually receptive females.

But why do aggressive behavior and the neural and hormonal systems underlying this behavior exist at all? What are the ultimate causes of aggressive behavior? From an evolutionary or functional point of view, ag-

gressive behavior in breeding males is *adaptive*. It confers reproductive success, and reproductive success promotes the perpetuation of genes that control aggressive behavior. In red deer, aggressive males are more likely to secure and mate with receptive females and thereby increase the proportion of males in subsequent generations that carry genes for aggressiveness. Unaggressive male red deer are less likely to secure mates, and their genes become poorly represented in the population. This does not mean that male aggression is "good" from an ethical or moral point of view. Rather, the behavior is adaptive in an evolutionary context.

Aggressive behavior is said to be sexually selected because it is invoked by competition for mating opportunities. **Sexual selection,** a special case of natural selection, yields traits that promote reproductive success in the sex with the greater potential reproductive rate. In deer, the female reproductive rate is limited by gestation and nursing, but the male reproductive rate is limited only by available females. In some birds, the male reproductive rate is slower than that in females because the males brood over the nest to hatch the eggs while the females seek other males with which they mate. In this case, female birds show greater aggression than males. In either case, any trait that confers an advantage in securing mates will be selected for in the sex with the greatest reproductive potential. These traits are not limited to behavioral proclivities such as aggression but include physical traits such as body size and coloration.

CHROMOSOMES AND GENES

Natural selection operates on **genes,** which are segments of deoxyribonucleic acid (DNA) molecules that form the fundamental hereditary unit. The genes we receive from our parents and transmit to our offspring are carried by **chromosomes,** structures in the nucleus of each cell in the body. Most body cells contain 46 chromosomes. At conception, the human being receives 23 chromosomes from the father's sperm and 23 chromosomes from the mother's ovum. These 46 chromosomes form 23 pairs, which are duplicated each time the cells divide (see Figure 2-16). As shown in Figure 2-17, the DNA molecule looks like a twisted ladder or a double-stranded helix (spiral).

Each gene gives coded instructions to the cell, directing it to perform a specific function (usually to manufacture a particular protein). Although all cells in the body carry the same genes, each cell is specialized because only 5% to 10% of the genes in any given cell are active. In the process of developing from a fertilized egg, each cell switches on some genes and switches off all others. When "nerve genes" are active, for example, a cell develops as a neuron because the genes are directing the cell to make the products that allow it to perform neural

Figure 2-16
Chromosomes
This photo (greatly enlarged) shows the 46 chromosomes of a normal human female. In a human male, pairs 1 through 22 would be the same as those in the female, but pair 23 would be XY rather than XX.

functions (which would not be possible if irrelevant genes, such as "muscle genes," were not switched off).

Genes, like chromosomes, exist in pairs. One gene of each pair comes from the sperm chromosomes, and one gene comes from the ovum chromosomes. Thus, a child receives only half of each parent's total genes. The total number of genes in each human chromosome is about 1,000, perhaps higher. Because the number of genes is so high, two human beings, even siblings, are extremely unlikely to inherit exactly the same set of genes. The only exception is identical twins, who, because they developed from the same fertilized egg, have exactly the same genes.

DOMINANT AND RECESSIVE GENES Either gene of a gene pair can be *dominant* or *recessive*. When both members of a gene pair are dominant, the individual manifests the form of the trait specified by these dominant genes. When one gene is dominant and the other recessive, the dominant gene again determines the form of the trait. Only if the genes contributed by both parents are recessive is the recessive form of the trait expressed. In the case of the genes determining eye color, for example, blue is recessive and brown is dominant. Thus, a blue-eyed child may have two blue-eyed parents, one blue-eyed parent and one brown-eyed parent (who carries a recessive gene for blue eyes), or two brown-eyed parents (each of whom carries a

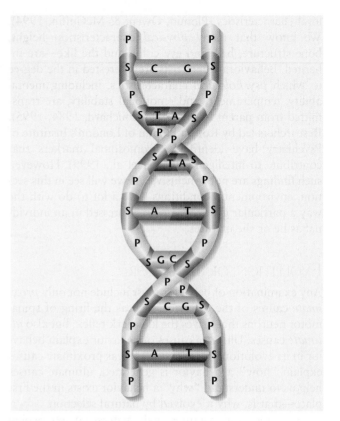

Figure 2-17
Structures of the DNA Molecule
Each strand of the molecule is made up of an alternating sequence of sugar (S) and phosphate (P); the rungs of the twisted ladder are made up of four bases (A, G, T, C). The double nature of the helix and the restriction on base pairings make possible the self-replication of DNA. In the process of cell division, the two strands of the DNA molecule come apart, with the base pairs separating, and one member of each base pair remains attached to each strand. Each strand then forms a new complementary strand using excess bases available in the cell. An A attached to a strand attracts a T, and so forth. By this process, two identical molecules of DNA come to exist where previously there was one.

recessive gene for blue eyes). A brown-eyed child, in contrast, never has two blue-eyed parents. Some other characteristics that are carried by recessive genes are baldness, albinism, hemophilia, and susceptibility to poison ivy.

Most human characteristics are not determined by the actions of a single gene pair, but there are some striking exceptions in which a single gene has enormous importance. Of special interest from a psychological viewpoint are diseases like phenylketonuria (PKU) and Huntington's disease (HD), both of which involve deterioration of the nervous system and associated behavioral and cognitive problems. Geneticists have identified the genes that cause both of these disorders.

PKU results from the action of a recessive gene inherited from both parents. The infant cannot digest an

© The Everett Collection

The famous folksinger Woody Guthrie died of Huntington's disease at the age of 55.

essential amino acid (phenylalanine), which then builds up in the body, poisons the nervous system, and causes irreversible brain damage. Children with PKU are severely retarded and usually die before reaching age 30. If the PKU disorder is discovered at birth and the infant is immediately placed on a diet that controls the level of phenylalanine, the chances of survival with good health and intelligence are fairly high. Until the PKU gene was located, the disorder could not be diagnosed until an infant was at least 3 weeks old.

A single dominant gene causes HD. The long-term course of the disease is degeneration of certain areas in the brain and progressive deterioration over 10 to 15 years. Individuals with HD gradually lose the ability to talk and control their movements, and they show marked deterioration in memory and mental ability. The disease usually strikes when a person is 30 to 40 years old; before then, there is no evidence of the disease.

Now that the Huntington's disease gene has been isolated, geneticists can test individuals at risk for the disease and determine whether they carry the gene. As yet, there is no cure for HD, but the protein produced by the gene has been identified and may provide a key to treating the disease.

SEX-LINKED GENES A normal female has two similar-looking chromosomes in pair 23, called *X chromosomes*. A normal male has one X chromosome in pair 23 and one that looks slightly different, called a *Y chromosome* (refer back to Figure 2-16). Thus, the normal female chromosome pair is XX, and the normal male pair is XY.

Women, who have two X chromosomes, are protected from recessive traits carried on the X chromosome. Men, who have only one X chromosome and one Y chromosome, express more recessive traits because a gene that is carried on one of these chromosomes will not be countered by a dominant gene on the other. Genetically determined characteristics and disorders that are linked to the 23rd chromosome pair are called *sex-linked traits* or *disorders*. For example, color blindness is a recessive sex-linked trait. A male is color-blind if the X chromosome he received from his mother carries the gene for color blindness. Females are less likely to be color-blind, because a color-blind female has to have both a color-blind father and a mother who is either color-blind or carries a recessive gene for color blindness.

GENETIC STUDIES OF BEHAVIOR

Single genes determine some traits, but many genes combine to determine most human characteristics; they are *polygenic*. Traits such as intelligence, height, and emotionality do not fall into distinct categories but show continuous variation. Most people are neither dull nor bright. Intelligence is distributed over a broad range, with most individuals located near the middle. Sometimes a specific genetic defect can result in mental retardation, but in most cases a large number of genes influence the factors underlying the different abilities that determine a person's intellectual potential. Of course, as we will discuss shortly, what happens to this genetic potential depends on environmental conditions (Plomin, Owen, & McGuffin, 1994).

SELECTIVE BREEDING One method of studying the inheritance of particular traits in animals is **selective breeding.** In selective breeding, animals that are high or low in a certain behavioral or physical trait are mated with each other. For example, in an early study of the inheritance of learning ability in rats, females that did poorly in learning to run a maze were mated with males that did poorly, and females that did well were mated with males that did well. The offspring of these matings were tested on the same maze. After a few rodent generations, "bright" and "dull" strains of rats were produced (see Figure 2-18). Such breeding may not necessarily yield more or less intelligent animals, however. A less fearful animal, for example, would be expected to perform better in the maze because it would be more likely to explore the apparatus.

Selective breeding has been used to demonstrate the inheritance of a number of behavioral characteristics. Dogs have been bred to be excitable or lethargic; chickens, to be aggressive and sexually active; fruit flies, to be more or less attracted to light; and mice, to be more or less attracted to alcohol. If a trait is influenced by heredity, changing it through selective breeding should be possible.

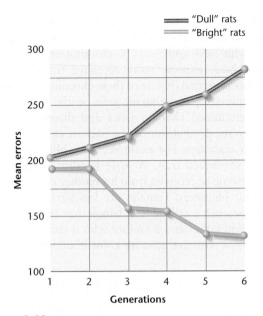

Legend:
"Dull" rats
"Bright" rats

Figure 2-18
Inheritance of Maze Learning in Rats
Mean error scores of "bright" (green line) and "dull" (purple line) rats selectively bred for maze-running ability. (After Thompson, 1954)

If selective breeding does not alter a trait, we assume that the trait is dependent primarily on environmental factors (Plomin, 1989).

TWIN STUDIES Because breeding experiments with human beings are obviously unethical, we must look instead at similarities in behavior among individuals who are related. Certain traits often run in families. But family members not only are linked genetically but also share the same environment. If musical talent "runs in the family," we do not know whether inherited ability or parental emphasis on music is the primary influence.

Sons of alcoholic fathers are more likely than others to develop alcoholism. Do genetic tendencies or environmental conditions play the major role? In an effort to answer questions of this sort, psychologists have turned to studies of twins, especially twins who have been adopted and raised in separate environments.

Identical twins develop from a single fertilized egg and therefore share exactly the same genes (they are referred to as *monozygotic* because they come from a single zygote, or fertilized egg). Fraternal twins develop from different egg cells and are no more alike genetically than ordinary siblings. They are referred to as *dizygotic* because they come from two zygotes. Studies that compare identical and fraternal twins help sort out the influences of environment and heredity. Identical twins are more similar in intelligence than fraternal twins, even when they are separated at birth and reared in different homes (see Chapter 13). Identical twins are also more similar than fraternal twins in some personality characteristics and in susceptibility to schizophrenia (see Chapter 15). A recent study shows that the amount of gray matter in the brain, as measured with MRI, is more correlated in identical twins than in fraternal twins, and it is also correlated with intelligence (Thompson et al., 2001). That is, smarter individuals have more gray matter in their brains, and the amount of gray matter appears to be strongly related to genetic factors (Plomin & Kosslyn, 2001).

One surprising finding from studies of adopted children suggests that genetic influences may become stronger as people age. The psychological traits of young children are not particularly similar to those of either their biological parents or their adoptive parents. As they grow older, we might expect them to become more like their adoptive parents in traits such as general cognitive ability and verbal ability and less like their biological parents. Contrary to this expectation, as adopted

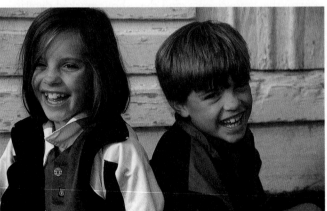

Identical twins are referred to as monozygotic because they develop from a single fertilized egg. Fraternal or dizygotic twins develop from different egg cells and therefore are no more similar genetically than ordinary siblings.

children approach age 16, they become more similar to their biological parents than to their adopted parents in these traits (Plomin, Fulker, Corley, & Defries, 1997), suggesting an emerging role of genetic influences.

MOLECULAR GENETICS OF BEHAVIOR In recent years, some researchers have suggested that certain human traits, such as some aspects of personality, are influenced by specific genes, which are thought to affect particular neurotransmitter receptors (Zuckerman, 1995). In most studies of this sort, family members who have a certain psychological trait are identified and compared with family members who lack that trait. Using techniques of molecular genetics, the researchers attempt to find genes or chromosome segments that are correlated with the presence of the trait under study. For example, a combination of traits referred to as "novelty seeking" (that is, a tendency to be impulsive, exploratory, and quick-tempered, as measured by scores on personality scales) has been linked to a gene that controls the D4 receptor for dopamine (Benjamin et al., 1996).

Occasionally this type of analysis has been applied to very specific behavioral traits. As mentioned earlier, sons of alcoholic fathers are more likely to be alcoholics themselves than are people chosen at random. When they drink alcohol, sons of alcoholics also tend to release more endorphin (the natural opiate neurotransmitter related to reward) than other people (Gianoulakis, Krishnan, & Thavundayil, 1996), suggesting a possible biological predisposition toward alcoholism.

But these analyses can sometimes be misleading and must be viewed with caution. For example, it was once claimed that a gene for the D2 dopamine receptor occurred only in severe alcoholics and thus was a genetic basis for alcoholism. More recent studies of this gene, however, indicate that it also occurs in individuals who pursue many other types of pleasure and may be linked to drug abuse, obesity, compulsive gambling, and other forms of "unrestrained behavior" (Blum, Cull, Braverman, & Comings, 1996). Our understanding of the role of this gene, and of its relationship to behavior, clearly has changed in the few years since its discovery and may change again as further evidence emerges. These studies highlight the need to await further confirmation before concluding that the genetic basis for behavior of any kind has been identified. In several cases, what appeared at first to be a clear genetic explanation was later found to be spurious.

ENVIRONMENTAL INFLUENCES ON GENE ACTION The inherited potential with which an individual enters the world is very much influenced by the environment the infant encounters. One example is diabetes. The tendency to develop diabetes is hereditary, although the exact method of transmission is unknown. In diabetes, the pancreas does not produce enough insulin to burn carbohy-drates and thus provide energy for the body. Scientists assume that genes determine the production of insulin. But people who carry the genetic potential for diabetes do not always develop the disease. If one identical twin has diabetes, the other twin develops the disorder in only about half the cases. Not all of the environmental factors that contribute to diabetes are known, but one variable that is fairly well established is obesity. An overweight person requires more insulin to metabolize carbohydrates than a thin person does. Consequently, an individual who carries the genes for diabetes is more likely to develop the disorder if he or she is overweight.

Schizophrenia presents a similar situation. As we will see in Chapter 15, substantial evidence suggests that this disorder has a hereditary component. If one identical twin is schizophrenic, chances are high that the other twin will exhibit some signs of mental disturbance. But whether or not the other twin develops full-blown schizophrenia depends on a number of environmental factors. Genes may predispose a person to schizophrenia, but the environment in which he or she grows up shapes the actual outcome.

◆ Interim Summary

- Chromosomes and genes, segments of DNA molecules that store genetic information, transmit an individual's hereditary potential.
- Behavior depends on the interaction between heredity and environment: An individual's genes set the limits of his or her potential, but what happens to that potential depends on the environment in which he or she grows up.

◆ Critical Thinking Questions

1. Every year seems to bring the discovery of a new gene for alcoholism or for drug dependence, schizophrenia, sexual orientation, impulsiveness, or some other complex psychological trait. But it often turns out after further studies that the gene is related to the trait in some people but not in everyone. And often the gene also turns out to be related to other behavioral traits in addition to the one to which it was originally linked. Can you think of any reasons why genes might affect psychological traits in this way? In other words, why is there not a perfect one-to-one match between the presence of a gene and the strength of a particular psychological trait?

2. Genes have an important influence on brain and behavior. But are genes responsible for everything? Can you think of examples of behavior that is not genetically programmed? How is this behavior transmitted across generations?

Is Aggressive Behavior Biologically or Environmentally Based?

AGGRESSIVE BEHAVIOR CAN BE BIOLOGICALLY BASED

L. Rowell Huesmann, University of Michigan

Neuroanatomical, neurophysiological, endocrine, and other physiological abnormalities affect the likelihood of aggressive behavior. Although these factors do not seem to directly cause violent behavior in humans, children's biological differences interact with their early exposure to different learning environments (or biosocial interactions) to create individual differences in their social behavior.

Biosocial interactions early in life seem to be particularly critical for the development of habitual aggressive behavior. Anger is first experienced well before a child is a year old, and physical aggression (hitting, pushing) is common among 2-year-olds. On the average, the more aggressive a 6-, 7-, or 8-year-old is, the more aggressive the adult (Huesmann, Eron, Lefkowitz, & Walder, 1984). Biological differences influence how young children behave and learn, as well as how individuals respond emotionally to certain situations that often stimulate violence.

What are some of the biological factors that may predispose some people toward behaving aggressively?

First, a variety of neuroanatomical differences seem to influence aggression. Along with the prefrontal cortex, the *hypothalamus* and the *amygdala* appear to be particularly important loci for anatomical differences affecting aggression. Electrical stimulation and lesions in these nuclei can increase or decrease a person's propensity to behave aggressively (see Moyer, 1976). Anatomical differences in any of these areas caused by trauma, tumors, and the like affect aggressive tendencies. However, whether noticeable changes in aggressiveness ac-

tually occur seems to depend on situational factors as well. For example, electrical stimulation studies with animals have shown that the same stimulation that triggers aggression against a small opponent may not trigger aggression against a larger opponent.

Second, individuals with lower levels of serotonin—a neurotransmitter involved in inhibiting impulsive responses to frustration—in their brains seem to be more at risk to behave aggressively (Knoblich & King, 1992). If serotonin is depleted in animals (such as through a diet or drugs), the treated animals then behave more aggressively. Linnoila and colleagues (1983) have found that men imprisoned for impulsive violent crimes have lower levels of serotonin than nonimpulsive violent offenders do. In addition, children with low serotonin levels are more likely to behave aggressively (see Knoblich & King, 1992).

Third, higher levels of testosterone before birth and in early childhood seem to cause the development of a neurophysiology more predisposed to aggression. Higher levels of testosterone at any moment seem to increase the likelihood of an individual behaving aggressively at that moment. Reinisch (1981) found that girls whose mothers were treated with a hormone similar to testosterone while they were pregnant grow up to be more aggressive than comparable control subjects. Similarly, adolescent boys who have more testosterone behave more aggressively when provoked (Olweus et al., 1988). However, the effects are not one way. Studies have also found that dominating another or aggressing against another increases

testosterone in males (Booth et al., 1989).

Other biological factors in addition to the three I have mentioned undoubtedly also play a role in aggression (such as characteristic arousal level), but these three serve well to illustrate how biology interacts with environment to affect aggressiveness. What causes the biological differences? Genetic variation is clearly important. Studies of twins raised apart from birth show a much higher correlation for aggression between identical twins than between fraternal same-sex twins (e.g., Tellegen et al., 1988). Large longitudinal studies of boys adopted at birth have also shown a concordance between the natural father and an adopted son in their having been convicted of a violent crime (Mednick, Reznick, Hocevar, & Baker, 1984). These genetic influences may well express themselves through the biological differences I have discussed— testosterone, serotonin, or limbic system neuroanatomy— or through another mechanism. Whatever the exact origin, these biological predispositions undoubtedly influence how interactions with the environment mold the child's social scripts, beliefs, and schemas, and how people respond cognitively and emotionally to provoking and frustrating environmental stimuli.

L. Rowell Huesmann

Is Aggressive Behavior Biologically or Environmentally Based?

AGGRESSIVE BEHAVIOR CAN BE ENVIRONMENTALLY BASED
Russell Geen, University of Missouri–Columbia

The roles of learned and innate factors in human aggression cannot be described in an either-or way. Virtually every psychologist who investigates the problem recognizes that both factors are involved and that differences in viewpoint involve the relative emphasis placed on each.

Evidence for the importance of learning in aggression comes from two major sources. One is controlled studies of behavior in experimental and natural settings. Experimental studies have shown that aggression is susceptible to influence by rewards and punishments in the same way as many other operant behaviors. In addition, human aggression varies according to how much the aggressor thinks that such behavior will lead to desirable outcomes and to the worth of those outcomes to the aggressor (Perry, Perry, & Boldizar, 1990). That behavior is a function of the expectancy of rewards and the value of those rewards to the person has long been accepted as a basic premise of social learning theory. Research has also shown that aggressive antisocial behav-

Russell Geen

ior can be traced back to early experiences in the home involving family members. One group of researchers who have studied this problem conclude that "the basic training for patterns of antisocial behavior prior to adolescence takes place in the home, and family members are the primary trainers" (Patterson, Reid, & Dishion, 1992). Children begin by learning that fighting, yelling, and throwing temper tantrums can be effective means of securing desired outcomes from other family members, and such behavior eventually generalizes to larger-scale aggressive antisocial behavior both in and outside the home.

The other source of evidence for the social learning of aggression is studies that reveal differences in violence as a function of cultural and social variables. There is, for example, considerable evidence of systematic variation in the occurrence of violent acts across different national cultures. Residents of some countries show a more pervasive tendency to think of violence as means of solving problems than do people living in other nations (Archer & McDaniel, 1995). Other studies indicate the existence of regional subcultural differences in aggression within the United States. For example, homicide rates among white, non-Hispanic males living in rural or small-town environments in the

southern part of the country are higher than corresponding rates in similar settings in other regions, a finding that has been attributed to different local norms for aggressive behavior (Cohen & Nisbett, 1994).

To set nature against nurture in a discussion of human aggression is to create a false dichotomy. Geen (1990) has suggested that both learning and heredity are best understood as background variables that create a level of potential for aggression without being proximal antecedents. Aggressive behavior is a response to situational conditions that provoke and arouse the person to attack. Even when a person is disposed to aggress and capable of behaving aggressively, a specific situation must elicit the act. The probability that such behavior will occur, and also the intensity of the behavior, will vary according to both the nature of the provocation and the level of potential for aggression set by the several background variables. Certainly people born with dispositions to be violent will be more aggressive when attacked than those lacking such dispositions, and people who have acquired strong aggressive tendencies through social learning will react more aggressively than those who have not. Heredity and social learning are complementary factors in human aggression.

1. The basic unit of the nervous system is a specialized type of cell called a *neuron.* Projecting from the cell body of a neuron are short branches called *dendrites* and a slender tubelike extension called the *axon.* Stimulation of the dendrites and cell body leads to a neural impulse that travels down the length of the axon. Sensory neurons transmit signals from sense organs to the brain and spinal cord; motor neurons transmit signals from the brain and spinal cord to muscles and glands. A nerve is a bundle of elongated axons belonging to hundreds or thousands of neurons.

2. A stimulus moves along a neuron as an electrochemical impulse that travels from the dendrites to the end of the axon. This traveling impulse, or action potential, is caused by depolarization, an electrochemical process in which the voltage difference across cell mechanisms is changed at successive points along the neuron.

3. Once started, an action potential travels down the axon to many small swellings at the end of the axon called *terminal buttons.* These terminal buttons release chemical substances called *neurotransmitters,* which are responsible for transferring the signal from one neuron to an adjacent one. The neurotransmitters diffuse across the synapse, a small gap between the juncture of the two neurons, and bind to receptors in the cell membrane of the receiving neuron. Some neurotransmitters have an excitatory effect, and others are inhibitory. If the excitatory effects on the receiving neuron become large relative to the inhibitory effects, depolarization occurs, and the neuron fires an all-or-none impulse.

4. There are many different kinds of neurotransmitter-receptor interactions, and they help explain a range of psychological phenomena. The most important neurotransmitters include acetylcholine, norepinephrine, dopamine, serotonin, gamma-aminobutyric acid (GABA), and glutamate.

5. The nervous system is divided into the central nervous system (the brain and spinal cord) and the peripheral nervous system (the nerves connecting the brain and spinal cord to other parts of the body). Subdivisions of the peripheral nervous system are the somatic system (which carries messages to and from the sense receptors, muscles, and the surface of the body) and the autonomic system (which connects with the internal organs and glands).

6. The human brain is composed of three functional divisions: the central core, the limbic system, and the cerebrum. The central core includes the medulla, which is responsible for respiration and postural reflexes; the cerebellum, which is concerned with motor coordination; the thalamus, a relay station for incoming sensory information; and the hypothalamus, which is important

in emotion and in maintaining homeostasis. The reticular formation, which crosses through several of the other central core structures, controls the organism's state of arousal and consciousness.

7. The limbic system controls some of the instinctive behaviors regulated by the hypothalamus, such as feeding, attacking, fleeing, and mating. It also plays an important role in emotion and memory.

8. The cerebrum is divided into two cerebral hemispheres. The convoluted surface of these hemispheres, the cerebral cortex, plays a critical role in higher mental processes such as thinking, learning, and decision making. Certain areas of the cerebral cortex are associated with specific sensory inputs or control of specific movements. The remainder of the cerebral cortex consists of association areas concerned with memory, thought, and language.

9. Techniques have been developed to obtain detailed pictures of the human brain without causing the patient undue distress or damage. They include computerized axial tomography (CAT or CT), magnetic resonance imaging (MRI), and positron emission tomography (PET).

10. When the corpus callosum (the band of nerve fibers connecting the two cerebral hemispheres) is severed, significant differences in the functioning of the two hemispheres can be observed. The left hemisphere is skilled in language and mathematical abilities. The right hemisphere can understand some language but cannot communicate through speech. Instead, it has a highly developed spatial and pattern sense.

11. The term *aphasia* is used to describe language deficits caused by brain damage. People with damage to Broca's area have difficulty enunciating words correctly and speak in a slow, labored way. People with damage to Wernicke's area can hear words but do not know their meaning.

12. The autonomic nervous system has sympathetic and parasympathetic divisions. Because it controls the action of the smooth muscles and the glands, the autonomic system is particularly important in emotional reactions. The sympathetic division is active during excitement, and the parasympathetic system is dominant during quiescence.

13. The endocrine glands secrete hormones into the bloodstream that travel through the body, acting in various ways on cells of different types. The pituitary has been called the "master gland" because it controls the secretion activity of other endocrine glands. The adrenal glands are important in determining mood, energy level, and ability to cope with stress.

14. An individual's hereditary potential, which is transmitted by the chromosomes and genes, influences his or her psychological and physical characteristics. Genes

are segments of DNA molecules, which store genetic information. Some genes are dominant, some recessive, and some sex-linked. Most human characteristics are polygenic; that is, they are determined by many genes acting together rather than by a single gene pair.

15. Selective breeding (mating animals that are high or low in a certain trait) is one method of studying the influence of heredity. Another means of sorting out the effects of environment and heredity is twin studies, in which the characteristics of identical twins (who share the same heredity) are compared with those of fraternal twins (who are no more alike genetically than ordinary siblings). Behavior depends on the interaction between heredity and environment: An individual's genes set the limits of his or her potential, but what happens to that potential depends on the environment in which he or she grows up.

CORE CONCEPTS

neuron
dendrite
axon
synapse
neurotransmitter
nerve
nucleus
ganglion
glial cell
action potential
ion channel
resting membrane potential
saltatory conduction
receptors
reuptake
degradation

central nervous system
peripheral nervous system
somatic system
autonomic system
hindbrain
midbrain
forebrain
central core
limbic system
cerebrum
medulla
cerebellum
thalamus
hypothalamus
homeostasis
reticular formation

hippocampus
amygdala
cerebral cortex
hemispheres
lobes
magnetic resonance imaging
aphasia
sympathetic nervous system
parasympathetic nervous system
hormones
behavior genetics
sexual selection
genes
chromosomes
selective breeding

 # WEB RESOURCES

http://psychology.wadsworth.com/atkinson14e

Take a quiz, try the activities and exercises, and explore web links.

http://psych.hanover.edu/Krantz/neurotut.html

The undergraduate level tutorials will help you review the basic neural functions. Then test yourself by using the available interactive quizzing.

http://www.med.harvard.edu/AANLIB/home.html

This Whole Brain Atlas houses a multitude of photos of the brain. The images range from photos of normal brains to the brains of patients with a brain tumor or Alzheimer's disease.

 InfoTrac Online Library
http://www.infotrac-college.com/wadsworth

Use InfoTrac College Edition to find popular and scientific articles by using the search terms below or your own relevant terms.

- Brain imaging
- Central nervous system
- Cerebral cortex
- Neural transmission
- Neurons

CD-ROM LINKS

 Psych Odyssey
Check out CD Chapter 3, Biological Bases of Behavior
A. Cellular Structures and Functions
B. The Brain: Structures and Function

 Psyk.trek 2.0
Check out CD Unit 2, Biological Bases of Behavior
2a. The Neuron and the Neural Impulse
2b. Synaptic Transmission
2c. Looking Inside the Brain: Research Methods
2d. The Hindbrain and the Midbrain
2e. The Forebrain: Subcortical Structures
2f. The Cerebral Cortex
2g. Right Brain/Left Brain

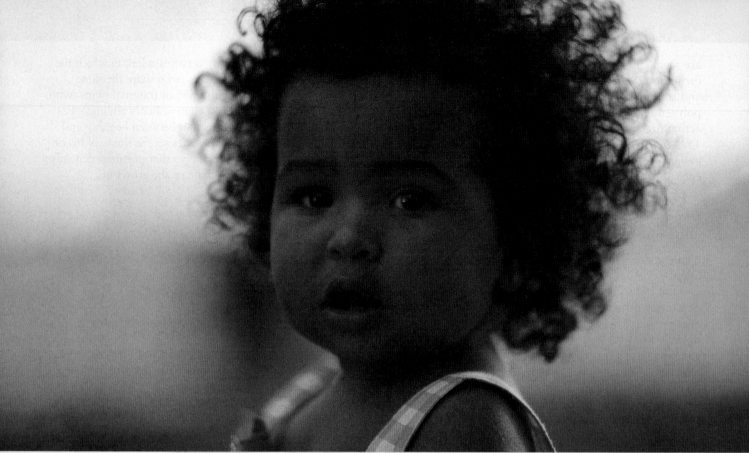

© Marco Cauz/CORBIS

PSYCHOLOGICAL DEVELOPMENT

3

It is parents' night at the beginning of the school year at Lincoln Elementary School. Mrs. Vohland, the kindergarten teacher, has given the parents of her new class a short presentation of the kinds of activities they will be doing over the academic year. The parents are milling around the room, looking at their children's artwork, and getting to know each other. A few parents approach Mrs. Vohland to introduce themselves or thank her for her presentation. One intense-looking father named Philip walks up to Mrs. Vohland and begins to ask her a series of pointed questions about her goals for the children. When will they learn to read? Will they have mastered addition and subtraction by the end of the year? Will his son be able to write short paragraphs by first grade? Mrs. Vohland tries to explain that kindergarten is for developing the building blocks of reading, arithmetic, and writing. Some chil-

dren will be very advanced by the end of the year, and some will not, because children develop at different paces. Philip is not satisfied with her answer, though, and informs Mrs. Vohland that his son has tested as "bright" and he expects him to have accomplished all these goals by the end of kindergarten.

When Philip finally lets her go, Mrs. Vohland takes a deep breath and begins to tidy her desk. Another father, Sam, approaches. He also looks a bit intense, and Mrs. Vohland braces herself for another onslaught of questions. Sam begins by saying that he is concerned about his son, who apparently has also been labeled as "bright" by some early intelligence tests. Sam's concerns, however, are quite different from Philip's. "I just want him to have a normal childhood. He's only 5, and the hard work will come later. I want him to have fun and to enjoy school. I'm worried you might push him too hard because he's supposedly smart."

Parents, obviously, can have very different expectations for their children. Particularly with a first child, these expectations are often based on their own personal experiences as a child, or what they've read in the media or heard from friends. In addition, children vary greatly in their pace of development. In this chapter, we describe the progress of "normal" development, but keep in mind the variations from this norm across children, families, and cultures.

Of all mammals, human beings require the longest period of maturation

and learning before they are self-sufficient. In general, the more complex an organism's nervous system, the longer the organism takes to reach maturity. A lemur (a primitive primate) can move about on its own shortly after birth and is soon able to fend for itself. An infant monkey is dependent on its mother for several months, a chimpanzee for several years. But even a chimpanzee—one of our closest relatives—will be a functioning adult member of its species long before a human of the same age.

Developmental psychologists are concerned with how and why different aspects of human functioning develop and change across the life span. They focus on physical development, such as changes in height and weight and the acquisition of motor skills; cognitive development, such as changes in thought processes, memory, and language abilities; and personality and social development, such as changes in self-concept and interpersonal relationships. The development of particular psychological abilities and functions is treated in more detail in later chapters. In this chapter we provide a general overview of psychological development across the life span and consider two central questions: (1) How do biological factors interact with events in the child's environment to determine the course of development (often called the *nature-nurture question*)? and (2) Is development best understood as a gradual, continuous process of change or as a series of abrupt, qualitatively distinct stages?

NATURE AND NURTURE

The question of whether heredity ("nature") or environment ("nurture") is more important in determining the course of human development has been debated for centuries. The 17th-century British philosopher John Locke rejected the prevailing notion that babies were miniature adults who arrived in the world fully equipped with abilities and knowledge and simply had to grow for these inherited characteristics to appear. On the contrary, Locke believed that the mind of a newborn infant is a tabula rasa (Latin for "blank slate"). What gets written on this slate is what the baby experiences—what he or she sees, hears, tastes, smells, and feels. According to Locke, all knowledge comes to us through our senses. It is provided entirely by experience; there is no built-in knowledge.

Charles Darwin's theory of evolution (1859), which emphasizes the biological basis of human development, led many theorists to emphasize heredity. With the rise of behaviorism in the 20th century, however, the environmentalist position once again dominated. Behaviorists like John B. Watson and B. F. Skinner argued that human nature is completely malleable: Early training can turn a child into any kind of adult, regardless of his or her heredity. Watson stated this argument in its most extreme form:

> Give me a dozen healthy infants, well-formed, and my own specified world to bring them up in, and I'll guarantee to take any one at random and train him to be any type of specialist I might select—doctor, lawyer, artist, merchant-chief, and, yes, even beggar-man and thief, regardless of his talents, penchants, tendencies, abilities, vocations, and race of his ancestors. (1930, p. 104)

Today most psychologists agree not only that both nature and nurture play important roles but also that they interact continuously to guide development. The newborn infant has an estimated 100 billion neurons in his or her brain but relatively few connections between them. The connections between neurons develop rapidly after birth, and the infant brain triples in weight in the first 3 years after birth (DiPietro, 2001). Brain development is heavily influenced both by genetic factors and by the stimulation or deprivation a child receives from the environment in the early years.

Even forms of development that seem to be determined by innate biological timetables can be affected by environmental events. At the moment of conception, a re-

Both John Locke and Charles Darwin influenced the nature-nurture debate, but in different ways. Locke emphasized the role of the senses in the acquisition of knowledge, arguing that knowledge is provided only by experience. Darwin emphasized the biological basis of human development, leading to renewed interest in the role of heredity.

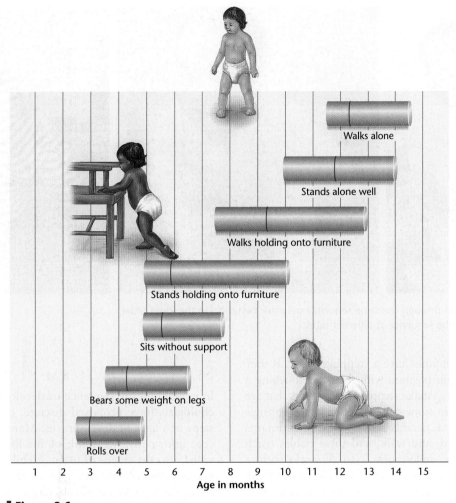

▎Figure 3-1
Motor Development
The bars indicate the age range in which most infants develop the behavior indicated.

Walks alone

Stands alone well

Walks holding onto furniture

Stands holding onto furniture

Sits without support

Bears some weight on legs

Rolls over

| 1 | 2 | 3 | 4 | 5 | 6 | 7 | 8 | 9 | 10 | 11 | 12 | 13 | 14 | 15 |

Age in months

markable number of personal characteristics are already determined by the genetic structure of the fertilized ovum. Our genes program our growing cells so that we develop into a person rather than a fish or a chimpanzee. They determine our sex, the color of our skin, eyes, and hair, and our overall body size, among other things. These genetically determined characteristics are expressed through the process of **maturation**—an innately determined sequence of growth and change that is relatively independent of external events. The human fetus develops according to a fairly fixed schedule, and fetal behavior, such as turning and kicking, also follows an orderly sequence that depends on the stage of growth. However, if the uterine environment is seriously abnormal in some way, maturational processes can be disrupted. For example, if the mother contracts rubella during the first 3 months of pregnancy (when the fetus's basic organ systems are developing according to the genetically programmed schedule), the infant may be born deaf, blind, or brain-dam-

aged, depending on which organ system was in a critical stage of development at the time of infection. Maternal malnutrition, smoking, and consumption of alcohol and drugs are other environmental factors that can affect the normal maturation of the fetus.

Motor development after birth also illustrates the interaction between genetically programmed maturation and environmental influences. Virtually all children go through the same sequence of motor behaviors in the same order: rolling over, sitting without support, standing while holding onto furniture, crawling, and then walking (see Figure 3-1). But they go through the sequence at different rates, and developmental psychologists have long wondered about the importance of learning and experience in such differences. Although early studies suggested that the answer was no (Dennis & Dennis, 1940; Gesell & Thompson, 1929; McGraw, 1935/1975), later studies indicate that practice or extra stimulation can accelerate the appearance of motor behaviors to some extent. For

Virtually all children go through the same sequence of motor behaviors in the same order, but they go through the sequence at different rates.

example, newborn infants have a stepping reflex. If they are held in an upright position with their feet touching a solid surface, their legs make stepping movements that are similar to walking. In some cultures, such as the Kipsigis people of rural Kenya, parents actively teach their infants how to sit up, stand, and walk, and these babies reach these developmental milestones 3 to 5 weeks before American babies (Cole & Cole, 2001). In contrast, among the Ache, a nomadic people from eastern Paraguay, children get little experience with locomotion on their own because the forest they live in is so dense. These children begin walking almost a full year later than children in the United States (although they catch up to, and probably surpass, them in motor skills by mid-childhood).

The development of speech provides another example of the interaction between genetically determined characteristics and experience. In the course of normal development, all human infants learn to speak, but not until they have attained a certain level of neurological development. With rare exceptions, infants less than a year old cannot speak in sentences. But children reared in an environment where people talk to them and reward them for making speechlike sounds talk earlier than children who do not receive such attention. For example, children in middle-class American homes begin to talk at about 1 year of age. Children reared in San Marcos, a remote village in Guatemala, have little verbal interaction with adults and do not utter their first words until they are more than 2 years old (Kagan, 1979). Note that the environment affects the *rate* at which children acquire the skills, not the ultimate skill level.

STAGES OF DEVELOPMENT

In explaining the sequence of development, several psychologists have proposed discrete, qualitatively distinct steps or stages of development. Many of us use this concept informally. We think of the life span as being divided into the stages of infancy, childhood, adolescence, and adulthood. Parents might say that their adolescent is going through a "rebellious stage." Developmental psychologists, however, have a more precise concept in mind: The concept of **stages** implies that behaviors at a given stage are organized around a dominant theme or a coherent set of characteristics, behaviors at one stage are qualitatively different from behaviors at earlier or later stages, and all children go through the same stages in the same order. Environmental factors may speed up or slow down development, but the order of the stages does not vary. A child cannot enter a later stage without going through an earlier one first. As we will see later in the chapter, however, not all psychologists agree that development proceeds according to a fixed sequence of qualitatively distinct stages.

Closely related to the concept of stages is the idea of **critical periods** in human development—crucial time periods in a person's life when specific events occur if development is to proceed normally. Critical periods have been identified for some aspects of physical development in the human fetus. For example, the period 6 to 7 weeks after conception is critical for normal development of the sex organs. Whether the primitive sex organ develops into a male or female sexual structure depends on the presence of male hormones, regardless of the XX or XY arrangement of chromosomes. The absence of male hormones means that female sex organs will develop in either case. If male hormones are injected later in development, they cannot reverse the changes that have already taken place.

During postnatal development there is a critical period for the development of vision. If children who are born with cataracts have them removed before age 7, their vision develops fairly normally. But if a child goes through the first 7 years without adequate vision, extensive permanent disability results (DeHart, Sroufe, & Cooper, 2000).

The existence of critical periods for *psychological* development is less well established. It is probably more accurate to say that there are **sensitive periods**—periods that are optimal for a particular kind of development. If a certain behavior is not well established during this sensitive period, it may not develop to its full potential. For example, the first year of life appears to be a sensitive period for the formation of close interpersonal attachments (Rutter, Quinton, & Hill, 1990). The preschool years may be especially significant for intellectual development and language acquisition (DeHart et al., 2000). Children who have not had enough exposure to language before age 6 or 7 may fail to acquire it altogether (Goldin-Meadow, 1982). The experiences of children during such sensitive periods may shape their future course of development in a manner that will be difficult to change later.

◆ Interim Summary

- Two central questions in developmental psychology are (1) How do biological factors ("nature") interact with environmental experiences ("nurture") to determine the course of development? and (2) Is development best understood as a continuous process of change or as a series of qualitatively distinct stages?

- Some developmental psychologists believe that development occurs in a sequence of periods in which (1) behaviors at a given stage are organized around a dominant theme or a coherent set of characteristics, (2) behaviors at one stage are qualitatively different from behaviors at earlier or later stages, and (3) all children go through the same stages in the same order.

- An individual's genetic heritage is expressed through the process of maturation: innately determined sequences of growth or other changes in the body that are relatively independent of the environment.

- Critical or sensitive periods are times during development when specific experiences must occur for psychological development to proceed normally.

◆ Critical Thinking Questions

1. Why do you think some parents are very concerned that their children develop basic skills faster than other children the same age? What effect do you think this has on the child's development?

2. Some theorists have claimed that there are sensitive periods for the development of attachments between an infant and his or her caregiver. What would the implications of such sensitive periods be, if they do exist?

CAPACITIES OF THE NEWBORN

At the end of the 19th century, psychologist William James suggested that the newborn child experiences the world as a "buzzing, blooming confusion," an idea that was still prevalent as late as the 1960s. We now know that newborn infants enter the world with all of their sensory systems functioning and are well prepared to learn about their new environment.

Because babies cannot explain what they are doing or tell us what they are thinking, developmental psychologists have had to design some ingenious procedures to study the capacities of infants. The basic method is to change the baby's environment in some way and observe the responses. For example, an investigator might present a tone or a flashing light and see if there is a change in heart rate or if the baby turns its head or sucks more vigorously on a nipple. In some instances, the researcher presents two stimuli at the same time to determine whether infants look longer at one than at the other. If they do, it indicates that they can tell the stimuli apart and perhaps that they prefer one over the other. In this section we describe some research findings on infant capacities, beginning with studies of infants' vision.

VISION

Newborns have poor visual acuity, their ability to change focus is limited, and they are very nearsighted. The computer-manipulated picture in Figure 3-2 (left) shows how a mother's face may look to an infant. By 7 or 8 months of age, infants' visual acuity is close to that of adults (Cole & Cole, 2001). Newborns spend a lot of time actively looking about. They scan the world in an organized way and pause when their eyes encounter an object or some change in their **visual field,** which is the

▌ Figure 3-2
Visual Acuity
The newborn's poor visual acuity makes the mother's face look fuzzy (left) rather than clear (right), even when viewed from close up.

full scope of what they can see. They are particularly attracted to areas of high contrast, such as the edges of an object. Instead of scanning the entire object, as an adult would, they keep looking at areas that have the most edges. They also prefer complex patterns over plain ones and patterns with curved lines over patterns with straight lines.

The possibility that there is **facial preference**—an inborn, unlearned preference for faces—initially aroused great interest. Newborns do tend to track a moving face-like pattern farther than a scrambled or blank face, but this preference declines sharply between 4 and 6 weeks of age. Later research showed that infants are not attracted to faces per se but to stimulus characteristics such as curved lines, high contrast, edges, movement, and complexity—all of which faces possess (Aslin, 1987; Banks & Salapatek, 1983). Newborns look mostly at the outside contour of a face, but by 2 months they focus on the inside of the face—the eyes, nose, and mouth. By 3 months, infants can recognize photographs of their mothers and prefer pictures of them to pictures of strangers. By 5 months, infants can remember the faces of strangers.

HEARING

Even fetuses 26 to 28 weeks old move in response to a sharp sound. Newborn infants turn their heads toward the source of a sound. Interestingly, the head-turning response disappears at about 6 weeks and does not reemerge until 3 or 4 months, at which time the infants also search with their eyes for the source of the sound. The temporary disappearance of the head-turning response probably represents a maturational transition from a reflexive response controlled by subcortical areas of the brain to a voluntary attempt to locate the source of the sound. By 4 months, infants reach toward the source of a sound in the dark. By 6 months, they show a marked increase in their responsiveness to sounds that are accompanied by visual stimuli and are able to pinpoint the location of a sound more precisely, an ability that continues to improve into their second year (Ashmead, Davis, Whalen, & Odom, 1991; Field, 1987; Hillier, Hewitt, & Morrongiello, 1992).

Newborn infants can also detect the difference between very similar sounds, such as two tones that are only one note apart on the musical scale (Olsho et al., 1982), and they can distinguish between the human voice and other kinds of sounds. They can also differentiate various characteristics of human speech. For example, 1-month-old infants can tell the difference between similar sounds such as "pa" and "ba." Interestingly, infants can distinguish between some speech sounds better than adults can. These are sounds that adults "hear" as identical because there is no distinction between them in their native language (Aslin, Pisoni, & Jusczyk, 1983). For example, "ra" and "la" are separate sounds in English but not in Japanese. Japanese infants can distinguish between them, but Japanese adults cannot.

By 6 months the child has picked up enough information about the language to begin to "screen out" sounds that it does not use (Kuhl, Williams, Lacerda, Stevens, & Lindblom, 1992). Thus, human infants appear to be born with perceptual mechanisms that are already tuned to the properties of human speech that will help them learn language (Eimas, 1975).

TASTE AND SMELL

Infants can discriminate between tastes shortly after birth. They prefer sweet-tasting liquids over liquids that are salty, bitter, sour, or bland. The characteristic response of the newborn to a sweet liquid is a relaxed expression resembling a slight smile, sometimes accompanied by lip-licking. A sour solution produces pursed lips and a wrinkled nose. In response to a bitter solution, the baby opens its mouth with the corners turned down and sticks out its tongue in what appears to be an expression of disgust.

Newborns can also discriminate among odors. They turn their heads toward a sweet smell, and heart rate and respiration slow down; these are indicators of attention. Noxious odors, such as those of ammonia or rotten eggs, cause them to turn their heads away; their heart rate and respiration accelerate, indicating distress. Infants are able to discriminate among even subtle differences in smells. After nursing for only a few days, an infant will consistently turn its head toward a pad saturated with its mother's milk in preference to one saturated with another mother's milk (Russell, 1976). Only breast-fed babies show this ability to recognize the mother's odor (Cernoch & Porter, 1985). When bottle-fed babies are given a choice between the smell of their familiar formula and that of a lactating breast, they choose the breast (Porter, Makin, Davis, & Christensen, 1992). There seems to be an innate preference for the odor of breast milk. In general, the ability to distinguish among smells has a clear adaptive value: It helps infants avoid noxious substances and thereby increase their chances of survival.

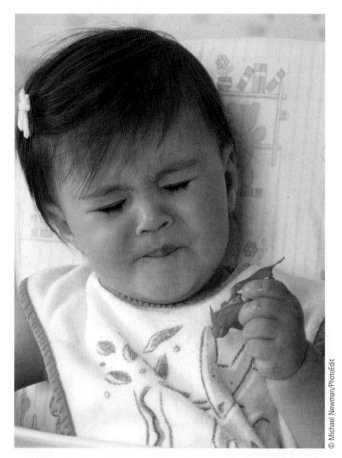

Infants show their likes and dislikes for certain tastes at a very young age using universal facial expressions, such as the expression for disgust.

LEARNING AND MEMORY

It was once thought that infants could neither learn nor remember, but this is not the case. Evidence for early learning and remembering comes from several classic studies. In one, infants only a few hours old learned to turn their heads right or left, depending on whether they heard a buzzer or a tone. To taste a sweet liquid, the baby had to turn to the right when a tone sounded and to the left when a buzzer sounded. After only a few trials, the babies were performing without error—turning to the right when the tone sounded and to the left when the buzzer sounded. The experimenter then reversed the situation so that the infant had to turn the opposite way when either the buzzer or the tone sounded. The babies mastered this new task quickly (Siqueland & Lipsitt, 1966).

By the time they are 3 months old, infants have good memories. When a mobile over an infant's crib was attached to one of the baby's limbs by a ribbon,

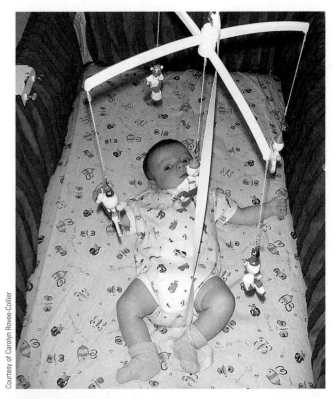

▌Figure 3-3
A Study of Infant Memory
A study showed that 3-month-old infants could easily learn to move a mobile by pulling on a ribbon attached to their leg; the infants remembered this new behavior when tested in the same situation eight days later. (From Rovee-Collier, C. (1999). The development of infant memory. *Current Directions in Psychological Science, 8,* 80–85.)

▌Figure 3-4
Preference for Sounds
A newborn can indicate a preference for certain sounds—such as the mother's voice—by sucking more vigorously on a nipple when it causes the preferred sounds to be played through the earphones.

3-month-old infants quickly discovered which arm or leg would move the mobile. When the infants were placed in the same situation 8 days later, they remembered which arm or leg to move (Rovee-Collier, 1999) (see Figure 3-3).

More startling is evidence that infants remember sensations they experienced before birth, while still in the mother's uterus. We noted earlier that newborn infants can distinguish the sound of the human voice from other sounds. They also prefer the human voice over other sounds. A few days after birth, infants can learn to suck on an artificial nipple in order to turn on recorded speech or vocal music, and they suck more vigorously to hear speech sounds than to hear nonspeech sounds or instrumental music (Butterfield & Siperstein, 1972). They also prefer heartbeat sounds and female voices over male voices, and they prefer their mother's voice to other women's voices. But they do not prefer their father's voice to other men's voices (Brazelton, 1978; DeCasper & Fifer, 1980; DeCasper & Prescott, 1984) (see Figure 3-4).

These preferences appear to stem from the infant's prenatal experience with sounds. For example, the mother's voice can also be heard in the uterus, which would appear to explain why a newborn infant prefers her voice over others. Perhaps most surprising is evidence that the fetus may actually be learning to discriminate among some of the sounds of individual words. In an extraordinary experiment, pregnant women read aloud passages from children's stories each day during the last 6 weeks of pregnancy. For example, some women read the first 28 paragraphs of the Dr. Seuss book *The Cat in the Hat.* Others read the last 28 paragraphs of the same story, but with the main nouns changed so that it was about the "dog in the fog" instead of the "cat in the hat." By the time the infants were born, they had heard one of the selected stories for a total of about 3½ hours.

Two or 3 days after the infants were born, they were permitted to suck on a special pacifier wired to record sucking rates (like the apparatus shown in Figure 3-4). Sucking on the pacifier turned on a tape recording of either their mother's voice or an unfamiliar woman's voice reading aloud either the story the infants had heard before birth or the story they had not heard previously. As in previous experiments, the infants showed by their sucking rates that they preferred their mother's voice to the stranger's. The startling finding, however, was that they also preferred the familiar story over the unfamiliar one—even when the two stories were read by the stranger (DeCasper & Spence, 1986).

In sum, the research we have described challenges the view of the newborn as experiencing the world as "buzzing, blooming confusion," as well as the view that the child enters the world as a "blank slate." Clearly, the infant enters the world well prepared to perceive and learn.

Massage Therapy for At-Risk Babies

Massage therapy is one of the oldest forms of medical treatment. It was first described in China during the 2nd century B.C. and became popular around the same time in India and Egypt (Field, 1998). In modern times, techniques like massage therapy have been replaced with pharmaceuticals. Still, among proponents of "alternative medicine," massage is still commonly used to treat a variety of ailments, including anxiety.

Is massage therapy useful? Tiffany Field and her colleagues at the Touch Research Institute at the University of Miami School of Medicine have embarked on a program of research to scientifically test the efficacy of massage in the treatment of young children with a variety of medical and emotional problems. They define massage as the manipulation of deep tissue with the presumed stimulation of pressure receptors. They have focused on disorders or conditions that they theorized could be positively affected by such techniques, by facilitating physical growth, reducing pain, increasing alertness, enhancing immune function, and diminishing stress, anxiety, and depression (Field, 1998, 2001).

Many studies of massage therapy have focused on children who have failed to grow normally because of prematurity, exposure to cocaine or HIV, or other conditions. In these studies, children are randomly assigned to receive regular massages from their parents or to be in a control group that receives attention but no massage. In one study of preterm infants in a neonatal intensive care unit, infants given 15-minute massages three times a day for 10 days gained 47% more weight than control infants (see the figure; Field et al., 1986; Scafidi et al., 1990). The infants receiving massage were also hospitalized for 6 days less at a hospital cost savings of $10,000 per infant. Measures of norepinephrine and epinephrine revealed more normal developmental increases over the

period of the study in the massaged infants than in the control infants, and the massaged infants had better scores on measure of neonatal behavior. At 1 year of age, the massaged infants still weighed more than the control infants and performed better on measures of mental, motor, and behavioral development (Scafidi et al., 1990). Similar results have been obtained for infants exposed to cocaine or HIV in the womb (Scafidi & Field, 1996; Wheeden et al., 1993)

Full-term infants also seem to benefit from massage. In one study of full-term 1- to 3-month-old infants born to adolescent mothers, infants were given 15 minutes a day of either massage or rocking for a total of 12 days over a 6-week period. During the massage sessions, the massaged infants spent more time in active alert states, cried less, and had lower salivary cortisol levels, suggesting lower stress levels. At the end of the 6-week treatment, the massaged infants had gained more weight, improved more on emotionality, sociability, and soothability,

showed better face-to-face interactions, had lower urinary stress hormones, and had higher serotonin levels than the control infants (Field, Grizzle, Scafidi, Abrams, & Richardson, 1996).

Children with juvenile rheumatoid arthritis often suffer chronic pain. Anti-inflammatory agents can relieve the pain but only so much, and some drugs are addictive. One study that had parents provide their arthritic children with daily massages found that these children experienced less anxiety, showed lower stress hormones, and reported less pain over a 1-month period than children who received only training in muscle relaxation (Field, Hernandez-Reif, Seligman et al., 1997). Positive results of massage therapy have also been found with children with asthma by reducing stress hormones and subjective states of anxiety that can trigger asthma attacks (Field et al., 1998).

What is the mechanism for the effects of massage therapy, particularly across such a wide variety of conditions? The

(continued)

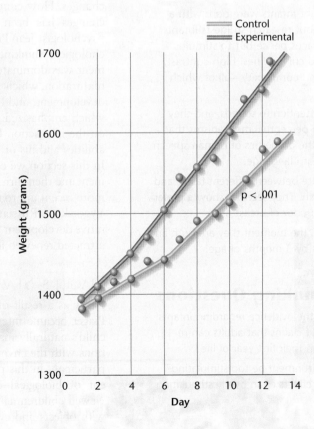

Mean daily weight gain in preterm infants who received massage therapy and control infants who did not. (From T. Field, "Massage Therapy Facilitates Weight Gain in Preterm Infants," *Current Directions in Psychological Science, 10,* pp. 51–53. © 1986 Blackwell Publishers.)

answer is not known yet, but it seems likely that reductions in stress-related hormones and in subjective states of anxiety and depression play an important role. The old notion that massage increases blood flow has not been consistently supported in recent studies (Field, 1998). Some of the positive effects of massage for children probably come from improvements in the relationship between the children and their parents, who are delivering the massage. Parents who provide massages to their children in these studies report that their own anxiety and depression levels decrease, and they feel they are having a more positive role in their child's illness than before (Field, Hernandez-Reif, Shaw et al., 1997). This may lead to a general improvement in the home environment and family life that has widespread effects on children's well-being.

Whatever the mechanisms, if massage therapy continues to be shown to reliably improve children's functioning across certain conditions, it represents an inexpensive and safe form of intervention.

 For more information, go online with InfoTrac. Use your own term or search:

- Infant massage
- Massage and pain

◆ Interim Summary

- Early theorists believed that all sensory preferences and abilities had to be learned, but research over the last several decades has established that infants are born with their sensory systems intact and prepared to learn about the world.

- Newborns have poor vision and cannot see as well as an adult until about age 2.

- Some theorists thought infants were born with a preference for faces, but research suggests infants are not attracted to faces per se but to stimulus characteristics such as curved lines, high contrast, edges, movement, and complexity—all of which faces possess.

- Even newborns pay attention to sounds, and they seem to be born with perceptual mechanisms that are already tuned to the properties of human speech that will help them learn language.

- Infants can discriminate between different tastes and odors shortly after birth. They seem to show a preference for the taste and odor of breast milk.

- Infants can learn from the moment they are born and show good memories by 3 months of age.

◆ Critical Thinking Questions

1. What do you think the evidence regarding infants' memories says about claims that adults can remember events from their first year of life?

2. Can an infant's environment be too stimulating? What might be the effects of an overly stimulating environment?

COGNITIVE DEVELOPMENT IN CHILDHOOD

Although most parents are aware of the intellectual changes that accompany their children's physical growth, they would have difficulty describing the nature of these changes. How contemporary psychologists describe these changes has been profoundly influenced by the Swiss psychologist Jean Piaget (1896–1980). Prior to Piaget, psychological thinking about children's cognitive development was dominated by two perspectives, the biological-maturation, which emphasized the "nature" component of development, and the environmental-learning perspective, which emphasized "nurture." In contrast, Piaget focused on the interaction between the child's naturally maturing abilities and his or her interactions with the environment. In this section we outline Piaget's stage theory of development and then turn to a critique of that theory and to some more recent approaches. We also discuss the work of Lev Vygotsky, a Russian psychologist whose ideas about cognitive development, originally published in the 1930s, have attracted renewed interest in recent years.

PIAGET'S STAGE THEORY

Partly as a result of his observations of his own children, Piaget became interested in the relationship between the child's naturally maturing abilities and his or her interactions with the environment. He saw the child as an active participant in this process, rather than as a passive recipient of biological development or external stimuli. He viewed children as "inquiring scientists" who experiment with objects and events in their environment to see what

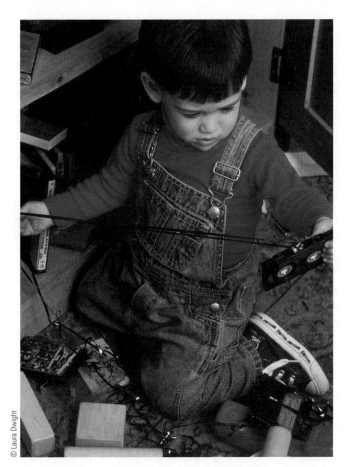

Piaget argued that children learn about the world by doing "experiments" with unknown objects or concepts.

CONCEPT REVIEW TABLE
Piaget's Stages of Cognitive Development

The ages given are averages. They may vary considerably depending on intelligence, cultural background, and socioeconomic factors, but the order of the progression is assumed to be the same for all children. Piaget has described more detailed phases within each stage; only a general characterization of each stage is given here.

Stage	Characterization
1. Sensorimotor (birth-2 years)	Differentiates self from objects
	Recognizes self as agent of action and begins to act intentionally; for example, pulls a string to set a mobile in motion or shakes a rattle to make a noise
2. Preoperational (2-7 years)	Learns to use language and to represent objects by images and words
	Thinking is still egocentric: has difficulty taking the viewpoint of others
	Classifies objects by a single feature; for example, groups together all the red blocks regardless of shape or all the square blocks regardless of color
3. Concrete operational (7-11 years)	Can think logically about objects and events
	Achieves conservation of number (age 6), mass (age 7), and weight (age 9)
	Classifies objects according to several features and can order them in series along a single dimension, such as size
4. Formal operational (11 years and up)	Can think logically about abstract propositions and test hypotheses systematically
	Becomes concerned with the hypothetical, the future, and ideological problems

will happen. ("What does it feel like to suck on the teddy bear's ear?" "What happens if I push my dish off the edge of the table?") The results of these "experiments" are used to construct **schemas**—theories about how the physical and social worlds operate. Upon encountering a novel object or event, the child attempts to **assimilate** it—understand it in terms of a preexisting schema. Piaget argued that if the new experience does not fit the existing schema, the child—like any good scientist—will engage in **accommodation**—modifying a schema to fit new information, thereby extending the child's theory of the world (Piaget & Inhelder, 1969). For example, if a boy's schema for firefighter is a male adult who wears a big, bulky uniform, but he sees a picture of a woman in a firefighter's uniform, he may first refuse to believe that women can be firefighters. He may argue that the woman in the picture must be playing "dress-up." Upon further evidence of women firefighters, however, the boy may engage in accommodation of his schema for firefighters, accepting that firefighters can be women, too.

Piaget's first job as a postgraduate student in psychology was as an intelligence tester for Alfred Binet, the inventor of the IQ test (see Chapter 12). In the course of

this work, he began wondering why children made the kinds of errors they did. What distinguished their reasoning from that of adults? He observed his own children closely as they played, presenting them with simple scientific and moral problems and asking them to explain how they arrived at their answers. Piaget's observations convinced him that children's ability to think and reason progresses through a series of qualitatively distinct stages. He divided cognitive development into four major stages, each of which has a number of substages. The major stages are the sensorimotor stage, the preoperational stage, the stage of concrete operations, and the stage of formal operations (see Concept Review Table).

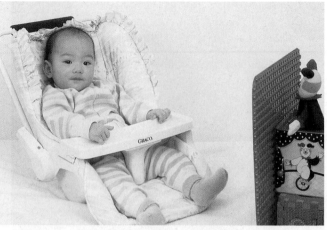

▌Figure 3-5
Object Permanence
When the toy is hidden by a screen, the infant acts as if the toy no longer exists. From this observation, Piaget concluded that the infant had not yet acquired the concept of object permanence.

THE SENSORIMOTOR STAGE Piaget designated the first 2 years of life as the **sensorimotor stage,** when infants are busy discovering the relationships between their actions and the consequences of those actions. They discover, for example, how far they have to reach to grasp an object and what happens when they push their dish over the edge of the table. In this way they begin to develop a concept of themselves as separate from the external world.

An important discovery during this stage is the concept of **object permanence,** the awareness that an object continues to exist even when it is not present. If a cloth is placed over a toy that an 8-month-old is reaching for, the infant immediately stops reaching and appears to lose interest in the toy. The baby seems neither surprised nor upset, makes no attempt to search for the toy, and acts as if the toy had ceased to exist (see Figure 3-5). In contrast, a 10-month-old will actively search for an object that has been hidden under a cloth or behind a screen. The older baby, having attained the concept of object permanence, seems to realize that the object exists, even though it is out of sight. But even at this age, search is limited. The infant who has had repeated success in retrieving a toy hidden in a particular place will continue to look for it in that spot even after watching an adult conceal it in a new location. Not until about 1 year of age will a child consistently look for an object where it was last seen, regardless of what happened on previous trials.

THE PREOPERATIONAL STAGE By about $1\frac{1}{2}$ to 2 years of age, children have begun to use symbols. Words can represent things or groups of things, and one object can represent another. A 3-year-old may treat a stick as a horse and ride it around the room, a block of wood can become a car, and one doll can become a father and another a baby. But although 3- and 4-year-olds can think in symbolic terms, their words and images are not yet organized in a logical manner. During this **preoperational stage** of cognitive development, the child does not yet comprehend certain rules or operations. An **operation** is a mental routine for separating, combining, and otherwise transforming information in a logical manner. For example, if water is poured from a tall, narrow glass into a short, wide one, adults know that the amount of water has not changed because they can reverse the transformation in their minds. They can imagine pouring the water from the short glass back into the tall glass, thereby arriving back at the original state. In the preoperational stage of cognitive development, a child's understanding of reversibility and other mental operations is absent or weak. As a result, according to Piaget, preoperational children have not yet attained **conservation**—the understanding that the amount of a substance remains the same even when its form is changed. They fail to understand that the amount of water is conserved—remains the same—when it is poured from the tall glass into the short one (see Figure 3-6).

Piaget believed that preoperational thinking is dominated by visual impressions. A change in the visual appearance of the clay influences the child more than less obvious but more essential qualities, such as mass or weight. This reliance on visual impressions is illustrated by an experiment on the conservation of number. If two

▌Figure 3-6
The Concept of Conservation
A 4-year-old acknowledges that the two short, wide glasses contain the same amount of liquid. However, when the contents of one glass is poured into a tall, thin glass, she says that it contains more liquid. Not until she is several years older will she state that the two different-shaped glasses contain the same amount of liquid.

rows of checkers are matched one for one against each other, young children will say, correctly, that the rows have the same number of checkers (see Figure 3-7). If the checkers in one row are brought closer together to form a cluster, 5-year-olds say that there are now more checkers in the straight row—even though no checkers have been removed. The visual impression of a long row of checkers overrides the numerical equality that was obvious when the checkers appeared in matching rows. In contrast, 7-year-olds assume that if the number of objects was equal before, it must remain equal. At this age,

numerical equality has become more significant than visual impression.

Another key characteristic of preoperational children, according to Piaget, is **egocentrism.** Preoperational children are unaware of perspectives other than their own—they believe that everyone else perceives the environment the same way they do (Piaget, 1950a). To demonstrate this, Piaget created the "three-mountain problem." A child is allowed to walk around a table on which are arranged three mountains of different heights. Then the child stands on one side of the table while a

▌Figure 3-7
Conservation of Number
When the two rows of ten checkers are evenly spaced, most children report that they contain the same amount. When one row is then spread out into a larger space, children under age 6 or 7 say that the original row contains fewer checkers.

doll is placed on the table at various locations (and therefore has a different view of the three mountains than the child). The child is asked to choose a photograph that shows what the doll is seeing. Before the age of 6 or 7, most children choose the photograph that illustrates their own perspective on the three mountains (Piaget & Inhelder, 1948/1956).

Piaget believed that egocentrism explains the rigidity of preoperational thought. Because young children cannot appreciate points of view other than their own, they cannot revise their schemas to take into account changes in the environment. This is why they are unable to reverse operations or conserve quantity.

OPERATIONAL STAGES Between the ages of 7 and 12, children master the various conservation concepts and begin to perform other logical manipulations. They can place objects in order on the basis of a dimension such as height or weight. They can also form a mental representation of a series of actions. Five-year-olds can find their way to a friend's house but cannot direct you there or trace the route with paper and pencil. They can find their own way because they know that they have to turn at certain places, but they have no overall picture of the route. In contrast, 8-year-olds can readily draw a map of the route. Piaget calls this period the **concrete operational stage:** Although children are using abstract terms, they are doing so only in relation to concrete objects—objects to which they have direct sensory access.

At about the age of 11 or 12, children arrive at adult modes of thinking. In the **formal operational stage,** the person is able to reason in purely symbolic terms. In one test for formal operational thinking, the child tries to discover what determines how long a pendulum will swing back and forth (its period of oscillation). Given a length of string suspended from a hook and several weights that can be attached to the lower end, the child can vary the length of the string, change the attached weight, and alter the height from which the bob is released. Children who are still in the concrete operational stage experiment by changing some of the variables but not in a systematic way. Average adolescents, however, set up a series of hypotheses and test them systematically. They reason that if a particular variable (weight) affects the period of oscillation, the effect will appear only if they change one variable and hold all others constant. If this variable seems to have no effect on how long the pendulum swings, they rule it out and try another. Considering all the possibilities—working out the consequences for each hypothesis and confirming or denying these consequences—is the essence of formal operational thought.

A CRITIQUE OF PIAGET'S THEORY

Piaget's theory was a major intellectual achievement that revolutionized the way we think about children's cognitive development. However, new, more sophisticated methods of testing the intellectual functioning of infants and preschool children reveal that Piaget underestimated their abilities. Many of the tasks designed to test stage theories actually require several skills, such as attention, memory, and specific factual knowledge. Children may have the ability being tested but be unable to perform the task because they lack one of the other required skills.

Take the example of object permanence. As we saw earlier, when infants younger than 8 months are shown a toy that is then hidden or covered while they watch, they act as if the toy no longer exists and do not attempt to search for it. Note, however, that successful performance on this test requires children not only to understand that the object still exists but also to remember where the object was hidden and to show through some physical action that they are searching for it. Because Piaget believed that early cognitive development depends on sensorimotor activities, he did not consider the possibility that the infant might know that the object still exists but be unable to show this knowledge through searching behavior.

In a study designed to test this possibility, children were not required to actively search for the hidden object. As shown in the far left section of Figure 3-8, the apparatus was a screen hinged at one edge to the top of a table. At first the screen lay flat on the table. As the infant watched, the screen was slowly rotated away from the infant through a complete 180-degree arc until it was again flat on the table. The screen was then rotated in the opposite direction, toward the infant.

When the infants were first shown the rotating screen, they looked at it for almost a full minute, but after repeated trials they lost interest and turned their attention elsewhere. At that point a brightly painted box appeared on the table beyond the hinge, where it would be hidden as the screen moved into its upright position. (The infant was actually seeing a reflected image of a box, not the actual box.) As shown in Figure 3-8, the infants were then shown either a possible event or an impossible event. One group of infants saw the screen rotate from its starting position until it reached the point where it should bump against the box. At that point the screen stopped and then moved back to its starting position. The other group saw the screen rotate to the upright position but then continue to rotate all the way to the other side of the 180-degree arc, just as though no box was in the way. The investigators reasoned that if the infants thought the

a) Habituation event
Infants are shown a rotating screen until they no longer attend to it.

b) Test events
In these test events, a box is placed where it can be hidden by the screen. The infants then see either a possible event (the screen rotates until it would hit the box and then returns to its starting position) or an impossible event (the screen appears to pass right through the box). Infants attend more to the impossible event, indicating that they realize that the hidden box still exists.

▌**Figure 3-8**
Testing Object Permanence
(Adapted from Baillargeon, R., "Object Performance in 3½ and 4½-Month-Old Infants," from *Developmental Psychology, 23*:655–664. Copyright © 1987. Reprinted by permission of the Academic Press.)

box still existed even when the screen hid it, they would be surprised when it seemed to pass through the box—an impossible event. The infants would then look at the screen longer than they would when the screen seemed to bump into the box before returning to its starting point. This is exactly what happened. Even though the impossible event was perceptually identical to an event that they had seen repeatedly and lost interest in, the infants found it more interesting than a physically possible event that they had never seen before—the screen stopping halfway through the arc and then reversing direction (Baillargeon, Spelke, & Wasserman, 1985).

Because the infants in this experiment were only 4½ months old, they displayed object permanence 4 to 5 months earlier than Piaget's theory predicts. Replications of this study have found that some infants as young as 3½ months display object permanence (Baillargeon, 1987; Baillargeon & DeVos, 1991).

More recent experiments using Piaget's conservation tasks have also yielded evidence that children's mental capacities develop earlier than he thought. In one study of number conservation, two sets of toys were lined up in one-to-one correspondence (as in Figure 3-6). The experimenter then said, "These are your soldiers and these are my soldiers. What's more, my soldiers, your soldiers, or are they both the same?" After the child answered this question correctly, the experimenter spread out one of the rows of toys and repeated the question. As Piaget and others had previously reported, 5-year-old children failed to conserve, stating that the spread-out row contained more soldiers. But then the investigator introduced a second set of conditions. Instead of describing the toys as individual soldiers, she said, "This is my army and this is your army. What's more, my army, your army, or are they both the same?" With this simple change of wording, most of the children were able to conserve, judging the two "armies" to be the same size, even when one of them was spread out. When children are prompted to interpret the display as an aggregate or collection rather than as a set of individual items, their judgments of equality are less likely to be influenced by irrelevant perceptual transformations (Markman, 1979).

Other research has identified more factors that can influence the development of concrete operational thought. For example, the experience of going to school seems to promote mastery of Piagetian tasks (Artman & Cahan, 1993). This and other evidence suggest that concrete operational reasoning may not be a universal stage of development that emerges during middle childhood but, instead, a product of the cultural setting, schooling, and the specific wording of questions and instructions.

ALTERNATIVES TO PIAGET'S THEORY

Developmental psychologists generally agree that these kinds of findings show that Piaget underestimated children's abilities, and his theory has been challenged on many grounds. However, there is no consensus on the best alternative to pursue. Some psychologists favor information-processing approaches, and others have pursued knowledge-acquisition and sociocultural approaches.

INFORMATION-PROCESSING APPROACHES We have already noted that many of the experiments challenging

Piaget's views were inspired by investigators who view cognitive development as the acquisition of several separate **information-processing skills—** specific skills at gathering and analyzing information from the environment. Accordingly, they think that the standard Piagetian tasks fail to separate these skills from the skill that the task is supposed to assess. But they disagree among themselves about exactly how their views challenge Piaget's theory. For example, they disagree on the important question of whether development is best understood as a series of qualitatively distinct stages or as a continuous process of change. Some think that the entire notion of stages should be abandoned (Klahr, 1982). In their view, the separate skills develop smoothly and continuously rather than in a series of discrete stages. But other information-processing theorists think that gradual changes in information-processing skills do in fact lead to discontinuous, stagelike changes in children's thinking (Case & Okamoto, 1996). These theorists are sometimes referred to as neo-Piagetians. Other neo-Piagetians agree that there are genuine stages but only within more narrow domains of knowledge. For example, a child's language skills, mathematical understanding, social reasoning, and so forth may all develop in a stagelike fashion, but each domain proceeds at its own pace relatively independently of the others (Mandler, 1983).

KNOWLEDGE-ACQUISITION APPROACHES Some developmental psychologists think that after infancy, children and adults have essentially the same cognitive processes and capacities and that the primary difference between them is the adult's more extensive knowledge base. By **knowledge** they mean not just a larger collection of facts but a deeper understanding of how facts in a particular domain are organized.

The distinction between facts and the organization of facts is shown in a study that compared a group of 10-year-old chess experts competing in a tournament with a group of college students who were chess amateurs. When asked to memorize and recall lists of random numbers, the college students easily outperformed the 10-year-olds. But when tested on their ability to recall actual positions of the chess pieces on the board, the 10-year-old chess experts did better than the 18-year-old chess amateurs (Chi, 1978). The relevant difference between the two groups is not different stages of cognitive development or different information-processing abilities, but domain-specific knowledge. Because the 10-year-olds had a deeper grasp of the underlying structure of chess, they could organize and reconstruct the arrangements from memory by "chunking" the separate

Studies of young chess experts suggest their greater store of knowledge about chess allows them to process information about appropriate moves more efficiently, giving them the upper hand in competitions with older but less expert chess players.

pieces of information into larger meaningful units (for example, a king-side attack by white) and eliminating from consideration implausible placements of the pieces. (We discuss experts versus amateur problem solvers in Chapter 9.)

Increasing knowledge of the world, rather than a qualitative shift in cognitive development, may also account for children's increasing ability to solve Piaget's conservation tasks as they grow older. For example, a child who does not know that mass or number is the critical feature that defines "more clay" or "more checkers" is likely to judge that the quantity has changed when only its visual appearance has changed. An older child may simply have learned the essential defining feature of "more." If this hypothesis is correct, children who fail to show conservation in one domain may show conservation in another, depending on their understanding of the domain. For example, in a study kindergarten children were told about a series of "operations" that doctors or scientists had performed. Some operations altered an animal so that it looked like a different animal; other operations altered an animal so that it looked like a plant (see Figure 3-9). Children were told that

> the doctors took a horse [shows child picture of horse] and did an operation that put black and white stripes all over its body. They cut off its mane and braided its tail. They trained it to stop neighing like a horse, and they trained it to eat wild grass instead of oats and hay. They also trained

▌Figure 3-9
Early Testing of Conservation
Children are told that doctors or scientists operated on an animal until it looked like a different animal (horse to zebra) or until it looked like a plant (porcupine to cactus). Children who say that the animal is "really" the new animal or plant are failing to show conservation; children who say that the animal is still "really" the original animal are showing conservation.

it to live in the wilds in Africa instead of in a stable. When they were all done, the animal looked just like this [shows picture of zebra]. When they were finished, was this animal a horse or a zebra? (Keil, 1989, p. 307)

When asked about operations that transformed one kind of animal into another, a majority of the children failed to conserve. About 65% agreed that the horse had been genuinely changed into a zebra. But when faced with the transformation of an animal into a plant, only about 25% agreed that a porcupine had been genuinely changed into a cactus (Keil, 1989). Studies like these demonstrate that in some domains preoperational children can ignore dramatic changes in visual appearance because they have learned that an invisible but essential defining feature of the object has remained unchanged.

SOCIOCULTURAL APPROACHES Although Piaget emphasized the child's interactions with the environment, the environment he had in mind was the immediate physical environment. The social and cultural context plays virtually no role in Piaget's theory. Yet much of what children must learn is the particular ways their culture views reality, what roles different people—and different sexes—are expected to play, and what rules and norms govern social relationships in their particular culture. In these areas there are no universally valid facts or correct views of reality. According to those who take a **sociocultural approach to development,** the child should be seen not as a physical scientist seeking "true" knowledge but as a newcomer to a culture who seeks to become a native by learning how to look at social reality through the lens of that culture (Rogoff, 2000).

Culture can influence children's development in several ways (Cole & Cole, 2001):

1. By providing the opportunity for specific activities: Children learn by observation, experience, or at least hearing about an activity. For example, because water is scarce in the desert, children of the Kung of the Kalahari Desert are unlikely to learn about conservation by pouring water from one glass to another, but children growing up in Seattle or Paris are unlikely to learn how to find water-bearing roots in the desert.

2. By determining the frequency of certain activities: For example, traditional dancing is important in Balinese culture, so children growing up in Bali become skilled dancers, but Norwegian children become expert skiers or skaters.

3. By how they relate different activities: For example, in cultures in which making pottery is important, children associate molding clay with interaction with their parents and perhaps with selling pots in the market. In cultures where making pottery is not important, children may view molding clay only as a nursery school pastime.

4. By controlling the child's role in the activity: In many cultures, meat is obtained in a supermarket, and children (and their parents) play no role in trapping, killing, and preparing the animal from which the meat comes. In other cultures, children learn from a young age how to hunt, kill, and prepare animals for family meals.

The origins of this view of cognitive development can be seen in the work of the Russian scholar Lev Vygotsky (1934/1986). Vygotsky believed that we develop understanding and expertise primarily through what might be described as apprenticeship—we are guided by more knowledgeable individuals, who help us understand more and more about our world and develop new skills. He also distinguished between two levels of cognitive development: the child's actual level of development, as expressed in problem-solving ability, and the child's level of potential development, which is determined by the kind of problem solving the child can do when guided by an adult or a more knowledgeable peer. According to Vygotsky, we need to know both the actual and potential levels of development in a particular child to fully understand that child's level of cognitive development and provide appropriate instruction.

Because language is the primary means by which humans exchange social meanings, Vygotsky viewed language development as central to cognitive development. In fact, he regarded language acquisition as the most important aspect of children's development (Blanck, 1990). Language plays an important role in developing new skills and knowledge. As adults and peers help children master new tasks, the communication between them becomes part of the children's thinking. The children then use their language ability to guide their own actions as they practice the new skill. What Piaget referred to as egocentric speech Vygotsky considered an essential component of cognitive development: Children speak to themselves to give themselves guidance and direction. This kind of self-instruction is termed *private speech*. You can observe this process in a child who gives herself instructions about how to perform a task, such as tying her shoes, that she previously heard from an adult (Berk, 1997).

THEORY OF MIND

As adults, we behave and think in ways that reflect our understanding that other people have minds—they think, they have expectations and beliefs, they have their own assumptions, and so on. Much of our behavior toward other people is based on our understanding of what they are thinking. For example, we have a date to meet a friend for coffee at 2 P.M. but realize that the meeting we are in is not going to be finished until 2:30 P.M. Knowing the friend expects us to be at the coffee house at 2 P.M., we take a break from the meeting to call our friend and tell her we are going to be late. We also occasionally reflect on our own thinking process by, for example, evaluating what we think about a situation or wondering how we could have been mistaken in a belief. This thinking about thinking is referred to as **metacognition.**

In recent years, psychologists have become interested in how metacognition, or more generally an individual's **theory of mind,** develops. These researchers have studied children's knowledge about basic mental states, such as desires, percepts, beliefs, knowledge, thoughts, intentions, and feelings (Flavell, 1999). The following study is typical in research on theory of mind and illustrates the basic developmental finding (Flavell, 1999).

> An experimenter shows a 5-year-old child a candy box with pictures of candy on it and asks her what she thinks is in it. "Candy," she replies. Then the child gets to look inside and discovers to her surprise that it actually contains crayons, not candy. The experimenter then asks her what another child who had not yet seen inside the box would think it contained. "Candy," the child answers, amused at the deception. The experimenter then tries the same procedure with a 3-year-old. The response to the initial question is the expected "Candy," but the response to the second is surprising—an unamused "Crayons." Even more surprising is that in response to further questioning, the 3-year-old claims that she had initially thought that there were crayons in the box and had even said that there were.

The basic interpretation of this finding is that preschoolers do not yet have a theory of mind, a conception that other people have minds and thoughts different from their own, and therefore do not understand that people can have beliefs different from their own or different from reality.

How does a child's theory of mind develop? Bartsch and Wellman (1995) argue that the developmental sequence has three steps. First, about age 2, children have an elementary conception of simple desires, emotions, and perceptual experiences. They understand that people can have wants and fears, and can see and feel things, but they do not understand that people mentally represent both objects and their own desires and beliefs. Second, at about age 3, children begin to talk about beliefs and thoughts as well as desires, and they seem to understand that beliefs can be false as well as true and can differ from one person to another. Yet, they still continue to explain their own actions and others' actions by appealing to desires rather than beliefs. Finally, at about age 4, children begin to understand that people's thoughts and beliefs affect their behaviors and that people can have beliefs that simply do not reflect reality.

One of the most interesting applications of research on theory of mind is the study of **autism,** a serious disorder in which children can seem unresponsive to others and tend to have significant problems in communicating with others. Henry Wellman (1994) has suggested that autistic children lack a fundamental theory of mind, which robs them of the ability to understand others' feelings, desires, and beliefs. As a result, people can seem like any other object to an autistic child. This contributes to the autistic child's apparent lack of interest in others and retreat into an inner world. Author Temple Grandin,

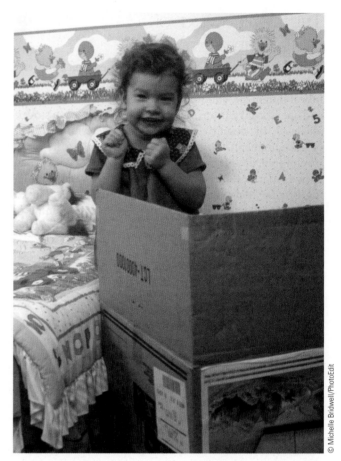

Theory of mind studies suggest that very young children tend to think that everyone else has the same perspective on the world—including what is in a closed box—as they do.

who has autism but has still achieved much in her life, describes it this way:

> Social interactions that come naturally to most people can be daunting for people with autism. As a child, I was like an animal that had no instincts to guide me; I just had to learn by trial and error. I was always observing, trying to work out the best way to behave, but I never fit in. I had to think about every social interaction. When other students swooned over the Beatles, I called their reaction an ISP—interesting sociological phenomenon. I was a scientist trying to figure out the ways of the natives. I wanted to participate, but did not know how. . . .
>
> All my life I have been an observer, and I have always felt like someone who watches from the outside. I could not participate in the social interactions of high school life. . . . My peers spent hours standing around talking about jewelry or some other topic with no real substance. What did they get out of this? I just did not fit in. I never fit in with the crowd, but I had a few friends who were interested in the same things, such as skiing and riding horses. Friendship always revolved around what I did rather than who I was. (Grandin, 1995, p. 132).

THE DEVELOPMENT OF MORAL JUDGMENT

In addition to studying the development of children's thought, Piaget was interested in how children develop **moral judgment**, children's understanding of moral rules and social conventions. He believed that children's overall level of cognitive development determined their moral judgment. On the basis of observations he made of children of different ages playing games with rules, such as marbles, he proposed that children's understanding of rules develops in a series of four stages (Piaget, 1932/1965). The first stage emerges at the beginning of the preoperational period. Children at this stage engage in "parallel play," in which each child follows a private set of idiosyncratic rules. For example, a child might sort marbles of different colors into groups or roll all the big ones across the room, followed by all the small ones. These "rules" give the child's play some regularity, but they are frequently changed and serve no collective purpose such as cooperation or competition.

Beginning about age 5, the child develops a sense of obligation to follow rules, treating them as absolute moral imperatives handed down by some authority such as God or the child's parents. Rules are permanent, sacred, and not subject to modification. Obeying them to the letter is more important than any human reason for changing them. For example, children at this stage reject the suggestion that the position of the starting line in the marble game might be changed to accommodate younger children who might want to play.

At this stage, children judge an act more by its consequences than by the intentions behind it. Piaget told children several pairs of stories. In one pair, a boy broke a teacup while trying to steal some jam when his mother was not home; another boy, who was doing nothing wrong, accidentally broke a whole trayful of teacups. "Which boy is naughtier?" Piaget asked. Preoperational children tended to judge as naughtier the person in the stories who did the most damage, regardless of the intentions or motivation behind the act.

In Piaget's third stage of moral development, the child begins to appreciate that some rules are social conventions—cooperative agreements that can be arbitrarily changed if everyone agrees. Children's moral realism also declines: When making moral judgments, children in this stage give weight to subjective considerations such as a person's intentions, and they see punishment as a human choice rather than as inevitable, divine retribution.

The beginning of the formal operational stage coincides with the fourth and final stage in children's understanding of moral rules. Youngsters show an interest in generating rules to deal even with situations they have never encountered. This stage is marked by an ideological mode of moral reasoning, which addresses wider social issues rather than just personal and interpersonal situations.

The American psychologist Lawrence Kohlberg extended Piaget's work on moral reasoning to adolescence and adulthood (Kohlberg, 1969, 1976). He looked for universal stages in the development of moral judgments by presenting research participants with moral dilemmas in the form of stories. In one story, a man whose dying wife needs a drug he cannot afford pleads with a pharmacist to let him buy the drug at a cheaper price. When the pharmacist refuses, the man decides to steal the drug. Participants are asked to discuss the man's action.

By analyzing answers to several such dilemmas, Kohlberg arrived at six developmental stages of moral

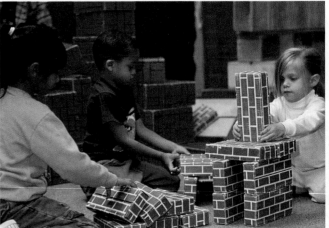

Although young children participate in parallel play with one another, only when they become older do they begin to understand the rules that govern social interaction.

CONCEPT REVIEW TABLE
Stages of Moral Reasoning

Kohlberg believed that moral judgment develops with age according to these stages. (Kohlberg, L. (1969), "Stages of Moral Reasoning," from "Stage and Sequence: The Cognitive Development Approach to Socialization," in *Handbook of Socialization Theory and Research*, D. A. Goslin (ed.). Reprinted by permission of Rand McNally.)

Level I:	Preconventional Morality

| Stage 1 | Punishment orientation (Obeys rules to avoid punishment) |
| Stage 2 | Reward orientation (Conforms to obtain rewards, to have favors returned) |

Level II:	Conventional Morality

| Stage 3 | Good-boy/good-girl orientation (Conforms to avoid disapproval of others) |
| Stage 4 | Authority orientation (Upholds laws and social rules to avoid censure of authorities and feelings of guilt about not "doing one's duty") |

Level III:	Postconventional Morality

| Stage 5 | Social-contract orientation (Actions guided by principles commonly agreed on as essential to the public welfare; principles upheld to retain respect of peers and, thus, self-respect) |
| Stage 6 | Ethical principle orientation (Actions guided by self-chosen ethical principles, which usually value justice, dignity, and equality; principles upheld to avoid self-condemnation) |

judgment, which he grouped into three levels: preconventional, conventional, and postconventional (see Concept Review Table). The answers are scored on the basis of the reasons given for the decision, not on the basis of whether the action is judged to be right or wrong. For example, agreeing that the man should have stolen the drug because "If you let your wife die, you'll get in trouble" or disagreeing because "If you steal the drug, you'll be caught and sent to jail" are both scored at Level I, or **preconventional.** In both instances, the man's actions are evaluated as right or wrong on the basis of anticipated punishment.

Kohlberg believed that all children are at Level I until about age 10, when they begin to evaluate actions in terms of other people's opinions, which characterizes the **conventional** level. Most youngsters can reason at this level by age 13. Following Piaget, Kohlberg argued that only individuals who have achieved formal operational thought are capable of the abstract thinking that is necessary for Level III, **postconventional** morality, in which actions are evaluated in terms of higher-order ethical principles. The highest stage, Stage 6, requires the ability to formulate abstract ethical principles and uphold them in order to avoid self-condemnation.

Kohlberg reported that fewer than 10% of his adult participants showed the kind of "clear-principled" Stage 6 thinking that is exemplified by the following response of a 16-year-old to the story described earlier: "By the

law of society [the man] was wrong. But by the law of nature or of God the druggist was wrong and the husband was justified. Human life is above financial gain. Regardless of who was dying, if it was a total stranger, man has a duty to save him from dying" (Kohlberg, 1969, p. 244). Before he died, Kohlberg eliminated Stage 6 from his theory; Level III is now sometimes simply referred to as high-stage principled reasoning.

Kohlberg presented evidence for this sequence of stages in children from several cultures, including the United States, Mexico, Taiwan, and Turkey (Colby, Kohlberg, Gibbs, & Lieberman, 1983; Nisan & Kohlberg, 1982). On the other hand, there is evidence that people use different rules for different situations and that the stages are not sequential (Kurtines & Greif, 1974). The theory has also been criticized as "male centered" because it places a "masculine" style of abstract reasoning based on justice and rights higher on the moral scale than a "feminine" style of reasoning based on caring and concern for the integrity and continuation of relationships (Gilligan, 1982).

Piaget's assertion that young children cannot distinguish between social conventions (rules) and moral prescriptions has also been challenged. In one study, 7-year-old children were given a list of actions and asked to indicate which ones would be wrong even if there were no rules against them. There was widespread agreement among these children that lying, stealing, hitting, and selfishness would be wrong even if there were no rules against them. In contrast, they thought that there was nothing wrong with chewing gum in class, addressing a teacher by his or her first name, boys entering the girls' bathroom, or eating lunch with one's fingers—as long as there were no rules against these acts (Nuccli, 1981).

◆ Interim Summary

- Piaget's theory describes stages in cognitive development. They proceed from the sensorimotor stage (in which an important discovery is object permanence), through the preoperational stage (when symbols begin to be used) and the concrete operational stage (when conservation concepts develop), to the formal operational stage (when hypotheses are tested systematically in problem solving).

- New methods of testing reveal that Piaget's theory underestimates children's abilities, and several alternative approaches have been proposed.

- Information-processing approaches view cognitive development as reflecting the gradual development of processes such as attention and memory.

- Other theorists emphasize increases in domain-specific knowledge.

- Still others, including Vygotsky, focus on the influence of the social and cultural context.

- Much of the newest research in children's cognitive development focuses on children's theory of mind, or understanding that other people have beliefs and expectations that can be different from their own and different from reality.

- Piaget believed that children's understanding of moral rules and judgments develops along with their cognitive abilities. Kohlberg extended Piaget's work to include adolescence and adulthood. He proposed three levels of moral judgment: preconventional, conventional, and postconventional.

◆ Critical Thinking Questions

1. What does Piaget's theory suggest about the likely success of academic programs for elementary school children that attempt to "accelerate" children's cognitive development? What do newer theories of cognitive development suggest about these programs?

2. What level of moral reasoning seems to be implied by campaigns designed to discourage young people from using drugs or being sexually active? Can you think of campaign themes that would appeal to a higher stage of moral reasoning?

PERSONALITY AND SOCIAL DEVELOPMENT

Soon after Christine brought baby Mike home from the hospital, she noticed that he seemed different from her first child, Maggie, at the same age. Maggie had been an easy baby to deal with—Christine's mother and sisters had been amazed at how quickly she fell into a regular sleeping and eating schedule, and how easily she adapted to changes. It seemed she could fall asleep anywhere, and she didn't seem to mind being passed around from relative to relative at the family's large, noisy holiday gatherings. Mike wasn't really difficult to deal with, but it took a bit more time and patience to get him on a regular schedule. Every new experience, from his first bath to his first taste of strained peas, met with mild but clear protest from Mike. But Christine soon discovered that if she soothed him, kept trying, and gave him a little time, he eventually adjusted to each new thing. (Adapted from DeHart et al., 2000, p. 213)

Like Christine, parents are often surprised that their second child has a very different personality from their first. As early as the first weeks of life, infants show individual differences in activity level, responsiveness to changes in their environment, and irritability. One infant cries a lot; another cries very little. One endures diapering or bathing without much fuss; another kicks and thrashes. One is responsive to every sound; another is oblivious to all but the loudest noises. Infants even differ in "cuddliness": Some seem to enjoy being cuddled and mold themselves to the person holding them; others stiffen and squirm (Rothbart & Bates, 1998). The term **temperament** is used to refer to such mood-related personality characteristics.

TEMPERAMENT

The observation that temperamental differences arise early in life challenges the traditional view that all of an infant's behaviors are shaped by its environment. Parents of a fussy baby, for example, tend to blame themselves for their infant's difficulties. But research with newborns has shown that many temperamental differences are inborn and that the relationship between parent and infant is reciprocal—in other words, the infant's behavior also shapes the parent's response. An infant who is easily soothed, who snuggles and stops crying when picked up, increases the parent's feelings of competence and attachment. An infant who stiffens and continues to cry, despite efforts to comfort it, makes the parent feel inadequate and rejected. The more responsive a baby is to the stimulation provided by the parent (snuggling and quieting when held, attending alertly when talked to or played with), the easier it is for parent and child to establish a loving bond.

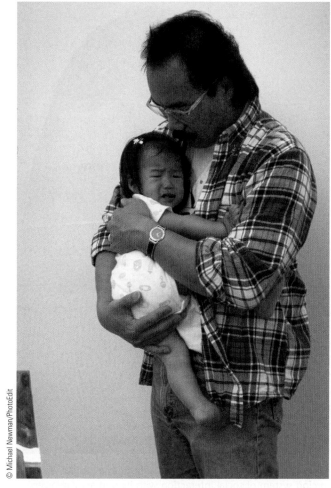

Some infants are more readily soothed than others. Such differences are due to differences in temperament.

A pioneering study of temperament began in the 1950s with a group of 140 middle- and upper-class infants. The initial data were gathered through interviews with parents and were later supplemented by interviews with teachers and by scores on tests administered to the children. The infants were scored on nine traits, which were later combined to define three broad temperament types. Infants who were playful, were regular in their sleeping and eating patterns, and adapted readily to new situations were classified as having an **easy temperament** (about 40% of the sample). Infants who were irritable, had irregular sleeping and eating patterns, and responded intensely and negatively to new situations were classified as having a **difficult temperament** (about 10% of the sample). Infants who were relatively inactive, tended to withdraw from new situations in a mild way, and required more time than easy infants to adapt to new situations were classified as having a **slow to warm up temperament** (about 15% of the sample). The re-

maining 35% of the infants were not rated high or low on any of the defining dimensions (Thomas, Chess, Birch, Hertzig, & Korn, 1963).

Of the original sample, 133 individuals were followed into adult life and again assessed on temperament and psychological adjustment. The results provide mixed evidence for the continuity of temperament. On the one hand, temperament scores across the first 5 years of these children's lives showed significant correlations: Children with "difficult" temperaments were more likely than "easy" children to have school problems later on. Adult measures of both temperament and adjustment were also significantly correlated with measures of childhood temperament obtained at ages 3, 4, and 5. On the other hand, all the correlations were low (about .3), and when considered separately, most of the nine traits measured showed little or no continuity across time (Chess & Thomas, 1984; Thomas & Chess, 1986, 1977).

This early research on the stability of temperament was criticized on several methodological grounds. It relied heavily on parents' reports of their infants' temperaments, and there is reason to believe that parents can be biased in their judgments, either rating their baby more positively or negatively than observers rate the baby. Later research, using both parents' reports and direct observation of children's behavior, suggests that the stability of temperamental characteristics shown in the early infant years is low. That is, a child's temperament at 2 months of age doesn't resemble very closely that child's temperament at age 5 years. But assessments of temperament made once a child is at least in the toddler years do predict the child's emotional and behavioral characteristics later in life (Rothbart & Bates, 1998). In one study, 79 children were categorized at 21 months as either extremely inhibited or uninhibited. At age 13, those who had been categorized as inhibited at 21 months of age scored significantly lower on a test of externalizing, delinquent behavior and aggressive behavior (Schwartz, Snidman, & Kagan, 1996). Other research has found that the tendency to approach or avoid unfamiliar events, which is an aspect of temperament, remains moderately stable over time (Kagan & Snidman, 1991). There is evidence that temperament is at least somewhat influenced by heredity. Several studies show more similarity in temperament between identical twins than between fraternal twins (Rothbart & Bates, 1998). This greater similarity between identical twins than fraternal twins suggests that genes play a role in temperament, because identical twins share the same genetic makeup, but fraternal twins are no more alike genetically than any other two siblings.

Researchers emphasize that continuity or discontinuity of temperament is a function of the interaction between the child's genotype (inherited characteristics) and the environment. In particular, they believe that the key to healthy development is a good fit between the child's temperament and the home environment. When parents of a difficult child provide a happy, stable home life, the child's negative, difficult behaviors decline with age (Belsky, Fish, & Isabella, 1991). Thomas and Chess cite the case of Carl, who displayed a very difficult temperament from the first few months of life through age 5. Because Carl's father took delight in his son's "lusty" temperament and allowed for his initial negative reactions to new situations, Carl flourished and became increasingly "easy." At age 23 he was clearly classified into the "easy" temperament group. Nevertheless, Carl's original temperament often emerged briefly when his life circumstances changed. For example, when he started piano lessons in late childhood, he showed an intense negative response, followed by slow adaptability and eventual positive, zestful involvement. A similar pattern emerged when he entered college (Thomas & Chess, 1986).

Strong evidence for an interaction between genes and environment in producing a child's temperament comes from a study of twins raised apart since early in life (Plomin, 1994). Identical twins raised apart showed some similarity in their tendencies to be inhibited and to show negative emotions, which could be considered aspects of temperament. Yet, the similarity of these twins raised apart was significantly less than the similarity of identical twins raised together, suggesting that environment does play a role.

EARLY SOCIAL BEHAVIOR

By 2 months of age, the average child smiles at the sight of its mother's or father's face. Delighted with this response, parents go to great lengths to encourage it. Indeed, the infant's ability to smile at such an early age may have evolved precisely because it strengthened the parent-child bond. Parents interpret these smiles to mean that the infant recognizes and loves them, and this encourages them to be even more affectionate and stimulating in response. A mutually reinforcing system of social interaction is thus established and maintained.

Infants all over the world begin to smile at about the same age, suggesting that maturation plays an important role in determining the onset of smiling. Blind babies also smile at about the same age as sighted infants, indicating that smiling is an innate response (Eibl-Eibesfeldt, 1970).

By their 3rd or 4th month, infants show that they recognize and prefer familiar members of the household by smiling or cooing more when seeing these familiar faces or hearing their voices, but they are still fairly receptive to strangers. At about 7 or 8 months, however, many infants begin to show wariness or distress at the

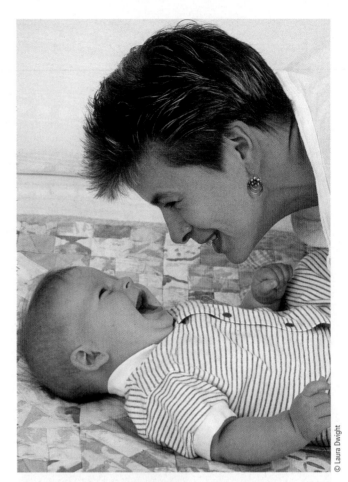

© Laura Dwight

The infant's ability to smile may contribute to a mutually reinforcing system of social interaction with its primary caregivers.

approach of a stranger and protest strongly when left in an unfamiliar setting or with an unfamiliar person. Parents are often disconcerted when their formerly gregarious infant, who had always happily welcomed the attentions of a babysitter, now cries inconsolably when they prepare to leave—and continues to cry for some time after they have left. Although not all infants show this stranger anxiety, the number of infants who do increases dramatically from about 8 months of age until the end of the first year. Similarly, distress over separation from the parent reaches a peak between 14 and 18 months and then gradually declines. By the time they are 3 years old, most children are secure enough in their parents' absence to interact comfortably with other children and adults.

The waxing and waning of these two fears appears to be only slightly influenced by conditions of child rearing. The same general pattern has been observed among American children reared entirely at home and among those attending a day care center. Figure 3-10 shows that although the percentage of children who cry when their

African Bushmen (n = 25)
Guatemalan Indian (n = 34)
Israeli Kibbutz (n = 122)
Antigua, Guatemala (n = 36)

■ **Figure 3-10**
Children's Stress at Mother's Departure
Even though the percentages of children who cry when their mothers leave the room varies from one culture to another, the age-related pattern of onset and decline of such distress is similar across cultures. (Reprinted by permission of the publisher from *Infancy: Its Place in Human Development* by Jerome Kagan, R. B. Kearsley and P. R. Zelazo, p. 107, Cambridge, Mass.: Harvard University Press, Copyright © 1978 by the President and Fellows of Harvard College.)

mother leaves the room varies in different cultures, the age-related pattern of onset and decline is very similar (Kagan, Kearsley, & Zelazo, 1978).

How do we explain the systematic timing of these fears? Two factors seem to be important in both their onset and their decline. One is the growth of memory capacity. During the second half of the first year, infants become better able to remember past events and to compare past and present. This makes it possible for the baby to detect, and sometimes fear, unusual or unpredictable events. The emergence of stranger anxiety coincides with the emergence of fear of a variety of stimuli that are unusual or unexpected. A weird-looking mask or a jack-in-the-box that brings smiles to a 4-month-old often causes an 8-month-old to look apprehensive and distressed. As children learn that strangers and unusual objects are not generally harmful, such fears gradually diminish.

Memory development is probably also involved in **separation anxiety,** the child's distress when a caretaker is not nearby. The infant cannot "miss" the parent unless he or she can recall that parent's presence a minute earlier and compare it with the parent's absence now. When the parent leaves the room, the infant is aware that something is amiss, and this can lead to distress. As the child's memory of past instances of separation improves, the child becomes better able to anticipate the return of the absent parent, and anxiety declines.

The second factor is the growth of **autonomy,** the child's independence from caretakers. One-year-olds are still highly dependent on the care of adults, but children 2 or 3 years old can head for the snack plate or toy shelf on their own. They can also use language to communicate their wants and feelings. Dependence on caregivers in general and on familiar caregivers in particular decreases, and the parent's presence becomes less critical for the child.

ATTACHMENT

The term **attachment** is used to describe an infant's tendency to seek closeness to particular people and to feel more secure in their presence. Psychologists at first theorized that attachment to the mother developed because she was the source of food, one of the infant's most basic needs. But some facts did not fit. For example, ducklings and baby chicks feed themselves from birth, yet they still follow their mothers about and spend a great deal of time with them. The comfort they derive from the mother's presence cannot come from her role in feeding. A well-known series of experiments with monkeys also showed that there is more to mother-infant attachment than nutritional needs (Harlow & Harlow, 1969).

Infant monkeys were separated from their mothers shortly after birth and placed with two artificial "mothers" constructed of wire mesh with wooden heads. The torso of one mother was bare wire; the other was covered with foam rubber and terry cloth, making it cuddly and easy to cling to (see Figure 3-11). Either mother could be equipped to provide milk by means of a bottle attached to its chest.

The experiment sought to determine whether the young monkey would cling to the mother that was always the source of food. The results were clear-cut: No matter which mother provided food, the infant monkey spent its time clinging to the terry-cloth mother. This purely passive but soft-contact mother was a source of security. For example, the obvious fear of the infant monkey placed in a strange environment was allayed if the infant could make contact with the cloth mother. While holding on to the cloth mother with one hand or foot, the monkey was willing to explore objects that were otherwise too terrifying to approach.

Although contact with a cuddly, artificial mother provides an important aspect of "mothering," it is not enough for satisfactory development. Infant monkeys raised with artificial mothers and isolated from other monkeys during the first 6 months of life showed bizarre behavior in adulthood. They rarely engaged in normal interaction with other monkeys later on (either cowering in fear or showing abnormally aggressive behavior), and their sexual responses were inappropriate. When female

Figure 3-11
A Monkey's Response to an Artificial Mother
Although it is fed via a wire mother, the infant spends more time with the terry-cloth mother. The terry-cloth mother provides a safe base from which to explore strange objects.

● **Table 3-1**
Episodes in the Strange Situation Procedure

1. A mother and her child enter the room. The mother places the baby on the floor, surrounded by toys, and goes to sit at the opposite end of the room.

2. A female stranger enters the room, sits quietly for a minute, converses with the mother for a minute, and then attempts to engage the baby in play with a toy.

3. The mother leaves the room unobtrusively. If the baby is not upset, the stranger returns to sitting quietly. If the baby is upset, the stranger tries to soothe him or her.

4. The mother returns and engages the baby in play while the stranger slips out of the room.

5. The mother leaves again, this time leaving the baby alone in the room.

6. The stranger returns. If the baby is upset, the stranger tries to comfort him or her.

7. The mother returns and the stranger slips out of the room.

monkeys that had been deprived of early social contact were successfully mated (after considerable effort), they made poor mothers, tending to neglect or abuse their first-born infants—although they became better mothers with their later children. Note, however, that these monkeys were deprived of all social contact. Monkeys with artificial mothers do fine as adults if they are allowed to interact with their peers during the first 6 months.

Although generalizing from research on monkeys to human development requires care, there is evidence that the human infant's attachment to the primary caregiver serves the same functions. Most of the work on attachment in human infants originated with the psychoanalyst John Bowlby in the 1950s and 1960s. Bowlby became interested in attachment while watching the behaviors of infants and young children who were in residential nurseries and hospital wards and therefore sep-

arated from their mothers. His research convinced him that a child's failure to form a secure attachment to one or more persons in the early years is related to an inability to develop close personal relationships in adulthood (Bowlby, 1973).

Mary Ainsworth, one of Bowlby's associates, made extensive observations of children and their mothers in Uganda and the United States and then developed a laboratory procedure for assessing the security of a child's attachments from about 12 to 18 months of age (Ainsworth, Blehar, Waters, & Wall, 1978). This procedure, called *the strange situation*, is a series of episodes in which a child is observed as the primary caregiver leaves and returns to the room (see Table 3-1). Throughout this sequence, the baby is observed through a one-way mirror and several observations are recorded: the baby's activity level and play involvement, crying and other distress signs, proximity to and attempts to gain the attention of the mother, proximity to and willingness to interact with the stranger, and so on. On the basis of their behaviors, babies are categorized into one of the following three groups:

Securely attached. Regardless of whether they are upset at the mother's departures (episodes 3 and 5), babies who are classified as securely attached seek to interact with her when she returns. Some are content simply to acknowledge her return from a distance while continuing to play with the toys. Others seek physical contact with her. Still others are completely preoccupied with the mother throughout the entire session, showing intense distress when she leaves. In all, 60% to 65% of American babies fall into this category.

Insecurely attached: avoidant. These babies avoid interacting with the mother during the reunion episodes. Some ignore her almost entirely; others display mixed attempts to interact and avoid interacting. Avoidant babies may pay little attention to the mother when she is in the room and often do not seem distressed when she leaves. If they are distressed, they are as easily comforted by the stranger as by the mother. About 20% of American babies fall into this category.

Insecurely attached: ambivalent. Babies are classified as ambivalent if they show resistance to the mother during the reunion episodes. They simultaneously seek and resist physical contact. For example, they may cry to be picked up and then squirm angrily to get down. Some act very passive, crying for the mother when she returns but not crawling toward her, and then showing resistance when she approaches. About 10% of American babies fall into this category.

PARENTING STYLES

Because some babies did not seem to fit any of these categories, more recent studies have included a fourth category, **disorganized** (Main & Solomon, 1986). Babies in this category often show contradictory behaviors. For example, they may approach the mother while taking care not to look at her, approach her and then show dazed avoidance, or suddenly cry out after having settled down. Some seem disoriented, appear emotionless, or look depressed. About 10% to 15% of American babies fall into this category, with the percentages much higher among babies who are maltreated or whose parents are being treated for mental disorders.

In attempting to account for differences in attachment among babies, researchers have directed most of their attention to the behavior of the primary caregiver, usually the mother. The main finding is that a caregiver's **sensitive responsiveness** to the baby's needs produces secure attachment. Mothers of securely attached babies usually respond promptly when the baby cries and behave affectionately when they pick up the baby. They also tailor their responses to the baby's needs (Clarke-Stewart, 1973). In feeding, for example, they use an infant's signals to determine when to begin and end feeding, and they attend to the baby's food preferences. In contrast, mothers of babies who are insecurely attached respond according to their own needs or moods rather than according to signals from the baby. For example, they respond to the baby's cries for attention when they feel like cuddling the baby but ignore such cries at other times (Stayton, 1973).

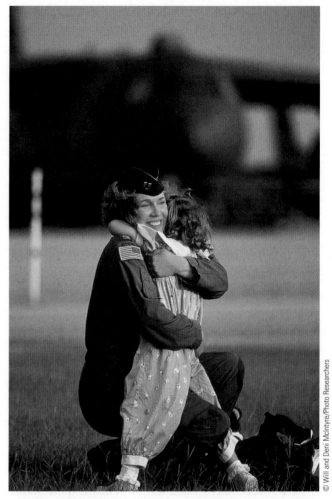

Studies of attachment have focused on children's responses to their caregivers after the caregiver has been away for some period of time.

Not all developmental psychologists agree that the caregiver's responsiveness is the major cause of an infant's attachment behaviors. They call attention to the baby's own inborn temperament (Campos, Barrett, Lamb, Goldsmith, & Stenberg, 1983; Kagan, 1984). Perhaps the temperaments that make some babies "easy" also make them more securely attached than do the temperaments of "difficult" babies. And, as noted earlier, a parent's response to a child is often itself a function of the child's own behavior. For example, mothers of difficult babies tend to spend less time playing with them (Green, Fox, & Lewis, 1983). Attachment patterns may reflect this interaction between a baby's temperament and the parents' responsiveness.

In reply, attachment theorists point to evidence that supports the "sensitive responsiveness" hypothesis. For example, in the first year of life, an infant's crying changes much more than the mother's responsiveness to the crying does. Moreover, the mother's responsiveness over a 3-month period predicts the infant's crying over the next 3 months significantly better than the infant's crying predicts the mother's subsequent responsiveness to crying. In short, the mother appears to influence the infant's crying more than the infant influences the mother's responsiveness to crying (Bell & Ainsworth, 1972). In general, the mother's behavior appears to be the most important factor in establishing a secure or insecure attachment (Isabella & Belsky, 1991).

Other research may resolve this debate. Recall that the attachment classification is based not on the baby's distress when the mother leaves but on how the baby reacts when she returns. It appears that an infant's temperament predicts the former but not the latter (Frodi & Thompson, 1985; Vaughn, Lefever, Seifer, & Barglow, 1989). Babies with easy temperaments typically are not distressed when the mother leaves. When she returns, they tend to greet her happily—showing secure attachment—or show the avoidant type of insecure attachment. Babies with difficult temperaments typically are distressed when the mother leaves. When she returns, they tend to seek her out and cling to her—showing secure attachment—or show the ambivalent type of insecure attachment (Belsky & Rovine, 1987). Children's overall reaction to the departure and return of their primary caregiver is a function of both the caregiver's responsiveness to the child and the child's temperament.

LATER DEVELOPMENT

A baby's attachment classification remains quite stable when retested several years later—unless the family experiences major changes in life circumstances (Main & Cassidy, 1988; Thompson, Lamb, & Estes, 1982). Stressful life changes are likely to affect parental responsiveness to the baby, which, in turn, affects the baby's feelings of security.

Early attachment patterns also appear to be related to how children cope with new experiences. In one study, 2-year-olds were given a series of problems requiring the use of tools. Some of the problems were within the child's capacity; others were quite difficult. Children who had been rated as securely attached at 12 months approached the problems with enthusiasm and persistence. When they encountered difficulties, they seldom cried or became angry. Rather, they sought help from adults. Children who had earlier been rated as insecurely attached behaved quite differently. They easily became frustrated and angry, seldom asked for help, tended to ignore or reject directions from adults, and quickly gave up trying to solve the problems (Matas, Arend, & Sroufe, 1978).

These and similar studies suggest that children who are securely attached by the time they enter their sec-

ond year are better equipped to cope with new experiences. However, we cannot be certain that the quality of children's early attachments is directly responsible for their later competence in problem solving. Parents who are responsive to their children's needs in infancy probably continue to provide effective parenting during early childhood—encouraging autonomy and efforts to cope with new experiences, yet ready with help when needed. A child's competence may therefore reflect the current state of the parent-child relationship rather than the relationship that existed 2 years earlier. Moreover, children's temperament—which, as we saw earlier, affects their behavior in the strange situation procedure—might also influence their competence as preschoolers.

EFFECTS OF DAY CARE

Research on the importance of early attachment experiences in children's development has raised questions about the impact of day care on children's long-term well-being. Day care is a controversial subject in the United States because many people have doubts about its effects on very young children and many Americans believe that children should be cared for at home by one of their parents, usually their mothers. But in a society with most mothers in the labor force, day care is a reality; in fact, more 3- and 4-year-olds (43%) attend day care than are cared for in either their own home or another home (35%).

A prominent critic of day care, developmental psychologist Jay Belsky, has published research suggesting that day care has negative effects on children's development (Belsky, 1986; Belsky, Woodworth, & Crnic, 1996). He has found that infants who receive more than 20 hours of nonmaternal care per week are more likely to be classified as insecurely attached to their mothers in the strange situation task, less compliant in meeting adults' demands, and more aggressive in interactions with peers.

In response to such evidence, the U.S. government initiated a massive study of the influence of various types of day care during infancy and childhood (NICHD Early Child Care Research Network, 1996, 1997). Researchers in 10 locations around the United States collected data on the characteristics of the children's families and the quality of care they received. Overall, the results of this research showed that children who spend 30 or more hours in day care per week are not distinguishable from those who spend less than 10 hours in comparable circumstances.

The quality of the day care facilities did have a major impact on children's well-being and development, however. In low-quality facilities, one caregiver cares for a large number of children, caregivers are inadequately

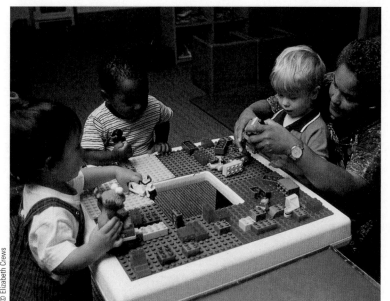

The quality of day care plays a more important role on its impact on children's development than the amount of time children spend in daycare.

trained, and there is a high turnover of caregivers. Children who spent more time in such facilities fared worse on a number of cognitive and emotional tasks than children who spent less time there or who were in high-quality facilities. Unfortunately, almost half the facilities studied were found to have low-quality caregiving. Low-quality day care was an especially great risk factor for cognitive and social difficulties when it was paired with problems in the child's home life, such as having an insensitive mother or being poor.

Other research on day care has confirmed that the quality of day care plays a major role in determining its impact on children. Children who receive high-quality day care from an early age have been found to be more socially competent in elementary school (Andersson, 1992; Field, 1991; Howes, 1990) and more assertive (Scarr & Eisenberg, 1993) than children who enter day care later. Good-quality day care can reduce the effects of growing up in a highly stressed home life (Phillips, Voran, Kisker, Howes, & Whitebrook, 1994).

In sum, children are not significantly affected by nonmaternal care. Any negative effects tend to be emotional, and positive effects are more likely to be social. Cognitive development is usually affected either positively or not at all. However, these findings apply to day care of reasonable quality. Poor-quality care can have negative effects on children, regardless of their home environment. Day care centers that are well equipped and have a high ratio of caregivers to children have positive effects on children's development.

GENDER IDENTITY AND SEX TYPING

Most children acquire a **gender identity,** a firm sense of themselves as either male or female. But most cultures elaborate the biological distinction between male and female into a sprawling network of beliefs and practices that permeate virtually every domain of human activity. Different cultures may define the socially correct behaviors, roles, and personality characteristics differently, and these expectations may change over time within a culture. But whatever its current definition, each culture still strives to transform male and female infants into "masculine" and "feminine" adults.

The term **sex typing** refers to the acquisition of behaviors and characteristics that a culture considers appropriate to one's sex. Note that gender identity and sex typing are not the same thing. A girl may have a firm acceptance of herself as female yet not avoid all behaviors that are labeled masculine.

But are gender identity and sex typing simply the product of cultural prescriptions and expectations, or are they partly a product of "natural" development? In this section we will examine four theories that attempt to answer this question.

PSYCHOANALYTIC THEORY The first psychologist to attempt a comprehensive account of gender identity and sex typing was Sigmund Freud (1933/1964). Psychoanalytic theory and its limitations are discussed in more detail in Chapter 13, but here we present a brief overview of aspects of the theory that are relevant to gender identity and sex typing.

According to Freud, children begin to focus on the genitals at about age 3. He called this the beginning of the phallic stage of psychosexual development. Specifically, both sexes become aware that boys have a penis and that girls do not. During this same stage, they also begin to have sexual feelings toward their opposite-sex parent and feel jealous and resentful of their same-sex parent; Freud called this the *Oedipal conflict* (after the ancient Greek legend of Oedipus, who killed his father and married his mother). As they mature further, both sexes eventually resolve this conflict by identifying with their same-sex parent and modeling their behaviors, attitudes, and personality attributes on that parent in an attempt to be like him or her—sex typing (Freud, 1925/1961). Psychoanalytic theory has always been controversial, and many critics have pointed out that there is no empirical evidence to support the conclusion that a child's discovery of genital sex differences or identification with the same-sex parent determines gender identity

Psychoanalytic and social learning theories have very different explanations for why children imitate their same-sex parents.

and sex typing (Kohlberg, 1966; Maccoby & Jacklin, 1974; McConaghy, 1979).

SOCIAL LEARNING THEORY In contrast to psychoanalytic theory, social learning theory has a much more straightforward account of sex typing. It emphasizes the rewards and punishments that children receive for sex-appropriate and sex-inappropriate behaviors, respectively, and the ways children learn sex-typed behavior by observing adults (Bandura, 1986; Mischel, 1966; Perry & Bussey, 1984). Observational learning also enables children to imitate same-sex adults and thereby acquire sex-typed behaviors.

Two broader points about social learning theory are worth noting. Unlike psychoanalytic theory, social learning theory treats sex-typed behaviors as any other learned behaviors. No special psychological principles or processes must be proposed to explain how children become sex typed. Second, if there is nothing special about sex-typed behaviors, then sex typing itself is neither inevitable nor unmodifiable. Children become sex typed because sex happens to be the basis on which their culture chooses to base reward and punishment. If a culture becomes less sex typed in its ideology, children become less sex typed in their behavior.

Considerable evidence supports the social learning account of sex typing. Parents do differentially reward and punish sex-appropriate and sex-inappropriate behaviors, as well as serve as the child's first models of masculine and feminine behavior. From infancy on, most parents dress boys and girls differently and provide them with different toys. Observations in the homes of preschool children have found that parents reward their daughters for dressing up, dancing, playing with dolls, and simply following them around but criticize them for manipulating objects, running, jumping, and climbing. In contrast, parents reward their sons for playing with blocks but criticize them for playing with dolls, asking for help, or even volunteering to be helpful (Fagot, 1978). Parents demand more independence of boys and have higher expectations of them. They also respond less quickly to boys' requests for help and focus less on the

Some theorists argue that parents impose sex-roles on their children by insisting they behave in sex-stereotyped behaviors, such as girls competing in beauty contests.

interpersonal aspects of a task. And finally, parents punish boys both verbally and physically more often than they punish girls (Maccoby & Jacklin, 1974).

In reacting differently to boys and girls, some researchers suggest, parents may not be imposing their own stereotypes on them but simply reacting to innate differences between the behaviors of the two sexes (Maccoby, 1998). Even as infants, boys demand more attention than girls do, and research suggests that human males are innately more physically aggressive than human females (Maccoby & Jacklin, 1974), which could be why parents punish boys more often. There may be some truth to this, but it is also clear that adults approach children with stereotyped expectations that lead them to treat boys and girls differently. For example, adults viewing newborn infants through the window of a hospital nursery believe that they can detect sex differences. Infants thought to be boys are described as robust, strong, and large featured; identical-looking infants thought to be girls are described as delicate, fine featured, and "soft" (Luria & Rubin, 1974).

Fathers appear to be more concerned with sex-typed behavior than mothers are, particularly with their sons. They react more negatively than mothers by interfering with the child's play or expressing disapproval when their sons play with "feminine" toys. Fathers are less concerned when their daughters engage in "masculine" play, but they still show more disapproval than mothers do (Langlois & Downs, 1980). But if parents and other adults treat children in sex-stereotyped ways, children themselves are the real "sexists." Peers enforce sex stereotyping

much more severely than parents. Boys, in particular, criticize other boys when they see them engaged in "girls'" activities. They are quick to call another boy a sissy if he plays with dolls, cries when he is hurt, or shows concern toward another child in distress. In contrast, girls seem not to object to other girls who play with "boys' " toys or engage in masculine activities (Langlois & Downs, 1980).

Although social learning theory plausibly explains many phenomena of sex typing, there are some observations that the theory cannot easily explain. First, it treats the child as a passive recipient of environmental forces: Society, parents, peers, and the media all "do it" to the child. This view of the child is inconsistent with the observation that children themselves construct and enforce their own exaggerated version of society's gender rules more insistently than most of the adults in their world. Second, there is an interesting developmental pattern to the child's view of gender rules. For example, a majority of 4-year-olds and 9-year-olds believe that there should be no sex-based restrictions on one's choice of occupation: Let women be doctors and men be nurses if they wish. Between these ages, however, children hold more rigid opinions. Most 6- and 7-year-olds believe that there *should* be sex-based restrictions on occupations.

Do these observations sound familiar? If you think these children sound like Piaget's preoperational moral realists, you are right. That is why Kohlberg (1966) developed a cognitive-developmental theory of sex typing based directly on Piaget's theory of cognitive development.

COGNITIVE-DEVELOPMENTAL THEORY Although 2-year-olds can identify their own sex in a photograph of themselves and are usually able to identify the sex of a stereotypically dressed man or woman in a photograph, they cannot accurately sort photographs into "boys" and "girls" or predict another child's toy preferences on the basis of sex (Thompson, 1975). At about 2½ years, however, a more conceptual awareness of sex and gender begins to emerge, and at this point cognitive-developmental theory becomes relevant. In particular, the theory proposes that gender identity plays a critical role in sex typing. The sequence is "I am a girl [boy]; therefore I want to do girl [boy] things" (Kohlberg, 1966). In other words, it is the motive to behave consistently with one's gender identity—not to obtain external rewards—that prompts children to behave in sex-appropriate ways. As a result, they willingly take on the task of sex typing themselves—and their peers.

According to cognitive-developmental theory, gender identity itself develops slowly over the years from 2 to 7, in accordance with the principles of the preoperational stage of cognitive development. In particular, preoperational children's overreliance on visual impressions and their resulting inability to conserve an object's identity when its appearance changes become relevant to their concept of sex. Thus, 3-year-olds can separate pictures of boys and girls, but many of them cannot say whether they themselves will be a mommy or a daddy when they grow up (Thompson, 1975). The understanding that a person's sex remains the same despite changes in age and appearance is called *gender constancy* and is analogous to conservation of quantity with water, clay, and checkers.

Substantial evidence supports Kohlberg's general sequence of sex-role identity development (Szkrybalo & Ruble, 1999). The notion that sex-role identity becomes stable only after gender constancy is in place has not been supported. Children have strong and clear preferences for activities deemed appropriate for their sex long before they attain gender constancy (Maccoby, 1998). In addition, Kohlberg's theory, as well as social learning theory, fails to address the fundamental question of why children should organize their self-concepts around their maleness or femaleness in the first place. Why should sex have priority over other potential categories of self-definition? It is this question that the next theory, gender schema theory, was designed to answer (Bem, 1985).

GENDER SCHEMA THEORY Both social learning theory and cognitive-developmental theory provide reasonable explanations for how children might acquire information about their culture's rules and norms for sex-appropriate behaviors, roles, and personality characteristics. But the culture is also teaching the child a much deeper lesson—that the distinction between male and female is so important that it should be used as a lens through which all other aspects of culture are viewed. Consider, for example, the child who first enters a day care center offering a variety of new toys and activities. The child could use many potential criteria in deciding which toys and activities to try. Should she consider indoor or outdoor activities? Does he prefer a toy that involves artistic production or one that requires mechanical manipulation? How about an activity that can be done with other children or one that can be done in solitude? But of all the potential criteria, the culture emphasizes one above all others: "Be sure to consider first and foremost whether the toy or activity is appropriate for your sex." At every turn, the child is encouraged to look at the world through the lens of gender—in other words, in terms of the **gender schema,** or set of beliefs about gender (Bem, 1993, 1985, 1981).

Parents and teachers do not directly teach children about the gender schema. Instead, the lesson is embedded in the daily practices of the culture. Consider, for example, a teacher who wishes to treat children of both sexes equally. She lines them up at the drinking fountain by alternating boys and girls. If a boy is selected to be hall monitor on Monday, a girl will be hall monitor on Tuesday. Equal numbers of boys and girls must be selected for the class play. This teacher believes that she is teaching her students the importance of gender equality. She is right, but she is also unwittingly teaching them the importance of gender. The students learn that no matter how unrelated to gender an activity might seem, one cannot engage in it without paying attention to the distinction between boys and girls.

Children also learn to apply the gender schema to themselves, to organize their self-concepts around their maleness or femaleness, and to judge their self-worth in terms of their answer to the question, Am I masculine or feminine enough? For these reasons, gender schema theory is a theory of gender identity as well as of sex typing.

Gender schema theory, then, is one possible answer to the question of why children organize their self-concepts around their maleness or femaleness. Like cognitive-developmental theory, gender schema theory views the developing child as an active agent in his or her own socialization. But like social learning theory, gender schema theory implies that sex typing is neither inevitable nor unmodifiable. According to this theory, children become sex typed because sex happens to be a major focus around which their culture chooses to organize its view of reality. The theory implies that if the culture becomes less sex typed, children will become less sex typed in their behaviors and self-concepts.

◆ Interim Summary

- Some early social behaviors, such as smiling, reflect innate responses that appear at about the same time in all infants, including blind infants. The emergence of many later social behaviors—including wariness of strangers and distress over separation from primary caregivers—appears to depend on the child's developing cognitive skills.

- An infant's tendency to seek closeness to particular people and to feel more secure in their presence is called *attachment*. Attachment can be assessed in a procedure called *the strange situation*, a series of episodes in which a child is observed as the primary caregiver leaves and returns to the room.

- Securely attached infants seek to interact with a caretaker who returns from an absence.

- Insecurely attached: avoidant infants avoid a caretaker returning from an absence.

- Insecurely attached: ambivalent infants show resistance to a caretaker returning from an absence.

- Disorganized infants show contradictory behaviors (sometimes avoidant, sometimes approaching) to a caretaker returning from an absence.

- Research on the effects of day care on children's well-being and attachments suggests that low-quality day care may be detrimental but high-quality day care is not and may counteract the effects of poor home environments.

- Gender identity is the degree to which one regards oneself as male or female. It is distinct from sex typing, the acquisition of characteristics and behaviors that society considers appropriate for one's sex.

- Freud's psychoanalytic theory holds that gender identity and sex typing develop from children's early discovery of the genital differences between the sexes and children's eventual identification with the same-sex parent.

- Social learning theory emphasizes the rewards and punishments that children receive for sex-appropriate and sex-inappropriate behaviors, as well as a process of identification with same-sex adults that is based on observational learning.

- A cognitive-developmental theory of gender identity and sex typing holds that once children can identify themselves as male or female, they are motivated to acquire sex-typed behaviors. Their understanding of sex and gender corresponds to Piaget's stages of cognitive development, especially their understanding of gender constancy—the realization that a person's sex remains constant despite changes of age and appearance.

- Gender schema theory seeks to explain why children base their self-concept on the male-female distinction in the first place. It emphasizes the role of culture in teaching children to view the world through the lens of gender.

◆ Critical Thinking Questions

1. Some psychologists have suggested that our childhood attachment styles can influence the kinds of romantic relationships we form as adults. What forms might the attachment styles discussed in this chapter assume in an adult romantic relationship? Can you relate your own adult "attachment styles" to your childhood attachment style or to features of your childhood environment?

2. Would your parents have characterized your infant personality as easy, difficult, or slow to warm up? Which aspects of your current personality seem to be primarily a reflection of your inborn temperament, which aspects seem to reflect the way you were raised, and which aspects seem to reflect a blend or interaction between nature and nurture?

ADOLESCENT DEVELOPMENT

Adolescence refers to the period of transition from childhood to adulthood. It extends roughly from age 12 to the late teens, when physical growth is nearly complete. During this period, the young person becomes sexually mature and establishes an identity as an individual apart from the family.

SEXUAL DEVELOPMENT Puberty, the period of sexual maturation that transforms a child into a biologically mature adult capable of sexual reproduction, takes place over a period of 3 or 4 years. It starts with a period of very rapid physical growth (the so-called adolescent growth spurt) accompanied by gradual development of the reproductive organs and secondary sex characteristics (breast development in girls, beard growth in boys, and the appearance of pubic hair in both sexes).

Menarche, the first menstrual period, occurs relatively late in puberty—about 18 months after a girl's growth spurt has reached its peak. The first menstrual periods tend to be irregular, and ovulation (the release of a mature egg) does not usually begin until a year or so after menarche. A boy's first ejaculation typically occurs about 2 years after the growth spurt begins. The first seminal fluid does not contain sperm; the number of sperm and their fertility gradually increase.

There is wide variation in the age at which puberty begins and the rate at which it progresses. Some girls attain menarche before age 11, others as late as 17, and the average age is about 12 years. Boys, on the average, experience their growth spurt and mature about 2 years later than girls. They begin to ejaculate semen with live sperm sometime between the ages of 12 and 16; the average age is $14\frac{1}{2}$. The wide variation in the timing of puberty is strikingly apparent in 7th- and 8th-grade classrooms. Some of the girls look like mature women with fully developed breasts and rounded hips; others still have the size and shape of little girls. Some of the boys are gangly adolescents; others look much as they did at the age of 9 or 10. (See the discussion of hormonal changes at puberty in Chapter 10.)

PSYCHOLOGICAL EFFECTS OF PUBERTY Conventional wisdom holds that adolescence is a period of "storm and stress," characterized by moodiness, inner turmoil, and rebellion. Modern research has largely not supported this view (Steinberg & Morris, 2001). Many adolescents do experiment with worrisome behavior, but experimentation leads to enduring problems in only a small subset of adolescents. Many adolescents experiment with alcohol during high school or do something that is against

There is wide variation in the age at which puberty begins and the rate at which it progresses. As a result, some adolescents may be much taller and more physically mature than others of the same age.

the law, but most of them do not develop an alcohol problem or a criminal career (Farrington, 1995). In addition, those adolescents who do show serious behavioral or emotional problems tend to have a history of similar problems during childhood. For example, most adolescent delinquents had recurrent problems with the law from an early age (Moffitt, 1993). Similarly, most adolescents who become seriously depressed suffered from anxiety or other types of psychological distress as children (Zahn-Waxler et al., 2000).

Some of the upsurge in problems in adolescence may be linked directly to the hormonal changes of puberty (Buchanan, Eccles, & Becker, 1992), but most are related to the personal and social effects of physical changes and, most important, the timing of those changes. Being an early or late maturer (1 year earlier or later than average) affects adolescents' satisfaction with their appearance and their body image. In general, 7th- and 8th-grade boys who have reached puberty report positive moods more often than their prepubertal male classmates, and they tend to be more satisfied with their weight and their overall appearance than later-maturing

boys—a reflection of the importance of strength and physical prowess for males in our society. But early-maturing boys also tend to have less self-control and emotional stability than later-maturing boys. They are more likely to smoke, drink, use drugs, and get into trouble with the law (Williams & Dunlop, 1999). In contrast, late-maturing boys feel worst about themselves in 7th grade but typically end up as the healthiest group by their senior year in high school (Petersen, 1989).

Early maturation has the opposite effect on the self-esteem of girls. Compared with later maturers, earlier maturers experience more depression and anxiety, have lower self-esteem, and are generally less satisfied with their weight and appearance (Caspi & Moffit, 1991; Ge et al., 1996). They tend to be embarrassed that their bodies are more womanly than those of their female classmates—particularly because current standards for female attractiveness emphasize a lean look. Although early maturers also achieve early popularity, this is partly because they are seen as sexually precocious. They are also more likely to have conflicts with their parents, to drop out of school, and to have both emotional and behavioral problems (Caspi & Moffitt, 1991; Stattin & Magnusson, 1990). Nevertheless, early adolescence is relatively trouble-free for most males and females.

Parents often report a lot of storm and stress in their relationships with their adolescents, and here the research largely backs up the common lore (Steinberg & Morris, 2001). Bickering and squabbling between parents and their offspring increase in adolescence, and there is a decline in how close parents and adolescents feel to each other (Larson & Richards, 1991). Adolescents typically pull away from their parents in an attempt to forge their own individual identities, and many parents are distressed by this withdrawal (Silverberg & Steinberg, 1990). In most families, however, the period of increased conflict in early adolescence is followed by the establishment of a new parent-adolescent relationship that is less volatile and more egalitarian. Parents who remain authoritative—warm and supportive but firm and clear about rules and their enforcement—tend to have adolescents who come through the adolescent years with the least enduring problems (Steinberg & Morris, 2001). In contrast, adolescents whose parents are authoritarian (with rigid rules and little obvious warmth in their dealings with their children) or overly permissive tend to encounter more emotional and behavioral problems (Baumrind, 1980).

IDENTITY DEVELOPMENT The psychoanalyst Erik Erikson believed that the major task confronting the adolescent is to develop a sense of identity, to find answers to the questions "Who am I?" and "Where am I going?" Although Erikson coined the term **identity crisis** to refer to this active process of self-definition, he believed that it is an integral part of healthy psychosocial development. Similarly, most developmental psychologists believe that adolescence should be a period of role experimentation for young people to explore various behaviors, interests, and ideologies. Many beliefs, roles, and ways of behaving may be tried on, modified, or discarded in an attempt to shape an integrated concept of the self.

Adolescents try to synthesize these values and appraisals into a consistent picture. If parents, teachers, and peers project consistent values, the search for identity is easier. In a simple society in which adult models are few and social roles are limited, the task of forming an identity is relatively easy. In a society as complex as ours, it is a difficult task for many adolescents. They are faced with an almost infinite array of possibilities regarding how to behave and what to do in life. As a result, there are large differences among adolescents in how the development of their identity proceeds. Moreover, any particular adolescent's identity may be at different stages of development in different areas of life (for example, sexual, occupational, and ideological).

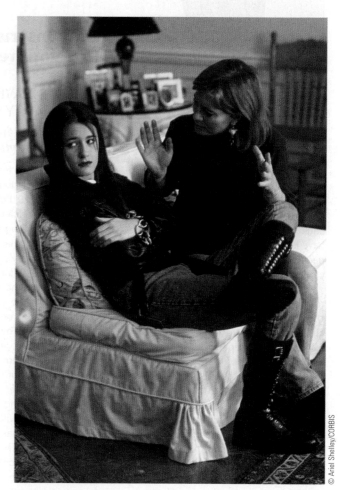

In most families, conflict between teens and parents is short-lived.

Ideally, the identity crisis should be resolved by the early or mid-twenties so that the individual can move on to other life tasks. When the process is successful, the individual is said to have achieved an identity—a coherent sense of sexual identity, vocational direction, and ideological worldview. Until the identity crisis is resolved, the individual has no consistent sense of self or set of internal standards for evaluating his or her self-worth in major areas of life. Erikson called this unsuccessful outcome **identity confusion.**

Erikson's theory about adolescent identity development has been tested and extended by other researchers (see Steinberg & Morris, 2001). On the basis of open-ended interviews, James Marcia (1966, 1980) arrived at four identity statuses or positions, based on whether the person perceives an identity issue and whether a resolution has been reached:

Identity achievement. Individuals in this status have passed through an identity crisis, a period of active questioning and self-definition. They are committed

Text continued p. 102

How Instrumental Are Parents in the Development of Their Children?

PARENTS HAVE NO LASTING INFLUENCE ON THE PERSONALITY OR INTELLIGENCE OF THEIR CHILDREN

Judith Rich Harris, award-winning psychologist and author *(The Nurture Assumption)*

Your parents took good care of you when you were little. They taught you many things. They are leading players in your memories of childhood. All these things could be true, and yet your parents may have left no lasting impression on your personality or intelligence or on the way you behave when they're not around.

Hard to believe? Try, for a moment, to put aside your preconceptions and consider the evidence. Consider, for example, the studies (discussed in Chapter 12) designed to separate the effects of genes from those of the home environment. These studies show that if you eliminate the similarities due to genes, two people who grew up in the same home are not noticeably more alike in personality or intelligence than two people picked at random from the same population. Almost all the similarities between brothers or sisters reared together are due to the genes they have in common. If they are adoptive siblings, they are no more alike than adopted people reared in different homes. On average, an adopted child reared by agreeable parents is no nicer than one reared by grouches, and one reared by parents who love books is no smarter than one reared by parents who love soap operas.

Because these results don't fit the popular theories of child development, many psychologists ignore them or try to explain them away. But results that don't fit the theories have been piling up (Harris, 1995, 1998). A recent study showed that children who spent most of their first three years in day-care centers do not differ in behavior or adjustment from children who spent that time at home (NICHD Early Child Care Research Network, 1998). Children who must vie with their siblings for their parents' attention do not differ in personality from only children (Falbo & Polit, 1986). Boys and girls behave as differently today as they did a generation ago, even though today's parents try hard to treat their sons and daughters alike (Serbin, Powlishta, & Gulko, 1993). Children who speak Korean or Polish at home but English with their peers end up as English speakers. The language learned outside the home takes precedence over the one their parents taught them, and they speak it without an accent (Harris, 1998).

But what about the evidence that dysfunctional parents tend to have dysfunctional offspring and that children who are treated with affection tend to turn out better than children who are treated harshly? The trouble with this evidence is that it comes from studies that provide no way to distinguish genetic from environmental influences or causes from effects. Are the offspring's problems due to the unfavorable environment provided by the dysfunctional parents or to personality characteristics inherited from them? Did the hugs cause the child to develop a pleasant personality, or did her pleasant personality make her parents want to hug her? Judging from studies that use more advanced techniques, it appears that the problems were at least partly inherited and that the child's pleasant personality evoked the hugs (Plomin, Owen, & McGuffin, 1994; Reiss, 1997).

There is no question that parents influence the way their children behave at home, and this is another source of confusion. Is the way children behave at home a good indication of how they'll behave in the classroom or the playground? When researchers discover that children behave differently in different social contexts, they usually assume that the way they behave with their parents is somehow more important or longlasting than the way they behave elsewhere. But the children who speak Korean or Spanish at home and English outside the home use English as their primary language in adulthood. A boy whose cries evoke sympathy when he hurts himself at home learns not to cry when he hurts himself on the playground, and as an adult he seldom cries. A child who is dominated by her older sibling at home is no more likely than a firstborn to allow herself to be dominated by her peers. Children learn separately how to behave at home and outside the home, and it's their outside-the-home behavior they bring with them to adulthood—which makes sense, since they are not going to spend their adult lives in their parents' house.

The notion that children are in a great hurry to grow up and that they see their own world as a pale imitation of the adult world is an adult-o-centric one. A child's goal is not to be like her mother or his father— it's to be a successful child. Children have to learn how to get along in the

Judith Rich Harris

world outside the home, and out there the rules are different. Children are not putty in their parents' hands.

How Instrumental Are Parents in the Development of Their Children?

PARENTS ARE INSTRUMENTAL IN THE DEVELOPMENT OF THEIR CHILDREN
Jerome Kagan, Harvard University

The development of the skills, values, and social behaviors that maximize adaptation to the society in which a particular child grows requires the orchestration of many relatively independent forces. The most important of these include the temperamental biases that the child inherits; the class, ethnic, and religious affiliations of the child's family; relationships with siblings; the historical era in which childhood is spent; and always the behaviors and personality of the parents.

Parental influences on the child assume two different forms. Parental actions with the child are the most obvious. Parents who regularly talk and read to their children usually produce children with the largest vocabularies, the highest intelligence scores, and the best academic grades (Gottfried, Fleming, & Gottfried, 1998; Ninio, 1980). Parents who reason with their children while making requests for obedience usually end up with more civil children (Baumrind, 1967). The power of the family is seen in the results of a study of over 1,000 children from 10 different cities in the United States who were studied extensively by a team of scientists. Some of these children were raised at home, and some attended daycare centers for varied amounts of time. The main result

Jerome Kagan

was that the family had the most important influence on the three-year-old child's personality and character (NICHD Early Child Care Research Network, 1998). One of the most important illustrations of the power of parental behavior is the fact that some children who were orphaned and made homeless by war were able to regain intellectual and social skills they failed to develop during their early privation if they were adopted by nurturant families (Rathbun, DiVirglio, & Waldfogel, 1958).

Parents also influence their children through their own characteristics. Children come to conclusions about themselves, often incorrect, because they assume that since they are the biological offspring of their mother and father, they possess some of the qualities that belong to their parents. This emotionally tinged belief is called *identification,* and it is the basis for national pride and loyalty to ethnic and religious groups. Thus, if a parent is perceived by her child as affectionate, just, and talented, the child assumes that she, too, probably possesses one or more of these desirable traits and, as a result, feels more confident than she has a right to, given the evidence. By contrast, the child who perceives a parent who is rejecting, unfair in doling out punishment, and without talent feels shame because he assumes that he probably is in possession of some of these undesirable characteristics (Kagan, 1998).

Support for this last claim is fact that all children become upset if someone criticizes their family. The anxiety or anger that follows such criticism is

strong because children assume, unconsciously, that any criticism of their parents is also a criticism of them.

The provocative suggestion in Harris's "The Nurture Assumption" that parents have minimal influences on their children's personality and character, while peers have a major influence, is undermined by two sets of facts. First, peers are of little influence until the child is five or six years of age, but six-year-olds from varied cultures or children living in different historical eras are very different in their behavior and personality. Puritan children living in New England in the 17th century were more obedient than contemporary Boston children because of parental behaviors toward them.

Second, children select friends who share their values and interests. A child who values schoolwork will choose friends with similar interests. If such a child becomes an academically successful adult, it is not logical to assume that this outcome is due to the influence of friends because the child chose that type of friend in the first place.

It is rare to find a belief that all societies, ancient and modern, share. I know of no society that claimed that the family's influence on the child's mind was without much significance. This degree of consensus implies that it might be a universal truth. To declare that parents have little influence on children, in light of the scientific evidence and every parent's daily experiences, is a little like declaring on a foggy September morning that all the trees have disappeared because you cannot see them.

to ideological positions that they have worked out for themselves, and they have decided on an occupation. They have begun to think of themselves as a future doctor, not just a pre-med chemistry major. They have reexamined their family's religious and political beliefs and discarded those that don't seem to fit their identity.

Foreclosure. Those in this status are also committed to occupational and ideological positions, but they show no signs of having gone through an identity crisis. They have accepted their family's religion without question. When asked about politics, they often say that they have never given it much thought. Some of them seem committed and cooperative; others seem rigid, dogmatic, and conforming. They give the impression that they would be lost if a major event challenged their unexamined rules and values.

Moratorium. These young people are in the midst of an identity crisis. They are actively seeking answers but have not resolved the conflicts between their parents' plans for them and their own interests. They may express a set of political or religious beliefs with great intensity for a while, only to abandon them after a period of reconsideration. At best, they seem sensitive, ethical, and open-minded; at worst, they appear anxiety-ridden, self-righteous, and vacillating (Scarr, Weinberg, & Levine, 1986).

Identity diffusion. This is Marcia's term for what Erikson calls identity confusion. Some individuals in this category have had an identity crisis; others have not. In either case, they still have no integrated sense of themselves. They say that it might be "interesting" to go to law school or start a business, but they are not taking steps in either direction. They say that they are not interested in religion or politics. Some seem cynical, and others shallow and confused. Some, of course, are still too young to have reached the identity development of adolescence.

As expected, the percentage of adolescents who have attained identity achievement increases steadily from before high school to the late college years, as the percentage remaining in identity diffusion steadily decreases (Waterman, 1985).

More contemporary research has focused on the development of self-concept from the perspective of cognitive theories (see Chapter 1), rather than based on Erikson's stages of identity development. As adolescents mature cognitively, they develop more abstract characterizations of themselves. They begin to view themselves more in terms of personal beliefs and standards and less according to social comparisons (Harter, 1998). Adolescents' self-concepts vary across different situations, so that they see themselves differently when they are with

parents than when they are with peers (Harter, 1998). They often engage in behaviors that do not represent how they really see themselves, especially among classmates or in romantic relationships.

In early adolescence, self-esteem is somewhat unstable but becomes more stable during later adolescence (Harter, 1998). African American adolescents tend to have higher self-esteem than white adolescents (Gray-Little & Hafdahl, 2000), and males have higher self-esteem than females (Kling et al., 1999). Not surprisingly, however, across both genders and most ethnic groups, higher self-esteem is related to parental approval, peer support, adjustment, and success in school (DuBois et al., 1998).

During adolescence and early adulthood, many minority youth struggle with their ethnic identity, and their resolution of this struggle can come in many forms (Phinney & Alipuria, 1990; Sellers et al., 1998). Some minority youth assimilate into the majority culture by rejecting their own culture. Some live in the majority culture but feel estranged. Some reject the majority culture and focus only on their own culture. And some try to find a balance between the majority culture and their own culture, a resolution sometimes referred to as biculturalism.

◆ Interim Summary

- Puberty has significant effects on an adolescent's body image, self-esteem, moods, and relationships; but most adolescents make it through this period without major turmoil.

- According to Erikson's theory, forming a personal sense of identity is the major task of the adolescent period.

- Identity crisis is the phrase coined by Erikson to describe the active period of self-definition characteristic of adolescence.

- Identity confusion is the unsuccessful outcome of identity crisis. The adolescent has no consistent sense of self or set of internal standards for evaluating his or her self-worth in major areas of life.

◆ Critical Thinking Questions

1. Using the categories of identity achievement, foreclosure, moratorium, and identity diffusion, can you identify how and when your religious, sexual, occupational, and political identities have developed and changed over time?

2. What experiences might influence the development of a minority youth's ethnic identity? For example, what experiences might lead a youth to develop a bicultural identity, and what experiences might lead a youth to reject majority culture?

1. Two central questions in developmental psychology are: (a) How do biological factors ("nature") interact with environmental experiences ("nurture") to determine the course of development? and (b) Is development best understood as a continuous process of change or as a series of qualitatively distinct stages?

2. Some developmental psychologists believe that development occurs in a sequence of periods in which (a) behaviors at a given stage are organized around a dominant theme or a coherent set of characteristics, (b) behaviors at one stage are qualitatively different from behaviors at earlier or later stages, and (c) all children go through the same stages in the same order. Critical or sensitive periods are times during development when specific experiences must occur for psychological development to proceed normally.

3. Early theorists believed that all sensory preferences and abilities had to be learned, but research over the last several decades has established that infants are born with their sensory systems intact and prepared to learn about the world.

4. Newborns have poor vision and cannot see as well as an adult until about age 2. Some theorists thought infants were born with a preference for faces, but research suggests infants are not attracted to faces per se but to stimulus characteristics such as curved lines, high contrast, edges, movement, and complexity—all of which faces possess. Even newborns pay attention to sounds. They seem to be born with perceptual mechanisms that are already tuned to the properties of human speech that will help them learn language. Infants can discriminate between different tastes and odors shortly after birth. They seem to prefer the taste and odor of breast milk. Infants can learn from the moment they are born and show good memories by 3 months of age.

5. Piaget's theory describes stages in cognitive development. These proceed from the sensorimotor stage (in which an important discovery is object permanence), through the preoperational stage (when symbols begin to be used) and the concrete operational stage (when conservation concepts develop), to the formal operational stage (when hypotheses are tested systematically in problem solving). New methods of testing reveal that Piaget's theory underestimates children's abilities, and several alternative approaches have been proposed.

6. Information-processing approaches view cognitive development as reflecting the gradual development of processes such as attention and memory. Other theorists emphasize increases in domain-specific knowledge. Still others, including Vygotsky, focus on the influence of the social and cultural context. Much of the newest research in children's cognitive development focuses on children's theory of mind, or understanding that other people have beliefs and expectations that can be different from their own and different from reality.

7. Piaget believed that children's understanding of moral rules and judgments develops along with their cognitive abilities. Kohlberg extended Piaget's work to include adolescence and adulthood. He proposed three levels of moral judgment: preconventional, conventional, and postconventional.

8. An infant's tendency to seek closeness to particular people and to feel more secure in their presence is called *attachment*. Attachment can be assessed in a procedure called *the strange situation,* a series of episodes in which a child is observed as the primary caregiver leaves and returns to the room. Securely attached infants seek to interact with a caretaker who returns from an absence. Insecurely attached: avoidant infants avoid a caretaker who returns from an absence. Insecurely attached: ambivalent infants show resistance to a caretaker who returns from an absence. Disorganized infants show contradictory behaviors (sometimes avoidant, sometimes approaching) to a caretaker who returns from an absence.

9. Research on the effects of day care on children's well-being and attachments suggests that low-quality day care may be detrimental, but high quality day care is not and may counteract the effects of poor home environments.

10. Gender identity is the degree to which one regards oneself as male or female. It is distinct from sex typing, the acquisition of characteristics and behaviors that society considers appropriate for one's sex. Freud's psychoanalytic theory holds that gender identity and sex typing develop from the children's early discovery of the genital differences between the sexes and children's eventual identification with the same-sex parent. Social learning theory emphasizes the rewards and punishments that children receive for sex-appropriate and sex-inappropriate behaviors, as well as a process of identification with same-sex adults that is based on observational learning. A cognitive-developmental theory of gender identity and sex typing holds that once children can identify themselves as male or female, they are motivated to acquire sex-typed behaviors. Their understanding of sex and gender corresponds to Piaget's stages of cognitive development, especially their understanding of gender constancy—the realization that a person's sex remains constant despite changes of age

and appearance. Gender schema theory seeks to explain why children base their self-concepts on the male-female distinction in the first place. It emphasizes the role of culture in teaching children to view the world through the lens of gender.

11. Puberty has significant effects on an adolescent's body image, self-esteem, moods, and relationships, but most adolescents make it through this period without major turmoil.

12. According to Erikson's theory, forming a personal sense of identity is the major task of the adolescent period. Identity crisis is Erikson's phrase to describe the active period of self-definition characteristic of adolescence. Identity confusion is the unsuccessful outcome of identity crisis in which the adolescent has no consistent sense of self or set of internal standards for evaluating his or her self-worth in major areas of life.

CORE CONCEPTS

maturation
stages
critical period
sensitive periods
visual field
facial preference
schemas
assimilate
accommodation
sensorimotor stage
object permanence
preoperational stage
operation
conservation
egocentrism
concrete operational stage
formal operational stage
information-processing skills

knowledge
sociocultural approach to
    development
metacognition
theory of mind
autism
moral judgment
preconventional level of moral
    development
conventional level of moral
    development
postconventional level of moral
    development
temperament
easy temperament
difficult temperament
slow to warm up temperament
separation anxiety

autonomy
attachment
securely attached
insecurely attached: avoidant
insecurely attached: ambivalent
disorganized
sensitive responsiveness
gender identity
sex typing
gender schema
adolescence
puberty
menarche
identity crisis
identity confusion

WEB RESOURCES

http://psychology.wadsworth.com/
atkinson14e

Take a quiz, try the activities and exercises, and explore web links.

http://home.att.net/xchar/tna/

This site is maintained by Seeing Both Sides author Judith Rich Harris and further explains her controversial book that highlights her belief in the importance of peers and the relative unimportance of parenting styles.

http://www.personal.psu.edu/faculty/n/x/nxd10/adolesce.htm

Find out more about adolescence here. You can search from a multitude of topics, including cognitive and social transitions, identity, and sexuality, or explore the case studies.

 ### InfoTrac Online Library
http://www.infotrac-college.com/
wadsworth

Use InfoTrac College Edition to find popular and scientific articles by using the search terms below or your own relevant terms.

- Cognitive development
- Developmental psychology
- Gender roles
- Moral development
- Psychosocial development
- Temperament

CD-ROM LINKS

 ### Psych Odyssey
Check out CD Chapter 10, Cognitive Development
A. Theories of Cognitive Development
B. Cognitive Development During Infancy
C. Cognitive Development During Childhood
D. Cognitive Development During Adolescence
See also CD Chapter 11, Social Development
A. Personality Development
B. A Developing Sense of Self
C. Moral Development

 ### Psyk.trek 2.0
Check out CD Unit 9, Human Development
9a Prenatal Development
9b Erikson's Theory of Personality Development
9c Piaget's Theory of Cognitive Development
9d Kohlberg's Theory of Moral Development

© Jerry Tobias/ CORBIS

SENSORY PROCESSES

Imagine yourself sitting late at night on a deserted beach. Although the image is one of profound serenity, there is in reality an enormous amount of information impinging on you from the world: Light from the sky, dim though it may seem, is entering your eyes. The sounds of the waves, soft though they may seem, are entering your ears. The sand you're sitting in is pushing up on your body, the smell of the sea is wafting into your nose, and the taste of the wine you just drank still lingers in your mouth.

And this is just the environmental information you're aware of! In addition, there's lots more information that you're unaware of. The microwave transmitter on the hill behind you, the radio station on the other side of town, and the cell phone of a talkative passer-by are all issuing electromagnetic radiation that, while enveloping you, isn't touching your consciousness. Across the street a pet owner blows his dog whis-

tle, sending a high-frequency shriek that, while very salient to the dog (and to any bats in the vicinity), is inaudible to you. Likewise, particles in the air and in your mouth and subtle pressures on your skin are there and constitute information but do not register.

The point here is that, even in the calmest of circumstances, the world is constantly providing us with a vast informational tapestry. We need to assimilate and interpret at least some of this information to appropriately interact with the world. This need raises two design considerations. First, which aspects of the environmental information register with our senses and which don't? Why do we see electromagnetic radiation in the form of green light but not electromagnetic radiation in the form of x-rays or radar waves? Second, How do the sense organs work to efficiently acquire the information that is acquirable?

The first question, while fascinating, is beyond the scope of this book. Steven Pinker in his recent classic, *How the Mind Works,* discusses it from an evolutionary perspective. We will, however, provide a hint of how to address it by noting that different organisms have evolved different ways of coping with the world. Bats, for example, have considerably poorer sight than we do but considerably better hearing, which they use as we use sight to create a continually updated model of the three-dimensional space and the objects within it. Similarly, dogs have considerably poorer vision than we do, but a much better sense of smell—

which they profitably use not only to understand the makeup of the present world but also to figure out what has happened there in the past. ("Hmmm. From the smell of this fire hydrant, it appears that my friend Spot was here about an hour ago.")

Our senses are our input systems, and constitute the means by which we determine the nature of the environment within which we exist and behave. In this chapter we discuss some of the major properties of the senses. Some of the research we review deals with psychological phenomena, and other studies address the biological bases of these phenomena. In virtually no other area of psychology have the biological and psychological approaches worked together so fruitfully.

Both approaches often make a distinction between sensation and perception. At the psychological level, sensations are fundamental, raw experiences associated with stimuli (for example, your sense of sight may register a large red object). The perceptual level is the integration and meaningful interpretation of these raw sensory experiences ("It's a fire engine"). At the biological level, sensory processes involve the sense organs and the neural pathways that emanate from them, which are concerned with the initial stages of acquiring stimulus information. Perceptual processes involve higher levels of the cortex, which are more related to meaning. This chapter is about sensation, and Chapter 5 concerns perception.

The distinction between sensation and perception, while useful for organizing chapters, is somewhat arbitrary. Psychological and biological events that occur early in the processing of a stimulus sometimes affect interpretation of the stimulus. Moreover, from the perspective of the nervous system, there is no sharp break between the initial uptake of stimulus information by the sense organs and the brain's use of that information to ascribe meaning. In fact, one of the brain's most important features is that, in addition to taking in sensory information, it is constantly sending messages from its highest levels back to the earliest stages of sensory processing. These **back projections** are activities that modify the way sensory input is processed (Damasio, 1994; Rolls, 2000; Wandell, 1995; Zeki, 1993).

This chapter is organized around the different senses: vision, hearing, smell, taste, and touch, including pressure, temperature, and pain. In everyday life, several senses are often involved in any given act. We see a peach, feel its texture, taste and smell it as we bite into it, and hear the sounds of chewing. For purposes of analysis, however, we consider the senses one at a time. Before beginning our study of individual senses, or sensory modalities, we will discuss some properties that are common to all senses.

CHARACTERISTICS OF SENSORY MODALITIES

Two characteristics are common to all sensory modalities. The first, sensitivity, describes sensory modalities at a psychological level, and the second, sensory coding, describes them at a biological level.

SENSITIVITY

It is a matter of common sense that the more intense a stimulus, the more strongly it affects the relevant sense organ: A bright light affects the visual system more than a dimmer light, a loud sound affects the auditory system more than a soft sound, and so on.

This commonsense observation is analogous to the equally commonsense observation that a dropped apple will fall downward. And just as Newton (supposedly) began from the dropped-apple observation to develop a detailed and quantitative theory of gravity, sensory psychologists have long sought to detail and quantify the relation between physical stimulus intensity and the resulting sensation magnitude.

ABSOLUTE THRESHOLDS A basic way of assessing the sensitivity of a sensory modality is to determine the **absolute threshold:** the minimum magnitude of a stimulus

● **Table 4-1**
Minimum Stimuli

Approximate minimum stimuli for various senses. *(Galanter, E. (1962). "Contemporary Psychophysics," from Roger Brown & collaborators (eds.),* New Directions in Psychology, *Vol. 1. Reprinted by permission of Roger Brown.)*

Sense	Minimum Stimulus
Vision	A candle flame seen at 30 miles on a dark, clear night
Hearing	The tick of a clock at 20 feet under quiet conditions
Taste	One teaspoon of sugar in 2 gallons of water
Smell	One drop of perfume diffused into the entire volume of six rooms
Touch	The wing of a fly falling on your cheek from a distance of 1 centimeter

that can be reliably discriminated from no stimulus at all—for example, the weakest light that can be reliably discriminated from darkness. Our sensory modalities are extremely sensitive to the presence of, or a change in, an object or event. For five of the senses, Table 4-1 provides an estimate of the minimal stimulus they can detect. The most noticeable aspect of these minimums is how low they and how sensitive the sensory modalities are.

These values were determined by using **psychophysical procedures,** experimental techniques for measuring the relation between the physical magnitude of some stimulus (such as the physical intensity of a light) and the resulting psychological response (how bright the light appears to be). In one common psychophysical procedure, the experimenter first selects a set of stimuli whose magnitudes vary around the threshold (for example, a set of dim lights whose intensities vary from invisible to barely visible). Over a series of trials, the stimuli are presented one at a time in random order, and the observer is instructed to say yes if the stimulus appears to be present and no if it does not. Each stimulus is presented many times, and the percentage of yes responses is determined for each stimulus magnitude.

Figure 4-1 depicts hypothetical data from this kind of experiment: a graph called a **psychophysical function,** which shows performance as a function of stimulus intensity. Here, the percentage of yes responses rises smoothly as stimulus intensity (defined here in terms of hypothetical "units") increases. When performance is characterized by such a graph, psychologists have agreed to define the absolute threshold as the value of the stimulus at which it is detected 50% of the time. For the data displayed in Figure 4-1, the stimulus is detected 50% of the time when the stimulus's intensity is about 28 units, so 28 units is defined to be absolute threshold.

❙ Figure 4-1
Psychophysical Function from a Detection Experiment
Plotted on the vertical axis is the percentage of times the participant responds, "Yes, I detect the stimulus"; on the horizontal axis is the measure of the magnitude of the physical stimulus. Such a graph may be obtained for any stimulus dimension to which an individual is sensitive.

Our sensory modalities are extremely sensitive in detecting the presence of an object—even the faint light of a candle in a distant window. On a clear night, a candle flame can be seen from 30 miles away!

A classic and particularly elegant experiment of this sort was reported by Hecht, Schlaer, and Pirenne (1942), who endeavored to determine the absolute threshold for vision and, in the process, demonstrated that human vision is nearly as sensitive as is physically possible. As every physics student knows, a **photon** is the smallest unit of light energy. Hecht and his colleagues showed that a person can detect a flash of light that contains only 100 photons, a fact that is impressive in and of itself. On a typical day, many billions of photons are entering your eye every second. What is even more impressive is that Hecht and his colleagues went on to show that only 7 of these 100 photons actually contact the critical molecules in the eye that are responsible for translating light into the nerve impulses that correspond to vision (the rest are absorbed by other parts of the eye). Furthermore, each of these 7 photons affects a different molecule. The critical receptive unit of the eye (a molecule), therefore, is sensitive to a single photon. This is what it means to say that "human vision is as sensitive as is physically possible."

ANOTHER KIND OF THRESHOLD: DETECTING CHANGES IN INTENSITY Measuring absolute threshold entails determining by how much stimulus intensity must be raised from zero in order to be distinguishable from zero. By how much must stimulus intensity be raised from some **standard**, defined to be some arbitrary level, to distinguish the new, higher level from the base level. This is measurement

of change detection. In a typical change-detection study, observers are presented with a pair of stimuli. One of them is the standard to which other stimuli are compared. The others are comparison stimuli. On each presentation of the pair, observers are asked to respond to the comparison stimulus with "more" or "less." What is being measured is the difference threshold or **just noticeable difference (jnd)**, the minimum difference in stimulus magnitude necessary to tell two stimuli apart.

Imagine measuring the visual system's sensitivity to changes in the brightness of a light. Typical results are shown in Figure 4-2. In this experiment the standard (a 50-watt bulb) was presented along with each comparison stimulus (ranging from 47 watts to 53 watts, in 1-watt steps) dozens of times. We have plotted the percentage of times in which each comparison stimulus was judged to be "brighter" than the standard. To determine the jnd, two points are estimated, one at 75% and the other at 25% on the "percent brighter" axis. Psychologists have agreed that half of this distance in stimulus intensity units is the just noticeable difference. In this case, then, the estimated jnd is (51 – 49)/2 = 1 watt. If an individual's sensitivity to change is high, meaning that he or she can notice tiny differences between stimuli, the estimated value of the jnd will be small. If sensitivity is not as high, the estimated jnd will be larger.

This kind of experiment was first carried out in the 19th century by two German scientists: Ernst Heinrich Weber, a physiologist, and Gustav Fechner, a physicist.

Figure 4-2
Results from an Experiment on Change Detection
Plotted on the vertical axis is the percentage of times the participant responds, "Yes, I detect more than the standard"; on the horizontal axis is the measure of the magnitude of the physical stimulus. The standard stimulus in this example is in the center of the range of stimuli. Such a graph may be obtained for any stimulus dimension for which an individual is sensitive to differences.

Their seminal finding was that the larger the value of the standard stimulus, the less sensitive the sensory system is to changes in intensity. Actually, under a wide range of circumstances, the relation is more precise: *The intensity by which the standard must be increased to be noticed is proportional to the intensity of the standard.* For example, if a room contained 20 lit candles and you could just detect the addition of one candle (5% more), then if the room contained 100 candles, an additional (5% × 100) 5 candles would be required for you to be able to detect the change. This proportional relation has come to be known as the Weber-Fechner law, and the constant of proportionality (5% in our light bulb example) is referred to as the **Weber fraction**.

Table 4-2 shows typical jnds for different sensory qualities, expressed in terms of the Weber fraction (note that we used 5% for simplicity in our light bulb example, but the actual Weber fraction for light is about 8%). Table 4-2 shows, among other things, that we are generally more sensitive to changes (we can detect a smaller increase) in light and sound than is the case with taste and smell. These values can be used to predict how much a stimulus must be changed from any level of intensity for people to notice the changes reliably. For example, a theater manager who wished to produce a subtle but noticeable change in the level of lighting on a stage might increase the lighting level by 10%. This change would be

● **Table 4-2**
Just Noticeable Differences (jnd) for Various Sensory Qualities

(expressed as the percentage change required for reliable change detection)

Quality	Just Noticeable Difference (jnd)
Light intensity	8%
Sound intensity	5%
Sound frequency	1%
Odor concentration	15%
Salt concentration	20%
Lifted weights	2%
Electric shock	1%

a 10-watt increase if a 100-watt bulb was used to begin with, but it would mean a 1,000-watt increase if 10,000 watts were already flooding the stage.

SUPRATHRESHOLD SENSATION Knowledge of sensory thresholds in vision and other sensory modalities is important in understanding how sense organs are designed. For example, that a molecule of light-sensitive pigment in the eye responds to a single photon of light is an important clue in understanding how the light-sensitive pigments work. However, most of our everyday visual behavior takes place in the context of **suprathreshold conditions,** conditions in which stimulus intensity is above threshold. Beginning with Weber and Fechner in the mid-19th century, scientists have been investigating the relation between suprathreshold stimulus intensities and corresponding sensory magnitudes by presenting stimuli of various intensities to humans and attempting to measure the magnitude of the humans' responses to them.

Imagine yourself in the following experiment. You sit in a dimly lit room looking at a screen. On each of a series of trials, a small spot of light appears on the screen. The spot differs in physical intensity from one trial to the next. Your job is to assign a number on each trial that reflects how intense that trial's light spot appears to you. So to a very dim light you might assign a 1, and to a very bright light, you might assign 100. Figure 4-3 shows typical data from such an experiment.

In the mid-20th century, the Harvard psychologist S. S. Stevens carried out an intensive investigation of suprathreshold sensation by using this kind of experiment. To interpret his data, Stevens derived a law, bearing his name, from two assumptions. The first assumption is the correctness of the Weber-Fechner law, that a jnd above some standard stimulus is some fixed percent-

Figure 4-3
Psychophysical Data from a Magnitude-Estimation Experiment
Plotted on the vertical axis is the average magnitude estimate given by the observer; on the horizontal axis is the measure of the magnitude of the physical stimulus. Such a graph may be obtained for any stimulus dimension the observer can perceive.

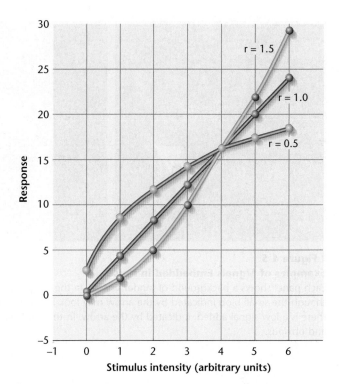

Figure 4-4
Psychophysical Data from a Magnitude-Estimation Experiment
Here different curves are shown for different sensory modalities that entail different exponents. An exponent less than 1.0 produces a concave-down curve, an exponent of 1.0 produces a linear curve, and an exponent greater than 1.0 produces a concave-up curve.

age of the standard. The second assumption is that psychological intensity is appropriately measured in units of jnds (just as distance is appropriately measured in meters or weight is appropriately measured in grams). This means, for example, that the difference between 4 and 7 jnds (3 jnds) would to an observer be the same as the difference between 10 and 13 jnds (also 3). We will skip the mathematical derivations and go straight to the bottom line: Stevens' Law, implied by these assumptions, is that perceived psychological magnitude (Ψ) is a **power function** of physical magnitude (Φ). By this is meant that the relation between Ψ and Φ is (basically) $\Psi = \phi^r$ where r is an **exponent**—a unique number that characterizes the function of each sensory modality. The function shown in Figure 4-3 is a power function with an exponent of 0.5 (which means that $\Psi = \phi^{.5}$; that is, Ψ is equal to the square root of ϕ).

Stevens and others have reported thousands of experiments in support of the proposition that the relation between physical and psychological intensity is a power function. A power function is quite different, depending on whether r, the exponent, is less than or greater than 1.0. As illustrated in Figure 4-4, a power function with a less-than-1 exponent, such as that corresponding to loudness, is concave down, and increasing levels of physical intensity lead to progressively smaller increases in sensation. In contrast, a power function with a greater-than-1 exponent, such as that corresponding to electric shock, is concave up, and increasing levels of physical intensity lead to progressively greater increases in sensa-

tion. Exactly why the exponents differ among the sensory modalities is not known. However, relatively benign sensory modalities such as light intensities have less-than-1 exponents, and relatively harmful sensory modalities such as electric shock have greater-than-1 exponents. This configuration probably serves adaptive purposes. For relatively "benign" modalities such as light intensity, the relation between physical intensity and the psychological response simply conveys useful information that may or may not be immediately relevant. However, a modality like pain signals the need for immediate action. If your finger accidentally comes in contact with a red-hot coal, this highly pain-evoking stimulus must produce a very high response; otherwise, loss of life or limb could result!

SIGNAL-DETECTION THEORY

Signal-detection theory is a standard way of understanding how errors are made in many diverse situations. Think about the kind of experiment in which light threshold is determined by presenting lights of various

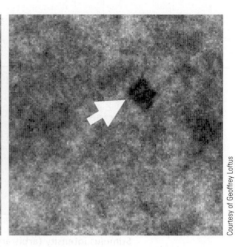

❚ Figure 4-5
Examples of Signals Embedded in Noise
Each panel shows a background of random noise. In the left panel, there is no signal, although the small blob indicated by the arrow may look like a signal. In the middle panel, there is a low signal added, indicated by the arrow. In the right panel, the signal is strong and obvious.

intensities and asking the observer to report, "Yes, I see the light" or "No, I don't." Unless the experiment is carried out extremely carefully (as was done by Hecht and his colleagues), interpreting results presents a serious problem. Observers may sometimes may say, "Yes, I detect a light" when actually they don't, but only think they see it. To deal with this problem, the experimental procedure is modified somewhat: Instead of presenting lights of varying intensities on all trials, there are some trials in which nothing is presented. With this modification, it is possible to estimate how inclined the observers are to say they detect something when we know they can't, because nothing is there to detect.

An example is a medical malpractice lawsuit that was filed in the late 1990s. A radiologist, Dr. A, examined a chest x-ray of a patient, Mr. P, during a routine medical exam. Sadly, there was a small but cancerous tumor in Mr. P's chest, undetected by Dr. A, that, 3 years later, had grown substantially and resulted in Mr. P's death. Mr. P's family filed the lawsuit against Dr. A, asserting that the tumor had been detectable in the original x-ray and that Dr. A should have detected it. During the ensuing trial, Mr. P's family called upon another radiologist, Dr. B, as an expert witness. As part of his preparation, Dr. B first viewed recent x-rays, taken just before Mr. P's death, in which the tumor, large and ominous at that point, was clearly visible. Dr. B then viewed the original x-ray—the one seen by Dr. A—and easily "detected" the then-smaller tumor that Dr. A had missed. Dr. B's conclusion was that, because he, Dr. B, was able to detect the tumor in the original x-ray, Dr. A should

have also detected it, and Dr. A, in missing it, was therefore negligent.

This case raises several interesting issues in the domain of sensation and perception. One, roughly characterized as "hindsight is 20-20," is discussed in the next chapter. In this chapter we will focus on another issue, the distinction between **sensation**, which is determined by the perceptual strength of the stimulus, and **bias**, which is a criterion, set by the observer, for making a particular response. To understand this distinction, consider the task of a radiologist trying to determine whether the x-ray is normal or whether it shows the presence of a tumor. In scientific lingo, this task is one of trying to detect a **signal**, which is what the observer is trying to detect, embedded in **noise**, which is anything in the environment irrelevant to what the observer is trying to detect. This concept is illustrated in Figure 4-5. There are three panels, each of which has the same background of random visual noise. Suppose that your task was to decide whether there was a small, black, generally diamond-shaped blob embedded somewhere in this noise. This task is strongly analogous to the radiologist's task of finding a poorly defined tumor in an x-ray.

Consider first the left panel of Figure 4-5, which has only noise. (We know this is true because we created it that way.) Would you indicate that the signal was present? There is not much evidence for the small diamond, as indeed there should not be, but there is, however, a random collection of noise over at the right, indicated by the yellow arrow, that *could* be the sought-after signal. Perhaps you might incorrectly choose it—or maybe you would correctly decide that there is only noise. In the middle panel, a weak signal is indicated by the arrow. In this case, you might correctly choose it or still feel that it is only noise and incorrectly claim there to be only noise. Finally, the right panel shows a strong signal, which you would probably correctly detect as a signal.

HITS AND FALSE ALARMS Now suppose that you are given a whole series of stimuli like the ones in Figure 4-5. Some, like the left panel, contain only noise, and others, like the right panel, contain noise plus signal. Your task is to say yes to those containing signal and no to those containing only noise. In this situation, a **hit** is a response of correctly responding yes when a signal is present, and a **false alarm** is the response of incorrectly responding yes when only noise is present. Over all trials, the proportion of hits is referred to the **hit rate,** and the proportion of false alarms is referred to as the **false-alarm rate.**

Carrying out this task perfectly is not possible. To see why, look at the left panel of Figure 4-5, which contains only noise. You might, upon inspecting it, think it contains a signal—for instance, the small dark blob pointed at by the arrow, which is part of the noise but resembles the kind of black blob you are seeking. So you might reasonably respond yes to it, in which case you would be incorrect. You would have made a false alarm.

In this kind of signal-detection experiment, we could measure the proportion of noise-only trials that result in an incorrect yes response, the false-alarm rate. We can also measure the proportion of noise-plus-signal trials that result in a correct yes response, the hit rate.

We now have a powerful tool to investigate the sensitivity of some sense organ. We know that if no signal is there to be detected, the observer says yes anyway with some probability equal to the false-alarm rate. So we infer that the observer does detect a signal only when the hit rate exceeds the false-alarm rate. If the hit rate exceeds the false-alarm rate by a lot, we infer that sensitivity is high. If the hit rate exceeds the false-alarm rate by only a little, we infer that sensitivity is low. If the hit rate equals the false-alarm rate, we infer that sensitivity is zero.

SENSITIVITY AND BIAS Notice that observers are at liberty to choose what their false-alarm rate will be. Imagine two hypothetical observers, Charlotte and Linda, who are equally good at detecting signals but who differ in an important way. Charlotte is a "conservative" observer who requires a lot of evidence to claim that a signal is present. Charlotte says yes infrequently, which means she has a low false-alarm rate but also a low hit rate. In contrast, Linda is a "liberal" observer who claims "signal" given the slightest shred of evidence for a signal. Linda, in other words, says yes frequently,

which endows her with a high false-alarm rate but also a high hit rate.

The most useful characteristic of a signal-detection analysis is that it allows separation of bias (referred to as β) and sensitivity (referred to as d', pronounced "dee-prime"). In our Charlotte-Linda example, Charlotte and Linda would be determined to have equal sensitivities, even though they have quite different bias values.

Let's go back to the medical malpractice lawsuit. Notice that there are two observers: Dr. A and Dr. B. The suit alleges that Dr. A has poor sensitivity—poor ability to detect a tumor—compared with Dr. B, and for this reason (essentially) Dr. A is alleged to have been negligent. However, we can now see that this conclusion does not necessarily follow from the fact that Dr. A did not detect the original tumor and Dr. B did. It is equally plausible that Dr. B simply had more of a bias to say, "Yes, I detect a tumor" than did Dr. A. This explanation actually makes a good deal of sense. Psychologists have discovered that, in a signal-detection situation, one of the factors that influence bias is expectation: Reasonably enough, the greater the observer's expectation that a signal will be present, the greater the observer's bias to respond yes. And, of course, Dr. B had good reason to expect the presence of a tumor, whereas Dr. A did not.

SENSORY CODING

Given some understanding of the sensitivity of the different senses, we can explore the biological bases of sensation, beginning with **sensory coding,** how stimuli are transmitted from the sensory receptors to the brain.

The brain has a formidable problem in sensing the world. Each sense responds to a certain kind of stimulus—light energy for vision, mechanical energy for hearing and touch, chemical energy for smell and taste. But the brain speaks only the language of electrical signals associated with neural discharges. Somehow, each sensory modality must first perform **transduction.** It must translate physical energy into electrical signals that can make their way to the brain. This is accomplished by specialized cells in the sense organs called *receptors.* For instance, the receptors for vision are located in a thin layer of tissue on the inside of the eye. Each visual receptor contains a chemical that reacts to light, which in turn triggers a series of steps that results in a neural impulse. The receptors for hearing are fine hair cells located deep in the ear, and vibrations in the air bend these hair cells to create a neural impulse. Similar descriptions apply to the other sensory modalities.

A receptor is a specialized nerve cell or neuron (see Chapter 2). When it is activated, it passes its electrical signal to connecting neurons. The signal travels until it reaches its receiving area in the cortex, with different sensory modalities sending signals to different receiving

Oscilloscope

Microelectrode

Amplifier

Light

Receptive
field

Screen

▌Figure 4-6
Single-Cell Recording
An anesthetized monkey is placed in a device that holds its
head in a fixed position. A stimulus, often a flashing or moving
bar of light, is projected onto the screen. A microelectrode implanted in the visual system of the monkey monitors activity
from a single neuron, and this activity is amplified and displayed on an oscilloscope.

areas. Somewhere in the brain the electrical signal results
in the conscious sensory experience that, for example,
underlies responses in a psychophysical experiment.
When we experience a touch, the experience is occurring
in the brain, not the skin. However, the electrical impulses in the brain that mediate the experience of touch
are themselves caused by electrical impulses in touch receptors located in the skin. Similarly, our experience of a
bitter taste occurs in the brain, not the tongue, but the
brain impulses that mediate the taste experience are
themselves caused by electrical impulses in taste receptors on the tongue. In this way our receptors play a major role in relating external events to conscious experience. Numerous aspects of our conscious perceptions are
caused by specific neural events in the receptors.

CODING OF INTENSITY AND QUALITY Our sensory
systems evolved to pick up information about objects
and events in the world. What kind of information do
we need to know about an event such as a brief flash of
a bright red light? Two properties of any stimulus are its
intensity, or how strong the stimulus is, and its **quality,**
what the stimulus is like. Clearly, it would be useful to

know its intensity (bright), quality
(red), duration (brief), location,
and time of onset. Each of our sensory systems provides some information about these attributes, although most research has
focused on the attributes of intensity and quality.

When we see a bright red
color patch, we experience the
quality of redness at an intense
level. When we hear a faint, high-
pitched tone, we experience the quality of the pitch at a nonintense level.
The receptors and their neural pathways
to the brain must therefore code both intensity and quality. How do they do this?
Researchers who study these coding processes need a way of determining which neurons are activated by which stimuli. The usual
means is to record the electrical activity of single
cells in the receptors and neural pathways to the
brain while some subject (which, in the case of
single-cell recording, is generally an animal such as a cat
or a monkey) is presented with various inputs or stimuli.
Such means can determine exactly which attributes of a
stimulus a particular neuron is responsive to.

Figure 4-6 shows a typical single-cell recording experiment for vision, although the procedure is similar for
studying other senses. Before the experiment, the animal
(in this case a monkey) has undergone a surgical procedure in which thin wires are inserted into selected areas
of its visual cortex. The thin wires are microelectrodes,
insulated except at their tips, that can be used to record
electrical activity of the neurons they are in contact with.
They cause no pain, and the monkey moves around and
lives quite normally. During the experiment, the monkey
is placed in a testing apparatus, and the microelectrodes
are connected to recording and amplifying devices. The
monkey is then exposed to various visual stimuli. For
each stimulus, the researcher can determine which neurons respond to it by observing which microelectrodes
produce sustained outputs. Because the electrical outputs are tiny, they must be amplified and displayed on an
oscilloscope, which converts the electrical signals into a
graph of the changing electrical voltage. Most neurons
emit a series of nerve impulses that appear on the oscilloscope as vertical spikes. Even in the absence of a signal
(a noise-only situation), many cells respond at a slow
rate. If a signal to which the neuron is sensitive is presented, the cells respond faster. This is the most fundamental neural correlate of the signal-detection situation.

With the aid of single-cell recordings, researchers
have learned a good deal about how sensory systems

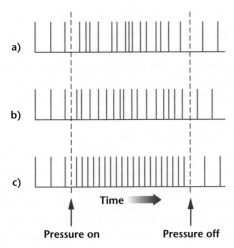

▍ Figure 4-7
Coding Intensity
Responses of a nerve fiber from the skin to (a) soft, (b) medium, and (c) strong pressure applied to the fiber's receptor. Increasing the stimulus strength increases both the rate and the regularity of nerve firing in this fiber.

code intensity and quality. The primary means for coding the intensity of a stimulus is via the number of neural impulses in each unit of time—that is, the rate of neural impulses. If someone lightly touches your arm, a series of electrical impulses is generated in a nerve fiber. If the pressure is increased, the impulses remain the same size but increase in number per unit of time (see Figure 4-7). The same is true for other sensory modalities. In general, the greater the intensity of the stimulus, the higher the neural firing rate, and the greater the firing rate, the greater the perceived magnitude of the stimulus.

One alternative for coding the intensity of a stimulus is by the **temporal pattern**, or spacing sequence of the electrical impulses. At low intensities, nerve impulses are further apart in time, and the length of time between impulses is variable. At high intensities, though, the time between impulses may be quite constant (see Figure 4-7). Another alternative is coding by number of neurons activated: The more intense the stimulus, the more neurons are activated.

Coding the quality of a stimulus is more complex. The key idea behind coding quality was proposed by Johannes Müller in 1825. Müller suggested that the brain can distinguish between information from different sensory modalities—such as lights and sounds—because they involve different sensory nerves (some nerves lead to visual experiences, others to auditory experiences, and so on). Müller's idea of specific nerve energies was supported by subsequent research demonstrating that neural pathways originating in different receptors terminate in different areas of the cortex. It is now generally agreed that the brain codes the qualitative differ-

ences between sensory modalities according to the specific neural pathways involved.

But what about the distinguishing qualities within a sense? How do we tell red from green or sweet from sour? Again, the coding is probably based on the specific neurons involved. We can distinguish between sweet and sour tastes, for example, because each kind of taste has its own nerve fibers. Sweet fibers respond primarily to sweet tastes, sour fibers primarily to sour tastes, and ditto for salty fibers and bitter fibers.

Specificity is not the only plausible coding principle. A sensory system may also use the pattern of neural firing to code the quality of a sensation. A particular nerve fiber may respond maximally to a sweet taste, but it may, to varying degrees, respond to other tastes as well. One fiber may respond best to sweet tastes, less to bitter tastes, and even less to salty tastes; a sweet-tasting stimulus would thus lead to activity in a large number of fibers, with some firing more than others. This particular pattern of neural activity would be the system's code for a sweet taste. A different pattern would be the code for a bitter taste. As shown when we discuss the senses in detail, both specificity and patterning are used in coding the quality of a stimulus.

◆ Interim Summary

- At the psychological level, sensations are experiences associated with simple stimuli, as yet unassociated with anything meaningful.

- The senses include seeing, hearing, smell, taste, pressure and temperature, pain, and the body senses.

- For all senses, sensitivity to stimulus intensity is measured by the absolute threshold (the minimum amount of stimulus energy that can be reliably detected) or the difference threshold (the minimum difference between two stimuli that can be reliably detected).

- The psychophysical function is the relation between stimulus intensity and the magnitude of sensation for above-threshold stimuli.

- Sensation is often viewed as the process of detecting a signal that is embedded in noise. In some cases, a signal may be "detected" even when only noise is present—a false alarm. Correctly detecting a signal that is present is a hit.

- The use of signal-detection theory allows the process of detecting a stimulus to be separated into two numbers, one representing the observer's sensitivity to the signal and the other representing the observer's bias to respond "signal present."

- Every sense modality must recode or transduce its physical energy into neural impulses.

1. How might you use measurements of the just noticeable difference (jnd) in loudness to describe the change in the auditory environment caused by the addition of a new airline to your local airport? Would you be able to explain your measurement method to a panel of concerned citizens?

2. In the text we described a radiologist, Dr. A, who was accused of missing a tumor in an x-ray, and Dr. B., the expert witness in the resulting lawsuit, who claimed that the tumor was clearly visible. Dr. B's implicit conclusion is that Dr. A is not as good as detecting tumors as is he, Dr. B. State clearly why Dr. B's conclusion is flawed given the available information, and design two experiments: the first addressing the issue of whether Dr. B perceives tumors better than Dr. A and the second addressing how easy it would be for radiologists in general to have detected the original tumor missed by Dr. A.

VISION

Humans are generally credited with the following senses: (1) vision, (2) hearing, (3) smell, (4) taste, (5) touch (or the skin senses), and (6) the body senses (which are responsible for sensing the position of the head relative to the trunk, for example). Because the last—the body senses—do not always give rise to conscious sensations of intensity and quality, we will not consider them further in this chapter.

Only vision, hearing, and smell are capable of obtaining information at a distance from us, and of this group, vision is the most finely tuned in humans. In this section we discuss the nature of the stimulus energy to which vision is sensitive, the visual system and particularly how its receptors carry out the transduction process, and how the visual modality processes information about intensity and quality.

LIGHT AND VISION

Each sense responds to a particular form of physical energy, and for vision the physical stimulus is light. Light is a form of electromagnetic energy, energy that emanates from the sun and the rest of the universe and constantly bathes our planet. Electromagnetic energy includes not only light but also cosmic rays, x-rays, ultraviolet and infrared rays, and radio and television waves. Think of electromagnetic energy as traveling in waves, with wavelengths (the distance from one crest of a wave to the next) varying tremendously from the shortest cosmic rays

(4 trillionths of a centimeter) to the longest radio waves (several miles). Our eyes are sensitive to only a tiny portion of this continuum: wavelengths of approximately 400 to 700 nanometers (a nanometer is a billionth of a meter). Visible electromagnetic energy—light—therefore makes up only a very small part of electromagnetic energy.

THE VISUAL SYSTEM

The human visual system consists of the eyes, several parts of the brain, and the pathways connecting them. (Go back to Figure 2-14 for a simplified illustration of the visual system.) The eye contains two systems, one for forming the image and the other for transducing the image into electrical impulses. The critical parts of these systems are illustrated in Figure 4-8.

An analogy is often made between an eye and a camera. Although this analogy is misleading for many aspects of the visual system, it is appropriate for the image-forming system, which focuses light reflected from an object to form an image of the object on the **retina,** which is a thin layer of tissue at the back of the eyeball

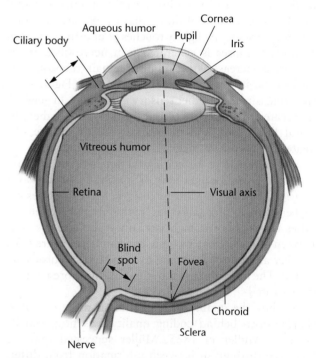

▌ Figure 4-8
Top View of the Right Eye
Light entering the eye on its way to the retina passes through the cornea, the aqueous humor, the lens, and the vitreous humor. The amount of light entering the eye is regulated by the size of the pupil, a small hole toward the front of the eye formed by the iris. The iris consists of a ring of muscles that can contract or relax, thereby controlling pupil size. The iris gives the eyes their characteristic color (blue, brown, and so forth).

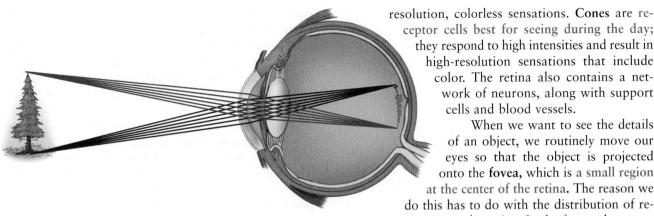

Figure 4-9
Image Formation in the Eye
Some of the light from an object enters the eye, where it forms an image on the retina. Both the cornea and the lens bend the light rays, as would a lens in a telescope. Based purely on optical considerations we can infer that the retinal image is inverted.

resolution, colorless sensations. **Cones** are receptor cells best for seeing during the day; they respond to high intensities and result in high-resolution sensations that include color. The retina also contains a network of neurons, along with support cells and blood vessels.

When we want to see the details of an object, we routinely move our eyes so that the object is projected onto the **fovea**, which is a small region at the center of the retina. The reason we do this has to do with the distribution of receptors across the retina. In the fovea, the receptors are plentiful and closely packed; outside the fovea, on the periphery of the retina, there are fewer receptors. More closely packed receptors mean higher resolution, as, analogously, a computer monitor set to more pixels per inch (such as one set to 1024×768) has a higher resolution than when it is set to fewer pixels per inch

(see Figure 4-9). The image-forming system itself consists of the cornea, the pupil, and the lens. Without them, we could see light but not pattern. The cornea is the transparent front surface of the eye: Light enters here, and rays are bent inward by it to begin the formation of the image. The lens completes the process of focusing the light on the retina (see Figure 4-9). To focus on objects at different distances, the lens changes shape. It becomes more spherical for near objects and flatter for far ones. In the eyes of myopic (nearsighted) people, the lens does not become flat enough to bring far objects into focus, although it focuses well on near objects. In the eyes of hyperopic (farsighted) people, the lens does not become spherical enough to focus on near objects, although it focuses well on far objects. As people with otherwise normal vision get older (into their 40s), the lens loses much of its ability to change shape or focus at all. Such optical defects can, of course, generally be corrected with eyeglasses or contact lenses.

The **pupil**, the third component of the image-forming system, is a circular opening whose diameter varies in response to the level of light present. It is largest in dim light and smallest in bright light, which helps to ensure that enough light passes through the lens to maintain image quality at different light levels.

All of these components focus the image on the retina. There the transduction system takes over. The heart of the system is the receptors. There are two types of receptor cells, rods and cones, so called because of their distinctive shapes, shown in Figure 4-10. The two kinds of receptors are specialized for different purposes. **Rods** are receptor cells designed for seeing at night; they operate at low intensities and lead to low-

| Amacrine cell | Bipolar cell | Rod |
| Ganglion cell | Horizontal cell | Cone |

Light

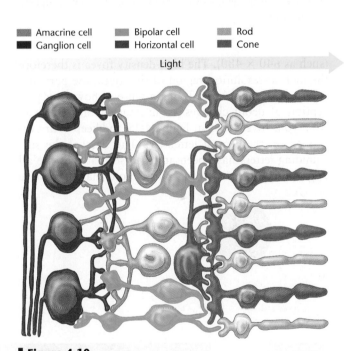

Figure 4-10
A Schematic Picture of the Retina
This is a schematic drawing of the retina based on an examination with an electron microscope. The bipolar cells receive signals from one or more receptors and transmit those signals to the ganglion cells, whose axons form the optic nerve. Note that there are several types of bipolar and ganglion cells. There are also sideways or lateral connections in the retina. Neurons called *horizontal cells* make lateral connections at a level near the receptors; neurons called *amacrine cells* make lateral connections at a level near the ganglion cells. (J. E. Dowling and B. B. Boycott (1969) "Organization of the Primate Retina" from *Proceedings of the Royal Society of London*, Series B, Vol. I66, pp. 80–111. Adapted by permission of the Royal Society of London.)

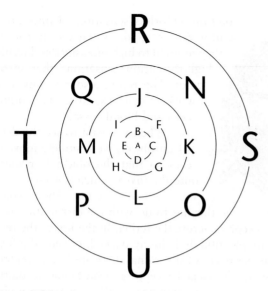

❚ Figure 4-11
Visual Acuity Decreases in the Periphery
Letter sizes have been scaled so that when the central *A* is looked at directly, all the other letters are approximately equally easy to read.

(such as 640 × 480). The high-density fovea is therefore the highest-resolution region of the fovea, the part that is best at seeing details. To get a sense of how your perception of detail changes as an image is moved away from your fovea, look at Figure 4-11 and keep your eyes trained on the central letter (*A*). The sizes of the surrounding letters have been adjusted so that they are all approximately equal in visibility. Note that to achieve

❚ Figure 4-12
Locating Your Blind Spot
(a) With your right eye closed, stare at the cross in the upper right-hand corner. Put the book about a foot from your eye and move it forward and back. When the blue circle on the left disappears, it is projected onto the blind spot. (b) Without moving the book and with your right eye still closed, stare at the cross in the lower right-hand corner. When the white space falls in the blind spot, the blue line appears to be continuous. This phenomenon helps us understand why we are not ordinarily aware of the blind spot. In effect, the visual system fills in the parts of the visual field that we are not sensitive to; thus, they appear to be a part of the surrounding field.

equal visibility, the letters on the outer circle must be about 10 times larger than the central letter.

Given that light reflected from an object has made contact with a receptor cell, how does the receptor transduce the light into electrical impulses? The rods and cones contain photopigments, chemicals that absorb light. Absorption of light by the photopigments starts a process that eventuates in a neural impulse. Once this transduction step is completed, the electrical impulses must make their way to the brain via connecting neurons. The responses of the rods and cones are first transmitted to bipolar cells and from there to other neurons called *ganglion cells* (refer to Figure 4-10). The long axons of the ganglion cells extend out of the eye to form the optic nerve to the brain. Where the optic nerve leaves the eye, there are no receptors, and we are therefore blind to a stimulus in this region (see Figure 4-12). We do not notice this hole in our visual field—known as the blind spot—because the brain automatically fills it in (Ramachandran & Gregory, 1991; Tong & Engel, 2001).

SEEING LIGHT

SENSITIVITY Our sensitivity to light is determined by the rods and cones. Three critical differences between rods and cones explain a number of phenomena involving brightness, which is a light's perceived intensity. The first difference is that rods and cones are activated under different levels of light. In broad daylight or in a well-lit room, only the cones are active, and the rods send no meaningful neural signals. At night under a quarter moon or in a very dimly lit room, only the rods are active.

A second difference is that cones and rods are specialized for different tasks, which can be seen in the way they are connected to ganglion cells. The left side of Figure 4-13 shows three adjacent cones, each of which is connected to a single ganglion cell. If a cone receives light, it increases the activity of its corresponding ganglion cell. Each ganglion cell is connected to its nearest neighbor by a connection that decreases the activity of that neighboring cell; it is also connected to the visual area of the brain by a long axon. Together these axons form the optic nerve. The right side of the figure shows three adjacent rods, each of which is connected to three

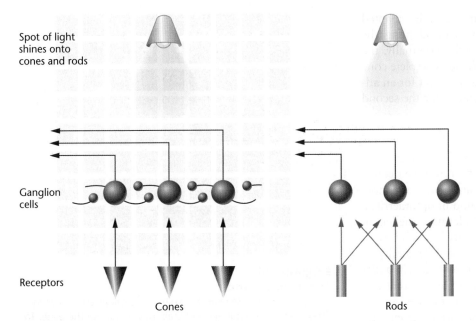

Spot of light shines onto cones and rods

Ganglion cells

Receptors

Cones

Rods

Figure 4-13
How Cones and Rods Connect to Ganglion Cells
This diagram shows a single spot of light shining onto a cone and a rod. To simplify matters, we have omitted several other types of cells located between receptors and ganglion cells. Arrows represent a signal to increase neuronal firing. Dots represent a signal to decrease neuronal firing. The long arrows emanating from the ganglion cells are axons that become part of the optic nerve.

ganglion cells. Here, however, there are no connections among ganglion cells that decrease neural activity.

To understand the implications of these wiring differences, suppose that a single spot of light is presented to either the cones or the rods. When it is presented to the cones, only one of the ganglion cells, corresponding to the location of the spot, responds. When a spot of light is presented only to the rods, however, it causes up to three ganglion cells to increase their activity. This combined activity helps to ensure that the signal reaches the brain, but there would be uncertainty about the exact location of the spot of light. The connections among ganglion cells associated with cones enhance detailed form perception under well-lit conditions; the convergence of many rods on a single ganglion cell enhances sensitivity to light under low lighting conditions. Practically speaking, you can do tasks requiring high resolution, such as reading fine print, only in good lighting, where the cones are active.

A third difference is that rods and cones are concentrated in different locations on the retina. The fovea contains many cones but no rods. The periphery, on the other hand, is rich in rods but has relatively few cones. Figure 4-11 showed one consequence of the smaller number of cones in the periphery. Viewing stars at night shows a consequence of the distribution of rods. To see a dim star as clearly as possible, you have to look slightly to one side of the star. This ensures that the light from the star activates the maximum possible number of rods.

DARK ADAPTATION Imagine yourself entering a dark movie theater from a bright street. At first you can see hardly anything in the dim light reflected from the screen. In a few minutes you can see well enough to find a seat. Eventually you can recognize faces in the dim light. This change in your ability to see in the dark is referred to as **dark adaptation.** As you spend time in the dark, the eye's pupil enlarges. More importantly, though, photochemical changes in the receptors increase the receptors' sensitivity to light.

Figure 4-14 illustrates a **dark-adaptation curve,** which shows how the absolute threshold decreases with the length of time the person is in darkness. The curve has two limbs. The upper limb reflects adaptation of the cones,

Figure 4-14
The Course of Light Adaptation
Subjects look at a bright light until the retina has become light adapted. When the subjects are then placed in darkness, they become increasingly sensitive to light, and their absolute thresholds decrease. This is called *light adaptation.* The graph shows the threshold at different times after the adapting light has been turned off. The green data points correspond to threshold flashes whose color could be seen; the purple data points correspond to flashes that appeared white regardless of the wavelength. Note the sharp break in the curve at about 10 minutes; this is called the *rod-cone break.* A variety of tests show that the first part of the curve is due to cone vision and the second part to rod vision. (Data are approximate, from various determinations.)

which takes place quite rapidly. Cones are fully adapted within about 5 minutes. While the cones are adapting, the rods are also adapting, but more slowly. Eventually, the rod adaptation catches up with the already-complete cone adaptation, but the rods then continue to adapt for an additional 25 minutes or so, which accounts for the second limb of the dark-adaptation curve.

SEEING PATTERNS

Visual acuity refers to the eye's ability to resolve details. Of the several ways of measuring visual acuity, the most common is the familiar eye chart found in optometrists' offices. This chart was devised by Herman Snellen in 1862. **Snellen acuity** is acuity measured relative to a viewer who does not need to wear glasses. An acuity of 20/20 indicates that a person can identify letters at a distance of 20 feet that a typical person can read at that distance. An acuity of 20/100 means that the viewer can read at 20 feet only those letters that are large enough for a typical viewer to read at a distance of 100 feet. In this case, visual acuity is less than normal.

The Snellen chart is not always the best way to measure acuity. First, it is not feasible for young children or other people who do not know how to read. Second, the method is designed to test acuity only for objects seen at a distance (20 feet), not acuity for reading and other close tasks. Third, the method does not distinguish between spatial acuity (the ability to see details of form) and **contrast acuity** (the ability to see differences in brightness). Figure 4-15 shows typical forms used in tests of visual acuity, with arrows pointing to the critical detail to be detected. Notice that each detail is merely a region of the field where brightness changes from light to dark (Coren, Ward, & Enns, 1999).

The sensory experience associated with viewing a pattern is determined by the way visual neurons register information about light and dark. The most primitive element of a visual pattern is the edge, or contour, the region of transition from light to dark or vice versa. One of the

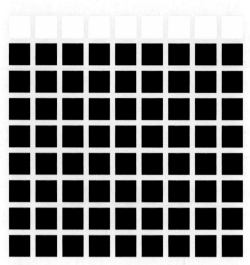

▍ Figure 4-16
The Hermann Grid
The gray smudges seen at the white intersections are illusionary. They are seen by your eye and brain but are not on the page. To convince yourself that they are not really there, move your eyes to the different intersections You will note that there is never a gray smudge at the intersection you are looking at directly. They appear in only intersections that fall on your peripheral visual field.

earliest influences on the registration of edges occurs because of the way ganglion cells in the retina interact (see Figure 4-13). The effects of these interactions can be observed by viewing a pattern known as the Hermann grid, shown in Figure 4-16. You can see gray smudges at the intersections of the white spaces separating the black squares. A disconcerting aspect of looking at this pattern is that the very intersection you are gazing at does not appear to be filled with a gray smudge; only the other intersections give the illusion of the gray smudge.

This illusion is the direct result of the connections producing decreased activity among the neighbors of active ganglion cells. A ganglion cell that is centered on one of the white intersections of the grid is receiving signals that decrease its rate of firing from neighboring ganglion cells on four sides (the cells centered in the white spaces above, below, to the right, and to the left of the intersection). A ganglion cell that is positioned on one of the white rows or columns, on the other hand, is receiving signals that decrease its rate of firing from neighboring cells on only two sides. The intersections appear darker than the white rows or columns because of the larger number of signals to decrease the rate of firing being received by ganglion cells centered there.

But why do the smudges appear only off to the side, not at the intersection you are directly looking at? The range over which the signals are sent is much smaller at the fovea than in the periphery. This arrangement contributes to greater visual acuity at the fovea than in the periphery.

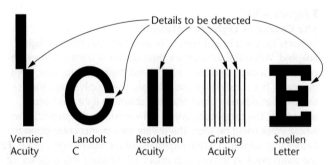

▍ Figure 4-15
Some Typical Forms Used in Tests of Visual Acuity
Arrows point to the details to be discriminated in each case.

A prism breaks up light into different wavelengths. Short wavelengths appear blue, medium wavelengths green, and long wavelengths red.

Seeing Color

All visible light (in fact, all electromagnetic radiation from gamma rays to radar waves) is alike except for wavelength. Our visual system does something wonderful with wavelength: It turns it into color, with different wavelengths resulting in different colors. Short wavelengths (450–500 nanometers) appear blue, medium wavelengths (500–570 nanometers) appear green, and long wavelengths (about 650–780 nanometers) appear red (see Figure 4-17). Our discussion of color perception considers only wavelength. This is adequate when the origin of a color sensation is an object that emits light, such as the sun or a light bulb. Usually, however, the origin of a color sensation is an object that reflects light when it is illuminated by a light source. In these cases, our perception of the object's color is determined partly by the wavelengths that the object reflects and partly by other factors, such as the surrounding context of colors. A rich variety of other colors in the spatial neighborhood of an object enables the viewer to see the correct color of an object even when the wavelengths reaching the eye from that object do not faithfully record the object's characteristic color (Brainard, 1999; Land, 1986; Maloney & Wandell, 1986). Your ability to see your favorite blue jacket as navy despite wide variations in the ambient lighting is called **color constancy**. We discuss this topic more fully in Chapter 5.

COLOR APPEARANCE Seeing color is a subjective experience in the sense that "color" is a construction of the brain based on an analysis of wavelengths of light. However, it is also objective in that any two viewers with the same kinds of color receptors (cones) appear to construct "color" in the same way. The most common way of referring to the various color experiences of a typical viewer is to organize them on three dimensions: hue, brightness, and saturation. **Hue** refers to the quality best described by the color's name, such as red or greenish yellow. **Brightness** refers to how much light appears to be reflected from a colored surface, with white the brightest possible color and black the dimmest. **Saturation** refers to the purity of the color. A fully saturated color, such as crimson, appears to contain no gray, and an unsaturated color, such as pink, appears to be a mix-

(480) Blue	(521) Green	(573) Yellow
400 nm	500 nm	600 nm	700 nm
Violet (380-450)	Blue-green	Yellow-green	Orange	Red (650-780)

❚ Figure 4-17
The Solar Spectrum
The numbers given are the wavelengths of the various colors in nanometers (nm).

▌Figure 4-18
The Color Solid
The three dimensions of color can be represented on a double cone. Hue is represented by points around the circumference, saturation by points along the radius, and brightness by points on the vertical axis. A vertical slice taken from the color solid will show differences in the saturation and lightness of a single hue. (Courtesy Macbeth/Munsell Color, New Windsor, NY)

ture of red and white. Albert Munsell, an artist, proposed a scheme for specifying colored surfaces by assigning them one of 10 hue names and two numbers, one indicating saturation and the other brightness. The colors in the **Munsell system** are represented by the color solid (see Figure 4-18). (The Concept Review Table summarizes the key characteristics of light and sound.)

Given a means of describing colors, we can ask how many colors we are capable of seeing. Within the 400–700 nanometer range to which humans are sensitive, we can discriminate among 150 hues, which suggests that we can distinguish among about 150 wavelengths. On the average, we can discriminate between two wavelengths that are only 2 nanometers apart; that is, the jnd for wavelengths is 2 nanometers. Given that each of the 150 discriminable colors can have many different values of lightness and saturation, the estimated number of colors we can discriminate is more than 7 million! Moreover, according to estimates by the National Bureau of Standards, we have names for about 7,500 of these colors. These numbers give some indication of the importance of color to our lives (Coren, Ward, & Enns, 1999).

COLOR MIXTURE All the hues we can tell apart can be generated by mixing together only three basic colors. This was demonstrated many years ago with the **color-matching experiment,** which measures an observer's inclination to see two physically different lights as having the same color. Suppose that we project different-colored lights to the same region of the retina. The result of this light mixture will be a new color. For example, a pure yellow light of 580 nanometers will appear yellow. However, a mixture of a 650-nanometer light (red), a 500-nanometer light (green), and a 450-nanometer light (blue) can be created that looks identical—literally *identical*—to the pure yellow light. This matching process can be carried out for any pure visible light whatsoever. A pair of such matching lights—that is, two lights with different physical makeups that appear identical—are called **metamers.**

Metamers provide important clues for understanding how the visual system works. The means by which a system, such as the visual system, constructs metamers reveals how the system *loses information.* In our example, the information about whether the stimulus is a mixture or a pure light is lost when they are both perceived to be the same yellow color. Although losing information may seem to be a bad thing, it is not. As we noted earlier in the chapter, we are at any instant being bombarded by an immense amount of information from the world. We do not need all of this information, or even the majority of it, to survive and flourish in the environment. If we do not elim-

CONCEPT REVIEW TABLE
The Physics and Psychology of Light and Sound

Stimulus	Physical Attribute	Measurement Unit	Psychological Experience
Light	Wavelength	Nanometers	Hue
	Intensity	Photons	Brightness
	Purity	Level of Gray	Saturation
Sound	Frequency	Hertz	Pitch
	Amplitude	Decibels	Loudness
	Complexity	Harmonics	Timbre

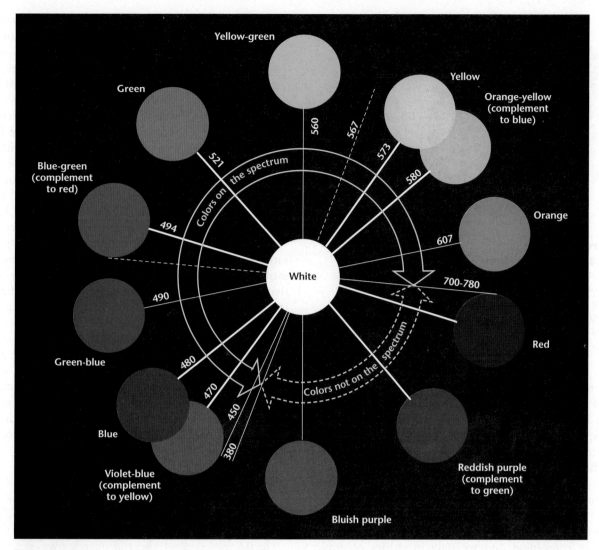

▌Figure 4-19
The Color Circle
A simple way to represent color mixture is by means of the color circle. The spectral colors (colors corresponding to wavelengths in our region of sensitivity) are represented by points around the circumference of the circle. The two ends of the spectrum do not meet; the space between them corresponds to the nonspectral reds and purples, which can be produced by mixtures of long and short wavelengths. The inside of the circle represents mixtures of lights. Lights toward the center of the circle are less saturated (or whiter); white is at the very center. Mixtures of any two lights lie along the straight line joining the two points. When this line goes through the center of the circle, the lights, when mixed in proper proportions, will look white. Such pairs of colors are called *complementary colors.*

inate much of it, we would constantly be overwhelmed by information overload. It is this information-elimination process that creates metamers. That three and exactly three primary colors are needed to match—that is, form a metamer of—any arbitrary color provides an important clue about how the visual system is constructed.

IMPLICATIONS OF THE MATCHING-BY-THREE-PRIMARIES LAW One implication of this arrangement for color mix-

ing is its important practical uses. Color reproduction in television or photography, for example, relies on the fact that a wide range of colors can be produced by mixing only three primary colors. Examined with a magnifying glass, your television screen is composed of tiny dots of only three colors (blue, green, and red). Additive color mixture occurs because the dots are so close together that their images on your retina overlap. (See Figure 4-19 for a way of representing color mixtures.)

Figure 4-20
Testing for Color Blindness
Two plates used in color blindness tests. In the left plate, individuals with certain kinds of red-green blindness see only the number 5;others see only the 7; still others, no number at all. Similarly, in the right plate, people with normal vision see the number 15, whereas those with red-green blindness see no number at all.

A second implication has to do with our understanding of color deficiencies. Although most people can match a wide range of colors with a mixture of three primaries, others can match a wide range of colors by using mixtures of only two primaries. Such people, referred to as **dichromats,** have deficient color vision. They confuse some colors that people with normal vision (trichromats) can distinguish among. But dichromats can still see color. Not so for monochromats, who are unable to discriminate among different wavelengths at all. **Monochromats** are truly color-blind and see only in shades of gray. (Screening for color blindness is done with tests like that shown in Figure 4-20, a simpler procedure than conducting color mixture experiments.) Most color deficiencies are genetic in origin. As noted in Chapter 2, color blindness occurs much more frequently in males (2%) than in females (0.03%), because the critical genes for this condition are recessive genes located on the X chromosome (Miyahara, Pokorny, & Smith, 1996; Nathans, 1987).

THEORIES OF COLOR VISION Two major theories of color vision have been suggested. The first was proposed by Thomas Young in 1807, long before scientists even knew about the existence of cones. Fifty years later, Hermann von Helmholtz further developed Young's theory. According to the Young-Helmholtz or **trichromacy theory,** even though we can discriminate among many different colors, there are only three types of receptors for color. We now know that these receptors are the cones. Each type of cone is sensitive to a wide range of

wavelengths but is most responsive within a narrower region. As shown in Figure 4-21, the short-wavelength cone is most sensitive to short wavelengths (blues), the medium-wavelength cone is most sensitive to medium wavelengths (greens and yellows), and the long-wavelength cone is most sensitive to long wavelengths (reds). The joint action of these three receptors determines the sensation of color. That is, a light of a particular wavelength stimulates the three receptors to different degrees, and the specific ratios of activity in the three receptors leads to the sensation of a specific color. The trichromatic theory holds that the quality of color is coded by the pattern of activity of three receptors rather than by specific receptors for each color.

The trichromatic theory explains the facts about color vision—and, most important, explains the result of the color-matching experiment—mentioned previously (see Wandell, 1995). First, we can discriminate among different wavelengths because they lead to different responses in the three receptors. Second, the law of three primaries follows directly from the trichromatic

Figure 4-21
The Trichromatic Theory
Response curves for the short-, medium-, and long-wave receptors proposed by trichromatic theory. These curves enable us to determine the relative response of each receptor to light of any wavelength. In the example show here, the response of each receptor to a 500-nanometer light is determined by drawing a line up from 500 nanometers and noting where this line intersects each curve. (Reprinted from "Spectral Sensitivity of the Foveal Cone Photopigments Between 400 and 500 nm," in *Vision Search, 15,* pp. 161–171. © 1975, with permission from Elsevier Science.)

theory. We can match a mixture of three widely spaced wavelengths to any color because the three widely spaced wavelengths activate the three different receptors, and activity in these receptors results in perception of the test color. (Now we see the significance of the number three.) Third, the trichromatic theory explains the various kinds of color deficiencies by positing that one or more of the three types of receptors is missing: Dichromats are missing one type of receptor, and monochromats are missing two of the three types of receptors. In addition to accounting for these long-known facts, trichromatic theory led biological researchers to a successful search for the three kinds of cones that are familiar to us today.

Despite its successes, the trichromatic theory cannot explain some well-established findings about color perception. In 1878 Ewald Hering observed that all colors may be described as consisting of one or two of the following sensations: red, green, yellow, and blue. Hering also noted that nothing is perceived to be reddish green or yellowish blue; rather, a mixture of red and green may look yellow, and a mixture of yellow and blue may look white. These observations suggested that red and green form an opponent pair, as do yellow and blue, and that the colors in an opponent pair cannot be perceived simultaneously. Further support for the notion of opponent pairs comes from studies in which an observer first stares at a colored light and then looks at a neutral surface. The observer reports seeing a color on the neutral surface that is the complement of the stared-at color (see Figure 4-22).

These phenomenological observations led Hering to propose an alternative to trichromacy theory, **opponent-color theory.** Hering believed that the visual system contains two types of color-sensitive units. One type responds to red or green, the other to blue or yellow. Each unit responds in opposite ways to its two opponent colors. The red-green unit, for example, increases its response rate when a red is presented and decreases it when a green is presented. Because a unit cannot respond in two ways at once, if two opponent colors are presented, white is perceived (see Figure 4-11). Opponent-color theory is able to explain Hering's observations about color and account for why we see the hues that we do. We perceive a single hue—red or green or yellow or blue—whenever only one type of opponent unit is out of balance, and we perceive combinations of hues when both types of units are out of balance. Nothing is perceived as red-green or as yellow-blue because a unit cannot respond in two ways at once. Moreover, the theory explains why people who first view a colored light and then stare at a neutral surface report seeing the complementary color. If the person first stares at red, for example, the red component of the unit becomes fatigued, and consequently the green component comes into play.

Each theory—trichromatic and opponent-color—can explain some facts but not others. For decades the two theories were viewed as competing, but eventually researchers proposed a two-stage theory in which the three types of receptors identified by the trichromatic theory feed into the color-opponent units at a higher level in the visual system (Hurvich & Jameson, 1974). The two-stage theory suggests that there should be neurons in the visual system that function as color-opponent units and operate on visual information after the retina (which contains the three kinds of receptors of trichromatic theory). In fact, such color-opponent neurons have been discovered in the **thalamus,** a neural way station between the retina and the visual cortex (DeValois & Jacobs, 1984). These cells are spontaneously active, increasing their activity rate in response to one range of wavelengths and decreasing it in response to another. Some cells at a higher level in the visual system fire more rapidly if the retina is stimulated by a blue light and less

▌ Figure 4-22
Complementary Afterimages
Look steadily for about a minute at the dot in the center of the colors, and then transfer your gaze to the dot in the gray field at the right. You should see a blurry image with colors that are complementary to the original. The blue, red, green, and yellow are replaced by yellow, green, red, and blue.

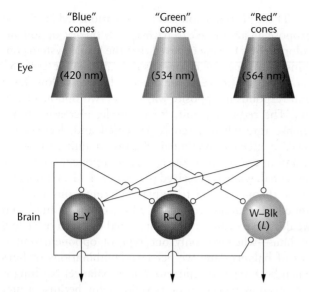

Figure 4-23
How the Trichromatic and Opponent-Process Theories May Be Related
This diagram shows three types of receptors connected to produce opponent-process neural responses at a later stage in processing. The numbers in the cones indicate wavelengths of maximum sensitivity. The lines with arrows represent connections that increase activity; the lines with dots represent connections that decrease activity. Note that this is only a small part of the whole system. Another set of opponent-process units has the reverse arrangement of increasing and decreasing connections.

rapidly when the retina is exposed to a yellow light. Such cells seem to constitute the biological basis of the blue-yellow opponent pair. A summary neural wiring diagram that shows how the trichromatic and opponent-process theories may be related is presented in Figure 4-23.

This research on color vision is a striking example of successful interaction between psychological and biological approaches to a problem. Trichromatic theory suggested that there must be three kinds of color receptors, and subsequent biological research established that there were three kinds of cones in the retina. Opponent-color theory said that there must be other kinds of units in the visual system, and biological researchers subsequently found opponent-color cells in the thalamus. Successful integration of the two theories required that the trichromatic cells feed into the opponent-color ones, and this, too, was confirmed by subsequent biological research. Outstanding work at the psychological level in these cases pointed the way for biological discoveries. It is no wonder that many scientists have taken the analysis of color vision as a prototype for the analysis of other sensory systems.

◆ Interim Summary

- The stimulus for vision is light, which is electromagnetic radiation in the range from 400 to 700 nanometers. The transduction system is in the retina, which contains the rods and cones, which are the visual receptors.

- Different wavelengths of light lead to sensations of different colors. Color vision is understood via the trichromatic theory, which holds that perception of color is based on the activity of three types of receptors (cones), each of which is most sensitive to wavelengths in a different region of the spectrum.

- There are four basic color sensations: red, yellow, green, and blue. Opponent-color theory proposes that there are red-green and yellow-blue opponent processes, each of which responds in opposite ways to its two opponent colors.

- Trichromatic and opponent-color theories have been successfully combined through the proposal that they operate at different neural locations in the visual system.

◆ Critical Thinking Questions

1. Think of an eye as analogous to a camera. What features of the eye correspond to which features of a camera?

2. Pilots preparing for flying at night often wear red goggles for an hour or so prior to their flight. Why do you suppose they do this?

3. From an evolutionary standpoint, can you think of reasons why some animals' eyes consist almost entirely of rods, other animals' eyes have only cones, and those of still others, such as humans, have both cones and rods?

HEARING

Along with vision, hearing is our major means of obtaining information about the environment. For most of us, it is the primary channel of communication as well as the vehicle for music. Hearing happens because small changes in sound pressure can move a membrane in our inner ear back and forth.

Like our discussion of vision, here we first consider the nature of the physical stimulus to which hearing is sensitive, then describe the auditory system with particular emphasis on how the receptors carry out the transduction process, and finally consider how the auditory system codes the intensity of sound and its quality.

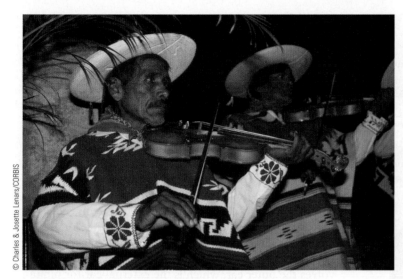
Musical instruments produce complex patterns of sound pressure. These are referred to as the sound's timbre.

SOUND WAVES

Sound originates from the motion or vibration of an object, as when the wind rushes through the branches of a tree. When something moves, the molecules of air in front of it are pushed together. These molecules push other molecules and then return to their original position. In this way, a wave of pressure changes (a sound wave) is transmitted through the air, even though the individual air molecules do not travel far. This wave is analogous to the ripples set up by throwing a stone into a pond.

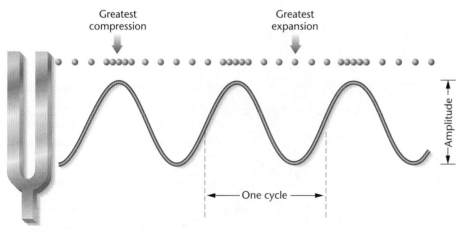

Greatest compression

Greatest expansion

Amplitude

One cycle

Figure 4-24
A Pure Tone
As the tuning fork vibrates, it produces a pure tone, which is made up of successive air-compression waves that form a sine-wave pattern. The amplitude of the wave corresponds to the wave's intensity, while the number of waves per second is its frequency. Using a technique called *Fourier analysis,* any arbitrary sound wave can be decomposed into the sum of sine waves of different frequencies and intensities.

A **sound wave** may be described by a graph of air pressure as a function of time. A pressure-versus-time graph of one type of sound is shown in Figure 4-24. The graph depicts a sine wave, familiar to anyone who has taken trigonometry. Sounds that correspond to sine waves are pure tones. An important dimension of a pure tone is the tone's **frequency,** which is the number of cycles per second (or **hertz**) at which the molecules move back and forth (see Figure 4-24). Frequency is the basis of our perception of **pitch,** which is the degree to which a sound is low or high. High-frequency tones take the form of high-frequency sine waves (like the 5,000 hertz sine wave shown in Figure 4-24); lower-frequency tones take the form of low-frequency sound waves (such as the 500 cycle/second sine wave shown in Figure 4-24). Sine waves are important in the analysis of hearing because, as proved by the French mathematician Fourier, any complex sound can be decomposed into pure tones and represented as a weighted sum of a series of different-frequency sine waves.

A second aspect of a pure tone is its **amplitude,** the pressure difference between the peak and the trough in a pressure-versus-time graph (see Figure 4-24). Amplitude underlies our sensation of **loudness,** which is how intense a sound appears to be. Sound amplitude is usually specified in a **decibel scale,** a logarithmic scale of loudness. An increase of 10 decibels corresponds to a 10-fold increase in amplitude above the sound's threshold; 20 decibels, a 100-fold increase; 30 decibels, a 1,000-fold increase; and so forth. For example, a soft whisper in a quiet library is approximately 30 decibels, a noisy restaurant may have a level of 70 decibels, a rock concert may be near 120 decibels, and a jet taking off may be over 140 decibels. Consistent exposure to sound levels at or above 100 decibels is associated with permanent hearing loss.

A final aspect of sound is timbre, which refers to our experience of the complexity of a sound. Almost none of the sounds we hear every day is as simple as the pure tones we have been discussing. (The exceptions are tuning forks and some electronic instruments.) Sounds produced by acoustical instruments, automobiles, the human voice, other animals, and wa-

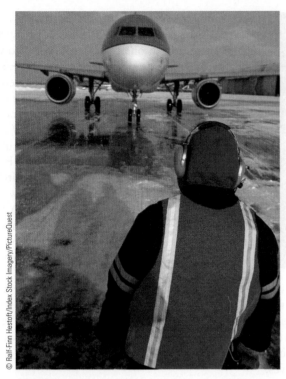

Prolonged exposure to loud noises can cause permanent hearing loss. This is why airport workers always wear ear protectors.

terfalls are characterized by complex patterns of sound pressure. The difference in timbre is, for example, what makes a middle C produced by a violin sound different from a middle C produced by a trombone.

THE AUDITORY SYSTEM

The **auditory system** is the ears, parts of the brain, and the various connecting neural pathways. Our primary concern is the ears, including not only the appendages on the sides of the head but also the entire hearing organ, most of which lies within the skull (see Figure 4-25).

Like the eye, the ear contains two systems. One system amplifies and transmits the sound to the receptors, where the other system takes over and transduces the sound into neural impulses. The transmission system involves the **outer ear,** which is the external ear (or pinna,) along with the auditory canal, and the **middle ear,** which is the eardrum and a chain of three bones, the malleus, incus, and stapes. The transduction system is housed in a part of the inner ear called the *cochlea,* which contains the receptors for sound.

Figure 4-26 details the transmission system. The outer ear aids in the collection of sound, funneling it through the auditory canal to a taut membrane, the

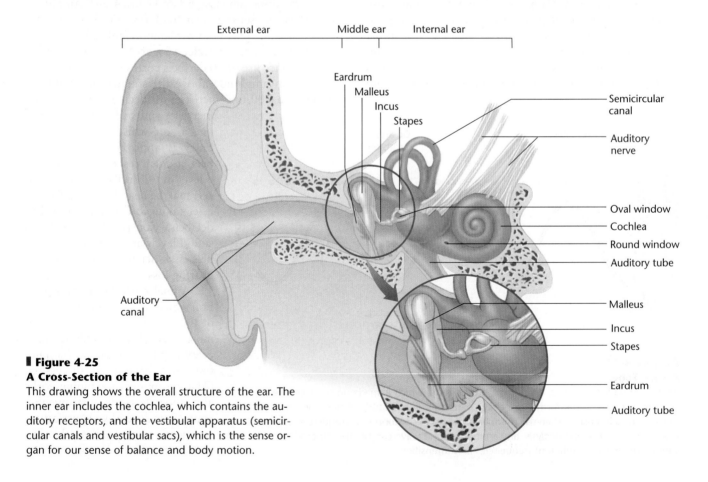

▌ Figure 4-25
A Cross-Section of the Ear
This drawing shows the overall structure of the ear. The inner ear includes the cochlea, which contains the auditory receptors, and the vestibular apparatus (semicircular canals and vestibular sacs), which is the sense organ for our sense of balance and body motion.

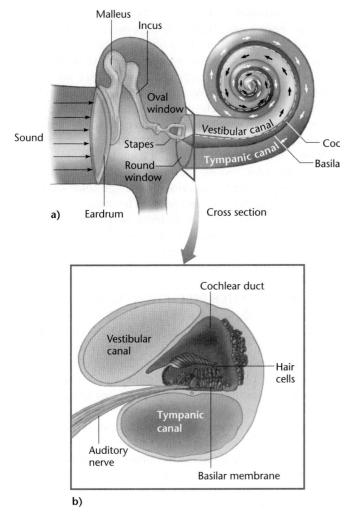

Figure 4-26
A Schematic Diagram of the Middle and Inner Ear
(a) Movement of the fluid within the cochlea deforms the basilar membrane and stimulates the hair cells that serve as the auditory receptors. (b) A cross-section of the cochlea showing the basilar membrane and the hair cell receptors. (From *Sensation and Perception*, 3/e, by S. Coren and L. Ward, © 1989. Used by permission of John Wiley and Sons, Inc.)

eardrum. The eardrum, the outermost part of the middle ear, is caused to vibrate by sound waves funneled to it through the auditory canal. The middle ear's job is to transmit these vibrations of the eardrum across an air-filled cavity to another membrane, the **oval window**, which is the gateway to the inner ear and the receptors. A mechanical bridge made up of three small bones, the **malleus, incus,** and **stapes,** accomplishes this transmission. The vibrations of the eardrum move the first bone, which then moves the second, which in turn moves the third, which results in vibrations of the oval window. This mechanical arrangement not only transmits the sound wave but greatly amplifies it as well.

Now consider the transduction system. The **cochlea** is a coiled tube of bone. It is divided into sections of fluid by membranes, one of which, the **basilar membrane,** supports the auditory receptors (Figure 4-26). The receptors are called **hair cells** because they have hairlike structures that extend into the fluid of the ear. Pressure at the oval window (which connects the middle and inner ear) leads to pressure changes in the cochlear fluid, which in turn causes the basilar membrane to vibrate, resulting in a bending of the hair cells and an electrical impulse. Through this complex process, a sound wave is, at last, transduced into an electrical impulse. The neurons that synapse with the hair cells have long axons that form part of the auditory nerve. Most of these auditory neurons connect to single hair cells. There are about 31,000 auditory neurons in the auditory nerve, many fewer than the 1 million neurons in the optic nerve (Yost & Nielson, 1985). The auditory pathway from each ear goes to both sides of the brain and has synapses in several nuclei before reaching the auditory cortex.

HEARING SOUND INTENSITY

Recall that our vision is more sensitive to some wavelengths than to others. A similar phenomenon occurs in hearing. We are more sensitive to sounds of intermediate frequency than we are to sounds near either end of our frequency range. Figure 4-27 shows the absolute threshold for sound intensity as a function of frequency. Many people have some deficit in hearing

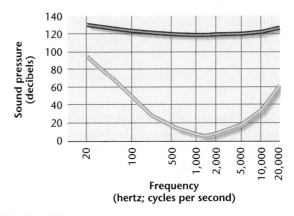

Figure 4-27
Absolute Threshold for Hearing
The lower curve shows the absolute intensity threshold at different frequencies. Sensitivity is greatest in the vicinity of 1,000 hertz. The upper curve describes the threshold for pain. (Data are approximate, from various determinations.)

and consequently have a threshold higher than those shown in the figure. There are two basic kinds of hearing deficits. In one kind, conduction loss, thresholds are elevated roughly equally at all frequencies as the result of poor conduction in the middle ear. In the other kind, sensory-neural loss, the threshold elevation is unequal, with large elevations at higher frequencies. This pattern is usually a consequence of inner ear damage, often involving some destruction of the hair cells, which are unable to regenerate. Sensory-neural loss occurs in many older people and explains why the elderly often have trouble hearing high-pitched sounds. Sensory-neural loss is not limited to the elderly, though. It also occurs in young people who are exposed to excessively loud sound. Rock musicians, airport runway crews, and pneumatic drill operators commonly suffer major, permanent hearing loss. For example, Pete Townshend, the well-known guitarist of the 1970s rock group The Who, suffered severe sensory-neural loss because of his continuous exposure to loud rock music. He has since alerted many young people to this danger.

It is natural to assume that the perceived intensity of a sound is the same at both ears, but in fact there are subtle differences. A sound originating to the right, for example, will be heard as more intense by the right ear than by the left ear. The head causes a "sound shadow" that decreases the intensity of the sound reaching the far ear. This difference does not interfere with our ability to hear, but we take advantage of it to localize where the sound is coming from. It is as if we said, "If the sound is more intense at my right ear than at my left ear, it must be coming from my right side." Likewise, a sound originating on the right side arrives at the right ear a split-second before it reaches the left ear (and vice versa for a sound originating on the left). We also take advantage of this difference to localize the sound ("If the sound arrived at my right ear first, it must be coming from the right").

HEARING PITCH

One of the primary psychological qualities of a sound is its pitch, a sensation based on the frequency of a sound. As frequency increases, so does pitch. Young adults can detect pure tone frequencies between 20 and 20,000 hertz, with the jnd less than 1 hertz at 100 hertz and increasing to 100 hertz at 10,000 hertz.

With sound, as with light, we rarely have opportunities to hear pure sensory stimuli. Recall that for the visual system we usually see mixtures of wavelengths rather than a pure stimulus—a light of only one wavelength (an exception is the light emitted by a laser). A

similar situation characterizes the auditory system. We rarely hear a pure tone. Instead, we are usually confronted by a sound made up of a mixture of tones. However, here the light-sound analogy begins to break down. When we mix wavelengths of light, we see an entirely new color, but when we mix pure tones together, often we can still hear each of the components separately, especially if the tones are widely separated in frequency. When the frequencies are close together, the sensation is more complex but still does not sound like a single, pure tone. In color vision, the fact that a mixture of three lights results in the sensation of a single color led to the idea of three types of receptors. The absence of a comparable phenomenon in hearing suggests that, rather than there being relatively few receptors specialized for relatively few different frequencies, sound-frequency receptors must form more of a continuum.

THEORIES OF PITCH PERCEPTION As with color vision, two kinds of theories have been proposed to account for how the ear codes frequency into pitch. The first was suggested in 1886 by Lord Rutherford, a British physicist. Rutherford proposed that a sound wave causes the entire basilar membrane to vibrate and that the rate of vibration determines the rate of impulses of nerve fibers in the auditory nerve. A 1,000-hertz tone causes the basilar membrane to vibrate 1,000 times per second, which causes nerve fibers in the auditory nerve to fire at 1,000 impulses per second, and the brain interprets this as a particular pitch. Because this theory proposes that pitch depends on how sound varies with time, it is called a **temporal theory.**

Rutherford's hypothesis was quickly discovered to be overly simplistic when experiments determined that nerve fibers have a maximum firing rate of about 1,000 impulses per second. If Rutherford's hypothesis were correct, we could not perceive the pitch of tones whose frequency exceeds 1,000 hertz—which, of course, we *can* do. Weaver (1949) proposed a way to salvage Rutherford's hypothesis. Weaver argued that frequencies above 1,000 hertz could be coded by different groups of nerve fibers, each group firing at a slightly different pace. If one group of neurons is firing at 1,000 impulses per second, for example, and then 1 millisecond later a second group of neurons begins firing at 1,000 impulses per second, the combined rate of impulses per second for the two groups is 2,000 impulses per second. This version of temporal theory received support from the discovery that the *pattern* of nerve impulses in the auditory nerve follows the waveform of the stimulus tone, even though individual cells do not respond on every cycle of the wave (Rose, Brugge, Anderson, & Hind, 1967).

While clever, this hypothesis is still insufficient. The ability of nerve fibers to follow the waveform breaks down at about 4,000 hertz—yet we can hear pitch at much higher frequencies. There must be another means of coding the quality of pitch, at least for high frequencies, and the second kind of theory of pitch perception deals with this question. It dates back to 1683, when the French anatomist Joseph Guichard Duverney proposed that frequency is coded into pitch mechanically by **resonance,** the degree to which a sound of a particular frequency reverberates over a mathematically matched distance (Green & Wier, 1984). To appreciate this proposal, consider an example of resonance. When a tuning fork is struck near a piano, the piano string that is tuned to the frequency of the fork begins to vibrate. To say that the ear works the same way is to say that the ear contains a structure like a stringed instrument, with different parts tuned to different frequencies, so that when a frequency is presented to the ear the corresponding part of the structure vibrates. This idea proved to be roughly correct, and the structure turned out to be the basilar membrane.

In the 1800s the ubiquitous Hermann von Helmholtz (remember him from color-vision theory?) developed this hypothesis further, eventually proposing the **place theory of pitch perception,** which holds that each specific place along the basilar membrane will lead to a particular pitch sensation. The fact that there are many such places on the membrane is consistent with there being many different receptors for pitch. Place theory does not imply that we hear with our basilar membrane. Rather, the places on the membrane that vibrate most determine which neural fibers are activated, and that determines the pitch we hear. This is an example of a sensory modality coding quality according to the specific nerves involved.

How the basilar membrane actually moves was not established until the 1940s, when Georg von Békésy measured its movement through small holes drilled in the cochleas of guinea pigs and human cadavers. Von Békésy's findings required a modification of place theory: Rather than behaving like a piano with separate strings, the basilar membrane behaves more like a bed sheet being shaken at one end. Specifically, von Békésy showed that the whole membrane moves for most frequencies but that the place of maximum movement depends on the specific frequency sounded. High frequencies cause vibration at the near end of the basilar membrane; as frequency increases, the vibration pattern moves toward the oval window (von Békésy, 1960). For this and other research on hearing, von Békésy received a Nobel prize in 1961.

Like temporal theories, place theories explain many pitch-perception phenomena, but not all. A major difficulty for place theory arises with low-frequency tones. With frequencies below 50 hertz, all parts of the basilar membrane vibrate about equally. This means that all the receptors are equally activated, which implies that we have no way of discriminating between different frequencies that are below 50 hertz. In fact, we can discern frequencies as low as 20 hertz. Overall, place theories have problems explaining our perception of low-frequency tones, and temporal theories have problems dealing with high-frequency tones. These difficulties led to the idea that pitch depends on both place and temporal pattern, with temporal theory explaining our perception of low frequencies and place theory explaining our perception of high frequencies. It is not clear, however, where one mechanism leaves off and the other takes over. Indeed, frequencies between 1,000 and 5,000 hertz might be handled by both mechanisms (Coren, Ward, & Enns, 1999).

Because our ears and eyes are so important to us in our day-to-day lives, many efforts have been made to develop replacements for individuals who suffer irreparable damage to these organs. Some of these efforts are described in the Cutting Edge Research feature.

◆ Interim Summary

- The stimulus for hearing is a wave of pressure changes (a sound wave).
- Sound waves are transduced by the outer and middle ear, causing the basilar membrane to vibrate, which results in a bending of the hair cells that produces a neural impulse.
- Pitch, the most striking quality of sound, increases with the frequency of the sound wave.
- There are two theories of pitch perception: temporal theories and place theories. These theories are not mutually exclusive. Temporal theory explains perception of low frequencies, and place theory accounts for perception of high frequencies.

◆ Critical Thinking Questions

1. Consider the relation between the eye and the ear. Each organ is made up of various components that perform various functions. What are the correspondences between the eye components and the ear components in terms of the functions they perform?

2. Why do you suppose that high-frequency sounds are heard poorly by older adults rather than low- or medium-frequency tones?

CUTTING-EDGE RESEARCH
Artificial Ears and Eyes

The science fiction fantasy of replacing defective sense organs with artificial ones is becoming a reality. Researchers have been working on artificial replacements (called *prostheses*) for damaged eyes and ears for several years.

Research on auditory prostheses has concentrated on devices that electrically stimulate the auditory nerve. They are designed to aid people whose hair cells have been destroyed but whose auditory nerve is intact and functional. Most of these devices insert an electrode through the round window into the cochlea to stimulate the neurons along basilar membrane; this is known as a cochlear implant. The implant is a series of electrodes placed at different points inside the cochlea. A small microphone is worn by the deaf person, along with a microchip that analyzes the frequencies and sends a small electrical signal to the appropriate place inside the cochlea. This stimulation mimics the way traveling waves stimulate the hair cells for various frequencies (Schindler & Merzenich, 1985).

Cochlear implants have now been placed in more than 10,000 profoundly deaf people. Most of the recipients can discriminate among frequencies of sounds quite well (Townshend, Cotter, Van Compernolle, & White, 1987), and many can recognize speech sounds, especially when a specialized speech preprocessor is included on the microchip to isolate certain speech-relevant fre-

quency changes (Blamey, Dowell, Brown, Clark, & Seligman, 1987). Interestingly, there may be a "critical period" or optimum time to implant these devices. Deaf children who received one before age 5 were able to learn speech more easily than children who received one at a later age (Tye-Murray, Spencer, & Woodworth, 1995). However, among adults, those who have become deaf later in life seem to benefit more than those who have been deaf from an early age (Busby, Tong, & Clark, 1993). The advantage for very young children is probably due to the fact that their brain centers for hearing and speech are still undergoing major developmental changes. In adults, the older they are when they become deaf, the greater the opportunity they have had to hear a variety of speech sounds, which prepares them to understand the strange new sounds generated by the implant.

There is some promise that cochlear implants will eventually allow a full range of hearing experience for people with this form of deafness (Miller & Spelman, 1990). There is even hope for people who lack a functioning auditory nerve, because more central implants, placed farther along the pathway to the brain, are currently being tested (Shannon & Otto, 1990).

The development of artificial eyes for the blind has not progressed as far as the development of artificial ears. The problem is not a matter of acquiring the optical image; a video camera can do this well. Rather, the problem is how to put the image information into the visual system in a form that the brain can use. Research has focused on direct elec-

trical stimulation of the visual cortex in volunteers who are either blind or undergoing brain surgery. If we know what a person sees when different places in the cortex are electrically stimulated, it should be possible to evoke different visual experiences by controlling the stimulation. The next step would be to use a video camera to form an image of the scene in front of the blind person and then evoke an experience of that scene in the brain.

Results thus far suggest that we are a long way from developing an artificial eye. When a small region of the visual cortex is stimulated with a weak electrical signal, the person experiences rudimentary visual sensations. These have been described as small spots of light ranging in size from that of a grain of rice to that of a coin. Most are white, but some are colored. If several places in the visual cortex are stimulated simultaneously, the corresponding spots are usually experienced together. Although multiple stimulation of the visual cortex provides the basis for a crude form of pattern vision (Dobelle, Meadejovsky, & Girvin, 1974), it is questionable whether this approach will lead to a successful prosthesis for damaged eyes. The neural input to the visual cortex is so complicated that it is unlikely to be adequately duplicated by artificial means.

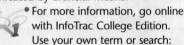 For more information, go online with InfoTrac College Edition. Use your own term or search:

- Acoustic nerve
- Cochlear implants
- Deafness
- Ear

OTHER SENSES

Senses other than vision and hearing lack the richness of patterning and organization that have led sight and hearing to be called the "higher senses." Still, these other senses are vitally important. Smell, for example, is one of the most primitive and most important of the senses, probably because smell has a more direct route to the brain than any other sense. The receptors, which

are in the nasal cavity, are connected to the brain without synapses. Moreover, unlike the receptors for vision and hearing, the receptors for smell are exposed directly to the environment—they are right there in the nasal cavity with no protective shield in front of them. (In contrast, the receptors for vision are behind the cornea, and those for hearing are protected by the outer and middle ear.) Because smell is clearly an important sen-

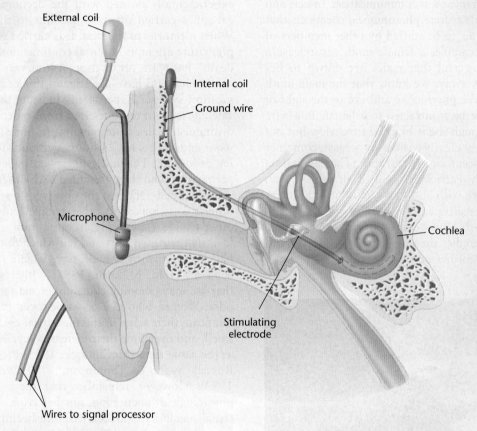

External coil

Internal coil

Ground wire

Microphone

Cochlea

Stimulating electrode

Wires to signal processor

The Cochlear Implant
This diagram illustrates the auditory prosthesis developed by William House and his associates. Sound is picked up by a microphone and filtered by a signal processor (not shown) worn outside the body. The electrical waveform produced by the processor is transmitted by radio waves through the skull to the electrode inside the brain.

sory modality, we begin our discussion of the other senses with it.

SMELL

Smell aids in the survival of our species. It is needed to detect spoiled food or escaping gas, and loss of the sense of smell can lead to a dulled appetite. Smell is even more essential for the survival of many other animals. Not surprisingly, then, a larger area of the cortex is devoted to smell in other species than in our own. In fish, the olfactory cortex makes up almost all of the cerebral hemispheres; in dogs, about 33%; in humans, only about 5%. These variations are related to differences in sensitivity to smell. Taking advantage of the superior smell capability of dogs, both the U.S. Postal Service and the Bureau of Customs have trained them to check unopened packages for heroin. Specially trained police dogs can sniff out hidden explosives.

Because smell is so well developed in other species, it is often used as a means of communication. Insects and some other animals secrete **pheromones,** chemicals that float through the air to be sniffed by other members of the species. For example, a female moth can release a pheromone so powerful that males are drawn to her from several miles away. We know that the male moth responds only to the pheromone and not to the sight of the female because he is attracted to a female in a wire container even though she is blocked from view but not to a female that is clearly visible in a glass container from which the scent cannot escape. (The fascinating novel *Perfume,* by Patrick Süskind, dealt with a man who, although born with absolutely no odor of his own, was exquisitely sensitive to all odors of the world. To others he seemed to have "extrasensory" powers, such as the ability to predict the imminent arrival of an unseen person by his or her odor.)

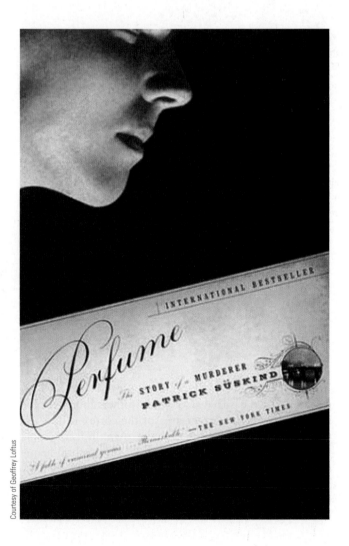

Courtesy of Geoffrey Loftus

Insects use smell to communicate death as well as "love." After an ant dies, the chemicals formed from its decomposing body stimulate other ants to carry the corpse to a refuse heap outside the nest. If a living ant is experimentally doused with the decomposition chemicals, it is carried off by other ants to the refuse heap. When it returns to the nest, it is carried out again. Such premature attempts at burial continue until the "smell of death" has worn off (Wilson, 1963).

Do humans have a vestige of this primitive communication system? Experiments indicate that we can use smell at least to tell ourselves from other people and to distinguish males from females. In one study, observers wore undershirts for 24 hours without showering or using deodorant. The undershirts were collected by the experimenter, who then presented each observer with three shirts to smell. One was the observer's own shirt, and the other two belonged to other people, one male and the other female. Based only on odor, most observers could identify their own shirt and tell which of the other shirts had been worn by a male or a female (Russell, 1976; Schleidt, Hold, & Attili, 1981). Other studies suggest that we may communicate subtler matters by means of odor. Women who live or work together seem to communicate their stage in the menstrual cycle by means of smell, and over time their menstrual cycles tend to begin at the same time (McClintock, 1971; Preti et al., 1986; Russell, Switz, & Thompson, 1980; Weller & Weller, 1993). However, remember that these are effects on physiological functioning, not behavior. Although menstrual regularity is associated with healthy reproductive functioning and fertility, it does not have a direct influence on human behavior. Indeed, many researchers now believe that the behavioral effects of pheromones on humans are likely to be indirect, because social and learning factors influence our behavior more than they do that of other mammals (Coren, Ward, & Enns, 1999).

THE SMELL SYSTEM The volatile molecules given off by a substance are the stimuli for smell. The molecules leave the substance, travel through the air, and enter the nasal passage (see Figure 4-28). The molecules must also be soluble in fat, because the receptors for smell are covered with a fatlike substance.

The **olfactory system** is the receptors in the nasal passage, certain regions of the brain, and interconnecting neural pathways. The receptors for smell are located high in the nasal cavity. When the cilia (hairlike structures) of these receptors come into contact with volatile molecules, an electrical impulse results. This is the transduction process (see Bozza & Mombaerts, 2001, for a description of the neural encoding). This impulse travels along nerve fibers to the **olfactory bulb,** a region of the brain that lies just below the frontal lobes. The olfactory

Frontal lobe of cerebrum

Olfactory tract

Olfactory bulb

Olfactory nerves

Olfactory epithelium

Cilia

a)

Substance being smelled

b)

▌Figure 4-28
Olfactory Receptors

(a) Detail of a receptor interspersed among numerous supporting cells. (b) The placement of the olfactory receptors in the nasal cavity.

bulb in turn is connected to the **olfactory cortex on the inside of the temporal lobes.** (Interestingly, there is a direct connection between the olfactory bulb and the part of the cortex known to be involved in the formation of long-term memories; perhaps this is related to the idea that a distinctive smell can be a powerful aid in retrieving an old memory.)

SENSING INTENSITY AND QUALITY Human sensitivity to the intensity of a smell depends on the substance involved. Absolute thresholds can be as low as 1 part per 50 billion parts of air. Still, we are far less sensitive to smell than other species. Dogs, for example, can detect substances in concentrations 100 times lower than those that can be detected by humans (Marshall, Blumer, & Moulton, 1981). Our relative lack of sensitivity is not due to our having less sensitive olfactory receptors. Rather, we just have fewer of them by about a factor of 100: roughly 10 million receptors for humans versus 1 billion for dogs.

Although we rely less on smell than do other species, we are capable of sensing many different qualities of odor. Estimates vary, but a healthy person appears to be able to distinguish among 10,000 to 40,000 different odors, with women generally doing better than men (Cain, 1988). Professional perfumers and whiskey blenders can probably do even better—discriminating among perhaps 100,000 odors (Dobb, 1989). Moreover, we know something about how the olfactory system codes the quality of odors at the biological level. The sit-

uation is most unlike the coding of color in vision, for which three kinds of receptors suffice. In smell, many kinds of receptors—an estimate of 1,000 kinds of olfactory receptors is not unreasonable—seem to be involved (Buck & Axel, 1991). Rather than coding a specific odor, each kind of receptor may respond to many different odors (Matthews, 1972). So quality may be partly coded by the pattern of neural activity, even in this receptor-rich sensory modality.

Dogs are far more sensitive to smells than humans, and for this reason they were used in the aftermath of the World Trade Center disaster for the search-and-rescue operation and bomb detection.

Humans vary in their sensitivity to different tastes. Some people, like this coffee taster, are able to discriminate among very subtle differences in the tastes of particular substances.

TASTE

The sense of taste gets credit for a lot of experiences that it does not provide. We say that a meal "tastes" good; but when our ability to smell is eliminated by a bad cold, food seems to lack taste and we may have trouble telling red wine from vinegar. Still, taste is a sense in its own right. Even with a bad cold, we can tell salted from unsalted food.

In what follows, we refer to the taste of particular substances, but note that the substance being tasted is not the only factor that determines its taste. Our genetic makeup and experience also affect taste. For example, people vary in their sensitivity to the bitter taste in caffeine and saccharin, and this difference appears to be genetically determined (Bartoshuk, 1979, 2000). The role of experience is illustrated by people living in the Karnataka province of India, who eat many sour foods and experience citric acid and quinine (the taste of tonic water) as pleasant tasting. Most Westerners experience the opposite sensations. This particular difference seems to be a matter of experience, for Indians raised in Western countries find citric acid and quinine unpleasant tasting (Moskowitz, Kumraich, Sharma, Jacobs, & Sharma, 1975).

THE TASTE SYSTEM The stimulus for taste is a substance that is soluble in saliva. The gustatory system includes **taste receptors** that are located on the tongue, throat, and roof of the mouth, as well as parts of the brain and interconnecting neural pathways. In what follows, we focus on the receptors on the tongue. These taste receptors occur in clusters, called *taste buds*, on the bumps of the tongue and around the mouth. At the ends of the taste buds are short, hairlike structures that extend outward and make contact with the solutions in the mouth. The contact results in an electrical impulse, the transduction process. The electrical impulse then travels to the brain.

SENSING INTENSITY AND QUALITY Sensitivity to different taste stimuli varies from place to place on the tongue. Although any substance can be detected at almost any place on the tongue (except the center), different tastes are best detected in different regions. Sensitivity to salty and sweet substances is best near the front of the tongue, sensitivity to sour substances along the sides, and sensitivity to bitter substances is best on the soft palate (see Figure 4-29). In the center of the tongue is a region that is insensitive to taste (the place to put an unpleasant pill). Although absolute thresholds for taste are generally very low, jnds for intensity are relatively high (Weber's constant is often about 0.2). If you are increasing the amount of spice in a dish, you usually must add more than 20% to be able to taste the difference.

Recent research suggests that "tongue maps," such as the one in Figure 4-29, may be oversimplified in that they suggest that if the nerves leading to a particular region were cut, all sensation would be lost. However, this does not occur because taste nerves inhibit one another. Damaging one nerve abolishes its ability to inhibit others. If you cut the nerves to a particular region, you also reduce the inhibitory effect, and the result is little change in the everyday experience of taste (Bartoshuk, 1993).

There is an agreed-upon vocabulary for describing tastes. Any taste can be described as one or a combination of the four basic taste qualities: sweet, sour, salty, and bitter (McBurney, 1978). These four tastes are best revealed in sucrose (sweet), hydrochloric acid (sour), sodium chloride (salty), and quinine (bitter). When people are asked to describe the tastes of various substances

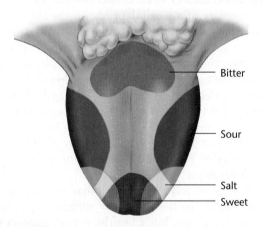

▌Figure 4-29
Taste Areas
Although any substance can be detected anywhere on the tongue—except in the center—different areas are maximally sensitive to different tastes. The area labeled "sweet," for example, is most sensitive to sweet tastes. (E. H. Erickson, "Sensory Neural Patterns in Gustation," from Zotterman (ed.) *Olfaction and Taste*, Vol. 1, p. 205–213. Copyright © 1963, with kind permission of Elsevier Science, Ltd.)

in terms of just the four basic tastes, they have no trouble. Even if they are given the option of using additional qualities of their own choice, they tend to stay with the four basic tastes (Goldstein, 1989).

The gustatory system codes taste in terms of both the specific nerve fibers activated and the pattern of activation across nerve fibers. There appear to be four types of nerve fibers, corresponding to the four basic tastes. Although each fiber responds somewhat to all four basic tastes, it responds best to just one of them, and it makes sense to talk of "salty fibers" whose activity signals saltiness to the brain. There is a remarkable correspondence between our subjective experience of taste and its neural coding.

PRESSURE AND TEMPERATURE

Traditionally, touch was thought to be a single sense. Today, it is considered to include three distinct skin senses, one responding to pressure, another to temperature, and the third to pain. This section briefly considers pressure and temperature, and the next discusses pain.

PRESSURE The stimulus for sensed pressure is physical pressure on the skin. Although we are not aware of steady pressure on the entire body (such as air pressure), we can discriminate among variations in pressure over the surface of the body. Some parts of the body are more sensitive than others at sensing the intensity of pressure. The lips, nose, and cheek are the most sensitive, while the big toe is least sensitive. These differences are closely related to the number of receptors that respond to the stimulus at each of these locations. In sensitive regions, we can detect a force as small as 5 milligrams applied to a small area. However, like other sensory systems, the pressure system shows profound adaptation effects. If you hold a friend's hand for several minutes without moving, you will become insensitive to its pressure and cease to feel it.

When we are actively exploring the environment through touch, the motor senses contribute to our experience. Through active touch alone we can readily identify familiar objects such as coins and keys (Klatzky, Lederman, & Metzger, 1985).

TEMPERATURE The stimulus for temperature is the temperature of our skin. The receptors are neurons just under the skin. In the transduction stage, cold receptors generate a neural impulse when there is a decrease in skin temperature, and warm receptors generate an impulse when there is an increase in skin temperature (Duclaux & Kenshalo, 1980; Hensel, 1973). Therefore, different qualities of temperature can be coded primarily by the specific receptors activated. However, this specificity of neural reaction has its limits. Cold receptors respond not only to low temperatures but also to very high

After being in a swimming pool for a while, our temperature sense adapts to the change in temperature. However, when first dangling a foot into the water, we can detect the cooler temperature.

temperatures (above 45 degrees centigrade or 113 degrees Fahrenheit). Consequently, a very hot stimulus will activate both warm and cold receptors, as you may have experienced when you accidentally plunged your foot into a very hot bath.

Because maintaining body temperature is crucial to survival, we must be able to sense small changes in our skin temperature. When the skin is at its normal temperature, we can detect a warming of only 0.4 degrees centigrade and a cooling of just 0.15 degrees centigrade (Kenshalo, Nafe, & Brooks, 1961). Our temperature sense adapts completely to moderate changes in temperature, so that after a few minutes the stimulus feels neither cool nor warm. This adaptation explains the strong differences of opinion about the temperature of a swimming pool between those who have been in it for a while and those who are first dangling a foot in it.

PAIN

Of all our senses, none captures our attention like pain. We may sometimes take a blasé view of the other senses, but it is hard to ignore pain. Yet for all the discomfort it causes, we would be at risk without a sense of pain. Children would not learn not to touch a hot stove or to stop chewing their tongues. In fact, some people are born with a rare genetic disorder called *congenital insensitivity to pain* that makes them insensitive to pain, and they typically die young, owing to tissue deterioration resulting from wounds that could have been avoided if they had been able to feel pain.

THE PAIN SYSTEM Any stimulus that is intense enough to cause tissue damage is a stimulus for pain. It may be pressure, temperature, electric shock, or chemical irritants. Such a stimulus causes the release of chemical substances in the skin, which in turn stimulate distinct high-threshold receptors (the transduction stage). These receptors are neurons with specialized free nerve endings, and researchers have identified several types (Brown & Deffenbacher, 1979). With regard to variations in the quality of pain, perhaps the most important distinction is between the kind of pain we feel immediately upon suffering an injury, called **phasic pain,** and the kind we experience after the injury has occurred, called *tonic pain.* Phasic pain is typically a sharp, immediate pain that is brief in duration (it rapidly rises and falls in intensity), whereas **tonic pain** is typically a dull and long-lasting pain. If you sprain your ankle, you immediately feel a sharp undulating pain (phasic pain), but after a while you start to feel the steady pain caused by the swelling (tonic pain). The two kinds of pain are mediated by two distinct neural pathways, and these pathways eventually reach different parts of the cortex (Melzack, 1990).

NONSTIMULUS DETERMINANTS OF PAIN More than any other sensation, the intensity and quality of pain are influenced by factors other than the immediate stimulus, such as the person's culture, expectations, and previous experience (see, for example, Arntz, Dresson, & De Jong, 1994; Price, 2000). The striking influence of culture is illustrated by some rituals non-Western societies engage in that seem unbearably painful to Westerners. A case in point is the hook-swinging ceremony practiced in some parts of India:

> The ceremony derives from an ancient practice in which a member of a social group is chosen to represent the power of the gods. The role of the chosen man (or "celebrant") is to bless the children and crops in a series of neighboring villages during a particular period of the year. What is remarkable about the ritual is that steel hooks, which are attached by strong ropes to the top of a special cart, are shoved under his skin and muscles on both sides of his back [see Figure 4-30]. The cart is then moved from village to village. Usually the man hangs on to the ropes as the cart is moved about. But at the climax of the ceremony in each village, he swings free, hanging only from the hooks embedded in his back, to bless the children and crops. Astonishingly, there is no evidence that the man is in pain during the ritual; rather, he appears to be in a "state of exaltation." When the hooks are later removed, wounds heal rapidly without any medical treatment other than the application of wood ash. Two weeks later the marks on his back are scarcely visible. (Melzack, 1973)

Clearly, pain is as much a matter of mind as of sensory receptors.

Phenomena like the one just described have led to the **gate control theory of pain** (Melzack & Wall, 1982, 1988). According to this theory, the sensation of pain requires not only that pain receptors on the skin be active but also that a "neural gate" in the spinal cord be open and allow the signals from the pain receptors to pass to the brain (the gate closes when critical fibers in the spinal cord are activated). Because the neural gate can be closed by signals sent down from the cortex, the perceived intensity of pain can be reduced by the person's mental state, as in the hook-swinging ceremony. What exactly is the "neural gate"? It appears to involve a region of the midbrain called the **periaqueductal gray,** or PAG for short. Neurons in the PAG are connected to other neurons that inhibit cells that would normally carry the pain signals arising in the pain receptors. So when the PAG neurons are active, the gate is closed; when the PAG neurons are not active, the gate is open.

Interestingly, the PAG appears to be the main place where strong painkillers such as morphine affect neural processing. Morphine is known to increase neural activity in the PAG, which should result in a closing of the neural gate, so the well-known analgesic effects of morphine fit with the gate control theory. Moreover, our body produces certain chemicals, called *endorphins,* that act like morphine to reduce pain, and these chemicals, too, are believed to create their effect by acting on the PAG to close the neural gate.

❚ Figure 4-30
Culture and Pain
Two steel hooks are inserted in the back of the celebrant in the Indian hook-swinging ceremony. *Right:* The celebrant hangs onto the ropes as a cart takes him from village to village. As he blesses the village children and crops, he swings freely suspended by the hooks in his back. (D. D. Kosambi (1967) "Living Prehistory in India," from *Scientific American 215*:105. Copyright © 1967 by D. D. Kosambi. Reprinted by permission of Dr. Meera Kosambi and Mr. Jijoy B. Surka.)

▌Figure 4-31
A Typical Acupuncture Chart
The numbers indicate sites at which needles can be inserted and then either twisted, electrified, or heated. An impressive analgesia results in many cases.

Other striking phenomena fit with gate control theory. One is stimulation-produced analgesia, in which stimulation of the PAG acts like an anesthetic. A rat can undergo abdominal surgery with only PAG stimulation as the anesthetic, with the rat showing no sign of experiencing pain (Reynolds, 1969). A milder version of this phenomenon is familiar to all of us: Rubbing a hurt area relieves pain, presumably because pressure stimulation is closing the neural gate. A phenomenon related to stimulation-produced analgesia is the reduction in pain resulting from acupuncture, a healing procedure developed in China in which needles are inserted into the skin at critical points. Twirling these needles has been reported to eliminate pain entirely, making it possible to perform major surgery on a conscious patient (see Figure 4-31). Presumably, the needles stimulate nerve fibers that lead to a closing of the pain gate.

At the psychological level, then, we have evidence that drugs, cultural beliefs, and various nonstandard medical practices can dramatically reduce pain. However, all of these factors may stem from a single biological process. Here, then, is a case in which research at the biological level may unify findings at the psychological level.

The interplay between the psychological and biological research on pain is typical of the successful interaction between these two approaches to sensation. As we commented at the beginning of the chapter, in perhaps no other area of psychology have the biological and psychological

approaches worked so well together. Again and again we have seen that neural events in receptors can explain phenomena at the psychological level. In discussing vision, we showed how variations in sensitivity and acuity—which are psychological phenomena—can be understood as the direct consequence of how different kinds of receptors (rods versus cones) connect to ganglion cells. Also with regard to vision, we pointed out how psychological theories of color vision led to discoveries at the biological level (for example, three kinds of cone receptors). In the case of hearing, the place theory of frequency perception was initially a psychological theory, and it led to research in the physiology of the basilar membrane. If ever anyone needed justification for intertwining psychological and biological research, the study of sensation provides it.

◆ Interim Summary

- The stimuli for smell are the molecules given off by a substance, which travel through the air and activate olfactory receptors located high in the nasal cavity.

- The stimulus for taste is a substance that is soluble in saliva; many of the receptors occur in clusters on the tongue (taste buds).

- Two of the skin senses are pressure and temperature. Sensitivity to pressure is greatest at the lips, nose, and cheeks, and least at the big toe. We are very sensitive to temperature and able to detect a change of less than 1 degree centigrade. We code different kinds of temperatures primarily by whether hot or cold receptors are activated.

- Any stimulus that is intense enough to cause tissue damage is a stimulus for pain. Phasic pain is typically brief and rapidly rises and falls in intensity; tonic pain is typically long-lasting and steady. Sensitivity to pain is greatly influenced by factors other than the noxious stimulus, including expectations and cultural beliefs.

◆ Critical Thinking Questions

1. Some people have described sensory experiences that cross over between two sensory systems. Called *synesthesia,* this apparently can occur both through natural causes and under the influence of a psychoactive drug. For example, people have reported being able to see the "color" of music or being able to hear the "tunes" associated with different smells. On the basis of what you know about sensory coding, can you think of what might cause such experiences?

2. How would your life change if you did not have a sense of pain? How would it change if you did not have a sense of smell? Which do you think would be worse, and why?

SEEING BOTH SIDES

Should Opioids Be Used for Treating Chronic Pain?

OPIOIDS ARE AN APPROPRIATE TREATMENT FOR CHRONIC PAIN
Robert N. Jamison, Harvard Medical School

Pain is a serious problem in the United States and throughout the rest of the world. About a third of the American population, or more than 80 million people, are severely affected by pain. Pain is the major reason people visit their primary care physicians; in fact, 70 million people see a physician each year because of pain. Chronic pain can affect all aspects of your life, interfering with sleep, employment, social life, and daily activities. Persons who have chronic pain frequently report depression, anxiety, irritability, sexual problems, and decreased energy. A restricted lifestyle causes changes in and concern about finances and the future. The treatments used for short-term pain often do not work well for pain that lasts a long time. Despite medical advances, chronic pain has remained a stubborn, debilitating problem for many individuals (Jamison, 1996).

Controversy remains about the use of opioid analgesics for chronic pain. Most physicians and health care professionals are reluctant to support the use of opioid medication for patients with chronic pain because of concerns about efficacy, adverse effects, tolerance, diversion, and addiction. It has been suggested that some patients become psychologically dependent after long-term opioid use. Some clinicians believe that opioid analgesics contribute to psychological distress, poor treatment outcome, impaired cognition, and a fostered reliance on the health care system. The scientific literature has not supported these fears

(American Academy of Pain Medicine and American Pain Society, 1996).

Most of the concerns about opioid therapy for chronic pain are based on an ill-founded notion that long-term use of narcotics always causes harm. Researchers and clinicians cite the relatively low incidence of abuse and addiction among patients with chronic pain and report that tolerance appears not to develop in those patients with stable pain pathophysiology (Portenoy, 1990). They suggest that the potential for increased functioning and improved quality of life significantly outweighs the risk of abuse. Investigators have also suggested that chronic opioid therapy may decrease the cost of rehabilitation programs for pain patients while improving outcome.

My colleagues and I initiated a prospective study of opioid therapy for chronic noncancer back pain (Jamison et al., 1998). The aim of this study was to examine the long-term safety and efficacy of chronic opioid therapy in a randomized trial of patients with back pain. All participants were randomly assigned to one of three treatment regimens: (1) a non-narcotic pain reliever, (2) a few short-acting narcotics a day, or (3) as much short- and long-acting narcotic medication as needed. The patients were followed for a year and then tapered off the medication. The results suggested that opioid therapy had a positive effect on pain and mood. Most important, opioid therapy for chronic back pain was used without significant risk of abuse,

and we found that individuals in the long-term opioid trial were compliant in coming off the opioid medication without signs of dependency or addiction.

The results of our studies and others point to the overwhelming evidence that addiction rarely occurs when morphine and other opioids are used for pain. This has been found to be true in both human and animal studies. Further studies will help to identify those individuals who benefit the most from opioid therapy. We remain hopeful that future breakthroughs will help those who suffer from back pain, headaches, arthritis, and pain associated with cancer. In the meantime, millions of people continue to live and die in needless pain. Many who request medication for their noncancer pain are mistaken as street addicts or drug abusers. Further education is needed to eradicate prejudices about the use of narcotics for pain. We know that, when used intelligently, opioids can help to significantly diminish pain. As pointed out by Ronald Melzack, an internationally recognized psychologist and pain researcher, social action is needed in promoting the use of opioids for pain to attack this "needless tragedy" (Melzack, 1990).

Robert N. Jamison

Should Opioids Be Used for Treating Chronic Pain?

WHY OPIOIDS SHOULD NOT BE USED FOR TREATING CHRONIC PAIN

Dennis C. Turk, University of Washington School of Medicine

Since the 4th century BC, there has been little question as to the effectiveness of opioids for the treatment of acute pain—pain of relatively brief duration, such as that following surgery. The long-term use of opioids for chronic pain, however, has swung from common use, to resistance, and back again. In the 1960s and 1970s two trends challenged the thinking about the medical use of opioids.

Behavioral scientist Wilbert Fordyce (1976) extended the principles of operant conditioning to chronic pain. He suggested that it is impossible to know how much pain someone experiences other than by what they tell you verbally or demonstrate by their behaviors. He suggested that these "pain behaviors" (overt expressions of pain, distress, and suffering) were observable and thus capable of being responded to by family members and physicians. Fordyce also suggested that opioid medications could serve as a negative reinforcement for pain behaviors. That is, if the patient took opioid medication as is commonly prescribed, "as needed," the pain behaviors would increase in order to obtain the pain-relieving effects of the medication. Fordyce suggested that elimination of the opioid medication would contribute to extinction of the pain behaviors.

Turk and Okifuji (1997) showed that physicians were more likely to prescribe opioids for chronic pain if patients were depressed, complained that pain impacted greatly on their lives, and showed a large number of pain behaviors (grimacing, limping), even though there were no differences in actual physical pathology or pain severity. Thus, the opioids were being prescribed for emotional distress, not specifically for pain or disease. The reinforcing properties of the opioids could thereby maintain the patients' complaints and even experience of pain.

The second development that challenged the use of opioids for chronic pain was the social movement in the 1970s to combat drug abuse ("Just say no to drugs"). Unfortunately, the campaign to reduce the inappropriate use of drugs was extended into clinical areas and the use of opioids in the treatment of pain. Thus, even appropriate uses of opioids were influenced by concerns about abuse.

Fears of addiction, tolerance, and side effects became prominent. The compulsive use of the drug results in physical, psychological, and social harm to the user, and use continues despite this harm. Physical dependence is a pharmacological property of a drug characterized by the occurrence of withdrawal following abrupt discontinuation of the substance or administration of a drug antagonist. Physical dependence develops with continued use of many drugs, not just opioids. One concern with the use of opioids is that with long-term use patients will require escalating doses of the medication to obtain the same level of pain relief. At times, it is difficult to distinguish the need for increased dosage due to tolerance from the progression of a disease process that might be increasing the pain severity.

Beginning in the mid-1980s, however, several authors (Melzack, 1990; Portenoy & Foley, 1986) began to question the generalization from illicit to the medical use of opioids. They suggested that if the use of opioids produced symptomatic improvement in chronic pain patients, then long-term use would be a reasonable treatment, and the failure to treat pain sufferers with appropriate and available opioids would be unethical.

Studies have evaluated the effectiveness of long-term use of opioids in the treatment of chronic pain (see Turk, 1996). The conclusions are limited, however, because few studies have been randomized controlled trials in which the physician and patient were unaware of the type of medication being prescribed. Moreover, the trials for so-called "chronic opioid therapy" have averaged only 6 weeks. Although many of the studies of long-term use of opioids for chronic pain report significant reductions in pain severity without significant problems, some studies have noted particular problems with abuse and intolerable side effects (Turk, 1996). Even when pain is reduced, no studies have found any significant improvement in physical functioning. Moreover, some studies of chronic pain patients have reported that both pain severity and physical functioning are improved following withdrawal from opioids (Flor, Fydrich, & Turk, 1992).

Furthermore, there has been a growing concern about neurotoxicity of long-term use of opioids leading to permanent changes in the nervous system that, paradoxically, might sensitize peripheral nerves, leading to reduction in the threshold for perceiving pain—"hyperalgesia" (Mao, Price, & Mayer, 1995).

The results of the available studies raise serious concerns about the long-term use of opioids: (1) there are only short-term research studies where the patients and physicians were blind to the drug being prescribed; (2) few studies have shown any improvement in the patients' physical functioning; (3) there is no experience with the medical uses of opioids extending over decades; (4) some studies have reported significant problems with addiction and side-effects; (5) long-term use of opioids may lead to permanent changes in the nervous system that may make people hypersensitive to pain; and (6) the outcomes of pain clinics have demonstrated *reduction of pain* associated with *reduction of opioids*.

The central question is not whether chronic pain patients should ever be treated with opioids but, rather, what are the characteristics of patients who are able to reduce pain and suffering and improve physical and psychological functioning without significant problems caused by long-term use? At the present time it seems premature to recommend that opioids be used on a long-term basis for a significant number of patients.

1. At the psychological level, sensations are experiences associated with simple stimuli. At the biological level, sensory processes involve the sense organs and connecting neural pathways and are concerned with the initial stages of acquiring stimulus information. The senses include vision; audition (hearing); olfaction (smell); gustation (taste); the skin senses, which include pressure, temperature, and pain; and the body senses.

2. One property that can be used to describe all senses is sensitivity. Sensitivity to stimulus intensity is measured by the absolute threshold, which is the minimum amount of stimulus energy that can be reliably detected. Sensitivity to a change in intensity is measured by the difference threshold or jnd, the minimum difference between two stimuli that can be reliably detected. The amount of change needed for detection to occur increases with the intensity of the stimulus and is approximately proportional to it (the Weber-Fechner law).

3. Another property of great interest is the relation between stimulus intensity and the magnitude of sensation for above-threshold stimuli. This relation is captured in Stevens's power law, which states that perceived stimulus magnitude is a power function of physical stimulus magnitude. The exponent of the power function differs for different sensory modalities; for most, like sound intensity, the exponent is less than 1.0, which means that the function relating perceived to physical intensity is concave down. For others, like pain intensity, the exponent is greater than 1.0, which means that the function relating perceived to physical intensity is concave up.

4. Sensation is often viewed as the process of detecting a signal that is embedded in noise. In some cases, a signal may be "detected" even when only noise is present, referred to as a false alarm. Correctly detecting a signal that is present is called a *hit*. The use of signal-detection theory allows the process of detecting a stimulus to be decomposed into two separate numbers: one representing the observer's sensitivity to the signal and the other representing the observer's bias to respond "signal present." Signal-detection theory not only is useful as a fundamental scientific tool but also has important practical applications, such as evaluating the performance of a radiologist trying to detect abnormalities in noisy x-rays.

5. Every sense modality must recode or transduce its physical energy into neural impulses. This transduction process is accomplished by the receptors. The receptors and connecting neural pathways code the intensity of a stimulus primarily by the rate of neural impulses and their patterns. They code the quality of a stimulus according to the specific nerve fibers involved and their pattern of activity.

6. The stimulus for vision is light, which is electromagnetic radiation in the range from 400 to 700 nanometers. Each eye contains a system for forming the image (including the cornea, pupil, and lens) and a system for transducing the image into electrical impulses. The transduction system is in the retina, which contains the visual receptors—the rods and cones.

7. Cones operate at high light intensities, lead to sensations of color, and are found mainly in the center (or fovea) of the retina. Rods operate at low intensities, lead to colorless sensations, and are found mainly in the periphery of the retina. Our sensitivity to the intensity of light is mediated by certain characteristics of the rods and cones. Of particular importance is the fact that rods connect to a larger number of ganglion cells than do cones. Because of this difference in connectivity, visual sensitivity is greater when it is based on rods than when it is based on cones, but visual acuity is greater when it is based on cones than when it is based on rods.

8. Different wavelengths of light lead to sensations of different colors. The appropriate mixture of three lights of widely separated wavelengths can be made to match almost any color of light. This fact and others led to the development of trichromatic theory, which holds that perception of color is based on the activity of three types of receptors (cones), each of which is most sensitive to wavelengths in a different region of the spectrum.

9. There are four basic color sensations: red, yellow, green, and blue. Mixtures of these make up our experiences of color, except that we do not see reddish greens and yellowish blues. This can be explained by the opponent-color theory, which proposes that there are red-green and yellow-blue opponent processes, each of which responds in opposite ways to its two opponent colors. Trichromatic and opponent-color theories have been successfully combined through the proposal that

they operate at different neural locations in the visual system.

10. The stimulus for audition (hearing) is a wave of pressure changes (a sound wave). The ear includes the outer ear (the external ear and the auditory canal), the middle ear (the eardrum and a chain of bones), and the inner ear. The inner ear includes the cochlea, a coiled tube that contains the basilar membrane, which supports the hair cells that serve as the receptors for sound. Sound waves transmitted by the outer and middle ear cause the basilar membrane to vibrate, resulting in a bending of the hair cells that produces a neural impulse.

11. Pitch, the most striking quality of sound, increases with the frequency of the sound wave. The fact that we can hear the pitches of two different tones sounded simultaneously suggests there may be many receptors that respond to different frequencies. Temporal theories of pitch perception postulate that the pitch heard depends on the temporal pattern of neural responses in the auditory system, which itself is determined by the temporal pattern of the sound wave. Place theories postulate that each frequency stimulates a particular place along the basilar membrane more than it stimulates other places and that the place where the maximum movement occurs determines which pitch is heard. There is room for both theories, as temporal theory explains perception of low frequencies and place theory accounts for perception of high frequencies.

12. Olfaction (smell) is even more important to nonhuman species than to humans. Many species use specialized odors (pheromones) for communication, and humans seem to possess a vestige of this system. The stimuli for smell are the molecules given off by a substance. The molecules travel through the air and activate olfactory receptors located high in the nasal cavity. There are many kinds of receptors (on the order of 1,000). A normal person can discriminate among 10,000 to 40,000 different odors, with women generally doing better than men.

13. Gustation (taste) is affected not only by the substance being tasted but also by genetic makeup and experience. The stimulus for taste is a substance that is soluble in saliva. Many of the receptors occur in clusters on the tongue (taste buds). Sensitivity varies from one place to another on the tongue. Any taste can be described as one or a combination of the four basic taste qualities: sweet, sour, salty, and bitter. Different qualities of taste are coded partly in terms of the specific nerve fibers activated—different fibers respond best to one of the four taste sensations—and partly in terms of the pattern of fibers activated.

14. Two of the skin senses are pressure and temperature. Sensitivity to pressure is greatest at the lips, nose, and cheeks and least at the big toe. We are very sensitive to temperature and can detect a change of less than 1 degree centigrade. We code different kinds of temperatures primarily by whether hot or cold receptors are activated.

15. Any stimulus intense enough to cause tissue damage is a stimulus for pain. There are two distinct kinds of pain, which are mediated by different neural pathways. Phasic pain is typically brief and rapidly rises and falls in intensity; tonic pain is typically long-lasting and steady. Sensitivity to pain is greatly influenced by factors other than the noxious stimulus, including expectations and cultural beliefs. These factors seem to exert their influence by opening or closing a neural gate in the spinal cord and midbrain; pain is felt only when pain receptors are activated and the gate is open.

CORE CONCEPTS

back projections
absolute threshold
psychophysical procedures
psychophysical function
photon
standard
just noticeable difference (jnd)
Weber fraction
suprathreshold conditions
power function
exponent (of a power function)
signal-detection theory
sensation
bias
signal
noise
hits
false alarm
hit rate
false-alarm rate
sensory coding
transduction
intensity
quality
temporal pattern
retina

pupil
rods
cones
fovea
dark adaptation
dark-adaptation curve
visual acuity
Snellen acuity
contrast acuity
color constancy
hue
brightness
saturation
Munsell system
color-matching experiment
metamers
dichromat
monochromat
trichromacy theory
opponent-color theory
thalamus
sound wave
frequency
hertz
pitch
amplitude (of a tone)

loudness
decibel scale
timbre
auditory system
outer ear
middle ear
eardrum
oval window
malleus
incus
stapes
cochlea
basilar membrane
hair cells
temporal theory (of sound)
resonance
place theory of pitch perception
pheromones
olfactory system
olfactory bulb
olfactory cortex
taste receptors
phasic pain
tonic pain
gate control theory of pain
periaqueductal gray

WEB RESOURCES

http://psychology.wadsworth.com/
atkinson14e

Take a quiz, try the activities and exercises, and explore web links.

http://hstat.nlm.nih.gov/hq/Hquest/db/local.nih.
cdc.nihcdc95.cdc100/screen/DocTitle/s/61504

This comprehensive site will help you explore the many aspects of cochlear implants. Click on the Interactive Table of Contents and search through topics like the benefits and limitations of implants and learn more about future research.

http://www.exploratorium.edu/learning_studio/
cow_eye/index.html

Did you ever want to dissect a cow eye? Well, here's your chance! You will soon see a similarity between the cow eye and the human eye.

 InfoTrac Online Library
http://www.infotrac-college.com/
wadsworth

Use InfoTrac to find popular and scientific articles with the search terms below or your own relevant terms.
- Cochlear implants
- Human vision
- Signal detection

CD-ROM LINKS

 Psych Odyssey

Check out CD Chapter 4, Sensation and Perception

A. Vision

 Psyk.trek 2.0

Check out CD Unit 3, Sensation and Perception

3a Light and the Eye
3b The Retina
3c Vision and the Brain
3h The Sense of Hearing

© Renee Lynn/CORBIS

PERCEPTION

5

The Tent and the Bear

On a warm Saturday in the early 1990s, two young men—we'll call them Alex and Ken—left their homes near Bozeman, Montana, for a day's hunting trip. As they walked along an abandoned logging road, their conversation touched on various hunting-related topics, but mostly they talked about bears. Alex had seen a bear the previous weekend, and both men were apprehensive about these dangerous creatures. They knew that their hunting rifles were powerful, but they were well aware that bears were equally powerful. The hunters maintained a constant vigil.

It was almost midnight by the time Alex and Ken retraced their path along the logging road bound for home. There was no moon; the woods were quiet and dark. The two hunters were tired from their day's efforts. As they rounded a curve, they suddenly became aware of a low growling sound they perceived to come from a large, dimly illuminated animal quivering slowly but ominously in the middle of the road, about 50 yards away. Terrified, they raised their rifles and fired. The growling noise and the quivering abruptly ceased. An instant later, an unmistakably human scream pierced the night. The hunters' relief at having killed the bear was replaced by confusion and dismay as they realized that the bear wasn't a bear at all. It was a tent in which two campers had been sleeping. One of the campers now lay dead from a bullet wound, and the other knelt beside him, shrieking in horror.

An investigation carried out in the aftermath of this terrible event revealed that Ken's bullets had passed harmlessly through the tent, and that a bullet from Alex's gun killed the camper. Accordingly, Alex went to trial, accused of negligent homicide. The tragedy of the killing was mirrored in the courtroom by Alex's overwhelming sorrow about what had happened. There was one critical fact, however, about which both Alex and Ken were certain: They had perceived a bear, not a tent that night. "We never would have shot if we had had any idea that it wasn't a bear," they both swore. The prosecution dismissed these assertions as ridiculous and desperate lies. The bullet-riddled tent itself was placed in the center of the court-room and the prosecutors asked the jury, "How could the defendant have possibly mistaken this rectangular yellow tent for a furry brown bear?"

How indeed? On the face of it, the prosecution's question seems quite reasonable. There, sitting in the courtroom for all to behold, was a big yellow tent, appearing not at all like a bear. However, a half-century's research on perception—visual perception in this instance—suggests that under the circumstances it wasn't at all unreasonable for Ken and Alex to have perceived the tent to be a bear. In this chapter we will elaborate on why this is so, demonstrating in the process how the raw sensations that we discussed in Chapter 4 become translated into the perceptions that are directly responsible for our behavior.

© The MacNeil River State Game Sanctuary, photo by Jon C. Pascal

Our perceptual systems work well in providing perceptions that closely map reality. But sometimes, the systems fail dramatically. How could this yellow tent be incorrectly perceived as a dangerous bear?

147

To get a feel for what we mean by this, let's start with a couple of demonstrations. Look first at the left panel of Figure 5-1. Do you recognize an object? If you are like most people (and have not seen this demonstration previously), your answer would be no. Now look at the right panel of Figure 5-1. What does it say? Again, if you're normal and haven't seen this demonstration before, you probably read, "I LOVE PARIS IN THE SPRINGTIME." In both cases you had perceptions—of meaningless black-and-white blobs in one instance and of a common cliché in the other—that somehow derived from the basic, objective stimulus, the light that entered your eyes and befell your retina. In both instances, however, there are interesting and systematic disconnects between the raw data and the ensuing perception. Does that "I love Paris" statement really say what you thought it did? Look at it again, this time reading it very slowly and word by word. You will see that it actually says, "I LOVE PARIS IN THE THE SPRING-TIME." What about those meaningless blobs in the left panel of Figure 5-1? Look at Figure 5-38 on page 187 and then return here. Are you back? The left panel of Figure 5-1 is no longer meaningless, is it? Indeed, if you are like most people, it is difficult for you to believe that it ever *was* meaningless. The stimulus entering your eyes is identical to what it was before, but the perception is entirely different: The black-and-white blobs are now organized into a meaningful object.

These demonstrations are designed to convince you that, although information may enter our senses in bits and pieces, that is not how we perceive the world. We perceive a world of objects and people, a world that gracefully presents us with integrated wholes, rather than chaotically bombarding us with piecemeal sensations. Only under unusual circumstances, or when we are drawing or painting, do we notice the individual features and parts of stimuli. Most of the time we see three-dimensional objects and hear words and music.

WHAT IS THE USE OF PERCEPTION?

Any living organism must solve an unending series of problems presented by its environment. The complexity of the problems and associated sophistication of the solutions depend on the nature and complexity of the organism. If you are a daffodil, for example, the problems you must deal with are (relatively) simple. You must figure out where your roots should go on the basis of the soil structure you're planted in, determining in the process the soil's texture and the distribution of moisture and nutrients. Additionally, you must determine which way to orient yourself on the basis of where the sun is.

But that's about it for daffodils. Humans, it won't surprise you to hear, are more complex. With respect to perception, the most important differences between daffodils and humans are these: First, a human is *mobile*. The vast majority of us must make our way through the environment, determining in the process the potential routes that we could take and the obstacles that must be surmounted for each route. Second, a human *manipulates objects*. We turn the steering wheel on a car, sign our names with a pen, and hurl a baseball across home plate. Third, a human makes decisions on the basis of **symbols**, such as written or spoken words or hieroglyphics.

I

LOVE

PARIS IN THE

THE SPRINGTIME

▌**Figure 5-1**
Raw Data and the Resulting Perception
Left panel: Do you see a meaningful object? (Look at Figure 5-38 on page 187 if you need help.) *Right panel:* What does the phrase say?

Fourth, a human makes and executes complex *plans* to deal with sudden unexpected events. We catch a glimpse of a dark form holding a sharp knife in a dark alley; we evaluate our options and cross to the other side of the street, where we can seek safety in the crowd there.

How do we do this? One possibility is that the information from the environment—or more specifically, its two-dimensional representation on our retina—is all that is really necessary to live a normal life. The psychologist J. J. Gibson offered a **theory of ecological optics,** which specified just that. According to Gibson, the vast richness of optical information from the world—the change in texture with distance, the shifting of objects' images relative to one another as one walks by them, and so on—are sufficient, in real life anyway, to solve all vision-related problems that the world presents us.

Although ingenious and sophisticated, Gibson's theory has been rejected by most perception scientists as insufficient. Instead, they argue, humans require a continually updated image or a **model of the environment,** a representation of the world within our brains that we use to consciously perceive, make decisions, and behave. Two ingredients are necessary to formulate and maintain such a model. The first is some means of acquiring raw information about the environment. In Chapter 4, we discussed how our sense organs are used to accomplish this. But acquiring raw information is not sufficient to build a model, any more than acquiring a stack of wood is sufficient to build a house. In addition, we need a means of organizing all this raw information into some kind of coherent structure. Such a means requires, among other things, *assumptions* about how the world is put together—birds are usually to be found above horses, stoves are usually to be found near refrigerators, a scene is usually illuminated by a single kind of light source, and so on. Perception is the use of such assumptions to integrate incoming sensory information into a model of the world, based upon which we make decisions and take action. Usually this process works pretty efficiently, and, for example, a yellow tent in the environment produces a model—a perception—of a yellow tent in our mind. Sometimes it doesn't work so well, and a yellow tent in the environment produces the perception of a bear in our mind, and we shoot it. Generally speaking, each sensory modality—seeing, hearing, and so on—has both a sense organ that acquires the raw information from the environment and a more central system in the brain for transforming this information into organized percepts.

Perception is sufficiently complex that any classification of it must be somewhat arbitrary. For organizational purposes, however, it is useful to divide perceptual issues into five categories. First via the process of *attention* a decision must be made about *which* incoming information is to be further processed, and which is to be discarded. (Should I be eavesdropping on the conversation on my left, which seems to be about my spouse, or the conversation on my right, which seems to involve hot stock tips?) Second, the system must be able to determine *where* objects of interest are. (Is that potentially dangerous object at arm's length, on my left, hundreds of yards straight ahead, or where?) Third, the perceptual system must be able to determine *which* objects are out there. (Is that a tent or a bear that I'm looking at?) Fourth, the system must be able to *abstract* the critical features of a recognized object. (A couch that has wrinkles and bumps in it would be reasonably perceived and described as "rectangular" even though its shape isn't a perfect rectangle.) This abstraction ability is closely related to the fifth category of perceptual issues, that of perceptual *constancy.* The perceptual system must maintain certain features of objects (such as the rectangular shape of a door even when the door's angle is such that it forms a trapezoid on your retina).

In the next five sections, we will discuss these five issues: attention, localization, recognition, abstraction, and constancy. We will then discuss some of the biological correlates of these perceptual processes. Finally, we consider the development of perception. Throughout the chapter, we focus primarily on visual perception, because this is the area that has been most investigated. Keep in mind, though, that the goals of localization, recognition, and constancy apply to all sensory modalities. With regard to recognition, for example, we can use our hearing to recognize a Mozart sonata, our sense of smell to recognize McDonald's fries, our sense of touch to recognize a quarter in our pants pocket, and our body senses to recognize that we are upright in a dark room.

◆ Interim Summary

- The study of perception deals with the question of how organisms process and organize incoming raw sensory information in order to (1) form a coherent representation or model of the world within which the organism dwells and (2) use that representation to solve naturally occurring problems, such as navigating, grasping, and planning.

- Five major functions of the perceptual system are (1) determining which part of the sensory environment to attend to, (2) localizing, or determining *where* objects are, (3) recognizing, or determining *what* objects are, (4) *abstracting* the critical information from objects, and (5) keeping the appearance of objects *constant,* even though their retinal images are changing. Another area of study is how our perceptual capacities develop.

1. Suppose a frog has only two things that it needs to do in life: Catch little bugs and avoid big predators. What kind of a model of the environment would the frog need to maintain? What would be the nature of the perceptual systems it needs to do this?

2. Why do you think that perception is imperfect? Why, for example, would a designer design a perceptual system that would allow a tent to be mistaken for a bear? What purpose might such imperfections serve?

Figure 5-2
Eye Movements in Viewing a Picture
Next to the picture of the girl is a record of the eye movements made by an individual inspecting the picture. (D. L. Yarbuss (1967) "Eye Movements and Vision," Plenum Publishing Corporation. Reproduced by permission of the publisher)

ATTENTION

We began the previous chapter by underscoring the fact that at any given instant our sense organs are being bombarded with a vast amount of information from the environment. As you sit reading, stop for a moment and attend to the various stimuli that are reaching you. There is, in your visual field, more than just the pages of this book. Perhaps your left shoe is feeling a little tight. What sounds do you hear? What odors are there in the air?

Meanwhile, the human bombardee is generally engaged in trying to *accomplish some task*. This task could be as simple as drinking a cup of coffee, as complex as doing brain surgery, or something in between, like trying to digest the information in this book. Whatever the task, only a tiny portion of the incoming stream of information is relevant to it. The vast majority is irrelevant. This state of affairs implies that the sensory systems and the brain must have some means of *screening* the incoming information—allowing through only the information relevant to the task at hand and filtering out the irrelevant information. If such a screening process did not exist, the irrelevant information would overwhelm the relevant information, and we would never get anything done.

Indeed, when we look at the sensory organs and certain parts of the brain, we discover that a major design feature is filters that allow them to screen and select incoming information along various dimensions. Roughly speaking, the sum total of all these filters is what is known as attention. Our various filters are adjusted to screen out all but the information that is required for the task at hand.

SELECTIVE ATTENTION

How exactly do we direct our attention to objects of interest? The simplest means is by physically reorienting our sensory receptors. For vision, this means moving our eyes until the object of interest falls on the fovea, which, as you will recall from Chapter 4, is the most sensitive region of the retina—the region designed to process visual detail.

EYE MOVEMENTS Studies of visual attention often involve observing an observer looking at a picture or scene. If we watch the person's eyes, it is evident that they are not stationary. Instead, visual scanning takes the form of **fixations,** which are brief periods during which the eyes are relatively stationary, separated by **saccades,** which are quick jumps of the eye from one place to the next. Each fixation lasts approximately 300 milliseconds (about a third of a second), and saccades are very fast (on the order of 20 milliseconds). It is during the fixation periods that visual information is acquired from the environment, and vision is essentially suppressed during saccades.

By monitoring a person's eye fixation pattern over a scene, we can gain considerable insight about the sequencing of the person's visual attention. There are a number of techniques for recording eye movements, but all of them eventually produce a video of the scene being viewed, superimposed on which is the sequence of eye fixations, as shown in Figure 5-2. Generally speaking, the points on which the eyes fixate are not random, but rather are the areas of the scene that contain the most information. The exact definition of "information" is beyond the scope of this book (and indeed beyond the scope of most research in psychology), but in this context it refers roughly to those areas that are most likely to distinguish the scene from any similar scene. For example, as shown in Figure 5-2, a person looking at a face makes many fixations on the eyes, nose, and mouth—those features that most efficiently distinguish one face from another.

Numerous researchers have demonstrated the relation between fixations and pictorial information by presenting a picture containing an object that was either unusual or not unusual within some background context (Henderson, Weeks, & Hollingworth, 1999; Hollingworth & Henderson, 2000; Loftus & Mackworth, 1978; Pashler, 2001). For instance, one observer might be shown a picture of a farmyard with a tractor in the middle of it, while another observer would see the same farmyard picture but with an octopus rather than the tractor. Eye fixations were directed earlier and more frequently to the unusual object (the octopus) than to the normal object (the tractor).

WEAPON FOCUS A useful practical application of this kind of eye movement research concerns what **weapon focus,** which refers to **rapt attention on a weapon in the scene.** More specifically, victims of armed crimes are often able to very accurately describe what the weapon looked like but seem to know relatively little about other aspects of the scene, such as the appearance of the person who was wielding the weapon, suggesting that attention was primarily focused on the weapon. Laboratory studies have generally confirmed this anecdotal evidence (see Loftus, Loftus, & Messo, 1987; Steblay, 1992; Pickel, 1998). In one study, for instance, eye movements were recorded while observers looked at a slide sequence, one of which showed a person handling a critical object that was either benign (a checkbook) or threatening (a knife). More eye fixations occurred on the critical object compared with the rest of the scene when the object was threatening than when it was benign. Correspondingly, observers were less able to recognize other aspects of the scene when they had viewed a threatening object as compared with a benign object.

Laboratory studies undoubtedly underestimate the attention-demanding power of a weapon in the real-life situations they are meant to explore. In both the real-life and the laboratory situations, a weapon is unusual and would be expected to draw attention on that basis. However, the real-life situation has the added component that the weapon constitutes crucial environmental information relevant to what becomes the threatened individual's immediate task: survival.

DIRECTED ATTENTION WITHOUT EYE MOVEMENTS We can also selectively attend to some visual stimulus without moving our eyes. In experiments that demonstrate this, observers have to detect when an object occurs. On each trial, the person stares at a blank field and then sees a brief **cue,** which is a directing stimulus such as a small arrow that directs the subject to attend either to the left or to the right. An object is then presented either in the location indicated by the cue or to the opposite location. The interval between the cue

and object is too brief for observers to move their eyes, yet they can detect the object faster in the cued location than when it occurs than elsewhere. Presumably, they are attending to the cued location even though they cannot move their eyes there (Posner & Raichle, 1994).

AUDITORY ATTENTION

Attention is **multimodal.** It can move within a modality, such as from one visual stimulus to another, or between modalities (like shifting our attention from watching the road while driving to listening to the person who just called our cell phone). Much of the original research on attention was done on auditory attention (e.g., Cherry, 1953). A real-life analogue of Cherry's work is a crowded party. The sounds of many voices bombard our ears. However, we can use purely mental means to selectively attend to the desired message. Some of the cues that we use to do this are the direction the sound is coming from, the speaker's lip movements, and the particular characteristics of the speaker's voice (pitch and intonation). Even in the absence of any of these cues, we can (though with difficulty) select one of two messages to follow on the basis of its meaning.

ATTENTION, PERCEPTION, AND MEMORY

With some caveats (to be described in Chapter 8), a general rule has emerged about the relation between attention and later memory: We are consciously unaware of and remember little, if anything, about nonattended information. In the auditory domain, a procedure known as **shadowing,** or repeating back one auditory message,

Although we may hear a number of conversations around us, as at a cocktail party, we remember very little of what we do not attend to. This is known as selective listening.

Distraction via Virtual Reality Diminishes Severe Pain

While drinking around a campfire with friends, 17-year-old Mark Powers was badly burned by an exploding a can of gasoline. Deep flash burns to his face, chest, back, stomach, upper legs, and right arm covered more than 33% of his body. He required skin grafting on his neck, chest, back, and stomach.

Although opioid painkillers reduced his pain as he lay motionless in his hospital bed, they were much less effective during wound-care procedures. While having his wounds cleaned, Mark like most burn patients, continued to experience severe to excruciating pain, as well as numerous unpleasant side effects from the drugs. In response, Hunter Hoffman from the University of Washington's Human Interface Technology Laboratory and David Patterson from Seattle's Harborview Hospital Burn Center originated a new psychological pain-control technique—one that relied on diverted attention in a virtual-reality (VR) setting—to supplement the usual drugs.

Diverting attention is particularly useful with burn pain because pain perception has a strong psychological component. As described in Chapter 4, pain, like any sensory input, consists of a specific signal, in this case, a train of nerve impulses from pain receptors in the skin. However, as we discuss in this chapter, perception, which is the interpretation of sensory input, is not entirely determined by the sensory input. This potential disconnect between sensation and perception is particularly salient with pain. The same incoming pain signal can be interpreted as painful or not painful, depending on what the patient is thinking and doing.

This notion is often couched within the context a gate control theory of pain. The idea here is that higher-order thought processes, such as attentional distraction, can initiate feedback signals from the cortex to the spinal cord that inhibit the intensity of incoming pain signals. In other words, in addition to influencing the way patients interpret incoming pain signals, distraction may actually reduce the intensity of the incoming pain signals.

Burn patients are unable to rise from their beds during wound care and are not generally able to interact with any sort of interesting, attention-attracting environment. Enter VR, which allows the patient to enter any world imaginable without physically going anywhere. A VR computer set up in the hospital room sends video output to two miniature LCD screens positioned in front of the patient's eyes by using a specially designed helmet. The computer monitors the patient's head position and feeds this information into the computer. When the patient moves his or her head (for example, looks up), the computer updates the artificial environment accordingly (in this case, changes the image from a virtual river to a virtual sky). These real-time changes in sensory input, in response to patients' actions, afford the illusion of actually being in the computer-generated environment. In principle, a person's perception within VR can perfectly mimic the perception of a person within the real world (as spectacularly envisioned by the science-fiction writer, Neal Stephenson in his novel *Snow Crash*).

An incoming pain signal requires conscious attention to be perceived as pain. But being drawn into another world— one of virtual reality—drains a substantial amount of attentional resources,

is used to demonstrate this. The observer wears stereo earphones, and entirely different messages are played to the two different ears. The person is asked to repeat (or "shadow") one of the messages as it is heard. After a few minutes, the messages are turned off, and the listener is asked about the unshadowed message. The listener's report of the message is usually limited to the physical characteristics of the sound in the unshadowed ear— whether the voice was high or low, male or female, and so forth. The listener can say almost nothing about the content of the message and, indeed, does not even notice when the language changes from English to French and then back again (Moray, 1969). Loftus (1972) reports an analogous finding in vision. He showed two pictures, side by side, but asked the observer to look at only one of them (and monitored the observer's eye movements to ensure compliance). The finding was that later memory was considerable for the attended picture but nil for the unattended picture.

The fact that we can report so little about auditory messages that we do not attend to initially led researchers to the idea that nonattended stimuli are filtered out completely (Broadbent, 1958). However, there is now considerable evidence that our perceptual system processes nonattended stimuli to some extent (in vision as well as audition), even though those stimuli rarely reach consciousness. We are very likely to hear the sound of our own name, for instance, even when it is spoken softly in a nonattended conversation. This could not happen if the entire nonattended message was lost at lower levels of the perceptual system. Therefore, lack of attention does not block messages entirely; rather, it attenuates them, much like a volume control that is turned down but not off (Treisman, 1969).

leaving less available to process pain signals. The attentional "spotlight" that would normally be focused on the pain is lured instead into the virtual world. For many patients undergoing VR treatment, their pain—particularly the normally excruciating pain associated with the care and cleansing of their wounds—becomes little more than an annoyance, distracting them from their primary goal of exploring the virtual world.

In a preliminary case study (Hoffman, Doctor, Patterson, Carrougher and Furness, 2000), two patients with severe burns went into a VR environment of a virtual kitchen complete with countertops, a window looking out at a partly cloudy sky, cabinets, and doors. Patients could perform actions—pick up a teapot, plate, toaster, plant, or frying pan—by inserting their cyberhand into the virtual object and clicking a grasp button on their 3-D mouse. Each patient could pick up a virtual wiggly-legged spider that possessed solidity and weight, created via a mixed-reality force feedback technique developed by Hoffman.

The VR treatments have shown a great deal of promise with the two initial patients. Patient 1 had five staples removed from a burn skin graft while playing Nintendo (a control condition), and six staples removed from the same skin graft while in VR. He reported dramatic reductions in pain in the VR compared with the Nintendo condition. Patient 2 (Mark Powers, described earlier), even with his severe and extensive burns, showed the same pattern.

Hoffman, Patterson, and Carrougher (2000) have found additional support that VR reduces burn pain. Twelve severely burned patients reported substantial pain reduction during physical therapy when in VR compared with conventional treatment. In addition to distracting the patients, VR can probably be used in behavioral reinforcement techniques to motivate patients to perform necessary but normally very painful stretching motions. For example, while playing in a VR game they could get virtual fuel for their virtual jet by gripping and ungripping their healing hand 10 times.

With funding from the Paul Allen Foundation for Medical Research and the National Institutes of Health, Hoffman and Patterson are now developing several new attention-grabbing virtual environments specifically designed for treating pain. Patients fly through an icy canyon with a river and frigid waterfall, or they shoot snowballs at snowmen and igloos (with animated impacts). The technology for these advances in pain reduction is proceeding apace with the psychological advances. Hoffman and University of Washington instrument maker Jeff Magula have recently completed a custom optic fiber VR helmet that uses photons instead of electrons, so burn patients can get VR while sitting in the water-filled scrubtanks. Hoffman and colleagues are optimistic that virtual reality can provide a much needed psychological pain-control technique that could prove valuable for treating other patient populations in pain due to cancer procedures, childbirth, dentistry, and physical therapy during recovery from knee surgery. Their project nicely demonstrates the growing interdisciplinary alliance between research in psychology on the one hand and real-world problems in medicine on the other. Further details about the work can be found at www.vrpain.com.

 For more information, go online with InfoTrac College Edition. Use your own term or search:

- Virtual reality and pain
- Patterson, David
- Pain perception

◆Interim Summary

- Selective attention is the process by which we select some stimuli for further processing while ignoring others.

- In vision, the primary means of directing our attention are eye movements. Most eye fixations are on the more informative parts of a scene.

- Selective attention also occurs in audition. Usually we are able to selectively listen by using cues such as the direction from which the sound is coming and the voice characteristics of the speaker.

- Our ability to selectively attend is mediated by processes that occur in the early stages of recognition as well as by processes that occur only after the message's meaning has been determined.

◆ Critical Thinking Questions

1. It seems quite clear that attention can be monitored by watching where a person looks. Suppose you hypothesize that selective visual attention could go from one place to another in the environment even with the eyes held still. How would you test this hypothesis?

2. How does selective attention aid perception under everyday circumstances? What would the consequences of driving a car in a city where no one had the ability to attend selectively? What kinds of accidents might occur more frequently than occur now? Would any kinds of accidents be apt to occur *less* frequently?

LOCALIZATION

Earlier, we described various problems that humans must solve for which localization of information is relevant. The most important such problems are (1) navigating our way around the often cluttered environment (think about what is required just to make your way from your bed to your kitchen sink without running into anything) and (2) grasping an object (to smoothly guide your fingers in quest of picking up your pen, you must know accurately where the pen is to begin with).

To know where the objects in our environment are, we first have to separate the objects from one another and from the background. Then the perceptual system can determine the position of the objects in a three-dimensional world, including their distance from us and their patterns of movement. In this section we discuss each of these perceptual abilities in turn.

SEPARATION OF OBJECTS

The image projected on our retina is a mosaic of varying brightnesses and colors. Somehow our perceptual system organizes that mosaic into a set of discrete objects projected against a background. This kind of organization was of great concern to Gestalt psychologists. (Recall from Chapter 1 that Gestalt psychology began in Germany early in the 20th century.) The Gestalt psychologists emphasized the importance of perceiving whole objects or forms and proposed principles to explain how we organize objects.

FIGURE AND GROUND The most elementary form of perceptual organization is that in a stimulus with two or more distinct regions, we usually see part of it as a figure and the rest as ground (or background). The regions seen as a **figure** contain the objects of interest, which appear more solid than the ground and appear in front of it. The **ground** is the region that appears to be behind the figure (for example, Singh & Hoffman, 2001). Figure 5-3a shows that figure-ground organization can be ambiguous. When you look at this pattern, you might see a pair of silhouette faces gazing at each other, or you might see an ornate vase. The vase appears white against a black ground, whereas the faces are black against a white ground. Notice that as you look at Figure 5-3b for a few moments, the two pattern organizations alternate in consciousness, demonstrating that the organization into figure and ground is in your mind, not in the stimulus. Notice also that the faces and the vase never appear to-

a)   b)   c)

❚ Figure 5-3
Reversible Figure and Ground
Three patterns in which either a white vase or a pair of black faces can be seen. Note that it is impossible to see both organizations at the same time, even though you know that both are possible percepts. When the white area is smaller (a), the vase is more likely to be seen; when the black area is smaller (c), the faces are more likely to be seen.

gether. You "know" that both are possible, but you cannot "see" both at the same time. Generally speaking, the smaller an area or a shape, the more likely it is to be seen as figure, as demonstrated in Figures 5-3a, b, and c. It is easier to see the vase when the white area is smaller, and it is easier to see the faces when the black area is smaller (Weisstein & Wong, 1986). These figure-ground principles are not restricted to simple stimuli. As shown in Figure 5-4, they apply to quite complex pictures as well.

Although vision is the most salient source of figure-ground relations, we can also perceive figure-ground relations in other senses. For example, we may hear the

Salvador Dali, *Slave Market with Disappearing Bust of Voltaire*, 1950, The Salvador Dali Museum, St. Petersburg, Fla

❚ Figure 5-4
The Slave Market with a Disappearing Bust of Voltaire
A reversible figure is in the center of this painting by Salvador Dali (1940). Two nuns standing in an archway reverse to form a bust of Voltaire.

song of a bird against a background of outdoor noises or the melody played by a violin against the harmonies of the rest of the orchestra.

GROUPING OF OBJECTS We see not only objects against a ground but also objects in a particular *grouping* as well. Even simple patterns of dots fall into groups when we look at them. To illustrate this, look at the matrix of dots in Figure 5-5a. These dots are equally spaced up and down, so they can be seen as organized in rows or columns or even as lying along diagonal paths. This is therefore an ambiguous pattern that follows similar principles to those illustrated in Figures 5-3 and 5-4. Only one organization is seen at a time, and at intervals this organization spontaneously switches to another.

The Gestalt psychologists proposed a number of determinants of grouping for these kinds of dot patterns. For instance, if the vertical distance between dots is reduced, as in Figure 5-5b, columns will most likely be seen. This is **grouping by proximity.** Varying the color or shape of the elements allows organization on the basis of **similarity** by grouping like with like (Figures 5-5c and d). If we move the dots to form two intersecting wave lines of dots, we are grouping by good continuation (Figure 5-5e), and if we enclose a space with lines of dots, we will tend to see grouping by closure. In this last case, we see a diamond positioned between two vertical lines, even though the pattern could be two familiar letters stacked on each other (*W* on *M*) or even facing each other (*K* and a mirror-image *K*). This illustrates the powerful nature of the Gestalt grouping determinants. These determinants create the most stable, consistent, and simple forms possible within a given pattern.

Modern research on visual grouping has shown that the Gestalt determinants have a strong influence on perception. For example, in one series of studies, visual targets that were part of larger visual groupings based on proximity were much harder to detect than the same targets seen as standing outside the group (Banks & Prinzmetal, 1976; Prinzmetal, 1981). In another set of studies, targets that were unlike nontargets in color and shape were easier to find than targets that were similar (Treisman, 1986). Even the similarity among the various nontargets has an important effect: Targets are easier to find as the similarity of nontargets increases, allowing the target to pop out as a figure distinct from the background (Duncan & Humphreys, 1989). Finally, there are reliable illusions associated with the Gestalt determinants, and people judge distances among the elements within perceptual groups to be smaller than the same distances when they are between elements in different groups (Coren & Girgus, 1980; Enns & Girgus, 1985). All of these results show that visual grouping plays a large role in the way we organize our visual experience.

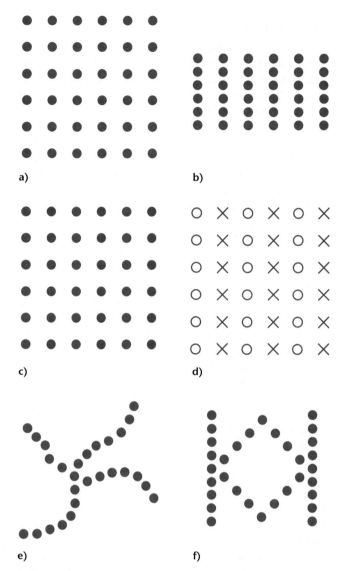

▮ Figure 5-5
Gestalt Determinants of Grouping
(a) Equally spaced dots can be seen as rows, columns, or even diagonals. (b) Grouping into columns by proximity. (c) Grouping into columns by color similarity. (d) Grouping into columns by shape similarity. (e) Grouping by good continuation. (f) Grouping by closure.

Although perceptual grouping has been studied mainly in visual perception, the same determinants of grouping appear in audition. Proximity clearly operates in audition (though it is proximity in time rather than in space). For example, four drumbeats with a pause between the second and third beats will be heard as two pairs. Similarity and closure are also important in hearing tones and more complex stimuli (Bregman, 1990).

PERCEIVING DISTANCE

To know where an object is, we must know its distance or depth. Although perceiving an object's depth seems effortless, it is actually a remarkable achievement because we have no direct access to the depth dimension. A retina is a two-dimensional surface onto which a three-dimensional world is projected. The retina therefore directly reflects height and width, but depth information is lost and must somehow be reconstructed on the basis of **depth cues**, different kinds of visual information that, logically or mathematically, provide information about some object's depth. Depth cues can be classified as binocular or monocular.

BINOCULAR CUES Why are we and other animals equipped with two eyes rather than just one? There are two reasons. Some animals, such as fish, have eyes on either side of the head, which allow them to see a very large percentage of the world around them without moving their heads or their bodies. Other animals, for including humans, have two eyes in the front of their heads, both pointing in the same direction. Humans can see less of the world at any given instant than fish, but they can use their two eyes to perceive depth. (Try covering one eye, and then sit as a passenger in a car driving in stop-and-go traffic. It's a scary experience, because you have much less sense than you normally would of how close you are to cars and other objects in front of you.)

The two eyes' ability to jointly infer depth comes about because the eyes are separated in the head, and each eye has a slightly different view of the same scene. You can easily demonstrate this by holding your right index finger close to your face and examining it first with only one eye open and then with only the other eye open. The term **binocular disparity** refers to the difference in the views seen by each eye. The disparity is largest for objects at close range and becomes smaller as the object recedes into the distance. Beyond 3 to 4 meters (10 to 12 feet), the difference in the views seen by each eye is so small that binocular disparity loses its effectiveness as a cue for depth. However, for many everyday tasks, such as reaching for objects and navigating around obstacles, the difference is a powerful cue for depth.

In humans and other animals with binocular vision, the visual part of the brain uses binocular disparity to assign objects to various locations in space, depending on how far apart the two images of an object are when compared. If the images of an object are in the same place in the two views, the brain assumes that this is the location on which both eyes are fixating. If the difference between the images is large, as it is for the two views of your finger held close to your face, the brain concludes that the object is much closer.

In addition to helping us see depth in the everyday world, binocular disparity can fool the eye into seeing depth when none is really present. A stereoscope displays a slightly different photograph to each eye. In Victorian times, these devices were proudly displayed in the sitting rooms of middle-class homes, much as widescreen television sets might be today. Yet the stereoscope is not just a curious antique. The same principle of binocular disparity is used today in children's View-Master toys, in special effects 3-D movies for which glasses with colored or light-polarizing filters are worn, and in the popular Magic Eye poster art. The principle behind all of these illusions is shown in Figure 5-6.

a) What the eyes normally do when viewing a picture, such as the row of flowers, is to converge on the point in space belonging to the picture plane. In this case, both eyes will receive the identical image and the surface will look flat.

▌Figure 5-6
The Magic of 3-D Vision in Pictures

b) Every 3-D illusion involving pictures is based on fooling the eyes so that they converge to a different point in space. In this case, the two eyes will receive slightly different images. If the brain is fooled into thinking that the different images belong to the same scene, small differences (disparity) in the images will be resolved by assigning objects to different locations in depth.

MONOCULAR CUES Binocular cues are limited to objects that are relatively close. What about objects that are farther away—distant clouds, cityscapes, or mountains? Here, binocular cues are relatively ineffective and other cues, known as monocular cues, must be used, and the task of the visual system is not straightforward. Essentially, the system has to make use of a hodgepodge of available information in the environment to come to a conclusion, much as a detective must sift through a hodgepodge of available evidence to figure out who the murderer is. Figure 5-7 illustrates some of the monocular cues that follow.

1. **Relative size.** If an image contains an array of similar objects that differ in size, the viewer interprets the smaller objects as being farther away (see the lightposts in Figure 5-7).

2. **Interposition.** If one object is positioned so that it obstructs the view of the other, the viewer perceives the overlapping object as being nearer (see the buildings in Figure 5-7).

3. **Relative height.** Among similar objects, those that appear closer to the horizon are perceived as being farther away (see the chimneys in Figure 5-7).

4. **Perspective.** When parallel lines in a scene appear to converge in the image, they are perceived as vanishing in the distance (see the street in Figure 5-7).

5. **Shading and shadows.** The configuration of shading and shadows provides information about an object's depth. Whenever a surface in a scene is blocked from receiving direct light, a shadow is cast. If that shadow falls on a part of the same object that is blocking the light, it is called an *attached shadow* or simply shading. If it falls on another surface that does not belong to the object casting the shadow, it is called a *cast shadow*. Both kinds of shadows are important cues to depth in the scene, giving us information about object shapes, distances between objects, and the location

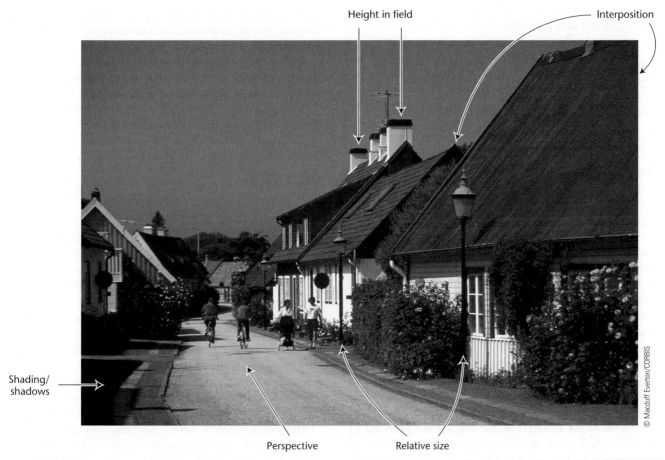

▮ Figure 5-7
Monocular Distance Cues in a Picture
Artists use some or all of these cues in combination to portray depth on a two-dimensional surface. All of these cues are present in a photograph of a natural scene and are also present on the retinal image in the eye.

of the light source in a scene (Coren, Ward, & Enns, 1999).

6. **Relative motion.** The different speeds of two objects can be a depth cue. Have you ever noticed that if you are moving quickly—perhaps on a fast-moving train—nearby objects seem to move quickly in the opposite direction while more distant objects move more slowly (though still in the opposite direction)? Extremely distant objects, such as the moon, appear not to move at all. The difference in the speeds with which these objects appear to move—motion parallax—provides a cue to their distance from us.

Cultural differences appear to affect depth cues. For example, in a comparison of children and college students in the United States and Zimbabwe, Weir & Seacrest (2000) found that ease of problems solved by weight or distance cues did not differ by age among Zimbabweans as it did among U.S. students (and as would be expected by common sense). Such cultural differences again appear when we discuss illusions.

PERCEIVING MOTION

To move around our environment effectively, we need to know not only the locations of stationary objects but also the trajectories of moving ones. We need to know, for example, that the car coming toward us from a block away will not yet have arrived at the intersection before we have crossed the street. We must, that is, be able to perceive motion.

STROBOSCOPIC MOTION What causes us to perceive motion? The simplest idea is that we perceive that an object is in motion whenever its image moves across the retina. This answer turns out to be too simple, though, for we can see motion even when nothing moves on the retina. This phenomenon, shown in Figure 5-8, was demonstrated in 1912 by Wertheimer in his studies of stroboscopic motion. **Stroboscopic motion** is produced most simply by flashing a light in darkness and then, a few milliseconds later, flashing another light near the location of the first light. The light will seem to move from one place to the other in a way that is indistinguishable from real motion.

Wertheimer's demonstration of stroboscopic motion is not just an idle academic exercise. The phenomenon is crucial to great deal of present-day visual-display technology. A prime example is the motion we perceive in movies, which is stroboscopic motion. A movie is, as most people realize, simply a series of still photographs (or frames), each slightly different from the preceding one. As the frames are successively displayed on the screen, the discrete frame-to-frame differences in, say, the position of Arnold Schwarzenegger's hand during a

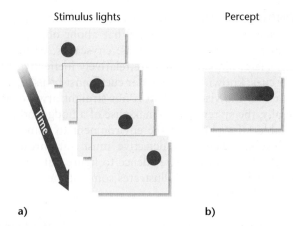

Figure 5-8
Stroboscopic Motion
The sequence of still frames in (a), shown at the appropriate intervals, results in the percept shown in (b). The illusion of continuous motion resulting from successively viewed still pictures is the basis of motion in movies, video, and television.

fight scene, are seen as motion—stroboscopic motion to be sure, but motion that is perceived pretty much exactly as normal, continuous motion.

REAL MOTION Of course, our visual system is also sensitive to real motion—that is, movement of an object through all intermediate points in space. However, the analysis of such motion under everyday conditions is amazingly complex. Some paths of motion on the retina must be attributed to movements of the eye over a stationary scene (as occurs when we are reading). Other motion paths must be attributed to moving objects (as when a bird enters our visual field). Moreover, some objects whose retinal images are stationary must be seen to be moving (as when we follow the flying bird with our eyes), and some objects whose retinal images are moving must be seen as stationary (as when the stationary background traces motion across the retina because our eyes are pursuing a flying bird).

Accordingly, our analysis of motion is highly relative. We are much better at detecting motion when we can see an object against a structured background (relative motion) than when the background is a uniform color and only the moving object can be seen (absolute motion). Certain patterns of relative movement can even be powerful cues to the shape and identity of three-dimensional objects. For example, researchers have found that the motion displays illustrated in Figure 5-9 are sufficient to enable viewers to easily identify the activity of a human figure, even though there are only 12 (or even fewer) points of light moving relative to one another (Johansson, von Hofsten, & Jansson, 1980). In other studies using these displays, viewers were able to

Time

a) This is an example of the types of displays used by investigators to study patterns of humans in motion. Positions of lights affixed to individuals are indicated.

b) A sequence of movement positions made by a dancing couple.

▌**Figure 5-9**
Patterns of Human Motion

identify their friends and even tell whether the model was male or female after seeing only the lights attached to the ankles (Cutting, 1986).

Another important phenomenon in the study of real motion is **selective adaptation.** This is a loss in sensitivity to motion that occurs when we view motion; the adaptation is selective in that we lose sensitivity to the motion viewed and to similar motions, but not to motion that differs significantly in direction or speed. If we look at upward-moving stripes, for example, we lose sensitivity to upward motion, but our ability to see downward motion is not affected (Sekuler, 1975). Like other types of adaptation, we do not usually notice the loss of sensitivity, but we do notice the aftereffect produced by adaptation. If we view a waterfall for a few minutes and then look at the cliff beside it, the cliff will appear to move upward. Most motions will produce such aftereffects, always in the opposite direction from the original motion.

How does the brain implement the perception of real motion? Some aspects of real motion are coded by specific cells in the visual cortex. These cells respond to some motions and not to others, and each cell responds best to one direction and speed of motion. The best evidence for the existence of such cells comes from studies

California Museum of Photography, University of California, Riverside

The Holmes-Bates stereoscope, invented by Oliver Wendell Holmes in 1861 and manufactured by Joseph Bates, creates a vivid perception of depth.

with animals in which the experimenter records the responses of single cells in the visual cortex while the animal is shown stimuli with different patterns of motion. Such single-cell recording studies have found cortical cells that are tuned to particular directions of movement.

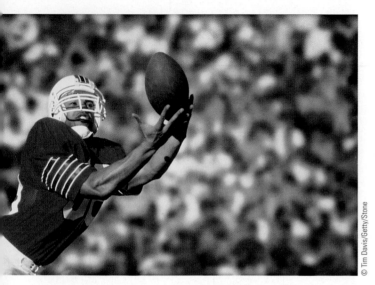

To catch the ball and avoid being tackled, football players must be able to perceive motion accurately.

There are even cells that are specifically tuned to detect an object moving toward the head, an ability that is clearly useful for survival (Regan, Beverley, & Cynader, 1979).

These specialized motion cells provide a possible explanation for selective adaptation and the motion aftereffect. Presumably, selective adaptation to an upward motion, for example, occurs because the cortical cells that are specialized for upward motion have become fatigued. Because the cells that are specialized for downward motion are functioning as usual, they will dominate the processing and cause the aftereffect of downward motion.

However, there is more to the neural basis of real motion than the activation of specific cells. We can see motion when we track a luminous object moving in darkness (such as an airplane at night). Because our eyes follow the object, the image is almost motionless on the retina, yet we perceive a smooth, continuous motion. Why? The answer seems to be that information about how our eyes are moving is sent from motor regions in the front of the brain to the visual cortex and influences the motion we see. In essence, the motor system is informing the visual system that it is responsible for the lack of regular motion on the retina, and the visual system then corrects for this lack. In more normal viewing situations, there are both eye movements and large retinal-image movements. The visual system must combine these two sources of information to determine the perceived motion. You can demonstrate a consequence of this arrangement by gently pushing up on your eyeball through your lower lid. The world appears to move because the world is moving across your retina, but the

normal signals from the motor regions are absent. The only interpretation the brain can make is that the world itself is moving.

◆Interim Summary

- To localize objects, we must first separate them and then organize them into groups.
- Localization involves determining an object's position in the up-down and left-right dimensions. This is relatively easy because the required information is part of our retinal image.
- Localizing an object also requires that we know its distance from us. This form of perception, known as depth perception, is not so easy because it's not available in the retinal image. We have a variety of depth cues, both monocular and binocular, that allow us to do this.
- Localizing an object sometimes requires that we know the direction in which an object is moving. This can be done either with real motion or with stroboscopic motion.

◆ Critical Thinking Questions

1. Imagine what your visual experience might be like if you suddenly became unable to see motion. In other words, suppose you saw things happening like a slide show rather than like a movie. How does motion perception contribute to your experience of a coherent world, and in what ways would the world become incoherent without a perception of motion?

2. Rank all the distance-perception cues from most important to least important. The main part of your answer should describe why you believe some distance-perception cues are more or less important than others. This, of course, requires a *definition* on your part of what it means for a distance-perception cue to be "important."

RECOGNITION

The perceptual system needs to determine not only where relevant objects are in the scene but also *what* they are. This is the process of recognition. Ideally, if a cat crosses our path, we should be able to recognize it as a cat, not as a skunk or a hula hoop. Similarly, if a benign tent is in front of us, we should not recognize it as a dangerous bear. (From an evolutionary perspective, however, we would be better off misperceiving a tent for a bear than a bear for a tent. Our visual system has prob-

In the early stages of recognition, the perceptual system uses information on the retina to describe the object in terms of primitive components like lines and edges. In later stages, the system compares this description to those of various categories of objects stored in the visual memory, such as "dogs."

ably evolved to be biased to perceive objects as dangerous, even if sometimes they are not.)

Recognizing an object entails several subproblems. First, we have to acquire fundamental or *primitive* bits and pieces of information from the environment and assemble them properly. For example, if we acquire the information that there's something red and something green and a circle and a square, we must somehow figure out that it's the circle that's red and the square that's green, not vice versa. Second, we have to figure out what the objects actually are. In the simple example we've just described, we somehow have to figure out that it's a square there to begin with. A more complex task would be to figure out that the combination of lines, angles, and shapes that we're looking at constitutes a human face, and a yet more complex task would be to figure out

that the face belongs to a particular person, like Michael Jordan.

We'll discuss these various functions of recognition by starting with the **binding problem:** how activity in different parts of the brain, corresponding to different primitives such as color and shape, are combined into a coherent perception of an object. Next, we'll talk about how we actually recognize what an object *is*.

THE BINDING PROBLEM: PREATTENTIVE AND ATTENTIVE PROCESSES

Attention is the process of selecting from the vast amount of incoming information what is processed and eventually perceived consciously. Attention has also been conceptualized as having the role of binding together different features of an incoming stimulus. An excellent illustration of what we mean is the **illusory conjunction,** which is an incorrect combination of two separate attributes of an object. Suppose an observer is shown very briefly (such as a 20th of a second) a stimulus such as the one in Figure 5-10—a small red circle, a large green square, and a medium-size blue triangle—and asked to report what was seen. The observer is typically able to report the three shapes and the three colors—but sometimes incorrectly reports which color went with which shape. The observer might report that the square was red, not green, and the perceived conjunction of shape (square) and color (red) is illusory. People often experience a rough analogy of this phenomenon while reading: They might conjoin part of one word on one line of text (say, the *Se* from *Senate*) with part of another word on a different line (the *attle* from *rattled*) and perceive that they see the word *Seattle* in the text—thereby misconjoining the primitive features of shape and location.

FEATURE INTEGRATION THEORY Illusory conjunctions suggest that information from the visual world is preattentively encoded along separate dimensions—in the example, shape and color are encoded separately—and then integrated in a subsequent *attentive* processing stage. This idea is, indeed, at the heart of **feature-integration**

▌Figure 5-10
Illusory Conjunction
When images are flashed briefly, observers often miscombine shape and color. This is known as *illusory conjunction.*

theory, a cornerstone of understanding object perception that was initially proposed by Anne Treisman (Treisman, 1986; Treisman & Gelade, 1993). The general idea is that in a first, preattentive stage, **primitive features,** qualities such as shape and color, are perceived, and in the second, *attentive* stage, focused attention is used to properly "glue" the features together into an integrated whole. Illusory conjunctions occur when stimulus duration is sufficient for the primitives to be obtained but not sufficient for the longer, attentional gluing stage.

A standard experimental procedure for distinguishing primitive features from "glued-together" features is a **visual search task** in which the observer's task is to determine whether some target object is present in a cluttered display (Chelazzi, Duncan, Miller, & Desimone, 1998; Palmer, Verghese, & Pavel, 2000). In a typical visual search task (Figure 5-11), the task is to find a green *L*. In the left panel of Figure 5-11, the task is simple. The green *L* pops out from the collection of red *T*s and red *L*s. In the right panel, however, the task of finding the same green *L* is considerably more difficult when the background is a collection of red *L*s and green *T*s. The reason, according to feature integration theory, is that color is a primitive feature: In the left panel, you can simply scan the information all at once. What is red and what is green perceptually separate, and the presence of the one green object—the target green *L*—is apparent. In the right panel, in contrast, you cannot distinguish the target from the background on the basis of the primitive attribute of color. Instead, you must attend to each letter, binding together the color and the shape, before you can determine whether that letter is or is not the target.

PROBLEMS WITH FEATURE INTEGRATION THEORY

Feature integration theory has enjoyed a great deal of support over the past couple of decades. In recent times, however, it has come under attack from the perspectives of both theoretical parsimony and biological plausibility. The major problem is that, using visual search and related procedures, scientists have unveiled too many presumed "primitives" to be realistic. A particularly lucid description of the problems with the theory is provided by Di Lollo, Kawahara, Suvic, and Visser (2001). They go on to describe an alternative, **dynamic control theory,** whose central premise is that, "instead of an early, hard-wired system sensitive to a small number of visual primitives, there is a malleable system whose components can be quickly reconfigured to perform different tasks at different times, much as the internal pattern of connectivity in a computer is rearranged dynamically by enabling and disabling myriad gates under program control" (p. 11). Essentially, the system rearranges itself for different tasks—as opposed to there being many subsystems for each possible task.

Determining What an Object Is

Attentive versus preattentive processing is concerned with the problem of determining which visual characteristics belong to the same object. A second problem is using the resulting information to determine what an object actually *is*. Here, shape plays a critical role. We can recognize a cup, for example, regardless of whether it is large or small (a variation in size), brown or white (a variation in color), smooth or bumpy (a variation in texture), or presented upright or tilted slightly (a variation in orientation). In contrast, our ability to recognize a cup is

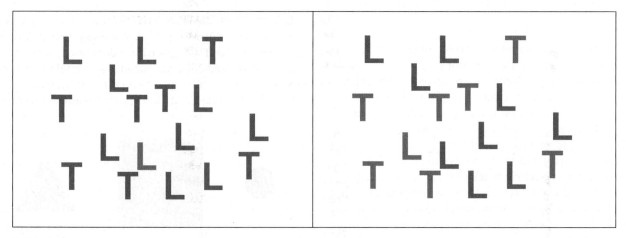

▌ Figure 5-11
A Visual Search Task
Find the green *L*. This is any easy task in the left panel, where popout takes place, but a difficult task in the right panel, where each stimulus requires focal attention.

Stimuli

Nerve
impulses

off   on   off   on   off   on

❚ Figure 5-12
The Response of a Simple Cell
This figure illustrates the response of a simple cortical cell to a
bar of light. The stimulus is on the top, the response on the
bottom; each vertical spike on the bottom corresponds to one
nerve impulse. When there is no stimulus, only an occasional
impulse is recorded. When the stimulus is turned on, the cell
may or may not respond, depending on the position and orientation of the light bar. For this cell, a horizontal bar produces
no change in response, a bar at 45 degrees produces a small
change, and a vertical bar produces a very large change.

strikingly affected by variations in shape. If part of the
cup's shape is hidden, we may not recognize it at all, but
we can recognize many objects about as well from simple
line drawings, which preserve only the shapes of the objects, as from detailed color photographs, which preserve
many other attributes of the objects as well (Biederman
& Ju, 1988).

Here also, visual processing can be divided into earlier and later stages. In early stages, the perceptual system uses information on the retina, particularly variations in intensity, to describe the object in terms of
primitive components such as lines, edges, and angles.
The system uses these components to construct a description of the object. In later stages, the system compares this description to those of various categories of
objects stored in visual memory and selects the best
match. To recognize a particular object as the letter *B*,
for example, is to say that the object's shape matches
that of *B*'s better than it matches that of other letters.

The Neural Basis of Behavior

FEATURE DETECTORS IN THE CORTEX
Much of what is known about the primitive features of
object perception comes from biological studies of
other species (such as cats and monkeys) that use single-

cell recordings in the visual cortex.
These studies examine the sensitivity of specific cortical neurons
when different stimuli are presented to the regions of the retina
associated with those neurons.
Such a retinal region is called a *receptive field*.

These single-cell studies were
pioneered by David Hubel and
Torstein Wiesel (1968), who, in
1981, won a Nobel prize for their
work. Hubel and Wiesel identified
three types of cells in the visual
cortex that can be distinguished by the features to
which they respond. **Simple cells** respond when the eye
is exposed to a line stimulus (such as a thin bar or
straight edge between a dark and a light region) at a
particular orientation and position within its receptive
field. Figure 5-12 illustrates how a simple cell responds
to a vertical bar and to bars tilted away from the vertical. The largest response is obtained for a vertical bar,
and the response decreases as the orientation varies
from the optimal one. Other simple cells are tuned to
other orientations and positions. A **complex cell** *also
responds to a bar or edge in a particular orientation
but does not require that the stimulus be at a particular
place within its receptive field*. It responds continuously
as the stimulus is moved across that field. **Hypercomplex cells** require not only that the stimulus be in a particular orientation but also that it be of a particular
length. If a stimulus is extended beyond the optimal
length, the response decreases and may cease entirely.
Since Hubel and Wiesel's initial reports, investigators
have found cells that respond to shape features other
than single bars and edges. For example, there are hypercomplex cells that respond to corners or angles of a
specific length (DeValois & DeValois, 1980; Shapley &
Lennie, 1985).

All of these cells are referred to as feature detectors. Because the edges, bars, corners, and angles to
which these detectors respond can be used to approximate many shapes, the feature detectors might be
thought of as the building blocks of shape perception.
As we will see later, though, this proposal seems to be
truer of simple shapes like letters than of complex
shapes like those of tables and tigers. ❚

RELATIONS AMONG FEATURES There is more to a description of a shape than just its features: The relations
among features must also be specified. The importance
of such relations is illustrated in Figure 5-13, where it is
evident that, for example, the features of a right angle
and a diagonal line must be combined in a specific way

Component		Component		Whole	Emergent
Feature A	+	Feature B	=	Object	Property

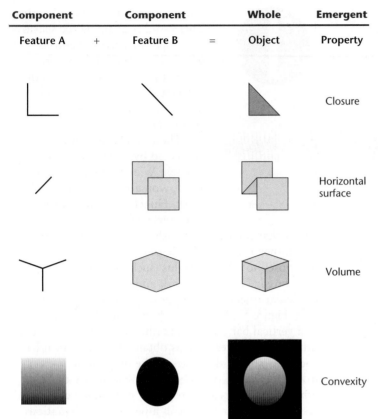

Closure

Horizontal surface

Volume

Convexity

▌Figure 5-13
Relationships Between Features
When simple two-dimensional features such as lines, angles, and shapes are combined, the resulting pattern is highly dependent on the spatial relations between the component features. In addition, new features are created. These emergent features have a perceptual reality, even though they involve complex spatial relations.

to result in a triangle. Likewise, a **Y** intersection and a hexagon must be specifically aligned to result in the drawing of a cube. Gestalt psychologists had these kinds of relations between features in mind when they emphasized that "the whole is different from the sum of its parts."

One way the whole is different is that it creates new perceptual features that cannot be understood by simply examining the component parts. Figure 5-13 shows four such **emergent features,** *which* owe their existence to the configuration of other features. Emergent features come from very specific spatial relations among more elementary features but nevertheless often behave just like simpler features in perceptual tasks, such as target detection and visual search (Enns & Prinzmetal, 1984; Enns & Rensink, 1990; He & Nakayama, 1992). These results indicate that the visual system performs many sophisti-

cated analyses of shape before the results of these analyses are made available to consciousness.

LATER STAGES OF RECOGNITION: NETWORK MODELS

Now that we have some idea of how an object's shape is described, we can consider how that description is matched to shape descriptions stored in memory to find the best match and to decide what an object is.

SIMPLE NETWORKS Much of the research on the matching stage has used simple patterns, specifically, handwritten or printed letters or words. Figure 5-14 illustrates a proposal about how we store shape descriptions of letters. The basic idea is that letters are described in terms of certain features, and that knowledge about what features go with what letter is contained in a network of connections. Such proposals are referred to as **connectionist models.** In the context of psychology, they were popularized in a series of publications by Jay McClelland and David Rumelhart (e.g., McClelland & Rumelhart, 1981) and have since been applied to diverse subareas, including language (Berent, 2001), working memory (Caplan & Waters, 2002), and facial expressions of emotion (Mignault, 2001). These models are appealing in that it is easy to conceive how networks could be realized in the brain with its array of interconnected neurons. Connectionism offers a bridge between psychological and biological models.

The bottom level of the network in Figure 5-14 contains the features ascending diagonal, descending diagonal, vertical line, and right-facing curve. The top level

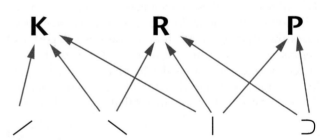

▌Figure 5-14
A Simple Network
The bottom level of the network contains the features (ascending diagonal, descending diagonal, vertical line, and right-facing curve), the top level contains the letters, and a connection between a feature and a letter means that the feature is part of the letter. Because the connections are excitatory, when a feature is activated, the activation spreads to the letter.

contains the letters themselves. We will refer to each of these features and letters as a *node* in the *network*. A connection between a feature and a letter node means that the feature is part of the letter. Connections ending in arrowheads are **excitatory connections.** If the feature is activated, the activation spreads to the letter (in a manner analogous to the way electrical impulses spread in a network of neurons).

To see how this network can be used to recognize (or match) a letter, consider what happens when the letter *K* is presented. It activates the features of ascending diagonal, descending diagonal, and vertical line. All three of these features activate the node for *K*, two of them—the descending diagonal and vertical line—activate the node for *R*, and one of them—the vertical line—activates the node for *P*. Only the *K* node has all of its features activated, and consequently it is selected as the best match.

This model is too simple to account for many aspects of recognition, however. Consider what happens when the letter *R* is presented. It activates the features of descending diagonal, vertical line, and right-facing curve. Now the nodes for both *R* and *P* have all their features activated, and the model has no way of deciding which of the two categories provides a better match. What the model needs to know is that the presence of a descending diagonal means that the letter cannot be a *P*. This kind of negative knowledge is included in the **augmented network** in Figure 5-15, which has everything the original network had, plus **inhibitory connections** (symbolized by solid circles at their ends) between features and letters that do not contain those features. When a feature is connected to a letter by an inhibitory connection, activating the feature decreases activation of the letter. When *R* is presented to the network in Figure 5-15, the descending diagonal inhibits the *P* node and decreases its overall level of activation. Now the *R* node will receive the most activation and, consequently, will be selected as the best match.

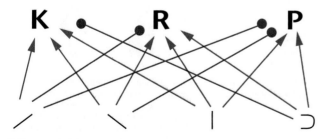

▌Figure 5-15
An Augmented Network
The network contains inhibitory connections between features and letters that do not contain these features, as well as excitatory connections.

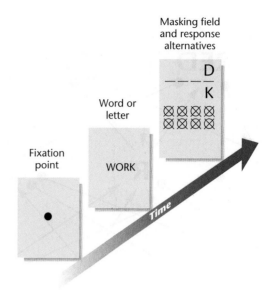

▌Figure 5-16
Perception of Letters and Words
This figure illustrates the sequence of events in an experiment that compares the perceptibility of a letter presented alone or in the context of a word. First, participants saw a fixation point, followed by a word or a single letter, which was present for only a few milliseconds. Then the experimenter presented a stimulus that contained a visual mask in the positions where the letters had been, plus two response alternatives. The task was to decide which of the two alternatives occurred in the word or letter presented earlier. (After Reicher, 1969)

NETWORKS WITH FEEDBACK The basic idea behind the model we just considered—that a letter must be described by the features it lacks as well as by the features it contains—does not explain a pervasive and interesting finding: A letter is easier to perceive when it is presented as part of a word than when it is presented alone. For example, as shown in Figure 5-16, if observers are briefly presented with either the single letter *K* or the word *WORK,* they are more accurate in identifying whether a *K* or *D* was present when the display contained a word than when it contained only a letter.

To account for this result, our network of feature-letter connections has to be altered in a few ways. First, we have to add a level of words to our network, and along with it excitatory and inhibitory connections that go from letters to words, as shown in Figure 5-17. In addition, we have to add excitatory connections that go from words down to letters. These **top-down feedback connections**—connections that go from the higher levels to the lower levels—explain why a letter is more perceptible when presented briefly in a word than when presented briefly alone. When *R* is presented alone, for example, the features of vertical line, descending diagonal,

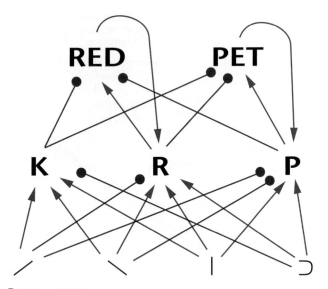

▌ Figure 5-17
A Network with Top-Down Activation
The network contains excitatory and inhibitory connections between letters and words (as well as between features and letters), and some of the excitatory connections go from words to letters.

and right-facing curve are activated, and this activation spreads to the node for R. Because the letter was presented very briefly, not all the features may have been fully activated, and the activation culminating at the R node may not be sufficient for recognition to occur. In contrast, when R is presented in *RED*, there is activation not only from the features of R to the R node but also from the features of E and D to their nodes. All of these partially activated letters then partially activate the *RED* node, which in turn feeds back activation to its letters via its top-down connections.

The upshot is that there is an additional source of activation for R when it is presented in a word—namely, activation coming from the word—and this is why it is easier to recognize a letter in a word than when it is presented alone. Many other findings about letter and word patterns have been shown to be consistent with this connectionist model (McClelland & Rumelhart, 1981). Models like these have also been used successfully in machines designed to read handwriting and recognize speech (Coren, Ward, & Enns, 1999).

RECOGNIZING NATURAL OBJECTS AND TOP-DOWN PROCESSING

We know quite a bit about recognition of letters and words, but what about more natural objects—animals, plants, people, furniture, and clothing? In this section we examine how we recognize such objects.

FEATURES OF NATURAL OBJECTS The shape features of natural objects are more complex than lines and curves and more like simple geometric forms. These features must be capable of combining to form the shape of any recognizable object (just as lines and curves can combine to form any letter). The features of objects must also be such that they can be determined or constructed from more primitive features, such as lines and curves, because, as noted earlier, primitive features are the only information available to the system in the early stages of recognition.

It has been suggested that the features of objects include a number of geometric forms, such as arcs, cylinders, cones, blocks, and wedges, as illustrated in Figure 5-18a. These features, referred to as **geons** (short for "geometric ions"), were identified by Biederman (1987), who argues that a set of 36 geons, such as those in Figure 5-18a, combined according to a small set of spatial relations, is sufficient to describe the shapes of all objects that people can possibly recognize. To appreciate this point, as shown in Figure 5-18b you can form an object by combining any two geons—and the number of possi-

a) Geons

Wedges, cubes, cylinders, cones, and arcs may be features of complex objects.

b) Objects

When the features (geons) are combined, they form natural objects. Note that when the arc (geon 5) is connected to the side of the cylinder (geon 3), it forms a cup; when connected to the top of the cylinder, it forms a pail.

▌ Figure 5-18
A Possible Set of Features (Geons) for Natural Objects
(From L. Biederman, *Computer Vision, Graphics, and Image Processing*, 32, pp. 29–73, © 1985 Academic Press. Used with permission.)

ble such two-geon objects is $36 \times 36 = 1,296$. Likewise, the number of possible three-geon objects is $36 \times 36 \times 36 = 46,656$. Two or three geons are sufficient to create almost 50,000 objects, and we have yet to consider objects made up of 4 or more geons. Moreover, geons like those in Figure 5-18a can be distinguished solely in terms of primitive features. For example, geon 2 in Figure 5-18a (the cube) differs from geon 3 (the cylinder) in that the cube has straight edges but the cylinder has curved edges; straight and curved edges are primitive features.

Evidence that geons are features comes from experiments in which observers try to recognize briefly presented objects. The general finding is that recognition of an object is good to the extent that the geons of the object are perceptible. In one study, part of the shape of an object was deleted in such a way that the deletion either interfered with recovering the geons (see the right column of Figure 5-19) or did not (see the middle column). Recognition of the objects was much better when there was no interference with the geons.

As usual, the description of an object includes not just its features but also the relations among them. This is evident in Figure 5-18b. When the arc is connected to the side of the cylinder, it forms a cup. When it is connected to the top of the cylinder, it forms a pail. Once the description of an object's shape is constructed, it is compared with an array of geon descriptions stored in memory to find the best match. This matching process between the description of an object's shape and the descriptions stored in memory resembles the process described earlier for letters and words (Hummel & Biederman, 1992).

THE IMPORTANCE OF CONTEXT A key distinction in perception is between bottom-up and top-down processes. **Bottom-up processes** are driven solely by the input—the raw, sensory data—whereas **top-down processes** are driven by a person's knowledge, experience, attention, and expectations. Recognizing the shape of an object solely on the basis of its geon description involves only bottom-up processes. A viewer starts with primitive features of the input, determines the geon configuration of the input, and then makes this description available to shape descriptions stored in memory. In contrast, recognizing that the object is a lamp partly on the basis of its being on a night table next to a bed involves some top-down processes. Other information is used besides the input regarding shape. Although most of the processes considered thus far in this chapter are bottom-up ones, top-down processes also play a major role in object perception.

Top-down processes, in the form of expectations, underlie the powerful effects of context on our perception of objects and people. You expect to see your

▌Figure 5-19
Object Recognition and Geon Recovery
Items used in experiments on object recognition. The left column shows the original intact versions of the objects. The middle column shows versions of the objects in which regions have been deleted, but the geons are still recoverable. The right column shows versions of the objects in which regions have been deleted and the geons are not recoverable. Recognition is better for the middle versions than for the rightmost versions. (After L. Biederman, *Computer Vision, Graphics, and Image Processing*, 32, pp. 29–73, © 1985 Academic Press. Used with permission.)

chemistry lab partner, Sarah, every Tuesday at 3 P.M., and when she enters the lab at that moment you hardly need to look to know who it is. Your prior knowledge has led to a powerful expectation, and little input is needed for recognition. But should Sarah suddenly appear in your hometown during Christmas vacation, you may have trouble recognizing her. She is out of context. Your expectations have been violated, and you must resort to extensive bottom-up processing to recognize her (we experience this as "doing a double take"). As this example makes clear, when the context is appropriate (that is, it predicts the input object), it facilitates perception. When the context is inappropriate, it impairs perception.

The effects of context are particularly striking when the stimulus object is ambiguous and can be perceived in more than one way. The ambiguous figure in Figure 5-20

Figure 5-20
An Ambiguous Stimulus
An ambiguous drawing that can be seen either as a young woman or as an old woman. Most people see the old woman first. The young woman is turning away, and we see the left side of her face. Her chin is the old woman's nose, and her necklace is the old woman's mouth. (From E. G. Boring (1930) "A New Ambiguous Figure," from *American Journal of Psychology, 42*:444–445.)

can be perceived either as an old woman or as a young woman. If you have been looking at unambiguous pictures that resemble the young woman in the figure (that is, if young women are the context), you will tend to see the young woman first in the ambiguous picture. This effect of temporal context is illustrated with another set of pictures in Figure 5-21. Look at the pictures as you would at a comic strip, from left to right and top to bottom. The pictures in the middle of the series are ambiguous. If you view the figures in the sequence just suggested, you will tend to see the ambiguous pictures as a man's face. If you view the figures in the opposite order, you will tend to see the ambiguous pictures as a young woman.

The stimulus object need not be ambiguous to demonstrate the effect of context. Suppose a person is first shown a picture of a scene and is then briefly given a picture of an unambiguous object to identify. Identification will be more accurate if the object is appropriate to the scene. For example, after looking at a kitchen scene, the person will correctly identify a briefly presented loaf of bread more often than a briefly presented mailbox (Palmer, 1975).

Because of top-down processing, our motives and desires can affect our perceptions. If we are very hungry, a quick glance at a red ball on our kitchen table may register as an apple. Our desire for food has led us to think

Figure 5-21
Effects of Temporal Context
What you see here depends on the order in which you view the pictures. If you start at the beginning and work forward, the middle pictures will appear to be a young woman. In other words, your initial perception perseverates. (From G. H. Fisher (1967) "Perception of Ambiguous Stimulus Materials," from *Perception & Psychophysics, 2*:421–422. Reprinted by permission of the Psychonomic Society.)

about food, and these expectations have combined with the input (a red, round object) to yield the percept of an apple. Motives can also have a negative effect on perception. If we believe a man to be a child molester, for example, we are more likely to misperceive his innocent touching of a child as sexual in nature.

Context effects and top-down processing also occur with letters and words and are a major part of reading. Both the number of eye fixations we make on text and the durations of these fixations are greatly influenced by how much we know about the text—and therefore by the amount of top-down processing we can invoke. When the material is unfamiliar, there is little top-down processing. In such cases we tend to fixate on every word, except for function words like *a*, *of*, and *the*. As the material becomes more familiar, we can bring our prior knowledge to bear on it, and our fixations become shorter and more widely spaced (Just & Carpenter, 1980; Rayner, 1978).

Top-down processing occurs even in the absence of context if the input is sufficiently sparse or degraded. Suppose that at a friend's apartment you enter her dark kitchen and see a smallish black object in the corner. You think the object could be your friend's cat, but the perceptual input is too degraded to convince you. So you think of a particular feature of the cat, such as its tail, and selectively attend to the region of the object that is likely to contain that feature if it is indeed a cat (Kosslyn & Koenig, 1992). This processing is top-down because you have used specific knowledge—the fact that cats have tails—to generate an expectation, which is then combined with the visual input. Situations like this are common in everyday life. Sometimes, however, the input is very degraded, and the expectations we form are way off the mark. Sometimes we finally realize that our would-be cat in the kitchen is really our friend's purse.

FAILURE OF RECOGNITION

Recognizing an object is usually so automatic and effortless that we take it for granted, but the process sometimes breaks down. We have already seen that in normal people recognition can fail in simple situations (as with illusory conjunctions) and in more complex situations (as when a tent is mistaken for a bear). Recognition also fails routinely in people who have suffered from certain kinds of brain damage (due to accidents or diseases such as strokes). The general term for such breakdowns or disorders in recognition is **agnosia.**

Of particular interest is a type of agnosia called *associative agnosia.* In this syndrome, patients with damage to temporal lobe regions of the cortex have difficulty recognizing objects only when they are presented visually. For example, the patient may be unable to name a comb when presented with a picture of it but can name it when allowed to touch it. The deficit is exemplified by the following case:

> For the first three weeks in the hospital the patient could not identify common objects presented visually and did not know what was on his plate until he tasted it. He identified objects immediately on touching them [but] when shown a stethoscope, he described it as "a long cord with a round thing at the end," and asked if it could be a watch. He identified a can opener as "could be a key." Asked to name a cigarette lighter, he said, "I don't know." He said he was "not sure" when shown a toothbrush. Asked to identify a comb, he said, "I don't know." For a pipe, he said, "some type of utensil, I'm not sure." Shown a key, he said, "I don't know what that is; perhaps a file or a tool of some sort." (Reubens & Benson, 1971)

What aspects of object recognition have broken down in associative agnosia? Because these patients often do well on visual tasks other than recognition—such as drawing objects or determining whether two pictured objects match—the breakdown is likely to be in the later stages of recognition, in which the input object is matched to stored object descriptions. One possibility is that the stored object descriptions have been lost or obscured in some way (Damasio, 1985).

Some patients with associative agnosia have problems recognizing certain categories but not others. These category-specific deficits are of considerable interest because they may tell us something new about how normal recognition works. The most frequent category-specific deficit is loss of the ability to recognize faces, called *prosopagnosia.* (We discussed this condition briefly in Chapter 1.) When this deficit occurs, there is always brain damage in the right hemisphere and often some damage in homologous regions of the left hemisphere as well. The condition is illustrated by the following case:

> He could not identify his medical attendants. "You must be a doctor because of your white coat, but I don't know which one you are. I'll know if you speak." He failed to identify his wife during visiting hours. . . . He failed to identify pictures of Churchill, Hitler, and Marilyn Monroe. When confronted with such portraits he would proceed deductively, searching for the "critical" detail which would yield the answer. (Pallis, 1955)

A second kind of category deficit is loss of the ability to recognize words, called *pure alexia* (typically accompanied by damage in the left occipital lobe). Patients with this deficit typically have no difficulty recognizing natural objects or faces. They can even identify individual letters. What they cannot do is recognize visually presented words. When presented with a word, they attempt to read it letter by letter. It can take as long as 10 seconds for them to recognize a common word, with the amount of time needed increasing with the number of letters in the word (Bub, Blacks, & Howell, 1989).

Other types of category-specific deficits involve impairment in the ability to recognize living things such as animals, plants, and foods. In rare cases, patients are unable to recognize nonliving things, such as household tools (Warrington & Shallice, 1984).

Some of the suggested explanations of category-specific deficits have implications for normal recognition. One hypothesis is that the normal recognition system is organized around different classes of objects—one subsystem for faces, another for words, a third for animals, and so on—and these subsystems are localized in different regions of the brain. A patient who suffers only restricted brain damage may show a loss of one subsystem but not others. Damage in a specific part of the right hemisphere, for example, might disrupt the face-recognition subsystem but leave the other subsystems intact (Damasio, 1990; Farah, 1990).

◆Interim Summary

- Recognizing an object requires that the various features associated with the object (such as shapes and colors) be correctly bound together, a process that requires attention.

- Recognizing an object amounts to assigning it to a category and is based mainly on the object's shape.

- Matching can be explained by a connectionist model or network.

- The shape features of natural objects are more complex than lines; they are similar to simple geometric forms such as cylinders, cones, blocks, and wedges. A particular set of such forms is a geon.

- Bottom-up recognition processes are driven solely by the input, whereas top-down recognition processes are driven by a person's knowledge and expectations.

◆ Critical Thinking Questions

1. At the beginning of this chapter, we described a tent that was tragically mistaken for a bear. Why do you think this misperception happened? What could the hunters have done to avoid the misperception?

2. Do you think there is a fundamental difference between recognizing a natural object, such as an eagle, and recognizing an artificial object, such as a stop sign? Give reasons for your answers.

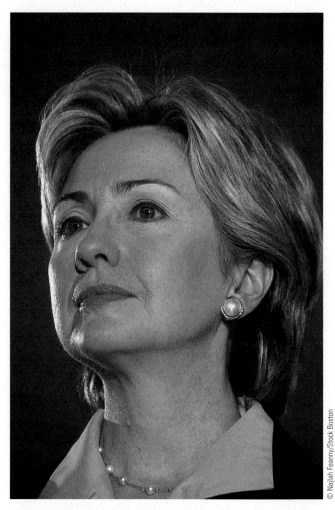

The former first lady, Hillary Rodham Clinton.

ABSTRACTION

Abstraction is the process of reducing the vast amount of information that comes in from the physical world through our senses to a more manageable set of categories.

To see what we mean, note that the **physical description** of an object is a listing of all the information necessary to completely reproduce the object. Many stimuli studied in the scientific laboratory—patches of light, squares, single letters—are relatively simple, and their physical descriptions are likewise simple. However, the physical description of most real-life, natural objects is enormously complicated. Look at Hillary Clinton's face. The visual detail that exists within it seems almost infinite. As you look closer and closer at her skin, for example, tiny blemishes and irregularities become apparent. Each individual hair on her head is positioned just so. The shadowing across her features, while subtle, is enormously complex. To write a complete description of her face, in other words, would take an extremely long time. Really, the only way you could do it would be to create a bitmap of her face, and even then the completeness of the description would be limited by the bitmap's resolution.

In real life, these limitations don't usually present a problem because you don't need that much detail to solve the problems assigned to you by the world. In a typical instance, you would need only as much detail as is necessary to (1) recognize her face to begin with and (2) determine from her expression what kind of mood she is in. (Caricaturists know this quite well; with a few deft strokes of their pen, they can capture the likeness and expression of a person with remarkable clarity.) This situation is not, of course, unique to faces. Whether you are looking at a hairpin or a pencil sharpener or an armchair or anything else, you rarely if ever need to know all the infinite visual detail. Rather, you need to know only enough to carry out whatever task is requiring you to perceive the object to begin with.

To get a feel for this, look at the two drawings in Figure 5-22. Both were created with a computer drawing program. The face on the left was drawn freehand, and the one on the right was drawn as a "copy" of the one on the left, using nothing but the drawing program's oval and line tools. Clearly, the left-hand original contains considerably more detail, but both give the same impression—of a slightly bewildered-looking individual.

When these two versions of the face were saved as files, the original, freehand version required 30,720 bytes of memory, but the "abstracted" version required only 902 bytes—a savings of about 97%! Clearly, it is more efficient in many respects to perceive and encode in memory an abstraction of the object rather than an exact representation of the object itself. As we noted earlier, object recognition is well conceptualized as the construction of objects with a "drawing program," where the primitives are geons.

A nice example of how perception of a real-life object is schematized in this manner was reported by Carmichael, Hogan, and Walter (1932), who presented ambiguous stimuli such as those in Figure 5-23 (middle column, labeled "Stimulus Figures"), along with a *label* that told the observers what they were looking at. For instance, while viewing the stimulus in the top middle column, some observers were told they were looking at "curtains in a window," and others were told they were looking at "a diamond in a rectangle." The observers were later asked to reproduce what they had seen. Examples are shown in the left and right columns of Figure 5-23. As you can see, what the subjects perceived and stored in memory corresponded very strongly to what they considered themselves to be looking at.

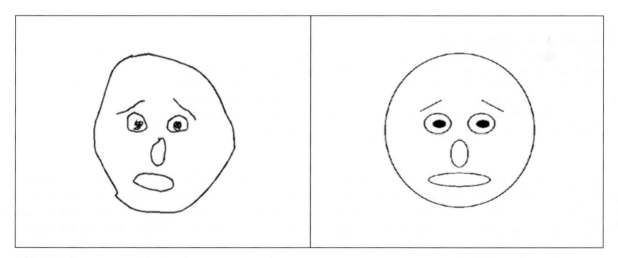

❚ Figure 5-22
The Process of Abstraction
Two versions of the same sad face. The one on the left was drawn freehand, and the one on the right was drawn with "abstracting" tools such as ovals and lines. The left face takes up considerably more disk space than the right, which illustrates one of the virtues of abstracting for any visual-processing device, including biological visual systems.

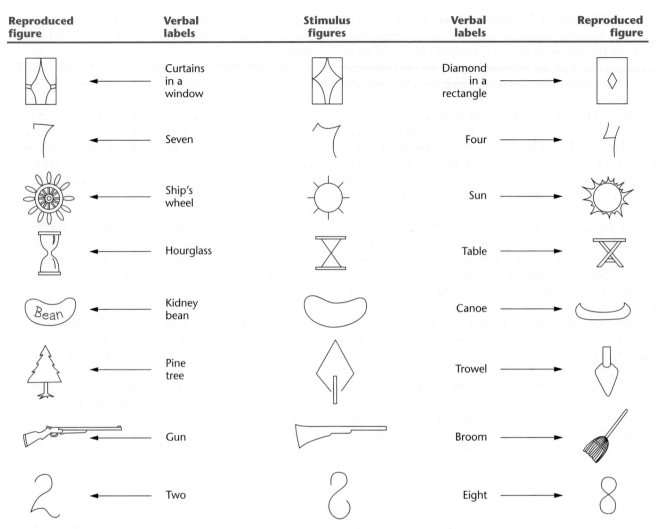

Reproduced figure	Verbal labels	Stimulus figures	Verbal labels	Reproduced figure
	Curtains in a window		Diamond in a rectangle	
	Seven		Four	
	Ship's wheel		Sun	
	Hourglass		Table	
	Kidney bean		Canoe	
	Pine tree		Trowel	
	Gun		Broom	
	Two		Eight	

▌ **Figure 5-23**
Verbal Labels and Abstraction
Carmichael, Hogan, and Walter (1932) showed people the kind of ambiguous stimuli shown in the middle panel. Observers were given one of the two verbal labels shown in the second and fourth columns. The subjects' later reconstructions of what they had seen conformed to the verbal label, as shown in the first and fifth columns. This experiment indicates that subjects remember not what they literally saw but rather abstract the fundamental information from it.

A more recent and quite different demonstration of abstraction was reported by Intraub and Richardson (1989). Here, observers were shown pictures of objects such as those in the top panels of Figure 5-24. The general finding was that when the observers later redrew the pictures, they enlarged the boundaries, as shown in the bottom panels of Figure 5-24. The conclusion again is that, rather than perceiving, storing, and later remembering a more-or-less literal image of what they had seen, the observers abstracted the important information (here the object's context as well as the object itself).

The notion of abstraction harks back to our discussion of color metamers in Chapter 4. Recall that color metamers are different physical stimuli (for instance, a pure yellow light on the one hand and a red-green mixture on the other) that lead to exactly the same color perception. In this instance, the visual system is throwing away the information corresponding to the physical difference between the stimuli. Abstraction entails much the same thing. The information corresponding to the exact physical description (the "bitmap") of the stimulus is lost, and what is retained is the critical information that is needed.

▌ Figure 5-24
Boundary Extension and Abstraction
Subjects tend to remember having seen a greater expanse of a scene than was shown to them in a photograph. For example, when drawing the close-up view in panel A from memory, the subject's drawing (panel C) contained extended boundaries. Another subject, shown a wider-angle view of the same scene (panel B), also drew the scene with extended boundaries (panel D). (Reprinted by permission from Intraub and Richardson (1989), p. 182)

◆Interim Summary

- Abstraction is the process of converting the raw sensory information acquired by the sense organs (for example, patterns of straight and curved lines) into abstract categories that are prestored in memory (for example, letters or words).

- Abstracted information takes less space and is therefore faster to work with than raw information. A useful analogy is between a bitmapped computer image of a face versus an abstracted image of the same face that is made up of preformed structures such as ovals and lines.

◆Critical Thinking Question

1. In Chapter 4, we talked about metamers. Can you see a relation between metamers and the process of abstraction? What is it?

PERCEPTUAL CONSTANCIES

You walk into a movie and discover, somewhat to your annoyance, that all the seats in the middle section of the theatre are taken and you are forced to sit far over on the left side. As the movie begins, however, you forget about your seating locale and just lose yourself in the movie's plot, its characters, and its stunning special effects. All visual aspects of the movie appear to be entirely normal—and yet they're not. Because you're sitting off to the side, at an angle to the screen, the image of the movie screen on your retina is not a rectangle. Rather, it's a trapezoid, and all the visual images you see on the screen are analogously distorted. And yet this doesn't really bother you, and you see everything as normal. How can this be? In this section we describe a truly remarkable ability of the perceptual systems, the maintenance of **constancy**, which refers to the brain's ability to maintain a perception of the

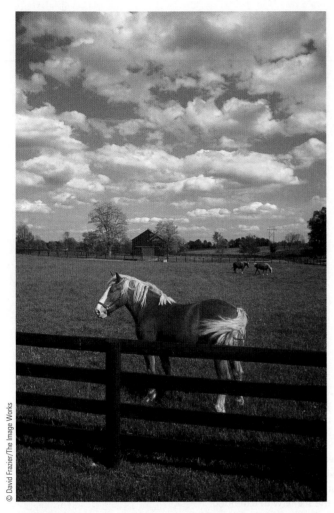

Perceptual constancy enables us to determine how far away objects are.

underlying physical characteristics of an object, such as shape, size or color, even when the sensory manifestations of these objects change drastically.

To understand the idea of constancies, we must first understand the relation and distinction between the inherent physical characteristics of an object and the information available to our perceptual systems about an object. A movie screen, for example, is rectangular; that's a physical characteristic of it. But the image of it on your retina can be rectangular or trapezoidal, depending on the angle from which you view it. A black cat seen in bright light is objectively lighter (it reflects more light to you) than a white cat in dim light, yet somehow, in any kind of light, we maintain the perception that the black cat is actually black and the white cat is actually white. An elephant seen from far away projects a smaller image on the retina than a gopher seen from close up, yet somehow, no matter what the distance, we maintain the perception that the elephant is

larger than the gopher. In general, what we perceive is (and this almost sounds like magic) a perception of what an object is actually like rather than a perception based solely on the "objective" physical information that arrives from the environment.

Although constancy is not perfect, it is a salient aspect of visual experience, and it should be. Otherwise, sometimes elephants would be smaller than mice, and a black cat would sometimes be lighter colored than a white cat, depending on the whims of the particular situation. If the shape and color of an object changed every time either we or it moved, the description of the object that we construct in the early stages of recognition would also change, and recognition would become an impossible task.

COLOR AND BRIGHTNESS CONSTANCY

Suppose I tell you that I am thinking of two numbers whose product is 36, and I ask you to tell me what the two original numbers are. Your reasonable response would be that you don't have enough information to answer: The numbers I'm thinking of could be 2 and 18, 6 and 6, 72 and ½, or any of an infinite number of other pairs.

Impossible though this task seems, it is, in a very real sense, what the visual system does when it maintains lightness and color constancy. Suppose you are looking at something, say, a piece of red paper, and asked to name its color. Color constancy refers to the fact that you would report the paper to be red whether you were inside a room lit by an incandescent bulb, which illuminates the paper with one particular set of wavelengths, or outside in the noonday sun, which illuminates the paper with a very different set of wavelengths.

It stands to reason that the perceived redness of the red paper is based on the **available wavelengths,** the wavelengths of the light that is reflected off the paper reaching your eyes. Let's now consider the physics of where these available wavelengths come from. First, the paper is illuminated by the **source wavelengths** coming from some light source, which could be, among many other things, an incandescent bulb inside or the sun outside. Second, the red paper itself is characterized by a **reflectance characteristic,** which determines how the paper reflects some wavelengths more than others (in particular, it reflects mostly wavelengths corresponding to red and less of other wavelengths). Now in a very real, mathematical sense, the available wavelengths reaching your eyes are the *product* of the source wavelengths and the reflectance characteristic. Realizing this puts us in a position to define color constancy, which is the ability of the visual system to perceive the reflectance characteristic—an inherent property of the object—no matter what the

❚ Figure 5-25
Shape Constancy
The various retinal images produced by an opening door are quite different, yet we perceive a door of constant rectangular shape.

source wavelengths. In this sense, the visual system is presented with a product—the available wavelengths—and somehow figures out one of the factors, the reflectance characteristic. The incandescent bulb and the sun provide very different source wavelengths and—because the reflectance characteristic of the red paper doesn't change—very different available wavelengths therefore reach the eye. Yet somehow the visual system is able to divide the source wavelengths out of the available wavelengths to arrive at the correct reflectance characteristic in both cases. This achievement is analogous to your somehow figuring out that the first number I'm thinking of (analogous to the source wavelengths) is 12, which means that the other number (analogous to the reflectance characteristic) must be $^{36}/_{12}$ or 3.

Brightness constancy is similar to color constancy. It refers to the fact that the perceived lightness of a particular object changes very little, if at all, even when the intensity of the source (and thus the amount of light reflected off the object) changes dramatically. A black velvet shirt can look just as black in sunlight as in shadow, even though it reflects thousands of times more light when it is directly illuminated by the sun.

How does the visual system manage these tricks? A clue comes about by examining the circumstances under which constancy *fails*. Suppose you put the black shirt behind an opaque black screen and view the shirt through a peephole in the screen. The screen reduces what you see through the opening to just the actual light reflected from the shirt, independent of its surroundings. Now, when it is illuminated, the shirt looks white because the light that reaches your eye through the hole is more intense than the light from the screen itself.

When we perceive objects in natural settings, rather than through peepholes, many other objects are usually visible. Color and brightness constancy depend on the relations among the intensities of light reflected from the different objects. By using our past knowledge of object colors in general, our visual system is able to correct for the effect of the source illumination (both the source intensity and the source wavelengths) and arrive at the brightness and the color of the objects we see (Gilchrist, 1988; Land, 1977; Maloney & Wandell, 1986).

SHAPE CONSTANCY

One example of shape constancy is the noneffect of sitting to one side of a movie theater. Another is illustrated in Figure 5-25. When a door swings toward us, the shape of its image on the retina goes through a series of changes. The door's rectangular shape produces a trapezoidal image, with the edge toward us wider than the hinged edge. Then the trapezoid grows thinner, until finally all that is projected on the retina is a vertical bar the thickness of the door. Nevertheless, we perceive an unchanging door swinging open. The fact that the perceived shape is constant while the retinal image changes is an example of shape constancy.

SIZE CONSTANCY

The most thoroughly studied of all the perceptual constancies is size constancy. An object's perceived size remains relatively constant no matter how far away it is. As an object moves farther away from us, we generally do not see it as decreasing in size. Hold a quarter 1 foot in front of you and then move it out to arm's length. Does it appear to get smaller? Not noticeably. Yet, as shown in Figure 5-26, the retinal image of the quarter when it is 24 inches away is only about half the size of its retinal image when it is 12 inches away.

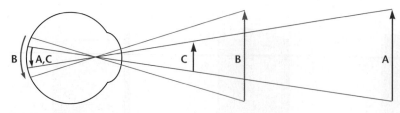

Figure 5-26
Retinal Image Size
This figure illustrates the geometric relationship between the physical size of an object and the size of its image on the retina. Arrows A and B represent objects of the same size, but one is twice as far from the eye as the other. As a result, the retinal image of A is about half the size of the retinal image of B. The object represented by arrow C is smaller than that of A, but its location closer to the eye causes it to produce a retinal image the same size as A.

DEPENDENCE ON DEPTH CUES The example of the moving quarter indicates that when we perceive the size of an object, we consider something in addition to the size of the retinal image. That additional something is the perceived distance of the object. As long ago as 1881, Emmert showed that size judgments depend on distance. Emmert used an ingenious method that involved judging the size of afterimages.

Observers were first asked to fixate on the center of an image for about a minute (see Figure 5-27 for an example of such an image). Then they looked at a white screen and saw an afterimage of what they had just seen.

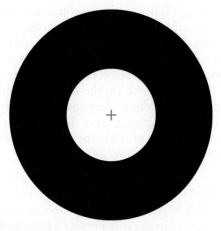

Figure 5-27
Emmert's Experiment
Hold the book at normal reading distance under good light. Fixate on the cross in the center of the figure for about a minute, and then look at a distant wall. You will see an afterimage of the two circles that appears larger than the stimulus. Then look at a piece of paper held close to your eyes. The afterimage will appear smaller than the stimulus. If the afterimage fades, blinking can sometimes restore it.

Their task was to judge the size of the afterimage; the independent variable was how far away the screen was. Because the retinal size of the afterimage was the same regardless of the distance of the screen, any variations in judgments of the size of the afterimage had to be due to its perceived distance. When the screen was far away, the afterimage looked large; when the screen was near, the afterimage looked small. Emmert's experiment is so easy to do that you can perform it on yourself.

On the basis of such experiments, Emmert proposed the size-distance invariance principle: that the perceived size of an object increases with both the retinal size of the object and the perceived distance of the object. It explains size constancy as follows: When the distance to an object increases, the object's retinal size decreases, but if distance cues are present, perceived distance will increase. Hence, the perceived size will remain approximately constant. When a person walks away from you, the size of her image on your retina becomes smaller, but her perceived distance becomes larger. These two changes cancel each other out, and your perception of her size remains relatively constant.

ILLUSIONS

Walk into the Haunted House at Disneyland. As you nervously make your way down the first corridor, you see masklike faces staring at you from the walls. As you move past them, the masks appear to physically swivel, ever gazing at you. Although disconcerted, you marvel at this effect, figuring that the masks must somehow be mounted on little motors that are sensitive to your approach and movement.

In reality, the masks are stationary, and only in your perception do they move. If you somehow managed to turn on the lights and inspect the masks, an oddity would immediately become apparent. You are actually looking at the inside of the mask rather than the outside, as is normal. But, under the poor viewing conditions of the haunted house, you don't realize this. Your visual system makes the assumption that you are looking at a face from the outside, just as you usually do, but if this is so, the geometry of the situation requires you to perceive the face to be rotating as you shift position relative to it.

This is an easy demonstration that you can do for yourself. Go to a costume store and find a cheap mask—one that just goes on the front of your face, not the pull-it-down-over-your-head type. Have a friend hold the mask up across the room so that the inside of the mask is facing you. Particularly if you cover one eye, you will perceive the face as coming out at you rather than going

The moon looks much larger when it is near the horizon than when it is high in the sky, even though in both locations its retinal image is the same size.

in from you as is actually the case. Once you have that perception, you will find that as you shift back and forth, the mask will appear to rotate.

The perceived-to-be-rotating mask is an example of an **illusion,** *a perception of something that differs systematically from physical reality.* The mask illusion, like many illusions, arises because of the visual system's attempts to maintain constancy—in this case, its assumption that a face is, like most faces, is being viewed from the outside rather than from the inside.

CONSTANCIES AND ILLUSIONS We have noted that the various constancies serve an important purpose: They allow us to perceive fundamental characteristics of the world around us even when the information arriving at our sense organs (our retinas in the examples we've discussed) change dramatically as a result of different source wavelengths, different source intensities, different distances from the object, or different viewing angles. For better or for worse, however, these constancies also lead to numerous optical illusions.

The size-distance principle is fundamental to understanding a number of size illusions. An example is the moon illusion. When the moon is near the horizon, it looks as much as 50% larger than when it is high in the sky, even though the moon's retinal image is a tiny bit larger when it is directly overhead, because it is a little bit closer than when on the horizon. (Similarly, a low-flying bird is closer when it is directly overhead than when you first see it on the horizon.) One explanation of this illusion is that the perceived distance to the horizon is judged to be greater than the distance to the zenith. Because the visual angle remains almost constant as the moon rises from horizon to zenith, however, the visual system must conclude that the moon itself is larger at the distant horizon than at the nearer zenith (Kaufman & Rock, 1989). One way to reduce the effectiveness of the depth cues that indicate the horizon moon is far away is to view the moon upside down. You can turn your back to the moon, bend over, and view the moon through your legs. If you have a photo of the moon on the horizon, you can simply turn the picture upside down (Coren, 1992).

Another size illusion is created by the Ames room (named after its inventor, Adelbert Ames). Figure 5-28 shows how the Ames room looks to an observer seeing it through a peephole. The boy in the right-hand corner of the room appears much bigger than the girl in the left-hand corner of the room. Yet the girl is actually taller! In this case, size constancy has broken down. Why? The

▌ Figure 5-28
The Ames Room
A view of how the Ames room looks to an observer viewing it through the peephole. The sizes of the boy and the girl depend on which one is in the left-hand corner of the room and which one is in the right-hand corner. The room is designed to wreak havoc with our perceptions. Because of the perceived shape of the room, the relative sizes of the boy and the girl seem impossibly different.

reason lies in the construction of the room. Although the room looks like a normal rectangular room through the peephole, it is actually shaped so that its left corner is almost twice as far away as its right corner (see the diagram in Figure 5-29). The boy on the left is much farther away than the one on the right and consequently projects a smaller retinal image. We do not correct for this

Peephole

▌ Figure 5-29
The True Shape of the Ames Room
This figure shows the true shape of the Ames room. The boy on the left is actually almost twice as far away as the boy on the right. However, this difference in distance is not detected when the room is viewed through the peephole. (After Goldstein, 1984)

difference in distance, though, because the lines in the room lead us to believe that we are looking at a normal room and therefore assume that both boys are the same distance from us. Again, the visual system's only interpretation of the boy subtending a smaller angle but being no farther away is that the boy is smaller. In essence, our assumption that the room is normal blocks our application of the size-distance invariance principle, and consequently size constancy breaks down.

The Ames-room effect in Figure 5-28 was used to great advantage by the movie director Peter Jackson in his *Lord of the Rings* trilogy. These movies involved different classes of creatures (e.g., hobbits, dwarves, elves, and humans), who, in keeping with J. R. R. Tolkien's original books, needed to appear to be very different sizes (for example, hobbits are only about half as tall as humans), even though the different beings were played by actors of similar heights. Some of these effects achieved by computer-graphics techniques, but for the most part they were achieved by illusion. For example, Aragorn, a human, was filmed apparently walking alongside Frodo, a hobbit. However, during the filming, Viggo Mortensen playing Aragorn was in the foreground, close to the camera, while Elijah Wood playing Frodo was actually in the background, approximately twice as far from the camera as Mortensen.

CROSS-MODAL ILLUSIONS We have demonstrated that many illusions occur because of incorrect assumptions made by the perceptual systems. Illusions can also occur because of conflicting information. One example, the **McGurk effect** (McGurk & MacDonald, 1976) results from conflicting auditory and visual information. In particular, an observer watches a video in which the speaker's lips form the sound "ga-ga," while the simultaneous sound track provides speech that is normally perceived as "ba-ba." The conjunction of these conflicting sources of information, surprisingly, produces the perception of "da-da." Thus, the speaker integrates the visual and auditory information with an entirely unexpected, "illusory" result.

CONSTANCIES IN ALL SENSORY MODALITIES

Although all the examples of constancy that we have described are visual, constancies also occur in the other senses. For example, a person will hear the same tune even if the frequencies of all its notes are doubled. Whatever the sensory modality, constancies depend on relations between features of the stimulus—between retinal size and distance in the case of size constancy, between the intensity of two adjacent regions in the case of lightness constancy, and so forth.

◆Interim Summary

- Another major function of the perceptual system is to achieve perceptual constancy—to keep the appearance of objects the same in spite of large changes in the stimuli received by the sense organs.
- The major constancies are color (and brightness), shape, and size.
- Constancies occur in all sensory modalities.
- Various kinds of perceptual illusions can be explained by the perceptual system's insistence on maintaining constancies.

◆ Critical Thinking Questions

1. In what way is the behavior of a visual artist influenced by color and shape constancy? Can you think of ways in which perceptual constancies actually make the artist's task more difficult than it would be without constancy?

2. Do you think that the moon illusion would be more pronounced if the moon were seen rising over a flat, featureless plane or behind a city skyline? Suppose you were on a boat approaching the city. Would the moon illusion be more pronounced if you were closer to the city or farther from the city?

The Neural Basis of Behavior

DIVISIONS OF LABOR IN THE BRAIN

In the past decade, taking pictures of the brain without surgery has brought exciting discoveries about the human brain and the neural processes underlying perception. This field is called **brain imaging** and includes techniques such as event-related potentials (ERPs), positron emission tomography (PET), and functional magnetic resonance imaging (fMRI). These are very active areas—probably among the most active in all of psychology (see, for example, Behrmann & Haimson, 1999; Colby & Goldberg, 1999; Farah, 2000; Kastner, De Weerd, Desimone, & Ungerleider, 1998; Kastner & Ungerleider, 2000).

We have already touched on some of this knowledge. In this section, we will describe a little more of what has been discovered. We will begin by talking about the neural basis of attention, and then we will turn to the visual cortex, a crucial way station for incoming visual information.

THE NEURAL BASIS OF ATTENTION

Recent years have produced major breakthroughs in our understanding of the neural basis of attention, particularly visual attention. The research of interest has concerned two major questions: (1) What brain structures mediate the psychological act of selecting an object to attend to? and (2) How does the subsequent neural processing differ for attended and nonattended stimuli?

TWO BRAIN SYSTEMS IN ATTENTION The brain appears to contain two separate systems that mediate selective attention. The first, which represents the perceptual features of an object, such as its location in space, its shape, and its color, is responsible for selecting one object among many on the basis of the features associated with that object. This is referred to as the **posterior system** because the brain structures involved—the parietal and temporal cortex, along with some subcortical structures—are located in the back of the brain. The second system, designed to control when and how these features will be used for selection, is referred to as the **anterior system** because the structures involved—the frontal cortex and a subcortical structure—are located in the front of the brain. In short, we can select an object for attention by focusing on its location, its shape, or its color. Although the actual selection of these features occurs in the posterior part of the brain, the selection process is guided by the anterior part of brain. Because of this function, some researchers refer to the anterior system as the "chief executive officer," or CEO, of selective attention.

Some critical findings about the posterior system come from PET scans of humans while they are engaged in selective-attention tasks. When observers are instructed to shift their attention from one location to another, the cortical areas that show the greatest increase in blood flow—and, hence, neural activity—are the parietal lobes of both hemispheres (Corbetta, Miezin, Shulman, & Petersen, 1993). Moreover, when people with brain damage in these regions are tested on attentional tasks, they have great difficulty shifting attention from one location to another (Posner, 1988). So, the regions that are active when a normal brain accomplishes the task turn out to be the same areas that are damaged when a patient cannot do the task. When single-cell recording studies are done with nonhuman primates, cells in the same brain regions are active when attention must be switched from one location to the next (Wurtz, Goldberg, & Robinson, 1980). Taken together, these findings strongly indicate that activity in parietal regions of the brain mediates attending to locations. There is comparable evidence for the involvement of temporal regions in attending to the color and shape of objects (Moran & Desimone, 1985).

NEURAL PROCESSING ON ATTENDED OBJECTS

Once an object has been selected for attention, what changes in neural processing occur? Consider an experiment in which a set of colored geometric objects is presented and the observer is instructed to attend only to the red ones and to indicate when a triangle is presented. The anterior system directs the posterior system to focus on color, but what else changes in the neural processing of each stimulus? The regions of the visual cortex that process color become more active than they would be if the observer was not selectively attending to color. More generally, the regions of the brain that are relevant to the attribute being attended to (color, shape, texture, motion, and so forth) show amplified activity (Posner & Dehaene, 1994). There is also evidence that brain regions that are relevant to unattended attributes are inhibited (La Berge, 1995; Posner & Raichle, 1994).

PET studies provide some of the best evidence for this amplification of attributes that are attended to. In one experiment (Corbetta, Miezin, Shulman, & Petersen, 1991), observers whose brains were being scanned viewed moving objects of varying color and form. In one condition, the individuals were instructed to detect changes among the objects in motion, and in other conditions they were instructed to detect changes among the objects in color or shape. Motion is the attribute attended to in the first condition, and color or shape in the other conditions. As shown in Figure 5-30, even though the physical stimuli were identical in all the conditions, posterior cortical areas known to be involved in the processing of motion were more active in the first condition, whereas areas involved in color or shape processing were more active in the other conditions. Attention, then, amplifies what is relevant, not only psychologically but biologically as well.

THE VISUAL CORTEX

At a general level, the **visual cortex,** which is the part of the brain that is concerned with vision, operates according to the principle of division of labor: Different

Figure 5-30
PET Images Reveal Differences in Cortical Activity
The image on the top right is from the condition in which participants attended to changes in color, whereas the images in the bottom row are from the conditions in which individuals attended to changes in shape or speed. (M. Corbetta, F. M. Miezen, S. Dobmeyer, D. L. Shulman, S. E. Persen, "Attentional Modulation of Neural Processing of Shape, Color and Velocity in Humans," *Science* V. 248 p. 1558, 1990; Reprinted by permission of the American Association for the Advancement of Science.)

regions of the visual cortex are specialized to carry out different perceptual functions (Kosslyn & Koenig, 1992; Zeki, 1993). More than 100 million neurons in the cortex are sensitive to visual input. Everything we know about them and the way they function has been learned through a few techniques. In studies involving animals, what we know is based largely on research in which electrical impulses are recorded (using microelectrodes) from single cells, as discussed in Chapter 4. Modern techniques for conducting such research owe much to the pioneering work of Hubel and Wiesel, mentioned earlier.

In studies involving humans, much of what we know comes from "natural experiments"—that is, cases of brain injury and disease that cast light on how visual behaviors relate to specific regions of the brain. Researchers in this area include neurologists (medical doctors who specialize in the brain) and neuropsychologists (psychologists who specialize in treating and studying patients with brain injury). An excellent introduction to this area is presented in *The Man Who Mistook His Wife for a Hat*, alluded to in Chapter 1.

The most important region of the brain for visual processing is the primary visual cortex, or V1. Its location at the back, or posterior, part of the brain is

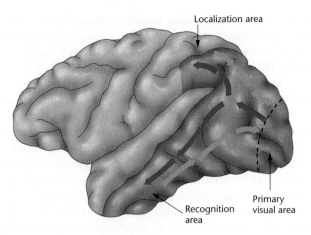

Figure 5-31
Two Cortical Visual Systems
The arrows going from the back of the brain toward the top depict the localization system; the arrows going from the back toward the bottom of the brain depict the recognition system.
(After Mortimer Mishkin, Leslie G. Ungerleider, & Kathleen A. Macko (1983), "Object Vision and Spatial Vision: Two Cortical Pathways, "*Trends in Neuroscience, 6(10)*:414–417.)

stretched over the back of the cortex, with its center directly over the rearmost part of the cortex.

Neurons in the primary visual cortex are sensitive to many features in a visual image, such as brightness, color, orientation, and motion. However, one of the most important features of these neurons is that they are each responsible for analyzing only a very tiny region of the image. In the foveal part of the image, this can be as small as less than 1 millimeter seen at arm's length. These neurons also communicate with one another only in very small regions. The benefit of this arrangement is that the entire visual field can be analyzed simultaneously and in great detail. What is missing from this analysis, however, is the ability to coordinate information that is not close together in the image—that is, to see the forest in addition to the trees.

To accomplish this task, cortical neurons send information from V1 to the many other regions of the brain that analyze visual information. Each of these regions specializes in a particular task, such as analyzing

shown in Figure 5-31. This is the first location in the cerebral cortex to which neurons sending signals from the eye are connected. All the other visually sensitive regions of the cortex (more than 30 such locations have been identified) are connected to the eyes through V1.

As has so often been the case, the function of V1 was discovered long before the development of modern recording or imaging techniques. It first became obvious when physicians examined patients who had suffered localized head injuries through accident or war. As shown in Figure 5-32, tissue damage (technically referred to as a lesion) to a specific part of V1 was linked to blindness in very specific parts of the visual field (technically, a scotoma). Note that this form of blindness is not caused by damage to the eyes or the optic nerve; it is entirely cortical in origin. For example, the very center of the visual field—the fovea—suffers a scotoma if a lesion occurs at the extreme rear of V1. Scotomas in more peripheral portions of the visual field are caused by lesions farther forward in V1. It is as though a map of the visual field has been

Figure 5-32
The Visual Consequences of Various Kinds of Lesions in the Primary Visual Cortex (V1)
The "map" of the visual field is upside down and mirror reversed.

DAMAGE	VISUAL FIELD LOSS
a) Half-field lesion	
b) Local lesion	
c) Quarter-field lesion	

Occipital pole

Calcarine fissure

color, motion, shape, and location. These more specialized regions are also in constant contact with V1, so that the neural communication between regions is better thought of as a conversation than as a command (Damasio, 1990; Zeki, 1993). One of the most important divisions of labor in visual analysis by the brain is between localization and recognition.

RECOGNITION VERSUS LOCALIZATION SYSTEMS

Research findings show that localization and recognition are carried out by different regions of the visual cortex. *Recognition* of objects depends on a branch of the visual system that includes the primary visual cortex and a region near the bottom of the cerebral cortex. In contrast, as illustrated in Figure 5-31, *localization* of objects depends on a branch of the visual system that includes the primary visual cortex and a region of the cortex near the top of the brain. Studies with nonhuman primates show that if the recognition branch of an animal's visual system is impaired, the animal can still perform tasks that require it to perceive spatial relations between objects (one in front of the other, for example) but cannot perform tasks that require discriminating between the actual objects, such as a cube from

a cylinder. If the location branch is impaired, the animal can distinguish a cube from a cylinder but cannot figure out where the objects are in relation to each other (Mishkin, Ungerleider, & Macko, 1983).

More recent research has used brain imaging to document the existence of separate object and location systems in the human brain. One widely used technique is PET (discussed in Chapter 2). A observer who has had a radioactive tracer injected into her bloodstream is placed in a PET scanner while she performs various tasks. The scanner measures increases in radioactivity in various brain regions, which indicate increases in blood flow to those regions. The regions that show the most increase in blood flow are the ones that mediate performance of the task.

In one such study, observers performed two tasks, one a test of face recognition, which depends on the brain region for object recognition, and the other a test of mental rotation, which requires localization. In the face-recognition task, observers saw a target picture with two test faces beneath it during each trial. One of the test faces was the person depicted by the target, except for changes in orientation and lighting, and the other was the face of a different person. As shown in Figure 5-33a, the observer's task was to decide which test face was the same as the target. While the observer was engaging in this task, there was increased blood flow in the recognition branch of the cortex (the branch terminating near the bottom of the cortex) but not in the localization branch (the branch terminating near the top of the cortex).

The mental rotation task produced very different results. In this task, on each trial observers saw a target display of a dot at some distance from a double line, and beneath the target were two test displays. As shown in Figure 5-33b, one test display was the same as the target, except that it had been rotated; the other test display contained a different configuration of the dot and lines. While engaging in this task, observers showed increased blood flow in the localization branch of the cortex but not in the recognition branch. Localization and recognition, therefore, are carried out in entirely different regions of the visual cortex (Grady et al., 1992; Haxby et al., 1990).

 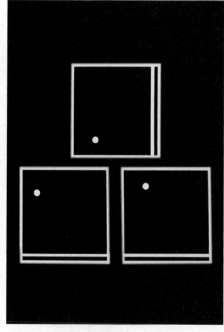

▌ Figure 5-33
Recognition and Localization Tasks
Sample items from the face-matching (left) and dot-location (right) matching tasks.
(Reprinted from *Journal of Cognitive Neruroscience*, pp. 23–24, Fig. 5-2, p. 30, vol. 4:1, Winter 1992, by permission of the MIT Press, Cambridge, MA)

The division of labor in the visual cortex does not end with the split between localization and recognition. Rather, the different kinds of information that are used in localization—eye movements, motion analysis, and depth perception, for example—are themselves processed by different subregions of the localization branch of the cortex. Similarly, the various kinds of information used in recognition—shape, color, and texture—also have specialized subregions devoted to their analysis (Livingstone & Hubel, 1988; Zeki, 1993). The upshot is that the visual cortex has numerous "processing modules," each of which is specialized for a particular task. The more we learn about the neural basis of other sensory modalities (and other psychological functions as well), the more this modular, division-of-labor approach seems to hold.

◆ Interim Summary

- Two separate brain systems seem to mediate the psychological act of selecting an object to attend to. The posterior system selects objects on the basis of location, shape, or color, and the anterior system is responsible for guiding this process, depending on the goals of the viewer.

- The visual cortex operates according to the principle of division of labor. Localization is mediated by a region near the top of the cortex, and recognition by a region near the bottom of the cortex.

- Recognition processes are further subdivided into separate modules such as color, shape, and texture.

◆ Critical Thinking Questions

1. Why do you think the brain seems to solve many problems by dividing the work among specialized regions? What advantages may be gained by this approach? What problems might be caused by this division of labor?

2. Some people are skeptical about the value of studying perception and behavior from a biological perspective. Given what you have learned about vision and visually guided behavior, how would you argue against such skeptics?

PERCEPTUAL DEVELOPMENT

An age-old question about perception is whether our abilities to perceive are learned or innate—the familiar nature-nurture problem. Contemporary psychologists no longer believe that this is an either-or question. No one doubts that both genetics and learning influence perception; rather, the goal is to pinpoint the contribution of each and to spell out their interactions. For the modern researcher, the question "Must we learn to perceive?" has given way to more specific questions: (1) What discriminatory capacities do infants have (which tells us something about inborn capacities), and how does this capacity change with age under normal rearing conditions? (2) If animals are reared under conditions that restrict what they can learn (referred to as controlled stimulation), what effects does this have on their later discriminatory capacity? (3) What effects does rearing under controlled conditions have on perceptual-motor coordination?

DISCRIMINATION BY INFANTS

Perhaps the most direct way to find out what human perceptual capacities are inborn is to see what capacities an infant has. At first, you might think that this research should consider only newborns, because an inborn capacity should be present from the first day of life. This idea turns out to be too simple, though. Some inborn capacities, such as perception of form, can appear only after more basic capacities, such as the ability to register details, have developed. Other inborn capacities may require some kind of environmental input for a certain length of time for the capacity to mature. Thus, the study of inborn capacities traces perceptual development from the first minute of life through the early years of childhood.

METHODS OF STUDYING INFANTS What an infant perceives is hard to determine because it cannot talk or follow instructions and has a fairly limited set of behaviors. To study infant perception, a researcher needs to find a form of behavior through which an infant indicates what it can discriminate. As shown in Figure 5-34, one such behavior is an infant's tendency to look at some objects more than at others; psychologists make use of this behavior in a technique known as the **preferential looking method** (Teller, 1979). Two stimuli are presented to the infant side by side. The experimenter, who is hidden from the infant's view, looks through a partition behind the stimuli and, by watching the infant's eyes, measures the amount of time that the infant looks at each stimulus. (Usually the experimenter uses a television camera to record the infant's viewing pattern.) During the experiment, the positions of the stimuli are switched randomly. If an infant consistently looks at one stimulus more than at the other, the experimenter concludes that the infant can tell them apart—that is, discriminate between them.

A related technique is the **habituation method** (Frantz, 1966; Horowitz, 1974). It takes advantage of the fact that although infants look directly at novel objects,

Figure 5-34
Testing the Visual Preferences of an Infant

PERCEIVING FORMS To be able to perceive an object, a person must first be able to discriminate one part of it from another, an ability referred to as visual acuity. Acuity is often assessed by varying both the contrast in a pattern (the difference in brightness between dark and light regions) and the spatial frequency of the pattern (the number of times a pattern is repeated within a given area). For any particular level of contrast, there are always some spatial frequencies that cannot be resolved by the visual system because they are too fine. At the other extreme, other spatial frequencies cannot be seen because they change over too large an area.

The method typically used to study acuity in infants is preferential looking, with a pattern of stripes as one stimulus and a uniform gray field as the other. Initially the stripes are relatively wide, and the infant prefers to look at the pattern rather than at the uniform field. Then the researcher decreases the width of the stripes until the infant no longer shows a preference. Presumably at this point the infant can no longer discriminate a stripe from its surroundings, because the pattern of stripes no longer has perceptible parts and looks like a uniform field. When first studied at about 1 month of age, infants can see some patterns, but their acuity is very low. Acuity increases rapidly over the first 6 months of life, and then it increases more slowly, reaching adult levels between 1 and 2 years of age (Courage & Adams, 1990a, 1990b; Teller & Movshon, 1986).

What do studies like this tell us about the infant's perceptual world? At 1 month, infants can distinguish among relatively large objects but cannot distinguish fine details. Their vision is sufficient to perceive some general characteristics of an object, including some facial features (which create something like a pattern of dark and light stripes). Figure 5-35 uses the results of acuity experiments to simulate what 1-, 2-, and 3-month-old in-

they soon become bored with the same object—that is, they habituate. Suppose that an object is presented for a while and then replaced by a new object. To the extent that the second object is perceived as identical or highly similar to the first one, the infant should spend little time looking at it. Conversely, to the extent that the second object is perceived as substantially different from the first one, the infant should spend a lot of time staring at it. By these means, an experimenter can determine whether two physical displays look the same to an infant.

Using these techniques, psychologists have studied a variety of perceptual capacities in infants. Some of these capacities are needed to perceive forms and are used in the task of recognition. Others, particularly depth perception, are involved in the task of localization. Still others are involved in the task of keeping the appearance of perceived objects constant.

Figure 5-35
Visual Acuity and Contrast Sensitivity
Simulations of what 1-, 2-, and 3-month-old infants see when they look at a woman's face from a distance of about 6 inches and a photograph of what an adult sees. The simulations of infant perception were obtained by first determining an infant's contrast sensitivity and then applying this contrast-sensitivity function to the photograph. (From *Sensations and Perception* by E. Bruce Goldstein, © 1989, 1984, 1980 Wadsworth Publishing Co.)

fants see when viewing a woman's face from a distance of 6 inches. At 1 month, acuity is so poor that it is difficult to perceive facial expressions (indeed, newborns look mostly at the outside contours of a face). By 3 months, acuity has improved to the point where an infant can decipher facial expressions. No wonder that infants seem so much more socially responsive at 3 months than at 1 month!

Being able to discriminate dark from light edges is essential for seeing forms, but what about other aspects of object recognition? Our sensitivity to some of the shape features of objects is manifested very early in life. When presented with a triangle, even a 3-day-old infant directs its eye movements toward the edges and vertices rather than looking randomly over the form (Salapatek, 1975). Also, infants find some shapes more interesting than others. As noted in Chapter 3, they tend to look more at forms that resemble human faces, apparently because of a preference for some of the features of faces, such as curved rather than straight contours (Fantz, 1970, 1961). By 3 months, an infant can recognize something about the mother's face, even in a photograph, as revealed by an infant's preference for looking at a photograph of the mother rather than one of an unfamiliar woman (Barrera & Maurer, 1981).

PERCEIVING DEPTH Depth perception begins at about 3 months but is not fully established until about 6 months. At about 4 months, infants begin to reach for the nearer of two objects, where nearness is signaled by binocular disparity (Granrud, 1986). A month or two later, they begin to reach for objects that are apparently nearer on the basis of monocular depth cues such as relative size, linear perspective, and shading cues (Coren, Ward, & Enns, 1999).

Further evidence of the development of monocular depth perception comes from studies using a "visual cliff" (Figure 5-36), a board placed across a sheet of glass, with a surface of patterned material located directly under the glass on the shallow side and at a distance of a few feet below the glass on the deep side. (The appearance of depth in Figure 5-36—the "cliff"—is created by an abrupt change in the texture gradient.) An in-

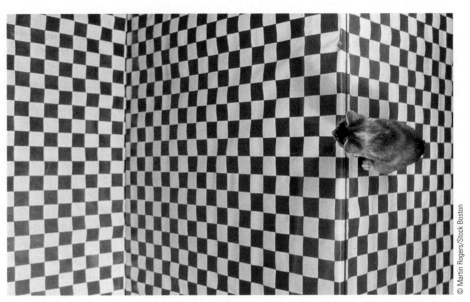

▌Figure 5-36
The Visual Cliff
The "visual cliff" is an apparatus used to show that infants and young animals are able to see depth by the time they are able to move about. The apparatus consists of two surfaces, both displaying the same checkerboard pattern and covered by a sheet of thick glass. One surface is directly under the glass; the other is several feet below it. When placed on the center board between the deep side and the shallow side, the kitten refuses to cross to the deep side but will readily move off the board onto the shallow side. (After Gibson & Walk, 1960)

fant who is old enough to crawl (6–7 months) is placed on the board; a patch is placed over one eye to eliminate binocular depth cues. When the mother calls or beckons from the shallow side, the infant consistently crawls toward her, but when the mother beckons from the deep side, the infant will not cross the cliff. From this we know that when an infant is old enough to crawl, depth perception is relatively well developed.

PERCEIVING CONSTANCIES Like the perception of form and depth, the perceptual constancies, particularly shape and size constancy, start to develop in the first few months of life (Kellman, 1984). Consider an experiment on size constancy that used the habituation method. Four-month-old infants were first shown one teddy bear for a while and then shown a second one. The second bear was either (1) identical in physical size to the original one but presented at a different distance so that it produced a different-sized retinal image or (2) different in physical size from the original bear. If the infants had developed size constancy, they should perceive bear 1 (same physical size) as identical to the one they saw originally and spend little time looking at it compared with the amount of time spent looking at bear 2 (which was actually bigger than the original). And this is exactly what happened (Granrud, 1986).

CONTROLLED STIMULATION

We turn now to the question of how specific experiences affect perceptual capacities. To answer this question, researchers have systematically varied the kind of perceptual experiences a young organism has and then looked at the effects of this experience on subsequent perceptual performance.

ABSENCE OF STIMULATION The earliest experiments on controlled stimulation sought to determine the effects of rearing an animal in the total absence of visual stimulation. The experimenters kept animals in the dark for several months after birth, until they were mature enough for visual testing. The idea behind these experiments was that if animals have to learn to perceive, they would be unable to perceive when first exposed to the light. The results turned out as expected. Chimpanzees that were reared in darkness for their first 16 months could detect light but could not discriminate among patterns (Riesen, 1947). However, subsequent studies showed that prolonged rearing in the dark does more than prevent learning. It also causes deterioration of neurons in various parts of the visual system. A certain amount of light stimulation turns out to be necessary to maintain the visual system. Without any light stimulation, nerve cells in the retina and visual cortex begin to atrophy (Binns & Salt, 1997; Movshon & Van Sluyters, 1981).

Although these findings do not tell us much about the role of learning in perceptual development, they are important in themselves. In general, when an animal is deprived of visual stimulation from birth, the longer the period of deprivation, the greater the deficit. Adult cats, on the other hand, can have a patch over one eye for a long period without losing vision in that eye. These observations led to the idea that there is a critical period for the development of inborn visual capacities. (A critical period is a stage in development during which the organism is optimally ready to acquire certain abilities.) Lack of stimulation during a critical period for vision can permanently impair the visual system (Cynader, Timney, & Mitchell, 1980).

LIMITED STIMULATION Researchers no longer deprive animals of stimulation for a long time. Instead, they study the effects of rearing animals that receive stimuli in both eyes, but only certain kinds of stimuli. They have raised kittens in an environment where they see only vertical stripes or only horizontal stripes. The kittens become blind to stripes in the orientation—horizontal or vertical—that they do not experience. And single-cell recording studies show that many cells in the visual cortex of a "horizontally reared" cat respond to horizontal stimuli and none responds to vertical stimuli, whereas the opposite pattern is found in the visual cortex of "vertically reared" cat (Blake, 1981; Movshon & Van Sluyters, 1981). This blindness seems to be caused by the degeneration of cells in the visual cortex.

Of course, researchers do not deprive humans of normal visual stimulation, but sometimes this happens naturally or as a consequence of medical treatment. For example, after eye surgery the eye that was operated on is usually covered with a patch. If the patient is a child in the first year of life, the acuity of the patched eye is reduced (Awaya et al., 1973). There is apparently a **critical period** early in the development of the human visual system similar to that in animal. If stimulation is restricted during this period, the system will not develop normally. The critical period is much longer in humans than in animals. It may last as long as 8 years, but the greatest vulnerability occurs during the first 2 years of life (Aslin & Banks, 1978).

None of these facts indicates that we have to learn to perceive. Rather, certain kinds of stimulation are essential for the maintenance and development of perceptual capacities that are present at birth. However, learning does have an effect on perception. For evidence of such effects, we need only consider our ability to recognize common objects. The fact that we can recognize a familiar object more readily than an unfamiliar one—a dog versus an aardvark, for example—must certainly be due to learning. If we had been reared in an environment rich in aardvarks and sparse in dogs, we would have recognized the aardvark more readily than the dog.

ACTIVE PERCEPTION When it comes to coordinating perceptions with motor responses, learning plays a major role. The evidence comes from studies in which observers receive normal stimulation but are prevented from making normal responses to that stimulation. Under such conditions, perceptual-motor coordination does not develop.

In one classic study, two kittens that had been reared in darkness had their first visual experience in the "kitten carousel" illustrated in Figure 5-37. As the active kitten walked, it moved the passive kitten riding in the carousel. Although both kittens received roughly the same visual stimulation, only the active kitten had this stimulation produced by its own movement. And only the active kitten successfully learned sensory-motor coordination. For example, when picked up and moved toward an object, only the active kitten learned to put out its paws to ward off a collision.

Similar results have been obtained with humans. In some experiments, people wear prism goggles that distort the directions of objects. Immediately after putting on these goggles, they temporarily have trouble reaching

Figure 5-37
The Importance of Self-Produced Movements
Both kittens received roughly the same visual stimulation, but only the active kitten had this stimulation produced by its own movement. (R. Held and A. Held (1963) "Movement Produced in the Development of Visually Guided Behavior," from *Journal of Comparative and Physiological Psychology, 56*:872–876. Copyright © 1963 by the American Psychological Association. Adapted with permission.)

for objects and often bump into things. If they move about and attempt to perform motor tasks while wearing the goggles, they learn to coordinate their movements with the actual location of objects rather than with their apparent locations. On the other hand, a person who is pushed in a wheelchair does not adapt to the goggles. Apparently, self-produced movement is essential to prism adaptation (Held, 1965).

In sum, the evidence indicates that we are born with considerable perceptual capacities. The natural development of some of these capacities may require years of normal input from the environment. But there clearly are learning effects on perception as well, which are particularly striking when perception must be coordinated with motor behavior.

This chapter, like the preceding one, includes many examples of the interplay between psychological and biological approaches. Throughout the chapter, we have encountered cases in which specific psychological functions are implemented by specific cells or brain regions. We have seen that specialized cells are used to perceive motion and that separate parts of the brain are used to register the visual features of location, shape, and color. Still other regions of the brain are involved in determining which of these features will be used to control behaviors and actions. Such examples illustrate how significant the findings of biological research can be in the study of psychological processes.

Figure 5-38
After looking at this picture, look back at the left panel of Figure 5-1 (page 148). Now what do you see?

◆Interim Summary

- Research on perceptual development is concerned with the extent to which perceptual capacities are inborn and the extent to which they are learned through experience.

- To determine inborn capacities, researchers study the discrimination capacities of infants with methods such as preferential looking and habituation.

- Perceptual constancies begin to develop as early as 6 months.

- Animals raised in darkness suffer permanent visual impairment, and animals raised with a patch over one eye become blind in that eye, suggesting a critical period early in life when lack of normal stimulation produces deficiency in an innate perceptual capacity.

◆ Critical Thinking Questions

1. Do you think that in general infants are more or less able to perceive the world than their parents think? How would you devise tests to answer this question?

2. How would you devise an experiment to determine whether 3-month-old infants are able to distinguish red from green? In your experiment, you should use the preferential-looking method. However, even an infant who cannot perceive red from green and sees both as gray may perceive a random green object as lighter or darker than a random red object. This fact will make your experiment more of a challenge to devise.

Is Perceptual Development an Innate or Socially Acquired Process?

PERCEPTUAL DEVELOPMENT IS AN INNATE PROCESS
Elizabeth S. Spelke, Massachusetts Institute of Technology

Human beings have a striking capacity to learn from one another. This capacity already is evident in the 1-year-old child, who can learn the meaning of a new word by observing just a few occasions of its use and who can learn the functions of a new object simply by watching another person use it. The rapid and extensive learning that occurs in early childhood suggests that much of what humans come to know and believe is shaped by our encounters with other things and people. But is our very ability to perceive things and people itself the result of learning? Or does perception originate in intrinsically generated growth processes and develop in relative independence of one's encounters with things perceived?

For two millennia, most of the thinkers who have pondered this question have favored the view that humans learn to perceive and that the course of development proceeds from meaningless, unstructured sensations to meaningful, structured perceptions. Research on human infants nevertheless provides evidence against this view. For example, we now know that newborn infants perceive depth and use depth information as adults do, to apprehend the true sizes and shapes of objects. Newborn infants divide the speech stream into the same kinds of sound patterns as do adults, focusing in particular on the set of sound contrasts used by human languages. Newborn infants distinguish human faces from other patterns and orient to faces preferentially. Finally, newborn infants are sensitive to many of the features of objects that adults use to distinguish one thing from another, and they appear to combine featural information in the same kinds of ways as do adults.

How does perception change after the newborn period? With development, infants perceive depth, objects, and faces with increasing precision. Infants also come to focus on the speech contrasts that are relevant to their own language in preference to speech contrasts relevant to other languages. (Interestingly, this focus appears to result more from a decline in sensitivity to foreign language contrasts than from an increase in sensitivity to native language contrasts.) Finally, infants become sensitive to new sources of information about the environment, such as stereoscopic information for depth, configural information for object boundaries, and new reference frames for locating objects and events. These developments bring greater precision and richness to infants' perceptual experience, but they do not change the infant's world from a meaningless flow of sensation to a meaningful, structured environment.

The findings from studies of human infants gain further support from studies of perceptual development in other animals. Since the pioneering work of Gibson and Walk, we have known that depth perception develops without visual experience in every animal tested: Innate capacities for perceiving depth allow newborn goats to avoid falling off cliffs, and they allow dark-reared rats and cats to avoid bumping into approaching surfaces. More recent studies reveal that newborn chicks perceive the boundaries of objects much as human adults do, and they even represent the continued existence of objects that are hidden. Studies of animals' developing brains reveal that both genes and intrinsically structured neural activity are crucial to the development of normally

functioning perceptual systems, but encounters with the objects of perception—external things and events—play a much lesser role. As with human infants, normal visual experience enriches and attunes young animals' perceptual systems, and abnormal visual experience may greatly perturb their functioning. Like human infants, however, other animals do not need visual experience to transform their perceptual world from a flow of unstructured sensations into a structured visual layout.

In sum, perception shows considerable structure at birth and continuity over development. This continuity may help to explain why young human infants are so adept at learning from other people. Consider an infant who watches an adult twist a lid off a jar while saying, "Let's open it." If the infant could not perceive the lid and jar as distinct movable and manipulable objects, she would not be able to make sense of the adult's action. If she could not perceive the sounds that distinguish *open* from other words, she could not begin to learn about this distinctive utterance. And if she could not perceive the person as an agent in some way like herself, then watching the person's action and listening to his speech would reveal nothing about what the infant herself could learn to do or say. Infants' prodigious abilities to learn, therefore, may depend critically on equally prodigious, unlearned abilities to perceive.

Elizabeth S. Spelke

Is Perceptual Development an Innate or Socially Acquired Process?

PERCEPTUAL DEVELOPMENT IS AN ACQUIRED PROCESS
Mark Johnson, University of London

Most developmental scientists now agree that both nature and nurture are essential for the normal development of perception. However, there is still much dispute about the extent to which either nature or nurture is the more important factor. Points of view on this issue are more than just philosophical musings; they affect the kinds of experiments that are undertaken. I argue here that classifying particular aspects of perceptual development as either innate or learned presents us with an overly passive view in which either genes or environment imposes structure on the developing brain. In contrast, I suggest that perceptual development is better characterized as an activity-dependent process involving complex and subtle interactions at many levels.

To begin to illustrate my point, let's consider some recent neurobiological work on the prenatal development of the visual cortex in rodents. The neurons studied in these experiments are those involved in binocular vision. Experiments show that the prenatal tuning of these neurons arises through their response to internally generated waves of electrical activity from the main inputs to the visual cortex, the lateral geniculate nucleus and eye (Katz & Shatz, 1996). In other words, the response properties of these visual cortical neurons are shaped by a kind of "virtual environment" generated by cells elsewhere in the brain and

Mark Johnson

eye. Although the term *innate* can be stretched to cover this example of development, we could equally well describe this process as the cortical cells "learning" from the input provided by their cousins in the LGN and eye. Further, after birth the same cortical neurons continue to be tuned in the same way, except that now their input also reflects the structure of the world outside the infant. When we examine development in detail, it becomes harder to argue, as some theorists do (Spelke, 1998), that "innate knowledge" is fundamentally different from learning.

Another example of the role of activity-dependent processes in perceptual development comes from the ability to detect and recognize faces. Because regions of the human cortex are specialized for processing faces, some have argued that this ability is innate. However, experiments with infants reveal a more complex story (Johnson, 1997). The tendency for newborns to look more toward faces turns out to be based on a very primitive reflex-like system that is triggered by a stimulus as simple as three high-contrast blobs in the approximate locations of the eyes and mouth. This simple bias is sufficient to ensure that newborns look much more at faces than at other objects and patterns over the first weeks of life. One consequence of this is that developing circuits on the visual recognition pathway of the cortex get more input related to faces and thus are shaped by experience with this special type of visual stimulus. We can now study this process by using new brain-imaging methods. Such studies have shown that the brains of young infants show less localized and less specialized processing

of faces in the cortex than do the brains of adults. It is not until age 1 year that infants show the same patterns of brain specialization for processing faces as adults, by which time they have had as much as 1,000 hours of exposure to human faces.

Another example comes from the study of infants' eye movements to visual targets. Although newborns are capable of some primitive reflexive eye movements, only much later in the first year can they make most of the kinds of complex and accurate saccades seen in adults. One view is that the very limited ability present in newborns is just sufficient to allow them to practice and develop new brain circuits for the more complex integration of visual and motor information necessary for adult eye movements. And practice they do! Even by 4 months, babies have already made more than 3 million eye movements. Once again, it appears that infants actively contribute to their own subsequent development.

These considerations should make us skeptical about the many claims for innate perceptual abilities based on experiments with babies of 4 months and older. In fact, when the same experiments were done with younger infants, quite different results have often been obtained, suggesting dramatic changes in perceptual abilities over the first few weeks and months after birth (Haith, 1998).

Infants are not passively shaped by either their genes or their environment. Rather, perceptual development is an activity-dependent process in which, during postnatal life, the infant plays an active role in generating the experience it needs for subsequent development.

1. Perception involves the translation of information acquired by our senses into meaningful experience. Perception can be thought of as continually updating and maintaining an internal model of the environment within which we live. It is via this model that we operate functionally and safely in our environment.

2. Attention is used to screen out the vast amount of information impinging on us at any given time from the environment and let through only the small amount of information that is relevant to carrying out the task at hand. The process of selective attention involves deciding which information to screen out and which to allow through for further processing. Selective attention can operate within all our senses; however, the most studied kinds of selective attention involve vision (e.g., you can move your eyes to attend to different places in the environment) and audition (e.g., you can selectively attend to what's coming into one ear or the other).

3. Localizing an object requires that we know its distance from us. This form of perception, known as depth perception, is usually thought to be based on depth cues. Monocular depth cues include relative size, interposition, relative height, linear perspective, shading, and motion parallax. A binocular depth cue is binocular disparity, which results from the fact that any object produces slightly different images on the two retinas.

4. Localizing an object sometimes requires that we know the direction in which an object is moving. Motion perception can be produced in the absence of an object moving across our retina. One example of this phenomenon is stroboscopic motion, in which a rapid series of still images induces apparent movement; another example is induced motion, in which movement of a large object induces apparent movement of a smaller stationary object. Perception of real motion (movement of a real object through space) is implemented by specific cells in the visual system, as indicated by single-cell recordings and experiments on selective adaptation.

5. Recognizing an object amounts to assigning it to a category and is based mainly on the shape of the object. In early stages of recognition, the visual system uses retinal information to describe the object in terms of features like lines and angles; neurons that detect such features (feature detectors) have been found in the visual cortex. In later stages of recognition, the system matches the description of the object with shape descriptions stored in memory to find the best match.

6. Matching can be explained by a connectionist model or network. The bottom level of the network contains features and the next level contains letters; an excitatory connection between a feature and a letter means that the feature is part of a letter, while an inhibitory connection means that the feature is not part of the letter. When a letter is presented, it activates some features in the network, which pass their activation or inhibition up to letters; the letter that receives the most activation is the best match to the input. The

network can be expanded to include a level of words and to explain why a letter is easier to recognize when presented in a word than when presented alone.

7. The shape features of natural objects are more complex than lines; they are similar to simple geometric forms such as cylinders, cones, blocks, and wedges. A limited set of such forms may be sufficient in combination to describe the shapes of all objects that people can recognize.

8. Bottom-up recognition processes are driven solely by the input, whereas top-down recognition processes are driven by a person's knowledge and expectations. Top-down processes underlie context effects in perception: The context sets up a perceptual expectation, and when this expectation is satisfied, less input information than usual is needed for recognition.

9. Abstraction is the process of ignoring idiosyncratic information corresponding to a sensed object, (for example, the particular orientation of a chair) and assigning the sensed object to a generic category (like "chair" or "something you can sit on"). Because abstracted information is more compact than literal information, it takes less storage space, and can be processed more efficiently.

10. Perceptual constancies refer to visual system's efforts to perceive an object's innate physical characteristics, such as its size, shape, and color—even though the sensory representations of these characteristics may vary with the object's distance or orientation, or the nature of the lighting source. Perceptual constancies are the source of many illusions, such as the well-known moon illusion.

11. Like any other psychological process, perception and all its attributes are carried out by brain functions.

The parts of the brain that carry out visual processes are becoming clarified via techniques such as single-cell recording and neural imaging. It is known that different brain regions are used to carry out the processes of recognition on the one hand and localization on the other.

12. Research on perceptual development is concerned with the extent to which perceptual capacities are inborn and the extent to which they are learned through experience. To determine inborn capacities, researchers study the discrimination capacities of infants using methods such as preferential looking and habituation. Acuity, which is critical to recognition, increases rapidly during the first 6 months of life and then increases more slowly. Depth perception begins to appear at about 3 months but is not fully established until about 6 months. Perceptual constancies begin to develop as early as 6 months.

13. Animals raised in darkness suffer permanent visual impairment, and animals raised with a patch over one eye become blind in that eye. Adult animals do not lose vision even when deprived of stimulation for long periods. These results suggest that there is a critical period early in life during which lack of normal stimulation produces deficiency in an innate perceptual capacity. If stimulation early in life is controlled in such a way that certain kinds of stimuli are absent, both animals and people become insensitive to the stimuli of which they have been deprived; again, this effect does not have much to do with learning. Perceptual-motor coordination must be learned, however. Both animals and people require self-produced movement to develop normal coordination.

CORE CONCEPTS

symbols
theory of ecological optics
model of the environment
fixations
saccades
weapon focus
cue
multimodal attention
shadowing
figure
ground
grouping by proximity
grouping by similarity
depth cues
binocular disparity (as a depth cue)
relative size (as a depth cue)
interposition (as a depth cue)
relative height (as a depth cue)
perspective (as a depth cue)
shading and shadows (as a depth cue)

relative motion (as a depth cue)
stroboscopic motion
selective adaptation
binding problem
illusory conjunction
feature-integration theory
primitive features
visual search task
dynamic control theory
simple cells
complex cells
hypercomplex cells
emergent features
connectionist models
excitatory connections
augmented network
inhibitory connections
top-down feedback connections
geons
bottom-up processes

top-down processes
agnosia
abstraction
physical description (of an object)
constancy
available wavelengths
source wavelengths
reflectance characteristic
illusion
McGurk effect
brain imaging
posterior system (for attention)
anterior system (for attention)
visual cortex
preferential looking method
habituation method
critical period

WEB RESOURCES

http://psychology.wadsworth.com/
atkinson14e

Take a quiz, try the activities and exercises, and explore web links.

http://www.yorku.ca/eye/thejoy.htm

Click on Fun Things in Vision and tease your senses while you learn more about perception. Then explore perception-specific topics like size perception, shape constancy, and more.

http://www.exploratorium.edu/imagery/
exhibits.html

Some more examples of illusions can be found on this site from the Exploratorium in San Francisco.

http://psych.hanover.edu/Krantz/sen_tut.html

This site offers you a collection of tutorials related to sensation and perception.

 InfoTrac Online Library
http://www.infotrac-college.com/
wadsworth

Use InfoTrac College Edition to find popular and scientific articles by using the search terms below or your own relevant terms.

Gestalt psychology
Optical illusions

CD-ROM LINKS

 Psych Odyssey

Check out CD Chapter 4, Sensation and Perception

B. Visual Perception

 Psyk.trek 2.0

Check out CD Unit 3, Sensation and Perception

3d Perception of Color
3e Gestalt Psychology
3f Depth Perception
3g Visual Illusions

© Peter Holst/The Image Bank/Getty

CONSCIOUSNESS

Veronica was sitting in a diner with her friend Gina, listening to Gina's recounting of a party she went to the night before. For a while, Veronica was interested in what Gina was saying, but as Gina went on and on about what a mutual acquaintance of theirs was wearing, Veronica lost interest, looked down at her watch, and then let her mind begin to drift. Suddenly, Gina said sharply, "Veronica! You haven't heard a word I've said!" Indeed, Veronica had not heard what Gina had said, and when she looked down at her watch, she was stunned to see that 10 minutes had passed.

Sound like a familiar experience? If so, you are in good company. One survey of a random sample of adults found that more than 80% acknowledged they had had the experience of missing part of a conversation because their mind "wandered" (Ross, 1997). Some similar experiences that people acknowledged included not being sure whether they had done something or only thought about it (73%), remembering the past so vividly that they seemed to be reliving it (60%), not being sure if they remembered an event or it was just a dream (55%), and driving a car and realizing that they didn't remember part of the trip (48%). These experiences might be referred to as altered states of consciousness. To most psychologists, an **altered state of consciousness** exists whenever there is a change from an ordinary pattern of mental functioning to a state that seems different to the person experiencing the change. Although this definition is not very precise, it reflects the fact that states of consciousness are personal and therefore subjective. Altered states of consciousness can vary from the distraction of a vivid daydream to the confusion and perceptual distortion caused by drug intoxication. In this chapter, we will look at some altered states of consciousness that are experienced by everyone (sleep and dreams), as well as some that result from special circumstances (meditation, hypnosis, and the use of drugs).

ASPECTS OF CONSCIOUSNESS

Discussions about the nature of conscious experience and the functions of consciousness will appear throughout this book as we consider perception, memory, language, problem solving, and other topics. At this point, a general theory of consciousness that provides a framework for considering these various topics would be helpful. Such an approach, however, is not feasible because there is no generally agreed-upon theory. Rather, there are almost as many theories of consciousness as there are individuals who have theorized about the topic. This state of affairs may be discouraging for some readers, particularly those whose prior exposure to science has been in areas where the facts are crystal clear and the theories are well established. Yet what can be more exciting or challenging than venturing into territory that is still uncharted? As important discoveries are being made—in neurophysiology, evolutionary biology, genetics, and various fields of psychology—many observers believe that an explanation of consciousness is tantalizingly close (Crick, 1994). In the absence of a general theory, our discussion of consciousness can do little more than introduce some terms and concepts that will provide a perspective on the topic as it surfaces in later chapters.

What is consciousness? The early psychologists equated "consciousness" with "mind." They defined *psychology* as "the study of mind and consciousness" and used the introspective method to study consciousness. As noted in Chapter 1, both introspection as a method for investigation and consciousness as a topic for investigation fell from favor with the rise of behaviorism in the early 1900s. John Watson and his followers believed that if psychology was to become a science, its data must be objective and measurable. Behavior could be publicly observed, and various responses could be objectively measured. In contrast, an individual's private experiences might be revealed through introspection but could not be directly observed by others or objectively measured. If psychology dealt with overt behavior, it would be dealing with public events rather than private events, which are observable only to the person experiencing them.

Behaviorism did not require as radical a change as its pronouncements seemed to imply. The behaviorists themselves dealt with private events when their research required them to do so. They accepted verbal responses as a substitute for introspection when the participant's own experiences were studied. What participants said was objective, regardless of the underlying subjective condition. Still, many psychologists continued to believe that when people said they experienced a series of colored afterimages after staring at a bright light, they

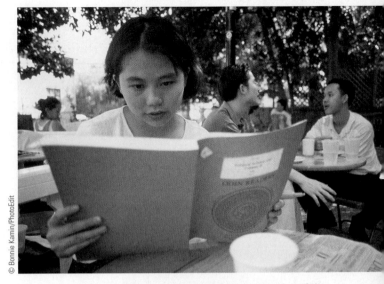

When we concentrate, we are unaware of background stimuli such as other people's conversations. This ability to select stimuli to focus on enables us to avoid information overload.

probably did see colors in succession. That is, their words were not the whole story. While behaviorists could deal with many phenomena in terms of verbal responses, their preoccupation with observable behavior caused them to neglect interesting psychological problems (such as dreaming, meditation, and hypnosis) because the subjective aspects made those topics irrelevant to them (Ericsson & Simon, 1993).

By the 1960s, psychologists began to recognize that various aspects of consciousness are too pervasive and important to be neglected. This does not mean that psychology must again be defined exclusively as the study of consciousness; it means only that it cannot afford to neglect consciousness. Confining psychology to the study of observable behavior is too limiting. If we can theorize about the nature of consciousness, and that theory leads to testable predictions about behavior, then such theorizing is a valuable contribution to understanding how the mind works.

CONSCIOUSNESS

Many textbooks define consciousness as the individual's current awareness of external and internal stimuli—that is, of events in the environment and of body sensations, memories, and thoughts. This definition identifies only one aspect of consciousness and ignores the fact that we are also conscious when we try to solve a problem or deliberately select one course of action over others in response to environmental circumstances and personal goals. We are conscious not only when we monitor our environment (internal and external) but also when we seek to control ourselves and our environment. In short, **consciousness** involves (1) monitoring ourselves and our environment so that percepts, memories, and thoughts are represented in awareness, and (2) controlling ourselves and our environment so that we are able to initiate and terminate behavioral and cognitive activities (Kihlstrom, 1984).

MONITORING Processing information from the environment is the main function of the body's sensory systems. It leads to awareness of what is going on in our surroundings as well as within our own bodies. However, we could not possibly attend to all of the stimuli that impinge on our senses without experiencing information overload. Our consciousness, therefore, focuses on some stimuli and ignores others. Often the information selected has to do with changes in our external or internal worlds. While concentrating on this paragraph, for example, you are probably unaware of numerous background stimuli. But should there be a change—the lights dim, the air begins to smell smoky, or the noise of the air conditioner ceases—you would suddenly be aware of such stimuli.

Our attention is selective. Some events take precedence over others in gaining access to consciousness and in initiating action. Events that are important to survival usually have top priority. If we are hungry, it is difficult for us to concentrate on studying; if we experience a sudden pain, we push all other thoughts out of consciousness until we do something to make the pain go away.

CONTROLLING Another function of consciousness is to plan, initiate, and guide our actions. Whether the plan is simple and readily completed (such as meeting a friend for lunch) or complex and long-range (such as preparing for a career), our actions must be guided and arranged to coordinate with events around us. In planning, events that have not yet occurred can be represented in consciousness as future possibilities. We may envision alternative "scenarios," make choices, and initiate the appropriate activities (Johnson-Laird, 1988).

Not all actions are guided by conscious decisions, nor are the solutions to all problems carried out at a conscious level. One of the tenets of modern psychology is that mental events involve both conscious and nonconscious processes and that many decisions and actions are conducted entirely outside of consciousness. The solution to a problem may occur out of the blue without our being aware that we have been thinking about it. And once we have the solution, we may be unable to offer an introspective account of how the solution was reached. Decision making and problem solving often occur at a nonconscious level, but this does not mean that all such behaviors occur without conscious reflection. Consciousness not only monitors ongoing behavior but plays a role in directing and controlling that behavior as well.

PRECONSCIOUS MEMORIES

We cannot focus on everything that is going on around us at any given time, nor can we examine our entire store of knowledge and memories of past events. At any given moment, we can focus attention on only a few stimuli. We ignore, select, and reject all the time, so that the contents of consciousness are continually changing. Nevertheless, objects or events that are not the focus of attention can still have some influence on consciousness. For example, you may not be aware of hearing a clock strike the hour. But after a few strokes you become alert, and then you can go back and count the strokes that you did not know you heard. Another example of peripheral attention (or nonconscious monitoring) is the lunch-line effect (Farthing, 1992). You are talking with a friend in a cafeteria line, ignoring other voices and general noise, when the sound of your own name in another conversation catches your attention. Clearly, you would not have detected your name in the other conversation if you had not, in some sense, been monitoring that conversation. You were not consciously aware of the other conversation until a special signal drew your attention to it. A considerable body of research indicates that we register and evaluate stimuli that we do not consciously perceive (Greenwald, 1992; Kihlstrom, 1987). These stimuli are said to influence us subconsciously, or to operate at a nonconscious level of awareness.

Many memories and thoughts that are not part of your consciousness at this moment can be brought to consciousness when needed. At this moment, you may not be conscious of your vacation last summer, but the memories are accessible if you wish to retrieve them, and then they become part of your consciousness. The term **preconscious memories** is used to refer to memories that are accessible to consciousness. They include specific memories of personal events as well as the information accumulated over a lifetime, such as your knowledge of the meaning of words, the layout of the streets of a city, or the location of a particular country. They also include knowledge about learned skills like the procedures involved in driving a car or the sequence of steps in tying a shoelace. These procedures, once mastered, generally operate outside conscious awareness, but when our attention is called to them, we are capable of describing the steps involved.

THE UNCONSCIOUS

One of the earliest theories of consciousness—and one that has been subject to considerable criticism over the years—is the psychoanalytic theory of Sigmund Freud. Freud and his followers believed that there is a portion of the mind, the **unconscious**, that contains some memories, impulses, and desires that are not accessible to

"Good morning, beheaded—uhm I mean beloved."

consciousness. Freud believed that some emotionally painful memories and wishes are repressed—that is, diverted to the unconscious, where they may continue to influence our actions even though we are not aware of them. Repressed thoughts and impulses cannot enter our consciousness, but they can affect us in indirect or disguised ways—through dreams, irrational behaviors, mannerisms, and slips of the tongue. The term **Freudian slip** is commonly used to refer to unintentional remarks that are assumed to reveal hidden impulses. Saying, "I'm sad you're better" when you intended to say, "I'm glad you're better" is an example of such a slip.

Freud believed that unconscious desires and impulses are the cause of most mental illnesses. He developed the method of psychoanalysis, which attempts to draw the repressed material back into consciousness and, in so doing, cure the individual (see Chapter 16). Most psychologists accept the idea that there are memories and mental processes that are inaccessible to introspection and accordingly may be described as unconscious. However, many would argue that Freud placed undue emphasis on the emotional aspects of the unconscious and not enough on other aspects. They would include in the unconscious a large array of mental processes that we depend on constantly in our everyday lives but to which we have no conscious access (Kihlstrom, 1987). For example, during perception, the viewer may be aware of two objects in the environment but have no awareness of the mental calculations that she performed almost instantaneously to determine that one is closer or larger than the other (see Chapter 5). Although we have conscious access to the outcome of these mental processes—we are aware of the size and distance of the object—we have no conscious access to their operations (Velmans, 1991).

A study of the stereotypes people hold about the elderly (for example, that they are slow and weak) provided a striking demonstration of how cues from the environment can influence our behavior without our conscious

knowledge. Participants were first given a "language test" in which they had to decipher a number of scrambled sentences. Some participants were given sentences that contained words such as forgetful, Florida, and bingo—words that the researchers believed would subconsciously evoke or "prime" the elderly stereotype in their minds. Control participants saw sentences that did not contain these words. After the language test was completed, each participant was thanked and allowed to leave. A research assistant—who did not know whether the participant was in the experimental group or the control group—surreptitiously measured how long it took the participant to walk down the 40-foot hallway to the exit. The researchers found that participants who had been primed with the elderly stereotype words walked more slowly than control participants. (The word *slow* had not appeared in the sentences.) Interviews with the participants showed that they had no awareness of this influence on their behavior (Bargh, Chen, & Burrows, 1996).

AUTOMATICITY AND DISSOCIATION

An important function of consciousness is control of our actions. However, some activities are practiced so often that they become habitual or automatic. Learning to drive a car requires intense concentration at first. We have to concentrate on coordinating the different actions (shifting gears, releasing the clutch, accelerating, steering, and so forth) and can scarcely think about anything else. However, once the movements become automatic, we can carry on a conversation or admire the scenery without being conscious of driving—unless a potential danger quickly draws our attention to the operation of the car. This habituation of responses that initially required conscious attention is termed **automaticity.**

Skills like driving a car or riding a bike, once they are well learned, no longer require our attention. They become automatic and allow a relatively uncluttered consciousness to focus on other matters. Such automatic processes may have negative consequences on occasion—for example, when a driver cannot remember landmarks passed along the way.

The more automatic an action becomes, the less it requires conscious control. Another example is the skilled pianist who carries on a conversation with a bystander while performing a familiar piece. The pianist is exercising control over two activities—playing and talking—but does not think about the music unless a wrong key is hit, alerting her attention to it and temporarily disrupting the conversation. You can undoubtedly think of other examples of well-learned, automatic activities that require little conscious control. One way of interpreting this is to say that the control is still there (we can focus on automatic processes if we want to) but has been dissociated from consciousness.

The French psychiatrist Pierre Janet (1889) originated the concept of **dissociation,** in which under certain conditions some thoughts and actions become split off, or dissociated, from the rest of consciousness and function outside of awareness. Dissociation differs from Freud's concept of repression because the dissociated memories and thoughts are accessible to consciousness. Repressed memories, in contrast, cannot be brought to consciousness. They have to be inferred from signs or symptoms such as slips of the tongue.

When faced with a stressful situation, we may temporarily put it out of our minds in order to function effectively; when bored, we may lapse into reverie or daydreams. These are mild examples of dissociation that involve dissociating one part of consciousness from another. More extreme examples of dissociation are demonstrated by cases of dissociative identity disorder, or multiple personality, which is discussed in detail in Chapter 15.

◆Interim Summary

- A person's perceptions, thoughts, and feelings at any given moment constitute that person's consciousness.

- An altered state of consciousness is said to exist when mental functioning seems changed or out of the ordinary to the person experiencing the state. Some altered states of consciousness, such as sleep and dreams, are experienced by everyone; others result from special circumstances, such as meditation, hypnosis, or drug use.

- The functions of consciousness are (1) monitoring ourselves and our environment so that we are aware of what is happening within our bodies and in our surroundings and (2) controlling our actions so that they are coordinated with events in the outside world. Not all events that influence consciousness are at the center of our awareness at a given moment. Memories of personal events and accumulated knowledge, which are accessible but are not currently part of a person's consciousness, are called *preconscious memories.* Events that affect behavior, even though we are not aware of perceiving them, influence us subconsciously.

- According to psychoanalytic theory, some emotionally painful memories and impulses are not available to consciousness because they have been repressed— that is, diverted to the unconscious. Unconscious thoughts and impulses influence our behavior even though they reach consciousness only in indirect ways—through dreams, irrational behavior, and slips of the tongue.

- The notion of automaticity refers to the habituation of responses that initially required conscious attention, such as driving a car.

◆ Critical Thinking Questions

1. Many amateur pianists memorize a piece for a recital by playing it over and over again until they can play it automatically, without paying attention to it. Unfortunately, they still often get stuck or forget parts of it during the actual recital. In contrast, some professional pianists deliberately memorize the music away from the piano, so that their "mind, not just their fingers" knows the piece. What does this imply about automatic processes and the controlling function of consciousness?

2. Freud argued that certain desires or thoughts remain in the unconscious because making them conscious arouses anxiety in the individual. What might be some other reasons that certain desires or thoughts might remain out of conscious awareness to us?

SLEEP AND DREAMS

We begin our discussion of consciousness with a state that seems to be its opposite: sleep. But although sleep might seem to have little in common with wakefulness, there are similarities between the two states. The phenomenon of dreaming indicates that we think while we sleep, although the type of thinking we do in dreams differs in various ways from the type we do while awake. We form memories while sleeping, as we know from the fact that we can remember dreams. Sleep is not entirely quiescent: Some people walk in their sleep. People who are asleep are not entirely insensitive to their environment: Parents are awakened by their baby's cry. Nor is sleep entirely planless: Some people can decide to wake at a given time and do so. In this section we explore several facets of sleep and dreaming.

 The Neural Basis of Behavior

STAGES OF SLEEP

Some people are readily roused from sleep; others are hard to wake. Research begun in the 1930s (Loomis, Harvey, & Hobart, 1937) has produced sensitive techniques for measuring the depth of sleep and determining when dreams are occurring (Dement & Kleitman, 1957). This research uses devices that measure electrical changes on the scalp associated with spontaneous brain activity during sleep, as well as eye movements that occur during dreaming. The graphic recording of the electrical changes, or brain waves, is called an *elec-*

① Electrodes on the scalp record the patterns of brain waves.

② Electrodes near the person's eyes record eye movement.

③ Electrodes on the chin record tension and electrical activity in the muscles.

④ A neutral electrode on the ear completes the circuit through amplifiers.

⑤ Amplifiers produce graphical records of the various patterns.

▌ **Figure 6-1**
Arrangement of Electrodes for Recording the Electrophysiology of Sleep
This diagram shows the way electrodes are attached to the person's head and face in a typical sleep experiment.

troencephalogram, or EEG (see Figures 6-1 and 6-2). The EEG measures the rapidly fluctuating average electrical potential of thousands of neurons lying on the surface of the cortex under the electrode. It is a rather crude measure of cortical activity, but it has proved very useful in sleep research.

Analysis of the patterns of brain waves suggests that there are five stages of sleep: four differing depths of sleep and a fifth stage, known as rapid eye movement (or REM) sleep. When a person closes his or her eyes and relaxes, the brain waves characteristically show a regular pattern of 8 to 12 hertz (cycles per second); these are known as alpha waves. As the individual drifts into Stage 1 sleep, the brain waves become less regular and are reduced in amplitude. Stage 2 is characterized by the appearance of spindles—short runs of rhythmical responses of 12 to 16 hertz—and an occasional sharp rise and fall in the amplitude of the

whole EEG (referred to as a K-complex). The still deeper Stages 3 and 4 are characterized by slow waves (1 to 2 hertz), which are known as delta waves. Generally, it is hard to wake the sleeper during Stages 3 and 4, although he or she can be aroused by something personal, such as a familiar name or a child crying. A more impersonal disturbance, such as a loud sound, may be ignored.

SUCCESSION OF SLEEP STAGES After an adult has been asleep for an hour or so, another change occurs. The EEG becomes very active (even more so than when the person is awake), but the person does not wake up. The electrodes placed near the person's eyes detect rapid eye movements so pronounced that one can even watch the sleeper's eyes move around beneath the closed eyelids. This stage is known as **REM sleep;** the other four sleep stages are known as **non-REM (or NREM) sleep.**

These various stages of sleep alternate throughout the night. Sleep begins with the NREM stages and has several sleep cycles, each containing some REM and some NREM sleep. Figure 6-3 illustrates a typical night's sleep for a young adult. As you can see, the person goes from wakefulness into a deep sleep (Stage 4) very rapidly. After about 70 minutes, Stage 3 recurs briefly, immediately followed by the first REM period of the night. Notice that the deeper stages (3 and 4) occurred during the first part of the night, whereas most REM sleep occurred in the last part. This is the typical pattern: The deeper stages tend to disappear in the second half of the night as REM becomes more prominent. There are usually four or five distinct REM periods over the course of an 8-hour night, with an occasional brief awakening as morning arrives.

The pattern of the sleep cycles varies with age. Newborn infants, for instance, spend about half their sleeping time in REM sleep. This proportion drops to 20% to 25% of total sleep time by age 5 and remains fairly constant until old age, when it drops to 18% or less. Older people tend to experience less Stage 3 and 4 sleep (sometimes these stages disappear) and more frequent and longer nighttime awakenings. A natural kind of insomnia seems to set in as people grow older (Gillin, 1985).

REM AND NREM COMPARED During NREM sleep, eye movements are virtually absent, heart and breathing rates decrease markedly, the muscles are relaxed, and the brain's metabolic rate decreases 25% to 30% compared with wakefulness. In contrast, during REM sleep, very rapid eye movements occur in bursts lasting 10 to 20 seconds, the heart rate increases, and the brain's metabolic rate increases somewhat compared with wakefulness. Further, during REM sleep we are almost completely paralyzed—only the heart, diaphragm, eye muscles, and smooth muscles (such as the muscles of the

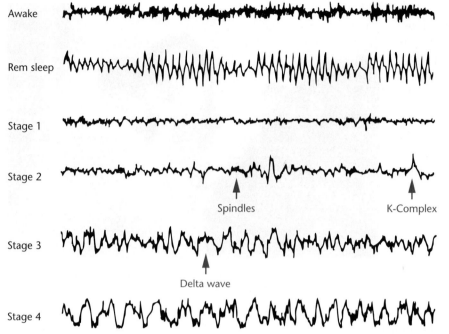

Awake

Rem sleep

Stage 1

Stage 2

Spindles   K-Complex

Stage 3

Delta wave

Stage 4

Figure 6-2
Electrophysiological Activity During Sleep
This figure represents EEG recordings during wakefulness and during the various stages of sleep. The Awake Stage (relaxed with eyes closed) is characterized by alpha waves (8–12 hertz). Stage 1 is basically a transition from wakefulness to the deeper stages of sleep. Stage 2 is defined by the presence of sleep spindles (brief bursts of 12–16 hertz waves) and K-complexes (a sharp rise and fall in the brainwave pattern). Stages 3 and 4 are marked by the presence of delta waves (1–2 hertz), and the only difference between these two stages is the amount of delta waves found. Stage 3 is scored when 20% to 50% of the record contains delta waves, and Stage 4 when the percentage of delta waves is 50% or more.

intestines and blood vessels) are spared. To summarize, NREM sleep is characterized by a very relaxed body, whereas REM sleep is characterized by a brain that appears to be wide awake in a virtually paralyzed body.

Physiological evidence indicates that in REM sleep the brain is largely isolated from its sensory and motor channels. Stimuli from other parts of the body are blocked from entering the brain, and there are no motor outputs. Nevertheless, the brain is still very active, spontaneously driven by the discharge of giant neurons that originate in the brain stem. These neurons extend into parts of the brain that control eye movements and motor activities. During REM sleep, the brain registers the fact that the neurons normally involved in walking and seeing are activated, even though the body itself is doing neither of these things (Hobson, 1994).

Sleepers who are awakened during REM sleep almost always report having a dream, but when awakened during NREM sleep they report a dream only about 50% of the time (Antrobus, 1983; Cavallero, Cicogna, Natale, & Occionero, 1992; Foulkes & Schmidt, 1983). The dreams reported when a person is

Figure 6-3
The Succession of Sleep Stages
This graph provides an example of the sequence and duration of sleep stages during a typical night. The individual went successively through Stages 1 to 4 during the first hour of sleep. He then moved back through Stage 3 to REM sleep. Thereafter, he cycled between NREM and REM periods, with two brief awakenings at about 3½ and 6 hours of sleep.

roused from REM sleep tend to be visually vivid with emotional and illogical features. They represent the type of experience we typically associate with the word *dream*. The longer the period of REM sleep before arousal, the longer and more elaborate the reported dream. In contrast, NREM dreams are neither as visual nor as emotionally charged as REM dreams, and they are more directly related to what is happening in the person's waking life. As indicated by the types of dreams we report and the frequency of reporting a dream, mental activity is different in REM and NREM periods.

SLEEP THEORY

Why are we awake at certain times and asleep at others? Two leading sleep researchers, Dale Edgar and William Dement (1992), have proposed an **opponent-process model of sleep and wakefulness.** According to this model, the brain possesses two opponent processes that govern the tendency to fall asleep or remain awake. They are the homeostatic sleep drive and the clock-dependent alerting process.

The **homeostatic sleep drive** is a physiological process that strives to obtain the amount of sleep required for a stable level of daytime alertness. It is active throughout the night, but it also operates during the daytime. Throughout the day, the need to sleep is continuously building. If we have slept too little the previous night, the tendency to fall asleep during the day will be significant.

The **clock-dependent alerting process** is the process in the brain that arouses us at a particular time each day. It is controlled by the so-called biological clock, which consists of two tiny neural structures located in the center of the brain. This "clock" controls a series of psychological and physiological changes, including rhythms of alertness, that are termed **circadian rhythms** because they occur approximately every 24 hours (the term comes from the Latin words *circa,* meaning "around," and *dies,* "day"). The biological clock is affected by exposure to light: Daylight signals it to stop the secretion of **melatonin,** a hormone that induces sleep.

The two opponent processes—homeostatic sleep drive and the clock-dependent alerting process—interact to produce our daily cycle of sleep and wakefulness. Whether we are asleep or awake at any given time depends on the relative strength of the two processes. During the day, the clock-dependent alerting process usually overcomes the drive for sleep, but during the evening our alertness decreases as the urge to sleep becomes stronger. Late in the evening, the biological clock becomes inactive and we fall asleep. ▌

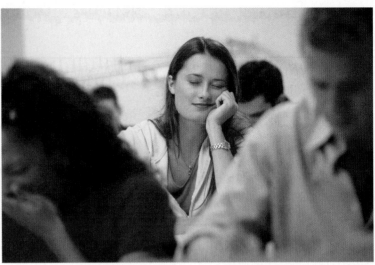

Sleep deprivation is a common cause of underperformance among students.

SLEEP DISORDERS

About 90% of adults sleep 6 to 9 hours per night, with the largest number sleeping 7½ to 8 hours. Although some people sleep only 6 to 7 hours, most of these people have measurable signs of sleepiness during the daytime, even if they do not realize it. It appears that most adults require 8 to 9 hours of sleep to be free from daytime sleepiness (Kryger, Roth, & Dement, 1994). A **sleep disorder** exists when inability to sleep well produces impaired daytime functioning or excessive sleepiness. In this section we look at some common types of sleep disorders.

DEPRIVATION Whether they are aware of it or not, most people occasionally or chronically deprive themselves of adequate sleep. Consider a few examples:

Thirty percent of high school and college students fall asleep in class at least once a week.

Thirty-one percent of all drivers have fallen asleep at the wheel at least once.

Fatigue is the primary factor that detrimentally affects the ability of pilots.

The nuclear accidents at Chernobyl and Three Mile Island occurred in the early morning hours, when night-shift workers were fatigued and missed, or were confused by, warning signals on their control panels (Gallup Organization, 1995; Maas, 1998; Pasztor, 1996).

Gallup surveys have found that 56% of the adult population reports daytime drowsiness as a problem. According to a leading sleep researcher, many of these individuals are "waking zombies" carrying years of ac-

© Chuck Savage/Corbis Stock Market

● **Table 6-1**
Advice for a Good Night's Sleep

There is considerable agreement among researchers and clinicians on how to avoid sleep problems. These recommendations are summarized in the table; some are based on actual research, and others are simply the best judgments of experts in the field. (G. M. Pion (1991) "Psychologists Wanted: Employment Trends Over the Past Decade," in R. R. Kilbur (ed.) *How to Manage Your Career in Psychology,* copyright © 1991 by the American Psychological Association. Reprinted by permission.)

Regular Sleep Schedule Establish a regular schedule of going to bed and getting up. Set your alarm for a specific time every morning and get up at that time no matter how little you may have slept. Be consistent about naps. Take a nap every afternoon or not at all; when you take a nap only occasionally, you probably will not sleep well that night. Waking up late on weekends can also disrupt your sleep cycle.

Alcohol and Caffeine Having a stiff drink of alcohol before going to bed may put you to sleep, but it disturbs the sleep cycle and can cause you to wake up early the next day. In addition, stay away from caffeinated drinks like coffee or cola for several hours before bedtime. Caffeine works as a stimulant even on those people who claim they are not affected by it, and the body needs 4 to 5 hours to halve the amount of caffeine in the bloodstream at any one time. If you must drink something before bedtime, try milk; there is evidence to support the folklore that a glass of warm milk at bedtime induces sleep.

Eating Before Bedtime Don't eat heavily before going to bed, since your digestive system will have to do several hours of work. If you must eat something before bedtime, have a light snack.

Exercise Regular exercise will help you sleep better, but don't engage in a strenuous workout just before going to bed.

Sleeping Pills Be careful about using sleeping pills. All of the various kinds tend to disrupt the sleep cycle, and long-term use inevitably leads to insomnia. Even on nights before exams, avoid using a sleeping pill. One bad night of sleep tends not to affect performance the next day, but hangover from a sleeping pill may.

Relax Avoid stressful thoughts before bedtime and engage in soothing activities that help you relax. Try to follow the same routine every night before going to bed; it might involve taking a warm bath or listening to soft music for a few minutes. Find a room temperature at which you are comfortable and maintain it throughout the night.

When all fails If you are in bed and have trouble falling asleep, don't get up. Stay in bed and try to relax. But if that fails and you become tense, then get up for a brief time and do something restful that reduces anxiety. Doing push-ups or some other form of exercise to wear yourself out is not a good idea.

---

cumulated "sleep debt." He points out that "a one-hour sleep loss every night for an entire week is equivalent to having pulled one all-nighter" (Maas, 1998, p. 53). A common sign of sleep deprivation is inability to get through the day without a temporary loss in energy and alertness, usually occurring in mid-afternoon. Many people attribute this state to a heavy meal, a low dose of alcohol, or environmental conditions such as sitting in a warm room and listening to a dull lecture. But these factors do not cause sleepiness—they merely reveal the presence of sleep debt. With adequate sleep, a normal person is alert throughout the day, even when engaged in unstimulating, sedentary activities.

Sleep researchers have demonstrated that alertness significantly increases when people who normally get 8 hours of sleep get an additional 2 hours of sleep. Although most people can operate satisfactorily on 8 hours of sleep, they are not at their best. Moreover, they lack a

safety margin to make up for the times when they get less than that amount of sleep. The loss of as little as an hour of sleep increases the likelihood of inattentiveness, mistakes, illness, and accidents (Maas, 1998).

Even if you cannot arrange to get 10 hours of sleep a night, you can avoid excessive sleep debt by getting 8 or 9 hours of restful sleep. Table 6-1 suggests techniques that can be used to ensure a good night's sleep.

INSOMNIA The term **insomnia** refers to complaints about a symptom, namely, dissatisfaction with the amount or quality of one's sleep. Whether or not a person has insomnia is a largely subjective matter. Many people who complain of insomnia are found to have perfectly normal sleep when they are studied in a sleep laboratory, whereas others who do not complain of insomnia have detectable sleep disturbances (Trinder, 1988). This does not mean that insomnia is not a real condition, only that subjective reports of sleeplessness do not always correlate well with more objective measures.

A perplexing feature of insomnia is that people seem to overestimate the amount of sleep lost. One study that monitored the sleep of people who identified themselves as insomniacs found that only about half were actually awake as much as 30 minutes during the night (Carskadon, Mitler, & Dement, 1974). The problem may be that some people remember only time spent awake and think they have not slept because they have no memory of doing so.

NARCOLEPSY AND APNEA Two relatively rare but severe sleep disorders are narcolepsy and apnea. A person with **narcolepsy** has recurring, irresistible attacks of drowsiness and may fall asleep at any time—while writing a letter, driving a car, or carrying on a conversation. If a student falls asleep while a professor is lecturing, that may be perfectly normal, but a professor who falls asleep while lecturing may be suffering from narcolepsy. Such episodes can occur several times a day in severe cases and last from a few seconds to 30 minutes. Narcoleptics have difficulty keeping jobs because of their daytime sleepiness and are potentially dangerous if they are driving a car or operating machinery when an attack occurs. Approximately one in a thousand individuals suffers from debilitating narcolepsy, and the incidence of milder, unrecognized cases may be much higher.

Essentially, narcolepsy is the intrusion of REM episodes into daytime hours. During attacks, victims go quickly into a REM state, so rapidly, in fact, that they may lose muscle control and collapse before they can lie down. Moreover, many report experiencing hallucinations during an attack as reality is replaced by vivid REM dreams. Narcolepsy runs in families, and there is evidence that a specific gene or combination of genes makes an individual susceptible to the disorder (Hobson, 1988; Mignot, 1998).

In **apnea**, the individual stops breathing while asleep. There are two reasons for apnea attacks. One reason is that the brain fails to send a "breathe" signal to the diaphragm and other breathing muscles, thus causing breathing to stop. The other reason is that muscles at the top of the throat become too relaxed, allowing the windpipe to partially close and thereby forcing the breathing muscles to pull harder on incoming air, which causes the airway to completely collapse. During an apnea episode, the oxygen level of the blood drops dramatically, leading to the secretion of emergency hormones. This reaction causes the sleeper to awaken in order to begin breathing again.

Most people have a few apnea episodes each night, but people with severe sleep problems may have several hundred episodes per night. With each one, they wake up to resume breathing, but these arousals are so brief

In an experiment by noted sleep researcher William Dement, a narcoleptic dog suddenly falls asleep. About 1 in 1,000 humans suffers from this debilitating sleep disorder.

that the person generally is unaware of them. The result is that people who suffer from apnea can spend 12 or more hours in bed each night and still be so sleepy the next day that they cannot function and may even fall asleep in the middle of a conversation (Ancoli-Israel, Kripke, & Mason, 1987). Sleep apnea is common among older men. Sleeping pills, which make arousal more difficult, lengthen periods of apnea (during which the brain is deprived of oxygen) and may prove fatal.

DREAMS

Dreaming is an altered state of consciousness in which picture stories are constructed based on memories and current concerns, or on fantasies and images. Investigators do not yet understand why people dream at all, much less why they dream what they do. However, modern methods of study have answered a great many questions about dreaming. Some of them are explored here.

DOES EVERYONE DREAM? Although many people do not recall their dreams in the morning, evidence from studies of REM sleep suggests that nonrecallers often do as much dreaming as recallers. If you take people who swear that they have never dreamed, put them in a dream research laboratory, and wake them from REM sleep, they may recall dreams at rates comparable to those of other people. If someone says, "I never dream," what they may mean is "I can't recall my dreams."

Some evidence does suggest, however, that preschool children do not dream and that elementary school age children dream much less often than adults (Foulkes, 1999). In addition, adults with certain types of brain damage also do not appear to dream (Solms, 1997). Some people may indeed not dream.

Researchers have proposed several hypotheses to account for differences in dream recall among people who clearly do dream. One possibility is that nonrecallers simply have more difficulty than recallers in remembering their dreams. Another hypothesis suggests that some people wake up relatively easily in the midst of REM sleep and therefore recall more dreams than those who sleep more soundly. The most generally accepted model of dream recall supports the idea that what happens on awakening is the crucial factor. According to this hypothesis, unless a distraction-free waking period occurs shortly after dreaming, the memory of the dream is not consolidated—that is, the dream cannot be stored in memory (Hobson, 1988; Koulack & Goodenough, 1976).

Other researchers argue that a person's motivation to recall dreams and interest in dreams is a good predictor of ability to recall dreams (Blagrove & Akehurst, 2000; Tonay, 1993). If upon awakening we make an effort to remember what we were dreaming at the time, some of the dream content will be recalled at a later time. Otherwise, the dream will fade quickly. We may know that we have had a dream but will be unable to remember its content. If you are interested in remembering your dreams, keep a notebook and pencil beside your bed. Tell yourself that you want to wake up when you have a dream. When you do, immediately try to recall the details and write them down. As your dream recall improves, look for patterns. Underline anything that strikes you as odd and tell yourself that the next time something similar happens, you are going to recognize it as a sign that you are dreaming. (Of course, you will lose some sleep if you follow this regimen!)

HOW LONG DO DREAMS LAST? Some dreams seem almost instantaneous. The alarm clock rings, and we awaken to complex memories of a fire breaking out and fire engines arriving with their sirens blasting. Because the alarm is still ringing, we assume that the sound must have produced the dream. Research suggests, however, that a ringing alarm clock or other sound merely reinstates a complete scene from earlier memories or dreams. This experience has its parallel during wakefulness, when a single cue may tap a rich memory. The length of a typical dream can be inferred from a REM study in which participants were awakened and asked to act out what they had been dreaming (Dement & Wolpert, 1958). The time it took them to pantomime the dream was almost the same as the length of the REM sleep period, suggesting that the incidents in dreams commonly last about as long as they would in real life.

DO PEOPLE KNOW WHEN THEY ARE DREAMING? The answer to this question is "sometimes yes." People can be taught to recognize that they are dreaming, yet their awareness does not interfere with the spontaneous flow of the dream. For example, people have been trained to press a switch when they notice that they are dreaming (Salamy, 1970).

Some people have **lucid dreams,** in which events seem so normal (lacking the bizarre and illogical character of most dreams) that the dreamers feel as if they are awake and conscious. Lucid dreamers report doing various "experiments" within their dreams to determine whether they are awake or dreaming. They also report an occasional "false awakening" within a dream. For example, one lucid dreamer discovered that he was dreaming and decided to call a taxicab as an indication of his control over events. When he reached into his pocket to see if he had some change to pay the driver, he thought that he woke up. He then found the coins scattered about the bed. At this point he really awoke and found himself lying in a different position and, of course, without any coins (Brown, 1936). Note, however, that relatively few people achieve lucidity with any regularity (Squier & Domhoff, 1998).

CAN PEOPLE CONTROL THE CONTENT OF THEIR DREAMS? Psychologists have demonstrated that some control of dream content is possible by changing people's environment or making suggestions to people in the presleep period and then analyzing the content of their dreams. In one study, researchers tested the effect of wearing red goggles for several hours before going to sleep. Although the researchers made no actual suggestion and the participants did not understand the purpose of the experiment, many participants reported that their visual dream worlds were tinted red (Roffwarg, Herman, Bower-Anders, & Tauber, 1978). In a study of the effect

We all like to have good dreams, but it is generally very difficult to control the content of our dreams.

of an overt predream suggestion, participants were asked to try to dream about a personality characteristic that they wished they had. Most of the participants had at least one dream in which the intended trait could be recognized (Cartwright, 1974). Despite these findings, most studies find little evidence that dream content can actually be controlled (Domhoff, 1985).

THEORIES OF DREAMING

One of the earliest theories of the function of dream sleep was suggested by Sigmund Freud. In *The Interpretation of Dreams* (1900), Freud proposed that dreams provide a "royal road to a knowledge of the unconscious activities of the mind." He believed that dreams are a disguised attempt at wish fulfillment. By this he meant that the dream touches on wishes, needs, or ideas that the individual finds unacceptable and have been repressed to the unconscious (for example, sexual longings for the parent of the opposite sex). These wishes and ideas are the latent content of the dream. Freud used the metaphor of a censor to explain the conversion of latent content into manifest content (the characters and events that make up the actual narrative of the dream). In effect, Freud said, the censor protects the sleeper, enabling him or her to express repressed impulses symbolically while avoiding the guilt or anxiety that would occur if they were to appear consciously in undisguised form.

According to Freud, the transformation of latent content into manifest content is done by "dream work," whose function is to code and disguise material in the unconscious in such a way that it can reach consciousness. However, sometimes dream work fails, and the resulting anxiety awakens the dreamer. The dream essentially expresses the fulfillment of wishes or needs that are too painful or guilt-inducing to be acknowledged consciously (Freud, 1933).

Subsequent research challenged several aspects of Freud's theory. After surveying dozens of studies of dreaming, Fisher and Greenberg (1977, 1996) concluded there is good evidence that the content of dreams has psychological meaning, but there is none that supports Freud's distinction between manifest and latent content. Although most psychologists would agree with Freud's general conclusion that dreams focus on emotional concerns, they question the concept of "dream work" and the idea that dreams represent wish fulfillment.

Since Freud's time, a variety of theories have been advanced to explain the role of sleep and dreams. Evans (1984), for example, views sleep, particularly REM sleep, as a period when the brain disengages from the external world and uses this "off-line" time to sift through the information that was input during the day and to incorporate it into memory (see also Crick & Mitchinson, 1983).

We are not consciously aware of the processing that occurs during REM sleep. During dreaming, however, the brain comes back online for a brief time, and the conscious mind observes a small sample of the modification and reorganization of information that is taking place. The brain attempts to interpret this information the same way it would interpret stimuli coming from the outside world, giving rise to the kinds of pseudo-events that characterize dreams. According to Evans, dreams are nothing more than a small subset of the vast amount of information that is being scanned and sorted during REM sleep, a momentary glimpse by the conscious mind that we remember if we awaken. Evans believes that dreams can be useful in making inferences about the processing that occurs during REM sleep but that they represent an extremely small sample on which to base such inferences.

Other researchers take different approaches. Hobson (1997), for example, notes that dreaming is characterized by formal visual imagery (akin to hallucination), inconstancy of time, place, and person (akin to disorientation), and inability to recall (akin to amnesia). Dreaming thus resembles delirium. It has also been suggested that dreams may have a problem-solving function (Cartwright, 1978, 1992, 1996), but this theory has been challenged on methodological grounds (Antrobus, 1993; Foulkes, 1993). Moreover, the content of dreams tends to differ according to the culture, gender, and personality of the dreamer, suggesting that dreams have some psychological meaning (Domhoff, 1996; Hobson, 1988). Dream content may reflect personal conflicts, but dreams do not necessarily function to resolve those conflicts (Squier & Domhoff, 1998).

Only about half of all dreams include even one element related to events of the previous day (Botman & Crovitz, 1992; Hartmann, 1968; Nielson & Powell, 1992). Moreover, systematic analyses of dream content have found that rates of aggression are higher than rates of friendly interactions; in fact, the murder rate in dreams is 2,226 per 100,000 characters, far above real-world rates (Hall & Van de Castle, 1966)! In addition, there are more negative than positive emotions in dreams. Overall, dreams cannot be viewed as simple extensions of the previous day's activities. On the other hand, researchers have repeatedly found great consistency in what people dream about over years or decades. G. William Domhoff and Adam Schneider (1998) report that

> Our analyses of lengthy dream journals reveal that there is an astonishing degree of consistency in what a person dreams about over several months or years, even 40 or 50 years in the two longest dream series analyzed to date. There are also striking continuities between dream findings and waking life, making possible accurate predictions about the concerns and interests of the dreamers. These findings suggest that dreams have "meaning."

Analyses of dreams have also found significant age, gender, and cross-cultural similarities and differences in their content, leading some theorists to propose that dreaming is a cognitive process (Antrobus, 1991; Domhoff, 1996; Foulkes, 1985). An early researcher in this field pointed out that dreams seem to express conceptions and concerns (Hall, 1947, 1953). However, dreaming differs from waking thought in that it lacks intentionality and reflectiveness (Blagrove, 1992, 1996; Foulkes, 1985), and these theorists think that dreaming is unlikely to have a problem-solving function. Instead, it is a cognitive activity, as evidenced by the continuity between dream content and waking thoughts and behavior. As Domhoff notes, "The concerns people express in their dreams are the concerns they have in waking life. What they dream about is also what they think about or do when they are awake" (1996, p. 8). Parents dream of their children, aggressive dream content is more common among people under age 30 than in older people, and women are more often victims of aggression. These patterns support what Domhoff and others refer to as the "continuity theory" of dreaming, in which dreaming is an imaginative process that reflects the individual's conceptions, concerns, and emotional preoccupations.

◆ Interim Summary

- Sleep, an altered state of consciousness, is of interest because of the rhythms evident in sleep schedules and in the depth of sleep. These rhythms are studied with the aid of the electroencephalogram (EEG).

- Patterns of brain waves show four stages (depths) of sleep, plus a fifth stage characterized by rapid eye movements (REMs). These stages alternate throughout the night. Dreams occur more often during REM sleep than during the other four stages (NREM sleep).

- The opponent-process model of sleep proposes that two opposing processes—the homeostatic sleep drive and the clock-dependent alerting process—interact to determine our tendency to fall asleep or remain awake. Whether we are asleep or awake at any given time depends on the relative forces exerted by the two processes.

- There are a variety of sleep disorders, including sleep deprivation, insomnia, narcolepsy, and apnea.

- Freud attributed psychological causes to dreams, distinguished between their manifest and latent content, and suggested that dreams are wishes in disguise.

- Other theories see dreaming as a reflection of the information processing that the brain is doing while asleep.

- Recently some theorists have concluded that dreaming is a cognitive process that reflects the individual's conceptions, concerns, and emotional preoccupations.

◆ Critical Thinking Questions

1. How might dream theories explain instances when people appear to have dreamed of an event they were not expecting before it actually happens?

2. What personality characteristics do you think might be related to the tendency to remember your dreams?

MEDITATION

Meditation refers to achieving an altered state of consciousness by performing certain rituals and exercises, such as controlling and regulating breathing, sharply restricting one's field of attention, eliminating external stimuli, assuming yogic body positions, and forming mental images of an event or symbol. The result is a pleasant, mildly altered subjective state in which the individual feels mentally and physically relaxed. After extensive practice, some individuals may have mystical experiences in which they lose self-awareness and gain a sense of being involved

The rituals of meditation include regulating breathing, restricting one's field of attention, eliminating external stimuli, and forming mental images of an event or symbol. Traditional forms of meditation follow the practices of yoga.

in a wider consciousness, however defined. The belief that such meditative techniques may cause a change in consciousness goes back to ancient times and is represented in every major world religion. Buddhists, Hindus, Sufi Muslims, Jews, and Christians all have literature describing rituals that induce meditative states.

Traditional forms of meditation follow the practices of yoga, a system of thought based on the Hindu religion, or Zen, which is derived from Chinese and Japanese Buddhism. Two common meditation techniques are opening-up meditation, in which the person clears his or her mind in order to receive new experiences, and concentrative meditation, in which the benefits are obtained by actively attending to some object, word, or idea. Following is a typical description of opening-up meditation:

> This approach begins with the resolve to do nothing, to think nothing, to make no effort of one's own, to relax completely and let go of one's mind and body . . . stepping out of the stream of ever-changing ideas and feelings which your mind is in, watch the onrush of the stream. Refuse to be submerged in the current. Changing the metaphor . . . watch your ideas, feelings, and wishes fly across the firmament like a flock of birds. Let them fly freely. Just keep a watch. Don't let the birds carry you off into the clouds. (Chauduri, 1965, pp. 30–31)

Here is a corresponding statement for concentrative meditation:

> The purpose of these sessions is to learn about concentration. Your aim is to concentrate on the blue vase. By concentration I do not mean analyzing the different parts of the vase, but rather, trying to see the vase as it exists in itself, without any connections to other things. Exclude all other thoughts or feelings or sounds or body sensations. (Deikman, 1963, p. 330)

After a few sessions of concentrative meditation, people typically report a number of effects: an altered, more intense perception of the vase; some time shortening, particularly in retrospect; conflicting perceptions, as if the vase fills the visual field and does not fill it; decreasing effectiveness of external stimuli (less distraction and eventually less conscious registration); and an impression of the meditative state as pleasant and rewarding.

Experimental studies of meditation provide only limited insight into the alterations of consciousness that a person can achieve when meditative practice and training extend over many years. In his study of a centuries-old Tibetan Buddhist text, Brown (1977) has described the complex training required to master the technique. He has also shown that cognitive changes can be expected at different levels of meditation. (In this type of meditation, people proceed through five levels until they reach a thoughtless, perceptionless, selfless state known as concentrative *samadhi*.)

Meditation may reduce arousal (especially in easily stressed individuals) and may be valuable for people suffering from anxiety and tension. We discuss the use of meditation to relieve stress-related disorders in Chapter 14. Some researchers argue that the benefits of meditation come largely from relaxation of the body (Holmes, 1984). Indeed, one study in which EEG readings were recorded for people practicing transcendental meditation found that most of the participants spent considerable portions of their meditation periods in physiological sleep (Younger, Adriance, & Berger, 1975). Other researchers suggest that the psychological benefits of meditation may be due to learning to put aside repetitive and troubling thoughts (Teasdale et al., 2000).

◆ Interim Summary

- Meditation represents an effort to alter consciousness by following planned rituals or exercises such as those of yoga or Zen.

- The result is a somewhat mystical state in which the individual is extremely relaxed and feels divorced from the outside world.

◆ Critical Thinking Questions

1. People who make a daily practice of meditating often say they are calmer and better able to respond to stress throughout the day as a result of meditating. If this is true, what might account for these effects?

2. There is some evidence that meditation can improve physical health. What might be the mechanisms for these effects, if true?

HYPNOSIS

Of all the altered states of consciousness discussed in this chapter, none has raised more questions than hypnosis. Once associated with the occult, hypnosis has become the subject of rigorous scientific investigation. As in all fields of psychological investigation, uncertainties remain, but by now many facts have been established. In this section we explore what is known about this controversial phenomenon.

INDUCTION OF HYPNOSIS

In **hypnosis,** a willing and cooperative individual (the only kind that can be hypnotized under most circumstances) relinquishes some control over his or her behavior to the hypnotist and accepts some distortion of reality. The hypnotist uses a variety of methods to induce this condition. For example, the person may be asked to concentrate on a small target (such as a thumbtack on the wall) while gradually becoming relaxed. The hypnotist may suggest that the person is becoming sleepy because, like sleep, hypnosis is a relaxed state in which a person is out of touch with ordinary environmental demands. But sleep is only a metaphor. The person is told that he or she will not really go to sleep but will continue to listen to the hypnotist.

The same state can be induced by methods other than relaxation. A hyperalert hypnotic trance is characterized by increased tension and alertness. For example, in one study, participants riding a stationary bicycle while receiving suggestions of strength and alertness were as responsive to hypnotic suggestions as relaxed participants (Banyai & Hilgard, 1976). This result denies the common equation of hypnosis with relaxation, but it is consistent with the trance-induction methods used by the whirling dervishes of some Muslim religious orders.

Modern hypnotists do not use authoritarian commands. Indeed, with a little training, people can hypnotize themselves (Ruch, 1975). The person enters the hypnotic state when the conditions are right; the hypnotist merely helps set the conditions. The following changes are characteristic of the hypnotized state:

Planfulness ceases. A deeply hypnotized individual does not like to initiate activity and would rather wait for the hypnotist to suggest something to do.

Attention becomes more selective than usual. A person who is told to listen only to the hypnotist's voice will ignore any other voices in the room.

Enriched fantasy is readily evoked. People may find themselves enjoying experiences at places that are distant in time and space.

Reality testing is reduced and reality distortion accepted. A person may uncritically accept hallucinated experiences (for example, conversing with an imagined person who is believed to be sitting in a nearby chair) and will not check to determine whether that person is real.

Suggestibility is increased. An individual must accept suggestions in order to be hypnotized at all, but whether suggestibility is increased under hypnosis is a matter of some dispute. Careful studies have found some increase in suggestibility following hypnotic induction, though less than is commonly supposed (Ruch, Morgan, & Hilgard, 1973).

Posthypnotic amnesia is often present. When instructed to do so, an individual who is highly responsive to hypnotism will forget all or most of what took place during the hypnotic session. When a prearranged release signal is given, the memories are restored.

A therapist induces a hypnotic state. Not all individuals are equally responsive to hypnosis.

Not all individuals are equally responsive to hypnosis, as Figure 6-4 indicates. Roughly 5% to 10% of the population cannot be hypnotized even by a skilled hypnotist, and the remainder show varying degrees of suscep-

Figure 6-4
Individual Differences in Hypnotizability
Participants were hypnotized, then given 12 different hypnotic suggestions. Their response to each suggestion was scored as present or absent, and the present responses were totaled for each participant to yield a score ranging from 0 (no responses) to 12 (responded to all). Most individuals fell in the middle ranges. (After Hilgard, 1965)

tibility. However, a person who is hypnotized on one occasion probably will be equally susceptible on another occasion (Hilgard, 1965; Piccione, Hilgard, & Zimbardo, 1989).

HYPNOTIC SUGGESTIONS

Suggestions given to a hypnotized individual can result in a variety of behaviors and experiences. The person's motor control may be affected, new memories may be lost or old ones reexperienced, and current perceptions may be radically altered.

CONTROL OF MOVEMENT Many hypnotized individuals respond to direct suggestion with involuntary movement. For example, if a person stands with arms outstretched and hands facing each other and the hypnotist suggests that the person's hands are attracted to each other, the hands will soon begin to move together, and the person will feel propelled by some external force. Direct suggestion can also inhibit movement. If a suggestible individual is told that an arm is stiff (like a bar of iron or an arm in a splint) and then is asked to bend the arm, it will not bend, or more effort than usual will be needed to make it bend. This response is less common than suggested movement.

A **posthypnotic response** occurs when people who have been roused from hypnosis respond with movement to a prearranged signal by the hypnotist. Even if the suggestion has been forgotten, they will feel a compulsion to carry out the behavior. They may try to justify such behavior as rational, even though the urge to perform it is impulsive. For example, a young man searching for a rational explanation of why he opened a window when the hypnotist took off her glasses (the prearranged signal) remarked that the room felt a little stuffy.

POSTHYPNOTIC AMNESIA At the suggestion of the hypnotist, events occurring during hypnosis may be "forgotten" until a signal from the hypnotist enables the individual to recall them. This is called **posthypnotic amnesia.** People differ widely in their susceptibility to posthypnotic amnesia, as Figure 6-5 shows. The items to be recalled in this study were 10 actions that the participants performed while hypnotized. A few participants forgot none or only one or two items; most participants forgot four or five items. However, a sizable number of participants forgot all 10 items. Many studies of posthypnotic amnesia have shown similar results. The group of participants with the higher recall is larger and presumably represents the average hypnotic responders; the participants who forgot all 10 items have been described as "hypnotic virtuosos."

Differences in recall between the two groups do not appear to be related to differences in memory capacity:

Figure 6-5
The Distribution of Posthypnotic Amnesia
Individuals performed 10 actions while hypnotized and were then given posthypnotic amnesia instructions. When asked what occurred during hypnosis, these individuals varied in the number of actions they failed to recall: The level of forgetting for a given individual ranged from 0 to 10 items. The experiment involved 491 people, and the graph plots the number of people at each level of forgetting. The plot shows a bimodal distribution for posthypnotic amnesia, with peaks at 4 and 10 items forgotten. (After Cooper, 1979)

Once the amnesia is canceled at a prearranged signal from the hypnotist, highly amnesic participants remember as many items as those who are less amnesic. Some researchers have suggested that hypnosis temporarily interferes with the person's ability to retrieve a particular item from memory but does not affect actual memory storage (Kihlstrom, 1987).

POSITIVE AND NEGATIVE HALLUCINATIONS Some hypnotic experiences require a higher level of hypnotic talent than others. The vivid and convincing perceptual distortions of hallucinations, for instance, are relatively rare in hypnotized individuals. Two types of suggested hallucinations have been documented: **positive hallucinations,** in which the person sees an object or hears a voice that is not actually present; and **negative hallucinations,** in which the person does not perceive something that normally would be perceived. Many hallucinations have both positive and negative components. For example, in order to not see a person sitting in a chair (a negative hallucination), an individual must see the parts of the chair that would ordinarily be blocked from view (a positive hallucination).

Hallucinations can also occur as a result of posthypnotic suggestion. For example, individuals may be told that upon being aroused from the hypnotic state they will find themselves holding a rabbit that wants to be petted

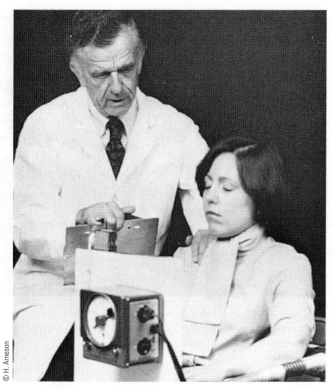

Previously when her hand was in the icewater, the woman felt no pain following suggestions of hypnotic anesthesia. By placing a hand on her shoulder, however, Dr. Hilgard tapped a "hidden observer" that reported the pain that the subject had felt at some level.

and that the rabbit will ask, "What time is it?" Seeing and petting the rabbit will seem natural to most people. But when they find themselves giving the correct time of day, they are surprised and try to provide an explanation for the behavior: "Did I hear someone ask the time? It's funny, it seemed to be the rabbit asking, but rabbits can't talk!"

Negative hallucinations can be used to control pain. In many cases, hypnosis eliminates pain even though the source of the pain—a severe burn or a bone fracture, for example—continues. The failure to perceive something (pain) that would normally be perceived qualifies this response as a negative hallucination. The pain reduction need not be complete for hypnosis to be useful in giving relief. Reducing pain by 20% can make the patient's life tolerable. Experimental studies have shown that the amount of pain reduction is closely related to the degree of measured hypnotizability (Crasilneck & Hall, 1985; Hilgard & Hilgard, 1975).

THE HIDDEN OBSERVER

The concept of a **hidden observer** originated with Hilgard's (1986) observation that in many hypnotized individuals, a part of the mind that is not within awareness seems to be watching the person's experience as a whole. This finding has been described as follows:

> The circumstances of Hilgard's discovery of a doubled train of thought in hypnosis were suitably dramatic. He was giving a classroom demonstration of hypnosis using an experienced subject who, as it happened, was blind. Hilgard induced deafness, telling him that he would be able to hear when a hand was put on his shoulder. Cut off from what was going on around him, he became bored and began to think of other things. Hilgard showed the class how unresponsive he was to noise or speech, but then the question arose as to whether he was as unresponsive as he seemed. In a quiet voice, Hilgard asked the subject whether, though he was hypnotically deaf, there might be "some part of him" that could hear; if so, would he raise a forefinger? To the surprise of everyone—including the hypnotized subject—the finger rose.
>
> At this, the subject wanted to know what was going on. Hilgard put a hand on his shoulder so he could hear, promised to explain later, but in the meantime asked the subject what he remembered. What he remembered was that everything had become still, that he was bored and had begun thinking about a problem in statistics. Then he felt his forefinger rise, and he wanted to know why.
>
> Hilgard then asked for a report from "that part of you that listened to me before and made your finger rise," while instructing the hypnotized subject that he would not be able to hear what he himself said. It turned out that this second part of the subject's awareness had heard all that went on and was able to report it. Hilgard found a suitable metaphor to describe this detached witness—the hidden observer. (Hebb, 1982, p. 53)

Thus, the hidden observer metaphor refers to a mental structure that monitors everything that happens, including events that the hypnotized individual is not consciously aware of perceiving. The presence of the hidden observer has been demonstrated in many experiments (Kirsch & Lynn, 1998). In studies of pain relief, for example, participants are able to describe how the pain feels, using automatic writing or speaking, at the same time that their conscious system accepts and responds to the hypnotist's suggestion of pain relief. Hilgard and his colleagues have compared this phenomenon to everyday experiences in which an individual divides attention between two tasks, such as driving a car and conversing at the same time or making a speech and simultaneously evaluating one's performance as an orator.

Although hidden observer experiments have been replicated in many laboratories and clinics, they have been criticized on methodological grounds. Skeptics argue that implied demands for compliance may have produced the results (see, for example, Spanos, 1986; Spanos & Hewitt, 1980). In an experiment designed to determine the role of compliance, researchers have shown that the responses of the truly hypnotized can be distinguished from those of the merely compliant. They asked participants of proven low hypnotizability to simulate hypnosis while highly responsive participants behaved naturally. The experimenter did not know to which group each participant belonged. The simulators did conform to the implied demands in the way they were expected to, but their reports of the subjective experiences differed significantly from those of individuals who were actually hypnotized (Hilgard, Hilgard, MacDonald, Morgan, & Johnson, 1978; Zamansky & Bartis, 1985).

HYPNOSIS AS THERAPY Hypnosis is used to treat a number of physiological and psychological disorders (see reviews by Lynn, Kirsch, Barabasz, Cardena, & Patterson, 2000; Pinnell & Covino, 2000). In medicine, hypnosis has been used to reduce anxiety related to medical and dental procedures, asthma, gastrointestinal diseases, and the nausea associated with cancer treatment and used for general pain management. In treatment for psychological disorders, hypnosis has been used to help people overcome addictions. The most controversial use of hypnosis is in the treatment of emotional problems. Proponents of the therapeutic use of hypnosis suggest that it allows therapists to uncover repressed memories that are behind psychological problems, but several researchers caution against the use of hypnosis in psychotherapy (see Ofshe & Waters, 1994; Loftus & Ketchum, 1994). They argue that hypnosis amounts to no more than a therapist planting false memories in the minds of clients, including memories of horrendous abuse experiences that never happened. We discuss the rather substantial evidence for the claims of these opponents in Chapter 8.

◆ Interim Summary

- Hypnosis is a responsive state in which individuals focus their attention on the hypnotist and his or her suggestions.
- Some people are more readily hypnotized than others, although most people show some susceptibility.
- Characteristic hypnotic responses include enhanced or diminished control over movements, distortion of memory through posthypnotic amnesia, and positive and negative hallucinations.
- Reduction of pain is one of the beneficial uses of hypnosis.

◆ Critical Thinking Questions

1. Do you think you would be a good hypnotic subject or not? Why?
2. If it is true that hypnosis only plants false ideas in the minds of suggestible people, does this mean the phenomenon of hypnosis is not real?

© Paul A. Souders/CORBIS

Although alcohol and tobacco are legal, they are included in the category of psychoactive drugs because they affect behavior, consciousness, and mood.

PSYCHOACTIVE DRUGS

In addition to meditation and hypnosis, drugs can be used to alter a person's state of consciousness. Since ancient times, people have used drugs to stimulate or relax, to bring on sleep or prevent it, to enhance ordinary perceptions, or to produce hallucinations. The word *drug* can be used to refer to any substance (other than food) that chemically alters the functioning of an organism. The term **psychoactive drugs** refers to drugs that affect behavior, consciousness, and/or mood. These drugs include not only illegal "street" drugs such as heroin and marijuana but also legal drugs such as tranquilizers and stimulants. Familiar, widely used drugs such as alcohol, nicotine, and caffeine are also included in this category.

Whether a particular drug is legal or not does not reflect the risks and dangers associated with the drug. For example, caffeine (coffee) is totally accepted, and its use is unregulated; nicotine (tobacco) is minimally regulated and at present is not even under the jurisdiction of the Food and Drug Administration; alcohol is subject to numerous regulations but is legal; and marijuana is illegal. Yet it could be argued that of all these substances nicotine is the most harmful, because it is responsible for about 360,000 deaths per year. We could well ask whether nicotine would even be made a legal drug if someone tried to introduce it today.

The Concept Review table lists and classifies the psychoactive drugs that are most frequently used and abused. Drugs that are used to treat mental disorders

CONCEPT REVIEW TABLE
Psychoactive Drugs That Are Commonly Used and Abused

Only a few examples of each class of drug are given. The generic name (for example, psilocybin) or the brand name (Xanax for alprazolam; Seconal for secobarbital) is used, depending on which is more familiar.

Depressants (Sedatives)

Alcohol (ethanol)

Barbiturates
  Nembutal
  Seconal

Minor tranquilzers
  Miltown
  Xanax
  Valium

Inhalants
  Paint thinner
  Glue

Opiates (Narcotics)

Opium and its derivatives
  Codeine
  Heroin
  Morphine

Methadone

Stimulants

Amphetamines
  Benzedrine
  Dexedrine
  Methedrine

Cocaine

Nicotine

Caffeine

Hallucinogens

LSD

Mescaline

Psilocybin

PCP (Phencyclidine)

Cannabis

Marijuana

Hashish

Figure 6-6
Cumulative Probability of Using Illegal Drugs in Four Generations
People born in more recent generations are much more likely to have used an illegal drug at some time in their lives than people born in earlier generations. (From L. A. Warner, R. C. Kessler, M. Hughes, J. C. Anthony, & C. B. Nelson. (1995). Prevalence and correlates of drug use and dependence in the United States. *Archives of General Psychiatry, 52,* 219–229.)

(see Chapter 16) also affect mood and behavior and thus might be considered psychoactive. They are not included here, however, because they are seldom abused. By and large, their effects are not immediate and usually are not experienced as particularly pleasant. An exception is the minor tranquilizers, which may be prescribed to treat anxiety disorders and are sometimes abused. Caffeine and nicotine are also listed in the table. Although both substances are stimulants and can have negative effects on health, they do not significantly alter consciousness and hence are not discussed in this section.

The prevalence of illegal substance use and abuse increased substantially in the last four decades. People who were teenagers in the 1960s and more recent generations are much more likely to have tried illegal substances such as marijuana, cocaine, or heroin at some time in their lives than their parents or grandparents (see Figure 6-6). Most people who ever use an illegal substance do so before the age of 20. Surveys find that more than half of adolescents have tried an illegal substance (including marijuana) by age 17 (NIDA, 2002).

Much substance use by adolescents and young adults is experimental. Typically, young people try alcohol or marijuana and maybe even heroin or cocaine a few times but do not use them chronically or continue to use them as they grow older. Some substances, however, have such powerful reinforcing effects on the brain that many people who try these substances, even experimentally, find themselves craving more of the substance and have a difficult time resisting taking the substance. In addition, some people have a greater vulnerability to becoming "hooked" psychologically or physically on substances, so even a little experimentation may be dangerous for them.

The drugs listed in the Concept Review table are assumed to affect behavior and consciousness because they act on the brain in specific biochemical ways. With repeated use, an individual can become dependent on any of them. **Drug dependence** has three key characteristics: (1) **tolerance**—with continued use, the individual must take more and more of the drug to achieve the same effect; (2) **withdrawal**—if use of the drug is discontinued, the person experiences unpleasant physical and psychological reactions; and (3) compulsive use—the individual takes more of the drug than intended, tries to control his or her drug use but fails, and spends a great deal of time trying to obtain the drug.

CUTTING-EDGE RESEARCH
Finding the Gene for Smoking

Most of the research on why some people smoke cigarettes has focused on the societal pressures that lead people to begin smoking. Yet, some recent research on smoking has focused on genetic contributors to smoking behavior and the risk of nicotine addiction (Pomerleau & Kardia, 1999).

The first reports suggesting that genes play a role in smoking were published 40 years ago by Fisher (1958), who found that identical twins, who share the same genetic makeup, are much more alike in their smoking behavior than nonidentical twins, who are no more alike genetically than any two siblings. Several subsequent publications confirmed this finding. Hughes (1986) summarized the data from 18 twin studies of smoking and concluded that 53% of the variation in smoking behavior was attributable to genetic causes.

Just how genes might affect smoking behavior was not known, however, until advanced technologies for genetic research began to be applied in studies of smoking. This new research is focusing on the neurotransmitter dopamine because the reinforcing properties of nicotine are probably due, in part, to the fact that nicotine stimulates dopamine release and inhibits the reuptake of dopamine, thereby increasing levels of dopamine at the synapse (Perkins & Stitzer, 1998). Genetic variation in the dopamine receptor gene (labeled DRD2) and the dopamine transporter gene (labeled SLC6A3) may influence concentrations of dopamine at the synapse and responses to dopamine, thereby influencing how reinforcing nicotine is (Pomerleau & Kardia, 1999). People with certain polymorphisms in the DRD2 or SLC6A3 genes that result in more dopamine at the synapse appear less likely to become smokers than people without these polymorphisms (Lerman et al., 1999). In addition, smokers with the SLC6A3 polymorphism are more likely to quit smoking

than those without it (Sabol et al., 1999).

This is likely to be only one of many pathways by which genes influence smoking (Pomerleau & Kardia, 1999). For example, there are nicotinic acetylcholine receptors that are the point of entry for nicotine into the central nervous system and moderate the reinforcing effects of nicotine (Picciotto et al., 1998). At present, there are no genetic probes available to study polymorphisms in these nicotine receptors in humans, but this looks like a good target for future research. The hope of investigators in this area is that greater understanding of the genetics of smoking behavior will lead to better identification of people at risk and the development of better treatments, including new drugs, to help people stop smoking.

 For more information, go online with InfoTrac College Edition. Use your own term or search:

- Dopamine and smoking
- Genes and addiction
- Smoking gene

The degree to which tolerance develops and the severity of withdrawal symptoms vary from one drug to another. Tolerance for opiates, for example, develops fairly quickly, and heavy users can tolerate a dosage that would be lethal to a nonuser. In contrast, marijuana smokers seldom build up much tolerance. Withdrawal symptoms are common and easily observed following heavy and sustained use of alcohol, opiates, and sedatives. They are common, but less apparent, for stimulants, and nonexistent after repeated use of hallucinogens (American Psychiatric Association, 2000).

Although tolerance and withdrawal are the primary characteristics of drug dependence, they are not necessary for a diagnosis. A person who shows a pattern of compulsive use without any signs of tolerance or withdrawal, as some marijuana users do, would still be considered drug dependent.

Drug dependence is usually distinguished from **drug abuse,** continued use of a drug, despite serious consequences, by a person who is not dependent on it (that is, shows no symptoms of tolerance, withdrawal, or com-

pulsive craving). For example, someone whose overindulgence in alcohol results in repeated accidents, absence from work, or marital problems (without signs of dependence) is said to abuse alcohol.

In this section we look at several types of psychoactive drugs and the effects they may have on those who use them.

DEPRESSANTS

Depressants are drugs that depress the central nervous system. They include tranquilizers, barbiturates (sleeping pills), inhalants (volatile solvents and aerosols), and ethyl alcohol. Of these, the most frequently used and abused is alcohol, and we will focus on it here.

ALCOHOL AND ITS EFFECTS People in most societies consume alcohol in some form. Alcohol can be produced by fermenting a wide variety of materials: grains such as rye, wheat, and corn; fruits such as grapes, apples, and plums; and vegetables such as potatoes. Through the

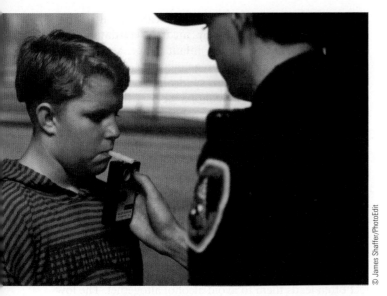

A device called a *Breathalyzer* is used to determine whether an underage person or a driver has been drinking. It measures the amount of alcohol in the air the person exhales, providing an index of the amount of alcohol in the blood.

© James Shaffer/PhotoEdit

process of distillation, the alcoholic content of a fermented beverage can be increased to obtain "hard liquor" such as whiskey or rum.

The alcohol used in beverages is called ethanol and consists of relatively small molecules that are easily and quickly absorbed into the body. Once a drink is swallowed, it enters the stomach and small intestine, where there is a heavy concentration of small blood vessels. These give the ethanol molecules ready access to the blood. Once they enter the bloodstream, they are rapidly carried throughout the body and to all of its organs. Although the alcohol is fairly evenly distributed through the whole body, its effects are likely to be felt most immediately in the brain because a substantial portion of the blood that the heart pumps at any given time goes to the brain and the fatty tissue in the brain absorbs alcohol very well (Kuhn, Swartzwelder, & Wilson, 1998).

Measuring the amount of alcohol in the air we exhale (as in a breath analyzer) gives a reliable index of the amount of alcohol in the blood. Consequently, it is easy to determine the relationship between blood alcohol concentration (BAC) and behavior. At concentrations of 0.03% to 0.05% in the blood (30 to 50 milligrams of alcohol per 100 milliliters of blood), alcohol produces light-headedness, relaxation, and release of inhibitions. People say things that they might not ordinarily say and tend to become more sociable and expansive. Self-confidence may increase, but motor reactions begin to slow. In combination, these effects make it dangerous to drive after drinking.

At a BAC of 0.10%, sensory and motor functions become noticeably impaired. Speech becomes slurred, and people have difficulty coordinating their movements. Some people become angry and aggressive; others grow silent and morose. At a level of 0.20% the drinker is seriously incapacitated, and a level above 0.40% may cause death. In most states, the legal definition of intoxication is a BAC of 0.10% (one-10th of 1%).

How much can a person drink without becoming legally intoxicated? The relationship between BAC and alcohol intake is not a simple one. It depends on a person's sex, body weight, and speed of consumption. Age, individual metabolism, and experience with drinking are also factors. Although the effects of alcohol intake on BAC vary a great deal, the average effects are shown in Figure 6-7. It is not true that beer or wine is less likely to make someone drunk than so-called hard drinks. A

Drinks in a two-hour period
(1.2 ozs. 80-proof liquor or 12 ozs. beer)

Weight												
100	1	2	3	4	5	6	7	8	9	10	11	12
120	1	2	3	4	5	6	7	8	9	10	11	12
140	1	2	3	4	5	6	7	8	9	10	11	12
160	1	2	3	4	5	6	7	8	9	10	11	12
180	1	2	3	4	5	6	7	8	9	10	11	12
200	1	2	3	4	5	6	7	8	9	10	11	12
220	1	2	3	4	5	6	7	8	9	10	11	12
240	1	2	3	4	5	6	7	8	9	10	11	12

Be careful driving
bac to .05%

Driving impaired
.05%–.09%

Do not drive
.10% & UP

Figure 6-7
BAC and Alcohol Intake
Approximate values of blood-alcohol concentration as a function of alcohol consumption in a 2-hour period. For example, if you weigh 180 pounds and had 4 beers in 2 hours, your BAC would be between 0.05% and 0.09%, and your driving ability would be seriously impaired. Six beers in the same 2-hour period would give you a BAC above 0.10%—the level accepted as proof of intoxication. (Data from the National Highway and Traffic Safety Administration.)

4-ounce glass of wine, a 12-ounce can of beer, and 1.2 ounces of 80-proof whiskey have about the same alcohol content and about the same effect.

ALCOHOL USAGE Many college students view drinking as an integral part of social life. It promotes conviviality, eases tension, releases inhibitions, and generally adds to the fun. Nevertheless, social drinking can create problems in terms of lost study time, poor performance on exams "the morning after," and arguments or accidents while intoxicated. Clearly the most serious problem is accidents: Alcohol-related automobile accidents are the leading cause of death among 15- to 24-year-olds. When the legal drinking age was lowered from 21 to 18 in a number of states, traffic fatalities among 18- and 19-year-olds increased by from 20% to 50%. All states have since raised their minimum drinking age, and the number of traffic accidents has decreased significantly.

About two-thirds of American adults report that they drink alcohol. At least 10% of them have social, psychological, or medical problems resulting from alcohol use. Probably half of that 10% are dependent on alcohol. Heavy or prolonged drinking can lead to serious health problems. High blood pressure, stroke, ulcers, cancers of the mouth, throat, and stomach, cirrhosis of the liver, and depression are some of the conditions associated with regular use of substantial amounts of alcohol.

Despite the fact that it is illegal for anyone under age 21 to purchase alcoholic beverages, experience with alcohol is almost universal among young people (51% of eighth graders have tried it, 80% of high school seniors, and 91% of college students; NIDA, 2002). More disturbing is the widespread "binge drinking" (having five or more drinks in a row). Binge drinking on college campuses is common. One study of students at a large public university in the Midwest found that 45% said they engage in binge drinking, defined as 5 or more drinks in one setting for males and 4 or more for females, at least occasionally (Wahlberg, 1999). Binge drinking is especially common among members of fraternities and sororities, with 76% of students saying they binge drink, and 15% having engaged in binge drinking at least six times in the previous 2 weeks. Lost study time, missed classes, injuries, unprotected sex, and trouble with police are some of the problems reported by college students who engage in binge drinking. Because of these problems, an increasing number of universities no longer permit alcohol on campus. The Drug Free School and Campuses Act, passed by Congress in 1989, requires institutions to make alcohol education programs and counseling services available to students and employees.

Alcohol can also cause damage to a developing fetus. Pregnant women who drink heavily are twice as likely to suffer repeated miscarriages and to produce low-birth-weight babies. A condition called **fetal alcohol syndrome** is characterized by mental retardation and multiple deformities of the infant's face and mouth, caused by drinking during pregnancy. The amount of alcohol needed to produce this syndrome is unclear, but as little as a few ounces of alcohol a week is thought to be detrimental (Streissguth et al., 1999).

CULTURAL DIFFERENCES IN ALCOHOL DISORDERS There are marked differences across cultures in the use of alcohol and in rates of alcohol-related problems (see Table 6-2). Low rates of alcohol-related problems in China and Taiwan may be due in part to the absence, in 50% of people of Asian descent, of an enzyme that eliminates the first breakdown product of alcohol, acetaldehyde. When these individuals consume alcohol, they experience a flushed face and heart palpitations, and the discomfort of this effect often leads them to avoid alcohol altogether. The low rates of alcohol-related disorders in Asia have also been attributed to the Confucian moral ethic, which discourages drunken behavior, and to the fact that alcohol is seen as appropriate for meals and ceremonial occasions but not for personal indulgence (Helzer & Canino, 1992).

In recent years, however, there have been substantial increases in alcohol use and related problems among businessmen in Asia. This may explain, in part, the high rates of alcohol-related problems in South Korea (see Table 6-2), where drinking among business associates after work is common. These nightly parties often involve drinking contests lasting until some of the contestants have to be carried home.

Although the United States may not have the highest rates of alcohol dependence in the world, alcohol depen-

● **Table 6-2**
Lifetime Prevalence of Alcohol Dependence in Various Cultures

The rates of alcohol dependence vary greatly across cultures.

Culture	Percentage
South Korea	22.00
New Zealand	19.00
Canada	18.00
Germany	13.00
Puerto Rico	13.00
Mainland United States	8.00
Taiwan	6.00
China	0.45

Source: Data from Helzer, Bucholz, and Robins, 1992.

● Table 6-3
Drinking Patterns of Some Groups in the United States (Percentages of People)

Heavy drinkers are those who regularly consumed seven or more drinks at least one evening a week for a period of several months but who never had any social, legal, or medical problems related to alcohol or any withdrawal symptoms. Problem drinkers are those who have had at least one alcohol-related problem in their lives but who have not had enough to qualify for a diagnosis of alcohol abuse or dependency.

	Total Abstention	Social Drinkers	Heavy Drinkers	Problem Drinkers	Abuse/ Dependecy
Mexican Americans born in the United States	7	52	3	14	23
Immigrant Mexican Americans	23	44	1	19	13
Puerto Ricans	20	69	7	10	13

Source: Data from Canino, Burnam, and Chetano, 1992.

dence and abuse are the most common disorders in the United States, with about 24% of the population reporting symptoms that qualify them for a diagnosis of dependence or abuse at some time in their lives (Kessler et al., 1994; note that Table 6-3 lists lifetime prevalences for alcohol dependence only; alcohol abuse requires only that there be chronic negative social consequences to drinking). There are substantial differences among ethnic groups within the United States in alcohol use and abuse. Notice in Table 6-3 the much higher rate of alcohol abuse and dependence in Mexican Americans born in the United States than in those who immigrated to the United States. Some theorists have argued that the more an immigrant group becomes assimilated to dominant U.S. culture, the more at risk they are for mental health problems in general and particularly for the common mental health problems of this culture (see Gaw, 1993). Assimilation is considered to rob immigrants of their ties to their heritage and extended social networks and to lead them to identify with a culture that will never accept them fully. Mexican Americans born in the United States tend to be more assimilated than more recent immigrants, which may help to explain why they show greater rates of alcohol-related problems.

One group in the United States that appears at high risk for alcohol abuse and dependence are Native Americans (Manson, Shore, Baron, Ackerson, & Neligh, 1992). For example, a study of adult members of a Pacific Northwest reservation community found that 27% qualified for a diagnosis of alcohol dependence. Deaths related to alcohol are as much as five times more common among Native Americans than in the general U.S. population (Manson et al., 1992). Hospital records indicate that alcohol-related illnesses are three times higher among Native Americans than among all people in the United States and twice the rates for other ethnic minority groups in the United States. The higher rates of

alcohol-related problems among Native Americans have been tied to their excessive rates of poverty and unemployment, lower education levels, and greater sense of helplessness and hopelessness.

GENDER AND AGE DIFFERENCES IN ALCOHOL DISORDERS In a community survey done in the United States, 72% of adult men said they had consumed at least one alcoholic beverage in the last year, compared to 62% of adult women (NIDA, 2002). About 11% of American men and 4% of American women meet the criteria for alcohol dependence in any given year (Kessler et al., 1994). Males are more likely than females to drink in all cultures, but the size of the gender difference differs by culture (Helzer & Canino, 1992). The gender gap in alcohol use is much greater among men and women who subscribe to traditional gender roles, which condone drinking for men but not for women (Huselid & Cooper, 1992). Similarly, in ethnic minority groups of the United States in which traditional gender roles are more widely accepted, such as Hispanics and recent Asian immigrants, the gender gap in drinking is greater than it is among whites, largely because of high percentages of women in the minority groups completely abstaining from alcohol.

Elderly people are less likely than others to abuse or be dependent on alcohol, probably for several reasons. First, with age, the liver metabolizes alcohol at a slower rate, and the lower percentage of body water increases the absorption of alcohol. As a result, older people can become intoxicated faster and experience the negative effects of alcohol more severely and quickly. Second, as people grow older, they may become more mature in their choices, including the choice about drinking alcohol to excess. Third, older people have grown up under stronger prohibitions against alcohol use and abuse and in a society with more stigma associated with alcoholism, leading them to curtail their use of alcohol more than younger people do. Finally, people who have used alcohol excessively for many years may die from alcohol-related diseases before they reach old age.

Recent studies of adolescents and young adults find widespread abuse of alcohol (Lewinsohn, Rohde, & Seeley, 1996; Nelson & Wittchen, 1998), particularly among males. For example, one study of more than 3,000 14- to 24-year-olds found that 15% of the males and about 5% of the females could be diagnosed with alcohol abuse (Nelson & Wittchen, 1998). Alcohol dependence was lower, with about 10% of the males and 3% of the females qualifying for the diagnosis. Over time, about half of the adolescents and young adults who abused alcohol stopped abusing alcohol, but abusers of alcohol were much more likely than nonabusers to become dependent on alcohol eventually.

OPIATES

Opium and its derivatives, collectively known as **opiates,** are drugs that diminish physical sensation and the capacity to respond to stimuli by depressing the central nervous system. (These drugs are commonly called *narcotics,* but *opiates* is a more accurate term; the term *narcotics* is not well defined and covers a variety of illegal drugs.) Opiates are used in medical settings to reduce pain, but their ability to alter mood and reduce anxiety has led to widespread illegal consumption. Opium, which is the air-dried juice of the opium poppy, contains a number of chemical substances, including morphine and codeine. Codeine, a common ingredient in prescription painkillers and cough suppressants, is relatively mild in its effects (at least at low doses). Morphine and its derivative, heroin, are much more potent. Most illegal opiate use involves heroin because it is more concentrated and can be concealed and smuggled more easily than morphine.

All opiate drugs bind to the same molecules in the brain, known as opiate receptors. The differences among these drugs depend on how quickly they reach the receptors and how much it takes to activate them—that is, their potency. The rate at which opiates enter the body depends on how they are taken. When opiates are smoked or injected, they reach peak levels in the brain within minutes. The faster this occurs, the greater the danger of death by overdose. Drugs that are "snorted" are absorbed more slowly because they must pass through the mucous membranes of the nose to the blood vessels beneath (Kuhn, Swartzwelder, & Wilson, 1998).

HEROIN USAGE Heroin is an opiate that can be injected, smoked, or inhaled. At first it produces a sense of well-being. Experienced users report a special thrill, or "rush," within a minute or two after an intravenous injection. Some describe this sensation as intensely pleasurable, similar to an orgasm. Young people who sniff heroin report that they forget everything that troubles them. Following this, the user feels "fixed," or gratified, and has no awareness of hunger, pain, or sexual urges. The person may "go on the nod," alternately waking and drowsing while comfortably watching television or reading a book. Unlike a person who is intoxicated by alcohol, a heroin user can readily produce skilled responses to tests of agility and intelligence and seldom becomes aggressive or assaultive.

The changes in consciousness produced by heroin are not very striking; there are no exciting visual experiences or feelings of being transported elsewhere. It is the change in mood—the feeling of euphoria and reduced anxiety—that prompts people to start using the drug. However, heroin is very addictive; even a brief period of usage can create physical dependence. After a person has been smoking or "sniffing" (inhaling) heroin for a while, tolerance builds up, and this method no longer produces the desired effect. In an attempt to re-create the original high, the individual may progress to "skin popping" (injecting under the skin) and then to "mainlining" (injecting into a vein). Once the user starts mainlining, stronger and stronger doses are required to produce the high, and the physical discomforts of withdrawal from the drug become intense (chills, sweating, stomach cramps, vomiting, headaches). Additional motivation to continue using the drug stems from the need to avoid physical pain and discomfort.

The hazards of heroin use are many; the average age at death for frequent users is 40 (Hser, Anglin, & Powers, 1993). Death is caused by suffocation resulting from depression of the brain's respiratory center. Death from an overdose is always a possibility because the concentration of street heroin fluctuates widely, and the user can never be sure of the potency of the powder in a newly purchased supply. Heroin use is generally associated with a serious deterioration of personal and social life. Because maintaining the habit is costly, the user often becomes involved in illegal activities to acquire money to purchase the drug.

Additional dangers of heroin use include AIDS (acquired immune deficiency syndrome), hepatitis, and other infections associated with unsterile injections. Sharing needles used to inject drugs is an extremely easy way to be infected with the AIDS virus; blood from an infected person can be trapped in the needle or syringe and injected directly into the bloodstream of the next person who uses the needle. Sharing of needles and syringes by people who inject drugs is a primary means by which the AIDS virus is spreading today.

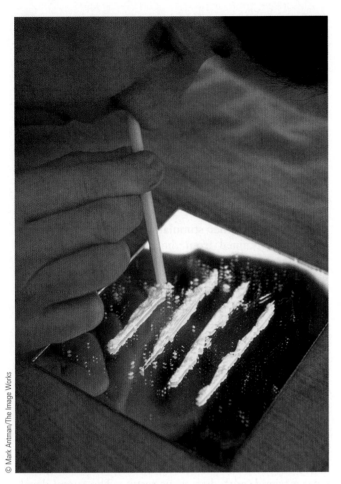

Cocaine is a powerful drug that users often inhale or snort through their noses.

OPIOID RECEPTORS In the 1970s, researchers made a major breakthrough in understanding opiate dependence with the discovery that opiates act on very specific neuroreceptor sites in the brain. Neurotransmitters travel across the synaptic junction between two neurons and bind to neuroreceptors, triggering activity in the receiv-

ing neuron (see Chapter 2). The molecular shape of the opiates resembles that of a group of neurotransmitters called *endorphins*. Endorphins bind to opioid receptors, producing sensations of pleasure as well as reducing discomfort (Julien, 1992). Heroin and morphine relieve pain by binding to opioid receptors that are unfilled (see Figure 6-8). Repeated heroin use causes a drop in endorphin production; the body then needs more heroin to fill the unoccupied opioid receptors in order to reduce pain. The person experiences painful withdrawal symptoms when heroin is discontinued because many opioid receptors are left unfilled. In essence, the heroin has replaced the body's own natural opiates (Koob & Bloom, 1988).

These findings have led to the development of drugs that operate by modulating the opioid receptors. These drugs are of two basic types: agonists and antagonists. **Agonists** bind to the opioid receptors to produce a feeling of pleasure and thereby reduce the craving for opiates, but they cause less psychological and physiological impairment than the opiates. **Antagonists** also lock onto the opioid receptors but in a way that does not activate them; the drug serves to "block" the receptors so that the opiates cannot gain access to them. Antagonists produce no feeling of pleasure and the craving is not satisfied (see Figure 6-8).

Methadone is the best-known agonist drug used in treating heroin-dependent individuals. It is addictive in its own right, but it produces less psychological impairment than heroin and has few disruptive physical effects. When taken orally in low doses, it suppresses the craving for heroin and prevents withdrawal symptoms. **Naltrexone**, an antagonist drug, blocks the action of heroin because it has a greater affinity for the opioid receptors than does heroin itself. Naltrexone is often used in hospital emergency rooms to reverse the effects of a heroin overdose, but it has not proved generally effective as a treatment for heroin dependence. Interestingly, naltrexone does reduce the craving for alcohol. Alcohol causes

▌Figure 6-8
Drug Abuse Medications
Methadone and naltrexone block the effects of heroine by binding to the same neuronal receptors that heroin binds to.

the release of endorphins, and naltrexone, by blocking opioid receptors, reduces the pleasurable effects of alcohol and hence the desire for it (Winger, Hoffman, & Woods, 1992).

STIMULANTS

In contrast to depressants and opiates, **stimulants** are drugs that increase alertness and general arousal. They increase the amount of monoamine neurotransmitters (norepinephrine, epinephrine, dopamine, and serotonin) in the synapse. The effects resemble what would happen if every one of the neurons that released a monoamine fired at once. The result is to arouse the body both physically, by increasing heart rate and blood pressure, and mentally, causing the person to become hyperalert (Kuhn, Swartzwelder, & Wilson, 1998).

AMPHETAMINES Amphetamines are powerful stimulants; they are sold under such trade names as Methedrine, Dexedrine, and Benzedrine and known colloquially as "speed," "uppers," and "bennies." The immediate effects of consuming such drugs are an increase in alertness and a decrease in feelings of fatigue and boredom. Strenuous activities that require endurance seem easier after taking amphetamines. As with other drugs, the ability of amphetamines to alter mood and increase self-confidence is the principal reason for their use. People also use them to stay awake.

Low doses that are taken for limited periods to overcome fatigue (for example, when driving at night) seem to be relatively safe. However, as the stimulating effects of amphetamines wear off, there is a period when the user feels depressed, irritable, and fatigued and may be tempted to take more of the drug. Tolerance develops quickly, and the user needs increasingly larger doses to produce the desired effect. Because high doses can have dangerous side effects—agitation, confusion, heart palpitations, and elevated blood pressure—medications containing amphetamines should be used with caution.

When tolerance develops to the point at which oral doses are no longer effective, many users inject amphetamines into a vein. Large intravenous doses produce an immediate pleasant experience (a "flash" or "rush"). This sensation is followed by irritability and discomfort, which can be overcome only by an additional injection. If this sequence is repeated every few hours over a period of days, it will end in a "crash," a deep sleep followed by a period of lethargy and depression. The amphetamine abuser may seek relief from this discomfort by turning to alcohol or heroin.

Long-term amphetamine use is accompanied by drastic deterioration of physical and mental health. The user, or "speed freak," may develop symptoms that are indistinguishable from those of acute schizophrenia (see Chapter 15), including persecutory delusions (the false belief that people are persecuting you or out to get you) and visual or auditory hallucinations. The delusions may lead to unprovoked violence. For example, during an epidemic of amphetamine use in Japan in the early 1950s (when amphetamines were sold without prescription and advertised for "elimination of drowsiness and repletion of the spirit"), 50% of the murders that occurred in a 2-month period were related to amphetamine abuse (Hemmi, 1969).

COCAINE Like other stimulants, **cocaine,** or "coke," a substance obtained from the dried leaves of the coca plant, increases energy and self-confidence; it makes the user feel witty and hyperalert. Early in the 20th century, cocaine was widely used and easy to obtain. In fact, it was an ingredient in the original recipe of Coca-Cola. Its use then declined, but in the 1980s and 1990s its popularity increased, even though it is now illegal.

Cocaine can be inhaled or "snorted," or made into a solution and injected directly into a vein. It can also be converted into a flammable compound, "crack," which is smoked. One of the earliest studies of the effects of cocaine was conducted by Freud (1885). In an account of his own use of cocaine, he was at first highly favorable to the drug and encouraged its use. However, he changed his mind about the drug after using it to treat a friend, with disastrous results. The friend developed severe dependence on the drug, demanded everlarger dosages, and was debilitated until his eventual death.

Despite earlier reports to the contrary, and as Freud soon discovered, cocaine is highly addictive. In fact, it has become more addictive and dangerous with the emergence of crack. Tolerance develops with repeated use, and withdrawal effects, although not as dramatic as those associated with opiates, do occur. The restless irritability that follows the euphoric high becomes, with repeated use, a feeling of depressed anguish. The down is as bad as the up was good and can be alleviated only by more cocaine (see Figure 6-9).

Heavy cocaine users can experience the same abnormal symptoms as people who use amphetamines heavily. A common visual hallucination is flashes of light ("snow lights") or moving lights. Less common—but more disturbing—is the feeling that bugs ("cocaine bugs") are crawling under one's skin. The hallucination may be so strong that the individual will use a knife to cut out the bugs. These experiences occur because cocaine is causing the sensory neurons to fire spontaneously (Weiss, Mirin, & Bartel, 1994).

a) A nerve impulse causes the release of neurotransmitters that carry the signal across the synapse to a receiving neuron. Some of the neurotransmitters are then reabsorbed into the originating neuron (reuptake process), while the rest are broken up chemically and made inactive (degradation process). These processes are discussed in Chapter 2.

b) Research findings indicate that cocaine blocks the reuptake process for three neurotransmitters (dopamine, serotonin, and norepinephrine) that are involved in the regulation of mood.

❚ **Figure 6-9**
Molecular Effects of Cocaine

HALLUCINOGENS

Hallucinogens, or psychedelics, are drugs whose main effect is to change perceptual experience. They typically change the user's perception of both the internal and the external world. Usual environmental stimuli are experienced as novel events; for example, sounds and colors seem dramatically different. Time perception is so altered that minutes may seem like hours. The user may experience auditory, visual, and tactile hallucinations and reduced ability to differentiate between self and surroundings.

Some hallucinogenic drugs are derived from plants, such as mescaline from cactus and psilocybin from mushrooms. Others are synthesized in the laboratory, such as LSD (lysergic acid diethylamide) and PCP (phencyclidine).

LSD LSD, or "acid," is a colorless, odorless, tasteless substance that is often sold dissolved on sugar cubes or pieces of paper. It is a potent drug that produces halluci-

nations at very low doses. Some users have vivid hallucinations of colors and sounds, and others have mystical or semireligious experiences. Anyone can have an unpleasant, frightening reaction ("bad trip"), even those who have had many pleasant LSD experiences. Another adverse LSD reaction is the flashback, which may occur days, weeks, months, or even years after the last use of the drug. During a flashback, the individual experiences illusions or hallucinations similar to those experienced during use of the drug. Because LSD is almost completely eliminated from the body within 24 hours after it is taken, the flashback is probably a restoration of memories of the prior experience.

More threatening to the LSD user is the loss of reality orientation that can be caused by the drug. This alteration in consciousness can lead to irrational and disoriented behavior and, occasionally, to a panic state in which users feel they cannot control what they are doing or thinking. People have jumped from high places to their deaths when in this state. LSD was popular during the 1960s, but its use subsequently declined, probably as a result of widespread reports of severe drug reactions. There are, however, some indications of renewed interest in LSD and other hallucinogens (Johnston, O'Malley, & Bachman, 1995).

PCP PCP is sold as a hallucinogen (under such street names as "angel dust," "Shermans," and "superacid") but is technically classified as a dissociative anesthetic. It may cause hallucinations, but it also makes the user feel dissociated or apart from the environment. PCP was first synthesized in 1956 for use as a general anesthetic. It had the advantage of eliminating pain without producing a deep coma. However, its legal manufacture was discontinued when doctors found that the drug produced agitation, hallucinations, and a psychotic-like state resembling schizophrenia in many patients. Because the ingredients are cheap and the drug is relatively easy to manufacture in a kitchen laboratory, PCP is widely used as an adulterant in more expensive street drugs. Much of what is sold as THC (the active ingredient of marijuana) is really PCP.

PCP can be taken in liquid or pill form, but more often it is smoked or snorted. In low doses, it produces insensitivity to pain and an experience similar to a moderately drunken state—confusion, loss of inhibition, and poor psychomotor coordination. Higher doses produce a disoriented, comalike condition. Unlike the person who experiences LSD, the PCP user is unable to observe his or her drug-induced state and frequently has no memory of it.

CANNABIS

Cannabis is a psychoactive substance that creates a high feeling, cognitive and motor impairments, and sometimes hallucinations. The cannabis plant has been harvested since ancient times for its psychoactive effects. The dried leaves and flowers are used to produce **marijuana,** the form of cannabis most often used in this country, and the solidified resin of the plant, called **hashish** ("hash"), a form of cannabis commonly used in the Middle East. Marijuana and hashish are usually smoked but may also be taken orally, mixed with tea or food. The active ingredient in both substances is THC (tetrahydrocannabinol). Taken orally in small doses (5–10 milligrams), THC produces a mild high; larger doses (30–70 milligrams) produce severe and longer-lasting reactions that resemble those of hallucinogenic drugs. As with alcohol, the reaction often has two stages: a period of stimulation and euphoria, followed by a period of tranquility and sleep.

When marijuana is smoked, THC is rapidly absorbed by the rich blood supply of the lungs. Blood from the lungs goes directly to the heart and then to the brain,

causing a high within minutes. However, THC also accumulates in other organs, such as the liver, kidneys, spleen, and testes. The amount of THC reaching the body varies according to how the user smokes: A cigarette allows for the transfer of 10% to 20% of the THC in the marijuana, whereas a pipe allows about 40% to 50% to transfer. A water pipe, or bong, traps the smoke until it is inhaled and therefore is a highly efficient means of transferring THC. Once in the brain, the THC binds to cannabinoid receptors, which are especially numerous in the hippocampus. Because the hippocampus is involved in the formation of new memories, it is not surprising that marijuana use inhibits memory formation (Kuhn, Swartzwelder, & Wilson, 1998).

Regular users of marijuana report a number of sensory and perceptual changes: a general euphoria and sense of well-being, some distortions of space and time, and changes in social perception. Not all marijuana experiences are pleasant. Sixteen percent of regular users report anxiety, fearfulness, and confusion as a "usual occurrence," and about one-third report that they occasionally experience such symptoms as acute panic, hallucinations, and unpleasant distortions in body image. Individuals who use marijuana regularly (daily or almost daily) often report both physical and mental lethargy, and about a third show mild forms of depression, anxiety, or irritability (American Psychiatric Association, 2000). Marijuana smoke contains even larger amounts of known carcinogens than tobacco (but marijuana users tend to smoke less than cigarette smokers, and their total intake of these substances is lower).

Marijuana use interferes with performance on complex tasks. Motor coordination is significantly impaired by low to moderate doses, and reaction time for automobile braking and the ability to negotiate a twisting road course are adversely affected (Institute of Medicine, 1982). These findings make it clear that driving under the influence of the drug is dangerous. The number of automobile accidents related to marijuana use is difficult to determine because, unlike alcohol, THC declines rapidly in the blood, quickly going to the fatty tissues and organs of the body. A blood analysis performed 2 hours after a heavy dose of marijuana may show no signs of THC, even though an observer would judge the person to be clearly impaired.

The effects of marijuana may persist long after the subjective feelings of euphoria or sleepiness have passed. A study of aircraft pilots using a simulated flight-landing task found that performance was significantly impaired as much as 24 hours after smoking one marijuana cigarette containing 19 milligrams of THC—despite the fact that the pilots reported no awareness of any aftereffects on their alertness or performance (Yesavage, Leier,

Concept Review Table
Effects of Major Psychoactive Drugs

Alcohol	Lightheadedness, relaxation, release of inhibitions
	Increased self-confidence
	Slowing of motor reactions
Heroin	Sense of well-being
	Feeling of euphoria
	Reduced anxiety
Amphetamines	Drowsiness
	Increased alertness
	Decreased fatigue and boredom
Cocaine	Increased energy and self-confidence
	Euphoric high
	Restless irritability
	High likelihood of dependence
LSD	Hallucinations
	Mystical experiences
	"Bad trips"
	Flashbacks
PCP	Feelings of dissociation from the environment
	Insensitivity to pain
	Confusion
	Loss of inhibition
	Poor coordination
Cannabis	Stimulation and euphoria followed by tranquility and sleep
	Sense of well-being
	Distortions of space and time
	Changes in social perception
	Impaired motor coordination
	Disruption of memory

Denari. & Hollister, 1985). These findings have led to concern about marijuana use by people whose jobs affect public safety.

Marijuana has two clear effects on memory (de Wit, Kirk, & Justice, 1998). First, it makes short-term memory more susceptible to interference. People under the influence of marijuana may lose the thread of a conversation or forget what they are saying in the middle of a sentence because of momentary distractions. Second, marijuana disrupts learning by interfering with the transfer of new information from short-term to long-term memory. These findings suggest that it is not a good idea to study while under the influence of marijuana; later recall of the material will be poor.

The Concept Review Table summarizes the effects of the major psychoactive drugs described in this section. By and large, these are short-term effects. The long-term effects of most drugs other than nicotine and alcohol are

largely unknown. However, the history of these two common drugs should lead us to be cautious in the use of any drug over a long period.

◆ Interim Summary

- Psychoactive drugs have long been used to alter consciousness and mood.

- Depressant drugs, such as alcohol, tranquilizers, and inhalants, depress the central nervous system. The most commonly used depressant is alcohol.

- Opiates, such as heroin and morphine, reduce perceptions of pain and induce euphoria, followed by a sense of drowsiness. Severe intoxication can lead to respiratory difficulties, unconsciousness, and coma.

- Stimulants, such as amphetamines and cocaine, activate those parts of the brain that register reward or pleasure, and they produce euphoria, energy, and a sense of self-esteem. Withdrawal from stimulants can cause depression, restlessness, and dangerous physiological symptoms.

- Hallucinogens, such as LSD and PCP, produce perceptual changes such as sensory distortions and hallucinations.

- Cannabis, such as marijuana and hashish, creates a high feeling, cognitive and motor impairments, and, in some people, hallucinations.

- Repeated use of any of these drugs can result in drug dependence, which is characterized by tolerance, withdrawal, and compulsive use.

- Drug abuse refers to continued use of a drug, despite serious consequences, by a person who has not reached the stage of dependence.

◆ Critical Thinking Questions

1. Laws that criminalize some psychoactive drugs (marijuana, cocaine) but not others (alcohol, tobacco) do not seem well matched to the drugs' actual dangers. If you were to redesign our country's drug policies from scratch, basing them only on current scientific knowledge, which drugs would you want to discourage most vigorously (or criminalize)? Which drugs would you worry about least?

2. It has been demonstrated that the ancient Asian medical practice of acupuncture, in which needles are inserted into the skin at different "acupuncture points," stimulates the brain's production of endorphins. How might this explain why acupuncture seems to help people overcome dependence on heroin?

PSI PHENOMENA

A discussion of consciousness would not be complete without considering some extraordinary claims about the mind that have long attracted widespread public attention. Of particular interest are questions about whether human beings (1) can acquire information in ways that do not involve stimulation of the known sense organs or (2) can influence physical events by purely mental means. These questions are the source of controversy over the existence of **psi,** anomalous processes of information and/or energy transfer that cannot currently be explained in terms of known biological or physical mechanisms. The phenomena of psi are the subject matter of **parapsychology** ("beside" or "beyond" psychology) and include the following:

1. *Extrasensory perception (ESP).* Response to external stimuli without any known sensory contact.
   a. *Telepathy.* Transference of thought from one person to another without the mediation of any known channel of sensory communication (for example, identifying a playing card that is merely being thought of by another person).
   b. *Clairvoyance.* Perception of objects or events that do not provide a stimulus to the known senses (for example, identifying a concealed playing card whose identity is unknown to anyone).
   c. *Precognition.* Perception of a future event that could not be anticipated through any known inferential process (for example, predicting that a particular number will come up on the next throw of a pair of dice).
2. *Psychokinesis (PK).* Mental influence over physical events without the intervention of any known physical force (for example, willing that a particular number will come up on the next throw of a pair of dice).

EXPERIMENTAL EVIDENCE

Most parapsychologists consider themselves to be scientists who apply the usual rules of scientific inquiry to admittedly unusual phenomena. Yet the claims for psi are so extraordinary, and so similar to what are widely regarded as superstitions, that some scientists consider psi to be impossible and reject the legitimacy of parapsychological inquiry. Such a priori judgments are out of place in science. The real question is whether the empirical evidence is acceptable by scientific standards. Many psychologists who are not yet convinced that psi has been demonstrated are nonetheless open to the possibility that new evidence might emerge that would be more persuasive. For their part, many parapsychologists believe that several recent experimental procedures either provide that evidence already or hold the potential for doing so. We shall examine one of the most promising of these, the ganzfeld procedure.

The **ganzfeld procedure** tests for telepathic communication between a participant who serves as the "receiver" and another participant who serves as the "sender." The receiver is sequestered in an acoustically isolated room and placed in a mild form of perceptual isolation: Translucent Ping-Pong ball halves are taped over the eyes, and headphones are placed over the ears; diffuse red light illuminates the room, and white noise is played through the headphones. (White noise is a random mixture of sound frequencies similar to the hiss made by a radio tuned between stations.) This homogeneous visual and auditory environment is called the *ganzfeld,* a German word meaning "total field."

The sender sits in a separate acoustically isolated room, and a visual stimulus (picture, slide, or brief videotape sequence) is randomly selected from a large pool of similar stimuli to serve as the "target" for the session. While the sender concentrates on the target, the receiver attempts to describe it by providing a continuous verbal report of his or her mental imagery and free associations. Upon completion of the session, the receiver is presented with four stimuli, one of which is the target, and asked to rate the degree to which each matches the imagery and associations experienced during the ganzfeld session. A "direct hit" is scored if the receiver assigns the highest rating to the target stimulus.

More than 90 experiments have been conducted since this procedure was introduced in 1974; the typical experiment involves about 30 sessions in which a receiver attempts to identify the target transmitted by the sender. An overall analysis of 28 studies (with a total of 835 ganzfeld sessions conducted by investigators in 10 different laboratories) reveals that participants were able to select the correct target stimulus 38% of the time. Because a participant must select the target from four alternatives, we would expect a success rate of 25% if only chance were operating. Statistically, this result is highly significant. The probability that it could have arisen by chance is less than one in a billion (Bem & Honorton, 1994).

The receiver (left) and the sender (right) in a ganzfeld experiment.

THE DEBATE OVER THE EVIDENCE

In 1985 and 1986, the *Journal of Parapsychology* published an extended examination of the ganzfeld studies, focusing on a debate between Ray Hyman, a cognitive psychologist and critic of parapsychology, and Charles Honorton, a parapsychologist and major contributor to the ganzfeld database. They agree on the basic quantitative results but disagree on its interpretation (Honorton, 1985; Hyman, 1994, 1985; Hyman & Honorton, 1986) In what follows, we use their debate as a vehicle for examining the issues involved in evaluating claims of psi.

THE REPLICATION PROBLEM In scientific research, a phenomenon is not considered established until it has been observed repeatedly by several researchers. Accordingly, the most serious criticism of parapsychology is that it has failed to produce a single reliable demonstration of psi that can be replicated by other investigators. Even the same investigator testing the same individuals over time may obtain statistically significant results on one occasion but not on another. The ganzfeld procedure is no exception; fewer than half (43%) of the 28 studies analyzed in the debate yielded statistically significant results.

The parapsychologists' most effective response to this criticism actually comes from within psychology itself. Many statisticians and psychologists are dissatisfied with psychology's focus on statistical significance as the sole measure of a study's success. As an alternative, they are increasingly adopting **meta-analysis,** a statistical technique that treats the accumulated studies of a particular phenomenon as a single grand experiment and each study as a single observation. Any study that obtains positive results—even though it may not be statistically significant itself—contributes to the overall strength and reliability of the phenomenon rather than simply being dismissed as a failure to replicate (Glass, McGaw, & Smith, 1981; Rosenthal, 1984). From this perspective, the ganzfeld studies provide impressive replicability: 23 of the 28 studies obtained positive results, an outcome whose probability of occurring by chance is less than one in a thousand. An additional 11 replications using computerized procedures yielded results consistent with the original set of 28 studies (Bem & Honorton, 1994).

A more recent meta-analysis of 40 additional ganzfeld studies, conducted between 1987 and 1999, revealed that the ganzfeld procedure continues to replicate (Bem, Palmer, & Broughton, 2001). At first glance, these more recent studies appeared to yield weaker results than did the earlier studies. Further analysis, however, showed that the 29 replications that had adhered to the standard procedure yielded results comparable to the previous studies, whereas the replications that had departed from the standard (for example, by using musical selections as targets) produced weaker results. Such a finding is neither bad nor unexpected. Many psi researchers now believe that the basic procedure is sufficiently well established to warrant extending it into unknown territory, even though this inevitably produces some unsuccessful experiments. When such replications are lumped into a meta-analysis with standard replications, weaker overall results are to be expected. This implies that future meta-analyses need to take this into account, lest the ganzfeld procedure become a victim of its own success.

The ability of a particular experiment to replicate an effect also depends on how strong the effect is and how many observations are made. If an effect is weak, an experiment with too few participants or observations will fail to detect it at a statistically significant level—even though the effect actually exists. If the ganzfeld effect actually exists and has a true direct-hit rate of 38%, then statistically we should expect studies with 30 ganzfeld sessions (the average for the 28 studies discussed earlier) to obtain a statistically significant psi effect only about one-third of the time (Utts, 1986).

In short, it is unrealistic to demand that any real effect be replicable at any time by any competent investigator. The replication issue is more complex than that, and meta-analysis is proving to be a valuable tool for dealing with some of those complexities.

INADEQUATE CONTROLS The second major criticism of parapsychology is that many, if not most, of the experiments have inadequate controls and safeguards. Flawed procedures that would permit a participant to obtain the communicated information in normal sensory fashion, either inadvertently or through deliberate cheating, are particularly fatal. This is called the *problem of sensory leakage*. Inadequate procedures for randomizing (randomly selecting) target stimuli are another common problem.

Methodological inadequacies plague all sciences, but the history of parapsychology contains several instances of promising results that collapsed when the procedures were examined from a critical perspective (Akers, 1984). One common charge against parapsychology is that whereas preliminary, poorly controlled studies often obtain positive results, as soon as better controls and safeguards are introduced, the results disappear.

Once a flaw is discovered in a completed experiment, there is no persuasive way of arguing that the flaw did not contribute to a positive outcome. The only remedy is to redo the experiment correctly. In a database of several studies, however, meta-analysis can evaluate the criticism empirically by checking to see if, in fact, the more poorly controlled studies obtained more positive results than the better controlled studies did. If there is a correlation between a procedural flaw and positive results across the studies, there is a problem. In the case of the ganzfeld database, both critic Hyman and parapsychologist Honorton agree that flaws of inadequate secu-

rity and possible sensory leakage do not correlate with positive results. Hyman claimed to find a correlation between flaws of randomization and positive results, but both Honorton's analysis and two additional analyses by nonparapsychologists dispute his conclusion (Harris & Rosenthal, 1988; Saunders, 1985). Moreover, the previously noted successful series of 11 computer-automated studies were specifically designed to control for flaws identified in the original database (Bem & Honorton, 1994).

THE FILE-DRAWER PROBLEM Suppose that each of 20 investigators independently decides to conduct a ganzfeld study. Even if there were no genuine ganzfeld effect, there is a reasonable probability that at least one of these investigators would obtain a statistically significant result by pure chance. That lucky investigator would then publish a report of the experiment, but the other 19 investigators—all of whom obtained "null" results—are likely to become discouraged, put their data in a file drawer, and move on to something more promising. As a result, the scientific community would learn about the one successful study but have no knowledge of the 19 null studies buried in file drawers. The database of known studies would thus be seriously biased toward positive studies, and any meta-analysis of that database would arrive at similarly biased conclusions. This is known as the *file-drawer problem*.

The file-drawer problem is a tricky one because by definition it is impossible to know how many unknown studies are languishing in file drawers. Nevertheless, parapsychologists offer two defenses against the charge that this problem constitutes a serious challenge to their findings. First, they point out that the *Journal of Parapsychology* actively solicits and publishes studies that report negative findings. Moreover, the community of parapsychologists is relatively small, and most investigators are aware of ongoing research in the field. When conducting meta-analysis, parapsychologists scout out unpublished negative studies at conventions and through their personal networks.

But their major defense is statistical, and again meta-analysis provides an empirical approach to the problem. By knowing the overall statistical significance of the known database, it is possible to compute the number of studies with null results that would have to exist in file drawers to cancel out that significance. In the case of the ganzfeld database, there would have to be more than 400 unreported studies with null results—the equivalent of 12,000 ganzfeld sessions—to cancel out the statistical significance of the 28 studies analyzed in the debate (Honorton, 1985). It is generally agreed, therefore, that the overall significance of the ganzfeld studies cannot reasonably be explained by the file-drawer effect (Hyman & Honorton, 1986).

Rather than continue their debate, Hyman and Honorton issued a joint communiqué in which they set forth their areas of agreement and disagreement and made a series of suggestions for the conduct of future ganzfeld studies (Hyman & Honorton, 1986). Their debate and the subsequent discussion provide a valuable model for evaluating disputed domains of scientific inquiry.

ANECDOTAL EVIDENCE

In the public's mind, the evidence for psi is primarily personal experiences and anecdotes. From a scientific standpoint, such evidence is unpersuasive because it suffers from the same problems that jeopardize the experimental evidence—nonreplicability, inadequate controls, and the file-drawer problem.

The replication problem is acute because most such evidence consists of single occurrences. A woman announces a premonition that she will win the lottery that day—and she does. You dream about an unlikely event, which actually occurs a few days later. A "psychic" correctly predicts the assassination of a public figure. Such incidents may be subjectively compelling, but there is no way to evaluate them because they are not repeatable.

The problem of inadequate controls and safeguards is decisive because such incidents occur under unexpected and ambiguous conditions. There is thus no way of ruling out alternative interpretations such as coincidence (chance), faulty memories, and deliberate deception.

Finally, the file-drawer problem also occurs with anecdotal evidence. The lottery winner who announced ahead of time that she would win is prominently featured in the news. But the thousands of others with similar premonitions who did not win are never heard from; their "evidence" remains in the file drawer. It is true that the probability of this woman's winning the lottery was very low. But the critical criterion in evaluating this case is not the probability that she would win but the probability that any one of the thousands who thought they would win would do so. That probability is much higher. Moreover, this woman has a personal file drawer that contains all the past instances in which she had similar premonitions but did not win.

The same reasoning applies to precognitive dreams (dreams that anticipate an unlikely event, which actually occurs a few days later). We tend to forget our dreams unless and until an event happens to remind us of them. We thus have no way of evaluating how often we might have dreamed of similar unlikely events that did not occur. We fill our database with positive instances and unknowingly exclude the negative instances.

Perhaps the fullest file drawers belong to the so-called psychics who make annual predictions in the tabloid newspapers. Nobody remembers the predictions that fail, but everybody remembers the occasional direct hits. In fact, these psychics are almost always wrong (Frazier, 1987; Tyler, 1977).

◆ Interim Summary

- Psi is the idea that people can acquire information about the world in ways that do not involve stimulation of known sense organs or can influence physical events by purely mental means.

- The phenomena of psi include extrasensory perception (ESP) in its various forms (telepathy, clairvoyance, precognition) and psychokinesis, movement of objects by the mind.

- The ganzfeld procedure tests for telepathic communication between a participant who serves as the "receiver" and another participant who serves as the "sender."

- There is an ongoing debate over the replicability of psi phenomena and the methods used in studies attempting to demonstrate the phenomena.

◆ Critical Thinking Questions

1. What "extrasensory" experiences have you had personally? Can you think of alternative explanations for these experiences?

2. The file drawer problem is ubiquitous in science. Why do you think some researchers believe it's a special problem in research on psi phenomena?

Is the Psi Phenomenon Real?

SKEPTICISM TOWARD PSI IS LARGELY UNFOUNDED
Daryl Bem, Cornell University

If some of the experimental evidence for psi, discussed in the text, is as impressive as it seems, why hasn't it become part of established science? Why do most scientists continue to be skeptical?

EXTRAORDINARY CLAIMS

Most scientists believe that extraordinary claims require extraordinary evidence. A study reporting that students who study harder get higher grades will be believed even if the study was seriously flawed because the data fit well with our understanding of how the world works. But the claim that two people in a ganzfeld study communicate telepathically is more extraordinary; it violates most people's a priori beliefs about reality. We therefore rightly demand a higher measure of proof from parapsychologists because their claims, if true, would require us to radically revise our model of the world—something that we should not undertake lightly. In this way, science is justifiably conservative. Many open-minded non-parapsychologists are genuinely impressed by the ganzfeld studies, for example, but it is reasonable for them to ask for more evidence before committing themselves to the reality of psi.

Extraordinariness is a matter of degree. Telepathy seems less extraordinary to most of us than precognition because we are already familiar with the invisible transmission of information through space. We may not understand how television pictures get to our living rooms, but we know that they do so. Why should telepathy seem that much more mysterious? Precognition, on the other hand, seems more extraordinary because there are no familiar phenomena in which information flows backward in time.

SKEPTICISM ON THE PART OF PSYCHOLOGISTS

Psychologists are a particularly skeptical group. A survey of more than 1,000 college professors found that about 66% believe that ESP is either an established fact or a likely possibility. Moreover, these favorable views were expressed by a majority of professors in the natural sciences (55%), the social sciences excluding psychology (66%), and the arts, humanities, and education (77%). The comparable figure for psychologists was 34% (Wagner & Monnet, 1979).

There are several reasons for the skepticism of psychologists. First, they are familiar with past instances of extraordinary claims that turned out to be based on flawed experimental procedures, on faulty inference, or even on fraud and deception. Over the history of research on parapsychology, in a number of cases research claims have later proved to be based on fraudulent data. Those who follow developments in this field have so often encountered charlatans—some of whom are very clever—that they have good reason to be skeptical of new claims (Gardner, 1981; Randi, 1982).

Second, psychologists know that popular accounts of psychological findings are frequently exaggerated. For example, the remarkable findings from research on asymmetries in the human brain have spawned a host of pop psychology books and media reports containing unsubstantiated claims about left-brained and right-brained individuals. Irresponsible reports about states of consciousness—including hypnosis and psi—appear daily in the media. It is worth noting, therefore, that when the college professors in the survey cited earlier were asked to name the sources for their beliefs about ESP, the frequently cited sources were reports in newspapers and magazines.

Third, like most professional scholars, academic psychologists tend to be most familiar with the research in their own areas of specialization. Because contemporary research on psi is not usually summarized in the professional journals, handbooks, or introductory textbooks, most psychologists are not aware of recent research in the area. In fact, you are now more familiar with the ganzfeld studies than most academic psychologists.

Finally, research in cognitive and social psychology has sensitized psychologists to the biases and shortcomings in our abilities to draw valid inferences from our everyday experiences (see Chapter 17). This makes them particularly skeptical of anecdotal reports of psi, where, as we saw before, our judgments are subject to many kinds of errors. Clearly, much of the skepticism of psychologists toward psi is well founded. Some of it is not, however. The research using the ganzfeld procedure has withstood considerable scrutiny and warrants serious consideration.

Is the Psi Phenomenon Real?

PSI OR MURPHY'S LAW?
Ray Hyman, Professor Emeritus, University of Oregon

Professor Bem, in making the case for the existence of psi, focuses on the data from the ganzfeld procedure. He suggests that if scientists took the time to scrutinize the results from the more than 90 ganzfeld experiments, they would no longer be so skeptical about the existence of psi. I seriously doubt this. I believe that if scientists, including psychologists, did take the time to examine the evidence, they would discover the same problems that I did. Where Bem and the parapsychologists see robustness, consistency, and replicability, I find only lack of robustness, inconsistency, and lack of replicability.

Bem divides the results of the ganzfeld procedure into three databases: (1) the 28 experiments that Honorton used in his 1985 meta-analysis (Honorton, 1985); (2) the 10 experiments using the autoganzfeld experiments (Bem and Honorton, 1994); and (3) the updated database of 40 recent experiments (Bem, Palmer, & Broughton, 2001).

Bem claims that the results of the latter two databases replicate the findings from the original 28 experiments. For example, the average hit rate was 38% in the first meta-analysis, 32% in the autoganzfeld experiments, and 30% in the new database of 40 experiments. Because these all differ "significantly" from the chance hit rate of 25%, Bem and the parapsychologists claim impressive replicability. However, this is problematical for several reasons. The variation in outcomes within the original and the new databases is much greater than it should be if we assume that all the studies were conducted in such a way that they consist of binomial trials from the same population. Because of this, the average effect size for these two databases is an arbitrary and meaningless composite. Much of the heterogeneity of outcomes in the first database, for example, is due to the fact that laboratories differed significantly from one another in their results. The laboratories also differed greatly in how many trials they contributed to the database. If, say, the laboratory that consistently obtained negative effect sizes had contributed proportionately more trials to the database, this could have markedly reduced the overall average hit rate. If, on the other hand, the laboratory that consistently produced the large effect sizes had contributed even more trials, the average effect would be much higher.

It is unrealistic to pretend that the outcomes in the original and the new ganzfeld databases represent a random sample from a well-defined population. It does not make sense to use the composite effect size for such heterogeneous outcomes as a meaningful estimate of some true effect size. The alternative is to try and find out what is causing the observed variation among experimental outcomes. Indeed, for each of the databases, parapsychologists have claimed to find personality, attitudinal, and stimulus variables that correlate with some of this variance. However, these patterns of correlations do not replicate from one database to the next. See Hyman (1994) for several examples of inconsistencies between the original ganzfeld and the autoganzfeld databases. See Milton and Wiseman (1999) for examples of how the most recent database fail to provide support for patterns found in the earlier two databases.

Bem and his colleagues (Bem et al., 2001) do not discuss these glaring examples of failures to replicate, but, instead, emphasize a new possible correlate of some of the variation among effect sizes. They report that the more a given study resembles the original ganzfeld studies in methodology, the more likely it is to obtain a positive and significant effect size. This observation relies upon a weak and nonsignificant correlation between rated "standardness" of a study and its effect size. Because this weak relationship was suggested by looking at the data, we cannot conclude that it is real. Even if this relationship turns out to be real, it does not help much. This is because it accounts for only a small percentage of the unexplained variance. Additionally, it would suggest that psi can only manifest itself under limited and rather specific experimental arrangements. Such limited generality would take away much of its interest.

Most scientists interpret successful replication of results as a replication of the same pattern among the variables. However, most of these patterns have conspicuously failed to replicate across databases. Indeed, the only consistent finding seems to be a great deal of heterogeneity in outcome from one study to another. So far, the parapsychologists have failed to find a reason for inconsistent patterns in the data. Almost surely, a variety of different factors are causing this variability. We cannot rule out the possibility that something like psi might be one of these many different sources of variability among effect sizes. Until the parapsychologists find a way to actually produce consistent and replicable patterns across independent experiments, the claim that the experiments support the existence of something called *psi* is little more than saying that psi is another name for Murphy's Law.

CHAPTER SUMMARY

1. A person's perceptions, thoughts, and feelings at any given moment constitute that person's consciousness. An altered state of consciousness is said to exist when mental functioning seems changed or out of the ordinary to the person experiencing the state. Some altered states of consciousness, such as sleep and dreams, are experienced by everyone; others result from special circumstances such as meditation, hypnosis, or the use of drugs.

2. The functions of consciousness are (a) monitoring ourselves and our environment so that we are aware of what is happening within our bodies and in our surroundings and (b) controlling our actions so that they are coordinated with events in the outside world. Not all events that influence consciousness are at the center of our awareness at a given moment. Memories of personal events and accumulated knowledge, which are accessible but not currently part of one's consciousness, are called *preconscious memories*. Events that affect behavior, even though we are not aware of perceiving them, influence us subconsciously.

3. According to psychoanalytic theory, some emotionally painful memories and impulses are not available to consciousness because they have been repressed—that is, diverted to the unconscious. Unconscious thoughts and impulses influence our behavior even though they reach consciousness only in indirect ways—through dreams, irrational behavior, and slips of the tongue.

4. The notion of automaticity refers to the habituation of responses that initially required conscious attention, such as driving a car.

5. Sleep, an altered state of consciousness, is of interest because of the rhythms evident in sleep schedules and in the depth of sleep. These rhythms are studied with the aid of the electroencephalogram (EEG). Patterns of brain waves show four stages (depths) of sleep, plus a fifth stage characterized by rapid eye movements (REMs). These stages alternate throughout the night. Dreams occur more often during REM sleep than during the other four stages (NREM sleep).

6. The opponent-process model of sleep proposes that two opposing processes—the homeostatic sleep drive and the clock-dependent alerting process—interact to determine our tendency to fall asleep or remain awake. Whether we are asleep or awake at any given time depends on the relative forces exerted by the two processes. There are a variety of sleep disorders, including sleep deprivation, insomnia, narcolepsy, and apnea.

7. Freud attributed psychological causes to dreams, distinguishing between their manifest and latent content and suggesting that dreams are wishes in disguise. Other theories see dreaming as a reflection of the information processing that the brain is doing while asleep. Recently some theorists have concluded that dreaming is a cognitive process that reflects the individual's conceptions, concerns, and emotional preoccupations.

8. Meditation represents an effort to alter consciousness by following planned rituals or exercises such as those of yoga or Zen. The result is a somewhat mystical state in which the individual is extremely relaxed and feels divorced from the outside world.

9. Hypnosis is a responsive state in which individuals focus their attention on the hypnotist and his or her suggestions. Some people are more readily hypnotized than others, although most people show some susceptibility. Characteristic hypnotic responses include enhanced or diminished control over movements, distortion of memory through posthypnotic amnesia, and positive and negative hallucinations. Reduction of pain is one of the beneficial uses of hypnosis.

10. Psychoactive drugs have long been used to alter consciousness and mood. They include depressants, such as alcohol, tranquilizers, and inhalants; opiates, such as heroin and morphine; stimulants, such as amphetamines and cocaine; hallucinogens, such as LSD and PCP; and cannabis, such as marijuana and hashish.

11. Repeated use of any of these drugs can result in drug dependence, which is characterized by tolerance, withdrawal, and compulsive use. Drug abuse refers to continued use of a drug, despite serious consequences, by a person who has not reached the stage of dependence.

12. There is considerable controversy over psi, the idea that people can acquire information about the world in ways that do not involve stimulation of known sense organs or can influence physical events by purely mental means. The phenomena of psi include extrasensory perception (ESP) in its various forms (telepathy, clairvoyance, precognition) and psychokinesis, movement of objects by the mind.

CORE CONCEPTS

altered states of consciousness
consciousness
preconscious memories
unconscious
Freudian slip
automaticity
dissociation
REM sleep
non-REM sleep (or NREM sleep)
opponent-process model of sleep
    and wakefulness
homeostatic sleep drive
clock-dependent alerting process
circadian rhythm
melatonin
sleep disorder
insomnia
narcolepsy

apnea
dreaming
lucid dreams
meditation
hypnosis
posthypnotic response
posthypnotic amnesia
positive hallucinations
negative hallucinations
hidden observer
psychoactive drugs
drug dependence
tolerance
withdrawal
drug abuse
depressants
fetal alcohol syndrome
opiates

heroin
agonists
antagonists
methadone
naltrexone
stimulants
amphetamines
cocaine
hallucinogens
LSD
PCP
cannabis
marijuana
hashish
psi
parapsychology
ganzfeld procedure
meta-analysis

 WEB RESOURCES

http://psychology.wadsworth.com/
atkinson14e

Take a quiz, try the activities and exercises, and explore web links.

http://www.circadian.com/learning_center/

Are you sleepy all the time? Are you having trouble concentrating? Check out this circadian learning center and learn more about how circadian rhythms, your biological clock, and sleep habits affect you throughout the day.

http://www.inmet.com/~dlb/hypnosis/
hypnosis.html

Peruse a plethora of different links related to consciousness.

 InfoTrac Online Library

http://www.infotrac-college.com/
wadsworth

Use InfoTrac College Edition to find popular and scientific articles by using the search terms below or your own relevant terms.

- Dreams
- Drugs and Behavior
- Insomnia
- Narcolepsy
- Psychotropic drugs
- REM sleep

CD-ROM LINKS

 Psych Odyssey

A. Check out CD Chapter 5, Consciousness
    Sleep
B. Drug-Induced Alterations in Consciousness

 Psyk.trek 2.0

4a Biological Rhythms
4b Sleep
4c Abused Drugs and Their Effects
4d Drugs and Synaptic Transmission

© Taxi/Getty Images

LEARNING AND CONDITIONING

7

Learning pervades our lives. It is involved not only in mastering a new skill or academic subject but also in emotional development, social interaction, and even personality development. We learn what to fear, what to love, how to be polite, how to be intimate, and so on. Given the pervasiveness of learning, it is not surprising that we have already discussed many instances of it—how, for example, children learn to perceive the world around them, to identify with their own sex, and to control their behavior according to adult standards. Despite the prevalence of learning in shaping our behavior, we tend not to be aware of much of the learning that happened in our lives. Indeed, you can readily demonstrate this yourself—but you'll need an experimental subject—perhaps your roommate.

First, take a few moments to observe the person's behavior. Once you have a sense for how the person is behaving, pick a behavior that you want to increase in frequency. Let's say your roommate is running his fingers through his hair, and you want him to do that more. (We'll assume your roommate is male, but this demonstration will also work for a female.) Well, the most straightforward way to get him to play with his hair more would be to ask him to do it more—but that might seem strange, and it would defeat the purpose of demonstrating learning that happens outside of awareness. In fact, you can increase the time your roommate spends playing with his hair without letting him know that his behavior has changed. Every time your roommate runs his fingers through his hair, do something that is pleasing to him. For example, you could smile and compliment him on his appearance by saying, "Hey, you are looking really good today." If he touches his hair again, compliment him again, and continue complimenting him whenever he engages in hair touching. What you will soon learn is that the frequency with which your roommate touches his hair will increase greatly (assuming that he is pleased with your compliments). What is amazing is that your roommate will probably have no idea that his behavior has dramatically changed. In fact, you can ask him why he is touching his hair so much. His answer will probably be quite interesting, and in all likelihood he will not attribute it to your compliments.

Of course, the change in your roommate's behavior is an example of learning. In this chapter, we will engage in a systematic analysis of learning that will give you insight into how experience alters behavior. You will come to understand why you were able to alter your roommate's behavior and what factors are responsible for this and other types of learning. To start, let's consider some basic principles of learning and conditioning. **Learning** may be defined as a relatively permanent change in behavior that occurs as the result of experience. Behavior changes that are due to maturation or to temporary conditions of the organism (such as fatigue or drug-induced states) are not included. Not all cases of learning are the same, though. There are two basic kinds of learning: nonassociative learning and associative learning. **Nonassociative learning** involves learning about a single stimulus, and it includes habituation and sensitization. **Habituation** is a type of nonassociative learning that is characterized by a decreased behavioral response to an innocuous stimulus. For example, the sound of a horn might startle you when you first hear it. But if the horn toots repeatedly in a short time, the amount that you startle to each sound progressively decreases. In contrast, **sensitization** is a type of nonassociative learning whereby there is an increase in a behavioral response to an intense stimulus. Sensitization typically occurs when noxious or fearful stimuli are presented to an organism. For example, the acoustic startle response to a horn is greatly enhanced if you enter a dark alley right before the loud sound. Both habituation and sensitization are relatively short-lived, lasting for minutes to hours. However, providing many spaced presentations of stimuli can yield longer-lasting learning.

Although these types of learning are quite simple, they are exceptionally important for tuning what an organism attends to in the world. Indeed, the fact that nonassociative learning can be demonstrated in all animals, ranging from single-celled paramecia to humans, is a testament to the importance of this form of learning. We will revisit nonassociative learning in the Neural Basis of Behavior section on Learning and Conditioning.

Associative learning is much more complicated than nonassociative learning, because it involves learning relationships among events. It includes classical conditioning, instrumental conditioning, and complex learning, among others. Classical and instrumental conditioning both involve forming associations—that is, learning that certain events go together. In classical conditioning, an organism learns that one event follows another. For example, a baby learns that the sight of a breast will be followed by the taste of milk. In instrumental conditioning, an organism learns that a response it makes will be followed by a particular consequence. For example, a young child learns that striking a sibling will be followed by disapproval from his or her parents. Complex learning involves something in addition to forming associations—for example, learning the route from your dorm room to the campus movie theater. Of course, there cannot be learning without memory, and memory will be the focus of the following chapter (Chapter 8).

There are other forms of learning as well, such as imprinting, modeling and imitation, and vicarious learning. These are discussed in later chapters. In this chapter we focus primarily on conditioning and complex learning. First, though, we need to consider how the various perspectives on psychology have been applied to the study of learning.

PERSPECTIVES ON LEARNING

Recall from Chapter 1 that three of the most important perspectives on psychology are the behaviorist, cognitive, and biological perspectives. As much as any area in psychology, the study of learning has involved all three of these perspectives.

Much of the early work on learning, particularly conditioning, was done from a behaviorist perspective. Researchers studied how nonhuman organisms learn an association between stimuli or an association between a stimulus and a response. The focus was on external stimuli and responses, in keeping with the behaviorist dictum that behavior is better understood in terms of external causes than mental ones. The behaviorist approach to learning made other key assumptions as well. One was that simple associations of the classical or instrumental kind are the building blocks of all learning. It follows that something as complex as acquiring a language is presumably a matter of learning many associations (Staats, 1968). Another assumption was that the same basic laws of learning operate, regardless of what is being learned or who is doing the learning—a rat learning to run a maze or a child mastering arithmetic (Skinner, 1971, 1938). These views led behaviorists to focus on how the behaviors of nonhuman organisms, particularly rats and pigeons, are influenced by rewards and punishments in simple laboratory situations.

The findings and phenomena uncovered in this work continue to form the basis of much of what we know about associative learning. But as we will see, the behaviorist assumptions have had to be modified in light of subsequent work. Understanding conditioning, not to mention complex learning, requires us to consider what the organism knows about the relations between stimuli and response (even when the organism is a rat or a pigeon), which ushers in the cognitive perspective. And in cases of complex learning, strategies, rules, and the like must be considered in addition to associations. Again, this requires us to adopt a cognitive approach. Moreover, it now appears that no single set of laws underlies learning in all situations and by all organisms. In particular, different mechanisms of learning seem to be involved in different species, which brings in the biological perspective. The upshot is that the contemporary study of learning requires an integrated approach that considers all three of the perspectives just mentioned.

◆ Interim Summary

- Learning is a relatively permanent change in behavior that is the result of experience.

- There are four basic kinds of learning: (1) habituation, (2) classical conditioning, (3) instrumental conditioning, and (4) complex learning.

◆ Critical Thinking Questions

1. The ubiquity of learning questions whether any behavior is innate. Indeed, one could make the argument that all behavior is learned. Do you agree with this view? Why or why not?

2. Several paradigms of thought have influenced the design and interpretation of learning experiments. For example, behaviorists have focused on observable changes in behavior that occur with experience, and cognitivists study the architecture of mental representations that yield learned behavior. Why are these different approaches important? How has the emergence of biopsychology influenced the study of learning?

Ivan Pavlov with his assistants.

CLASSICAL CONDITIONING

Classical conditioning is a learning process in which a previously neutral stimulus becomes associated with another stimulus through repeated pairing with that stimulus. The study of classical conditioning began in the early years of the 20th century, when Ivan Pavlov, a Russian physiologist who had already won the Nobel Prize for research on digestion, turned his attention to learning. While studying digestion, Pavlov noticed that a dog began to salivate at the mere sight of a food dish. Although any dog will salivate when food is placed in its mouth, this dog had learned to associate the sight of the dish with the taste of food. Pavlov had happened upon a case of associative learning, in which relationships between events are learned, and he decided to see whether a dog could be taught to associate food with other things, such as a light or a tone.

PAVLOV'S EXPERIMENTS

In Pavlov's basic experiment, a researcher first attaches a *fistula* or tube to the dog's salivary gland to measure salivary flow. Then the dog is placed in front of a pan into which meat powder can be delivered automatically. A researcher turns on a light in a window in front of the dog (or, in some forms of the experiment, rings a bell or turns on a metronome). After a few seconds, some meat powder is delivered to the pan and the light is turned off. The dog is hungry, and the recording device registers copious salivation. This salivation is an **unconditioned response** (UCR, an innate or unlearned response elicited by the UCS), for no learning is involved in order for meat to evoke salivation. By the same token, the meat powder is an **unconditioned stimulus** (UCS, a stimulus that automatically elicits a response without prior conditioning). After a few presentations of the light followed by meat powder, the dog will salivate in response to the light, even if no meat powder is delivered. This anticipatory salivation is a **conditioned response** (CR, learned response), and the light is a **conditioned stimulus** (CS, learned stimulus). In other words, the CR is a learned response evoked by a CS that has come to predict the occurrence of the UCS. The Concept Review Table summarizes the different elements of classical conditioning. Although the light was originally a neutral stimulus—one that would not ordinarily trigger a salivary response—the dog has learned to associate the light with food and to respond to it by salivating. Pavlov's experiment is diagrammed in Figure 7-1.

In Pavlov's experiments, the form of the CR often mimicked the form of the UCR—it was salivation in both cases. Some investigators concluded that the CS simply substitutes for the UCS in order to generate the CR. However, in addition to salivating to the CS, Pavlov's dogs also showed other responses to the light, such as tail wagging, jumping, and barking. These responses are not similar to the UCR and indicate that the

CONCEPT REVIEW TABLE
Stimuli and Responses in Classical Conditioning

Stimulus/Response	Description
Unconditioned stimulus (UCS)	A stimulus that automatically elicits a response, typically via a reflex, without prior conditioning
Unconditioned response (UCR)	The response originally given to the unconditioned stimulus, used as the basis for establishing a conditioned response to a previously neutral stimulus
Conditioned stimulus (CS)	A previously neutral stimulus that comes to elicit a conditioned response through association with an unconditioned stimulus
Conditioned response (CR)	The learned or acquired response to a stimulus that did not evoke the response originally (i.e., a conditioned stimulus)

Before Conditioning

CS (light) → No response or irrelevant response

UCS (food) → UCR (salivation)

After Conditioning

CS (light) → CR (salivation)

▮ Figure 7-1
A Diagram of Classical Conditioning
The association between the UCS and the UCR exists at the beginning of the experiment and does not have to be learned. The association between the CS and the UCS is learned. It arises through the pairing of the conditioned and unconditioned stimuli. (An association may also be learned between the conditioned stimulus and the conditioned response.)

dogs learn much more than a simple stimulus-response (light-salivation) association. Indeed, evidence indicates that the animals learn a predictive relationship between the CS and UCS, which allows the CS to generate many different behaviors that anticipate UCS delivery.

PHENOMENA AND APPLICATIONS

LEARNING CURVES: ACQUISITION AND EXTINCTION
Over the years, psychologists have devised many variations of Pavlov's conditioning experiments. To appreciate these variations, we need to note some critical aspects of the conditioning experiment. Each paired presentation of

the conditioned stimulus (CS) and the unconditioned stimulus (UCS) is called a *trial*. The trials when the organism is learning the association between the two stimuli are the *acquisition stage* of conditioning. During this stage, repeated pairings of the CS (light) and UCS (food) strengthen the association between the two, as illustrated by the increase in the magnitude of the CR in the left-hand curve of Figure 7-2. The largest change in the magnitude of the CR happens in the earliest conditioning trials, and there is little change in the CR late in training. If the UCS is subsequently omitted, the CR will gradually diminish, and extinction occurs, as illustrated by the right-hand curve in Figure 7-2. **Extinction** represents learning that the CS no longer predicts the UCS. Extinction is not the "unlearning" of the original CS-UCS association; in fact, extinction involves the formation of a new CS–"no UCS" memory that inhibits expression of the CS-UCS association. The preservation of the original CS-UCS association after extinction training is reflected by **spontaneous recovery**. The original CR returns as time passes following extinction.

CONDITIONING IN DIFFERENT SPECIES Classical conditioning is pervasive in the animal kingdom and occurs in both humans and organisms as primitive as the nematode, *Caenorhabditis elegans* (a parasitic worm). For example, nematodes can learn that an olfactory CS predicts an aversive acetic acid solution (the UCS), which causes withdrawal (the UCR), and they come to show learned withdrawal responses (the CR). Numerous human responses can also be classically conditioned. To illustrate, consider the plight of cancer patients who are undergoing chemotherapy to stop the growth of their tumors. Chemotherapy involves injecting toxic substances (the UCS) into the patient, who as a result often becomes nau-

▮ Figure 7-2
Acquisition and Extinction of a Conditioned Response
The curve in the panel on the left depicts the acquisition phase of an experiment. Drops of saliva in response to the CS (before the onset of the UCS) are plotted on the vertical axis; the number of trials is plotted on the horizontal axis. After 16 acquisition trials, the experimenter switched to extinction; the results are presented in the panel at the right. (Adapted from *Conditioned Reflexes*, by E. P. Pavlov. Copyright © 1927 by Oxford University Press. Reprinted by permission of Oxford University Press.)

seated (the UCR). After a number of chemotherapy sessions, patients sometimes become nauseated and sick upon entering the treatment room. The repeated pairing of the chemotherapy (the UCS) and the sight of the treatment room (the CS) has led them to associate the room with the chemotherapy, which results in the intestinal upset before their treatment even begins (the CR). A related phenomenon arises with young cancer patients who are given ice cream before the chemotherapy session. The ice cream may have been intended to lighten the child's distress about the impending treatment, but unfortunately the ice cream becomes conditioned to the chemotherapy experience. Now the ice cream is the CS and the chemotherapy the UCS. The result is that the children become less likely to eat ice cream, even outside the chemotherapy setting (Bernstein, 1978, 1999).

Classical conditioning also plays a role in emotional responses like fear. Suppose that a rat in an enclosed compartment is periodically subjected to electric footshock. Just before the shock occurs, a tone sounds. After repeated pairings of the tone (the CS) and the shock (the UCS), the tone alone will produce reactions in the rat that indicate fear, including freezing and crouching. In addition, its blood pressure increases. The rat has been conditioned to be fearful when exposed to what was previously a neutral stimulus. Humans, too, can be conditioned to be fearful (Jacobs & Nadel, 1985; Watson & Rayner, 1920). Indeed, classical conditioning of fear seems to be at the root of several anxiety disorders, such as post-traumatic stress disorder and panic disorder (Bouton, Mineka, & Barlow, 2001).

SECOND-ORDER CONDITIONING This far in our discussion of conditioning, the UCS has always been a biologically significant stimulus such as food or shock. However, other stimuli can acquire the power of a UCS by being consistently paired with a biologically significant UCS. Recall the example of a dog exposed to a light (CS) followed by food (UCS), where the light comes to elicit a conditioned response. Once the dog is conditioned, the light itself acquires the power of a UCS. If the dog is now put in a situation in which it is exposed to a tone (CS₂) followed by the light (but no food) on each trial, the tone alone will eventually elicit a CR, even though it has never been paired with food. (There must also be other trials in which the light is again paired with food; otherwise, the originally conditioned relation between light and food will be extinguished.) The ability of the tone to produce a CR after being paired with the light, which itself predicts the UCS, is called **second-order conditioning**. In second-order conditioning, a CS comes to produce a CR, despite never having been paired with an UCS.

The existence of second-order conditioning greatly increases the scope of classical conditioning, especially in humans, for whom biologically significant UCSs occur relatively infrequently. Now all that is needed for conditioning to occur is the pairing of one stimulus with another, if the latter has previously been paired with a biologically significant event. Consider again the example of chemotherapy. Suppose that for a particular young patient the taste of ice cream has become conditioned to the side effects of chemotherapy, such as nausea (a biologically significant event). If the child is repeatedly presented with other stimuli, such as the taste of carrots, followed by ice cream, the patient may start to experience unpleasant feelings in response to the carrots alone.

GENERALIZATION AND DISCRIMINATION When a CR has been associated with a particular stimulus, similar stimuli will evoke the same response. Suppose that a person is conditioned to have a mild emotional reaction to the sound of a tuning fork producing a tone of middle C. (The emotional reaction is measured by the *galvanic skin response*, or GSR, which is a change in the electrical activity of the skin that occurs during emotional stress.) That person will also show a change in GSR in response to higher or lower tones without further conditioning (see Figure 7-3). The more similar the new stimuli are to the original CS, the more likely they are to evoke the conditioned response. This principle, called **generaliza-**

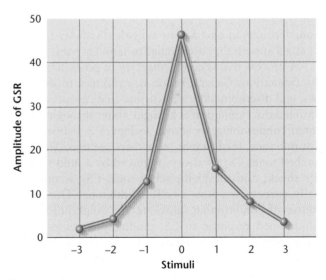

▌ Figure 7-3
The Gradient of Generalization
Stimulus 0 denotes the tone to which the galvanic skin response (GSR) was originally conditioned. Stimuli +1, +2, and +3 represent test tones of increasingly higher pitch; stimuli –1, –2, and –3 represent tones of lower pitch. Note that the amount of generalization decreases as the difference between the test tone and the training tone increases. ("The Sensory Generalization of Conditioned Responses with Varying Frequencies of Tone," from *Journal of General Psychology*, Vol. 17, p. 125–148, 1937. Reprinted by permission of the Helen Dwight Reid Educational Foundation.)

Figure 7-4
Conditioned Discrimination
The discriminative stimuli were two tones of clearly different pitch (CS_1 = 700 hertz and CS_2 = 3,500 hertz). The unconditioned stimulus, an electric shock applied to the left forefinger, occurred only on trials when CS_1 was presented. The strength of the conditioned response, in this case the GSR, gradually increased following CS_1 and extinguished following CS_2. (Adapted from "Differential Classical Conditioning: Verbalization of Stimulus Contingencies," by M. J. Fuhrer & P. E. Baer, reprinted by permission from *Science*, Vol. 150, December 10, 1965, pp. 1479–1481. Copyright © 1965 by American Association for the Advancement of Science.)

tion, accounts in part for an individual's ability to react to novel stimuli that are similar to familiar ones.

A process that is complementary to generalization is discrimination. Generalization is a reaction to similarities, and **discrimination** is a reaction to differences. Conditioned discrimination is brought about through differential conditioning, as shown in Figure 7-4. Instead of just one tone, for instance, now there are two. The low-pitched tone, CS_1, is always followed by a mild forefinger shock, and the high-pitched tone, CS_2, is not. Initially, participants show a GSR to both tones. During the course of conditioning, however, the amplitude of the conditioned response to CS_1 gradually increases while the amplitude of the response to CS_2 decreases. Through this process of differential reinforcement, participants are conditioned to discriminate between the two tones. The high-pitched tone, CS_2, has become a signal to inhibit the learned response.

Generalization and discrimination occur frequently in everyday life. A young child who has learned to associate the sight of her pet dog with playfulness may initially approach all dogs. Eventually, through discrimination, the child may expect playfulness only from dogs that look like hers. The sight of a threatening dog has come to inhibit the child's response to approaching dogs.

INHIBITORY CONDITIONING The examples of conditioning we have discussed to this point are called **excitatory conditioning**, the ability of a CS to increase the probability or magnitude of a given behavior. Another important form of learning in classical conditioning is **inhibitory conditioning**, the ability of a CS to decrease the probability or magnitude of a behavioral response. Inhibitory learning occurs, for example, when a CS that has come to predict the occurrence of a UCS is presented alone, as occurs during extinction. Inhibitory conditioning also occurs when a CS that predicts a UCS is presented with a new CS on trials in which the UCS is omitted. For example, when a tone that predicts forefinger shock is presented together with a light (a *compound* CS presentation) in the absence of shock, the light becomes a conditioned inhibitor; that is, the light comes to predict the absence of shock. Inhibition is indexed by the ability of the light to reduce the conditional responding that would normally be produced by the excitatory tone when the cues are presented in compound. Inhibition is also reflected in the slow rate of acquisition of conditional responding to the light CS when the light is presented with a UCS after inhibitory training. Inhibitory conditioning is conceptually important because it indicates that associative learning is bidirectional and can cause either increases or decreases in behavior.

PREDICTABILITY AND COGNITIVE FACTORS

Up to this point, we have analyzed classical conditioning solely in terms of external or environmental events. One stimulus is consistently followed by another, and the organism comes to associate them with each other. Although this behaviorist view was dominant for many years, some researchers have argued that the critical factor behind conditioning is what the animal knows (Bolles, 1972; Tolman, 1932). In this cognitive view, classical conditioning gives an organism new knowledge about the relationship between two stimuli; given the CS, the organism has learned to expect the UCS (Rescorla, 1988). In what follows, we consider the role played by cognitive factors in classical conditioning.

CONTIGUITY VERSUS PREDICTABILITY Since Pavlov's time, researchers have tried to determine the critical factor needed for classical conditioning to occur. Pavlov and others believed that the critical factor was temporal contiguity of the CS and UCS. That is, the two stimuli must occur close together in time for an association to develop. However, an alternative, more cognitive, view is that the CS must be a reliable predictor of the UCS. In other words, for conditioning to occur, there must be a higher probability that the UCS will occur when the CS

▌Figure 7-5
Rescorla's Experiment
For each group, the events for 16 trials are presented. On some trials the CS occurs and is followed by the UCS (CS + UCS); on other trials the CS or UCS occurs alone; and on still other trials, neither the CS nor the UCS occurs. The boxes to the far right give a count of these trial outcomes (CS+UCS, CS only, UCS only, or neither stimulus) for the two groups. The number of CS + UCS trials is identical for both groups, as is the number of trials on which only the CS occurs. But the two groups differ in the number of trials on which the UCS occurred alone (never in Group A and as frequently as any other type of trial in Group B). A conditioned response to CS developed readily for Group A but did not develop at all for Group B. (R. A. Rescorla (1967) "Pavlovian Conditioning & Its Proper Control Procedures," from *Psychological Review*, Vol. 74:71–80. Copyright © 1967 by the American Psychological Association.)

has been presented than when it has not. The UCS must be predictable.

In a path-breaking experiment, Rescorla (1968) contrasted contiguity and predictability. On certain trials he exposed rats to shock (the UCS), and on some of these trials he preceded the shock with a tone (the CS). The procedures for two of the groups in the experiment are illustrated in Figure 7-5. The number of temporally contiguous pairings of tone and shock was the same in both groups. The variable Rescorla manipulated was the occurrence of shocks in the absence of tones. All shocks were preceded by tones in Group A. In Group B, shocks were equally likely in the presence and absence of the tone. The tone was highly predictive of the shock in Group A but had no predictive power in Group B.

The predictive power of the tone proved to be critical: Rats in Group A exhibited conditioning to the tone CS, whereas those in Group B did not (as determined by whether the rats exhibited a conditioned fear response to the tone). In other groups in the experiment (not shown in Figure 7-5), the strength of the conditioning was directly related to the predictive value of the CS in signaling the occurrence of the UCS. Subsequent experiments support the conclusion that the predictive relationship between the CS and the UCS is more important than either temporal contiguity or the frequency with which the CS and UCS are paired (Rescorla, 1972, 1988).

What a rat is doing in the preceding experiment may be compared with what you do in everyday life in deter-

mining what events predict other events. For example, if you walk into your kitchen and find a mess on the counter that you didn't make, then you begin to look for events that predict the occurrence of the messes. You might have observed that the mess appeared after your friends, Joe and Sally, were in the kitchen. On subsequent occasions, you might observe that there is rarely a mess when Sally has been in the kitchen, but there is always a mess when Joe has been in the kitchen. Like the rat in the preceding experiment that has to predict the occurrence of shock, you try to predict the kitchen messes. And like you, the rat does not focus on events that merely occur along with shock (such as the sight of the experimental apparatus). Rather, the rat looks for an event that tends to occur only prior to shock but not at other times (and therefore is truly predictive of the shock, as the tone is for Group A).

PREDICTABILITY AND EMOTION Predictability is also important for emotional reactions. If a particular CS reliably predicts that pain is coming, the absence of that CS predicts that pain is *not* coming and the organism can relax. The CS therefore is a "danger" signal, and its absence is a "safety" signal. When such signals are erratic, the emotional toll on the organism can be devastating. When rats have a reliable predictor that shock is coming, they respond with fear only when the danger signal is present; if they have no reliable predictor, they appear to be continually anxious and may even develop ulcers (Seligman, 1975).

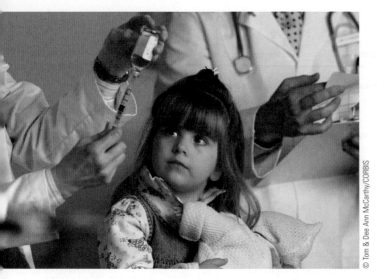

If a doctor gives a child a danger signal by saying that a procedure will hurt, the child will be fearful until the procedure is over. In contrast, if the doctor always tells a child that "it won't hurt," when in fact it sometimes does, the child has no danger or safety signals and may become terribly anxious whenever in the doctor's office.

There are clear parallels to human emotionality. If a dentist gives a child a danger signal by saying that a procedure will hurt, the child will be fearful until the procedure is over. In contrast, if the dentist always tells a child that "it won't hurt," when in fact it sometimes does, the child has no danger or safety signals and may become terribly anxious whenever in the dentist's office. As adults, many of us have experienced the anxiety of being in a situation where something disagreeable is likely to happen but no warnings exist for us to predict it. Unpleasant events are, by definition, unpleasant, but unpredictable unpleasant events are downright intolerable. (Further discussion of this point is included in Chapter 14.)

BIOLOGICAL CONSTRAINTS

We mentioned earlier in the chapter that different species sometimes learn the same thing by different mechanisms. These mechanisms were discovered by researchers studying animals' behavior in their natural environment. They reveal that what an organism can learn through conditioning is constrained by its biology.

THE ETHOLOGICAL APPROACH Ethologists, like behaviorists, are concerned with the behavior of animals, but ethologists place greater emphasis on evolution and genetics than on learning. This emphasis has led them to take a distinctive approach to learning—to assume that it is rigidly constrained by an animal's genetic endowment and to show that different species learn different things in

different ways. (Early behaviorists, on the other hand, assumed that the laws of learning were the same for all species.) As ethologists put it, when an animal learns, it must conform to a genetically determined "behavioral blueprint." Just as an architectural blueprint imposes constraints on the kinds of functions that a building may serve, so a behavioral blueprint imposes genetic constraints on the kinds of associations that an organism may learn. To some extent animals are "preprogrammed" to learn particular things in particular ways.

CONSTRAINTS ON CLASSICAL CONDITIONING Some of the best evidence for constraints on classical conditioning comes from studies of taste aversion learning. Consider first the basic phenomenon of a learned taste aversion. In a typical study, a rat is permitted to drink a flavored solution—say, vanilla. After drinking it, the rat is made ill with a nauseating injection of lithium chloride (LiCl). When the rat recovers, it is again presented with the vanilla solution. Now the rat scrupulously avoids the solution because it has learned to associate the vanilla taste with feeling ill. Such avoidance is an instance of classical conditioning: The initial taste of the solution is the CS, the feeling of being sick is the UCS, and after conditioning the taste signals that sickness is on its way.

According to early behaviorist ideas, a light or a sound might be expected to play the same signaling role as taste. That is, if a light is as effective a stimulus as taste, then an association between a light and feeling sick should be no more difficult to establish than one between a taste and feeling sick. But the facts turn out to be otherwise, as shown in the experiment by Garcia and Koelling (1966) diagrammed in Table 7-1. In the first stage of the experiment, an experimental group of rats is allowed to lick at a tube that contains a flavored solution. Each time the rat licks the tube, a click and a light are presented. The rat experiences three stimuli simultaneously—the taste of the solution, as well as the light and the click. In the second stage of the experiment, rats in the experimental group are mildly poisoned. Which stimuli—the taste or the light-plus-click—will become associated with feeling sick? To answer this question, in the third and final stage, rats in the experimental group are again presented with the tube. Sometimes the solution in the tube has the same flavor as before but there is no light or click, and at other times the solution has no flavor but the light and click are presented. The animals avoid the solution when they experience the taste, but not when the light-plus-click is presented. Therefore, the rats have associated only taste with feeling sick. These results cannot be attributed to taste being a more potent CS than light-plus-click, as shown by the control condition of the experiment, which is diagrammed at the bottom of Table 7-1. In the second stage, instead of being mildly poisoned, the rat is shocked. In the

● Table 7-1
An Experiment on Constraints and Taste Aversion

The design of an experiment showing that taste is a better signal for sickness than shock, whereas light-plus-sound is a better signal for shock than sickness. *(J. Garcia and R. A. Koelling (1966) "The Relation of Cue to Consequence in Avoidance Learning," Psychonomic Science, 4:123–124. Reprinted by permission of the Psychonomic Society.)*

Group	Conditioned Stimuli	Unconditioned Stimulus	Result
Group-Poison	Sweet taste; light+click	Lithium chloride → sickness	Taste → suppress drinking Light + click → no suppression
Group-Shock	Sweet taste; light+click	Footshock → fear	Taste → no suppression Light + click → suppression

final stage, the animal avoids the solution only when the light-plus-click is presented, not when it experiences the taste alone (Garcia & Koelling, 1966).

So, taste is a better signal for sickness than for shock, and light-plus-click is a better signal for shock than for sickness. Why does this selectivity of association exist? It does not fit with the early behaviorist idea that equally potent stimuli can be substituted for one another. Because taste and light-plus-click can both be effective CSs, and being sick and being shocked are both effective UCSs, it should have been possible for either CS to become associated with either UCS. On the other hand, selectivity of association fits perfectly with the ethological perspective and its emphasis on an animal's evolutionary adaptation to its environment. In their natural habitat, rats rely on taste to select their food. Consequently, there may be a genetically determined relationship between taste and intestinal reactions that fosters an association between taste and sickness but not between light and sickness. Moreover, in a rat's natural environment, pain resulting from external factors like cold or injury is invariably due to external stimuli. Consequently, there may be a built-in relationship between external stimuli and "external pain," which fosters an association between light and shock but not one between taste and shock.

If rats learn to associate taste with sickness because it fits with their natural means of selecting food, another species with a different means of selecting food might have trouble learning to associate taste with sickness. This is exactly what happens. Birds naturally select their food on the basis of looks rather than taste, and they readily learn to associate a light with sickness but not to associate a taste with sickness (Wilcoxin, Dragoin, & Kral, 1971). Here, then, is a perfect example of different species learning the same thing—what causes sickness— by different means. In short, if we want to know what may be conditioned to what, we cannot consider the CS and UCS in isolation. Rather, we must focus on the two in combination and consider how well that combination reflects built-in relationships. This conclusion differs considerably from the assumption that the laws of learning are the same for all species and situations. In fact, several recent theorists have explored classical conditioning by using a behavior systems approach that considers the evolutionary history of the behaviors under study (Fanselow, 1994).

◆ Interim Summary

- In classical conditioning, a conditioned stimulus (CS) that consistently precedes an unconditioned stimulus (UCS) comes to serve as a signal for the UCS and will elicit a conditioned response (CR) that often resembles the unconditioned response (UCR).

- For classical conditioning to occur, the CS must be a reliable predictor of the UCS; that is, there must be a higher probability that the UCS will occur when the CS has been presented than when it has not.

- The ability of stimuli to become associated in a classical conditioning experiment is constrained by biology and evolution.

◆ Critical Thinking Questions

1. In classical conditioning, it is generally believed that associations between the CS and UCS, rather than the CS and UCR, are the essence of conditioning. Can you think of an experiment that might differentiate these possibilities?

2. Some anxiety disorders in humans may be mediated by classical conditioning. For example, patients with panic disorder often experience panic attacks in situations that they have experienced before. Further, panic attacks can be precipitated when bodily sensations reminiscent of panic, such as increases in heart rate, occur during exercise. Can you describe the onset of panic attacks in terms of classical conditioning? What are the CS, UCS, CR, and UCR?

INSTRUMENTAL CONDITIONING

In classical conditioning, the CR often (but not always) resembles the normal response to the UCS. Salivation, for example, is a dog's normal response to food. But when you want to teach an organism something novel—such as teaching a dog a new trick—you cannot use classical conditioning. What UCS would make a dog sit up or roll over? To train the dog, you must first persuade it to do the trick (or an approximation of the trick) and then reward the animal with either approval or food. If you keep doing this, eventually the dog will learn the trick (in fact, the dog learns that the trick predicts food or approval). Much real-life learning occurs by this means, which is referred to as operant or instrumental conditioning.

In **instrumental conditioning**, certain responses are learned because they operate on, or affect, the environment. An organism does not just react to stimuli, as in classical conditioning, but also behaves in ways designed to produce certain changes in its environment. That is, the organism's behavior is instrumental in obtaining desired outcomes. Alone in a crib, a baby may kick and twist and coo spontaneously. When left by itself in a room, a dog may pad back and forth, sniff, or perhaps pick up a ball, drop it, and play with it. Neither organism is responding to a specific external stimulus. Rather, they are operating on their environment. Once the organism performs a certain behavior, however, the likelihood that the action will be repeated depends on its consequences. The baby will coo more often if each coo is followed by parental attention, and the dog will pick up the ball more often if this action is followed by petting or a treat. If we think of the baby as having parental attention as a goal and the dog as having food as a goal, operant conditioning amounts to learning that a particular behavior leads to attaining a particular goal (Rescorla, 1987). Like classical conditioning, instrumental conditioning involves learning relationships between events (such as relationships between responses and outcomes).

THE LAW OF EFFECT

The study of instrumental conditioning began at the turn of the 20th century with a series of experiments by E. L. Thorndike (1898). Thorndike, who was greatly influenced by Darwin's theory of evolution, was trying to show that learning in animals is continuous, like learning in humans. A typical experiment proceeded as follows. A hungry cat is placed in a cage whose door is held fast by a simple latch, and a piece of fish is placed just outside the cage. Initially, the cat tries to reach the food by extending its paws through the bars. When this fails, the cat moves about the cage, engaging in a variety of behaviors. At some point it inadvertently hits the latch, frees itself, and eats the fish. The researchers then place the cat back in its cage and put a new piece of fish outside. The cat goes through roughly the same set of behaviors until once more it happens to hit the latch. The procedure is repeated again and again. Over a number of trials, the cat eliminates many of its irrelevant behaviors, and eventually it opens the latch and frees itself as soon as it is placed in the cage. The cat has learned to open the latch to obtain food.

It may sound as if the cat is acting intelligently, but Thorndike argued that there is little "intelligence" operating here. There is no moment in time when the cat seems to have an insight about the solution to its problem. Instead, the cat's performance improves gradually over a series of trials. The cat appears to be engaging in trial-and-error behavior, and when a reward immediately follows one of those behaviors, the learning of the action is strengthened. Thorndike referred to this strengthening as the **law of effect**. He argued that in instrumental learning, the law of effect selects from a set of random responses only those that are followed by positive consequences. The process is similar to evolution, in which genes that promote survival or fitness are selected across generations (Schwartz, 1989).

SKINNER'S EXPERIMENTS

B. F. Skinner was responsible for changes in how researchers conceptualize and study instrumental conditioning. His method of studying instrumental conditioning was simpler than Thorndike's—he examined only one response at a time—and it has been widely accepted.

LEARNING CURVES: ACQUISITION AND EXTINCTION

In a Skinnerian experiment, a hungry animal—usually a rat or a pigeon—is placed in a box like the one shown in Figure 7-6, which is popularly called a *Skinner box* or operant chamber. The inside of the box is bare except for a protruding bar with a food dish beneath it. A small light above the bar can be turned on at the experimenter's discretion. Left alone in the box, the rat moves about, exploring. Occasionally it inspects the bar and presses it. The rate at which the rat first presses the bar is the *baseline level*. After establishing the baseline level, the experimenter activates a food magazine located outside the box. Now, every time the rat presses the bar, a small food pellet is released into the dish. The rat eats the food pellet and soon presses the bar again. The food reinforces bar pressing, and the rate of pressing increases dramatically. If the food magazine is disconnected and pressing the bar no longer delivers food, the rate of bar pressing diminishes. An instrumental response that is not

▌Figure 7-6
Apparatus for Instrumental Conditioning
This photograph shows a Skinner box with a magazine for delivering food pellets. The computer is used to control the experiment and record the rat's responses.

B. F. Skinner was a pioneer in the study of instrumental conditioning.

reinforced undergoes extinction, just as a classically conditioned response does.

Instrumental conditioning increases the likelihood of a response by following the behavior with a *reinforcer* (often something like food or water). Because the bar is always present in the Skinner box, the rat can respond to it as frequently or infrequently as it chooses. The organism's rate of response is therefore a useful measure of the instrumental learning; the more frequently the response occurs during a given time interval, the greater the learning.

In instrumental conditioning, an environmental event that follows behavior produces either an increase or a decrease in the probability of that behavior. **Reinforcement** refers to the process whereby the delivery of an appetitive stimulus or the removal of an aversive stimulus increases the probability of a behavior. Note that there may be either a positive contingency between the behavior and reinforcement (for example, bar pressing is followed by food) or a negative contingency (for example, bar pressing terminates or prevents shock). **Positive reinforcement** describes a behavior that produces an appetitive stimulus, and **negative reinforcement** occurs when behavior prevents an aversive stimulus. For example, the likelihood that you will remember to bring your sweetheart flowers on Valentine's Day will increase

if your boyfriend or girlfriend is especially affectionate when you remember to give him or her flowers. Likewise, you are more likely to avoid your apartment if you frequently fight with your roommates. In the former case, an appetitive stimulus (affection) increases behavior (flower giving), and in the latter case removal of an aversive stimulus (fighting) also increases behavior (avoidance of apartment).

Punishment is the converse of reinforcement (see Aversive Conditioning later in this chapter). It is the process by which delivery of an aversive stimulus or the removal of an appetitive stimulus decreases the probability of a behavior. Again, note that there may be either a positive contingency between the behavior and punishment (such as bar pressing is followed by shock) or a negative contingency (such as bar pressing terminates or prevents food delivery). In the first case, behavior produces an aversive stimulus, and in the second case, which is also called **omission training**, behavior prevents an appetitive stimulus. For example, the likelihood that you bring your date chocolate on Valentine's Day will decrease if he or she gets mad at you for offering the caloric gift. Likewise, the probability that you argue with your parents will decrease if they ground you for the evening when you do. In the former example, an aversive stimulus (anger) decreases behavior (chocolate giving), and in the latter example the removal of an appetitive stimulus (going out at night) also decreases behavior (arguing

CONCEPT REVIEW TABLE
Types of Reinforcement and Punishment

Type	Definition	Effect	Example
Positive reinforcement	Delivery of a pleasant or appetitive stimulus that follows a behavioral response	Increases the likelihood of the behavioral response	If studying is followed by a high grade on an exam, then the incidence of studying before exams will increase.
Negative reinforcement	Removal of an unpleasant or aversive stimulus after a behavior response	Increases the likelihood of the behavioral response	If leaving your dorm room removes you from a noisy roommate, then the time you spend away from your room will increase
Punishment	Presentation of an unpleasant or aversive stimulus after a behavioral response	Decreases the likelihood of the behavioral response	If your professor embarrasses you for asking a question in class, then the likelihood you will ask questions in class will decrease
Omission training	Removal of a pleasant or appetitive stimulus after a behavioral response	Decreases the likelihood of the behavioral response	If your girl- or boyfriend withholds affection whenever you watch TV, the time you spend in front of the TV will decrease

with parents). Reinforcement produces "good" outcomes, and punishment produces "bad" outcomes. As we have seen, a "good" outcome can be either the delivery of something wanted (positive reinforcer) or the withholding of something aversive (negative reinforcer). Likewise, a "bad" outcome can be either the delivery of something aversive (punishment) or the withholding of something wanted (omission training). (See the Concept Review table.)

IMPLICATIONS FOR CHILD REARING Although rats and pigeons have been the favored experimental subjects, instrumental conditioning applies to many species, including our own. Indeed, instrumental conditioning has a good deal to tell us about child rearing. A particularly illuminating example is the following case. A young boy had temper tantrums if he did not get enough attention from his parents, especially at bedtime. Because the parents eventually responded to the tantrums, their attention probably reinforced the boy's behavior. To eliminate the tantrums, the parents were advised to go through the normal bedtime ritual and then ignore the child's protests, painful though that might be. If the reinforcer (attention) was withheld, the behavior should be extinguished—which is just what happened. The time the child spent crying at bedtime decreased from 45 minutes to not at all over a period of only 7 days (Williams, 1959). This is an example of omission training because withholding something the boy wanted (parental attention) *decreased* the behavioral response (bedtime crying) that was contingent upon punishment.

Another application of instrumental conditioning to child rearing focuses on the temporal relationship between a response and its reinforcer. Laboratory experiments have shown that immediate reinforcement is more effective than delayed reinforcement. The more time that elapses between an instrumental response and a reinforcer, the weaker the response. Many developmental psychologists have noted that delay of reinforcement is an important factor in dealing with young children. If a child acts kindly to a pet, for example, praising the child immediately rather than waiting until later will best strengthen the behavior. Similarly, if a child hits someone without provocation, this aggressive behavior is more likely to be eliminated if the child is punished immediately.

SHAPING Suppose that you want to use instrumental conditioning to teach your dog a trick—for instance, to get the mail from the slot in your front door. You cannot wait until the dog does this naturally and then reinforce it, because you may wait forever. When the desired behavior is truly novel, you have to condition it by taking advantage of natural variations in the animal's actions. To train a dog to get the mail, you can give the animal a food reinforcer each time it approaches the door, requiring it to move closer and closer to the mail for each reinforcer until finally the dog mouths and grabs the mail. This technique, called **shaping**, is reinforcing only variations in response that deviate in the direction desired by the experimenter.

Animals can be taught elaborate tricks and routines by means of shaping. Two psychologists and their staff trained thousands of animals of many species for television shows, commercials, and county fairs (Breland & Breland, 1966). One popular show featured "Priscilla,

Pigeon sitting

Pigeon pecking key

Pigeon rewarded

▌**Figure 7-7**
Search and Rescue by Pigeons
The Coast Guard has used pigeons to search for people lost at sea. Shaping methods are used to train the pigeons to spot the color orange—the international color for life jackets. Three pigeons are strapped into a Plexiglas chamber attached to the underside of a helicopter. The chamber is divided into thirds so that each bird faces in a different direction. When a pigeon spots an orange object, or any other object, it pecks a key that buzzes the pilot. The pilot then heads in the direction indicated by the bird that responded. Pigeons are better suited than people for the task of spotting distant objects at sea. They can stare over the water for a long time without suffering eye fatigue, they have excellent color vision, and they can focus on a 60- to 80-degree area, whereas a person can focus only on a 2- to 3-degree area. (After Simmons, 1981)

the Fastidious Pig." Priscilla turned on the TV set, ate breakfast at a table, picked up dirty clothes and put them in a hamper, vacuumed the floor, picked out her favorite food, and took part in a quiz program by answering questions from the audience by flashing lights that indicated yes or no. She was not an unusually bright pig; in fact, because pigs grow so fast, a new "Priscilla" was trained every 3 to 5 months. The ingenuity was not the pig's but the experimenters', who used instrumental conditioning and shaped the pig's behavior to produce the desired result. Shaping has been used to train pigeons to locate people lost at sea (see Figure 7-7), and porpoises have been trained to retrieve underwater equipment.

Importantly, the Brelands' work also indicated that not all behaviors could be shaped. For example, they had great difficulty training raccoons to drop coins into a piggy bank to receive a food reward. Rather than drop the coins in the bank to obtain a food reinforcer, the raccoons would rub them together incessantly, drop them in the bank, pull them out again, and continue rubbing them together. This behavior, of course, resembles the behavior that raccoons normally display to natural food items. The behavioral predisposition of the raccoon to vigorously manipulate an object associated with food mitigated instrumental conditioning of a novel food-reinforced response. Instrumental conditioning, like classical conditioning, operates under biological constraints.

PHENOMENA AND APPLICATIONS

A number of phenomena greatly increase the generality of instrumental conditioning and show its applications to human behavior. Here we look briefly at some of them.

CONDITIONED REINFORCERS Most of the reinforcers we have discussed are called *primary* because they satisfy basic drives. If instrumental conditioning occurred only with primary reinforcers, it would not occur very often because primary reinforcers are not that common. However, virtually any stimulus can become a *secondary* or *conditioned reinforcer*, which is a stimulus that has been consistently paired with a primary reinforcer.

A minor variation in the typical instrumental conditioning experiment illustrates how conditioned reinforcement works. When a rat in a Skinner box presses a lever, a tone sounds momentarily and is followed shortly by delivery of food (the food is a primary reinforcer; the tone will become a conditioned reinforcer). After the animal has been conditioned in this way, the experimenter begins the extinction process, so that when the rat presses the lever, neither the tone nor the food occurs. In time, the animal ceases to press the lever. Then the tone is reconnected but not the food magazine. When the animal discovers that pressing the lever turns on the tone, its rate of pressing increases markedly, overcoming the extinction even though no food is delivered. The tone has acquired a reinforcing quality of its own through classical conditioning. Because the tone was reliably paired with food, it came to signal food.

Our lives abound with conditioned reinforcers. Two of the most prevalent are money and praise. Presumably, money is a powerful reinforcer because it has been paired so frequently with so many primary reinforcers—we can buy food, drink, and comfort, to mention just a few of the obvious things. And mere praise can sustain many activities without even the promise of a primary reinforcer.

GENERALIZATION AND DISCRIMINATION Again, what was true for classical conditioning holds for instrumental conditioning as well: Organisms generalize what they have learned, and generalization can be curbed by discrimination training. If a young child is reinforced by her parents for petting the family dog, she will soon generalize this petting response to other dogs. Because this can be dangerous (the neighbors might have a vicious watchdog), the child's parents may provide some discrimination training so that she is reinforced when she pets the family dog but not the neighbor's.

Discrimination training will be effective to the extent that there is a discriminative stimulus (or set of them) that clearly distinguishes cases in which the response should be made from those in which it should be suppressed. Our young child will have an easier time learning which dog to pet if her parents can point to an aspect of dogs that signals friendliness (a wagging tail, for example). In general, a discriminative stimulus will be useful to the extent that its presence predicts that a response will be followed by reinforcement and its absence predicts that the response will not be followed by reinforcement (or vice versa). Just as in classical conditioning, the predictive power of a stimulus seems to be critical to conditioning.

SCHEDULES OF REINFORCEMENT In real life, not every instance of a behavior is reinforced. For example, hard work is sometimes followed by praise, but often it goes unacknowledged. If instrumental conditioning occurred only with continuous reinforcement, it might play a limited role in our lives. Once a behavior is established, however, it can be maintained when it is reinforced only a fraction of the time. This phenomenon, partial reinforcement, can be illustrated in the laboratory by a pigeon that learns to peck at a key for food. Once this instrumental response is established, the pigeon continues to peck at a high rate, even if it receives only occasional reinforcement. In some cases, pigeons that were rewarded with food an average of once every 5 minutes (12 times an hour) pecked at the key as often as 6,000 times per hour—500 pecks per pellet of food received! Moreover, extinction following the maintenance of a response on partial reinforcement is much slower than extinction following the maintenance of a response on continuous reinforcement. Extinction of pecking in pigeons reinforced every 5 minutes takes days, whereas pigeons reinforced continuously extinguish in a matter of minutes. This phenomenon is known as the *partial-reinforcement effect.* It makes intuitive sense because there is less difference between extinction and maintenance when reinforcement during maintenance is only partial.

When reinforcement occurs only some of the time, we need to know exactly how it is scheduled—after every third response? After every 5 seconds? It turns out that the schedule of reinforcement determines the pattern of responding. There are four basic schedules of reinforcement (see the Concept Review table). Some

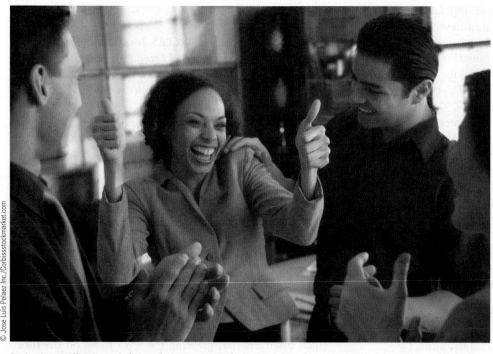

Praise is an effective reinforcer for many people.

CONCEPT REVIEW TABLE
Schedules of Reinforcement

Schedule	Procedure
Ratio schedules	
Fixed ratio (FR)	Reinforcement is provided after a fixed number of responses.
Variable ratio (VR)	Reinforcement is provided after a certain number of responses, with the number varying unpredictably.
Interval schedules	
Fixed interval (FI)	Reinforcement is provided after a certain amount of time has elapsed since the last reinforcement.
Variable interval (VI)	Reinforcement is provided after a certain amount of time has elapsed since the last reinforcement, with the duration of the interval varying unpredictably.

schedules are called **ratio schedules,** because reinforcement depends on the number of responses the organism makes. It's like being a factory worker who gets paid for piecework. The ratio can be either fixed or variable. On a **fixed ratio schedule** (called an *FR schedule*), the number of responses that have to be made is fixed at a particular value. If the number is 5 (FR 5), 5 responses are required for reinforcement; if it is 50 (FR 50), 50 responses are required; and so on. In general, the higher the ratio, the higher the rate at which the organism responds, particularly when the organism is initially trained on a relatively low ratio (say, FR 5) and then is continuously shifted to progressively higher ratios, culminating, say, in FR 100. It is as if our factory worker initially got $5 for every 5 hems sewn, but then times got tough and he needed to do 100 hems to get $5. But perhaps the most distinctive aspect about behavior under an FR schedule is the pause in responding right after the reinforcement occurs (see the left side of Figure 7-8). It is hard for the factory worker to start on a new set of hems right after he has just finished enough to obtain a reward.

On a **variable ratio schedule** (a VR schedule), the organism is still reinforced only after making a certain number of responses, but that number varies unpredictably. In a VR 5 schedule, the number of responses needed for reinforcement may sometimes be 1, at other times 10, with an average of 5. Unlike the behavior that occurs under FR schedules, there are no pauses when the organism is operating under a VR schedule (see the left

side of Figure 7-8), presumably because the organism has no way of detecting how far it is from a reinforcement. A good example of a VR schedule in everyday life is the operation of a slot machine. The number of responses (plays) needed for reinforcement (payoff) keeps varying, and the operator has no way of predicting when reinforcement pattern will occur. VR schedules can generate very high rates of responding (as casino owners appear to have figured out).

Other schedules of reinforcement are called **interval schedules,** because under these schedules reinforcement is available only after a certain time interval has elapsed (and the animal makes a response). Again, the schedule can be either fixed or variable. On a **fixed interval schedule** (an FI schedule), the organism is reinforced for its first response after a certain amount of time has passed since its last reinforcement. On an FI 2 (minutes) schedule, for example, reinforcement is available only when 2 minutes have elapsed since the last reinforced response; responses made during that 2-minute interval have no effect. One distinctive aspect of responding on an FI schedule is a pause that occurs immediately after reinforcement. (This post-reinforcement pause can be even longer than the one that occurs under FR schedules.) Another distinctive aspect of responding on an FI schedule is an increase in the rate of responding as the end of the interval approaches, producing a pattern often described as a scallop (see the right side of Figure 7-8). A good example of an FI sched-

▌ Figure 7-8
Typical Patterns of Responding on the Four Basic Schedules of Reinforcement
Each curve plots an animal's cumulative number of responses as a function of time; the slope of the curve thus indicates the animal's rate of responding. The short tick marks on each line indicate the moment the responses occurred. The curves on the left are for ratio schedules. In the curve for the FR schedule, note the horizontal segments, which correspond to pauses (they show no increase in the cumulative number of responses). The curves on the right are for interval schedules. In the curve for the FI schedule, again the horizontal segments correspond to pauses. (Adapted from Barry Schwartz, *Psychology of Learning and Behavior,* 3/e, with the permission of W. W. Norton & Co., Inc.)

Gamblers who play the slot machines are reinforced with pay-offs on a variable ratio schedule. Such a schedule can generate very high rates of responding.

ule in everyday life is mail delivery, which comes just once a day (FI 24 hours) or in some places twice a day (FI 12 hours). Right after your mail is delivered, you would not check it again, but as the end of the mail-delivery interval approaches, you will start checking again.

On a **variable interval schedule** (a VI schedule), reinforcement still depends on a certain interval having elapsed, but the interval's duration varies unpredictably. In a VI 10 (minute) schedule, for example, sometimes the critical interval is 2 minutes, sometimes 20 minutes, and so on, with an average of 10 minutes. Unlike the variations in responding under an FI schedule, organisms tend to respond at a uniform high rate when the schedule is a VI 1 (see the right side of Figure 7-8). For an example of a VI schedule in everyday life, consider redialing a phone number after hearing a busy signal. To receive reinforcement (getting your call through), you have to wait some time interval after your last response (dialing), but the length of that interval is unpredictable.

AVERSIVE CONDITIONING

We have talked about reinforcement as if it is almost always positive (food, for example). But negative or aversive events, such as shock or a painful noise, are often used in instrumental conditioning. There are different kinds of aversive conditioning, depending on whether the aversive event is used to weaken an existent response or learn a new response.

PUNISHMENT In punishment training, a response is followed by an aversive stimulus or event, which results in the response being weakened or suppressed on subse-

quent occasions. Suppose that a child who is learning to use crayons starts drawing on the wall (the undesirable response). If he is slapped on the hand when he does this (the punishment), he will learn not to do so. Similarly, if a rat that is learning to run a maze is shocked whenever it chooses a wrong path, it will soon learn to avoid its past mistakes. In both cases, punishment is used to decrease the likelihood of an undesirable behavior.

Although punishment can suppress an unwanted response, it has several disadvantages. First, its effects are not as informative as the results of reward. Reward essentially says, "Repeat what you have done"; punishment says, "Stop it!" but fails to give an alternative. As a result, the organism may substitute an even less desirable response for the punished one. Second, the by-products of punishment may be unfortunate. Through classical conditioning, punishment often leads to dislike or fear of the punishing person (parent, teacher, or employer) and the situation (home, school, or office) in which it occurred. Finally, an extreme or painful punishment may elicit aggressive behavior that is more serious than the original undesirable behavior.

These cautions do not mean that punishment should never be employed. It can effectively eliminate an undesirable response if it is consistent and delivered immediately after the undesired response, and if an alternative response is rewarded. Rats that have learned to take the shorter of two paths in a maze to reach food will quickly switch to the longer one if they are shocked when taking the shorter path. The temporary suppression produced by punishment provides an opportunity for the rat to learn to take the longer path. In this case, punishment is an effective means of redirecting behavior because it is informative, which seems to be the key to the humane and effective use of punishment. A child who gets a shock from an electrical appliance may learn which connections are safe and which ones are hazardous.

ESCAPE AND AVOIDANCE Aversive events can also be used in the learning of new responses. Organisms can learn to make a response to terminate an ongoing aversive event, as a child learns to turn off a faucet to stop hot water from flowing into the bathtub. This is *escape learning*. Organisms can also learn to make a response to prevent an aversive event from even starting, as we learn to stop at red lights to prevent accidents (and traffic tickets). This is *avoidance learning*.

Often, escape learning precedes avoidance learning. For example, a rat is placed in a box consisting of two compartments divided by a barrier. On each trial, the animal is placed in one of the compartments. At some point a warning tone is sounded, and 5 seconds later the floor of that compartment is electrified. To get away from the shock, the animal must jump over the barrier into the other compart-

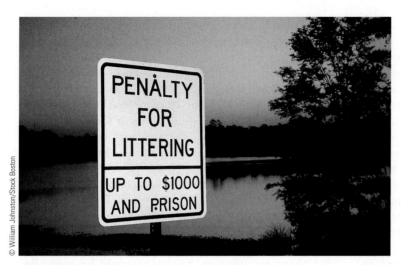

The threat of punishment is an effective motivator.

ment. Initially, the rat jumps over the barrier only when the shock starts—this is escape learning. With practice, it learns to jump upon hearing the warning tone, thereby avoiding the shock entirely—this is avoidance learning.

Avoidance learning has generated a great deal of interest, in part because there is something very puzzling about it. What exactly is reinforcing the avoidance response? In the experiment just described, what reinforces the animal for jumping over the barrier? Intuitively, it seems to be the absence of shock, but this is a nonevent. How can a nonevent serve as a reinforcer? One solution to this puzzle holds that there are two stages in the learning taking place. The first stage involves classical conditioning. Through repeated pairings of the warning (the CS) and the punishing event or shock (the UCS), the animal learns a fear response to the warning. The second stage involves instrumental conditioning. The animal learns that a particular response (jumping over the barrier) removes an aversive event, fear. In short, what first appears to be a nonevent is actually fear, and we can think of avoidance as escape from fear (Mowrer, 1947; Rescorla & Solomon, 1967).

Control and Cognitive Factors

Our analysis of instrumental conditioning has tended to emphasize environmental factors: A response is consistently followed by a reinforcing event, and the organism learns to associate the response with the reinforcement. However, the cognitive theory of avoidance suggests that cognitive factors may play an important role in instrumental conditioning, just as they do in classical conditioning. As we will see, it is often useful to view the organism in an instrumental conditioning situation as acquiring new knowledge about relationships between responses and reinforcers.

CONTINGENCY VERSUS CONTROL As with classical conditioning, we want to know what factor is critical for instrumental conditioning to occur. Again, one of the options is temporal contiguity: An instrumental response is conditioned whenever it is immediately followed by reinforcement (Skinner, 1948). A more cognitive option, closely related to predictability, is that of control: An instrumental response is conditioned only when the organism interprets the reinforcement as being controlled by its response. Some important experiments by Maier and Seligman (1976) provide more support for the control view than for the temporal contiguity view. (See also the discussion of control and stress in Chapter 15.) Their basic experiment has two stages. In the first stage, some rats learn that whether they receive a shock or not depends on (is controlled by) their behavior, while other rats learn that they have no control over the shock. Think of the rats as being tested in pairs. Both members of a pair are in a harness that restricts their movements, and occasionally they receive an electric shock. One member of the pair, the "control" rat, can turn off the shock by pushing a nearby panel with its nose; the other member of the pair, the "yoked" rat, cannot exercise any control over the shock. Whenever the control rat is shocked, so is the yoked rat, and whenever the control rat turns off the shock, the yoked rat's shock is also terminated. The control and yoked rats therefore receive the same number of shocks.

To find out what the rats learned in the first stage, a second stage is needed. In this stage, the experimenter places both rats in a new apparatus—a box divided into two compartments by a barrier. On each trial a tone is first sounded, indicating that the compartment the animal currently occupies is about to be subjected to an electric shock. To avoid the shock, the rat must learn to jump the barrier into the other compartment when it hears the warning tone. Control rats learn this response rapidly. But the yoked rats are another story. Initially, the yoked rats make no movement across the barrier, and as trials progress, their behavior becomes increasingly passive, finally lapsing into utter helplessness. Why? Because during the first stage the yoked rats learned that shocks were not under their control, and this belief in noncontrol made conditioning in the second stage impossible. If a belief in noncontrol makes instrumental conditioning impossible, a belief in control may be what makes it possible. Many other experiments support the notion that instrumental conditioning occurs only when the organism perceives reinforcement as being under its control (Seligman, 1975). See Chapter 15 for a detailed discussion of learned helplessness.

CONTINGENCY LEARNING We can also talk about these findings in terms of contingencies. We can say that instrumental conditioning occurs only when the organism perceives a *contingency* between its responses and reinforcement. In the first stage of the preceding study, the relevant contingency is between pushing a panel and the absence of shock. Perceiving this contingency amounts to determining that the likelihood of avoiding shock is greater when the panel is pushed than when it is not. Dogs that do not perceive this contingency in the first stage of the study appear not to look for any contingency in the second stage. This contingency approach makes it clear that the results of research on instrumental conditioning fit with the findings about the importance of predictability in classical conditioning: Knowing that a CS predicts a UCS can be interpreted as showing that the organism has detected a contingency between the two stimuli. In both classical and instrumental conditioning, what the organism seems to learn is a contingency between two events: In classical conditioning, a behavior is contingent on a particular stimulus; in instrumental conditioning, a behavior is contingent on a particular anticipated response.

Our ability to learn contingencies develops very early. In a study of 3-month-old infants, each infant was lying in a crib with its head on a pillow. Beneath each pillow was a switch that closed whenever the infant turned its head. For infants in the control group, whenever they turned their heads and closed the switch, a mobile on the opposite side of the crib was activated. For these infants, there was a contingency between head turning and the mobile moving—the mobile being more likely to move with a head turn than without. These infants quickly learned to turn their heads, and they reacted to the moving mobile with signs of enjoyment (they smiled and cooed). The situation is quite different for infants in the experimental group. For these infants, the mobile was made to move roughly as often as it did for infants in the control group, but whether it moved or not was not under their control: There was no contingency between head turns and the mobile movements. These infants did not learn to turn their heads more frequently, and after a while they showed no signs of enjoying the moving mobile. The mobile appears to have gained its reinforcing character when its movement could be controlled and lost it when its movement could not be controlled.

BIOLOGICAL CONSTRAINTS

As with classical conditioning, biology imposes constraints on what may be learned through instrumental conditioning (see Shaping earlier in this chapter). These constraints involve relationships between responses and reinforcers. Consider pigeons in two experimental situations: reward learning, in which the animal acquires a response that is reinforced by food, and escape learning, in which the animal acquires a response that is reinforced by the termination of shock. In the case of reward, pigeons learn much faster if the response is pecking a key than if it is flapping their wings. In the case of escape, the opposite is true: Pigeons learn faster if the response is wing flapping than if it is pecking (Bolles, 1970).

These seem inconsistent with the assumption that the same laws of learning apply to all situations, but they make sense from an ethological perspective. The reward case with the pigeons involved eating, and pecking (but not wing flapping) is part of the birds' natural eating activities. A genetically determined connection between pecking and eating is reasonable. Similarly, the escape case involved a danger situation, and the pi-

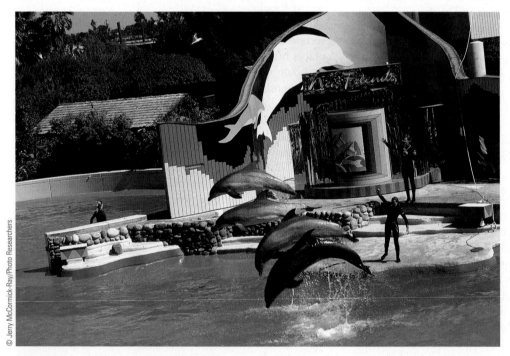

© Jerry McCormick-Ray/Photo Researchers

Instrumental conditioning and shaping are used in training animals to perform tricks of various kinds.

geon's natural reactions to danger include flapping its wings (but not pecking). Birds are known to have a small repertoire of defensive reactions, and they will quickly learn to escape only if the relevant response is one of these natural reactions.

The ethological research just discussed reveals a new way in which biological and psychological approaches can interact. Ethological concepts help us make sense of previous psychological findings. In this case, they explain why pigeons learn faster in a reward learning situation if the response is pecking but learn faster in an escape learning situation if the response is wing flapping.

◆ Interim Summary

- In instrumental conditioning, animals learn that their behavior has consequences. For example, a rat may learn to press a lever to obtain food reinforcement. The rate of response is a useful measure of response strength. The rate and pattern of responding during instrumental conditioning is determined by schedules of reinforcement.

- Reinforcers increase the probability of a response, whereas punishers decrease the probability of behavioral responses. Reinforcers and punishers can be arranged in either positive or negative contingencies with a particular behavior.

◆ Critical Thinking Questions

1. Suppose that you are taking care of an 8-year-old who won't make his bed and, in fact, doesn't seem to know how to begin the task. How might you use instrumental conditioning techniques to teach him to make his bed?

2. Sometimes a person may be fearful of a neutral object, such as loose buttons, but not know why. How could you explain this phenomenon in terms of principles presented in this chapter?

COMPLEX LEARNING

According to the cognitive perspective, the crux of learning—and of intelligence in general—lies in an organism's ability to mentally represent aspects of the world and then operate on these mental representations rather than on the world itself. In many cases, corresponding to classical and instrumental conditioning, what is mentally represented is an association between stimuli or events. In other cases, what is represented seems more complex. It might be a map of one's environment or an abstract concept like the notion of cause. Also, the operations performed on mental representa-

tions are sometimes more complex than associative processes. The operations may take the form of a mental trial and error, in which the organism tries out different possibilities in its mind. Or the operations may be a strategy in which we take some mental steps only because they make possible subsequent steps. The idea of a strategy in particular seems at odds with the assumption that complex learning is built out of simple associations. In what follows, we consider some learning phenomena that point to the need to consider nonassociative representations and operations. Some of these phenomena involve animals, and others involve humans performing tasks that are similar to conditioning.

COGNITIVE MAPS AND ABSTRACT CONCEPTS

An early advocate of the cognitive approach to learning was Edward Tolman, whose research dealt with the problem of rats learning their way through complex mazes (Tolman, 1932). In his view, a rat running through a complex maze was not learning a sequence of right- and left-turning responses but rather was developing a **cognitive map**—a mental representation of the layout of the maze.

More recent research provides strong evidence for this view. Consider the maze diagrammed in Figure 7-9. It is a central platform with eight identical arms radiating outward. On each trial, the researcher places food at the end of each arm. The rat needs to learn to visit each arm (and obtain the food there) without returning to those it has already visited. Rats learn to do so remarkably well; after 20 trials, they virtually never return to an arm they have already visited. (Rats do this even when the maze has been doused with aftershave lotion to mask the odor cues about which arms still have food.) Most important, a rat rarely employs the strategy that would occur to humans—such as always going through the arms in an obvious order (say, clockwise). Instead, the rat visits the arms randomly, indicating that it has not learned a rigid sequence of responses. What, then, has it learned? Probably it has developed a maplike representation of the maze that specifies the spatial relations between arms, and on each trial it makes a mental note of which arm it has visited (Olton, 1979, 1978).

More recent studies of primates provide even stronger evidence for complex mental representations. Particularly striking are those showing that chimpanzees can acquire abstract concepts that were once believed to be the sole province of humans. In a typical study, chimpanzees learn to use plastic tokens of different shapes, sizes, and colors as words. For example, they might learn that one token refers to "apples" and another to "paper," even though there is no physical resemblance between the

Figure 7-9
A Maze for Studying Cognitive Maps
With food placed at the end of every arm, the rat's problem is to find all the food without retracing its steps. The pattern shown here reflects perfect learning: This rat visited each arm of the maze only once, eating whatever it found there; it did not go back to an empty arm even one time. (From *Brain, Mind, and Behavior* by Bloom and Lazerton. Copyright © 1988 by Educational Broadcasting Corporation. Used with permission of W. H. Freeman and Company.)

token and the object. The fact that chimpanzees can learn these references suggests that they understand concrete concepts such as "apple" and "paper." More impressive, they can also learn abstract concepts such as "same," "different," and "cause." Chimpanzees can learn to use their

Using the technique developed by Premack, an experimenter tests a chimpanzee's ability to use language by manipulating plastic chips that represent specific words.

"same" token when presented with either two "apple" tokens or two "orange" ones, and their "different" token when presented with one "apple" and one "orange" token. Likewise, chimpanzees seem to understand causal relations. They apply the token for "cause" when shown scissors and some cut paper but not when shown scissors and some intact paper (Premack, 1985; Premack & Premack, 1983).

INSIGHT LEARNING

While many early researchers tried to study complex learning with species far removed from humans, such as rats and pigeons, others assumed that the best evidence for complex learning would come from research with primates. Wolfgang Köhler's work with chimpanzees, carried out in the 1920s, remains particularly important. The problems that Köhler set for his chimpanzees left some room for insight, because no parts of the problem were hidden from view. (In contrast, the workings of a food dispenser in a Skinner box are hidden from the animal's view.) Typically, Köhler placed a chimpanzee in an enclosed area with a desirable piece of fruit, often a banana, out of reach. To obtain the fruit, the animal had to use a nearby object as a tool. Usually the chimpanzee solved the problem in a way that suggested that the animal had some insight. The following description by Köhler is typical:

> Sultan [Köhler's most intelligent chimpanzee] is squatting at the bars but cannot reach the fruit which lies outside by means of his only available short stick. A longer stick is deposited outside the bars, about two meters on one side of the object and parallel with the grating. It cannot be grasped with the hand, but it can be pulled within reach by means of the small stick. [See Figure 7-10 for an illustration of a similar multiple stick problem.] Sultan tries to reach the fruit with the smaller of the two sticks. Not succeeding, he tears at a piece of wire that projects from the netting of his cage, but that too is in vain. Then he gazes about him (there are always in the course of these tests some long pauses, during which the animals scrutinize the whole visible area). He suddenly picks up the little stick once more, goes up to the bars directly opposite to the long stick, scratches it towards him with the "auxiliary," seizes it, and goes with it to the point opposite the objective (the fruit), which he secures. From the moment that his eyes fall upon the long stick, his procedure forms one consecutive whole, without hiatus, and although the angling of the bigger stick by means of the smaller is an action that could be complete and distinct in itself, yet observation shows that it follows, quite suddenly, on an interval of hesitation and doubt—staring about—which undoubtedly has a relation to the final objective, and is immediately merged in the final action of the attainment of the end goal. (Köhler, 1925, pp. 174–175)

In several respects, the performance of these chimpanzees is unlike the responses of Thorndike's cats or

Figure 7-10
The Multiple Stick Problem
Using the shorter sticks, the chimpanzee pulls in a stick long enough to reach the piece of fruit. It has learned to solve this problem by understanding the relationship between the sticks and the piece of fruit.

Skinner's rats and pigeons. For one thing, the solution was sudden rather than the result of a gradual trial-and-error process. Another point is that once a chimpanzee solved a problem, thereafter it would solve the problem with few irrelevant moves. This is most unlike a rat in a Skinner box, which continues to make irrelevant responses for many trials. Also, Köhler's chimpanzees could readily transfer what they had learned to a novel situation. In one problem, Sultan was not caged, but some bananas were placed too high for him to reach, as shown in Figure 7-11. To solve the problem, Sultan stacked some boxes that were strewn around him, climbed the "platform," and grabbed the bananas. In subsequent problems, if the fruit was again too high to reach, Sultan found other objects to use in constructing a platform. In some cases, Sultan used a table and a small ladder, and in one case Sultan pulled Köhler himself over and used the experimenter as a platform!

The chimpanzee's solution has three critical aspects: its suddenness, its availability once discovered, and its transferability. These aspects are at odds with trial-and-error behaviors of the type observed by Thorndike, Skinner, and their students. Instead, the chimpanzee's solutions may reflect a mental trial and error. The animal forms a mental representation of the problem, manipulates components of the representation until it hits upon a solution, and then enacts the solution in the real world. The solution appears sudden because the researchers do not have access to the chimpanzee's mental processes. The solution is available thereafter because a mental representation persists over time. And the solution is transferable because the representation is either abstract enough to cover more than the original situation or malleable enough to be extended to a novel situation.

Köhler's work suggests that complex learning often involves two phases. In the initial phase, problem solv-

Figure 7-11
A Chimpanzee Constructing a Platform
To reach the bananas hanging from the ceiling, the chimpanzee stacks boxes to form a platform.

"Deep Blue," IBM's chess-playing computer, applied artificial intelligence to defeat chess master Garry Kasparov. Kasparov believed that the computer had actually learned to formulate strategy rather than simply following the rules for playing chess that were programmed into it.

ing is used to arrive at a solution. In the second phase, the solution is stored in memory and retrieved whenever a similar problem situation presents itself. Hence, complex learning is intimately related to memory and thinking (the topics of the next two chapters). Moreover, this two-phase structure characterizes not just chimpanzee learning but many cases of complex learning in humans. Indeed, it has been incorporated into artificial intelligence programs that try to simulate human learning (Rosenbloom, Laird, Newell, &McCarl, 1991).

Prior Beliefs

Research on animal learning has tended to emphasize the learning of perfectly predictable relations. In most studies of classical conditioning, the CS is followed by the UCS 100% of the time. But in real life the relationships between stimuli or events usually are less than perfectly predictable. The study of associative learning with less than perfect relationships has been conducted mainly with humans. Many of these studies have used tasks that are quite novel and do not make much contact with the learner's prior beliefs. In such cases, participants are very sensitive to the degree of the objective relationship between the stimuli (Shanks & Dickinson, 1987; Wasserman, 1990). But our concern here is with studies that use tasks that *do* make contact with the learner's prior beliefs. These studies show that prior beliefs can determine what is learned, which indicates that learning involves processes in addition to those that form associations between inputs.

In these studies, a different pair of stimuli—say, a picture and a description of a person—is presented on each trial, and the participant's task is to learn the relationship between the members of the pairs—say, that pictures of tall men tend to be associated with brief descriptions. Some striking evidence for the role of prior beliefs comes from cases in which, objectively, there is no relationship between the stimuli, yet participants "learn" such a relationship. In one experiment, participants were concerned with the possible relationship between the drawings that mental patients made and the symptoms the patients displayed. On each trial, participants were presented with a patient's drawing of a person and one of six symptoms, including "suspiciousness of other people" and "concerned with being taken care of." The participant's task was to determine whether any aspects of the drawings were associated with any of the symptoms. In fact, the six symptoms had been randomly paired with the drawings so that there was no association between them. Yet participants consistently reported such associations, and the relationships they reported were ones that they probably believed before participating in the experiment—for example, that large eyes are associated with suspiciousness or that a large mouth is associated with a desire to be taken care of by others. These nonexistent but plausible relationships are referred to as *spurious associations* (Chapman & Chapman, 1969).

In the preceding study, prior beliefs about the stimuli determined what was "learned." Because prior beliefs are part of one's knowledge, these results attest to the cognitive nature of such learning. However, the study does not say anything about how learning proceeds when there is in fact an objective association to be learned. This issue was analyzed in the following research.

On each of a set of trials, participants were presented with two measures of an individual's honesty taken from two completely different situations. For example, one measure might have been how often a young boy copied another student's homework in school, and the second an indication of how often that same boy was dishonest at home. Most people believe (erroneously) that two measures of the same trait (such as honesty) will always be highly correlated. This is the critical prior belief. In fact, the objective relationship between the two measures of honesty varied across different conditions of the experiment, sometimes being quite low, and the participants' task was to estimate the strength of this relationship by choosing a number between 0 (which indicated no relation) and 100 (a perfect relation). The results showed that participants consistently overestimated the strength of the relationship. Their prior belief that an honest person is honest in all situations led them to see more than was there (Jennings, Amabile, & Ross, 1982).

In the preceding study, sometimes the learner's prior beliefs were not in agreement with the objective association to be learned. In these cases, beliefs and data were in conflict. In such situations, people typically go with their prior beliefs. If they believe that two measures of an individual's honesty should be highly related, for example, they may "detect" such a relationship even when there is no objective association. However, as the data (the objective association) are made increasingly salient, our prior beliefs are overcome, and we learn what is in fact there (Alloy & Tabachnik, 1984).

The results of these studies are reminiscent of what we called *top-down processing* in perception (see Chapter 5), in which perceivers combine their expectations of what they are likely to see with the actual input to yield a final percept. In top-down processing in learning, the learner combines prior belief about an associative relationship with the objective input about that relationship to yield a final estimate of the strength of that relationship.

The effects of prior beliefs on learning have important implications for education. In particular, when teaching someone about a topic—for example, the biology of digestion—the student's prior beliefs about the subject matter cannot be ignored. The student often tries to assimilate the new information to the earlier beliefs. Educationally, it may be best to get these prior beliefs out in the open so that the instructor can confront them if they are in fact erroneous (Genter & Stevens, 1983).

In sum, this line of research demonstrates the importance of prior beliefs in human learning and strengthens the case for a cognitive approach to learning. In a way, however, the research also has a connection to the ethological approach to learning. Just as rats and pigeons may be constrained to learn only associations that evolution has prepared them for, so we humans seem to be constrained to learn associations that our prior beliefs have prepared us for. Without prior constraints of some sort, perhaps there would simply be too many potential associations to consider, and associative learning would be chaotic, if not impossible.

◆ Interim Summary

- According to the cognitive perspective, the crux of learning is an organism's ability to represent aspects of the world mentally and then operate on these mental representations rather than on the world itself.

- When learning relationships between stimuli that are not perfectly predictive, people often invoke prior beliefs.

◆ Critical Thinking Questions

1. Do you believe that there are differences between how we learn facts and how we learn motor skills? If so, what are some of those differences?

2. When a rat learns to swim for a food reward in a T-shaped maze, it will remember the location of the reward (say, in the left arm of the T) if the maze is drained and the rat is allowed to run for the food. What does this tell you about the nature of the learning that has occurred?

As we have seen in this chapter, recent studies of brain anatomy and physiology have led to new insight into how the brain executes complex functions, such as learning and memory. For example, neurons in the hippocampus are important for complex learning and memory in both rodents and humans. In particular, NMDA receptors participate in strengthening communication between hippocampal neurons though long-term potentiation. Can we take this knowledge to build a smarter brain? Recent work in mice by Joe Z. Tsien and colleagues at Princeton University suggest that we can (Tsien, 2000).

Tsien and colleagues have used recently developed molecular techniques to manipulate the genetic makeup of mice. First, they created mutated mouse DNA that affected the way NMDA receptors were manufactured in brain cells. They then introduced this modified DNA into a newly fertilized mouse egg. After the egg developed into an adult mouse, that mouse possessed some cells that carried the mutated DNA. By breeding these mice through many generations, they were able to generate a "transgenic" mouse that expressed the mutated DNA in all of its cells. Tsien and colleagues found that these transgenic mice, which they termed *Doogie*, expressed a high level of a special type of NMDA receptor in the hippocampus as adults. As a result, it was much easier to induce hippocampal long-term potentiation (LTP), and once induced the LTP was much greater than that observed in normal mice. Other aspects of neuronal morphology and synaptic transmission in the hippocampus appeared normal; the mice seemed to have a selective enhancement in synaptic plasticity.

The key question is how these animals would perform in learning and memory tasks. Not surprisingly, Doogie mice were found to perform better than normal mice in many tasks (hence the name Doogie, the nickname of the boy-wonder doctor portrayed by Neil Patrick Harris on the television program *Doogie Howser, M.D.*). For example, Doogie mice learned to find a hidden platform in a pool of water faster than normal mice, and they also learned more readily to fear places that predicted aversive foot shock. Inter-estingly, the smart mice also learned to rapidly suppress their fear of places paired with shock when shock delivery was halted. So the Doogie mice are much better at learning the predictive relationships between stimuli in learning tasks than genetically normal mice.

What are the implications of this discovery for humans? Although it is unethical to modify the human genome to manufacture desired traits, such as intelligence, the findings in mice provide information that may aid learning and memory in adult humans. For example, drugs that enhance the function of the hippocampal NMDA receptors manufactured by Doogie mice might be used for the treatment of learning disabilities or for patients with Alzheimer's disease. Moreover, such drugs might be used to enhance memory in nondisabled individuals. In either case, the mouse studies have paved the way for a deeper understanding of the cellular basis of human learning and memory.

 For more information, go online with InfoTrac College Edition. Use your own term or search:

- Smart brain
- Tsien, Joe

The Neural Basis of Behavior

LEARNING AND CONDITIONING

The biology of neurons and their interconnections, which proved so important in our analysis of sensation and perception, is also relevant to the study of learning, especially classical conditioning and simple forms of learning such as habituation.

Researchers believe that the neural basis of learning consists of changes in the nervous system, and increasingly they are looking for these changes at the level of neural connections. To appreciate their ideas, you need to recall from Chapter 2 the basic structure of a neural connection and how it transmits an impulse. An impulse is transmitted from one neuron to another by the axon of the sending neuron. Because the axons are separated by the synaptic gap, the sender's axon secretes a neurotransmitter, which diffuses across the gap and stimulates the receiving neuron. More precisely, when the neural impulse travels down the sender's axon, it triggers terminals at the end of the axon to release the neurotransmitter, and this neurotransmitter is picked up by receptors on the receiving neuron. This entire structure is called a *synapse*. The key ideas regarding learning are (1) that some change in the synapse is the neural basis of learning and (2) that the effect of this change is to make the synapse more (or less) efficient.

HABITUATION AND SENSITIZATION

To understand the neural basis of complex psychological phenomena, such as learning and memory, it is best to examine simple forms of learning and memory. Perhaps the most elementary form of learning is nonassociative learning, in which organisms learn about a sin-

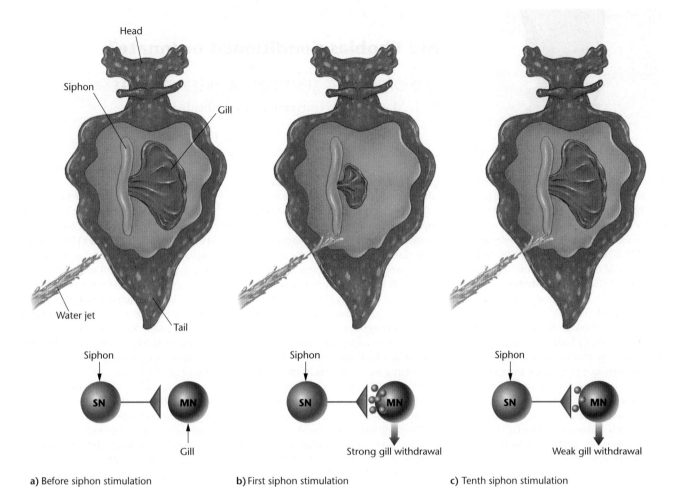

a) Before siphon stimulation   b) First siphon stimulation   c) Tenth siphon stimulation

▌Figure 7-12
Habituation and Sensitization in *Aplysia californica*
(a) Before mechanical stimulation of the siphon, the gill is extended. (b) When water is squirted on the siphon for the first time during habituation training, the gill withdraws vigorously. A simple circuit involving siphon sensory neurons (SN) that form excitatory synaptic contacts onto motor neurons (MN) mediates gill withdrawal. (c) After the 10th siphon stimulus, the magnitude of gill withdrawal is small. The gill withdrawal response has habituated. Habituation is mediated by a decrease in presynaptic neurotransmitter release at the SN-MN synapse.

gle stimulus. Habituation and sensitization are examples of this type of learning. During habituation, a behavioral response, such as orienting to an unfamiliar sound, decreases over successive presentations of that stimulus. During sensitization, a behavioral response increases during presentations of intense stimuli, such as very loud noises. In both cases, learned changes in behavior can persist for hours to days.

To study these learning processes at the neural level, a team of researchers led by Nobel Prize winner Eric Kandel has chosen to work with an organism with a very simple nervous system: the marine slug, *Aplysia californica* (Kandel, Schwartz, & Jessell, 1991). *Aplysia* has proven to be an excellent experimental model to study nonassociative learning, because it has a simple and accessible nervous system. Learning in *Aplysia* has

been studied by measuring the gill withdrawal reflex, which can be elicited by gentle mechanical stimulation of the gill or surrounding tissue. The gill withdrawal reflex is a defensive response that protects the fragile gill from injury.

When the gill is lightly stimulated with a water jet, the gill is withdrawn. However, repeated stimulation of the gill produces weaker and weaker withdrawal responses. Researchers have shown that this habituation learning is accompanied by a decrease in the amount of neurotransmitter secreted by gill sensory neurons onto a motor neuron that controls gill withdrawal (Figure 7-12).

The gill withdrawal reflex also exhibits sensitization. If an intense stimulus, such as an electric shock to the tail or head is administered, then the light touch to the gill will elicit a much larger withdrawal response. Like

Are Phobias Conditioned or Innate?

CONDITIONING SENSITIZES A PREEXISTING FEAR
N. J. Mackintosh, University of Cambridge

John Watson, the founding father of behaviorism, believed that the human infant had only a handful of innate fears—two of the main ones being a fear of loud noises and a fear of loss of support. All other fears, he argued, were learned as a result of conditioning. And to prove his point, Watson and his student, Rosalie Rayner, demonstrated the conditioning of fear in an 11-month-old infant, Albert B (Watson & Rayner, 1920). Albert was initially happy to reach out and touch any small animal brought close to him, but after seven conditioning trials on which a white rat (the CS) was presented and, if Albert reached toward it, a steel bar was sharply struck immediately behind him (the UCS), Albert began to cry and withdraw from the rat. The fear conditioned to the rat generalized to other stimuli—a rabbit, a dog, and a sealskin coat. Since then, hundreds of laboratory experiments have shown that the pairing of an arbitrary and initially neutral CS with an aversive event, such as a brief electric shock or very loud noise, will establish a conditioned fear reaction to that CS.

Watson and Rayner's study has often been cited (see Harris, 1979) as evidence that adult phobias, whether of snakes or spiders, open spaces or confined places, are based on one or more past episodes of conditioning in which, for example, a snake has been associated with some aversive consequence. There are several difficulties with this simple application of conditioning theory—one of which, it is worth noting (if only to defend Watson and Rayner against a charge of gross cruelty), is that little Albert never showed much more than mild fretting and withdrawal, even when the rat was allowed to crawl over him, and that even this modest level of fear showed little generalization when he was tested in a different room.

Studies of "vicarious conditioning" have shown that the mere sight of a nonspecific showing a fear reaction to a particular CS can act as a sufficient UCS to reinforce the conditioning of fear to that CS. Wild-born rhesus monkeys tend to be afraid of snakes. This is not an innate fear, because laboratory-born infant rhesus monkeys show no such fear. But a single experience of watching an adult displaying a fear reaction to a snake will condition a fear of snakes in the infant (Mineka, 1987). Here, then, may be one way in which parents can, unwittingly, influence the behavior of their children.

The traditional behaviorist view was that any detectable stimulus can become associated with any consequence. On the face of it, this implies another serious problem for a conditioning account of phobias, because by far the most common phobias are those directed toward animals or social situations, rather than to the myriad other objects or events (electrical outlets, the sight of one's own blood) that are more likely to have been associated with painful consequences. Does this mean that the predisposition to phobias is genetically determined? Not if that is taken to imply that we are all born with an innate fear of spiders—or else we would all have a spider phobia. Surely, it is at least in part the differences among our individual experiences that cause one person to develop a phobia of spiders, another, one of snakes, and another, none at all. But why just of spiders, snakes, and so on? Some conditioning experiments have suggested some answers to this question.

In a series of studies, Ohman and his colleagues have shown that conditioned GSRs in people are more resistant to extinction when the CS is a picture of a snake or spider than when it is a picture of flowers or mushrooms (Ohman, 1986). Cook and Mineka (1990) have provided evidence of similar selective fear in monkeys. Infant monkeys developed a fear of snakes after watching a video clip of an adult monkey displaying fear reactions to a snake but showed no fear of flowers after watching a cleverly edited video clip showing an adult monkey apparently having a panic attack at the sight of a flower.

Results such as these have been widely interpreted as evidence of a biological predisposition to associate certain classes of stimuli with certain consequences. In the evolutionary history of early hominids or other African primates, snakes and spiders were potentially dangerous, but flowers and mushrooms were not. For the learning theories, there are other questions left unanswered. Ohman's experiments have established only that fear of snakes extinguishes more slowly than fear of flowers, not that it is acquired more rapidly in the first place. Other experiments have shown that pictures of snakes are just as easily established as safety signals as are pictures of flowers (McNally & Reiss, 1984). Cook and Mineka's infant monkeys, having watched a video of adults showing fear reactions to flowers but not to snakes, *did* then show significant fear of a live snake (although no fear of flowers). Some of these findings suggest that what is happening is sensitization of a preexisting fear to certain classes of stimuli under conditions of stress or threat, rather than more rapid conditioning of fear (Lovibond, Siddle, & Bond, 1993).

Are Phobias Conditioned or Innate?

PHOBIAS ARE AN INNATE DEFENSE MECHANISM
Michael S. Fanselow, University of California, Los Angeles

The emotional experience of fear can be overwhelmingly powerful. Why does it exist? The reason must lie in the fact that fear serves some biologically important function. Fear in the face of a serious threat organizes our resources to protect against that threat. From such a vantage, fear becomes a behavioral system that evolved for the purpose of defense against environmental threats. For many animal species, one of the most serious threats is becoming the food of another species. If one fails to defend against a predator, the ability for future contributions to the gene pool is nil, and it is not surprising that very effective systems for defending against a predator have evolved. Certain brain regions are dedicated to this function, and those brain regions serve fear in species ranging from at least mice and rats to monkeys and humans. If natural selection is responsible for fear, it seems reasonable that genetic factors shape this experience.

So fear is in part defined by its biological function. But to be useful to a behavioral scientist, there need to be two other aspects to the definition. The conditions that give rise to fear must be specified—what turns on the defensive behavioral system. Also, the behaviors that result as a consequence of fear must be detailed. Natural selection has shaped the answer to these questions with genetic encoding of what we are born to fear, what we come to fear, and how we behave when afraid.

Defending against predation is urgent. You must react quickly with effective behavior. Slow, trial-and-error learning by reinforcement simply will not do.

A species that relied on such learning would likely be the subject of a paleontologist rather than a psychologist. First, you must recognize threats quickly. Animals have an uncanny ability to recognize their natural predators. In one study, deer mice were trapped on two sides of the Cascade Mountains of Washington. Snakes are a natural predator of the eastern mice but not of the western mice. On the other hand, western mice have to contend with weasels. The mice were bred for one generation in the laboratory, and their offspring were tested for fear of a range of predators and nonpredators. Although these animals had no experience outside the lab and had never encountered a predator before, they displayed defensive responses specifically to the predators of their parents' habitat. This innate "phobia" is not lost when selection pressure is eased; even the highly domesticated laboratory rat shows fear on its first encounter with a cat. Although it is not possible to perform such experiments with humans, the fact that phobias are far more common for some stimuli than for others suggests that we have similar dispositions.

This is not to say that fear of environmental stimuli is never learned. But this learning is genetically constrained and specialized. Learning of fear is rapid and occurs with a single aversive experience, reflecting the evolutionary urgency of defense. Despite the rapidity of this learning, the sort of stimuli we learn to fear is heavily constrained. In the famous "little Albert study" described by Dr. Mackintosh, Watson and Rayner conditioned a baby boy to fear a white rat by pairing it with a loud noise. But although fear of a rat is easily acquired, the same methods do not result in conditioned fear to many other stimuli. Similar predispositions are found in other primates, for as Dr. Mackintosh also explained, monkeys readily learn to become afraid of snakes but not of flowers. Even when a researcher chooses a domesticated laboratory rat and uses a seemingly arbitrary stimulus such as electric shock, there is selectivity in association formation. Rats more readily learn to fear noises than lights, which fare better as safety signals.

If fear has to protect us against a very imminent threat, we are unlikely to have the opportunity to learn what behaviors are effective and what behaviors are not. The trial-and-error learner is doomed. Rather, specialized defensive behaviors are already programmed into the species, and they are executed as soon as fear is activated. A rat freezes the first time it encounters a cat—cats are attracted to moving targets. This is a response to fear, as the rat will show the same freezing response to a noise that has been paired with shock. Although rats are known to be adept lever pressers when asked to work for food, they are horrendous if asked to make the same response to avoid shock. Of course, manipulation of small objects probably never did much for the rats' ancestors when they were faced with a predator. Similarly, I speculate that I would be more likely to solve a complex calculus problem if the inducement was a fine wine rather than avoidance of an armed attacker.

habituation, sensitization learning involves a change in synaptic transmission between sensory and motor neurons that control the gill. In this case, the intense stimulus causes an increase in the amount of neurotransmitter secreted by the sensory neuron. This increase depends on the activation of interneurons that release serotonin onto the gill sensory neurons. These findings provide relatively direct evidence that elementary learning is mediated by synaptic changes at the neuronal level.

CLASSICAL CONDITIONING

What about associative learning? Do synaptic changes like the ones just described mediate classical conditioning? The fact that classical conditioning is similar to sensitization—both involve changing one's response to a weak stimulus on the basis of a stronger stimulus—suggests that the two kinds of learning might have a similar neural basis. Indeed, researchers have proposed a neural model of classical conditioning in *Aplysia* that is remarkably similar to that for sensitization (Hawkins & Kandel, 1984). Incredible progress has also been made in understanding the neural mechanisms of classical conditioning in mammals, including humans. Two experimental models have been used with great success: eyeblink conditioning and fear conditioning.

EYEBLINK CONDITIONING When a stimulus, such as an air puff (the UCS), is directed at the eye, it elicits a reflexive blink. This unconditional eyeblink response can be conditioned if a CS, such as a tone, precedes the puff. After training, the CS will come to elicit eyeblink CRs even when the air puff is not presented.

Detailed mapping studies in rabbits by Richard Thompson and colleagues have revealed the neural circuitry in this form of classical conditioning (Thompson & Krupa, 1994). The essential site of synaptic plasticity appears to reside in the cerebellum. Animals with cerebellar lesions cannot learn or remember the conditioned eyeblink (although they show normal eyeblink UCRs). Interestingly, eyeblink conditioning is associated with changes in synaptic transmission in the cerebellum. This change is called **long-term depression** and is associated with a long-lasting decrease in synaptic transmission at synapses in the cerebellar cortex. This change occurs in the pathway that transmits information about the CS to cerebellar cortical neurons. The decrease in CS transmission in the cerebellar cortex results in a behavioral CR because the cerebellar cortex normally inhibits the CR-producing part of the eyeblink conditioning circuit.

FEAR CONDITIONING As we saw in earlier in this chapter, emotional responses such as fear are easily conditioned. Laboratory work with rats has yielded important insights into the brain mechanisms of this sort of learning. In this model, rats are conditioned to fear a place or a cue that has been paired with an aversive stimulus, such as foot shock. Fear is often assessed by measuring freezing behavior—the immobility that rodents show when they are afraid.

As in the eyeblink conditioning paradigm, a specific brain area is essential for learning and remembering fearful experiences. In this case, it is the amygdala, a limbic system structure deep within the temporal lobes that is important for emotions, including fear (Klüver & Bucy, 1937). The amygdala receives sensory information from thalamic and cortical brain areas, associates these stimuli, and translates these associations into fear responses mediated by the hypothalamus, midbrain, and medulla (Figure 7-13). Animals with amygdala damage cannot learn or remember fear memories (Davis, 1997; Fendt & Fanselow, 1999; Maren, 2001; Maren & Fanselow, 1996). Moreover, neurons in the amygdala exhibit many changes during new fear learning. For example, amygdala neurons increase their activity in response to CSs that have been associated with aversive UCSs. It appears that learning in the amygdala is mediated by **long-term potentiation** (LTP) (see Cellular Basis of Learning later in this chapter), which is a persistent increase in synaptic transmission in pathways that send CS information to the amygdala (Rogan & LeDoux, 1996). Hence, in both eyeblink conditioning and fear conditioning, changes in synaptic transmission in defined brain areas are responsible for the behavioral changes that accompany associative learning.

Another study shows that what holds for other mammals applies to humans as well (Bechara et al., 1995). This study involved a human patient, referred to as S.M., who had a rare disorder (Urbach-Wiethe

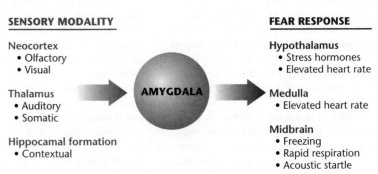

▌ Figure 7-13
Neural Circuit for Classical Fear Conditioning
The amygdala receives sensory information from many sensory areas, including the thalamus, neocortex, and hippocampus. The amygdala associates this information during fear conditioning and then generates fear CRs by projecting to brain areas, such as the midbrain, hypothalamus, and medulla, that mediate a number of different fear responses.

disease) that results in degeneration of the amygdala. S.M. was exposed to a fear-conditioning situation in which a neutral visual stimulus (the CS) was predictably followed by the sound of a loud horn (the UCS). Despite repeated trials, S.M. showed no evidence of fear conditioning. Yet S.M. had no trouble recalling the events associated with the fear conditioning, including the relationship between the conditioned and unconditioned stimuli. Another patient, who had a normal amygdala but had suffered damage to a brain structure involved in the learning of factual material, showed normal fear conditioning but was unable to recall the events associated with the conditioning. The two patients had the opposite problems, indicating that the amygdala is involved in the learning of fear, not learning in general.

Cellular Basis of Learning

As we have seen, learning results in changes in synaptic transmission in both slugs and mammals. We have not been very specific about what causes these changes in synaptic transmission. There are several possibilities. One is that learning results in an increase in the amount of neurotransmitter secreted by the sending neuron, perhaps because of an increase in the number of axon terminals that secrete the neurotransmitter. Alternatively, there may be no increase in the amount of neurotransmitter sent, but there may be an increase in the number of postsynaptic receptors. Other possibilities are that the synapse could change in size or that entirely new synapses could be established. All of these changes are examples of **synaptic plasticity,** or changes in the morphology and/or physiology of synapses involved in learning and memory. Indeed, learning may be accompanied by the growth of new neurons (see Chapter 2, Cutting Edge Research).

A critical advance in understanding the cellular basis of memory was the finding that synapses in several brain areas can exhibit long-lasting increases in synaptic transmission under some conditions (Berger, 1984; Bliss & Lømo, 1973). For example, rapid electrical stimulation of synapses in the hippocampus causes an enhancement in the magnitude of synaptic responses that lasts for days or even weeks (Figure 7-14). This phenomenon, termed *long-term potentiation* or LTP, requires a special type of neurotransmitter receptor, the NMDA receptor (Malinow, Otmakhov, Blum, & Lisman, 1994; Zalutsky & Nicoll, 1990). The NMDA receptor is unlike other receptors, in that two conditions must be satisfied for the receptor to open. First, presynaptic glutamate must bind to the NMDA receptor, and, second, the postsynaptic membrane in which the receptor resides must be strongly depolarized. Once opened, the NMDA receptor allows a very large number of calcium ions to flow into the neuron. That influx of ions appears to cause a long-term change in the membrane of the neuron, making it more responsive to the initial signal when it recurs at a later time (see Figure 7-14). Interestingly, activation of NMDA receptors could arise during classical conditioning, in which weak (CS) and strong (UCS) inputs converge onto single neurons. In this case, LTP would be induced at synapses transmitting CS information because conditioning would result in both presynaptic activity (during the CS) and postsynaptic depolarization (during the UCS) in the neurons upon which CS and UCS information converge (Maren & Fanselow, 1996).

Such a mechanism, in which two divergent signals strengthen a synapse, provides a possible explanation of how separate events become associated in memory. For example, learning someone's name requires that you make an association between the person's appearance and his or her name. LTP strengthens synapses so that the sight of the person will prompt you to recall the person's name. In classical fear conditioning, an association is established between a relatively neutral CS and an aversive UCS. The NMDA mechanism thus offers an intriguing theory to explain how events are associated in memory—a theory that current research is actively pursuing (Maren, 1999).

◆ Interim Summary

- Habituation is mediated by a decrease in synaptic transmission, and sensitization by an increase in transmission. Regression and growth, respectively, of synapses are also involved in these types of learning.

- Synapses in the mammalian brain are involved in storing information during learning. Increases in synaptic transmission, such as long-term potentiation, are part of these learning processes.

◆ Critical Thinking Questions

1. The induction of long-term potentiation requires that presynaptic activity and postsynaptic depolarization happen together in time. However, we have seen that classical conditioning requires more than co-occurrence of stimuli—the CS has to predict the US. How does this affect your willingness to accept LTP as a model for classical conditioning?

2. The cellular mechanisms of learning appear to be similar in a wide range of animal species. For example, learning in the sea slug and the rat are mediated by changes in synaptic transmission. Why are these learning mechanisms so similar?

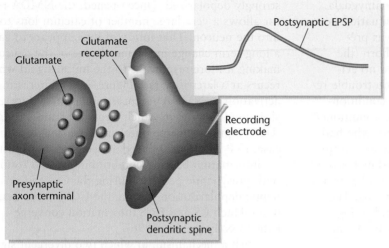

a) Before high-frequency stimulation

Glutamate
Glutamate receptor
Postsynaptic EPSP
Recording electrode
Presynaptic axon terminal
Postsynaptic dendritic spine

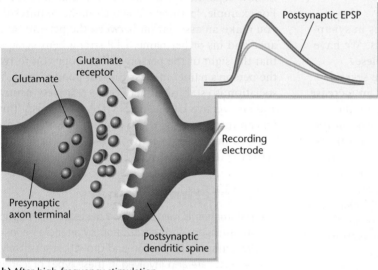

b) After high-frequency stimulation

Glutamate
Glutamate receptor
Postsynaptic EPSP
Recording electrode
Presynaptic axon terminal
Postsynaptic dendritic spine

c) EPSP amplitude

EPSP amplitude (mV)
HFS
Time (min)

❚ **Figure 7-14**
Long-term Potentiation in Hippocampus

(a) Before high-frequency stimulation (HFS), presynaptic glutamate release activates postsynaptic glutamate receptors to produce an excitatory postsynaptic potential (EPSP). (b) After high-frequency stimulation of the presynaptic neuron, the postsynaptic EPSP is greatly increased in amplitude. This increase is due to an enhancement of presynaptic neurotransmitter release and an increase in the number of postsynaptic glutamate receptors. (c) Graph illustrating the amplitude of the EPSP before and after HFS. Long-term potentiation is indicated by the persistent increase in EPSP amplitude.

1. Learning may be defined as a relatively permanent change in behavior that is the result of practice. There are four basic kinds of learning: (a) habituation, in which an organism learns to ignore a familiar and inconsequential stimulus; (b) classical conditioning, in which an organism learns that one stimulus follows another; (c) instrumental conditioning, in which an organism learns that a particular response leads to a particular consequence; and (d) complex learning, in which learning involves more than the formation of associations.

2. Early research on learning was done from a behaviorist perspective. It often assumed that behavior is better understood in terms of external causes than internal ones, that simple associations are the building blocks of all learning, and that the laws of learning are the same for different species and different situations. These assumptions have been modified in light of subsequent work. The contemporary analysis of learning includes cognitive factors and biological constraints, as well as behaviorist principles.

3. In Pavlov's experiments, if a conditioned stimulus (CS) consistently precedes an unconditioned stimulus (UCS), the CS comes to serve as a signal for the UCS and will elicit a conditioned response (CR) that often resembles the unconditioned response (UCR). Stimuli that are similar to the CS also elicit the CR to some extent, although discrimination training can curb such generalization. These phenomena occur in organisms as diverse as flatworms and humans.

4. Cognitive factors also play a role in conditioning. For classical conditioning to occur, the CS must be a reliable predictor of the UCS; that is, there must be a higher probability that the UCS will occur when the CS has been presented than when it has not.

5. According to ethologists, what an animal learns is constrained by its genetically determined "behavioral blueprint." Evidence for such constraints on classical conditioning comes from studies of taste aversion. Although rats readily learn to associate the feeling of being sick with the taste of a solution, they cannot learn to associate sickness with a light. Conversely, birds can learn to associate light and sickness but not taste and sickness.

6. Instrumental conditioning deals with situations in which the response operates on the environment rather than being elicited by an unconditioned stimulus. The earliest systematic studies were performed by Thorndike, who showed that animals engage in trial-and-error behavior and that any behavior that is fol-

lowed by reinforcement is strengthened; this is known as the law of effect.

7. In Skinner's experiments, typically a rat or pigeon learns to make a simple response, such as pressing a lever, to obtain reinforcement. The rate of response is a useful measure of response strength. Shaping is a training procedure that is used when the desired response is novel; it involves reinforcing only variations in response that deviate in the direction desired by the experimenter.

8. A number of phenomena can increase the generality of instrumental conditioning. One is conditioned reinforcement, in which a stimulus associated with a reinforcer acquires its own reinforcing properties. Other relevant phenomena are generalization and discrimination; organisms generalize responses to similar situations, although this generalization can be brought under the control of a discriminative stimulus. Finally, there are schedules of reinforcement. Once a behavior is established, it can be maintained when it is reinforced only part of the time. Exactly when the reinforcement comes is determined by its schedule; the basic types of reinforcement schedules are fixed ratio, variable ratio, fixed interval, and variable interval schedules.

9. There are three kinds of aversive conditioning. In punishment, a response is followed by an aversive event, which results in the response being suppressed. In escape, an organism learns to make a response in order to terminate an ongoing aversive event. In avoidance, an organism learns to make a response to prevent the aversive event from even starting.

10. Cognitive factors play a role in instrumental conditioning. For instrumental conditioning to occur, the organism must believe that reinforcement is at least partly under its control; that is, it must perceive a contingency between its responses and the reinforcement. Biological constraints are also a factor in instrumental conditioning. There are constraints on what reinforcers can be associated with what responses. With pigeons, when the reinforcement is food, learning is faster if the response is pecking a key rather than flapping the wings, but when the reinforcement is termination of shock, learning is faster when the response is wing flapping rather than pecking a key.

11. According to the cognitive perspective, the crux of learning is an organism's ability to represent aspects of the world mentally and then operate on these mental representations rather than on the world itself. In complex learning, the mental representations depict more

than associations, and the mental operations may constitute a strategy. Studies of complex learning in animals indicate that rats can develop a cognitive map of their environment, as well as acquire abstract concepts such as cause. Other studies demonstrate that chimpanzees can solve problems through insight and then generalize the solutions to similar problems.

12. When learning relationships between stimuli that are not perfectly predictive, people often invoke prior beliefs. This can lead to the detection of relationships that are not objectively present (spurious associations). When the relationship is objectively present, having a prior belief about it can lead to overestimating its predictive strength; when an objective relationship conflicts with a prior belief, the learner may favor the prior belief. These effects demonstrate top-down processing in learning.

13. The neural mechanisms of nonassociative forms of learning have been studied in invertebrate slugs. Habituation is mediated by a decrease in synaptic transmission, and sensitization by an increase in transmission. Regression and growth, respectively, of synapses are also involved in these types of learning.

14. Synapses in the mammalian brain take part in storing information during learning. The cerebellum is particularly important for motor conditioning, and the amygdala is essential for emotional conditioning. Increases in synaptic transmission, termed long-term potentiation, are involved in these learning processes.

CORE CONCEPTS

learning

nonassociative learning

habituation

sensitization

associative learning

classical conditioning

unconditioned response

unconditioned stimulus

conditioned response

conditioned stimulus

extinction

spontaneous recovery

second-order conditioning

generalization

discrimination

excitatory conditioning

inhibitory conditioning

instrumental conditioning

law of effect

reinforcement

positive reinforcement

negative reinforcement

punishment

omission training

shaping

conditioned reinforcer

ratio schedules

fixed ratio schedule

variable ratio schedule

interval schedules

fixed interval schedule

variable interval schedule

cognitive map

long-term depression

long-term potentiation

synaptic plasticity

WEB RESOURCES

http://psychology.wadsworth.com/
atkinson14e

Take a quiz, try the activities and exercises, and explore web links.

http://www.as.wvu.edu/~sbb/comm221/
chapters/pavlov.htm

By now we should know what Pavlov's dogs do when they hear a bell, but do we know what an average teacher does when he hears a bell? Monitor the hall, of course! Learn more about how classical conditioning can influence your actions.

http://psych.athabascau.ca/html/prtut/
reinpair.htm

Professor Grant at Athabusa University discusses positive reinforcement on this site. After you have read the information, try the practice exercise to test your knowledge.

http://www.nobel.se/medicine/laureates/1904/
pavlov-bio.html

Here you will find everything you everwanted to know about the life of Ivan Pavlov.

InfoTrac Online Library
http://www.infotrac-college.com/
wadsworth

Use InfoTrac College Edition to find popular and scientific articles by using the search terms below or your own relevant terms.

- Classical conditioning
- Habituation
- Operant conditioning
- Schedule of reinforcement

CD-ROM LINKS

Psych Odyssey

Check out CD Chapter 6, Learning
  A. Classical Conditioning
B. Operant Conditioning

Psyk.trek 2.0

Check out CD Unit 5, Learning
  5a Overview of Classical Conditioning
5b Basic Processes in Classical Conditioning
5c Overview of Operant Conditioning
5d Schedules of Reinforcement
5e Reinforcement and Punishment
5f Avoidance and Escape Learning

© Firefly Productions/CORBIS

MEMORY

CHAPTER OUTLINE

A Memory Error with Far-Reaching Consequences

In December of 1986, Ronald Cotton went on trial in Burlington, North Carolina, accused of brutally raping a college student named Jennifer Thompson. Ms. Thompson testified that during her ordeal, which occurred in the nighttime darkness of her apartment bedroom, she intently studied the rapist's face. In a *New York Times* Op Ed column, written 15 years later, she stated, "I looked at his hairline; I looked for scars, for tattoos, for anything that would help me identify him." Based on what she presumed to be the resulting very strong memory of her attacker's appearance, she confidently identified Mr. Cotton as the man who raped her. Based on Ms. Thompson's identification, Mr. Cotton, despite a strong alibi for the night in question, was convicted and was sentenced by an Alamance County Superior Court to serve life plus 54 years.

On the face of it, it would seem that the jury did the right thing in convicting Mr. Cotton: Alibi or no, Ms. Thompson's identification was pretty convincing. She described the vivid memory she had formed of her attacker's appearance, she eventually picked Mr. Cotton out of a collection of police photos, she picked him again out of a police lineup, and her trial testimony left the jury with no doubt that she believed she had picked the right man. As she later wrote, "I knew this was the man. I was completely confident. I was sure. . . . If there was the possibility of a death sentence, I wanted him to die. I wanted to flip the switch."

As the years passed, Ronald Cotton appealed his conviction from his jail cell, always maintaining his innocence. Eventually, another man, a prison inmate named Bobby Poole, was discovered to have boasted to his cellmates about having committed the rape for which Mr. Cotton had been convicted. As a precaution, Jennifer Thompson was shown Mr. Poole and asked about the possibility that he, not Mr. Cotton, could have been her attacker. Ms. Thompson stuck to her guns, proclaiming confidently, "I have never seen this man [Bobby Poole] in my life. I have no idea who he is."

But Jennifer Thompson was wrong, both in her identification of Ronald Cotton and in her rejection of Bobby Poole as the man who raped her. After serving 11 years in prison, Mr. Cotton was exonerated of the crime by the emerging science of DNA matching. Moreover, the same evidence confirmed that Bobby Poole was indeed the rapist. Jennifer Thompson, finally convinced of her false memory but profoundly shocked by it, became a strong advocate of extreme caution when convicting a defendant solely on the basis of someone's memory.

In their landmark book, *Actual Innocence*, Barry Scheck, Peter Newfeld, and Jim Dwyer described the Innocence Project, a program devoted to using DNA evidence as a means of exonerating the falsely accused. In their accounts of Ronald Cotton's and dozens of others' similar plights, the authors note, "In a study of DNA exonerations, by the Innocence Project, 84% of the wrongful convictions rested, at least in part, on mistaken identification by an eyewitness or victim," and go on to point out that "dramatic as these results are, they only confirm a century of social science research and judicial fact finding." It is, in large part, this research with which we are concerned in this chapter. Our memories are usually more or less correct—if they weren't, we'd have a tough go of it through life. However, they are incorrect more often than we might think, and sometimes the consequences of incorrect memories are dramatic.

A moment's thought should convince you that memory is the most critical mental facility we possess with regard to our ability to operate as humans. We make almost all decisions about what to do based on memory of one sort or another. Even a person deprived of the sensory input that most of us take for granted—a blind and deaf person like Helen Keller—is entirely capable of living a superbly fulfilling life. In contrast, as is attested by anyone who knows a person ravaged by Alzheimer's disease, even with normal sensory input, lack of memory is profoundly debilitating.

It is not surprising, therefore, that memory is the focus of a great of research, both in psychology and in the biological sciences, and in this chapter we describe a small portion of that research. To appreciate the scientific study of memory, however, we need to understand how researchers divide the field into manageable units.

THREE IMPORTANT DISTINCTIONS

ENCODING → **STORAGE** → **RETRIEVAL**
Put into memory | Maintain in memory | Recover from memory

■ **Figure 8-1**
Three Stages of Memory
Theories of memory attribute forgetting to a failure at one or more of these stages. (A. W. Melton (1963) "Implication of Short-Term Memory for a General Theory of Memory" from *Journal of Verbal Learning and Verbal Behavior*, 2:1-21. Adapted by permission of the Academic Press.)

Psychologists today make three major distinctions about memory. The first concerns three stages of memory: encoding, storage, and retrieval. The second deals with different memories for storing information for short and long periods. The third distinction is about different memories being used to store different kinds of information (for example, one system for facts and another for skills). For each of these distinctions, there is evidence that the entities being distinguished—say, working versus long-term memory—are mediated in part by different structures in the brain.

THREE STAGES OF MEMORY

Suppose that you are introduced to another student and told that her name is Barbara Cohn. That afternoon you see her again and say something like, "You're Barbara Cohn. We met this morning." Clearly, you have remembered her name. But how exactly did you remember it?

This memory feat can be broken into three stages (see Figure 8-1). First, when you were introduced, you somehow entered Barbara Cohn's name into memory. This is the **encoding stage,** when environmental information is translated into and stored as a meaningful entity. You transformed a physical input (sound waves) corresponding to her spoken name into the kind of code or representation that memory accepts, and you "placed" that representation in memory. You likewise transformed

another physical input, the pattern of light corresponding to her face, into a memory for her face, and you connected the two representations. Second, you retained—or stored—the information corresponding to her name and her face during the time between the two meetings. This is the **storage stage,** when stored information is maintained over time. Third, based on the stored representation of her face, you recognized her in the afternoon as someone you had met in the morning and, based on this recognition, you recovered her name from storage. All of this is the **retrieval stage,** when you attempt to pull from your memory information that you previously encoded and stored there.

Memory can fail at any of these three stages. Had you been unable to recall Barbara's name at the second meeting, this could have reflected a failure in encoding (you didn't properly store her face to begin with), in storage (you forgot her name somewhere along the way), or retrieval (you hadn't connected her name to her face in such a way that you could conjure up one from the other). Much of current research on memory attempts to specify the mental operations that occur at each of the three stages of memory and to explain how these operations can go awry and result in memory failure.

Recent studies suggest that the different stages of memory are mediated by different structures in the brain. The most striking evidence comes from brain-scanning studies that involve **positron emission tomography (PET)** or **functional magnetic resonance imaging (fMRI),** in which measures of brain activity are recorded while participants are engaged in tasks. These experiments involve two parts. In the first, which focuses on encoding, participants study a set of verbal items—for example, pairs consisting of categories and uncommon instances (furniture-sideboard). In the second, which focuses on retrieval, participants have to recognize or recall the items when cued with the category name. In both parts, the most striking finding is that during encoding most of the activated brain regions are in the left hemisphere, whereas during retrieval most of the activated brain areas are in the right hemisphere (Shallice et al., 1994; Tulving et al., 1994a, 1994b). The distinction between encoding and retrieval has a clear-cut biological bias.

Memory has three stages. The first stage, encoding, consists of placing a fact in memory. This occurs when we study. The second stage is storage, when the fact is retained in memory. The third stage, retrieval, occurs when the fact is recovered from storage—for example, when we take an exam.

Argentinian pianist Daniel Barenboim in concert. Recent evidence indicates that we use a different long-term memory for storing skills like the ability to play the piano than we do for retaining facts.

THREE MEMORY STORES

The three stages of memory do not operate the same way in all situations. Memory processes differ between situations that require us to store material (1) for less than a second, (2) for a matter of seconds, and (3) for longer intervals ranging from minutes to years.

THE ATKINSON-SHIFFRIN THEORY The basis for the distinction between different memories corresponding to different time intervals was formalized by Richard Atkinson and Richard Shiffrin in 1968. The basic tenets of the **Atkinson-Shiffrin theory** are as follows:

1. Information arriving from the environment is first placed into what is termed **sensory store**, which has three main characteristics (Massaro & Loftus, 1996). First, sensory store contains all the information from the environment captured by the sense organs. Second, sensory store is transient. This means that information from sensory store decays over a time period ranging a few tenths of a second (for visual sensory store) to a few seconds (for auditory sensory store). Third, the small portion of information in sensory store that is attended to (see Chapter 5) is transferred out of sensory store into the next major component of the system, short-term store.

2. **Short-term store** is, as just indicated, the next repository of information, into which attended information from sensory store is placed, has five main characteristics. First, it can be roughly identified with consciousness; that is, information in short-term store is information that you are conscious of. Second, information in short-term store is readily accessible. It can be used as the foundation for making decisions or carrying out tasks in times of seconds or less. Third, all else being equal, information in short-term store will decay (will be forgotten) over a period of approximately 20 seconds. Fourth, information can be prevented from decaying if it is rehearsed: **Rehearsal** refers to repeating some information over and over (Sperling, 1967), Fifth, information in short-term store can undergo other forms of processing, collectively known as **elaboration** (for example, being transformed into a suitable visual image), when it is transferred from short-term store into the third repository of information, long-term store.

3. **Long-term store** is the large repository of information that we maintain of all information that is generally available to us. Long-term store has three main characteristics. First, as just indicated, information enters it, via various kinds of elaborative processes, from short-term store. Second, as far as researchers have discovered, the size of long-term store is unlimited. Third, information is acquired from long-term store via the process of retrieval and placed back into short-term store, where it can be manipulated and used to carry out the task at hand.

DIFFERENT MEMORIES FOR DIFFERENT KINDS OF INFORMATION

Until about two decades ago, psychologists generally assumed that the same memory system was used for all kinds of memories. For example, the same long-term memory was presumably used to store both one's recollection of a grandmother's funeral and the skills one needs to ride a bike. Recent evidence indicates that this assumption is wrong. In particular, we seem to use a different long-term memory for storing facts (such as who the current president is) than we do for retaining skills (such as how to ride a bicycle). The evidence for this difference, as usual, includes both psychological and biological findings; these are considered later in the chapter.

The kind of memory situation that we understand best, **explicit memory,** is one in which a person consciously recollects an event as occurring in a particular time and place. In contrast, **implicit memory** is one in which a person unconsciously remembers information of various sorts—for example, information required to carry out some physical task such as throwing a baseball.

◆ Interim Summary

- There are three stages of memory: encoding, storage, and retrieval.

- There is increasing biological evidence for these distinctions. Recent brain-scanning studies of long-term memory indicate that most of the brain regions activated during encoding are in the left hemisphere and that most of the regions activated during retrieval are in the right hemisphere.

- There are three kinds of memory that differ in terms of their temporal characteristics: Sensory memory lasts over a few hundreds of milliseconds; short-term store (now called *working memory*) operates over seconds; long-term store operates over times ranging from minutes to years.

- Explicit memory is conscious, and implicit memory is unconscious.

◆ Critical Thinking Questions

1. Suppose that a friend complained to you, "I have a terrible memory"? What questions might you ask or what tests might you do to find out exactly which aspects of memory (if any) underlie your friend's reported deficiencies?

2. How would you measure memory if it's not conscious?

SENSORY MEMORY

The information initially acquired from the environment via the sense organs is placed into a short-lasting memory called *sensory memory*. We have briefly described sensory memory: It holds a large amount of information, it holds a fairly faithful representation of the sensory information that enters the sense organ, and it is short-lasting. When you have the dramatic experience of seeing an otherwise dark world briefly lit up by a lightning flash, you are experiencing the sensory memory corresponding to vision, called *iconic memory*.

There are probably sensory memories corresponding to all sensory modalities, but, as with sensation and perception, those that have been studied most extensively are the ones corresponding to vision (iconic memory) and to audition (echoic memory). For purposes of brevity, we will, in what follows, concentrate on the most-studied sensory memory, iconic memory.

In 1960, George Sperling published a seminal paper based on his Harvard doctoral dissertation. Sperling began with the observation that when people were briefly presented with a large amount of information—say 12 digits arranged as three rows of four columns per row—they typically could report only about 4 or 5 of the digits. This number of immediately recallable items, known as the **span of apprehension**, had been known for almost a century and was assumed to represent the maximum amount of information a person could acquire from such an informational array. However, people had two intuitions that indicated that things were not quite so simple. The first was that they were able to see more than they could report but that they quickly forgot it: "By the time we are able to write down 4 or 5 digits," they complained, "we can't remember the rest of the display any more." The second intuition was that the image of the display appeared to *persist* longer than the display itself. Both these intuitions are easy to demonstrate: Go into a pitch-dark closet with a book, open the book to a random page, and fire a flash with a camera (the picture doesn't matter, just the flash). You will find that you can "see" much of the text in the book, but you won't be able to report much of it. Moreover, although the flash lasts only microseconds, your image of the book will appear to last for about half a second.

Sperling tested these intuitions using an ingenious experimental procedure called a **partial-report procedure**, which is demonstrated in Figure 8-2. In this procedure, an array of letters was flashed to observers for a brief period—about a 20th of a second. The number of letters in the array was varied, and the letters were arranged in rows. In Figure 8-2 (left panel), there are three rows of four digits per row. There were two report conditions. In the standard, **whole-report condition**, the observer simply reported as many letters as possible. In the new, **partial-report condition**, the observer had to report only one, randomly chosen row of letters. An **auditory cue** presented immediately after the array told the observer which row was to be reported: A high tone indicated the top row, a medium tone indicated the middle row, and a low tone indicated the bottom row. In the partial-report condition, Sperling estimated how many letters the observer had available by multiplying the average numbers of letters the observer was able to report from the indicated row by the number of rows. If the observer could report three letters from the indicated row, for example, the inference was

■ Figure 8-2
The Partial-Report Experiment
The left panel shows the stimulus configuration: three rows of four letters per row. A high, medium, or low tone (cue) signals the observer to report the top, middle, or bottom row. The middle and right panels show data from this kind of experiment. The middle panel shows that as the number of letters in the display increases, whole-report performance levels off at 4.5 letters; however, partial-report performance continues to increase, thereby demonstrating the basic existence of a large-capacity sensory memory. The right panel shows that as the delay between the array's offset and the signaling tone increases, partial-report performance declines, reflecting the rapid decay of sensory memory. The bar at the far right of the right panel graph represents whole-report performance—about 4.5 letters.

that he or she must have had three letters available from each of the three rows (the observer didn't know which row to report until after the array was physically gone) or 3 × 3 = 9 letters in all. The middle panel of Figure 8-2 shows the results of this experiment. As the number of letters in the array increased, the number of reported letters leveled out at about 4.5 for the whole-report condition—simply a replication of past results. However, in the partial-report condition, the number of letters reported continued to rise with number of letters presented, thereby implying that the observers' first intuition was correct: They had more letters available than they were able to report in the traditional whole-report condition.

In a second experiment, Sperling kept the number of letters in the array constant—12 in our example—but varied the delay between the offset of the letter array and the auditory row-indicating cue, using a partial-report procedure. As can be seen in the right panel of Figure 8-2, the results were dramatic. As the cue delay interval increased, the estimated number of letters available dropped with cue interval up to around 300 ms. The implication is that iconic memory fades away over a period of about a third of a second.

VISIBLE PERSISTENCE: THE TEMPORAL INTEGRATION EXPERIMENT

Soon after Sperling's seminal work came a series of experiments demonstrating the essentially visual aspects of iconic memory. These experiments are best exemplified by a paradigm invented by Erikson & Collins (1967) and elaborated on by Di Lollo and his colleagues (Di Lollo, 1980; Hogben & Di Lollo, 1974). In Di Lollo's version of this **temporal-integration paradigm**, 24 dots are presented in 24 of the 25 squares of an imaginary 5 × 5 array, and the observer's task is to report the location of the missing dot (see Figure 8-3a). Even when the array is shown briefly, the missing dot's location can be easily reported; however, the trick is that the 24-dot stimulus was presented as two "frames" of 12 dots per frame, separated in time. Figure 8-3b shows result of this experiment. When the time between the two frames was brief, the missing dot location could be reported with high probability. However, performance declined precipitously as the interframe interval increased up to about 150 ms. The interpretation was that as the first frame's iconic memory decreased over time, the first frame became less visible and could be less easily integrated with the image of the second frame.

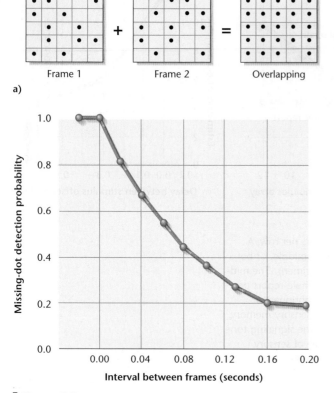

Frame 1   Frame 2   Overlapping

a)

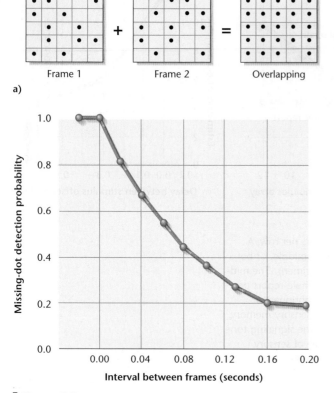

Figure 8-3
The Temporal-Integration Task
(a) The stimulus configuration. Two frames of 12 dots per frame form, when overlapping, a 5 × 5 array of dots with one dot missing. (b) Data from this kind of experiment are plotted. As the interval between the two frames increases, performance declines, demonstrating the quick decline of the visible persistence necessary to visually integrate the two frames.

PARTIAL REPORT, VISIBLE PERSISTENCE, AND A THEORY THAT INTEGRATES THEM

Initially, the partial-report paradigm and the temporal integration paradigm were thought to measure pretty much the same thing. It soon became clear, however, that there were two separate aspects of iconic memory. The first aspect was that which allowed information to be extracted. The second part was that which was *visible*—that part of which the person is consciously aware. It also became clear that these two aspects of iconic store had somewhat different characteristics (Coltheart, 1980), which meant that the two tasks were not simply two measures of the same thing. A theory was proposed to integrate both paradigms, as well as to integrate work on sensation and perception on the one hand and work on memory on the other

(Loftus & Irwin, 1998). The basics of this theory are as follows.

1. A briefly presented visual stimulus (such as an array of letters or an array of dots or the world lit up by a lightning flash) triggers a **sensory response** in the nervous system. This response can be conceptualized as the magnitude of nervous activity, which rises and then falls, as shown in Figure 8-4: Response magnitude rises with the onset of the stimulus, continues to rise for a short time after the offset of the stimulus, and then decays to zero.

2. The amount of information acquired from the stimulus (that, for example, can be used as a basis for responding in Sperling's experiments) is related to the area under the sensory-response function.

3. The visibility of the stimulus is related to the rate at which the observer is acquiring information from the stimulus.

This last point, equating visibility to information-acquisition rate, is not quite so odd as it might seem at first glance. Have you ever had the experience of day-dreaming while driving a car and then suddenly realizing that you had not been conscious of any of the scenery that you were passing? This is tantamount to

Stimulus offset (40 milliseconds)

Figure 8-4
Sensory Response Magnitude
A sensory response function generated by a stimulus presented for 40 milliseconds. The magnitude of the assumed neural response is plotted as a function of time since the onset of the stimulus. The area under the curve determines information acquired from the stimulus, and the height of the curve at any given point largely determines how visible the stimulus is.

saying that your conscious awareness of the passing scenery—its visibility—depends on the degree to which you were acquiring information from it: No information acquisition, no visibility.

◆ Interim Summary

- Sensory memory has a very large capacity but decays in a very short time. Information within sensory memory that is attended to is transferred to the next memory, working memory.

- Visible persistence is information that maintains a persisting, conscious, visual representation over a period of several tenths of a second.

- A sensory response function is a concept that allows integration of sensory memory and visible persistence.

◆ Critical Thinking Questions

1. In what ways is Sperling's partial-report experiment analogous to a professor's testing you on the material learned in a class? In what ways are the experiment and the exam process different?

2. Do you think that the partial-report experiment or the temporal-integration experiment more closely measures the contents of consciousness? Explain the reasons for your answer.

WORKING MEMORY

As noted earlier, sensory memory contains an enormous amount of quickly decaying information. As illustrated by the Doonesbury cartoon, only information that is attended to is transferred from sensory memory to the next memory store. Atkinson and Shiffrin referred to this memory store as short-term store. More recently, however, short-term store, the information that is attended to, has been renamed working memory and has been found to have a degree of complexity far outstripping the relatively simple role assigned to it when it was originally postulated.

Working memory involves the three stages of encoding, storage, and retrieval. Let us look more closely at each of these stages as they relate to working memory.

ENCODING

To encode information into working memory, we must attend to it. Because we are selective about what we attend to (see Chapter 5), our working memory will contain only what has been selected. This means that much of what we are exposed to never even enters working

memory and, of course, will not be available for later retrieval. Indeed, many "memory problems" are really lapses in attention. For example, if you bought some groceries and someone later asked you the color of the checkout clerk's eyes, you might be unable to answer, not because of a failure of memory but because you had not paid attention to the clerk's eyes in the first place.

PHONOLOGICAL CODING When information is encoded into memory, it is entered in a certain code or representation. For example, when you look up a phone number and retain it until you have dialed it, in what form do you represent the digits? Is the representation a **visual code**—a mental picture of the digits? Is it a **phonological code**—the sounds of the names of the digits? Or is it a **semantic code** based on some meaningful association that the digits have? Research indicates that we can use any of these possibilities to encode information into working memory, although we favor a phonological code when we are trying to keep the information active through rehearsal—that is, by repeating an item over and over. Rehearsal is a particularly popular strategy when the information consists of verbal items such as digits, letters, or words. So in trying to remember a phone number, we are most likely to encode the number as the sounds of the digit names and to rehearse these sounds to ourselves until we have dialed the number.

In a classic experiment that provided evidence for a phonological code, researchers briefly showed participants a list of six consonants (for example, RLBKSJ). When the letters were removed, they had to write all six letters in order. Although the entire procedure took only a second or two, participants occasionally made errors. When they did, the incorrect letter tended to be similar in sound to the correct one. For the list mentioned, a participant might have written RLTKSJ, replacing the B with the similar-sounding T (Conrad, 1964). This finding supports the hypothesis that the participants encoded each letter phonologically (for example, "bee" for B), sometimes lost part of this code (only the "ee" part of the sound remained), and then responded with a letter ("tee") that was consistent with the remaining part of the code. This hypothesis also explains why it is more difficult to recall the items in order when they are acoustically similar (for example, TBCGVE) than when they are acoustically distinct (RLTKSJ).

VISUAL CODING If need be, we can also maintain verbal items in a visual form, but experiments indicate that the visual code fades quickly. When a person must store nonverbal items (such as pictures that are difficult to describe and therefore difficult to rehearse phonologically), the visual code becomes more important. Although most of us can maintain some kind of visual image in working memory, a few people are able to maintain images that are almost photographic in clarity. This ability occurs mainly in children. Such children can look briefly at a picture and, when it is removed, still experience the image before their eyes. They can maintain the image for as long as several minutes and, when questioned, provide a wealth of detail, such as the number of stripes on a cat's tail (see Figure 8-5). Such children seem to be reading the details directly from an eidetic (or photographic) image (Haber, 1969). Eidetic imagery is very rare, though. Some studies with children indicate that only about 5% report long-lasting visual images that possess sharp detail. Moreover, when the criteria for possessing true photographic imagery are made more stringent—for example, being able to read an imaged page of text as easily from the bottom up as from the top down—the frequency of eidetic imagery becomes minuscule, even among children (Haber, 1979). The visual code in working memory, then, is something short of a photograph.

Figure 8-5
Testing for Eidetic Images
This test picture was shown to elementary school children for 30 seconds. After the picture was removed, one boy saw in his eidetic image "about 14" stripes in the cat's tail. The painting, by Marjorie Torrey, appears in Lewis Carroll's *Alice in Wonderland*, abridged by Josette Frank. (From *Alice in Wonderland*, abridged by Josette Frank, Random House, 1955)

When you look up a phone number and retain it until you have dialed it, do you retain it visually, phonologically, or semantically?

TWO WORKING MEMORY SYSTEMS The existence of both phonological and visual codes led researchers to argue that working memory has two distinct stores or buffers. One is a **phonological buffer,** which briefly stores information in an acoustic code; the second is a **visual-spatial sketchpad,** which briefly stores information in a visual or spatial code (Baddeley, 1986). Some recent brain-scanning studies indicate that the two buffers are mediated by different brain structures.

In one experiment, on every trial participants saw a sequence of letters in which both the identity and the position of the letter varied from one item to another (see Figure 8-6). On some trials, participants had to attend only to the identity of the letters; their task was to determine whether each letter presented was identical to the one presented three back in the sequence. On other trials, participants had to attend only to the position of

the letters; their task was to determine whether each letter's position was identical to the position of the letter presented three back in the sequence (see Figure 8-6). Essentially, what varied was whether the participants were storing verbal information (the identities of the letters) or spatial information (the positions of the letters). Presumably, the verbal information was being kept in the acoustic buffer and the spatial information in the visual-spatial buffer.

On both the identity and the spatial trials, PET measures of brain activity were recorded. The results indicated that the two buffers are in different hemispheres. On trials in which participants had to store verbal information (acoustic buffer), most of the brain activity was in the left hemisphere; on trials in which participants had to store spatial information (visual-spatial buffer), most of the brain activity was in the right hemisphere. The

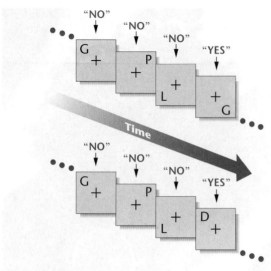

▌ Figure 8-6
An Experiment on Acoustic and Visual Buffers
Participants had to decide whether each item was identical to the one three back in the sequence. The top half of the figure shows a typical sequence of events in which participants had to attend only to the identity of the letters, along with the responses required to each item. The bottom half of the figure shows the trial events when individuals had to attend only to the position of the letters, along with the responses required to each item. (After Smith et al., 1995)

two buffers seem to be distinct systems (Smith, Jonides, & Koeppe, 1996). This finding is not very surprising, considering the brain's tendency toward hemispheric specialization, as discussed in Chapter 2.

STORAGE

Perhaps the most striking fact about working memory is that its capacity is very limited. On the average, the limit is seven items, give or take two (7 ± 2). Some people store as few as five items; others can retain as many as nine. It may seem strange to give such an exact number to cover all people when it is clear that individuals differ greatly in memory ability. These differences, however, are due primarily to long-term memory. For working memory, most normal adults have a capacity of 7 ± 2. This constancy has been known since the earliest days of experimental psychology. Hermann Ebbinghaus, who began the experimental study of memory in 1885, reported results showing that his own limit was seven items. Some 70 years later, George Miller (1956) was so struck by the consistency of this finding that he referred to it as the "magic number seven," and we now know that the limit holds in non-Western cultures as well as Western ones (Yu et al., 1985).

Psychologists determined this number via a **digit-span task:** showing people various sequences of unrelated items (digits, letters, or words) and asking them to recall the items in order. The items are presented rapidly, and the individual does not have time to relate them to information stored in long-term memory. The number of items recalled reflects only the storage capacity of the individual's working memory. On the initial trials, participants have to recall just a few items—say, three or four digits—which they can easily do. In subsequent trials, the number of digits increases until the experimenter determines the participant's memory span—the maximum number of items (almost always between five and nine) that the participant can recall in perfect order. This task is so simple that you can easily try it yourself. The next time you come across a list of names (a directory in a business or university building, for example), read through the list once and then look away and see how many names you can recall in order. It will probably be between five and nine.

CHUNKING As just noted, the digit-span task discourages individuals from connecting the items to be remembered to information in long-term memory. When such connections are possible, performance on the memory-span task can change substantially. To illustrate this change, suppose that you were presented with the letter string SRUOYYLERECNIS. Because your memory span is 7 ± 2, you would probably be unable to repeat the entire 14-letter sequence. If, however, you noticed that these letters spell the phrase SINCERELY YOURS in reverse order, your task would become easier. By using this knowledge, you have decreased the number of items that must be held in working memory from 14 to 2 (the 2 words). But where did this spelling knowledge come from? From long-term memory, where knowledge about words is stored. You can use long-term memory to perform what is known as **chunking,** or recoding new material into larger, more meaningful units and storing those units in working memory. Such units are called *chunks*, and the capacity of working memory is best expressed as 7 ± 2 chunks (Miller, 1956). Chunking can occur with numbers as well. The string 149-2177-620-02 is beyond our capacity, but 1492-1776-2002 is well within it. The general principle is that we can boost our working memory by regrouping sequences of letters and digits into units that can be found in long-term memory (Bower & Springston, 1970).

FORGETTING We may be able to hold on to seven items briefly, but in most cases they will soon be forgotten. Forgetting occurs either because the items "decay" over time or because they are displaced by new items.

Information in working memory may simply decay as time passes. We may think of the representation of an item as a trace that fades within a matter of seconds. One of the best pieces of evidence for this hypothesis is that our working memory span holds fewer words when the words take longer to say. For example, the span is less for long words such as *harpoon* and *cyclone* than for shorter words such as *bishop* and *pewter* (try saying the words to yourself to see the difference in duration). Presumably this effect arises because as the words are presented we say them to ourselves, and the longer it takes to do this, the more likely it is that some of the words' traces will have faded before they can be recalled (Baddeley, Thompson, & Buchanan, 1975).

The other major cause of forgetting in working memory is the displacement of old items by new ones. The notion of displacement fits with the idea that working memory has a fixed capacity. Being in working memory may correspond to being in a state of activation. The more items we try to keep active, the less activation there is for any one of them. Perhaps only about seven items can be simultaneously maintained at a level of activation that permits all of them to be recalled. Once seven items are active, the activation given to a new item will be taken away from items that were presented earlier. Consequently, those items may fall below the critical level of activation needed for recall (Anderson, 1983).

RETRIEVAL

Let us continue to think of the contents of working memory as being active in consciousness. Intuition suggests that access to this information is immediate. You do not have to dig for it; it is right there. Retrieval, then, should not depend on the number of items in consciousness. But in this case, intuition is wrong.

Research has shown that the more items there are in working memory, the slower retrieval becomes. Most of the evidence for this comes from a type of experiment introduced by Sternberg (1966) and referred to as a **Sternberg memory-scanning task.** On each trial of the experiment, a participant is shown a set of digits, the memory list, that he or she must temporarily maintain in working memory. It is easy for the participant to do so because the memory list contains between one and six digits. The memory list is then removed from view and a probe digit is presented. The participant must decide whether the probe was on the memory list. For example, if the memory list is 3 6 1 and the probe is 6, the participant should respond yes; given the same memory list and a probe of 2, the participant should respond no. Participants rarely make an error on this task. What is of interest, however, is the decision time, which is the elapsed

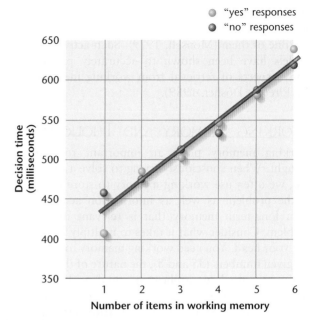

■ Figure 8-7
Retrieval as a Search Process
Decision times increase in direct proportion to the number of items in short-term memory. Green circles represent yes responses; purple circles, no responses. The times for both types of decision fall along a straight line. Because the decision times are so fast, they must be measured with equipment that permits accuracy in milliseconds (thousandths of a second). (Adapted from "High Speed Scanning in Human Memory," reprinted with permission from *Science*, vol. 153, August 5, 1966, pp. 652–654 by S. Sternberg. Copyright © 1966 by the American Association for the Advancement of Science.)

time between the onset of the probe and the participant's pressing of a yes or a no button. Figure 8-7 presents data from such an experiment, indicating that decision time increases directly with the length of the memory list. What is remarkable about these decision times is that they fall along a straight line. This means that each additional item in working memory adds a fixed amount of time to the retrieval process—approximately 40 milliseconds, or $\frac{1}{25}$ of a second. The same results are found when the items are letters, words, auditory tones, or pictures of people's faces (Sternberg, 1975).

The most straightforward interpretation of these results is that retrieval requires a **serial search** of working memory—a search in which the items are examined one at a time. This search presumably operates at a rate of 40 milliseconds per item, which is too fast for people to be aware of it (Sternberg, 1966). However, thinking of working memory as a state of activation leads to a different interpretation of the results. Retrieval of an item in working memory may depend on the activation of that item reaching a critical level. That is, one decides that a probe is in working memory if it is above a critical level of activation, and the more items are in working memory, the less activation there is for any one of them (Monsell, 1979). Such **activation models** have been shown to accurately predict many aspects of retrieval from working memory (McElree & Dosher, 1989).

WORKING MEMORY AND THOUGHT

Working memory plays an important role in thought. When consciously trying to solve a problem, we often use working memory to store parts of the problem as well as information accessed from long-term memory that is relevant to the problem. Consider what it takes to multiply 35 by 8 in your head. You need working memory to store the given numbers (35 and 8), the nature of the operation required (multiplication), and arithmetic facts such as $8 \times 5 = 40$ and $8 \times 3 = 24$. Not surprisingly, performance on mental arithmetic declines substantially if you have to remember simultaneously some words or digits. Try doing the mental multiplication just described while remembering the phone number 745-1739 (Baddeley & Hitch, 1974). Because of its role in mental computations, researchers often conceptualize working memory as a kind of blackboard on which the mind performs computations and posts the partial results for later use (Baddeley, 1986).

Other research shows that working memory is used not only in doing numerical calculations but also in solving a wide range of complex problems. An example of such problems is geometric analogies, which are sometimes used in tests of intelligence (Ravens, 1965). An illustration of a geometric analogy is presented in Figure 8-8. Try to solve it to get an intuitive idea of the role of working memory in problem solv-

"Can we hurry up and get to the test? My short-term memory is better than my long-term memory."

© 1985, reprinted courtesy of Bill Hoest and *Parade* Magazine.

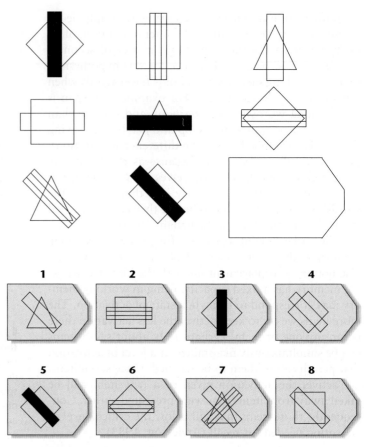

Figure 8-8
Illustration of a Geometric Analogy
The task is to inspect the forms in the top matrix in which the bottom right entry is missing, and to determine which of the eight alternatives given below is the missing entry. To do this, you have to look across each row and determine the rules that specify how the forms vary, and then do the same thing for each column. (P. A. Carpenter, M. A. Just, and P. Shell (1990), "What one intelligence test measures: a theoretical account of the processing in the Raven Progressive Matrices Test," *Psychological Review,* 97(3):404–431. Adapted by permission of the American Psychological Association.)

Answer: Option 8.

ing. You may note that you need working memory to store (1) the similarities and differences that you observe among the forms in a row and (2) the rules that you come up with to account for these similarities and differences and that you then use to select the correct answer. It turns out that the larger one's working memory, the better one does on problems like these (even though there is relatively little variation among people in the capacity of their working memory). Moreover, when computers are programmed to simulate people solving problems such as the one in Figure 8-8, one of the most important determinants of how well the program does is the size of the working memory created by the programmer. There seems to be little doubt that part of the difficulty of many complex problems is the load they place on working memory (Carpenter, Just, & Shell, 1990).

Working memory is also crucial for language processes like following a conversation or reading a text. When reading for understanding, often we must consciously relate new sentences to some prior material in the text. This relating of new to old seems to occur in working memory because people who have more working-memory capacity score higher than others on reading comprehension tests (Daneman & Carpenter, 1980; Just & Carpenter, 1992).

TRANSFER FROM WORKING MEMORY TO LONG-TERM MEMORY

From what we have seen so far, working memory serves two important functions. It stores material that is needed for short periods, and it serves as a work space for mental computations. Another possible function is serving as a way station to long-term memory. That is, information may reside in working memory while it is being encoded or transferred into long-term memory (Atkinson & Shiffrin, 1971a and 1971b; Raaijmakers & Shiffrin, 1992). Although there are a number of different ways to implement the transfer, one way that has been the subject of considerable research is rehearsal, the conscious repetition of information in working memory. Rehearsal apparently not only maintains the item in working memory but also causes it to be transferred to long-term memory. The term *maintenance rehearsal* is used to refer to active efforts to hold information in working memory; *elaborative rehearsal* refers to efforts to encode information in long-term memory.

Some of the best evidence for the way station function of working memory comes from experiments on free recall. In a free-recall experiment, participants first see a list of perhaps 40 unrelated words that are presented one at a time. After all the words have been presented, participants must immediately recall them in any order (hence the designation "free"). The results from such an experiment are shown in Figure 8-9. The chance of correctly recalling a word is graphed as a function of the word's position in the list. The part of the curve to the left in the graph is for the first few words presented, and the part to the right is for the last few words presented.

Presumably, at the time of recall, the last few words presented are still likely to be in working memory, whereas the remaining words are in long-term memory. We would expect recall of the last few words to be high because items in working memory can be re-

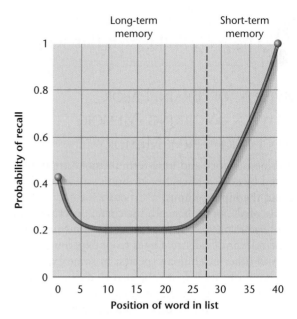

▌ Figure 8-9
Results of a Free Recall Experiment

The probability of recall varies with an item's position in a list, with the probability being highest for the last five or so positions, next highest for the first few positions, and lowest for the intermediate positions. Recall of the last few items is based on short-term memory, whereas recall of the remaining items is based on long-term memory. (B. B. Murdock (1962) "The Serial Position Effect in Free Recall," from *Journal of Experimental Psychology*, 64:482–488. Copyright © 1962 by the American Psychological Association. Adapted by permission.)

trieved easily. Figure 8-9 shows that this is indeed the case. But recall for the first words presented is also quite good. Why? This is where rehearsal enters the picture. When the first words were presented, they were entered into working memory and rehearsed. Because there was little else in working memory, they were rehearsed often and therefore were likely to be transferred to long-term memory. As more items were presented, working memory quickly filled up and the opportunity to rehearse and transfer any given item to long-term memory decreased. So only the first few items presented enjoyed the extra opportunity for transfer, which is why they were later recalled so well from long-term memory.

In sum, working memory is a system that can hold roughly 7 ± 2 chunks of information in either a phonological or a visual format. Information is lost from working memory through either decay or displacement and is retrieved from this system by a process that is sensitive to the total number of items being kept active at any given time. Last, working memory is used to store and process information that is needed during problem solving, and therefore it is critical for thought.

DIVISION OF BRAIN LABOR BETWEEN WORKING MEMORY AND LONG-TERM MEMORY

Working memory and long-term memory are implemented by somewhat different brain structures. In particular, the **hippocampus,** a structure located near the middle of the brain beneath the cortex, is critical for long-term memory but not for working memory. Much of the relevant evidence comes from experiments with rats and other nonhuman species. In some experiments, one group of rats is first subjected to damage to the hippocampus and the surrounding cortex, and a second group is subjected to damage in a completely different region, the front of the cortex. Both groups of rats then have to perform a delayed-response task. On each trial, first one stimulus (such as a square) is presented, and then, after a delay, a second stimulus (such as a triangle) is presented. The animal has to respond only when the second stimulus differs from the first. How well the animal performs on this task depends on the kind of brain damage it has suffered and the length of the delay between the two stimuli.

When the delay is long (15 seconds or more), animals with damage to the hippocampus perform poorly, but those with damage in the front of the cortex perform relatively normally. Because a long delay between stimuli requires long-term memory for storage of the first stimulus, these results fit with the idea that the hippocampus is critical for long-term memory. When the delay between the two stimuli is short (just a few seconds), the opposite results occur. Now animals with damage in the front of the cortex perform poorly, and those with hippocampal damage perform relatively normally. Because a short delay between stimuli requires working memory for storage of the first stimulus, these results indicate that regions in the frontal cortex are involved in working memory. Hence, different regions of the brain are involved in working memory and long-term memory (Goldman-Rakic, 1987; Zola-Morgan & Squire, 1985).

What evidence is there for this distinction in humans? Patients who happen to have suffered damage in certain brain regions provide an "experiment of nature." Specifically, some patients have suffered damage to the hippocampus and surrounding cortex and consequently show a severe memory loss. Because the hippocampus is located in the middle of the temporal lobe, these patients are said to have medial-temporal lobe amnesia. Such patients have profound difficulty remembering material for long intervals but rarely have any trouble remembering material for a few seconds. A patient with medial-temporal lobe amnesia may be unable to recognize his doctor when she enters the room—even though the patient has seen this doctor every day for years—yet will have no trouble repeating the physician's name when she is reintroduced (Milner, Corkin, & Teuber, 1968). Such a patient has a severe impairment in long-term memory but a normal working memory.

Other patients, however, show the opposite problem. They cannot correctly repeat a string of even three words, yet they are relatively normal when tested on their long-term memory for words. Such patients have an impaired working memory but an intact long-term memory. And their brain damage is never in the medial temporal lobe (Shallice, 1988). Thus, for humans as well as other mammals, working memory and long-term memory are mediated by different brain structures.

Recent research using brain-scanning techniques has revealed that neurons in the **prefrontal lobes, just behind the forehead,** hold information for short-term use, such as a phone number that is about to be dialed. These neurons appear to act like a computer's random access memory (RAM) chips, which hold data temporarily for current use and switch quickly to other data as needed. These cells are also able to draw information from other regions of the brain and retain it as long as it is needed for a specific task (Goldman-Rakic, cited in Goleman, 1995). ∎

◆ Interim Summary

- Information in working memory tends to be encoded acoustically, although we can also use a visual code.

- The most striking fact about working memory is that its storage capacity is limited to 7 ± 2 items, or chunks.

- Retrieval slows down as the number of items in working memory increases.

- Working memory is used in solving various kinds of problems, such as mental arithmetic, geometric analogies, and answering questions about text.

◆ Critical Thinking Questions

1. Why do you think that phonological encoding is such a major part of how working memory is organized?

2. How might an increase in the size of your working memory affect your performance on a standardized test of comprehension like the SAT? Try to explain how underlying comprehension processes might be affected.

LONG-TERM MEMORY

Long-term memory is involved when information has to be retained for intervals as brief as a few minutes (such as a point made earlier in a conversation) or as long as a lifetime (such as an adult's childhood memories). In experiments on long-term memory, psychologists have generally studied forgetting over intervals of minutes, hours, or weeks, but a few studies have involved years or even decades. Experiments that use intervals of years often involve the recall of personal experience (autobiographical memory) rather than the recall of laboratory materials. In what follows, studies using both kinds of material are intermixed because they seem to reflect many of the same principles.

Our discussion of long-term memory will again distinguish among the three stages of memory—encoding, storage, and retrieval—but this time there are two complications. First, unlike the situation with working memory, important interactions between encoding and retrieval occur in long-term memory. In view of these interactions, we will consider some aspects of retrieval in our discussion of encoding and present a separate discussion of interactions between encoding and retrieval. The other complication is that it is often difficult to know whether forgetting from long-term memory is due to a loss from storage or to a failure in retrieval. To deal with this problem, we will delay our discussion of storage until after we have considered retrieval so that we have a clearer idea of what constitutes good evidence for a storage loss.

ENCODING

ENCODING MEANING For verbal material, the dominant long-term memory representation is neither acoustic nor visual. Instead, it is based on the meanings of the items. Encoding items according to their meaning occurs even when the items are isolated words, but it is more striking when they are sentences. Several minutes after hearing a sentence, most of what you can recall or recognize is the sentence's meaning. Suppose that you heard the sentence "The author sent the committee a long letter." The evidence indicates that 2 minutes later you would do no better than chance in telling whether you had heard that sentence or one that has the same meaning: "A long letter was sent to the committee by the author" (Sachs, 1967).

Encoding of meaning is pervasive in everyday memory situations. When people report on complex social or political situations, they may misremember many of the specifics (who said what to whom, when something was said, who else was there) yet can accurately describe the basic situation. In the Watergate scandal of the early 1970s, for example, the chief government witness (John Dean) was subsequently shown to have made many mistakes about what was said in particular situations, yet his overall testimony is generally thought to accurately describe the events that occurred (Neisser, 1982).

Although meaning may be the dominant way of representing verbal material in long-term memory, we sometimes code other aspects as well. We can, for example, memorize poems and recite them word for word. In such cases we have coded not only the meaning of the poem but the exact words themselves. We can also use a phonological code in long-term memory. When you get a phone call and the other party says, "Hello," you often recognize the voice. In a case like this, you must have coded the sound of that person's voice in long-term memory. Visual impressions, tastes, and smells are also coded in long-term memory. Overall, long-term memory has a preferred code for verbal material (namely, meaning), but other codes can be used as well.

ADDING MEANINGFUL CONNECTIONS Often the items we need to remember are meaningful, but the connections between them are not. In such cases memory can be improved by creating real or artificial links between the items. For example, people who are learning to read music must remember that the five lines in printed music are referred to as EGBDF. Although the symbols themselves are meaningful (they refer to notes on a keyboard), their order seems arbitrary. What many learners do is convert the symbols into the sentence "Every Good Boy Does Fine"; the first letter of each word names each symbol, and the relationships between the words in the sentence supply meaningful connections between the symbols. These connections aid memory because they provide retrieval paths between the words. Once the word "Good" has been retrieved, for example, there is a path or connection to "Boy," the next word that must be recalled.

One of the best ways to add connections is to elaborate on the meaning of the material while encoding it. The more deeply or elaborately one encodes the meaning, the better the resulting memory will be (Craik & Tulving, 1975). If you have to remember a point made in a textbook, you will recall it better if you concentrate on its meaning rather than on the exact words. And the more deeply and thoroughly you expand on its meaning, the better you will recall it.

An experiment by Bradshaw and Anderson (1982) illustrates some of these points. Participants read facts about famous people that they would later have to recall, such as "At a critical point in his life, Mozart made a journey from Munich to Paris." Some facts were elaborated according to either their causes or their consequences, as in "Mozart wanted to leave Munich to avoid a romantic entanglement." Other facts were presented

When we forget information in long-term memory, it doesn't mean that the information itself is lost. We may be able to retrieve the information if something reminds us of it. This is one reason that families maintain photograph albums.

alone. Later the participants were tested on their memory of just the facts (not the elaborations). Participants recalled more facts with elaborations than facts that had been presented alone. Presumably, in adding the cause (or consequence) to their memory representation, they set up a retrieval path from the cause to the target fact in the following manner:

Mozart journeyed from Munich to Paris.

Mozart wanted to avoid a romantic entanglement in Munich.

At the time of recall, participants could either retrieve the target fact directly or retrieve it indirectly by following the path from its cause. Even if they forgot the target fact, they could infer it if they retrieved the cause.

Results like these establish an intimate connection between understanding and memory. The better we understand some material, the more connections we see between its parts. Because these connections can serve as retrieval links, the better we understand items, the more we remember.

RETRIEVAL

Many cases of forgetting from long-term memory result from loss of access to the information rather than from loss of the information itself. Poor memory often reflects a retrieval failure rather than a storage failure. (Note that this is unlike working memory, in which forgetting is a result of decay or displacement, and retrieval is thought to be relatively error free.) Trying to retrieve an

item from long-term memory is like trying to find a book in a large library. Failure to find the book does not necessarily mean that it is not there. You may be looking in the wrong place, or the book may simply be misfiled.

EVIDENCE FOR RETRIEVAL FAILURES Our everyday experience provides considerable evidence for retrieval failures. At some point, all of us have been unable to recall a fact or experience, only to have it come to mind later. How many times have you taken an exam and not been able to recall a specific name, only to remember it later? Another example is the "tip-of-the-tongue" phenomenon, in which a particular word or name lies tantalizingly outside our ability to recall it (Brown & McNeill, 1966). We may feel tormented until a search of memory (dredging up and then discarding words that are close but not quite right) finally retrieves the correct word.

A more striking example of retrieval failure occurs when a person undergoing psychotherapy retrieves a memory that had previously been forgotten. Although we lack firm evidence for such occurrences, they suggest that some seemingly forgotten memories are not lost but merely difficult to get at.

For stronger evidence that retrieval failures can cause forgetting, consider the following experiment. Participants were asked to memorize a long list of words. Some of the words were names of animals, such as *dog, cat, horse;* some were names of fruits, such as *apple, orange, pear;* some were names of furniture; and so on (see Table 8-1). At the time of recall, the participants were divided into two groups. One group was supplied with retrieval cues such as "animal," "fruit," and so on; the other group, the control group, was not. The group that was given the retrieval cues recalled more words than the control group. In a subsequent test, when both groups were given the retrieval cues, they recalled the same number of words. The initial difference in recall between the two groups must have been due to retrieval failures.

In sum, the better the retrieval cues available, the better our memory. This principle explains why we usually do better on a recognition test of memory than on a recall test. In a **recognition test,** we are asked whether we have seen a particular item before (for example, "Was Bessie Smith one of the people you met at the wedding?"). The test item itself is an excellent retrieval cue for our memory of that item. In contrast, in a **recall test,** we have to produce the memorized items using minimal retrieval cues (for example, "Recall the name of the woman you met at the party"). Because the retrieval cues in a recognition test are generally more useful than those in a recall test, performance is usually better on recognition tests (such as multiple-choice exams) than on recall tests (such as essay exams) (Tulving, 1974).

● Table 8-1
Examples From a Study of Retrieval Failures

Participants who were not given the retrieval cues recalled fewer words from the memorized list than other participants who were given the cues. This finding shows that problems at the retrieval stage of long-term memory are responsible for some memory failures. (E. Tulving and Z. Pearlstone (1976) "Availability and Accessibility," from *Journal of Memory and Language*, 5:381–391. Reprinted by permission of Academic Press.)

List to Be Memorized

dog	cotton	oil
cat	wool	gas
horse	silk	coal
cow	rayon	wood
apple	blue	doctor
orange	red	lawyer
pear	green	teacher
banana	yellow	dentist
chair	knife	football
table	spoon	baseball
bed	fork	basketball
sofa	pan	tennis
knife	hammer	shirt
gun	saw	socks
rifle	nails	pants
bomb	screwdriver	shoes

Retrieval Cues

animals	cloth	fuels
fruit	color	professions
furniture	utensils	sports
weapons	tools	clothing

INTERFERENCE Among the factors that can impair retrieval, the most important is **interference.** If we associate different items with the same cue, when we try to use that cue to retrieve one of the items (the target item), the other items may become active and interfere with our recovery of the target. For example, if your friend Dan moves and you finally learn his new phone number, you will find it difficult to retrieve the old number. Why? Because you are using the cue "Dan's phone number" to retrieve the old number, but instead this cue activates the new number, which interferes with recovery of the old one. (This is referred to as retroactive interference.) Or suppose that your reserved space in a parking garage, which you have used for a year, is changed. At first, you may find it difficult to retrieve your new parking location

from memory. Why? Because you are trying to learn to associate your new location with the cue "my parking place," but this cue retrieves the old location, which interferes with the learning of the new one (proactive interference). In both examples, the power of retrieval cues ("Dan's phone number" or "my parking place") to activate particular target items decreases with the number of other items associated with those cues. The more items are associated with a cue, the more overloaded it becomes and the less effective it is in aiding retrieval.

Interference can operate at various levels, including the level of whole facts. In one experiment, participants first learned to associate various facts with the names of professions. For example, they learned the following associations:

The banker:
(1) was asked to address the crowd,
(2) broke the bottle, and
(3) did not delay the trip.

The lawyer:
(1) realized that the seam was split, and
(2) painted an old barn.

The occupational names *banker* and *lawyer* were the retrieval cues. Because *banker* was associated with three facts and *lawyer* was associated with just two, *banker* should have been less useful than *lawyer* in retrieving any of its associated facts (*banker* was the more overloaded cue). When participants were later given a recognition test, they did take longer to recognize any one of the facts learned about the banker than any one of those learned about the lawyer. In this study, then, interference slowed the speed of retrieval. Many other experiments show that interference can lead to a complete retrieval failure if the target items are weak or the interference is strong (Anderson, 1983). Indeed, it has long been thought that interference is a major reason why forgetting from long-term memory increases with time: The relevant retrieval cues become more and more overloaded with time.

Figure 8-10 shows one of the first experiments that demonstrated forgetting, which was reported by Ebbinghaus (1885). Ebbinghaus, who used himself as a subject, studied lists of 13 syllables, which he repeated until he was able to recall the list without error on two successive trials. Then, after intervals ranging from 20 minutes to 31 days, he tested himself by determining how long it took him to relearn the list to the original level; the less the forgetting, the fewer trials should be needed to relearn the list. The figure plots a measure of ease of relearning (called *savings*) as a function of time; it suggests that one forgets a lot about an event within the first few hours but that after that the rate of forgetting slows down. Although this curve is representative of memory for unrelated verbal

Figure 8-10
Forgetting as a Function of Time
A forgetting curve graphs the decline in recall as a function of time. This graph was one of the first forgetting graphs ever, reported by Ebbinghaus (1885).

material, different kinds of curves are found with different kinds of material (Bahrick & Phelphs, 1987). In all cases, interference is thought to play some role in the changes in forgetting with time.

MODELS OF RETRIEVAL In attempting to explain interference effects, researchers have developed a variety of models of retrieval. As with retrieval from short-term memory, some models of long-term-memory retrieval are based on a search process, whereas others are based on an activation process.

The interference effects in the banker-lawyer experiment fit nicely with the idea that retrieval from long-term memory may be thought of as a search process (Raaijmakers & Shiffrin, 1981). To illustrate, consider how the sentence "The banker broke the bottle" might be recognized (see Figure 8-11). The term *banker* accesses its representation in memory, which localizes the search to the relevant part of long-term memory. There, three paths need to be searched to verify that "broke the bottle" was one of the facts learned about the banker. In contrast, if the test sentence is "The lawyer painted an old barn," there are only two paths to be searched. Because the duration of a search increases with the number of paths to be considered, retrieval will be slower for the "banker" sentence than for the "lawyer" one.

An alternative way to think about the retrieval process is in terms of activation. When trying to recognize "The banker broke the bottle," for example, the participant activates the representation for *banker*, and the activation then spreads simultaneously along the three paths emanating from *banker* (see Figure 8-11). When sufficient activation reaches "broke the bottle," the sentence can be recognized. Interference arises because the activation from the banker representation must be subdivided among the paths emanating from it. The more facts are associated with *banker*, the thinner the activation will be on each path and the longer it will take for sufficient activation to reach any particular fact. Thinking of retrieval in terms of spreading activation can also account for why interference slows retrieval (Anderson, 1983).

Figure 8-11
Retrieval as a Search Process Versus an Activation Process
When the sentence "The banker broke the bottle" is presented, the term *banker* accesses the banker representation in long-term memory. Once at this representation, there are three paths to be searched. When the sentence "The lawyer painted an old barn" is presented, *lawyer* accesses the lawyer representation, from which there are two paths to be searched. Alternatively, the term *banker* may activate the banker representation, and this activation then spreads simultaneously along the three paths (and similarly for the "lawyer" example).

FORGETTING—LOSS OF INFORMATION FROM STORAGE

The fact that some forgetting is due to retrieval failures does not imply that *all* forgetting is. It seems most unlikely that everything we ever learned is still there in memory waiting for the right retrieval cue. Some information is almost certainly forgotten—lost from storage (Loftus & Loftus, 1980).

Some evidence of storage loss comes from people who receive **electroconvulsive therapy** to alleviate severe depression (a mild electric current applied to the brain produces a brief epileptic-like seizure and momentary unconsciousness; see Chapter 16). In such cases the patient loses some memory for events that occurred in the months just prior to the shock but not for earlier events (Squire & Fox, 1980). These memory losses are unlikely to be due to retrieval failures because if the shock disrupted retrieval, all memories should be affected, not just the recent ones. More likely, the shock disrupts storage processes that consolidate new memories over a period of months or longer, and information that is not consolidated is lost from storage.

Most research on storage in long-term memory is done at the biological level. Researchers have made substantial progress in determining the neuroanatomical bases of consolidation. It appears that the critical brain structures involved are the hippocampus and the cortex surrounding the hippocampus (including the entorhinal, perirhinal, and parahippocampal cortices, which are involved in the exchange of information between the hippocampus and much of the cerebral cortex). The hippocampus's role in consolidation seems to be that of a cross-referencing system, linking together aspects of a particular memory that are stored in separate parts of the brain (Squire, 1992). Although a global memory loss in humans usually occurs only when the surrounding cortex as well as the hippocampus is impaired, damage to the hippocampus alone can result in severe memory disturbance. This fact was demonstrated by a study that started with an analysis of a particular patient's memory problems (due to complications from coronary bypass surgery) and ended with a detailed autopsy of his brain after his death. The autopsy revealed that the hippocampus was the only brain structure that was damaged (Zola-Morgan, Squire, & Amaral, 1989).

A study using monkeys provides the best evidence we have that the function of the hippocampus is to consolidate relatively new memories. A group of experimental monkeys learned to discriminate between items in 100 pairs of objects. For each pair, there was food under one object, which the monkey got only if it chose that object. Because all the objects differed, the monkeys essentially learned 100 different problems. Twenty of the problems were learned 16 weeks before the researchers removed the monkeys' hippocampus; additional sets of 20 problems were learned either 12, 8, 4, or 2 weeks before the hippocampal surgery. Two weeks after the surgery, the researchers tested the monkeys' memory with a single trial of each of the 100 pairs. The key finding was that the experimental monkeys remembered discriminations that they had learned 8, 12, or 16 weeks before surgery as well as normal control monkeys did, but they remembered the discriminations learned 2 or 4 weeks before surgery less well than the control monkeys did. Moreover, the experimental monkeys actually remembered less about the discriminations learned 2 to 4 weeks before surgery than about the discriminations learned earlier. These results suggest that memories need to be processed by the hippocampus for a period of a few weeks, for it is only during this period that memory is impaired by removal of the hippocampus. Permanent long-term memory storage is almost certainly localized in the cortex, particularly in the regions where sensory information is interpreted (Squire, 1992; Zola-Morgan & Squire, 1990). ▍

INTERACTIONS BETWEEN ENCODING AND RETRIEVAL

In describing the encoding stage, we noted that operations carried out during encoding, such as elaboration, make retrieval easier. Two other encoding factors also increase the chances of successful retrieval: (1) organizing the information at the time of encoding and (2) ensuring that the context in which information is encoded is similar to that in which it will be retrieved.

ORGANIZATION The more we organize the material we encode, the easier it is to retrieve. Suppose you were at a conference where you met various professionals—doctors, lawyers, and journalists. When you later try to recall their names, you will do better if you initially organize the information by profession. Then you can ask yourself, "Who were the doctors I met? Who were the lawyers?" and so forth. A list of names or words is far easier to recall when we encode the information into categories and then retrieve it on a category-by-category basis (Bower, Clark, Winzenz, & Lesgold, 1969).

CONTEXT It is easier to retrieve a particular fact or episode if you are in the same context in which you en-

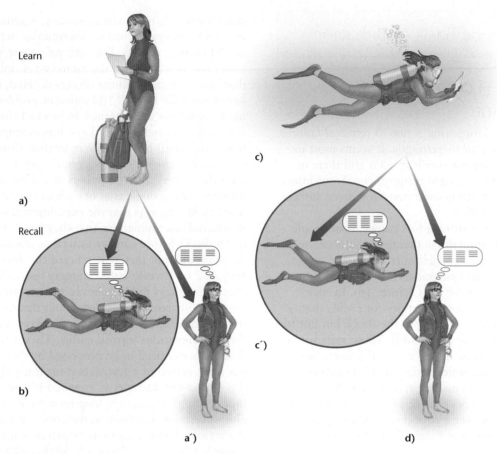

Learn

a)

Recall

b)

a′)

c)

c′)

d)

▌Figure 8-12
Effects of Environmental Context on Retrieval
In an experiment to demonstrate how context affects retrieval, one group of deep-sea divers learned a list of words while they were on the beach (panel a), and another group of divers learned the list while they were beneath 15 feet of water (panel c). Later, each group was divided in half and tried to recall the words either in the same environment in which they had learned them (panels a′ and c′) or in a different environment (panels b and d).
(D. Godden and A. D. Baddeley (1975) "Context-Dependent Memory in Two Natural Environments: On Land & Under Water," from *British Journal of Psychology*, 66:325–331.)

coded it (Estes, 1972). For example, it is a good bet that your ability to retrieve the names of your classmates in the first and second grades would improve if you were to walk through the corridors of your elementary school. Similarly, your ability to retrieve an emotional moment with a close friend—for example, an argument with her in a restaurant—would be greater if you were back in the place where the incident occurred. This may explain why we are sometimes overcome with a torrent of memories when we visit a place where we once lived. The context in which an event was encoded is one of the most powerful retrieval cues. Figure 8-12, for example, shows the procedure of an experiment in which the effect of context was demonstrated (Godden & Baddeley, 1975). In this experiment, it did not matter overall whether the divers originally learned the to-be-remembered words on land or under water. However, divers tested in an environment

that was different from the one in which they had learned the words recalled 40% less than did divers who learned and recalled in the same environment. Reinstating the original learning context made an enormous difference for retrieval efficiency!

Context is not always external to the individual. It can include what is happening inside us when we encode information—that is, our internal state. For example, individuals who learned a list of words while under the influence of marijuana recalled more of the words when tested in the same drug-induced state than when tested in a nondrugged state, and individuals who learned the list in a nondrugged state recalled more words when tested in a nondrugged state than when tested in a drug-induced state (Eich, 1980). Such cases are referred to as state-dependent learning because memory is partly dependent on the internal state prevailing during learning. Feelings evoked by the altered state seem to serve as cues for retrieving information encoded while in that state. The evidence for this phenomenon is controversial, but it does suggest that memory does improve when our internal state during retrieval matches our internal state during encoding (Eich, 1980).

EMOTIONAL FACTORS IN FORGETTING

So far we have treated memory as if it were entirely separate from emotion. But don't we sometimes remember or forget material because of its emotional content? There has been a great deal of research on this question. The results suggest that emotion can influence long-term memory in five distinct ways: rehearsal, flashbulb memories, retrieval interference via anxiety, context effects, and repression.

REHEARSAL The simplest idea is that we tend to think about emotionally charged situations, negative as well as positive, more than we think about neutral ones. We rehearse and organize exciting memories more than we do blander ones. For example, you may forget where you saw this or that movie, but if a fire breaks out while you are in a theater, that incident will dominate your thoughts for a while. You will describe the setting over and over to friends, as well as think about the setting over and over to yourself, thereby rehearsing and organizing it. Because we know that rehearsal and organization can improve retrieval from long-term memory, it is not surprising that many researchers have found that memory is better for emotional situations than for unemotional ones (Neisser, 1982; Rapaport, 1942).

FLASHBULB MEMORIES The second way emotion can affect memory is via flashbulb memories. A **flashbulb**

Many people think they can remember exactly where they were and what they were doing when they heard about the shocking death of Lady Diana, Princess of Wales.

memory is a vivid and relatively permanent record of the circumstances in which one learned of an emotionally charged, significant event. An example is the explosion of the space shuttle *Challenger* in 1986, which was witnessed by millions of people on television. Many people in their twenties remember exactly where they were when they learned of the *Challenger* disaster and exactly who told them about it, even though these are the kinds of details that we usually forget quickly. Americans age 30 or older may have flashbulb memories of the assassination attempt on Ronald Reagan in 1981, and those age 40 or older may have such memories of the assassinations of John F. Kennedy and Martin Luther King Jr. in the 1960s. According to a published report, a century ago Americans had flashbulb memories of the assassination of Abraham Lincoln. When Colegrove (1899) interviewed 179 people, 127 of them were able to give full particulars as to where they were and what they were doing when they heard of Lincoln's assassination.

The problem with early studies of flashbulb memories, such as Colegrove's, is that there was no way of assessing whether they were correct. One man, for example, described detailed memories of a powerful 1960 earthquake in Chile, recalling being woken up early in the morning by the violent shaking of his house and noticing, among other things, that his grandfather clock had stopped at 6 A.M. sharp. Many years later, he discovered that the earthquake had actually taken place in early afternoon: Although the earthquake was certainly real, his vivid flashbulb memories of its taking place in the morning were not. Later we discuss the reconstructive processes that lead to such vivid but incorrect memories. For the moment, remember that when flashbulb memories are carefully studied in conjunction with a record of what actually happened, flashbulb memories turn out to be susceptible to decay and interference, just like other kinds of memories (Curci, Oliver, Finkenauer, & Gisle, 2001; Neisser & Harsch, 1993; Schmock, Buffalo, & Squire, 2000; Sierra & Berrios, 2000).

RETRIEVAL INTERFERENCE VIA ANXIETY There are also cases in which negative emotions hinder retrieval, which brings us to the third way emotion can affect memory. An experience that many students have at one time or another illustrates this process: You are taking an exam, and you are not very confident about it. You can barely understand the initial question, let alone answer it. Signs of panic appear. Although the second question really isn't hard, the anxiety triggered by the previous question spreads to this one. By the time you look at the third question, you might have difficulty even if the question asked something as mundane as your phone number. You're in a complete panic.

What is happening to memory here? Failure to deal with the first question produced anxiety. Anxiety is often accompanied by extraneous thoughts, such as "I'm going to flunk out" or "Everybody will think I'm stupid." These thoughts fill our consciousness and interfere with attempts to retrieve information that is relevant to the question, and this may be why memory fails. According to this view, anxiety does not directly cause memory failure. Rather, it causes, or is associated with, extraneous thoughts, and these thoughts cause memory failure by interfering with retrieval (Holmes, 1974).

CONTEXT EFFECTS Emotion may also affect memory through a context effect. As noted earlier, memory is best when the context at the time of retrieval matches that at the time of encoding. Because our emotional state during learning is part of the context, if the material we are learning makes us feel sad, perhaps we can best retrieve that material when we feel sad again. Experimenters have demonstrated such an emotional-context effect. Participants agreed to keep diaries for a week, recording every emotional incident that occurred and noting whether it was pleasant or unpleasant. One week after they handed in their diaries, the participants returned to the laboratory and were hypnotized. Half the participants were put in a pleasant mood and the other half in an unpleasant mood. All were asked to recall the incidents recorded in their diaries. For participants in a pleasant mood, most of the incidents they recalled had been rated as pleasant at the time that they were experienced; for participants in an unpleasant mood at retrieval, most of the incidents recalled had been rated as unpleasant. As expected, recall was best when the dominant emotion during retrieval matched that during encoding (Bower, 1981).

REPRESSION Thus far, all of the means by which emotions can influence memory rely on principles already discussed: rehearsal, interference, and context effects. Another view of emotion and memory, Freud's theory of the unconscious, brings up new principles. Freud proposed that some emotional experiences in childhood are so traumatic that allowing them to enter consciousness many years later would cause the individual to be totally overwhelmed by anxiety. Such traumatic experiences are said to be repressed, or stored in the unconscious, and they can be retrieved only when some of the emotion associated with them is defused. Repression therefore represents the ultimate retrieval failure: Access to the target memories is actively blocked. This notion of active blocking makes the repression hypothesis qualitatively different from the ideas about forgetting discussed earlier. (For a discussion of Freud's theory, see Chapter 13.)

Repression is such a striking phenomenon that we would, of course, like to study it in the laboratory, but it

has proved difficult to do this. To induce true repression in the laboratory, the experimenter must cause the participant to experience something extremely traumatic, but this obviously would be unethical. The studies that have been done have exposed participants to mildly upsetting experiences, and the results have been mixed (Baddeley, 1990; Erdelyi, 1985).

In sum, long-term memory is a system that can hold information for days, years, or decades, typically in a code based on meaning, although other codes are possible. Retrieval of information from this system is sensitive to interference; many apparent "storage losses" are really retrieval failures. Storage in this system involves consolidation, a process that is mediated by the hippocampal system. Many aspects of long-term memory can be influenced by emotion; such influences may reflect selective rehearsal, retrieval interference, the effects of context, or two special mechanisms: flashbulb memories and repression.

◆ Interim Summary

- Information in long-term memory is usually encoded according to its meaning.
- Many cases of forgetting in long-term memory are due to retrieval failures (the information is there but cannot be found).
- Some forgetting from long-term memory is due to a loss from storage, particularly when there is a disruption of the processes that consolidate new memories.
- The biological locus of consolidation includes the hippocampus and surrounding cortex. Recent research suggests that consolidation takes a few weeks to be completed.
- Retrieval failures in long-term memory are less likely when the items are organized during encoding and when the context at the time of retrieval is similar to the context at the time of encoding.
- Retrieval processes can also be disrupted by emotional factors.

◆ Critical Thinking Questions

1. We reviewed various proposals about how emotion affects explicit long-term memory. Some of these proposals imply that emotion helps memory, whereas others suggest that emotion hurts memory. How can you reconcile these apparent differences?

2. Suppose that you were interested in helping people improve their ability to store information in long-term memory and retrieve information from it. What techniques might you suggest in light of what you have learned in this section?

IMPLICIT MEMORY

To this point, we have been concerned mainly with situations in which people remember personal facts. In such cases, memory is a matter of consciously recollecting the past and is said to be expressed explicitly. But there seems to be another kind of memory, one that is often manifested in skills and shows up as an improvement in the performance of some perceptual, motor, or cognitive task without conscious recollection of the experiences that led to the improvement. For example, with practice we can steadily improve our ability to recognize words in a foreign language, but at the moment that we are recognizing a word, and thereby demonstrating our skill, we need not have any conscious recollection of the lessons that led to our improvement. In such cases, memory is expressed implicitly (Schacter, 1989).

MEMORY IN AMNESIA

Much of what is known about implicit memory has been learned from people who suffer **amnesia,** or partial loss of memory. Amnesia may result from very different causes, including accidental injuries to the brain, strokes, encephalitis, alcoholism, electroconvulsive shock, and surgical procedures (for example, removal of the hippocampus to reduce epilepsy). Whatever its cause, the primary symptom of amnesia is a profound inability to remember day-to-day events and hence to acquire new factual information. This is referred to as **anterograde amnesia,** and it can be extensive. There is an intensively studied patient, identified as N.A., who is unable to participate in a normal conversation because at the least distraction he loses his train of thought. Another patient, identified as H.M., reads the same magazines over and over and continually needs to be reintroduced to doctors who have been treating him for decades.

H.M. is the most famous of the brain-damaged patients whose memory functioning has been studied extensively (Milner, 1970; Squire, 1992). At the age of 27, H.M., who suffered from severe epilepsy, underwent surgery to remove portions of the temporal lobe and limbic system on both sides of his brain. The surgery left him unable to form new memories, although he could remember events that had occurred prior to the surgery.

H.M. can retain new information as long as he focuses on it, but as soon as he is distracted, he forgets the information, and he is unable to recall it later. On one occasion, for example, he kept the number 584 in mind for 15 minutes, using the following mnemonic system:* "5, 8, 4 add to 17. You remember 8, subtract from 17 and it leaves 9. Divide 9 by half and you get 5 and 4, and

*Mnemonic systems, or systems for aiding memory, are discussed later in the chapter.

there you are—584" (quoted in Milner, 1970). A few minutes later, however, H.M.'s attention shifted, and he could no longer remember either the number or his method for remembering it.

A secondary symptom of amnesia is **retrograde amnesia,** which is inability to remember events that occurred prior to the injury or disease. The extent of such retrograde amnesia varies from one patient to another. Aside from retrograde and anterograde memory losses, the typical amnesiac appears relatively normal: He or she has a normal vocabulary, the usual knowledge about the world (at least before the onset of the amnesia), and generally no loss of intelligence.

SKILLS AND PRIMING A striking aspect of amnesia is that not all kinds of memory are disrupted. Although amnesiacs generally are unable to either remember old facts about their lives or learn new ones, they have no difficulty remembering and learning perceptual and motor skills. There is apparently a different memory for facts than for skills. More generally, explicit and implicit memory (which encode facts and skills, respectively) seem to be different systems.

The skills that are preserved in amnesia include motor skills, such as tying one's shoelaces or riding a bike, and perceptual skills, such as normal reading or reading words that are projected into a mirror (and hence reversed). Consider the ability of reading mirror-reversed words. To do this well takes practice. (Try holding this book in front of a mirror and reading it.) Amnesiacs improve with practice at the same rate as normal participants, although they may have no memory of having participated in earlier practice sessions (Cohen & Squire, 1980). They show normal memory for the skill but vir-

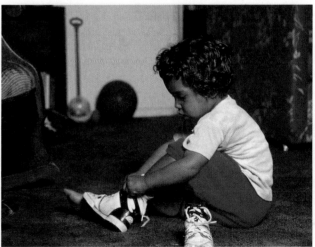

Memory for skills such as tying one's shoelaces is referred to as implicit memory.

tually no memory for the learning episodes that developed it (the latter being facts).

A similar pattern emerges when prior exposure to a stimulus facilitates or primes later processing of that stimulus. This pattern is illustrated in the experiment outlined in Table 8-2. In Stage 1 of the experiment, amnesiac and normal participants were given a list of words to study. In Stage 2, stems of words on the list and stems of words not on the list were presented, and the participants tried to complete them (see Table 8-2). The normal participants performed as expected, completing more stems when they were drawn from words on the list than when they were drawn from words not on the list. This difference, due to facilitation by prior exposure to a stimulus, is referred to as **priming** because the words presented in Stage 1 facilitated or primed performance on the stem completion problems presented in Stage 2. Significantly, amnesiacs also completed more stems in Stage 2 when they were drawn from words on the list than when they were drawn from words not on the list. In fact, the degree of priming for amnesiacs was exactly the same as for normal participants. This finding indicates that when memory is manifested implicitly, as in priming, amnesiacs perform normally.

In Stage 3 of the experiment, the original words were presented again, along with some novel words, and participants had to recognize which words had appeared on the list. Now amnesiacs remembered far fewer words than normals. Thus, when memory is tested explicitly, as in recognition, amnesiacs perform far below normals.

There is an interesting variation of the preceding study that further strengthens its conclusion. Suppose that in Stage 2 participants are instructed that they will perform better on the stem-completion task if they try to think of the words presented earlier. This instruction makes stem completion into an explicit memory task (because conscious recollection is being emphasized). Now amnesiacs show substantially less priming than normal participants (Graf & Mandler, 1984).

CHILDHOOD AMNESIA One of the most striking aspects of human memory is that everyone suffers from a particular kind of amnesia: Virtually no one can recall events from the first years of life, even though this is the time when experience is at its richest. This curious phenomenon was first discussed by Freud (1905), who called it **childhood amnesia.**

Freud discovered the phenomenon by observing that his patients were generally unable to recall events from their first 3 to 5 years of life. At first you might see nothing unusual about this, because memory for events declines with time, and for adults there has been a lot of intervening time since early childhood. But childhood amnesia cannot be reduced to normal forgetting. Most 30-year-olds can recall a good deal about their high school years, but it is a rare 18-year-old who can tell you anything about his or her third year of life. Yet the time interval—about 15 years—is roughly the same in each case.

In some studies, people have been asked to recall and date their childhood memories. For most people, their first memory is of something that occurred when they were age 3 or older, and a few individuals report memories prior to the age of 1. A problem with these reports, however, is that we can never be sure that the "remembered" event actually occurred (the person may have reconstructed what he or she thought happened). This problem was overcome in an experiment in which participants were asked a total of 20 questions about a childhood event that was known to have occurred—the birth of a younger sibling—the details of which could be verified by another person. The questions asked of each participant dealt with events that occurred when the mother left to go to the hospital (for example, "What time of day did she leave?"), when the mother was in the hospital ("Did you visit her?"), and when the mother and infant returned home ("What time of day did they come home?"). The participants were college students, and their ages at the time that their siblings were born varied from 1 to 17 years. The results are shown in Figure 8-13. The number of questions answered is plotted as a function of the participant's age when the sibling was born. If the sibling was born before the participant was 3 years old, the person could not recall a thing about it. If the birth occurred after that, recall increased

● Table 8-2
Procedure for an Experiment to Study Implicit Memory in Amnesia

(Reprinted from Neuropsychologia, *Vol. 16. pp. 169–172 by W. K. Warrington and L. Weiskrantz, "Further Analysis of the Proper Learning Effect in Amnesiac Parents." Copyright © 1978, with permission from Elsevier Science, Ltd.)*

Stage 1	Example
Present list of words for study	MOTEL

Stage 2	
Present stems of list words and nonlist words for completion. Number of list words completed minus number of nonlist words completed = Priming	MOT BLA

Stage 3	
Present original list of words plus new words for recognition	MOTEL STAND

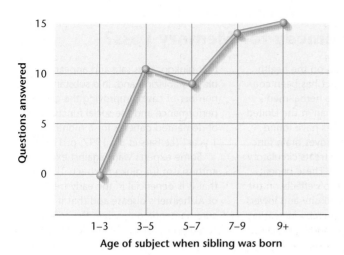

Figure 8-13
Recall of an Early Memory
In an experiment on childhood amnesia, college-age individuals were asked 20 questions about the events surrounding the birth of a younger sibling. The average number of questions answered is plotted as a function of the individual's age when the sibling was born. If the birth occurred before the fourth year of life, no individual could recall a thing about it. If the birth occurred after that, recall increased with age at the time of the event. (After Sheingold & Tenney, 1982)

with age at the time of the event. These results suggest almost total amnesia for the first 3 years of life. More recent research, however, suggests that such recall may be improved if more cues are given and the cues are more specific (Fivush & Hamond, 1991). Still, the bulk of the evidence indicates that we should be skeptical about reports of memory from the first few years of life. (The dip from ages 3 to 5 to ages 5 to 7 is probably just due to random fluctuations in the data).

What causes childhood amnesia? A generally accepted explanation is that childhood amnesia is due to a massive difference between how young children encode experience and how adults organize their memories. Adults structure their memories in terms of categories and schemas ("She's that kind of person," "It's that kind of situation"), but young children encode their experiences without embellishing them or connecting them to related events. Once a child begins to form associations between events and to categorize those events, early experiences become lost (Schachtel, 1982).

What causes the shift from early childhood to adult forms of memory? One factor is biological development. The hippocampus, which is known to be involved in consolidating memories, is not mature until roughly a year or two after birth. Therefore, events that take place in the first 2 years of life cannot be sufficiently consolidated and consequently cannot be recalled later.

Other causes of the shift to adult memory are better understood at the psychological level. These include cognitive factors, particularly the development of language and the beginning of schooling. Both language and the kind of thinking emphasized in school provide new ways of organizing experiences, ways that may be incompatible with the way the young child encodes experiences. Interestingly, language development reaches an early peak at age 3, schooling often begins at age 5, and the age span from 3 to 5 is the time when childhood amnesia seems to end.

A VARIETY OF MEMORY SYSTEMS

On the basis of work with various brain-damaged patients, researchers have proposed that both explicit and implicit memory come in various forms. One such proposal is presented in the Concept Review table. The basic distinction is between explicit and implicit memory. (Recall that explicit memory involves consciously recollecting the past, and implicit memory shows up as improved performance of a skill without conscious recollection of the lessons that led to it.) With regard to implicit memory, a further distinction is made between perceptual-motor skills, such as reading mirror-reversed words, and priming, as occurs in word-stem completions. The reason for assuming that skills and priming may involve different memory stores is that there are patients with brain damage (individuals in the early stages of Alzheimer's disease) who are able to learn motor skills but show less priming than normal. In contrast, other brain-damaged patients (individuals with Huntington's disease) show normal priming but

CONCEPT REVIEW TABLE
Propopsed Classification of Memory Stores

Squire et al. (1990) propose that there are several different memory systems. The basic distinction is between explicit and implicit memory (which they refer to as *declarative* and *nondeclarative*, respectively).

Explicit (Declarative) Memory	Implicit (Nondeclarative) Memory
Episodic	Skills
Semantic	Priming
	Conditioning
	Nonassociative

An Herbal Remedy for Memory Loss?

It has been called "the elixir of youth" and "memory mate." It has been found effective by both ancient healers and modern scientists. These days it is receiving a great deal of attention in the medical journals as well as the popular press.

This much-heralded substance is an extract from the ginkgo tree, an ornamental tree often planted along city streets. The Chinese have used ginkgo nuts for thousands of years to increase sexual energy and as a remedy for diseases ranging from venereal disease to cancer. Modern medical researchers have found evidence that ginkgo extract can be effective in treating a variety of ailments, including asthma, depression, impotence, and retinal damage. Perhaps most significant is the potential of gingko for the treatment of memory loss due to Alzheimer's disease, multi-infarct dementia (ministrokes), and normal aging.

Much of the research on the health benefits of gingko extract has been conducted in Europe, where herbal medicine is more accepted than in the United States. Laboratory studies have found that gingko extract improves brain functioning and prevents or treats circulatory disorders such as stroke. These benefits stem largely from ginkgo's effects on the blood: It thins blood viscosity and lowers platelet adhesiveness, thereby increasing blood flow to the brain and extremities. It also regulates blood vessel elasticity. Because of these effects, it can counteract some of the most common conditions associated with aging, particularly decreased blood flow to the brain, which can adversely affect memory, concentration, and intellectual ability.

Laboratory studies of the effects of ginkgo extract on memory are usually set up as double-blind studies in which some participants receive ginkgo extract while others receive a placebo. The results have shown small but significant positive effects of ginkgo extract on short-term memory, degenerative dementia of the Alzheimer type, and multi-infarct dementia. One group of researchers concluded

that ginkgo "was safe and appears capable of stabilizing and, in a substantial number of cases, improving the cognitive performance and the social functioning of demented patients for 6 months to 1 year" (Le Bars et al., 1997, p. 1327).

Some experts warn against excessive enthusiasm for ginkgo extract. They note that it is beneficial in the early treatment of Alzheimer's disease and that it can cure dementia only when the condition is caused by lack of blood flow to the brain. Claims that ginkgo extract is an "elixir of youth" are clearly overstated. Others note that ginkgo extract has not been subjected to extensive clinical trials, nor has it received approval from the Food and Drug Administration. Nevertheless, the evidence from controlled research lends support to the ancient Chinese belief that ginkgo can increase health and longevity.

 For more information, go online with InfoTrac College Edition. Use your own term or search:

- Ginkgo
- Ginkgo and memory
- Herbs and memory

---

have difficulty learning new motor skills (Schacter, 1989).

The concept review also distinguishes between two kinds of explicit memory. **Episodic memory** refers to memory of personal episodes, and **semantic memory** refers to memory of facts and general truths. Your memory of your high school graduation is an episodic fact, and so is your memory for what you had for dinner last night. In each of these cases, the episode is encoded with respect to you, the individual (your graduation, your dinner, and so on), and often with respect to a specific time and place as well. In contrast, semantic facts, such as your memory or knowledge that the word *bachelor* means an unmarried man and that September has 30 days, are encoded in relation to other knowledge rather than in relation to yourself, and there is no coding of time and place (Tulving, 1985). This distinction between semantic and episodic memory fits with the fact that al-

though amnesiacs have severe difficulty remembering personal episodes, they seem relatively normal in their general knowledge.

IMPLICIT MEMORY IN NORMAL INDIVIDUALS

Studies using normal individuals also suggest separate systems for explicit and implicit memories. There seem to be fundamental differences in how these two kinds of memories are implemented in the brain. The critical evidence comes from brain-scanning experiments (PET). In one experiment (Squire et al., 1992), participants first studied a list of 15 words and then were exposed to three different conditions. The implicit-memory condition was the stem-completion task. Half the stems were drawn from the 15 words originally studied, and the other half were new; participants were instructed to complete the stems with the first words that came to mind. The second condition of interest involved explicit memory. Again, word stems were presented, but now participants were instructed to use them to recall words from the initial list of 15. The third condition was a control. Word stems were presented, and participants were instructed to complete them with the first words that came to mind, but none of the stems were drawn from the words initially studied. The control condition therefore requires no memory. Participants performed all three of these tasks while their brains were being scanned.

Consider first what the brain is doing during the explicit-memory task. From the material presented in the first section of this chapter, we might expect that (1) the hippocampus is involved (remember, this structure is critical in forming long-term memories) and (2) most of the brain activity will be in the right hemisphere (because the task emphasized retrieval, and long-term retrieval involves mainly right-hemisphere processes). This is exactly what was found. More specifically, when brain activity in the explicit-memory condition was compared with that in the control condition, there was increased activation of hippocampal and frontal regions in the right hemisphere.

Now consider the implicit-memory condition. Compared with the control condition, it showed decreases in activation rather than increases. Priming is reflected in less-than-usual neural activity, as if there has been a "greasing of the neural wheels." Implicit memory, then, has the opposite neural consequences of explicit memory, demonstrating a biological difference between the two kinds of memory.

This evidence points once again to the interconnections between biological and psychological research. In fact, throughout this chapter we have seen instances of the role of biological evidence in explaining psychological phenomena. In many cases, the psychological evidence was obtained first and used to direct subsequent biological research. For example, the cognitive distinction between short-term and long-term memory was made in papers published about a century ago, but only relatively recently have biologically oriented researchers been able to demonstrate some of the neural bases for this key distinction. Biological research is contributing to other areas of the study of memory as well. We now know something about the biological basis of storage in explicit long-term memory and about storage in the visual and verbal buffers of short-term memory. Such knowledge not only is useful in its own right but also may prove helpful in combating the ravages of memory brought about by diseases of aging such as stroke and Alzheimer's.

◆ Interim Summary

- Explicit memory refers to the kind of memory manifested in recall or recognition, when we consciously recollect the past. Implicit memory refers to the kind of memory that manifests itself as an improvement on some perceptual, motor, or cognitive task, with no conscious recollection of the experiences that led to the improvement.

- Although explicit memory—particularly recall and recognition of facts—breaks down in amnesia, implicit memory is usually spared. This suggests that there may be separate storage systems for explicit and implicit memory.

- Research with normal individuals also suggests that there may be separate systems for explicit and implicit memory.

- Brain-scanning studies with normal individuals show that explicit memory is accompanied by increased neural activity in certain regions, whereas implicit memory is accompanied by a decrease in neural activity in critical regions.

◆ Critical Thinking Questions

1. On the basis of what you have learned about explicit long-term memory, how would you go about studying for an exam that emphasizes factual recall?

2. We noted that childhood amnesia is related to the development of the hippocampus. What psychological factors might also contribute to childhood amnesia? (Think of things that change dramatically around age 3.)

CONSTRUCTIVE MEMORY

Our description of memory processes so far might leave the impression that a good metaphor for creating, maintaining, and using information in long-term store would be creating, maintaining, and using a videotape. Consider the correspondences:

1. Information is acquired and placed into memory via sensation, perception, and attention in the same way as information is acquired and placed onto a videotape via a video camera.

2. Information is forgotten from long-term store in the same way as videotapes gradually become degraded.

3. Information cannot be retrieved from long-term store in the same way, as it is difficult to find a par-

ticular scene on a home video—particularly if there are a lot of scenes on the video and/or it has been a long time since you last retrieved and viewed the scene.

Despite these apparent similarities, it would be a grave mistake to use a video recorder as the primary metaphor for understanding memory, because there is a very important and fundamental difference between how memory works and how a videotape works. Unlike a videotape, memory is a **constructive** and **reconstructive process.** The memory for an event can and does depart systematically from the objective reality that gave rise to it, both at the time it is formed (via constructive processes) and then later over time (via reconstructive memory). This crucial difference leads to some of the most interesting and counterintuitive aspects of memory. It almost certainly, for example, underlies Jennifer Thompson's seemingly strange and certainly catastrophic memory misidentification of the man who raped her. In the sections that follow, we will first recount a personal anecdote that nicely illustrates the reconstructive nature of memory and then trace the reconstructive nature of memory from original perception through long-term retrieval. Finally, we will briefly discuss the already alluded-to relevance of reconstructive memory to the legal system.

PIAGET'S CHILDHOOD MEMORY

The renowned Swiss developmental psychologist, Jean Piaget, once described a vivid memory from his childhood:

> . . . one of my first memories would date, if it were true, from my second year. I can still see, most clearly, the following scene, in which I believed until I was about fifteen. I was sitting in my pram, which my nurse was pushing in the Champs Elysees, when a man tried to kidnap me. I was held in by the strap fastened round me while my nurse bravely tried to stand between me and the thief. She received various scratches, and I can still see vaguely those on her face. Then a crowd gathered, a policeman with a short cloak and a white baton came up, and the man took to his heels. I can still see the whole scene, and can even place it near the tube station.

A vivid memory indeed! Why then did Piaget believe in it only "until I was about fifteen"? What happened then?

> When I was about fifteen, my parents received a letter from my former nurse saying that she had been converted to the Salvation Army. She wanted to confess her past faults, and in particular, to return the watch she had been given as a reward [for saving Baby Jean from the kidnapper]. She had made up the whole story, faking the scratches. I, therefore, must have heard, as a child, the account of this story, which my parents believed, and projected into the past in the form of a visual memory.

Piaget discovered that this memory, vivid though it seemed, was not merely incorrect but fabricated from whole cloth. When you think about it, the implications of this anecdote are far-reaching: At least some of what we firmly believe to be true is probably fiction. As we will discuss later, this implication is not quite as disturbing as it might seem at first glance, because (1) it takes a special set of circumstances to create a false memory that is this dramatic, and (2) even when such memories are created, they generally do not have any serious real-world consequences. Be that as it may, some false memories, like Jennifer Thompson's, can sometimes have devastating consequences.

How do such memories come about? The answer is that they arise from a combination of constructive processes, which can be divided into those occurring at the time of original encoding of the to-be-remembered event and those occurring after the memory of the remembered event has already been formed.

CONSTRUCTIVE PROCESSES AT THE TIME OF MEMORY ENCODING

Memory encoding refers to processes that occur when the long-term memory representation of some event is being established. From the perspective of establishing a long-term representation, encoding has two stages: initial perception (transfer of information into short-term store) and then whatever processes are entailed in the transfer of information from short-term store to long-term store. Construction of a false memory can occur at either or both of these stages.

CONSTRUCTIVE PERCEPTION In Chapter 5, we discussed the systematic ways in which what is perceived does not necessarily correspond to what is objectively out in the world. In many instances, perception is determined not only by the "bottom-up" processing of raw, objective, sensory data but also by the "top-down" influences of history, knowledge, and expectations. What does this mean for later memory? What is perceived forms the basis for the initial memory; therefore, if what is originally perceived differs systematically from the objective world, the perceiver's initial memory—and probably later memories as well—of what happened will likewise be distorted.

To illustrate such **constructive perception,** we first turn to another personal anecdote, this one from one of the authors of this book (GL). In 1973, GL was visiting a friend who showed him a "music box," consisting of a cube, approximately 6 inches on a side, with translucent faces. The box was connected to a stereo system, and as music played, colored lights inside the box lit up in various sequences. With particular light combinations, certain images became clearly visible on the box's translucent sides. For instance, there was a Viet Cong soldier on one side, a picture of Bob Dylan on another side, and a picture of the Beatles on yet a third side. Intrigued by this sequence of images, GL and his friend became curious about how they were formed. They supposed that pictures from news magazines had been clipped and affixed to the inside of the box's translucent sides in such a way that they became visible only with certain combinations of colored lights. At length, they took the box apart to investigate. To their amazement, they discovered that there was nothing but random splatters of paint on the translucent sides. The vivid images they had perceived were not there in the world; rather, they had been constructed out of randomness. And, even though GL and his friend discovered that their perceptions were illusory, GL maintains to this day a vivid memory of the music-box images that his perceptual system so artfully constructed.

A good example of how constructive perception can demonstrated in the scientific laboratory is found in a phenomenon known as perceptual interference, which was originally described in a 1964 *Science* article by Jerome Bruner and Mary Potter. They showed observers pictures of common objects (say, a rocket) and asked the observers to name the object. The catch was that the objects began by being out of focus—sufficiently out of focus that they were pretty much unrecognizable—and then were gradually brought into focus. There were two main conditions in the experiment. In the very-out-of-focus (VOF) condition, the objects started out very out of focus, and in the moderately-out-of-focus (MOF) condition, the objects started out only moderately out of focus. The **perceptual interference** finding was that the objects had to eventually be more focused for the observers to recognize them in the VOF condition than in the MOF condition.

Why was this? The hypothesis offered by Bruner and Potter was that, upon seeing any out-of-focus object, an observer would generate hypotheses about what the object was (for instance, an observer might initially hypothesize an out of focus rocket to be a pencil). Once a hypothesis was generated, the hypothesis itself largely drove the observer's perception. As the object became more and more focused, the observer would continue to hold the incorrect perception even past the focus level that would allow another observer who *hadn't* generated any incorrect expectations to perceive the object correctly. Because observers in the VOF condition had more opportunity to form incorrect hypotheses than observers in the MOF condition, it would require a greater degree of focus for eventual correct recognition for the VOF than for the MOF observers.

GENERATION OF INFERENCES As we have pointed out, perception is not sufficient to form a lasting memory of some event. Other processes have to occur to transfer information corresponding to the event from short-term store to long-term store. **Constructive processes** can occur here in the form of **inferences.**

Let's illustrate using memory for verbal material. Even when we read something as simple as a sentence, we often draw inferences from it and store them along with the sentence in long-term store. This tendency is particularly strong when reading text because inferences are often needed to connect different lines. Consider the following story, which was presented to participants in an experiment.

1. Provo is a picturesque kingdom in France.
2. Corman was heir to the throne of Provo.
3. He was so tired of waiting.
4. He thought arsenic would work well.

When reading this story, participants draw inferences at certain points. At line 3, they infer that Corman wanted to be king, which permits them to connect line 3 to the preceding line. But this is not a necessary inference (Corman could have been waiting for the king to receive him). At line 4, participants infer that Corman had decided to poison the king, so they can connect this line to what preceded it. Again, the inference is not a necessary one. (There are people other than the king to poison, and there are other uses of arsenic.) When participants' memories were later tested for exactly which lines had been presented, they had trouble distinguishing the story lines from the inferences we just described. It is hard to keep what was actually presented separate from what we added to it (Seifert, Robertson, & Black, 1985).

POST-EVENT MEMORY RECONSTRUCTION

Earlier we cautioned against thinking of a videotape as an metaphor for memory. A better metaphor would be file folder (either a physical, cardboard folder or a computer folder) containing the components of some complex enterprise we're working on—say, the material for a novel we're writing, which would include our notes, our chapters in progress, our photographs, and so on. Every time we open this folder, the contents of it change in some fashion as our work progresses. And so it is with our memory for some event: Every time we revisit some memory in our minds, the memory changes in some fashion. We may, as we do during memory formation, generate inferences and store these inferences as part of our memory. We may strip away information that doesn't seem to make sense in light of other facts we know or we've learned. We may add new information that is suggested to us by others. All of these kinds of processes fall into the category of **post-event memory reconstruction.**

INTERNALLY GENERATED INFERENCES There are many ways in which people can make inferences that they then incorporate into their memory. A recent example reported by Hannigan and Reinitz (2001) described inference in visual memory. In their experiment, observers viewed a slide sequence depicting some common activity, such as shopping in a supermarket. As part of the sequence, they saw scenes depicting some relatively unusual situation (such as oranges scattered over the supermarket floor). Later, the observers confidently asserted that they had seen a picture that reasonably depicted a possible cause of this situation (such as a slide of a woman pulling an orange from the bottom of the pile), although in fact they had never seen the slide. These and related results strongly suggest that, in these situations, viewers make inferences about what must have happened and then incorporate the results of such inferences into their memory of the event.

Inferences can also be made based on **schemas, mental representations of a class of people, objects, events, or situations.** Stereotypes, on which we will focus momentarily, are a kind of schema because they represent classes of people (for example, Italians, women, athletes). Schemas can also be used to describe our knowledge about how to act in certain situations.

For example, most adults have a schema for how to eat in a restaurant (enter the restaurant, find a table, get a menu from the waiter, order food, and so on). Perceiving and thinking in terms of schemas enables us to process large amounts of information swiftly and economically. Instead of having to perceive and remember all the details of each new person, object, or event we encounter, we can simply note that it is like a schema already in our memory and encode and remember only its most distinctive features. The price we pay for such "cognitive economy," however, is that an object or event can be distorted if the schema used to encode it does not fit well.

Bartlett (1932) was perhaps the first psychologist to systematically study the effects of schemas on memory. He suggested that memory distortions much like those that occur when we fit people into stereotypes can occur when we attempt to fit stories into schemas. Research has confirmed Bartlett's suggestion. For example, after reading a brief story about a character going to a restaurant, people are likely to recall statements about the character eating and paying for a meal, even though those actions were never mentioned in the story (Bower, Black, & Turner, 1979).

Situations in which memory is driven by schemas seem a far cry from the simpler situations discussed earlier in the chapter. Consider, for example, memory for a list of unrelated words. Here memory processes appear more bottom-up. They function more to preserve the input than to construct something new. However, there is

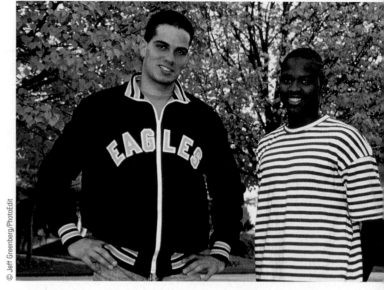

The stereotype of the "typical jock" may interfere with our encoding of information about these college students, who could have entirely different characteristics from those included in the stereotype.

a constructive aspect even to this simple situation, for techniques such as using imagery add meaning to the input. Similarly, when we read a paragraph about a schema-based activity, we must still preserve some of its specifics if we are to recall it correctly. The two aspects of memory—to preserve and to construct—may always be present, although their relative emphasis may depend on the exact situation.

As noted, one important kind of schema is a **social stereotype,** which concerns personality traits or physical attributes of a whole class of people. We may, for example, have a stereotype of the typical German (intelligent, meticulous, serious) or of the typical Italian (artistic, carefree, fun loving). These descriptions rarely apply to many people in the class and can often be misleading guides for social interaction. Our concern here, however, is not with the effects of stereotypes on social interaction (see Chapter 18 for a discussion of this) but with their effects on memory.

When presented with information about a person, we sometimes stereotype that person (for example, "He's your typical Italian") and combine the information presented with that in our stereotype. Our memory of the person thus is partly constructed from the stereotype. To the extent that our stereotype does not fit the person, our recall can be seriously distorted. A British psychologist provides a firsthand account of such a distortion:

In the week beginning 23 October, I encountered in the university, a male student of very conspicuously Scandinavian appearance. I recall being very forcibly impressed by the man's Nordic, Viking-like appearance—his fair hair, his blue eyes, and long bones. On several occasions, I recalled his appearance in connection with a Scandinavian correspondence I was then conducting and thought of him as the "perfect Viking," visualizing him at the helm of a longship crossing the North Sea in quest of adventure. When I again saw the man on 23 November, I did not recognize him, and he had to introduce himself. It was not that I had forgotten what he looked like but that his appearance, as I recalled it, had become grossly distorted. He was very different from my recollection of him. His hair was darker, his eyes less blue, his build less muscular, and he was wearing spectacles (as he always does). (Hunter, 1974, pp. 265–266)

The psychologist's stereotype of Scandinavians seems to have so overwhelmed any information he actually encoded about the student's appearance that the result was a highly constructed memory. It bore so little resemblance to the student that it could not even serve as a basis for recognition.

EXTERNALLY PROVIDED SUGGESTIONS Post-event reconstruction may also occur as a result of information provided by others. A classic experiment, reported by Elizabeth Loftus and John Palmer (1974) illustrates this process. In the experiment, a group of subjects were shown a film of a car accident (one car running into another). After the film, the subjects were asked a series of questions about the accident that they had just seen. The subjects were divided into two subgroups that were treated identically except for a single word in one of the questions. In particular, the "hit" group was asked the following question about speed: "How fast was the car going when it hit

In remembering what happened in a traffic accident, we may use general knowledge (such as our knowledge of rules of the road or of the meaning of traffic signals) to construct a more detailed memory.

the other car?" The corresponding question asked to the "smashed" group was, "How fast was the car going when it smashed into the other car?" Other than that, the "hit" and "smashed" groups were treated identically.

The first finding to emerge from this experiment was that the "smashed" group provided a higher speed estimate than the "hit" group (roughly 10.5 mph versus 8 mph). This is interesting, in that is demonstrates the effects of leading questions on the answers that are given. More relevant to the issue of post-event reconstruction, however, was the next part of procedure. All subjects returned approximately a week later and were asked some additional questions about the accident. One of the questions was "Did you see any broken glass?" In fact, there had been no broken glass, so the correct answer to the question was no. However, the subjects who had originally been asked about speed with the verb *smashed* were substantially more likely to incorrectly report the presence of broken glass than were subjects who had originally been asked about speed using the verb *hit*.

The interpretation of this finding is that the verb *smashed* constituted post-event information. Upon hearing this word, the subjects reconstructed their memory for the accident to be consistent with a violent accident in which two cars "smashed" into one another. Integration into their memory of the broken glass was one consequence of such reconstruction. That is how the nonexistent broken glass appeared in those subjects' memories a week later.

How powerful is the effect of suggestive information? This study, along with thousands of others that have replicated its basic result over the past quarter-century, demonstrates the ease of structuring a situation such that a real event is remembered incorrectly with respect to incidental details. Is it possible that, in like fashion, a memory of an entire fictional event could be created? This seems less likely, based on intuition and common sense, yet intuition and common sense are incorrect in this regard.

To begin with, there are anecdotes of false memories similar to Piaget's described earlier. Even more dramatically, there are occasional reports by people who claim to have experienced events that would be generally considered to be impossible, such as being abducted and experimented on by aliens. Given that these people actually believe these experiences occurred, they would likely constitute prima facie evidence of false memories for complete events. However, interpretation of such anecdotal reports is problematic. First, implausible though such events are, we cannot completely rule out the possibility that they actually occurred. Second, and of somewhat more concern, we do not know that the witnesses are being truthful. One could argue that a few publicity-seeking members of the population carefully make up and stick to such stories to gain attention.

More persuasive scientific evidence comes from recent laboratory studies in which memories of entirely fictional events have been shown to be implantable under controlled conditions. For example, Hyman, Husband, & Billings (1995) reported a study in which college students were asked whether they remembered a relatively unusual and entirely fictional event (for example, attending a wedding reception and accidentally spilling a punch bowl on the parents of the bride) that subjects were told occurred when they were relatively young (around 5 years old). Initially, no one remembered these events. However following two interviews about the "event," a substantial proportion of the students (20% to 25%) reported quite clear "memories" for parts or all of the events. Indeed, many of the students began "remembering" details that had never been presented to them (and which, of course, could not have corresponded to objective reality). For example, one subject initially had no recall of the wedding event, but by the second interview, stated, "It was an outdoor wedding, and I think we were running around and knocked something over like the punch bowl or something and, um, made a big mess and of course got yelled at for it." Other studies (Loftus, Coan & Pickrell, 1996; Loftus & Pickrell, 1995) have reported similar findings, and another study (Garry, Manning, Loftus, & Sherman, 1996) has reported that such memories can be induced by merely having people *imagine* fictional renderings of their pasts.

In these studies, subjects appear to be using post-event information provided by the experimenters to create memories of entire events that never occurred. In addition, the process of imagining these events spontaneously led to additional, self-generated post-event information, involving additional details, which then also was incorporated.

As noted, not all subjects in these experiments actually remembered these false events. In general, the percentage of people remembering was approximately 25%. The Hyman and associates (1995) study reported some personality correlates of false memory creation. The first was the score on the Dissociative Experiences Scale, which measures the extent to which a person has lapses in memory and attention or fails to integrate awareness, thought, and memory. The second correlate was the score on the Creative Imagination Scale, which is a measure of hypnotizability and can also be construed as a self-report measure of the vividness of visual imagery.

CONSTRUCTIVE MEMORY AND THE LEGAL SYSTEM

As we have suggested in several of our discussions and examples, constructive memory is particularly important in the legal system, where cases are frequently won or lost—and defendants are or are not meted out punishments ranging from prison sentences to death—on the basis of a witness's memory of what did or did not happen. A dramatic example of the consequences of a false memory is the years spent by Ronald Cotton languishing in prison as a result of Jennifer Thompson's false memory of who raped her. This is by no means an isolated incident but, sadly, one of many known cases and countless unknown cases of miscarriages of justice caused by false memories. In this section, we specifically describe the importance of memory in the legal system.

CONFIDENCE AND ACCURACY A scientist studying memory in the scientific laboratory has the luxury of knowing whether a participant's memory is correct or incorrect. The scientist, having created the event that the witness is trying to remember, is in a position to compare the participant's response to objective reality. In the real world, however—particularly the real world of a witness whose memory is crucial to the outcome of some legal case—no one has the ability to judge objectively whether the witness is correct or incorrect, because there is no objective record of the original event (with a few exceptions, such as a crime captured on video, as in the infamous Rodney King case). Therefore, the main indicator of whether a witness is correct is the witness's *confidence* that his or her memory is accurate: A witness who says, "I'm 100% sure that that's the man who raped me" is judged to be more likely correct than a witness who says, "I'm 75% sure that that's the man who raped me." A critical question for the legal system is: How good is a witness's confidence as an index of the witness's memory? Common sense says that it's pretty good. Does scientific evidence back this up?

The answer is that although in both the scientific laboratory and in normal everyday life, high confidence is often predictive of high accuracy, psychologists have also delineated the circumstances in which—contrary to common sense—this normal predictive power vanishes. Such circumstances include (1) some original event that causes poor encoding to begin with (because of short duration, poor lighting, lack of appropriate attention, or any of a number of other factors), (2) some form of post-event reconstruction (such as inferences or information suggested by others), and (3) the motivation and opportunity to rehearse the reconstructed memory (Penrod & Cutler, 1995; Wells, Ferguson, & Lindsay, 1981).

In the best-known study of this phenomenon, 45 experiments that had measured the relationship between confidence in some memory and the accuracy of that memory were examined. In approximately half of those studies, there was the positive relation between confidence and accuracy that our intuitions would lead us to believe: Higher confidence was associated with higher accuracy. In the other half of the experiments, however, there was *no* relation (or, in some instances, even a negative relation) between confidence and accuracy (Deffenbacher, 1980).

Which result was found depended on the overall circumstances surrounding the formation of the memory. Favorable circumstances (such as good lighting, no stress, and no post-event information) led to the expected positive relation between confidence and accuracy. However, unfavorable circumstances led to no relation or a negative relation between confidence and accuracy.

The reason is that when encoding circumstances are poor, initial memory is filled with gaps. Suppose, for example, that a person experiences a near-accident in a car (say, is almost hit by another car). Because of the brevity and stress of the situation, the person probably would not remember many details—for example, the make or color of the other car, or whether there was a passenger in the car. These would be *gaps* in the person's memory. But because the event was salient, the person would rehearse the event in his or her mind. In the process of rehearsing, the memory gaps would tend to fill in. Such filling in could be random, it could be due to expectations, it could be due to post-event information—it could be due to many things, few of them likely to be accurate. The resulting memory would therefore be generally inaccurate. But the rehearsal of this inaccurate memory leads to a *strong* memory, in which the person would have relatively high confidence (Leippe, 1980).

An important practical conclusion issues from these studies. When a witness expresses great confidence in some memory (such as the identification of a defendant as the remembered culprit in some crime), the jury would do well to learn of the events that led up to this confident memory. If the circumstances for forming the original memory were good and there was little cause for post-event memory reconstruction, the jury can reasonably accept the high confidence as evidence of the memory's accuracy. If, on the other hand, the circumstances for forming the original memory were poor, and there were apparent sources of potentially false for post-event memory reconstruction, the jury should discount the witness's high confidence as an index of the memory's accuracy.

The legal system is finally beginning to take these research findings into account. In April 2001, the state of New Jersey adopted new general guidelines for identification procedures that were based largely on the kind of research that we have just described. In an accompanying memo, New Jersey Attorney General James Farmer noted that it is important to guard against identification procedures that may invest a witness with a false sense of confidence, and goes on to say, "Studies have established that the confidence level that witnesses demonstrate regarding their identifications is the primary determinant of whether jurors accept identifications as accurate and reliable."

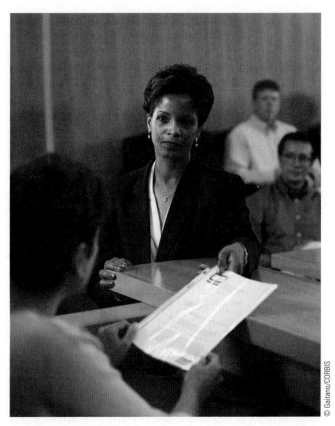

A very confident eyewitness, while persuasive to a jury, may nevertheless be completely incorrect.

SUGGESTIVE INFORMATION AND CHILDREN'S MEMORIES Young children appear to be particularly susceptible to suggestive information, especially while they are being interviewed. Ceci and Bruck (1993) describe a variety of studies demonstrating this kind of suggestibility. The problem is particularly acute because children are often interviewed about crimes by interviewers who, wittingly or unwittingly, provide a great deal of suggestive information in the course of the interview.

An example of a recently reported experiment demonstrating the consequences of this sort of confirmatory interview technique worked as follows. First, a trained social worker was given a fact sheet about a particular event in which a child had participated. This fact sheet contained both actual actions that had happened during the event, and false actions—actions that had not occurred. The social worker was then asked to interview the child about the event. She was asked specifically not to ask leading questions.

Several results emerged from this procedure. First, the child being interviewed eventually recalled the false actions with a good deal of confidence, thereby indicating that the interviewer had "infected" the child with her preconceptions about what had happened. Second, other professionals couldn't tell which of the things the child recalled were the real actions and which were falsely implanted. In this instance, the interview itself—unbiased though the professional interviewer tried to make it—was obviously effective in conveying the interviewer's preexisting biases to the child *and* actually altering the child's memory about what happened—indeed, altering it in such a fashion that other professionals couldn't tell what in the child's memory was based on actual experience and which was based on after-the-fact suggested information.

FORCED CONFESSIONS A growing body of work has demonstrated that interrogation techniques carried out by police and other investigators have been able to produce genuinely false memories (and confessions) of crimes that the suspects can be objectively shown to have not committed (Kassin, 1997; Leo, 1996; Ofshe, 1992). Researchers have demonstrated that false memories can be created in the minds of innocent people by techniques that include, but are not limited to, (1) being told that there is unambiguous evidence (such as fingerprints) proving their culpability, (2) being told that they were drunk or were otherwise impaired so that they wouldn't have remembered the crime, (3) being told that awful crimes are repressed and if they try hard they will be able to "recover" these repressed memories, and (4) that they are suffering from multiple personality disorder and that the crime was committed by another of their personalities.

Richard Ofshe (1992) provides a dramatic, indisputable example of such a sequence of false memories. In a well-known case (described in a series of *New Yorker* articles), Paul Ingram, a high-ranking employee of the Thurston County (Washington) Sheriff's Department, was accused by his two daughters of having raped and abused them over many years as part of a series of satanic cult rituals. Ingram initially claimed innocence, but following a lengthy series of police interrogations began to admit to the crimes and also began to have increasingly vivid "memories" of the details. Ofshe, a sociologist at the University of California at Berkeley with expertise in cult-related matters, was retained by the prosecution to advise them in the Ingram case. In the course of his investigation, Ofshe concluded that (1) there was zero evidence of the presumed cult activity that constituted the foundation of the accusations against Ingram and (2) that many of Ingram's "memories"—detailed though they were, and confident of their validity as Ingram was—could not logically be true, but rather were almost certainly created as a result of the intense suggestion provided during interrogations by police officers and other authority figures. To confirm his false-memory hypothesis, Ofshe carried out an experiment wherein he accused Ingram of a specific event that all other participants agreed did not happen. (This fictional event consisted of Ingram's successfully demanding that his son and daughter have sex with one another and observing them do so.) Ingram initially reported not remembering this event. However, upon intensely thinking about the possibility of it having happened, in conjunction with the accusation by a trusted authority figure (Ofshe), Ingram began to not only "remember" the fabricated event itself but also generate minute details about how the event unfolded. Ingram eventually claimed this memory to be very real to him. Even when stupendous efforts by all parties (Ofshe, the police, and all other interrogators) were eventually made to convince Ingram that the event was not real but part of an experiment, Ingram still steadfastly and sincerely refused to cease believing that the incident had actually occurred. Eventually, however, following the cessation of the intense interrogation, Ingram began to question and recant the memories that he had originally formed. The Ingram case, although probably the most public and dramatic of false memories created by interrogation, is not an isolated anomaly.

JENNIFER THOMPSON'S MEMORY We conclude this section by returning to the case of Jennifer Thompson. Why was it that Thompson both misidentified Ronald Cotton and failed to identify the actual rapist? Although we don't know the answers to these questions with absolute certainty, we can, on the basis of what is known about reconstructive memory, certainly make some educated guesses.

To begin with, the circumstances surrounding the original event—the rape—were far from optimal from the perspective of Ms. Thompson's being able to memorize the rapist's appearance. It was dark, Ms. Thompson was terrified, and her attention was probably on what was most important at the moment—trying to avoid being raped and/or to escape—than on what her attacker looked like. Therefore, it is likely that her original memory was poor.

Why then did Ms. Thompson identify Mr. Cotton to begin with? This is unclear. However, based on other evidence, the police believed that he was the culprit and may well have suggested this to her during her original identification of him from mug shots. Once she had identified him in this fashion, however, she reidentified him in a live lineup—but one containing Mr. Cotton, whose picture she had already seen, along with five other individuals who were completely unfamiliar to her. It is therefore no surprise that she picked out Mr. Cotton from the lineup. The important thing, however, is that Mr. Cotton's picture that she selected during the original identification, along with Mr. Cotton himself, whom she selected from the lineup, provided a fertile source of post-event information—information that allowed Ms. Thompson to reconstruct her memory for the original event such that her originally hazy memory of the original rapist was transformed into a very vivid memory of Mr. Cotton. This reconstruction had three important consequences. First, it formed the basis for Ms. Thompson's very confident in-court identification that proved to be the basis for Mr. Cotton's conviction. Second, it prevented her from correctly recognizing Bobby Poole as the man who had actually been there. Finally, it evidently formed the basis for Ms. Thompson's recollection of how well she had studied the rapist to begin with. Notice how she described this process: "I looked at his hairline; I looked for scars, for tattoos, for anything that would help me identify him." But did she? If so, why did she recognize the wrong man? The answer is probably that after having constructed an excellent memory of Ronald Cotton as a result of seeing him during the identification procedures, she constructed an accompanying memory of the process by which her image of him was formed.

◆ Interim Summary

- Unlike a videotape, a memory is constructed and reconstructed on the basis of expectations and knowledge: It shows systematic departures from the objective reality that underlies it.

- Memory reconstruction can occur at the time the memory is originally formed or at varying times after its formation.

- Memory reconstruction forms the basis for memories that, although systematically incorrect, seem very real and are recounted with a great deal of confidence.

◆ Critical Thinking Questions

1. Suppose that on their 10th anniversary, Jason and his wife, Kate, are discussing their wedding. Jason laughingly recounts the story of how Kate's mother accidentally stumbled over the food table and spilled a bottle of champagne. Kate, not so laughingly, claims that it was Jason's mother who had the embarrassing accident. Use what is known about constructive and reconstructive memories to construct a sequence of events that might have led to this disagreement.

2. It is generally agreed that the accuracy of memory declines over time. Describe two separate reasons for why this occurs. (*Hint:* You learned about one in the previous section and about the other in this section).

IMPROVING MEMORY

Having considered the basics of working memory and long-term memory, we are ready to tackle the question of how memory can be improved, focusing primarily on explicit memory. First we will consider how to increase the working memory span. Then we will turn to a variety of methods for improving long-term memory. These methods work by increasing the efficiency of encoding and retrieval.

CHUNKING AND MEMORY SPAN

For most of us, the capacity of working memory cannot be increased beyond 7 ± 2 chunks. However, we can enlarge the size of a chunk and thereby increase the number of items in our memory span. We demonstrated this point earlier: Given the string 149-2177-620-02, we can recall all 12 digits if we recode the string into three chunks—1492-1776-2002—and store them in working memory. Although recoding digits into familiar dates works nicely in this example, it will not work with most digit strings because we have not memorized enough significant dates. But if a recoding system could be developed that worked with virtually any string, working memory span for numbers could be dramatically improved.

Psychologists have studied an individual who discovered such a general-purpose recoding system and used it to increase his memory span from 7 to almost 80 random digits (see Figure 8-14). This person, referred to as S.F., had average memory abilities and average intelligence for a college student. For a year and a half he engaged in a memory-span task for about 3 to 5 hours per week. During this extensive practice, S.F., a good long-distance runner, devised the strategy of recoding sets of four digits into running times. For example, S.F. would recode 3492 as "3:49.2—world class time for the mile," which for him was a single chunk. Because S.F. was familiar with many running times (that is, he had them stored in long-term memory), he could readily chunk most sets of four digits. When he could not (for example, 1771 cannot be a running time because the third digit is too large), he tried to recode the four digits into either a familiar date or the age of some person or object known to him.

Use of these recoding systems enabled S.F. to increase his memory span from 7 to 28 digits (because each of S.F.'s seven chunks contains four digits). He then built up his memory span to nearly 80 digits by organizing the running times in a hierarchy. Thus, one chunk in S.F.'s working memory might have pointed to three running times; at the time of recall, S.F. would go

Figure 8-14
Number of Digits Recalled by S.F.
S.F. greatly increased his memory span for digits by devising a recoding system that used chunking and hierachical organization. Total practice time was about 215 hours. (Adapted from "Acquisition of a Memory Skill," reprinted by permission from *Science*, Vol. 208, 1980, pp. 1181–1182 by I. A. Ericsson, et al. Copyright © 1980 by American Association for the Advancement of Science.)

from this chunk to the first running time and produce its four digits, then move to the second running time in the chunk and produce its digits, and so on. One chunk was therefore worth 12 digits. In this way S.F. achieved his remarkable memory span. The expansion of his memory capacity was due to increasing the size of a chunk (by relating the items to information in long-term memory), not to increasing the number of chunks that working memory can hold. When he switched from digits to letters, his memory span went back to seven—that is, seven letters (Ericsson, Chase, & Faloon, 1980).

This research on working memory is fairly recent. Interest in expanding long-term memory has a longer history and is the focus of the rest of this section. We will look first at how material can be encoded to make it easier to retrieve and then consider how the act of retrieval itself can be improved.

IMAGERY AND ENCODING

We mentioned earlier that we can improve the recall of unrelated items by adding meaningful connections between them at the time of encoding, for these connections will facilitate later retrieval. **Mental images** have been found to be particularly useful for connecting pairs of unrelated items, and for this reason imagery is the major ingredient in many mnemonic systems, or systems for aiding memory.

A well-known mnemonic system is the **method of loci** (*loci* is the Latin word for "places"). This method works especially well with an ordered sequence of arbitrary items, such as unrelated words. The first step is to commit to memory an ordered sequence of places—such as the locations you would come upon during a slow walk through your house. You enter through the front door into a hallway, move next to the bookcase in the living room, then to the television in the living room, then to the curtains at the window, and so on. Once you can easily take this mental walk, you are ready to memorize as many unrelated words as there are locations on your walk. You form an image that relates the first word to the first location, another image that relates the second word to the second location, and so on. If the words are items on a shopping list—for example, *bread, eggs, beer, milk,* and *bacon*—you might imagine a slice of bread nailed to your front door, an egg hanging from the light cord in the hallway, a can of beer in the bookcase, a milk commercial playing on your television, and curtains made from giant strips of bacon (see Figure 8-15). Once you have memorized the items in this way, you can easily recall them in order by simply taking your mental walk again. Each location will retrieve an image, and each image will retrieve a word. The method clearly works and is a favorite among people who perform memory feats professionally.

Figure 8-15
A Mnemonic System
The method of loci aids memory by associating items (here, entries on a shopping list) with an ordered sequence of places.

Table 8-3
The Key-Word Method

Examples of key words used to link Spanish words to their English translations. For example, when the Spanish word muleta is pronounced, part of it sounds like the English word "mule." Thus, "mule" could be used as the key word and linked to the English translation by forming an image of a mule standing erect on a crutch.

Spanish	Key Word	English
caballo	(eye)	horse
charco	(charcoal)	puddle
muleta	(mule)	crutch
clavo	(claw)	nail
lagartija	(log)	lizard
payaso	(pie)	clown
hiio	(eel)	thread
tenaza	(tennis)	pliers
jabon	(bone)	soap
carpa	(carp)	tent
pato	(pot)	duck

Caballo ➞ eye ➞ Horse

Pato ➞ pot ➞ Duck

Figure 8-16
Foreign Language Learning
Mental images can be used to associate spoken Spanish words with corresponding English words. Here, possible images for learning the Spanish words for "horse" and "duck" are illustrated.

Imagery is also used in the key word method for learning words in a foreign language. (See Table 8-3.) Suppose that you had to learn that the Spanish word *caballo* means "horse." The key word method has two steps. The first is to find a part of the foreign word that sounds like an English word. Because *caballo* is pronounced, roughly, "cob-eye-yo," "eye" could serve as the key word. The next step is to form an image that connects the key word and the English equivalent—for example, a giant eye being kicked by a horse (see Figure 8-16). This should establish a meaningful connection between the Spanish and English words. To recall the meaning of *caballo,* you would first retrieve the key word *eye* and then the stored image that links it to "horse." The key word method may sound complicated, but studies have shown that it is very helpful in learning the vocabulary of a foreign language (Atkinson, 1975; Pressley, Levin, & Delaney, 1982).

ELABORATION AND ENCODING

We have seen that the more we elaborate items, the more we can subsequently recall or recognize them. This phenomenon arises because the more connections we establish between items, the larger the number of retrieval possibilities. The practical implications of these findings are straightforward: If you want to remember a particular fact, expand on its meaning. Suppose you read a newspaper article about an epidemic in Brooklyn that health officials are trying to contain. To expand on this, you could ask yourself questions about the causes and consequences of the epidemic: Was the disease carried by a person or by an animal? Was it transmitted through the water supply? To contain the epidemic, will officials go so far as to stop outsiders from visiting Brooklyn? How long is the epidemic likely to last? Questions about the causes and consequences of an event are especially effective because each question sets up a meaningful connection, or retrieval path, to the event.

CONTEXT AND RETRIEVAL

Because context is a powerful retrieval cue, we can improve our memory by restoring the context in which the learning took place. If your psychology class always meets in a particular room, your recall of the lecture material may be better when you are in that room than when you are in a different building because the context of the room serves as a cue for retrieving the lecture material. Most often, though, when we have to remember something, we cannot physically return to the context in which we learned it. If you are having difficulty remembering the name of a high school classmate, you are not about to go back to your high school just to recall it.

However, you can try to re-create the context mentally. To retrieve the long forgotten name, you might think of different classes, clubs, and other activities that you participated in during high school to see whether any of these bring to mind the name you are seeking. When participants used these techniques in an actual experiment, they were often able to recall the names of high school classmates that they were sure they had forgotten (Williams & Hollan, 1981).

ORGANIZATION

We know that organization during encoding improves subsequent retrieval. This principle can be put to great practical use: We are capable of storing and retrieving a massive amount of information if we organize it appropriately.

Some experiments have investigated organizational devices that can be used to learn many unrelated items. In one study, participants memorized lists of unrelated words by organizing the words in each list into a story, as illustrated in Figure 8-17. When tested for 12 such lists (a total of 120 words), participants recalled more than 90% of the words. Control participants, who did not use an organizational strategy, recalled only about 10% of the words! The performance of the experimental participants appears to be a remarkable memory feat, but anyone armed with an organizational strategy can do it.

At this point, you might concede that psychologists have devised some ingenious techniques for organizing lists of unrelated items. But, you argue, what you have to remember are not lists of unrelated items but stories

you were told, lectures you have heard, and readings like the text of this chapter. Isn't this kind of material already organized, and doesn't this mean that the previously mentioned techniques are of limited value? Yes and no. Yes, this chapter is more than a list of unrelated sentences, but—and this is the essential point—there is always a problem of organization with any lengthy material. Later you may be able to recall that elaborating meaning aids learning, but this may not bring to mind anything about, for example, acoustic coding in short-term memory. The two topics do not seem to be intimately related, but there is a relationship between them: Both deal with encoding phenomena. The best way to see that relationship is to note the headings and subheadings in the chapter, because these show how the material in the chapter is organized.

An effective way to study is to keep this organization in mind. You might, for example, try to capture part of the chapter's organization by sketching a hierarchical tree like the one shown in Figure 8-18. You can use this hierarchy to guide your memory search whenever you have to retrieve information about this chapter. It may be even more helpful, though, to make your own hierarchical outline of the chapter. Memory seems to benefit most when the organization is done by the person who needs to remember the material.

PRACTICING RETRIEVAL

Another way to improve retrieval is to practice it—that is, to ask yourself questions about what you are trying to learn. Suppose that you have 2 hours to study an assignment that can be read in approximately 30 minutes. Reading and rereading the assignment four times is generally less effective than reading it once and asking yourself questions about it. You can then reread selected parts to clear up points that were difficult to retrieve the first time around, perhaps elaborating these points so that they become well connected to one another and to the rest of the assignment. Attempting retrieval is an efficient use of study time. This was demonstrated long ago by experiments using material similar to that actually learned in courses (see Figure 8-19).

A procedure akin to practicing retrieval may be useful in implicit memory situations. The procedure, referred to as mental practice, consists of imagining the rehearsal of a perceptual motor skill without actually moving any part of the body. For example, you might imagine yourself swinging at a tennis ball, making mental corrections when the imagined swing seems faulty, without moving your arm. Such mental practice can improve performance of the skill, particularly if the mental practice is interspersed with actual physical practice (Swets & Bjork, 1990).

A LUMBERJACK DARTed out of a forest, SKATEd around a HEDGE past a COLONY of DUCKs. He tripped on some FURNITURE, tearing his STOCKING while hastening toward the PILLOW where his MISTRESS lay.

A VEGETABLE can be a useful INSTRUMENT for a COLLEGE student. A carrot can be a NAIL for your FENCE or BASIN. But a MERCHANT of the QUEEN would SCALE that fence and feed the carrot to a GOAT.

One night at DINNER I had the NERVE to bring my TEACHER. There had been a FLOOD that day, and the rain BARREL was sure to RATTLE. There was, however, a VESSEL in the HARBOR carrying this ARTIST to my CASTLE.

▌ Figure 8-17
Organizing Words Into a Story
Three examples in which a list of 10 unrelated words is turned into a story. The capitalized items are the words on the list.
(After Bower & Clark, 1969)

Figure 8-18
A Hierarchical Tree
Creating hierarchical trees of chapters in textbooks can help students retrieve information about those chapters. This tree represents the organization of part of this chapter.

◆ Interim Summary

- Although we cannot increase the capacity of working memory, we can use recoding schemes to enlarge the size of a chunk and thereby increase the memory span.

- One way to improve encoding and retrieval is to use imagery, which is the basic principle underlying mnemonic systems such as the method of loci and the key word method.

- Other ways to improve encoding (and subsequent retrieval) are to elaborate the meaning of the items and to organize the material during encoding (hierarchical organization seems preferable).

◆ Critical Thinking Questions

1. Suppose that an actor has a very long speech to memorize. How might she best go about such memorization?

2. Given what we know about context and retrieval, what would be the most efficient way to study for a statistics exam?

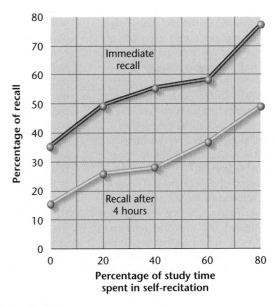

Figure 8-19
Practicing Retrieval
Recall can be improved by spending a large proportion of study time attempting retrieval rather than silently studying. Results are shown for tests given immediately and 4 hours after completing study. (After Gates, 1917)

Are Repressed Memories Valid?

REPRESSED MEMORIES ARE A DANGEROUS BELIEF

Elizabeth F. Loftus, University of Washington

In a land transformed by science, pseudo-scientific beliefs live on. It was a set of wild, wacky, and dangerous beliefs that led to serious problems for Nadean Cool, a 44-year-old nurse's aide in Appleton, Wisconsin. Nadean had sought therapy in late 1986 to help her cope with her reaction to a traumatic event that her daughter had experienced. During therapy, her psychiatrist used hypnosis and other methods to dig out allegedly buried memories of abuse. In the process, his patient became convinced that she had repressed memories of being in a satanic cult, of eating babies, of being raped, of having sex with animals, and of being forced to watch the murder of her 8-year-old friend. She came to believe that she had more than 120 separate personalities—children, adults, angels, and even a duck—all because, she was told, she had experienced such severe childhood sexual and physical abuse. In addition to hypnosis and other suggestive techniques, the psychiatrist also performed exorcisms on Nadean, one of which lasted 5 hours, replete with the sprinkling of holy water and screams for Satan to leave Nadean's body. When Nadean came to realize that false memories had been planted, she sued for malpractice. Her case settled, mid-trial, in early 1997, for $2.4 million. (See Loftus & Ketcham, 1994, for more cases like Nadean's.)

Hundreds of people, mostly women, have developed memories in therapy of extensive brutalization that they claimed they repressed, and they later retracted these. How do we know that the abuse memories aren't real and the retractions false? One clue is that the women would sometimes develop memories that were psychologically or biologically impossible, such as detailed memories of abuse occurring at the age of 3 months or memories of being forced to abort a baby by coat hanger when physical evidence confirmed virginity.

How is it possible for people to develop such elaborate and confident false memories? In the early 1970s, I began to do studies on the "misinformation effect." When people witness an event and are later exposed to new and misleading information about that event, their recollections often become distorted. The misinformation invades us, like a Trojan horse, precisely because we do not detect its influence.

Later studies showed that suggestive information not only can alter the details of a recent experience but also can plant entirely false beliefs and memories in the minds of people (Loftus & Pickrell, 1995; Hyman et al., 1995; Porter, Yuille & Lehman, 1999). In some studies, as many as half the individuals who underwent suggestive interviewing came to develop either full or partial false childhood memories. Hypnotic interventions have been particularly successful ways of feeding people suggestive material and getting them to accept it. Inducing people to briefly imagine that something occurred to them in childhood can increase people's belief that something similar to the imagined experience happened to them (Garry, Manning, Loftus, & Sherman, 1996).

It might be tempting to dismiss these studies because they are so unlike the therapy world. However, some recent efforts have taken great pains to mimic a therapy environment (Mazzoni & Loftus, 1998). In this research, subjects reported on their very early childhood experiences on two separate occasions. In between, some subjects underwent dream interpretation with a clinical psychologist. Regardless of the content of the dream, the clinician suggestively interpreted their dream to mean that they had had a particular experience before age 3 (such as lost for an extended time in a public place or faced a great danger to their lives). Weeks later, when subjects were again questioned about their childhoods, most of them had become more confident that they had been lost or had faced a great danger. Their confidence was sometimes quite high, even though they had initially denied having the experience, and even though it would be relatively unlikely that they would have concrete, detailed episodic memories for experiences that actually had happened to them this early in life (consider childhood amnesia).

Of course, simply because we can plant false childhood memories in subjects in no way implies that memories that arise after suggestion, imagination, or dream interpretation are all necessarily false. In no way does this invalidate the experiences of the many thousands of individuals who have truly been abused and are later in life reminded of the experience. We do need to keep in mind, however, that without corroboration, there is little that even the most experienced evaluator can use to differentiate the true memories from those suggestively planted. Apart from bearing on the controversy about repressed memories that has plagued our society for more than a decade, the modern research does reveal important ways in which our memories are malleable, and it reveals much about the rather flimsy curtain that sometimes separates memory and imagination.

Are Repressed Memories Valid?

REPRESSED MEMORIES CAN BE VALID
Kathy Pezdek, Claremont Graduate University

In recent years, a number of critical questions have been raised regarding the credibility of adults' memory for their childhood experiences. At the heart of these claims is the view that it is relatively easy to plant memories for events that did not occur.

Let me say up front that surely there have been some false memories for sexual abuse, and surely some therapeutic techniques are more likely to foster false memories than others. Further, it is surely possible to find some individuals who are so highly suggestible that one could readily get them to believe anything. However, the claim by those who promote the suggestibility explanation for recovered memories assumes an extremely strong construct of memory suggestibility. The truth is that the cognitive research on the suggestibility of memory simply does not support the existence of a suggestibility construct that is sufficiently robust to explain this phenomenon.

How do cognitive psychologists study the suggestibility of memory? This text refers to an experiment by Loftus, Schooler, & Wagenaar (1985) in which

Kathy Pezdek

participants were more likely to think that they saw broken glass in the film of a traffic accident (broken glass was not present in the film) if they had been asked a previous question that included the word *smashed* rather than *hit*. This finding is real, but it involves an insignificant detail of an insignificant

event, and even so, across a number of studies using this paradigm, the difference in the rate of responding positively to the question about the broken glass, for example, in the control (*hit*) versus the misled (*smashed*) condition is typically only 20% to 30%. Although this suggestibility effect is a real one, it is neither large nor robust.

What evidence supports the conclusion that a memory can be planted for an event that never occurred? The most frequently cited study in this regard is the "lost in the mall" study by Loftus and Pickrell (1995). These researchers had 24 volunteers suggest to offspring or younger siblings that they had been lost in a shopping mall as a child. Six of the 24 participants reported full or partial memory of the false event. However, these results would not be expected to generalize to the situation of having a therapist plant a false memory for incest. Being lost while shopping is not such a remarkable memory implant. Children are often warned about the dangers of getting lost, have fears about getting lost, are commonly read classic tales about children who get lost (such as Hansel and Gretel, Pinocchio), and, in fact, do get lost, if only for a few frightening minutes. Therefore, it would be expected that most children would have a preexisting script for getting lost that would be accessed by the suggestion of a particular instance of getting lost in the Loftus study. In sharp contrast, it is hardly likely that most children would have a preexisting script for incestuous sexual contact.

My graduate students and I recently conducted a study to test whether Loftus's findings regarding planting a false memory generalize to less plausible

events (Pezdek, Finger, & Hodge, 1997). In this study, 20 volunteers read descriptions of one true event and two false events to a younger sibling or close relative. The plausible false event described the relative being lost in a mall while shopping; the implausible false event described the relative receiving a rectal enema. After being read each event, participants were asked what they remembered about the event. Only three of the false events were "remembered" by any of the participants, and all were the plausible event regarding being lost in the mall. No one believed the implausible false event. Implausible events such as parent-child intercourse or receiving an enema are simply unlikely to be suggestively planted in memory because children do not have preexisting scripts for these events.

At a broader level, it is also important to consider that although the "false memory debate" most often concerns reported memories for childhood sexual abuse, this is only one of the many sources of psychogenic amnesia for which memory recovery has been reported. It is well documented that combat exposure and other violent events can produce psychogenic amnesia (for a review, see Arrigo & Pezdek, 1997). Those who doubt the reality of repressed memory for sexual abuse need to explain psychogenic amnesia for these other types of trauma as well.

In conclusion, cognitive research offers little support for the claim that implausible false events such as childhood sexual abuse are easily planted in memory. Although there are some techniques that can be used to suggestively plant bizarre false memories in some highly suggestive individuals, there is no evidence that this is a widespread phenomenon.

CHAPTER SUMMARY

1. There are three stages of memory: encoding, storage, and retrieval. Encoding refers to the transformation of information into the kind of code or representation that memory can accept; storage refers to retention of the encoded information; and retrieval refers to the process by which information is recovered from memory. The three stages may operate differently in situations that require us to store material for a matter of seconds (working memory) and in situations that require us to store material for longer intervals (long-term memory). Moreover, different long-term memory systems seem to be involved in storing facts, which are part of explicit memory, and skills, which are part of implicit memory.

2. There is increasing biological evidence for these distinctions. Recent brain-scanning studies of long-term memory indicate that most of the brain regions activated during encoding are in the left hemisphere and that most of the regions activated during retrieval are in the right hemisphere. Evidence from both animal studies and studies of humans with brain damage indicates that different brain regions may mediate working memory and long-term memory. In particular, in both humans and other mammals, damage to the hippocampal system impairs performance on long-term memory tasks but not on working memory tasks.

3. There are three kinds of memory that differ in terms of their temporal characteristics: Sensory memory lasts over a few hundreds of milliseconds; short-term store (now called *working memory*) operates over seconds; long-term store operates over times ranging from minutes to years.

4. Sensory memory has a very large capacity but decays in a very short time. Information within sensory memory that is attended to is transferred to the next memory, working memory.

5. Information in working memory tends to be encoded acoustically, although we can also use a visual code. The most striking fact about working memory is that its storage capacity is limited to 7 ± 2 items, or chunks. Although we are limited in the number of chunks we can remember, we can increase the size of a chunk by using information in long-term memory to recode incoming material into larger meaningful units. Information can be lost or forgotten from working memory. One cause of forgetting is that information decays with time; another is that new items displace old ones.

6. Retrieval slows down as the number of items in working memory increases. Some have taken this result to indicate that retrieval involves a search process, and others have interpreted the result in terms of an activation process.

7. Working memory is used in solving various kinds of problems, such as mental arithmetic, geometric analogies, and answering questions about text. However, working memory does not seem to be involved in the understanding of relatively simple sentences. Working memory may also serve as a way station to permanent memory, in that information may reside in working memory while it is being encoded into long-term memory.

8. Information in long-term memory is usually encoded according to its meaning. If the items to be remembered are meaningful but the connections between them are not, memory can be improved by adding meaningful connections that provide retrieval paths. The more one elaborates the meaning of material, the better memory of that material will be.

9. Many cases of forgetting in long-term memory are due to retrieval failures (the information is there but cannot be found). Retrieval failures are more likely to occur when there is interference from items associated with the same retrieval cue. Such interference effects suggest that retrieval from long-term memory may be accomplished through a sequential search process or a spreading activation process.

10. Some forgetting from long-term memory is due to a loss from storage, particularly when there is a disruption of the processes that consolidate new memories. The biological locus of consolidation includes the hippocampus and surrounding cortex. Recent research suggests that consolidation takes a few weeks to be completed.

11. Retrieval failures in long-term memory are less likely when the items are organized during encoding and when the context at the time of retrieval is similar to the context at the time of encoding. Retrieval processes can also be disrupted by emotional factors. In some cases, anxious thoughts interfere with retrieval of the target memory; in others, the target memory may be actively blocked (repressed). In still other cases, emotion can enhance memory, as in flashbulb memories.

12. Explicit memory refers to the kind of memory manifested in recall or recognition, in which we consciously recollect the past. Implicit memory refers to the kind of memory that manifests itself as an improvement on some perceptual, motor, or cognitive task, with no conscious recollection of the experiences that led to the improvement. Although explicit memory—particularly recall and recognition of facts—breaks down in amnesia, implicit memory is usually spared. This suggests that there may be separate storage systems for explicit and implicit memory.

13. Research with normal individuals also suggests that there may be separate systems for explicit and implicit memory. Much of this research has relied on a measure of implicit memory called *priming* (for example, the extent to which prior exposure to a list of words later facilitates completing stems of these words). Some studies reveal that an independent variable that affects explicit memory (amount of elaboration during encoding) has no effect on priming, and other studies show that a variable that affects implicit memory has no effect on explicit memory. Brain-scanning studies with normal individuals show that explicit memory is accompanied by increased neural activity in certain regions, whereas implicit memory is accompanied by a decrease in neural activity in critical regions.

14. Unlike a videotape, a memory is constructed and reconstructed on the basis of expectations and knowledge: It shows systematic departures from the objective reality that underlies it. This kind of reconstruction can occur at the time the memory is originally formed or at varying time periods following its formation. This kind of reconstruction forms the basis for memories that, although systematically incorrect, seem very real and are recounted with a great deal of confidence.

15. Although we cannot increase the capacity of working memory, we can use recoding schemes to enlarge the size of a chunk and thereby increase the memory span. Long-term memory for facts can be improved at the encoding and retrieval stages. One way to improve encoding and retrieval is to use imagery, which is the basic principle underlying mnemonic systems such as the method of loci and the key word method.

16. Other ways to improve encoding (and subsequent retrieval) are to elaborate the meaning of the items and to organize the material during encoding (hierarchical organization seems preferable). The best ways to improve retrieval are to attempt to restore the encoding context at the time of retrieval and to practice retrieving information while learning it.

CORE CONCEPTS

encoding stage
storage stage
retrieval stage
positron emission tomography
  (PET)
functional magnetic resonance
  imaging (fMRI)
Atkinson-Shiffrin theory (of
  memory)
sensory store
short-term store
rehearsal
elaboration
long-term store
explicit memory
implicit memory
span of apprehension
partial-report procedure
whole-report condition
partial-report condition

auditory cue
temporal-integration paradigm
sensory response
working memory
visual code
phonological code
semantic code
phonological buffer
visual-spatial sketchpad
digit-span task
chunking
Sternberg memory-scanning task
serial search (of memory)
activation models (of memory
  scanning)
hippocampus
prefrontal lobes
recognition test
recall test
interference

electroconvulsive therapy
flashbulb memory
amnesia
anterograde amnesia
retrograde amnesia
priming
childhood amnesia
episodic memory
semantic memory
constructive processes
reconstructive processes
constructive perception
perceptual interference
inferences
post-event memory reconstruction
schemas
social stereotype
mental images
method of loci

WEB RESOURCES

http://psychology.wadsworth.com/
atkinson14e

Take a quiz, try the activities and exercises, and explore web links.

http://www.exploratorium.edu/memory/index.html

Think you have a good memory? Put it to the test on this site! You can also explore an interactive dissection of a sheep brain, which will help you see where memory processes take place.

http://olias.arc.nasa.gov/cognition/tutorials/
index.html

This is another fun site hosted by NASA that allows you to explore issues in cognitive psychology. There are interactive exercises involving recognition, recall, interference, and short-term memory.

http://www.apa.org/

If you want to find the most recent articles on memory, type *memory* into the search blank of this site. Happy researching!

 InfoTrac Online Library
http://www.infotrac-college.com/
wadsworth

Use InfoTrac to find popular and scientific articles by using the search terms below or your own relevant terms.
- Encoding
- Explicit and implicit memory
- Long-term memory
- Retrieval cues
- Short-term memory

CD-ROM LINKS

 Psych Odyssey
Check out Chapter 7, Memory
  A. The Atkinson-Schiffrin Model of Memory
B. Memory Deficiencies
C. Improving Memory

 Psyk.trek 2.0
Check out Unit 6, Memory and Thought
  6a Memory Encoding
6b Memory Storage
6c Physiology of Memory

© Mug Shots/Corbis

LANGUAGE AND THOUGHT

9

In the 1970s, many Americans began jogging for exercise. Some of these joggers reported experiencing a "runner's high," a feeling of intense euphoria that presumably came with intense exercise. What could be causing this? At about the same time, neuroscientists discovered a new class of endogenous chemicals (chemicals produced by the body) that act like morphine, which came to be called "endorphins" (for endogenous morphine). Many scientists then made the induction that intense exercise leads to an increase in endorphins, which in turn is responsible for a runner's high. This hypothesis became extremely well known. Alas, further biological work challenged the endorphin theory of a runner's high. Although endorphin levels in the blood do indeed rise with exercise, the endorphins produced do not pass from the circulating blood into the brain, so they could not be the cause of the mood changes (Kolata, 2002).

This is a nice example of scientific thinking. First, some fact about a mood change (a runner's high) is reduced to an alteration in body chemistry (increased endorphins). But further work shows that the change in body chemistry does not affect the right organ. The episode involves many aspects of thinking and language. New concepts (like endorphins) are introduced, reasoning with these concepts is used to generate a hypothesis, and then subsequent tests of the hypothesis undermine it. And all of the concepts, claims, and counterclaims are expressed in language.

The greatest accomplishments of our species stem from our ability to entertain complex thoughts such as those in this example, to communicate them, and to act on them. Thinking includes a wide range of mental activities. We think when we try to solve a problem that has been presented to us in class, and we think when we daydream while waiting for a class to begin. We think when we decide what groceries to buy, plan a vacation, write a letter, or worry about a troubled relationship.

We begin this chapter with a discussion of language, the means by which thoughts are communicated. Then we consider the development or acquisition of language. The remaining sections of this chapter discuss major topics in propositional thinking. We begin by focusing on concepts, the building blocks of thought, and discuss their use in classifying objects. This is the study of concepts and categorization. Then we consider how thoughts are organized to arrive at a conclusion. This is the study of reasoning. Next we turn to the imaginal mode of thought, and in the final section we discuss thought in action—the study of problem solving—and consider the uses of both propositional and imaginal thought.

LANGUAGE AND COMMUNICATION

Language is our primary means of communicating thought. Moreover, it is universal: Every human society has a language, and every human being of normal intelligence acquires his or her native language and uses it effortlessly. The naturalness of language sometimes lulls us into thinking that language use requires no special explanation. Nothing could be further from the truth. Some people can read, and others cannot; some can do arithmetic, and others cannot; some can play chess, and others cannot. But virtually everyone can master and use an enormously complex linguistic system. In contrast, even the most sophisticated computers have severe problems in interpreting speech, understanding written text, or speaking in a productive way. Yet most normal children perform these linguistic tasks effortlessly. Why this should be so is among the fundamental puzzles of human psychology.

LEVELS OF LANGUAGE

Language use has two aspects: production and comprehension. In **the production of language,** we start with a thought, somehow translate it into a sentence, and end up with sounds that express the sentence. In **the comprehension of language,** we start by hearing sounds, attach meanings to the sounds in the form of words, combine the words to create a sentence, and then somehow extract meaning from it. Language use seems to involve moving through various levels, as shown in Figure 9-1. At the highest level are sentence units, including sentences and phrases. The next level is that of words and parts of words that carry meaning (the prefix *non* or the suffix *er,* for example). The lowest level contains speech sounds. The adjacent levels are closely related: The

▌Figure 9-1
Levels of Language
At the highest level are sentence units, including phrases and sentences. The next level is words and parts of words that carry meaning. The lowest level contains speech sounds.

phrases of a sentence are built from words and prefixes and suffixes, which in turn are constructed from speech sounds. **Language** is therefore a multilevel system for relating thoughts to speech by means of word and sentence units (Chomsky, 1965).

There are striking differences in the number of units at each level. All languages have only a limited number of speech sounds; English has about 40 of them. But rules for combining these sounds make it possible to produce and understand thousands of words (a vocabulary of 70,000 words is not unusual for an adult; see Bloom, 2000). Similarly, rules for combining words make it possible to produce and understand millions of sentences (if not an infinite number of them). So two of the basic properties of language are that it is structured at multiple levels and that it is productive. Rules allow us to combine units at one level into a vastly greater number of units at the next level. Every human language has these two properties.

LANGUAGE UNITS AND PROCESSES

Let's now consider the units and processes involved at each level of language. In surveying the relevant material, we usually take the perspective of a person comprehending language, a listener, though occasionally we switch to that of a language producer, or speaker.

SPEECH SOUNDS If you could attend to just the sounds someone makes when talking to you, what would you hear? You would not perceive the person's speech as a continuous stream of sound but rather as a sequence of **phonemes,** or discrete speech categories. For example, the sound corresponding to the first letter in *boy* is an instance of a phoneme symbolized as /b/. (Note that phonemes may correspond to letters, but they are speech sounds, not letters.) In English, we divide all speech sounds into about 40 phonemes.

We are good at discriminating among different sounds that correspond to different phonemes in our language but poor at discriminating among different sounds that correspond to the same phoneme. Consider, for example, the sound of the first letter in *pin* and the sound of the second letter in *spin* (Liberman, Cooper, Shankweiler, & Studdert-Kennedy, 1967). They are the same phoneme, /p/, and they sound the same to us, even though they have different physical characteristics. The /p/ in *pin* is accompanied by a puff of air, but the /p/ in *spin* is not (try holding your hand a short distance from your mouth as you say the two words). Our phonemic categories act as filters that convert a continuous stream of speech into a sequence of familiar phonemes.

Every language has a different set of phonemes, which is one reason we often have difficulty learning to pronounce foreign words. Another language may use phonemes that do not appear in ours. It may take us a while even to hear the new phonemes, let alone produce them. For example, in Hindi the two different /p/ sounds just described correspond to two different phonemes, so Hindu speakers appreciate differences that we do not. Another language may not make a distinction between two sounds that our language treats as two phonemes. In Japanese, the English sounds corresponding to r and l (/r/ and /l/) are perceived as the same phoneme—which leads to the frequent confusion between words like *rice* and *lice*.

When phonemes are combined in the right way, we perceive them as words. Each language has its own rules about which phonemes can follow others. In English, for example, /b/ cannot follow /p/ at the beginning of a word (try pronouncing *pbet*). The influence of such rules is revealed when we listen. We are more accurate in perceiving a string of phonemes whose order conforms to the rules of our language than a string whose order violates these rules. The influence of these rules is even more striking when we take the perspective of a speaker. For example, we have no difficulty pronouncing the plurals of nonsense words that we have never heard before. Consider *zuk* and *zug*. In accordance with a simple rule, the plural of *zuk* is formed by adding the phoneme /s/, as in *hiss*. In English, however, /s/ cannot follow g at the end of a word, so to form the plural of *zug* we must use another rule—one that adds the phoneme /z/, as in *fuzz*. We may not be aware of these differences in forming plurals, but we have no difficulty producing them. It is as if we "know" the rules for combining phonemes, even though we are not consciously aware of the rules: We conform to rules that we cannot verbalize.

WORD UNITS What we typically perceive when listening to speech are not phonemes but words. Unlike phonemes, words carry meaning. However, they are not the only smallish linguistic units that convey meaning. Suffixes such as *ly* or prefixes such as *un* also carry meaning. They can be added to words to form more complex words with different meanings, as when *un* and *ly* are added to *time* to form *untimely*. The term **morpheme** is used to refer to any small linguistic unit that carries meaning.

Most morphemes are themselves words. Most words denote some specific content, such as *house* or *run*. A few words, however, primarily serve to make sentences grammatical. Such grammatical words, or **grammatical morphemes**, include what are commonly referred to as articles and prepositions, such as *a, the, in, of, on,* and *at*. Some prefixes and suffixes also play primarily a grammatical role. These grammatical morphemes include the suffixes *ing* and *ed*.

Grammatical morphemes may be processed differently than content words. One piece of evidence for this is forms of brain damage in which the use of grammatical morphemes is impaired more than the use of content words (Zurif, 1995). Also, as we will see later, grammatical morphemes are acquired in a different way than content words.

The most important aspect of a word is, of course, its **meaning.** A word can be viewed as the name of a concept, and its meaning is the concept it names. Some words are ambiguous because they name more than one concept. *Club,* for example, names both a social organization and an object used for striking. Sometimes we may be aware of a word's ambiguity, as when we hear the sentence "He was interested in the club." In most cases, however, the sentence context makes the meaning of the word sufficiently clear that we do not consciously experience any ambiguity—for example, "He wanted to join the club." Even in these cases, though, there is evidence that we unconsciously consider both meanings of the ambiguous word for a brief moment. In one experiment, a participant was presented a sentence such as "He wanted to join the club," followed immediately by a test word that the participant had to read aloud as quickly as possible. Participants read the test word faster if it was related to *either* meaning of *club* (for example, *group* or *struck*) than if it was unrelated to either meaning (for example, *apple*). This suggests that both meanings of *club* were activated during comprehension of the sentence and that either meaning could prime related words (Swinney, 1979; Tanenhaus, Leiman, & Seidenberg, 1979).

SENTENCE UNITS As listeners, we usually effortlessly combine words into **sentence units,** which include sentences as well as phrases. An important property of these units is that they can correspond to parts of a thought, or proposition. Such correspondences allow a listener to "extract" propositions from sentences.

To understand these correspondences, first you have to appreciate that any **proposition** can be divided into a subject and a predicate (a description). In the proposition "Audrey has curly hair," "Audrey" is the subject and "has curly hair" is the predicate. In the proposition "The tailor is asleep," "the tailor" is the subject and "is asleep" is the predicate. And in "Teachers work too hard," "teachers" is the subject and "work too hard" is the predicate. Any sentence can be broken into phrases so that each phrase corresponds either to the subject or the predicate of a proposition or to an entire proposition. For example, intuitively we can divide the simple sentence "Irene sells insurance" into two phrases, "Irene" and "sells insurance." The first phrase, called a **noun phrase** because it centers on a noun, specifies the subject of an underlying proposition. The second phrase,

Figure 9-2
Phrases and Propositions
The first step in extracting the propositions from a complex sentence is to decompose the sentence into phrases. This decomposition is based on rules like "Any sentence can be divided into a noun phrase and a verb phrase."

a **verb phrase,** gives the predicate of the proposition. For a more complex example, consider the sentence "The serious scholar reads books." This sentence can be divided into two phrases, the noun phrase "the serious scholar" and the verb phrase "reads books." The noun phrase expresses an entire proposition, "scholars are serious"; the verb phrase expresses part (the predicate) of another proposition, "scholars read books" (see Figure 9-2). Again, sentence units correspond closely to proposition units, which provides a link between language and thought.

When listening to a sentence, people seem to first divide it into noun phrases, verb phrases, and the like, and then to extract propositions from these phrases. There is a good deal of evidence for our dividing sentences into phrases and treating the phrases as units, with some of the evidence coming from memory experiments. In one study, participants listened to sentences such as "The poor girl stole a warm coat." Immediately after each sentence was presented, participants were given a probe word from the sentence and asked to say the word that came after it. People responded faster when the probe and the response words came from the same phrase ("poor" and "girl") than when they came from different phrases ("girl" and "stole"). So each phrase acts as a unit in memory. When the probe and response are from the same phrase, only one unit needs to be retrieved (Wilkes & Kennedy, 1969).

Analyzing a sentence into noun and verb phrases, and then dividing these phrases into smaller units like nouns, adjectives, and verbs, is syntactic analysis. **Syntax deals with the relationships between words in phrases and sentences.** Syntax primarily serves to structure the parts of a sentence so we can tell what is related to what. For example, in the sentence "The green bird ate a red snake," the syntax of English tells us that the bird did the eating and not the snake, that the bird was green but not the snake, that the snake was red but not the bird, and so on. Furthermore, in an example like "The dogs

that the man owned were lazy," the syntax helps us to identify the man as doing the owning (by word order) and the dogs as being lazy (by word order and number agreement). In identifying the verb and noun phrases of a sentence and how they are related, we are identifying what is what, and who did what to whom.

In the course of understanding a sentence, we usually perform such a syntactic analysis effortlessly and unconsciously. Sometimes, however, our syntactic analysis goes awry, and we become aware of the process. Consider the sentence "The horse raced past the barn fell." Many people have difficulty understanding this sentence. Why? Because on first reading, we assume that "The horse" is the noun phrase and "raced past the barn" is the verb phrase, which leaves us with no place for the word *fell*. To understand the sentence correctly, we have to repartition it so that the entire phrase "The horse raced past the barn" is the noun phrase and "fell" is the verb phrase (that is, the sentence is a shortened version of "The horse who was raced past the barn fell") (Garrett, 1990; Garrod & Pickering, 1999).

EFFECTS OF CONTEXT ON COMPREHENSION AND PRODUCTION

Figure 9-3 presents an amended version of our levels-based description of language. It suggests that producing a sentence is the inverse of understanding a sentence.

To understand a sentence, we hear phonemes, use them to construct the morphemes and phrases of the sen-

Figure 9-3
Levels of Understanding and Producing Sentences
In producing a sentence, we translate a propositional thought into the phrases and morphemes of a sentence and translate these morphemes into phonemes. In understanding a sentence, we go in the opposite direction—we use phonemes to construct the morphemes and phrases of a sentence and from these units extract the underlying propositions.

tence, and finally extract the proposition from the sentence unit. We work from the bottom up. To produce a sentence, we move in the opposite direction: We start with a propositional thought, translate it into the phrases and morphemes of a sentence, and finally translate these morphemes into phonemes.

Although this analysis describes some of what occurs in sentence understanding and production, it is oversimplified because it does not consider the context in which language processing occurs. Often the context makes what is about to be said predictable. After comprehending just a few words, we jump to conclusions about what we think the entire sentence means (the propositions behind it) and then use our guess about the propositions to help understand the rest of the sentence. In such cases, understanding proceeds from the highest level down, as well as from the lowest level up (Adams & Collins, 1979).

Indeed, sometimes language understanding is nearly impossible without some context (what topic is being talked about). To illustrate, try reading the following paragraph:

> The procedure is actually quite simple. First you arrange things into different groups. Of course, one pile may be sufficient, depending on how much there is to do. If you have to go somewhere else due to lack of facilities, that is the next step; otherwise you are pretty well set. It is important not to overdo things. That is, it is better to do too few things at once than too many. In the short run this may not seem important, but complications can easily arise. A mistake can be expensive as well. At first the whole procedure will seem complicated. Soon, however, it will become just another facet of life. (After Bransford & Johnson, 1973)

In reading the paragraph, you no doubt had difficulty understanding exactly what it was about. But given the context of "washing clothes," you can now use your background knowledge about washing clothes to interpret all the cryptic parts of the passage. The "procedure" referred to in the first sentence is that of "washing clothes," the "things" referred to in the first sentence are "clothes," the "different groups" are "groups of clothing of different colors," and so on. Your understanding of the paragraph, if you reread it, should now be excellent.

In addition to background knowledge, another salient part of the context is the other person (or persons) we are communicating with. In understanding a sentence, it is not enough to understand its phonemes, morphemes, and phrases. We must also understand the speaker's intention in uttering that particular sentence. For example, when someone at dinner asks you, "Can you pass the potatoes?" you usually assume that the speaker's intention was not to find out whether you are physically capable of lifting the potatoes but, rather, to

Language production depends on context. You would probably use different language when giving directions to a tourist than when telling a neighbor where a particular restaurant or store is located.

induce you to actually pass the potatoes. However, had your arm been in a sling, given the identical question, you might assume that the speaker's intention was to determine your physical capability. In both cases, the sentence (and proposition) is the same. What changes is the speaker's intention in uttering that sentence (Grice, 1975). There is abundant evidence that people determine the speaker's intention as part of the process of comprehension (Clark, 1984).

There are similar effects in the production of language. If someone asks you, "Where is the Empire State Building?" you will say different things depending on the physical context and the assumptions you make about the questioner. If the question is asked of you in Detroit, for example, you might answer, "In New York." If the question is asked in Brooklyn, you might say, "Near midtown Manhattan." If the question is asked in Manhattan, you might say, "On 34th Street." In speaking, as in understanding, we must determine how the utterance fits the context.

The Neural Basis of Behavior

LANGUAGE

Recall from Chapter 2 that there are two regions of the left hemisphere of the cortex that are critical for language: Broca's area, which lies in the posterior part of the frontal lobes, and Wernicke's area, which lies in the temporal region. Damage to either of these areas—or to some in-between areas—leads to specific kinds of aphasia (a breakdown in language) (Dronkers, Redfern, & Knight, 2000).

The disrupted language of a patient with **Broca's aphasia** (a patient with damage to Broca's area) is illustrated by the following interview, in which *E* designates the interviewer (or experimenter) and *P,* the patient:

E: Were you in the Coast Guard?

P: No, er, yes, yes . . . ship . . . Massachu . . . chusetts . . . Coast Guard . . . years. [Raises hands twice with fingers indicating "19"]

E: Oh, you were in the Coast Guard for 19 years.

P: Oh . . . boy . . . right . . . right.

E: Why are you in the hospital?

P: [Points to paralyzed arm] Arm no good. [Points to mouth] Speech . . . can't say . . . talk, you see.

E: What happened to make you lose your speech?

P: Head, fall, Jesus Christ, me no good, str, str . . . oh Jesus . . . stroke.

E: Could you tell me what you've been doing in the hospital?

P: Yes sure. Me go, er, uh, P. T. nine o'cot, speech . . . two times . . . read . . . wr . . . ripe, er, rike, er, write . . . practice . . . get-ting better. (Gardner, 1975, p. 61)

The speech is very disfluent (halting and hesitant). Even in simple sentences, pauses and hesitations are plentiful. This is in contrast to the fluent speech of a patient with **Wernicke's aphasia** (a patient with damage in Wernicke's area):

Boy, I'm sweating, I'm awful nervous, you know, once in a while I get caught up. I can't mention the tarripoi, a month ago, quite a little, I've done a lot well, I impose a lot, while, on the other hand, you know what I mean, I have to run around, look it over, trebin and all that sort of stuff. (Gardner, 1975, p. 68)

In addition to fluency, there are other marked differences between Broca's and Wernicke's aphasias. The speech of a Broca's aphasic consists mainly of content words. It contains few grammatical morphemes and complex sentences and, in general, has a telegraphic quality that is reminiscent of the two-word stage of language acquisition (see The Development of Language later in this chapter). In contrast, the language of a Wernicke's aphasic preserves syntax but is remarkably devoid of content. There are clear problems in finding the right noun, and occasionally words are invented for the occasion (as in the use of *tarripoi* and *trebin*). These observations suggest that Broca's aphasia involves a disruption at the syntactic stage and that Wernicke's aphasia involves a disruption at the level of words and concepts.

These characterizations of the two aphasias are supported by research findings. In a study that tested for a syntactic deficit, participants had to listen to a sentence on each trial and show that they understood it by selecting a picture (from a set) that the sentence described. Some sentences could be understood without using much syntactic knowledge. For example, given "The bicycle the boy is holding is broken," we can figure out that it is the bicycle that is broken and not the boy, solely from our knowledge of the concepts involved. Understanding other sentences requires extensive syntactic analysis. In "The lion that the tiger is chasing is fat," we must rely on syntax (word order) to determine that it is the lion who is fat and not the tiger. On the sentences that did not require much syntactic analysis, Broca's aphasics did almost as well as normal participants, scoring close to 90% correct. But with sentences that required extensive analysis, Broca's aphasics fell to the level of guessing (for example, given the sentence about the lion and tiger, they were as likely to select the picture with a fat tiger as the one with the fat lion). In contrast, the performance of Wernicke's aphasics did not depend on the syntactic demands of the sentence. Thus, Broca's aphasia, but not Wernicke's, seems to be partly a disruption of syntax (Caramazza & Zurif, 1976). The disruption is not total, though, in that Broca's aphasics are capable of handling certain kinds of syntactic analysis (Grodzinsky, 1984; Zurif, 1995).

Other experiments have tested for a conceptual deficit in Wernicke's aphasia. In one study, participants were presented with three words at a time and asked to select the two that were most similar in meaning. The words included animal terms, such as *dog* and *crocodile,* as well as human terms, such as *mother* and *knight.* Normal participants used the distinction between humans and animals as the major basis for their selections; given *dog, crocodile,* and *knight,* for example, they selected the first two. Wernicke's patients, however, ignored this basic distinction. Although Broca's aphasics showed some differences from normals, their selections at least respected the human-animal distinction. A conceptual deficit thus is more pronounced in Wernicke's aphasics than in Broca's aphasics (Zurif, Carramazza, Myerson, & Galvin, 1974).

In addition to Broca's and Wernicke's aphasias, there are numerous other kinds of aphasias (Benson, 1985). One of these is referred to as conduction aphasia. In this condition, the aphasic seems relatively normal in tests of both syntactic and conceptual abilities but has severe problems when asked to repeat a spoken sentence. A neurological explanation of this curious disorder is that the brain structures mediating basic aspects of comprehension and production are intact but that the neural connections between these structures are damaged. The patient can understand what is said because Wernicke's area is intact and can produce fluent speech because Broca's area is intact but cannot transmit what was understood to the speech center because the connecting links between the areas are damaged (Geschwind, 1972).

This research presupposes that each kind of aphasia is caused by damage to a specific area of the brain. This idea may be too simple. In reality, the particular region mediating a particular linguistic function may vary from one person to another. The best evidence for such individual differences comes from findings of neurosurgeons preparing to operate on patients with incurable epilepsy. The neurosurgeon needs to remove some brain tissue but first has to be sure that this tissue is not mediating a critical function such as language. Accordingly, prior to surgery and while the patient is awake, the neurosurgeon delivers small electric charges to the area in question and observes their effects on the patient's ability to name things. If electrical stimulation disrupts the patient's naming, the neurosurgeon knows to avoid this location during the operation.

These locations are of great interest to students of language. Within a single patient, these language locations seem to be highly localized. A language location might be less than 1 centimeter in all directions from locations where electrical stimulations do not disrupt language. But—and this is the crucial point—different brain locations have to be stimulated to disrupt naming in different patients. For example, one patient's naming may be disrupted by electrical stimulation to locations in the front of the brain but not by stimulation in the back of the brain, whereas another patient might show a different pattern (Ojemann, 1983). If different areas of the brain mediate language in different people, presumably the areas associated with aphasias also vary from one person to another. ▮

◆ Interim Summary

- Language is structured at three different levels: (1) sentence units, (2) words and parts of words that carry meaning, and (3) speech sounds.
- The three levels of language are interconnected. Sentence units are built from words (and parts of words), and words are constructed from speech sounds.
- A phoneme is a category of speech sounds. Every language has its own set of phonemes—with different sets for different languages—and rules for combining them into words.
- A morpheme is the smallest unit of language that carries meaning. Most morphemes are words, but others are prefixes and suffixes that are added to words.
- Syntactic rules are used for combining words into phrases and phrases into sentences.
- The areas of the brain that mediate language lie in the left hemisphere and include Broca's area and Wernicke's area.

◆ Critical Thinking Questions

1. Now that you have some idea of the units and levels of language (such as phonemes, words, semantics, and syntax), apply these notions to learning a second language. Which components do you think will be easiest and hardest to learn? Why?

2. Background knowledge is clearly important for understanding language. Do you think there is a particular region of the brain that mediates such knowledge? Why or why not?

THE DEVELOPMENT OF LANGUAGE

Our discussion of language should suggest the immensity of the task confronting children. They must master all levels of language—not only the proper speech sounds but also how those sounds are combined into thousands of words and how those words can be combined into sentences to express thoughts. It is a wonder that virtually all children in all cultures accomplish so much in a mere 4 to 5 years. We will first discuss *what* is acquired at each level of language and then *how* it is acquired—specifically, the roles played by learning and innate factors.

WHAT IS ACQUIRED?

Development occurs at all three levels of language. It starts at the level of phonemes, proceeds to the level of words and other morphemes, and then moves on to the level of sentence units, or syntax. In what follows, we adopt a chronological perspective, tracing the child's development in both understanding and producing language.

PHONEMES AND COMBINATIONS OF PHONEMES Recall that adult listeners are good at discriminating among different sounds that correspond to different phonemes in their language but poor at discriminating among different sounds that correspond to the same phoneme in their language. Remarkably, children come into the world able to discriminate among different sounds that correspond to different phonemes in *any* language. What changes over the first year of life is that infants learn which phonemes are relevant to their language and lose their ability to discriminate between sounds that correspond to the same phoneme in their language. (In essence, they lose the ability to make distinctions that will be of no use to them in understanding and producing their language.) These remarkable facts were determined through experiments in which infants who were sucking on pacifiers were presented with pairs of sounds in succession. Because infants suck more in response to a novel stimulus than in response to a familiar one, their rate of sucking can be used to tell whether they perceive two successive sounds as the same or different. Six-month-old infants increase their rate of sucking when the successive sounds correspond to different phonemes in any language, but 1-year-olds increase their rate of sucking only when the successive sounds correspond to different phonemes in their own language. Thus, a 6-month-old Japanese child can distinguish /l/ from /r/ but loses this ability by the end of the first year of life (Eimas, 1985).

Although children learn which phonemes are relevant during their first year of life, it takes several years for them to learn how phonemes can be combined to form words. When children first begin to talk, they occasionally produce "impossible" words like *dlumber* for *lumber*. They do not yet know that in English /l/ cannot follow /d/ at the beginning of a word. By age 4, however, children have learned most of what they need to know about phoneme combinations.

WORDS AND CONCEPTS At about 1 year of age, children begin to speak. One-year-olds already have concepts for many things (including family members, household pets, food, toys, and body parts), and when they begin to

Children between 18 and 30 months of age learn to combine words in phrases and sentences.

speak, they are mapping these concepts onto words that adults use. The beginning vocabulary is roughly the same for all children. Children 1 to 2 years old talk mainly about people ("Dada," "Mama," "baby"), animals ("dog," "cat," "duck"), vehicles ("car," "truck," "boat"), toys ("ball," "block," "book"), food ("juice," "milk," "cookie"), body parts ("eye," "nose," "mouth"), and household implements ("hat," "sock," "spoon").

Although these words name some of the young child's concepts, they by no means name them all. Consequently, young children often have a gap between the concepts they want to communicate and the words they have at their disposal. To bridge this gap, children aged 12 to 30 months old **overextend** their words—they **apply words to neighboring concepts**. For example, a 2-year-old child might use the word *doggie* for cats and cows as well as dogs. (The child is not unsure of the word's meaning. If presented with pictures of various animals and asked to pick the "doggie," the child makes the correct choice.) Overextensions begin to disappear at about age 2½, presumably because the child's vocabulary begins to increase markedly, thereby eliminating many of the gaps (Clark, 1983; Rescorla, 1980).

Thereafter, the child's vocabulary development virtually explodes. At 1½ years, a child might have a vocabulary of 25 words; at 6 years, the child's vocabulary is about 15,000 words. To achieve this incredible growth, children have to learn new words at the rate of almost 10 per day (Miller & Gildea, 1987; Templin, 1957). Children seem to be attuned to learning new words. When they hear a word they do not know, they may assume that it maps onto one of their concepts that is not yet labeled, and they use the context in which the word was spoken to find that concept (Clark, 1983; Markman, 1987).

FROM PRIMITIVE TO COMPLEX SENTENCES Between the ages of 1½ and 2½, the acquisition of phrase and sentence units, or syntax, begins. Children start to combine single words into two-word utterances such as "There cow" (in which the underlying proposition is "There's the cow"), "Jimmy bike" ("That's Jimmy's bike"), or "Towel bed" ("The towel's on the bed"). There is a telegraphic quality about this two-word speech. The child leaves out the grammatical words (such as *a, an, the,* and *is*), as well as other grammatical morphemes (such as the suffixes *ing, ed,* and *s*) and puts in only the words that carry the most important content. Despite their brevity, these utterances express most of the basic intentions of speakers, such as locating objects and describing events and actions.

Children progress rapidly from two-word utterances to more complex sentences that express propositions more precisely. Thus, "Daddy hat" may become "Daddy wear hat" and finally "Daddy is wearing a hat." Such expansions of the verb phrase appear to be the first complex constructions that occur in children's speech. The next step is the use of conjunctions like *and* and *so* to form compound sentences ("You play with the doll, and I play with the blocks") and the use of grammatical morphemes like the past tense *ed*. The sequence of language development is remarkably similar for all children.

Learning Processes

How do children acquire language? Clearly, learning must play a role, which is why children raised in English-speaking households learn English while children raised in French-speaking households learn French. Innate factors must also play a role, which is why all the children in a household learn language but none of the pets do (Gleitman, 1986). In this section, we discuss learning, and innate factors are considered in the next section. In both discussions, we emphasize sentence units and syntax, for it is at this level of language that the important issues about language acquisition are illustrated most clearly.

IMITATION AND CONDITIONING One possibility is that children learn language by imitating adults. Although imitation plays some role in the learning of words (a parent points to a telephone, says, "Phone," and the child tries to repeat the word), it cannot be the principal means by which children learn to produce and understand sentences. Young children constantly utter sentences that they have never heard an adult say, such as "All gone milk." Even when children in the two-word

stage of language development try to imitate longer sentences (for example, "Mr. Miller will try"), they produce their usual telegraphic utterances ("Miller try"). In addition, the mistakes children make (for instance, "Daddy taked me") suggest that they are trying to apply rules, not simply trying to copy what they have heard adults say (Ervin-Tripp, 1964).

A second possibility is that children acquire language through conditioning. Adults may reward children when they produce a grammatical sentence and reprimand them when they make mistakes. For this to work, parents would have to respond to every detail in a child's speech. However, Brown, Cazden, & Bellugi (1969) found that parents do not pay attention to how the child says something as long as the statement is comprehensible. Also, attempts to correct a child (and, hence, apply conditioning) are often futile. Consider an example:

CHILD: Nobody don't like me.

MOTHER: No, say, "nobody likes me."

CHILD: Nobody don't like me.

MOTHER: No, now listen carefully; say "nobody likes me."

CHILD: Oh! Nobody don't LIKES me. (McNeill, 1966, p. 49)

HYPOTHESIS TESTING The problem with imitation and conditioning is that they focus on specific utterances. However, children often learn something general, such as a rule. They seem to form a hypothesis about a rule of language, test it, and retain it if it works.

Consider the morpheme *ed*. As a general rule in English, *ed* is added to the present tense of verbs to form the past tense (as in *cook-cooked*). Many common verbs, however, are irregular and do not follow this rule (*go-went, break-broke*). Many of these irregular verbs express concepts that children use from the beginning. So, at an early point, children use the past tense of some irregular verbs correctly (presumably because they learned them by imitation). Then they learn the past tense for some regular verbs and discover the hypothesis "add *ed* to the present tense to form the past tense." This hypothesis leads them to add the *ed* ending to many verbs, including irregular ones. They say things like "Annie goed home" and "Jackie breaked the cup," which they have never heard before. Eventually, they learn that some verbs are irregular and stop overgeneralizing their use of *ed* (Pinker, 1994).

How do children generate these hypotheses? There are a few operating principles that all children use as a guide to forming hypotheses. One is to pay attention to the ends of words. Another is to look for prefixes and suffixes that indicate a change in meaning. A child armed with these two principles is likely to hit upon the hypothesis that *ed* at the end of verbs signals the past tense, because *ed* is a word ending associated with a change in meaning. A third operating principle is to avoid exceptions, which explains why children initially generalize their *ed*-equals-past-tense hypothesis to irregular verbs. Some of these principles appear in Table 9-1, and they seem to hold for all of the 40 languages studied by Slobin (1985).

In recent years, there has been a challenge to the idea that learning a language involves learning rules. Some researchers argue that the mere fact that a regular pattern is overextended does not guarantee that these errors are caused by following a rule. Marcus (1996), for example, believes that children's grammar is structured similarly to adults'. But because children have had less exposure to correct forms, their memories for irregular forms like *broke* are weaker. Whenever they cannot recall such a form, they add *ed,* producing an overextension. Other researchers have argued that what looks like an instance of learning a single rule may in fact be a case of learning numerous associations. Consider again a child learning the past tense of verbs in English. Instead of learning a rule about adding *ed* to the present tense of a verb, perhaps children are learning associations between the past tense ending *ed* and various phonetic properties of verbs that can go with *ed.* The phonetic properties of a verb include properties of the sounds that make up the verb, such as whether it contains an *alk* sound at the end. A child may unconsciously learn that verbs containing an *alk* sound at the end—such as *talk, walk,* and *stalk*—are likely to take *ed* as a past tense ending. This proposal has in fact been shown to account for some aspects of learn-

ing verb endings, including the finding that at some point in development children add the *ed* ending even to irregular verbs (Rumelhart & McClelland, 1987).

However, other aspects of learning verb endings cannot be explained in terms of associations between sounds. For example, the word *break* and the word *brake* (meaning to a stop a car) are identical in sound, but the past tense of the former is *broke,* whereas that of the latter is *braked.* So a child must learn something in addition to sound connections. This additional knowledge seems best cast in terms of rules (for example, "If a verb is derived from a noun—as in the case of *brake*—always add *ed* to form the past tense"). Another piece of evidence that verb endings can involve rules (for regular verbs) or memorized past tenses (for exceptions) comes from studies of aphasics. Recall that Broca's aphasics have difficulty with the grammatical aspects of language, and they also have more problems with regular verbs (which are handled by rules) than with irregular ones. Furthermore, **anomic aphasics,** who primarily have problems in retrieving and recognizing words, have more problems with irregular verbs (which require memory) than with regular verbs (Ullman et al., 1997). Language learning thus seems to involve rules as well as associations and memory (Pinker, 1991; Pinker & Prince, 1988).

INNATE FACTORS

As noted earlier, some of our knowledge about language is inborn, or innate. There are, however, some controversial questions about the extent and nature of this innate knowledge. One question concerns its richness. If our innate knowledge is very rich or detailed, the process of language acquisition should be similar for different languages, even if the opportunities for learning differ among cultures. Is this the case? A second question about innate factors involves critical periods. Innate behavior will be acquired more readily if the organism is exposed to the right cues during a critical time period. Are there such critical periods in language acquisition? A third question concerns the possible uniqueness of our innate knowledge about language. Is the ability to learn a language system unique to the human species? We will consider these three questions in turn.

THE RICHNESS OF INNATE KNOWLEDGE All children, regardless of their culture and language, seem to go through the same sequence of language development. At age 1 year, the child speaks a few isolated words; at about age 2, the child speaks two- and three-word sentences; at age 3, sentences become more grammatical; and at age 4, the child's speech sounds much like that of an adult. Because cultures differ markedly in the opportunities they provide for children to learn from adults—

in some cultures parents are constantly speaking to their children, whereas in others parents verbally ignore their children—the fact that this sequence is so consistent across cultures indicates that our innate knowledge about language is very rich.

Indeed, our innate knowledge of language seems to be so rich that children can go through the normal course of language acquisition even when there are no language users around them to serve as models or teachers. A group of researchers studied six deaf children of hearing parents who had decided not to have their children learn sign language. Before the children received any instruction in lip reading and vocalization, they began to use a system of gestures called *home sign*. Initially, their home sign was a kind of simple pantomime, but eventually it took on the properties of a language. For example, it was organized at both the morphemic and syntactic levels, including individual signs and combinations of signs. In addition, these deaf children (who essentially created their own language) went through the same stages of development as normal hearing children. The deaf children initially gestured one sign at a time and later put their pantomimes together into two- and three-concept "sentences." These striking results attest to the richness and detail of our innate knowledge (Feldman, Goldin-Meadow, & Gleitman, 1978).

CRITICAL PERIODS Like other innate behaviors, language learning has some critical periods. This is particularly evident when it comes to acquiring the sound system of a new language—learning new phonemes and the rules for combining them. We have already noted that infants less than 1 year old can discriminate among phonemes of any language but lose this ability by the end of their first year, so the first months of life are a critical period for homing in on the phonemes of one's native language. There also seems to be a critical period for acquiring the sound system of a second language. After a few years of learning a second language, young children are more likely than adults to speak it without an accent, and they are better able to understand the language when it is spoken in noisy conditions (Lenneberg, 1967; Snow, 1987). Furthermore, when adults learn a second language, they typically retain an accent that they can never unlearn, no matter how many years they speak the new language (think of Arnold Schwarzenegger).

More recent research indicates that there is also a critical period for learning syntax. The evidence comes from studies of deaf people who know American Sign Language (ASL), which is a full-blown language and not a pantomime system. The studies of interest involved adults who had been using ASL for 30 years or more but varied in the age when they had learned the language.

Research has shown that there is a critical period for learning syntax. Deaf people can use American Sign Language more effectively if they learn it at an early age.

Although all the participants were born to hearing parents, some were native signers who were exposed to ASL from birth, others first learned ASL between ages 4 and 6 when they enrolled in a school for the deaf, and still others did not encounter ASL until after they were 12 (their parents had been reluctant to let them learn a sign language rather than a spoken one). If there is a critical period for learning syntax, the early learners should have shown greater mastery of some aspects of syntax than the later learners, even 30 years after acquisition. This is exactly what the researchers found. With respect to understanding and producing words with multiple morphemes—such as *untimely,* which consists of the morphemes *un, time,* and *ly*—native signers did better than those who learned ASL when entering school, who in turn did better than those who learned ASL after age 12 (Meier, 1991; Newport, 1990).

Indirect evidence for the existence of a critical period for language acquisition can be seen in cases of children who have experienced extreme isolation. A famous case of social isolation in childhood is that of Genie, a girl whose father was psychotic and whose mother was blind and highly dependent. From birth until she was discovered by child welfare authorities at age 11, Genie was strapped to a potty chair in an isolated room of her parents' home.

Before she was discovered, Genie had had almost no contact with other people. She had virtually no language ability. Efforts to teach her to speak had limited results. She was able to learn words, but she could not master the rules of grammar that come naturally to younger children. Although tests showed that she was highly intelligent, her language abilities never progressed beyond those of a third-grader (Curtiss, 1977; Rymer, 1992a, 1992b).

CAN ANOTHER SPECIES LEARN HUMAN LANGUAGE?
Some experts believe that our innate capacity to learn language is unique to our species (Chomsky, 1972; Pinker, 1994). They acknowledge that other species have communication systems but argue that these are qualitatively different from ours. Consider the communication system of the chimpanzee. Chimpanzees' vocalizations and gestures are limited in number, and the productivity of their communication system is very low compared with that of human language, in which a relatively small number of phonemes can be combined to create thousands of words, which in turn can be combined to create an unlimited number of sentences.

Another difference is that human language is structured at several levels, whereas chimpanzee communications are not. In particular, in human language there is a clear distinction between the level of words or morphemes, which have meaning, and the level of sounds, which do not. There is no hint of such a duality of structure in chimpanzee communication; every symbol carries meaning.

Still another difference is that chimpanzees do not vary the order of their symbols to vary the meaning of their messages as we do. For instance, for us, "Jonah ate the whale" means something quite different from "The whale ate Jonah." There is no evidence for a comparable difference in chimpanzee communications.

The fact that chimpanzee communication is impoverished compared with our own does not prove that chimpanzees lack the capacity for a more productive system. Their system may be adequate for their needs. To determine whether chimpanzees have the same innate capacity we do, we must see whether they can learn our language.

In one of the best-known studies of the teaching of language to chimps, Gardner and Gardner (1972) taught a female chimpanzee named Washoe signs adapted from American Sign Language. Sign language was used because chimps lack the vocal equipment to pronounce human sounds. Training began when Washoe was about 1 year old and continued until she was 5. During this time, Washoe's caretakers communicated with her only by means of sign language. They first taught her signs by means of shaping procedures, waiting for her to make a gesture that resembled a sign and then reinforcing her. Later, Washoe learned signs simply by observing and imitating. By age 4, Washoe could produce 130 different signs and understand even more. She could also generalize a sign from one situation to another. For example,

she first learned the sign for "more" in connection with "more tickling" and then generalized it to indicate "more milk."

Other chimpanzees have acquired comparable vocabularies. Some studies used methods of manual communication other than sign language. For example, Premack (1971; 1985) taught a chimpanzee named Sarah to use plastic symbols as words and to communicate by manipulating these symbols. In a series of similar studies, Patterson (1978) taught sign language to a gorilla named Koko, starting when Koko was 1 year old. By age 10, Koko had a vocabulary of more than 400 signs (Patterson & Linden, 1981).

Do these studies prove that apes can learn human language? There seems to be little doubt that the apes' signs are equivalent to our words and that the concepts behind some of the signs are equivalent to ours. But many experts question whether these studies show that apes can learn syntax and learn to combine signs in the same way that humans combine words into a sentence. For example, not only can we combine the words *man, John, hurt,* and *the* into the sentence "The man hurt John," but we can also combine the same words in a different order to produce a sentence with a different meaning, "John hurt the man." Although the studies just described provide some evidence that apes can combine signs into a sequence resembling a sentence, there is little evidence that apes can alter the order of the signs to produce a different sentence (Brown, 1986; Slobin, 1979).

Even the evidence that apes can combine signs into a sentence has come under attack. In their early work, researchers reported cases in which an ape produced what seemed to be a meaningful sequence of signs, such as "Gimme flower" and "Washoe sorry" (Gardner & Gardner, 1972). As data accumulated, however, it became apparent that, unlike human sentences, the utterances of an ape are often highly repetitious. An utterance like "You me banana me banana you" is typical of the signing chimps but would be most odd for a human child. In the cases in which an ape utterance is more like a sentence, the ape may simply have imitated the sequence of signs made by its human teacher. Some of Washoe's most sentence-like utterances occurred when she was answering a question. For example, the teacher signed, "Washoe eat?" and Washoe signed, "Washoe eat time." Washoe's combination of signs may have been a partial imitation of her teacher's combination, which is not how human children learn to combine words (Terrace, Petitto, Sanders, & Bever, 1979).

The evidence considered thus far supports the conclusion that, although apes can develop a humanlike vocabulary, they cannot learn to combine their signs in the systematic way humans do. However, studies by

Greenfield and Savage-Rumbaugh (such as 1990) seem to challenge this conclusion. The researchers worked with a pygmy chimpanzee, whose behavior is thought to be more like that of humans than the behavior of the more widely studied common chimpanzee. The pygmy chimpanzee, a 7-year-old named Kanzi, communicated by manipulating symbols that stand for words. Unlike previous studies, Kanzi learned to manipulate the symbols in a relatively natural way, for example, by listening to his caretakers as they uttered English words while pointing to the symbols. Most important, after a few years of language training, Kanzi demonstrated some ability to vary word order to communicate changes in meaning. For example, if Kanzi was going to bite his half-sister Mulika, he would signal, "Bite Mulika," but if his sister bit him, he would sign, "Mulika bite." Kanzi thus seems to have some syntactic knowledge, roughly that of a 2-year-old human.

These results are tantalizing, but they need to be interpreted with caution. For one thing, Kanzi is so far among the few chimpanzees who have shown any syntactic ability, and we might question how general the results are. For another thing, although Kanzi may have the linguistic ability of a 2-year-old, it took him substantially longer to get to that point than it does a human. But perhaps the main reason to be skeptical about the possibility of any ape's developing comparable linguistic abilities to a human has been voiced by Chomsky (1991):

> If an animal had a capacity as biologically advantageous as language but somehow hadn't used it until now, it would be an evolutionary miracle, like finding an island of humans who could be taught to fly.

◆ Interim Summary

- Infants appear to be preprogrammed to learn phonemes, but they need several years to learn the rules for combining them.
- When children begin to speak, they first learn words that name concepts that are familiar in their environment. Then they move on to sentences. They begin with one-word utterances, progress to two-word telegraphic speech, and then elaborate their noun and verb phrases.
- Children learn language in part by testing hypotheses (often unconsciously). These hypotheses tend to be guided by a small set of operating principles, which call the children's attention to critical characteristics of utterances, such as word endings.
- Innate factors also play a major role in language acquisition. There are numerous findings that support this claim. For one, all children in all cultures seem to go through the same stages in acquiring their language. For another, like other innate behaviors, some language abilities are learned only during a critical period.

◆ Critical Thinking Questions

1. Do you think there is a critical period for learning word meanings? Why or why not?
2. What do you think would happen if parents explicitly taught children language the way that most researchers have taught apes human language. Would it speed up, slow down, or leave unchanged the process of language acquisition?

The chimpanzee on the left has been trained to communicate by using a keyboard. The one on the right has learned a kind of sign language; here he makes the sign for "toothbrush."

CONCEPTS AND CATEGORIZATION: THE BUILDING BLOCKS OF THOUGHT

Thought can be conceived of as a "language of the mind." Actually, there may be more than one language. One mode of thought corresponds to the stream of sentences that we seem to "hear in our mind." It is referred to as **propositional thought** because it expresses a proposition or claim. Another mode, **imaginal thought**, corresponds to images, particularly visual ones, that we can "see" in our minds. Research on thinking in adults has emphasized these two modes, particularly the propositional mode.

We can think of a proposition as a statement that expresses a factual claim. "Mothers are hard workers" is one proposition. "Cats are animals" is another. It is easy to see that such a thought consists of concepts—such as "mothers" and "hard workers" or "cat" and "animal"—combined in a particular way. To understand propositional thought, however, we first need to understand the concepts that compose it.

FUNCTIONS OF CONCEPTS

A **concept** represents an entire class; it is the set of properties that we associate with a particular class. Our concept of "cat," for example, includes the properties of having four legs and whiskers. Concepts serve some major functions in mental life. One of those functions is to divide the world into manageable units (cognitive economy). The world is full of so many different objects that if we treated each one as distinct, we would soon be overwhelmed. For example, if we had to refer to every single object we encountered by a different name, our vocabulary would have to be gigantic—so immense that communication might become impossible. (Think what it would be like if we had a separate name for each of the 7 million colors among which we can discriminate!) Fortunately, we do not treat each object as unique. Rather, we see it as an instance of a concept. Many different objects are seen as instances of the concept "cat," many others as instances of the concept "chair," and so on. By treating different objects as members of the same concept, we reduce the complexity of the world that we have to represent mentally.

Categorization refers to the process of assigning an object to a concept. When we categorize an object, we treat it as if it has many of the properties associated with the concept, including properties that we have not directly perceived. A second major function of concepts is

that they allow us to predict information that is not readily perceived (referred to as predictive power). For example, our concept of "apple" is associated with such hard-to-perceive properties as having seeds and being edible, as well as with readily perceived properties like being round, having a distinctive color, and coming from trees. We may use the visible properties to categorize some object as an "apple" (the object is red, round, and hangs from a tree) and then infer that the object has the less visible properties as well (it has seeds and is edible). Concepts enable us to go beyond directly perceived information (Anderson, 1991; Bruner, 1957).

We also have concepts of activities, such as "eating"; of states, such as "being old"; and of abstractions, such as "truth," "justice," or even the number 2. In each case we know something about the properties that are common to all members of the concept. Widely used concepts like these are generally associated with a one-word name. This allows us to communicate quickly about experiences that occur frequently. We can also make up concepts on the spot to serve some specific goal. For example, if you are planning an outing, you might generate the concept "things to take on a camping trip." These kinds of goal-driven concepts facilitate planning. Although such concepts are used relatively infrequently, and accordingly have relatively long names, they still provide us with some cognitive economy and predictive power (Barsalou, 1985).

PROTOTYPES

The properties associated with a concept seem to fall into two sets. One set of properties makes up the **prototype** of the concept. They are the properties that describe the best examples of the concept. In the concept "grandmother," for example, your prototype might include such properties as a woman who is in her 60s, has gray hair, and loves to spend time with her children. The prototype is what usually comes to mind when we think of the concept. But although the prototype properties may be true of the typical grandmother, they clearly are not true of all instances (think of a woman in her late 30s who, like her daughter, had a child while a teenager). This means that a concept must contain something in addition to a prototype. This additional something is a **core** that comprises the properties that are most important for being a member of a concept. Your core of the concept "grandmother" would probably include the properties of being a female parent of a parent, the properties that are essential for being a member of the concept (Armstrong, Gleitman, & Gleitman, 1983).

As another example, consider the concept "bird." Your prototype likely includes the properties of flying and chirping—which works for the best examples of

Do flying and chirping make a bird? Your prototype for "bird" probably includes these features. However, they do not apply to certain kinds of birds, such as penguins.

"bird," such as robins and blue jays, but not for other examples, such as ostriches and penguins. Your core would probably specify something about the biological basis of birdhood—having certain genes or, at least, having parents that are birds.

Note that in both our examples—"grandmother" and "bird"—the prototype properties are salient but not perfect indicators of concept membership, whereas the core properties are more central to concept membership. However, there is an important difference between a concept like "grandmother" and a concept like "bird." The core of "grandmother" is a definition, and it is easily applied. Anyone who is a female parent of a parent must be a "grandmother," and it is relatively easy to determine whether someone has these defining properties. Concepts like this one are said to be well defined. Categorizing a person or object into a well-defined category involves determining whether it has the core or defining properties. In contrast, the core of "bird" is hardly a

definition—we may know only that genes are somehow involved, for example—and the core properties are hidden from view. If we happen upon a small animal, we can hardly inspect its genes or inquire about its parentage. All we can do is check whether it does certain things, such as fly and chirp, and use this information to decide whether it is a bird. Concepts like "bird" are said to be fuzzy. Deciding whether an object is an instance of a fuzzy concept often involves determining its similarity to the concept's prototype (Smith, 1995). Most natural concepts seem to be fuzzy. They lack true definitions, and categorization of these concepts relies heavily on prototypes.

Some instances of fuzzy concepts have more prototype properties than other instances. Among birds, for example, a robin will have the property of flying, whereas an ostrich will not. The more prototype properties an instance has, the more typical of the concept it is considered to be. In the case of "bird," most people rate a robin as more typical than a chicken, and a chicken as more typical than an ostrich; in the case of "apple," they rate red apples as more typical than green ones (since red seems to be a property of the concept "apple"); and so on. The degree to which an instance is typical has a major effect on its categorization. When people are asked whether a pictured animal is a "bird," a robin produces an immediate yes, whereas a chicken requires a longer decision time. When young children are asked the same question, a robin will almost inevitably be classified correctly, whereas a chicken will often be declared a nonbird. Typicality also determines what we think of when we encounter the name of the concept. Hearing the sentence "There is a bird outside your window," we are far more likely to think of a robin than a vulture, and what comes to mind will obviously influence what we make of the sentence (Rosch, 1978).

UNIVERSALITY OF PROTOTYPES FORMATION Are our prototypes determined mainly by our culture, or are they universal? For some concepts, such as "grandmother," culture clearly has a major impact on the prototype. But for more natural concepts, prototypes are surprisingly universal.

Consider color concepts such as "red." This is a fuzzy concept (no ordinary person knows its defining properties) and one with a clear prototype: People in our culture agree on which hues are typical reds and which hues are atypical. People in other cultures agree with our choices. Remarkably, this agreement is found even among people whose language does not include a word for "red." When speakers of these languages are asked to pick the best example from an array of red hues, they make the same choices we would. Even though the range of hues for what they would call "red" may differ from ours, their idea of a typical red is the same as ours (Berlin & Kay, 1969).

Other research suggests that the Dani, a New Guinea people whose language has terms only for "black" and "white," perceive color variations in exactly the same way as English-speaking people, whose language has terms for many colors. Dani individuals were given a set of red color patches to remember; the patches varied in how typical they were of "red." Later the participants were presented with a set of color patches and asked to decide which ones they had seen before. Even though they had no word for "red," they recognized more typical red colors better than less typical ones. This is exactly what American participants do when performing a comparable task (Rosch, 1974). Color prototypes thus appear to be universal.

More recent experiments suggest that prototypes for some animal concepts may also be universal. The experiments compared U.S. students and Maya Itza participants. (Maya Itza is a culture of the Guatemalan rainforest that is relatively insulated from Western influences.) The U.S. participants were from southeastern Michigan, which happens to have a number of mammalian species that are comparable to those found in the Guatemalan rainforest. Both groups were presented with the names of these species. They were first asked to group them into sets that go together, then to group those sets into higher-order groups that were related, and so on until all the species were in one group corresponding to "mammals." These groupings were determined by the similarity of the prototypes: In the first pass, participants would group together only species that seemed very similar. By making these groupings, each participant created a kind of tree, with the initial groupings at the bottom and "mammal" at the top; this tree reflects the taxonomy of animals.

The trees or taxonomies created by the Maya Itza were quite similar to those created by the U.S. students; in fact, the correlation between the average Itza and U.S. trees was about +60. Moreover, both the Itza and U.S. taxonomies were highly correlated with the actual scientific taxonomy. Apparently, all people base their prototypes of animals on properties that they can easily observe (overall shape, or distinctive features like coloring, a bushy tail, or a particular movement pattern). These properties are indicators of the evolutionary history of the species, on which the scientific taxonomy is based (Lopez, Atran, Medin, Cooley, & Smith, 1997).

One can also think of cases where the contents of animal concepts differ across cultures. If in some culture ostriches are plentiful but robins are not, that culture may well have a different prototype for "bird" than does our culture. However, the principles by which prototypes are formed—such as focusing on frequently encountered features of instances of the concept—may well be universal.

HIERARCHIES OF CONCEPTS

In addition to knowing the properties of concepts, we also know how concepts are related to one another. For example, "apples" are members (or a subset) of a larger concept, "fruit"; "robins" are a subset of "birds," which in turn are a subset of "animals." These two types of knowledge (properties of a concept and relationships between concepts) are represented in Figure 9-4 as a hierarchy. As Figure 9-4 makes clear, an object can be identified at different levels. The same object is at once a "Golden Delicious apple," an "apple," and a "fruit." However, in any hierarchy one level is the **basic** or preferred one for classification, the level at which we first categorize an object. For the hierarchy in Figure 9-4, the level that contains "apple" and "pear" would be the basic one. Evidence for this claim comes from studies in

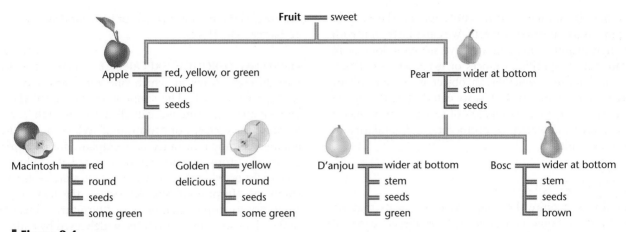

▌Figure 9-4
Hierarchy of Concepts
Words that begin with a capital letter represent concepts; lowercase words depict properties of these concepts. The green lines show relationships between concepts, and the red lines connect properties and concepts.

which people are asked to name pictured objects with the first names that come to mind. People are more likely to call a pictured Golden Delicious apple an "apple" than either a "Golden Delicious apple" or a "fruit." Basic-level concepts are special in other respects as well. As examples, they are the first ones learned by children, they are used more frequently, and they have shorter names (Mervis & Rosch, 1981).

It seems, then, that we first divide the world into basic-level concepts. What determines which level is basic? The answer appears to be that the basic level has the most distinctive properties. In Figure 9-4, "apple" has several properties that are distinctive—not shared by other kinds of fruit (for example, red and round are not properties of "pear"). In contrast, "Golden Delicious apple" has few distinct properties; most of its properties are shared by "MacIntosh apple," for example. And "fruit," which is at the highest level of Figure 9-4, has few properties of any kind. Thus, we first categorize the world at what turns out to be the most informative level (Murphy & Brownell, 1985).

DIFFERENT CATEGORIZATION PROCESSES

We are constantly making categorization decisions. We categorize every time we recognize an object, every time we diagnose a problem ("That's a power failure"), and so on. How do we use concepts to categorize our world? The answer depends on whether the concept is well defined or fuzzy.

For well-defined concepts like "grandmother," we may determine how similar a person is to our prototype ("She's sixtyish and has gray hair, so she looks like a grandmother"). But if we are trying to be accurate, we can determine whether the person has the defining properties of the concept ("Is she the female parent of a parent?"). The latter amounts to applying a rule: "If she's the female parent of a parent, she's a grandmother." There have been many studies of such rule-based categorization of well-defined concepts, and they show that the more properties there are in the rule, the slower and more error-prone the categorization process (Bourne, 1966). This may be due to processing the properties one at a time.

For fuzzy concepts like "bird" and "chair," we do not know enough defining properties to use rule-based categorization, so we often rely on similarity instead. As already mentioned, one thing we may do is determine the similarity of an object to the prototype of the concept ("Is this object similar enough to my prototype to call it a chair?"). The evidence that people categorize objects in this fashion comes from experiments that involve three steps (Smith, 1995):

1. First the researcher determines the properties of a concept's prototype and of various instances of that concept. (The researcher might ask one group of participants to describe the properties of their prototypical chair and of various pictures of chairs.)
2. Then the researcher determines the similarity between each instance (each pictured chair) and the prototype by identifying their shared properties. This results in a similarity-to-prototype score for each instance.
3. Finally, the researcher shows that the similarity-to-prototype score is highly correlated with how accurately and quickly participants can correctly categorize that instance. This shows that similarity-to-prototype plays a role in categorization.

There is another kind of similarity calculation that we can use to categorize objects. We can illustrate it with our chair example. Because we have stored in long-term memory some specific instances or exemplars of chairs, we can determine whether an object is similar to our stored chair exemplars. If it is, we can declare that it is a chair. Thus, we have two means of categorization based on similarity: similarity to prototypes and similarity to stored exemplars.

ACQUIRING CONCEPTS

How do we acquire the multitude of concepts that we know about? Some concepts, such as the concepts of "time" and "space," may be inborn. Others have to be learned.

LEARNING PROTOTYPES AND CORES We can learn about a concept in different ways. Either we are explicitly taught something about the concept or we learn it through experience. Which way we learn depends on what we are learning. Explicit teaching is likely to be the means by which we learn cores of concepts, and experience seems to be the usual means by which we acquire prototypes. Someone explicitly tells a child that a "robber" is someone who takes another person's possessions with no intention of returning them (the core), and the child's experiences may lead him or her to expect robbers to be shiftless, disheveled, and dangerous (the prototype).

Children must also learn that the core is a better indicator of concept membership than the prototype is, but it takes a while for them to learn this. In one study, children aged 5 to 10 were presented with descriptions of items and asked to decide whether they belonged to particular well-defined concepts. We can illustrate the study with the concept of "robber." One description given for "robber" depicted a person who matched its prototype but not its core:

> A smelly, mean old man with a gun in his pocket who came to your house and takes your TV set because your parents didn't want it anymore and told him he could have it.

Another description given for "robber" was of a person who matched its core but not its prototype:

> A very friendly and cheerful woman who gave you a hug, but then disconnected your toilet bowl and took it away without permission and no intention to return it.

The younger children often thought that the prototypical description was more likely than the core description to be an instance of the concept. Not until age 10 did children show a clear shift from the prototype to

the core as the final arbitrator of concept decisions (Keil & Batterman, 1984).

LEARNING THROUGH EXPERIENCE There are at least two different ways in which one can learn a concept through experience. The simplest way is called the *exemplar strategy*, and we can illustrate it with a child learning the concept of "furniture." When the child encounters a known instance or exemplar—for example, a table—she stores a representation of it. Later, when she has to decide whether a new item—say, a desk—is an instance of "furniture," she determines the new object's similarity to stored exemplars of "furniture," including tables. This strategy seems to be widely used by children, and it works better with typical instances than with atypical ones. Because the first exemplars a child learns tend to be typical ones, new instances are more likely to be correctly classified to the extent that they are similar to typical instances. Thus, if a young child's concept of "furniture" consisted of just the most typical instances (say, table and chair), he could correctly classify other instances that looked similar to the learned exemplars, such as desk and sofa, but not instances that looked different from the learned exemplars, such as lamp and bookshelf (Mervis & Pani, 1981). The exemplar strategy remains part of our repertory for acquiring concepts, as there is substantial evidence that adults often use it in acquiring novel concepts (Estes, 1994; Nosofsky & Johansen, 2000).

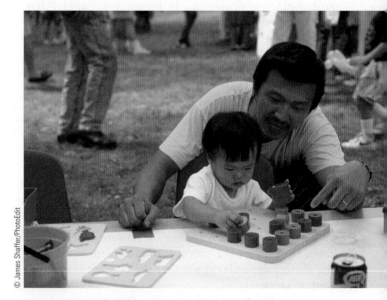

Parents can teach children to name and classify objects. Later, when the child sees another object, he may determine whether it is in the same category as the stored exemplar.

But as we grow older we start to use another strategy, hypothesis testing. We inspect known instances of a concept, searching for properties that are relatively common to them (for example, many pieces of "furniture" are found in living spaces), and we hypothesize that these common properties are what characterize the concept. We then analyze novel objects for these critical properties, maintaining our hypothesis if it leads to a correct categorization about the novel object and revamping it if it leads us astray. This strategy thus focuses on abstractions—properties that characterize sets of instances rather than just single instances—and is tuned to finding core properties, because they are the ones that are common to most instances (Bruner, Goodenow, & Austin, 1956). What properties we look for, though, may be biased by any specific knowledge we have about the objects themselves. If a child thinks furniture always has a flat surface, this piece of prior knowledge may overly restrict the hypothesis that is generated. (See Figure 9-5 for an example of this kind of bias in hypothesis testing.)

Category 1

Category 2

▌Figure 9-5
Biases in Concept Learning
In an experiment on concept learning, two groups of adult participants were presented with children's drawings. One group of participants was told that Category 1 drawings had been done by creative children and Category 2 drawings by noncreative children, and another group was told that Category 1 drawings had been done by city children and Category 2 drawings by farm children. The two groups offered different kinds of hypotheses about the categories. The creative-noncreative group produced more hypotheses about the two categories that emphasized the amount of detail in the drawing; in contrast, the farm-city group produced more hypotheses about the two categories that emphasized the clothing in the drawing. Moreover, the same feature (for example, the object pointed to in the fourth figure in Category 1) was sometimes interpreted differently by the two groups. (E. J. Wesniewski and D. L. Nedin (1991) "Harpoons & Logistics: The Interaction of Theory & Similarity in Rule Induction," in *Concept Formation: Knowledge & Experience in Unsupervised Learning*, ed. by D. Fisher, M. Pazzani, & P. Langley. Copyright © 1991 by Morgan & Kaufman Publishers, Inc. Reprinted by permission of the publisher.)

The Neural Basis of Behavior

CONCEPTS AND CATEGORIZATION

Although we have emphasized the difference between well-defined and fuzzy concepts, research at the neurological level indicates that there are important differences just among fuzzy concepts. In particular, the brain seems to store concepts of animals and concepts of artifacts in different neural regions. We mentioned some of the evidence for this in our discussion of perception in Chapter 5. There we noted that there are patients who are impaired in their ability to recognize pictures of animals but relatively normal in their recognition of pictured artifacts such as tools, whereas other patients show the reverse pattern. Recent research shows that what holds for pictures holds for words as well. Many of the patients who are impaired in naming pictures also cannot tell what the corresponding word means. For example, a patient who cannot name a pictured giraffe also cannot tell you anything about giraffes when presented with the word *giraffe*. The fact that the deficit appears for both words and pictures indicates that it has to do with concepts: The patient

has lost part of the concept "giraffe" (McCarthy & Warrington, 1990). There is an alternative to the idea that concepts of animals and artifacts are stored in different regions of the brain. Concepts of animals may contain more perceptual features (what does it look like?) than functional features (what can it be used for?), whereas concepts of artifacts may have more functional than perceptual features. When brain damage affects perceptual regions more than functional ones, we would expect patients to show more impairment with animal than artifact concepts; when damage affects functional or motor regions of the brain more than perceptual regions, we would expect the opposite pattern (Farah & McClelland, 1991). The choice between this perceptual-functional hypothesis and the separate-regions-for-separate-concepts one remains controversial (Caramazza, 2000; Martin, Ungerleider, & Haxby, 2000).

Other research has focused on processes of categorization. One line of research suggests that determining the similarity between an object and a concept's prototype involves different brain regions than determining the similarity between an object and stored exemplars of the concept. The logic behind these studies is as follows: The exemplar process involves retrieving items from long-term memory. As we saw in Chapter 8, such retrieval depends on brain structures in the medial temporal lobe. It fol-

lows that a patient with damage in these regions of the brain will be unable to effectively categorize objects by using a process that involves exemplars, although the patient might be relatively normal in the use of prototypes. This is exactly what researchers have found.

One study tested patients with medial-temporal lobe damage as well as normal individuals on two different tasks. One task required participants to learn to sort dot patterns into two categories (see Figure 9-6 for examples), and the other task required participants to learn to sort paintings into two categories corresponding to two different artists. Independent evidence indicated that only the painting task relied on retrieval of explicit exemplars. The patients learned the dot pattern concepts as easily as the normal participants, but they performed far worse than the normal participants in acquiring the painting concepts (Kolodny, 1994). Thus, use of exemplars depends on the brain structures that mediate long-term memory, but use of prototypes in categorization must depend on other structures. Other research has fo-

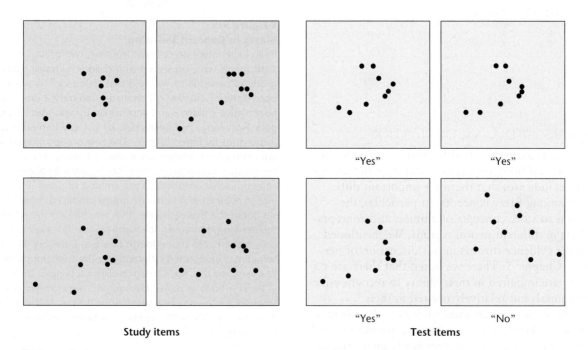

Study items   **Test items**

"Yes" "Yes"

"Yes" "No"

▌ **Figure 9-6**
Examples of Dot Patterns Used to Study Categorization in Amnesiac Patients
Individuals learned that the study items all belonged to one category and then had to decide whether each of the test items belonged to that category. The test items that belong to the category (the ones labeled "yes") do not match the study items directly. Rather, the test items that belong to the category are sufficiently similar to a prototype of the study items—roughly an average of the dot positions of the study items—to justify a "yes" response. (Adapted from Squire & Knowlton, 1995)

cused on a patient who is essentially incapable of committing any new information to long-term memory (he cannot learn new exemplars), yet he performs normally on the dot pattern task. Clearly, prototype-based categorization does not depend on the structures that mediate long-term memory (Squire & Knowlton, 1995).

The preceding discussion shows that there are neural differences between categorization based on prototypes and categorization based on stored exemplars. What about categorization based on rules? A recent study shows that rule use involves different neural circuits than similarity processes. Two groups of participants were taught to categorize imaginary animals into two categories corresponding to whether the animals were from Venus or Saturn. One group learned to categorize the animals on the basis of a complex rule: "An animal is from Venus if it has antennae ears, curly tail, and hoofed feet; otherwise it's from Saturn." The second group learned to categorize the animals by relying solely on their memory. (The first time they saw an animal, they would have to guess, but on subsequent trials they would be able to remember its category.) Then both groups were given novel animals to categorize while having their brains scanned. The rule group continued to categorize by rule, but the memory group had to categorize a novel animal by retrieving the stored exemplar that was most similar to it and then selecting the category associated with that exemplar.

For the memory group, most of the brain areas that were activated were in the visual cortex at the back of the brain. This fits with the idea that these participants were relying on retrieval of visual exemplars. Participants in the rule group also showed activation in the back of the brain, but they showed activation in some frontal regions as well. These regions are often damaged in patients who have trouble doing rule-based tasks. Categorization based on rules therefore relies on different neural circuitry than does categorization based on similarity (Patalano, Smith, Jonides, & Koeppe, 2002).

This research provides yet another example of the interplay between biological and psychological approaches to a phenomenon. Categorization processes that have been viewed as different at the psychological level—such as using exemplars versus using rules—have now been shown to involve different brain mechanisms. This example follows a pattern that we have encountered several times in earlier chapters: A distinction first made at the psychological level is subsequently shown to hold at the biological level as well. ▪

◆ Interim Summary

- Thought occurs in both propositional and imaginal modes. The key component of a proposition is a concept, the set of properties that we associate with a class.

- A concept includes both a prototype (properties that describe a best example) and a core (properties that are most important for being a member of the concept). Core properties play a major role in processing well-defined concepts like "grandmother," whereas prototype properties dominate in fuzzy concepts like "bird."

- Children often learn a new concept by using an exemplar strategy: A novel item is classified as an instance of a concept if it is sufficiently similar to a known exemplar of the concept. As children grow older, they also use hypothesis testing as a strategy for learning concepts.

- Different neural regions may mediate different kinds of concepts. For example, perceptual regions of the brain may be more involved in representing animals from artifacts, whereas functional and motor regions of the brain may play a larger role in representing artifacts than animals. Different neural regions may also be involved in different categorization procedures.

◆ Critical Thinking Questions

1. We have discussed some cases in which prototypes seem to be universal—that is, largely unaffected by culture. Can you think of cases in which prototypes would be greatly influenced by culture? If so, give some examples.

2. A critical finding is that some neurological patients are impaired in their animal concepts but not in their artifact concepts, whereas other patients show the reverse pattern. Aside from differences in the number of perceptual and function features contained in animals and artifact concepts, can you think of another explanation of the critical finding with patients?

REASONING

When we think in terms of propositions, our sequence of thoughts is organized. The kind of organization of interest to us here manifests itself when we try to reason. In such cases, our sequence of thoughts often takes the form of an argument, in which one proposition corresponds to a claim, or conclusion, that we are trying to draw. The remaining propositions are reasons for the claim or premises for the conclusion.

DEDUCTIVE REASONING

LOGICAL RULES According to logicians, the strongest arguments demonstrate **deductive validity**, meaning that it is impossible for the conclusion of the argument to be false if its premises are true (Skyrms, 1986). An example of such an argument is the following:

1. a. If it's raining, I'll take an umbrella.
   b. It's raining.
   c. Therefore, I'll take an umbrella.

How does the reasoning of ordinary people line up with that of the logician? When asked to decide whether an argument is deductively valid, people are quite accurate in their assessments of simple arguments like this one. How do we make such judgments? Some theories of deductive reasoning assume that we operate like intuitive logicians and use logical rules in trying to prove that the conclusion of an argument follows from the premises. Consider the following rule:

If you have a proposition of the form "If p then q," and another proposition p, then you can infer the proposition q.

Presumably, adults know this rule (perhaps unconsciously) and use it to decide that the previous argument is valid. Specifically, they identify the first premise ("If it's raining, I'll take an umbrella") with the "If p then q" part of the rule. They identify the second premise ("It's raining") with the p part of the rule, and then they infer the q part ("I'll take an umbrella").

Rule following becomes more conscious if we complicate the argument. Presumably, we apply our sample rule twice when evaluating the following argument:

2. a. If it's raining, I'll take an umbrella.
   b. If I take an umbrella, I'll lose it.
   c. It's raining.
   d. Therefore, I'll lose my umbrella.

Applying our rule to propositions a and c allows us to infer "I'll take an umbrella," and applying our rule again to proposition b and the inferred proposition allows us to infer "I'll lose my umbrella," which is the conclusion.

One of the best pieces of evidence that people are using rules like this is that the number of rules an argument requires is a good predictor of the argument's difficulty. The more rules are needed, the more likely it is that people will make an error and the longer they will take when they do make a correct decision (Rips, 1983, 1994).

a) Hypothesis: If a card has a vowel on one side, it has an even number on the other side.

b) Hypothesis: If a person is drinking beer, he or she must be over 19.

▌Figure 9-7
Content Effects in Deductive Reasoning
(a) An illustration of the problem in which participants had to decide which two cards should be turned over to test the hypothesis. (b) An illustration of the problem in which participants had to decide which cards to turn over to test the hypothesis.
(After Griggs & Cox, 1982; Wason & Johnson-Laird, 1972)

EFFECTS OF CONTENT Logical rules do not capture all aspects of deductive reasoning. Such rules are triggered only by the *logical form* of propositions, yet our ability to evaluate a deductive argument often depends on the *content* of the propositions as well. We can illustrate this point with the following experimental problems. Participants are presented four cards. In one version of the problem, each card has a letter on one side and a digit on the other (see Figure 9-7a). The participant must decide which cards to turn over to determine whether the following claim is correct: "If a card has a vowel on one side, then it has an even number on the other side." While most participants correctly choose the "E" card, fewer than 10% of them also choose the "7" card, which is the other correct choice. (To see that the "7" card is critical, note that if it has a vowel on its other side, the claim is disconfirmed.)

Performance improves dramatically, however, in another version of the problem (see Figure 9-7b). Now the claim that participants must evaluate is "If a person is drinking beer, he or she must be over 19." Each card has a person's age on one side and what he or she is drinking on the other. This version of the problem is logically equivalent to the preceding version (in particular, "Beer" corresponds to "E," and "16" corresponds to "7"), but now most participants make the correct choices (they turn over the "Beer" and "16" cards). The content of the propositions affects their reasoning.

Results like these imply that we do not always use logical rules when solving deduction problems. Rather, sometimes we use rules that are less abstract and more relevant to everyday problems—pragmatic rules. An example is the permission rule, which states that "If a particular action is to be taken, often a precondition must be satisfied." Most people know this rule and use it when presented with the drinking problem in Figure 9-7b; that is, they would think about the problem in terms of permission. Once activated, the rule would lead people to look for failures to meet the relevant precondition (being under age 19), which in turn would lead them to choose the "16" card. In contrast, the permission rule would not be triggered by the letter-number problem in Figure 9-7a, so there is no reason for people to choose the "7" card. Thus, the content of a problem affects whether a pragmatic rule is activated, which in turn affects the correctness of the reasoning (Cheng, Holyoak, Nisbett, & Oliver, 1986).

In addition to applying rules, participants may sometimes solve the drinking problem by setting up a concrete representation of the situation—a mental model. They may, for example, imagine two people, each with a number on his back and a drink in his hand. They may then inspect this mental model and see what happens, for example, if the drinker with "16" on his back has a beer in his hand. According to this idea, we reason in terms of mental models that are suggested by the content of the problem (Johnson-Laird, 1989).

The two procedures just described—applying pragmatic rules and constructing mental models—have one thing in common. They are determined by the content of the problem, in contrast to the application of logical rules, which should not be affected by problem content. Our sensitivity to content often prevents us from operating as logicians in solving a problem.

INDUCTIVE REASONING

LOGICAL RULES Logicians have noted that an argument can be good even if it is not deductively valid. Such arguments are **inductively strong,** meaning that it is improbable that the conclusion is false if the premises are true (Skyrms, 1986). An example of an inductively strong argument is as follows:

3. a. Mitch majored in accounting in college.
   b. Mitch now works for an accounting firm.
   c. Therefore, Mitch is an accountant.

This argument is not deductively valid (Mitch may have tired of accounting courses and taken a night watchman's job). Inductive strength, then, is a matter of probabilities, not certainties, and (according to logicians) inductive logic should be based on the theory of probability.

We make and evaluate inductive arguments all the time. In doing so, do we rely on the rules of probability theory as a logician or mathematician would? One relevant probability rule is the base-rate rule, which states that the probability of something being a member of a class (such as Mitch being a member of the class of accountants) is greater the more class members there are (that is, the higher the base rate of the class). Our sample argument about Mitch being an accountant can be strengthened by adding the premise that Mitch joined a club in which 90% of the members are accountants.

Another relevant probability rule is the conjunction rule: The probability of a proposition cannot be less than the probability of that proposition combined with another proposition. For example, the probability that "Mitch is an accountant" cannot be less than the probability that "Mitch is an accountant and makes more than $60,000 a year." The base-rate and conjunction rules are rational guides to inductive reasoning—they are endorsed by logic—and most people will defer to them when the rules are made explicit. However, in rough-and-tumble everyday reasoning, people frequently violate these rules, as we are about to see.

HEURISTICS A **heuristic** is a short-cut procedure that is relatively easy to apply and can often yield the correct answer, but not inevitably so. People often use heuristics in everyday life because they have found them useful. However, as the following discussion shows, they are not always dependable.

In a series of ingenious experiments, Tversky and Kahneman (1973, 1983; Kahneman & Tversky, 1996) have shown that people violate some basic rules of probability theory when making inductive judgments. Violations of the base-rate rule are particularly common. In one experiment, one group of participants was told that a panel of psychologists had interviewed 100 people—30 engineers and 70 lawyers—and written personality descriptions of them. These participants were then given a few descriptions and asked to indicate the probability that the person described was an engineer. Some descriptions were prototypical of an engineer (for example, "Jack shows no interest in political issues and spends his free time on home carpentry"), and others were neutral (for example, "Dick is a man of high ability and promises to be quite successful"). Not surprisingly, these participants rated the prototypical description as more likely to be that of an engineer.

Another group of participants was given the identical instructions and descriptions, except they were told that the 100 people were 70 engineers and 30 lawyers (the reverse of the first group). The base rate of engineers therefore differed greatly between the two groups. This difference had virtually no effect: Participants in the second group gave essentially the same ratings as those in the first group. For example, participants in both groups rated the neutral description as having a 50-50 chance of being that of an engineer (whereas the rational move would have been to rate the neutral description as more likely to be in the profession with the higher base rate). Participants completely ignored the information about base rates (Tversky & Kahneman, 1973).

People pay no more heed to the conjunction rule. In one study, participants were presented with the following description:

Linda is 31 years old, single, outspoken, and very bright. In college, she majored in philosophy . . . and was deeply concerned with issues of discrimination.

Participants then estimated the probabilities of the following two statements:

4. Linda is a bank teller.
5. Linda is a bank teller and is active in the feminist movement.

Statement 5 is the conjunction of statement 4 and the proposition "Linda is active in the feminist movement." In flagrant violation of the conjunction rule, most participants rated statement 5 as more probable than statement 4. This is a fallacy because every feminist bank teller is a bank teller, but some female bank tellers are not feminists, and Linda could be one of them (Tversky & Kahneman, 1983).

Participants in this study based their judgments on the fact that Linda seems more similar to a feminist bank teller than to a bank teller. Although they were asked to estimate probability, participants instead estimated the similarity of the specific case (Linda) to the prototype of the concepts "bank teller" and "feminist bank teller." Estimating **similarity** is used as a **heuristic** for estimating

probability. People use the similarity heuristic because similarity often relates to probability yet is easier to calculate. Use of the similarity heuristic also explains why people ignore base rates. In the engineer-lawyer study described earlier, participants may have considered only the similarity of the description to their prototypes of "engineer" and "lawyer." Given a description that matched the prototypes of "engineer" and "lawyer" equally well, participants judged that engineer and lawyer were equally probable. Reliance on the similarity heuristic can lead to errors even by experts.

Reasoning by similarity shows up in another common reasoning situation, that in which we know some members of a category have a particular property and have to decide whether other members of the category have that property as well. In one study, participants had to judge which of the following two arguments seemed stronger:

6. a. All robins have sesamoid bones.
   b. Therefore all sparrows have sesamoid bones.

   versus

7. a. All robins have sesamoid bones.
   b. Therefore all ostriches have sesamoid bones.

Not surprisingly, participants judged the first argument to be stronger, presumably because robins are more similar to sparrows than they are to ostriches. This use of similarity appears rational, inasmuch as it fits with the idea that things that have many known properties in common are likely to share unknown properties as well. But the veneer of rationality fades when we consider participants' judgments on another pair of arguments:

7. a. All robins have sesamoid bones.
   b. Therefore all ostriches have sesamoid bones (same as the preceding argument).

   versus

8. a. All robins have sesamoid bones.
   b. Therefore all birds have sesamoid bones.

Participants judged the second argument to be stronger, presumably because robins are more similar to the prototype of birds than they are to ostriches. But this judgment is a fallacy. On the basis of the same evidence (that robins have sesamoid bones), it cannot be more likely that all birds have some property than that all ostriches do, because ostriches are in fact birds. Again, our similarity-based intuitions can sometimes lead us astray (Osherson, Smith, Wilkie, Lopez, & Shafir, 1990).

Similarity is not our only strong heuristic. Another is the **causality heuristic.** People estimate the probability of a situation by the strength of the causal connections between the events in the situation. For example, people judge statement 10 to be more probable than statement 9:

9. Sometime during the year 2004, there will be a massive flood in California in which more than 1,000 people will drown.
10. Sometime during the year 2004, there will be an earthquake in California, causing a massive flood in which more than 1,000 people will drown.

Judging statement 10 to be more probable than statement 9 is another violation of the conjunction rule (and hence another fallacy). This time, the violation arises because in statement 10 the flood has a strong causal connection to another event, the earthquake, whereas in statement 9 the flood alone is mentioned and has no causal connections.

So, our reliance on heuristics often leads us to ignore some basic rational rules, including the base-rate and conjunction rules. But we should not be too pessimistic about our level of rationality. For one thing, the similarity and causality heuristics probably lead to correct decisions in most cases. Another point is that under the right circumstances we can appreciate the relevance of certain logical rules to particular problems and use them appropriately (Gigerenzer, 1996; Nisbett, Kranz, Jepson, & Kunda, 1983). For example, in reading and thinking about this discussion, you were probably able to see the relevance of the base-rate and conjunction rules to the problems at hand.

 The Neural Basis of Behavior

REASONING

We noted that many psychologists accept the logicians' distinction between deductive and inductive reasoning, but not all do. Some researchers who believe that mental models underlie deductive reasoning further hold that mental models are used in inductive reasoning and that consequently there is no qualitative difference between deductive and inductive reasoning (for example, see Johnson-Laird, 1997). The question of whether there are two kinds of reasoning or one is a fundamental issue, and recently it has been studied at the neural level. A number of brain-imaging experiments have been carried out, but for our purposes it suffices to focus on a single study by Osherson and colleagues (1998).

These researchers used PET to image peoples' brains while they performed a deductive reasoning or an inductive reasoning task. In both tasks, participants had to evaluate arguments like the following:

A. None of the bakers plays chess.
Some of the chess players listen to opera.
(therefore) Some of the opera listeners are not bakers.

B. Some of the computer programmers play the piano. No one who plays the piano watches soccer matches. (therefore) Some computer programmers watch soccer matches.

In the deductive task, participants were asked to distinguish valid arguments (conclusion must be true if the premises are) from invalid arguments (possible for conclusion to be false even if premises are true). Participants were first given some training on this valid-invalid distinction. In these cases, A is valid, and B is not. The task is not easy, as the researchers wanted to ensure that their participants' reasoning powers were fully engaged. In the induction task, individuals were asked whether the conclusion had a greater chance of being true than false, given that the premises were true. For argument A, the answer has to be yes—because the argument is deductively valid. For argument B, the answer is more up for grabs. But what is important is that in both cases participants are reasoning in terms of "chances of being true"; that is, they're reasoning about probabilities (regardless of how they compute them).

A number of brain areas were active during deductive but not inductive reasoning, and a number of areas showed the reverse pattern. These results are consistent with the hypothesis that deductive and inductive reasoning are mediated by different mechanisms. More specifically, only when reasoning deductively were a number of areas in the right hemisphere activated, some of which were toward the back of the brain. These activations might reflect the participants use of spatial representations (like Venn diagrams) in trying to answer the difficult validity question. In contrast, when reasoning inductively, some of the major brain activations were in the left hemisphere, in a region of the frontal cortex that is known to be involved in estimation problems (such as How many camels are there in California?). Estimation often involves rough assessments of probabilities (such as What's the chance of a medium-sized city having a zoo?).

Other imaging studies of deductive versus inductive reasoning (Goel, Gold, Kapur, & Houle, 1998) have also found distinctive areas involved in the two kinds of reasoning, although the areas found were not always the same as those obtained in the previous study. The difference in the areas activated in the two studies may reflect the use of very different materials, but the fact that both experiments show different neural patterns for deductive and inductive reasoning supports the idea that two different reasoning mechanisms are involved. These studies provide a beginning of an understanding of reasoning at the neural level.

Decision Making and the Brain

Closely related to the topic of reasoning is the study of decision making, particularly situations in which people choose among options whose outcomes are uncertain. For example, "Should I major in premedical, where I will have a middling chance to get into a decent medical school and then make a lot of money, or instead should I major in psychology where my chance of getting into a decent graduate school are a bit better but my income will be less?" In studying decision making, researchers make their studies more tractable by replacing such complex options with options that contain just the essential information. For example, do you prefer Option A, in which you have an 70% chance of winning $4 and a 30% chance of losing $2, or Option B, in which you have a 50% chance of winning $4 and a 50% chance of losing $1?

Studies like this generally shown that people make choices that maximize their **utility** (roughly, the subjective value of money to them). Recently, researchers have discovered that neurological patients with a brain damage in a particular part of the frontal lobes have problems making good decisions (ones that maximize utility), even though they have retained normal intelligence, language, and memory. The area of the frontal lobes involved is what is referred to as the ventrolateral prefrontal cortex. It includes an area that 50 years ago was thought to underlie personality and was sometimes the target of "frontal lobotomies" in mental patients (a dubious surgical procedure that is no longer used). Rather than the "seat of personality," the ventrolateral cortex is now seen as involved in decision making, and studies of ventrolateral patients have begun to inform us about the neural bases of decision making.

Some of the experiments involve a gambling task, which unfolds as follows. Participants—ventrolateral patients and controls—sit in front of four decks of cards that look alike. Initially, they are given $2,000 in play money and in-

structed that the game requires a long series of card selections, one at a time, from any of the four decks, until they are told to stop. After turning each card, the participant receives some money, the amount varying from deck to deck. In addition, after turning certain of the cards, the subject are both given money and have to pay a penalty, which varies from deck to deck and from position to position within a given deck. Participants are told that the goal of the game is to maximize their profit and that they are free to switch from any deck to another at any time and as often as they like. It turns out that turning any card from deck A or B yields $100, whereas turning any card from decks C or D yields $50. However, the penalties are higher in the high-paying decks (A and B) than in the low-paying decks (C and D). In fact, the penalties are so much stiffer in the high- than the low-paying decks that over the long haul it is better to always choose from the low-paying decks. Decks C and D are the "advantageous" decks, and A and B are the "disadvantageous" decks.

The game was played for 100 trials. It takes a while to figure out that the overall payoff is probably higher with the advantageous decks C and D, and so for the first 20 trials all participants choose more from the disadvantageous decks (remember they are yielding $100 on every trial, whereas the penalties happen on only some trials). But by the second 20 trials, the normal controls have developed "hunches" that C and D are better choices. From there on, their hunches develop into an articulate hypothesis (the penalties in the disadvantageous decks are severe enough to negate the higher payoffs), and their choice of the advantageous decks continues to grow. The picture is very different for the ventrolateral patients. Over the course of the 100 trials, they rarely develop any hunches about the task and continue to favor the disadvantageous decks. They are incapable of learning to defray high payoffs to protect themselves from even higher losses. This deficit in decision making is not due simply to having brain damage. When patients were tested who had brain damage that spared the ventrolateral area of interest, they per-

formed the task the same as the normal participants (Bechera, 2000).

So there is something special about the ventrolateral cortex and decision making. Damasio (1994) has proposed that the ventrolateral cortex is the cortical region that receives signals from the autonomic nervous system and forms associations between these "gut" feelings and cognitive states—"I've got a feeling that choosing Deck A will hurt me." Damasio refers to these associations as "somatic markers" and argue that ventrolateral patients can't form these markers, can't have gut-level hunches, and never learn which are the advantageous decks. Furthermore, the ventrolateral cortex sends feedback signals back to the autonomic nervous system, and ventrolateral patients have some deficiencies in their ability to generate anticipatory autonomic responses.

Support for the latter ideas comes from studies that measure autonomic responses during the gambling task (Bechera, Tranel, Damasio, & Damasio, 1996). The autonomic response measure was the galvanic skin response (GSR), which indirectly measures emotional reactivity. Both normal controls and ventrolateral patients are alike in that they show increases in GSRs when they actually receive a reward or a penalty, But the patients and the controls differ in an important respect: As controls became familiar with the task, they began to generate GSRs prior to the selection of some cards, whereas the ventrolateral patients entirely failed to generate such anticipatory GSRs. Further, for the controls the anticipatory GSR was greater when they were considering selecting from the disadvantageous deck than the advantageous deck. A large anticipatory feeling of anxiety could serve as a useful cue for the controls that they were considering a bad decision, whereas no such autonomic cue was available to the ventrolateral patients.

Apparently our guts are involved in our decisions about uncertain outcomes, and in a useful way.

For more information, go online with InfoTrac College Edition. Use your own term or search:

- Decision-making and the brain
- Decision-making and gambling

- In reasoning, some arguments are deductively valid, which means that it is impossible for the conclusion to be false if the premises are true. When evaluating such an argument, we sometimes use logical rules, and other times use heuristics—rules of thumb that operate on the content of propositions, not their logical form.

- Other arguments are inductively strong, which means that it is improbable that the conclusion is false if the premises are true. When evaluating such an argument, often we ignore the principles of probability theory and rely on similarity and causality heuristics.

- Research on the neural bases of reasoning supports the distinction between deductive and inductive reasoning. When people are presented with the same arguments, different parts of the brain become active when people evaluate deductive validity versus inductive strength.

◆ **Critical Thinking Questions**

1. With regard to inductive reasoning, what kind of training might people be given to increase their use of the base-rate and conjunction rules in real-life reasoning situations?

2. How could you use a brain-imaging experiment to see if there is a neural distinction between reasoning by formal procedures (logical rules, probability rules) and reasoning by heuristics?

IMAGINAL THOUGHT

Earlier we mentioned that, in addition to propositional thought, we can also think in an imaginal mode, particularly in terms of visual images. In this section we take a closer look at such visual thinking.

We seem to do some of our thinking visually. Often we retrieve past perceptions, or parts of them, and operate on them the way we would operate on a real percept. To appreciate this point, try to answer the following three questions:

1. What shape are a German shepherd's ears?
2. What new letter is formed when an uppercase *N* is rotated 90 degrees?
3. How many windows are there in your parents' living room?

When answering the first question, most people report that they form a visual image of a German shep-

herd's head and "look" at the ears to determine their shape. When answering the second question, people report first forming an image of a capital *N* and then mentally "rotating" it 90 degrees and "looking" at it to determine its identity. And when answering the third question, people report imagining the room and then "scanning" the image while counting the windows (Kosslyn, 1983; Shepard & Cooper, 1982).

These examples are based on subjective impressions, but they and other evidence suggest that imagery involves the same representations and processes that are used in perception (Finke, 1985). Our images of objects and places have visual detail: We see the German shepherd, the *N*, or our parents' living room in our "mind's eye." Moreover, the mental operations that we perform on these images seem to be analogous to the operations we carry out on real visual objects. We scan the image of our parents' room in much the same way that we would scan a real room, and we rotate our image of the *N* the way we would rotate the real object.

IMAGINAL OPERATIONS

We have noted that the mental operations performed on images seem to be analogous to those that we carry out on real visual objects. Numerous experiments provide objective evidence for these subjective impressions.

One operation that has been studied intensively is **mental rotation.** In a classic experiment, participants saw the capital letter *R* on each trial. The letter was presented either normally or backward, and either in its usual vertical orientation or rotated by various degrees (see Figure 9-8). The participants had to decide whether the letter was normal or backward. The more the letter had been rotated from its vertical orientation, the longer it took the participants to make the decision (see Figure 9-9). This finding suggests that participants made their decisions by rotating the image of the letter in their minds until it was vertical and then checking to determine whether it was normal or backward.

Another operation that is similar in imagery and perception is that of scanning an object or array. In an experiment on scanning an image, participants first studied the map of a fictional island that contained seven key locations. The map was removed, and participants were asked to form an image of it and fixate on a particular location (for example, the tree in the southern part of the island) (Figure 9-10). Then the experimenter named another location (for example, the tree at the northern tip of the island). Starting at the fixated location, the participants were to scan their images until they found the named location and to push a button upon "arriving"

Figure 9-8
Study of Mental Rotation
Examples of the letters presented to participants in studies of mental rotation. On each presentation, participants had to decide whether the letter was normal or backward. Numbers indicate deviation from the vertical in degrees. (L. A. Cooper & R. N. Shepard (1973) "Chronometric Studies of the Rotation of Mental Images," in *Visual Information Processing*, ed. by W. G. Chase. Adapted by permission of Academic Press.)

Figure 9-10
Scanning Mental Images
The person scans the image of the island from south to north, looking for the named location. It appears as though the individual's mental image is like a real map and that it takes longer to scan across the mental image if the distance to be scanned is greater. (S. M. Kosslyn, et al., (1978) "Scanning Mental Images," from "Visual Images Preserve Metric Spatial Information: Evidence from Studies of Image Scanning," in *Journal of Experimental Psychology*, 4:47–60. Copyright © 1978 by the American Psychological Association. Adapted by permission.)

Figure 9-9
Decision Times in the Mental Rotation Study
The time taken to decide whether a letter had normal or reversed orientation was greatest when the rotation was 180 degrees so that the letter was upside down. (L. A. Cooper & R. N. Shepard (1973) "Chronometric Studies of the Rotation of Mental Images," in *Visual Information Processing*, ed. by W. G. Chase. Adapted by permission of Academic Press.)

there. The greater the distance between the fixated location and the named one, the longer the participants took to respond. Indeed, the time people took to scan the image increased linearly with the imagined distance, which suggests that they were scanning their images in much the same way that they scan real objects.

Another commonality between imaginal and perceptual processing is that both are limited by **grain size.** On a television screen, for instance, the grain of the picture tube determines how small the details of a picture can be and still remain perceptible. Although there is no such screen in the brain, we can think of our images as occurring in a mental medium whose grain limits the amount of detail we can detect in an image. If this grain size is fixed, smaller images should be more difficult to inspect than larger ones. A good deal of evidence supports this claim. In one experiment, participants first formed an image of a familiar animal—for example, a cat. Then they were asked to decide whether the imaged object had a particular property. Participants made decisions faster for larger properties, such as the head, than for smaller ones, such as the claws. In another study, participants were asked to form an image of an animal at different relative sizes—small, medium, or large. They were then asked to decide whether their images had a particular property. Their decisions were faster for larger images than for smaller ones. In imagery as in perception, the larger the image, the more readily we can see the details of an object (Kosslyn, 1980).

The Neural Basis of Behavior

IMAGERY

Perhaps the most persuasive evidence that imagery is like perception would be demonstrations that the two are mediated by the same brain structures. In recent years, a substantial amount of evidence of this sort has accumulated.

Some of the evidence comes from studies of brain-damaged patients and shows that any problem the patient has in visual perception is typically accompanied by a parallel problem in visual imagery (Farah, Hammond, & Levine, 1988). A particularly striking example is patients who suffer damage in the parietal lobe of the right hemisphere and as a result develop **visual neglect** of the left side of the visual field. Though not blind, these patients ignore everything on the left side of their visual field. A male patient, for example, may neglect to shave the left side of his face. The Italian neurologist Bisiach (Bisiach & Luzzatti, 1978) found that this visual neglect extends to imagery. He asked patients with visual neglect to imagine a familiar square in their native Milan as it looks while standing in the square facing the church. The patients reported most objects on their right but few on their left. When asked to imagine the scene from the opposite perspective, while standing in front of the church and looking out into the square, the patients neglected the objects they had previously reported (which were now on the left side of the image). These patients manifested the same kind of neglect in imagery that they did in perception, which suggests that the damaged brain structures normally mediate imagery as well as perception.

Some studies have used brain-scanning methods to demonstrate that in normal individuals the parts of the brain involved in perception are also involved in imagery. In one experiment, participants performed both a mental arithmetic task ("Start at 50 and count down, subtracting by 3's") and a visual imagery task ("Visualize a walk through your neighborhood, making alternating right and left turns starting at your door"). While a participant was doing each task, the amount of

blood flow in various areas of his or her cortex was measured. There was more blood flow in the visual cortex when participants engaged in the imagery task than when they engaged in the mental arithmetic task. Moreover, the pattern of blood flow during the imagery task was like that normally found in perceptual tasks (Roland & Friberg, 1985).

A PET experiment by Kosslyn and associates (1993) provides a striking comparison of the brain structures involved in perception and imagery. While having their brains scanned, participants performed two different tasks, a perception task and an imagery task. In the perception task, first a block capital letter was presented on a background grid and then an X was presented in one of the grid cells. The participant's task was to decide as quickly as possible whether the X fell on part of the block letter (see Figure 9-11). In the imagery task, the background grid was again presented, but without a block capital letter. Under the grid was a lowercase letter, and participants had been previously instructed to generate an image of the capital version of the lowercase letter and project it onto the grid. Then an X was presented in one of the grid cells, and participants were asked to determine whether the X fell on part of the imagined block letter. Not surprisingly, the perception task resulted in heightened neural activity in parts of the visual cortex, but so did the imagery task. Indeed, the imagery task resulted in increased activity in brain structures that are among the first regions of the cortex to receive visual information.

Imagery is like perception from the early stages of cortical processing. Moreover, when the neural activa-

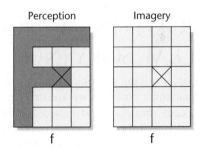

Perception   Imagery

f   f

▌ Figure 9-11
Imagery and Perception
Tasks used to determine whether visual imagery involves the same brain structures as visual perception. In the perception task, participants must decide whether the X fell on part of the block letter. In the imagery task, participants generate an image of the block letter and then decide whether the X fell on part of the (image of the) block letter. The person knows which letter to image because the lowercase version of it is presented below the grid. (The lowercase version is also presented in the perception task, just to keep things comparable.) (From Robert J. Sternberg, *Beyond IQ: A Triarchic Theory of Human Intelligence*, © 1985 by Robert J. Sternberg. Reprinted by permission of Cambridge University Press.)

tions from the two tasks were directly compared, there was more activation in the imagery task than in the perception task, presumably reflecting the fact that the imagery task required more "perceptual work" than the perception task. These results leave little doubt that imagery and perception are mediated by the same neural mechanisms. Here again, biological research has provided evidence to support a hypothesis that was first proposed at the psychological level. ▮

◆ Interim Summary

- Thoughts that are manifested as visual images contain the kind of visual detail found in perception.
- Mental operations that are performed on images (such as scanning and rotation) are like those carried out on perceptions.
- Imagery is like perception because both are mediated by the same parts of the brain. Brain-scanning experiments indicate that the specific regions involved in an imagery task are the same as those involved in a perceptual task.

◆ Critical Thinking Questions

1. In this section we discussed visual imagery. By analogy, how would you find evidence for auditory imagery?
2. How could you use brain-scanning experiments to determine whether individual differences in imaging ability are related to neural differences?

THOUGHT IN ACTION: PROBLEM SOLVING

For many people, solving a problem epitomizes thinking itself. When solving a problem, we are striving for a goal but have no ready means of obtaining it. We must break down the goal into subgoals and perhaps divide these subgoals further into smaller subgoals, until we reach a level that we have the means to obtain (Anderson, 1990).

We can illustrate these points with a simple problem. Suppose that you need to figure out the combination of an unfamiliar lock. You know only that the combination has four numbers and that whenever you come across a correct number you will hear a click. Your overall goal is to find the combination. Rather than trying four numbers at random, most people divide the overall goal into four subgoals, each corresponding to finding one of the four numbers in the combination. Your first subgoal is to find the first number, and you have a procedure for accomplishing this—turning the lock slowly while listening

for a click. Your second subgoal is to find the second number, for which you can use the same procedure, and so on for the remaining subgoals.

The strategies that people use to decompose goals into subgoals is a major issue in the study of problem solving. Another issue is how people represent a problem mentally, which also affects how readily we can solve the problem. The following discussion considers both of these issues.

PROBLEM-SOLVING STRATEGIES

Much of what we know about strategies for breaking down goals derives from the research of Newell and Simon (1972). Typically, the researchers ask participants to think aloud while trying to solve a difficult problem. They then analyze the participants' verbal responses for clues to the underlying strategy. Specifically, the researchers use the verbal responses as a guide in programming a computer to solve the problem. The output can be compared with aspects of people's performance on the problem—for example, the sequence of moves—to see whether they match. If they match, the computer program offers a theory of a problem-solving strategy. A number of general-purpose strategies have been identified in this way.

One strategy is to reduce the difference between our current state in a problem situation and our goal state, in which a solution is obtained. Consider again the combination-lock problem. Initially, our current state includes no knowledge of any of the numbers, and our goal state includes knowledge of all four numbers. We therefore set up the subgoal of reducing the difference between these two states, and identifying the first number accomplishes this subgoal. Our current state now includes knowledge of the first number. There is still a difference between our current state and our goal state. We can reduce this difference identifying the second number, and so on for the third and fourth numbers. The key idea behind **difference reduction** is that we set up subgoals that, when obtained, put us in a state that is closer to our goal.

A similar but more sophisticated strategy is **means-ends analysis**. We compare our current state to the goal state in order to find the most important difference between them, and eliminating this difference becomes our main subgoal. We then search for a means or procedure to achieve this subgoal. If we find such a procedure but discover that something in our current state prevents us from applying it, we introduce a new subgoal of eliminating this obstacle. Many commonsense problem-solving situations involve this strategy. Here is an example:

> I want to take my son to nursery school. What's the [most important] difference between what I have and what I want? One of distance. What [procedure] changes distance? My automobile. My automobile won't work. What

is needed to make it work? A new battery. What has new batteries? An auto repair shop. (After Newell & Simon, 1972, as cited in Anderson, 1990, p. 232)

Means-ends analysis is more sophisticated than difference reduction because it allows us to take action even if it results in a temporary decrease in similarity between our current state and the goal state. In the example just presented, the auto repair shop may be in the opposite direction from the nursery school. Going to the shop temporarily increases the distance from the goal, yet this step is essential for solving the problem.

Another strategy is to **work backward** from the goal, a particularly useful strategy in solving mathematical problems like the one illustrated in Figure 9-12. The problem is this: Given that ABCD is a rectangle, prove that AD and BC are the same length. In working backward, we might proceed as follows:

> What could prove that AD and BC are the same length? I could prove this if I could prove that the triangles ACD and BDC are congruent. I can prove that ACD and BDC are congruent if I could prove that two sides and an included angle are equal. (After Anderson, 1990, p. 238)

We reason from the goal to a subgoal (proving the triangles congruent), from that subgoal to another subgoal (proving the sides and angle equal), and so on, until we reach a subgoal that we have a ready means of obtaining.

The three strategies that we have considered—difference reduction, means-ends analysis, and working backward—are extremely general and can be applied to virtually any problem. These strategies, which are often referred to as weak methods, do not rest on any specific knowledge and may even be innate. People are especially likely to rely on these weak methods when they are first learning about an area and are working on problems whose content is unfamiliar. When people gain expertise in an area, they develop more powerful domain-specific procedures (and representations), which come to dominate the weak methods (Anderson, 1987). (The steps in problem solving by weak methods are listed in Table 9-2.)

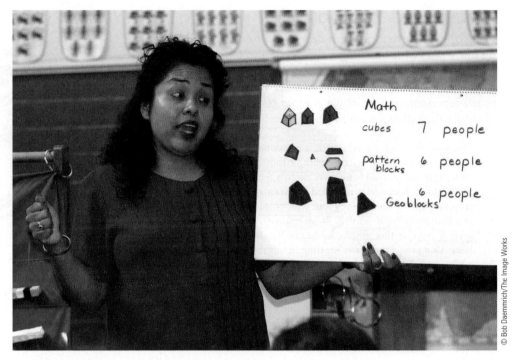

Learning aids help students visualize a math problem.

▌ Figure 9-12
An Illustrative Geometry Problem
Given that ABCD is a rectangle, prove that the line segments AD and BC are the same length.

● **Table 9-2**
Steps in Problem Solving

---

1. Represent the problem as a proposition or in visual form.
2. Determine the goal.
3. Break down the goal into subgoals.
4. Select a problem-solving strategy and apply it to achieve each subgoal.

Representing the Problem

Being able to solve a problem depends not only on our strategy for breaking it down but also on how we represent it. Sometimes a propositional representation works best, and at other times a visual representation or image is more effective. Consider the following problem:

> One morning, exactly at sunrise, a monk began to climb a mountain. A narrow path, a foot or two wide, spiraled around the mountain to a temple at the summit. The monk ascended at varying rates, stopping many times along the way to rest. He reached the temple shortly before sunset. After several days at the temple, he began his journey back along the same path, starting at sunrise and again walking at variable speeds with many pauses along the way. His average speed descending was, of course, greater than his average climbing speed. Prove that there exists a particular spot along the path that the monk will occupy on both trips at precisely the same time of day. (Adams, 1974, p. 4)

In trying to solve this problem, many people start with a propositional representation. They may even try to write out a set of equations. The problem is far easier to solve when it is represented visually. All you need do is visualize the upward journey of the monk superimposed on the downward journey. Imagine one monk starting at the bottom and the other at the top. No matter what their speed, at some time and at some point along the path the two monks will meet. Thus, there must be a spot along the path that the monk occupied on both trips at precisely the same time of day. (Note that the problem did not ask you where the spot was.)

Some problems can be readily solved by manipulating either propositions or images. Look at this simple problem: "Ed runs faster than David but slower than Dan; who's the slowest of the three men?" To solve this problem in terms of propositions, note that we can represent the first part of the problem as a proposition that has "David" as subject and "is slower than Ed" as predicate. We can represent the second part of the problem as a proposition with "Ed" as subject and "is slower than Dan" as predicate. We can then deduce that David is slower than Dan, which makes David the slowest. To solve the problem by means of imagery, we might imagine the three men's speeds as points on a line, like this:

Then we can simply "read" the answer directly from the image. Apparently some people prefer to represent

Figure 9-13
Materials for the Candle Problem
Given the materials depicted, how can you support a candle on a door? The solution is shown on page 348. (After Glucksberg & Weisberg, 1966)

such problems as propositions, and others tend to represent them visually (Johnson-Laird, 1985).

In addition to the issue of propositions versus images, there are questions about what is represented. Often we have difficulty with a problem because we fail to include something important in our representation or because we include something in our representation that is not an important part of the problem. We can illustrate this point with an experiment. One group of participants was given the problem of supporting a candle on a door, using only the materials depicted in Figure 9-13. The solution was to tack the box to the door and use the box as a platform for the candle. Most participants had difficulty with the problem, presumably because they represented the box as a container, not as a platform (this difficulty is often referred to as **functional fixedness**). Another group of participants was given the identical problem except that the contents of the box were removed. These participants had more success in solving the problem, presumably because they were less likely to include the box's container property in their representation and more likely to include its supporter property. Studies like this provide an inkling of why many experts believe that arriving at a useful representation of a problem is half the solution to the problem.

Experts Versus Novices

In a given content area (physics, geography, or chess, for instance), experts solve problems qualitatively differently than novices do. These differences are due to differences in the representations and strategies used by experts and novices. Experts have many more specific representations stored in memory that they can bring to bear on a problem. A master chess player, for example, can look for 5 seconds at a configuration of over 20 pieces and reproduce it perfectly; a novice in this situation can reproduce only the usual 7 ± 2 items (see Chapter 8). Experts can accomplish this memory feat because through years of practice they have developed representations of many possible configurations of chess pieces that permit them to encode a complex configuration in just a few chunks. Further, these representations are presumably what underlies their superior chess game. A master may have stored as many as 50,000 configurations and has learned what to do when each one arises. Master chess players can essentially "see" possible moves and do not have to think them out the way novices do (Chase & Simon, 1973; Simon & Gilmartin, 1973).

Even when they are confronted with a novel problem, experts represent it differently than novices do. This point is illustrated by studies of problem solving in physics. An expert (say, a physics professor) represents a problem in terms of the physical principle that is needed for solution:

For example, "This is one of those every-action-has-an-equal-and-opposite-reaction problems." In contrast, a novice (say, a student taking a first course in physics) tends to represent the same problem in terms of its surface features—for example, "This is one of those inclined-plane problems" (Chi, Feltovich, & Glaser, 1982).

The tendency to focus on the superficial features of a problem also shows up when novices solve a problem by using an analogy. When we do not know much about a particular domain and have to solve a problem in it, frequently we think of superficially similar problems that we have encountered to use as analogies. In one illustrative study on this phenomenon (Ross, 1984), people had to learn new ways to edit text on a computer. During the learning phase, people were often reminded by superficial similarities of an earlier text edit and used this to figure out how to do the current edit. For example, people learned two different methods for inserting a word into text, with one method illustrated on a shopping list and the other method illustrated on a restaurant review. Later, they had to insert a word in either another shopping list or restaurant review. People were more likely to use the method they had learned with the similar text (given a shopping list, they tended to insert a word by

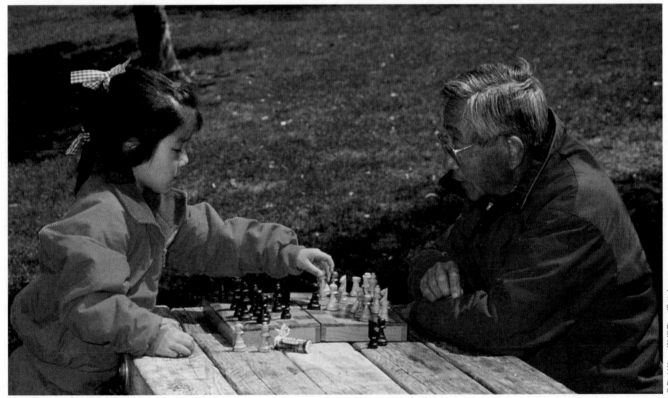

Experts solve problems in qualitatively different ways than novices do. Experts such as chess masters have many more specific representations stored in memory that they can bring to bear on a problem.

Does Language Direct Thought, or Does Thought Direct Language?

HOW LANGUAGE CAN DIRECT THOUGHT
Dan I. Slobin, University of California, Berkeley

No one would disagree with the claim that language and thought interact in many significant ways. There is disagreement, however, about the proposition that each language has its own influence on the thought and action of its speakers. On the one hand, anyone who has learned more than one language is struck by the many ways in which languages differ. On the other hand, we expect human beings everywhere to have similar ways of experiencing the world.

There are two issues here: linguistic relativity and linguistic determinism. Relativity is easy to demonstrate. While speaking any language, you have to pay attention to the meanings that are grammatically marked in that language. For example, in English you must mark the verb to indicate the time of occurrence of an event you are speaking about: "It's raining," "It rained," and so forth. Turkish, however, like many Native-American languages, has more than one past tense, depending on one's source of knowledge of the event. There are two past tenses—one to report direct experience and the other to report events that you know about only by inference or hearsay. If you were out in the rain last night, you will say, "It rained last night," using the form that indicates you were a witness to the rain, but if you wake up in the morning and see the wet street and garden, you are obliged to use the other past-tense form—the one that indicates that you were not a witness to the rain itself.

Differences of this sort have long fascinated linguists and anthropologists, who have provided hundreds of facts about "exotic" languages—for example, that the form of a verb of handling can depend on the shape of an object that is being handled (Navajo). But it must be pointed out that "nonexotic" languages also have their surprises. For example, in English it is not appropriate to say, "Richard Nixon has worked in Washington," but it is perfectly okay to say, "Bill Clinton has worked in Washington." Why? English restricts the present-perfect tense ("has worked") to assertions about people who are alive. Exotic!

Proponents of linguistic determinism argue that such differences between languages influence the ways people think—perhaps the ways in which whole cultures are organized. Among the strongest statements of this position are those by Benjamin Lee Whorf and his teacher, Edward Sapir, in the first half of the 20th century—the Sapir-Whorf hypothesis—for the theory of linguistic relativity and determinism. How can such bold claims be substantiated? If one takes the hypothesis seriously, it should be possible to show that Turks are more sensitive to evidence than are Americans, but that Americans are more aware of death than Turks. Clearly, the hypothesis cannot be supported on so grand a level. Rather, experimental psychologists and cognitive anthropologists have sought to find small differences, on controlled tasks, between speakers of various languages.

The results have been mixed. In most cases, human thought and action are overdetermined by an array of causes, so the structure of language may not play a central causal role. Linguistic determinism can best be demonstrated in situations in which language is the principal means of drawing people's attention to particular aspects of experience. Some of the most convincing empirical research to demonstrate some degree of linguistic determinism is being conducted under the direction of Stephen C. Levinson. For example, Levinson and his collaborators distinguish between languages that describe spatial relations in terms of the body (such as English "right/left," "front/back") and those that orient to fixed points in the environment (such as "north/south/east/west" in some aboriginal Australian languages). In a language of the second type, one would refer, for example, to "your north shoulder" or "the west end of the table"; in narrating a past event, one would have to remember how the actions related to the compass points. To speak this type of language, you always have to know where you are with respect to the compass points, whether you are speaking or not. And Levinson's group has shown, in extensive cross-linguistic and cross-cultural studies, that this is, in fact, the case.

Dan I. Slobin

Much more research needs to be done, but it is evident that language is only one of the factors shaping human thought and action. However, because language is so pervasive—and because we must always make cognitive decisions while speaking—the hypothesis of linguistic determinism will continue to attract scientific attention. (For a lively debate on many of these issues, read Gumperz & Levinson, 1996.)

Does Language Direct Thought, or Does Thought Direct Language?

HOW THOUGHT CAN INFLUENCE LANGUAGE

Eleanor Rosch, University of California, Berkeley

Are we trapped by our language into a particular view of the world? According to the most dramatic form of the hypothesis of linguistic determinism (Whorf, 1956), the grammar of each language embodies a complete metaphysic (a worldview). For example, English has nouns and verbs, Nootka has only verbs, and Hopi divides the world into the two principles of manifest and unmanifest. Whorf claims that such linguistic differences mold the minds of speakers into mutually incomprehensible ways of thinking.

What evidence do we have for the effect of linguistic differences on thought? At the level of metaphysic, Whorf used bizarre-sounding literal translations from Native American languages to make his case. But literal translations from any language, even familiar ones such as French or German, sound equally strange. At the level of whole societies, language, culture, and thought cannot be separated experimentally. Even in the case where a difference in worldview or metaphysic has been documented, such as in the Eastern meditation traditions, a people's ability to understand those traditions has been found to depend on the practices they do, not on

Eleanor Rosch

the languages they speak or learn (Rosch, 1997).

A less-sweeping Whorfian claim is that grammatical form classes (such as nouns and verbs in English or shape classifiers in Navajo) affect aspects of thought such as classification or memory. Here we can do experiments, but the findings have been largely negative. For example, grammatical classes do not aid memory the way semantic classes (meaning units such as plants or animals) do. And speaking a language with shape classifiers does not assure that one will prefer to classify items by shape rather than by color. Perhaps grammatical form classes become so automatically processed that they lose much of their semantic meaningfulness for speakers. Or perhaps there is a separate module of thinking, specifically for speaking, which does not necessarily interact with the rest of the meaning system (Slobin, 1996).

Most research on the language and thought issue has been at the still narrower level of vocabulary items. Do the Inuit really have many words for snow, and do the words as such, rather than the snow, affect their thought? But even vocabulary is not easy to isolate from other factors. Languages have names for things in their environments (such as microchip), words that map important social and cultural distinctions (such as separate terms for older brother and younger brother), ways of referring to distinctions not encoded by single vocabulary items (skiers find many ways to refer to different kinds of snow), and

changes in vocabulary to reflect social change (the disappearance of the polite *thou* and familiar *you* distinction in English). Color categories were once thought to be an ideal domain for vocabulary research because one can measure both color (using the physics of light) and aspects of thought (such as color memory) independently of language. However, the findings have suggested that most facts about both color vocabulary and cognition are determined by the human visual system, with only a secondary role played by language (Hardin & Maffi, 1997; Rosch, 1974). As Slobin has indicated, location words are the domain in which there is the most persuasive evidence for effects of a linguistic reference system on thinking. But note that this is a circumscribed domain and that the pragmatics of location (finding objects and finding one's way around) are adequately conveyed by all systems.

What can we learn from all this? Certainly, language differences are intriguing and important, but they do not exist in isolation. Posing scientific questions as a dichotomy of isolated extremes on which contributors must take adversarial positions, as in a courtroom or political debate, may be more a matter of our culture (Peng & Nisbett, 1999; Tannen, 1998) than of good science that leads to lasting knowledge. We need to learn to think about the relation of language and thought, as well as other polarities in psychology, in terms of interesting, but complex, mutually determining units.

The solution to the candle problem.

using the method originally illustrated with a shopping list). Early in learning, we are guided by superficial similarities among problems.

Experts and novices also differ in the strategies they employ. In studies of physics problem solving, experts generally try to formulate a plan for attacking the problem before generating equations, whereas novices typically start writing equations with no general plan in mind (Larkin, McDermott, Simon, & Simon, 1980). Another difference is that experts tend to reason from the givens of a problem toward a solution, but novices tend to work in the reverse direction (the working-backward strategy). This difference in the direction of reasoning has also been found in studies of how physicians solve problems. More expert physicians tend to reason in a forward direction—

from symptom to possible disease—but the less expert tend to reason in a backward direction—from possible disease to symptom (Patel & Groen, 1986).

The characteristics of expertise just discussed—a multitude of representations, representations based on principles, planning before acting, and working forward—make up some of the domain-specific procedures that come to dominate the weak methods of problem solving discussed earlier.

◆ Interim Summary

- Problem solving requires breaking down a goal into subgoals that can be obtained more easily.

- Strategies for breaking a goal into subgoals include reducing differences between the current state and the goal state; means-ends analysis (eliminating the most important differences between the current and goal states), and working backward.

- Some problems are easier to solve by using a visual representation, and others can be more readily solved by using a propositional representation. Numerous problems can be solved equally well by visual or propositional representations.

- Expert problem solvers differ from novices in four ways: They have more representations to bring to bear on the problem, they represent novel problems in terms of solution principles rather than surface features, they form a plan before acting, and they tend to reason forward rather than backward.

◆ Critical Thinking Questions

1. Think of some activity (an academic subject, game, sport, or hobby) in which you have gained some expertise. How would you characterize the changes that you went through in improving your performance? How do these changes line up with those described in the chapter?

2. How can the findings about expertise in problem solving be used in teaching people professional skills, like teaching medical students about a new specialty?

CHAPTER SUMMARY

1. Language, our primary means for communicating thoughts, is structured at three levels. At the highest level are sentence units, including phrases that can be related to thoughts or propositions. The next level is words and parts of words that carry meaning. The lowest level contains speech sounds. The phrases of a sentence are built from words (and parts of words), whereas the words themselves are constructed from speech sounds.

2. A phoneme is a category of speech sounds. Every language has its own set of phonemes and rules for combining them into words. A morpheme is the smallest unit that carries meaning. Most morphemes are words; others are prefixes and suffixes that are added to words. A language also has syntactic rules for combining words into phrases and phrases into sentences. Understanding a sentence requires not only analyzing phonemes, morphemes, and phrases but also using context and understanding the speaker's intention. The areas of the brain that are responsible for language lie in the left hemisphere and include Broca's area (frontal cortex) and Wernicke's area (temporal cortex).

3. Language development occurs at three different levels. Infants come into the world preprogrammed to learn phonemes, but they need several years to learn the rules for combining them. When children begin to speak, they learn words that name familiar concepts. In learning to produce sentences, they begin with one-word utterances, progress to two-word telegraphic speech, and then elaborate their noun and verb phrases.

4. Children learn language at least partly by testing hypotheses. Children's hypotheses appear to be guided by a small set of operating principles, that call their attention to critical characteristics of utterances, such as word endings. Innate factors also play a role in language acquisition.

5. Our innate knowledge of language seems to be very rich and detailed, as suggested by the fact that all children seem to go through the same stages in acquiring a language. Like other innate behaviors, some language abilities are learned only during a critical period. It is a matter of controversy whether our innate capacity to learn language is unique to our species. Many studies suggest that chimpanzees and gorillas can learn signs that are equivalent to our words, but they have difficulty learning to combine these signs in the systematic (or syntactic) way in which humans combine words.

6. Thought occurs in different modes, including propositional and imaginal. The basic component of a proposition is a concept, the set of properties we associate with a class. Concepts provide cognitive economy by allowing us to code many different objects as instances of the same concept and also permit us to predict information that is not readily perceptible.

7. A concept includes both a prototype (properties that describe the best examples) and a core (properties that are most essential for being a member of the concept). Core properties play a major role in well-defined concepts like "grandmother"; prototype properties dominate in fuzzy concepts like "bird." Most natural concepts are fuzzy. Concepts are sometimes organized into hierarchies; in such cases, one level of the hierarchy is the basic or preferred level for categorization.

8. Children often learn a concept by following an exemplar strategy. With this technique, a novel item is classified as an instance of a concept if it is sufficiently similar to a known exemplar of the concept. As children grow older, they use hypothesis testing as another strategy for learning concepts. Different categorization processes have been shown to involve different brain mechanisms.

9. In reasoning, we organize our propositions into an argument. Some arguments are deductively valid: It is impossible that the conclusion of the argument is false if its premises are true. When evaluating a deductive argument, we sometimes try to prove that the conclusion follows from the premises by using logical rules. Other times, however, we use heuristics—rules of thumb—that operate on the content of propositions rather than on their logical form.

10. Some arguments are inductively strong: It is improbable that the conclusion is false if the premises are

true. In generating and evaluating such arguments, we often ignore some of the principles of probability theory and rely instead on heuristics that focus on similarity or causality.

11. Not all thoughts are expressed in propositions; some are manifested as visual images. Such images contain the kind of visual detail found in perceptions. The mental operations performed on images (such as scanning and rotation) are like the operations carried out on perceptions. Imagery seems to be like perception because it is mediated by the same parts of the brain. Brain damage that causes the perceptual problem visual neglect also causes comparable problems in imagery. Experiments using brain-scanning techniques indicate that the specific brain regions involved in an imagery task are the same as those involved in a perceptual task.

12. Problem solving requires breaking down a goal into subgoals that are easier to obtain. Strategies for doing this include reducing differences between the current state and the goal state, means-ends analysis (eliminating the most important differences between the current and goal states), and working backward. Some problems are easier to solve by using a propositional representation; for other problems, a visual representation works best.

13. Expert problem solvers differ from novices in four basic ways: They have more representations to bring to bear on the problem, they represent novel problems in terms of solution principles rather than surface features, they form a plan before acting, and they tend to reason forward rather than working backward.

CORE CONCEPTS

production of language
comprehension of language
language
phoneme
morpheme
grammatical morpheme
meaning
sentence unit
proposition
noun phrase
verb phrase
syntax
Broca's aphasia

Wernicke's aphasia
overextension
anomic aphasic
propositional thought
imaginal thought
concept
categorization
prototype
core
basic level
deductive validity
pragmatic rules
mental model

inductive strength
heuristic
similarity heuristic
causality heuristic
utility
mental rotation
grain size
visual neglect
difference reduction
means-ends analysis
work backward
functional fixedness

WEB RESOURCES

http://psychology.wadsworth.com/
atkinson14e

Take a quiz, try the activities and exercises, and explore web links.

http://www.brown.edu/Departments/Anthropology/apelang.html

To learn more about primates and their language abilities, check out this extensive collection of links.

http://www.ilovelanguages.com/

Everything you ever wanted to know about languages.

 InfoTrac Online Library
http://www.infotrac-college.com/
wadsworth

Use InfoTrac College Edition to find popular and scientific articles by using the search terms below or your own relevant terms.
- Animal communication
- Decision-making heuristics
- Language development
- Problem solving

CD-ROM LINKS

 Psych Odyssey

Check out CD Chapter 8, Language and Thought
A. Do Animals Use Language?
B. Language: Hemispheric Differences
C. Language Acquisition: Babbling
D. The Nature of Thought
E. Strategies and Obstacles in Problem Solving
F. Judgment and Decision Making

 Psyk.trek 2.0

Check out CD Unit 6, Memory and Thought
6d Problem solving
6e Decision making

© R. W. Jones/Corbis

MOTIVATION

CHAPTER OUTLINE

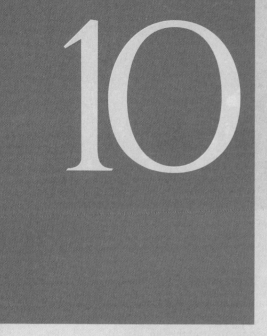

You're driving along the highway, trying to get to an important job interview on time. You were running late this morning, so you skipped breakfast. Now you are starving. It seems as if every billboard on the highway is advertising food—egg and ham muffins, juicy hamburgers, cool, sweet juice. Your stomach rumbles and you try to ignore it, but that is impossible. Every mile you go, you are that much hungrier. You nearly rear-end the car in front of you as you stare at a billboard advertising pizza. In short, you have been overwhelmed by the motivational state known as hunger.

A **motivation** is a condition that energizes behavior and gives it direction. It is experienced subjectively as a conscious desire—the desire for food, for drink, for sex. Most of us can choose whether or not to act on our desires. We can force ourselves to forgo what we desire, and we can make ourselves

do what we would rather not do. Perhaps we can even deliberately choose not to think about the desires that we refuse to act on. But it is considerably more difficult—perhaps impossible—to control our motivations directly. When we are hungry, it is hard not to want food. When we are hot and thirsty, we cannot help wanting a cool breeze or a cold drink. Conscious choice appears to be the consequence, rather than the cause, of our motivational states. So what does control motivation, if not rational choice?

The causes of motivation range from physiological events within the brain and body to our culture and social interactions with the other individuals who surround us. This chapter will discuss the control of basic motivations such as thirst, hunger, and sex. To a large extent these motivations arise from our biological heritage and reveal general principles about how motivation and reward work to give direction to behavior. Social aspirations and cultural influences on motivation will be discussed later.

For basic motivations like hunger, thirst, and sex, psychologists have traditionally distinguished between two types of theories of motivation. The difference concerns where the motivation comes from, what causes it, and how the motivation controls behavior. On the one hand are **drive theories**,

which emphasize the role of internal factors in motivation. Some internal drives, such as those related to hunger or thirst, have been said to reflect basic physiological needs. For motivations like sex or aggression, drive factors seem less tied to absolute physiological needs. After all, does one ever need to aggressively attack another in the same way that one needs to eat or drink? Still, aggression and sex have been said to have drive aspects, both in the sense that internal factors such as hormonal state often appear important and in the sense that they may have evolved originally to fulfill basic ancestral needs.

On the other hand are **incentive theories** of motivation, which emphasize the motivational role of external events or objects of desire. Food, drink, sexual partners, targets of attack, relationships with others, esteem, money, and the rewards of success—all are incentives. Incentives are the objects of motivation. After all, our motivations don't operate in a vacuum—when we want, we want something. The nature of that something pulls us in one direction or another. The goal might be tasty food, water to drink, a partner for interaction, expulsion of an intruder, or possession of a disputed resource. Many incentives also serve as rewards. They can produce pleasure and reinforce behavior that leads to them.

The causes of motivation range from physiological events such as thirst to social aspirations and cultural influences such as those that create the desire to excel.

Some incentives are **primary reinforcers,** meaning that they are able to act as rewards independently of prior learning. For example, a sweet taste or a sexual sensation may be pleasant the first time it is experienced. Other incentives are **secondary reinforcers,** meaning that they have gained their status as rewards at least partly through learning about their relationship to other events. For example, money or a good grade can be effective incentives, based on our cultural experience with them and with the success and status they represent. For animals, a conditioned stimulus that has been paired with food can serve as an effective reward. In every case, learning is crucial to the formation of secondary reinforcers. Although less important, learning may even play a part in modulating the effectiveness of some primary reinforcers. For example, you may have been hungry when you were born—but you weren't born with any idea of the foods that are now your favorites. Incentive theories of motivation focus especially on the relationship of learning and experience to the control of motivation.

Incentive and drive theories provide different perspectives on the control of motivation. But the difference between the theoretical perspectives is primarily in their points of view, and there actually is no conflict between the two. It is widely acknowledged that both types of processes exist for almost every kind of motivation (Toates, 1986). But it is easier to focus on one type of control and thoroughly understand it before switching to the other. For this reason, we will consider incentive processes in the first section and then turn to drive pro-

cesses in the second section. In the third section, we will integrate the two perspectives, because both incentive and drive factors operate together in real life, and they often interact (see Figure 10-1). Consider again the example that opened this chapter. A drive factor (your hunger) enhanced the motivational effect of incentives (the billboards depicting food). In fact, the taste of food becomes more pleasant to most people when they are hungry and less pleasant when they have eaten enough (Cabanac, 1979). Have you ever skipped lunch to better enjoy an evening feast? Or been scolded for snacking because it would "ruin your dinner"? Conversely, incentive factors can awaken drive states. Have you ever walked through the delicious aroma from a bakery or restaurant and suddenly realized that you were hungry?

REWARD AND INCENTIVE MOTIVATION

Motivation typically directs behavior toward a particular incentive that produces pleasure or alleviates an unpleasant state: food, drink, sex, and so forth. In other words, **incentive motivation**—or wanting something—is typically associated with affect—or liking that same something. Precisely speaking, the term **affect** refers to the entire range of consciously experienced pleasure and displeasure. Yet in discussing motivation and reward, we typi-

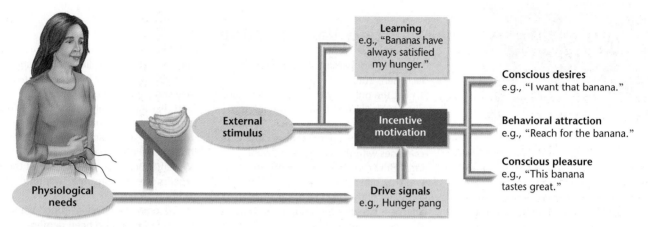

▌Figure 10-1
A Model of Basic Motives
An external stimulus, such as the sight of food, is compared to the memory of its past reward value. At the same time, physiological signals of hunger and satiety modulate the potential value at the moment. These two types of information are integrated to produce the final incentive motivation for the external stimulus, which is manifested in behavior and conscious experience. (Adapted from Toates, 1986)

cally emphasize the pleasure half of the continuum, the part that corresponds with liking. The sheer pervasiveness of affect in our experience of life has led some to suggest that pleasure has evolved to serve a basic psychological role (Cabanac, 1992). That role is to shape behavior by helping to define a psychological "common currency" that reflects the value of each action we perform. Pleasure tends to be associated with stimuli that increase our ability to survive or our offspring's ability to survive. These include tasty food, refreshing drink, and sexual reproduction. Painful or frustrating consequences are associated with events that threaten our survival: physical damage, illness, or loss of resources. The rewarding or affective consequences of an action, in other words, generally reflect whether that action is worth repeating.

But to guide future actions, momentary pleasures and displeasures need to be learned, remembered, and attributed to relevant objects and events, imbuing those objects and events with **incentive salience**, meaning that these objects and events have become linked with anticipated affect, which grabs attention and steers seeking behavior. So, however closely interwoven incentive motivation and pleasurable rewards are in our conscious experiences of the world, this does not mean that "wanting" and "liking" are the same thing (Berridge, 1999). Indeed, as you will see in the Cutting-Edge Research box and drug addiction section, they can diverge under special circumstances. One clear distinction concerns the timing of wanting and liking. **Wanting** is the anticipation of pleasure, as in the cravings that you experience when you think ahead to a delicious meal. **Liking**, by contrast,

is the pleasure that you experience in the moment that you begin to eat that meal. Liking something in the past usually contributes to wanting it in the future. This even occurs in short time spans, such as when a nibble of food whets your appetite for more. Through such processes, affective rewards (liking) can fuel incentive motivation (wanting).

Wanting, in particular, appears to have evolved as a way for the brain to guide action in the future by keeping track of the good or bad consequences of past actions. If wanting is a kind of common currency for the value of diverse events, it makes sense that the brain should have a way of translating our different "wants" into an equivalent "dollar value." There is indeed evidence that the brain may have a neural "common currency" for reward. It is even possible that all rewards are desired precisely because they activate the same brain systems. This neural currency appears to be related to the level of activity within the **brain's dopamine system** (see Figure 10-2). The neurons of this system lie in the upper brain stem and send their axons through the nucleus accumbens and up to the prefrontal cortex. As their name implies, these neurons use the neurotransmitter dopamine to convey their message.

The brain's dopamine system is activated by many kinds of natural rewards, or primary reinforcers, such as tasty food or drink or a desired sexual partner. The same neurons are also activated by many drugs that humans and animals find rewarding, such as cocaine, amphetamine, and heroin. The ability of virtually every reward, whether natural or artificial, to activate

CUTTING-EDGE RESEARCH
Wanting Versus Liking

If liking something in the past nearly always means that you will want it again in the future, how can researchers be sure that the brain's dopamine system accounts for wanting, but not liking? This has been a tough distinction to make. Indeed, in much earlier work, the two concepts (wanting and liking) were fused together into the simpler notion of rewards. As early as the 1950s, researchers discovered that electrical stimulation of certain areas of the brain (namely, the hypothalamus) was a powerful reward, evidenced by the fact that animals and people would work in order to get it again (Olds, 1956). Animals and people clearly wanted and avidly sought out brain stimulation or other natural rewards—like food or sex—when paired with brain stimulation. This was taken as evidence that brain stimulation was itself a reward, both pleasurable (liked) and desired (wanted). The targeted brain sites were even dubbed "pleasure centers" by many. And because dopamine neurons appeared to be crucial links within the so-called pleasure centers (Valenstein, 1976), for many decades—and continuing to this day—scientists

have linked dopamine with pleasant affect (Isen, 2002).

But the only way that researchers can distinguish "liking" from "wanting" is to use separate measures for each. Seeking out repeated experiences more closely coincides with the concept of "wanting." How can we index "liking" in a way that differentiates it from "wanting"? Recall that liking—or pleasurable affect—is experienced during consumption, not in anticipation of it. Facial and bodily movements often reveal the experience of pleasure. Consider the case of eating good food. We humans can generally tell when someone else—even an infant—likes the taste of something. When something tastes good, we tend to smile and lick our lips. Likewise, when something tastes bad, we tend to frown with our mouths open and our upper lips raised. It turns out that nonhuman primates and many other mammals, including rats, share some of these same facial expressions for good- and bad-tasting foods (Steiner, Glaser, Hawilo, & Berridge, 2001) (see Figure).

If rewarding brain stimulation truly induces pleasure, then it should increase seeking as well as expressions of pleasure. Newly armed with separate measures of "wanting" and "liking," researchers tested this proposition. They found that electrically stimulating the brain's dopamine system motivated ani-

mals to seek rewards like food, despite the fact that, as they become satiated, they show increasing distaste for the food (Berridge & Valenstein, 1991). The same pattern of results is found when drugs (like amphetamines) are injected into the brain's dopamine system (Wyvell & Berridge, 2000). Both of these experiments demonstrate "wanting" without "liking."

The opposite effect—"liking" without "wanting"—has also been demonstrated. Researchers injected a particular chemical neurotoxin into anesthetized rats, which selectively destroyed neurons in the brain's dopamine system but left all other neurons healthy and functioning. Once recovered from their operations, these rats were uninterested in food, water, or any other reward. They even voluntarily starved to death unless fed through a tube. Wanting was thus destroyed along with the dopamine neurons. But not so for liking. If sweet or bitter tastes were infused into the animals' mouths, they showed the same facial and bodily expressions as intact rats (Berridge & Robinson, 1998).

So, paying close attention to laboratory rats' facial expressions of pleasure and displeasure proved to be the key to unlocking the tight association between wanting and liking. From this new research, we can conclude that the brain's dopamine system accounts for "wanting" a diverse array of natural and artificial incentives. Other brain systems—like the opiate system—have been found to underlie "liking" (Berridge, 1999).

 For more information, go online with InfoTrac College Edition. Use your own term or search:

- Brain and reward
- Dopamine

Courtesy K.C. Berridge

Displays of Liking in Humans and Animals

These photos show human infant, primate, and rat affective displays to sweet and bitter tastes. Displays of "liking" include tongue protrusions to a sweet taste (*top photographs*). Displays of "disliking" include the gape (*bottom photographs*). (After Berridge, 1999, and Steiner et al., 2001)

Figure 10-2
Dopamine Pathway Activated by Incentive Motivation
The brain's dopamine system is activated by rewarding stimuli and appears to underlie incentive motivation, or the feeling of "wanting." The neurotransmitter dopamine travels along the pathway from the ventral tegmental area (VTA) to the nucleus accumbens, and then on to the prefrontal cortex. (Adapted from NIDA, 2001)

these neurons has led some psychologists to conclude that activity in this neural system constitutes the brain's common currency for tracking future rewards (Wise, 1982). Keep in mind, though, that the functioning of the brain's dopamine system is more closely linked to incentive motivation, or wanting. Rather than creating sensations of pleasure or liking per se, its activity appears to dispose individuals to want to repeat the event that caused the dopamine infusion, regardless of whether that event produces pleasure or displeasure. The Cutting Edge Research section describes the path-breaking studies that provide evidence for this distinction.

DRUG ADDICTION AND REWARD

Addiction is a powerful motivation for some people. The craving for certain drugs, such as opiates (heroin or morphine), psychostimulants (amphetamine or cocaine) or synthetic street versions of these drugs, and certain other drugs (alcohol, nicotine), can become overwhelming (Leshner, 1997). Addicts may crave their drug so strongly that they will sacrifice job, family life and relationships, home, and even freedom to obtain it.

Taking a drug once, or even once in a while, does not constitute addiction. Many Americans have sampled at least one of the drugs just mentioned without becom-

ing addicted. Even regular use (for example, often drinking wine with dinner) need not reflect addiction. **Addiction** occurs only when a pattern of compulsive and destructive drug-taking behavior has emerged; often the person compulsively craves the drug. What causes the transformation from trying out a drug, or engaging in social or recreational use, into addiction?

Some drugs are especially powerful in their ability to produce addiction. Three major factors operate together to make psychoactive drugs more addictive than other incentives, although not all of these factors need be present for addiction to occur. The first is the ability of most addictive drugs to overactivate incentive systems in the brain. Because drugs act directly on brain neurons, they can produce levels of activity in the dopamine system that far surpass those produced by natural incentives. Euphoric drugs activate both pleasure (liking) and incentive (wanting) systems, perhaps because they activate both opiate and dopamine neural systems. Once experienced, the memory of such intense pleasure is a potent temptation to regain it again and again.

But the memory of pleasure by itself would not be sufficient to produce addiction, at least for many people, without additional factors. The second factor is the ability of addictive drugs, if taken repeatedly, to produce unpleasant withdrawal syndromes. As a drug is taken again and again, the pleasure systems that it activates may become increasingly resistant to activation in an effort to regain their normal balanced state. This is, in part, the cause of **tolerance**, the need for a greater amount of a drug to achieve the same euphoria. In addition, after repeated exposure to the drug, the brain may activate processes that have consequences exactly opposite to those of the drug. These processes may help the brain remain in a balanced state when the drug is taken, but by themselves they are experienced as highly unpleasant. If the addict stops using the drug, the lack of activity in resistant pleasure systems and the activation of unpleasant drug-opposite processes can produce **withdrawal,** an intensely aversive reaction to the cessation of drug use. This aversive state presents addicts with another motive to resume taking the drug, at least for as long as the withdrawal state lasts—typically several weeks.

Finally, addictive drugs may produce permanent changes in brain incentive systems that cause cravings even after withdrawal is over. Repeated use of drugs like cocaine, heroin, or amphetamine, which activate the brain's dopamine systems, causes these neurons to become hyperactive or sensitized. **Neural sensitization** may be permanent, and it means that these dopamine neurons will be activated more highly by drugs and drug-related stimuli. Because the brain's dopamine system appears to mediate incentive motivation (wanting) more than pleasure (liking), its hyperactivation in addicts may cause exaggerated craving for the drug, even when drug experiences are no longer particularly positive (Robinson & Berridge, 2001). Neural sensitization lasts much longer than withdrawal. This may be why recovered addicts are in danger of relapse into drug use, even after they have completed detoxification programs.

The combination of these factors sheds light on why psychoactive drugs, more than many other incentives, are able to produce addictions. These drugs directly activate brain pleasure and incentive systems to unmatched levels, produce withdrawal syndromes that drive a recovering addict back to the drug, and permanently hyperactivate the brain's dopamine system that causes drugs to be craved. This combination is hard to resist.

© Joel Gordon

◆ Interim Summary

- Motivational states direct and energize behavior. They arise from two sources: internal drive factors and external incentive factors.

- Incentive motivation (wanting something) is typically associated with pleasurable affect (liking that same something). Although some incentives—such as a sweet food when we are hungry—are powerful motivators by themselves, most incentives are established through learning.

- The brain's dopamine system appears to underlie incentive motivation, or the experience of "wanting." Artificial activation of these neurons by drugs or electrical brain stimulation causes increased motivation for both natural and artificial incentives, and changes in these systems, produced by repeatedly taking drugs that activate it, may partly cause the compulsive cravings of addiction.

◆ Critical Thinking Questions

1. Research suggests that wanting and liking are separable psychological systems. Think of a time in your own life when you experienced wanting without liking (perhaps having to do with food). What caused the two to diverge?

2. Many addictive drugs change the brain's dopamine system, making these neurons hyperactive or sensitized. Because there is no known way to reverse these changes, it's reasonable to conclude that the brains of recovering addicts have been permanently altered. Knowing this, how can recovering addicts avoid relapse? How would you design an effective treatment program to prevent relapse?

Addictive drugs can permanently change the brain's dopamine system, which creates a hyperactive craving for drugs. This is why objects and events associated with drug use continue to have strong incentive salience and produce cravings, even after recovering addicts have chosen to live drug-free.

HOMEOSTASIS AND DRIVES

Our lives depend on keeping certain things the same. If the temperature of your brain changed by more than several degrees, you would quickly become unconscious. If the proportion of water in your body rose or fell by more than a few percent, your brain and body could not function and you would risk death. Humans and animals walk a tightrope of balance between physiological extremes. Like delicate and finely tuned machines, we cannot work unless our internal environment is in balance. But unlike most machines, we've been designed to maintain this balance ourselves. Even when the outside world changes, our internal states remain relatively stable.

A great deal of basic motivation is directed toward helping to maintain our internal balance. To keep our internal world within the narrow limits of physiological survival, we have active control processes to maintain **homeostasis,** a constant internal state (*homeo* means "equal," and *stasis* means "static" or "constant"). A homeostatic control process is a system that actively works to maintain a constant state (that is, homeostasis).

Homeostatic control processes can be psychological, physiological, or mechanical. A familiar example is the thermostat that runs your furnace or air conditioner. Thermostats are designed to maintain temperature homeostasis. When you set your thermostat to a particular temperature, that temperature is the goal value or set point. A **set point** is the value that the homeostatic system tries to maintain. If the winter room temperature falls below the value you set, the thermostat is triggered: The discrepancy between its goal and the actual temperature causes it to activate the furnace. If the summer room temperature rises above the thermostat's set temperature for cooling, the thermostat activates the air conditioner. A thermostat coupled to both furnace and air conditioner can be used to keep your room at a stable temperature even as the seasons change. Many physiological processes work like thermostats: They activate motivations that help maintain homeostasis.

TEMPERATURE AND HOMEOSTASIS

If the temperature of your brain dropped by 10° C, you would lose consciousness. If your brain temperature rose more than 10° C above normal, you would die. Even though you may have been in very hot or cold weather, your brain remained largely protected within a narrow range of several degrees centigrade. Homeostatic control systems, both physiological and psychological, are the reason for this constancy.

Physiological responses such as sweating and shivering are part of the reason your brain temperature remains so constant. These physiological responses provide cooling in the form of evaporation and heating in the form of muscle activity. Psychological reactions also come into play as you begin to feel uncomfortably hot. You may find yourself wanting to shed clothing, have a cool drink, or find shade. But what turns on these physiological and psychological responses?

When you are under the hot sun, your entire body becomes hot. Conversely, if you remain too long unprotected in the cold, your entire body becomes hypothermic (too cold). But only within your brain is the change of temperature actually detected. Neurons at several sites in the brain, especially within the preoptic (front) region of the hypothalamus at the base of the brain, are essentially neural thermostats (Satinoff, 1983). They begin to operate differently as their own temperature changes. These neurons serve as both the thermometer and the homeostatic set point within your body. When their temperatures diverge from their normal levels, their metabolism alters, and this changes their activity or firing patterns. This triggers physiological reactions such as perspiration or shivering, which help correct your body temperature. In addition, it triggers your sensation of being too hot or too cold, which makes you want to seek shade or put on a coat, behavioral solutions to the same problems.

When you are too hot, a cool breeze can feel good. Likewise, when you are too cold, a warm bath feels pleasant. But as your own internal temperature changes, your perception of these outside events also changes. Although ordinarily your entire body changes temperature by a degree or two when you are in situations that make you feel very hot or cold, it is only the slight change in your brain temperature that causes the change in the way you feel. The brain can be fooled into feeling hot or cold by merely changing the temperature of a relatively few neurons in the hypothalamus. For example, cooling of the hypothalamus alone (by painlessly pumping cold liquid through a small loop of tubing that has been surgically implanted into the hypothalamus) motivates a rat to press a bar to turn on a heat lamp that warms its skin—even though its overall body temperature has not been lowered (Satinoff, 1964). The hypothalamic neurons have detected a change in their own temperature away from the normal set point.

Most of us have experienced a temporary change in set point. An illness can temporarily raise brain set points to several degrees above normal. Then the temperature they "seek" becomes higher, and a fever results. Physiological reactions that elevate body temperature are activated. You shiver, and your body temperature begins to rise above normal. But in spite of the rise in temperature, you may still feel cold—even in a warm room—until your hypothalamic neurons rise all the way to their elevated set point.

THIRST AS A HOMEOSTATIC PROCESS

Satisfying thirst is an important homeostatic process. **Thirst** is the psychological manifestation of the need for water, which is essential for survival. What controls this process?

After going without water or exercising intensively, the body begins to deplete two kinds of fluid reservoirs as water is gradually eliminated through perspiration, respiration, or urination. The first type of reservoir is made up of water contained within the cells. This water is mixed with the protein, fat, and carbohydrate molecules that form the structure and contents of the cell. The water inside your cells is your intracellular reservoir. The second type of reservoir is made up of water that is outside the cells. This water is contained in blood and other body fluids and is called the *extracellular reservoir*.

Extracellular thirst results when our bodies lose water because we have gone without drinking or have exercised intensively. Water is extracted from the body by the kidneys in the form of urine, excreted by sweat glands in the skin, or breathed out of the lungs as vapor, and in each case it comes most directly from the blood supply. The loss reduces the volume of extracellular fluid that remains; in turn, the loss of blood volume produces a reduction in blood pressure. You will not feel this slight change in blood pressure, but pressure receptors within your kidneys, heart, and major blood vessels detect it and activate sensory neurons that relay a signal to the brain. Neurons in the hypothalamus next send an impulse to the pituitary gland, causing it to release antidiuretic hormone (ADH) into the bloodstream. ADH causes the kidneys to retain water from the blood as they filter it. Rather than send this water on to become urine, the kidneys deliver it back to the blood. This happens whenever you go without drinking for more than several hours. For example, you may have noticed that your urine appears more concentrated in color at such times (for instance, when you wake up after a night's sleep). In addition, the brain sends a neural signal to the kidneys that causes them to release the hormone renin. Renin interacts chemically with a substance in the blood to produce yet another hormone, angiotensin, which activates neurons deep within the brain, producing the desire to drink.

You may recall that this entire chain of events is triggered by a drop in blood pressure caused by dehydration. Other events that cause dramatic loss of blood pressure can also produce thirst. For example, soldiers wounded on the battlefield or injured people who have bled extensively may feel intense thirst. The cause of their craving is the activation of pressure receptors, which triggers the same chain of renin and angiotensin production, resulting in the experience of thirst (Fitzsimons, 1990).

Intracellular thirst is caused by osmosis—the tendency of water to move from zones where it is plentiful to zones where it is relatively rare. It is primarily the concentration of "salt" ions of sodium, chloride, and potassium that determine whether water is plentiful or rare. As the body loses water, these concentrations begin to rise in the bloodstream. In essence, the blood becomes saltier. The higher concentrations within the blood cause water to migrate from the relatively dilute insides of body cells—including neurons—toward the blood. In a process something like sucking up a puddle of water with a paper towel, water is pulled out of the neurons and other cells. Neurons within the hypothalamus become activated when higher salt concentrations in the blood pull water from them, causing them to become dehydrated. Their activation produces "osmotic" or intracellular thirst, producing the desire to drink. Drinking replaces water in the blood, reducing the concentration of salt, which in turn allows water to return to neurons and other cells. That is why people become thirsty after eating salty food—even though they might not have lost water.

◆ Interim Summary

- Drive factors tend to promote homeostasis: the preservation of a constant internal state.

- Homeostasis involves (1) a set point, or goal value, for the ideal internal state, (2) a sensory signal that measures the actual internal state, (3) a comparison between the set point and the sensory signal, and (4) a response that brings the actual internal state closer to the set point goal.

- Temperature regulation is an example of homeostasis. The regulated variable is the temperature of the blood, and sensors for this are located in various parts of the body, including the hypothalamus. Adjustments are either automatic physiological responses (e.g., shivering) or voluntary behavioral ones (e.g., putting on a sweater).

- Thirst is another homeostatic motive that operates on two regulated variables, extracellular fluid and intracellular fluid. Loss of extracellular fluid is detected by blood-pressure sensors, neurons in major veins and organs that respond to a drop in pressure. Loss of intracellular fluid is detected by osmotic sensors, neurons in the hypothalamus that respond to dehydration.

◆ Critical Thinking Questions

1. Here we've discussed how two internal factors—extracellular thirst and intracellular thirst—motivate drinking. What other factors might motivate drinking? To what extent do you think social and cultural factors motivate drinking?

2. Now that you have been exposed to both incentive and drive perspectives on motivation, compare and contrast them. Can you envision either incentives or drives operating in isolation? Why or why not?

Most bar owners know that salty foods trigger osmotic or intracellular thirst and thus induce customers to drink more.

HUNGER

The control of hunger involves many of the same homeostatic concepts as thirst, but eating is much more complex than drinking. When we're thirsty, we generally need only water, and our thirst is directed toward anything that will provide it. But there are lots of different things to eat. We need to eat a number of different kinds of things (proteins, carbohydrates, fats, minerals) to be healthy. We need to select the proper balance of foods that contain these things. Evolution has given our brains ways of helping us select the foods we need (and avoid eating things that might poison us). Some of these ways involve the basic taste preferences we were born with. Others involve mechanisms for learning preferences for particular foods and aversions to others.

Flavor is the most important factor in food preferences. Flavor contains both taste and odor components, but taste has been more important in human evolution. Humans are born "programmed" with likes and dislikes for particular tastes. Even infants respond to sweet tastes with lip-smacking movements and facial expressions indicative of pleasure (Steiner, 1979). They respond to bitter tastes by turning away and pulling their faces into expressions of disgust. Apes, monkeys, and a number of other species respond in the same way. Food manufacturers capitalize on our natural "sweet tooth" to devise sweet foods that spur many people to overeat.

Why do we find sweet foods and drinks so attractive? Evolutionary psychologists have suggested that it is because sweetness is an excellent "label" that told our ancestors, foraging among unknown plants, that a particular food or berry was rich in sugar, a class of digestible carbohydrate. Eating sweet foods is an excellent way to gain calories, and calories were not abundant in our evolutionary past. A similar labeling explanation has been advanced for our dislike of bitterness. The naturally bitter compounds that occur in certain plants can make those plants toxic to humans. Bitterness, in other words, is a label for a natural type of poison that occurs commonly. Ancestors who avoided bitter plants may have been more successful at avoiding such poisons (Rozin & Schulkin, 1990).

A second way of developing food preferences is through an array of learning and social learning mechanisms. One of these is preference based on the consequences of ingesting food with a particular taste. Experience with the nourishing consequences of a food leads to gradual liking for its taste through a process that is essentially a form of classical conditioning (Booth, 1991). Experience with other forms of taste-consequence pairings may also be the basis for developing preferences for tastes that are initially not pleasant, such as alcohol or coffee. In other words, the positive psychological or

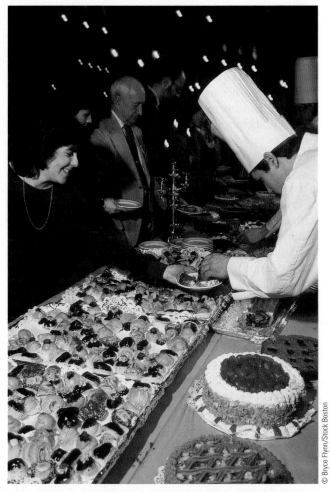

Evolutionary psychologists argue that sweet foods, like these pastries, are so compelling to us because "sweetness" conveyed to our ancestors that a particular food was rich in sugar and calories. Of course, sugars were more rare in our ancestor's environment than they are for us today.

physical effects of alcohol or caffeinated coffee may cause us to develop preferences for these foods, even if we initially do not like their taste. The same kind of process can work in the opposite direction to produce strong dislike for a particular food. If your first sample of a tasty food or drink is followed sometime later by nausea or vomiting, you may find that the food is not tasty the next time you try it. The food hasn't changed, but you have, because your new associative memories cause the food to subsequently be experienced as unpleasant. This process is called **conditioned aversion**.

INTERACTIONS BETWEEN HOMEOSTASIS AND INCENTIVES

Whatever particular foods we choose, it is clear that we must eat to maintain energy homeostasis. Body cells burn fuel to produce the energy required for the tasks they perform. Physical exercise causes muscle cells to burn extra fuel to meet the metabolic needs placed on them by energetic movement. By burning more fuel, they draw on stores of calories that have been deposited as body fat or other forms of "stored energy." As you read this, the neurons of your brain are also burning fuel to meet the metabolic needs created as they fire electrical impulses and make and release neurotransmitters. The main fuel used by these brain neurons is glucose, a simple sugar. Without fuel, neurons cannot work. Unfortunately, your brain doesn't use more glucose when you "exercise it" by thinking hard. Those neurons are always active and always consuming glucose, whether you are thinking hard or not. Concentrated thought or other psychological events may slightly alter the pattern of glucose use, but not the total amount.

Glucose is present in many fruits and other foods. It can also be manufactured by the liver out of other sugars or carbohydrates. Once you've eaten a meal, a great deal of glucose will be absorbed into your bloodstream through the process of digestion. Even more will be created by your liver as it converts other forms of nutrients. In this way, a meal replenishes the fuel needed by your brain neurons and your body's other cells.

Because our cells need fuel, we might expect hunger to be solely a homeostatic motivation controlled entirely by the need to keep sufficient sources of energy available. Indeed, homeostasis is the dominant principle operating in the control of hunger. Deficits in available fuels can trigger hunger, and surpluses can inhibit it. But even though homeostasis is crucial to understanding the control of hunger, incentive factors are equally important. In fact, we can't understand hunger unless we look at the interaction between homeostasis and incentives.

The importance of interactions between homeostatic drive reduction and the taste and other incentive stimuli of food was made clear by a classic experiment by Miller and Kessen (1952). These investigators trained rats to run down a short path for a milk reward. In one case, the rats received milk as a reward in the ordinary way: They drank it. In the other case, the rats received exactly the same amount of milk, but in a more direct way: The milk was gently pumped into their stomachs through a tube passed into an artificial opening, or fistula, that had been implanted weeks before. Both of these rewards provided exactly the same number of calories. Both reduced the rats' fuel deficit to the same degree. But the rats learned to run for the milk reward much better when they were allowed to drink it. The milk was not a powerful motivator when it was pumped directly into the stomach, even though it reduced hunger just as well as when it went into the mouth. The rats needed to *both* taste the reward *and* have it reduce hunger.

The importance of such interactions between oral incentives and drive reduction has been demonstrated in many ways since that original experiment (Toates, 1986). Food that bypasses the normal route of voluntary tasting and swallowing is not strongly motivating for either animals or humans. For example, people who are fed entirely by means of intravenous or intragastric infusions of nutrients often find these "meals" unsatisfying. They may feel an intense desire to have some food that they can put into their mouths—even if they are required to spit it out again after chewing it. The strong desire for oral stimulation—above and beyond the satisfaction of caloric needs—is also reflected in our widespread use of artificial sweeteners, which provide flavor without calories. Food incentives, in the form of the sensory experience involved in eating palatable foods and drinks, thus are as crucial to appetite as caloric drive reduction.

Learning is also an important part of the interaction between physiological hunger signals and the incentive stimuli of eating. Dramatic demonstrations can be seen in animals in which the act of eating is uncoupled from the ordinary caloric consequences by the implantation of a stomach fistula, which allows food to leave the stomach as well as to be put into it. If the fistula cap is removed, whatever is eaten will fall out rather than be digested. This is called **sham feeding** because the meal is a sham in the sense that it provides no calories. Sham-fed animals eat normal amounts and then stop. Why do they stop rather than continue eating? The answer becomes clear if one observes food intake during subsequent meals: The animals gradually increase the amount eaten as they learn that the meal conveys fewer calories than it once did (Van Vort & Smith, 1987). If the fistula cap is replaced so that everything is digested as it normally would be, the animals eat the "too large" amount for their next few meals. Gradually, their meal size declines to normal levels as they learn that the food apparently is rich in calories once again. These observations have led to the hypothesis of **conditioned satiety**—that the fullness we feel after a meal is at least in part a product of learning (Booth, 1987).

Humans also are capable of conditioned satiety. In one experiment, people were asked to eat several meals of a distinctive food that was rich in calories and of another food that was low in calories. Later, when the participants were again given the two foods, which were apparently the same as before but with the caloric content made equal, they found the food that had originally been higher in calories more satiating (Booth, 1990).

A final form of interaction between food incentives and homeostatic drive is the phenomenon called *alliesthesia* (Cabanac, 1979), in which food (especially sweet food) tastes better when one is hungry. More generally, **alliesthesia** means that any external stimulus that corrects an internal trouble is experienced as pleasurable. For example, when people are asked to rate the palatability of sweet drinks either after a meal or after several hours without food, they give higher palatability ratings to the same drink when they are hungry than when they have recently eaten.

PHYSIOLOGICAL HUNGER CUES

You may have noticed that when you are hungry your stomach sometimes growls. At such moments, the stomach walls are engaged in muscular contractions, creating the burbling movements of its contents that you hear. Stomach contractions are most frequent when you are hungry and likely to feel that your stomach is empty. The association of these contractions with feelings of hunger led early investigators to hypothesize that pressure sensors in the stomach detect emptiness and trigger both contractions and the psychological experience of hunger. Later, psychologists and physiologists found that this coincidence is really just that—a coincidence. Stomach sensations from contractions are not the real cause of hunger. In fact, people who have had their stomachs surgically removed for medical reasons, so that food passes directly to the intestines, can still have strong feelings of hunger.

The stomach does have receptors that are important to changes in hunger, but these receptors are primarily chemical in nature. They have more to do with feelings of satiety than with feelings of hunger. They are activated by sugars and other nutrients in stomach contents and send a neural signal to the brain.

The physiological signal for hunger is more directly related to the real source of calories for neurons and other cells: levels of glucose and other nutrients in the body. The brain itself is its own sensor for deficiencies in available calories. You may remember that neurons in the brain use glucose as their principal source of energy. Neurons in particular parts of the brain, especially the brain stem and hypothalamus, are especially sensitive to glucose levels. When the level falls too low, the activity of these neurons is disrupted. This signals the rest of the brain, producing hunger. Such hunger can be produced artificially in laboratory animals even just after a meal. If chemicals that prevent neurons from burning glucose as a fuel are infused into an animal's brain, the animal will suddenly seek out food. Its brain has been fooled into sensing a lack of glucose, even though glucose was actually present, because the neurons have been disrupted in the same way as they are when glucose is low.

PERIPHERAL SIGNALS To some degree, hunger is what we feel when we have no feeling of satiety. As long as caloric food is in our stomach or intestine, or calorie stores are high within our body, we feel relatively sated. When these decline, hunger ensues. The control of hunger is therefore the reverse of the control of satiety.

Many physical systems contribute to the feeling of satiety after a meal. The first system is made up of the parts of the body that process food first: the stomach and intestine. Both the physical expansion of the stomach and the chemicals within the food activate receptors in the stomach's walls. These receptors relay their signal to the brain through the vagus nerve, which carries signals from many other body organs as well. A second kind of satiety message comes from the duodenum, the part of the intestines that receives food directly from the stomach. This signal is sent to the brain as a chemical rather than through a nerve. When food reaches the duodenum, it causes it to release a hormone (cholecystokinin, or CCK) into the bloodstream. CCK helps promote physiological digestion, but it also has a psychological consequence. It travels through the blood until it reaches the brain, where it is detected by special receptors. This produces feelings of satiety. Hungry animals can be fooled into false satiety if microscopic amounts of CCK are infused into their brains shortly after they have begun a meal (Smith & Gibbs, 1994).

Perhaps surprisingly, the brain's most sensitive signal of nutrient availability comes from neuronal receptors that are separate both from the brain and from food: neuronal receptors in the liver (Friedman, 1990). Receptors in the liver are highly sensitive to changes in blood nutrients after digestion. These signals are also sent to the brain through the vagus nerve. A hungry animal will stop eating almost immediately after even a tiny amount of nutrients are infused into the blood supply that goes directly to the liver.

Why should the brain rely on nutrient signals from the liver rather than on its own detectors? The answer may be that the liver can more accurately measure the various types of nutrients used by the body. The brain detects chiefly glucose, but other forms of nutrients, such as complex carbohydrates, proteins, and fats, can be measured, stored, and sometimes converted into other nutrients by the liver. Its role as a general "currency exchange" for various nutrients may allow the liver to make the best estimate of the total energy stores available to the body.

The Neural Basis of Behavior

INTEGRATION OF HUNGER SIGNALS

Signals for hunger and satiety are processed by the brain in two stages to produce the motivation to eat.

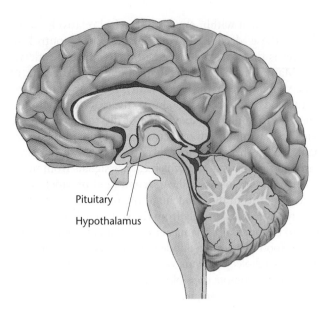

▌Figure 10-3
The Hypothalamus and Pituitary

Damage to the ventromedial hypothalamus produces overeating and obesity.

First, signals from hunger receptors in the brain itself and satiety signals relayed from the stomach and liver are added together in the brain stem to detect the overall level of need (Grill & Kaplan, 1990). This "integrated hunger assessment" is also connected in the brain stem to the sensory neural systems that process taste. Taste neurons in the brain stem may change their responsiveness during some forms of hunger and satiety (Scott & Mark, 1986), which may be part of the reason that food tastes more palatable when we are hungry.

To become the conscious experience we know as hunger, and to stimulate the seeking of food, the hunger signal of the brain stem must be processed further in the forebrain. A key site for this processing is the hypothalamus (see Figure 10-3). Hunger is affected in two dramatically different ways by manipulations of two parts of the hypothalamus: the lateral hypothalamus (the parts on each side) and the ventromedial hypothalamus (the lower ["ventral"] and middle ["medial"] portion). Destruction of the lateral hypothalamus produces an apparent total lack of hunger, at least until the rest of the brain recovers and compensates (Teitelbaum & Epstein, 1962). This phenomenon is called the **lateral hypothalamic syndrome.** Animals that have had small lesions made in their lateral hypothalamus may simply ignore food. They may even reject it as though it tasted bad (for example, grimace and vigorously spit it out). Unless they are fed artificially, they will starve to death. Nearly the exact opposite pattern of behavior is seen with the **ventromedial hypothalamic syndrome.** Lesions of the ventromedial hypothalamus produce extreme ap-

petites. Animals with such lesions eat voraciously and consume large quantities of food, especially if it is palatable. Not surprisingly, they gain weight until they become quite obese, up to double their normal body weight.

Other manipulations of these brain sites also appear to change hunger. For example, electrical stimulation of the lateral hypothalamus produces overeating: the exact opposite of a lesion of the lateral hypothalamus (and the same effect as a lesion of the ventromedial hypothalamus). An animal with a stimulating electrode in its lateral hypothalamus may begin to look for food and eat as soon as the stimulation begins—and to stop eating once it ends. Conversely, stimulation of the ventromedial hypothalamus will stop a hungry animal's ordinary eating.

Neurochemical stimulation of the hypothalamus works in similar ways. For example, certain compounds such as neuropeptide Y, or opiate drugs such as morphine, can stimulate feeding when they are injected into the ventromedial hypothalamus. These drugs may temporarily stimulate hunger or make food taste better. Other drugs, such as amphetamines, can halt feeding when injected into parts of the lateral hypothalamus. Many prescription diet drugs are chemically similar to amphetamines. Such drugs might inhibit appetite by acting on neurons in the hypothalamus.

Around 1960, when the importance of the lateral hypothalamus and ventromedial hypothalamus to hunger were discovered, psychologists tended to view these sites simply as hunger or satiety centers. Since then, it has become clear that the concepts of "hunger center" or "satiety center" are too simplistic, for a number of reasons. One is that these sites are not the

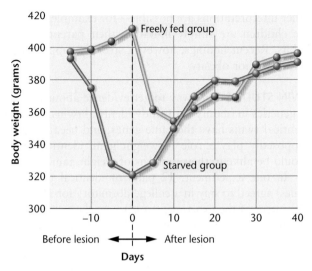

▌Figure 10-4
Body Weight and the Lateral Hypothalamus
Before lesioning of the lateral hypothalamus, one group of rats was starved and another group was allowed to feed freely. After surgery, the starved animals increased their food intake and gained weight while the freely fed group lost weight. Both groups stabilized at the same weight level. (After Powley & Keesey, 1970)

sole centers for hunger or satiety in the brain. They interact with many other brain systems to produce their effects. In fact, some of the same effects can be produced by manipulating related brain systems instead of the hypothalamus. For example, many of the effects of manipulating the lateral hypothalamus can be duplicated by manipulating the brain's dopamine system, which simply passes through the hypothalamus. Like

lateral hypothalamic lesions, lesions in this dopamine-containing bundle of axons eliminate feeding. In fact, many early studies of lateral hypothalamic lesions actually destroyed both the dopamine systems and the neurons in the lateral hypothalamus itself. Conversely, the elicitation of feeding by electrical stimulation and by many drugs also depends partly on activation of the brain's dopamine system. Thus, rather than just one or two centers, many neuroanatomical and neurotransmitter systems are involved in appetite and satiety.

One consequence of having many neural systems for appetite is that it is not possible to abolish eating by destroying just one site. Even in animals with lateral hypothalamic lesions, appetite will return eventually. If the rats are artificially fed for several weeks or months after the lesion, they will begin to eat again, but they will eat only enough to maintain their lower body weight. They seem to have reached homeostasis at a lower set point. In fact, rats can be "protected" from the usual loss of eating that would follow a lateral hypothalamic lesion if they are put on a diet before the lesion that lowers their body weight (see Figure 10-4). This indicates that hypothalamic lesions don't actually destroy hunger. Instead, they may raise or lower the homeostatic set point for body weight that ordinarily controls hunger. Changing the set point is like resetting a thermostat: The system attempts to achieve the new body weight. The effect of ventromedial hypothalamic lesions also conforms to this idea. Animals with those lesions do not gain weight infinitely. Eventually they stop at a new, obese body weight. At that point, they eat only enough to maintain the new set point. But if they are put on a diet and drop below that set point, they will resume overeating in order to regain that body weight when they are finally given the opportunity (see Figure 10-5). Once they regain that level of obesity, they will halt once again. ▌

OBESITY

We have emphasized homeostatic processes in hunger, but eating behavior shows several departures from homeostasis. Some people's body weight is not as constant as the homeostatic viewpoint suggests. The most frequent deviation from homeostatic regulation of eating—at least for humans—is obesity. **Obese** is defined as being 30% or more in excess of one's ap-

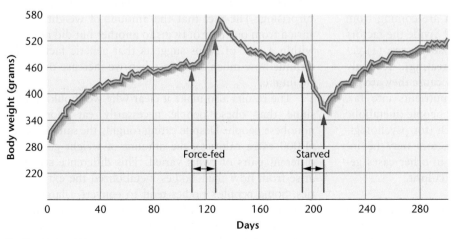

▌Figure 10-5
Effects of Forced Feeding and Starvation on Rats with VMH Lesions
Following lesioning of the ventromedial hypothalamus, the rat overeats and gains weight until it stabilizes at a new, obese level. Forced feeding or starvation alters the weight level only temporarily; the rat returns to its stabilized level. (After Hoebel & Teitelbaum, 1966)

propriate body weight. Currently in the United States, obesity is considered an epidemic, with roughly 27% of Americans meeting the criteria, a percentage that has nearly doubled in the past 20 years. The prevalence of obesity also varies among different groups. Physical obesity occurs about equally in both sexes, but the psychological perception of being overweight is more common among women. More than 50% of American women, compared with more than 35% of men, consider themselves overweight (Brownell & Rodin, 1994; Horm & Anderson, 1993). In the United States, obesity is more prevalent in lower-class socioeconomic groups than in higher-class ones. However, in developing countries the reverse is true: The higher people's socioeconomic status, the more likely they are to be obese (Logue, 1991; Stunkard, 1996).

Obesity is a major health hazard. It contributes to a higher incidence of diabetes, high blood pressure, and heart disease. As if this were not bad enough, in our culture obesity can also be a social stigma, as obese people are often perceived as being indulgent and lacking in willpower (Crandall, 1994; Crocker, Cornwell, & Major, 1993). This allegation can be most unfair because, as we will see, in many cases obesity is due to genetic factors rather than overeating. Given the problems associated with obesity, it is not surprising that each year millions of people spend billions of dollars on diets and drugs to lose weight.

Most researchers agree that obesity is a complex problem that can involve metabolic, nutritional, psychological, and sociological factors. Obesity probably is not a single disorder but a variety of disorders that all have fatness as their major symptom (Rodin, 1981). Asking how one becomes obese is like asking how one gets to Pittsburgh—there are many ways to do it, and which one you "choose" depends on where you are coming from (Offir, 1982). In what follows, we will divide the factors that lead to weight gain into two broad classes: (1) genetics and (2) calorie intake (overeating). Roughly speaking, people may become obese because they are genetically predisposed to metabolize nutrients into fat, even if they don't eat more than other people (metabolic reasons), or because they eat too much (for psychological or sociological reasons). Both factors may be involved in some cases of obesity, and in other cases genetics or overeating alone may be the culprit.

GENETIC FACTORS It has long been known that obesity runs in families. In families in which neither parent is obese, only about 10% of the children are obese; if one parent is obese, about 40% of the children are also obese; and if both parents are obese, approximately 70% of the children are also obese (Gurney, 1936). These statistics suggest a biological basis of obesity, but

other interpretations are possible—for example, perhaps the children are simply imitating their parents' eating habits. Recent findings, however, strongly support a genetic basis for obesity.

TWIN STUDIES One way to get evidence about the role of genetics in obesity is to study identical twins. Because identical twins have the same genes, and because genes supposedly play a role in weight gain, identical twins should be alike in their patterns of weight gain.

In one experiment, 12 pairs of identical twins (all males) agreed to stay in a college dormitory for 100 days. The intent of the experiment was to get the twins to gain weight. Each man ate a diet that contained 1,000 extra calories per day. For men, 1,000 extra calories is the rough equivalent of eating four very large meals a day, instead of three regular meals. Also, the men's physical activity was restricted. They were not allowed to exercise and instead spent much of their time reading, playing sedentary games, and watching television. By the end of the 100 days, all of the men had gained weight, but the amount gained ranged from 9 to 30 pounds. However—and this is the key point—there was hardly any variation in the amount gained by the members of each pair of twins (the variation occurred between pairs of twins). In other words, identical twins gained almost identical amounts. Moreover, identical twins tended to gain weight in the same places. If one member of a pair of twins gained weight in his middle, so did the other; if one member of another pair of twins gained weight on his hips and thighs, so did the other (Bouchard, Lykken, McGue, Segal, & Tellegen, 1990).

These results make it clear that both calorie intake and genetics contribute to weight gain. The fact that all the men in the study gained weight shows that increased calories translates into increased weight, which is hardly surprising. The fact that the amount of weight gained varied from one pair of twins to another but did not vary within a pair of twins suggests that genetic factors determine how much we gain when we increase our calorie intake.

The results also make it clear why we should not assume that obese people necessarily eat more than nonobese people. Despite eating roughly the same amount (1,000 extra calories), the amount of weight gained by different pairs of twins varied. This difference seems to arise from how their bodies metabolized the extra calories. Some people's bodies tend to convert a larger proportion of calories into fat stores, and others are likely to burn off the same calories through different metabolic processes, regardless of how much is eaten (Ravussin et al., 1988).

A critic might object to making too much of the study just described. Identical twins not only have identical genes but also grow up in very similar environments. Perhaps environmental factors were responsible for the identical twins being alike in weight gain. We need to study identical twins who have been reared apart and see how similar the members of a pair are in weight gain. This was done in a study conducted in Sweden (Stunkard et al., 1990). The researchers studied the weights of 93 pairs of identical twins reared apart, as well as that of 153 pairs of identical twins reared together. Members of a pair of twins reared apart were found to be remarkably similar in weight; indeed, they were as similar in weight as members of pairs of twins reared together. Clearly, genes are a major determinant of weight and weight gain.

FAT CELLS Given that genes play a role in weight gain, we want to know some details of that role. In particular, what are the digestive and metabolic processes that are affected by genes and that mediate weight gain? One answer involves fat cells, where all body fat is stored. There are between 30 billion and 40 billion fat cells in the bodies of most normal adults, but the degree of excess weight carried by ordinary American adults varies by more than the 25% to 33% this figure would suggest. The additional variation comes from the size, rather than the mere number, of fat cells: The more calories one eats and fails to burn off, the larger existing fat cells become.

In one study, obese participants were found to have three times as many fat cells as normal participants (Knittle & Hirsch, 1968). In other studies, researchers have shown that rats with double the usual number of fat cells tend to be twice as fat as control rats. And when researchers cut some of the fat cells out of young rats so that they had only half as many fat cells as their littermates, those rats grew up to be only half as fat as their littermates (Faust, 1984; Hirsch & Batchelor, 1976). Because there is a link between genes and the number of fat cells, and another link between the number of fat cells and obesity, through this chain, genes are connected to obesity.

DIETING AND SET POINTS When people take diet drugs, a variety of things can happen. The drug might suppress appetite directly, which would reduce the feeling of hunger. Another drug might suppress the set point—the point at which body weight is set and that the body strives to maintain—rather than suppress appetite directly. For example, it has been suggested that diet drugs such as fenfluramine have this effect (Stunkard, 1982). Such an effect would be equivalent to direct appetite suppression as long as body weight was higher than the lowered set point. Once body weight fell to the lower level, appetite would return to just the degree needed to remain at that weight. When a person stopped taking the drug, the set point would return to its higher

level, and the person would regain the weight that had been lost. Finally, some drugs, such as nicotine, may help people lose weight by elevating the metabolic rate of cells, causing them to burn more calories than they ordinarily would.

One reason that the set point hypothesis has become popular among psychologists is the strong tendency for obese adults, both humans and animals, to return to their original body weight after ceasing dieting. In contrast to the young rats just described, even surgical removal of fat deposits by liposuction appears not to produce permanent weight loss when it is performed on adult rats: The adults regain the fat elsewhere. This also appears to be true of liposuction performed on obese human adults (Vogt & Belluscio, 1987).

Some investigators have suggested that once adult levels of fat tissue have been reached, they are maintained at that level. The brain may detect changes in the level of body fat and influence hunger accordingly (Weigle, 1994). For example, an "obesity gene" in mice is thought to control the ability of fat cells to produce a chemical "satiety signal" (Zhang et al., 1994). Mice that lack this gene become obese. Ordinarily, the more body fat one has, the more satiety signal is released into the blood. Whether human obesity involves a disruption in this satiety factor or gene is not yet known. But the possibility that the level of fat stores is kept constant may help explain why some obese people find it difficult not to regain weight that they lost through dieting.

In sum, there are various routes by which genes can be responsible for excessive weight gain, including having many and large fat cells, having a high set point, and having a low metabolic rate.

OVEREATING Although physiological factors such as fat regulation and metabolic rate are important determinants of body weight, there is no question that overeating can also cause obesity. The psychological factors that contribute to overeating include the breakdown of conscious restraints and emotional arousal.

BREAKDOWN OF CONSCIOUS RESTRAINTS Some people stay obese by going on eating binges after dieting. An obese man may break a 2-day diet and then overeat so much that he eventually consumes more calories than he would have, had he not dieted at all. Because the diet was a conscious restraint, the breakdown of control is a factor in increased calorie intake.

To gain a more detailed understanding of the role of conscious restraints, researchers have developed a questionnaire that asks about diet, weight history, and concern with eating (for example, How often do you diet? Do you eat sensibly in front of others, yet overeat when alone?). The results show that almost everyone—

whether thin, average, or overweight—can be classified into one of two categories: people who consciously restrain their eating and people who do not. In addition, regardless of their actual weight, the eating behavior of restrained eaters is closer to that of obese individuals than to that of unrestrained eaters (Herman & Polivy, 1980; Ruderman, 1986).

A laboratory study shows what happens when restraints are dropped. Restrained and unrestrained eaters (both of normal weight) were required to drink either two milkshakes, one milkshake, or none; they then sampled several flavors of ice cream and were encouraged to eat as much as they wanted (Herman & Mack, 1975). The more milkshakes the unrestrained eaters were required to drink, the less ice cream they consumed later. In contrast, the restrained eaters who had been preloaded with two milkshakes ate more ice cream than did those who drank one milkshake or none. Thus, individuals who are trying to restrain their eating by ignoring their ordinary impulse to eat more may also come to ignore the feelings of satiety that would ordinarily halt their desire to eat. Ironically, then, this is why conscious efforts to diet often backfire.

EMOTIONAL AROUSAL Overweight individuals often report that they tend to eat more when they are tense or anxious, and experimental results support these reports. Obese participants eat more in a high-anxiety situation than they do in a low-anxiety situation, but normal-weight participants eat more in situations of low anxiety (McKenna, 1972). Other research indicates that any kind of emotional arousal seems to increase food intake in some obese people. In one study, overweight and normal-weight participants saw a different film in each of four sessions. Three of the films aroused various emotions: one was distressing, one amusing, and one sexually arousing. The fourth film was a boring travelogue. After viewing each of the films, the participants were asked to taste and evaluate different kinds of crackers. The obese participants ate significantly more crackers after viewing any of the arousing films than they did after seeing the travelogue. Normal-weight individuals ate the same amount of crackers regardless of which film they had seen (White, 1977).

The ability of emotional stress to elicit eating has been observed in other animals, too. This may mean that stress can activate basic brain systems that, under some conditions, result in overeating (Rowland & Antelman, 1976).

DIETING AND WEIGHT CONTROL Although genetic factors may limit the amount of weight we can comfortably lose, overweight people can still lose weight by following a weight-control program. For a program to be

successful, though, it must involve something other than just extreme dieting.

LIMITATIONS OF DIETING Unfortunately, most dieters are not successful, and those who succeed in shedding pounds often gain weight again after ceasing dieting. This state of affairs seems to be partly due to two deep-seated reactions to a temporary deprivation of food (which is what a diet is). The first reaction, as we've seen, is that deprivation per se can lead to subsequent overeating. In some experiments, rats were first deprived of food for 4 days, then allowed to feed until they regained their normal weights, and finally allowed to eat as much food as they wanted. These rats ate more than control rats with no history of deprivation. Thus, prior deprivation leads to subsequent overeating, even after the weight lost as a result of the deprivation has been regained (Coscina & Dixon, 1983).

The second reaction of interest is that deprivation *decreases* metabolic rate, and as you may recall, the lower one's metabolic rate, the fewer calories expended, and the higher one's weight. Consequently, the calorie reduction during dieting is partly offset by the lowered metabolic rate, making it difficult for dieters to meet their goals. The reduced metabolic rate caused by dieting may also explain why many people find it harder and harder to lose weight with each successive diet: The body responds to each bout of dieting with a reduction in metabolic rate (Brownell, 1988).

Both reactions to dieting—binge eating and lowered metabolic rate—are understandable in evolutionary terms. Until very recently in human history, whenever people experienced deprivation it was because of a scarcity of food in the environment. One adaptive response to such scarcity is to overeat and store in our bodies as much food as possible whenever it is available. Natural selection may have favored the ability to overeat following deprivation, which explains the overeating reaction. A second adaptive response to a scarcity of food in the environment is for organisms to decrease the rate at which they expend their limited calories, so natural selection may have favored the ability to lower one's metabolic rate during deprivation. This explains the second reaction of interest. Over the millennia, these two reactions have served our species well in times of famine, but once famine is not a concern–as in most economically developed countries today–they prevent obese dieters from losing weight permanently (Polivy & Herman, 1985).

WEIGHT CONTROL PROGRAMS To lose weight and keep it off, it seems that overweight individuals need to establish a new set of permanent eating habits (as opposed to temporary dieting) and engage in a program of exercise. Some support for this conclusion is provided by the following study, which compared various methods for treating obesity (Craighead, Stunkard, & O'Brien, 1981; Wadden et al., 1997).

For 6 months, obese individuals followed one of three treatment regimens: (1) behavior modification of eating and exercise habits, (2) drug therapy using an appetite suppressant (fenfluramine), and (3) a combination of behavior modification and drug therapy. Participants in all three treatment groups were given information about exercise and extensive nutritional counseling, including a diet of no more than 1,200 calories per day. Participants in the behavior modification groups were taught to become aware of situations that prompted them to overeat, to change the conditions associated with their overeating, to reward themselves for appropriate eating behavior, and to develop a suitable exercise regimen. In addition to the three treatment groups, there were two control groups: One consisted of participants waiting to take part in the study, and the other of participants who saw a physician for traditional treatment of weight problems.

Table 10-1 presents the results of the study. The participants in all three treatment groups lost more weight than the participants in the two control groups, with the group combining behavior modification and drug therapy losing the most weight and the behavior-modification-only group losing the least. However, during the year after treatment, a striking reversal developed. The behavior-modification-only group regained far less weight than the two other treatment groups; these participants maintained an average weight loss of nearly 20 pounds by the end of the year, whereas the weight losses for the drug-therapy-only group and the combined-treatment group regained roughly two-thirds of the weight they had initially lost.

What caused this reversal? An increased sense of self-efficacy or self-control may have been a factor. Participants who received the behavior-modification-only treatment could attribute their weight loss to their own efforts, thereby strengthening their resolve to continue controlling their weight after the treatment ended. Participants who received an appetite suppressant, on the other hand, probably attributed their weight loss to the medication and did not develop a sense of self-control. Another possible factor stems from the fact that the medication had decreased the participants' feelings of hunger, or temporarily lowered their set point, and consequently participants in the drug-therapy-only group and the combined-treatment group may not have been sufficiently prepared to cope with the increase in hunger they felt when the medication was stopped.

ANOREXIA AND BULIMIA

Although obesity is the most common eating problem, the opposite problem has also surfaced in the form of anorexia nervosa and bulimia. Both of these disorders involve a pathological desire not to gain weight and disproportionately strike women.

Anorexia nervosa is an eating disorder characterized by extreme, self-imposed weight loss—at least 15% of the individual's minimum normal weight. Some anorexics in fact weigh less than 50% of their normal weight. Despite the extreme loss of weight and the resulting problems, the typical anorexic denies that there is a problem and refuses to gain weight. In fact, anorexics frequently think that they look too fat. For females to be diagnosed as anorexic, in addition to the weight loss, they must also have stopped menstruating. The weight loss can lead to a number of dangerous side effects, including emaciation, susceptibility to infection, and other symptoms of undernourishment. These side effects can lead to death.

Anorexia is relatively rare. Its incidence in the United States is about 1% (Fairburn, Welch, & Hay, 1993). However, this incidence represents more than a doubling since the 1960s, and the frequency may still be rising (McHugh, 1990). Anorexia is 20 times more likely to occur in women than in men, and the majority of anorexics are young women between their teens and their thirties. Typically, anorexics are entirely focused on food, carefully calculating the amount of calories in anything they might consume. Sometimes this concern reaches the point of obsession, as when one anorexic commented to her therapist, "Of course I had breakfast; I ate my Cheerio," or when another said, "I won't lick a postage stamp—one never knows about calories" (Bruch, 1973). The obsession with food and possible

● **Table 10-1**
Weight Loss Following Different Treatments

Weight loss in pounds at the end of six months of treatment and on a follow-up one year later. Participants in the two control groups were not available for the one-year follow up. (L. W. Craighead, A. J. Stankard, & R. M. O'Brien (1981) "Behavior Therapy and Pharmcotherapy for Obesity," in Archives of General Psychiatry, 38:763–768. Copyright © 1981 by the American Medical Association.)

	Weight loss after treatment	Weight loss one year later
Treatment groups		
Behavior modification only	24.0	19.8
Drug therapy only	31.9	13.8
Combined treatment	33.7	10.1
Control groups		
Waiting list	2.9 (gain)	—
Physician office visits	13.2	—

weight gains leads some anorexics to become compulsive exercisers as well, sometimes exercising vigorously several hours a day (Logue, 1991).

Bulimia is an eating disorder characterized by recurrent episodes of binge eating (rapid consumption of a large amount of food in a discrete period of time), followed by attempts to purge the excess by means of vomiting or laxatives. The binges can be frequent and extreme. A survey of bulimic women found that most women binged at least once per day (usually in the evening) and that an average binge involved consuming some 4,800 calories (often sweet or salty carbohydrate foods). However, because of the purges that follow the binges, a bulimic person's weight may stay relatively normal, which allows bulimics to keep their eating disorder hidden. But this behavior can have a high physiological cost. Vomiting and use of laxatives can disrupt the balance of potassium in the body, which can result in problems like dehydration, cardiac arrhythmias, and urinary infections.

Like anorexia, bulimia primarily afflicts young women. But bulimia is more frequent than anorexia, with an estimated 5% to 10% of American women affected to some degree, with rates as high as 20% reported on college campuses. Rather than being restricted to the upper classes, bulimia is found in all racial, ethnic, and socioeconomic groups in our society.

Researchers have suggested a variety of causes for anorexia and bulimia, including social, biological, and personality or family factors. It is probably necessary for several of these factors to occur together for any individual to develop an eating disorder.

SOCIOCULTURAL CAUSES Many psychologists have proposed that social and cultural factors play major roles in anorexia and bulimia. In particular, they point to American society's emphasis on thinness in women. This emphasis has increased markedly in the past 40 years, which fits with the observation that the incidence of eating disorders has also increased during that period. An indication of this trend is the change in what people regard as a "perfect" woman's figure. The photos (below) place Jayne Mansfield, who was widely thought to have an ideal figure in the 1950s, next to a photo of actress Jennifer Lopez, who reflects today's ideal. Lopez is clearly much thinner than Mansfield, especially in the hips and thighs, the region of the body with which most women experience deep dissatisfaction.

But how exactly do media images of the "ideal" female body sink in and account for high rates of disordered eating? Insight into this process is offered by **objectification theory,** a sociocultural account of how being raised in a culture that sexually objectifies the female body (both within the visual mass media and within actual interpersonal encounters) fundamentally alters girls' and women's self-views and well-being (Fredrickson & Roberts, 1997). Sexual objectification occurs any time a person is treated first and foremost as a body valued for its sexual use to (or consumption by) others. Sexual objectification is a dehumanizing form of interpersonal regard. It reduces the targeted person's full humanity to the status of an object for the observer's benefit.

The first psychological consequence of repeated exposure to cultural practices of sexually objectifying female bodies, the theory holds, is that girls and women learn to internalize an objectifying observer's perspective on their own body. This preoccupation with physical appearance is termed *self-objectification* (see the Concept

Jane Mansfield (*left*) represented the perfect female figure for the 1950s, whereas Jennifer Lopez (*right*) represents the perfect female figure today.

CONCEPT REVIEW TABLE
Objectification Theory

Objectification theory outlines the causes, features, and consequences of self-objectification, defined as a preoccupation with appearance characterized by vigilant appearance monitoring. (After Fredrickson et al., 1998)

Theory Outline	Theory Elements

Causes	Cultural practices of sexual objectification
	   in media messages
	   in interpersonal encounters

Features	Internalized observer's perspective on self Vigilant appearance monitoring Disrupted mental resources

Consequences	Psychological experiences
	   increased shame
	   increased anxiety
	   decreased positive emotions
	   insensitivity to bodily cues
	
	Health and mental health risks
	   disordered eating
	   depression
	   sexual dysfunction

Review table). In brief, **self-objectification** means that a person thinks about and values her own body more from a third-person perspective, focusing on observable body attributes ("How do I look?"), rather than from a first-person perspective, focusing on privileged, or unobservable body attributes ("How do I feel?"). Self-objectification is conceptualized both as a relatively stable trait—with some girls and women self-objectifying more than others—and as a temporary state—with some situations pulling for self-objectification more than others.

Objectification theory claims that self-objectification causes a range of psychological and emotional reactions. First and foremost, self-objectification leads to a form of self-consciousness characterized by vigilant monitoring of the body's outward appearance. This preoccupation with appearance can disrupt a person's stream of consciousness and thereby limit the mental resources that she can devote to other activities. It also creates a predictable set of emotional reactions, including increased shame and anxiety and diminished positive emotions and sexual pleasure. Over time, these emotional reactions can accumulate and compound, which explains why certain health and mental health problems dispro-

portionately afflict girls and women. Chief among these problems are various forms of disordered eating, which includes anorexia and bulimia, as well as restrained eating (dieting) more generally. But the theory doesn't stop there. It accounts for gender differences in depression and sexual dysfunction as well (see the Concept Review Table).

Risks for these three problems—disordered eating, depression, and sexual dysfunction—not only coincide with gender but also coincide with age. Intriguingly, the risks change in step with observable life-course changes in the female body: They first emerge for girls in early adolescence and lessen for women in late middle age. Objectification theory notes that women are most targeted for sexual objectification during their years of reproductive potential and uses this fact to explain these changing risk patterns over the life course.

Initial survey studies with college women showed that self-objectification, feelings of shame about one's body, and disordered eating were all associated with one another (Noll & Fredrickson, 1998). But those are simply correlations. How do we know that self-objectification is a cause of disordered eating, and not just a consequence or a symptom? A series of clever laboratory experiments provided the necessary evidence. In these studies, participants—male and female college students—believed they were partaking in a study on consumer decisions. Under this guise, they sampled various products and rated how those products made them feel. When it came time to try on and evaluate a garment (in a private "dressing room"), participants were randomly assigned to try on either a bulky sweater or a swimsuit (each was available in a range of sizes). For both men and women, trying on the swimsuit produced a self-conscious state of self-objectification. But that's where any similarity between men and women ended. Later came a difficult math test (presented as another study altogether). Men performed equally well on the math test regardless of what they were wearing. Women, by contrast, performed worse on the test when wearing less, consistent with the claim that self-objectification causes a disruption of mental resources. Still later came a taste test. After redressing in their own clothes, participants were asked to taste and evaluate a candy bar. Regardless of what they wore—swimsuit or sweater—most men ate the entire candy bar. The pattern of eating evident among the women, by contrast, was greatly affected by wearing the swimsuit. As the theoretical model reviewed in Concept Review Table 10-1 predicts, women who wore the swimsuit experienced state self-objectification as well as shame about their current body. The emotional reaction of shame in turn predicted restrained eating, perhaps as a way to correct the shameful mismatch between their own body and the ultra-thin cultural ideals (Fredrickson, Roberts, Noll, Quinn, & Twenge, 1998). These results provide causal evidence in support of objectification theory, which aims to detail the psychological and emotional processes through which exposure of objectifying messages can "get under the skin" and produce disordered eating.

BIOLOGICAL CAUSES Clearly, though, not everyone who is exposed to cultural messages of sexual objectification develops an eating disorder. Certain biological vulnerabilities may increase the tendency to develop eating disorders. One hypothesis is that anorexia is caused by malfunctions of the hypothalamus, the part of the brain that helps regulate eating. Anorexic individuals show lowered functioning of the hypothalamus and abnormalities in several of the neurochemicals that are important to the functioning of the hypothalamus (Fava, Copeland, Schweiger, & Herzog, 1989). With regard to bulimia, there may be a deficiency in the neurotransmitter serotonin, which plays a role in both mood regulation and appetite (Mitchell & deZwann, 1993).

FAMILIAL CAUSES Personality and family factors may also play a role in anorexia and bulimia. Many young women with eating disorders come from families that demand "perfection" and extreme self-control but do not allow expressions of warmth or conflict (Bruch, 1973; Minuchin, Rosman, & Baker, 1978). Some young women may seek to gain some control over, and expressions of concern from, their parents by controlling their eating habits, eventually developing anorexia. Others may turn to binge eating when they feel emotionally upset or painfully aware of their low self-esteem (Polivy & Herman, 1993).

Therapies designed to help people with eating disorders regain healthy eating habits and deal with the emotional issues they face have proven useful (Agras, 1993; Fairburn & Hay, 1992). Drugs that regulate serotonin levels can also be helpful, particularly for people with bulimia (Mitchell & deZwann, 1993). Anorexia and bulimia are serious disorders, however, and people who have them often continue to have significant problems for several years.

◆ Interim Summary

- Humans have both innate and learned taste preferences and aversions that guide choice of foods. Homeostatic hunger signals, which arise when the body is low in calorie-containing fuels such as glucose, produce appetite partly by causing the individual to perceive food incentives as more attractive and pleasant.

- Hunger is largely controlled by homeostatic deficit and satiety signals. Certain neurons in the brain, especially in the brain stem and hypothalamus, detect shortages in glucose and trigger hunger. Other nutrient detectors, especially in the liver, detect increasing energy stores and trigger satiety. A satiety signal, in the form of the hormone cholecystokinin, is also released from the intestines to help stop hunger and eating.

- Two regions of the brain are critical to hunger: the lateral hypothalamus and the ventromedial hypothalamus. Destruction of the lateral hypothalamus leads to undereating; destruction of the ventromedial hypothalamus leads to overeating.

- People become obese primarily because (1) they are genetically predisposed to be overweight or (2) they overeat (for psychological reasons). The influence of genes is mediated by their effect on fat cells, metabolic rate, and set points. As for overeating and obesity, obese people tend to overeat when they break a diet, eat more when emotionally aroused, and are more responsive to external hunger cues than normal-weight individuals.

- In treating obesity, extreme diets appear ineffective because deprivation leads to subsequent overeating and to a lowered metabolic rate. What seems to work best is to establish a new set of permanent eating habits and engage in a program of exercise.

- Anorexia nervosa is characterized by extreme, self-imposed weight loss. Bulimia is characterized by recurrent episodes of binge eating, followed by attempts to purge the excess by means of vomiting and laxatives. Possible causes of these eating disorders include personality factors such as low self-esteem, social factors such as a cultural emphasis on thinness and pervasive cultural messages that objectify the female body, and biological factors such as low serotonin levels.

◆ Critical Thinking Questions

1. A potent negative emotion, such as feeling ashamed of one's body, can contribute to both overeating and obesity, as well as to undereating and various eating disorders. Why is this so? Describe the pathways to each deviation from normal eating. What do you think determines which pathway is followed?

2. The text describes a number of problems associated with dieting, or restrained eating. Why does dieting continue to be very popular? What sociocultural factors come into play?

GENDER AND SEXUALITY

Like thirst and hunger, sexual desire is a powerful motivation. There are, however, some important differences. Sex is a social motive—it typically involves another person—whereas the survival motives concern only the individual. In addition, sex does not involve an internal deficit that needs to be regulated and remedied for the organism to survive. Consequently, social motives do not lend themselves to a homeostatic analysis.

With regard to sex, two critical distinctions should be kept in mind. The first stems from the fact that, although we begin to mature sexually at puberty, the basis for our sexual identity is established in the womb. We therefore distinguish between adult sexuality (that is, beginning with changes at puberty) and early sexual development. The second distinction is between the biological and environmental determinants of sexual behaviors and feelings. For many aspects of sexual development and adult sexuality, a fundamental question is the extent to which the behavior or feeling in question is a product of biology (particularly hormones), environment and learning (early experiences and cultural norms), or interactions between biological and environmental factors.

If the embryonic sex glands produce enough androgen, the fetus will develop male genitals. Shown here is a male fetus 4 months after conception.

EARLY SEXUAL DEVELOPMENT

To have gratifying social and sexual experiences as adults, most individuals need to develop an appropriate **gender identity,** in which males come to think of themselves as males and females as females. This development is quite complex and actually begins before birth. For the first couple of months after conception, only the chromosomes of a human embryo indicate whether it will develop into a boy or a girl. Up to this stage, both sexes are identical in appearance and have tissues that will eventually develop into either testes or ovaries, as well as a genital tubercle that will become either a penis or a clitoris. But between 2 and 3 months after conception, a primitive sex gland, or gonad, develops into testes if the embryo is genetically male or into ovaries if the embryo is genetically female (see Chapter 2). Once testes or ovaries develop, they produce the sex hormones, which then control the development of the internal reproductive structures and the external genitals. The sex hormones are even more important for prenatal development than they will be for the expression of adult sexuality.

The critical hormone in genital development is androgen. If the embryonic sex glands produce enough androgen, the newborn will have male genitals; if there is insufficient androgen, the newborn will have female genitals

even if it is genetically male. Conversely, if androgens are added artificially, the newborn will have male genitals even if it is genetically female. In other words, the presence or absence of a male (Y) chromosome normally influences sexual development simply by determining whether the embryo will secrete androgens. The anatomical development of the female embryo does not require female hormones, only the absence of male hormones. In short, nature will produce a female unless androgen intervenes.

The influence of androgen, called **androgenization,** extends far beyond anatomy. After it has molded the genitals, androgen begins to operate on the brain cells. Studies with rats provide evidence that prenatal androgen changes the volume and detailed structure of cells in the fetus's hypothalamus, an organ that regulates motivation in humans as well as in rats (Money, 1989). These effects of androgen essentially masculinize the brain and may be responsible for some masculine traits and behaviors that appear months or years later, such as higher levels of aggressiveness.

In a series of experiments, pregnant monkeys were injected with androgen, and their female offspring were observed in detail. These offspring showed some anatomical changes (penises instead of clitorises) and also acted differently than normal females. They were more aggressive in play, more masculine in sexual play, and less intimidated by approaching peers (Goy, 1968; Phoenix, Goy, & Resko, 1968). These findings indicate that some gender-typical behaviors (such as greater aggression in males) are partly hormonally determined in nonhuman animals.

Early hormonal abnormalities can also have the opposite consequence. They can "feminize" the later sexual behavior of males. A striking example is "maternal stress": a change in the sexual behavior of male rats whose mothers experienced high emotional stress during pregnancy (Ward, 1992). High levels of stress in a pregnant mother rat triggers hormonal events that result in a decrease in the amount of androgens produced by the male embryo's testes. That, in turn, results in a reduction of androgen reaching the developing brain. The hypothalamus and other brain regions appear to develop differently in such embryos. When these male rats become adults, they show less male sexual behavior and may even show female patterns of copulation movement if they are mounted by another male.

It is not known whether similar effects on brain development or behavior occur in humans. Although some believe that these experiments may provide insights into the basis of human heterosexual versus homosexual orientation, there are differences between the results of these animal experiments and human behavior. For example, male rats born to maternally stressed mothers tend to show less sexual behavior of any kind than ordinary male rats, but this is not true of gay men compared with heterosexual men. Nevertheless, these examples illustrate the importance of early hormonal environment for the later sexual behavior of nonhuman animals, and they raise the possibility that prenatal hormones may be important for human sexual motivation as well.

HORMONES VERSUS ENVIRONMENT

In humans, much of what is known about the effects of prenatal hormones and early environment has been uncovered by studies of individuals who, for various reasons, were exposed to the prenatal hormones that would ordinarily be experienced by one sex but then were raised in a social role that would ordinarily typify the other sex. In most such cases, the assigned label and the sex role in which the individual is raised have a much greater influence on gender identity than the individual's genes and hormones.

For example, many thousands of women born during the 1950s and 1960s were exposed to an antimiscarriage drug, diethylstilbestrol, that had unexpected hormonelike effects on brain development. Ordinarily, the testosterone (the major androgen) secreted by a

male embryo's testes is converted in the brain into a substance similar to diethylstilbestrol. Pregnant women who took the drug therefore unknowingly exposed their fetus to a chemical environment similar to that experienced by the developing brain of a normal male. For male fetuses, this would have little consequence: Their brains were already exposed to male patterns of chemical stimulation. But the female fetuses were exposed to a malelike chemical stimulation for the period when their mothers took the drug. For the overwhelming majority of these daughters, the prenatal exposure had no detectable effect. Most girls who were exposed prenatally to diethylstilbestrol went on to grow up like other girls and to become indistinguishable from women with normal prenatal experience. Social environment, in other words, appears to have had a much greater influence on the sexual and gender development of these women than prenatal hormones.

But this is not to say that prenatal chemical environment had absolutely no effect. Researchers have detected several subtle differences that characterize at least some of the women exposed to diethylstilbestrol. For example, a slightly higher proportion of these women appear to be homosexual or bisexual than would ordinarily be expected. Sexual orientation is not identical to gender identity, but in this case a slight effect of prenatal hormones on both may be reflected. (Sexual orientation is discussed in detail later in this section.) Similarly, these women show slightly lower ratings on some measures of "maternal interest," such as finding infants attractive, even though they are not different from other women by most other measures of parental, sexual, or social behavior and attitudes (Ehrhardt et al., 1989). Such studies suggest that although prenatal hormonal events may have some subtle consequences for later sexual and social development, their effect is much weaker in humans than in nonhuman animals. For humans, social and cultural factors appear to be dominant (Money, 1980).

There are, however, some studies that point to the opposite conclusion. The most famous of these occurred several years ago in remote villages of the Dominican Republic. It involved 18 genetic males who, owing to a condition known as androgen insensitivity, were born with internal reproductive organs that were clearly male but with external genitals that were closer to those of females, including a clitoris-like sex organ. In androgen insensitivity, the gonads develop as normal testes and begin to secrete testosterone and other androgens. However, the receptor systems that would be activated by androgens are missing from at least some of the body tissues that would ordinarily be masculinized by the hormones. Even though androgens are secreted and are present in the bloodstream of such a boy, they do not produce the male pattern of genital and physical development. All 18 of the infants studied had been raised as girls, which was at odds with both their genes and their prenatal hormonal environment. When they reached puberty, the surge of male hormones produced the usual bodily changes and turned their clitoris-like sex organs into penis-like organs. The vast majority of these males-reared-as-females rapidly turned into males. They seemed to have little difficulty adjusting to a male gender identity. They went off to work as miners and woodsmen, and some found female sexual partners. In this case, biology triumphed over environment (Imperato-McGinley, Peterson, Gautier, & Sturla, 1979).

There is controversy, however, about these Dominican boys who appeared to be girls. They do not seem to have been raised as ordinary girls (which is not surprising, in that they had ambiguous genitals). Rather, they seemed to have been treated as half-girl, half-boy, which could have made their subsequent transition to males easier (Money, 1987).

In other cases, the results of conflict between prenatal hormones and social rearing are less clear. In the most dramatic example, identical twin boys had a completely normal prenatal environment. But at the age of 8 months, one of the boys had his penis completely severed in what was supposed to be a routine circumcision. Ten months later, the parents authorized surgery to turn their child into a little girl—the testes were removed and a vagina was given preliminary shape. The child was then given female sex hormones and raised as a girl. Within a few years, the child seemed to have assumed a female gender identity: She preferred more feminine clothes, toys, and activities than her twin brother did. Because she appeared to be a normal girl in many ways, most investigators concluded that this was a case in which social environment had won out.

However, studies of the child at the time she reached puberty revealed that the outcome was more complex (Diamond, 1982). As a teenager, she was unhappy and appeared to be confused about her sexuality, even though she had not been told about her original sex or the sex-change operation she had undergone. In interviews, she refused to draw a picture of a woman and instead would draw only a man. Aspects of her body language, such as her walking gait and patterns of posture and movement, were masculine in appearance. Socially, she had considerably more than the usual degree of difficulty in forming relationships with her peers.

A recent follow-up on this individual found that he eventually rejected the female gender identity and has successfully lived as a male since then (Diamond & Sigmundson, 1997). In the long run, the attempt to control his gender identity through socialization and to raise him as a "normal girl" was unsuccessful. It is difficult to know the precise source of the difficulty he experienced in emotional and social adjustment at puberty. Explanations include the possibility that his early brain development as a male placed constraints on his later ability to adapt to a female gender identity.

What can we conclude about gender identity? Clearly, prenatal hormones and environment are both major determinants of gender identity and typically work in harmony. When they clash, as they do in some individuals, most experts believe that environment will dominate. But this is a controversial area, and expert opinion may change as additional data are gathered.

ADULT SEXUALITY

Changes in body hormone systems occur at puberty, which usually begins between the ages of 11 and 14 (see Figure 10-6). The hypothalamus begins to secrete chemicals called *gonadotropin releasing factors;* these stimulate the pituitary gland, which lies immediately below the hypothalamus. The pituitary secretes sex hormones, called

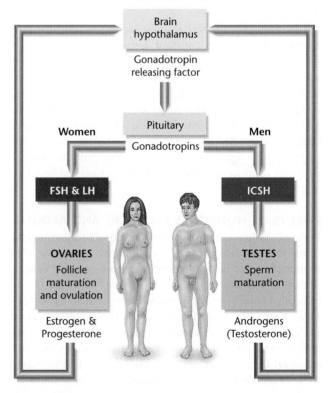

▌ **Figure 10-6**
The Hormonal System Involved in Sex
By way of hormones, the hypothalamus directs the pituitary, which in turn directs the gonads to secrete the sex hormones.

gonadotropins, into the bloodstream. These circulate through the body and reach the gonads—ovaries in females and testes in males—which generate egg or sperm cells. Gonadotropins activate the gonads, causing them to secrete additional sex hormones into the bloodstream.

In women, the hypothalamus releases its gonadotropin-releasing factors on a monthly cycle, rising and falling approximately every 28 days. This stimulates the pituitary to secrete two gonadotropins: follicle-stimulating hormone (FSH) and luteinizing hormone (LH), also on a monthly cycle. These hormones activate the ovaries. Follicle-stimulating hormone stimulates the ovaries to generate follicles, clusters of cells in the ovaries that allow fertile eggs to develop. Once a follicle is generated, it begins to secrete the female hormone, estrogen. Estrogen is released into the bloodstream to affect the body's sexual development and, in many species of animals, to activate sexual motivation in the brain. The second gonadotropin, luteinizing hormone, is released from the pituitary slightly later than follicle-stimulating hormone. Luteinizing hormone causes ovulation, the release of a mature fertile egg cell from the follicle. When the follicle releases its egg, it also secretes a second female hormone, progesterone, which prepares the uterus for implantation of a fertilized egg and, in some species of animals, also activates sexual motivation in the brain.

In men, the hypothalamus secretes gonadotropin-releasing factor in a constant fashion rather than in a monthly cycle. This causes the male pituitary to constantly release its gonadotropin, called *interstitial cell stimulating hormone* (ICSH), into the bloodstream. ICSH causes male testes to produce mature sperm cells and dramatically boost secretion of androgens, especially testosterone. Testosterone and other androgens stimulate the development of male physical characteristics and, in most species of animals, act on the brain to activate sexual desire.

EFFECTS OF HORMONES ON DESIRE AND AROUSAL
In many species, sexual arousal is closely tied to variations in hormonal levels. In humans, however, hormones play less of a role. One way to assess the contribution of hormones to sexual arousal is to study the effects of removing the gonads, a procedure called *gonadectomy.* (In males, removal of the testes is called *castration.*) In experiments with animals such as rats and guinea pigs, castration results in rapid decline and eventual disappearance of sexual activity. For humans, of course, there are no controlled experiments. Psychologists rely instead on observations of males with serious illnesses (such as cancer of the testes) who have undergone chemical castration (use of synthetic hormones to suppress or block the use of androgen). These

studies typically show that some men lose interest in sex but others continue to lead a normal sex life (Money, Weideking, Walker, & Gain, 1976; Walker, 1978). Apparently androgen contributes to sexual desire only in some cases.

Another way to measure the contribution of hormones to sexual desire and arousal in men is to look for a relationship between hormonal fluctuation and sexual interest. For example, is a man more likely to feel aroused when his testosterone level is high? It turns out that testosterone level may have no effect on copulatory function—as indicated by the ability to have an erection—but does increase desire, as indicated by sexual fantasies (Davidson, 1988). The major determinants of sexual desire in men, however, seem to be emotional factors. For males as well as females, the most common cause of low desire in couples seeking sex therapy is marital conflict (Goleman, 1988).

Sexual desire is even less dependent on hormones in women. This contrasts with nonprimate species, in which female sexual behavior is highly dependent on sexual hormones. In all other animals, removal of the ovaries results in cessation of sexual activity. A castrated female ceases to be receptive to the male and usually resists sexual advances. The major exception is the human female. Following menopause (when the ovaries have ceased to function), most women do not experience diminished sexual desire. In fact, some women show increased interest in sex after menopause, possibly because they are no longer concerned about becoming pregnant. There is evidence to indicate that women's sexual desire is facilitated by trace amounts of sex hormones in the bloodstream (Sherwin, 1988a). However, the level required is so low that it may be exceeded in most women and hence not play a significant role in changes in desire.

Studies of the relationship between hormonal fluctuation and sexual arousal in premenopausal females lead to a similar conclusion: Normal changes in hormones control arousal in other animals but not in humans. In female mammals, hormones fluctuate cyclically, with accompanying changes in fertility. During the first part of the mammalian cycle (while the egg is being prepared for fertilization), the ovaries secrete estrogen, which prepares the uterus for implantation and also tends to arouse sexual interest. After ovulation occurs, both progesterone and estrogen are secreted. This fertility or estrous cycle is accompanied by a variation in sexual motivation in most mammalian species. Most female animals are receptive to sexual advances by a male only during the period of ovulation, when the estrogen level is at its highest; during this time, the female is said to be "in heat." Among primates, however, sexual activity is less strongly influenced by the fertility cycle. Monkey, ape, and chimpanzee females copulate during all phases of the cycle, although ovulation is still the period of most intense sexual activity. In the human female, sexual desire and arousal seem to be affected much more by social and emotional factors.

In sum, the degree of hormonal control over sexual behavior is lower in humans than in other animals. Still, even for humans there may be some hormonal control, as witnessed by the relationship between testosterone levels and sexual desire in men.

The Neural Basis of Behavior

NEURAL CONTROL In one sense, the primary sex organ is the brain. The brain is where sexual desire originates and where sexual behavior is controlled. In humans, the sexual function of the brain extends to the control of sexual thoughts, images, and fantasies. Within the brain, sexual hormones can influence neural function in adult individuals. Next, we discuss how sexual hormones also influence the physical growth and connection patterns of neurons in early life for all mammalian species, including humans, and in adults for at least some species (Breedlove, 1994).

The nervous system is affected by sexual hormones at many levels. At the level of the spinal cord, neural circuits control the movements of copulation. In males, these include erection of the penis, pelvic movements, and ejaculation. All of these actions can be elicited in a reflex fashion in men whose spinal cords have been severed by injury and who have no conscious body sensations. Similarly, clinical studies of women with spinal injury indicate that vaginal secretions in response to genital stimulation and pelvic movements may be controlled by neural reflex circuits within the spinal cord (Offir, 1982).

Higher levels of the brain, especially the hypothalamus, contain the neural systems that are important to more complex aspects of sexual behavior. For example, sexual pursuit and copulation can be elicited in both males and females of many animal species by electrical stimulation of hypothalamic regions. Even in humans, stimulation of brain regions near the hypothalamus has been reported to induce intense sexual feelings and desire (Heath, 1972). Conversely, lesions of the hypothalamus can eliminate sexual behavior in many species, including humans. ▮

Sexual play among snow monkeys. Normal heterosexual behavior in primates depends not only on hormones and the development of specific sexual responses but also on an affectional bond with a member of the other sex.

EARLY EXPERIENCES The environment also influences adult sexuality. Early experience is a major determinant of the sexual behavior of many mammals and can affect specific sexual responses. For instance, in their play, young monkeys exhibit many of the postures required later for copulation. When wrestling with their peers, infant male monkeys display hindquarter grasping and thrusting responses that are components of adult sexual behavior. Infant female monkeys retreat when threatened by an aggressive male infant and stand steadfastly in a posture similar to the stance required to support the weight of the male during copulation. These presexual responses appear as early as 60 days of age and become more frequent and refined as the monkey matures. Their early appearance suggests that they are innate responses to specific stimuli, and the modification and refinement of these responses through experience indicate that learning plays a role in the development of the adult sexual pattern.

Experience also affects the interpersonal aspect of sex. Monkeys raised in partial isolation (in separate wire cages, where they can see other monkeys but cannot have contact with them) are usually unable to copulate at maturity. The male monkeys are able to perform the mechanics of sex: They masturbate to ejaculation at about the same frequency as normal monkeys. But when confronted with a sexually receptive female, they do not seem to know how to assume the correct posture for copulation. They are aroused, but they aimlessly grope the female or their own bodies. Their problem is not just a deficiency of specific responses. These monkeys have social or affectional problems. Even in nonsexual situations, they are unable to relate to other monkeys, exhibiting either fear and flight or extreme aggression. Apparently, normal heterosexual behavior in primates depends not only on hormones and the development of specific sexual responses but also on an affectional bond with a member of the other sex. This bond is an outgrowth of earlier interactions with the mother and peers, through which the young monkey learns to trust, to expose its delicate parts without fear of harm, to accept and enjoy physical contact with others, and to be motivated to seek the company of others (Harlow, 1971).

Although we must be cautious about generalizing these findings to human sexual development, clinical observations of human infants suggest certain parallels. Human infants develop their first feelings of trust and affection through a warm and loving relationship with their primary caretaker (see Chapter 3). This basic trust is a prerequisite for satisfactory interactions with peers. And affectionate relationships with other youngsters of both sexes lay the groundwork for the intimacy required for sexual relationships among adults.

CULTURAL INFLUENCES Culture also influences the expression of sexual desire. Unlike that of other primates, human sexual behavior is strongly determined by culture. For example, every society places some restrictions on sexual behavior. Incest (sexual relations within the family) is prohibited in almost all cultures. Other aspects of sexual behavior—sexual activity among children, homosexuality, masturbation, and premarital sex—are permitted in varying degrees by different societies. Among preliterate cultures, acceptable sexual activity varies widely. Some very permissive societies encourage autoerotic activities and sex play among children of both sexes and allow them to observe adult sexual activity. The Chewa of Africa, for example, believe that if children are not allowed to exercise themselves sexually, they will be unable to produce offspring later. The Sambia of New Guinea have institutionalized bisexuality: From prepuberty until marriage, a boy lives with other males and engages in homosexual practices (Herdt, 1984).

In contrast, very restrictive societies try to control preadolescent sexual behavior and prevent children from learning about sex. The Cuna of South America believe that children should be totally ignorant about sex until they are married; they do not even permit their children to watch animals give birth.

Although the most obvious way to study cultural differences is to investigate practices in different countries, one can also look at culture changes that occur

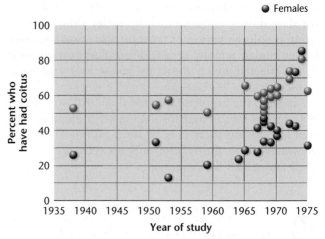

● Males
● Females

Figure 10-7
Reported Incidence of Premarital Coitus
Each data point represents findings from a study of the incidence of premarital sex among college men and women. Note the marked upward trend starting in the 1960s. (J. R. Hopkins (1977) "Sexual Behavior in Adolescence," in *Journal of Social Issues,* Vol. 33(2):67–85. Adapted with permission of the Society for the Psychological Study of Social Issues.)

within a country. One such change occurred in the United States and other Western countries between the 1940s and the 1970s. In the 1940s and 1950s, the United States and most other Western countries would have been classified as sexually restrictive. Traditionally, the existence of prepubertal sexuality had been ignored or denied. Marital sex was considered the only legitimate sexual outlet, and other forms of sexual expression (homosexual activities, premarital and extramarital sex) were generally condemned and often prohibited by law. Of course, many members of these societies engaged in such activities, but often with feelings of shame.

Over the years, sexual activities became less restricted. Premarital intercourse became more acceptable and more frequent. Among American college-educated individuals interviewed in the 1940s, 27% of the women and 49% of the men had engaged in premarital sex by age 21 (Kinsey, Pomeroy, & Martin, 1948; Kinsey, Pomeroy, Martin, & Gebhard, 1953). In contrast, several surveys of American college students conducted in the 1970s reported percentages ranging from 40% to over 80% for both males and females (Hunt, 1974; Tavris & Sadd, 1977). Over the past several decades, there has been a gradual trend toward initiating sex at an earlier age. Roughly 50% of both men and women report having had sexual intercourse by age 16 or 17

(Laumann, Gagnon, Michael, & Michaels, 1994). Figure 10-7 gives the reported incidence of premarital intercourse in studies conducted over a 35-year span. Note that the change in sexual behavior was greater among women than among men and that the biggest changes occurred in the late 1960s. These changes led many observers of the social scene in the 1970s to conclude that a "sexual revolution" had occurred.

Today it seems that the sexual revolution has been stymied by the fear of sexually transmitted diseases, particularly AIDS. Moreover, the "revolution" may have involved behavior more than feelings. In interviews of American college-student couples in the 1970s, only 20% thought that sex between casual acquaintances was completely acceptable (Peplau, Rubin, & Hill, 1977). In a similar vein, although women are becoming more like men with regard to sexual behavior, they continue to differ from men in certain attitudes toward sex before marriage. The majority of women who engage in premarital sex do so with only one or two partners with whom they are emotionally involved. Men, in contrast, are more likely to seek sex with multiple partners (Laumann et al., 1994). However, within a given 5-year period, the majority of both men and women are likely to have no more than one sexual partner (Laumann et al., 1994).

SEX DIFFERENCES Studies of heterosexuals have shown that young men and women differ in their attitudes about sex; women are more likely than men to view sex as part of a loving relationship. Related to this, differences between women and men have been reported in the nature of the type of event that is most likely to elicit sexual jealousy: emotional infidelity or sexual infidelity. Whether measured by self-reports or by autonomic reactions such as heart rate, women react more strongly to the prospect of emotional infidelity (the prospect of their partner's forming a romantic relationship with someone else), regardless of whether the infidelity involves an actual sexual act. By contrast, men react more strongly to the prospect of sexual infidelity, regardless of whether their partner's sexual liaison involves an emotional commitment (Buss, Larsen, Western, & Semmelroth, 1992).

Differences between the sexes apply to behavior as well as to attitudes. Women who engage in premarital sex are likely to have fewer sexual partners than men. Differences between male and female patterns of sexual behavior persist regardless of sexual orientation. For example, lesbian couples are likely to have sex less frequently than heterosexual couples, and gay male couples have sex more often than heterosexual couples. Such differences can be viewed as reflecting a continuum that extends from female-typical characteristics to male-typical characteristics (Buss, 1994).

SEXUAL ORIENTATION

An individual's **sexual orientation** is the degree to which he or she is sexually attracted to persons of the other sex and/or to persons of the same sex. Like Alfred Kinsey, the pioneering sex researcher of the 1940s, most behavioral scientists conceptualize sexual orientation as a continuum, ranging from exclusive heterosexuality to exclusive homosexuality. For example, on Kinsey's own 7-point scale, individuals who are attracted exclusively to persons of the other sex and who engage in sexual behavior only with such persons are at the heterosexual end of the scale (category 0); those who are attracted exclusively to persons of the same sex and who engage in sexual behavior only with such persons are at the homosexual end of the continuum (category 6). Individuals in categories 2 through 4 are usually defined as bisexual.

This oversimplifies the situation, however, because sexual orientation comprises several distinct components, including erotic attraction or sexual desire, sexual behavior, romantic attraction, and self-identification as a heterosexual, homosexual, or bisexual person. It is not uncommon for an individual to be at different points on the scale for different components. For example, many people who are sexually attracted to persons of the same sex have never participated in any homosexual behaviors, and many who have had frequent homosexual encounters do not identify themselves as homosexual or bisexual persons. To further complicate matters, individuals may shift over time on one or more of the components.

FREQUENCY OF DIFFERENT SEXUAL ORIENTATIONS In a survey of sexuality in the United States, 10.1% of adult men and 8.6% of adult women in a national random sample reported at least one of the following: (1) They were currently attracted "mostly" or "only" to persons of their own sex, (2) they found having sex with someone of the same sex "somewhat" or "very" appealing, or (3) they had engaged in sexual behavior with a person of the same sex since age 18 (Laumann et al., 1994). In terms of self-identification, 2.8% of the men and 1.4% of the women in the survey indicated that they considered themselves to be gay, lesbian, or bisexual. To get a sense of how common these attractions and self-identifications are, you might compare them to the percentage of people in the population who are left-handed (about 8%).

As the authors of the survey acknowledge, these percentages must be regarded as underestimates because many people are reluctant to report desires or behaviors that are still considered by some to be immoral or pathological. The problem was particularly acute in this survey because the interviews were conducted in the respondents' own homes, and other family members, including children, were also in the home at the time, although not necessarily in the room, during more than 20% of the interviews.

CAUSES OF SEXUAL ORIENTATION The common question "What causes homosexuality?" is scientifically misconceived because it implicitly assumes either that heterosexuality needs no explanation or that its causes are self-evident. Those who have thought about it at all are likely to conclude that because only heterosexual behavior results in reproduction, it must be the "natural" outcome of evolution, so only deviations from heterosexuality (such as homosexuality) pose a scientific puzzle. Freud himself did not agree: "[heterosexuality] is also a problem that needs elucidation and is not a self-evident fact based upon an attraction that is ultimately of a chemical nature" (1905/1962, pp. 11–12). It is because we agree with Freud that we have called this section of the chapter "sexual orientation" and not "homosexuality."

At issue once again is the nature-nurture question, which we introduced in Chapter 1 and discussed in the chapter on development (Chapter 3) and will discuss again in the chapter on individual differences (Chapter 12): To what extent is an adult's sexual orientation determined by earlier life experiences or to innate biological influences, such as genes or prenatal hormones?

The best data on earlier life experiences comes from an intensive, large-scale interview study of approximately 1,000 homosexual and 500 heterosexual men and women living in the San Francisco Bay area (Bell, Weinberg, & Hammersmith, 1981a). The study uncovered one—and only one—major factor that predicted a homosexual orientation in adulthood for both men and women: childhood gender nonconformity. As shown in Table 10-2, when asked what play activities they had or had not enjoyed as children, gay men and lesbians were significantly more likely than heterosexual men and women to report that they had not enjoyed activities typical of their sex and significantly more likely to report that they had enjoyed activities typical of the other sex. Gay men and lesbians were also more likely than their heterosexual counterparts to report that they had not been masculine (for men) or feminine (for women) as children. In addition to this gender nonconformity, gay men and lesbians were more likely to have had more friends of the other sex.

Two features of the data in Table 10-2 are worth noting. First, the findings are quite strong and similar for men and women: 63% of both gay men and lesbians had not enjoyed childhood activities typical of their sex, compared with only 10% to 15% of their heterosexual counterparts. Second, it is clear that women are more likely than men to have enjoyed activities typical of the other sex during childhood and to have had more childhood friends of the other sex. In fact, a majority of both the lesbians and the heterosexual women in this study were "tomboys"—that is, enjoyed boys' activities as children. It is the nonenjoyment of sex-typical activities that appears to be the best predictor of an adult homosexual orientation for both men and women. The overall finding that childhood gender nonconformity predicts an adult homosexual outcome has now been confirmed in several other studies (Bailey & Zucker, 1995), including several that followed gender-nonconforming boys into adolescence and adulthood and assessed their sexual orientations (Green, 1987; Zucker, 1990).

● **Table 10-2**
Gender Nonconformity in Childhood

In a large-scale interview study, gay men and lesbians were more likely than heterosexual men and women to report that they were gender nonconforming during childhood. *(A. P. Bell, M. A. Weinberg, & S. K. Hammerstein,* Sexual Preference: Its Development in Men & Women.*)*

Gender Nonconforming Preferences and Behaviors	Men		Women	
	Gay	Heterosexual	Lesbian	Heterosexual
Had not enjoyed sex-typical activities	63%	10%	63%	15%
Had enjoyed sex-atypical activities	48%	11%	81%	61%
Atypically sex-typed (masculinity/femininity)	56%	8%	80%	24%
Most childhood friends were other sex	42%	13%	60%	40%

In addition to the gender nonconformity finding, the San Francisco study also yielded many negative findings that were important because they disconfirmed common theories about the antecedents of a homosexual orientation. For example:

- A person's identification with the other-sex parent while growing up appears to have no significant impact on whether he or she turns out to be homosexual or heterosexual. This fails to confirm Freud's psychoanalytic theory (discussed in Chapter 13), as well as other theories based on the dynamics of the person's childhood family.

- Gay men and lesbians were no more likely than their heterosexual counterparts to report having their first sexual encounter with a person of the same sex. Moreover, they neither lacked heterosexual experiences during their childhood and adolescent years nor found such experiences unpleasant.

- A person's sexual orientation is usually determined by adolescence, even though he or she might not yet have become sexually active. Gay men and lesbians typically experienced same-sex attractions about 3 years before they had engaged in any "advanced" sexual activity with persons of the same sex.

These last two sets of findings indicate that, in general, homosexual feelings, not homosexual behaviors, are the crucial antecedents of an adult homosexual orientation. They thus disconfirm any simple behavioral learning theory of sexual orientation, including the popular, laypersons' version, which asserts that an individual can become gay by being "seduced" by a person of the same sex or by having an admired, openly gay teacher, parent, or clergyperson. Cross-cultural data are also consistent with this conclusion. For example, in the Sambian culture of New Guinea, cited earlier, all boys engage in exclusively homosexual behaviors from prepuberty through late adolescence. At that point, virtually all of them marry and become exclusively heterosexual (Herdt, 1984).

Finally, it is clear from all the studies that one's sexual orientation is not something that one simply chooses. Gay men and lesbians do not choose to have erotic feelings toward persons of the same sex any more than heterosexual persons choose to have erotic feelings toward persons of the other sex. As the accompanying essays in the Seeing Both Sides section illustrate, behavioral scientists do disagree over the nature-nurture question—whether the major determinants of sexual orientation are rooted in biology or experience—but the public often misconstrues the question to be whether sexual orientation is determined by variables beyond the individual's control or is freely chosen. That is not the same question.

Because most of the major theories of homosexuality based on childhood or adolescent experiences have not been supported by the evidence, many scientists now believe that the origins of both childhood gender nonconformity and adult homosexual orientation may lie in an individual's biology, possibly in the genes or prenatal hormones. In Seeing Both Sides, two contrasting views of the current biological evidence are presented. One view clearly puts "nature" over "nurture," emphasizing the roles of genes and hormones in causing both childhood gender nonconformity and adult homosexual orientation. The other view, by contrast, takes a "nature *and* nurture" approach (see Chapter 1). It presents a new theory called **exotic-becomes-erotic,** which posits a critical, albeit more limited role for biology in determining sexual orientation. The influence of nature comes first. The theory suggests that genes and hormones cause differences in childhood temperament and personality traits, which for some children can produce a dislike of sex-typical activities and a preference for sex-atypical activities. Next comes the influence of nurture. The theory asserts that engaging in sex-atypical activities places kids in the company of the other sex (rather than the same sex), who come to be seen as similar to the self. Later, when adult sexuality is awakened, the theory contends that people find those who are viewed as different from the self (exotic) to be most sexually attractive (erotic), who turn out to be members of their same sex.

The more general point within combined nature and nurture approaches is that just because a behavior might be advantageous from the standpoint of reproduction, it does not follow that evolution has "hardwired" it into the species (nature only). A similar case for the combined action of nature and nurture can be made for the notion of **imprinting,** which is the early rapid learning that allows a newborn (or newly hatched) animal to develop an attachment to its mother (see Chapter 7). Within the first hours of life, infants of many species are "programmed" to learn an emotional attachment to the closest social figure. Most often this is the mother, but if the first moving object seen is a human or a mobile toy, the imprinting process can produce attachment beyond species boundaries. Imprinting turns out to have consequences for later sexual behavior as well, because mate choices follow maternal imprinting. The imprinting instinct is genetic (nature), but as long as the environment (nurture) supports or promotes reproductively advantageous behavior often enough, attachment and reproductive behaviors need not necessarily get fully programmed into the genes. And just as ducklings encounter mother ducks most of the time, so, too, human societies see to it that men and women see each other as dissimilar often enough to ensure that the species will not perish from the earth.

Is Sexual Orientation Innate or Socially Determined?

SEXUAL IDENTITY COULD BE INNATE
J. Michael Bailey, Northwestern University

For many years, most psychologists assumed that homosexuality was a product of nurture, caused by pathological parent-child relationships or atypical conditioning experiences. However, scientific studies of these possibilities did not provide much support for them. (e.g., Bell, Weinberg, & Hammersmith, 1981). Parents of homosexual people were not very different from those of heterosexual people (and when they were, the direction of causation was unclear). Most homosexual people had homosexual desire long before they had any sexual experiences that could plausibly have led to unusual conditioning. As scientists became disenchanted with social explanations, their attention turned to theories that located the origins of sexual orientation within the person.

The best-established correlate of adult homosexuality is childhood gender nonconformity (Bailey & Zucker, 1995). On average, gay men were feminine boys and lesbians were masculine girls. Childhood gender nonconformity emerges in early childhood apparently despite, rather than because of, socialization pressures. Indeed, extremely feminine boys, who usually become gay men (Green, 1987), often suffer due to reactions to their atypical behavior. The association between sexual orientation and childhood gender nonconformity appears cross-culturally universal (Whitam & Mathy, 1986; Whitam & Mathy, 1991). Although we do not know the precise causes of childhood gender nonconformity, the general picture implicates innateness rather than learning.

More direct evidence comes from studies of siblings, including twins. Gay men tend to have more gay brothers compared with heterosexual men, and lesbians tend to have more lesbian sisters compared with heterosexual women (Bailey & Pillard, 1995). Studies of twins suggest that these patterns reflect genetic influences rather than the environment shared by family members. Identical twins tend to be more similar in their sexual orientations than fraternal twins (Bailey & Pillard, 1995). On the other hand, at least half the time if one identical twin is homosexual, the other twin is heterosexual. Although this establishes an important role for environment in sexual orientation development, environmental influences need not be social. Biological factors can also cause twin differences (Martin, Boomsma, & Machen, 1997). When identical twins have different sexual orientations, they often remember being different as children, implicating early environmental factors. The precise nature of the relevant environmental influences remains unclear, however.

More direct evidence for genetic influences has come from linkage studies that actually look at DNA (Hamer et al., 1993). Pairs of gay brothers tend to have inherited the same piece of the X chromosome, Xq28, more often than would be expected by chance. This suggests that a gene in that region affects male sexual orientation. Supporting this possibility, heterosexual men tend not to have inherited the same version of Xq28 as their gay brothers (Hu et al., 1995).

The most influential theory hypothesizes that there is an area of the brain that affects sexual orientation and that the development of this sexual orientation center depends on the early effects of hormones (Levay, 1996). Thus, according to the theory, gay men have feminine sexual orientation centers, and lesbians have masculine centers. Two cases of boys whose penises were accidentally destroyed early in life and who were subsequently reared as females are also relevant. As adults, both individuals were primarily attracted to women, consistent with their prenatal biology rather than postnatal rearing (Bradley, Oliver, Chernick, & Zuckner, 1998; Diamond & Sigmundson, 1996). One study actually compared the brains of gay men to those of heterosexual men and women, and found that one nucleus (a clump of related cells) was larger in the brains of heterosexual men than in those of gay men, whose brains looked like those of heterosexual women (LeVay, 1991). This nucleus was in the hypothalamus, which is known to be important for sexual behavior. The hypothalamus probably develops very early in humans, and thus this difference between gay and heterosexual men was unlikely to be caused by different experiences.

The origins of sexual orientation remain controversial, and there is much work to be done. Many of the most important findings (e.g., Hamet et al., 1993; LeVay, 1991) need to be replicated. At this point, a role for the social environment cannot be excluded, although little if

J. Michael Bailey

any empirical research has supported such a role. In contrast, the scientific search for innate origins has produced a steady stream of findings.

Is Sexual Orientation Innate or Socially Determined?

SEXUAL ORIENTATION COULD BE SOCIALLY DETERMINED
Daryl J. Bem, Cornell University

Dr. Bailey and I agree on the evidence showing a link or correlation between biological variables and sexual orientation. But, I propose an alternative interpretation of the biological evidence: the Exotic-Becomes-Erotic (EBE) theory of sexual orientation (Bem, 1996). The path proposed by this theory is illustrated in the figure.

A → B The theory proposes, first, that genetic, hormonal, and possibly other biological factors do not directly influence adult sexual orientation itself but, rather, influence a child's temperament and personality traits. Many personality traits have a strong genetic or heritable component, including such childhood temperaments as aggression and activity level.

B → C Temperaments such as these predispose a child to enjoy some activities more than others: A more aggressive or active child will enjoy rough-and-tumble play (boy-typical activities); another will prefer to socialize quietly (girl-typical activities). Thus, depending on the sex of the child, he or she will be genetically predisposed to be gender conforming or gender nonconforming. As shown in Table 10-2, children also tend to have friends who share their activity preferences; for example, the child—male or female—who shuns competitive team sports will avoid playing with boys and seek out girls as playmates.

C → D Accordingly, gender conforming children will feel more different from children of the other sex; gender nonconforming children will feel more different from children of the same sex—that is, to see them as relatively more "exotic" than children of the other sex.

D → E This feeling of being different creates heightened arousal. For the male-typical child, it may be felt as antipathy or contempt in the presence of girls ("girls are yucky"); for the female-typical child, it may be felt as timidity or apprehension in the presence of boys.

For most children, however, this arousal will probably not be consciously felt.

E → F This arousal is transformed in later years into sexual arousal or erotic attraction: Exotic becomes erotic. Evidence for this last step comes, in part, from studies in which heterosexual male participants who had been physiologically (but nonsexually) aroused were found to be more sexually attracted to a woman than were men who had not been physiologically aroused. In other words, general physiological arousal can be subsequently experienced as, interpreted as, or actually transformed into sexual arousal.

Evidence for the theory's claim that childhood gender nonconformity intervenes between biological variables and sexual orientation actually comes from the same studies that Dr. Bailey cites as showing the link between the two. For example, the studies of twins that he cites also found that pairs of identical twins were more similar than pairs of fraternal twins on childhood gender nonconformity. Similarly, the DNA studies found that pairs of gay brothers who share the same piece of the X chromosome are also more alike on gender nonconformity than are gay brothers who do not share it. A more recent analysis of data from a large study of Australian twins shows more directly that childhood gender nonconformity is, in fact, the intervening link between the genes and sexual orientation (Bem, 2000). In short, the studies showing a link between biological variables and an adult homosexual orientation are consistent with EBE theory's assertion that the biology leads first to gender-nonconforming interests and preferences in childhood and, only subsequently, to the adult homosexual orientation. Nevertheless, the studies do not prove that the theory is correct; Only additional research can help us to decide.

Finally, it should be noted that EBE theory applies as much to heterosexuality as to homosexuality. Because most societies emphasize the differences between males and females, most boys and girls will grow up feeling different from their other-sex peers and, hence, will come to be erotically attracted to them later in life. This is why heterosexuality is the most common orientation across time and culture.

GENDER AND SEXUALITY 383

Throughout this chapter, we have seen that psychological and biological causes are so closely intertwined in the control of many motivations that they merge into one stream of events. Not only can biological causes control psychological motivations like hunger and thirst, but psychological processes and experiences control motivation and may feed back to control physiological responses. For example, repeated use of an addictive drug may permanently change particular brain systems. More commonly, the particular foods and drinks we desire are established as objects of choice largely by learning, and even the degree of satiety produced by a stomach full of food is influenced by previous experience. Our social attachments are determined largely by the consequences of earlier social interactions with particular individuals. When it comes to many motivational processes, biology and psychology are not separate domains but, rather, two aspects of control that continually interact to direct motivational processes.

◆ Interim Summary

- Prenatal hormones contribute to sexual development. If the embryonic sex glands produce enough androgen hormones, the embryo will have a male pattern of genital and brain development. If androgens are low or missing, the embryo will have a female pattern of genital and brain development.

- For nonhuman animals, prenatal hormones appear to be powerful determinants of adult sexual behavior. For humans, prenatal hormones appear to be less important than postnatal social gender roles in determining adult sexual behavior.

- The female hormones (estrogen and progesterone) and male hormones (androgens) are responsible for the changes in the body that occur at puberty, but in contrast to other animals, they play a limited role in human sexual arousal. In primates and humans, early social experiences with parents and peers have a large influence on adult sexuality, and for humans, cultural norms are also influential.

- Recent studies have bolstered the claim that biological, genetic, hormonal, or neural factors may partly determine whether an individual will be heterosexual or homosexual, but the evidence is not conclusive. It is also unknown whether biological factors may influence sexual orientation directly or whether they instead contribute to other traits, such as gender conformity, that indirectly influence the development of sexual orientation.

◆ Critical Thinking Questions

1. How does sexual identity differ from sexual orientation?

2. Why do you think many people believe that sexual desire and activity in humans is strongly influenced by hormones when the evidence suggests that it is not?

1. Motivational states direct and activate behavior. They arise from two sources: internal drive factors and external incentive factors.

2. Incentive factors are goals in the outside world, such as food, water, sexual partners, and drugs. Incentives are the target of motivated behavior and are typically rewarding. Although some incentives—such as a sweet food when we are hungry—are powerful motivators by themselves, most incentives are established through learning.

3. Many types of natural rewards may activate the brain's dopamine system. Activity in these neurons may constitute the neural basis for all incentives or "wants." Artificial activation of these neurons by drugs or electrical brain stimulation causes increased motivation for both natural and artificial incentives. Changes in this system, produced by repeatedly taking drugs that activate it, may partly cause the compulsive craving of addiction.

4. Drive factors tend to promote homeostasis: the preservation of a constant internal state. Homeostasis involves several components: a goal value or set point for the ideal internal state, a sensory signal that measures the actual internal state, a comparison between the goal value and the sensory signal, and finally, a response that brings the actual internal state closer to the goal value.

5. Regulation of temperature is an example of homeostasis. The regulated variable is the temperature of the blood, and sensors for this are located in various parts of the body, including the hypothalamus. Adjustments are either automatic physiological responses (for example, shivering) or voluntary behavioral ones (such as putting on a sweater).

6. Thirst is another homeostatic motive. There are two regulated variables, intracellular fluid and extracellular fluid. Loss of intracellular fluid is detected by osmotic sensors, neurons in the hypothalamus that respond to dehydration. Loss of extracellular fluid is detected by blood-pressure sensors, neurons in major veins and organs that respond to a drop in pressure. Intracellular and extracellular signals act together to produce thirst.

7. Hunger has evolved to allow us to select an array of nutrients. Humans have innate taste preferences, such as for sweetness, and innate aversions, such as for bitterness, that guide our choice of foods. In addition, we may develop a wide variety of learned preferences and aversions. Homeostatic hunger signals, which arise when the body is low in calorie-containing fuels such as glucose, produce appetite partly by causing the indi-

vidual to perceive food incentives as more attractive and pleasant.

8. Hunger is largely controlled by homeostatic deficit and satiety signals. Certain neurons in the brain, especially in the brain stem and hypothalamus, detect shortages in glucose and trigger hunger. Other nutrient detectors, especially in the liver, detect increasing energy stores and trigger satiety. A satiety signal, in the form of the hormone cholecystokinin, is released from the intestines to help stop hunger and eating.

9. Two regions of the brain are critical to hunger: the lateral hypothalamus and the ventromedial hypothalamus. Destruction of the lateral hypothalamus leads to undereating; destruction of the ventromedial hypothalamus leads to overeating. Although these regions were originally thought to be centers for hunger and satiety, hunger is not destroyed by any lesion. Another interpretation of these effects is that the two regions of the hypothalamus exert reciprocal effects on the homeostatic set point for body weight. Damage to the lateral hypothalamus may lower the set point, and damage to the ventromedial hypothalamus may raise the set point. Diet drugs that alter appetite may work partly by affecting neurons in these regions of the hypothalamus.

10. People become obese primarily because: (1) they are genetically predisposed to be overweight or (2) they overeat (for psychological reasons). The influence of genes is mediated by their effect on fat cells, metabolic rate, and set points. As for overeating and obesity, obese people tend to overeat when they break a diet, eat more when emotionally aroused, and are more responsive to external hunger cues than normal-weight individuals. In treating obesity, extreme diets appear ineffective because the deprivation leads to subsequent overeating and to a lowered metabolic rate. What seems to work best is to establish a new set of permanent eating habits and engage in a program of exercise.

11. Anorexia nervosa is characterized by extreme, self-imposed weight loss. Bulimia is characterized by recurrent episodes of binge eating, followed by attempts to purge the excess by means of vomiting and laxatives. Possible causes of these eating disorders include personality factors such as low self-esteem, social factors such as a cultural emphasis on thinness and pervasive cultural messages that objectify the female body, and biological factors such as low serotonin levels.

12. Prenatal hormones contribute to sexual development. If the embryonic sex glands produce enough androgen hormones, the embryo will have a male pattern of genital and brain development. If androgens are low

or missing, the embryo will have a female pattern of genital and brain development. For nonhuman animals, prenatal hormones appear to be powerful determinants of adult sexual behavior. For humans, prenatal hormones appear to be much less important, although they may still play a role in later sexual behavior. In cases in which the hormonal exposure of the embryo is typical of one sex but the social role and gender after birth is more typical of the other sex (due to hormone imbalance, prenatal drugs, or a postnatal accident), the individual's development seems to correspond most closely to the postnatal social gender.

13. The female hormones (estrogen and progesterone) and male hormones (androgens) are responsible for the changes in the body that occur at puberty, but they play a limited role in human sexual arousal. In contrast, in other animals there is substantial hormonal control over sex. Early social experiences with parents and peers have a large influence on adult sexuality in primates and humans. For humans, other environmental determinants of adult sexuality include cultural norms. Although Western society has become increasingly flexible regarding female and male sex roles, men and women may still differ in their attitudes toward sex and relationships.

14. Recent studies have bolstered the claim that biological, genetic, hormonal, or neural factors may partly determine whether an individual will be heterosexual or homosexual, but the evidence is not conclusive. It is also unknown whether biological factors may influence sexual orientation directly or whether they instead contribute to other traits, such as gender conformity, that indirectly influence the development of sexual orientation.

CORE CONCEPTS

motivation
drive theories
incentive theories
primary reinforcers
secondary reinforcers
incentive motivation
affect
incentive salience
wanting
liking
brain's dopamine system
addiction
tolerance

withdrawal
neural sensitization
homeostasis
set point
thirst
extracellular thirst
intracellular thirst
conditioned aversion
sham feeding
conditioned satiety
alliesthesia
lateral hypothalamic syndrome

ventromedial hypothalamic
    syndrome
obese
anorexia nervosa
bulimia
objectification theory
self-objectification
gender identity
androgenization
sexual orientation
exotic-becomes-erotic
imprinting

WEB RESOURCES

http://psychology.wadsworth.com/
atkinson14e

Take a quiz, try the activities and exercises, and explore web links.

http://www.obesity-news.com/

This site contains a vast array of information about obesity research and weight loss drug development.

http://www.eating-disorders.com/

This site provides information about different eating disorders and discusses some of the underlying causes of the disorders. Here you can join a discussion, ask questions, or get inspiration and help.

http://www.indiana.edu/kinsey/

Provided by the pioneering Kinsey Institute, this site provides extensive coverage of sexuality and links to other sites dealing with "sexology."

 InfoTrac Online Library
http://www.infotrac-college.com/
wadsworth

Use InfoTrac to find popular and scientific articles using the search terms below or your own relevant terms.
- Anorexia
- Bulimia
- Compulsive behavior
- Homeostasis
- Obesity

CD-ROM LINKS

 Psych Odyssey

Check out CD Chapter 12, Motivation and Emotion

A. Motivation

 Psyk.trek 2.0

Check out CD Unit 8, Motivation and Emotion

8a Hunger
8b Achievement Motivation

EMOTION

11

In the 1970s, Ted Bundy lured a woman into a sexual encounter, then killed her. He did this again about 30 times. His desire was to possess a lifeless female form—comatose or dead—and just before his 1989 execution, he admitted to police detectives that he kept some of his victims in such a state for hours or days before he disposed of their bodies. He even photographed his victims and kept a stash of their skulls in his Seattle apartment. Bundy explained, "When you work hard to do something right, you don't want to forget it."

Ted Bundy did not feel remorse, guilt, or shame about violating standards of human decency. On the contrary, he was proud of himself. Later, when facing his own murder trial and probable death sentence, his examining psychiatrist uncovered further unusual emotions. He described Bundy as cheerful and jovial. He stated that although

Bundy "intellectually" understood the charges against him, "he sure didn't act like a man who was facing a death sentence. He was acting like a man who did not have a care in the world." Against the strong urgings of his legal advisors, Bundy even chose to serve as counsel in his own defense. As his psychiatrist later explained, "[Bundy] was not motivated by a need to help himself. He was motivated by the need to be the star of the show. . . . He was the producer of a play in which he was playing a big role. The defense and his future were of secondary importance to him." Ted Bundy had no fear for future consequences.

Emotions, it turns out, are so central to human experience and successful social encounters that we consider those who seem to have no emotions—like the serial killer who shows no shame or no fear—to be inhuman. We call such people cold-blooded. This label fits, because although we share basic motives such as hunger and sex with cold-blooded reptiles, we seem to share emotions only with other warm-blooded mammals (Panksepp, 1998).

People like Ted Bundy are, in fact, thought to have specific biological and social-cognitive deficits. They are said to have **antisocial personality disorder** (and are sometimes called *psychopaths* or *sociopaths*), **a disorder characterized by deficits in normal emotional responding—especially for shame, guilt, and fear—as well as deficits in empathy for the emotions of others** (Hare, 1999). And yet people like Ted Bundy are not completely devoid of emotions. Instead, "they seem to suffer a kind of emotional poverty that limits the range and depth of their feelings. While at times they appear cold and unemotional, they are prone to shallow and short-lived displays of feeling. . . .

Many clinicians have commented that the emotions of psychopaths are so shallow as to be of little more than 'proto-emotions'—primitive responses to immediate needs" (Hare, 1999, p. 52). In this chapter we will explore what Ted Bundy seemed to lack—the full array of meaningful human emotions.

Emotions and motives (discussed in Chapter 10) are closely related. Emotions can activate and direct behavior in the same way that basic motives do. They may also accompany motivated behavior: Sex, for example, is not only a powerful motive but also a potential source of joy. Despite their similarities, we need to distinguish between motives and emotions. One distinction is that emotions are triggered from the outside, whereas motives are activated from within. That is, emotions are usually aroused by external circumstances, and emotional reactions are directed toward these circumstances. Motives, in contrast, are often aroused by internal circumstances (such as a homeostatic imbalance) and are naturally directed toward particular objects in the environment (such as food, water, or a mate). Another distinction between motives and emotions is that a motive is usually elicited by a specific need, but an emotion can be elicited by a wide variety of stimuli (think of all the different things that can make you angry or happy).

These distinctions are not absolute. An external source can sometimes trigger a motive, as when the sight of food triggers hunger. And the discomfort caused by a homeostatic imbalance—severe hunger, for example—can arouse emotions. Nevertheless, emotions and motives are different enough in their sources, subjective experience, and effects on behavior that they merit separate treatment.

COMPONENTS OF EMOTION

An **emotion** is a complex, multicomponent episode that creates a readiness to act. An intense emotion has at least six components (Frijda, 1986; Lazarus, 1991b). Typically, an emotion begins with a **cognitive appraisal**, a person's assessment of the personal meaning of his or her current circumstances (see Figure 11-1). This appraisal process is considered the first component of an emotion. Cognitive appraisals, in turn, trigger a cascade of responses that represent other loosely connected components of an emotion. The component that we most frequently recognize is the **subjective experience** of the emotion—the affective state or feeling tone the emotion brings. A third and closely related component includes **thought and action tendencies**—urges to think and act in certain ways. When something sparks your interest, for instance, you want to explore it and learn more about it. When someone angers you, you may be tempted to aggress, either physically or verbally. A fourth component includes internal bodily reactions, especially those of the **autonomic nervous system,** the division of the peripheral nervous system that controls the heart and other smooth muscles (see Chapter 2). When you are afraid, for example, your heart may pound in your chest, and your palms may sweat. A fifth component of an emotion includes **facial expressions,** the muscle actions that move facial landmarks in particular ways. When you experience disgust, for example, you probably frown while also raising your upper lip and partially closing your eyes, as if to shut out the smell and sight of whatever offends you. The final component includes **responses to emotion,** meaning how people cope with or react to their own emotion or the situation that elicited it. The Concept Review table reviews these various components.

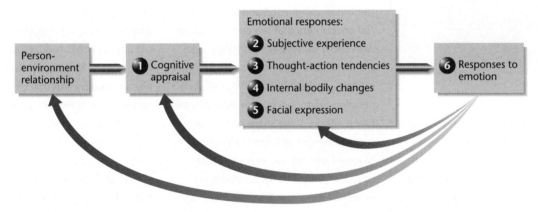

▌ Figure 11-1
Schematic Diagram of the Emotion Process
Six components of emotion are triggered by circumstances described by certain person-environment relationships. (After Lazarus, 1991b; Rosenberg, 1998)

CONCEPT REVIEW TABLE
Six Components of the Emotion Process

Cognitive appraisal	a person's assessment of the personal meaning of his or her current circumstances
Subjective experience	the affective state or feeling tone that colors private experience
Thought and action tendencies	urges to think or act in particular ways
Internal bodily changes	physiological responses, particularly those involving the autonomic nervous system such as changes in heart rate and sweat gland activity
Facial expression	muscle contractions that move facial landmarks—like cheeks, lips, noses, and brows—into particular configurations
Responses to emotion	how people regulate, react to, or cope with their own emotion or the situation that triggered it

None of these six components by itself is an emotion. Instead, they come together to create a particular emotion. Viewing emotion as a complex system helps distinguish emotions from closely related states, like moods. Emotions are distinct from moods in multiple ways. First, emotions typically have a clear cause. They are about something or someone (Oatley & Jenkins, 1996). You are angry *at* your sister. You are awestruck *by* the Grand Canyon. **Moods,** on the other hand, are often free-floating and diffuse affective states (Russell & Feldman Barrett, 1999). For unknown reasons, you feel irritable one day, and cheerful the next. This raises a second difference: Emotions are typically brief, lasting only seconds or minutes, but moods endure longer, lasting for hours, even days. A third difference is that emotions typically implicate the multiple component systems described previously, but moods may be salient only at the level of subjective experience (Rosenberg, 1998; Russell & Feldman Barrett, 1999). Finally, emotions are often conceptualized as fitting into discrete categories, like fear, anger, joy, and interest. Moods, by contrast, are often conceptualized as varying along the dimensions of pleasantness and arousal level (Russell & Feldman Barrett, 1999). This last point is still hotly debated, however. An example of this debate is provided in the Seeing Both Sides box later in this chapter.

Many emotion theorists take a systems perspective on emotion, in which the components of an emotion are seen as having reciprocal effects on each other. In other words, each component can influence the others. Whereas Figure 11-1 outlines the typical way that an emotion unfolds—through cognitive appraisal (Reisenzein, 1983)—laboratory experiments have shown that introducing another component of an emotion first—like physiological arousal or a facial expression—can jumpstart the entire, multicomponent emotion process. Let's say you race up four flights of stairs and arrive at your dorm room with your heart pounding. In that aroused state, you may be more likely to appraise an ambiguous remark from your roommate (such as "nice hair") as an insult and lash out. The critical questions in contemporary emotion research concern the detailed nature of each of the components of an emotion and the specific mechanisms by which they influence each other. For example, one set of questions concerns the functions of each component. Why do emotions color subjective experience? Why do they evoke bodily changes? Why do they show up on our faces? Another set of questions concerns how responses of the various components contribute to the intensity of an experienced emotion. Do you feel angrier when you experience more arousal of your autonomic nervous system? Indeed, could you even feel angry if you had no autonomic arousal? Similarly, does the intensity of your anger depend on your having a certain kind of thought or a certain kind of facial expression? In contrast to these questions about the intensity of an emotion, there are also questions about which components of an emotion are responsible for making the different emotions feel different. To appreciate the difference between questions about intensity and questions about differentiation, consider the possibility that autonomic arousal greatly increases the intensity of our emotions but that the pattern of arousal is roughly the same for several emotions. In this case, autonomic arousal could not differentiate among emotions.

These questions will guide us in this chapter as we consider cognitive appraisals, subjective experiences, bodily changes, and facial expressions. We will also consider people's responses to their own emotions and their attempts to regulate their emotional experiences. We then discuss gender and cultural variation in emotions. In the final section, we turn to aggression, which is at times a reflection of intense emotion and a topic of considerable societal importance. Throughout, we will be concerned primarily with the most intense and prototypic emotions, like anger, fear, sadness and disgust on the negative side and joy, interest, and contentment on the positive side. Even so, the ideas and principles that will emerge in our discussion are relevant to a variety of feelings.

◆ Interim Summary

- An emotion is a complex, multicomponent episode that creates a readiness to act.

- There are six components of emotions: cognitive appraisals, the subjective experiences of emotion, thought-action tendencies, internal bodily changes, facial expressions, and responses to the emotion.

- Emotions are distinct from moods in several ways. For instance, emotions have clear causes, are particularly brief, and implicate multiple components.

◆ Critical Thinking Questions

1. Reconsider Figure 11-1, which describes the six components of the emotion process. Do you think that all six components need to be present in order to call a given experience an emotion? Why or why not? What might be the rationale for including responses to emotion as the sixth component?

2. Drawing from your own day-to-day experiences, can you identify the difference between an emotion and a mood? Do emotions and moods feel different, subjectively?

COGNITIVE APPRAISAL AND EMOTION

You will notice in Figure 11-1 that the first box in the model mentions the **person-environment relationship.** This refers to the objective situation in which a person finds herself—her current circumstances in the world, or in relation to others. One such circumstance, for instance, is receiving an insult; another is facing a colorful sunset. These person-environment relationships are not themselves components of emotions, because they do not always or directly trigger emotions. For these circumstances to produce an emotion in us, we would need to interpret them as relevant to our personal goals or well-being. This interpretation process is cognitive appraisal. For instance, you might interpret receiving an insult as a threat to your honor. If so, you'd experience anger. In another instance, you might interpret that same insult as the meaningless ranting of an erratic person and experience no emotion whatsoever. Likewise, if you are a spiritual person, you might interpret the sunset as evidence of God's immense power and artistry and experience a mixture of awe and gratitude. On another evening, you might be frightened by the impending loss of daylight, because you're on a day hike (with no flashlight) and worry that you can't make it back to camp before dark. It is through this appraisal process, then, that we assess whether the current person-environment relationship impinges on our goals or well-being. If it does, the appraisal process translates the objective circumstance into a personally meaningful one. Personal meaning, in turn, determines the type of emotion we experience, as well as its intensity (Lazarus, 1991b).

Cognitive appraisals are largely responsible for differentiating the emotions. Indeed, we often emphasize cognitive appraisals when we describe the quality of an emotion. We say, "I was angry because she was unfair" or "I was frightened because I was abandoned." Assessments of unfairness and abandonment are clearly abstract beliefs that result from a cognitive process. These observations suggest that cognitive appraisals are often sufficient to determine the quality of emotional experience.

DISCOVERY OF APPRAISALS

The importance of this cognitive component within emotions was first spotlighted in a famous study in the early 1960s. Schachter and Singer (1962) suggested that if people could be induced to be in a general state of autonomic arousal, the quality of their emotion would be determined solely by their appraisal of the situation (see Figure 11-2a). This was called the **two-factor theory** of emotions. According to this theory, emotions were thought to result from the combination of two factors— an initial state of unexplained arousal plus a cognitive explanation (or appraisal) for that arousal. We will discuss the James-Lange Theory and the Facial Feedback Hypothesis (included in Figure 11-2) later in this chapter.

Participants in Schachter and Singer's study were given an injection of epinephrine, which typically causes autonomic arousal—an increase in heart and respiration rates, muscle tremors, and a jittery feeling. The experimenter then manipulated the information that the participants were given regarding the effects of the injection. Some participants were correctly informed about the arousal consequences of the drug, but others were given no information about the drug's physiological effects. The informed participants had an explanation for their sensations, whereas the uninformed participants did not. Schachter and Singer predicted that how the uninformed participants interpreted their symptoms would depend on the situation in which they were placed. Participants were left in a waiting room with another person, ostensibly another participant but actually a confederate of the experimenter. The confederate created either a happy situation (by making paper airplanes, playing basketball

a) Two-Factor Theory

Stimulus ➡ General physiological arousal ➡ Cognitive appraisal of arousal ➡ Subjective experience of the emotion

b) James-Lange Theory

Stimulus ➡ Physiological arousal specific to an emotion ➡ Subjective experience of the emotion

c) Facial Feedback Hypothesis

Facial expression ➡ Subjective experience of the emotion

❙ **Figure 11-2**
Classic Theories of Emotion
Early theories of emotion proposed different relationships between the components of emotion.

with wads of paper, and so on) or an angry situation (by complaining about the experiment, tearing up a questionnaire, and so on). The uninformed participants placed in the happy situation rated their feelings as happier than the informed participants in that situation did. Although the data were less clear for the angry situation, Schachter and Singer claimed that the uninformed participants were angrier than the informed participants. In other words, participants who had a physiological explanation for their arousal appeared to be less influenced by the situation than participants who did not have the explanation.

The Schachter and Singer experiment was extremely influential over the next two decades, but that influence may not have been justified (Reisenzein, 1983). The pattern of results in the study did not strongly support the experimenters' hypotheses, in that the differences between critical groups did not reach statistical significance and a control group did not react in a manner consistent with the hypotheses. In addition, the autonomic arousal may not have been the same in the happy and angry situations, and it certainly was not neutral. Follow-up experiments have found that participants rate their experiences more negatively (less happy or more angry) than the situation warrants, suggesting that the physiological arousal produced by epinephrine is experienced as somewhat unpleasant. Also, later experimenters have had difficulty reproducing the results obtained by Schachter and Singer (Marshall & Zimbardo, 1979; Maslach, 1979; Mezzacappa, Katkin, & Palmer, 1999). We need further evidence that completely neutral arousal may be mistakenly attributed to a particular emotion.

Another study supplied such evidence. Participants first engaged in strenuous physical exercise and then participated in a task, during which they were provoked by a confederate of the experimenter. The exercise created physiological arousal that was neutral and that persisted until the participant was provoked. This arousal should have combined with any arousal elicited by the provocation, resulting in a more intense response of anger. In fact, participants who had just exercised responded more aggressively to the provocation than those who did not (Zillmann & Bryant, 1974). Although these results do not support Schachter and Singer's two-factor theory per se, they do support a more limited effect, called the **misattribution of arousal.** This effect means that lingering physiological arousal—say, from running up four flights of stairs—can be mistakenly attributed to subsequent circumstances—like an ambiguous remark, "nice hair"—and intensify our emotional reactions to those circumstances. In the case of our earlier example, the lingering arousal could fuel anger. This effect has been replicated in many studies.

Schachter and Singer's famous study, along with the later work on the misattribution of arousal, is important because it created a central role for cognitive appraisals within the emotion process. Even so, the two-factor theory did little to explain how emotions unfold outside the laboratory (Reisenzein, 1983). This is because Schachter and Singer's first factor of unexplained physiological arousal may occur only rarely in real life. Think for a moment of the last time you were really afraid. Where were you? What happened? As you visualize the details of that experience, try to locate the moment when you experienced *unexplained* arousal. Suppose you experienced fear while snorkeling when you saw a shark. Although you did sense a huge adrenalin rush, that arousal was never unexplained. The shark was the explanation! Or more precisely, your appraisal that the shark endangered you was the explanation.

Departing from Schachter and Singer, most contemporary appraisal theorists would place the component of cognitive appraisal *before* the component of physiological arousal, not after it. But, as Schachter and Singer suggested, the perceived arousal and cognitive appraisal are not experienced as independent. Rather, the arousal is attributed to the appraisal—"My heart is racing because I'm so angry about what Mary said." So both arousal and appraisal contribute to the intensity of experience—and sometimes appraisal alone can determine the quality of experience.

THEMES AND DIMENSIONS OF APPRAISALS

The model of emotion presented in Figure 11-1 is consistent with various appraisal theories of emotion. All appraisal theories are alike in that they suggest that people's appraisals of situations (not their appraisals of physiological arousal) lead to the subjective experience of emotion, the arousal associated with it, and other components of the emotional response. Yet various appraisal theories differ in how they conceptualize the appraisal process. These theories can be divided into (1) **minimalist appraisal theories,** which reduce the number of appraisal dimensions to minimum, often based on fundamental themes, and (2) **dimensional appraisal theories,** which identify a range of appraisal dimensions thought to be sufficient to account for differences among emotions.

According to the minimalist appraisal theories, there are certain fundamental human transactions that yield specific emotions. One appraisal theorist, Richard Lazarus (1991b), identifies these fundamental transactions as core relational themes. A **core relational theme** represents the personal meaning that results from a particular pattern of appraisals about a specific person-environment relationship. It distills the appraisal process

Emotions and Their Cognitive Causes

Fifteen emotions and their associated core relational themes (appraisal patterns). *(After Lazarus, 1991b)*

Emotion	Core Relational Theme
Anger	A demeaning offense against me and mine
Anxiety	Facing uncertain, existential threat
Fright	Facing an immediate, concrete, and overwhelming physical danger
Guilt	Having transgressed a moral imperative
Shame	Having failed to live up to an ego ideal
Sadness	Having experienced an irrevocable loss
Envy	Wanting what someone else has
Jealousy	Resenting a third party for loss or threat to another's affection
Disgust	Taking in or being too close to an indigestible object or idea (metaphorically speaking)
Happiness	Making reasonable progress toward the realization of a goal
Pride	Enhancing our ego identity by taking credit for a valued object or achievement, either our own or that of some person or group with whom we identify
Relief	A distressing goal-incongruent condition has changed for the better or gone away
Hope	Fearing the worst but yearning for better
Love	Desiring or participating in affection, usually but not necessarily reciprocated
Compassion	Being moved by another's suffering and wanting to help

● Table 11-2
Primary Appraisal Dimensions and Their Consequences

Combinations of two appraisal dimensions and their associated emotions. *(After Roseman, 1984)*

	Occur	Not Occur
Desirable	Joy	Sorrow
Undesirable	Distress	Relief

to its essence. Table 11-1 lists several emotions (such as sadness) and the core relational themes that trigger them (for sadness, irrevocable loss). These fundamental themes and their associated emotions can be found in every human culture. Some circumstances are appraised the same by almost everyone. For example, for most humans and even most animals, being near a large hissing snake tends to be appraised as threatening. Even so, the types of circumstances that elicit the appraisal patterns listed in Table 11-1 may differ across cultures, a point we will return to in a later section.

The dimensional appraisal theories are concerned with specifying the various dimensions of appraisals and the emotional consequences of those dimensions. An example is given in Table 11-2. One dimension is the desirability of an anticipated event, and another is whether the event occurs. When we combine these two dimensions, we get four possible appraisals, each of which seems to produce a distinct emotion. (We are using only

four emotions in our example to try to keep things simple.) When a desired event (such as falling in love) occurs, we experience joy; when a desired event does not occur (the person we are in love with does not love us), we experience sorrow; when an undesired event (such as doing poorly on an exam) occurs, we experience distress; and when an undesired event does not occur (not doing poorly on an exam), we experience relief.

The preceding example makes use of only two dimensions, but most dimensional theories of appraisal assume that numerous dimensions are involved. For example, Smith and Ellsworth (1985, 1987) found that at least six dimensions were needed to describe 15 different emotions (including, for example, anger, guilt, and sadness). These dimensions were (1) the desirability of the situation (pleasant or unpleasant), (2) the amount of effort the person anticipates spending on the situation, (3) the certainty of the situation, (4) the amount of attention the person wants to devote to the situation, (5) the degree of control the person feels he or she has over the situation, and (6) the degree of control the person attributes to nonhuman forces in the situation. To illustrate how the last two dimensions operate, anger is associated with an unpleasant situation caused by another person, guilt is associated with an unpleasant situation we brought on ourselves, and sadness is associated with an unpleasant situation controlled by circumstances. So, if you and your friend miss a concert that you had your heart set on hearing, you will feel anger if you missed it because your friend carelessly misplaced the tickets, guilt if you misplaced the tickets, and sadness if the performance is canceled because of a performer's illness. The virtue of this kind of approach is that it specifies the appraisal process in detail and accounts for a wide range of emotional experiences.

Despite the widespread acceptance of appraisal theories of emotion, most of the early evidence for these theories rested on correlations between self-reported appraisals and self-reported emotions. The causal role of appraisals was thus not established (Parkinson & Manstead, 1992). A recent experiment supplied this missing evidence. Participants first completed a task in which they attributed a series of neutral events (such as check for the mail, wait for the bus) either to themselves (internal attribution condition) or to someone else (external attribution condition). They did this by generating either 20 sentences like "I check for the mail" and "I wait for the bus" or 20 like "He checks for the mail" and "He waits for the bus." Next, they faced an ambiguous negative situation: They had been told by one experimenter to proceed to the next room to complete the study. When they opened the door to the assigned room, a second experimenter cried out from within, "Get out! Didn't you read the sign on the door? You disturbed our experiment. Wait outside the door." How would people respond to this outburst? Would they feel guilty or get angry? Recall that guilt is associated with unpleasant circumstances you bring on yourself and anger is associated with unpleasant circumstances caused by another person. Results of the experiment showed that participants who were earlier primed to make internal attributions were more likely to express guilt and apologize, and those who were earlier primed to make external attributions were more likely to express anger and blame the other experimenter (Neumann, 2000). These findings demonstrate that cognitive appraisals precede and cause the other components of emotion.

CONSCIOUS AND UNCONSCIOUS APPRAISALS

Much debate among emotion theorists has centered on whether the appraisal process necessarily occurs consciously and deliberately. Some have argued that emotions can occur without any preceding conscious thought (Zajonc, 1984). Experiments on common phobias have tested this idea by presenting pictures of spiders and snakes to participants who (1) fear snakes, (2) fear spiders, or (3) have no phobias (Ohman, 2000). In one condition, the pictures were shown long enough for participants to consciously recognize them. In another condition, a procedure called **backward masking** was used, meaning that pictures were shown for only 30 milliseconds and then masked by a neutral picture so that participants were unaware of the picture's content. Phobics showed nearly identical physiological responses (increased sweat gland activity) to pictures of their phobic object, regardless of whether they consciously saw the spider or snake or not. These sorts of studies suggest that appraisals of threat can occur at unconscious levels, making people experience emotions for reasons unknown to them.

Most contemporary appraisal theories acknowledge that cognitive appraisals can occur automatically, outside conscious awareness. Debate continues, though, over how much of the appraisal process can occur un-

consciously. One recent suggestion is that only the most rudimentary appraisals of valence ("Are these circumstances good for me or bad for me?") and urgency ("How quickly must I respond?) are made outside of awareness. By contrast, more complex appraisals, such as agency ("Who is to blame?"), result from conscious information processing (Robinson, 1998).

In short, the cognitive appraisals within emotion processes are similar to other forms of cognition. They result in part from automatic processing, outside conscious awareness, and in part from controlled processing, of which we are aware (see Chapters 6 and 18 for similar dual-process perspectives). To illustrate, if from the corner of your eye you see something shaped like a snake, an automatic and unconscious appraisal process may make you jump before a more controlled and deliberate appraisal process can determine that the object in question is, in fact, a harmless piece of rope.

 The Neural Basis of Behavior

APPRAISALS IN THE BRAIN

Research on the brain circuits involved in emotion processes also supports the view that appraisals occur both consciously and unconsciously. One brain structure that plays a key role within emotion circuits is the **amygdala**, a small, almond-shaped mass that is located in the lower brain and is known to register emotional reactions. At one time, it was thought that the amygdala received all its inputs from the cortex and, hence, that those inputs always involved conscious appraisal. But research with rats uncovered connections between sensory channels and the amygdala that do not go through the cortex, and these direct connections may be the biological basis of unconscious appraisals (LeDoux & Phelps, 2000). The amygdala is capable of responding to an alarming situation before the cortex does, which suggests that sometimes we can experience an emotion before we know why.

Although the initial research on the amygdala's role in automatic emotions was based on rats, the neural pathways involved appear similar in humans. Brain imaging in humans (see Chapter 2) has also demonstrated a key role for the amygdala within emotions (Figure 11-3). Using the same backward masking technique described earlier, fearful facial expressions were shown to participants for about 30 milliseconds and then masked by neutral expressions on the same faces. Even though participants had no conscious awareness of the fearful faces, imaging data showed activation within the amygdala (Whalen et al., 1998). These data

Figure 11-3
Amygdala Activation During Unconscious Appraisals
This image shows a coronal slice of brain. Fearful and happy faces were shown to participants using a backward masking technique that prevented conscious awareness. Portrayed is the activation difference for masked fearful versus masked happy faces. The highlighted area represents greater activation in the amygdala for masked fearful faces. These findings suggest that the amygdala may play a role in the unconscious appraisal of emotionally-relevant stimuli. (From Whalen, Rauch, Etcoff, McInerney, Lee, & Jenike, (1998), "Masked Presentation of Emotional Facial Expressions Modulate Amygdala Activity Without Explicit Knowledge," *Journal of Neuroscience* 18, 411–418.)

suggest that the amygdala monitors emotion-eliciting stimuli at an automatic, nonconscious level. Interestingly, criminals with antisocial personality disorder, like Ted Bundy, described at the start of this chapter, show less activation in the amygdala during emotional processing than normal criminals or normal noncriminals (Kiehl et al., 2001), providing neurological evidence for an emotion-related deficit. ▮

◆ Interim Summary

- A cognitive appraisal is an interpretation of the personal meaning of certain circumstances (or person-environment relationships) that results in an emotion. Such appraisals affect both the intensity and the quality of an emotion.

- The classic two-factor theory of emotion predicted that when people are induced into a state of undifferentiated arousal, the quality of their emotional experience would be influenced by their appraisal of the situation. This theory, although popular, is not well supported by data. A related effect, known as the misattribution of arousal, has received better empirical support. It states that any lingering physiological arousal can be mistakenly attributed to subsequent circumstances and intensify our emotional reactions to those circumstances.

- One prominent minimalist appraisal theory emphasizes the importance of emotion-specific core relational themes, like a demeaning offense for anger (see Table 11-1). Dimensional appraisal theories focus on identifying the relevant dimensions of cognitive appraisal of emotion, like degrees of certainty or control.

- Cognitive appraisals can occur outside conscious awareness, and brain research identifies the amygdala as involved in automatic appraisals.

◆ Critical Thinking Questions

1. What is the relationship between a person-environment relationship and a cognitive appraisal (that is, the first two boxes in Figure 11-1)? Can you think of a specific person-environment relationship that has, at one time, led you to experience an emotion, whereas at another time it did not?

2. If the appraisal process can be outside awareness, sometimes we may experience emotions and not know why. How then, would that sort of an emotion differ from a mood, which also has no known cause?

SUBJECTIVE EXPERIENCES AND EMOTION

Although the initial appraisal process may occur outside conscious awareness, the subjective experience of emotions—the feeling component—is, by definition, within awareness. Recall the study of phobic people who were shown pictures of their phobic objects (spiders or snakes) via the backward masking technique that prevented conscious awareness. The results showed not only that people experienced bodily responses (increased sweat gland activity) to unseen feared objects but also that they reported feeling aversion, arousal, and lack of control, all consistent with the subjective experience of fear. So, one output of the appraisal process is a change in subjective experience. On the aversive side, we may feel angry, afraid, sad, disgusted, or perhaps some combination of these feelings. On the pleasant side, we may feel elated and joyful, serene and content, interested and engaged, or some other pleasant feeling like awe or gratitude.

What function do these inner feelings serve? A prominent view is that these feelings serve as feedback about the personal relevance of our current circumstances. When we feel a negative emotion, like fear or anger, the unpleasant feeling serves as a cue that something in our environment poses us a threat and that we may need to act fast to protect ourselves. When we feel a positive emotion, like joy or interest, the pleasant feeling signals that we are safe and satiated, and that we can feel free to play or explore. More generally, the feeling component of emotion is thought to guide behavior, decision making, and information processing (Clore, Gasper, & Garvin, 2001).

THOUGHT AND ACTION TENDENCIES

One way that feelings guide behavior and information processing is through the urges that accompany them. These urges are called *thought-action tendencies* (Fredrickson, 1998) or sometimes just action tendencies (Frijda, 1986; Lazarus, 1991b). Table 11-3 lists several emotions and the thought-action tendencies they instill. With negative emotions, people's thought-action tendencies become narrow and specific. In fear, for example, we feel the specific urge to escape the danger. By contrast, with positive emotions, people's thought-action tendencies become broad and more open to possibilities. In joy, for instance, we feel the urge to be playful in general. (See the Cutting-Edge Research box for a discussion of the related benefits of positive emotions.)

● Table 11-3
Emotions and their Associated Thought-Action Tendencies

Twelve emotions and the urges they spark. *(After Fredrickson, 1998, 2002; Fredrickson & Branigan, 2001; Frijda, 1986; Lazarus, 1991b)*

Emotion	Thought-Action Tendency
Anger	Attack
Fear	Escape
Disgust	Expel
Guilt	Make amends
Shame	Disappear
Sadness	Withdraw
Joy	Play
Interest	Explore
Contentment	Savor and integrate
Pride	Dream big
Gratitude	Be prosocial
Elevation	Become a better person

Certainly, people do not invariably act on the urges that accompany their emotions. Keep in mind that these are thought-action *tendencies*, not thoughts or actions per se. They merely describe people's ideas about possible courses of action, and whether these ideas narrow to a specific behavioral urge, as for negative emotions, or broaden to encompass a wide range of possibilities, as for positive emotions. Whether urges become actions depends on the complex interplay of impulse control, cultural norms, and other factors. Even so, many emotion theorists hold that having particular thought and action tendencies come to mind is what made emotions evolutionarily adaptive: For negative emotions, specific thought-action tendencies are thought to represent those actions that worked best in getting our ancestors out of life-or-death situations (Levenson, 1994; Tooby & Cosmides, 1990). For positive emotions, broadened thought-action tendencies are thought to build enduring personal resources—like health, optimism, and social support—which might have also made the difference between life and death for our ancestors (Fredrickson, 1998, 2001).

FEELINGS MODIFY ATTENTION AND LEARNING

We tend to pay more attention to events that fit our current feelings than to events that do not. As a consequence, we learn more about the events that fit, or are congruent with, our feelings. One experiment that demonstrates these phenomena involved three stages. In the first stage, participants were hypnotized and induced to be either happy or sad. In the second stage, the hypnotized participants read a brief story about an encounter between two men—a happy character and a sad one. The story vividly described the events of the two men's lives and their emotional reactions. After reading the story, participants were asked who they thought the central character was and with whom they identified. Participants who had been induced to feel happy identified more with the happy character and thought the story contained more statements about him; participants who had been induced to feel sad identified more with the sad character and thought the story contained more statements about him. These results indicate that participants paid more attention to the character and events that were congruent with their feelings than to those that were not (Bower, 1981). More recent experiments demonstrate that current feelings guide attention automatically, by producing faster reaction times to feeling-congruent events (Derryberry & Tucker, 1994).

The third stage of the hypnosis experiment provided evidence that participants also learned more about feeling-congruent events than about feeling-incongruent events. One day after reading the story, the participants, now in a

CUTTING-EDGE RESEARCH
Benefits of Positive Emotions

What good are positive emotions? This question seems almost silly because at one level the answer is obvious: Positive emotions feel good. This fact alone makes them rewarding and valuable experiences. End of story, right?

Unfortunately, for many years, this had been the end of the story. Any review of the scientific literature on emotions will reveal an overwhelming focus on negative emotions—like fear, anger, disgust, and shame—and only a tiny focus on positive emotions—like joy, contentment, interest, and love. So, although few would argue with Thomas

Jefferson's assumption in the U. S. Declaration of Independence that the pursuit of happiness is a worthy goal, until recently, few had pursued positive emotions scientifically.

This situation is changing, and a recent landmark study sounds a wake-up call about the profound benefits positive emotions may hold for us. This was a study of 180 Catholic nuns who donated their lives not only to God but also to science (see chart). As part of a larger study of aging and Alzheimer's disease, these nuns agreed to give scientists access to their archived work and medical records (and to donate their brains at death). The work archives included autobiographies handwritten in the 1930s and 1940s, when the nuns were in their early 20s and about to take their final vows. Researchers scored these essays for

emotional content, recording instances of positive emotion—like happiness, interest, love, and hope—and negative emotions—like sadness, fear, and lack of interest. No association was found between negative emotional content and mortality, perhaps because it was rather rare in these essays. But a strong inverse association was found between positive emotional content and mortality: Those nuns who expressed the most positive emotions lived up to 10 years longer than those who expressed the least positive emotions (Danner, Snowdon, & Friesen, 2001, see chart). This gain in life expectancy is considerably larger than the gain you'd get from quitting smoking. Imagine how long you'd live if you both quit smoking and accentuated the positive?

Although this study of nuns is compelling, it does not address *how* positive emotions provide benefits. Insight into the possible pathways is provided by a recent theory that describes the form and function of positive emotions, called the *broaden-and-build theory* of positive emotions (Fredrickson, 1998, 2001).

POSITIVE EMOTIONS BROADEN OUR THINKING AND ACTIONS
One virtue of negative emotions is that they spark strong urges to act in specific ways: to fight when angry, to flee when afraid, or to spit when disgusted (Lazarus, 1991b). Put differently, negative emotions narrow our thinking and actions. Positive emotions have a complementary effect; they broaden our thinking and actions. Joy creates the urge to play, interest the urge to explore, contentment the urge to savor, and love a recurring cycle of each of these urges. The virtue here is that positive emotions expand our typical ways of thinking and being in the world, pushing us to be more creative, more curious, or more connected to others (Fredrickson, 1998; Isen, 2002). A recent experiment supports this basic distinction between negative and positive emotions. Participants were shown one of five emotionally evocative film clips to induce one of two positive emotions (joy

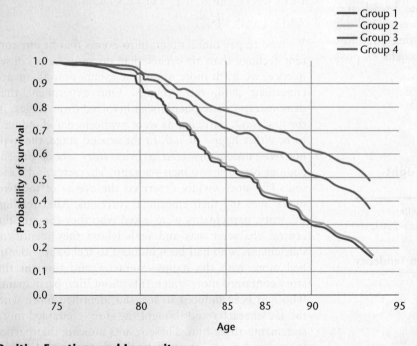

— Group 1
— Group 2
— Group 3
— Group 4

Positive Emotions and Longevity
Four groups of 45 nuns were formed by ranking the number of positive emotion sentences in the autobiographies they wrote in early life. Then, for each of the four groups, the probability of survival in late life was calculated. These survival curves are plotted. (Note that the survival curves for Groups 1 and 2—representing those nuns who expressed the least positive emotions—are virtually overlaid on each other.) (From D. D. Danner, D. A. Snowden, W. V. Friesen (2001). Positive emotions in early life and longevity: Finding from the nun study. *Journal of Personality and Social Psychology*, 80:804–813. Copyright © 2000 by the American Psychological Association. Reprinted with permission.)

or contentment), one of two negative emotions (fear or anger), or no emotion (the control condition). While in these states, participants listed all the things they would like to do right then. Compared with those experiencing no emotion, those experiencing fear or anger listed fewer things they'd like to do right then and named things consistent the specific action tendencies listed in Table 11-3 (for example, those who felt angry felt like being aggressive). By contrast, and again compared with those experiencing no emotion, those experiencing joy or contentment named more things they'd like to do right then, consistent with a broadened thought-action repertoire (Fredrickson & Branigan, 2002).

POSITIVE EMOTIONS BUILD OUR PERSONAL RESOURCES

Although emotions themselves are short-lived, they can have lasting effects on us.

By momentarily broadening our thinking and actions, positive emotions promote discovery of novel and creative ideas, actions, and social bonds. Playing, for instance, can build our physical and social resources, exploring can generate knowledge, and savoring can set our life priorities. Importantly, these outcomes often endure long after the initial positive emotion has vanished. In this way, positive emotions build up our store of resources to draw on in times of trouble, including physical resources (such as health and effective physical functioning), intellectual resources (such as a cognitive map for way finding), psychological resources (such as an optimistic outlook), and social resources (such as someone to turn to for help).

So, feeling good may do more for us than we typically acknowledge. The **broaden-and-build theory** states that **positive emotions broaden our typical**

ways of thinking and acting and, in turn, build our lasting personal resources, making us more complex and resilient people than we would be otherwise. The next time you're laughing with friends, pursuing an interest, or enjoying a walk through the park, consider that you may be cultivating more than just fleeting good feelings. You may also be optimizing your own long-term health and well-being (Fredrickson, 2000, 2002).

 For more information, go online with InfoTrac College Edition. Use your own term or search:

- Positive emotion

Positive emotionality may extend life expectancy.

neutral state, returned to the laboratory, where they were asked to recall the story. Participants recalled more about the character they had identified with: For the previously happy participants, 55% of the facts they recalled were about the happy character; for the previously sad participants, 80% of the facts they recalled were about the sad character (Bower, 1981).

Exactly how does the congruence between our current feelings and some new material affect the learning of that material? We know that we can learn new material better if we can relate it to information already in memory. Our feelings during learning may increase the availability of memories that fit that feeling, and such memories will be easier to relate to new material that also fits that feeling. Suppose that you hear a story about a student flunking out of school. If you are feeling sad when you hear the story, some of your memories about failure experiences (particularly academic failures) may be easily accessible, and the similarity of these memories to the new fact of someone flunking out of school will make it easy to relate them. In contrast, if you are feeling happy when you hear the story, your most accessible memories may be too dissimilar to a school failure to foster a relationship between the old memories and the new fact. So, our feelings influence what memories are more accessible, and those memories influence what is easy for us to learn at the moment (Bower, 1981; Isen, 1985).

FEELINGS MODIFY EVALUATIONS AND JUDGMENTS

Our feelings can affect our evaluations of other people. Everyday experiences provide numerous examples of this. When we are feeling happy, a friend's habit of constantly checking his appearance in a mirror may seem just an idiosyncrasy; when we are feeling irritable, we may dwell on how vain he is. Our feelings affect our evaluation of inanimate objects as well. In one experiment, participants were asked to evaluate their major possessions. Participants who had just been made grateful by receiving a small gift rated their televisions and cars more positively than did control participants who were feeling neutral (Isen, Shalker, Clark, & Karp, 1978).

Our feelings also affect our judgments about the frequency of various risks. Recent theorists have argued that such influence occurs because emotions activate tendencies to reproduce the same cognitive appraisals that initially produced the emotion (Lerner & Keltner, 2001; Siemer, 2001). Feeling fear, for instance, each leads us to appraise subsequent circumstances as uncertain and uncontrollable and thus cause us to see future risks as more likely. In contrast, feeling angry or happy, although feelings of different valence, leads us to appraise subsequent circumstances as certain and controllable and thus

causes us to see future risks as less likely (Johnson & Tversky, 1983; Lerner & Keltner, 2001). In an experiment testing this idea, participants were first induced to feel anger or fear by vividly recounting circumstances that made them angry or fearful. They were then asked to rate the degree to which the circumstances they described were under their control and how certain or uncertain they were about them. Finally, participants estimated their own chances of experiencing a range of positive and negative life events, like marrying someone wealthy or getting a sexually transmitted disease. The results are shown in Figure 11-4. Fear and anger had opposite effects on cognitive appraisal and on estimates of risk. Those feeling fear appraised their circumstances as uncertain and uncontrollable, and these appraisals in turn predicted more pessimistic risk assessments. Those feeling anger, by contrast, appraised their circumstances as certain and controllable, and these appraisals in turn

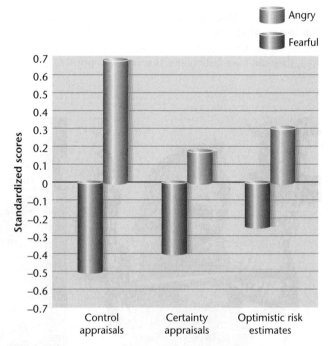

Figure 11-4
Fear, Anger, and Risk
Fear and anger had opposite effects on cognitive appraisals and risk estimates. Effect sizes are represented in standardized scores to put appraisals and risk estimates on the same scale. Compared with angry participants (green bars), fearful participants (purple bars) rated their circumstances as less under their control (left bars) and less certain (middle bars) and made more pessimistic estimates of future risks (right bars). Subsequent analyses confirmed that appraisals accounted for the effect of emotions on risk estimates. (From J. S. Lerner and D. Keltner (2001). "Fear, Anger, and Risk," in *Journal of Personality and Social Psychology*, 81:146–159. Copyright © 2001 by the American Psychological Association. Reprinted with permission.)

predicted more optimistic risk assessments (Lerner & Keltner, 2001).

Our feelings affect other types of judgment as well. In another experiment, participants were made either sad or angry by imagining themselves experiencing either a sad event or an angry one. They then were asked to evaluate the possible causes of hypothetical events, such as missing an important flight or losing money. Participants who were angry tended to attribute the hypothetical events to the mistakes of other people, but participants who were sad tended to attribute them to situations (for example, traffic congestion was the reason for missing a flight). So the angry participants were more ready to blame someone for negative events, whereas the sad participants were more willing to acknowledge that an unlucky situation might have caused the events (Keltner, Ellsworth, & Edwards, 1993).

Feeling afraid, then, makes the world seem more dangerous. Such a perception can reinforce the fearful feelings. In addition, as noted earlier, our feelings lead us to selectively attend to and learn feeling-congruent facts, which can also reinforce the initial emotion. A similar analysis applies to positive emotions. Positive emotions broaden our habitual modes of thinking, which may make it more likely that we find positive meaning in subsequent circumstances and then experience further positive emotions. So, the cognitive consequences of subjective experiences serve to perpetuate emotional states, which can produce downward spirals for negative emotions and upward spirals for positive ones (Fredrickson & Joiner, 2002).

◆ Interim Summary

- Subjective experiences of emotions, or feelings, guide behavior, decision making, and judgment.

- Different emotions carry urges to think and act in certain ways, called *thought-action tendencies*. These are summarized in Table 11-3.

- According to the broaden-and-build theory, positive emotions broaden people's momentary thought action repertoires, which, in turn, can build lasting resources for survival.

- Subjective experiences also steer memory, learning, and risk assessments.

◆ Critical Thinking Questions

1. Some theorists argue that the thought-action tendencies listed in Table 11-3 are the result of evolutionary processes. Why might this be the case?

2. What are some of the cognitive processes by which a particular emotion might perpetuate itself?

BODILY CHANGES AND EMOTION

When we experience certain emotions intensely, such as fear or anger, we may be aware of a number of bodily changes—including rapid heartbeat and breathing, dryness of the throat and mouth, perspiration, trembling, and a sinking feeling in the stomach (see Table 11-4). Many of the physiological changes that take place during emotional arousal result from activation of the sympathetic division of the autonomic nervous system (see Chapter 2). The **sympathetic nervous system** prepares the body for emergency action and is responsible for the following changes (which need not all occur at once):

1. Blood pressure and heart rate increase.
2. Respiration becomes more rapid.
3. The pupils dilate.

● Table 11-4
Symptoms of Fear in Combat Flying

Based on reports of combat pilots during World War II. *(From L. F. Shafer (1947) "Symptoms of Fear in Combat Flying," in* Journal of Consulting Psychology, *11:137–143.)*

During combat missions did you feel. . . ?	Sometimes	Often	Total
A pounding heart and rapid pulse	56%	30%	86%
That your muscles were very tense	53	30	83
Easily irritated or angry	58	22	80
Dryness of the throat or mouth	50	30	80
Nervous perspiration or cold sweat	53	26	79
Butterflies in the stomach	53	23	76
A sense of unreality—that this could not be happening to you	49	20	69
A need to urinate frequently	40	25	65
Trembling	53	11	64
Confused or rattled	50	3	53
Weak or faint	37	4	41
That right after a mission you were unable to remember the details of what had happened	34	5	39
Sick to the stomach	33	5	38
Unable to concentrate	32	3	35
That you had wet or soiled your pants	4	1	5

4. Perspiration increases while secretion of saliva and mucus decreases.
5. Blood-sugar level increases to provide more energy.
6. The blood clots more quickly in case of wounds.
7. Blood is diverted from the stomach and intestines to the brain and skeletal muscles.
8. The hairs on the skin become erect, causing goose pimples.

The sympathetic nervous system thus gears up the organism for energy output. As the emotion subsides, the **parasympathetic nervous system**—the energy-conserving system—takes over and returns the organism to its normal state.

These activities of the autonomic nervous system are themselves triggered by activity in certain regions of the brain, including the hypothalamus (which, as we saw in the last chapter, plays a major role in many biological motives) and the amygdala, which, as described earlier in this chapter, is implicated in the appraisal process. Impulses from these areas are transmitted to nuclei in the brain stem that control the functioning of the autonomic nervous system. The autonomic nervous system then acts directly on the muscles and internal organs to initiate some of the bodily changes described here. It also acts indirectly by stimulating the adrenal hormones to produce other bodily changes.

Note that the kind of heightened physiological arousal we have described is characteristic of those negative emotions that come with urges for specific actions requiring substantial physical energy (such as attack or flee; the role of this fight-or-flight response in threatening or stressful situations is discussed further in Chapter 14). Indeed, a core idea within many emotion theories is that thought-action tendencies infuse both mind and body.

So, for example, when you feel fear and experience the urge to escape, your body simultaneously reacts by mobilizing appropriate autonomic support for the possibility of running. According to this perspective, the function of the physiological changes evident during these potent negative emotions is to prepare the body for specific actions (Levenson, 1994).

Positive emotions, some have argued, produce few bodily changes because their associated thought-action tendencies are broad and not specific. So instead of producing the heightened arousal that supports specific actions, positive emotions may be particularly suited for helping people recover from any lingering arousal that follows negative emotions, an idea called the **undoing effect of positive emotions**. A recent experiment tested this idea. Participants were first asked to prepare a speech on "Why you are a good friend" under considerable time pressure. They were told that the speech would be videotaped and evaluated by their peers. This speech task produced feelings of anxiety, along with increases in blood pressure and heart rate. These physiological changes lingered on, even after participants were told that they would not have to deliver their speech after all. At this point, the participants were shown a randomly selected film clip that induced one of two positive emotions (joy or contentment), a negative emotion (sadness), or no emotion. Results are shown in Figure 11-5. Those who turned their attention to either of the two positive emotion films returned to their own baseline levels of cardiovascular activity faster than those who saw either the neutral or sad films (Fredrickson, Mancuso, Branigan, & Tugade, 2000). Cultivating positive emotions, then, appears to be a particularly good way to combat the lingering physiological aftereffects of negative emotions.

■ **Figure 11-5**
The Undoing Effect of Positive Emotions
Joy and contentment produce faster cardiovascular recovery from lingering negative emotional arousal than neutrality and sadness. (Adapted with permission from B. L. Fredrickson, R. A. Mancuso, C. Branigan, & M. M. Tugade (2000), "The Undoing Effect of Positive Emotions," in *Motivation and Emotion*, 24:237–258. © 2000 Kluwer Academic/Plenum Publishers.)

INTENSITY OF EMOTIONS

What is the relationship between the heightened physiological arousal experienced with some emotions and the subjective experience of those emotions? In particular, is our perception of our own arousal—called **visceral perception**—part of the experience of the emotion? One way to answer this question is to study the emotional life of individuals with spinal cord injuries. When the spinal cord is severed or lesioned, sensations below the point of injury cannot reach the brain. Because some of these sensations arise from the sympathetic nervous system, the injuries reduce the contributions of autonomic arousal to the experience of emotion.

In one study, army veterans with spinal cord injuries were divided into five groups according to the location on the spinal cord where the lesion occurred. In one group, the lesions were near the neck (at the cervical level), with no feedback from the sympathetic system to the brain. In another group, the lesions were near the base of the spine (at the sacral level), with at least partial feedback from the sympathetic nerves possible. The other three groups fell between these two extremes. The five groups thus represented a continuum of visceral perception: The higher the lesion on the spinal cord, the less the feedback of the autonomic nervous system to the brain (Hohmann, 1962).

The participants were interviewed to determine their feelings in situations of fear, anger, grief, and sexual excitement. Each person was asked to recall an emotion-arousing incident prior to the injury and a comparable incident following the injury and then to compare the intensity of their emotional experience in each case. The data for states of fear and anger are shown in Figure 11-6. The higher the lesion on the individual's spinal cord (that is, the less feedback coming from the autonomic nervous system), the greater the decrease in emotionality following injury. The same relationship was true for states of sexual excitement and grief. A reduction in autonomic arousal resulted in a reduction in the intensity of experienced emotion.

Comments by veterans with the highest spinal cord lesions suggested that they could react emotionally to arousing situations but that they did not really feel emotional. For example, "It's sort of a cold anger. Sometimes I act angry when I see some injustice. I yell and cuss and raise hell, because if you don't do it sometimes, I've learned people will take advantage of you; but it doesn't have the heat to it that it used to. It's a mental kind of anger." Or, "I say I am afraid, like when I'm going into a real stiff exam at school, but I don't really feel afraid, not all tense and shaky with the hollow feeling in my stomach, like I used to."

▌Figure 11-6
The Relationship Between Spinal Cord Lesions and Emotionality
People with spinal cord lesions compared the intensity of their emotional experiences before and after injury. Their reports were coded according to the degree of change: 0 indicates no change, a mild change ("I feel it less, I guess") is scored –1 for a decrease or +1 for an increase, and a strong change ("I feel it a hulluva lot less") is scored –2 or +2. Note that the higher the lesion, the greater the decrease in emotionality following injury.
(Adapted from G. W. Hohmann, "The effect of dysfunctions of the autonomic nervous system on experienced feelings and emotions," Paper read at the New School for Social Research, New York, October 1962.)

The study just described is important, but it is not entirely objective—the emotional situations varied from one participant to another and were described from hindsight. More recent studies with noninjured participants provide more experimental control. Across healthy individuals, people can be divided into those who are good at visceral perception—for instance, those who are good at detecting their own heartbeat—and those who are not. If visceral perception contributes to the intensity of emotions, then people who are good heartbeat detectors should report more intense subjective experiences of emotions and show more intense facial expressions. A study in which good and poor heartbeat detectors viewed film clips that elicited amusement, anger, and fear found that good detectors reported more intense experiences of each emotion (Wiens, Mezzacappa, & Katkin, 2000). A related study found that good heartbeat detectors showed more intense facial expressions to emotional pic-

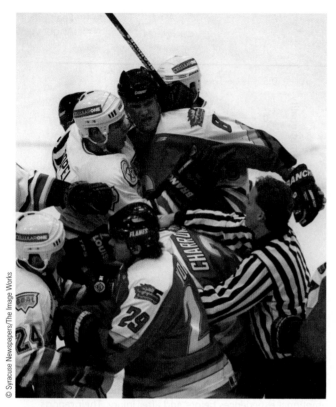

Physical arousal may intensify feelings of anger.

tures (Ferguson & Katkin, 1996). Together with the studies on spinal cord injuries, these studies suggest that visceral perception plays a role in the experience of the intensity of emotions (Schachter, 1964).

DIFFERENTIATION OF EMOTIONS

Clearly, autonomic arousal contributes to the intensity of emotional experience. But does it differentiate the emotions? In other words, is there one pattern of physiological activity for excitement, another for anger, still another for fear, and so on? This question dates back to **William James, the author of the very first psychology textbook, published in 1890.** He proposed that the perception of bodily changes *is* the subjective experience of emotion and that we could not have one without the other: "We feel sorry because we cry, angry because we strike, afraid because we tremble, and not that we cry, strike, or tremble, because we are sorry, angry, or fearful" (James, 1890/1950, p. 450). The Danish physiologist Carl Lange arrived at a similar conclusion at about the same time, so this view has come to be known as the James-Lange theory. It runs as follows: Because the perception of autonomic arousal (and perhaps of other bodily changes) constitutes the experience of an emo-

tion, and because different emotions feel different, there must be a distinct pattern of autonomic activity for each emotion. The **James-Lange theory** therefore holds that autonomic arousal differentiates the emotions (see Figure 11-2b).

This theory (particularly the part dealing with autonomic arousal) came under severe attack in the 1920s. The attack was led by the physiologist Walter Cannon (1927), who offered three major criticisms:

1. Because the internal organs are relatively insensitive structures and are not well supplied with nerves, internal changes occur too slowly to be the primary source of emotional feeling.
2. Artificially inducing the bodily changes associated with an emotion—for example, injecting a drug such as epinephrine—does not produce the experience of a true emotion. At most, it produces "as if" emotions: Injected participants remark, "I feel as if afraid."
3. The pattern of autonomic arousal does not seem to differ much from one emotional state to another. For example, anger makes our heart beat faster, but so does the sight of a loved one.

The third argument, then, explicitly denies that autonomic arousal can differentiate the emotions.

Psychologists have tried to rebut Cannon's third point as they develop increasingly accurate measures of the components of autonomic arousal. Although a few experiments in the 1950s reported distinct physiological patterns for different emotions (Ax, 1953; Funkenstein, 1955), until the 1990s most studies had found little evidence for different patterns of arousal being associated with different emotions. A study by Levenson, Ekman, and Friesen (1990), however, provided evidence of autonomic patterns that are distinct to different emotions. Participants produced emotional expressions for each of six emotions—surprise, disgust, sadness, anger, fear, and happiness—by following instructions about which particular facial muscles to contract. While they held an emotional expression for 10 seconds, the researchers measured their heart rate, skin temperature, and other indicators of autonomic arousal. A number of these measures revealed differences among the emotions (see Figure 11-7). Heart rate was faster for the negative emotions of anger, fear, and sadness than for happiness, surprise, and disgust, and the first three emotions themselves could be partially distinguished by the fact that skin temperature was higher in anger than in fear or sadness. So, even though both anger and the sight of a loved one make our heart beat faster, only anger makes it beat much faster; and although anger and fear have much in common, anger is hot and fear is cold (no wonder peo-

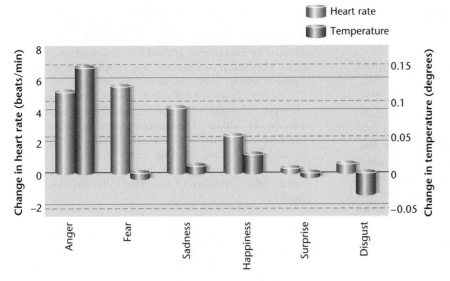

■ Figure 11-7
Differences in Arousal for Different Emotions
Changes in heart rate (orange) and right finger temperature (blue). For heart rate, the changes associated with anger, fear, and sadness were all significantly greater than those for happiness, surprise, and disgust. For finger temperature, the change associated with anger was significantly different from that for all other emotions. (Adapted from an article by P. Ekman, et al., "Autonomic Nervous System Activity Distinguishes Among Emotions," from *Science*, Vol. 221, pp. 1208–1210, September 16, 1983. Copyright © 1983 American Association for the Advancement of Science.)

ple describe their anger as their "blood boiling" and their fear as "bone-chilling" or as "getting cold feet").

Other research suggests that these distinctive arousal patterns may be universal. Levenson, Ekman, and colleagues studied the Minangkabau of Western Sumatra, a culture very different from Western culture. Again, participants produced facial expressions for various emotions—fear, anger, sadness, and disgust—while measures were taken of their heart rate, skin temperature, and other indicators of arousal. Although the magnitude of the physiological changes was less than that of the changes reported earlier for American individuals, the patterns of arousal for the different emotions were the same: Heart rate was faster for anger, fear, and sadness than for disgust, and skin temperature was highest for anger (Levenson, Ekman, Heider, & Friesen, 1992).

These results are important, but they do not provide unequivocal support for the James-Lange theory or for the claim that autonomic arousal is the only component that differentiates the emotions. The studies we have described demonstrated that there are some physiological differences between emotions (though some researchers

question this; see Cacioppo, Berntson, Larsen, Poehlmann, & Ito, 2000), not that those differences are perceived and experienced as qualitative differences between emotions. Even if autonomic arousal does help differentiate some emotions, it is unlikely that it differentiates all emotions. The difference between contentment and gratitude, for example, may not be found in autonomic reactions. Also, Cannon's first two arguments against the James-Lange theory still stand: Autonomic arousal is at times too slow to differentiate emotional experiences, and artificial induction of arousal does not yield a true emotion. For these reasons, many emotion theorists still believe that something other than autonomic arousal differentiates the emotions. As we discussed earlier, that something else (or part of it) is usually thought to be the individual's cognitive appraisal of the situation.

◆ Interim Summary

- Intense negative emotions involve physiological arousal caused by activation of the sympathetic division of the autonomic nervous system.

- Positive emotions appear to have an undoing effect on lingering negative emotional arousal.

- People with spinal cord injuries, which limit feedback from the autonomic nervous system, report experiencing less intense emotions. Other studies also suggest that visceral perception contributes to the intensity of emotions.

- The James-Lange theory states that autonomic arousal also differentiates the emotions, and recent evidence suggests that, to a degree, the pattern of arousal (for example, heartbeat, skin temperature) differs for different emotions.

◆ Critical Thinking Questions

1. Drawing from your own experiences of anger or fear, does your perception of bodily changes contribute to your judgment of the intensity of your emotion?

2. In what way is the James-Lange theory of emotions similar to Schachter and Singer's two-factor theory? In what way do these two theories differ?

FACIAL EXPRESSION AND EMOTION

The facial expression that accompanies an emotion clearly serves to communicate that emotion. Since the publication of Charles Darwin's 1872 classic, *The Expression of Emotion in Man and Animals*, psychologists have regarded the communication of emotion as an important function, one that has survival value for the species. Looking frightened may warn others that danger is present, and perceiving that someone is angry tells us that he or she may be about to act aggressively. Other research suggests that, in addition to their communicative function, emotional expressions contribute to the subjective experience of emotion, just as appraisals and bodily changes do. Facial expressions might at times even jumpstart the whole emotion process.

COMMUNICATION OF EMOTION THROUGH FACIAL EXPRESSIONS

Certain facial expressions seem to have a universal meaning, regardless of the culture in which an individual is raised. The universal expression of anger, for example, involves a flushed face, brows lowered and drawn together, flared nostrils, a clenched jaw, and bared teeth. When people from five countries (the United States, Brazil, Chile, Argentina, and Japan) viewed photographs showing facial expressions typical of happiness, anger, sadness, disgust, fear, and surprise, they had little difficulty identifying the emotion that each expression conveyed. Even members of remote groups that had had virtually no contact with Western cultures (the Fore and Dani peoples in New Guinea) were able to identify the emotions represented by facial expressions of people from Western cultures. Likewise, American college students who viewed videotapes of facial expressions of Fore natives identified the associated emotions accurately, although they sometimes confused fear and surprise (Ekman, 1982).

The universality of certain emotional expressions supports Darwin's claim that they are innate responses with an evolutionary history. According to Darwin, many of the ways in which we express emotion are inherited patterns that originally had some survival value. For example, the expression of disgust or rejection is based on the organism's attempt to rid itself of something unpleasant—perhaps even poisonous—that it has ingested. To quote Darwin (1872),

> The term "disgust," in its simplest sense, means something offensive to the taste. But as disgust also causes annoyance, it is generally accompanied by a frown, and often by gestures as if to push away or to guard oneself against the offensive object. Extreme disgust is expressed by movements around the mouth identical with those preparatory to the act of vomiting. The mouth is opened widely, with the upper lip strongly retracted. The partial closure of the eyelids, or the turning away of the eyes or of the whole body, are likewise highly expressive of disdain. These actions seem to declare that the despised person is not worth looking at, or is disagreeable to behold. Spitting seems an almost universal sign of contempt or disgust; and spitting obviously represents the rejection of anything offensive from the mouth.

The fact that facial expressions of emotions communicate important information is demonstrated even more powerfully when the facial expression of one person by itself changes the behavior of another person. Such evidence is provided by studies of infants' interactions with their mothers. In one study, infants who had just started to crawl were placed on an apparatus called a *visual cliff* (described in Chapter 5, and shown in Figure 5-36). The depth of the apparent cliff was not as deep as that used in studies of depth perception; instead, it was the size of an ordinary step, which made it less clear whether the drop posed a danger or not. When infants approached the edge of the cliff, they would look to their mother. In one condition, mothers had been instructed to make an expression of intense fear. In another, they were instructed to smile broadly. The mothers' facial expression resolved the infants' uncertainty about the danger: Babies whose mothers showed fear never crossed to the deep side, whereas 74% of those whose mothers smiled did (Sorce, Emde, Campos, & Klinnert, 1985).

Although facial expressions seem to be innately associated with particular emotions, certain aspects of them are learned. Emotional **display rules**, for instance, vary across cultures and specify the types of emotions people should express in certain situations and the behaviors appropriate for particular emotions. As an example, in some cultures people who lose a loved one are expected to feel sad and to express their sadness by openly crying and wailing for the loved one to return. In other cultures, bereaved people are expected to sing, dance, and be merry. In Europe, two men greeting each other on the street may embrace and kiss, but in the United States such displays of affection are often taboo for men. A laboratory study with participants from Japan and the United States demonstrated cultural similarities in expressions alongside differences in display rules. Participants from both cultures viewed a disgusting film clip either alone or in

Facial expressions are universal in the emotions they convey. Photographs of people from New Guinea and from the United States demonstrate that specific emotions are conveyed by the same facial expressions. Shown here are, from left to right, happiness, sadness, and disgust.

the presence of an authority figure. Although they showed nearly identical facial expressions when alone, when the authority was present, Japanese participants more often masked their disgust expressions with a smile (Ekman, 1972). Superimposed on the basic expressions of emotion, which appear to be universal, are conventional forms of expressions—a kind of language of emotion that is recognized by other members of the culture but potentially misunderstood by people from other cultures.

THE FACIAL FEEDBACK HYPOTHESIS

The idea that facial expressions, in addition to their communicative function, also contribute to our experience of emotions is called the **facial feedback hypothesis** (Tomkins, 1962). This hypothesis runs parallel to the James-Lange theory: Just as we receive feedback about (or perceive) our autonomic arousal, so do we receive feedback about our facial expressions, and this feedback can cause or intensify the experience of emotions. The hypothesis is illustrated in Figure 11-2c. Play around with this idea yourself. Make yourself smile, and hold that smile for several seconds. Did you begin to feel happy? Now, make yourself scowl and hold it. Does this make you feel tense or angry?

Testing the facial feedback hypothesis experimentally is trickier than making faces and telling how you feel. Experimenters need to rule out the possibility that participants report their feelings based on common knowledge about which expressions and feelings go together, like the knowledge that smiling and feeling happy go hand-in-hand. The trick is to get participants to smile without knowing it. In one such experiment, participants rated cartoons for funniness while holding a pen either in their teeth or in their lips. Holding a pen in your teeth forces your face into a smile, while holding it in your lips prevents a smile. (Try it!) Consistent with the facial feedback hypothesis, participants who held the pen in their teeth rated the cartoons as funnier than those who held the pen in their lips (Strack, Martin, & Stepper, 1988).

In addition to these studies, which show a direct connection between expression and experienced emotion, other experiments indicate that facial expressions may have an indirect effect on experienced emotion by increasing autonomic arousal. Such an effect was demonstrated in the experiment discussed earlier in which producing particular emotional expressions led to changes in heartbeat and skin temperature (Levenson, Ekman, & Friesen, 1990). We therefore need to add emotional expression to our list of factors that can initiate emotions. Even so, knowing that we can jump-start an emotion by making a facial expression does not mean that this is the typical way that emotions unfold. In daily life, appraisals of our current circumstances are still the most likely trigger of emotions, as described in Figure 11-1. Yet, when facing adversity, knowledge of the facial feedback hypothesis might inspire us to "grin and bear it," and studies have shown that doing so is linked with speedy physiological recovery (Fredrickson & Levenson, 1998).

◆ Interim Summary

- The facial expressions that accompany a subset of emotions have a universal meaning: People from different cultures agree on what emotion a person in a particular photograph is expressing.

- The communicative power of facial expressions is evident in parent-infant interactions. Mothers' facial expressions of fear or joy have been shown to dramatically alter their infants' behavior.

- Cultures may differ in the factors that elicit certain emotions and in display rules that specify how emotions should be experienced and expressed.

- In addition to their communicative functions, emotional expressions may contribute to the subjective experience of an emotion (the facial feedback hypothesis).

◆ Critical Thinking Questions

1. What effect does your smile have on others? What effect does your smile have on you?

2. How do the facial feedback hypothesis and Schachter and Singer's classic study relate to the model of emotion illustrated in Figure 11-1?

RESPONSES TO EMOTION: EMOTION REGULATION

Emotion regulation, or people's responses to their own emotions, can be considered a component in the emotion process because people—at least by middle childhood—almost always have reactions to their emotions and goals about what they would like to feel or express, and when. Sometimes people have the goal of maintaining or intensifying an emotion, whether positive or negative. For instance, you might wish to savor and prolong the joy you feel when you're with people you love. In another circumstance, you might want to work up your anger before registering a complaint to a merchant. Other times, people have the goal of minimizing or eliminating an emotion, again, whether positive or negative. Imagine feeling immensely proud of a personal achievement, perhaps getting into college. While on that pleasurable high, imagine running into a friend who was rejected from multiple colleges. Might you want to minimize your expressions of pride at that moment? Yet perhaps most commonly, people's goals are to minimize their negative emotions, like sadness or anger. You might have this goal to lift your own spirits, to shield another person from your negative expressions, or both.

So emotions and people's efforts to regulate them go hand-in-hand—so much so that we hardly have one without the other. Indeed, a considerable part of the socialization process is directed toward teaching children how and when to regulate their emotions. Parents teach their children, both directly and by example, when certain emotions are appropriate and when they are not. Take the example of receiving a disappointing gift (say, an ugly sweater) from your grandmother. Can you show your disappointment to your grandmother? Your parents hope that you won't, and eventually you learn not to. Why is this important? Evidence suggests that children's success in learning these lessons about emotion regulation predicts their social success more generally (Eisenberg, Cumberland, & Spinrad, 1998). For instance, experimenters who have given preschool children disappointing gifts in the lab have learned that kids' abilities to control their expressions of negative emotion are negatively correlated with their risks for later disruptive behavior problems (Cole, Zahn-Waxler, & Smith, 1994).

People control or regulate their emotions in many different ways. A recent study classified the different strategies that people use to improve their negative emotions as either cognitive or behavioral and as either diversion or engagement tactics (Parkinson & Totterdell, 1999). Table 11-5 lists these different kinds of strategies. Suppose you had a fight with your roommate, are angry, but want to feel better. You could disengage from your anger through sheer mental effort, by trying to think of nothing, or by distracting yourself by doing something fun or demanding, like playing your guitar or doing your calculus assignment. Alternatively, you could confront your feelings or the situation with an engagement strategy. Maybe you can reappraise the situation as better than you thought—if there's another reason your roommate was so irritable, you need not take it personally. Or

you can try to solve the underlying problem, by talking through the issues with your roommate. These tactics are not mutually exclusive. You might first use distraction to quell the heat of your anger and then later, when you have a cooler head, you might discuss the underlying problem with your roommate. In addition, these tactics are not always deliberately chosen. Like other cognitions and behavior, with repeated use, they can become automatic responses, outside of conscious awareness.

People's responses to their emotions—whether deliberate regulation strategies or automatic responses—can influence the other components of emotion, either directly or indirectly. This is why Figure 11-1 has feedback arrows leading from responses to emotion, on the right, to all the preceding boxes. This influence also underscores that an emotion is a process—one that unfolds and changes over time—and not a simple state that can be captured in a single snapshot. Imagine, for instance, that you are the first to arrive at the scene after a bicyclist is hit by a car. You notice the bicyclist's leg is broken because it's bent in an unnatural position. Here, your initial emotion of disgust might quickly transform into compassion as you reappraise the circumstance as one in which the injured bicyclist needs your help. So your emotions in this situation change over time, in part because of your responses to your own emotions ("I can't show my feelings of disgust to this suffering person"), and in part because the circumstances themselves change over time (e.g., the ambulance arrives, and you feel relieved).

Does it matter which strategy you use to regulate an emotion? Consider that ugly sweater again. One way to convince your grandmother that you appreciate the gift is to focus on what your face shows. You could actively suppress any facial signs of anger or sadness and instead make yourself smile and give Grandma a hug. Another strategy would be to focus on how you interpret the situation, reappraising it to be better than you first

● Table 11-5
Classification of Emotion Regulation Strategies

People use different cognitive and behavioral strategies to make themselves feel better (*After Parkinson & Totterdell, 1999*)

	Cognitive	Behavioral
Diversion		
Disengagement	Avoid thinking about the problem	Avoid the problematic situation
Distraction	Think about something pleasant or absorbing	Do something pleasant or demanding
Engagement		
Affect-directed	Reappraise	Vent feelings; seek comfort
Situation-directed	Think about how to solve the problem	Take action to solve the problem

thought. You might tell yourself (as your parents often did), "It's the thought that counts" and focus on the care and effort your grandmother invested in selecting or knitting that sweater. Doing so might naturally yield a smile and hug for Grandma. Although these two strategies for dealing with the ugly sweater might be equally convincing to your grandmother, the strategy of suppressing facial expressions has been shown to increase physiological arousal. Interestingly, it does so both for the person who is doing the suppressing (Gross & Levenson, 1997) and for the person with whom the suppresser is interacting (Gross, 2001). Reappraisals, by contrast, don't appear to take a physiological toll, because they change emotions, rather than stifle them.

Plus, recent research has shown that efforts to suppress facial expressions take a toll on cognitive functioning, too (Muraven, Tice, & Baumeister, 1998; Richards & Gross, 2000). In one study, participants were shown slides of men with recent or past injuries, many of them quite serious and therefore disgusting to view. During the slide presentation, participants heard each man's name, occupation, and type of accident. In one condition (suppression), participants were instructed to control their facial expressions by looking neutral and keeping still. In another condition (reappraisal), they were told to view the slides "with the detached interest of a medical professional" and to try to think so objectively that "you don't feel anything at all." For comparison, in a third condition, participants were simply told to view the slides carefully. Results showed that people instructed to suppress had poorer memory for the injured men's background information than those who simply watched. Those who reappraised showed no such memory deficit (Richards & Gross, 2000). This finding suggests that efforts to maintain composure by suppressing facial expressions may impair people's ability to navigate their social worlds. If, for instance, one person in a heated argument stonewalls and the other doesn't, they may end up with different memories of who said what, which in time could erode the relationship.

So reappraisal seems a better strategy for regulating emotions than suppressing facial expressions. Other research has shown that, at least in the short run, distraction techniques—like playing basketball or reading an absorbing novel—are better strategies than rumination techniques—like thinking over and over again about the causes and consequences of your sadness or anger. Rumination tends to heighten negative emotions, whereas distraction lessens them. Because of the effects of emotions on evaluations and judgments (described earlier), eventual efforts to solve underlying problems tend to be more successful once negative emotions have abated (Nolen-Hoeksema & Larson, 1999). We return to a discussion of rumination and its effects on depression and anxiety in Chapter 14.

◆ Interim Summary

- People almost always respond to or regulate their emotions, by either exaggerating or minimizing them, and the ability to do so predicts social success.

- Emotion regulation strategies have been classified as either cognitive or behavioral and as either diversion or engagement (see Table 11-5).

- Responses to emotion can influence other components of the emotion process. This is why Figure 11-1 has feedback arrows leading from "responses to emotion" to all preceding boxes.

- The strategies people use to regulate emotions can have unexpected repercussions. For instance, suppressing facial expression increases autonomic arousal and impairs memory.

◆ Critical Thinking Questions

1. Identify and describe an example from your own life in which you deliberately tried to regulate an emotion. How did you do it? Did your regulation strategy alter the other components of the emotion process? Which ones?

2. Research suggests that if you merely interact with a person who suppresses his own emotions, your own physiological arousal may increase. How might this happen?

EMOTIONS, GENDER, AND CULTURE

So far, in our discussion of the emotion process, we've emphasized how that process is similar for everybody. Yet emotional circumstances often bring out the differences between individuals and across groups. Sometimes those differences reflect personality and individuality (discussed in Chapters 12 and 13), and other times those differences reflect socialization histories, which vary by gender and culture. As we turn to issues of gender and culture in emotion processes, keep in mind that socialized differences and biological similarities both play key roles in the emotion process. As discussed in Chapter 1, it's not "nature *or* nurture" but rather "nature *and* nurture."

Looking back to Figure 11-1, you will notice that the emotion process begins with people's appraisals of their transactions with the environment and ends with their responses to their own emotions. One way to conceptualize the differences in emotion by gender and culture is to situate those differences as "front-end" or "back-end" differences. Front-end differences refer to those that begin with, or precede, the appraisal process. For instance, as we saw in our discussion of objectification theory (Chapter 10), to the extent that girls and women face circumstances that emphasize the importance of their weight and appearance, they may experience certain emotions—like shame—and certain emotional consequences—like depression and eating disorders—more frequently than do boys and men. By contrast, back-end differences refer to those linked to responses to emotion. People in some cultures, for instance, express fewer emotions socially, appearing stoic, whereas those in other cultures are very expressive and effusive. Using this perspective, we characterize the middle part of the process—the emotional responses of subjective experience, thought-action tendencies, bodily changes, and, to some extent, facial expressions—as relatively less influenced by gender and culture differences. This is clearly an oversimplification. For instance, we just discussed how responses to emotion serve to modify each and every other component of the emotion process. As such, any differences by gender or culture in responses to emotion also produce differences in these middle components. Even so, those differences in the middle components may be secondary to differences in front-end or back-end processes.

Gender Differences

First, note that people—men and women alike—hold strong beliefs about how emotions differ by gender. Women are stereotyped as the more emotional sex, experiencing and expressing emotions more often. The exceptions are anger and pride, which are among the few emotions held to be experienced and expressed more often by men (Plant, Hyde, Keltner, & Devine, 2000). How do these stereotypes map onto reality? Consolidating across multiple studies, psychologists have learned that men and women differ more in the *expression* of emotions—both facially and verbally—than in the subjective *experience* of emotions (Fischer, 2000). When gender differences in reports of subjective experience do emerge, they can often be traced back to differences in gender stereotypes. For instance, one study found that endorsement of the gender stereotypes was, for women, associated with reporting high-intensity emotions and, for men, associated with reporting low-intensity emotions (Grossman & Wood, 1993). This suggests that gender stereotypes color people's reports of their own experiences. Men might think, "I am a man, and men are not emotional, therefore I must not be emotional," and women might think, "I am a woman, and women are emotional, therefore I must be emotional." Studies have shown that stereotypes most color emotion reports when those reports are made at a global level ("How often do you feel sad or depressed")

or from hindsight ("How anxious were you during last week's exam?"). It turns out that gender differences in reported experience vanish when men and women report how they feel in the moment ("How anxious do you feel right now?"), presumably because in the moment, people are more focused on the specifics of their circumstances and feelings and less on how those feelings conform to their gendered beliefs about themselves (Feldman Barrett, Robin, Pietromonaco, & Eyssell, 1998).

These findings suggest that emotions may be a medium through which men and women (and boys and girls) "do gender"—behave in gender-appropriate ways. So just as females show femininity by paying attention to their appearance and diet, they may also show femininity by expressing the "feminine" emotions of sadness and fear and avoiding expression of the "masculine" emotions of anger and pride. Likewise, males may show their masculinity by showing the opposite pattern ("boys don't cry," men show "no fear"). Supporting this view, a study demonstrated that gender differences in emotional expression are linked to gender differences in the goals men and women have for regulating emotions. Women more readily expressed sadness and fear and were more likely to regulate their emotions to protect relationships. Men, in contrast, more readily expressed anger and were more likely to regulate their emotions to maintain or demonstrate their power (Timmers, Fischer, & Manstead, 1998).

The link between gender and power has led some psychologists to suggest that a gender hierarchy, in which women have relatively less power and status than men, is responsible for the observed gender differences in emotion. Women, as lower status, express the "powerless" emotions of sadness, anxiety, and fear (emotions that work to make one appear weak and helpless) and men, as higher status, express the "powerful" emotions of anger, pride, and contempt (emotions that work to maintain control and dominance; Fischer, 2000). Again, the distinction here targets emotion *expression*, not emotion experience. In one recent review of gender and anger, women were found to experience anger just as much as men—and in contexts of interpersonal relationships, even more. Even so, men appear angrier than women because they express their anger in prototypical ways—that is, with physical and verbal assaults. Women, in contrast, express their anger with tears, which may make it easier to dismiss their anger or mislabel it as sadness (Kring, 2000). Women also report being less comfortable than men in expressing their anger. Such gender differences in expressions of anger, then, may be what reinforce men as "powerful" and women as "powerless." Gender stereotypes also come into play: In a recent study, participants judged how angry or sad a person was who expressed an ambiguous blend of

Both of these photos show the same blend of two different emotion expressions. The brows are lowered and drawn together as they are for anger, while the lip corners are turned down as they are for sadness. Research has shown that when these and other anger-sadness blends appear on a man's face, people more often see the ambiguous blends as anger, but when the same blends appear on a woman's face, people more often see them as sadness (Plant et al., 2000). These findings suggest that gender stereotypes shape perceivers' interpretations of facial expressions.

anger and sadness. When the blended expression appeared on a man's face, it was seen as showing more anger; when it appeared on a woman's face, it was seen as showing more sadness (Plant et al., 2000).

To sum, gender differences in emotion may stem primarily from the back-end of the emotion process—from the ways that men and women regulate and express their emotions. These differences, in turn, most likely stem from gender differences in the way males and females are socialized—both by parents and by the culture more generally—to conform to gender stereotypes. Indeed, studies have shown that parents talk to their preschool children differently about emotions—for example, emphasizing sadness more with their daughters than with their sons (Fivush & Buckner, 2000). Such differences may set the stage for the emergence of gender differences in emotion regulation habits in later life. In other words, gender-specific lessons about appropriate emotion regulation are one way that boys and girls learn to be masculine or feminine, powerful or powerless.

CULTURAL DIFFERENCES

Psychologists studying cultural differences in emotion have mostly focused on how collectivism and individualism shape emotional experiences. Recall from Chapter 1 that **collectivism** refers to cultures that emphasize the fundamental connectedness and interdependence among people, and **individualism** refers to cultures that emphasize the fundamental separateness and independence of individuals. Many East Asian, Latin American, and African countries are identified as collectivist cultures, and the United States, Canada, Australia, and many Western European countries are identified as individualist cultures. Of course, not all citizens of these countries can be classified as collectivists or individualists. Variations by gender, social class, and ethnicity are common. Even so, differences along the dimension of collectivism-individualism appear critical to understanding cultural differences in emotions.

To understand why this is so, we can examine how variations in collectivism-individualism affect people's

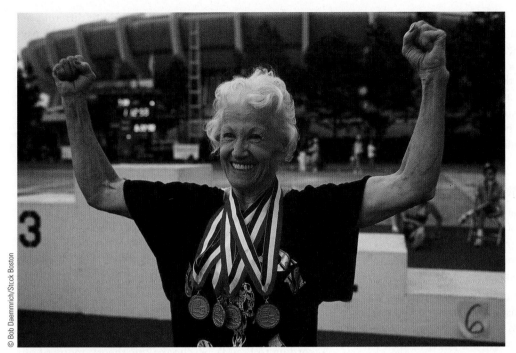

Happiness is more closely associated with individual achievements in individualist cultures and with good relationships in collectivist cultures.

© Bob Daemmrich/Stock Boston

views of self (Markus & Kitayama, 1991). In collectivist contexts, people's sense of self is embedded within relationships, with many personal goals reflecting this, including desires to fit in and create interpersonal harmony. In individualist contexts, by contrast, people's sense of self is bounded, or viewed as separate from close others, with many personal goals reflecting desires to be independent and unique. Continuing with the framework described earlier, cultural differences in personal goals can produce cultural differences in emotions through "front-end" differences in the emotion process. That is, if people in different cultures differ in their personal goals, especially regarding interpersonal relationships, so, too, will they differ in their appraisals of the personal meaning of their current circumstances, even when those circumstances are very similar. One study examined people's emotional reactions following errors in shared plans, like missing a scheduled meeting or get-together. In this study, Italians were selected to represent collectivism, and English-speaking Canadians were selected to represent individualism. As expected in collectivist cultures, Italians valued the relationship more than Canadians did. And when plans went wrong, Italians experienced more sorrow, whereas Canadians experienced more anger (Grazzani-Gavazzi & Oatley, 1999). Sorrow reflects collectivism in this circumstance

because the error is viewed as a shared loss. Anger, by contrast, reflects individualism because the error is viewed as a something the self deals with individually. So here, because relationships matter differently to people in collectivist and individualist cultures, the same circumstance—a broken plan—yields different emotions.

As another example, researchers have found that the circumstances that yield "good feelings" vary by culture. In Japan, a more collectivist culture, feeling good most frequently accompanies interpersonal engagement, like feeling friendly, whereas in the United States, a more individualist culture, feeling good most frequently accompanies interpersonal disengagement, like feeling superior or proud (Kitayama, Markus, & Kurokawa, 2000). This evidence suggests that people's sources of happiness depend on the ways in which their cultures value relationships and social worth—again, presumably because people's self-views and personal goals reflect collectivism or individualism.

So far we've discussed cultural differences in the "front-end" of the emotional process—that is, differences in the circumstances that yield emotions and differences in the appraisals of personal significance. Yet collectivism and individualism also affect the "back-end" of the emotional process, by prescribing which emotions can be expressed and when. We encountered one example of this earlier in discussing display rules for facial expressions. Compared with people from the United States, people from Japan more often mask experiences of disgust with smiles when in the presence of another. Relatedly, other studies find that pride is more acceptable to express in individualist cultures than in collectivist cultures (Fischer, Manstead, & Mosquera, 1999).

In addition to front-end differences in appraisals and back-end differences in responses to emotion, recent survey research on culture and emotion suggests that people's fundamental beliefs about emotions may differ in collectivist and individualist contexts (Mesquita, 2001). For instance, in individualist cultures, emotions are taken to reflect the subjective inner worlds of individuals and are thought to "belong to" a particular person (for instance, "Mark is angry"). By contrast, in collectivist cultures, emotions are taken to reflect objective reality and are thought to "belong to" relationships (for instance, "We are angry"). So, just as we said that emotions may be one medium through which people "do gender" or behave in gender-appropriate ways, emotions may also reinforce and sustain important cultural themes: Emotions appear to bind people together in collectivist cultures and to define individual uniqueness in individualist cultures.

◆ Interim Summary

- Emotions vary by gender and culture, perhaps most typically at the front-end of the emotion process (such as person-environment relations and cognitive appraisals) and the back-end of the emotion process (such as responses to emotion).

- Many gender differences can be linked to gender stereotypes about emotions, which assign "powerless" emotions, like sadness and fear, to women, and "powerful" emotions, like anger and pride, to men.

- Cultural differences in individualism versus collectivism also yield differences in emotion, with collectivism's greater focus on relationships affecting both appraisal processes and regulation strategies.

◆ Critical Thinking Questions

1. Revisit Figure 11-1 and explain the difference between "front-end" and "back-end" differences by gender and culture.

2. Are there likely to be aspects of the emotion process that do not vary by gender or culture? Why or why not?

AGGRESSION

As listed in Table 11-3, the action tendency associated with anger is to attack. People who act on this urge become either physically or verbally aggressive. Among the various thought-action tendencies associated with emotions, psychologists have singled out aggression for extensive study. This special attention is partly due to the social significance of aggression. At the societal level, in an age when nuclear weapons are widely available, a single aggressive act can spell worldwide disaster. At the individual level, many people experience aggressive thoughts and impulses frequently, and how they handle these thoughts has major effects on their health and interpersonal relations. Another reason psychologists have focused on aggression is that two ma-

jor theories of social behavior make quite different assumptions about the nature of aggression. Freud's psychoanalytic theory views aggression as a drive, but social-learning theory views it as a learned response. Research on aggression helps us evaluate these competing theories.

In the following discussion we first describe these different views, along with related research, and then consider how they differ with respect to the effects of portrayals of aggression in the mass media. Keep in mind that what we mean by **aggression** is behavior that is intended to injure another person (physically or verbally) or to destroy property. The key concept in this definition is intent. If a person accidentally steps on your foot in a crowded elevator and immediately apologizes, you would not interpret the behavior as aggressive; but if someone walks up to you as you sit at your desk and steps on your foot, you would not hesitate to label the act as aggressive.

AGGRESSION AS A DRIVE

According to Freud's psychoanalytic theory, many of our actions are determined by instincts, particularly the sexual instinct. When expression of these instincts is frustrated, an aggressive drive is induced. Later, psychoanalytic theorists broadened this **frustration-aggression hypothesis**, proposing that whenever a person's effort to reach a goal is blocked, an aggressive drive is induced that motivates behavior intended to injure the obstacle (person or object) causing the frustration (Dollard, Doob, Miller, Mowrer, & Sears, 1939). This proposal has two critical aspects. One is that the cause of aggression is frustration; the other is that aggression has the properties of a basic drive—being a form of energy that persists until its goal is satisfied, as well as being an inborn reaction like hunger or sex. As we will see, it is the drive aspect of the frustration-aggression hypothesis that has been particularly controversial.

If aggression is really a basic drive like hunger, we would expect other mammalian species to exhibit patterns of aggression that are similar to ours (just as they exhibit patterns of hunger that are similar to ours). The evidence for this has changed over the years. In the 1960s, early ethological research suggested that there was a major difference between humans and other species—namely, that animals had evolved mechanisms to control their aggressive instincts but humans had not (Ardrey, 1966; Lorenz, 1966). Subsequent research suggested, however, that animals may be no less aggressive than we are. The incidence of murder, rape, and infanticide among animals was shown to be much greater than previously thought.

One kind of murder occurs in border wars between chimpanzees (Goodall, 1978). In one well-documented case in the Gombe Stream National Park in Tanzania, a

Is aggression a drive or a learned response?

mate and kill it with exactly the same response that is exhibited by a wild rat (a hard bite to the neck that severs the spinal cord). The stimulation seems to trigger an innate killing response that was previously dormant. Conversely, if a neurochemical blocker is injected into the same brain site that induces rats to spontaneously kill mice on sight, the rats become temporarily peaceful (Smith, King, & Hoebel, 1970). In these cases, then, aggression has some properties of a drive, because it involves inborn reactions.

In some mammals, such instinctive patterns of aggression are controlled by the cortex and therefore are influenced more by experience. Monkeys living in groups establish a dominance hierarchy: One or two males become leaders, and the others position themselves at various lower levels in the hierarchy. When the hypothalamus of a dominant monkey is electrically stimulated, the monkey attacks subordinate males but not females. When a low-ranking monkey is stimulated in the same way, it cowers and behaves submissively (see Figure 11-8). Thus, aggressive behavior in a monkey is not automatically elicited by stimulation of the hypothalamus; the monkey's environment and past experiences also play a role. Humans are similar. Although we are equipped with neurological mechanisms that are tied to aggression, activation of these mechanisms is usually controlled by the prefrontal cortex, an area of the brain implicated in emotion regulation. Supporting this view, recent evidence suggests that the aspects of the prefrontal cortex are dysfunctional in individuals who show impulsive violence (Davidson, Putnam, & Larson, 2000). For others without this particular brain abnormality, the frequency with which aggressive behavior is expressed, the forms it takes, and the situations in which it is displayed are determined largely by experience and social influences.

Aggression as a Learned Response

Social-learning theory is concerned with human social interaction, but it has its origins in behaviorist studies of animal learning such as those discussed in Chapter 7. It focuses on the behavior patterns that people develop in response to events in their environment. Some social behaviors may be rewarded, and others may produce unfavorable results. Through the process of differential reinforcement, people eventually select the more successful behavior patterns. Although **social-learning theory shares basic principles of reinforcement with behaviorism, it differs from strict behaviorism in that it also emphasizes cognitive processes.** Because people can represent situations mentally, they are able to foresee the likely consequences of their actions and alter their behavior accordingly.

Social-learning theory further differs from strict behaviorism in that it stresses the role of **vicarious learning,**

gang of five male chimpanzees defended their territory against any strange male that wandered into it. If the gang encountered a group of two or more strangers, their response would be raucous but not deadly, but if there was only one intruder, one member of the gang might hold his arm, another a leg, while a third pounded the intruder to death. Or a couple of members of the gang would drag the intruder over the rocks until he died. In another chimpanzee border war observed during the 1970s, a tribe of about 15 chimpanzees destroyed a smaller neighboring group by killing the males one at a time. Female primates engage in as many aggressive acts as males, although their encounters are less deadly because their teeth are shorter and less sharp (Smuts, 1986).

Although observations like these bring animal aggression more in line with human aggression, there still are many differences. Humans wage wide-scale wars, for example.

Findings on the biological basis of aggression in animals provide evidence for an aggressive drive in at least some species. Some studies show that mild electrical stimulation of a specific region of the hypothalamus produces aggressive, even deadly, behavior in animals. When a cat's hypothalamus is stimulated via implanted electrodes, the animal hisses, its hair bristles, its pupils dilate, and it will strike at a rat or other objects placed in its cage. Stimulation of a different area of the hypothalamus produces quite different behavior: Instead of exhibiting any of these rage responses, the cat coldly stalks and kills a rat.

Similar techniques have produced aggressive behavior in rats. A laboratory-bred rat that has never killed a mouse, nor seen a wild rat kill one, may live quite peacefully in the same cage with a mouse. But if the rat's hypothalamus is stimulated, the animal will pounce on its cage-

Courtesy of Dr. Jose M.R. Delgado

Courtesy of Dr. Jose M.R. Delgado

▌ Figure 11-8
Brain Stimulation and Aggression
A mild electrical current is delivered to electrodes implanted in the monkey's hypothalamus via remote radio control. The animal's response (attack or flight) depends on its position in the dominance hierarchy of the colony.

or **learning by observation**. Many behavior patterns are learned by watching the actions of others and observing the consequences. A child who observes the pained expression of an older sibling in the dentist's chair will probably be fearful when the time comes for his or her first dental appointment. Social-learning theory emphasizes the role of models in transmitting both specific behaviors and emotional responses. It focuses on such questions as what types of models are most effective and what factors determine whether the observed behavior will actually be performed (Bandura, 1973, 1986).

With this emphasis on learning, it is no surprise that social-learning theory rejects the concept of aggression as a frustration-produced drive. The theory proposes instead that aggression is similar to any other learned response. Aggression can be learned through observation or imitation, and the more often it is reinforced, the more likely it is to occur. A person who is frustrated by a blocked goal or disturbed by a stressful event experiences an unpleasant emotion. The response that this emotion elicits will differ, depending on the kinds of responses the individual has learned to use in coping with stressful situations. The frustrated individual may seek help from others, behave aggressively, withdraw, try even harder to surmount the obstacle, or resort to drug or alcohol use. The chosen response will be the one that has relieved frustration most successfully in the past. According to this view, frustration provokes aggression

mainly in people who have learned to respond to adverse situations with aggressive behavior (Bandura, 1977).

Figure 11-9 shows how social-learning theory differs from psychoanalytic theory (that is, the frustration-aggression hypothesis) in conceptualizing aggression. Social-learning theory assumes that (1) aggression is just

Psychoanalytic Theory

Social-Learning Theory

▌ Figure 11-9
Two Views of Aggression
This diagram schematically represents the determinants of aggression according to psychoanalytic theory (the frustration-aggression hypothesis) and social-learning theory. From the viewpoint of social-learning theory, the emotional arousal caused by unpleasant experiences can lead to any number of different behaviors, depending on the behavior that has been reinforced in the past.

▍ Figure 11-10
Children's Imitation of Adult Aggression
Nursery school children observed an adult expressing various forms of aggressive behavior toward an inflated doll. After watching the adult, both boys and girls behaved aggressively toward the doll, performing many of the detailed acts of aggression that the adult had displayed, including lifting and throwing the doll, striking it with a hammer, and kicking it.

one of several reactions to the aversive experience of frustration and (2) aggression is a response with no drivelike properties, and consequently it is influenced by the anticipated consequences of behavior.

One source of evidence for social-learning theory comes from classic research showing that aggression, like any other response, can be learned through imitation. Preschool children who observed an adult expressing various forms of aggression toward a large inflated doll subsequently imitated many of the adult's actions, including unusual ones (see Figure 11-10). The experiment was expanded to include two filmed versions of aggressive modeling: one showing an adult behaving aggressively toward the doll, the other showing a cartoon character displaying the same aggressive behavior. The results were equally striking. Children who watched either of the two films behaved as aggressively toward the doll as children who had observed a live model displaying aggression. Figure 11-11 shows the measures of aggressive behavior for each of the groups and for two control groups who observed either no model or a nonaggressive model. The conclusion of such studies is that observation of either live or filmed models of aggression increases the viewer's likelihood of aggression. This may be part of the reason that children whose parents use physical punishment severely are likely to be more aggressive than average. The parents provide the model (Eron, 1987).

Imitative aggressive responses
All aggressive responses

█ Figure 11-11
Imitation of Aggression
Observing aggressive models (either live or on film) greatly increases the amount of aggressive behavior displayed by children, compared with observing a nonaggressive model or no model at all. Note that observation of the live model results in imitation of more specific aggressive acts, whereas observation of filmed (either real-life or cartoon) models instigates more aggressive responses of all kinds. (Adapted from A. Bandura, et al., "Imitation of Film-Mediated Aggressive Models," in *Journal of Abnormal Psychology*, 66:8. Copyright © 1963 by the American Psychological Association. Adapted by permission.)

Another piece of evidence for social-learning theory is that aggression is sensitive to reinforcement contingencies in the same manner that other learned responses are. A number of studies show that children are more likely to express the aggressive responses they learned by watching aggressive models when they are reinforced for such actions or when they observe aggressive models being reinforced. In one study, investigators observed children for 10 weeks, recording instances of aggression and the events that immediately followed them, such as positive reinforcers (the victim winced or cried), punishment of the aggression (the victim counterattacked), or neutral reactions (the victim ignored the aggressor). For the children who showed the highest overall level of aggression, the most common reaction to their aggressive act was positive reinforcement. For the children who showed the least aggression, punishment was a common reaction. Children who initially were not aggressive but who occasionally succeeded in stopping attacks through counter-aggression gradually began to initiate attacks of their own (their aggression was being positively reinforced). Clearly, the consequences of aggression play an impor-

tant role in shaping behavior (Patterson, Littman, & Bricker, 1967).

AGGRESSIVE EXPRESSION AND CATHARSIS

Studies that try to distinguish between aggression as a drive and aggression as a learned response often focus on **catharsis,** or purging an emotion by experiencing it intensely. If aggression is a drive, expression of aggression should be cathartic, resulting in a reduction in the intensity of aggressive feelings and actions (analogous to the way eating leads to a reduction of hunger-based feelings and actions). On the other hand, if aggression is a learned response, expression of aggression could result in an increase in such actions (if the aggression is reinforced). The available evidence favors the learned-response view.

Psychologists have conducted numerous laboratory studies to determine whether aggression decreases once it has been partially expressed. Studies of children indicate that participation in aggressive activities either increases aggressive behavior or maintains it at the same level. Experiments with adults produce similar results. When given repeated opportunities to shock another person (who cannot retaliate), college students become more and more punitive. Participants who are angry become even more punitive in successive attacks than participants who are not angry. If aggression were cathartic, the angry participants should reduce their aggressive drive by acting aggressively and become less punitive the more they engage in aggression (Berkowitz, 1965).

Some evidence about catharsis comes from real-life situations. In one case, California aerospace workers who had been laid off were interviewed about how they felt about their companies and supervisors and subsequently asked to describe their feelings in writing. If aggression were cathartic, men who expressed a lot of anger in the interviews should have expressed relatively little in the written reports. The results, however, showed otherwise: The men who let out anger in conversation expressed even more anger in their written reports. Another study looked at the relationship between the hostility of a country (vis-à-vis its neighboring countries) and the kinds of sports its citizens play. More belligerent countries were found to play more combative games. Again, aggression seems to breed more aggression rather than dissipate it (Ebbesen, Duncan, & Konecni, 1975).

These results argue against aggression being cathartic. However, there are circumstances in which the expression of aggression may decrease its incidence. For example, behaving aggressively may arouse feelings of anxiety that inhibit further aggression, particularly if the aggressors observe that their actions have led to injuries. But in these instances the effect on aggressive behavior can be explained by its consequences without concluding that an aggressive drive is being reduced. Also, although expressing hostile feelings in action does not usually reduce the aggression, it may make the person feel good. But this may happen because the person feels more powerful and more in control, rather than because the person has reduced an aggressive drive.

Most of the studies we have discussed deal with the consequences of directly expressing aggression. What about the effects of indirectly or vicariously expressing aggression by watching violence on television or in the movies or by playing violent video games? Is viewing violence or playing violent games cathartic, providing fantasy outlets for an aggressive drive? Or do they elicit aggression by modeling and reinforcing violent behavior? We have already seen that children imitate live or filmed aggressive behavior in an experimental setting, but how do they react in more natural settings? The increasing amount of media violence to which children are exposed makes this an important question.

Several experimental studies have controlled children's viewing of television. In one study, one group of children watched violent cartoons for a specified amount of time each day, and another group watched nonviolent cartoons for the same amount of time. The amount of aggression the children showed in their daily activities was carefully recorded. The children who watched violent cartoons became more aggressive in their interactions with peers, but the children who viewed nonviolent cartoons showed no change in interpersonal aggression (Steuer, Applefield, & Smith, 1971).

The study just described involves an experimental group and a control group. However, most studies that deal with children's viewing habits are correlational. They determine the relationship between amount of exposure to televised violence and the degree to which children use aggressive behavior to solve interpersonal conflicts. This correlation is clearly positive (Singer & Singer, 1981), even for children in Finland, which has a limited number of violent programs (Lagerspetz, Viemero, & Akademi, 1986). Yet correlations, you will recall, do not imply causal relationships. It may be that children who are aggressive prefer to watch violent television programs. That is, having an aggressive nature causes one to view violence, rather than vice versa.

To evaluate this alternative hypothesis, a study traced television viewing habits over a 10-year period. More than 800 children between the ages of 8 and 9 were studied. Investigators collected information about each child's viewing preferences and aggressiveness (as

rated by schoolmates). Boys who preferred programs that contain a considerable amount of violence were found to be much more aggressive in their interpersonal relationships than boys who preferred programs that contain little violence. So far, the evidence is similar to that found in previous studies. But 10 years later, more than half of the original participants were interviewed regarding their television preferences, given a test that measured delinquent tendencies, and rated by their peers for aggressiveness. Figure 11-12 shows that high exposure to violence on television at age 9 is positively related to aggressiveness in boys at age 19. Most important, the correlation remains significant even when statistical methods are used to control for degree of childhood aggressiveness, thereby reducing the possibility that the initial level of aggression determines both childhood viewing preferences and adult aggressiveness.

Interestingly, the results showed no consistent relationship between the television viewing habits of girls and their aggressive behavior at either age. This agrees with the results of other studies indicating that girls tend to imitate aggressive behavior much less than boys do unless they are specifically reinforced for doing so. In our society, girls are less likely to be reinforced for behaving aggressively. And because most of the aggressive roles on television are male, females are less likely to find aggressive models to imitate. For boys, however, the majority of studies point to the conclusion that viewing violence

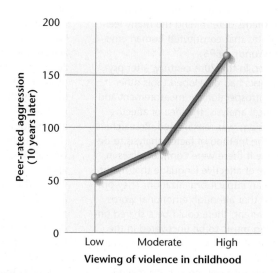

Figure 11-12
The Relationship Between Childhood Viewing of Violent Television and Adult Aggression
A preference for viewing violent television programs by boys at age 9 is positively correlated with aggressive behavior at age 19. (After Eron, Huesmann, Lefkowitz, & Walder, 1972)

What Is the Underlying Structure of Emotions?

THE DIMENSIONAL ORGANIZATION OF EMOTION
Peter J. Lang, University of Florida

There are thousands of words in all languages that describe emotional experience. When psychology first began to develop as a science, and its primary aim was to illuminate human consciousness, this myriad of emotion words implied as many different states of feeling. Confronted by a confusing, affective plethora, one of the field's great founders, Wilhelm Wundt, proposed that affective experience was determined by only a few underlying dimensions that could be independently analyzed by trained introspectionists. For example, an important characteristic of all emotional reactions was pleasantness, which could vary from very positive to very negative affect. Another dimension might define a feeling's degree of activation or excitement, increasing from calm to high arousal. Wundt proposed a kind of chemistry of consciousness: These two affective dimensions organized elements of sensation, with different combinations of elements determining the many feeling states that constituted human emotion (Wundt, 1896).

Later, in the 20th century, after psychologists had developed tools other than introspection for measurement and statistical analysis, the idea of affective dimensions was reexamined. Researchers used the method of factor analysis to determine if there were commonalities in the use of affective language that might reveal an implicit organization. They presumed that although emotional words are different, there could be a shared underlying music to be uncovered in the pattern of their use. Factor analysis is a correlational method defining such common variance—an underlying relatedness. For example, evaluative words like *happy, joyful, fun, liberating, free, warm,* and *sympathetic* show common variance and can be said to share a common implicit meaning—it's good, it's pleasant.

For several decades, researchers have repeatedly examined patterns of use in emotional language and consistently found two dominant, independent factors that appear to underlie much of affective report: (1) emotional valence, the degree of pleasantness or unpleasantness implicit in the report, and (2) the degree of experienced activation or arousal, varying from calm repose to high excitement. Whatever words are used to describe a feeling, the reaction can be scaled on these two simple dimensions, capturing the substantive meaning of any affective report (Mehrabian & Russell, 1974; Osgood, Suci, & Tannenbaum, 1957; Russell, 1980).

Recently, these factors were also shown to be significant for measures of emotion other than evaluative language. That is, the complex phenomena we call emotion also involves a change *in our actions* (how much we delay, approach, or avoid, and in how well we perform a task) and *in our physiology* (modifications of heart rate and other visceral events, muscle tension, and somatic reflexes). When participants respond to emotionally arousing stimuli we can record, along with affective judgments, many other response events—such as how long they choose to view the stimulus (a measure of interest), sweat gland activity, changes in brain waves, facial expressions, and heart rate. Curiously, if these varied data are submitted to factor analysis, two dominant factors again survive statistical test, affective valence and arousal—with particular physiological and behavioral measures indexing the different factors (Cuthbert, Schupp, Bradley, Birbaumer, & Lang, 2000; Lang, Greenwald, Bradley, & Hamm, 1993).

Why is this so? What is so fundamental about valence and arousal that these factorial dimensions should so frequently emerge?

The similarity of reaction in animals to situations we consider emotional suggests that affects are products of evolution. For example, in anticipation of a dangerous or painful event, the same behavioral and physiological changes reflexively occur in nearly all mammals—including humans. A neural network deep in the brain, basically the same in all complex organisms, orchestrates these responses. This circuit constitutes a kind of defense system that has evolved to ensure the survival of individuals and species. An analogous circuit organizes positive appetitive responses associated with nourishment, sexuality, and nurturance of young. In brief, the evolved brain appears to have two primary motivational systems—one dedicated to defense and the other to appetitive needs—both deploying varying patterns of reflexive responses, somatic and visceral (Davis & Lang, 2002).

Many years ago, Jerzy Konorski (1967) suggested that pleasant affects were prompted by engagement of the appetitive system and that the defense system determined unpleasant affects. In this general view, the affective valence factor reflects the motivational state, appetitive or defensive, underlying evaluative judgments, pleasant or unpleasant. Affective arousal reflects the vigor of motivational engagement—the reported intensity of either pleasant or unpleasant emotional experience. For example, threat at a distance engages the defense system, prompting increased vigilance and reports of moderate arousal. With greater proximity in time or space, there is greater probability of the dangerous event, emotional language is more intense, and the body increasingly mobilizes for action (Lang, Bradley, & Cuthbert, 1997).

In summary, the affective dimensions of valence and arousal are a useful way to organize emotional reactions, because they capture the underlying motivational strategy of organisms—direction and vigor—and given a stable context of measurement, they relate closely to activation of the brain's motive circuits and to affect's reflexive physiology.

What Is the Underlying Structure of Emotions?

AN ARGUMENT FOR DISCRETE EMOTIONS
Robert W. Levenson, University of California, Berkeley

A small set of prototypical challenges and problems that have enormous implications for human survival and thriving undoubtedly played a major role in the evolution of our emotions. Bonding with others, handling threats, dealing with loss, defending what is ours, avoiding noxious substances, and soothing self and others are all integral parts of the human condition. Their ubiquity and importance would have created enormous selection pressures favoring generalized solutions for each of these problems and challenges—solutions that have the highest likelihood of producing beneficial outcomes for the individual and for the social group. Emotions are these solutions, orchestrating configurations of motor behaviors; expressive signals in face and voice; changes in attention, perception, and information processing; and physiological adjustments that can be activated quickly and efficiently, often with little conscious intervention. Viewed in this way, emotions can be seen as time-tested solutions for timeless problems.

This group of problems and challenges and the associated emotional solutions are not distributed evenly across the landscape of human experience. Emotional solutions for dealing with problems of rotting food (disgust), loss of a loved one (sadness), or having a possession taken away (anger) differ more in kind and in configuration than in degree. Because of this, it is virtually impossible to find a single unipolar or bipolar dimensional structure that allows ordinal ranking of the most common emotions (such as anger, contempt, disgust, fear, happiness, sadness, surprise). Consider the pervasive "positive-negative" dimension. Although happiness is clearly more positive than the others in this set, subsequent ranking quickly becomes problem-

atic. Is disgust more negative than fear? Is fear more negative than anger? Or consider another oft-proposed dimension: "approach-avoidance." Although disgust can readily be placed at the extreme avoidance end of the scale, the other emotions are not so clear. Sadness, for example, sometimes drives us toward and sometimes away from others (and has a similar bimodal effect on the behavior of others toward us).

The same kinds of problems are also found at the level of individual components of the emotional response. Emotional appearance changes in the face (Ekman, 1972) poorly fit popular dimensional schemes. Consider trying to map brow changes onto the "positive-negative" dimension. Lowered and furrowed brows are associated with a negative emotion (anger), but raised brows are not part of the positive emotion (happiness) display. Rather, raised brows are either associated with surprise (if both inner and outer portions are raised), an emotion that is arguably neither positive nor negative, or with sadness (if only the inner portion is raised), an emotion that is clearly negative. Attempting to map lip movements onto this dimension creates similar problems. Lip corners move up bilaterally in a positive emotion (happiness) and move down in a negative emotion (sadness), but they also move up unilaterally in another negative emotion (contempt) and are stretched laterally in yet another negative emotion (fear). Autonomic nervous system responses present comparable difficulties. Heart rate increases are found in two negative emotions (anger, fear) but not in a third (disgust) (Levenson, 1992). These two negative emotions—alike in heart rate change—diverge in terms of temperature (warming in anger versus

cooling in fear), a difference found both in physiological studies of emotion and in common metaphoric manners of speaking (Lakoff, 1987).

These kinds of problems with the dimensional view lead me to conclude that a discrete view is the most parsimonious way to organize emotions. In this view, emotions are seen as having different *configurations* of behavior, expression, and physiology that represent generalized solutions to a small set of common problems and challenges. Nonetheless, humans are clearly capable of talking and thinking about emotions in dimensional ways. We respond to the ubiquitous question of "How are you feeling today?" by invoking a dimensional structure when we reply with "good" or "bad." However, even in this highly conventional case, a response of "bad" is likely to engender an additional question probing for more information as to whether we are sad or mad or afraid (or something comparably "discrete").

What would enable us to resolve the discrete versus dimensional question with greater certainty? Only the most sanguine of brain-mapping enthusiasts envisions our finding particular pieces of the human brain that are associated with particular discrete emotions or particular emotional dimensions. More likely, the war between discrete and dimensional views will continue to be waged with lower-tech tools. Based on current knowledge, it appears that humans can and do think and talk about emotions in both discrete and dimensional ways. However, the more we discover about the structure and function of emotions, the more difficult it becomes to apply dimensional rubrics, and the more compelling discrete models become.

Children often imitate what they see on television.

does increase aggressive behavior, particularly in young children. Indeed, this conclusion is supported by a meta-analysis of 28 studies of this issue (Wood, Wong, & Chachere, 1991). These findings argue against the idea of aggression as catharsis, as well as the view that aggression is a drive.

So the scientific evidence that viewing TV and movie violence increases aggression is very strong. Despite this evidence, the visual media are become increasingly violent and diverse and now include interactive media, like video games. Public concern about violent video games rose dramatically in the aftermath of school shootings in Paducah, Kentucky; Jonesboro, Arkansas; and Littleton, Colorado. The adolescent boys who committed these atrocities habitually played some of the bloodiest and most violent video games available. Given that children, adolescents, and college students (mostly male) spend considerable time playing violent video games, psychologists have become interested in whether playing these violent games also increases aggressive behavior in the real world. A meta-analysis of 54 recent studies provides clear evidence that it does—and also that playing these violent games increases aggressive thoughts, feelings, and arousal, and reduces prosocial helping behavior (Anderson & Bushman, 2001).

The results of research on media violence provide strong support for efforts to reduce the amount of aggression in media marketed to children. They also carry a message for parents. Not only should responsible parents closely monitor the type of television programs their children view and video games they play but also they should avoid praising aggressive actions, either by their children or by television characters. They also need to be aware of their powerful role in modeling behavior. If they behave aggressively, their children are likely to do so as well.

Our survey of aggression has by no means considered all of its possible causes. Common causes of anger and aggression include loss of self-esteem or a perception that another person has acted unfairly (Averill, 1983). We have not focused on either of these factors in our discussion of aggression as a drive versus aggression as a learned response. Also, many social conditions are involved in the instigation of aggression. Poverty, overcrowding, the actions of authorities such as the police, and cultural values are only a few. Some of these social influences will be considered in Chapter 17. In sum, aggression may often occur when a person is frustrated, but it does not always follow frustration. Many social conditions and cues either increase or decrease a person's tendency to act aggressively (Berkowitz, 1981).

The study of aggression makes it clear that an emotional reaction is a complex event. Similarly, each component of an emotion that we considered—cognitive appraisals, subjective experiences, bodily changes, facial expressions, and responses to emotion—is itself a complex event involving multiple factors, both biological and psychological. In fact, each of the perspectives on emotion described in this chapter has addressed how the biological components of emotion (such as physiological arousal and universal facial expressions) and the psychological components of emotion (such as cognitive appraisals) interact to produce the experience of emotion. Taken together, the research reviewed in this chapter suggests that in most cases the biological and psychological components of emotion probably have reciprocal influences on each other in a dynamic process that evolves over time. A situation may initially elicit a mild emotion, but as a person evaluates the situation more deeply, the emotion may intensify, and his physiological arousal may increase. The effects of the emotion on his memory for similar events from the past and on his appraisals of this event may further intensify his subjective experience of emotion. Over time, then, feedback loops between the biological and psychological components of an emotion can influence the development of the emotion. We will return to discussions of the feedback between the biological and psychological components of emotion when we discuss stress in Chapter 14 and emotional disorders in Chapters 15 and 16.

◆ Interim Summary

- The psychoanalytic hypothesis that aggression is a basic drive receives some support from studies showing a biological basis for aggression. In some animals, aggression is controlled by neurological mechanisms in the hypothalamus. Stimulation of the hypothalamus of a rat or cat can lead to rage or a killing response. In humans and certain other mammals, aggressive behavior is largely under cortical control and hence is affected by past experiences and social influences.

- According to social-learning theory, aggressive responses can be learned through imitation and increase in frequency when positively reinforced. Children are more likely to express aggressive responses when they are reinforced for such actions than when they are punished for the actions.

- Evidence indicates that aggression either increases subsequent aggressive behavior or maintains it at the same level, arguing against catharsis. When given repeated opportunities to shock another person who cannot retaliate, college students become more and more punitive.

- Indirect or vicarious expression of aggression also shows no evidence for catharsis: There is a positive relationship between the amount of media violence children consume and the extent to which they act aggressively.

◆ Critical Thinking Questions

1. How are responses to emotion—or attempts to regulate emotion—implicated in the biology and psychology of aggressive behavior?

2. Which types of studies suggest that media violence plays a causal role in increasing aggression?

CHAPTER SUMMARY

1. The components of emotion include cognitive appraisals, the subjective experience of emotion, thought-action tendencies, autonomic arousal, facial expressions, and responses to the emotion.

2. A cognitive appraisal is an interpretation of the personal meaning of a situation that results in an emotion. Such appraisals affect both the intensity and the quality of an emotion. When people are induced into a state of undifferentiated arousal, the quality of their emotional experience may be influenced by their appraisal of the situation. Cognitive appraisals can occur outside of conscious awareness, and brain research identifies the amygdala as involved in automatic appraisals.

3. Subjective experiences of emotions, or feelings, guide behavior, decision making, and judgment. Different emotions carry urges to think and act in certain ways, called *thought-action tendencies*. Feelings also steer memory, learning, and risk assessments.

4. Intense negative emotions involve physiological arousal caused by activation of the sympathetic division of the autonomic nervous system. Positive emotions have an undoing effect on lingering negative emotional arousal. People with spinal cord injuries, which limit feedback from the autonomic nervous system, report experiencing less intense emotions. Autonomic arousal may also help differentiate the emotions, because the pattern of arousal (for example, heartbeat, skin temperature) differs for different emotions.

5. The facial expressions that accompany a subset of emotions have a universal meaning: People from different cultures agree on what emotion a person in a particular photograph is expressing. Cultures may differ in the factors that elicit certain emotions and in rules for the proper display of emotion. In addition to their communicative functions, emotional expressions may contribute to the subjective experience of an emotion (the facial feedback hypothesis).

6. People almost always respond to or regulate their emotions by either exaggerating or minimizing them, and the ability to do so predicts social success. The strategies people use to regulate emotions can have unexpected repercussions. For instance, suppressing facial expression increases autonomic arousal and impairs memory.

7. Emotions vary by gender and culture. Many gender differences can be linked to gender stereotypes about emotions, which assign "powerless" emotions, like sadness and fear, to women, and "powerful" emotions, like anger and pride, to men. Cultural differences in individualism versus collectivism also yield differences in emotion, with collectivism's greater focus on relationships affecting both appraisal processes and regulation strategies.

8. The psychoanalytic hypothesis that aggression is a basic drive receives some support from studies showing a biological basis for aggression. In some animals, aggression is controlled by neurological mechanisms in the hypothalamus. Stimulation of the hypothalamus of a rat or cat can lead to a rage or killing response. In humans and certain other mammals, aggressive behavior is largely under cortical control and hence is affected by past experiences and social influences.

9. According to social-learning theory, aggressive responses can be learned through imitation and increase in frequency when positively reinforced. Children are more likely to express aggressive responses when they are reinforced for such actions than when they are punished for the actions.

10. Evidence indicates that aggression either increases subsequent aggressive behavior or maintains it at the same level. When given repeated opportunities to shock another person who cannot retaliate, college students become more and more punitive. The indirect or vicarious expression of aggression has similar effects: There is a positive relationship between the amount of media violence children consume and the extent to which they act aggressively.

CORE CONCEPTS

antisocial personality disorder
emotion
cognitive appraisal
subjective experience
thought and action tendencies
autonomic nervous system
facial expression
responses to emotion
moods
person-environment relationship
two-factor theory
misattribution of arousal

minimalist appraisal theories
dimensional appraisal theories
core relational theme
backward masking
amygdala
broaden-and-build theory
sympathetic nervous system
parasympathetic nervous system
undoing effect of positive emotions
visceral perception
William James
James-Lange theory

display rules
facial feedback hypothesis
emotion regulation
collectivism
individualism
aggression
frustration-aggression hypothesis
social-learning theory
vicarious learning
catharsis

WEB RESOURCES

http://psychology.wadsworth.com/
atkinson14e

Take a quiz, try the activities and exercises, and explore web links.

http://www.psy.ulaval.ca/~arvid/R2e.html

How *do* we study emotion? This site does an excellent job of answering this question.

http://www.apa.org/pubinfo/anger.html

Provided by the American Psychological Association, this is an interesting article about controlling anger.

http://www.eur.nl/fsw/research/happiness/
index.htm

This is the world database for happiness. Here you will find survey results from across the world, as well as a test bank for happiness and further readings about happiness.

InfoTrac Online Library
http://www.infotrac-college.com/
wadsworth

Use InfoTrac College Edition to find popular and scientific articles by using the search terms below or your own relevant terms.

- Aggressiveness (Psychology)
- Anger
- Emotion
- Happiness

CD-ROM LINKS

Psych Odyssey
Check out CD Chapter 12, Motivation and Emotion

B. Emotion

Psyk.trek 2.0
Check out CD Unit 8, Motivation and Emotion

8c Elements of Emotion
8d Theories of Emotion

© Getty Images/Stone

INTELLIGENCE

12

Tommy was born in December 1856 to Janet Woodrow, the daughter of a Presbyterian minister, and Joseph Ruggles Wilson, himself a Presbyterian minister who became a leader of the Presbyterian Church in the American South. Tommy's parents were educated people who highly valued learning. As a schoolboy, however, Tommy had great difficulty reading. Despite attending special schools, he still was not able to read until late childhood, around age 10 or 11. With a great deal of hard work, he was eventually able to qualify for admission to the College of New Jersey, which later became Princeton University. Even in college, however, Tommy did not excel at coursework.

To this point, you might predict that Tommy's chances for success in life were only moderate. We might say today that "he didn't look good on paper." Our modest predictions for

Tommy's future would be proven wrong, however. Tommy was Thomas Woodrow Wilson. After graduating from Princeton, he earned a law degree from the University of Virginia and a doctorate in political science from Johns Hopkins University.

During periods as a professor at Bryn Mawr College, Wesleyan University, and Princeton University, Wilson wrote nine books and became a respected essayist. He was named president of Princeton in 1902 and then won the race for governor of New Jersey in a landslide election in 1910. In 1912, he ran for president of the United States against the incumbent, President William Howard Taft, and won, becoming the 28th U.S. president. During his 8 years in office, Wilson led the United States through World War I and worked tirelessly to establish a lasting and meaningful peace in Europe. In 1919, he won the Nobel Peace prize for his efforts in establishing the League of Nations.

Based on his accomplishments across the course of his life, most people would say that Thomas Woodrow

Wilson was an intelligent man. If he had taken an intelligence test or some other kind of aptitude test as a boy, however, he might not have scored in the "intelligent" range. Wilson's life story raises important questions about what we mean by intelligence.

The concept of intelligence has been one of the most contentious across the history of psychology and continues to be so today. Even defining **intelligence** can be difficult because your definition reflects your theory of what it means to be intelligent, and theories of intelligence differ widely, as we will discuss later. Some theorists have argued that intelligence doesn't exist as a real entity, but simply is a label for what intelligence tests measure. Other theorists suggest that intelligence should be considered more broadly and that it involves the ability to learn from experience, think in abstract terms, and deal effectively with one's environment. We will consider various conceptualizations and theories of intelligence in this chapter. First, however, we discuss how intelligence is measured.

427

ASSESSMENT OF INTELLECTUAL ABILITIES

Many industrialized societies rely heavily on objective assessment of cognitive or intellectual abilities. Schoolchildren are often placed in instructional groups on the basis of their performances on such tests. Aptitude or ability tests are part of the admissions procedure in many colleges and most professional and graduate schools. In addition, many industries and government agencies select job applicants and place or promote employees on the basis of test scores. Beyond these practical concerns, methods of assessment are essential to theory and research on intelligence.

Because tests and other assessment instruments play important practical and scientific roles, it is essential that they measure accurately what they are intended to measure. Specifically, they must have reliability and validity. They also must be standardized, meaning that the conditions for taking the test are the same for all test-takers. For example, the instructions accompanying the test must be the same for everyone.

RELIABILITY

If a test or method of assessment has good **reliability,** it will yield reproducible and consistent results. If a test yielded different results when it was administered on different occasions or scored by different people, it would be unreliable. A simple analogy is a rubber yardstick. If we did not know how much it stretched each time we took a measurement, the results would be unreliable no matter how carefully we made each measurement.

Reliability is typically assessed by correlating two sets of scores. For example, the same test might be given to the same group of people on two occasions. If the test is reliable, their scores on the first occasion should correlate highly with their scores on the second. If they do, the test is said to have test-retest reliability or temporal stability.

In practice, of course, we would not usually want to give the same test to the same people twice. But there are many situations in which we would want to give equivalent forms of the same test—for example, when college-bound high school seniors want to take the Scholastic Assessment Test (SAT) more than once. To ensure that two forms of the same test yield equivalent scores, both forms are administered to the same population and the two forms are correlated. The test is said to have **alternative form reliability** if the two forms of the test correlate highly. Some of the questions on the SAT do not actually count toward the student's score but are being statistically evaluated so they can be used on future equivalent forms of the test.

Another common measure of reliability is **internal consistency,** the degree to which the separate questions or items on a test measure the same thing. This can be assessed by correlating the scores obtained by a group of individuals on each item with their total scores. Any item that does not correlate with the total score is an unreliable item that is failing to contribute to what the test is measuring. Discarding unreliable items "purifies" a test by increasing its internal consistency. As the number of reliable items on a test increases, the reliability of the test's total score also increases.

Most tests and assessment instruments are scored objectively, often by computer. But sometimes intellectual performance or social behavior must be subjectively evaluated. An essay examination is a familiar example. To assess the reliability of such subjective judgments, two or more sets of ratings by independent judges are correlated. For example, two observers might independently rate a group of nursery school children for aggression, or two or more judges might be asked to read past U.S. presidential inaugural addresses and rate them for optimism or count the number of negative references to Iraq. If the correlation between raters or judges is high, the method is said to possess **interrater agreement** or **interjudge reliability.**

In general, a well-constructed, objectively scored test of ability should have a reliability coefficient of .90 or greater. For subjective judgments, reliability coefficients of .70 can sometimes be satisfactory for research purposes, but inferences about particular individuals must be

Psychological tests are often used to evaluate job applicants.

made with great caution. But as noted earlier, the reliability of a test's total score increases as the number of reliable items on the test increases. We can apply the same reasoning to subjective judgments and increase the reliability of the method by adding more judges, raters, or observers. For example, if ratings by two observers correlate only .50, the researcher can add a third, comparable observer and thereby raise the interjudge reliability of their summed ratings to .75; adding a fourth rater would raise the reliability to .80.

VALIDITY

Reliability assesses the degree to which a test is measuring something, but high reliability does not guarantee that the test has good **validity**—that is, that it measures what it is intended to measure. For example, if the final examination in your psychology course contained especially difficult vocabulary words or trick questions, it might be a test of your verbal ability or test sophistication rather than of the material learned in the course. Such an examination might be reliable—students would achieve about the same scores on a retest, and the separate items might all be measuring the same thing—but it would not be a valid test of achievement for the course.

In some instances, the validity of a test can be assessed by correlating the test score with some external criterion. This correlation is called a *validity coefficient,* and this kind of validity is called **criterion or empirical validity.** For example, the relatively strong positive correlation between scores on the SAT and freshman grades in college is one indication of the test's validity. Because of sensitivity to race and sex discrimination, the courts are increasingly requiring companies and government agencies that use tests for personnel selection to provide evidence that those tests correlate with on-the-job performance—in other words, that they have criterion or empirical validity.

There may be aspects of intelligence for which it is not clear what the external criterion should be. How, for example, should a researcher assess the validity of a test for achievement motivation? One can think of a number of possibilities. The test could be given to business executives to see if it correlates with their salaries. Perhaps the test will correlate with teachers' ratings of their students' ambition. The problem is that there is no single criterion that the researcher is willing to accept as the ultimate "true" answer. It would be reassuring if the test correlated with executive salaries, but if it did not, the researcher would not be willing to judge the test to be invalid. This is known as the **criterion problem in assessment:** There is no measure of "truth" against which to validate the test. Accordingly, the researcher attempts instead to establish its **construct validity**—to show that

scores on the test correlate with outcomes that the theory says it should predict.

This is done through the research process itself. The researcher uses his or her theory both to construct the test and to generate predictions from the theory. Studies using the test are then conducted to test those predictions. To the extent that the results of several converging studies confirm the theory's predictions, both the theory and the test are validated simultaneously. Most often, mixed results suggest ways in which both the theory and the test need to be modified. For example, McClelland (1987) proposed a theory of achievement motivation that was supposed to identify and explain ambitious, high-achieving individuals in any area of activity. A test for assessing achievement motivation was designed and used to test predictions from the theory. Results from several studies indicated that the predictions were confirmed for men involved in entrepreneurial activities but not for women or for individuals involved in other kinds of activities, such as academic research. Accordingly, the theory was modified to apply primarily to entrepreneurial achievement, and the test was modified so that it was more valid for women.

EARLY INTELLIGENCE TESTS

The first attempt to develop tests of intellectual ability was made a century ago by Sir Francis Galton. A naturalist and mathematician, Galton developed an interest in individual differences after considering the evolutionary theory proposed by his cousin, Charles Darwin. Galton believed that certain families are biologically superior to others—that some people are innately stronger or smarter than others. Intelligence, he reasoned, is a question of exceptional sensory and perceptual skills, which are passed from one generation to the next. Because all information is acquired through the senses, the more sensitive and accurate an individual's perceptual apparatus, the more intelligent the person. (Galton's belief in the heritability of intelligence led him to propose that the human race's mental capacities could be enhanced through eugenics, or selective breeding. Fortunately, he is remembered more for his application of statistics to the study of intelligence than for his espousal of eugenics.)

In 1884, Galton administered a battery of tests (measuring variables such as head size, reaction time, visual acuity, auditory thresholds, and memory for visual forms) to more than 9,000 visitors at the London Exhibition. To his disappointment, he discovered that eminent British scientists could not be distinguished from ordinary citizens on the basis of their head size and that measurements such as reaction time were not related to other measures of intelligence. Although his test did not prove very useful, Galton did invent the correlation co-efficient, which—as we have already seen—plays an important role in psychology.

The first tests resembling modern intelligence tests were devised by the French psychologist Alfred Binet in the late 19th century. In 1881, the French government passed a law making school attendance compulsory for all children. Previously, slow learners had usually been kept at home, but now teachers had to cope with a wide range of individual differences. The government asked Binet to create a test that would detect children who were too slow intellectually to benefit from a regular school curriculum.

Binet assumed that intelligence should be measured by tasks that required reasoning and problem-solving abilities rather than perceptual-motor skills. In collaboration with another French psychologist, Théophile Simon, Binet published such a test in 1905 and revised it in 1908 and again in 1911.

Binet reasoned that a slow or dull child was like a normal child whose mental growth was retarded. On tests, the slow child would perform like a younger normal child, whereas the mental abilities of a bright child were characteristic of older children. Binet devised a scale of test items of increasing difficulty that measured the kinds of changes in intelligence ordinarily associated with growing older. The higher a child could go on the scale in answering items correctly, the higher his or her mental age (MA). The concept of mental age was critical to Binet's method. Using this method, the MA of a child could be compared with his or her chronological age (CA) as determined by date of birth.

THE STANFORD–BINET INTELLIGENCE SCALE

The test items originally developed by Binet were adapted for American schoolchildren by Lewis Terman at Stanford University. Terman standardized the administration of the test and developed age-level norms by giving the test to thousands of children of various ages. In 1916, he published the Stanford revision of the Binet tests, now referred to as the Stanford-Binet Intelligence Scale. It was revised in 1937, 1960, 1972, and most recently in 1986. Despite its age, the Stanford-Binet is still one of the most frequently used psychological tests.

Terman retained Binet's concept of mental age. Each test item was age-graded at the level at which a substantial majority of the children pass it. A child's mental age could be obtained by summing the number of items passed at each level. In addition, Terman adopted a convenient index of intelligence suggested by the German psychologist William Stern. This index is the intelligence

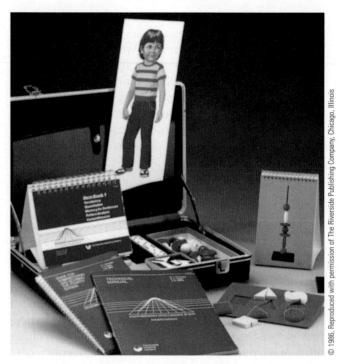

Test materials from the Stanford-Binet Intelligence Scale.

quotient (IQ), which expresses intelligence as a ratio of mental age to chronological age:

$$IQ = MA/CA \times 100$$

The number 100 is used as a multiplier so that the IQ will have a value of 100 when MA is equal to CA. If MA is lower than CA, the IQ will be less than 100; if MA is higher than CA, the IQ will be more than 100.

The most recent revision of the Stanford-Binet uses standard age scores instead of IQ scores. These can be interpreted in terms of percentiles, which show the percentage of individuals in the standardization group falling above or below a given score (Thorndike, Hagen, & Sattler, 1986). And although the concept of IQ is still used in intelligence testing, it is no longer actually calculated by using this equation. Instead, tables are used to convert raw scores on the test into standard scores that are adjusted so that the mean at each age equals 100.

IQ scores tend to fall in the form of a bell-shaped curve, with most people's scores hovering around 100, but some people's scores much higher or lower than 100. Figure 12-1 provides the percentages of the population who will fall in various ranges of IQ scores.

In line with the current view of intelligence as a composite of different abilities, the 1986 revision of the Stanford-Binet groups its tests into four broad areas: verbal reasoning, abstract/visual reasoning, quantitative reasoning, and short-term memory (Sattler, 1988). A separate score is obtained for each area. Table 12-1 gives some examples of items, grouped by area.

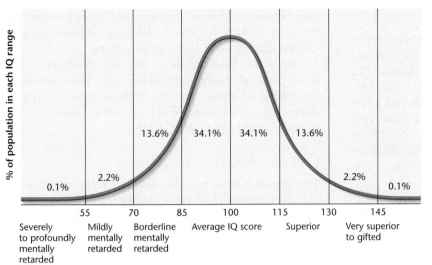

Figure 12-1
Frequency Distribution of IQ Scores
IQ scores fall into a normal distribution, with few scores at either the high or low extremes, and most scores falling around 100. (From A. Anastasia and S. Urbina, *Psychological Testing,* 7/e, © 1997 Prentice-Hall.)

● **Table 12-1**
Items From the Stanford-Binet Intelligence Scale

Typical examples of items from the 1986 Stanford-Binet Intelligence Scale for a 6- to 8-year-old.

Test	Description
Verbal Reasoning	
Vocabulary	Defines words, such as "dollar" and "envelope."
Comprehension	Answers questions, such as "Where do people buy food?" and "Why do people comb their hair?"
Absurdities	Identifies the "funny" aspect of a picture, such as a girl riding a bicycle on a lake or a bald man combing his hair.
Verbal Relations	Tells how the first three items in a sequence are alike and how they differ from the fourth: scarf, tie, muffler, shirt.
Quantitative Reasoning	
Quantitative	Performs simple arithmetic tasks, such as selecting a die with six spots because the number of spots equals the combination of a two-spot die and a four-spot die.
Number Series	Gives the next two numbers in a series, such as 20 16 12 8 __ __.
Equation Building	Builds an equation from the following array: 2 3 5 + = . One correct response would be 2 + 3 = 5.
Abstract/Visual Reasoning	
Pattern Analysis	Copies a simple design with blocks.
Copying	Copies a geometrical drawing demonstrated by the examiner, such as a rectangle intersected by two diagonals.
Short-Term Memory	
Bead Memory	Shown a picture of different-shaped beads stacked on a stick. Reproduces the sequence from memory by placing real beads on a stick.
Memory for Sentences	Repeats after the examiner sentences such as "It is time to go to sleep" and "Ken painted a picture for his mother's birthday."
Memory for Digits	Repeats after examiner a series of digits, such as 5-7-8-3, forward and backward.
Memory for Objects	Shown pictures of individual objects, such as a clock and an elephant, one at a time. Identifies the objects in the correct order of their appearance in a picture that also includes extraneous objects; for example, a bus, a clown, an *elephant,* eggs, and a *clock.*

The Wechsler Intelligence Scales

In 1939, David Wechsler developed a new test because he thought the Stanford-Binet depended too heavily on language ability and was not appropriate for adults. The **Wechsler Adult Intelligence Scale,** or WAIS (1939, 1955, 1981), is divided into two parts—a verbal scale and a performance scale—that yield separate scores as well as a full-scale IQ. The test items are described in Table 12-2. Wechsler later developed a similar test for children, the Wechsler Intelligence Scale for Children (WISC) (1958, 1974, 1991).

Items on the performance scale require the manipulation or arrangement of blocks, pictures, or other materials. The Wechsler scales also provide scores for each subtest, so the examiner has a clearer picture of the individual's intellectual strengths and weaknesses. For example, a discrepancy between verbal and performance scores prompts the examiner to look for specific learning problems such as reading disabilities or language handicaps.

Both the Stanford-Binet and the Wechsler scales show good reliability and validity. They have test-retest reliabilities of about .90, and both are fairly valid predictors of achievement in school, with validity coefficients of about .50 (Sattler, 1988).

Group Ability Tests

The Stanford-Binet and the Wechsler scales are individual ability tests. They are administered to a single individual by a specially trained tester. Group ability tests, in contrast, can be administered to a large number of people by a single examiner and are usually in pencil-and-paper form.

● **Table 12-2**

Tests Composing the Wechsler Adult Intelligence Scale

The tests of the Wechsler Intelligence Scale for Children are similar to those of the adult scale, with some modifications.

Test	Description
Verbal Scale	
Information	Questions tap a general range of information, for example, "What is the capital of Italy?"
Comprehension	Tests practical information and ability to evaluate past experience, for example, "Why do we put stamps on a letter to be mailed?"
Arithmetic	Verbal problems testing arithmetic reasoning.
Similarities	Asks in what way two objects or concepts (for example, *recipe* and *map*) are similar; assesses abstract thinking.
Digit Span	A series of digits presented auditorily (for example, 7-5-6-3-8) is repeated in a forward or backward direction; tests attention and rote memory.
Vocabulary	Assesses word knowledge.
Letter Number Sequencing	Orally presented letters and numbers in a mixed-up order must be reordered and repeated, first with the numbers in ascending order and then with the letters in alphabetical order; assesses working memory.
Performance Scale	
Digit Symbol	A timed coding task in which numbers must be associated with marks of various shapes; assesses speed of learning and writing.
Picture Completion	The missing part of an incompletely drawn picture must be discovered and named; assesses visual alertness, visual memory, and perceptual organization.
Block Design	Pictured designs must be copied with blocks; assesses ability to perceive and analyze patterns.
Picture Arrangement	A series of comic-strip pictures must be arranged in the right sequence to tell a story; assesses understanding of social situations.
Matrix Reasoning	A geometric shape that is similar in some way to a sample shape must be selected from a set of possible alternatives; assesses perceptual organization.
Object Assembly	Puzzle pieces must be assembled to form a complete object; assesses ability to deal with part-whole relationships.
Symbol Search	A series of paired groups of symbols are presented, a target group of two symbols and a search group. Examinee must determine if either target symbol appears in the search group; assesses processing speed.

The **Scholastic Assessment Test (SAT)** and the **American College Test (ACT)** are examples of group-administered general-ability tests that are familiar to most college students in the United States. Virtually all 4-year colleges require applicants to take one of these tests as a way of setting a common standard for students from high schools with different curricula and grading standards. The SAT has been undergoing major revisions in response to criticism, and there are plans to include essay components, among other changes, in upcoming versions. These changes were made in response to recent high school curriculum trends that place a premium on more sophisticated reading, writing, and mathematics skills.

Correlations between SAT scores and freshman grade point averages vary across studies, with a median correlation of about .38 for the verbal section of the SAT and .34 for the mathematics section (Linn, 1982). When these correlations are corrected for the fact that many students with very low scores do not end up attending college (and hence cannot be included in the calculation of the validity correlation), the resulting correlations are about .50. This means that about 44% of students in the top fifth of the distribution of SAT scores will also be in the top fifth of the distribution of freshman grade point averages, compared with only 4% of students in the bottom fifth of the SAT score distribution. SAT scores improve prediction considerably, but it is clear that the freshman grades of students with identical SAT scores will vary widely.

THE FACTORIAL APPROACH

Some psychologists view intelligence as a general capacity for comprehension and reasoning that manifests itself in various ways. This was Binet's assumption. Although his test contained many kinds of items, Binet observed that a bright child tended to score higher than dull children on all of them. He assumed, therefore, that the different tasks sampled a basic underlying ability. Similarly, despite the diverse subscales included the WAIS, Wechsler also believed that "intelligence is the aggregate or global capacity of the individual to act purposefully, to think rationally, and to deal effectively with his environment" (Wechsler, 1958).

Other psychologists, however, question whether there is such a thing as "general intelligence." They believe that intelligence tests sample a number of mental abilities that are relatively independent of one another. One method of obtaining more precise information about the kinds of abilities that determine performance on intelligence tests is **factor analysis,** a statistical technique that examines the intercorrelations among a number of tests and, by grouping those that are most highly correlated, reduces them to a smaller number of independent dimensions, called factors. The basic idea is that two tests that correlate very highly with each other are probably measuring the same underlying ability. The goal is to discover the minimum number of factors, or abilities, required to explain the observed pattern of correlations among an array of different tests.

It was the originator of factor analysis, Charles Spearman (1904), who first proposed that all individuals possess a general intelligence factor (called *g*) in varying amounts. A person could be described as generally bright or generally dull, depending on the amount of *g* he or she possessed. According to Spearman, the *g* factor is the major determinant of performance on intelligence tests. In addition, special factors, each called *s*, are specific to particular abilities or tests. For example, tests of arithmetic or spatial relationships would each tap a separate *s*. An individual's tested intelligence would reflect the amount of *g* plus the magnitude of the various *s* factors possessed by that individual. Performance in mathematics, for example, would be a function of a person's general intelligence and mathematical aptitude.

A later investigator, Louis Thurstone (1938), objected to Spearman's emphasis on general intelligence, suggesting instead that intelligence can be broken down into a number of primary abilities by using factor analysis. After many rounds of administering tests, factor-analyzing the results, purifying the scales, and retesting, Thurstone identified seven factors, which he used to construct his Test of Primary Mental Abilities.

Revised versions of this test are still widely used, but its predictive power is no greater than that of general intelligence tests such as the Wechsler scales. Thurstone's hope of discovering the basic elements of intelligence through factor analysis was not fully realized, for several reasons. For one, his primary abilities are not completely independent. Indeed, the significant intercorrelations among them provide support for the concept of a general intelligence factor underlying the specific abilities. For another, the number of basic abilities identified by factor analysis depends on the nature of the test items. Other investigators, using different test items and alternative methods of factor analysis, have identified from 20 to 150 factors representing the range of intellectual abilities (Ekstrom, French, & Harman, 1979; Ekstrom, French, Harman, & Derman, 1976; Guilford, 1982).

This lack of consistency in number and kinds of factors raises doubts about the value of the factorial approach. Nevertheless, factor analysis remains an important technique for studying intellectual performance (Lubinski, 2000), and we will encounter it again when we discuss personality traits in Chapter 13.

CULTURAL CONSIDERATIONS

Intelligence tests have come under fire in recent years for being biased in favor of middle- and upper-class European Americans and against members of cultural minorities (Helms, 1992). Educated European Americans may be more comfortable in taking intelligence tests because they are more familiar with the kinds of reasoning assessed on intelligence tests and because testers are often also European Americans. In contrast, different cultures within the United States and in other countries may emphasize other forms of reasoning over those assessed on intelligence tests and may not be comfortable with the testing situations of intelligence tests.

A classic example involves the interpretation of syllogisms, logical problems often used in intelligence tests. A typical syllogism runs like this: "All bears in the North are white. My friend saw a bear in the North. What color was that bear?" According to intelligence tests, the "right" answer is that the bear is white. A subject's ability to infer that the bear is white is taken as an indication of his or her deductive reasoning skills.

When researchers asked farmers in Central Asia to solve these syllogisms, however, they discovered that this form of reasoning violated a social norm that you never state something you do not know from firsthand experience (Luria, 1976, pp. 108–109):

> Experimenter: In the Far North, where there is snow, all bears are white. Novaya Zemlya is in the Far North and there is always snow there. What color are the bears there?
> Respondent: . . . We always speak only of what we see; we don't talk about what we haven't seen.
> E: But what do my words imply? (The syllogism is repeated.)
> R: Well, it's like this: our tsar isn't like yours, and yours isn't like ours. Your words can be answered only by someone who was there and if a person wasn't there, he can't say anything on the basis of your words.
> E: . . . But on the basis of my words—in the North, where there is always snow, the bears are white, can you gather what kind of bears there are in Novaya Zemlya?

Scores on the Scholastic Assessment Test are used to predict academic achievement in college. The correlation between SAT scores and freshman grad point averages is about .50.

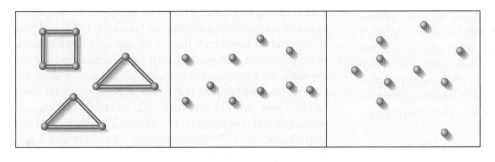

R: If a man was 60 or 80 and had seen a white bear and had told about it, he could be believed, but I've never seen one and hence I can't say. That's my last word.

This may have been interpreted as unintelligent by the rules of the test, but he was only following a social convention of his culture in his answer to the experimenter. Critics of intelligence tests argue that similar cultural clashes happen in subtler ways whenever persons not of the dominant, educated culture that created intelligence tests are asked to take these tests. A "culture-fair" test would have to include items that are equally applicable to all groups or items that are different for each culture but are psychologically equivalent for the groups being tested. An example of one such test is given in Figure 12-2. In general, attempts at culture-fair tests have proven disappointing.

◆ Interim Summary

- There are many different definitions of intelligence. Some theorists view it as simply what intelligence tests measure. Others view it as a set of general abilities, including the ability to learn from experience, think in abstract terms, and deal effectively with one's environment.

- A good test of intelligence must be reliable—it yields reproducible and consistent results. Alternate form reliability is shown when two forms of a test correlate highly with each other. A test has good internal consistency when various items on the test are correlated highly with each other. When more subjective assessments are used, judges rate the answers of respondents, and the researcher hopes to see interjudge reliability or interrater reliability.

- A test has good validity if it measures what it is intended to measure. Criterion or empirical validity is shown when the test is highly correlated with another test of the same construct. Construct validity is shown when the scores on the test predict outcomes that the researcher's theory suggests it should predict.

- The first successful intelligence tests were developed by the French psychologist Alfred Binet, who pro-

posed the concept of mental age. A bright child's mental age is above his or her chronological age; a slow child's mental age is below his or her chronological age. The concept of the intelligence quotient (IQ), the ratio of mental age to chronological age (multiplied by 100), was introduced when the Binet scales were revised to create the Stanford-Binet. Many intelligence test scores are still expressed as IQ scores, but they are no longer actually calculated according to this formula.

- Both Binet and Wechsler, the developer of the Wechsler Adult Intelligence Scale (WAIS), assumed that intelligence is a general capacity for reasoning.

- Similarly, Spearman proposed that a general factor (*g*) underlies performance on different kinds of test items. Factor analysis is a method for determining the kinds of abilities that underlie performance on intelligence tests.

◆ Critical Thinking Questions

1. Many colleges are now ceasing to use standardized tests such as the SAT or ACT to evaluate students seeking admission, arguing they are poor predictors of the students' overall success in college or in life. What do you think are the advantages and disadvantages of not using standardized tests in admissions procedures?

2. Do you think it is possible to create a culture-fair test of intelligence?

CONTEMPORARY THEORIES OF INTELLIGENCE

Until the 1960s, research on intelligence was dominated by the factorial approach. However, with the development of cognitive psychology and its emphasis on information-processing models (see Chapter 9), a new approach emerged. This approach is defined somewhat differently by different investigators, but the basic idea is to try to understand intelligence in terms of the cognitive processes that operate when we engage in intellectual activities (Sternberg & Kaufman, 1998). The information-processing approach asks:

1. What mental processes are involved in the various tests of intelligence?
2. How rapidly and accurately are these processes carried out?
3. What types of mental representations of information do these processes act upon?

Rather than trying to explain intelligence in terms of factors, this approach attempts to identify the mental processes that underlie intelligent behavior. It assumes that individual differences on a given task depend on the specific processes that different individuals bring into play and the speed and accuracy of those processes. The goal is to use an information-processing model of a particular task to identify appropriate measures of the processes used in performing the task. These measures may be as simple as the response to a multiple-choice item, or they may include response speed or the eye movements associated with the response. The idea is to use whatever information is needed to estimate the efficiency of each component process.

GARDNER'S THEORY OF MULTIPLE INTELLIGENCES

Howard Gardner (1993a) developed his theory of multiple intelligences as a direct challenge to what he calls the "classical" view of intelligence as a capacity for logical reasoning. Gardner was struck by the variety of adult roles in different cultures—roles that depend on a variety of skills and abilities yet are equally important to successful functioning in those cultures. His observations led him to conclude that there is not just one underlying mental capacity or g, but a variety of intelligences that work in combination. He defines an intelligence as the "ability to solve problems or fashion products that are of consequence in a particular cultural setting or community" (1993b, p. 15). It is these multiple intelligences that enable human beings to take on such diverse roles as physicist, farmer, shaman, and dancer (Gardner, 1993a).

Gardner is quick to point out that an intelligence is not a "thing," some sort of commodity inside the head, but "a potential, the presence of which allows an individual access to forms of thinking appropriate to specific kinds of content" (Kornhaber & Gardner, 1991, p. 155). According to **Gardner's theory of multiple intelligences,** there are seven distinct kinds of intelligence that are independent of one another, each operating as a separate system (or module) in the brain according to its own rules. These are (1) linguistic, (2) musical, (3) logical-mathematical, (4) spatial, (5) bodily-kinesthetic, (6) intrapersonal, and (7) interpersonal. These are described more fully in Table 12-3.

Gardner analyzes each kind of intelligence from several viewpoints: the cognitive operations involved, the appearance of prodigies and other exceptional individuals, evidence from cases of brain damage, manifestations in different cultures, and the possible course of evolutionary development. For example, certain kinds of brain damage can impair one type of intelligence and have no effect on the others. He notes that the capacities of adults in different cultures represent different combinations of the various intelligences. Although all normal people can apply all of the intelligences to some extent, each individual is characterized by a unique combination of relatively stronger and weaker intelligences (Walters & Gardner, 1985), which help account for individual differences.

As noted earlier, conventional IQ tests are good predictors of college grades, but they are less valid for predicting later job success or career advancement. Measures of other abilities, such as interpersonal intelligence, may help explain why some people with brilliant college records fail miserably in later life while lesser students become charismatic leaders (Kornhaber, Krechevsky, & Gardner, 1990). Gardner and colleagues therefore call for "intelligence-fair" assessments in schools that would allow children to demonstrate their abilities by other means besides paper-and-pencil tests, such as putting together gears to demonstrate spatial skills.

ANDERSON'S THEORY OF INTELLIGENCE AND COGNITIVE DEVELOPMENT

One criticism of Gardner's theory is that high levels of ability in any of the various intelligences is usually correlated with high ability in the others; that is, no specific intellectual capacity is wholly distinct from the others (Messick, 1992; Scarr, 1985). In addition, psychologist Mike Anderson points out that Gardner's multiple intelligences are ill-defined—they are "sometimes a behavior, sometimes a cognitive process, and sometimes a structure in the brain" (1992, p. 67). Anderson therefore has sought to develop a theory based on the idea of general intelligence proposed by Thurstone and others.

Gardner's Seven Intelligences

(Adapted from Gardner, Kornhaber, & Wake, 1996)

Type of Intelligence	Description
1. **Linguistic Intelligence**	The capacity for speech, along with mechanisms dedicated to phonology (speech sounds), syntax (grammar), semantics (meaning), and pragmatics (implications and uses of language in various settings).
2. **Musical Intelligence**	The ability to create, communicate, and understand meanings made of sound, along with mechanisms dedicated to pitch, rhythm, and timbre (sound quality).
3. **Logical-Mathematical Intelligence**	The ability to use and appreciate relationships in the absence of action or objects—that is, to engage in abstract thought.
4. **Spatial Intelligence**	The ability to perceive visual or spatial information, modify it, and re-create visual images without reference to the original stimulus. Includes the capacity to construct images in three dimensions and to move and rotate those images.
5. **Bodily-Kinesthetic Intelligence**	The ability to use all or part of the body to solve problems or fashion products; includes control over fine and gross motor actions and the ability to manipulate external objects.
6. **Intrapersonal Intelligence**	The ability to distinguish among one's own feelings, intentions, and motivations.
7. **Interpersonal Intelligence**	The ability to recognize and make distinctions among other people's feelings, beliefs, and intentions.

According to Gardner's theory of multiple intelligences, these three individuals are displaying different kinds of intelligence: logical-mathematical, musical, and spatial.

Anderson's theory of intelligence holds that individual differences in intelligence and developmental changes in intellectual competence are explained by different mechanisms. Differences in intelligence result from differences in the "basic processing mechanism" that implements thinking, which in turn yields knowledge. Individuals vary in the speed at which basic processing occurs. A person with a slower basic processing mechanism is likely to have more difficulty acquiring knowledge than a person with a faster processing mechanism. This is equivalent to saying that a low-speed processing mechanism produces low general intelligence.

Anderson notes, however, that there are some cognitive mechanisms that show no individual differences. For example, people with Down syndrome may not be able to add 2 plus 2 yet can recognize that other people hold beliefs and may act on those beliefs (Anderson, 1992). The mechanisms that provide these universal capacities are "modules." Each module functions independently, performing complex computations. Modules are not af-

Emotional Intelligence

New York Times writer Daniel Goleman popularized the term *emotional intelligence* in his 1995 book. He argued that understanding and control of your emotions is one of the most important keys to health and success in life. Goleman's book was based on important new work by psychologists such as Peter Salovey, John Mayer, and Reuven Bar-On showing that, indeed, people who are emotionally astute have a leg up on those of us who are not.

Mayer and Salovey (1997; Mayer, Salovey, & Caruso, 2000) suggest there are four critical components to emotional intelligence. The first is *accurate perception and expression* of emotions. Being able to read the emotions of others enables you to anticipate possible threats they might pose. For example, imagine you are in an argument with a coworker who is known to have a volatile temper. If you can accurately perceive that your coworker is getting extremely agitated, you will know that it may be time to back off and live to fight another day. If you don't accurately perceive your coworker's level of anger, you might end up with a bloody nose. Accurately perceiving and expressing others' emotions also helps you empathize with their position. In turn, you can modify your responses to other people, either to be more persuasive in arguing your point or to make them feel that you understand them well. This can make you an effective negotiator and a trusted friend to others.

Accurately perceiving and expressing your own emotions is the first step to responding appropriately to those emotions. People who don't realize they are anxious can have chronic physiological arousal that costs them physical wear and tear and impairs their health (see Chapter 14). People who don't realize they are sad may not take the necessary actions to change the sources of their sadness. People who don't realize they are angry may

suddenly and impulsively lash out at others, feeling out of control.

The second component of emotional intelligence is the ability to *access and generate emotions* in the service of thinking and problem solving. We often ask ourselves, "How do I feel about this?" in trying to make an important decision, such as what college to attend or what major to pursue. Being able to access our current feelings about an issue or to anticipate our future feelings, should we make a particular decision, gives us important information that should go into many decisions.

The third component of emotional intelligence is *understanding emotions and emotional meanings*. We may accurately perceive we are anxious, but if we don't understand why we are anxious, we can't do much about it. We often make incorrect attributions for our emotions, which can lead us to take unwise steps. For example, imagine you have been staying up late each night for many weeks to complete your school assignments and then getting up for early morning classes. Eventually, you begin to feel sad, lethargic, and unmotivated. You might conclude that you are feeling sad and unmotivated because you are pursuing the wrong major, or even that college is not for you. The true reason for your sadness, however, may well be sleep deprivation, which can cause depression-like symptoms (see Chapter 6). Attributing your sadness incorrectly to your college major rather than correctly to your lack of sleep could cause you to make some very bad decisions.

The final component of emotional intelligence is *emotional regulation*—being able to manage and regulate your emotions appropriately. This does not mean completely controlling the emotions you feel or express. Indeed, such emotional overcontrol is unhealthy. But letting your emotions rage unabated can also be unhealthy. The most obvious example is with anger. We all feel angry at times, but most of us know we can't express our anger at any time and in any way we wish (at least we can't get away with it). How we channel our anger is critical to our relationships to others and to our own health. People who completely sup-

press their anger can be exploited by others, and people who chronically express their anger in a hostile manner lose friends quickly. In contrast, people who can express the reasons for their anger in ways that others can hear and accept are more likely to both maintain their friendships and avoid being exploited. In addition, research we will review in Chapter 14 clearly shows that people who do not channel their anger appropriately experience more heart disease, probably because their cardiovascular system is chronically overaroused and overreactive.

Can you learn emotional intelligence? Many schools now have programs to teach young people how to recognize and better manage their anger, in hopes of reducing school violence, and some evaluations of these programs suggest they can be effective in teaching young people anger control (Graczyk et al., 2000; Topping, Holmes, & Bremner, 2000). Many a crusty corporate executive has also undergone emotional schooling to learn how to better empathize with employees and manage with a bigger heart, and it appears these programs can be successful (Cherniss, 2000). Much of what psychotherapy focuses on is helping people recognize, accurately label, and manage their emotions better, and many studies show psychotherapy to be effective in relieving a variety of psychological disorders (see Chapter 16). These same techniques are sometimes used to help cardiac patients better control anger and stress so as to improve their health (see Chapter 14). Thus, there is increasing evidence that emotional intelligence truly is important to success and well-being, and fortunately, those of us born emotionally challenged can become more intelligent. The empirical research specifically examining emotional intelligence is in its infancy, however, and we are sure to learn much more in years to come (Mayer et al., 2000).

 For more information, go online with InfoTrac College Edition. Use your own term or search:

- Emotional intelligence
- Emotional regulation

fected by the basic processing mechanism; they are virtually automatic. According to Anderson, it is the maturation of new modules that explains the increase of cognitive abilities in the course of development. For example, the maturation of a module devoted to language would explain the development of the ability to speak in complete sentences.

In addition to modules, according to Anderson, intelligence includes two "specific abilities." One of these deals with propositional thought (language mathematical expression) and the other with visual and spatial functioning. Anderson suggests that the tasks associated with these abilities are carried out by "specific processors." Unlike modules, which carry out very particular functions, each of the specific processors handles a broad class of problems or knowledge. Also unlike modules, specific processors are affected by the basic processing mechanism. A high-speed processing mechanism enables a person to make more effective use of the specific processors to score higher on tests and accomplish more in the real world.

Anderson's theory of intelligence thus suggests two different "routes" to knowledge. The first involves using the basic processing mechanism, which operates through the specific processors, to acquire knowledge. In Anderson's view, this is what we mean by "thinking," and it accounts for individual differences in intelligence (which, in his view, are equivalent to differences in knowledge). The second route involves the use of modules to acquire knowledge. Module-based knowledge, such as perception of three-dimensional space, comes automatically if the module has matured sufficiently, and this accounts for the development of intelligence.

Anderson's theory can be illustrated by the case of a 21-year-old man known as MA who suffered convulsions as a child and was diagnosed as autistic. As an adult, he could not talk and achieved very low scores on psychometric tests. However, he was found to have an IQ of 128 and had an extraordinary ability to detect prime numbers, doing so more accurately than a scientist with a degree in mathematics (Anderson, 1992). Anderson concludes that MA had an intact basic processing mechanism, which allowed him to think about abstract symbols, but had suffered damage to his linguistic modules, which hindered acquisition of everyday knowledge and communication.

STERNBERG'S TRIARCHIC THEORY

In contrast to Anderson's theory, Robert **Sternberg's triarchic theory** addresses experience and context as well as basic information-processing mechanisms (Sternberg,

1996). His theory has three parts or subtheories: the componential subtheory, which deals with thought processes; the experiential subtheory, which deals with the effects of experience on intelligence; and the contextual subtheory, which considers the effects of the individual's environment and culture. The most highly developed of these subtheories is the componential subtheory.

The componential theory considers the components of thought. Sternberg has identified three types of components:

1. Metacomponents are used to plan, control, monitor, and evaluate processing during problem solving. Sternberg (1996) has relabeled these as analytical abilities. For example, if you were going to cook Thanksgiving dinner, you would have to plan the menu and then monitor your progress toward getting all the ingredients, cooking each dish, and making sure everything was ready to serve at the same time.
2. Performance components carry out problem-solving strategies. Sternberg (1996) now calls these creative abilities. A skilled mechanic can use his creative abilities to devise a way to fix parts of a car that are not working.
3. Knowledge-acquisition components encode, combine, and compare information during the course of problem solving. Sternberg (1996) now calls these practical abilities. You are using your knowledge-acquisition or practical abilities as you read through this chapter and decide to commit certain pieces of information to memory.

These components are intertwined. Each comes into play during the problem-solving process, and none of them can operate independently. Sternberg illustrates the functioning of these components with analogy problems of the following kind:

lawyer is to client as doctor is to _____
(a) medicine   (b) patient

A series of experiments with such problems led Sternberg to conclude that the critical components were the encoding process and the comparison process. The participant encodes each of the words in the analogy by forming a mental representation of the word—in this case, a list of attributes of the word that are retrieved from long-term memory. For example, a mental representation of the word *lawyer* might include the following attributes: college-educated, versed in legal procedures, represents clients in court, and so on. Once the participant has formed a mental representation for each word in the analogy, the comparison process scans the representations looking for matching attributes that solve the analogy.

Other processes are involved in analogy problems, but Sternberg has shown that individual differences on this task are determined primarily by the efficiency of the encoding and comparison processes. The experimental evidence shows that individuals who score high on analogy problems (skilled performers) spend more time encoding and form more accurate mental representations than do individuals who score low on such problems (less-skilled performers). In contrast, during the comparison stage, the skilled performers are faster than the less-skilled performers in matching attributes, but both are equally accurate. So, the better test scores for skilled performers are based on the increased accuracy of their encoding process, but the time they require to solve the problem is a complicated mix of slow encoding speeds and fast comparisons (Galotti, 1989; Pellegrino, 1985).

The componential subtheory by itself does not provide a complete explanation of individual differences in intelligence. The experiential subtheory is needed to account for the role of experience in intelligent performance. According to Sternberg, differences in experience affect the ability to solve a given problem. A person who has not previously encountered a particular concept, such as a mathematical formula or an analogy problem, will have more difficulty applying that concept than someone who is experienced in the use of that concept. An individual's experience with a task or problem thus falls somewhere along a continuum that extends from totally novel to completely automatic (that is, totally familiar as a result of long experience).

Of course, a person's exposure to particular concepts depends to a large extent on the environment. This is where the contextual subtheory comes in. This subtheory is concerned with the cognitive activity needed to fit into particular environmental contexts (Sternberg, 1985; Sternberg, Castejon, Prieto, Hautamaeki, & Grigorenko, 2001). It focuses on three mental processes: adaptation, selection, and shaping of real-world environments. According to Sternberg, the individual first looks for ways to adapt, or fit into, the environment. If it is not possible to adapt, the individual tries to select a different environment or to shape the existing environment in order to fit into it better. A spouse who is unhappy in a marriage may not be able to adapt to the current circumstances. He or she may therefore select a different environment (for example, through separation or divorce) or try to shape the existing environment (for example, through counseling) (Sternberg, 1985).

CECI'S BIOECOLOGICAL THEORY

Some critics claim that Sternberg's theory has so many parts that it is not coherent (Richardson, 1986). Others note that it does not show how problem solving occurs in everyday contexts. Still others point out that it largely ignores the biological aspects of intelligence. Stephen Ceci (1990, 1996) has attempted to address these issues by building on Sternberg's theory while placing much more emphasis on context and its impact on problem solving.

Ceci's bioecological theory proposes that there are "multiple cognitive potentials," rather than a single underlying general intelligence or *g*. These multiple abilities, or intelligences, are biologically based and place limits on mental processes. Their emergence, however, is shaped by the challenges and opportunities in the individual's environment, or context.

In Ceci's view, context is essential to the demonstration of cognitive abilities. By "context," he means domains of knowledge as well as factors such as personality, motivation, and education. Contexts can be mental, social, or physical (Ceci & Roazzi, 1994). A particular individual or population may appear to lack certain mental abilities, but if given a more interesting and motivating context, the same individual or population can demonstrate a higher level of performance. To take just one example, in a famous longitudinal study of high-IQ children studied by Lewis Terman (Terman & Oden, 1959), high IQ was thought to be correlated with high achievement. But a closer look at the results revealed that children from upper-income families went on to become more successful adults than children from lower-income families. In addition, those who became adults during the Great Depression ended up less successful than those who became adults later, when there were more job opportunities. In Ceci's words, "The bottom line . . . is that the ecological niche one occupies, including individual and historical development, is a far more potent determinant of one's professional and economic success than is IQ" (1990, p. 62).

Ceci also argues against the traditional view that intelligence is related to a capacity for abstract thinking, regardless of the subject area. He believes that the ability to engage in complex thought is tied to knowledge gained in particular contexts or domains. Rather than being endowed with a greater capacity for abstract reasoning, intelligent people have enough knowledge in a particular domain to enable them to think in a complex way about problems in that area of knowledge (Ceci, 1990). In the course of working in a particular domain—for example, computer programming—the individual's knowledge base grows and becomes better organized. Over time, this

Research indicates that the more risk factors children are exposed to, the lower their IQs tend to be. (After Sameroff)

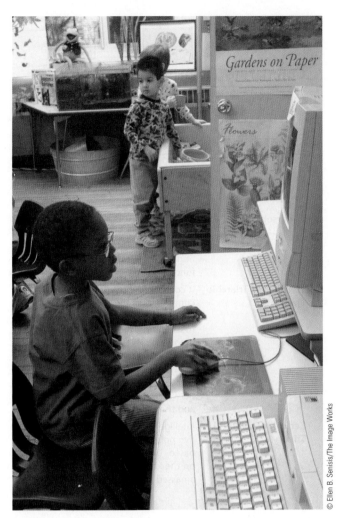

Learning environments enriched by technology are important ingredients to eventual success.

makes possible more intelligent performances—for example, more efficient programs.

In sum, according to Ceci, everyday or real-world intellectual performance cannot be explained by IQ alone or by some biological notion of general intelligence. Instead, it depends on the interaction between multiple cognitive potentials with a rich, well-organized knowledge base. For example, a child could be born with strong cognitive potentials, but if she was raised in an extremely impoverished intellectual environment, she might never develop these potentials. One longitudinal study provided evidence of the impact of environment on IQ. Sameroff and colleagues (1993) examined the relationship between the environment children were exposed to in early childhood and their IQs at ages 4 and 13. The more environmental risk factors a child was exposed to—such as lack of education or mental illness in his or her mother, minority status (which is associated with low standard of living and inferior schools), and large family size—the lower the child's IQ was (see Figure 12-3).

COMPARING THEORIES OF INTELLIGENCE

The four theories of intelligence discussed in this section differ in several ways (see the Concept Review Table on the next page). Gardner attempts to explain the wide variety of adult roles found in different cultures. He believes that this diversity cannot be explained by a single underlying intelligence and instead proposes that there are at least seven different intelligences, which are present in different combinations in each individual. To Gardner, an intelligence is an ability to solve problems or create products that are of value in a particular culture. In this view, the Polynesian mariner who is skilled at navigating by the stars, the figure skater who can successfully execute a triple axel, and the charismatic leader who can motivate throngs of followers are as "intelligent" as a scientist, mathematician, or engineer.

Anderson's theory attempts to explain several aspects of intelligence—not only individual differences but also the increase of cognitive abilities with development, the existence of specific abilities, and the existence of universal abilities that do not vary from one individual to another, such as the ability to see objects in three di-

CONCEPT REVIEW TABLE
Comparing Theories of Intelligence

The four theories of intelligence reviewed conceptualize intelligence quite differently.

Theory	Description
Gardner's Theory	Intelligence is an ability to solve problems or create products that are of value in a particular culture.
Anderson's Theory	Intelligence is a basic processing mechanism, along with specific processors that deal with propositional thought and visual and spatial functioning.
Sternberg's Triarchic Theory	It consists of three subtheories: the componential theory, which looks at internal information-processing mechanisms; the experiential subtheory, which takes into account the individual's experience with a task or situation; and the contextual subtheory, which explores the relationship between the external environment and the individual's intelligence.
Ceci's Bioecological Theory	Intelligence involves multiple cognitive potentials that are biologically based, but their expression depends on the knowledge an individual has amassed in a particular domain.

mensions. To explain these aspects, he proposes the existence of a basic processing mechanism, equivalent to Spearman's general intelligence or *g*, along with specific processors that deal with propositional thought and visual and spatial functioning. The existence of universal abilities is explained by the notion of "modules" whose functioning depends on maturation.

Sternberg's triarchic theory stems from the belief that earlier theories are not wrong but merely incomplete. It consists of three subtheories: the componential subtheory, which looks at internal information-processing mechanisms; the experiential subtheory, which takes into account the individual's experience with a task or situation; and the contextual subtheory, which explores the relationship between the external environment and the individual's intelligence.

Ceci's bioecological theory extends Sternberg's theory by examining the role of context in greater depth. Rejecting the idea of a single general capacity for abstract problem solving, Ceci proposes that intelligence rests on multiple cognitive potentials. These potentials are biologically based, but their expression depends on the knowledge an individual has amassed in a particular domain. Knowledge is crucial to intelligence, in Ceci's view.

Despite their differences, these theories have some aspects in common. They all attempt to take into account the biological basis of intelligence, be it a basic processing mechanism or a set of multiple intelligences, modules, or cognitive potentials. In addition, three of the theories place a strong emphasis on the contexts within which individuals operate—environmental factors that influence intelligence. Thus, the study of intelligence continues to explore the complex interaction between biological and environmental factors that is a central focus of psychological research today.

CROSS-CULTURAL PERSPECTIVES ON INTELLIGENCE

The theories of intelligence discussed thus far have reflected the views largely of Northern American and European cultures. These views are not shared by all cultures. Many cultures put more emphasis on social intelligence (Sternberg & Kaufman, 2001). For example, several African cultures emphasize responsible participation in the family, cooperativeness, and obedience as important to intelligence. In Zimbabwe, the word for "intelligence," *ngware,* actually means to be prudent and cautious, especially in social relationships (Sternberg, 2000). Similarly, some studies of China and Taiwan find that social competence and self-knowledge are important components of intelligence, according to citizens of these cultures (Yang & Sternberg, 1997). It is important to note that African and Asian cultures do not exclusively emphasize social intelligence but also recognize the importance of the cognitive skills.

◆ Interim Summary

- Gardner's theory of multiple intelligences suggests that there are seven distinct kinds of intelligence that are independent of one another, each operating as a separate system (or module) in the brain according to its own rules. These are (1) linguistic, (2) musical, (3) logical-mathematical, (4) spatial, (5) bodily-kinesthetic, (6) intrapersonal, and (7) interpersonal.

- Anderson's theory of intelligence suggests that differences in intelligence result from differences in the "basic processing mechanism" that implements thinking, which in turn yields knowledge.

- Sternberg's triarchic theory has three parts or subtheories: the componential subtheory, which deals with thought processes; the experiential subtheory, which deals with the effects of experience on intelligence; and the contextual subtheory, which considers the effects of the individual's environment and culture. According to his componential subtheory, three components of thought are critical in intelligence: metacomponents or analytical abilities, performance components or creative abilities, and knowledge-acquisition components or practical abilities.

- According to Ceci's bioecological theory of intelligence, everyday or real-world intellectual performance cannot be explained by IQ alone or by some biological notion of general intelligence. Instead, it depends on the interaction between multiple cognitive potentials with a rich, well-organized knowledge base.

- Other cultures tend to emphasize social intelligence more than Europe and North America do.

◆ Critical Thinking Questions

1. From your observations, what skills or abilities do you think are the most important components of intelligence?

2. Do you think there ever can be any theory of intelligence that applies universally, or is intelligence defined by the demands of particular cultures?

GENETICS AND INTELLIGENCE

Some of the fiercest debates over intelligence have focused on the contribution of genetics to determining the level of intelligence in individuals or groups. Advocates of particular political positions and social policies frequently argue either for or against the idea that intelligence is inherited (for example, Herrnstein & Murray, 1994). Because these debates reveal widespread public misunderstanding about the empirical issues involved, we will describe in some detail the reasoning and methods that behavioral scientists use to assess how genetic and environmental factors contribute to individual differences, including differences in intelligence.

We begin with Table 12-4, which lists (in descending order) the scores of a hypothetical examination taken by two groups of six students each. As shown in the last row, the average (mean) score of the students within each group is 82.0. But we can also see that the scores from Class A are much more spread out—that is, more variable—than the scores from Class B. In other words, the students in Class A are more different from one an-

● Table 12-4
Hypothetical Examination Scores of Two Groups of Students

Group A		Group B	
Alice	100	Greta	89
Bob	95	Harold	88
Carol	89	Ilene	83
Dan	83	John	80
Emily	67	Karen	77
Fred	58	Leon	75
Average	82.0	Average	82.0

other than the students in Class B. As explained in the Appendix, the degree to which the scores in a set differ from one another can be expressed mathematically by a quantity called their *variance*.

Now consider the scores for Class A. Why are they different from one another? Why do some students do better than others? What accounts for the variance we observe? One obvious possibility is that some students studied for the exam longer than other students did. To find out whether and to what extent this is true, we could conduct a hypothetical experiment in which we "controlled for" the variable of study time by requiring all students to study exactly 3 hours for the exam, no more and no less. If study time really does affect students' scores, what would happen to the variance of those scores?

First, some of the students who would have studied longer than 3 hours and done quite well will now do less well. For example, if Alice—who might have studied for 6 hours to achieve her perfect score of 100—had been permitted to study for only 3 hours, her score might have been more like Greta's score of 89. Second, some of the students who would have studied less than 3 hours and not done very well will now do better. Fred—who had time to only skim the reading for the exam—might have obtained a score higher than 58 if he had studied for 3 hours. Like Leon, he might at least have obtained a score of 75. In other words, if we controlled the study time of Class A, the students' scores would bunch closer together, looking more like Class B's scores—the variance of their scores would decrease. If we actually did this experiment and observed that the variance in Class A's scores decreased by, say, 60%, we could claim that study time had accounted for 60% of the variance in the original scores for this class. In this hypothetical example, then, a major reason the exam scores differed so much from one another in Class A is that students differed in the amount of time they spent studying.

Theoretically, we could test for other potential sources of variance in the same way. If we think that having a good breakfast might affect students' scores, we could feed all the students the same breakfast (or deny breakfast to all the students) and observe whether the variance of their scores is reduced as a result. In general, holding constant any variable that "makes a difference" will reduce the variance of the scores. In the extreme case, if we held all the relevant variables constant, the variance would diminish to zero: Every student would obtain the same score.

However, we cannot say what will happen to the mean of the scores when we hold a variable constant. For example, if the students in Class A had originally studied for the exam for only 2 hours on the average, by requiring them all to study for 3 hours we will raise the class average. If, however, the students had studied for 4 hours on the average, we will lower the class average by limiting everybody to only 3 hours of study time.

HERITABILITY

We are now prepared to ask the "genetics" question: To what extent do some students do better than others on the exam because they are genetically more capable? To put it another way, what percentage of the variance in exam scores is accounted for by genetic differences among the students? In general, the percentage of the variance in any trait that is accounted for by genetic differences among the individuals in a population is the trait's **heritability.** The more individual differences on a trait are due to genetic differences, the closer the heritability is to 100%. For example, height is heavily influenced by genetics: Its heritability ranges from about 85% to 95% across different studies.

Several studies of twins suggest IQ is partly heritable.

Now, however, we face a practical difficulty. We cannot experimentally determine how much of the variance in exam scores is accounted for by genetic differences the way we did for study time because that would require holding the genetic variable constant—that is, turning all the students into genetic clones. But we can take advantage of the fact that nature sometimes produces genetic clones in the form of identical twins. To the extent that identical twins are more alike on a trait than fraternal twins, we can infer that the trait has a genetic or heritable component (assuming that other factors, such as differential parental treatment, can be ruled out).

Across many twin studies the heritability of intelligence (as measured by intelligence tests) has been estimated to be between 60% and 80% (Lubinski, 2000). One difficulty in interpreting the results of twin studies is that identical twin pairs may be treated more alike than fraternal twin pairs, which may account for the greater similarity of their personalities. This is one reason that researchers at the University of Minnesota decided to study sets of twins who had been reared apart (Bouchard, 1994).

The participants in the Minnesota Study of Twins Reared Apart were assessed on a number of ability and personality measures. In addition, they participated in lengthy interviews, during which they were asked questions about such topics as childhood experiences, fears, hobbies, musical tastes, social attitudes, and sexual interests. These studies reveal that twins reared apart are just as similar to each other across a wide range of abilities as twins reared together (see Figure 12-4), permitting us to conclude with greater confidence that identical twins are more similar to each other on personality characteristics than fraternal twins because they are more similar genetically (Bouchard, Lykken, McGue, Segal, & Tellegen, 1990; Lykken, 1982; Tellegen et al., 1988).

MISUNDERSTANDINGS ABOUT HERITABILITY The recurring public debate over nature-nurture questions reveals widespread misunderstanding about the concept of heritability. Therefore, it is important to be clear about the following points:

- Heritability refers to a population, not to individuals. The heritability of a trait refers to differences among individuals within a population, not to percentages of a trait within an individual. To say that height has a heritability of 90% does not mean that 90% of your height came from your genes and 10% came from the environment. It means that 90% of the differences in height among individuals observed in a particular population is due to genetic differences among those individuals.

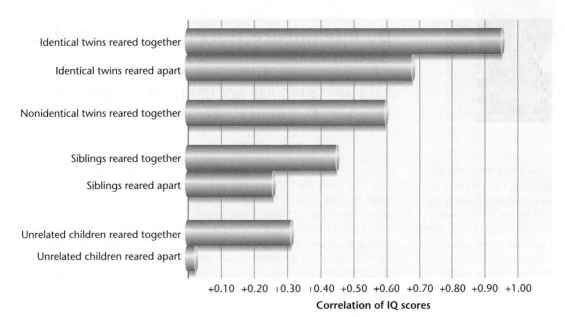

Identical twins reared together									
Identical twins reared apart									
Nonidentical twins reared together									
Siblings reared together									
Siblings reared apart									
Unrelated children reared together									
Unrelated children reared apart									

+0.10 +0.20 +0.30 +0.40 +0.50 +0.60 +0.70 +0.80 +0.90 +1.00

Correlation of IQ scores

▌ Figure 12-4
IQ Data From Twin Studies
Identical twins tend to have more similar IQs than nonidentical twins or other siblings, even when they were reared apart. (From "Familiar Studies of Intelligence: A Review," T. Bouchard, et al., *Science,* Vol. 212, #4498, p 1055–9, 29 May 1981. Copyright © 1981 American Association for the Advancement of Science. Used by permission of Thomas Bouchard.)

- The heritability of a trait is not a single, fixed number. Heritability refers to an attribute of a trait in a particular population at a particular point in time. If something happens to change the variance of a trait in a population, the heritability of the trait will also change. For example, if everyone in our society were suddenly given equal educational opportunities, the variance of intellectual performance in the society would decrease, and scores on standardized measures of intellectual ability would be more similar. (This is what happened in our hypothetical experiment in which everyone had to study the same length of time for the exam.) And because heritability is the percentage of variance that is due to inherited differences among individuals, the heritability would actually increase because the percentage of the variance due to an important environmental factor, education, would have decreased.

- Heritability does not tell us about the source of mean differences between groups. One of the most contentious and recurring debates in American society is over the question of whether average differences in the intelligence test scores of different ethnic groups are due to genetic differences between the groups. In the early 20th century the debate concerned the relatively low intelligence scores obtained by Hungarian, Italian, and Jewish immigrants when

they were tested upon arrival in the United States. The test scores of these immigrants led some researchers to conclude that the majority were "feebleminded" (Kamin, 1974). Today the debate concerns the lower scores obtained by African Americans and Hispanic Americans compared with white Americans (Herrnstein & Murray, 1994). In these debates, the heritability of intelligence is often used to support the genetic argument. But this claim is based on a logical fallacy, as illustrated by the following "thought experiment":

> We fill a white sack and a black sack with a mixture of different genetic varieties of corn seed. We make certain that the proportions of each variety of seed are identical in each sack. We then plant the seed from the white sack in fertile Field A, while the seed from the black sack is planted in barren Field B. We will observe that within Field A, as within Field B, there is considerable variation in the height of individual corn plants. This variation will be due largely to genetic factors (differences in the seed). We will also observe, however, that the average height of plants in Field A is greater than that of plants in Field B. That difference will be entirely due to environmental factors (the soil). The same is true of IQs: Differences in the average IQ of various human populations could be entirely due to environmental differences, even if within each population all variation were due to genetic differences (Eysenck & Kamin, 1981, p. 97).

Text continued on p. 448

Do Intelligence Tests Accurately Reflect Aptitude?

SATS AND GRES ARE ACCURATE MEASURES OF INTELLIGENCE
Douglas K. Detterman, Case Western Reserve University

How do you know if two measures are really the same thing? You compute a statistic called a *correlation* (ranging from 0 to 1.0) and the higher the correlation, the more similar two measures are. Mental tests called *aptitude, achievement, intelligence,* and *cognitive ability* tests are correlated so highly with one another that many experts believe they are really all the same. What any test of mental ability is called probably has more to do with social acceptability than what the test really measures. It is not surprising that these tests are highly correlated since, from Binet to the most recent computer-administered GRE, they were all designed to predict academic achievement.

A test is nothing more than a sample of behavior hopefully predictive of future behaviors. The easiest thing tests should predict is later behavior on the same test, known as the reliability of a test. Intelligence, aptitude, and achievement tests are the most highly reliable of all psychological tests. Individually administered intelligence tests correlate above .90 with a later administration of the same test. In 1932, a group-administered test was given to every Scottish school child. Recently, the same test was given to some that had taken the original test. The correlation of the two administrations over the 66-year span was .74 (Deary et al.). Compare this with the average reliability of .6 for height, weight, and blood pressure taken in a doctor's office. Most psychological tests of personality, psychopathology, or motivation are lucky to have test-retest reliabilities between .4 and .8.

Do tests predict anything useful? You bet! Anghoff and Johnson correlated the performance of over 20,000 students who had taken the SAT and then later taken the GRE. The correlation was .86. While the addition of gender and major raised the correlation to .93 or higher, college quality mattered little. Paying big bucks for a college education won't help to get you into graduate school, at least as far as test scores are concerned. Other academic criteria like grades or class rank are also predicted by these tests, but less well, because grades and class rank are less reliable themselves. Mental ability tests are highly predictive of many real-world criteria, from flying a jet fighter to becoming a good lawyer or musician. Occupations that have the highest average IQ are also the most socially desirable. Most importantly, mental tests predict academic achievement, the usual doorway to life achievement.

Then why do these tests get so much bad press? First, they are often used improperly. Although nearly all colleges require tests for admission, perhaps 80% of colleges admit nearly everyone who applies. Why do they require tests? I think they want to appear selective. Even for the 20% of colleges that are selective, many other factors than test scores weigh in the decision. Given two students with the same test scores, the one with the best chance of getting in a selective school will have the following characteristics: minority, athlete, attended selective private high school, family income over $70,000 per year and one parent had college education, legacy (a parent attended the college), parent is large donor to college (Bowen & Bok, 1998). Before tests, these sorts of factors were the only thing used for college admission. I think admissions would be fairer at selective schools if only test scores were used.

A second reason that people often get a bad impression of tests is that there are situations in which they cannot predict performance. When applicants are heavily selected for IQ, they will all be very similar in IQ, so IQ cannot contribute to performance. Our educational system selects for intelligence, and each step requires higher levels of academic achievement. You have probably noticed that things are harder in college than they were in high school. Here is the reason. The average IQ of a college graduate is over 110 while the average IQ of those who finish professional or graduate school is over 120. Intelligence will be only a small contributor to performance in medical or graduate school. Other things like hard work and personality will determine differences in success because everyone is smart. You have to be tall to play basketball. The NBA selects players for height and NBA players are much taller than the average person. But the correlation between height and points scored in the NBA is near zero. It is as silly to say that intelligence has nothing to do with performance in medical or graduate school as it is to say height has nothing to do with basketball.

Tests like the SAT and GRE are essentially tests of intelligence. They are highly reliable and predict real-world behaviors better than anything else we know about. Tests have often been misused and are not the measure of the basic worth of a human being. But when used properly, they can make selection decisions fairer and more accurate and can help students in designing their educational future.

Do Intelligence Tests Accurately Reflect Aptitude?

IQS, SATS, AND GRES ARE NOT MEASURES OF *GENERAL* INTELLIGENCE

Stephen J. Ceci, Cornell University

There is a funny anecdote about a man waiting for a bus. When a woman arrives pushing a pram with her baby in it, the man peers into the pram:

Man: My, what a lovely baby you have!

Woman: Oh don't go by that—you should see her photographs!

We all know individuals who seem more interested in photographs than in reality. For such persons, intelligence test scores (the photos) are more important than the attainments they are supposed to predict (the baby).

Thousands of "validity" studies show that tests of general intelligence predict a wide range of behaviors, imperfectly, but better than anything else we can measure: IQ scores predict freshman grades somewhat better than high-school grades and letters of reference do, and they also predict first-year graduate school grades better than do undergraduate grades and letters. But the prediction from IQ (or SATs or GREs) is modest, and many applicants' grades will differ from expectations based on such scores. Test makers argue that even modest predictability can help admissions officers make better decisions than they would by not using the tests (Hunt, 1996).

Stephen J. Ceci

For many years I chaired a graduate admissions committee. One of the saddest experiences is discovering the tremendous weight given to test scores such as the GRE. Granted, there are other considerations to distinguish among applicants who are similar in GRE scores and grades; however, at most universities applicants with very low scores won't get admitted unless the school needs to fill seats for financial reasons.

All who serve on admission committees can tell tales—about the applicant with great scores who turned out to be a loser, unable to think creatively and manage work effectively. Or about the occasional applicant with low scores who somehow manages to gain entrance and goes on to disprove the prediction by emerging as the top student. I am not claiming that measures of general intelligence such as the GREs, IQ scores, and SATs are worthless. But they are not perfect, and applicants who excel at them represent but one type of individual who could do well. Other types of applicants (e.g., those with well-honed real-world skills, interpersonal strengths, highly creative) are systematically excluded.

But my most serious complaint about tests of general intelligence is that they do not strike me as measures of general intelligence any more than a math or history achievement test strikes me as one. Like all achievement tests, the SATs, IQs, and GREs are susceptible to external influences, including coaching, quality of school attended, and parental educational level and income. It should come as no surprise to find that the number of math classes taken in school is a predictor of math scores on the SATs and GREs, *even after controlling for initial math aptitude.* This implies that although math scores add to the prediction of college or graduate-school grades, they may not measure inherent math ability any more than a score on a test of Russian proficiency would for someone who attended a school where Russian was not taught. Thus, I view tests of "general intelligence" as often little more than achievement tests, indexing how much knowledge one has gained. They tell us little about actual ability under different circumstances, particularly those situations that require thinking unlike the type required to answer test questions correctly. And such tests tell us little about potentially valuable talents that are not measured, such as creativity, practical intelligence, and the ability to organize, motivate, and manage oneself and others—skills that appear to be somewhat independent of so-called intelligence tests, and which have been demonstrated to predict important educational outcomes.

Recently, there has been a spate of studies about the predictive validity of SATs and GREs, and while such measures may predict first-year grades, their predictiveness wanes over the years. One recent study even reported that the GREs did not predict at all after the first year of graduate school—not second-, third-, or fourth-year grades, not creativity or quality of the doctoral research (Sternberg & Williams, 1997), although it's possible there will be a "sleeper effect," and intelligence scores could end up predicting later career achievements and earnings. These de facto achievement tests have many valid uses; however, it is unwise to refer to them as tests of "general intelligence" until they can be shown to tap a far wider array of abilities and achievements than they do. And until their predictiveness gets better, we should not confuse the baby with her photographs.

Environmental factors such as parental encouragement can influence intellectual ability—even though these abilities have high heritabilities.

• Heritability does not tell us about the effects of environmental changes on the average level of a trait. Another incorrect claim about heritability is that a trait with high heritability cannot be changed by a change in the environment. For example, it has been argued that it is futile to use preschool intervention programs to help disadvantaged children enhance their intellectual abilities because those abilities have high levels of heritability. But between 1946 and 1982 the height of young adult males in Japan increased by 3.3 inches, mainly owing to improved nutrition (Angoff, 1988). And yet height is one of the most heritable traits we possess. Then, as now, taller Japanese parents have taller children than do shorter Japanese parents. Similarly, IQ test scores have risen significantly over the last century in many cultures (Flynn, 1999). In sum, heritability is about variances, not average levels.

◆ Interim Summary

• Behavioral scientists typically quantify the extent to which a group of people differ from one another on some measure of a trait or ability by computing the variance of the scores obtained. The more the individuals in the group differ from one another, the higher the variance. Researchers can then seek to determine how much of that variance is due to different causes. The proportion of variance in a trait that is accounted for (caused by) genetic differences among the individuals is called the *heritability* of the trait.

• Heritabilities can be estimated by comparing correlations obtained on pairs of identical twins (who share all their genes) and correlations obtained on pairs of fraternal twins (who, on the average, share about half of their genes). If identical twin pairs are more alike on the trait than fraternal twin pairs, the trait probably has a genetic component. Heritabilities can also be estimated from the correlation between identical twin pairs who have been separated and raised in different environments. Any correlation between such pairs must be due to their genetic similarities.

• Heritability refers to differences among individuals; it does not indicate how much of a trait in an individual is due to genetic factors. It is not a fixed attribute of a trait: If something happens to change the variability of a trait in a group, the heritability will also change. Heritability indicates the variance within a group, not the source of differences between groups. Heritability does, however, indicate how much possible environmental changes might change the mean level of a trait in a population.

◆ Critical Thinking Questions

1. What are the political and social policy implications of claims that intelligence is largely due to genetic factors?

2. How might an individual's belief that his or her own level of intelligence is due to genetic factors influence his or her decisions about school or careers?

1. There are many different definitions of intelligence. Some theorists view it as simply what intelligence tests measure. Others view it as a set of general abilities, including the ability to learn from experience, think in abstract terms, and deal effectively with one's environment.

2. A good test of intelligence must be reliable—it must yield reproducible and consistent results. Alternate form reliability is shown when two forms of a test correlate highly with each other. A test has good internal consistency when various items on the test are correlated highly with each other. When more subjective assessments are used, judges rate the answers of respondents, and the researcher hopes to see interjudge reliability or interrater reliability.

3. A test has good validity if it measures what it is intended to measure. Criterion or empirical validity is shown when the test is highly correlated with another test of the same construct. Construct validity is shown when the scores on the test predict outcomes that the researcher's theory suggests it should predict.

4. The first successful intelligence tests were developed by the French psychologist Alfred Binet, who proposed the concept of mental age. A bright child's mental age is above his or her chronological age; a slow child's mental age is below his or her chronological age. The concept of the intelligence quotient (IQ), the ratio of mental age to chronological age (multiplied by 100), was introduced when the Binet scales were revised to create the Stanford-Binet. Many intelligence test scores are still expressed as IQ scores, but they are no longer actually calculated according to this formula.

5. Both Binet and Wechsler, the developer of the Wechsler Adult Intelligence Scale (WAIS), assumed that intelligence is a general capacity for reasoning.

6. Similarly, Spearman proposed that a general factor (g) underlies performance on different kinds of test items. Factor analysis is a method for determining the kinds of abilities that underlie performance on intelligence tests.

7. Gardner's theory of multiple intelligences suggests that there are seven distinct kinds of intelligence that are independent of one another, each operating as a separate system (or module) in the brain according to its own rules. These are (1) linguistic, (2) musical, (3) logical-mathematical, (4) spatial, (5) bodily-kinesthetic, (6) intrapersonal, and (7) interpersonal.

8. Anderson's theory of intelligence suggests that differences in intelligence result from differences in the "basic processing mechanism" that implements thinking, which in turn yields knowledge.

9. Sternberg's triarchic theory has three parts or subtheories: the componential subtheory, which deals with thought processes; the experiential subtheory, which deals with the effects of experience on intelligence; and the contextual subtheory, which considers the effects of the individual's environment and culture. According to his componential subtheory, three components of thought are critical in intelligence: metacomponents or analytical abilities, performance components or creative abilities, and knowledge-acquisition components or practical abilities.

10. According to Ceci's bioecological theory of intelligence, everyday or real-world intellectual performance cannot be explained by IQ alone or by some biological notion of general intelligence. Instead, it depends on the interaction between multiple cognitive potentials with a rich, well-organized knowledge base.

11. Other cultures tend to emphasize social intelligence more than Europe and North America do.

12. Behavioral scientists typically quantify the extent to which a group of people differ from one another on some measure of a trait or ability by computing the variance of the scores obtained. The more the individuals in the group differ, the higher the variance. Researchers can then seek to determine how much of that variance is due to different causes. The proportion of

variance in a trait that is accounted for (caused by) genetic differences among the individuals is called the *heritability* of the trait.

13. Heritabilities can be estimated by comparing correlations obtained on pairs of identical twins (who share all their genes) and correlations obtained on pairs of fraternal twins (who, on the average, share about half of their genes). If identical twin pairs are more alike on the trait than fraternal twin pairs, the trait probably has a genetic component. Heritabilities can also be estimated from the correlation between identical twin pairs who have been separated and raised in different environments. Any correlation between such pairs must be due to their genetic similarities.

14. Heritability refers to differences among individuals; it does not indicate how much of a trait in an individual is due to genetic factors. It is not a fixed attribute of a trait: If something happens to change the variability of a trait in a group, the heritability will also change. Heritability indicates the variance within a group, not the source of differences between groups. Heritability does, however, indicate how much possible environmental changes might change the mean level of a trait in a population.

CORE CONCEPTS

intelligence	criterion problem in assessment	*g*
reliability	construct validity	Gardner's theory of multiple
alternative form reliability	Stanford-Binet Intelligence Scale	intelligences
internal consistency	intelligence quotient (IQ)	Anderson's theory of intelligence
interrater agreement	Wechsler Adult Intelligence Scale	Sternberg's triarchic theory
interjudge reliability	Scholastic Assessment Test (SAT)	Ceci's bioecological theory
validity	American College Test (ACT)	heritability
criterion or empirical validity	Factor analysis	

WEB RESOURCES

http://psychology.wadsworth.com/ atkinson14e

Take a quiz, try the activities and exercises, and explore web links.

http://www.geocities.com/CapitolHill/1641/ iqown.html

Think you're a smart cookie? Put it to the test on this site.

http://www.mugu.com/cgi-bin/Upstream/Issues/ psychology/IQ/index.html

This site contains an interesting mix of links about intelligence.

 InfoTrac Online Library
http://www.infotrac-college.com/ wadsworth

Use InfoTrac to find popular and scientific articles by using the search terms below or your own relevant terms.

- Intelligence
- Intelligence tests

CD-ROM LINKS

 Psych Odyssey
Check out CD Chapter 9, Intelligence
A. The Nature of Intelligence
B. Context & Intelligence
C. Gender & Intelligence

 Psyk.trek 2.0
Check out CD Unit 7, Testing and Intelligence
7a Types of Psychological Tests
7b Key Concepts in Testing
7c Understanding IQ Scores
7d Heritability, Environment, and Intelligence

© John Feingersh/Corbis

PERSONALITY

13

were absentminded, flushed the toilet before using it, like to dip buttered toast in their coffee, and enjoyed surprising people by sneezing in elevators.

Many other sets of identical twins studied by the Minnesota researchers also displayed similarities. For example, the twins shown in the accompanying photo were separated at birth and not reunited until they were 31 years old, by which time both had become firefighters. What causes such similarities? Surely there aren't firefighting genes or genes for dipping toast or surprising people in elevators. Such similarities reflect the inherited components of more basic personality characteristics. Indeed, both similarities and differences among individuals provide challenges for psychology.

In many ways, every person is like every other person. The biological and psychological processes discussed in this book—development, consciousness, perception, learning, remembering, thinking, motivation, and emotion—are basically the same for all of us. But in other ways every person is different from every other person. Each of us has a distinctive pattern of abilities, beliefs, attitudes, motivations, emotions, and personality traits that makes each of us unique.

In this chapter we look at four theoretical approaches that dominated personality psychology in the 20th century: the psychoanalytic, behaviorist, humanistic, and cognitive approaches. We will also discuss evolutionary approaches, which have been applied to understand personality only in the last couple of decades. In reviewing these theories, we raise a question that has never been satisfactorily answered: To what degree are our beliefs, emotions, and actions free and in what ways are they determined by causes beyond our control? Are we basically good, neutral, or evil? Fixed or

These twins, separated at birth, showed remarkable similarities in interests and habits when they first met at age 31.

modifiable? Active or passive in controlling our destinies? What constitutes psychological health or lack of health? These are not empirical questions, and theories of personality do not attempt to answer them explicitly. But each theoretical approach contains implicit answers—a set of distinctive underlying assumptions about human nature. Historically, these more philosophical factors have been as important as the empirical data in provoking controversies and in winning converts for the competing accounts of personality.

We also return to a major theme that we introduced in Chapter 3: the interaction between nature and nurture. In Chapter 3 we discussed how innate biological factors interact with events in an individual's environment to determine the course of development, focusing particularly on factors that make us all alike. We considered, for example, how innately determined sequences of maturation cause all children to go through the same stages of development in the same sequence, regardless of differences in their environments. In this chapter we focus on the biological and environmental factors that make us different from one another—in other words, the factors that create individuality. First, however, we discuss how we measure personality.

Oskar Stohr and Jack Yufe are identical twins who were born in Trinidad and separated shortly after birth. Their mother took Oskar to Germany, where he was raised by his grandmother as a Catholic and a Nazi. Jack remained in Trinidad with his Jewish father, was raised as a Jew, and spent part of his youth on an Israeli kibbutz. The two families never corresponded.

When they were in their late forties, Oskar and Jack were brought together by researchers at the University of Minnesota who were studying sets of twins who had been raised apart. Although Oskar and Jack had met only once before, they showed some remarkable similarities. Both showed up for the study wearing mustaches, wire-rimmed glasses, and blue double-breasted suits. Their mannerisms and temperaments were similar, and they shared certain idiosyncrasies: Both liked spicy foods and sweet liqueurs,

ASSESSMENT OF PERSONALITY

Personality can be defined as the distinctive and characteristic patterns of thought, emotion, and behavior that make up an individual's personal style of interacting with the physical and social environment. When we are asked to describe an individual's personality, we are likely to use terms referring to personality traits—adjectives such as extraverted and conscientious. Personality psychologists have attempted to devise formal methods for describing and measuring personality, which go beyond our everyday use of trait terms in three ways. First, they seek to reduce the potential set of trait terms to a manageable set that will still encompass the diversity of human personality. Second, they attempt to ensure that their instruments for measuring personality traits are reliable and valid. Finally, they do empirical research to discover the relationships among traits and between traits and specific behaviors.

One way to begin the task of deriving a comprehensive but manageable number of traits is to consult a dictionary. It is assumed that through the process of linguistic evolution a language will encode most, if not all, of the important distinctions among individuals that make a difference in everyday life. Language embodies the accumulated experience of the culture, and the dictionary is the written record of that experience. In the 1930s two personality psychologists actually undertook this task. They found approximately 18,000 words that refer to characteristics of behavior—nearly 5% of all the words in the dictionary! Next, they reduced the list to about 4,500 terms by eliminating obscure words and synonyms. Finally, they organized the list into psychologically meaningful subsets (Allport & Odbert, 1936).

Subsequent researchers have used such trait terms to obtain personality ratings of individuals. Peers who know an individual well are asked to rate him or her on a scale for each trait. For example, a rater might be asked to rate the person on the trait of friendliness, using a seven-point scale ranging from "not at all friendly" to "very friendly." Often such scales are labeled at the two ends with opposite traits—for example, "domineering-submissive" or "conscientious-unreliable." Individuals can also be asked to rate themselves on the scales.

Raymond Cattell (1957, 1966) condensed the Allport-Odbert list to fewer than 200 traits and obtained both peer and self-ratings for each trait. He then used factor analysis to determine how many underlying personality factors could account for the pattern of correlations among the trait ratings. His analysis yielded 16 factors. A similar procedure was used by the British psychologist Hans Eysenck to arrive at two personality factors: introversion-extraversion and emotional instability-stability, which he calls neuroticism (Eysenck, 1953); he has since added a

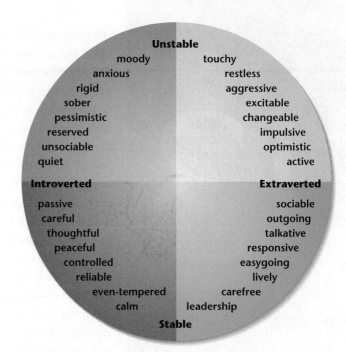

▌Figure 13-1
Eysenck's Personality Factors
This figure shows the two major factors that emerge from factor-analytic studies of the intercorrelations between traits by Eysenck and others. The Stable-Unstable axis defines the neuroticism factor; the Introverted-Extraverted axis defines the extraversion factor. The other terms around the circle indicate where other traits are placed with respect to these two factors.
(From H. J. Eysenck & S. Rachman (1965), *The Causes and Cures of Neurosis*, by H. J. Eysenck. Copyright © 1965 by H. J. Eysenck and S. Rachman. Reprinted by permission of EdiTS.)

third. **Introversion-extraversion** refers to the degree to which a person's basic orientation is turned inward toward the self or outward toward the external world. At the introversion end of the scale are individuals who are shy and prefer to work alone. They tend to withdraw into themselves, particularly in times of emotional stress or conflict. At the extraversion end are individuals who are sociable and prefer occupations that permit them to work directly with other people. In times of stress, they seek company. **Neuroticism** (instability-stability) is a dimension of emotionality, with moody, anxious, temperamental, and maladjusted individuals at the neurotic or unstable end, and calm, well-adjusted individuals at the other. Figure 13-1 shows how these two dimensions combine to organize a number of subtraits that are correlated with the factors.

How many basic personality factors are there? Even with a rigorous analytic procedure like factor analysis, there is no definitive answer. Cattell arrived at 16 factors, but Eysenck arrived at only 2 (or, now, 3). Other investigators have come up with different numbers. In our discussion of intelligence in Chapter 12, we encountered a similar situation when we noted that the number of factors

Extraverted people are not afraid to be the center of attention.

Despite these disagreements, a consensus is emerging among many trait researchers that five trait dimensions capture most of what we mean by personality—referred to as the "Big Five" (Ozer & Reise, 1994). Although the five factors were originally identified through a factor analysis of the Allport-Odbert trait list (Norman, 1963), the same five have emerged from a wide variety of personality tests (McCrae & Costa, 1999). There is still disagreement about how best to name and interpret the factors, but one reasonable way to summarize them is with the acronym OCEAN: Openness to experience, Conscientiousness, Extraversion, Agreeableness, and Neuroticism. The Concept Review Table displays some representative examples of the trait scales that characterize each of the five factors. Many personality psychologists consider the discovery and validation of the Big Five to be one of the major breakthroughs of contemporary personality psychology. Proponents of the Big Five argue that these core personality traits organize the myriad of more narrowly focused personality characteristics that have been discussed by other researchers (McCrae & Costa, 1999). In other words, they argue that all aspects of personality are subsumed under the Big Five.

CONCEPT REVIEW TABLE
Five Trait Factors

This table presents five trait factors that reliably emerge when a wide variety of assessment instruments are factor-analyzed. The adjective pairs are examples of trait scales that characterize each of the factors. *(After McCrae & Costa, 1987)*

Trait Factor	Representative Trait Scales
Openness	Conventional-Original
	Unadventurous-Daring
	Conservative-Liberal
Conscientiousness	Careless-Careful
	Undependable-Reliable
	Negligent-Conscientious
Extraversion	Retiring-Sociable
	Quiet-Talkative
	Inhibited-Spontaneous
Agreeableness	Irritable-Good natured
	Ruthless-Soft hearted
	Selfish-Selfless
Neuroticism	Calm-Worrying
	Hardy-Vulnerable
	Secure-Insecure

defining the concept of intelligence could be 1 (Spearman's general intelligence factor, g), 7 (Thurstone's primary mental abilities), or as many as 150 (Guilford, 1982).

Some of the discrepancy occurs because different traits are initially put into the analysis, some occurs because different types of data are being analyzed (for example, peer ratings versus self-ratings), and some occurs because different factor analytic methods are employed. But much of the disagreement is a matter of taste. A researcher who prefers a more differentiated or fine-grained description of personality will set a lower criterion for a factor and thus accept more factors, arguing that important distinctions would be lost if the factors were further merged. Another researcher, like Eysenck, will prefer to merge several lower-level factors into more general ones, arguing that the resulting factors will be more stable (that is, more likely to reemerge in other analyses). For example, when Cattell's 16 factors are factor analyzed, Eysenck's 2 factors emerge as superfactors. We can therefore think of a hierarchy of traits in which each broad general trait is composed of several subordinate, narrower traits.

PERSONALITY INVENTORIES

Most personality tests do not actually ask individuals to directly rate themselves on personality trait dimensions. Instead, individuals are asked a set of questions about how they react in certain situations. For example, they might be asked to indicate how much they agree or disagree with the statement "I often try new and foreign foods" or "I really like most people I meet." Questionnaires that assess personality—called **personality inventories**—ask the same questions of each person, and the answers are usually given in a form that can be easily scored, often by computer. Each item on a personality inventory is composed to exemplify a particular personality trait, and subsets of similar items are summed to give the individual a score on each trait scale. For example, the item "I often try new and foreign foods" is on the Openness to Experience scale of one inventory designed to measure the Big Five; the item "I really like most people I meet" is on the Extraversion scale.

Items on most personality inventories are initially composed according to the developer's theory of each trait and then retained or discarded from the final inventory, depending on whether they correlate or fail to correlate with other items on the same scale. Often a large number of trial items are placed on a preliminary form of the inventory, which is administered to a large number of people. Their responses are then factor-analyzed to determine which subsets of items intercorrelate and whether these subsets actually belong to the trait scale for which they were originally devised.

MINNESOTA MULTIPHASIC PERSONALITY INVENTORY (MMPI) A very different method of test construction, called the *criterion-keyed method* or *empirical construction*, was used to develop one of the most popular of all personality inventories, the **Minnesota Multiphasic Personality Inventory (MMPI)**. The original MMPI was developed to provide a pencil-and-paper version of a psychiatric interview (Hathaway & McKinley, 1943). It has more than 550 statements concerning attitudes, emotional reactions, physical and psychological symptoms, and experiences. The test taker responds to each statement by answering "true," "false," or "cannot say."

Here are four representative items:

I have never done anything dangerous for the thrill of it.

I daydream very little.

My mother or father often made me obey, even when I thought it was unreasonable.

At times my thoughts have raced ahead faster than I could speak them.

Instead of formulating items on the basis of a theory, designers of the MMPI gave hundreds of test items like these to groups of individuals. Each group was known to differ from the norm on a particular criterion. For example, to develop a scale of items that distinguish between paranoid and normal individuals, the same questions were given to two groups. The criterion group was individuals who had been hospitalized with the diagnosis of paranoid disorder; the control group was people who were similar to the criterion group in age, sex, socioeconomic status, and other important variables but had never been diagnosed as having psychiatric problems. Only the questions that discriminated between the psychiatric group and the control group were retained on the inventory. Questions that at face value might seem to distinguish normal from paranoid individuals (for instance, "I think that most people would lie to get ahead") may or may not do so when put to an empirical test. In fact, patients diagnosed as paranoid were significantly less likely to respond "true" to this statement than were normal individuals. On the final test, the responses to each item are scored according to the extent to which they correspond to answers given by the different criterion groups.

The MMPI was the first major inventory to incorporate a number of validity scales within it. These scales attempt to determine whether the person has answered the test items carefully and honestly. If an individual's score on any of these scales is too high, his or her scores on the content scales must be interpreted with particular caution or disregarded altogether. These scales have been helpful but not completely successful at detecting invalid scores. Table 13-1 lists the 3 validity and 10 content scales usually scored on the MMPI.

Because the MMPI is derived from differences between criterion and control groups, it does not really matter whether what the person says is true. What is important is the fact that he or she says it. If people with schizophrenia answer "true" and control participants answer "false" to the statement "My mother never loved me," their answers distinguish the two groups regardless of how their mothers actually behaved. This is an advantage of a test based on the criterion-keyed method over one based on a test constructor's assumption that certain answers indicate specific personality traits. The disadvantage is that one does not really have a theoretical understanding of the connection between the test responses and the personality characteristics they identify.

The MMPI, published in 1943, is based on research that began in 1939. There are now more than 8,000 published studies on the MMPI, and it has been translated into at least 150 languages. There are even several private companies that provide computer-based scoring and interpretation of the inventory.

Over the years, the MMPI has been criticized for the weak reliability and validity of some of its scales. It also

● Table 13-1
MMPI Scales

The first three scales are "validity" scales, which help determine whether the person has answered the test items carefully and honestly. For example, the F (Frequency) scale measures the degree to which infrequent or atypical answers are given. A high score on this scale usually indicates that the individual was careless or confused in responding. (However, high F scores often accompany high scores on the Schizophrenia scale, which measures bizarre thinking.) The remaining "clinical" scales were originally named for categories of psychiatric disorders, but interpretation now emphasizes personality attributes rather than diagnostic categories.

Scale Name	Scale Abbreviation	Interpretation of High Scores
Lie	L	Denial of common frailties
Frequency	F	Invalidity of profile
Correction	K	Defensive, evasive
Hypochondriasis	Hs	Emphasis on physical complaints
Depression	D	Unhappy, depressed
Hysteria	Hy	Reacts to stress by denying problems
Psychopathic Deviancy	Pd	Lack of social conformity; often in trouble with the law
Masculinity-Femininity	Mf	Feminine orientation (males); masculine orientation (females)
Paranoia	Pa	Suspicious
Psychoasthenia	Pt	Worried, anxious
Schizophrenia	Sc	Withdrawn, bizarre thinking
Hypomania	Ma	Impulsive, excitable
Social Introversion-Extraversion	Si	Introverted, shy

became evident that the original inventory was getting out of date and should be revised. But the enormous amount of existing data on the original version discouraged most researchers from undertaking such a daunting task. Nevertheless, it has been done. The MMPI-2, published in 1989, incorporates a number of significant revisions while maintaining the basic features of the original, including most of the original items.

The MMPI has been most valuable in distinguishing in a general way between abnormal and normal populations and can be used to evaluate the overall severity of a particular individual's disturbance (Meehl & Dahlstrom, 1960). It is less successful, however, in making finer distinctions among various forms of psychopathology.

Many criticisms have been raised about the use of the MMPI in culturally diverse samples, however (Dana, 1998). The norms for the original MMPI—the scores that were considered "healthy" scores—were based on samples of people in the United States that were not representative of people from a wide range of ethnic and racial backgrounds, age groups, and social classes. In response to this problem, the publishers of the MMPI established new norms based on more representative samples of communities across the United States. Still, there are concerns that the MMPI norms do not reflect variations across cul-

tures in what is considered normal or abnormal. In addition, the linguistic accuracy of the translated versions of the MMPI and the comparability of these versions to the English version have been questioned (Dana, 1998).

Although the MMPI was originally designed to identify people with serious personality disorders, it has been widely used to study normal populations. But because it does not adequately sample some of the traits that are useful in describing the normal personality, the California Psychological Inventory (CPI) was devised. The CPI uses many of the same items as the MMPI. Its scales measure such traits as dominance, sociability, self-acceptance, responsibility, and socialization. The comparison groups for some of the scales were obtained by asking high school and college students to identify classmates whom they would rate high or low on the trait in question. For the dominance scale, for example, the criterion group consisted of students who were described by their peers as high in dominance (aggressive, confident, self-reliant), and the control group consisted of students who were described by their peers as low in dominance (retiring, lacking in self-confidence, inhibited). Items that revealed a statistically significant difference between the criterion group and the control group formed the dominance scale. The CPI is still one of the most widely validated personality inventories available for use with normal populations (Megargee, 1972).

THE Q-SORT A special method for measuring personality traits is called the **Q-sort** (The Q was chosen arbitrarily and has no particular meaning). In this method, a rater or sorter describes an individual's personality by sorting a set of approximately 100 cards into piles. Each card contains a personality statement (for example, "Has a wide range of interests" and "Is self-defeating"). The rater sorts the cards into nine piles, placing the cards that are least descriptive of the individual in pile 1 on the left and those that are most descriptive in pile 9 on the right. The other cards are distributed in the intermediate piles, with those that seem neither characteristic nor uncharacteristic of the individual going into the middle pile (pile 5). Each Q item receives a score ranging from 1 to 9, with higher numbers indicating that the item is more characteristic of the person. (Some Q-sorts use fewer or more than nine piles, but the technique is the same.)

At first glance, this would seem no different from asking raters to rate an individual on a set of traits, using a 9-point rating scale. And in fact, the item scores can be used in this way if the researcher wishes. But there is an important difference. When filling out rating scales, the rater is implicitly comparing the individual with others (for example, a rating of "very friendly" implies that the individual is very friendly compared with other individuals). When performing a Q-sort, however, the rater is explicitly comparing each trait with other traits within the same individual (for example, placing the item "friendly" in pile 9 implies that, compared with other traits, friendliness stands out as particularly descriptive of the individual).

Researchers can compare two Q-sorts by computing the correlation between them, thereby assessing the degree to which two individuals are similar in their overall personality configurations. If the two Q-sorts are descriptions of the same individual at two different times, the correlation assesses the test-retest reliability of the Q-sort, or the continuity of the individual's overall personality profile over time. If two Q-sorts are descriptions of a single individual made by two raters, the correlation assesses the interjudge reliability of the Q-sort, or the degree to which two people perceive the individual in the same way. (For example, in marital counseling, it could be helpful to assess the degree to which two spouses agree or disagree in their perceptions of each other.) Finally, if one of the Q-sorts is a description of a hypothetical personality type, the correlation between an individual's Q-sort and the hypothetical sort assesses the degree to which the person is similar to that personality type. For example, one researcher asked clinical psychologists to construct Q-sorts of the hypothetical "optimally adjusted personality." The correlation between a person's Q-sort and this hypothetical sort can be directly interpreted as an adjustment score (Block 1961/1978).

By itself, the trait approach is not a theory of personality but a general orientation and set of methods for assessing stable characteristics of individuals. By themselves, personality traits do not tell us anything about the dynamic processes of personality functioning, and trait psychologists who have sought to develop theories of personality have had to look to other approaches to address the second major task of personality psychology: synthesizing the many processes that influence an individual's interactions with the physical and social environments—biology, development, learning, thinking, emotion, motivation, and social interaction—into an integrated account of the total person.

◆ Interim Summary

- To arrive at a comprehensive but manageable number of personality traits on which individuals can be assessed, investigators first collected all the trait terms found in a dictionary (about 18,000) and then reduced them to a smaller number. Ratings of individuals on these terms were factor-analyzed to determine how many underlying dimensions were needed to account for the correlations among the scales.

- Although different investigators arrive at different numbers of factors, most now believe that five factors provide the best compromise. These have been labeled the "Big Five" and form the acronym OCEAN: Openness to experience, Conscientiousness, Extraversion, Agreeableness, and Neuroticism.

- Personality inventories are questionnaires on which individuals report their reactions or feelings in certain situations. Responses to subsets of items are summed to yield scores on separate scales or factors within the inventory.

- Although items on most inventories are composed or selected on the basis of a theory, they can also be selected on the basis of their correlation with an external criterion—the criterion-keyed method of test construction. The best-known example is the Minnesota Multiphasic Personality Inventory (MMPI), which is designed to identify individuals with psychological disorders.

- The Q-sort is a method of assessing personality in which raters sort cards with personality adjectives into nine piles, placing the cards that are least descriptive of the individual in pile 1 on the left and those that are most descriptive in pile 9 on the right.

1. There are consistent differences between women and men in scores on some of the Big 5 personality traits. On which traits would you expect to find gender differences, and in what direction?

2. How would you rate yourself on the "Big Five" personality traits? Do you think your personality can be accurately described in this way? What important aspect of your personality seems to be left out of such a description? If you and a close friend (or a family member) were to describe your personality, on which characteristics would you be likely to disagree? Why? Are there traits on which you think this other person might actually be more accurate than you in describing your personality? If so, why?

THE PSYCHOANALYTIC APPROACH

Sigmund Freud, the creator of psychoanalytic theory, is one of the towering intellectual figures of the 20th century. The basic premise of **psychoanalytic theory** is that **much of what we think and do is driven by unconscious processes.** Despite its shortcomings as a scientific theory, the psychoanalytic account of personality remains the most comprehensive and influential theory of personality ever created. Its impact extends well beyond psychology, influencing the social sciences, the humanities, the arts, and society generally. Even though psychoanalytic theory plays a less central role in psychology today than it did 50 or 60 years ago, many of its ideas have been absorbed into the mainstream of psychological thinking. Even parents who have done nothing more than raise their children with the occasional guidance of psychiatrist Benjamin Spock's best-selling *Baby and Child Care* are more like Freudian psychologists than they realize.

Freud began his scientific career as a neurologist, using conventional medical procedures to treat patients suffering from various "nervous" disorders. Because those procedures often failed, he turned to the technique of hypnosis but soon abandoned it. Eventually he discovered the method of **free association,** in which a patient is instructed to say everything that comes to mind, regardless of how trivial or embarrassing it may seem. By listening carefully to these verbal associations, Freud detected consistent themes that he believed were manifestations of unconscious wishes and fears. He found similar themes in the recall of dreams and early childhood memories.

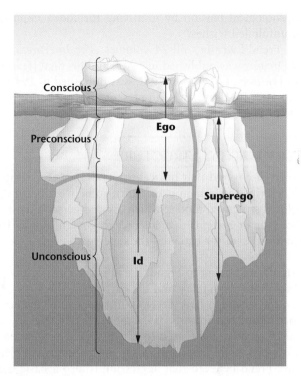

❚ Figure 13-2
Freud's Structural Model of the Mind
In Freud's "iceberg" model of the mind, all of the id and most of the ego and superego are submerged in the unconscious. Small parts of the ego and superego are either in the conscious or in the preconscious.

Freud compared the human mind to an iceberg (see Figure 13-2). The small part that shows above the surface of the water consists of the **conscious**—our current awareness—**and the** preconscious, all the information that is not currently "on our mind" but that we could bring into consciousness if called upon to do so (for example, the name of the president of the United States). The much larger mass of the iceberg below the water represents the **unconscious, a storehouse of impulses, wishes, and inaccessible memories that affect our thoughts and behavior.** Freud was not the first to discover unconscious mental influences—even Shakespeare includes them in his plays—but he gave them primary importance in the everyday functioning of the normal personality.

Closely allied with Freud's focus on unconscious processes was his belief in the determinism of human behavior. **Psychological determinism** is the doctrine that all thoughts, emotions, and actions have causes. Freud maintained not only that all psychological events are caused but also that most of them are caused by unsatisfied drives and unconscious wishes. In one of his earliest publications, *The Psychopathology of Everyday Life* (1901), he argued that dreams, humor, forgetting, and slips of the tongue ("Freudian slips") all serve to relieve psychological tension by gratifying forbidden impulses or unfulfilled wishes.

Freud's writings fill 24 volumes. *The Interpretation of Dreams* was published in 1900, and his final treatise, *An Outline of Psychoanalysis*, was published in 1940, a year after his death. We can present only the barest outline of Freud's theory of personality here.

PERSONALITY STRUCTURE

Freud discovered that his iceberg model was too simple to describe the human personality, so he went on to develop a structural model, which divided personality into three major systems that interact to govern human behavior: the id, the ego, and the superego.

THE ID According to Freud, the **id** is the most primitive part of the personality and the part from which the ego and the superego later develop. It is present in the newborn infant and consists of the most basic biological impulses or drives: the need to eat, to drink, to eliminate wastes, to avoid pain, and to gain sexual (sensual) pleasure. Freud believed that aggression is also a basic biological drive. In fact, he believed that the sexual and aggressive drives were the most important instinctual determinants of personality throughout life. The id seeks immediate gratification of these impulses. Like a young child, it operates on the pleasure principle: It continually strives to obtain pleasure and to avoid pain, regardless of the external circumstances.

THE EGO Children soon learn that their impulses cannot always be gratified immediately. Hunger will not be alleviated until someone provides food. Relief of bladder or bowel pressure must be delayed until the bathroom is reached. Certain impulses—playing with one's genitals or hitting someone—may be punished. A new part of the personality, the ego, develops as the young child learns to consider the demands of reality. The **ego** obeys the reality principle: The gratification of impulses must be delayed until the situation is appropriate. The ego thus is essentially the executive of the personality: It decides which id impulses will be satisfied and in what manner. The ego mediates among the demands of the id, the realities of the world, and the demands of the superego.

THE SUPEREGO The third part of the personality is the **superego,** which judges whether actions are right or wrong. More generally, the superego is the internalized representation of the values and morals of society. It is the individual's conscience, as well as his or her image of the morally ideal person (called the *ego ideal*).

The superego develops in response to parental rewards and punishments. Initially, parents control chil-

© 2002 by Sidney Harris

"VERY WELL I'LL INTRODUCE YOU. EGO MEET ID. NOW GET BACK TO WORK."

dren's behavior directly through reward and punishment. By incorporating parental standards into the superego, children bring behavior under their own control. Children no longer need anyone to tell them it is wrong to steal; their superego tells them. Violating the superego's standards, or even the impulse to do so, produces anxiety—beginning with anxiety over loss of parental love. According to Freud, this anxiety is largely unconscious but may be experienced as guilt. If parental standards are overly rigid, the individual may be guilt-ridden and inhibit all aggressive or sexual impulses. In contrast, an individual who fails to incorporate any standards for acceptable social behavior will feel few behavioral constraints and may engage in excessively self-indulgent or criminal behavior. Such a person is said to have a weak superego.

The three components of personality are often in conflict: The ego postpones the gratification that the id wants immediately, and the superego battles with both the id and the ego because behavior often falls short of the moral code it represents. In the well-integrated personality, the ego remains in firm but flexible control; the reality principle governs. In terms of his earlier iceberg model, Freud proposed that all of the id and most of the ego and superego are submerged in the unconscious and that small parts of the ego and superego are in either the conscious or the preconscious (see Figure 13-2).

PERSONALITY DYNAMICS

CONSERVATION OF ENERGY Freud was greatly influenced by the German physicist Hermann von Helmholtz, who argued that physiological events could be explained by the same principles that had been so successful in physics. Freud was particularly impressed by the principle of conservation of energy, which states that energy may be changed into different forms but is neither created nor destroyed. He proposed that humans are also closed energy systems. There is a constant amount of psychic energy for any given individual, which Freud called **libido** (Latin for "lust"), reflecting his view that the sexual drive was primary.

One corollary of the principle of conservation of energy is that if a forbidden act or impulse is suppressed, its energy will seek an outlet somewhere else in the system, possibly appearing in a disguised form. The desires of the id contain psychic energy that must be expressed in some way, and preventing the expression of those desires does not eliminate them. Aggressive impulses, for example, may be expressed in disguised form by racing sports cars, playing chess, or making sarcastic remarks. Dreams and neurotic symptoms are also manifestations of psychic energy that cannot be expressed directly.

ANXIETY AND DEFENSE Individuals with an urge to do something forbidden experience anxiety. One way of reducing this anxiety is to express the impulse in a disguised form that will avoid punishment either by society or by its internal representative, the superego. Freud and his daughter Anna Freud described several additional **defense mechanisms,** or strategies for preventing or reducing anxiety, and several are listed in the Concept Review Table.

CONCEPT REVIEW TABLE
Major Defense Mechanisms

Repression	Excluding from conscious awareness impulses or memories that are too frightening or painful.
Rationalization	Assigning logical or socially desirable motives to what we do so that we seem to have acted rationally.
Reaction formation	Concealing a motive from ourselves by giving strong expression to the opposite motive.
Projection	Assigning our own undesirable qualities to others in exaggerated amounts.
Intellectualization	Attempting to gain detachment from a stressful situation by dealing with it in abstract, intellectual terms.
Denial	Denying that an unpleasant reality exists.
Displacement	Directing a motive that cannot be gratified in one form into another channel.

We all use defense mechanisms at times. They help us over the rough spots until we can deal with stressful situations more directly. Defense mechanisms are maladaptive only when they become the dominant mode of responding to problems. We will discuss a few of the most common defense mechanisms here.

REPRESSION Freud considered repression to be the basic, and most important, defense mechanism. In **repression,** impulses or memories that are too frightening or painful are excluded from conscious awareness. Memories that evoke shame, guilt, or self-deprecation are often repressed. Freud believed that repression of certain childhood impulses is universal. In later life, individuals may repress feelings and memories that could cause anxiety because they are inconsistent with their self-concepts. Feelings of hostility toward a loved one and experiences of failure may be banished from conscious memory.

Repression is different from suppression. Suppression is the process of deliberate self-control, keeping impulses and desires in check (perhaps holding them in privately while denying them publicly) or temporarily pushing aside painful memories. Individuals are aware of suppressed thoughts but are largely unaware of repressed impulses or memories.

Freud believed that repression is seldom completely successful. The repressed impulses threaten to break through into consciousness; the individual becomes anxious (though unaware of the reason) and employs other defense mechanisms to keep the partially repressed impulses from awareness.

RATIONALIZATION When the fox in Aesop's fable rejected the grapes that he could not reach because they were sour, he illustrated a defense mechanism known as **rationalization.** Rationalization does not mean "to act rationally," as we might assume; it refers to the assignment of logical or socially desirable motives to what we do so that we seem to have acted rationally. Rationalization serves two purposes: It eases our disappointment when we fail to reach a goal ("I didn't want it anyway"), and it gives us acceptable motives for our behavior. If we act impulsively or on the basis of motives that we do not wish to acknowledge even to ourselves, we rationalize what we have done in order to place our behavior in a more favorable light.

In searching for the good reason rather than the true reason, individuals make a number of excuses. These excuses are usually plausible; they simply do not tell the whole story. For example, "My roommate failed to wake me" or "I had too many other things to do" may be true, but they may not be the real reasons for the individual's failure to perform the behavior in question. Individuals who are really concerned set an alarm clock or find the time to do what they are expected to do.

A classic experiment involving posthypnotic suggestion (see Chapter 6) demonstrates the process of rationalization. A hypnotist instructs a participant under hypnosis that when he wakes from the trance he will watch the hypnotist. Then, when the hypnotist takes off her glasses, the participant will raise the window but will not remember that the hypnotist told him to do this. Aroused from the trance, the participant feels a little drowsy but soon circulates among the people in the room and carries on a normal conversation, furtively watching the hypnotist. When the hypnotist casually removes her glasses, the participant feels an impulse to open the window. He takes a step in that direction but hesitates. Unconsciously, he mobilizes his desire to be a reasonable person. Seeking a reason for his impulse to open the window, he says, "Isn't it a little stuffy in here?" Having found the needed excuse, he opens the window and feels more comfortable (Hilgard, 1965).

REACTION FORMATION Sometimes individuals can conceal a motive from themselves by giving strong expression to the opposite motive. This tendency is called **reaction formation.** A mother who feels guilty about not wanting her child may become overindulgent and overprotective in order to assure the child of her love and assure herself that she is a good mother. In one case, a mother who wished to do everything for her daughter could not understand why the child was so unappreciative. At great sacrifice, she arranged for the daughter take expensive piano lessons and assisted her in the daily practice sessions. Although the mother thought she was being extremely kind, she was actually being very demanding—in fact, hostile. She was unaware of her own hostility, but when confronted with it, she admitted that she had hated piano lessons as a child. Under the conscious guise of being kind, she was unconsciously being cruel to her daughter. The daughter sensed what was going on and developed symptoms that required psychological treatment.

PROJECTION All of us have undesirable traits that we do not acknowledge, even to ourselves. A defense mechanism known as **projection** protects us from recognizing our own undesirable qualities by assigning them to other people in exaggerated amounts. Suppose that you have a tendency to be critical of or unkind to other people, but you would dislike yourself if you admitted this tendency. If you are convinced that the people around you are cruel or unkind, your harsh treatment of them is not based on your bad qualities—you are simply "giving them

what they deserve." If you can assure yourself that everybody else cheats on college examinations, your unacknowledged tendency to take some academic shortcuts seems not so bad. Projection is really a form of rationalization, but it is so pervasive that it merits discussion in its own right.

INTELLECTUALIZATION Intellectualization is an attempt to gain detachment from a stressful situation by dealing with it in abstract, intellectual terms. This kind of defense may be a necessity for people who must deal with life-and-death matters in their jobs. A doctor who is continually confronted with human suffering cannot afford to become emotionally involved with each patient. In fact, a certain amount of detachment may be essential for the doctor to function competently. This kind of intellectualization is a problem only when it becomes so pervasive that individuals cut themselves off from all emotional experiences.

DENIAL When an external reality is too unpleasant to face, an individual may engage in **denial,** refusing to acknowledge that the undesired reality exists. The parents of a terminally ill child may refuse to admit that anything is seriously wrong, even though they are fully informed of the diagnosis and the expected outcome. Because they cannot tolerate the pain that acknowledging reality would produce, they resort to denial. Less extreme forms of denial may be seen in individuals who consistently ignore criticism, fail to perceive that others are angry with them, or disregard all kinds of clues suggesting that their spouse is having an affair.

Sometimes, denying facts may be better than facing them. In a severe crisis, denial may give the person time

Emergency room physicians may need to develop many defenses to handle their high stress jobs.

to face the grim facts at a more gradual pace. For example, victims of a stroke or a spinal cord injury might give up altogether if they were fully aware of the seriousness of their condition. Hope gives them an incentive to keep trying. Soldiers who have faced combat or imprisonment report that denying the possibility of death helped them function. In such situations, denial clearly has an adaptive value. On the other hand, the negative aspects of denial are evident when people postpone seeking medical help. For example, a woman may deny that a lump in her breast may be cancerous and delay going to a physician until the condition has become life-threatening.

DISPLACEMENT Through the mechanism of **displacement,** a motive that cannot be gratified in one form is directed into a new channel. An example of displacement was provided in our discussion of anger that could not be expressed toward the source of frustration and was redirected toward a less threatening object. Freud felt that displacement was the most satisfactory way of handling aggressive and sexual impulses. The basic drives cannot be changed, but we can change the object toward which a drive is directed. Erotic impulses that cannot be expressed directly may be expressed indirectly in creative activities such as art, poetry, and music. Hostile impulses may find socially acceptable expression through participation in contact sports.

It seems unlikely that displacement actually eliminates the frustrated impulses, but substitute activities do help reduce tension when a basic drive is thwarted. For example, the activities of taking care of others or seeking companionship may help reduce the tension associated with unsatisfied sexual needs.

Some people may displace their aggressive impulses by engaging in aggressive sports.

PERSONALITY DEVELOPMENT

Freud believed that **during the first 5 years of life, the individual progresses through several developmental stages that affect his or her personality.** Applying a broad definition of sexuality, he called these periods **psychosexual stages.** During each stage, the pleasure-seeking impulses of the id focus on a particular area of the body and on activities connected with that area.

Freud called the first year of life the **oral stage** of psychosexual development. **During this period, infants derive pleasure from nursing and sucking and begin to put anything they can reach into their mouths.** Freud called the second year of life the beginning of the **anal stage** and believed that **during this period children find pleasure both in withholding and in expelling feces.** These pleasures come into conflict with parents who are attempting toilet training, the child's first experience with imposed control. In the **phallic stage,** from about age 3 to age 6, **children begin to derive pleasure from fondling their genitals.** They observe the differences between males and females and begin to direct their awakening sexual impulses toward the parent of the opposite sex.

Around the age of 5 or 6, according to Freud, **a boy's sexual impulses are directed toward his mother. This leads him to perceive his father as a rival for his mother's affection.** Freud called this situation the **Oedipal conflict,** after the ancient Greek myth in which Oedipus unwittingly kills his father and marries his mother. Freud also believed that the boy fears that his father will retaliate against these sexual impulses by castrating him. He labeled this fear castration anxiety and considered it to be the prototype for later anxieties provoked by forbidden internal desires. In a normal case of development, the boy simultaneously reduces this anxiety and vicariously gratifies his feelings toward his mother by identifying with his father—that is, by internalizing an idealized perception of his father's attitudes and values. The same process in a girl—resulting in her identifying with her mother—is analogous but more complicated.

Resolution of the Oedipal conflict ends the phallic stage, which is followed by the **latency period.** During this sexually quiescent time, which lasts from about age 7 to age 12, children become less concerned with their bodies and turn their attention to the skills needed for coping with their environment. Finally, adolescence and puberty usher in the **genital stage,** the mature phase of adult sexuality and functioning.

Freud believed that special problems at any stage could arrest, or fixate, development and have a lasting effect on personality. The individual's libido would remain attached to the activities appropriate for that stage. A person who was weaned very early and did not have enough sucking pleasure might become fixated at the oral stage. As an adult, he or she might be excessively de-

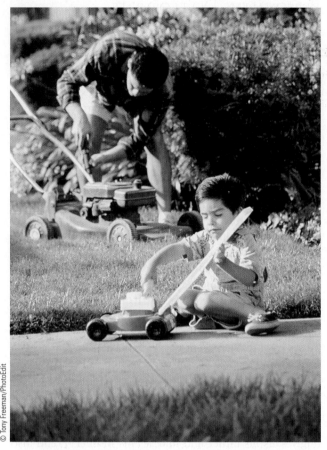

According to psychoanalytic theory, a child resolves the Oedipal conflict by identifying with the same-sex parent.

pendent on others and overly fond of oral pleasures such as eating, drinking, and smoking. Such a person is said to have an oral personality. A person fixated at the anal stage of psychosexual development may be abnormally concerned with cleanliness, orderliness, and saving and may tend to resist external pressure. Such a person is said to have an anal personality. Inadequate resolution of the Oedipal conflict can lead to a weak sense of morality, difficulties with authority figures, and many other problems.

MODIFICATIONS OF FREUD'S THEORIES

Freud modified his theories throughout his life. Like a good scientist, he remained open to new data, revising his earlier positions as new observations accumulated that could not be accommodated by the original theory. For example, quite late in his career he completely revised his theory of anxiety. Freud's theory has been further extended by his daughter Anna, who played a particularly important role in clarifying the defense mechanisms (1946/1967) and applying psychoanalytic theory to the practice of child psychiatry (1958).

Although Freud was open to new data, he was not open to dissenting opinions. He was particularly adamant that his colleagues and followers not question the libido theory and the centrality of sexual motivation in the functioning of personality. This dogmatism forced a break between Freud and many of his most brilliant associates, some of whom went on to develop rival theories that placed more emphasis on motivational processes other than sexuality. These former associates included Carl Jung and Alfred Adler, as well as later theorists such as Karen Horney, Harry Stack Sullivan, and Erich Fromm.

Of those who broke with Freud, perhaps the most famous was Carl Jung. Originally one of Freud's most dedicated followers, Jung eventually came to disagree profoundly with some aspects of Freud's theory and founded his own school of psychology, which he called *analytic psychology.* Jung believed that in addition to the personal unconscious described by Freud, there is a **collective unconscious,** a part of the mind that is common to all humans. The collective unconscious consists of primordial images or archetypes inherited from our ancestors. Among those archetypes are the mother, the father, the sun, the hero, God, and death. To gather evidence for the presence of these archetypes, Jung examined dreams, myths, and other cultural products, noting that certain images, such as that of a vulture, often appear in dreams and also in religious writings and ancient mythologies with which the dreamer is not familiar. Although Jung agreed with Freud on the existence of the unconscious, he believed that Freud's theory failed to explain the presence of common images or archetypes in the unconscious minds of all humans.

Another well-known "neo-Freudian" was the American psychologist Harry Stack Sullivan. Sullivan developed his own theory of personality on the basis of his experience with psychoanalysis. He placed primary emphasis on interpersonal relations, arguing that a personality "can never be isolated from the complex of interpersonal relations in which the person lives and has his being" (Sullivan, 1953, p. 10). In his view, people's responses to interpersonal experiences cause them to develop personifications—mental images of themselves and others. Images of the self fall into three categories: the good-me personification, the bad-me personification, and the not-me. The last category contains aspects of the self that are so threatening that the individual dissociates them from the self-system and maintains them in the unconscious. This concept is similar to Freud's concept of repression in that it requires a constant effort to keep these aspects of the self in the unconscious.

Like Freud, Sullivan believed that early childhood experiences play an important role in the development of personality. He believed, however, that the personality continues to develop after childhood. He identified seven

© Tony Freeman/PhotoEdit

Children must develop ways of handling their sometimes mixed feelings about their parents.

An important part of this new direction is **object relations theory,** which deals with a person's attachments and relationships to other people throughout life. Object relations theorists have not rejected the concept of the id or the importance of biological drives in motivating behavior, but they have an equal interest in such questions as degree of psychological separateness from parents, degree of attachment to and involvement with other people versus preoccupation with self, and the strength of the individual's feelings of self-esteem and competence.

Although we did not identify it as such, Erik Erikson's stage theory of development (discussed in Chapter 3) is an example of a revised psychoanalytic theory. Erikson himself was trained as a psychoanalyst by Anna Freud, and he perceived his own views as expanding rather than altering Freudian theory. Instead of viewing developmental stages in terms of their psychosexual functions, Erikson saw them as psychosocial stages involving primarily ego processes. For Erikson, the important feature of the first year of life is not that it focuses on oral gratification but that the child is learning to trust (or mistrust) the environment as a satisfier of needs. The important feature of the second year of life is not that it focuses on anal concerns such as toilet training but that the child is learning autonomy. Toilet training just happens to be a frequent arena of conflict in which the child's striving for autonomy clashes with new demands by parents. Erikson's theory also adds more stages in order to encompass the entire life span.

PROJECTIVE TESTS

Personality psychologists who follow in Freud's psychoanalytic tradition are particularly interested in assessing unconscious wishes, motivations, and conflicts. Accordingly, they prefer tests that resemble Freud's technique of free association, in which the individual is free to say whatever comes to mind. For this reason, they developed projective tests. A **projective test** presents an ambiguous stimulus to which the person may respond as he or she wishes. Because the stimulus is ambiguous and does not demand a specific response, it is assumed that the individual projects his or her personality onto the stimulus and thus reveals something about himself or herself. Projective tests have also been useful in areas of personality other than psychoanalytic theory. Two of the most widely used projective techniques are the Rorschach Test and the Thematic Apperception Test (TAT).

THE RORSCHACH TEST The **Rorschach Test,** developed by the Swiss psychiatrist Hermann Rorschach in the 1920s, is a series of 10 cards, each of which displays a rather complex inkblot like the one shown in Figure 13-3. Some of the blots are in color; some are black and white.

stages of personality development—infancy, childhood, the juvenile era, preadolescence, early adolescence, late adolescence, and adulthood—and maintained that each stage is largely socially determined. Although a person may go through a stage in a particular way because of certain biological factors, the primary influence is the typical situations he or she experiences at that age. Sullivan's view of development therefore differs considerably from Freud's biologically based theory.

These dissidents and more recent psychoanalytic theorists all place greater emphasis on the role of the ego. They believe that the ego is present at birth, develops independently of the id, and performs functions other than finding realistic ways of satisfying id impulses, including learning how to cope with the environment and making sense of experience. Ego satisfactions include exploration, manipulation, and competence in performing tasks. This approach ties the concept of the ego more closely to cognitive processes.

Figure 13-3
A Rorschach Inkblot
The person is asked to tell what he or she sees in the blot. It may be viewed from any angle.

The person is instructed to look at one card at a time and report everything the inkblot resembles. After the person has finished the 10 cards, the examiner usually goes over each response, asking the person to clarify some responses and indicate which features of the blot gave a particular impression.

The individual's responses may be scored in various ways. Three main categories are location (whether the response involves the entire inkblot or a part of it), determinants (whether the individual responds to the shape of the blot, its color, or differences in texture and shading), and content (what the response represents). Most testers also score responses according to frequency of occurrence; for example, a response is "popular" if many people assign it to the same inkblot.

Several elaborate scoring systems have been devised on the basis of these categories, but most of them have proved to be of limited predictive value. Consequently, many psychologists base their interpretations on an impressionistic evaluation of the response record, as well as on the individual's general reaction to the test situation (for example, whether the person is defensive, open, competitive, cooperative, and so on).

In 1974, a system was introduced that attempted to extract and combine the validated portions of all the scoring systems into one complete system. It has undergone extensive revision and is now supplemented by a computer scoring service and software for microcomputers (Exner & Weiner, 1995). This system is now widely used in clinical and forensic settings (Lillienfield, Wood, & Garb, 2000).

THE THEMATIC APPERCEPTION TEST Another popular projective test, the **Thematic Appercep-tion Test** (TAT), was developed at Harvard University by Henry Murray in the 1930s. The participant is shown as many as 20 ambiguous pictures of persons and scenes, similar to the one in Figure 13-4, and asked to make up a story about each picture. The individual is encouraged to give free rein to his or her imagination and to tell whatever story comes to mind. The test is intended to reveal basic themes that recur in a person's imaginings. (Apperception is a readiness to perceive in certain ways, based on prior experiences.) People interpret ambiguous pictures according to their apperceptions and elaborate stories in terms of preferred plots or themes that reflect personal fantasies. If particular problems are bothering them, those problems may become evident in a number of the stories or in striking deviations from the usual theme in one or two stories. For example, when shown a picture similar to the one in Figure 13-4, a 21-year-old male told the following story:

> She has prepared this room for someone's arrival and is opening the door for a last general look over the room. She is probably expecting her son home. She tries to place

Figure 13-4
The Thematic Apperception Test
This picture is similar to the pictures used on the Thematic Apperception Test. The pictures usually have elements of ambiguity so that the individual can "read into" them something from personal experience or fantasy.

everything as it was when he left. She seems like a very tyrannical character. She led her son's life for him and is going to take over again as soon as he gets back. This is merely the beginning of her rule, and the son is definitely cowed by this overbearing attitude of hers and will slip back into her well-ordered way of life. He will go through life plodding down the tracks she has laid down for him. All this represents her complete domination of his life until she dies. (Arnold, 1949, p. 100)

Although the original picture shows only a woman standing in an open doorway looking into a room, the young man's readiness to talk about his relationship with his mother led to this story of a woman's domination of her son. Facts obtained later confirmed the clinician's interpretation that the story reflected the man's own problems.

In analyzing responses to TAT cards, the psychologist looks for recurrent themes that may reveal the individual's needs, motives, or characteristic way of handling interpersonal relationships.

PROBLEMS WITH PROJECTIVE TESTS

Since the widespread adoption of Exner's scoring system for the Rorschach, hundreds of studies have been done to test the validity and reliability of results of the Rorschach based on this system (see Lillienfeld et al., 2000). Unfortunately, the Exner system appears to have done little to make the Rorschach a psychometrically sound test. The system too often misclassifies normal individuals as pathological, particularly individuals who are members of ethnic minority groups in the United States or from other cultures. The reliability of results from the Rorschach has generally been poor, in large part because the same responses may be evaluated quite differently by two trained examiners. And attempts to demonstrate the Rorschach's ability to predict behavior or discriminate between groups have met with limited success.

The TAT has fared somewhat better (Lillienfeld et al., 2000). When specific scoring systems are used (for example, to measure achievement motives or aggressive themes), interscorer reliability is fairly good (Winter, 1973). TAT measures have also proven useful in predicting some specific behaviors. For example, the need for power, as assessed by TAT responses, significantly predicted important life outcomes, such as the choice of a career that gave one influence over others, in two long-term studies of female college students (Winter, John, Stewart, Klohnen, & Duncan, 1998).

Many other projective tests have been devised. Some ask the individual to draw pictures of people, houses, trees, and so on. Others involve completing sentences that start with "I often wish . . . ," "My mother . . . ," or "I feel like quitting when they . . . ." In fact, any stimulus to which a person can respond in an individualistic way could be considered the basis for a projective test. But many projective tests have not been subjected to enough research to establish their usefulness in assessing personality, and those that have been researched have not proven to have consistently strong reliability or validity (Lillienfeld et al., 2000).

A PSYCHOANALYTIC PORTRAIT OF HUMAN NATURE

At the beginning of the chapter, we noted that each approach to personality carries with it a distinctive philosophy of human nature. To what extent are our actions free or determined? Good, neutral, or evil? Fixed or modifiable? Active or passive? What constitutes psychological health? Our description of Freud's theory has hinted at many of his views on these matters. Freud is often compared with Copernicus and Darwin. Like them, he was accused of undermining the stature and dignity of humanity. The astronomer Copernicus demoted the earth from its position as the center of the universe to one of several planets moving around a minor star; Darwin demoted the human species to one of numerous animal species. Freud took the next step by emphasizing that human behavior is determined by forces beyond our control, thereby depriving us of free will and psychological freedom. By emphasizing the unconscious status of our motivations, he deprived us of rationality; by stressing the sexual and aggressive nature of those motivations, he dealt the final blow to our dignity.

Freud saw the rise of the Nazis and the outbreak of World War II as natural consequences of the human aggressive drive when it is not held in check.

Psychoanalytic theory also paints a portrait of human nature as basically evil. Without the restraining forces of society and its internalized representative, the superego, humans would destroy themselves. Freud was a deeply pessimistic man. He was forced to flee from Vienna when the Nazis invaded in 1938, and he died in September 1939 just as World War II began. He saw these events as natural consequences of the human aggressive drive when it is not held in check.

According to psychoanalytic theory, our personalities are basically determined by inborn drives and by events in our environment during the first 5 years of life. Only extensive psychoanalysis can undo some of the negative consequences of early experiences, and it can do so only in limited ways. We also emerge from psychoanalytic theory as relatively passive creatures. Although the ego is engaged in an active struggle with the id and superego, we are passive pawns of this drama being played out in our unconscious. Finally, for Freud, psychological health consisted of firm but flexible ego control over the impulses of the id. As he noted, the goal of psychoanalysis was to ensure that "Where id is, there ego shall be" (1933).

AN EVALUATION OF THE PSYCHOANALYTIC APPROACH

Psychoanalytic theory is so broad in scope that it cannot simply be pronounced true or false. However, there can be no doubt of its impact on our culture, or of the value of some of its scientific contributions. For example, Freud's method of free association opened up an entirely new database of observations that had never before been explored systematically. In addition, the recognition that our behavior often reflects a compromise between our wishes and our fears accounts for many of the apparent contradictions in human behavior better than any other theory of personality. And Freud's recognition that unconscious processes play an important role in much of our behavior is almost universally accepted—although these processes are often reinterpreted in learning-theory or information-processing terms (Funder, 2001).

Nevertheless, as a scientific theory, the psychoanalytic account has been persistently criticized (Grünbaum, 1984). One of the main criticisms is that many of its concepts are ambiguous and difficult to define or measure objectively. Also, psychoanalytic theory assumes that very different behaviors may reflect the same underlying motive. For example, a man who had a hostile and uncaring father may become a hostile parent to his own children or overly protective of them. When opposite behaviors are claimed to result from the same underlying motive, it is difficult to confirm the presence or absence of the motive or to make predictions that can be empirically verified.

A more serious criticism concerns the validity of the observations that Freud obtained through his psychoanalytic procedure. Critics have pointed out that it often is not clear what Freud's patients told him spontaneously about past events in their lives, what he may have "planted" in their minds, and what he simply inferred. For example, Freud reported that many of his patients recalled being seduced or sexually molested as children. At first he believed them, but then he decided that these reports were not literally true but, rather, reflected the patients' own early sexual fantasies. He regarded this realization as one of his major theoretical insights. But one writer argued that Freud's original assumption about the reality of the seductions was probably more accurate, an argument that seems more reasonable in light of our increased awareness of child sexual abuse (Masson, 1984).

Other critics have gone further and suggested that Freud may have questioned his patients so persistently with leading questions and suggestions that they were led to reconstruct memories of seductions that never occurred—a hypothesis that Freud considered but rejected (Powell & Boer, 1994). Others charge that in many cases Freud simply inferred that seduction had occurred, even though the patient never reported such an incident; he actually substituted his theoretical expectations for data (Esterson, 1993; Scharnberg, 1993).

When Freud's theories have been empirically tested, the results have been mixed (Westen, 1998). Efforts to link adult personality characteristics to psychosexually relevant events in childhood have generally met with negative outcomes (Sears, Maccoby, & Levin, 1957; Sewell & Mussen, 1952). When relevant character traits are identified, they appear to be related to similar character traits in the parents (Beloff, 1957; Hetherington & Brackbill, 1963). Thus, even if a relationship were to be found between toilet-training practices and adult personality traits, it could have arisen because both are linked to parental emphasis on cleanliness and order. In such a case, a simple learning-theory explanation—parental reinforcement and the child's imitation of the parents' behavior—would be a more economical explanation of the adult traits than the psychoanalytic hypothesis.

This outcome should also remind us that Freud based his theory on observations of a very narrow range of people—primarily upper-middle-class men and women in Victorian Vienna who suffered from neurotic symptoms. In hindsight, many of Freud's cultural biases are obvious, particularly in his theories about women. For example, his theory that female psychosexual development is shaped largely by "penis envy"—a girl's feelings of inadequacy because she doesn't have a penis—is almost universally rejected as reflecting the sex bias of Freud and the historical period in which he lived. A little girl's personality development during the Victorian era was surely shaped more decisively by her awareness that she lacked the greater independence, power, and social status of her brother than by her envy of his penis.

Despite these criticisms, the remarkable feature of Freud's theory is how well it managed to transcend its narrow observational base. For example, many experimental studies of the defense mechanisms and reactions to conflict have supported the theory in contexts quite different from those in which Freud developed the theory (Blum, 1953; Erdelyi, 1985; Holmes, 1974; Sears, 1943, 1944). The structural theory (ego, id, and superego), the psychosexual theory, and the energy concept have not fared well over the years. Even some psychoanalytic writers are prepared to abandon them or to modify them substantially (Kline, 1972; Schafer, 1976). On the other hand, Freud's dynamic theory—his theory of anxiety and the mechanisms of defense—has withstood the test of time, research, and observation. A survey of psychoanalytically oriented psychologists and psychiatrists found widespread agreement with a number of ideas that were controversial when Freud first introduced them, including the importance of early childhood experiences in shaping adult personality and the centrality of both conflict and the unconscious in human mental life (Westen, 1998).

◆ Interim Summary

- Freud's psychoanalytic theory holds that many behaviors are caused by unconscious motivations. Personality is determined primarily by the biological drives of sex and aggression and by experiences that occur during the first 5 years of life.

- Freud's theory of personality structure views personality as composed of the id, the ego, and the superego. The id operates on the pleasure principle, seeking immediate gratification of biological impulses. The ego obeys the reality principle, postponing gratification until it can be achieved in socially acceptable ways. The superego (conscience) imposes moral standards on the individual. In a well-integrated personality, the ego remains in firm but flexible control over the id and superego, and the reality principle governs.

- Freud's theory of personality dynamics proposes that there is a constant amount of psychic energy (libido) for each individual. If a forbidden act or impulse is suppressed, its energy will seek an outlet in some other form, such as dreams or neurotic symptoms. The theory assumes that unacceptable id impulses cause anxiety, which can be reduced by defense mechanisms.

- Freud's theory of personality development proposes that individuals pass through psychosexual stages and must resolve the Oedipal conflict, in which the young child sees the same-sex parent as a rival for the affection of the opposite-sex parent. Over the years, Freud's theory of anxiety and defense mechanisms has fared better than his structural and developmental theories have.

- Psychoanalytic theory has been modified by later psychologists, notably Carl Jung and Harry Stack Sullivan. Jung proposed that, in addition to the personal unconscious described by Freud, there is a collective unconscious, a part of the mind that is common to all humans. Sullivan suggested that people's responses to interpersonal experiences cause them to develop personifications—mental images of themselves and others.

- Psychologists who take the psychoanalytic approach sometimes use projective tests, such as the Rorschach Test and the Thematic Apperception Test (TAT). Because the test stimuli are ambiguous, it is assumed that the individual projects his or her personality onto the stimulus, thereby revealing unconscious wishes and motives.

◆ Critical Thinking Questions

1. As this section makes clear, the value of Sigmund Freud's impact on psychology is hotly debated. What is your opinion on the value of Freud's legacy?

2. Can you identify some of your own assumptions about other people that are rooted in Freudian theory, whether you previously realized they were or not?

THE BEHAVIORIST APPROACH

In contrast to the psychodynamic approach to personality, the **behaviorist approach** emphasizes the importance of environmental, or situational, determinants of behavior. In this view, behavior is the result of a continuous interaction between personal and environmental variables. Environmental conditions shape behavior through learning; a person's behavior, in turn, shapes the environment. Persons and situations influence each other. To predict behavior, we need to know how the characteristics of the individual interact with those of the situation (Bandura, 1986, 2001).

SOCIAL LEARNING AND CONDITIONING

OPERANT CONDITIONING The effects of other people's actions—the rewards and punishments they provide—

are an important influence on an individual's behavior. Accordingly, one of the most basic principles of behavioral theory is **operant conditioning**—the type of learning that occurs when we learn the association between our behaviors and certain outcomes. The basic tenet of behaviorist theory is that people behave in ways that are likely to produce reinforcement and that individual differences in behavior result primarily from differences in the kinds of learning experiences a person encounters in the course of growing up.

Although individuals learn many behavior patterns through direct experience—that is, by being rewarded or punished for behaving in a certain manner—they also acquire many responses through **observational learning.** People can learn by observing the actions of others and noting the consequences of those actions. It would be a slow and inefficient process, indeed, if all of our behavior had to be learned through direct reinforcement of our responses. Similarly, the reinforcement that controls the expression of learned behaviors may be direct (tangible rewards, social approval or disapproval, or alleviation of aversive conditions), vicarious (observation of someone receiving reward or punishment for behavior similar to one's own), or self-administered (evaluation of one's own performance with self-praise or self-reproach).

Because most social behaviors are not uniformly rewarded in all settings, the individual learns to identify the contexts in which certain behavior is appropriate and those in which it is not. To the extent that a person is rewarded for the same response in many different situations, generalization takes place, ensuring that the same behavior will occur in a variety of settings. A boy who is reinforced for physical aggression at home, as well as at school and at play, is likely to develop an aggressive personality. More often, aggressive responses are differentially rewarded, and the individual learns to distinguish between situations in which aggression is appropriate and situations in which it is not (for example, aggression is acceptable on the football field but not in the classroom). For this reason, behaviorists challenge the usefulness of characterizing individuals with trait terms like *aggressive,* arguing that such terms obscure the cross-situational variability of behavior.

CLASSICAL CONDITIONING To account for emotion or affect, behaviorists add **classical conditioning**—the type of learning that occurs when specific situations become associated with specific outcomes—to their account of personality (see Chapter 7). For example, when a child is punished by a parent for engaging in some forbidden activity, the punishment elicits the physiological responses that we associate with guilt or anxiety. Subsequently, the child's behavior may itself elicit those responses, and the child will feel guilty when engaging in the forbidden be-

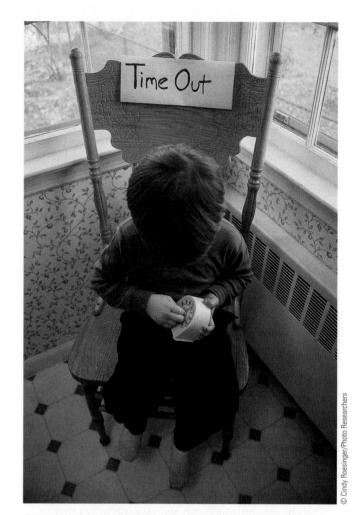

"Time-outs" are based on behaviorist principles.

havior. In the terminology of classical conditioning, we would say that the behavior becomes a conditioned stimulus by being paired with the unconditioned stimulus of punishment; the anxiety becomes the conditioned response. For the behaviorist, it is classical conditioning that produces the internalized source of anxiety that Freud labeled the superego.

INDIVIDUAL DIFFERENCES We noted earlier that personality psychology seeks to specify both the variables on which individuals differ from one another and the general processes of personality functioning. Trait approaches have focused on the first task, describing personality differences in detail while saying virtually nothing about personality functioning. Psychoanalytic theory has attempted to do both. In contrast, the behaviorist approach has focused primarily on process, devoting little attention to individual differences. Because this approach sees personality as the product of the individual's unique reinforcement history and emphasizes the degree to which behavior varies across situations, it has not attempted to classify individuals into types or to rate them on traits.

A BEHAVIORIST PORTRAIT OF HUMAN BEHAVIOR

Like the psychoanalytic approach, the behaviorist approach to personality is deterministic. In contrast to the psychoanalytic approach, however, it pays little attention to biological determinants of behavior and focuses on environmental determinants. People are not inherently good or evil but are readily modified by events and situations in their environment. As we noted in Chapter 3, John Watson, the founder of the behaviorist movement in the United States, claimed that he could raise an infant to be anything, regardless of the infant's "talents, penchants, tendencies, abilities, vocations, and race of his [or her] ancestors." Few behaviorists would take such an extreme view today. Nevertheless, behaviorists hold a strong optimism about our ability to change human behavior by changing the environment.

The human personality as described by behavioral theorists may be highly modifiable, but it still has a passive quality. We still seem to be shaped primarily by forces beyond our control. This view changed, however, as social-learning approaches (described later in this chapter) replaced traditional behaviorist theories, increasingly emphasize the individual's active role in selecting and modifying the environment, thereby permitting the person to become a causal force in his or her own life. As we will see, however, this role is not active enough for humanistic theorists. In particular, they do not believe that it is sufficient to define psychological health as merely optimal adaptation to the environment.

AN EVALUATION OF THE BEHAVIORIST APPROACH

Through its emphasis on specifying the environmental variables that evoke particular behaviors, behavioral theory has made a major contribution to both clinical psychology and personality theory. It has led us to see human actions as reactions to specific environments, and it has helped us focus on how environments control our behavior and how they can be changed to modify behavior. As we will see in Chapter 16, the systematic application of learning principles has proved successful in changing many maladaptive behaviors.

Behavioral theorists have been criticized for overemphasizing situational influences on behavior (Carlson, 1971). But the learning theorists' findings on the cross-situational consistency of personality have forced other

personality psychologists to reexamine their assumptions. The result has been a clearer understanding of the interactions between people and situations and an enhanced appreciation of each person's individuality. As we see in the next section, the cognitive theorists built on the work of behavioral theorists to introduce quite a different way of viewing personality.

◆ Interim Summary

- According to behaviorist theory, individual differences in behavior result primarily from differences in the kinds of learning experiences a person encounters in the course of growing up.
- Through operant conditioning, people learn to associate specific behaviors with punishment or reward. They can also learn these associations through observational learning.
- Through classical conditioning, people learn to associate specific situations with certain outcomes, such as anxiety.

◆ Critical Thinking Questions

1. Think about your own tendency to be friendly or unfriendly. To what extent is the situation important in determining your level of friendliness? What are some of the reinforcements and punishments you've had in your life that might have contributed to your tendency to be friendly or unfriendly?

2. Behavioral theorists view all types of human behavior as modifiable. Do you think there are any types of behavior that are not modifiable? Why or why not?

THE COGNITIVE APPROACH

Today most personality psychologists would not identify themselves as "pure" adherents to any one of the three approaches described so far, and the differences among the approaches are no longer as sharp as they once were. This is because most contemporary personality theorists have joined psychologists in other subfields in becoming more "cognitive." In fact, most contemporary experimental work in personality psychology begins from a cognitive base. The **cognitive approach** is not actually a "philosophy" of human nature in the way that the other approaches are. Rather, it is a general empirical approach and a set of topics related to how people process information about themselves and the world.

For the cognitive theorist, differences in personality stem from differences in the way individuals mentally represent information.

SOCIAL LEARNING THEORY

Social-learning theory has its roots in early behavioral theory but was considered a radical departure from behaviorism when it was first introduced. The social-learning perspective is aptly summarized in the following comment by Albert Bandura: "The prospects for survival would be slim indeed if one could learn only from the consequences of trial and error. One does not teach children to swim, adolescents to drive automobiles, and novice medical students to perform surgery by having them discover the requisite behavior from the consequences of their successes and failures" (1986, p. 20). According to **social-learning theorists,** internal cognitive processes influence behavior, as well as observation of the behaviors of others and the environment in which behavior occurs.

As early as 1954, Julian Rotter was introducing cognitive variables into the behaviorist approach (1954, 1982). Rotter proposed the concept of behavior potential, meaning the likelihood of a particular behavior occurring in a particular situation—for example, staying up all night to study for an exam. The strength of the behavior potential is determined by two variables: ex-

Albert Bandura developed social cognitive theory.

pectancy and reinforcement value. In the case of pulling an all-nighter, the likelihood of engaging in that behavior is greater if the student expects to receive a higher grade as a result. This expectation will depend on what happened the last time the student was in a similar situation. If studying all night resulted in a higher grade the last time, the student will expect the same result this time. In other words, the more often the student is reinforced for studying all night, the stronger his or her expectancy that the behavior will be reinforced in the future. As for reinforcement value, it depends on the degree to which we prefer one reinforcer over another. If a student prefers sleeping over receiving a higher grade, the likelihood of pulling an all-nighter decreases.

Bandura, one of the leading contemporary theorists in this area, has taken this approach even further, developing what he calls **social-cognitive theory** (1986, 2000). His theory emphasizes reciprocal determinism, in which external determinants of behavior (such as rewards and punishments) and internal determinants (such as beliefs, thoughts, and expectations) are part of a system of interacting influences that affect both behavior and other parts of the system (Bandura, 1986). In Bandura's model, not only can the environment affect behavior but also behavior can affect the environment. In fact, the relationship between environment and behavior is a reciprocal one: The environment influences our behavior, which then affects the kind of environment we find ourselves in, which may in turn influence our behavior, and so on.

Bandura notes that people use symbols and forethought in deciding how to act. When they encounter a new problem, they imagine possible outcomes and consider the probability of each. Then they set goals and develop strategies for achieving them. This is quite different from the notion of conditioning through rewards and punishments. Of course, the individual's past experiences with rewards and punishments will influence his or her decisions about future behavior.

Bandura also points out that most behavior occurs in the absence of external rewards or punishments. Most behavior stems from internal processes of self-regulation. As he expresses it, "Anyone who attempted to change a pacifist into an aggressor or a devout religionist into an atheist would quickly come to appreciate the existence of personal sources of behavioral control" (1977, pp. 128–129).

How do these internal, personal sources of control develop? According to Bandura and other social-learning theorists, we learn how to behave by observing the behavior of others or by reading or hearing about it. We do not have to actually perform the behaviors we observe; instead, we can note whether those behaviors were rewarded or punished and store that information in memory. When new situations arise, we can behave according to the expectations we have accumulated on the basis of our observation of models.

Bandura's social-cognitive theory thus goes beyond classical behaviorism. Rather than focusing only on how environment affects behavior, it examines the interactions among environment, behavior, and the individual's cognitions. In addition to considering external influences such as rewards and punishments, it considers internal factors such as expectations. And instead of explaining behavior simply in terms of conditioning, it emphasizes the role of observational learning.

Another prominent social-learning theorist, Walter Mischel, has attempted to incorporate individual differences into social learning theory by introducing the following set of cognitive variables:

1. Competencies: What can you do? Competencies include intellectual abilities, social and physical skills, and other special abilities.
2. Encoding strategies: How do you see it? People differ in the way they selectively attend to information, encode (represent) events, and group the information into meaningful categories. An event that is perceived by one person as threatening may be seen by another as challenging.
3. Expectancies: What will happen? Expectations about the consequences of different behaviors will guide the individual's choice of behavior. If you cheat on an examination and are caught, what do you expect the consequences to be? If you tell your friend what you really think of him or her, what will happen to your relationship? Expectations about our own abilities will also influence behavior: We may anticipate the consequences of a certain behavior but fail to act because we are uncertain of our ability to execute the behavior.
4. Subjective values: What is it worth? Individuals who have similar expectancies may choose to behave differently because they assign different values to the outcomes. Two students may expect a certain behavior to please their professor. However, this outcome is important to one student but not to the other.
5. Self-regulatory systems and plans: How can you achieve it? People differ in the standards and rules they use to regulate their behavior (including self-imposed rewards for success or punishments for failure), as well as in their ability to make realistic plans for reaching a goal. (After Mischel, 1973, 1993)

All of these person variables (sometimes referred to as cognitive social-learning person variables) interact with the conditions of a particular situation to determine what an individual will do in that situation.

KELLY'S PERSONAL CONSTRUCT THEORY

George Kelly (1905–1966) was another of the personality psychologists to first suggest that cognitive processes play a central role in an individual's functioning. Kelly noted that personality psychologists typically characterized an individual on dimensions that they themselves had constructed. He proposed instead that the goal should be to discover **personal constructs, the dimensions that individuals themselves use to interpret themselves and their social worlds.** These dimensions constitute the basic units of analysis in Kelly's personal construct theory (1955).

More generally, Kelly believed that individuals should be viewed as intuitive scientists. Like formal scientists, they observe the world, formulate and test hypotheses about it, and make up theories about it. They also categorize, interpret, label, and judge themselves and their world. And, like scientists, individuals can entertain invalid theories, beliefs that hinder them in their daily lives and lead to biased interpretations of events and persons, including themselves.

Like scientists trying to make predictions about events, people want to understand the world so that they can predict what will happen to them. Kelly argued that each individual uses a unique set of personal constructs in interpreting and predicting events. Those constructs tend to take an either-or form: A new acquaintance is either friendly or unfriendly, intelligent or unintelligent, fun or boring, and so on. But two people meeting the same individual may use different constructs in evaluating that individual—someone who seems friendly and intelligent to one person may seem unfriendly and unintelligent to another. These differences lead to differences in behavior—one person will respond positively to the new acquaintance while an-

According to Kelly, personal constructs take an either-or form. A new acquaintance is either friendly or unfriendly, intelligent or unintelligent, fun or boring.

other may avoid him or her. These differences in behavior produce differences in personality.

Because typical trait tests of personality do not meet Kelly's basic criterion that individuals must be assessed in terms of their personal constructs, he devised his own test for eliciting a person's personal constructs, the Role Construct Repertory Test or "Rep Test." On this test, clients fill in a matrix or grid like the one shown in Figure 13-5. Along the top of the grid is a list of people who are important to the individual. These might be supplied by the assessor or by the client, but they usually include "myself" and sometimes include "my ideal self." On each line of the grid, the assessor circles three of the cells. For example, in the first row of the figure the assessor has circled the cells in the columns labeled "myself," "my mother," and "my best friend." The client is asked to consider these three people and to place an X in the cells of the two who are most similar to each other but different from the third. As shown in the first row, this (male) client considers himself and his mother to be the most similar pair. He is then asked, "In what way are you and your mother alike but different from your best friend?" In this case the client has indicated that he and his mother are both witty. This description is his con-

struct. Next he is asked, "In what way is your friend different from you and your mother?" He has responded that his friend is humorless. This description is his contrast. For this client, then, the dimension witty-humorless is one of the personal constructs he uses to interpret his interpersonal world.

Note that a construct-contrast pair need not constitute logical opposites. For example, this client might have labeled himself and his mother as witty but then labeled his best friend as serious or introverted or prefers-to-listen-to-humor-rather-than-initiate-it. If that is how he construes the two sides of the dimension, then that is what Kelly wanted to know. The Rep Test is designed to assess the individual's constructs, not the psychologist's.

This procedure is repeated with several other triads in the set. By looking at the entire set, the investigator or therapist can explore a number of themes that seem to characterize the individual's interpretation of the world. For example, some clients will reveal through this procedure that they see the entire world in authoritarian terms; dimensions like strong-weak, powerful-powerless, and so forth might appear repeatedly. Or an individual might reveal that she always pairs herself with males on the construct end of dimensions while placing other women on the contrast end.

The Rep Test is a very general procedure and is not restricted to interpretations of other people. For example, an individual may be asked to consider triads of situations or events. (Which two are alike but different from the third? Taking an examination, going out on a blind date, encountering a spider.) The technique has proved valuable both for research on people's constructs and for counseling.

SELF-SCHEMAS

A **schema** is a cognitive structure that helps us perceive, organize, process, and utilize information (Markus, 1999). Through the use of schemas, each individual develops a system for identifying what is important in his or her environment while ignoring everything else. Schemas also provide a structure within which to organize and process information. For example, most people have developed a mother schema. When asked to describe their mother, it is easy for them because the information is organized into a well-defined cognitive structure. It is easier to describe one's mother than to describe a woman one has heard about but has never met.

Schemas are relatively stable over time and therefore result in stable ways of perceiving and utilizing information. They differ from one individual to another, causing people to process information differently and to behave in different ways. They thus can be used to explain differences in personality.

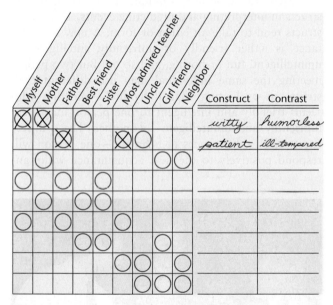

▌ Figure 13-5
The Role Construct Repertory Test
In each row, the individual compares three of the people listed at the top of the grid, placing an X under the two who are most alike. He or she then describes how they are alike by writing in the construct. Finally, the individual describes how the third person is different from the other two by writing in the contrast. This person indicates that he sees himself and his mother as being both witty and different from his best friend, who is seen as humorless. The procedure is repeated for each row in the matrix.

Perhaps the most important schema is the **self-schema**, which consists of "cognitive generalizations about the self, derived from past experience, that organize and guide the processing of self-related information" (Markus, 1977, p. 64). From an early age, we all develop a cognitive representation of who we are. The resulting self-schema is made up of the aspects of our behavior that are most important to us, and it plays a central role in the way we process information and interact with the world around us. For example, two people may both enjoy jogging and literature, but for one person exercise may be an important part of the self-schema, yet the other person's self-schema may place greater emphasis on being well-read. The first person is likely to spend more time jogging than reading, and the reverse is likely to be true of the second person.

The core of the self-schema is basic information, such as the person's name, physical appearance, and relationships with significant people. But more important from the standpoint of individual differences are particularistic features of the self-schema (Markus & Sentis, 1982; Markus & Smith, 1981). For the person whose self-schema includes an emphasis on exercise, for example, exercise is part of "who he or she is" and a part of the daily or weekly routine. For the person who enjoys jogging but does not view it as central, an occasional jog around the park will be sufficient. So, differences in self-schemas produce differences in behavior.

Self-schemas not only guide the perception and processing of information but also provide a framework for organizing and storing it. As with the mother schema mentioned earlier, we would expect people to retrieve information from memory more easily when they have a strong schema for it. This hypothesis was tested in an experiment in which college students were presented with a series of 40 questions on a video screen (Rogers, Kuiper,

& Kirker, 1977). The participants were asked to respond to each question by pressing a yes or no button as quickly as possible. Thirty of the questions could be answered easily without being processed through the self-schema. They asked whether a word was printed in big letters, rhymed with another word, or had the same meaning as another word. The other 10 questions required participants to decide whether a word described them, and the researchers proposed that in these cases the information had to be processed through the self-schema.

The participants were later asked to recall as many of the 40 words as they could. The results showed that when participants answered questions about themselves they were more likely to remember the information later. The researchers concluded that the participants processed this information through their self-schemas. Because information in the self-schema is easy to access, words referring to the self were easier to remember than words processed in other ways. In subsequent studies, when participants were asked whether a word described the experimenter (Kuiper & Rogers, 1979) or a celebrity (Lord, 1980), they did not recall those words as easily as words describing themselves. In sum, it appears that the superior organization and accessibility of information about ourselves makes information that is processed through the self-schema more accessible than information that is processed in other ways (Karylowski, 1990; Klein & Loftus, 1988; Klein, Loftus, & Burton, 1989).

Self-schemas differ considerably across cultures to the extent that some theorists argue that personality is a product of culture (Cross & Markus, 1999). For example, in North America we assume that the self is autonomous and separate from others and from situations and that we have individual choice over our actions and beliefs. In the North American conception of the self, a person's wishes, desires, interests, and abilities make up the self. We have the power and the responsibility to create the self we want to have, rather than allow external influences to shape our self-concepts. In contrast, in some Asian cultures, the self is not an entity separate from others but is thoroughly intertwined with one's obligations and relationships to others. The core issue in the development of the self is not to discover and express one's own wishes, desires, interests, and abilities, but to determine how one is meant to fit in with the social group and to shape oneself to best serve the social group.

An Evaluation of the Cognitive Approach

The cognitive approach has some strengths as well as some weaknesses. One positive aspect of the approach is that it is based on empirical research. As illustrated by the preceding descriptions of experiments, many cogni-

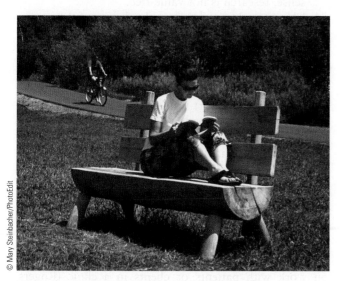

Your recreational activities reflect your self-schemas.

tive structures have been subjected to extensive study in controlled laboratory experiments. Another strength of cognitive theory is that it goes beyond the trait approach in explaining personality characteristics. Rather than simply identifying traits, cognitive theorists use cognitive structures to explain individual differences in behavior.

On the other hand, a frequent criticism of the cognitive approach is that it employs vague concepts. It is difficult to state specifically what a personal construct is or to be sure when a schema is being used, and it is not entirely clear how a personal construct differs from a schema or how any of these cognitive structures relate to memory and other aspects of information processing. Moreover, behaviorists might ask whether it is really necessary to use these concepts. Perhaps personality can be explained just as well without referring to cognitions.

◆ Interim Summary

- The cognitive approach to personality is based on the idea that differences in personality stem from differences in the way individuals mentally represent information.

- Albert Bandura developed social cognitive theory, which holds that internal cognitive processes combine with environmental pressures to influence behavior, and that cognitive processes and environment have reciprocal effects on each other.

- Walter Mischel has identified a number of cognitive person variables that affect people's reactions to the environment and behaviors in the environment.

- George Kelly's personal construct theory focuses on the concepts that individuals use to interpret themselves and their social world.

- Much research has focused on the self-schema, which consists of the aspects of a person's behavior that are most important to that person. Experiments have shown that people perceive information more readily and recall it better when it is relevant to their self-schemas.

◆ Critical Thinking Questions

1. Some theorists argue that our most important schemas for ourselves and others are often nonconscious—we don't even realize we hold them and might deny we hold them if asked explicitly. Can you think of some methods by which you might be able to tap into a person's nonconscious schemas?

2. What do you think are some of the most important developmental processes or events that contribute to the type of self-schema an individual develops?

THE HUMANISTIC APPROACH

During the first half of the 20th century, the psychoanalytic and behaviorist approaches were dominant in psychology. In 1962, however, a group of psychologists founded the Association of Humanistic Psychology. They saw humanistic psychology as a "third force," an alternative to the other two approaches. To define its mission, the association adopted four principles:

1. The experiencing person is of primary interest. Humans are not simply objects of study. They must be described and understood in terms of their own subjective views of the world, their perceptions of self, and their feelings of self-worth. The central question each person must face is "Who am I?" In order to learn how the individual attempts to answer this question, the psychologist must become a partner with that person.

2. Human choice, creativity, and self-actualization are the preferred topics of investigation. People are not motivated only by basic drives like sex or aggression or physiological needs like hunger and thirst. They feel a need to develop their potentials and capabilities. Growth and self-actualization should be the criteria of psychological health, not merely ego control or adjustment to the environment.

3. Meaningfulness must precede objectivity in the selection of research problems. Humanistic psychologists argue that we should study important human and social problems, even if that sometimes means adopting less rigorous methods. And while psychologists should strive to be objective in collecting and interpreting observations, their choice of research topics can and should be guided by values. In this sense, research is not value-free.

4. Ultimate value is placed on the dignity of the person. People are basically good. The objective of psychology is to understand, not to predict or control people.

Psychologists who share these values come from diverse theoretical backgrounds. For example, the trait theorist Gordon Allport was also a humanistic psychologist, and we have already pointed out that several psychoanalysts, such as Carl Jung, Alfred Adler, and Erik Erikson, held humanistic views of motivation that diverged from Freud's views. But it is Carl Rogers and Abraham Maslow whose theoretical views lie at the center of the humanistic movement.

CARL ROGERS

Like Freud, Carl Rogers (1902–1987) based his theory on work with patients or clients in a clinic (Rogers, 1951, 1959, 1963, 1970). Rogers was impressed with

Carl Rogers believed that individuals have an innate tendency to move toward growth, maturity, and positive change. He referred to this as the *actualizing tendency.*

what he saw as the individual's innate tendency to move toward growth, maturity, and positive change. He came to believe that the basic force motivating the human organism is the **actualizing tendency**—a tendency toward fulfillment or actualization of all the capacities of the organization. A growing organism seeks to fulfill its potential within the limits of its heredity. A person may not always clearly perceive which actions lead to growth and which do not. But once the course is clear, the individual chooses to grow. Rogers did not deny that there are other needs, some of them biological, but he saw them as subservient to the organism's motivation to enhance itself.

Rogers's belief in the primacy of actualization forms the basis of his nondirective or client-centered therapy. This method of psychotherapy assumes that every individual has the motivation and ability to change and that the individual is best qualified to decide the direction such change should take. The therapist's role is to act as a sounding board while the client explores and analyzes his or her problems. This approach differs from psychoanalytic therapy, during which the therapist analyzes the patient's history to determine the problem and devise a course of remedial action. (See Chapter 16 for a discussion of various approaches to psychotherapy.)

THE SELF The central concept in Rogers's theory of personality is the **self,** or self-concept (Rogers uses the terms interchangeably). The self (or real self) consists of all the ideas, perceptions, and values that characterize "I" or "me"; it includes the awareness of "what I am" and "what I can do." This perceived self, in turn, influences both the person's perception of the world and his or her behavior. For example, a woman who perceives herself as strong and competent perceives and acts upon the world quite differently than a woman who considers herself weak and ineffectual. The self-concept does not necessarily reflect reality: A person may be highly successful and respected but still view himself or herself as a failure.

According to Rogers, the individual evaluates every experience in relation to his or her self-concept. People want to behave in ways that are consistent with their self-image, and experiences and feelings that are not consistent are threatening and may be denied entry into consciousness. This is essentially Freud's concept of repression, although Rogers felt that such repression is neither necessary nor permanent. (Freud would say that repression is inevitable and that some aspects of the individual's experiences always remain unconscious.)

The more areas of experience a person denies because they are inconsistent with his or her self-concept, the wider the gap between the self and reality and the greater the potential for maladjustment. Individuals whose self-concepts do not match their feelings and experiences must defend themselves against the truth because the truth will result in anxiety. If the gap becomes too wide, the person's defenses may break down, resulting in severe anxiety or other forms of emotional disturbance. A well-adjusted person, in contrast, has a self-concept that is consistent with his or her thoughts, experiences, and behaviors; the self is not rigid but flexible, and it can change as it assimilates new experiences and ideas.

Rogers also proposed that each of us has an ideal self, our conception of the kind of person we would like to be. The closer the ideal self is to the real self, the more fulfilled and happy the individual becomes. A large discrepancy between the ideal self and the real self results in an unhappy, dissatisfied person.

Thus, two kinds of inconsistency can develop: between the self and the experiences of reality and between the real self and the ideal self. Rogers proposed some hypotheses about how these inconsistencies may develop. In particular, Rogers believed that people are likely to function more effectively if they are brought up with **unconditional positive regard**—being given the sense that they are valued by parents and others even when their feelings, attitudes, and behaviors are less than ideal. If parents offer only conditional positive regard—valuing the child only when he or she behaves, thinks, or feels correctly—the child's self-concept is likely to be distorted. For example, feelings of competition and hostility toward a younger sibling are natural, but parents disapprove of hitting a baby brother or sister and usually punish such actions. Children must somehow integrate this experience into their self-concept. They may decide that they are bad and feel ashamed. They may decide that their parents do not like them and feel rejected. Or they may deny their feelings and decide they do not want to hit the baby. Each of these attitudes distorts the truth. The third alternative is the easiest for children to accept, but in so doing they deny their real feelings, which then become unconscious. The more people are forced to deny their own feelings and accept the values of others, the more uncomfortable they will feel about themselves. Rogers suggested that the best approach is for the parents to recognize the child's feelings as valid while explaining the reasons that hitting is not acceptable.

MEASURING REAL-IDEAL SELF-CONGRUENCE Earlier, we described a method of assessment called the *Q-sort*, in which a rater or sorter is given a set of cards, each containing a personality statement (for example, "Is cheerful"), and asked to describe an individual's personality by sorting the cards into piles. The rater places statements that are least descriptive of the individual in a pile on the left and those that are most descriptive in a pile on the right. The other statements are distributed in the intermediate piles, thereby assigning each Q item a score corresponding to the pile in which it is placed. Researchers can compare two Q-sorts by computing a correlation between their item scores, thereby assessing the degree to which the two sorts are similar.

Rogers pioneered the use of the Q-sort as a way of examining the self-concept. His Q set contains statements like "I am satisfied with myself," "I have a warm emotional relationship with others," and "I don't trust my emotions." In Rogers's procedure, individuals first sort themselves as they actually are—their real self—and then sort themselves as they would like to be—their ideal self. The correlation between the two sorts reveals the degree of incongruence between the real and ideal selves. A low or negative correlation cor-

responds to a large discrepancy, implying feelings of low self-esteem and lack of worth.

By repeating this procedure several times during the course of therapy, Rogers could assess the effectiveness of therapy. In one study, correlations between self and ideal Q-sorts of individuals seeking therapy averaged −.01 before therapy but increased to + .34 after therapy. Correlations for a matched control group that did not receive therapy did not change (Butler & Haigh, 1954). In other words, the therapy had significantly reduced these individuals' perception of the discrepancy between their real selves and their ideal selves. Note that this could occur in two ways: An individual could change his or her concept of the real self so that it was closer to the ideal self or change his or her concept of the ideal self so that it was more realistic. Therapy can produce both kinds of changes.

More recently, psychologist Tory Higgins (1987) has shown that self-discrepancies such as those described by Rogers are associated with serious depression and anxiety.

ABRAHAM MASLOW

The psychology of Abraham Maslow (1908–1970) overlaps with that of Carl Rogers in many ways. Maslow was first attracted to behaviorism and carried out studies of primate sexuality and dominance. He was already moving away from behaviorism when his first child was born, after which he remarked that anyone who observes a baby cannot be a behaviorist. He was influenced by psychoanalysis but eventually became critical of its theory of motivation and developed his own theory. Specifically, he proposed that there is a **hierarchy of needs,** ascending from the basic biological needs to the more complex psychological motivations that become important only after the basic needs have been satisfied (see Figure 13-6). The needs at one level must be at least partially satisfied before those at the

▌ Figure 13-6
Maslow's Hierarchy of Needs
Needs that are low in the hierarchy must be at least partially satisfied before needs that are higher in the hierarchy become important sources of motivation. (After Abraham H. Maslow, "Hierarchy of Needs," from *Motivation and Personality.* Copyright © 1954 by Harper and Row Publishers, Inc. Reprinted by permission of Pearson Education, Inc., Upper Saddle River, NJ.)

Self-actualization needs: to find self-fulfillment and realize one's potential

Aesthetic needs: symmetry, order, and beauty

Cognitive needs: to know, understand, and explore

Esteem needs: to achieve, be competent, and gain approval and recognition

Belongingness and love needs: to affiliate with others, be accepted, and belong

Safety needs: to feel secure and safe, out of danger

Physiological needs: hunger, thirst, and so forth

next level become important motivators of action. When food and safety are difficult to obtain, efforts to satisfy those needs will dominate a person's actions, and higher motives will have little significance. Only when basic needs can be satisfied easily will the individual have the time and energy to devote to aesthetic and intellectual interests. Artistic and scientific endeavors do not flourish in societies in which people must struggle for food, shelter, and safety. The highest motive—self-actualization—can be fulfilled only after all other needs have been satisfied.

Maslow decided to study self-actualizers—men and women who had made extraordinary use of their potential. He began by studying the lives of eminent historical figures such as Spinoza, Thomas Jefferson, Abraham Lincoln, Jane Addams, Albert Einstein, and Eleanor Roosevelt. In this way he was able to create a composite picture of a self-actualizer. The distinguishing characteristics of such individuals are listed in Table 13-2, along with some of the behaviors that Maslow believed could lead to self-actualization.

Maslow then extended his study to a population of college students. Selecting students who fit his definition of self-actualizers, he found this group to be in the healthiest 1% of the population. These students showed no signs of maladjustment and were making effective use of their talents and capabilities (Maslow, 1970).

Many people experience what Maslow called **peak experiences:** transient moments of self-actualization. A peak experience is characterized by happiness and fulfillment—a temporary, nonstriving, non-self-centered state of goal attainment. Peak experiences may occur in different intensities and in various contexts, such as creative activities, appreciation of nature, intimate relationships, aesthetic perceptions, or athletic participation. After asking a large number of college students to describe any experience that came close to being a peak experience, Maslow attempted to summarize their responses. They spoke of wholeness, perfection, aliveness, uniqueness, effortlessness, self-sufficiency, and the values of beauty, goodness, and truth.

A HUMANISTIC PORTRAIT OF HUMAN NATURE

As a matter of principle, humanistic psychologists have been quite explicit about the principles underlying their approach to human personality. The four principles set forth by the Association of Humanistic Psychology, which we summarized earlier, draw sharp contrasts between the humanistic portrait of human personality and the portraits drawn by the psychoanalytic and behaviorist approaches.

Most humanistic psychologists do not dispute the claim that biological and environmental variables can influence behavior, but they emphasize the individual's own

● **Table 13-2**
Self-Actualization

Listed here are the personal qualities that Maslow found to be characteristic of self-actualizers and the behaviors he considered important to the development of self-actualization. *(A. H. Maslow (1967), "Self-actualization and beyond." In* Challenges of Humanistic Psychology, *J. F. T. Bugenthal (ed.). Copyright © 1967 by Abraham H. Maslow. Used with permission of McGraw-Hill Publishers.)*

Characteristics of Self-Actualizers

Perceive reality efficiently and can tolerate uncertainty

Accept themselves and others for what they are

Spontaneous in thought and behavior

Problem-centered rather than self-centered

Have a good sense of humor

Highly creative

Resistant to enculturation, although not purposely unconventional

Concerned for the welfare of humanity

Capable of deep appreciation of the basic experiences of life

Establish deep, satisfying interpersonal relationships with a few, rather than many, people

Able to look at life from an objective viewpoint

Behaviors Leading to Self-Actualization

Experience life as a child does, with full absorption and concentration

Try something new rather than sticking to secure and safe ways

Listen to your own feelings in evaluating experiences rather than to the voice of tradition or authority or the majority

Be honest; avoid pretenses or "game playing"

Be prepared to be unpopular if your views do not coincide with those of most people

Assume responsibility

Work hard at whatever you decide to do

Try to identify your defenses and have the courage to give them up

role in defining and creating his or her destiny, and they downplay the determinism that is characteristic of the other approaches. In their view, individuals are basically good, striving for growth and self-actualization. They are also modifiable and active. Humanistic psychologists set a particularly high criterion for psychological health. Mere ego control or adaptation to the environment is not enough. Only an individual who is growing toward self-actualization can be said to be psychologically healthy. In other words, psychological health is a process, not an end state.

Such assumptions have political implications. From the perspective of humanistic psychology, anything that retards the fulfillment of individual potential—that prevents any human being from becoming all he or she can be—should be challenged. For example, if women in the 1950s were happy and well adjusted to traditional sex roles, the criterion of psychological health defined by behaviorism was satisfied. But from the humanistic perspective, consigning all women to the same role is undesirable—no matter how appropriate that role might be for some women—because it prevents many from reaching their maximum potential. It is no accident that the rhetoric of liberation movements—such as women's liberation and gay liberation—echoes the language of humanistic psychology.

Albert Einstein and Eleanor Roosevelt were among the individuals Maslow identified as self-actualizers.

AN EVALUATION OF THE HUMANISTIC APPROACH

By focusing on the individual's unique perception and interpretation of events, the humanistic approach brings individual experience back into the study of personality. More than other theories we have discussed, the theories of Rogers and Maslow concentrate on the whole, healthy person and take a positive, optimistic view of human personality. Humanistic psychologists emphasize that they study important problems, even if they do not always have rigorous methods for investigating them. They have a point—investigating trivial problems just because one has a convenient method for doing so does little to advance the science of psychology. Moreover, humanistic psychologists have succeeded in devising new methods for assessing self-concepts and conducting studies that treat the individual as an equal partner in the research enterprise. Nevertheless, critics question the quality of the evidence in support of the humanists' claims. For example, to what extent are the characteristics of self-actualizers a consequence of a psychological process called *self-actualization* and to what extent are they merely reflections of the particular value systems held by Rogers and Maslow? Where, they ask, is the evidence for Maslow's hierarchy of needs?

Humanistic psychologists are also criticized for building their theories solely on observations of relatively healthy people. Their theories are best suited to well-functioning people whose basic needs have been met, freeing them to concern themselves with higher needs. The applicability of these theories to malfunctioning or disadvantaged individuals is less apparent.

Finally, some have criticized the values espoused by the humanistic theorists. Many observers believe that Americans are already obsessed with the individual and show little concern for the welfare of the larger society. A psychology that raises individual self-fulfillment and actualization to the top of the value hierarchy may provide a "sanction for selfishness" (Wallach & Wallach, 1983). Although Maslow lists concern for the welfare of humanity among the characteristics of self-actualizers (see Table 13-2) and some of the self-actualizers identified by Maslow—such as Eleanor Roosevelt and Albert Einstein—clearly possessed this characteristic, it is not included in the hierarchy of needs.

◆ Interim Summary

- The humanistic approach is concerned with the individual's subjective experience. Humanistic psychology was founded as an alternative to psychoanalytic and behaviorist approaches.

- Carl Rogers argued that the basic force motivating the human organism is the actualizing tendency—a tendency toward fulfillment or actualization of all the capacities of the self. When the needs of the self are denied, severe anxiety can result. Children come to develop an actualized self through the experience of unconditional positive regard from their caregivers.

- Abraham Maslow proposed that there is a hierarchy of needs, ascending from the basic biological needs to the more complex psychological motivations that become important only after the basic needs have been satisfied. The needs at one level must be at least partially satisfied before those at the next level become important motivators of action.

◆ **Critical Thinking Questions**

1. Several studies suggest that people in Asian cultures are not as concerned with individualism as Americans are and instead are more concerned with the collective welfare of their family and community. To what extent do you think this refutes humanistic perspectives on personality?

2. Do you think it's always a good idea to give a child unconditional positive regard? Why or why not?

THE EVOLUTIONARY APPROACH

One of the newest and most controversial theories in personality is really an application of a very old theory. Evolutionary theory, as proposed by Darwin (1859), has played an important role in biology for well over a century. Darwin ventured some ideas about the evolutionary roots of human behavior, but the modern field of evolutionary psychology began with the work of Wilson (1975) on "sociobiology." The basic premise of sociobiology and, later, **evolutionary psychology** is that behaviors that increased the organism's chances of surviving and leaving descendants would be selected for over evolutionary history and thus would become aspects of humans' personalities.

Not surprisingly, a good deal of the research on the application of evolutionary psychology to personality has focused on mate selection. Mating involves competition—among heterosexuals, males compete with males and females compete with females. What's being competed for differs between the sexes, however, because males and females have different roles in reproduction (Trivers, 1972). Because females carry their offspring for 9 months and then nurse and care for them after birth, they have a greater investment in each offspring and can produce fewer offspring in their lifetimes than men can. This puts a premium for the female on the quality of the genetic contribution of the males with whom she reproduces, as well as on signs of his ability and willingness to help care for his offspring. In contrast, the optimal reproductive strategy for males is to reproduce as often as possible, and they will primarily be looking for females who are available and fertile.

David Buss, Douglas Kenrick, and other evolutionary psychologists have investigated personality differences between males and females that they hypothesize are the result of these differences in reproductive strategies (Buss, 1999; Kenrick, 2001; Schmitt & Buss, 1996). They reasoned that women who are interested in mating should emphasize their youth and beauty, because these are signs of their fertility, but should be choosier than men about what partners they mate with. In contrast, men who are interested in mating should emphasize their ability to support their offspring and should be less choosy than women about their mating partners. A variety of findings have supported these hypotheses. When asked what they do to make themselves attractive to the opposite sex, women report enhancing their beauty through makeup, jewelry, clothing, and hairstyles. Women also report playing hard to get. Men report bragging about their accomplishments and earning potential, displaying expensive possessions, and flexing their muscles (Buss, 1988). Other studies have found that men are more interested in casual sex than women are (Buss & Schmitt, 1993) and are less selective in their criteria for one-night stands (Kenrick, Broth, Trost, & Sadalla, 1993).

One proxy for fertility is youth, and one proxy for economic resources is older age. Evolutionary theory suggests that men will be interested in mating with younger women, whereas women will be interested in mating with older men. These sex differences in mating preferences are have been found across 37 cultures (Buss, 1989). Kenrick and Keefe (1992) even found evidence for these mating preferences in singles ads placed in newspapers. In the ads, the older a man was, the more he expressed a preference for a younger woman. Women tended to express a preference for older men, regardless of the women's age.

Some theorists have extended evolutionary predictions far beyond mating preferences, arguing that men

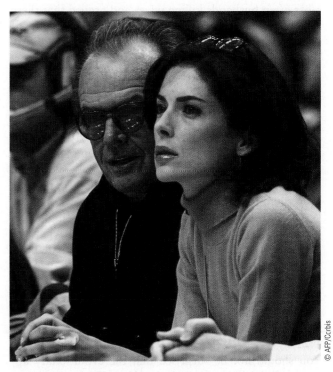

Evolutionary theory provides an explanation for why older men often seek women who are much younger than they are.

are more individualistic, domineering, and oriented toward problem solving than women because these personality characteristics increased males' ability to reproduce often over history and thus were selected for (Gray, 1992; Tannen, 1990). In contrast, women are more inclusive, sharing, and communal because these personality characteristics increased the chances of survival of their offspring and thus were selected for.

In some of their more controversial work, evolutionary theorists have argued that because of sex differences in mating strategies there should be sex differences in both sexual infidelity and the sources of jealousy. Whereas men's desire to mate frequently makes them more prone to sexual infidelity than women, their concern that they are not investing their resources in offspring who are not their own makes them more concerned about sexual infidelity of their female partners. This suggests that men will be more likely than women to cheat on their female partners and more jealous than women if their spouse or partner cheats on them. Several studies have found support for these hypotheses (Buss, Larsen, Westen, & Semmelroth, 1992).

When competition among males for available females becomes fierce, it can lead to violence, particularly among males who have fewer resources to compete with, such as unemployed males. Wilson and Daly (1985; Daly & Wilson, 1990) found that homicides between nonrelatives are most likely to be among young males, whom they argued were fighting over "face" and status. They further found that homicides within families are most often husbands killing wives and argued that these killings represent the male's attempt at controlling the fidelity of the female partner.

AN EVOLUTIONARY PORTRAIT OF HUMAN NATURE

The evolutionary portrait of human nature would appear to be a rather grim one. We are this way because it has been adaptive for the species to develop in this manner, and everything about our personalities and social behavior is coded in our genes. This would seem to leave little room for positive change.

Evolutionary theorists are the first to emphasize, however, that evolution is all about change—when the environment changes, only organisms that can adapt to that change will survive and reproduce. This change just happens more slowly than we might like it to.

AN EVALUATION OF THE EVOLUTIONARY APPROACH

You should not be surprised that the evolutionary approach has taken a great deal of heat. There are important social and political implications of the arguments and findings of these theorists. Some critics argue that evolutionary psychology simply provides a thinly veiled justification for the unfair social conditions and prejudices in today's world. If women are subordinate to men in economic and political power, it's because this was evolutionarily adaptive for the species. If men beat their wives and have extramarital affairs, they can't help it; it's in their genes. If some ethnic groups have more power and wealth in society, it's because their behaviors have been selected for over evolutionary history, and their genes are superior.

Evolutionary theorists have also taken heat from the scientific community. The early arguments of sociobiologists were highly speculative and not based on hard data. Some critics argued that their hypotheses were unfalsifiable or untestable. In the last decade, there has been an upsurge of empirical research attempting to rigorously test evolutionary theories of human behavior. Some theorists have steered away from controversial topics such as sex differences in personality or abilities to investigate the role of evolution in shaping the cognitive structures of the brain (Cosmides, 1989; Cosmides & Tooby, 1989).

Still, the question remains of whether an evolutionary explanation for a given finding—whether a human sex difference or some behavior or structure that all humans share—is necessary. It is easy to develop alternative explanations for most of the findings that evolutionary theorists tend to attribute to reproductive strategies (Eagly & Wood, 1999). For example, sex differences in personality characteristics could be due to sex differences in body size and strength (for instance, men are more dominant than women because their size allows them to be, whereas women are friendlier than men because they are trying not to get beaten up by men). The causes of behavior focused on by most alternative explanations are more proximal than evolutionary causes—the explanations don't rely on claims about what has been true for millions of years and make claims only about what has been true in the relatively recent past. For many findings touted by evolutionary theorists as consistent with evolutionary history, it is difficult to conceive of experiments that could help us decide between an evolutionary explanation and an alternative explanation that focuses on more proximal causes.

Evolutionary theory is attractive in its power to explain a wide range of behaviors, however. Not since the introduction of behaviorism has psychology had a new explanatory framework that might account for most aspects of human behavior. Many evolutionary theorists are vigorously pursuing more sophisticated and persuasive empirical tests of their hypotheses. Evolutionary psychology will clearly have an important influence on personality theories in years to come.

- Evolutionary psychology attempts to explain human behavior and personality in terms of the adaptiveness of certain characteristics for survival and reproductive success over human history.

- Evolutionary theory is consistent with some observed sex differences in mate preferences.

- It is a controversial theory, however, both for its social implications and for the difficulty of refuting arguments derived from this theory.

◆ **Critical Thinking Questions**

1. To what extent do you think the political implications of a psychological theory should be of concern to its proponents?

2. Do you think evolutionary theory can predict anything about how human behavior will change in the next few centuries?

THE GENETICS OF PERSONALITY

We end with another controversial and relatively recent approach to understanding the origins of personality—the argument that personality traits are largely determined by the genes an individual was born with. Some of the best evidence that genes play a role in personality comes from the Minnesota Study of Twins Reared Apart, which we described in Chapter 12 and highlighted at the beginning of this chapter. Recall from Chapter 12 that the participants in this study were assessed on a number of ability and personality measures. In addition, they participated in lengthy interviews during which they were asked questions about such topics as childhood experiences, fears, hobbies, musical tastes, social attitudes, and sexual interests. A number of startling similarities were found. The twins with the most dramatically different backgrounds are Oskar Stohr and Jack Yufe, described at the beginning of the chapter. Another pair of twins with fairly different backgrounds are both British homemakers. They were separated during World War II and raised by families that differed in socioeconomic status. Both twins, who had never met before, arrived for their interviews wearing seven rings on their fingers.

These studies reveal that twins reared apart are just as similar to each other across a wide range of personality characteristics as twins reared together, permitting us to conclude with greater confidence that identical twins are more similar to each other on personality characteristics

than fraternal twins because they are more similar genetically (Bouchard et al., 1990; Lykken, 1982; Tellegen et al., 1988).

For the most part, the correlations found in the Minnesota studies are in accord with results from many other twin studies. In general, the highest levels of heritability are found in measures of abilities and intelligence (60%–70%), the next highest levels are typically found in measures of personality (about 50%); and the lowest levels are found for religious and political beliefs and vocational interests (30%–40%).

Similar studies have examined the heritability of personality traits. For example, one study found that traits such as shyness and the tendency to become easily upset have heritabilities of between 30% and 50% (Bouchard et al., 1990; Newman, Tellegen, & Bouchard, 1998).

INTERACTIONS BETWEEN PERSONALITY AND ENVIRONMENT

GENOTYPE-ENVIRONMENT CORRELATION In shaping an individual's personality, genetic and environmental influences are intertwined from the moment of birth (McGuffin, Riley, & Plomin, 2001). First, it may take certain environments to trigger the effects of specific genes (Gottlieb, 2000). For example, a child born with a genetic tendency toward alcoholism may never become alcoholic if never exposed to alcohol. Second, parents give their biological offspring both their genes and a home environment, and both are functions of the parents' own genes. As a result, there is a built-in correlation between the child's inherited characteristics (genotype) and the environment in which he or she is raised. For example, because general intelligence is partially heritable, parents with high intelligence are likely to have children with high intelligence. But parents with high intelligence are also likely to provide an intellectually stimulating environment for their children—both through their interactions with them and through books, music lessons, trips to museums, and other intellectual experiences. Because the child's genotype and environment are positively correlated in this way, he or she will get a double dose of intellectual advantage. Similarly, children born to parents with low intelligence are likely to encounter a home environment that exacerbates whatever intellectual disadvantage they may have inherited directly.

Third, some parents may deliberately construct an environment that is negatively correlated with the child's genotype. For example, introverted parents may encourage participation in social activities to counteract the child's likely introversion: "We make an effort to have people over because we don't want Chris to grow up to be as shy as we are." Parents of a very active child may try to provide interesting quiet activities. But whether the correlation is positive or negative, the point is that

One way that genetics may influence personality is by influencing the neurochemistry of the brain and body. The functioning of the nervous system is affected by the amounts of various neurotransmitters available at any given time, which can vary quite widely. People also seem to differ in their average levels of those transmitters, and these differences seem to be related to particular personality traits.

Dopamine plays a role in the control of body movements and is involved in brain systems that cause the person to approach attractive objects and people. It therefore is thought to affect sociability and general activity level. Some researchers suggest that dopamine is related to extraversion and impulsivity (Depue & Collins, 1999).

Another important neurotransmitter is serotonin, which is also involved in impulsivity, and in moods such as anxiety and depression. The popular antidepressant drug Prozac is a selective serotonin reuptake inhibitor, and its effect is to raise serotonin levels. According to Peter Kramer, author of *Listening to Prozac,* the drug can actually give people new personalities. It can prevent a person from worrying needlessly and overreacting to minor stresses, thereby giving them a more cheerful outlook on life. People who have taken Prozac often report that they feel like "better people" who get more work done and are more attractive to members of the opposite sex.

Is it true that we can change our personalities by taking a pill such as Prozac? A group of scientists administered a Prozac-like drug called Paxil (paroxetine) for 4 weeks to 26 healthy volunteers who were free of depression. They chose Paxil because it is a relatively potent and specific inhibitor of serotonin reuptake compared with some of the other drugs in this category. They also administered a placebo to another group of healthy volunteers for 4 weeks. Neither the volunteers nor the researchers knew which type of pill an individual volunteer was taking. Personality and social behaviors were assessed in the volunteers 1 week and 4 weeks into the study by having them complete questionnaires and work together with other people on a puzzle task while being observed.

The volunteers who took Paxil became less irritable and hostile toward others and were more likely to engage in positive social behavior in the puzzle task than the volunteers who took the placebo. In addition, the higher the level of Paxil evident in the blood of the volunteers who took the drug, the more their irritability and hostility declined and the more their positive social behavior increased over the 4 weeks (Knutson et al., 1998).

These results seem to suggest that Paxil truly did change the personalities of the health volunteers. It seemed to do so, however, largely by changing their moods. The volunteers who took Paxil showed a significant reduction in negative mood, which fully accounted for the changes in their personalities and social behaviors. This suggests that Paxil may not have had a direct effect on personality but an indirect effect by relieving any negative mood the volunteers may have been experiencing.

Such an interpretation is fully in line with theorists who argue that a fundamental aspect of personality is mood or temperament, which influences the person's willingness to approach new challenges or to flee from them (Cloninger, Svrakic, & Przybeck, 1993; Gray, 1994). According to these theories, all personality traits derive from the individual's basic temperament, how the environment responds to that temperament (for example, did your parents punish you for being anxious or support you in overcoming anxiety?), and how your temperament leads you to make important choices in your life.

Research on the biological causes of personality is still developing. In the meantime, there are social implications to the findings summarized here: Do we want, as a society, to have people changing their personalities with pills?

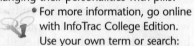

For more information, go online with InfoTrac College Edition. Use your own term or search:

- Prozac and personality
- Dopamine and personality

---

the child's genotype and environment are not simply independent sources of influence that add together to shape the child's personality. Finally, in addition to being correlated with the environment, a child's genotype shapes the environment in certain ways (Bouchard et al., 1990; Plomin, DeFries, & Loehlin, 1977; Scarr, 1996). In particular, the environment becomes a function of the child's personality through three forms of interaction: reactive, evocative, and proactive.

REACTIVE INTERACTION Different individuals who are exposed to the same environment interpret it, experience it, and react to it differently—a process known as **reactive interaction.** An anxious, sensitive child will experience and react to harsh parents differently than will a calm, resilient child, and the sharp tone of voice that provokes the sensitive child to tears might pass unnoticed by his sister. An extraverted child will attend to people and events around her, but her introverted brother will ignore them. A brighter child will get more out of being read to than a less bright child. In other words, each child's personality extracts a subjective psychological environment from the objective surroundings, and it is that subjective environment that shapes personality development. Even if parents provided exactly the same environment for all their children—which they

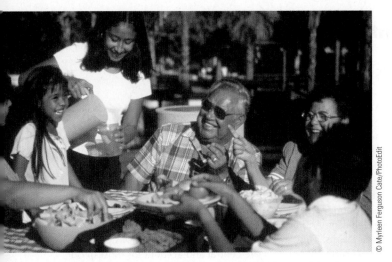
Outgoing children evoke different behavior from adults than shy children.

usually do not—it will not be psychologically equivalent for all of them. Reactive interaction occurs throughout life. One person will interpret a hurtful act as the product of deliberate hostility and react to it quite differently than a person who interprets the same act as the result of unintended insensitivity.

EVOCATIVE INTERACTION Every individual's personality evokes distinctive responses from others, which has been referred to as **evocative interaction.** An infant who squirms and fusses when picked up will evoke less nurturance from a parent than one who likes to be cuddled. Docile children will evoke a less controlling style of child rearing from parents than will aggressive children. For this reason, we cannot simply assume that an observed correlation between the child-rearing practices of a child's parents and his or her personality reflects a simple cause-and-effect sequence. Instead, the child's personality can shape the parents' child-rearing style, which, in turn, further shapes the child's personality. Evocative interaction also occurs throughout life: Gracious people evoke gracious environments; hostile people evoke hostile environments.

PROACTIVE INTERACTION As children grow older, they can move beyond the environments provided by their parents and begin to select and construct environments of their own. These environments, in turn, further shape their personalities. This process is referred to as **proactive interaction.** A sociable child will choose to go to the movies with friends rather than stay home alone and watch television because her sociable personality prompts her to select an environment that reinforces her sociability. And what she cannot select she will construct: If nobody invites her to the movies, she will organize the event

herself. As the term implies, proactive interaction is a process through which individuals become active agents in the development of their own personalities.

The relative importance of these three kinds of personality-environment interactions shifts over the course of development (Scarr, 1996; Scarr & McCartney, 1983). The built-in correlation between a child's genotype and his or her environment is strongest when the child is young and confined almost exclusively to the home environment. As the child grows older and begins to select and construct his or her own environment, this initial correlation decreases and the influence of proactive interaction increases. As we have noted, reactive and evocative interactions remain important throughout life.

SOME UNSOLVED PUZZLES Studies of twins have produced a number of puzzling patterns that still are not completely understood. For example, the estimate of heritability for IQ is higher when it is based on identical twin pairs reared apart than it is when based on a comparison of identical and fraternal twins pairs reared together. Moreover, the striking similarities of identical twins do not seem to diminish across time or separate rearing environments. In contrast, the similarities of fraternal twins (and nontwin siblings) diminish from childhood through adolescence, even when they are reared together. Instead, the longer they live together in the same home, the less similar they become (Scarr, 1996; Scarr & McCartney, 1983).

Some of these patterns would emerge if the genes themselves interact so that inheriting all one's genes in common (as identical twins do) is more than twice as effective as inheriting only half one's genes in common (as fraternal twins and nontwin siblings do). This could come about if a trait depends on a particular combination of genes. Consider, for example, the trait of having blue eyes (which we will oversimplify a bit to make the point). Suppose that two parents each have a blue-eye gene and a brown-eye gene. For one of their children to get blue eyes, the child must inherit a blue gene from the father and a blue gene from the mother; the three other combinations (brown-brown, brown-blue, blue-brown) will give the child brown eyes. In other words, any child of theirs has a one-in-four chance of getting blue eyes. But because identical twins inherit identical genes from their parents, they will also inherit the same combination of genes. If one gets blue eyes, so will the other. In contrast, if a fraternal twin inherits a blue gene from both parents, the chances that the other twin will also do so is still only one out of four and not one out of two. So, in this example, inheriting all one's genes in common is more than twice as effective as inheriting only half one's genes in common. There is evidence for this kind of gene-gene interaction for some personality traits, especially extraversion (Lykken, McGue, Tellegen,

Is Freud's Influence on Psychology Still Alive?

FREUD'S INFLUENCE ON PSYCHOLOGY IS ALIVE AND VIBRANT

Joel Weinberger, Adelphi University

Is Freud still alive? Of course Freud is dead. He died on September 23, 1939. No one asks whether Isaac Newton or William James is dead. For some odd reason this is reserved for Freud. If the question is whether psychoanalysis, the branch of psychology he founded, is dead, the answer is clearly no. Psychoanalysis survived Freud and thrives today. The American Psychological Association's division of psychoanalysis is the second largest division in the association. There now exist several schools of psychoanalysis, some of which Freud would probably not recognize. That is just what you would expect from a discipline whose founder is now 60 years dead.

Are Freud's ideas dead? They certainly are not. They have entered our common vernacular. They have entered and forever changed our culture. Think of the terms of *id, ego, superego, Freudian slip,* and so on. There are psychoanalytic writers, historians, psychiatrists, and of course, psychologists. The real question, I suppose, is whether Freud's ideas are still *valid.* The answer is that some are and some are not. A surprising number remain relevant, even central, to modern psychology. So I suppose the charge is to state which of his ideas remain valid. And that is what I will address.

Let's look at some of Freud's central ideas and see how they stack up with today's psychology. Freud said that all human motives could be traced back to biological sources, specifically to sex and aggression. There is a branch of psychol-

ogy now termed evolutionary psychology (Buss, 1994); there is also sociobiology (Wilson, 1975) and ethology (Hinde, 1982). All champion the importance of biological factors in our behavior. And all have data to back up their claims. This aspect of Freud's thinking is certainly not dead. As for the importance of sex and aggression? Just look at the best selling books, hit movies, and TV shows around you. What characterizes virtually all of them? Sex and violence. Hollywood and book publishers seem all to be Freudians, and so are the people who sample their wares.

Another idea of Freud's that was very controversial in his time was his notion that children have sexual feelings. Now that is simply commonplace knowledge.

Psychoanalysts have long held that one of the major factors accounting for the effectiveness of psychotherapy is the therapeutic relationship. For many years this was not accepted, particularly by the behaviorist school (Emmelkamp, 1994). We now know that this is a critical factor in therapeutic success (Weinberger, 1996). The related idea that we carry representations of early relationships around in our heads, an idea expanded upon by object relations theory (a school of psychoanalysis) and attachment theory (the creation of a psychoanalyst, John Bowlby), is also now commonly accepted in psychology.

The most central idea usually attributed to Freud is the importance of unconscious processes. According to Freud,

we are most often unaware of why we do what we do. For a long while, mainstream academic psychology rejected this notion. Now it seems to have finally caught up to Freud. Modern thinkers now believe that unconscious processes are central and account for most of our behavior. Discussion of unconscious processes permeate research in memory (Graf & Masson, 1993), social psychology (Bargh, 1997), cognitive psychology (Baars, 1988), and so on. In fact, it is now a mainstream belief in psychology. More specific notions of Freud's such as his ideas about defense have also received empirical support (Shedler, Mayman, & Manis, 1993; D. Weinberger, 1990). So have some of his ideas about unconscious fantasies (Siegel & Weinberger, 1997). There is even some work afoot to examine Freud's conceptions of transference (Andersen & Glassman, 1996; Crits-Christoph, Cooper, & Luborsky, 1990).

Of course, many of the particulars of Freud's thinking have been overtaken by events and have turned out to be incorrect. What thinker who died over 60 yeas ago has had all of his or her ideas survive intact, without change? In broad outline however, Freud's ideas are not only alive, they are vibrant. We should probably be testing more of them. Any notion that Freud should be ignored because some of his assertions have been shown to be false is just plain silly. It is throwing out the baby with the bath water. And, he is so much fun to read!

Is Freud's Influence on Psychology Still Alive?

FREUD IS A DEAD WEIGHT ON PSYCHOLOGY
John F. Kihlstrom, University of California, Berkeley

If the 20th century was "The American Century," it was also the century of Sigmund Freud (Roth, 1998), because Freud changed our image of ourselves. Copernicus showed that the Earth did not lie at the center of the universe, and Darwin showed that humans were descended from "lower" animals, but Freud claimed to show that human experience, thought, and action was determined not by our conscious rationality, but by irrational forces outside our awareness and control—forces which could only be understood and controlled by an extensive therapeutic process called *psychoanalysis.*

Freud also changed the vocabulary with which we understand ourselves and others. Before you ever opened this textbook, you already knew something about the id and the superego, penis envy and phallic symbols, castration anxiety and the Oedipus complex. In popular culture, psychotherapy is virtually identified with psychoanalysis. Freudian theory, with its focus on the interpretation of ambiguous events, lies at the foundation of "postmodern" approaches to literary criticism such as deconstruction. More than anyone else, Freud's influence on modern culture has been profound and long-lasting.

Freud's cultural influence is based, at least implicitly, on the premise that his theory is scientifically valid. But from a scientific point of view, classical Freudian psychoanalysis is dead as both a theory of the mind and a mode of therapy (Crews, 1998; Macmillan, 1996). No empirical evidence supports any specific proposition of psychoanalytic theory, such as the idea that development proceeds through oral, anal, phallic, and genital stages, or that little boys lust after their mothers and hate and fear their fathers. No empirical evidence indicates

that psychoanalysis is more effective, or more efficient, than other forms of psychotherapy, such as systematic desensitization or assertiveness training. No empirical evidence indicates that the mechanisms by which psychoanalysis achieves its effects, such as they are, are those specifically predicated on the theory, such as transference and catharsis.

Of course, Freud lived at a particular period of time, and it might be argued that his theories were valid when applied to European culture at that time, even if they are no longer apropos today. However, recent historical analyses show that Freud's construal of his case material was systematically distorted by his theories of unconscious conflict and infantile sexuality, and that he misinterpreted and misrepresented the scientific evidence available to him. Freud's theories were not just a product of his time: They were misleading and incorrect even as he published them.

Drew Westen (1988), a psychologist at Harvard Medical School, agrees that Freud's theories are archaic and obsolete, but argues that Freud's legacy lives on in a number of theoretical propositions that are widely accepted by scientists: the existence of unconscious mental processes; the importance of conflict and ambivalence in behavior; the childhood origins of adult personality; mental representations as a mediator of social behavior; and stages of psychological development. However, some of these propositions are debatable. For example, there is no evidence that childrearing practices have any lasting impact on personality. More important, Westen's argument skirts the question of whether *Freud's* view of these matters was correct. It is one thing to say that unconscious motives play a role in behavior. It is something quite different to say that our

every thought and deed is driven by repressed sexual and aggressive urges; that children harbor erotic feelings toward the parent of the opposite sex; and that young boys are hostile toward their fathers, who they regard as rivals for their mothers' affections. This is what *Freud* believed, and so far as we can tell *Freud* was wrong in every respect. For example, the unconscious mind revealed in laboratory studies of automaticity and implicit memory bears no resemblance to the unconscious mind of psychoanalytic theory (Kihlstrom, 1998).

Westen also argues that psychoanalytic theory itself has evolved since Freud's time, and that it is therefore unfair to bind psychoanalysis so tightly to the Freudian vision of repressed, infantile, sexual and aggressive urges. This is true, and it is a historical fact that so-called "ego psychology" helped preserve much of what was interesting in psychology during its "Dark Ages" of radical behaviorism (Kihlstrom, 1994). But again, this avoids the issue of whether *Freud's* theories are correct. Furthermore, it remains an open question whether these "neo-Freudian" theories are any more valid than are the classically Freudian views that preceded them. For example, it is not at all clear that Erik Erikson's stage theory of psychological development is any more valid than Freud's is.

While Freud had an enormous impact on 20th century culture, he has been a dead weight on 20th century psychology. The broad themes that Westen writes about were present in psychology before Freud, or arose more recently independent of his influence. At best, Freud is a figure of only historical interest for psychologists. He is better studied as a writer than as a scientist. Psychologists can get along without him.

& Bouchard, 1992; Pedersen, Plomin, McClearn, & Friberg, 1988). But personality-environment interactions could also be partially responsible for these patterns.

Consider identical twins. Because they have identical genotypes, they also react to situations in similar ways (reactive interaction), they evoke similar responses from others (evocative interaction), and their similar, genetically guided talents, interests, and motivations lead them to seek out and construct similar environments (proactive interaction). The important point is that these processes all operate whether the twins are reared together or apart. For example, two identical twins who were separated at birth will still be treated in similar ways by other people because they evoke similar responses from others.

Proactive interaction operates in the same way. Each twin's personality prompts him or her to select friends and environments that happen to be similar to the friends and environments chosen by the other twin. But friends and environments that are similar will treat each twin in similar ways. And so it goes. Because the twins begin with identical genotypic personalities, all the processes of personality-environment interaction act together to promote and sustain their similarity across time—even if they have not met since birth.

In contrast, the environments of fraternal twins and nontwin siblings increasingly diverge as they grow older—even within the same home. They are most alike in early childhood, when parents provide the same environment for both (although even here siblings will react somewhat differently and evoke different responses from the parents). But as soon as they begin to select and construct environments outside the home, their moderately different talents, interests, and motivations will take them down increasingly divergent paths, thereby producing increasingly divergent personalities.

SHARED VERSUS NONSHARED ENVIRONMENTS Twin studies allow researchers to estimate not only how much of the variation among individuals is due to genetic variation but also how much of the environmentally related variation is due to aspects of the environment that family members share (for example, socioeconomic status) as compared with aspects of the environment that family members do not share (for example, friends outside the family). Surprisingly, some studies suggest differences due to shared aspects of the environment seem to account for almost none of the environmental variation: After their genetic similarities are subtracted out, two children from the same family seem to be no more alike than two children chosen randomly from the population (Rowe, 1997; Scarr, 1992). This implies that the kinds of variables that psychologists typically study (such as child-rearing practices, socioeconomic status, and parents' education) are contributing virtually nothing to individual differences in personality. How can this be so?

One possible explanation might be that the reactive, evocative, and proactive processes act to diminish the differences between environments as long as those environments permit some flexibility of response. A bright child from a neglecting or impoverished home is more likely than a less bright sibling to absorb information from a television program (reactive interaction), to attract the attention of a sympathetic teacher (evocative interaction), and to go to the library (proactive interaction). This child's genotype acts to counteract the potentially debilitating effects of the home environment, and therefore he or she develops differently than a less bright sibling. Only if the environment is severely restrictive will these personality-driven processes be thwarted (Scarr, 1996; Scarr & McCartney, 1983). This explanation is supported by the finding that the most dissimilar pairs of identical twins reared apart are those in which one twin was reared in a severely restricted environment.

Although this explanation seems plausible, there is no direct evidence that it is correct. In recent years, several psychologists have pointed to methodological problems in research on the heritability of individual differences that may also account for the apparent lack of effects of the environment (Turkheimer, 1998). For example, almost all the data for these studies come from self-report questionnaires, but the validity of these questionnaires, particu-

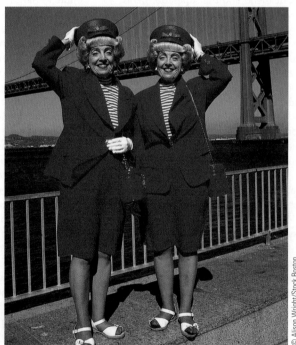

Because identical twins have identical genotypes, the process of personality-environment interaction act together to promote and sustain their similarity over time—even if they grow up in different environments.

larly as assessments of the environment of different children in the family, is questionable. In addition, the families who participate in these studies tend to be quite similar to each other in demographics—not representing the extremes of either good or bad environments. This would reduce the apparent contribution of the environment to children's abilities and personalities.

In any case, it appears that research will have to shift from the usual comparisons of children from different families to comparisons of children within the same families—with particular attention to the personality-environment interactions within those families. Similarly, more attention must be given to influences outside the family. One writer has suggested that the peer group is a far more important source of personality differences among children than the family (Harris, 1995).

◆ Interim Summary

- Evidence from twin studies suggests that genetic factors substantially influence personality traits.

- In shaping personality, genetic and environmental influences do not act independently but are intertwined from the moment of birth. Because a child's personality and his or her home environment are both a function of the parents' genes, there is a built-in correlation between the child's genotype (inherited personality characteristics) and that environment.

- Three dynamic processes of personality-environment interaction are (1) reactive interaction—different individuals exposed to the same environment experience it, interpret it, and react to it differently; (2) evocative interaction—an individual's personality evokes distinctive responses from others; and (3) proactive interaction—individuals select or create environments of their own. As a child grows older,

the influence of proactive interaction becomes increasingly important.

- Studies of twins have produced a number of puzzling patterns: Heritabilities estimated from identical twins reared apart are higher than estimates based on comparisons between identical and fraternal twins; identical twins reared apart are as similar to each other as identical twins reared together, but fraternal twins and nontwin siblings become less similar over time, even when they are reared together.

- These patterns are probably due in part to interactions among genes, so that having all one's genes in common is more than twice as effective as having only half of one's genes in common. Such patterns might also be due in part to the three processes of personality-environment interaction (reactive, evocative, and proactive).

- After their genetic similarities are subtracted out, children from the same family seem to be no more alike than children chosen randomly from the population. This implies that the kinds of variables that psychologists typically study (such as child-rearing practices and the family's socioeconomic status) contribute virtually nothing to individual differences in personality.

◆ Critical Thinking Questions

1. What are some ways that reactive, evocative, and proactive interaction might have influenced the development of your personality and abilities?

2. If you have siblings, what do you think are the best explanations for the similarities and differences you see between yourself and your siblings?

CHAPTER SUMMARY

1. Although different investigators arrive at different numbers of factors, most now believe that five factors provide the best compromise. These have been labeled the "Big Five" and form the acronym OCEAN: Openness to experience, Conscientiousness, Extraversion, Agreeableness, and Neuroticism.

Although items on most inventories are composed or selected on the basis of a theory, they can also be selected on the basis of their correlation with an external criterion—the criterion-keyed method of test construction. The best-known example is the Minnesota Multi-

phasic Personality Inventory (MMPI), which is designed to identify individuals with psychological disorders.

2. The Q-sort is a method of assessing personality in which raters sort cards with personality adjectives into nine piles, placing the cards that are least descriptive of the individual in pile 1 on the left and those that are most descriptive in pile 9 on the right.

3. Freud's psychoanalytic theory holds that many behaviors are caused by unconscious motivations. Personality is determined primarily by the biological drives of sex and aggression and by experiences that occur during

the first 5 years of life. Freud's theory of personality structure views personality as composed of the id, the ego, and the superego. The id operates on the pleasure principle, seeking immediate gratification of biological impulses. The ego obeys the reality principle, postponing gratification until it can be achieved in socially acceptable ways. The superego (conscience) imposes moral standards on the individual. In a well-integrated personality, the ego remains in firm but flexible control over the id and superego, and the reality principle governs.

4. Freud's theory of personality development proposes that individuals pass through psychosexual stages and must resolve the Oedipal conflict, in which the young child sees the same-sex parent as a rival for the affection of the opposite-sex parent. Over the years, Freud's theory of anxiety and defense mechanisms has fared better than his structural and developmental theories have.

5. Psychoanalytic theory has been modified by later psychologists, notably Carl Jung and Harry Stack Sullivan. Jung proposed that in addition to the personal unconscious described by Freud, there is a collective unconscious, a part of the mind that is common to all humans. Sullivan suggested that people's responses to interpersonal experiences cause them to develop personifications—mental images of themselves and others.

6. Psychologists who take the psychoanalytic approach sometimes use projective tests, such as the Rorschach Test and the Thematic Apperception Test (TAT). Because the test stimuli are ambiguous, it is assumed that the individual projects his or her personality onto the stimulus, thereby revealing unconscious wishes and motives.

7. Behavioral approaches assume that personality differences result from variations in learning experiences. Through operant conditioning, people learn to associate specific behaviors with punishment or reward. They can also learn these associations through observational learning. Through classical conditioning, people learn to associate specific situations with certain outcomes, such as anxiety.

8. The cognitive approach to personality is based on the idea that differences in personality stem from differences in the way individuals mentally represent information. Albert Bandura developed social cognitive theory, which holds that internal cognitive processes combine with environmental pressures to influence behavior and that cognitive processes and environment have reciprocal effects on each other. Walter Mischel has identified a number of cognitive person variables that affect people's reactions to the environment and behaviors in the environment. George Kelly's personal construct theory focuses on the concepts that individuals use to interpret themselves and their social world. Much research has focused on the self-schema, the aspects of a person's behavior that are most important to that person. Experiments have shown that

people perceive information more readily and recall it better when it is relevant to their self-schemas.

9. The humanistic approach is concerned with the individual's subjective experience. Humanistic psychology was founded as an alternative to psychoanalytic and behaviorist approaches. Carl Rogers argued that the basic force motivating the human organism is the actualizing tendency—a tendency toward fulfillment or actualization of all the capacities of the self. When the needs of the self are denied, severe anxiety can result. Children come to develop an actualized self through the experience of unconditional positive regard from their caregivers. Abraham Maslow proposed that there is a hierarchy of needs, ascending from the basic biological needs to the more complex psychological motivations that become important only after the basic needs have been satisfied. The needs at one level must be at least partially satisfied before those at the next level become important motivators of action.

10. Evolutionary psychology attempts to explain human behavior and personality in terms of the adaptiveness of certain characteristics for survival and reproductive success over human history. Evolutionary theory is consistent with some observed sex differences in mate preferences. It is a controversial theory, however, both for its social implications and for the difficulty of refuting arguments derived from this theory.

11. Evidence from twin studies suggests that genetic factors substantially influence personality traits. In shaping personality, genetic and environmental influences do not act independently but are intertwined from the moment of birth. Because a child's personality and his or her home environment are both a function of the parents' genes, there is a built-in correlation between the child's genotype (inherited personality characteristics) and that environment.

12. Three dynamic processes of personality-environment interaction are (1) reactive interaction—different individuals exposed to the same environment experience it, interpret it, and react to it differently; (2) evocative interaction—an individual's personality evokes distinctive responses from others; and (3) proactive interaction—individuals select or create environments of their own. As a child grows older, the influence of proactive interaction becomes increasingly important.

13. Studies of twins have produced a number of puzzling patterns: Heritabilities estimated from identical twins reared apart are higher than estimates based on comparisons between identical and fraternal twins. Identical twins reared apart are as similar to each other as identical twins reared together, but fraternal twins and nontwin siblings become less similar over time, even when they are reared together. These patterns are probably due in part to interactions among genes, so that having all one's genes in common is more than twice as effective as having only half of one's genes in

common. Such patterns might also be due in part to the three processes of personality-environment interaction (reactive, evocative, and proactive).

14. After their genetic similarities are subtracted out, children from the same family seem to be no more alike than children chosen randomly from the population. This implies that the kinds of variables that psychologists typically study (such as child-rearing practices and the family's socioeconomic status) contribute virtually nothing to individual differences in personality.

CORE CONCEPTS

personality
introversion-extraversion
neuroticism
the "Big Five"
personality inventories
Minnesota Multiphasic Personality
  Inventory
Q-sort
psychoanalytic theory
free association
conscious
preconscious
unconscious
psychological determinism
id
ego
superego
libido
defense mechanisms

repression
rationalization
reaction formation
projection
intellectualization
denial
displacement
psychosexual stages
oral stage
anal stage
phallic stage
Oedipal conflict
latency period
genital stage
collective unconscious
object relations theory
projective test
Rorschach Test
Thematic Apperception Test

behaviorist approach
operant conditioning
observational learning
classical conditioning
cognitive approach
social-learning theory
social cognitive theory
personal constructs
schema
self-schema
actualizing tendency
self
unconditional positive regard
hierarchy of needs
peak experiences
evolutionary psychology
reactive interaction
evocative interaction
proactive interaction

 # WEB RESOURCES

http://psychology.wadsworth.com/
atkinson14e

Take a quiz, try the activities and exercises, and explore web links.

London: http://www.freud.org.uk/
Vienna: http://freud.t0.or.at/freud/index-e.htm

Check out the chronology of Freud's life on the Vienna site or photos from the London museum, including Freud's famous couch.

http://pmc.psych.nwu.edu/

Why do people differ? This detailed site provides further insight into personality research, as well as a variety of further links to academic and nonacademic web pages.

 InfoTrac Online Library
http://www.infotrac-college.com/
wadsworth

Use InfoTrac College Edition to find popular and scientific articles by using the search terms below or your own relevant terms.

- Sigmund Freud
- Abraham Maslow
- Personality tests
- Personality traits

CD-ROM LINKS

 Psych Odyssey
Check out CD Chapter 15, Personality
A. The Nature of Personality
B. Psychodynamic Approaches

 Psyk.trek 2.0
Check out CD Unit 10, Personality Theory
10a Freudian Theory
10b Behaviorist Theory
10c Humanistic Theory
10d Biological Theory

© PhotoDisc/Getty Images

STRESS, HEALTH, AND COPING

14

Janet was feeling near the end of her rope. All day long she had endured one hassle after another. At breakfast, she spilled orange juice on the only clean blouse she had. When she got to work, there were 32 e-mail messages and 15 phone messages waiting for her. In the afternoon, her boss told her to prepare a financial report for the board meeting that was to occur at 9 A.M. the next morning, but her computer crashed and she could not access the financial records for her division. Tired and overwhelmed, when she got home, she called her mother for support, only to discover that her father had been hospitalized with chest pains. After hanging up, Janet felt disoriented, her heart was racing, and she began to get a migraine.

The kind of stress Janet was experiencing is familiar to many of us—silly mistakes that cause stress, the stress of a demanding boss, the stress in our per-

sonal relationships. Exposure to stress can lead to painful emotions like anxiety or depression. It can also lead to physical illnesses, both minor and severe.

Yet, people's reactions to stressful events differ widely: Some people faced with a stressful event develop serious psychological or physical problems, whereas other people faced with the same stressful event develop no problems and may even find the event challenging and interesting. In this chapter we discuss the concept of stress and the effects of stress on the mind and body. We also look at the differences between people's ways of thinking about and coping with stressful events, and how these differences contribute to adjustment.

Stress has become a popular topic. The media often attribute unusual behavior or illness to burnout due to stress or a nervous breakdown resulting from stress. For example, when a celebrity attempts suicide, it is often said that he or she was burnt out from the pressures of public life. On college campuses, "I'm so stressed out!" is a common claim. But what is stress? In general terms, **stress** refers to experiencing events

that are perceived as endangering one's physical or psychological well-being. These events are usually referred to as **stressors,** and people's reactions to them are termed **stress responses.**

There are some types of events that most people experience as stressful. We will describe the characteristics of such events and then describe the body's natural reaction to stress. This reaction is adaptive when it is possible to flee from or attack a stressor, but it can become maladaptive when a stressor is chronic or uncontrollable. Stress can have both direct and indirect effects on health.

The study of how stress and other social, psychological, and biological factors come together to contribute to illness is known as **behavioral medicine** or health psychology (Taylor, 1999). We will review research on how psychosocial factors interact with biological vulnerabilities to affect cardiovascular health and the functioning of the immune system. Finally, we will describe ways of managing stress to improve health.

CHARACTERISTICS OF STRESSFUL EVENTS

Countless events create stress. Some are major changes affecting large numbers of people—events such as war, nuclear accidents, and earthquakes. Others are major changes in the life of an individual—for instance, moving to a new area, changing jobs, getting married, losing a friend, suffering a serious illness. Everyday hassles can also be experienced as stressors—losing your wallet, getting stuck in traffic, arguing with your professor. Some stressors are acute: They only last a short time, such as when you are caught in an unusual traffic jam on the way to an important job interview. Other stressors are chronic: They go on for an extended period, even indefinitely, as when you are in an unsatisfying marriage. Finally, the source of stress can be within the individual, in the form of conflicting motives or desires.

Events that are perceived as stressful usually fall into one or more of the following categories: traumatic events outside the usual range of human experience, uncontrollable or unpredictable events, events that represent major changes in life circumstances, or internal conflicts. In this section we look briefly at each of these categories.

TRAUMATIC EVENTS

The most obvious sources of stress are **traumatic events**—situations of extreme danger that are outside the range of usual human experience. These include natural disasters, such as earthquakes and floods; disasters caused by human activity, such as wars and nuclear accidents; catastrophic accidents, such as car or plane crashes; and physical assaults, such as rape or attempted murder.

Many people experience a specific series of psychological reactions after a traumatic event (Horowitz, 1986). At first, survivors are stunned and dazed and appear to be unaware of their injuries or of the danger. They may wander around in a disoriented state, perhaps putting themselves at risk for further injury. For example, an earthquake survivor may wander through buildings that are on the verge of collapse. In the next stage, survivors are still passive and unable to initiate even simple tasks, but they may follow orders readily. For example, days after the assault, a rape survivor may not even think to prepare food to eat, but if a friend calls and insists that they go out for food, she will comply. In the third stage, survivors become anxious and apprehensive, have difficulty in concentrating, and may repeat the story of the catastrophe over and over again. The sur-

The causes of stress vary from one person to the next. What is overwhelming to one person may be exciting and challenging to another.

Victims of disasters such as hurricanes and tornados are often stunned and disoriented shortly after the disaster. Later they become more responsive but may still have trouble initiating even simple activities. They may remain anxious and distracted long after the disaster.

vivor of a car crash may become extremely nervous near a car, may be unable to go back to work because of inability to concentrate, and may repeatedly tell friends about the details of the crash.

One type of traumatic event that is tragically common in our society is sexual abuse. The impact of rape and other types of sexual violence on the victim's emotional and physical health appears to be great (Koss & Boeschen, 1998). Several studies have found that in the first 6 months after a rape or other assault, women and men show high levels of depression, anxiety, dismay, and many other indicators of emotional distress (Duncan, Saunders, Kilpatrick, Hanson, & Resnick, 1996; Kessler, Davis, & Kendler, 1997). For some people, this emotional distress declines over time. For others, however, emotional distress is long lasting.

In one study, Burnam and colleagues (1988) found that assault victims were twice as likely as others to have a diagnosable depressive disorder, anxiety disorder, or substance abuse disorder at some time after the assault. They were most likely to develop these disorders if they had been assaulted as a child. In fact, people who had been assaulted as children remained at higher risk for developing a psychological disorder throughout their lives.

Fortunately, most of us never experience traumatic events. More common events can lead to stress responses, however. Four characteristics of common events lead to their being perceived as stressful: controllability, predictability, major changes in life circumstances, and internal conflicts. Of course, the degree to

which an event is stressful differs for each individual. That is, people differ in the extent to which they perceive an event as controllable, predictable, and a challenge to their capabilities and self-concept, and it is largely these appraisals that influence the perceived stressfulness of the event (Lazarus & Folkman, 1984).

CONTROLLABILITY

The **controllability** of an event—the degree to which we can stop it or bring it about—influences our perceptions of stressfulness. The more uncontrollable an event seems, the more likely it is to be perceived as stressful (see Chapter 7). Major uncontrollable events include the death of a loved one, being laid off from work, and serious illness. Minor uncontrollable events include such things as having a friend refuse to accept your apology for some misdeed and being bumped off a flight because the airline oversold tickets. One obvious reason uncontrollable events are stressful is that if we cannot control them, we cannot stop them from happening.

As noted earlier, however, our perceptions of the controllability of events appear to be as important to our assessment of their stressfulness as the actual controllability of those events. Consider a study in which participants were shown color photographs of victims of violent deaths. The experimental group could terminate the viewing by pressing a button. The control participants saw the same photographs for the same length of time as the experimental group, but they could not terminate the exposure. (The length of time the control group saw the photographs was determined by the length of time the experimental group saw them.) The level of arousal or anxiety in both groups was determined by measuring galvanic skin response (GSR), a drop in the electrical resistance of the skin that is widely used as an index of autonomic arousal. The experimental group showed much less anxiety in response to the photographs than the control group, even though the two groups were exposed to the photographs for the same amount of time (Geer & Maisel, 1973).

The belief that we can control events appears to reduce the impact of the events, even if we never exercise that control. This was demonstrated in a study in which two groups of participants were exposed to a loud, extremely unpleasant noise. Participants in one group were told that they could terminate the noise by pressing a button, but they were urged not to do so unless it was absolutely necessary. Participants in the other group had no control over the noise. None of the participants who had a control button actually pressed it, so the noise exposure was the same for both groups. Nevertheless, performance on subsequent problem-solving tasks was significantly worse for the group that had no control, indicating that they were more disturbed by the noise than the group that had the potential for control (Glass & Singer, 1972).

PREDICTABILITY

The **predictability** of an event—the degree to which we know if and when it will occur—also affects its stressfulness. Being able to predict the occurrence of a stressful event—even if the individual cannot control it—usually reduces the severity of the stress. As discussed in Chapter 7, laboratory experiments show that both humans and animals prefer predictable aversive events over unpredictable ones. In one study, rats were given a choice between a signaled shock and an unsignaled shock. If the rat pressed a bar at the beginning of a series of shock trials, each shock was preceded by a warning tone. If the rat failed to press the bar, no warning tones sounded during that series of trials. All of the rats quickly learned to press the bar, showing a marked preference for predictable shock (Abbott, Schoen, & Badia, 1984). Humans generally choose predictable over unpredictable shocks, too. They also show less emotional arousal and report less distress while waiting for predictable shocks to occur, and they perceive predictable shocks as less aversive than unpredictable ones of the same intensity (Katz & Wykes, 1985).

How do we explain these results? One possibility is that a warning signal before an aversive event allows the person or animal to initiate some sort of preparatory process that acts to reduce the effects of a noxious stimulus. An animal receiving the signal that a shock is about to happen may shift its feet in such a way as to reduce the experience of the shock. A man who knows he is about to receive a shot in the doctor's office can try to distract himself to reduce the pain. A woman who hears warnings of an impending hurricane can board up her windows in an attempt to prevent damage to her house.

Another possibility is that with unpredictable shock, there is no safe period, but with predictable shock, the organism (human or animal) can relax to some extent until the signal warns that shock is about to occur (Seligman & Binik, 1977). A real-life example of this phenomenon occurs when a boss who tends to criticize an employee in front of others is out of town on a business trip. The boss's absence is a signal to the employee that it is safe to relax. In contrast, an employee whose boss criticizes him unpredictably throughout the day and never goes out of town may chronically feel stressed.

Some jobs, such as fire fighting and emergency-room medicine, are filled with unpredictability and are considered very stressful. Serious illnesses often are very unpredictable. One of the major problems faced by cancer patients who receive treatment is that they cannot be sure whether they have been cured until many years have passed. Every day they must confront the uncertainty of a potentially disastrous future. Even an event as overwhelmingly negative as torture can be affected by the extent to which victims feel that the episodes of torture are predictable. Victims who are able to predict the timing and type of torture they experience while being detained recover better once they are released than victims who perceive the torture as completely unpredictable (Basoglu & Mineka, 1992).

MAJOR CHANGES IN LIFE CIRCUMSTANCES

Two pioneering stress researchers, Holmes and Rahe (1967), argued that any life change that requires numerous readjustments can be perceived as stressful. In an attempt to measure the impact of life changes, they developed the Life Events Scale shown in Table 14-1. The scale ranks life events from most stressful (death of a spouse) to least stressful (minor violations of the law). To arrive at this scale, the investigators examined thousands of interviews and medical histories to identify the kinds of events that people found stressful. Because marriage appeared to be a critical event for most people, it was placed in the middle of the scale and assigned an arbitrary value of 50. The investigators then asked approximately 400 men and women of varying ages, backgrounds, and marital status to compare marriage with a number of other life events. They were asked such questions as "Does the event call for more or less readjustment than marriage?" They were then asked to assign a point value to each event on the basis of their evaluation of its severity and the time required for adjustment. These ratings were used to construct the scale in Table 14-1.

The Holmes and Rahe scale shown in Table 14-1 had a major influence on stress research, but it has also had many critics. Although positive events often require adjustment and hence are sometimes stressful, most research indicates that negative events have a much greater impact on psychological and physical health than positive events. In addition, the Holmes and Rahe scale assumes that all people respond to a given event in the same way, but there are large differences in how people are affected by events. Some of these differences are linked to age and cultural background (Masuda & Holmes, 1978). Also, some people do not find major changes or pressure situations stressful. Rather, they experience them as challenging and are invigorated by them. Later we will discuss characteristics of individuals

● Table 14-1
The Life Events Scale

This scale, also known as the Holmes and Rahe Social Readjustment Rating Scale, measures stress in terms of life changes. *(Reprinted with permission from T. H. Holmes & R. H. Rahe (1967) "The Social Readjustment Rating Scale," in the* Journal of Psychosomatic Research, *Vol. 11, No. 2, pp. 213–218. Copyright © 1967 Elsevier Science.)*

Life Event	Value
Death of spouse	100
Divorce	73
Marital separation	65
Jail term	63
Death of close family member	63
Personal injury or illness	53
Marriage	50
Fired from job	47
Marital reconciliation	45
Retirement	45
Change in health of family member	44
Pregnancy	40
Sex difficulties	39
Gain of a new family member	39
Business readjustment	39
Change in financial state	38
Death of a close friend	37
Change to a different line of work	36
Foreclosure of mortgage	30
Change in responsibilities at work	29
Son or daughter leaving home	29
Trouble with in-laws	29
Outstanding personal achievement	28
Wife begins or stops work	26
Begin or end school	26
Change in living conditions	25
Revision of personal habits	24
Trouble with boss	23
Change in residence	20
Change in school	20
Change in recreation	19
Change in church activities	19
Change in social activities	18
Change in sleeping habits	16
Change in eating habits	15
Vacation	13
Christmas	12
Minor legal violations	11

Although marriage is a happy event, it can also be stressful.

that affect whether they view situations as stressors or as challenges.

INTERNAL CONFLICTS

So far we have discussed only external events in which something or someone in the environment challenges our well-being. Stress can also be brought about by **internal conflicts—unresolved issues that may be either conscious or unconscious.** Conflict occurs when a person must choose between incompatible, or mutually exclusive, goals or courses of action. Many of the things people desire prove to be incompatible. You want to play on your college volleyball team but cannot put in the time required and still earn the grades necessary to apply to graduate school. You want to join your friends for a pizza party but are afraid you will fail tomorrow's exam if you don't stay home and study. You don't want to go to your uncle's for dinner, but you also don't want to listen to your parents' complaints if you turn down the invitation. In each case, the two goals are incompatible because the action needed to achieve one automatically prevents you from achieving the other.

Even if two goals are equally attractive—for example, you receive two good job offers—you may agonize over the decision and experience regrets after making a choice. This stress would not have occurred if you had been offered only one job.

Conflict may also arise when two inner needs or motives are in opposition. In our society, the conflicts that are most pervasive and difficult to resolve generally occur between the following motives:

Independence versus dependence. Particularly when we are faced with a difficult situation, we may want someone to take care of us and solve our problems. But we are taught that we must stand on our own.

At other times we may wish for independence, but circumstances or other people force us to remain dependent.

Intimacy versus isolation. The desire to be close to another person and to share our innermost thoughts and emotions may conflict with the fear of being hurt or rejected if we expose too much of ourselves.

Cooperation versus competition. Our society emphasizes competition and success. Competition begins in early childhood among siblings, continues through school, and culminates in business and professional rivalry. At the same time, we are urged to cooperate and to help others.

Expression of impulses versus moral standards. Impulses must be regulated to some degree in all societies. We noted in Chapter 3 that much of childhood learning involves internalizing cultural restrictions on impulses. Sex and aggression are two areas in which our impulses frequently come into conflict with moral standards, and violation of these standards can generate feelings of guilt.

These four areas present the greatest potential for serious conflict. Trying to find a workable compromise between opposing motives can create considerable stress.

◆ Interim Summary

- Stress refers to experiencing events that are perceived as endangering one's physical or psychological well-being. These events are usually referred to as stressors, and people's reactions to them are termed stress responses.

- Traumatic events are events outside the normal range of people's experience that are highly distressing. Traumas such as rape can lead to a wide range of emotional and physical problems.

- The controllability of a situation also affects how stressful it is. Our perceptions of controllability are as important as the actual controllability of the situation.

- Unpredictable events are often perceived as stressful.

- Some researchers argue that any major change can be stressful.

- Internal conflicts—unresolved issues that may be conscious or unconscious—can cause stress.

◆ Critical Thinking Questions

1. Consider the situations in your own life you find stressful. What are the characteristics of these situations that make them so stressful?

2. To what extent do you think the need for control is influenced by culture?

PSYCHOLOGICAL REACTIONS TO STRESS

Stressful situations produce emotional reactions ranging from exhilaration (when the event is demanding but manageable) to anxiety, anger, discouragement, and depression (see the Concept Review Table). If the stressful situation continues, our emotions may switch back and forth among any of these, depending on the success of our coping efforts. Let us take a closer look at some of the more common emotional reactions to stress.

ANXIETY

The most common response to a stressor is anxiety. People who live through events that are beyond the normal range of human suffering (natural disasters, rape, kidnapping) sometimes develop a severe set of anxiety-related symptoms known as **post-traumatic stress disorder** (PTSD).

There are four sets of symptoms of PTSD. The first set represents a deep detachment from everyday life. People report feeling completely numb to the world, as if they have no emotional reactions to anything. They feel estranged from others, as if they can no longer relate to even close family and friends. They also lose their interest in their former activities and may just sit around for hours at a time, apparently staring into nothingness. The second set of symptoms is a repeated reliving of the

CONCEPT REVIEW TABLE
Reactions to Stress

Psychological Reactions

Anxiety

Anger and aggression

Apathy and depression

Cognitive impairment

Physiological Reactions

Increased metabolic rate

Increased heart rate

Dilation of pupils

Higher blood pressure

Increased breathing rate

Tensing of muscles

Secretion of endorphins and ACTH

Release of extra sugar from the liver

trauma. People may dream every night of the trauma and become afraid to go to sleep. Even while awake, they may mentally relive the trauma so vividly that they begin to behave as if they were there. A former combat soldier, when he hears a jet flying low nearby, might hit the ditch, cover his head, and feel as though he is back in combat. A rape survivor might replay scenes from her trauma over and over and see the face of her attacker in other men. The third set of symptoms includes sleep disturbances, difficulty in concentrating, and overalertness. Trauma survivors may act as though they are always vigilant for signs of the trauma recurring. They may find it impossible to concentrate on anything, including their work, conversations, or driving a car. Even if they are not having recurrent nightmares, they may have restless nights and wake up exhausted. Another symptom of PTSD that is not part of these three core sets of symptoms is survivor guilt—some people feel terribly guilty about surviving a trauma when others did not, even if they could not have saved other people.

Post-traumatic stress disorder may develop immediately after the trauma, or it may be brought on by a minor stress experienced weeks, months, or even years later. It may last a long time. A study of victims of the 1972 flood that wiped out the community of Buffalo Creek, West Virginia, found that shortly after the flood, 63% of the survivors were suffering from PTSD symptoms. Fourteen years later, 25% still experienced PTSD symptoms (Green, Lindy, Grace, & Leonard, 1992). Similarly, a study of Florida children who survived Hurricane Andrew in 1992 found that nearly 20% were still suffering from PTSD a year after the disaster (LaGreca, Sliverman, Vernberg, & Prinstein, 1996). Another study of children in South Carolina who survived Hurricane Hugo in 1993 found that, 3 years after the hurricane, a third still experienced a sense of detachment and avoided thoughts or feelings associated with the hurricane. A quarter of the children were irritable and angry, and 20% experienced chronic physiological arousal (Garrison et al., 1995).

Traumas caused by humans, such as sexual or physical assault, terrorist attacks, and war, may be even more likely to cause PTSD than natural disasters, for at least two reasons. First, such traumas challenge our basic beliefs about the goodness of life and other people, and when these beliefs are shattered, PTSD is more likely to occur (Janoff-Bulman, 1992). Second, human-caused disasters often strike individuals rather than whole communities, and suffering through a trauma alone seems to increase a person's risk of experiencing PTSD.

Studies of rape survivors have found that about 95% experience post-traumatic stress symptoms severe enough to qualify for a diagnosis of the disorder in the first 2 weeks following the rape (see Figure 14-1). About 50% still qualify for the diagnosis 3 months after the rape. As

Figure 14-1
Post-Traumatic Symptoms in Rape
Almost all women who have been raped show symptoms of post-traumatic stress disorder severe enough to be diagnosed with PTSD in the first or second week following the rape. Over the 3 months following the rape, the percentage of women continuing to show PTSD declines. However, almost 50% of women continue to be diagnosed with PTSD 3 months after a rape. (After Foa & Riggs, 1995)

many as 25% still suffer from PTSD 4 to 5 years after the rape (Foa & Riggs, 1995; Resnick, Kilpatrick, Dansky, & Sanders, 1993).

Post-traumatic stress disorder became widely accepted as a diagnostic category because of difficulties experienced by Vietnam War veterans. Although stress reactions to the horrors of battle had been noted in earlier wars (in World War I it was called "shell shock" and in World War II "combat fatigue"), veterans of the Vietnam War seemed especially prone to develop the long-term symptoms we have described. The National Vietnam Veterans Readjustment Study found that nearly half a million Vietnam veterans still suffered from PTSD 15 years after their military service. Rates of PTSD were highest among Hispanic veterans, next highest among African American veterans, and lowest among European Americans (see Figure 14-2; Schlenger et al., 1992). A separate study of Native American Vietnam veterans found that as many as 70% still suffered symptoms of PTSD decades after the war ended (Manson et al., 1996). Veterans from ethnic minority groups may suffer more PTSD because they have the double jeopardy of war exposure and the stress of discrimination once they return to the United States.

Substance abuse, violence, and interpersonal problems are common correlates of post-traumatic stress disorder. In a study of 713 men who served in Vietnam, 16% reported having problems resulting from drinking

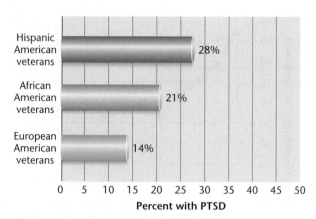

■ Figure 14-2
Rates of PTSD in Vietnam Veterans
A large study of Vietnam veterans showed higher rates of PTSD among veterans of color than among white veterans. (Adapted from W. E. Schlenger, R. A. Kolka, J. A. Fairbank, & R. L. Hough (1992), "The Prevalence of Post-Traumatic Stress Disorder in the Vietnam Generation: A Multi-Method, Multi-Source Assessment of Psychiatric Disorders," from *Journal of Traumatic Stress*, 5, 333–363.)

heavily, such as trouble at school or work, problems with friends, and passing out. Sixteen percent had been arrested at least once; and 44% said that they had war memories that they were still trying to forget (Yager, Laufer, & Gallops, 1984). The soldiers who fought in Vietnam were young (the average age was 19), and the conditions of warfare were unusual: absence of clear front lines, unpredictable attacks in dense jungle, difficulty distinguishing between Vietnamese allies and enemies, and lack of support for the war among the American public. To this day, some Vietnam veterans still reexperience in memories or in dreams those traumatic events. As one veteran wrote, "The war is over in history. But it never ended for me" (Marbly, 1987, p. 193).

More recent and ongoing wars and conflicts have resulted in PTSD, however, both for soldiers and for civil-

Post-traumatic stress disorder affects about one-sixth of Vietnam War veterans.

ians caught in these conflicts. For example, a study of veterans of the 1991 Persian Gulf War found that 13% were suffering from PTSD in the year after the war (Sutker, Davis, Uddo, & Ditta, 1995).

The wars in the former Yugoslavia begun in the 1990s were marked by "ethnic cleansing"—the torture and slaughter of thousands and displacement of millions of former Yugoslavians. This campaign was one of the most brutal in history, with many atrocities, concentration camps, organized mass rapes, and neighbors murdering neighbors. This woman's story is far too common:

> Case Study: A woman in her 40s worked the family farm in a rural village until the day the siege began, when mortar shells turned most of their house to rubble. A few months before, she and her husband had sent their son away to be with relatives in Slovenia. The morning after the shelling, the Chetniks—Serbian nationalist forces—came and ordered everyone to leave their houses at once. Many neighbors and friends were shot dead before the woman's eyes. She and her husband were forced to sign over the title to their house, car, and bank deposits—and watched as the looting began. Looters included neighbors who were their friends. Over the next few days they traveled back from the Muslim ghetto to their land to feed the animals. One day, as she and her husband stood in the garden, the Chetniks captured them. Her husband was taken away with other men. For the next 6 months she did not know if he was dead or alive. She spent days on transport trains with no food or water, where many suffocated to death beside her. On forced marches she had to step over the dead bodies of friends and relatives. Once her group was forced across a bridge that was lined with Chetnik machine gunners randomly shooting to kill and ordering them to throw all valuables over the edge into nets. She spent weeks in severely deprived conditions in a big tent with many women and children, where constant sobbing could be heard. When she herself could not stop crying she thought that something had broken in her head and that she had gone "crazy." Now she says, "I will never be happy again." When alone, everything comes back to her. But when she is with others or busy doing chores, she can forget. "My soul hurts inside, but I'm able to pull it together." She is able to sleep without nightmares only by using a nightly ritual: "I lie down and go through every step of the house in Bosnia—the stable, everything they took, the rugs, the horses, the doors. I see it all again." (Weine et al., 1995, p. 540)

A study of Bosnian refugees conducted just after they resettled in the United States found that 65% suffered from PTSD, with older refugees more vulnerable to PTSD than younger refugees (Weine et al., 1995; see also Cardozo, Vergara, Agani, & Cotway, 2000). A follow-up study of these refugees 1 year later found that 44% were still suffering from PTSD (Weine et al., 1998).

Many refugees from Bosnia and other war-torn countries report having been tortured before they es-

Many refugees suffer from PTSD, with older refugees more vulnerable to PTSD than younger refugees.

caped their homeland, and the experience of torture significantly increases the chances that an individual will develop PTSD (Basoglu & Mineka, 1998; Shrestha et al., 1998). Torture survivors who were political activists appear less prone to develop PTSD than those who were not political activists (Basoglu et al., 1997). Political activists appeared more psychologically prepared for torture than others because they expected at some time to be tortured, often had previous experience with torture, and had a belief system whereby torture was viewed merely as an instrument of repression.

ANGER AND AGGRESSION

Another common reaction to a stressful situation is anger, which may lead to aggression. Laboratory studies have shown that some animals behave aggressively in response to a variety of stressors, including overcrowding, electric shock, and failure to receive an expected food reward. If a pair of animals is shocked in a cage from which they cannot escape, they begin fighting when the shock starts and stop fighting when it ends.

Children often become angry and exhibit aggressive behavior when they experience frustration. As noted in Chapter 11, the frustration-aggression hypothesis assumes that whenever a person's efforts to reach a goal are blocked, an aggressive drive is induced that motivates behavior designed to injure the object—or person—causing the frustration. Although research has shown that aggression is not an inevitable response to frustration, it certainly is a frequent one. When one child takes a toy from another, the second child is likely to attack the first in an attempt to regain the toy. In the late 1980s, some adults frustrated by interminable traffic jams on hot Los Angeles freeways began shooting at one another. Fortunately, adults usually express their aggression verbally rather than physically; they are more likely to exchange insults than blows.

Direct aggression toward the source of frustration is not always possible or wise. Sometimes the source is vague and intangible. The person does not know what to attack but feels angry and seeks an object on which to vent these feelings. Sometimes the individual responsible for the frustration is so powerful that an attack would be dangerous. When circumstances block direct attack on the cause of frustration, aggression may be displaced: The aggressive action may be directed toward an innocent person or object rather than toward the actual cause of the frustration. A man who is reprimanded at work may take out unexpressed resentment on his family. A student who is angry at her professor for an unfair grade may blow up at her roommate. A child frustrated by experiences at school may resort to vandalism of school property.

APATHY AND DEPRESSION

Although aggression is a frequent response to frustration, the opposite response, withdrawal and apathy, is also common. If the stressful conditions continue and the individual is unable to cope with them, apathy may deepen into depression.

The theory of learned helplessness (Seligman, 1975) explains how experience with uncontrollable negative events can lead to apathy and depression (see also Chapter 7). A series of experiments showed that dogs placed in a shuttle box (an apparatus with two compartments separated by a barrier) quickly learn to jump to the opposite compartment to escape a mild electric shock delivered to their feet through a grid on the floor. If a light is turned on a few seconds before the grid is electrified, the dogs can learn to avoid the shock by jumping to the safe compartment when signaled by the light. However, if the dog has previously been confined in another enclosure where shocks were unavoidable and inescapable—so that nothing the animal did terminated the shock—it is very difficult for the dog to learn the avoidance response in a new situation. The animal simply sits and endures the shock in the shuttle box, even though an easy jump to the opposite compartment would eliminate discomfort. Some dogs never learn, even if the experimenter demonstrates the proper procedure by carrying them over the barrier. The experimenters concluded that the animals had learned through prior experience that they were helpless to avoid the shock and therefore gave up trying to do so, even in a new situation. The animals were unable to overcome this learned helplessness (Overmeier & Seligman, 1967).

Some humans also appear to develop **learned helplessness, characterized by apathy, withdrawal, and inaction, in response to uncontrollable events.** Not all do, however. The original learned helplessness theory has had to be modified to take into account the fact that although some people become helpless after uncontrollable events, others are invigorated by the challenge posed by such events (Wortman & Brehm, 1975). This modified theory will be discussed later in the chapter.

The original learned helplessness theory is useful, however, in helping us understand why some people seem to give up when they are exposed to difficult events. For example, the theory has been used to explain why prisoners in Nazi concentration camps did not rebel against their captors more often: They had come to believe that they were helpless to do anything about their situation and therefore did not try to escape. Similarly, women whose husbands beat them frequently may not try to escape. They often say that they feel helpless to do anything about their situation because they fear what their husbands would do if they tried to leave or because they do not have the economic resources to support themselves and their children.

COGNITIVE IMPAIRMENT

In addition to emotional reactions, people often show substantial cognitive impairment when faced with serious stressors. They find it hard to concentrate and to organize their thoughts logically. They may be easily distracted. As a result, their performance on tasks, particularly complex tasks, tends to deteriorate.

This cognitive impairment may come from two sources. High levels of emotional arousal can interfere with the processing of information, so the more anxious, angry, or depressed we are after experiencing a stressor, the more likely we are to exhibit cognitive impairment. Cognitive impairment may also result from the distracting thoughts that go through our heads when we are faced with a stressor. We contemplate possible sources of action, worry about the consequences of our actions, and berate ourselves for not being able to handle the situation better. For instance, while trying to complete a test, students who suffer from test anxiety tend to worry about possible failure and about their inadequacies. They can become so distracted by these negative thoughts that they fail to follow instructions and neglect or misinterpret information. As their anxiety mounts, they have difficulty retrieving facts that they have learned well.

Cognitive impairment often leads people to adhere rigidly to behavior patterns because they cannot consider alternative patterns. People have been trapped in flaming buildings because they persisted in pushing against exit doors that opened inward; in their panic, they failed to consider other possible means of escape. Some people resort to old, childlike behavior patterns that are not appropriate to the situation. A cautious person may become even more cautious and withdraw entirely, whereas an aggressive person may lose control and strike out heedlessly in all directions.

◆ Interim Summary

- Anxiety is a common response to stress. Some people develop a severe anxiety disorder called *post-traumatic stress disorder*.
- Some people become angry in response to stress and may become aggressive.
- Withdrawal, apathy, and depression may result from stress. Some people develop learned helplessness, which is characterized by passivity and inaction and an inability to see opportunities to control their environment.
- Some people develop cognitive impairment when stressed and become unable to think clearly.

◆ Critical Thinking Questions

1. What kinds of things can family members or friends do to help the survivor of a trauma cope as well as possible with the psychological aftermath of the trauma?

2. Do you think some people are especially prone to develop PTSD following a trauma? If so, why might they be more vulnerable?

 The Neural Basis of Behavior

PHYSIOLOGICAL REACTIONS TO STRESS

The body reacts to stressors by initiating a complex sequence of responses. If the perceived threat is resolved quickly, these emergency responses subside, but if the stressful situation continues, a different set of internal responses occurs as we attempt to adapt. In this section we examine these physiological reactions in detail.

THE FIGHT-OR-FLIGHT RESPONSE

Whether you fall into an icy river, encounter a knife-wielding assailant, or are terrified by your first parachute jump, your body responds in similar ways. Regardless of the stressor, your body automatically prepares to handle the emergency. Recall from Chapter 11 that this is called the **fight-or-flight response**—the body's mobilization to attack or flee from a threatening

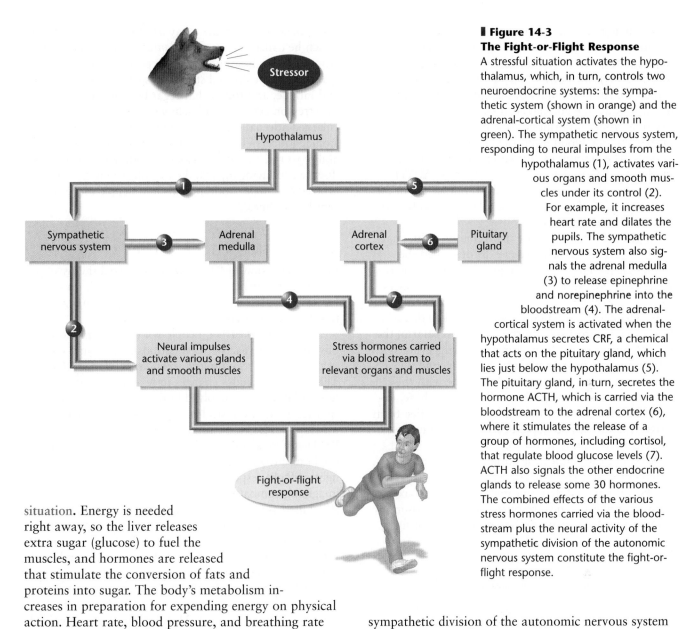

Figure 14-3
The Fight-or-Flight Response
A stressful situation activates the hypothalamus, which, in turn, controls two neuroendocrine systems: the sympathetic system (shown in orange) and the adrenal-cortical system (shown in green). The sympathetic nervous system, responding to neural impulses from the hypothalamus (1), activates various organs and smooth muscles under its control (2). For example, it increases heart rate and dilates the pupils. The sympathetic nervous system also signals the adrenal medulla (3) to release epinephrine and norepinephrine into the bloodstream (4). The adrenal-cortical system is activated when the hypothalamus secretes CRF, a chemical that acts on the pituitary gland, which lies just below the hypothalamus (5). The pituitary gland, in turn, secretes the hormone ACTH, which is carried via the bloodstream to the adrenal cortex (6), where it stimulates the release of a group of hormones, including cortisol, that regulate blood glucose levels (7). ACTH also signals the other endocrine glands to release some 30 hormones. The combined effects of the various stress hormones carried via the bloodstream plus the neural activity of the sympathetic division of the autonomic nervous system constitute the fight-or-flight response.

situation. Energy is needed right away, so the liver releases extra sugar (glucose) to fuel the muscles, and hormones are released that stimulate the conversion of fats and proteins into sugar. The body's metabolism increases in preparation for expending energy on physical action. Heart rate, blood pressure, and breathing rate increase, and the muscles tense. At the same time, certain unessential activities, such as digestion, are curtailed. Saliva and mucus dry up, thereby increasing the size of the air passages to the lungs, and an early sign of stress is a dry mouth. The body's natural painkillers, endorphins, are secreted, and the surface blood vessels constrict to reduce bleeding in case of injury. The spleen releases more red blood cells to help carry oxygen, and the bone marrow produces more white corpuscles to fight infection.

Most of these physiological changes result from activation of two neuroendocrine systems controlled by the hypothalamus: the sympathetic system and the adrenal-cortical system. The hypothalamus has been called the brain's stress center because of its dual function in emergencies. Its first function is to activate the sympathetic division of the autonomic nervous system (see Chapter 2). The hypothalamus transmits nerve impulses to nuclei in the brain stem that control the functioning of the autonomic nervous system. The sympathetic division of the autonomic system acts directly on muscles and organs to produce increased heart rate, elevated blood pressure, and dilated pupils. The sympathetic system also stimulates the inner core of the adrenal glands (the adrenal medulla) to release the hormones epinephrine (adrenaline) and norepinephrine into the bloodstream. Epinephrine has the same effect on the muscles and organs as the sympathetic nervous system (for example, it increases heart rate and blood pressure) and thus serves to perpetuate a state of arousal. Norepinephrine, through its action on the pituitary gland, is indirectly responsible for the release of extra sugar from the liver (see Figure 14-3).

The hypothalamus carries out its second function, activation of the adrenal-cortical system, by signaling the pituitary gland to secrete adrenocorticotropic hormone (ACTH), the body's "major stress hormone" (see Chapter 2). ACTH stimulates the outer layer of the adrenal glands (the adrenal cortex), resulting in the release of a group of hormones (the major one is cortisol) that regulate the blood levels of glucose and certain minerals. The amount of cortisol in blood or urine samples is often used as a measure of stress. ACTH also signals other endocrine glands to release about 30 hormones, each of which plays a role in the body's adjustment to emergency situations.

In groundbreaking work that remains influential today, researcher Hans Selye (1978) described the physiological changes we have just discussed as part of a **general adaptation syndrome,** a set of responses that is displayed by all organisms in response to stress. The general adaptation syndrome has three phases (see Figure 14-4). In the first phase, alarm, the body mobilizes to confront a threat by triggering sympathetic nervous system activity. In the second phase, resistance, the organism attempts to cope with the threat by fleeing it or fighting it. The third phase, exhaustion, occurs if the organism is unable to flee from or fight the threat and depletes its physiological resources in attempting to do so.

Selye argued that a wide variety of physical and psychological stressors can trigger this response pattern. He also argued that repeated or prolonged exhaustion of physiological resources, due to exposure to prolonged stressors that one cannot flee from or fight,

is responsible for a wide array of physiological diseases, which he called *diseases of adaptation.* He conducted laboratory studies in which he exposed animals to several types of prolonged stressors, such as extreme cold and fatigue, and found that regardless of the nature of the stressor, certain bodily changes inevitably occurred: enlarged adrenal glands, shrunken lymph nodes, and stomach ulcers. These changes decrease the organism's ability to resist other stressors, including infectious and disease-producing agents. As we will see later, chronic arousal can make both animals and people more susceptible to illness.

THE PHYSIOLOGY OF PTSD

In our discussion of PTSD, we emphasized the psychological consequences of trauma. Recent work on PTSD has also focused on apparent physiological changes that trauma survivors experience.

As we noted earlier, people with PTSD are more physiologically reactive to situations that remind them of their trauma (Southwick, Yehuda, & Wang, 1998). This activity includes changes in several neurotransmitters and hormones involved in the fight-or-flight response. In addition, studies using positron emission tomography (PET) have found some differences between PTSD sufferers and controls in activity levels in parts of the brain involved in the regulation of emotion and the fight-or-flight response (Charney et al., 1994). While imagining combat scenes, combat veterans with PTSD show increased blood flow in the anterior cingulate gyrus and the amygdala—areas of the brain that may play a role in emotion and memory. In contrast, combat veterans without PTSD did not show increases in blood flow in these regions while imagining combat scenes (see Figure 14-5; Shin et al., 1997). Some studies also show damage to the hippocampus among PTSD patients (Figure 14-6; Bremner, 1998). The hippocampus is involved in memory. Damage to it may result in some of the memory problems that PTSD sufferers report.

It is not clear whether these neurobiological abnormalities in PTSD sufferers is a cause or a consequence of their disorder. Deterioration of the hippocampus could be the result of extremely high levels of cortisol at the time of the trauma (Bremner, 1998). Interestingly, however, resting levels of cortisol among PTSD sufferers (when they are not being exposed to reminders of their trauma) tend to be lower than among people without PTSD (Yehuda, 2000). Because cortisol may act to shut down sympathetic nervous system activity after stress, the lower levels of cortisol among PTSD sufferers may result in prolonged activity of the sympathetic nervous system following stress. As a result, they may more easily develop a conditioned fear

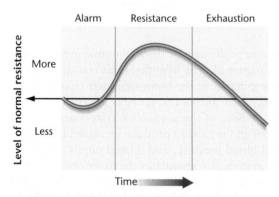

▌ Figure 14-4
The General Adaptation Syndrome
According to Hans Selye, the body reacts to a stressor in three phases. In the first phase, *alarm,* the body mobilizes to confront the threat, which temporarily expends resources and lowers resistance. In the *resistance* phase, the body actively confronts the threat, and resistance is high. If the threat continues, the body moves into the *exhaustion* phase.

■ **Figure 14-5**
PTSD and Blood Flow in the Brain
Studies using positron emission tomography show greater blood flow in the anterior cingulate and amygdala in combat veterans with PTSD than those without PTSD. (Shin, Kosslyn, Alpert, Rauch, Macklin, & Pitman (1997). "Visual Imagery and Perception in Posttraumatic Stress Disorder: A Positron Emission Tomographic Investigation." © *Archives of General Psychiatry 54*, 233–241.)

of stimuli associated with the trauma and subsequently develop PTSD. One longitudinal study assessed cortisol levels in people who had been injured in a traffic accident 1 to 2 hours previously (Yehuda, McFarlane, & Salev, 1998). Six months later, these people were evaluated for the presence of PTSD. Those who did develop the disorder had shown cortisol levels immediately after the trauma that were significantly lower than those who did not develop the disorder. Similar results were found in a study of rape survivors (Resnick et al., 1995). These data suggest that people who develop PTSD have lower baseline levels of cortisol before they experience their trauma and possibly that abnormally low cortisol levels contribute to the development of PTSD. ■

HOW STRESS AFFECTS HEALTH

Attempts to adapt to the continued presence of a stressor may deplete the body's resources and make it vulnerable to illness. The wear and tear on the body that results from chronic overactivity of the physiological response to stress is referred to as allostatic load. Chronic stress can lead to physical disorders such as ulcers, high blood pressure, and heart disease. It may also impair the immune system, decreasing the body's ability to fight invading bacteria and viruses. Indeed, doctors estimate that emotional stress plays an important role in more than half of all medical problems.

Psychophysiological disorders are physical disorders in which emotions are believed to play a central role. A common misconception is that people with psychophysiological disorders are not really sick and do not need medical attention. On the contrary, the symptoms of psychophysiological illness reflect physiological disturbances associated with tissue damage and pain. A peptic ulcer caused by stress is indistinguishable from an ulcer caused by a factor unrelated to stress, such as long-term heavy usage of aspirin.

Traditionally, research in psychophysiology focused on such illnesses as asthma, hypertension (high blood pressure), ulcers, colitis, and rheumatoid arthritis. Researchers looked for relationships between specific illnesses and characteristic attitudes toward, or ways of

■ **Figure 14-6**
PTSD and the Hippocampus
Studies using magnetic resonance imaging show deterioration in the hippocampus of people with PTSD (right scan) compared with people without PTSD (left scan). (From Bremner, 1998)

coping with, stressful life events. For example, individuals with hypertension were said to feel that life is threatening and that they must therefore be on guard at all times. Those suffering from colitis were believed to be angry but unable to express their anger. However, most studies that reported characteristic attitudes to be related to specific illnesses have not been replicated (Overmier & Murison, 1998). Thus, the hypothesis that people who react to stress in similar ways will be vulnerable to the same illnesses has generally not been confirmed. An important exception is research on coronary heart disease and Type A behavior patterns, as we will see shortly.

CORONARY HEART DISEASE The overarousal caused by chronic stressors may contribute to coronary heart disease. **Coronary heart disease** (CHD) occurs when the blood vessels that supply the heart muscles are narrowed or closed by the gradual buildup of a hard, fatty substance called plaque, blocking the flow of oxygen and nutrients to the heart. This can lead to pain, called *angina pectoris*, that radiates across the chest and arm. When the flow of oxygen to the heart is completely blocked, it can cause a myocardial infarction or heart attack.

Coronary heart disease is a leading cause of death and chronic illness. Nearly half of the deaths in the United States every year are caused by coronary heart disease, in many cases before the individual reaches age 65. There seems to be a genetic contribution to coronary heart disease: People with family histories of CHD are at increased risk for the disease. CHD is also linked to high blood pressure, high serum cholesterol, diabetes, smoking, and obesity.

People in high-stress jobs are at increased risk for CHD, particularly if their jobs are highly demanding but provide them little control (Schneiderman, Antoni, Saab, & Ironson, 2001). An example of such a job is an assembly line in which rapid, high-quality production is expected and the work is machine-paced rather than self-paced.

In one study, 900 middle-aged men and women were followed over a 10-year period and examined for the development of heart disease. Two independent methods— occupational titles and the participants' reports of their feelings about their jobs—were used to classify workers along the dimensions of job demand and job control. The results showed that both men and women in occupations classified as "high strain" (high demand combined with low control) had a risk of coronary heart disease 1.5 times greater than the risk faced by those in other occupations (Karasek, Baker, Marxer, Ahlbom, & Theorell, 1981; Karasek, Theorell, Schwartz, Pieper, & Alfredsson, 1982; Pickering et al., 1996).

A demanding family life in addition to a stressful job can adversely affect a woman's cardiovascular health. Employed women in general are not at higher risk for CHD than homemakers. However, employed mothers are more likely to develop heart disease. The likelihood of disease increases with the number of children for working women but not for homemakers (Haynes & Feinleib, 1980). Yet women who have flexibility in and control over their work, and a good income so that they can afford to hire help with housecleaning and child-care tasks, seem not to suffer as much either physically or psychologically from their role overload (Lennon & Rosenfield, 1992; Taylor, 1999).

One group that lives in chronically stressful settings and has particularly high rates of high blood pressure is low-income African-Americans. They often do not have adequate financial resources for daily living, may be poorly educated and therefore have trouble finding good jobs, or live in violent neighborhoods. All these conditions have been linked to higher blood pressure (Williams, 1995).

Experimental studies with animals have shown that disruption of the social environment can induce pathology that resembles coronary artery disease (Manuck, Kaplan, & Matthews, 1986; Sapolsky, 1990). Some of these experiments have been conducted with a type of macaque monkey whose social organization involves the establishment of stable hierarchies of social dominance: Dominant and submissive animals can be identified within a given group on the basis of the animals' social behavior. The introduction of unfamiliar monkeys into an established social group is a stressor that leads to increased aggressive behavior as group members attempt to reestablish a social dominance hierarchy (Manuck, Kaplan, & Matthews, 1986).

In these studies, some monkey groups remained stable with fixed memberships, and other groups were stressed by the repeated introduction of new members. After about 2 years under these conditions, the high-ranking or dominant males in the unstable social condition showed more extensive atherosclerosis than the subordinate males (Sapolsky, 1990).

THE IMMUNE SYSTEM A relatively new area of research in behavioral medicine is **psychoneuroimmunology,** the study of how the body's immune system is affected by stress and other psychological variables (Ader, 2001). By means of specialized cells called *lymphocytes,* the immune system protects the body from disease-causing microorganisms. It affects the individual's susceptibility to infectious diseases, allergies, cancers, and autoimmune disorders (that is, diseases such as rheumatoid arthritis, in which the immune cells attack the normal tissue of the body). There is no single index of the quality of an individual's immune functioning, or immunocompetence. The immune system is a complex one with many interacting components, and different investigators have chosen to focus on different components of the system.

Evidence from a number of areas suggests that stress affects the immune system's ability to defend the body (Schneiderman et al., 2001). One study indicates that the common belief that we are more likely to catch a cold when we are under stress is probably correct (Cohen, Tyrel, & Smith, 1991). Researchers exposed 400 healthy volunteers to a nasal wash containing one of five cold viruses or an innocuous salt solution. The participants answered questions about the number of stressful events they had experienced in the past year, the degree to which they felt able to cope with the demands of daily life, and the frequency with which they experienced negative emotions such as anger and depression. Based on these data, each participant was assigned a stress index ranging from 3 (lowest stress) to 12 (highest stress). The volunteers were examined daily for cold symptoms and for the presence of cold viruses or virus-specific antibodies in their upper respiratory secretions.

The majority of the virus-exposed volunteers showed signs of infection, but only about a third actually developed colds. The rates of viral infection and of actual cold symptoms increased in accordance with the reported stress levels. Compared with the lowest-stress group, volunteers who reported the highest stress were significantly more likely to become infected with the cold virus and almost twice as likely to develop a cold (see Figure 14-7). These results held even after controlling statistically for a number of variables that might influence immune functioning, such as age, allergies, cigarette and alcohol use, exercise, and diet. However, the two indicators of immunocompetence that were measured in this study did not show any specific change as a result of stress, so exactly how stress lowered the body's resistance to the cold virus remains to be determined.

This study is unusual in that the participants were exposed to a virus, lived in special quarters near the laboratory for a number of days both before and after exposure, and were carefully monitored. Such controlled conditions for studying the effects of stress on health are seldom feasible. Most studies look at individuals undergoing a particularly stressful event—such as academic pressure, bereavement, or marital disruption—and evaluate their immunocompetence (Cohen, 1996). For example, a study of people who survived Hurricane Andrew in 1992 found that those who experienced more damage to their homes or whose lives were more threatened by the storm showed poorer immune system functioning than people whose homes and lives had been safer (Ironson et al., 1997). Similarly, following the 1994 Northridge earthquake in the Los Angeles area, people whose lives had been more severely disrupted showed more decline in immune system functioning than those who had not experienced as much stress as a result of the earthquake (Solomon, Segerstrom, Grohr, Kemeny, & Fahey, 1997). People who worried more about the impact of the earthquake on their lives were especially likely to show detriments in natural killer cells, a type of T-cell that seeks out and destroys cells that have been infected with a virus (Segerstrom, Solomon, Kemeny, & Fahey, 1998). It doesn't take a natural disaster to affect people's immune systems. A study of dental students found that dental wounds healed 40% more slowly if the wounds were obtained a few days before a stressful exam than if the wounds were obtained during summer vacation (Marucha et al., 1998). The slow healing of wounds during exam period was associated with poorer immune system functioning.

One factor that appears to be important is the extent to which an individual can control stress. Recall that controllability is one of the variables that determines the severity of stress. A series of animal studies demonstrated that uncontrollable shock has a much greater effect on the immune system than controllable shock (Laudenslager, Ryan, Drugan, Hyson, & Maier, 1983; Visintainer, Volpicelli, & Seligman, 1982). In these experiments, rats were subjected to electric shock. One group could press a lever to turn off the shock. The other animals received an identical sequence of shocks, but their levers were ineffective (see Figure 14-8). In one study using this procedure, the investigators looked at how readily the rats' T-cells multiplied when challenged by an invader. (T-cells are lymphocytes that secrete

Figure 14-7
Stress and Colds
This graph shows the percentage of virus-exposed people who developed colds as a function of the degree of stress reported.
(After S. Cohen, D. A. J. Tyrrell, and A. P. Smith (1991) "Psychological Stress and Susceptibility to the Common Cold," *The New England Journal of Medicine*, 325:606–612. Used with permission from S. Cohen.)

Operative lever. The rat can terminate a shock by pressing the lever in front of him.

Inoperative lever. Lever presses by the rat have no effect.

To programmer

Simultaneous electrical shocks delivered to tails of rats

▌ Figure 14-8
Yoked Controls in a Stress Experiment
A series of electrical shocks are preprogrammed to be delivered simultaneously to the tails of the two male rats. The rat on the left can terminate a shock when it occurs by pressing the lever. The rat on the right has no control in the situation (lever is inoperative), but he is yoked to the first rat. That is, when the first rat receives a shock, the yoked rat simultaneously receives the same shock, and the shock remains on until the first rat presses his lever. The lever presses of the yoked rat have no effect on the shock sequence for either animal.

chemicals that kill harmful cells, such as cancer cells.) They found that the T-cells from rats that could control the shock multiplied as readily as those from rats that were not stressed at all. T-cells from rats exposed to uncontrollable shock, on the other hand, multiplied only weakly. Thus, shock (stress) interfered with the immune response only in rats that could not control it (Laudenslager et al., 1983).

In another study, the investigators implanted tumor cells into rats, gave them shocks, and recorded whether the rats' natural defenses rejected the cells or whether they developed into tumors. Only 27% of the rats that were given uncontrollable shocks rejected the tumors, but 63% of the rats that could turn the shocks off rejected the tumors—even though the rats received identical amounts of shock (Visintainer et al., 1982).

Perceptions of control also appear to mediate the influence of stress on the immune system in humans. In a study of the effects of marital separation or divorce on immune functioning, the partner who had initiated the separation (the one more in control of the situation) was less distressed, reported better health, and showed better immune system functioning than the other partner (Kiecolt-Glaser et al., 1988). Similarly, studies of women with breast cancer have found that those with a pessimistic perspective—that is, who felt that they had little control over events—were the most likely to develop new tumors over a 5-year period, even after the physical severity of their diseases was taken into account (Levy & Heiden, 1991; Watson et al., 1999).

Some of the best evidence that stress can affect the immune system comes from studies showing that at least some types of supportive psychological interventions can slow the progress of cancer (Baum & Posluszny, 1999). For example, several years ago researcher David Spiegel and colleagues began a study in which they randomly assigned women with metastatic breast cancer either to a series of weekly support groups or to no support groups (all of the women were receiving standard medical care for their cancers). The focus of the groups was on facing death and learning to live one's remaining days to the fullest. The researchers had no intention of affecting the course of the cancers and did not believe that it was possible to do so. They wanted only to improve the quality of life for the women in their study.

The researchers were quite surprised when, 48 months after the study began, all of the women who had not been in the support groups had died of their cancers whereas a third of the women in the support groups were still alive (Spiegel, Bloom, Kraemer, & Gottheil, 1989). The average survival time (from the time the study began) for the women in the support groups was about 40 months and about 19 months for the women who were not in the support groups. There were no differences between the groups, other than their participation in the weekly support meetings, that could explain the differences in average survival time. The two groups did not differ in the initial seriousness of their cancers, the type of therapy received, or other variables that might have affected their survival time. The researchers were forced to conclude that their intervention actually increased the number of months that the women in the support group lived (for similar results, see Helgeson et al., 1998; Richardson, Shelton, Krailo, & Levine, 1990).

How did the intervention affect the progress of these women's cancers? It is not clear, but the women in the support groups gained a great deal of psychological strength from the groups, which were intensely emotional and supportive. Members discussed their fear of dying, visited other members in the hospital, grieved when other members died, attended their funerals, and mourned the loss of abilities and friendships. In addition to sharing grief, the women in these groups derived tremendous strength from one another. They came to feel like experts in living, a wisdom that grew from their confrontation with death. They chose new life projects ranging from imparting values to their children to writing books of poetry (Spiegel, 1991). In addition, group members showed lower levels of emotional distress and learned how to control their physical pain better than women who did not participate in the support groups. Similarly, psychological interventions can substantially influence the time people need to recover from major surgery (see Kiecolt-Glaser, McGuire, Robles, & Glaser, 2002). When people are given information about what to expect before surgery and techniques for reducing pain after surgery, they show faster improvement after surgery, require less pain medication, stay in the hospital a shorter period, and have fewer postoperative complications.

The immune system is incredibly complicated, employing several different weapons that interact to defend the body. Much remains to be discovered about the immune system and even more about its relationship to the nervous system. Scientists once believed that the immune system operated quite independently, isolated from other physiological systems. But current studies are making it increasingly evident that the immune system and the nervous system have numerous anatomical and physiological connections. For example, researchers are discovering that lymphocytes have receptors for a number of neurotransmitters and that these immune system cells are equipped to receive messages from the nervous system that may alter the way they behave. The discovery of a link between neurotransmitters and the immune system is important because negative emotional states such as anxiety or depression can affect neurotransmitter levels.

In sum, as research on psychoneuroimmunology yields additional information about the links between the nervous and immune systems, we will gain a clearer understanding of how mental attitudes affect health.

HEALTH-RELATED BEHAVIORS Certain health-related behaviors can greatly increase our susceptibility to illness. Smoking is one of the leading causes of cardiovascular disease and emphysema. A high-fat diet contributes to many forms of cancer as well as to cardiovascular disease. People who do not regularly engage in a moderate amount of exercise are at increased risk for heart disease and earlier death (Baum & Posluszny, 1999). Excessive alcohol consumption can lead to liver disease and cardiovascular disease and may contribute to some cancers. And failure to use condoms during sex significantly increases the risk of contracting HIV. Scientists estimate that most of the diseases people die from in industrialized countries are heavily influenced by health-related behaviors (Taylor, 1999).

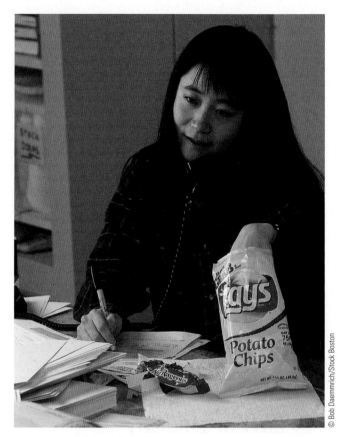

When we're stressed, we often engage in unhealthy behaviors.

When we are stressed, we may be less likely to engage in healthy behaviors. Students taking exams stay up all night, often for several nights in a row. They may skip meals and snack on junk food. Many men whose wives have died do not know how to cook for themselves and therefore may eat poorly or hardly at all. In their grief, some bereaved men increase their rates of alcohol consumption and smoking. People under stress cease normal exercise routines and become sedentary. Thus, stress may indirectly affect health by reducing rates of positive health-related behaviors and increasing rates of negative behaviors.

Engaging in unhealthy behaviors may also increase a person's subjective sense of stress. Drinking too much alcohol on a regular basis can interfere with cognitive functioning; a person who consumes excessive amounts of alcohol cannot think as clearly or quickly as one who does not drink excessively. Excessive drinking can also induce lethargy, fatigue, and a mild or moderate sense of depression that makes it difficult to overcome stressful situations or just keep up with the demands of everyday life.

Similarly, people who do not get enough sleep show impairments in memory, learning, logical reasoning, arithmetic skills, complex verbal processing, and decision making. Sleeping for only 5 hours per night for just two nights significantly reduces performance on math problems and creative thinking tasks. So, staying up late to prepare for an exam can actually decrease performance on the test (Dinges & Broughton, 1989).

Among people who already have a serious illness such as cancer or cardiovascular disease, stress can reduce their motivation or ability to engage in behaviors that are critical to their recovery or survival (Schneiderman et al., 2001). For example, they may skip appointments with their physician or fail to take necessary medications. They may not follow diets that are essential for their health; for example, a diabetic may not control sugar intake. Studies of persons infected with HIV disease suggest that those under more stress are more likely to engage in unprotected sexual activity or intravenous drug use (Fishbein et al., 1998).

In contrast, people who engage in a healthy lifestyle—eating a low-fat diet, drinking alcohol in moderation, getting enough sleep, and exercising regularly—often report that stressful events seem more manageable and that they feel more in control of their lives. Thus, engaging in healthy behaviors can help reduce the stressfulness of life as well as reducing the risk or progression of a number of serious diseases.

◆ Interim Summary

- The body reacts to stress with the fight-or-flight response. The sympathetic nervous system causes increased heart rate, elevated blood pressure, dilated pupils, and the release of extra sugar from the liver. The adrenal-cortical system causes the release of adrenocorticotropic hormone (ACTH), which stimulates the release of cortisol in the blood.

- These reactions are part of a general adaptation syndrome, a set of responses displayed by all organisms in response to stress. The syndrome consists of three phases: alarm, resistance, and exhaustion.

- Psychophysiological disorders are physical disorders in which emotions are believed to play a central role. For example, stress can contribute to coronary heart disease.

- Psychoneuroimmunology is the study of how psychological factors can affect the immune system. Stress may impair the functioning of the immune system, increasing the risk of immune-related disorders.

- Stress may affect health directly by creating chronic overarousal of the sympathetic division of the autonomic nervous system or the adrenal-cortical system or by impairing the immune system. People under stress also may not engage in positive health-related behaviors, and this may lead to illness.

◆ Critical Thinking Questions

1. How can we help people with a serious disease like cancer change in ways that might slow the progress of the disease without making them feel that they are being blamed for having the disease?

2. What are some of your unhealthiest behaviors? What prevents you from changing them?

PSYCHOLOGICAL FACTORS AND STRESS RESPONSES

As noted earlier, events that are uncontrollable or unpredictable, or that challenge our views of ourselves, tend to be experienced as stressful. Some people appear more likely than others to appraise events in these ways. There are three basic theories about why some people are prone to appraise events as stressful: the psychoanalytic, behavioral, and cognitive theories.

PSYCHOANALYTIC THEORY

Psychoanalysts distinguish between **objective anxiety**, which is a reasonable response to a harmful situation, and **neurotic anxiety**, which is anxiety out of proportion to the actual danger. Freud believed that neurotic anxiety stems from unconscious conflicts between unacceptable impulses and the constraints imposed by reality (see Chapter 13). Many impulses pose a threat to the individual because they are contradictory to personal or social values. A woman may not consciously acknowledge that she has strong hostile feelings toward her mother because these feelings conflict with her belief that a child should love her parents. If she acknowledged her true feelings, she would destroy her self-concept as a loving daughter and risk the loss of her mother's love and support. When she begins to feel angry toward her mother, the resulting anxiety serves as a signal of potential danger. Thus, this woman may experience even a minor conflict with her mother, such as a disagreement about where the family should go for vacation or what to have for dinner, as a major stressor. A woman who is not so conflicted in her feelings about her mother would experience such a conflict as a less severe stressor.

According to psychoanalytic theory, we all have unconscious conflicts. For some people, however, these conflicts are more numerous and severe, and as a result these people experience more events as stressful.

BEHAVIORAL THEORY

Although Freud saw unconscious conflicts as the internal source of stress responses, behaviorists have focused on ways in which individuals learn to associate stress responses with certain situations. People may also react to specific situations with fear and anxiety because those situations caused them harm or were stressful in the past. Some phobias develop through such classical conditioning (see Chapter 7). For example, a person whose car nearly slid off the road on the side of a steep mountain may now experience anxiety every time she is in a high place. Or a student who failed a final exam in a particular classroom may feel anxious the next year when he reenters that room to take another class.

Sometimes fears are difficult to extinguish. If your first reaction is to avoid or escape the anxiety-producing situation, you may not be able to determine when the situation is no longer dangerous. A little girl who has been punished for assertive behavior in the past may never learn that it is acceptable for her to express her wishes in new situations because she never tries. People can continue to have fears about particular situations because they chronically avoid the situation and therefore never challenge their fears.

COGNITIVE THEORY

A modification of the learned helplessness theory proposed by Abramson, Seligman, & Teasdale (1978) focuses on the attributions or causal explanations people give for important events. These researchers argued that when people attribute negative events to causes that are internal to them ("it's my fault"), are stable in time ("it's going to last forever"), and are global, affecting many areas of their lives, they are likely to show a helpless, depressed response to negative events. For example, if a man whose wife left him attributed the breakup of his marriage to his "bad" personality (an internal, stable, and global attribution), he would tend to lose self-esteem and expect future relationships to fail as well. In turn, he would show lowered motivation, passivity, and sadness. In contrast, if he made a less pessimistic attribution, such as attributing the failure of his marriage to incompatibility between himself and his wife, he would tend to maintain his self-esteem and motivation for the future.

Abramson and colleagues propose that people have consistent **attributional styles,** or styles of making attributions for the events in their lives, and that these styles influence the degree to which people view events as stressful and have helpless, depressed reactions to difficult events. A number of studies support this theory (Peterson & Bossio, 2001). In one study, researchers assessed the attributional styles of students a few weeks before a midterm exam. Just before the exam, they also asked the students

what grade they would consider a failure and what grade they would be happy with. After the students received their grades, they measured the students' levels of sadness and depression. Among students who received a grade below their standards, those who had a pessimistic attributional style were significantly more depressed than those who had a more optimistic attributional style (Metalsky, Halberstadt, & Abramson, 1987).

Pessimism is also linked to physical illness (Taylor, Kemeny, Reed, Bower, & Gruenewald, 2000). Students who are more pessimistic report more illness and make more visits to the health center than students with a more optimistic attributional style. In a 35-year study of men in the Harvard classes of 1939–1940, researchers found that men who had a pessimistic attributional style at age 25 were more likely to develop physical illness over the subsequent years than men with a more optimistic attributional style (Peterson, Seligman, & Vaillant, 1988). Other studies have found that pessimists recover more slowly from coronary bypass surgery and have more severe angina than optimists (Scheier et al., 1989).

How does pessimism affect health? People who are pessimistic tend to appraise events as more stressful. In turn, this greater sense of stress may contribute to poor health by causing the chronic arousal of the body's fight-or flight response, resulting in the type of physiological damage discussed earlier. Several studies have found evidence for this. In one, the blood pressure of pessimists and optimists was monitored daily for 3 days. The pessimists had chronically higher blood pressure levels than the optimists across the 3 days (Raikkonen et al., 1999).

The chronic physiological arousal associated with pessimism has also been linked to lowered immune system functioning. For example, a study of older adults found that those who were pessimistic had poorer im-

People who are pessimistic do not recover from illnesses or surgery as quickly as people who are optimistic.

mune system functioning than those who were optimistic (Kamen-Siegel, Rodin, & Seligman, 1991). A study of gay men who were HIV-positive found that those who blamed themselves for negative events showed more decline in immune functioning over 18 months than those who engaged in less self-blaming attributions (Segerstrom, Taylor, Kemeny, Reed, & Visscher, 1996). Another study of gay men found that among both HIV-positive and HIV-negative men, those who were more pessimistic and fatalistic were less likely to engage in healthy behaviors, such as maintaining a proper diet, getting enough sleep, and exercising (Taylor et al., 1992). This is particularly important for the HIV-positive men, because engaging in these behaviors can reduce the risk of developing AIDS. Thus, a pessimistic outlook may affect health directly, by reducing immune system functioning, or indirectly, by reducing a person's tendency to engage in health-promoting behavior.

HARDINESS Another line of research has focused on people who are most resistant to stress—who do not become physically or emotionally impaired even in the face of major stressful events (Kobasa, 1979; Kobasa, Maddi, & Kahn, 1982). This characteristic is referred to as **hardiness.** In one study, more than 600 men who were executives or managers in the same company were given checklists and asked to describe all of the stressful events and illnesses they had experienced over the previous 3 years. Two groups were selected for comparison. The first group scored above average on both stressful events and illness; the second group scored equally high on stress but below average on illness. Members of both groups then filled out detailed personality questionnaires. Analysis of the results indicated that the high-stress, low-illness men differed from the men who became ill under stress on three major dimensions: They were more actively involved in their work and social lives, they were more oriented toward challenge and change, and they felt more in control of events in their lives (Kobasa, 1979).

These personality differences could be the result rather than the cause of illness. For example, it is hard for people to be involved in work or in social activity when they are ill. The investigators therefore conducted a longitudinal study that considered the personality characteristics of business executives before they became ill and then monitored their life stress and the extent of their illnesses for 2 years. The results showed that the executives whose attitudes toward life could be rated high on involvement, feelings of control, and positive responses to change remained healthier over time than men who scored low on these dimensions (Kobasa, Maddi, & Kahn, 1982). The most important factors appear to be a sense of control and commitment to goals

(Cohen & Edwards, 1989). Other studies of women (Wiebe & McCallum, 1986) and persons symptomatic with HIV disease (Farber, Schwartz, Schaper, Moonen, & McDaniel, 2000) have also found that hardiness predicts better psychological and physical health.

The personalities of stress-resistant or hardy individuals are characterized by commitment, control, and challenge. These characteristics are interrelated with the factors that influence the perceived severity of stressors. For example, the sense of being in control of life events reflects feelings of competence and also influences the appraisal of stressful events. Challenge also involves cognitive evaluation, the belief that change is normal in life and should be viewed as an opportunity for growth rather than as a threat to security.

FINDING MEANING In a related line of work, researchers have been examining a somewhat surprising but heart-warming phenomenon: Many people confronted with a major trauma say that they feel their lives have changed in extremely positive ways as a result of their experiences. Studies of bereaved people, cancer patients, myocardial infarction patients, bone marrow transplant patients, stroke victims and their caregivers, and men testing positive for HIV find that, as a consequence of their experience, they feel their lives have more meaning and they have grown in important ways (Tennen & Affleck, 1999). Take, for example, this quote from a woman who recently lost someone she loved very dearly.

> I tend to look at it generally as if all the things that happen in my life are a gift, for whatever reason, or however they happen. It doesn't necessarily have to be only pleasant gifts, but everything that happens . . . there's a meaning. I've had a lot of suffering in my life . . . and through that I've learned a great deal. While I wouldn't want to go back and relive that, I'm grateful for it because it makes me who I am. There's a lot of joys and sorrows, but they all enrich life. (Alicia, quoted in Nolen-Hoeksema & Larson, 1999, p. 143)

People often say that they feel they grew in character as a result of their experience, discovering new strengths they didn't know they had. They also say they gained a healthier perspective on what is important in their lives and made major changes in their lives based on this new perspective. Many people report that their relationships with friends and family members are deeper and more meaningful now.

In turn, finding meaning or positive growth in a trauma seems to help people adjust, both physically and psychologically. Several studies have found that people who finding meaning or growth in traumatic events show less depression and anxiety after the event than others. For example, in a study of recently bereaved peo-

Finding meaning in a loss can help people cope with it.

ple, Davis and colleagues (1998) showed that those who found some meaning in their loss or felt they grew positively showed less depression and fewer symptoms of post-traumatic stress disorder than those who did not over the 18 months following their loss. It did not matter to psychological health what type of meaning or growth people found, as long as they found some sort of meaning or growth in their experience.

Some studies also suggest that finding meaning is related to the course of physiological disease. For example, Affleck and colleagues found that men who had had a heart attack and who felt they had grown personally as a result of the heart attack, such as changing their philosophy of life or values, were less likely to have a subsequent heart attack and had less cardiac disease over the next 8 years (Affleck, Tennen, Croog, & Levine, 1987). In a study of men who were HIV positive, Bower and colleagues found that those who had found some meaning in the loss of a friend or partner to AIDS maintained healthier immune systems (indexed by CD4 T helper cells) and were less likely to die from AIDS over a 2- to 3 follow-up period (Bower, Kemeny, Taylor, & Fahey, 1998).

Why are some people able to find meaning or growth in trauma and others do not? Optimism seems to play a role. Optimists are more likely to report positive changes, benefits, or growth following stressful events (see Taylor et al., 2000). Similarly, hardy people appear to perceive more benefits from their stressful experiences. For example, a study of U.S. soldiers participating in a peacekeeping mission to Bosnia showed that those who scored high on measures of hardiness during their deployment were more likely to believe they had obtained benefits, such as personal growth, from their work in Bosnia than those who were not hardy (Britt, Adler, & Bartone, 2001).

THE TYPE A PATTERN

A behavior pattern or personality style that has received a great deal of attention is the **type A pattern.** Over the years, physicians had noticed that heart attack victims tend to be hostile, aggressive, impatient individuals who were overinvolved in their work. In the 1950s, two cardiologists defined a set of behaviors that seemed to characterize patients with coronary heart disease, which were labeled the type A pattern (Friedman & Rosenman, 1974). People who exhibit this behavior pattern are extremely competitive and achievement oriented; they have a sense of time urgency, find it difficult to relax, and become impatient and angry when confronted with delays or with people whom they view as incompetent. Although outwardly self-confident, they are prey to constant feelings of self-doubt, and they push themselves to accomplish more and more in less and less time. Some common type A behaviors are listed in Table 14-2.

Type B people do not exhibit the characteristics listed for type A. They are able to relax without feeling guilty and work without becoming agitated. They lack a sense of time urgency, with its accompanying impatience, and are not easily roused to anger.

To examine the relationship between type A behavior and coronary heart disease, more than 3,000 healthy, middle-aged men were evaluated by means of a structured interview that was designed to be irritating. The interviewer kept the participant waiting without explanation and then asked a series of questions about being competitive, hostile, and pressed for time, such as "Do you ever feel rushed or under pressure?" "Do you eat quickly?" "Would you describe yourself as ambitious and hard driving or relaxed and easy-going?" and "Do you resent it if someone is late?" The interviewer interrupted, asked questions in a challenging manner, and made irrelevant remarks. The interview was scored more on the way the person behaved in answering the questions than on the answers themselves. For example, type A men spoke loudly in an explosive manner, talked over the interviewer so as not to be interrupted, appeared tense and tight-lipped, and described hostile incidents with great emotional intensity. Type B men sat in a relaxed manner, spoke slowly and softly, were easily interrupted, and smiled often.

After the participants had been classified as type A or type B, they were studied for $8\frac{1}{2}$ years. During that period, type A men had twice as many heart attacks or other forms of coronary heart disease as type B men. These results held up even after diet, age, smoking, and other variables were taken into account (Rosenman et al., 1976). Other studies confirmed this twofold risk and linked type A behavior to heart disease in both men and women (Kornitzer et al., 1982; Haynes, Feinleib, & Kannel, 1980). In addition, type A behavior correlates with severity of coronary artery blockage, as determined at autopsy or in x-ray studies of the inside of coronary blood vessels (Friedman et al., 1968; Williams et al., 1988).

In 1981, the American Heart Association concluded that type A behavior should be classified as a risk factor for coronary heart disease. However, two subsequent studies failed to find a link between type A behavior and heart disease (Case, Heller, Case, & Moss, 1985; Shekelle, Neaton, Jacobs, Hulley, & Blackburn, 1983). Although some researchers attribute this failure to the way type A individuals were assessed in these studies, others believe that the original definition of type A behavior is too diffuse. They argue that time urgency and competitiveness are not the most important components. Instead, the crucial variable may be hostility.

Several studies have found that a person's level of hostility is a better predictor of heart disease than his or her overall level of type A behavior. Accordingly, several studies have used personality tests rather than interviews to measure hostility. For example, a 25-year study of 118 male lawyers found that those who scored high in hostility on a personality inventory taken in law school were five times more likely to die before age 50 than other classmates (Barefoot et al., 1989). In a similar follow-up study of physicians, hostility scores obtained in medical school predicted the incidence of coronary heart disease, as well as mortality from all causes (Barefoot, Williams, & Dahlstrom, 1983). In both studies, this relationship was independent of the effects of smoking, age, and high blood pressure. There is some evidence that when anger is repressed or held in, it may be even more destructive to the heart than anger that is expressed (Spielberger et al., 1985; Wright, 1988).

How does type A behavior or hostility lead to coronary heart disease? A possible biological mechanism is the way the sympathetic nervous system responds to stress. When exposed to stressful experimental situations (for example, when faced with the threat of failure, harassment, or competitive task demands), most participants report feeling angry, irritated, and tense. However, participants who score high on hostility as a trait show much larger increases in blood pressure, heart rate, and secretion of stress-related hormones than participants with low hostility scores (Raeikkoenen, Matthews, Flory, & Owens, 1999; Suarez, Kuhn, Schanberg, Williams, & Zimmerman, 1998). The same results are found when type A participants are compared with type B participants. The sympathetic nervous systems of hostile and/or type A individuals appear to be hyperresponsive to stressful situations. All of these physiological changes can damage the heart and blood vessels.

Not surprisingly, hostile people also report higher degrees of interpersonal conflict and less social support than other people (Benotsch et al, 1997). Reductions in social support have direct negative effects on a number of objective and subjective indices of health (see Uchino, Uno, & Holt-Lunstad, 1999). Thus, hostility may have both di-

Type A people lose their temper easily

rect effects on cardiovascular health by increasing chronic arousal and indirect effects by lowering social support.

The good news about the type A behavior pattern is that it can be modified through well-established therapy programs, and people who are able to reduce their type A behavior show lowered risk of coronary heart disease. We will discuss this therapy later in the chapter.

◆ Interim Summary

- Psychoanalytic theory suggests that events are stressful when they arouse our unconscious conflicts.

- Behaviorists argue that people react to specific situations with fear and anxiety because those situations caused them harm or were stressful in the past.

- Cognitive theorists argue that people's attributions or causal explanations influence their stress responses. People who tend to attribute bad events to internal, stable, and global causes are more likely to develop learned helplessness after experiencing such events and to become ill.

- Hardy people tend to see stressful events as challenges and have a strong sense of personal control; these characteristics may protect against the development of illness in the face of stress.

- People who are able to find meaning in a traumatic event are less likely to develop emotional problems.

- People with the type A behavior pattern tend to be hostile, aggressive, impatient individuals who are overinvolved in their work. Studies of men and women show that people who exhibit this pattern are at increased risk for coronary heart disease.

◆ Critical Thinking Questions

1. What might be the benefits of the type A behavior pattern for people with this pattern?

2. What might make some cultures more prone to stress-related health problems than others?

COPING SKILLS

The emotions and physiological arousal created by stressful situations are highly uncomfortable, and this discomfort motivates the individual to do something to alleviate it. The term **coping** is used to refer to the process by which a person attempts to manage stressful demands, and it takes two major forms. A person can focus on the specific problem or situation that has arisen, trying to find some way of changing it or avoiding it in the future. This is called **problem-focused coping**. A person can also focus on alleviating the emotions associated with the stressful situation, even if the situation itself cannot be changed. This is called **emotion-focused coping** (Lazarus & Folkman, 1984). When dealing with a stressful situation, most people use both problem-focused and emotion-focused coping.

PROBLEM-FOCUSED COPING

There are many strategies for solving problems. First, you must define the problem. Then you can generate alternative solutions and weigh the costs and benefits of the alternatives. Eventually, you must choose between alternative solutions and then act upon your choice. Problem-focused strategies can also be directed inward: You can change something about yourself instead of changing the environment. You can change your goals, find alternative sources of gratification, or learn new skills in inward-directed strategies. How skillfully people employ these strategies depends on their range of experiences and capacity for self-control.

Suppose you receive a warning that you are about to fail a course required for graduation. You might confer with the professor, devise a work schedule to fulfill the requirements and then follow it, or you might decide that you cannot fulfill the requirements in the time remaining and sign up to retake the course in summer school. Both of these actions are problem-focused methods of coping.

People who tend to use problem-focused coping in stressful situations show lower levels of depression both during and after the stressful situation (Billings & Moos, 1984). Of course, people who are less depressed may find it easier to use problem-focused coping. But longitudinal studies show that problem-focused coping leads to shorter periods of depression, even taking into account people's initial levels of depression. In addition, therapies that teach depressed people to use problem-focused coping can be effective in helping them overcome their depression and react more adaptively to stressors (Nezu, Nezu, & Perri, 1989).

EMOTION-FOCUSED COPING

People engage in emotion-focused coping to prevent their negative emotions from overwhelming them and making them unable to take action to solve their problems. They also use emotion-focused coping when a problem is uncontrollable.

We try to cope with our negative emotions in many ways. Some researchers have divided these into behavioral strategies and cognitive strategies (Moos, 1988). Behavioral strategies include engaging in physical exercise, using alcohol or other drugs, venting anger, and seeking emotional support from friends. Cognitive strategies include temporarily setting the problem aside ("I decided it wasn't worth worrying about") and reducing the threat by changing the meaning of the situation ("I decided that her friendship wasn't that important to me"). Cognitive strategies often involve reappraising the situation. Obviously, we would expect some behavioral and cognitive strategies to be adaptive and others (such as drinking heavily) to merely cause more stress.

One strategy that appears to help people adjust emotionally and physically to a stressor is seeking emotional support from others. In a study of women who had just undergone surgery for breast cancer, Levy and colleagues (1990) found that those who actively sought social support had higher natural killer cell activity, indicating that their immune system was attacking the cancer more aggressively. Pennebaker (1990) has found that people who reveal personal traumas, such as being raped or having a spouse commit suicide, to supportive others tend to show more positive physical health both shortly after the trauma and in the long run.

The quality of the social support a person receives after experiencing a trauma strongly influences the impact of that support on the individual's health, however (Rook, 1984). Some friends or relatives can be burdens instead of blessings in times of stress. People whose social networks are characterized by a high level of conflict tend to show poorer physical and emotional health after a major stressor such as bereavement (Windholz, Marmar, & Horowitz, 1985). Conflicted social relationships may affect physical health through the immune system. Kiecolt-Glaser, Glaser, Cacioppo, and Malarkey (1998) found that newlywed couples who became hostile and negative toward each other while discussing a marital problem showed greater decreases in four indicators of immune system functioning than couples who remained calm and nonhostile in discussing marital problems. Couples who became hostile during these discussions also showed elevated blood pressure for a longer period than those who did not become hostile.

Some people engage in a more maladaptive way of coping with negative emotions: They simply deny that they have any negative emotions and push those emotions out of conscious awareness, a strategy that is referred to as repressive coping. People who engage in repressive coping tend to show more autonomic nervous system activity (such as a higher heart rate) in response to stressors than people who do not engage in repressive coping (Brown et al., 1996; Weinberg, Schwartz, & Davidson, 1979). Pushing emotions out of awareness may require real physical work, which results in chronic overarousal and, in turn, in physical illness.

Repressing important aspects of one's identity may also be harmful to one's health. An intriguing study showed that gay men who conceal their homosexual identity may suffer health consequences (Cole et al., 1996). Men who concealed their homosexuality were about three times more likely to develop cancer and certain infectious disease (pneumonia, bronchitis, sinusitis, tuberculosis) over a 5-year period than men who were open about their homosexuality (see Figure 14-9). All of these men were HIV-negative. But another study by the same researchers focused on HIV-positive gay men and found that the disease progressed faster in those who concealed their homosexuality than in those who did not (Cole et al., 1995). The differences in health between the men who were "out" and those who were "closeted" did not reflect differences in health-related behaviors (smoking, exercise). It may be that chronic inhibition of one's

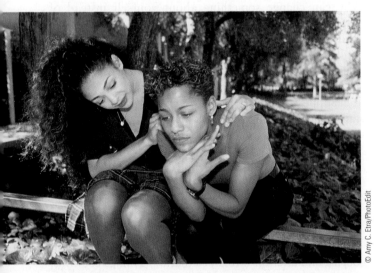

Talking with supportive friends about your problems can be an adaptive coping strategy.

© Amy C. Etra/PhotoEdit

Figure 14-9
Infectious Diseases as a Function of Concealing One's Sexual Orientation
Homosexual men who concealed their homosexuality from others were more prone to several infectious diseases. (From S. W. Cole, M. E. Kemeny, S. E. Taylor, and B. R. Visscher (1996), "Elevated Physical Health Risk Among Gay Men Who Conceal Their Homosexual Identity," *Health Psychology,* 15, pp. 243–251. Copyright © 1996 by the American Psychological Association. Reprinted with permission.)

identity, like chronic inhibition of emotions, can have direct effects on health.

In contrast, talking about negative emotions and important issues in one's life appears to have positive effects on health. In a large series of studies, Pennebaker (1990) has found that encouraging people to reveal personal traumas in diaries or essays improves their health. In one study, 50 healthy undergraduates were randomly assigned to write either about the most traumatic and upsetting events in their lives or about trivial topics for 20 minutes on 4 consecutive days. Blood samples were taken from the students on the day before they began writing, on the last day of writing, and 6 weeks after writing, and it was tested for several markers of immune system functioning. The number of times the students visited the college health center over the 6 weeks after the writing task was also recorded and compared with the number of health center visits the students had made before the study. As Figure 14-10 shows, students who revealed their personal traumas in essays showed more positive immune system functioning and visited the health center less frequently than students in the control group (Pennebaker, Kiecolt-Glaser, & Glaser, 1988). In contrast, the group who wrote about trivial events experienced a slight increase in health center visits and a decrease in lymphocyte response, for unknown reasons. Pennebaker (1997) believes that writ-

ing is helpful because it assists people in finding meaning in the events that happen to them and helps them understand them. Finding meaning and understanding then reduces the negative emotions people feel about events and may therefore reduce the physiological wear and tear associated with chronic negative emotions (see also Bower et al., 1998).

Positive social support may help people adjust better emotionally to stress by leading them to avoid ruminat-

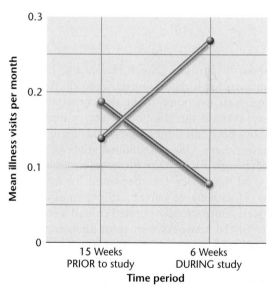

Figure 14-10
Students' Health After Writing About Traumas or Trivialities
Students who revealed personal traumas in a series of essays had stronger immune system functioning and fewer health care visits than students who wrote about trivial events in their essays. (After Pennebaker, Kiecolt-Glaser, & Glaser, 1988)

CUTTING-EDGE RESEARCH
Is Religion Good for Your Health?

Psychologists have had an ambivalent relationship with religion. In recent years, however, an increasing number of studies have suggested that religious people are happier and healthier, on average, than nonreligious people (for reviews, see Ellison & Levin, 1998). Actively religious people show lower mortality rates from a variety of diseases than nonreligious people (Oman & Reed, 1998). They are also generally in better physical health (Koenig et al., 1997). Religious beliefs may have an impact on health because they influence health behaviors. Many religions have prohibitions against unhealthy behaviors, such as excessive drinking, taking drugs, and smoking, and religious people do smoke and drink less than nonreligious people (Koenig et al., 1997). In addition, positive social support is linked to better health, and religious groups offer social support to their members.

There is a much longer tradition of researching the links between religion and mental health. In the past, many psychologists have viewed religion as bad for mental health. They argued that religious beliefs do not help people cope with adversity. Instead, they lead people to accept adversity as "God's will" rather than doing what they can to overcome that adversity. And, they said, if religious people look psychologically healthier in some studies, it is only because they are more prone to deny their psychological problems, or because these studies were biased in favor of finding a positive relationship between religion and psychological health.

It is true that many of the studies on religion and health done over the years were conducted by people who had a stake in the outcome of the study—religious people who wanted to find a positive relationship or nonreligious people who wanted to find a negative relationship. There is an increasing body of well-done psychological science, however, that is consistently finding that people who have a strong religious faith and are active in a religious community

recover better psychologically after traumas than nonreligious people (Ellison & Levin, 1998). For example, a study of parents who had lost an infant to sudden infant death syndrome found that those parents who were active in their churches were better able to cope with the loss of their child (McIntosh, Silver, & Wortman, 1993).

For now, just how religiosity affects mental and physical health is largely unknown (Ellison & Levin, 1998). In addition, most of the research to date has been on people who ascribe to Christian or Jewish beliefs, and little work has been done with people of other faiths. But old assumptions that religion is a danger to health and that religiosity is an unhelpful defense mechanism are being replaced by more open-minded views on the benefits religion offers to people.

 For more information, go online with InfoTrac College Edition. Use your own term or search:

- Religion health
- Religion and psychology

---

ing about the stressor (Nolen-Hoeksema, 1991). Rumination involves isolating ourselves to think about how bad we feel, worrying about the consequences of the stressful event or our emotional state, or repeatedly talking about how bad things are without taking any action to change them. One longitudinal study of recently bereaved people found that those who ruminated in response to their grief were depressed for longer periods (Nolen-Hoeksema & Larson, 1999). In addition, those who were more socially isolated or had a lot of conflict in their social networks were most likely to ruminate.

Another longitudinal study was conducted quite by accident. A group of researchers at Stanford University happened to have obtained measures of emotion-focused coping tendencies and levels of depression and anxiety in a large group of students 2 weeks before the major earthquake that hit the San Francisco Bay area in 1989. They remeasured the students' levels of depression and anxiety 10 days and 7 weeks following the earthquake. They also estimated how much environmental stress the students experienced as a result of the earthquake (that

is, injury to themselves, to their friends or family, and to their homes). The results showed that students who exhibited a ruminative style of coping with emotions before the earthquake were more likely to be depressed and anxious 10 days after the earthquake and 7 weeks later. This was true even after the students' levels of depression and anxiety before the earthquake were taken into account (Nolen-Hoeksema & Morrow, 1991). Students who engaged in dangerous activities, such as drinking alcohol, to avoid their negative moods also tended to remain depressed and anxious. In contrast, students who used pleasant activities to improve their mood and regain a sense of control experienced short and mild periods of depression and anxiety.

You might ask whether people who engage in ruminative coping are more likely to solve their problems. The available evidence suggests that the answer is no. People who engage in ruminative coping are less likely to engage in active problem solving in response to stressors. In contrast, people who use pleasant activities to take a breather from their negative moods are more likely to turn to active problem solving to deal with stressors (Nolen-Hoeksema & Larson, 1999; Nolen-Hoeksema & Morrow, 1991). In addition, people who use ruminative coping may actually do a poorer job of problem solving when they do try. Two laboratory studies have shown that depressed people who spend 10 minutes ruminating and then do a problem-solving task show poorer performance at problem solving than depressed people who are distracted for 10 minutes before attempting the problem-solving task (Lyubomirsky & Nolen-Hoeksema, 1995; Nolen-Hoeksema & Morrow, 1991). Rumination thus may get in the way of good problem solving.

◆ Interim Summary

- Coping strategies are divided into problem-focused strategies and emotion-focused strategies.

- People who take active steps to solve problems are less likely to experience depression and illness following negative life events.

- People who use rumination or avoidance strategies to cope with negative emotions show longer and more severe distress after negative events than people who seek social support or reappraise an event to cope with their emotions.

◆ Critical Thinking Questions

1. In what way might the environment in which a child is raised affect the development of his or her coping strategies?

2. How might you differentiate between people who repress or deny that they are distressed and people who really do not experience much distress in the face of difficult events?

MANAGING STRESS

In addition to seeking positive social support in times of stress, people can learn other techniques to reduce the negative effects of stress on the body and the mind. In this section, we discuss some behavioral and cognitive techniques that have been shown to help people reduce the effects of stress. We then discuss in detail how these techniques are applied to reduce type A behavior and coronary heart disease.

BEHAVIORAL TECHNIQUES

Among the behavioral techniques that help people control their physiological responses to stressful situations are biofeedback, relaxation training, meditation, and aerobic exercise.

BIOFEEDBACK In **biofeedback** training, individuals receive information (feedback) about an aspect of their physiological state and then attempt to alter that state. For example, in a procedure for learning to control tension headaches, electrodes are attached to the participant's forehead so that any movement in the forehead muscle can be electronically detected, amplified, and fed back to the person as an auditory signal. The signal, or tone, increases in pitch when the muscle contracts and decreases when it relaxes. By learning to control the pitch of the tone, the individual learns to keep the muscle relaxed. (Relaxation of the forehead muscle usually ensures relaxation of scalp and neck muscles as well.) After 4 to 8 weeks of biofeedback training, the participant learns to recognize the onset of tension and to reduce it without feedback from the machine (Thorpe & Olson, 1997).

RELAXATION TRAINING Relaxation training involves teaching people techniques to deeply relax their muscles and slow down and focus their thoughts. Physiological processes that are controlled by the autonomic nervous

Biofeedback has proven useful in reducing some chronic health problems.

Legend:
— Blood Pressure
— Heart Rate

Group 2 (increase)

Group 1 (decrease)

Change in heart rate (beats/min) or blood pressure (mm of Mercury)

Five-trial blocks

Group two participants received biofeedback (light and tone) whenever their blood pressure and heart rates *increased* simultaneously.

Group one participants received biofeedback (light and tone) whenever their blood pressure and heart rates *decreased* simultaneously.

■ **Figure 14-11**
Operant Conditioning of Blood Pressure and Heart Rate
Parrticipants in both groups achieved significant simultaneous control of blood pressure and heart rate during a single conditioning session. The group reinforced for lowering both functions (group 1) achieved increasingly greater control over trials; the group reinforced for raising both functions (group 2) was less consistent. (G. E. Schwartz (1975) "Biofeedback, Self-Regulation, and the Patterning of Physiological Processes," in *American Scientist,* 63:316. Reprinted by permission of The Scientific Research Society.)

system, such as heart rate and blood pressure, have traditionally been assumed to be automatic and not under voluntary control. However, laboratory studies have demonstrated that people can learn to modify heart rate and blood pressure (see Figure 14-11). The results of these studies have led to relaxation procedures for treating patients with high blood pressure (hypertension). One procedure is to show patients a graph of their blood pressure while it is being monitored and to teach them techniques for relaxing different muscle groups. Patients are instructed to tense their muscles (for example, to clench a fist or tighten the abdomen), release the tension, and notice the difference in sensation. By starting with the feet and ankle muscles and progressing through the body to the muscles that control the neck and face, patients learn to modify muscular tension. This combination of biofeedback with relaxation training has proved effective in lowering blood pressure for some individuals (Mukhopadhyay & Turner, 1997).

Reviews of numerous studies using biofeedback and relaxation training to control headaches and hypertension conclude that the most important variable is learning how to relax (Thorpe & Olson, 1997). Some people may learn to relax faster when they receive biofeedback. Others may learn to relax equally well when they receive training in muscle relaxation without any specific biofeedback. The usefulness of relaxation training seems to depend on the individual. Some people who are not conscientious about taking drugs to relieve high blood pressure are more responsive to relaxation training, whereas others who have learned to control their blood pressure through relaxation may eventually drop the procedure because they find it too time-consuming.

MEDITATION Meditation is an effective technique for inducing relaxation and reducing physiological arousal. Almost all studies of the phenomenon report a significant lowering of the respiratory rate, a decrease in oxygen consumption, and less elimination of carbon dioxide. The heart rate is lowered, blood flow stabilizes, and the concentration of lactate in the blood is decreased (Dillbeck & Orme-Johnson, 1987). Also, there are changes in EEG brain wave activity that suggest that cortical arousal is decreased during meditation, reflecting a reduced level of mental activity (Fenwick, 1987). Meditation has also proved effective in helping people with chronic feelings of anxiety, in improving self-esteem, and in reducing relapse in people prone to serious depression (Snaith, 1998). In a study of cancer patients, those who were taught to meditate showed significant reductions in symptoms of depression, anger, and anxiety and fewer cardiopulmonary and gastrointestinal symptoms than those who were not taught to meditate (Speca, Carlson, Goodey, & Angen, 2000).

However, a leading researcher in this field contends that the same effects can be achieved through simple rest. After a thorough study of the research evidence, he concludes that there are no consistent differences between meditating and resting participants in heart rate, respiration rate, oxygen consumption, blood flow, and other physiological measures (Holmes, 1984, 1985a, 1985b). So, simply resting may produce stress-reduction effects similar to those produced by meditation.

EXERCISE Another factor that is important in controlling stress is physical fitness. Individuals who regularly engage in aerobic exercise (any sustained activity that increases heart rate and oxygen consumption, such as jogging, swimming, or cycling) show significantly lower heart rates and blood pressure in response to stressful situations than others (Taylor, 1999). In turn, Brown (1991) found that physically fit people were much less likely to become physically ill following stressful events than people who were not fit. Because of these findings, many stress management programs also emphasize physical fitness.

COGNITIVE TECHNIQUES

People who are able to control their physiological or emotional responses through biofeedback and relaxation training in the laboratory will have more difficulty doing so in actual stressful situations, particularly if they continue to interact in ways that make them tense. Consequently, an additional approach to stress management focuses on changing the individual's cognitive responses to stressful situations. **Cognitive behavior therapy** attempts to help people identify the kinds of stressful situations that produce their physiological or emotional symptoms and alter the way they cope with these situations. For example, a man who suffers from tension headaches would be asked to keep a record of their occurrence and rate the severity of each headache and the circumstances in which it occurred. Next he would be taught how to monitor his responses to these stressful events and asked to record his feelings, thoughts, and behavior prior to, during, and following the event. After a period of self-monitoring, certain relationships often become evident among situational variables (for example, criticism by a supervisor or coworker), thoughts ("I can't do anything right"), and emotional, behavioral, and physiological responses (depression, withdrawal, and headache).

The next step is trying to identify the expectations or beliefs that might explain the headache reactions (for example, "I expect to do everything perfectly, so the slightest criticism upsets me" or "I judge myself harshly, become depressed, and end up with a headache"). The final and most difficult step is trying to change something about the stressful situation, the individual's way of thinking about it, or the individual's behavior. The options might include finding a less stressful job, recognizing that the need to perform perfectly leads to unnecessary anguish over errors, and learning to behave more assertively in interactions instead of withdrawing.

Biofeedback, relaxation training, exercise, and cognitive therapy have all proved useful in helping people control their physiological and emotional responses to stress. Some research suggests that the improvement is more likely to be maintained over time with a combination of cognitive and behavior therapy (Holroyd, Appel, & Andrasik, 1983). Because the complex demands of everyday life often require flexible coping skills, being able to relax may not be an effective method of coping with some of life's stresses. Programs for stress management frequently employ a combination of biofeedback, relaxation training, exercise, and cognitive modification techniques.

MODIFYING TYPE A BEHAVIOR

A combination of cognitive and behavioral techniques has been shown to reduce type A behavior (Friedman et al., 1994). The participants were more than 1,000 individuals who had experienced at least one heart attack. Participants in the treatment group were helped to reduce their sense of time urgency by practicing standing in line (a situation that type A individuals find extremely irritating) and using the opportunity to reflect on things that they do not normally have time to think about, to watch people, or to strike up a conversation with a stranger. Treatment also included helping participants learn to express themselves without exploding at people and to alter certain specific behaviors (such as interrupting others or talking or eating hurriedly). Therapists helped the participants reevaluate certain beliefs (such as the notion that success depends on the quantity of work produced) that might lead to urgent and hostile behavior. Finally, participants found ways to make their home and work environments less stressful (such as reducing the number of unnecessary social engagements).

The critical dependent variable in this study was the occurrence of another heart attack. By the end of the study 4½ years later, the experimental group had a heart attack recurrence rate almost half that of control participants who were not taught how to alter their lifestyles. Clearly, learning to modify type A behavior was beneficial to these participants' health (Friedman et al., 1994).

Like other research described in this chapter, this study was based on the premise that the mind and the body influence each other. Simple models of how stress affects health are being replaced by complex models that explain how biological, psychological, and social factors intertwine to create disease or health. As we have seen, the body has characteristic physiological reactions to stress. For people with preexisting biological vulnerabilities, such as a genetic predisposition to heart disease, these physiological reactions to stress can cause deterioration in health. Yet an individual's perception of stress is determined by characteristics of events in the environment and by his or her personal history, appraisals of the event, and coping styles. Thus, the extent to which the individual experiences psychological distress or ill health following potentially stressful situations is determined by the biological and psychological vulnerabilities and strengths he or she brings to these situations.

Is Unrealistic Optimism Good for Your Health?

UNREALISTIC OPTIMISM CAN BE BAD FOR YOUR HEALTH
Neil D. Weinstein, Rutgers University

Are you more likely or less likely to develop a drinking problem than the other people in your psychology class? How about your chances of getting a sexually transmitted disease (STD) or your chances of having a heart attack some day? When asked questions like these, few people admit to having above-average risk. Typically, 50% to 70% of a group claim that their risk is below average, another 30% to 50% say that their risk is average, but less than 10% acknowledge that their risk is above average.

Obviously, this cannot be correct. Your own risk of heart disease might actually be below average, but the number of people who make such a claim is simply too great for them all to be right. The "average" person has, by definition, an "average" risk. So when the people who claim below-average risk greatly outnumber those who say their risk is higher than average, something must be wrong with their risk judgments.

The data show that most of the individuals whose actions, family history, or environment put them at high risk either don't realize it or won't admit it. In general, we summarize these findings by saying that people are unrealistically optimistic about future risks. This unrealistic optimism is especially strong with risks that are somewhat under our own control, such as alcoholism, lung cancer, and STDs. Apparently, we are quite confident that we will do a better job of avoiding these problems than will our peers.

What unrealistic optimism demonstrates is that we are not impartial and open-minded when it comes to health risk information. Most of us want to be informed and make good decisions, but we also want to feel that our lifestyles are already healthful, that changes are not needed, and that we don't have to worry. Unfortunately, this search for a rosy interpretation can get us into trouble. If everything is fine as is, then we don't need to take precautions. We can continue to get drunk with our friends, eat as much pizza, fries, and hamburgers as we want, and use condoms only with sexual partners we know are promiscuous (curiously, we rarely think that any of them are). Most of the time, such risky behavior does not get us into trouble, but the odds of getting into trouble are certainly increased. The millions of college students who get STDs every year or who get into automobile accidents after too many beers are clear examples of people doing things that they know are supposed to be risky. But they have concluded that, for them, it will be okay. This is not ignorance; it is unrealistic optimism.

An especially upsetting example is college students who smoke cigarettes. They have all kinds of illusions to make them feel comfortable. They will smoke for only a couple of years and then they will quit. (Others may get hooked, but not them.) Their cigarettes are low in tar, or they don't inhale. They exercise a lot, which will counteract the effects of smoking. Smokers don't deny that cigarettes are bad for people. They just think the effects won't be bad for them. Typically, they say that their risk of heart disease, lung cancer, and emphysema is lower than that of other smokers and only "a little" above the risk of the average person.

Optimism does have its advantages. When people already have a severe illness and are coping with it—illnesses such as cancer or AIDS—maintaining optimism is important. It helps people put up with sometimes unpleasant treatments, and a positive mood may itself help by improving the body's ability to resist disease. Even being overly optimistic about the future is unlikely to lead someone who has a life-threatening disease to pretend that he or she is not sick or to

Neil Weinstein

stop treatment. However, the perils of unrealistic optimism are greater when the issue is preventing harm from occurring. If you think you can handle a car after a night of drinking, if none of your dates could carry an STD, or if, unlike your classmates, you can stop smoking any time you want, your unrealistic optimism is likely to lead to health consequences you will regret.

Is Unrealistic Optimism Good for Your Health?

UNREALISTIC OPTIMISM CAN BE GOOD FOR YOUR HEALTH
Shelley E. Taylor, University of California, Los Angeles

Is unrealistic optimism bad for your health? It seems like it should be. After all, if people believe they are relatively invulnerable to disorders ranging from tooth decay to heart disease, logically, shouldn't that interfere with practicing good health behaviors? Ample evidence suggests that most people are indeed unrealistically optimistic about their health. But, if anything, unrealistic optimism seems to be good for your health.

Consider the practice of health habits, such as wearing a seat belt, getting exercise, and avoiding harmful substances such as tobacco and alcohol. Rather than undermining such habits, as some have assumed, unrealistic optimism may actually lead people to practice better health habits.

Shelley E. Taylor

Aspinwall and Brunhart (1996) found that people with optimistic expectations about their health actually pay *more* attention to personally relevant risk-related information than pessimistic people, apparently so that they can take preventive action to offset those risks. People who are optimistic about their health may be so precisely because they practice better health habits than more pessimistic people (Armor & Taylor, 1998).

Perhaps the most persuasive evidence for beneficial health effects of unrealistic optimism has come from studies of gay men with the HIV virus. In one study, men who were unrealistically optimistic about their ability to avoid AIDS (such as believing that their bodies might shake off the virus) practiced more health-promoting behaviors than those who were less optimistic (Taylor, Kemeny, Aspinwall, Schneider, Rodriguez, & Herbert, 1992). Reed, Kemeny, Taylor, Wang, and Visscher (1994) found that, among men diagnosed with AIDS, maintaining an unrealistically optimistic outlook, as opposed to a realistic one, was associated with an increased length of life of nine months. In a parallel finding, Richard Schulz found that pessimistic cancer patients died earlier than those who were more optimistic (Schulz, Bookwala, Knapp, Scheier, & Williamson, 1996).

Optimists also seem to recover faster from illnesses. Leedham, Meyerowitz, Muirhead, and Frist (1995) found that optimistic expectations among heart transplant patients were associated with better mood, quality of life, and adjustment to illness. Similar findings are reported by Scheier and his associates (Scheier et al., 1989) in their study of people adjusting to coronary artery bypass surgery. What accounts for findings like these?

Optimism is associated with good coping strategies, as well as with good health habits. Optimists are active copers who try to solve problems rather than avoid them (e.g., Scheier & Carver, 1992). Optimistic people are also more interpersonally successful, and so they may do a better job of attracting social support. Social support is known to reduce the likelihood of illness and promote recovery, and so, optimistic people may recruit this special resource for dealing with stress and with illness.

Scientists are now realizing that optimism may create or be associated with a bodily state conducive to health or to rapid recovery from illness. Suzanne Segerstrom and her associates (Segerstrom, Taylor, Kemeny, & Fahey, 1998) studied a group of law students under intense academic stress during the first semester of law school. They found that the optimistic law students showed an immunological profile suggestive of greater resistance to illness and infection. Other studies are showing similar findings (Bower, Kemeny, Taylor, & Fahey, 1998).

Why do some people think that optimism is bad for your health? Some researchers have indicted unrealistic optimism as a culprit that promotes health risk without the evidence. For example, although smokers seemingly underestimate their risk for lung cancer, there is no evidence that their unrealistic optimism led them to smoke or justifies their continued smoking. Indeed, smokers are well aware that they are more vulnerable to lung disorders than are nonsmokers.

Does this mean that unrealistic optimism is always beneficial for your health or is beneficial to all people? Seymour Epstein and his associates (Epstein & Meier, 1989) have suggested that most optimists are "constructive optimists" who take active efforts to protect their health and safety. But a few optimists are "naïve optimists" who believe that everything will turn out all right without any active efforts on their part. If optimists are ever at risk for poorer health habits, it may be this small group of avoidant copers.

Before you write off unrealistic optimism as a state that blinds people to the realistic risks we all face, look at its benefits. It keeps people happier, healthier, and more likely to recover from illness.

- Biofeedback and relaxation training attempt to teach people how to control their physiological responses by learning to recognize tension and reduce it through deep muscle relaxation and concentration.

- Exercise can help people cope with stress over the long term.

- Cognitive behavior therapy attempts to help people recognize and modify their cognitive and behavioral responses to stress.

- Type A behavior can be changed through behavioral and cognitive techniques, resulting in reduced risk of coronary heart disease.

◆ **Critical Thinking Questions**

1. Some people claim to be "addicted to stress." If this is possible, what might it mean to be addicted to stress?

2. What do you expect would be the greatest challenges to helping a type A person change his or her behavior?

CHAPTER SUMMARY

1. Stress refers to experiencing events that are perceived as endangering one's physical or psychological well-being. These events are usually referred to as stressors, and people's reactions to them are termed stress responses. Traumatic events are usually perceived as stressful, as are uncontrollable and unpredictable events. Some researchers believe that any major change, as well as internal conflicts, can be stressful.

2. Some people become angry in response to stress and may become aggressive. Withdrawal, apathy, and depression may result from stress. Some people develop learned helplessness, which is characterized by passivity and inaction and the inability to see opportunities to control one's environment. Some people develop cognitive impairment when stressed and cannot think clearly.

3. The body reacts to stress with the fight-or-flight response. The sympathetic nervous system causes increased heart rate, elevated blood pressure, dilated pupils, and release of extra sugar from the liver. The adrenal-cortical system causes the release of adrenocorticotropic hormone (ACTH), which stimulates the release of cortisol in the blood.

4. These reactions are part of a general adaptation syndrome, a set of responses displayed by all organisms in response to stress. The syndrome consists of three phases: alarm, resistance, and exhaustion.

5. Stress may affect health directly by creating chronic overarousal of the sympathetic division of the autonomic nervous system or the adrenal-cortical system or by impairing the immune system. People under stress also may not engage in positive health-related behaviors, and this may lead to illness. Psychophysiological

disorders are physical disorders in which emotions are believed to play a central role. For example, stress can contribute to coronary heart disease. Psychoneuroimmunology is the study of how psychological factors can affect the immune system. Stress may impair the functioning of the immune system, increasing the risk of immune-related disorders.

6. Psychoanalytic theory suggests that events are stressful when they arouse our unconscious conflicts. Behaviorists argue that people react to specific situations with fear and anxiety because those situations caused them harm or were stressful in the past. Cognitive theorists argue that people's attributions or causal explanations influence their stress responses. People who tend to attribute bad events to internal, stable, and global causes are more likely to develop learned helplessness and become ill after experiencing such events.

7. Hardy people tend to see stressful events as challenges and have a strong sense of personal control, characteristics that may protect against the development of illness in the face of stress. People who are able to find meaning in a traumatic event are less likely to develop emotional problems.

8. People with the type A behavior pattern tend to be hostile, aggressive, impatient individuals who are overinvolved in their work. Studies of men and women show that people who exhibit this pattern are at increased risk for coronary heart disease.

9. Coping strategies are divided into problem-focused strategies and emotion-focused strategies. People who take active steps to solve problems are less likely to experience depression and illness following negative life

events. People who use rumination or avoidance strategies to cope with negative emotions show longer and more severe distress after negative events than people who seek social support or reappraise an event to cope with their emotions.

10. Biofeedback and relaxation training attempt to teach people how to control their physiological responses by learning to recognize tension and reduce it through deep muscle relaxation and concentration.

11. Exercise can help people cope with stress over the long term.

12. Cognitive behavior therapy attempts to help people recognize and modify their cognitive and behavioral responses to stress.

13. Type A behavior can be changed through behavioral and cognitive techniques, resulting in reduced risk of coronary heart disease.

CORE CONCEPTS

stress
stressor
stress response
behavioral medicine
traumatic event
controllability
predictability
internal conflicts
anxiety
post-traumatic stress disorder

learned helplessness
fight-or-flight response
general adaptation syndrome
psychophysiological disorders
coronary heart disease
psychoneuroimmunology
objective anxiety
neurotic anxiety
attributional style
hardiness

type A pattern
coping
problem-focused coping
emotion-focused coping
biofeedback
relaxation training
meditation
cognitive behavior therapy

 WEB RESOURCES

http://psychology.wadsworth.com/
atkinson14e

Take a quiz, try the activities and exercises, and explore web links.

http://wellness.uwsp.edu/Health_Service/Services/
stress.htm

How stressed are you? Answer the questions on this site and find out.

http://www.coolware.com/health/medical_
reporter/stress.html

Learn more about stress, health, and how to cope with the stress in your life.

http://sdoublet.freeyellow.com/problem.htm

This site provides an extensive discussion of the history of stress research.

 InfoTrac Online Library

http://www.infotrac-college.com/
wadsworth

Use InfoTrac College Edition to find popular and scientific articles by using the search terms below or your own relevant terms.

- Type A behavior
- Biofeedback
- Health psychology
- Meditation
- Posttraumatic stress disorder

CD-ROM LINKS

 Psych Odyssey

Check out CD Chapter 18, Health Psychology
A. Stress and Coping

 Psyk.trek 2.0

Check out CD Unit 11, Abnormal Behavior and Therapy
10f Types of Stress
10g Responding to Stress

PSYCHOLOGICAL DISORDERS

15

Mike was a 32-year-old father who had many concerns. When driving, he felt compelled to stop the car often to check whether he had run over people, although there was no reason to think he had. Before flushing the toilet, Mike inspected the toilet to be sure that a live insect had not fallen into it—he did not want to be responsible for killing any live creature. In addition, he repeatedly checked the doors, stoves, lights, and windows of his house, making sure that all were shut or turned off so that no harm, such as fire or burglary, would befall his family as the result of his "irresponsible" behavior. In particular, he worried about the safety of his 15-month-old daughter, repeatedly checking the gate to the basement to be sure

that it was locked. He did not carry his daughter while walking on concrete floors, in order to avoid killing her by accidentally dropping her. Mike performed these and many other checks for an average of 4 hours a day. (Adapted from Foa & Steketee, 1989, p. 189)

Most of us have concerns, but Mike's concerns seem extreme. Some people might say they are so extreme as to be abnormal, even crazy. In this chapter, we explore the concept of abnormality. We will see that sometimes the line between normal and abnormal is clear, but most of the time it is fuzzy. We will investigate in detail several specific types of abnormality and theories of

why some people develop psychological disorders and others do not.

A word of warning may be appropriate before we proceed. It is common for students studying abnormal psychology for the first time to diagnose mental disorders in themselves, just as medical students diagnose themselves as suffering from every new disease they read about. Most of us have had some of the symptoms we will be describing, and that is not cause for alarm. However, if you have been bothered by distressing feelings for a long time, it never hurts to talk to someone about them—perhaps someone in your school's counseling service or student health service.

DEFINING ABNORMALITY

What do we mean by "abnormal" behavior? By what criteria do we distinguish it from "normal" behavior? In this age of rapid technological advances, you might think that there would be some objective test—a blood test or brain scan—that could determine whether an individual has a mental disorder. There is no such test currently, however. Instead, we must rely on signs and symptoms, and on subjective criteria for deciding when those symptoms constitute abnormality. A number of different types of criteria for defining abnormality have been proposed.

DEVIATION FROM CULTURAL NORMS

Every culture has certain standards, or norms, for acceptable behavior, and behavior that deviates markedly from those norms is considered abnormal. Proponents of a **cultural relativist perspective** argue that we should respect each culture's definitions of abnormality for the members of that culture. By doing so, we do not impose one culture's standards for behavior on another. Opponents of this position point to a number of dangers, however (Szasz, 1971). Throughout history, societies have labeled individuals as abnormal to justify controlling or silencing them, as Hitler branded the Jews abnormal to justify the Holocaust. Another problem is that the concept of abnormality changes over time within the same society. Forty years ago, most Americans would have considered men wearing earrings abnormal. Today, such behaviors tend to be viewed as differences in

lifestyle rather than as signs of abnormality. Thus, ideas of normality and abnormality differ from one society to another and over time within the same society.

DEVIATION FROM STATISTICAL NORMS

The word **abnormal** means away from the norm. Many characteristics, such as height, weight, and intelligence, cover a range of values when measured over an entire population. Most people, for example, fall within the middle range of height, and a few are abnormally tall or abnormally short. One definition of abnormality therefore is based on deviation from statistical norms: Abnormal behavior is statistically infrequent or deviant from the norm. But according to this definition, a person who is extremely intelligent or extremely happy would be classified as abnormal. Thus, in defining abnormal behavior, we must consider more than statistical frequency.

MALADAPTIVENESS OF BEHAVIOR

Rather than defining abnormal behavior in terms of deviance from either statistical or societal norms, many social scientists believe that the most important criterion is how the behavior affects the well-being of the individual or the social group. According to this criterion, behavior is abnormal if it is **maladaptive**—that is, if it has adverse effects on the individual or on society. Some kinds of deviant behavior interfere with the welfare of the individual (a man who is so fearful of crowds that he cannot ride the bus to work, alcoholics who drink so heavily that they cannot hold a job, a woman who attempts suicide). Other forms of deviant behavior are harmful to society (an adolescent who has violent aggressive outbursts, a paranoid individual who plots to assassinate national leaders). If we use the criterion of maladaptiveness, all of these behaviors would be considered abnormal.

PERSONAL DISTRESS

A fourth criterion considers abnormality in terms of the individual's subjective feelings of **distress**—their feelings of anxiety, depression, or agitation, or experiences such as insomnia, loss of appetite, or numerous aches and pains. Most people who are diagnosed with a mental disorder feel acutely miserable. Sometimes personal distress may be the only symptom of abnormality, and the individual's behavior may appear normal to the casual observer.

Fashions change over time—just as definitions of abnormality do.

None of these definitions provides a completely satisfactory description of abnormal behavior. In most instances, all four criteria—social deviation, statistical frequency, maladaptive behavior, and personal distress—are considered in diagnosing abnormality.

WHAT IS NORMALITY?

Normality is even more difficult to define than abnormality, but most psychologists would agree that the characteristics in the following list indicate emotional well-being. (Note that these characteristics do not make sharp distinctions between the mentally healthy and the mentally ill. Rather, they represent traits that a normal person possesses to a greater degree than an individual who is diagnosed as abnormal.)

1. **Appropriate perception of reality.** Normal individuals are fairly realistic in appraising their reactions and capabilities and in interpreting what is going on in the world around them. They do not consistently misperceive what others say and do, and they do not consistently overrate their abilities and tackle more than they can accomplish, nor do they underestimate their abilities and shy away from difficult tasks.
2. **Ability to exercise voluntary control over behavior.** Normal individuals feel fairly confident about their ability to control their behavior. Occasionally they may act impulsively, but they are able to restrain their sexual and aggressive urges when necessary. They may fail to conform to social norms, but in such instances their decisions are voluntary rather than the result of uncontrollable impulses.
3. **Self-esteem and acceptance.** Well-adjusted people have some appreciation of their own worth and feel accepted by those around them. They are comfortable with other people and are able to react spontaneously in social situations. At the same time, they do not feel obligated to completely subjugate their opinions to those of the group. Feelings of worthlessness, alienation, and lack of acceptance are prevalent among individuals who are diagnosed as abnormal.
4. **Ability to form affectionate relationships.** Normal individuals are able to form close and satisfying relationships with other people. They are sensitive to the feelings of others and do not make excessive demands on others to gratify their own needs. Often, mentally disturbed people are so concerned with protecting their own security that they become extremely self-centered. Preoccupied with their own feelings and strivings, they seek affection but are unable to reciprocate. Sometimes they fear intimacy because their past relationships have been destructive.
5. **Productivity.** Well-adjusted people are able to channel their abilities into productive activity. They are

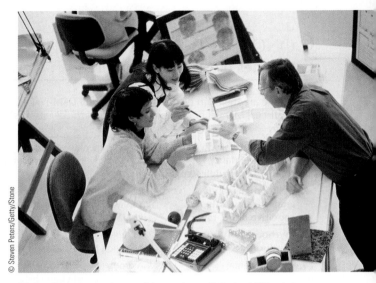

Well-adjusted people are able to channel their abilities into productive activity.

enthusiastic about life and do not need to drive themselves to meet the demands of the day. Chronic lack of energy and excessive susceptibility to fatigue are often symptoms of psychological tension resulting from unsolved problems.

CLASSIFYING ABNORMAL BEHAVIORS

A broad range of behaviors have been classified as abnormal. Some abnormal behaviors are acute and transitory, resulting from particularly stressful events, whereas others are chronic and lifelong. Each person's behavior and emotional problems are unique, and no two individuals behave in exactly the same manner or share the same life experiences. However, enough similarities exist for mental health professionals to classify cases into categories.

A good classification system has many advantages. If the various types of abnormal behavior have different causes, we can hope to uncover them by grouping individuals according to similarities in behavior and then looking for other ways in which they may be similar. A diagnostic label also enables those who work with disturbed individuals to communicate information more quickly and concisely. The diagnosis of schizophrenia indicates quite a bit about a person's behavior. Knowing that an individual's symptoms are similar to those of other patients is also helpful in deciding how to treat the patient. Disadvantages arise, however, if we allow a diagnostic label to carry too much weight. Labeling induces us to overlook the unique features of each case and expect the person to conform to the classification. We may also forget that a label for maladaptive behavior is not an explanation of that behavior.

CONCEPT REVIEW TABLE
Categories of Mental Disorders

Listed here are the main diagnostic categories of DSM-IV. Each category includes numerous subclassifications. *(From* Diagnostic and Statistical Manual of Mental Disorders, *Fourth Edition, Washington, DC: American Psychiatric Association, 1994.)*

1. Disorders usually first evident in infancy, childhood, or adolescence	Includes mental retardation, autism, attention deficit disorder with hyperactivity, separation anxiety, speech disorders, and other deviations from normal development.
2. Delirium, dementia, amnestic, and other cognitive diorders	Disorders in which the functioning of the brain is known to be impaired, either permanently or transiently; may be the result of aging, degenerative diseases of the nervous system (for example, syphilis or Alzheimer's disease), or the ingestion of toxic substances (for example, lead poisoning or drugs).
3. Psychoactive substance use disorders	Includes excessive use of alcohol, barbiturates, amphetamines, cocaine, and other drugs that alter behavior. Marijuana and tobacco are also included in this category, which is controversial.
4. Schizophrenia	A group of disorders characterized by loss of contact with reality, marked disturbances of thought and perception, and bizarre behavior. At some phase, delusions or hallucinations almost always occur.
5. Mood disorders	Disturbances of normal mood; the person may be extremely depressed, abnormally elated, or may alternate between periods of elation and depression.
6. Anxiety disorders	Includes disorders in which anxiety is the main symptom (generalized anxiety or panic disorders) or anxiety is experienced unless the individual avoids feared situations (phobic disorders) or tries to resist performing certain rituals or thinking persistent thoughts (obsessive-compulsive disorders). Also includes post-traumatic stress disorder.
7. Somatoform disorders	The symptoms are physical, but no organic basis can be found and psychological factors appear to play the major role. Included are conversion disorders (for example, a woman who resents having to care for her invalid mother suddenly develops a paralyzed arm) and hypochondriasis (excessive preoccupation with health and fear of disease when there is no basis for concern.) Does *not* include psychosomatic disorders that have an organic basis. (See Chapter 14)
8. Dissociative disorders	Temporary alterations in the functions of consciousness, memory, or identity due to emotional problems. Included are amnesia (the individual cannot recall anything about his or her history following a traumatic experience) and dissociative identity disorder (better known as multiple personality disorder, involving two or more independent personality systems existing within the same individual).
9. Sexual Disorders	Includes problems of sexual identity (for example, transsexualism), sexual performance (for example, impotence, premature ejaculation, and frigidity), and sexual aim (for example, sexual interest in children, sadism, and masochism).
10. Eating disorders	Self-induced starvation (anorexia) or patterns of binge eating followed by self-induced purging (bulimia).
11. Sleep disorders	Includes chronic insomnia, excessive sleepiness, sleep apnea, sleepwalking, and narcolepsy.
12. Factitious disorders	Physical or psychological symptoms that are intentionally produced or feigned. Differs from malingering in that there is no obvious goal, such as disability payments or the avoidance of military service. The best-studied form of this disorder is called Münchausen syndrome: The individual's plausible presentation of factitious physical symptoms results in frequent hospitalizations.
13. Impulse control disorder	Includes kleptomania (compulsive stealing of objects not needed for personal use or their monetary value), pathological gambling, and pyromania (setting fires for the pleasure or relief of tension derived thereby).
14. Personality disorders	Long-standing patterns of maladaptive behavior that constitute immature and inappropriate ways of coping with stress or solving problems. Antisocial personality disorder and narcissistic personality disorder are two examples.
15. Other conditions that may be the focus of clinical attention	This category includes many of the problems for which people seek help, such as marital problems, parent-child difficulties, and academic or occupational problems.

The classification does not tell us how the behavior originated or what causes it to continue.

The classification of mental disorders used by most mental health professionals in the United States is the *Diagnostic and Statistical Manual of Mental Disorders, 4th edition* (DSM-IV for short), which corresponds generally to the international system formulated by the World Health Organization. The major categories of mental disorders classified by DSM-IV are listed in the Concept Review Table. DSM-IV provides an extensive list of subcategories under each of these headings, as well as a description of the symptoms that must be present for the diagnosis to be applicable.

You have probably heard the terms *neurosis* and *psychosis* and may be wondering where they fit into the categories of mental disorders listed in the Concept Review Table. Traditionally, these terms denoted major diagnostic categories. **Neuroses** (the plural of *neurosis*) included a group of disorders characterized by anxiety, unhappiness, and maladaptive behavior that were seldom serious enough to require hospitalization. The individual could usually function in society, though not at full capacity. **Psychoses** (the plural of *psychosis*) included more serious mental disorders. The individual's behavior and thought processes were so disturbed that he or she was out of touch with reality, could not cope with the demands of daily life, and usually had to be hospitalized.

Neither neuroses nor psychoses appear as major categories in DSM-IV. There are several reasons for this departure from earlier classification systems, but the main one concerns precision of diagnosis. Both categories were fairly broad and included a number of mental disorders with quite dissimilar symptoms. Consequently, mental health professionals did not always agree on the diagnosis for a particular case. DSM-IV attempts to achieve greater consensus by grouping disorders according to very specific behavioral symptoms without implying anything about their origins or treatment. The intention is to describe observations of individuals who have psychological problems in a way that ensures accurate communication among mental health professionals. Consequently, DSM-IV includes many more categories than previous editions of the manual.

Although psychosis is no longer a major category, DSM-IV recognizes that people who are diagnosed as having schizophrenia, delusional disorders, and some mood disorders exhibit psychotic behavior at some point during their illness. Their thinking and perception of reality are severely disturbed, and they may have hallucinations (false sensory experiences, such as hearing voices or seeing strange visions) and/or delusions (false beliefs, such as the conviction that all thoughts are controlled by a powerful being from another planet). These issues will become clearer as we look more closely at some of the mental disorders listed in the Concept Review Table. We will examine anxiety disorders, mood disorders, schizophrenia, and two types of personality disorder. Alcoholism and drug dependence (both classified as psychoactive substance use disorders) are covered in Chapter 6.

Table 15-1 indicates the likelihood of the major mental disorders during one's lifetime. The study on which this table is based found that mental disorders are more common among people under age 45. Although the overall rates of disorders are not different in men and women, there are sex differences in the incidence of specific disorders. For example, men are twice as likely as women to abuse alcohol or other drugs. Antisocial personality disorders affect three times as many men as women, but more women suffer from mood and anxiety disorders.

Many cultures recognize mental disorders that do not correspond to any disorders listed in the DSM-IV (see Table 15-2). Some of these disorders may have the same underlying causes as certain disorders recognized by the DSM-IV but are manifested by different symptoms in other cultures. Other disorders may be truly unique to the cultures in which they are found. The presence of such culture-bound syndromes suggests that the disorders listed in DSM-IV represent only the disorders that occur in mainstream American culture rather than a universal list of disorders to which all humans are susceptible. This supports the views of those who argue that we cannot define abnormality without reference to the norms of a particular culture.

● Table 15-1
Lifetime Prevalence Rates of Selected Disorders

Listed here are the percentage of individuals in the U.S. population who have experienced one of these mental disorders during their lifetime. These percentages are based on interviews with a sample of 8,098 individuals, age 18 to 54, all around U.S. cities. (*From R. C. Kessler, K. A. McGonagle, S. Zhao, and C. B. Nelson (1994), "Lifetime and 12-month prevalence of DSM-III-R psychiatric disorders in the United States: Results from the National Comorbidity Study," Archives of General Psychiatry, 51(1):8–19. Copyright © 1994 by the American Medical Association.*)

Disorder	Rate
Anxiety disorders	24.9
Mood disorders	19.3
Schizophrenia and related disorders	0.7
Antisocial personality	3.5
Substance use disorder	26.6

Table 15-2
Culture-Bound Syndromes

Some cultures have syndromes or mental disorders that are found only in that culture and that do not correspond to any DSM-IV categories. (*Based on APA, 2000*)

Syndrome	Cultures Where Found	Symptoms
amok	Malaysia, Laos, Philippines, Papua New Guinea, Puerto Rico, Navajos	Brooding, followed by violent behavior, persecutory ideas, amnesia, exhaustion. More often seen in men than in women.
ataque de nervios	Latin America	Uncontrollable shouting, crying, trembling, heat in the chest rising to the head, verbal or physical aggression, seizures, fainting.
ghost sickness	American Indians	Nightmares, weakness, feelings of danger, loss of appetite, fainting, dizziness, hallucinations, loss of consciousness, sense of suffocation.
koro	Malaysia, China, Thailand	Sudden and intense anxiety that the penis (in males) or the vulva and nipples (in females) will recede into body and cause death.
latah	East Asia	Hypersensitivity to sudden fright, trance-like behavior. Most often seen in middle-aged women.
susto	Mexico, Central America	Appetite disturbances, sleep disturbances, sadness, loss of motivation, feelings of low self-worth following a frightening event. Sufferers believe that their soul has left their body.
taijin kyofusho	Japan	Intense fear that one's body displeases, embarrasses, or is offensive to others.

PERSPECTIVES ON MENTAL DISORDERS

Attempts to understand the causes of mental disorders generally fall under one of the three broad perspectives we have discussed throughout this book. The **biological perspective,** also called the *medical* or *disease model,* suggests that mental disorders are brain disorders. Researchers using this approach look for genetic irregularities that may predispose a person to develop a particular mental disorder by affecting the functioning of the brain. They also look for abnormalities in specific parts of the brain and dysfunction in neurochemical systems in the brain and other parts of the body. Proponents of this perspective generally favor the use of drugs to treat disorders.

There are a number of specific **psychological perspectives** that see mental disorders as problems in the functioning of the mind. The **psychoanalytic perspective** emphasizes unconscious conflicts, usually originating in early childhood, and the use of defense mechanisms to handle the anxiety generated by the repressed impulses and emotions. Bringing the unconscious conflicts and emotions into awareness presumably eliminates the need for the defense mechanisms and alleviates the disorder.

The **behavioral perspective** investigates how fears become conditioned to specific situations and the role of reinforcement in the origin and maintenance of inappropriate behaviors. This approach looks at mental disorders from the standpoint of learning theory and assumes that maladaptive behaviors are learned.

The **cognitive perspective** suggests that some mental disorders stem from disordered cognitive processes and

can be alleviated by changing these faulty cognitions. Rather than stressing hidden motivations, emotions, and conflicts, however, it emphasizes conscious mental processes. The way we think about ourselves, the way we appraise stressful situations, and our strategies for coping with them are all interrelated.

Cultural or **sociological perspectives** take the view that mental disorders are not situated in the brain or mind of the individual but in the social context in which the individual lives. Proponents of this perspective look to stresses in the physical and social environment, such as discrimination and poverty, that can interfere with people's functioning. They also pay attention to how culture shapes the types of mental disorders people are most susceptible to and how they manifest their distress.

The ideas embodied in these brief summaries will become clearer as we discuss them in relation to specific mental disorders. Each of these approaches has something important to say about mental disorders, but none has the complete answer. One way of integrating these factors is the **vulnerability-stress model,** which considers the interaction between a predisposition, which makes a person vulnerable for developing a particular disorder, and stressful environmental conditions encountered by that person. At the biological level, vulnerability might stem from genetic factors. This is evident in disorders in which having a close relative with the disorder increases a person's risk of developing it. At the psychological level, a chronic feeling of hopelessness and inadequacy might make an individual vulnerable to depression. Having a predisposition for a particular disorder does not guarantee that the person will develop the disorder. Whether the predisposition leads to an actual disorder often depends on the kinds of stressors, including poverty, malnutrition, frustration, conflicts, and traumatic life events, the individual encounters.

The key point of the vulnerability-stress model is that both vulnerability and stress are necessary. It helps explain why some people develop serious psychological problems when confronted with a minimum of stress while others remain healthy regardless of how difficult their lives may become.

◆ Interim Summary

- The diagnosis of abnormal behavior is based on social norms, statistical frequency, adaptiveness of behavior, and personal distress.

- Characteristics of good mental health include efficient perception of reality, control of behavior, self-esteem, ability to form affectionate relationships, and productivity.

- DSM-IV classifies mental disorders according to specific behavioral symptoms. Such a classification system helps communicate information and provides a basis for research. However, each case is unique, and diagnostic labels should not be used to pigeonhole individuals.

- Theories about the causes of mental disorders and proposals for treating them can be grouped according to those that focus on the brain and other biological factors; those that focus on the mind, including psychoanalytic, behavioral, and cognitive perspectives; and those that focus on sociocultural and environmental factors.

- The vulnerability-stress model emphasizes the interaction between a predisposition (biological and/or psychological) that makes a person vulnerable to a particular disorder and stressful environmental conditions encountered by the individual.

◆ Critical Thinking Questions

1. Studying any mental disorder from one theoretical perspective holds the danger that the investigator will be biased to look for particular causes of the disorder and to ignore other causes. But is it possible to study a mental disorder from a totally atheoretical perspective—that is, to approach the disorder with no presumptions about its likely causes? Why or why not?

2. People who are diagnosed with a mental disorder often say it is a relief to have a label for their distress. Why might this be true?

ANXIETY DISORDERS

Most of us feel anxious and tense in the face of threatening or stressful situations. Such feelings are normal reactions to stress. Anxiety is considered abnormal only when it occurs in situations that most people can handle with little difficulty. **Anxiety disorders** include a group of disorders in which anxiety either is the main symptom (generalized anxiety and panic disorders) or is experienced when the individual attempts to control certain maladaptive behaviors (phobic and obsessive-compulsive disorders). (Post-traumatic stress disorder, which involves anxiety following a traumatic event, was discussed in Chapter 14.) The following passage describes a person suffering from an anxiety disorder:

> Hazel was walking down a street near her home one day when she suddenly felt flooded with intense and frightening physical symptoms. Her whole body tightened up, she began sweating and her heart was racing, and she felt dizzy and disoriented. She thought, "I must be having a heart attack! I can't stand this! Something terrible is happening! I'm going to die." Hazel just stood frozen in the middle of the street until an onlooker stopped to help her.

There are four types of symptoms of anxiety, and Hazel was experiencing symptoms of each type. First, she had physiological or somatic symptoms: Her heart was racing, she was perspiring, and her muscles tensed. You may recognize these symptoms as part of the fight-or-flight response discussed in Chapter 14. This is the body's natural reaction to a challenging situation—the physiological changes of the fight-or-flight response prepare the body to fight a threat or to flee from it.

Second, Hazel had cognitive symptoms of anxiety: She was sure she was having a heart attack and dying. Third, Hazel had a behavioral symptom of anxiety: She froze, unable to move until help arrived. Fourth, she had the sense of dread and terror that make up the emotional symptoms of anxiety.

All of these symptoms can be highly adaptive when we are facing a real threat, such as a saber-toothed tiger in prehistoric times or a burglar today. They become maladaptive when there is no real threat to fight against or flee from. Hazel's symptoms were not triggered by a dangerous situation but came "out of the blue." Even when these symptoms do arise in response to some perceived threat, they can be maladaptive when they are out of proportion to the threat or persist after the threat has passed. Many people with anxiety disorders seem to view situations as highly threatening that most of us would consider benign, and they worry about those situations even when they are highly unlikely to occur. For example, people with social phobias are terrified of the possibility that they might embarrass themselves in public, and they therefore go to great lengths to avoid social situations.

● Table 15-3
Generalized Anxiety

The statements listed in this table are self-descriptions by individuals who have chronically high levels of anxiety. (*From Abnormal Psychology"* The Problem of Maladaptive Behavior, 7/e, by I. G. Sarason & B. R. Sarason. Copyright © 1993 by I. G. Sarason and B. R. Sarason. Adapted by permission of Prentice-Hall, Upper Saddle River, NJ.)

I am often bothered by the thumping of my heart.

Little annoyances get on my nerves and irritate me.

I often become suddenly scared for no good reason.

I worry continuously, and that gets me down.

I frequently get spells of complete exhaustion and fatigue.

It is always hard for me to make up my mind.

I always seem to be dreading something.

I feel nervous and high-strung all the time.

I often feel I cannot overcome my difficulties.

I feel constantly under strain.

In one form of anxiety disorder, **generalized anxiety disorder,** the person experiences a constant sense of tension and dread. Inability to relax, disturbed sleep, fatigue, headaches, dizziness, and rapid heart rate are the most common physical complaints. In addition, the individual continually worries about potential problems and has difficulty concentrating or making decisions. When the individual finally makes a decision, it becomes a source of further worry ("Did I foresee all the possible consequences?"). Some self-descriptions provided by people with chronically high levels of anxiety appear in Table 15-3. Other anxiety disorders, such as panic disorder, phobias, and obsessive-compulsive disorder, are characterized by more focused anxiety and are discussed in more detail in the rest of this section.

PANIC DISORDERS

Hazel's symptoms suggest that she experienced a **panic attack**—an episode of acute and overwhelming apprehension or terror. During panic attacks, the individual feels certain that something dreadful is about to happen. This feeling is usually accompanied by such symptoms as heart palpitations, shortness of breath, perspiration, muscle tremors, faintness, and nausea. The symptoms result from excitation of the sympathetic division of the autonomic nervous system (see Chapter 2) and are the same reactions that an individual experiences when extremely frightened. During severe panic attacks, the person fears that he or she will die.

As many as 40% of young adults have occasional panic attacks, especially during times of stress (King, Gullone, Tonge, & Ollendick, 1993). For most of these people, the panic attacks are annoying but isolated events that do not change how they live their lives. When panic attacks become a common occurrence and the individual begins to worry about having attacks, he or she may receive a diagnosis of **panic disorder.** Panic disorder is relatively rare: Only about 1.5% to 3.5% of the population will ever develop a panic disorder (American Psychiatric Association, 2000). Usually panic disorder appears sometime between late adolescence and the mid-30s. Without treatment, panic disorder tends to become chronic (Weiss & Last, 2001).

Panic-like symptoms may take a different form across cultures. People from Latino cultures, particularly in the Caribbean, sometimes experience a sudden rush of anxiety symptoms known as *ataque de nervios.* The symptoms of *ataque* include trembling, feelings of out of control, sudden crying, screaming uncontrollably, verbal and physical aggression, and sometimes seizure-like or fainting episodes and suicidal gestures (Lopez & Guarnaccia, 2000). When *ataque de nervios* comes out of the blue, it is often attributed to the stresses of daily living or to spiritual causes. A study of Puerto Ricans after the 1985 floods found that 16% of the victims reported experiencing an *ataque* (Guarnaccia Canino, Rubio-Stipec, & Bravo, 1993).

People with panic disorder may believe that they have a life-threatening illness, such as heart disease or susceptibility to stroke, even after such illnesses have been ruled out by medical examinations. They may go from one physician to another, searching for the one who can diagnose their ailments. They may also believe that they are "going crazy" or "losing control." If their symptoms go untreated, they may become depressed and demoralized.

About a third to half of people with panic disorder also develop agoraphobia (American Psychiatric Association, 2000). People with **agoraphobia** fear any place where they might be trapped or unable to receive help in an emergency. The emergency they most often fear is having a panic attack. The term *agoraphobia* comes from the ancient Greek words meaning "fear of the marketplace." People with agoraphobia fear being in a busy, crowded place such as a mall. They may also fear being in tightly enclosed spaces from which it can be difficult to escape, such as a bus, elevator, or subway, or being alone in wide-open spaces such as a meadow or a deserted beach. All of these places are frightening for people with agoraphobia because if a panic attack or some other emergency occurred, it would be very difficult for them to escape or get help. They may also fear that they will embarrass themselves when others see that they are having a panic attack, even though other people usually cannot tell when a person is having a panic attack.

People with agoraphobia avoid all the places they fear. They significantly curtail their activities, remaining in a few "safe" places, such as the area within a few blocks of home. Sometimes they can venture into "unsafe" places if a trusted family member or friend accompanies them. If they attempt to enter "unsafe" places on their own, however, they may experience a great deal of general anxiety beforehand and have a full panic attack when in the unsafe place. Hazel, whom we met earlier in the chapter, provides an example:

> Hazel continued to have panic attacks every few days, sometimes on the same street where she had the first panic attack, but increasingly in places where she'd never had a panic attack before. It seemed she was especially likely to have a panic attack if there were lots of people standing around her, and she became confused about how she would get out of the crowd if she began to panic. The only place Hazel had not had any panic attacks was in her apartment. She began to spend more and more time in her apartment and refused to go anyplace she had previously had a panic attack. After a few months, she had called in sick to work so often that she was fired. Yet, Hazel could not bring herself to leave her apartment at all. She had her groceries delivered to her so she wouldn't have to go out to get them. She would see friends only if they would come to her apartment. Hazel's savings were becoming depleted, however, because she had lost her job. Hazel began looking for a job that she could do from her apartment.

Although people can develop agoraphobia without panic attacks, the vast majority of people with agoraphobia do have panic attacks or panic-like symptoms in social situations (Craske & Barlow, 2001). Agoraphobia usually develops within a year of the onset of recurrent panic attacks. Obviously, the symptoms of agoraphobia can severely interfere with the ability to function in daily life. People with agoraphobia often turn to alcohol and other drugs to cope with their symptoms. Fortunately, we have learned a great deal about the causes of panic and agoraphobia in recent years.

UNDERSTANDING PANIC DISORDER AND AGORAPHOBIA

Many people who develop panic disorder probably have a genetic or other biological vulnerability to the disorder. Panic disorder runs in families (Foley et al., 2001; van den Heuvel, van de Wetering, Veltman, & Pauls, 2000). This does not mean, of course, that panic disorders are entirely hereditary, in that family members live in the same environment. However, the results of twin studies provide firmer evidence for an inherited predisposition for panic disorder. Recall that identical twins share the same heredity; thus, if a disorder is transmitted entirely genetically, when one identical twin suffers from the disorder, the other twin should be highly likely to suffer from the disorder. In contrast, fraternal twins are no more alike genetically than ordinary siblings, so that when one twin suffers from the disorder, the other twin should not be at greatly increased risk for the disorder.

Twin studies have shown than an identical twin is twice as likely to suffer panic disorder if the other twin does than is true for fraternal twins (Kendler, Neale, Kessler, & Heath, 1992, 1993; van den Heuvel et al., 2000).

One characteristic that may be inherited in people who are prone to panic attacks is an overreactive fight-or-flight response (McNally, 2001). A full panic attack can be induced easily by having such individuals engage in activities that stimulate the initial physiological changes of the fight-or-flight response. For example, when people with panic disorder purposely hyperventilate, breathe into a paper bag, or inhale a small amount of carbon dioxide, they experience an increase in subjective anxiety, and many will experience a full panic attack (see Figure 15-1; Bourin, Baker, & Bradwejn, 1998; Craske & Barlow, 2001). In contrast, people without a history of panic attacks may experience some physical discomfort while performing these activities, but they rarely experience a full panic attack.

a) After hyperventilating

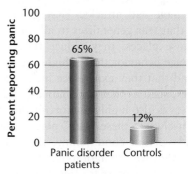

b) After inhaling carbon dioxide

▌ Figure 15-1
Panic Attacks of Patients and Controls
People with panic disorder are much more likely than people without panic disorder to have a panic attack when made to hyperventilate or inhale small amounts of carbon dioxide in laboratory experiments. (Adapted from R. M. Rapee, T. A. Brown, M. M. Anthony, & D. H. Barlow (1992), "Response to hyperventilation and inhalation of 5.5% carbon-dioxide-enriched air across the DSM-III-R anxiety disorders," *Journal of Abnormal Psychology,* 101, 538–552. Copyright © 1992 by the American Psychological Association. Adapted with permission.)

This overreactive fight-or-flight response may be the result of deficiencies in areas of the brain that regulate this response, especially the limbic system (Deakin & Graeff, 1991; Gray, 1982; Reiman, Lane, Ahern, Schwartz, & Davidson, 2000). Some studies show that people with panic disorder have low levels of the neurotransmitter serotonin in the limbic system and other brain circuits involved in the fight-or-flight response (Bell & Nutt, 1998). Serotonin deficiencies cause chronic hyperactivation of these areas of the brain, putting the individual on the verge of a panic attack most of the time.

An overreactive fight-or-flight response may not be enough to create a full panic disorder, however. Cognitive-behavioral theories of panic and agoraphobia suggest that people who are prone to panic attacks tend to pay very close attention to their bodily sensations, misinterpret bodily sensations in a negative way, and engage in catastrophic thinking (Bouton, Mineka, & Barlow, 2001; Clark, 1988; Craske & Barlow, 2001). In the case described earlier, when Hazel felt her muscles tightening, she began thinking, "I'm having a heart attack! I'm going to die!" Not surprisingly, these thoughts increased her emotional symptoms of anxiety, which in turn made her physiological symptoms worse—her heart rate increased even more, and her muscles felt even tighter. Interpreting these physiological changes catastrophically led to a full panic attack. Between attacks, Hazel is hypervigilant, paying close attention to any bodily sensation. Her constant vigilance causes her autonomic nervous system to be chronically aroused, making it more likely that she will have another panic attack.

How does agoraphobia develop out of panic disorder? According to the cognitive-behavioral theory, people with panic disorder remember vividly the places where they have had attacks. They greatly fear those places, and that fear generalizes to all similar places. By avoiding those places, they reduce their anxiety, and their avoidance behavior thus is highly reinforced. They may also find that they experience little anxiety in particular places, such as their own homes, and this reduction of anxiety is also highly reinforcing, leading them to confine themselves to these "safe" places. Thus, through classical and operant conditioning, their behaviors are shaped into what we call agoraphobia.

What evidence is there for this theory? Several laboratory studies support the contentions that cognitive factors play a strong role in panic attacks and that agoraphobic behaviors may be conditioned through learning experiences (McNally, 2001). In one study, researchers asked two groups of patients with panic disorder to wear masks through which they would inhale slight amounts of carbon dioxide. Both groups were told that, although inhaling a slight amount of carbon dioxide was not dangerous to their health, it could induce a panic attack.

One group was told that they could not control the amount of carbon dioxide that came through their masks. The other group was told that they could control how much carbon dioxide they inhaled by turning a knob. Actually, neither group had any control over the amount of carbon dioxide they inhaled, and both groups inhaled the same small amount. Eighty percent of the patients who believed that they had no control experienced a panic attack, but only 20% of those who believed that they could control the carbon dioxide had an attack. These results clearly suggest that beliefs about control over panic symptoms play a strong role in panic attacks (Sanderson, Rapee, & Barlow, 1989).

In a study focusing on agoraphobic behaviors, researchers examined whether people with panic disorder could avoid having a panic attack, even after inhaling carbon dioxide, by having a "safe person" nearby. Panic patients who were exposed to carbon dioxide with their safe person present were much less likely to experience the emotional, cognitive, and physiological symptoms of panic than panic patients who were exposed to carbon dioxide without their safe person present (see Figure 15-2; Carter, Hollon, Caron, & Shelton, 1995). These results show that the symptoms of panic become associated with certain situations and that operant behaviors such as sticking close to a "safe person" can be reinforced by the reduction of panic symptoms.

The biological and cognitive-behavioral theories of panic disorder and agoraphobia thus can be integrated

I Figure 15-2
Panic Symptoms in Panic Patients With and Without a Safe Person Available
Panic patients were much more likely to show symptoms of panic when a safe person was not with them. (After Carter, Hollon, Caron, & Shelton, 1995)

Biological predisposition to overreactive
fight-or-flight response

+

Cognitive predisposition to catastrophizing cognitions

Excessive fight-or-flight response easily triggered

Frequent panic attacks

Person avoids places associated with panic

Avoidance reinforced by reduction of anxiety

Agoraphobia develops

▌ **Figure 15-3**
A Vulnerability-Stress Model of Panic and Agoraphobia
A combination of biological vulnerability to an overreactive
fight-or-flight response plus cognitive vulnerability to catastrophizing cognitions may begin a chain of processes leading to
panic and agoraphobia.

into a vulnerability-stress model (Craske & Barlow,
2001; see Figure 15-3). People who develop panic disorder may have a genetic or biochemical vulnerability to
an overreactive fight-or-flight response, so that even
with only a slight triggering stimulus, their bodies experience all the physiological symptoms of the response.
For a full panic disorder to develop, however, it may be
necessary for these individuals to also be prone to catastrophizing these symptoms and worrying excessively
about having panic attacks. These cognitions further
heighten their physiological reactivity, making it even
more likely that they will experience a full fight-or-flight
response. Agoraphobia develops when they begin to
avoid places that they associate with their panic symptoms and confine themselves to places where they experience less anxiety. This vulnerability-stress model has
led to exciting breakthroughs in the treatment of panic
disorder and agoraphobia, which we will discuss in
Chapter 16.

PHOBIAS

A **phobia** is an intense fear of a stimulus or situation that
most people do not consider particularly dangerous. The
individual usually realizes that this fear is irrational but
still feels anxiety (ranging from strong uneasiness to
panic) that can be alleviated only by avoiding the feared
object or situation.

Many of us have one or two irrational fears—of
snakes, insects, and heights, for example. However, a
fear is usually not diagnosed as a phobic disorder unless
it interferes considerably with the person's daily life. Examples might include a woman whose fear of enclosed
places prevents her from entering elevators or a man
whose fear of crowds prevents him from attending the
theater or walking along congested sidewalks.

DSM-IV divides phobic disorders into three broad
categories: simple phobias, social phobias, and agoraphobia. A **simple phobia** is a fear of a specific object, animal, or situation. Irrational fears of snakes, germs, enclosed places, and darkness are examples. Some people
may develop a simple phobia but be normal in other respects. In more serious cases, the individual has a number of phobias that interfere with many aspects of life

One of the most common phobias is a snake phobia.

and may be intertwined with obsessive or compulsive behavior. People with **social phobias** feel extremely insecure in social situations and have an exaggerated fear of embarrassing themselves. Often they are afraid that they will betray their anxiety by such signs as hand tremors, blushing, or a quavering voice. These fears are usually unrealistic: Individuals who fear that they might shake do not do so; those who fear that they will stutter or quaver actually speak quite normally. Fear of public speaking or of eating in public are the most common complaints of socially phobic individuals.

People with social phobias will go to great lengths to avoid situations in which others might evaluate them. They may take jobs that are solitary and isolating to avoid other people. If they find themselves in a feared social situation, they may begin trembling and perspiring, feel confused and dizzy, have heart palpitations, and eventually have a full panic attack. They are sure that others see their nervousness and are judging them as inarticulate, weak, stupid, or "crazy."

Social phobia is quite common, with about 8% of the U.S. adult population qualifying for the diagnosis in a 12-month period and 1 in 8 people experiencing the disorder at some time in their lives (Kessler et al., 1998; Schneider et al., 1992). Social phobia typically begins in adolescence (Blazer, George, & Hughes, 1991) and tends to be a chronic problem if it is not treated (Kessler et al., 1998).

UNDERSTANDING PHOBIAS

Historically, phobias have been the subject of a major clash between psychodynamic theories and behavioral theories. Freud's theory of the development of phobias was one of his most famous and controversial. Freud argued that phobias result when people displace anxiety over unconscious motives or desires onto objects that symbolize those motives or desires. His classic example was the case of Little Hans, a 5-year-old who developed an intense fear of horses. Freud interpreted the boy's phobia in terms of Oedipal fears (see Chapter 13) through the following analysis: Hans was in love with his mother, jealously hated his father, and wanted to replace him (the Oedipal conflict); he feared that his father would retaliate by castrating him; the anxiety produced by this conflict was enormous because the wishes were unacceptable to the child's conscious mind; the anxiety was displaced onto an innocent object (a large horse that Hans had seen fall down and thrash about violently in the street).

Freud's evidence for his explanation of Hans's horse phobia consisted of Hans's answers to a series of rather leading questions about what he was "really" afraid of, along with the fact that Hans appeared to lose his horse phobia after his conversations with Freud. Freud suggested that Hans had gained insight into the true source of his phobia and that this insight had cured the phobia. Critics pointed out, however, that Hans never provided any spontaneous or direct evidence that his real concern was his father rather than the horse. They also noted that Hans's phobia diminished gradually over time rather than abruptly in response to some sudden insight.

Some of the severest critics of Freud's analysis of phobias were behaviorists (Watson & Raynor, 1920). They argued that phobias do not develop from unconscious anxieties but rather from classical and operant conditioning. Many phobias emerge after a traumatic experience—a child nearly drowns and develops a phobia of water, another child is bitten by a dog and develops a phobia of dogs, an adolescent who stumbles through a speech in class is laughed at by peers and develops a phobia of public speaking. In these cases, a previously neutral stimulus (water or dogs or public speaking) is paired with a traumatic event (drowning or biting or embarrassment) that elicits anxiety. Through classical conditioning, the previously neutral stimulus now is able to elicit the anxiety reaction. In addition, many people with such fears avoid the phobic object because avoidance helps reduce their anxiety, and the phobic behavior is maintained through operant conditioning.

Although some phobias appear to result from actual frightening experiences, others may be learned vicariously through observation (Bandura, 1969; Mineka, Davidson, Cook, & Keir, 1984). Fearful parents tend to produce children who share their fears. A child who observes parents react with fear to a variety of situations may develop the same reactions to those situations. Indeed, studies find that phobias clearly run in families (Kessler et al., 1998; Fyer, Mannuzza, Chapman, & Liebowitz, 1993). It is unclear whether this is due largely to children learning phobias from their parents or also partially due to genetic transmission of phobias. The first-degree relatives of people with phobias are three to four times more likely than others to also have a phobia, and twin studies suggest that this is due, at least in part, to genetics (Hettema et al., 2001). What is likely to be inherited is a fearful temperament rather than the phobia per se (Hudson & Rapee, 2000).

Behavioral theories have led to highly successful treatments for phobias, lending further support to these theories. In contrast, treatments based on psychodynamic theories of phobias tend to be unsuccessful, and current drug treatments tend to relieve phobic symptoms only in the short term.

OBSESSIVE-COMPULSIVE DISORDER

A man gets out of bed several times each night and checks all the doors to make sure they are locked. Upon returning to bed, he is tormented by the thought that he may have missed one. Another man takes three or four showers in succession, scrubbing his body thoroughly with a special disinfectant each time, fearful that he may be contaminated by germs. A woman has recurrent thoughts about stabbing her infant and feels panic-stricken whenever she has to handle scissors or knives. A teenage girl is always late to school because she feels compelled to repeat many of her actions (replacing her brush on the dresser, arranging the school supplies in her book bag, crossing the threshold to her bedroom) a set number of times, usually some multiple of the number 4.

All of these people have symptoms of **obsessive-compulsive disorder:** Their lives are dominated by repetitive acts or thoughts. Obsessions **are** persistent intrusions of unwelcome thoughts, images, or impulses that elicit anxiety. Compulsions **are** irresistible urges to carry out certain acts or rituals that reduce anxiety. Obsessive thoughts are often linked with compulsive acts (for example, thoughts of lurking germs, which lead to the compulsion to wash eating utensils many times before using them). Regardless of whether the repetitive element is a thought (obsession) or an act (compulsion), the central feature of the disorder is the subjective experience of loss of control. The victims struggle mightily to rid themselves of the troublesome thoughts or resist performing the repetitive acts but are unable to do so.

At times, all of us have persistently recurring thoughts ("Did I leave the gas on?") and urges to perform ritualistic behavior (arranging items on a desk in a precise order before starting an assignment). But for people with obsessive-compulsive disorders, such thoughts and acts occupy so much time that they seriously interfere with daily life. These individuals recognize their thoughts as irrational and repugnant but are unable to ignore or suppress them. They realize the senselessness of their compulsive behavior but become anxious when they try to resist their compulsions, and feel a release of tension once the acts are carried out.

Obsessive thoughts cover a variety of topics, but most often they are concerned with causing harm to oneself or others, fear of contamination, and doubt that a completed task has been accomplished satisfactorily (Hewlett, 2000; Rachman & Hodgson, 1980). Interestingly, the content of obsessions changes with the times. In earlier days, obsessive thoughts about religion and sex were common—for example, blasphemous thoughts or impulses to shout obscenities in church or expose one's genitals in public. These types of obsessions are less frequent today. And whereas obsessions about contamination used to focus on syphilis, AIDS has now become the object of many contamination fears (Rapaport, 1989).

Some people with an obsessive-compulsive disorder have intrusive thoughts without engaging in repetitious actions. However, the majority of patients with obsessive thoughts also exhibit compulsive behavior (Akhtar, Wig, Varma, Pershard, & Verma, 1975). Compulsions take a variety of forms, of which the two most common are washing and checking (Foa & Steketee, 1989). "Washers" feel contaminated when exposed to certain objects or thoughts and spend hours performing washing and cleaning rituals. "Checkers" check doors, lights, ovens, or the accuracy of a completed task 10, 20, or 100 times or repeat ritualistic acts over and over again. They believe that their actions will prevent future "disasters" or punishments. Sometimes these rituals are related to the anxiety-evoking obsessions in a direct way (for example, repeatedly checking to see if the stove has been turned off to avoid a possible fire); other rituals are not rationally related to the obsessions (for example, dressing and undressing in order to prevent one's spouse from having an accident). The common theme behind all of these repetitive behaviors is doubt. Obsessive-compulsive individuals cannot trust their senses or their judgment; they can't trust their eyes, even though they see no dirt, or really believe that the door is locked.

Obsessive-compulsive disorders are related to phobic disorders in that both involve severe anxiety and both may appear in the same patient. However, there are important differences. Phobic patients seldom ruminate about their fears, nor do they show ritualistic compulsive behavior. And the two disorders are evoked by different stimuli. Dirt, germs, and harm to others—common obsessive-compulsive preoccupations—seldom cause major problems for phobic individuals.

Obsessive-compulsive disorder often begins at a young age (Foa & Franklin, 2001). It tends to be chronic if left untreated. Obsessional thoughts are very distressing, and engaging in compulsive behaviors can take a great deal of time and be highly maladaptive (for example, washing one's hands so often that they bleed). People with this disorder thus are quite psychologically impaired. Between 1% and 3% of people develop obsessive-compulsive disorder at some time in their lives (Hewlett, 2000). The prevalence of OCD does not seem to differ greatly across countries that have been studied, including the United States, Canada, Mexico, England, Norway, Hong Kong, India, Egypt, Japan, and Korea (Escobar, 1993; Insel, 1984; Kim, 1993).

UNDERSTANDING OBSESSIVE-COMPULSIVE DISORDER

Considerable research evidence suggests that obsessive-compulsive disorder may have biological causes. Some family research suggests that disordered genes may play a role in determining who is vulnerable to OCD (Hettema et al., 2001; Nestadt et al., 2000). Most of the biological research on OCD, however, has focused on a critical circuit in the brain. People with this disorder may have defi-

▌ Figure 15-4
The Human Brain and OCD
This three-dimensional view of the human brain shows the locations of the orbital frontal cortex and the basal ganglia—areas implicated in obsessive-compulsive disorder. Among the basal ganglia's structures are the caudate nuclei, which filter powerful impulses that arise in the orbital frontal cortex so that only the most powerful ones reach the thalamus.

1992; Rapaport, 1990; Swedo, Pietrini, & Leonard, 1992). An elaborate circuit in the brain seems to be involved, beginning with the frontal cortex (see Figure 15-4). Impulses arise here and are carried to a part of the basal ganglia called the *caudate nucleus*. The strongest impulses then travel to the thalamus, where they may be acted upon. As a result, primitive impulses may break through into consciousness and motivate the execution of stereotyped behaviors much more often in people with obsessive-compulsive disorder than in normal individuals.

PET scans of people with obsessive-compulsive disorder show more activity in the areas of the brain involved in this primitive circuit than do PET scans of people without the disorder (Baxter, Schwartz, Guze, & Bergman, 1990) (see Figure 15-5; Saxena et al., 1998). In addition, people with the disorder often get some relief from their symptoms when they take drugs that regulate serotonin levels (Rapaport, 1991). Finally, patients who respond well to these drugs tend to show greater reductions in the rate of activity in these brain areas than patients who do not respond well to these drugs (Baxter et al., 1992; Swedo et al., 1992). Interestingly, OCD patients who respond to behavior therapies also tend to show decreases in activity in the caudate nucleus and thalamus (see Figure 15-6; Schwartz, Snidman, & Kagan, 1996).

ciencies in the neurotransmitter serotonin in the areas of the brain that regulate primitive impulses about sex, violence, and cleanliness—impulses that are often the focus of obsessions (Baxter, Schwartz, Bergman, & Szuba,

▌ Figure 15-5
A Normal Brain Versus an Obsessive-Compulsive Brain
This PET scan shows the metabolic differences between areas of the brain of a person with obsessive-compulsive disorder and the same areas in the brain of a normal person.

▌ Figure 15-6
OCD Pretreatment Versus Posttreatment
PET studies show decreases in metabolic activity in the caudate nucleus in OCD patients after they have received behavior therapy. (From Schwartz, Stoessel, Baxter, Martin, & Phelps, 1996)

As with panic disorder, however, people may go on to develop a full obsessive-compulsive disorder only if they also have certain cognitive and behavioral vulnerabilities in addition to a biological vulnerability. Cognitive and behavioral theorists suggest that people with obsessive-compulsive disorder have more trouble "turning off" intrusive thoughts because they have a tendency toward rigid, moralistic thinking (Rachman, 1993; Salkovskis, 1989). They are more likely to judge their negative, intrusive thoughts as unacceptable, and they become more anxious and guilty about these thoughts. This anxiety then makes it even harder to dismiss the thought (Clark & de Silva, 1985). People with obsessive-compulsive disorder may also believe that they should be able to control all thoughts and have trouble accepting the fact that everyone has negative thoughts occasionally (Clark & Purdon, 1993; Freeston, Ladouceur, Thibodeau, & Gagnon, 1992). They tend to believe that having these thoughts means they are going crazy, or they equate having the thought with actually engaging in the behavior ("If I'm thinking about hurting my child, I'm as guilty as if I actually did hurt my child"). Of course, this just makes them even more anxious when they have thoughts, because it's harder to dismiss them.

Compulsions may develop when the obsessional person discovers that some behavior temporarily quells the obsession and the anxiety it arouses. This reduction in anxiety reinforces the behavior, and a compulsion is born: Every time the person has the obsession, he or she will feel compelled to engage in the behavior to reduce anxiety.

Again, some of the best evidence in favor of cognitive and behavioral perspectives on obsessive-compulsive disorder can be seen in the fact that therapies based on these perspectives are helpful to people with the disorder, as we will discuss in Chapter 16. In contrast, psychodynamic theories of obsessive-compulsive disorder have not led to successful treatments. According to those theories, obsessions are unacceptable impulses (hostility, destructiveness, inappropriate sexual urges) that have been repressed and reappear in a disguised form. The individual feels that they are not a part of himself or herself, and may engage in compulsive acts to undo or atone for them. A mother who is obsessed with thoughts of murdering her child may feel compelled to check many times during the night to assure herself that the child is well. Compulsive rituals also serve to keep threatening impulses out of the individual's conscious awareness: A person who is continually busy has little opportunity to think improper thoughts or commit improper actions. According to psychodynamic theory, bringing the unconscious conflict to light and gaining insight into it should cure an obsessive-compulsive disorder. What little research has been done to test this theory, however, suggests that insight-oriented therapy does not cure obsessive-compulsive disorder in most cases.

In sum, biological and psychological factors probably combine in creating many of the anxiety disorders. Many people who develop these disorders probably have a genetic, neurological, or biochemical vulnerability to anxiety. But it may be necessary for them also to have a tendency toward catastrophizing and engaging in maladaptive avoidant behaviors that reduce anxiety for a full anxiety disorder to develop.

◆ Interim Summary

- Anxiety disorders include generalized anxiety (constant worry and tension), panic disorders (sudden attacks of overwhelming apprehension), phobias (irrational fears of specific objects or situations), and obsessive-compulsive disorders (persistent unwanted thoughts, or obsessions, combined with urges, or compulsions, to perform certain acts).

- Biological theories of anxiety disorders attribute them to genetic predispositions or to biochemical or neurological abnormalities. Most anxiety disorders run in families, and twin studies strongly suggest that panic disorder and obsessive-compulsive disorder have an inherited component.

- People who suffer panic attacks have an overreactive fight-or-flight response, perhaps because of serotonin deficiencies in the limbic system.

- People with obsessive-compulsive disorder may have serotonin deficiencies in areas of the brain that regulate primitive impulses.

- Cognitive and behavioral theorists suggest that people with anxiety disorders are prone to catastrophizing cognitions and to rigid, moralistic thinking. Maladaptive behaviors such as avoidant behaviors and compulsions arise through operant conditioning when the individual discovers that the behaviors reduce anxiety. Phobias may emerge through classical conditioning.

- Psychodynamic theories attribute anxiety disorders to unconscious conflicts that are disguised as phobias, obsessions, or compulsions.

◆ Critical Thinking Questions

1. Women are more likely than men to suffer from the anxiety disorders (except for obsessive-compulsive disorder). Can you generate some hypotheses for this gender difference?

2. Humans are much more likely to develop phobias of snakes and spiders than of guns or other modern weapons that are a greater danger to them. Can you generate an evolutionary explanation for this?

MOOD DISORDERS

Individuals with **mood disorders** may be severely depressed or manic (wildly elated), or may experience periods of depression as well as periods of mania. Mood disorders are divided into **depressive disorders,** in which the individual has one or more periods of depression without a history of manic episodes, and **bipolar disorders,** in which the individual alternates between periods of depression and periods of mania, usually with a return to normal mood between the two extremes. Manic episodes without some history of depression are uncommon.

DEPRESSION

> From the time I woke up on the morning until the time I went to bed at night, I was unbearably miserable and seemingly incapable of any kind of joy or enthusiasm. Everything—every thought, word, movement—was an effort. Everything that once was sparkling now was flat. I seemed to myself to be dull, boring, inadequate, thick brained, unlit, unresponsive, chill skinned, bloodless and sparrow drab. I doubted, completely, my ability to do anything well. It seemed as though my mind had slowed down and burned out to the point of being virtually useless. The wretched, convoluted, and pathetically confused mass of gray worked only well enough to torment me with a dreary litany of my inadequacies and shortcomings in character and to taunt me with the total, the desperate hopelessness of it all. (Jamison, 1995, p. 110)

Most of us have periods when we feel sad, lethargic, and uninterested in any activities—even pleasurable ones. Mild depressive symptoms are a normal response to many of life's stresses, especially important losses. Depression becomes a disorder when the symptoms become so severe that they interfere with normal functioning, and when they continue for weeks at a time. Depressive disorders are relatively common, with about 17% of people having an episode of severe depression such as Jamison describes at some time in their lives (Kessler et al., 1994). Women are twice as likely as men to develop depression (Nolen-Hoeksema, 2002).

Although depression is characterized as a mood disorder, it is truly a disorder of the whole person, affecting bodily functions, behaviors, and thoughts as well as emotions (see Figure 15-7). A person need not have all the symptoms of depression to be diagnosed with a disorder, but the more symptoms he or she has and the more intense they are, the more certain we can be that the individual is suffering from depression.

The emotional symptoms of depression are not the everyday blues that we all experience from time to time, but an unrelenting pain and despair. People also report that they have lost the ability to experience joy, even in response to the most joyous occasions, a symptom re-

Figure 15-7
The Symptoms of Depression
Depression includes emotional, cognitive, motivational, and physical symptoms.

ferred to as **anhedonia.** They say that they don't find interacting with family or friends, their work, or their hobbies enjoyable anymore.

The cognitive symptoms consist primarily of negative thoughts, with themes of worthlessness, guilt, hopelessness, and even suicide. Motivation is at a low ebb: The depressed person tends to be passive and has difficulty initiating activities. The following conversation between a patient and his therapist illustrates this passivity. The man, who had been hospitalized after a suicide attempt, spent his days sitting motionless in the lounge. His therapist decided to try to engage him in some activities:

> Therapist: I understand that you spend most of your day in the lounge. Is that true?
>
> Patient: Yes, being quiet gives me the peace of mind I need.
>
> Therapist: When you sit here, how's your mood?
>
> Patient: I feel awful all the time. I just wish I could fall in a hole somewhere and die.
>
> Therapist: Do you feel better after sitting for 2 or 3 hours?
>
> Patient: No, the same.
>
> Therapist: So you're sitting in the hope that you'll find peace of mind, but it doesn't sound like your depression improves.
>
> Patient: I get so bored.
>
> Therapist: Would you consider being more active? There are a number of reasons why I think increasing your activity level might help.

Some people suffer depression for years.

Patient: There's nothing to do around here.

Therapist: Would you consider trying some activities if I could come up with a list?

Patient: If you think it will help, but I think you're wasting your time. I don't have any interests. (Beck, Rush, Shaw, & Emery, 1979, p. 200)

The physical symptoms of depression include changes in appetite, sleep disturbances, fatigue, and loss of energy. Because a depressed person's thoughts are focused inward rather than toward external events, he or she may magnify minor aches and pains and worry about health.

As we see from this description of its symptoms, depression can be a debilitating disorder. Unfortunately, severe depression can also be long-lasting. One study of people with severe depression found that over a 9-year period they were symptom-free only 27% of the time (Judd et al., 1998). Even if they recover from one bout of depression, people remain at high risk for relapses into new episodes. There is some good news, however. Episodes of depression can be greatly shortened—and new episodes prevented—with either drug therapy or psychotherapy, as we discuss in Chapter 16.

BIPOLAR DISORDER

The majority of depressions occur without episodes of mania. But some people with a mood disorder will experience both depression and mania and hence can be diagnosed with bipolar disorder, also known as manic-depression. The individual alternates between depression and extreme elation. In some cases the cycle between depressive episodes and manic episodes is swift, with only a brief return to normality in between.

People experiencing **manic episodes** behave in a way that appears on the surface to be the opposite of depression. During mild manic episodes, they are energetic, enthusiastic, and full of self-confidence. They talk continually, rush from one activity to another with little need for sleep, and make grandiose plans, paying little attention to their practicality, as Jamison (1995, pp. 36–37) describes:

> I was a senior in high school when I had my first attack. At first, everything seemed so easy. I raced about like a crazed weasel, bubbling with plans and enthusiasms, immersed in sports, and staying up all night, night after night, out with friends, reading everything that wasn't nailed down, filling manuscript books with poems and fragments of plays, and making expansive, completely unrealistic plans for my future. The world was filled with pleasure and promise; I felt great. Not just great, I felt *really* great. I felt I could do anything, that no task was too difficult. My mind seemed clear, fabulously focused, and able to make intuitive mathematical leaps that had up to that point entirely eluded me. Indeed, they elude me still. At the time, however, not only did everything make perfect sense, but it all began to fit into a marvelous kind of cosmic relatedness. My sense of enchantment with the laws of the natural world caused me to fizz over, and I found myself buttonholing my friends to tell them how beautiful it all was. They were less than transfixed by my insights into the webbings and beauties of the universe although considerably impressed at how exhausting it was to be around my enthusiastic ramblings: You're talking too fast, Kay. Slow down, Kay. You're wearing me out, Kay. Slow down, Kay. And those times when they didn't actually come out and say it, I still could see it in their eyes: For God's sake, Kay, slow down.

This kind of energy, self-confidence, and enthusiasm may actually seem quite attractive to you, and indeed, many people in the midst of a manic episode do not want to get rid of their symptoms. At some point, however, manic symptoms often cross a line from joyful exuberance into hostile agitation. People may become angered by attempts to interfere with their activities and become abusive. Impulses (including sexual ones) are immediately expressed in actions or words. People may become confused and disoriented and may experience delusions of great wealth, accomplishment, or power. Eventually, most manic episodes revert into episodes of depression, sometimes extremely severe.

Bipolar disorders are relatively uncommon. Whereas about 21% of adult females and 13% of adult males in the United States have experienced depression, less than 2% of the adult population has had a bipolar disorder. Bipolar disorder, which appears to be equally common in men and women (Kessler et al., 1994), differs from other mood disorders in that it tends to occur at an earlier age, is more likely to run in families, responds to different medications, and almost always recurs if not treated.

UNDERSTANDING MOOD DISORDERS

As with the anxiety disorders, a combined biological and psychological model may best explain the mood disorders. Most people who develop depression—and particularly bipolar disorder—may have a biological vulnerability to these disorders. But the experience of certain types of life events, along with a tendency to think in negative ways, also clearly increases the likelihood of developing these disorders.

 The Neural Basis of Behavior

THE BIOLOGICAL PERSPECTIVE A tendency to develop mood disorders, particularly bipolar disorders, appears to be inherited (Wallace, Schneider, & McGuffin, 2002). Family history studies of people with bipolar disorder find that their first-degree relatives (parents, children, and siblings) have at least two to three times higher rates of both bipolar disorder and depressive disorders than relatives of people without bipolar disorder (Wallace et al., 2002; MacKinnon, Jamison, & De Paulo, 1997). Twin studies of bipolar disorder have also consistently suggested that the disorder has a genetic component. Indeed, the concordance rates between identical twins (the likelihood that both twins will have the disorder if one twin has the disorder) range from 50% to 100% across recent studies (Stoll, Renshaw, Yurgelun-Todd, & Cohen, 2000).

There is increasing evidence that depression, particularly recurrent depression, also is heritable. Family history studies find that first-degree relatives of people with depression have two to four times higher rates of depression than others (Sullivan, Neale, & Kendler, 2000). Interestingly, relatives of depressed people do not have any greater risk of developing bipolar disorder than relatives of people with no mood disorder. This suggests that bipolar disorder has a different genetic basis from that of depression. Twin studies also suggest that depression is heritable but to a lesser degree than bipolar disorder (Sullivan et al., 2000).

The specific role that genetic factors play in mood disorders is unclear. However, it seems likely that a biochemical abnormality is involved. The neurotransmitters norepinephrine and serotonin are believed to play an important role in mood disorders. Recall from Chapter 2 that neurotransmitters and their receptors interact like locks and keys (see Figure 15-8). Each neurotransmitter will fit into a particular type of receptor on the neuronal membrane. If there are the wrong number of receptors for a given type of neurotransmit-

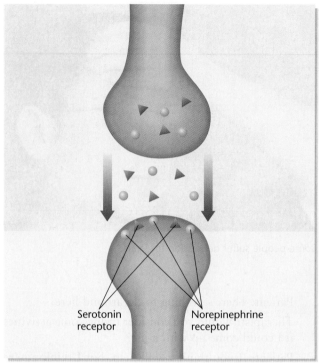

▲ Serotonin

● Norepinephrine

Figure 15-8
Neurotransmission in Depression
The neuronal receptors for norepinephrine and serotonin may not work efficiently in depressed people, so that norepinephrine and serotonin released from one neuron cannot bind to receptor sites on other neurons.

ter or the receptors for that neurotransmitter are too sensitive or not sensitive enough, the neurons do not efficiently use the available amounts of neurotransmitter. Several studies suggest that people with depression or bipolar disorder may have abnormalities in the number and sensitivity of receptor sites for serotonin and norepinephrine, particularly in areas of the brain that are involved in the regulation of emotion, such as the hypothalamus (Thase et al., 2002). In major depressive disorder, receptors for these neurotransmitters appear to be insensitive or too few in number. The picture is less clear for bipolar disorder, but it is likely that receptors for these neurotransmitters undergo poorly timed changes in sensitivity that are correlated with mood changes (Kujawa & Nemeroff, 2000).

The structure and functioning of the brain also appears to be altered in people with mood disorders. Neuroimaging studies using computed tomography (CT) scans and magnetic resonance imaging (MRI) have found deterioration in the prefrontal cortex of people with severe unipolar depression or bipolar dis-

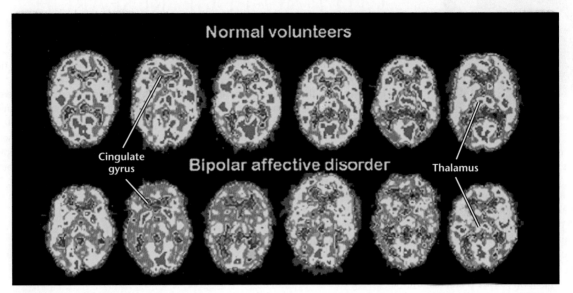

Figure 15-9
PET Scans of Bipolar Disorder
PET scans in six control subjects and six patients with bipolar disorder. Note decreases in relative metabolic rate in the cingulate gyrus and thalamus in bipolar subjects. (Courtesy of Monte S. Buschbaum, M.D., Mt. Sinai School of Medicine, New York)

order (Drevets, 2000; Liotti & Mayberg, 2001). This is associated with abnormalities in metabolism in this area of the brain, according to positron emission tomography (PET) studies (see Figure 15-9; Buchsbaum

Figure 15-10
Brain Functioning in Depression
This brain image shows increased metabolism in the medial thalamus of people with depression compared with those without depression. (Source: Drevets, W.C. (2000). Neuroimaging studies of mood disorders. *Biological Psychiatry, 48,* 813–829)

et al., 1997). The prefrontal cortex is involved in many aspects of cognitive functioning and in the regulation of emotion. The prefrontal cortex also has extensive connections with many other areas of the brain, including the thalamus, hypothalamus, amygdala, and hippocampus, which are involved in the regulation of responses to stress and in sleep, appetite, sexual drive, motivation, and memory. These areas of the brain show abnormalities in metabolism in people with the mood disorders as well (see Figure 15-10; Drevets et al., 1992, 1995). These structural and functional brain abnormalities could be precursors and causes of mood disorders, or they could be the result of biochemical processes in the mood disorders that have a toxic effect on the brain. We do not yet know the precise meaning of these abnormalities, but the rapid advances in neuroimaging technologies are sure to bring exciting new clues in the future.

THE COGNITIVE PERSPECTIVE Cognitive theories focus primarily on depression. According to these theories, people become depressed because they tend to interpret events in their lives in pessimistic, hopeless ways (Abramson, Metalsky, & Alloy, 1989; Beck et al., 1979; Peterson & Seligman, 1984). One of the most influential cognitive theorists, Aaron Beck, grouped the negative thoughts of depressed individuals into three categories, which he called the *cognitive triad:* negative thoughts about the self, about present experiences, and about the future. Negative thoughts about the self include the de-

The Biology of Suicide

The most disastrous consequence of depression is suicide. Not everyone who attempts or commits suicide is depressed, however, and suicidal thoughts and actions are alarmingly common. Nearly half of all teenagers in the United States say they know someone who has tried to commit suicide (see figure). One in five teenagers admits to attempting or seriously contemplating suicide (National Institute of Mental Health, 2000). Suicide is the ninth leading cause of the death in the United States and third leading cause among people 15 to 24 years of age (NIMH, 2000). More people die from suicide than from homicide.

Women attempt to commit suicide about three times more often than men do, but men succeed more often than women in killing themselves. The greater number of suicide attempts by women is probably related to the greater incidence of depression among women. The fact that men are more successful in their attempts is related to the choice of method. Until recently, women have tended to use less lethal means, such as cutting their wrists or overdosing on sleeping pills; men are more likely to use firearms or carbon

monoxide fumes or to hang themselves (Crosby, Cheltenham, & Sacks, 1999). However, with the marked increase in the number of women owning guns, suicide by firearms has now become women's method of first choice. Consequently, the fatality rate for women is changing. (Attempted suicides are successful 80% of the time when firearms are involved, but only 10% of drug or poison ingestions are

fatal—a powerful argument for not keeping firearms in the home.)

Within the United States, there are substantial differences between ethnic-racial groups in rates of suicide (McIntosh, 1991; NIMH, 2000). Whites have higher suicide rates than all other groups except for Native Americans, whose suicide rate is more than twice the national average. There are also cross-national differences in suicide

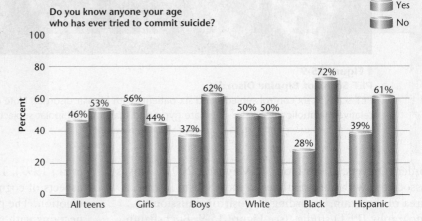

Do you know anyone your age who has ever tried to commit suicide?

Note: Hispanic may be of any race. There were too few Asian respondents to give separate percentages.

Based on surveys of 13- to 17-year-olds nationwide. The latest poll was conducted Oct. 11 to 14, 1999, with 1,038 teenagers. Those with no answer are not shown.

Teenager's Experience With Suicide
Percentages of teenagers in a national poll who answered "yes" or "no" to the question, "Do you know anyone your age who has ever tried to commit suicide?" (Source: *New York Times*, October 20, 1999, page 1)

pressed person's belief that he or she is worthless and inadequate. The depressed person's negative view of the future is one of hopelessness. Depressed people believe that their inadequacies and defects will prevent them from ever improving their situation.

Beck proposes that the depressed person's negative beliefs about self ("I am worthless," "I can't do anything right") are formed during childhood or adolescence through such experiences as loss of a parent, social rejection by peers, criticism by parents or teachers, or a series of tragedies. These negative beliefs are activated whenever a new situation resembles in some way—perhaps only remotely—the conditions in which the beliefs were learned, and depression may result. Moreover, according to Beck, depressed individuals make some systematic errors in thinking that lead them to misperceive reality in a way that contributes to their negative beliefs

about themselves. These cognitive distortions are listed in Table 15-4.

Another cognitive approach to depression, which focuses on the kinds of attributions, or causal explanations, that people make when bad things happen, was discussed in Chapter 14. This theory proposes that people who tend to attribute negative events to causes that are internal ("it's my fault"), are stable over time ("it's going to last forever"), and affect many areas of their lives are more prone to depression than individuals who have a less pessimistic attributional style (Abramson, Metalsky, & Alloy, 1989; Peterson & Seligman, 1984).

Critics of cognitive theories of depression have argued that these negative cognitions are symptoms or consequences of depression rather than causes. Although it is clear that depressed people have negative cognitions, there is less evidence that negative cognitive styles pre-rates, with higher rates in Hungary, Germany, Austria, Denmark, and Japan and lower rates in Egypt, Mexico, Greece, and Spain (WHO, 1992). The United States, Canada, and England have suicide rates that fall between these two extremes.

Among the reasons most frequently cited by those who have attempted suicide are depression, loneliness, ill health, marital problems, and financial or job difficulties (Jamison, 1999; NIMH, 1999).

Another psychological problem contributing to suicide, in addition to depression, is drug abuse. For example, a prospective study of suicide attempts found that 33% of attempters were identified as heavy drinkers, compared to less than 3% of nonattempters. When alcoholism co-occurs with depression, the risk of suicide is especially high (Waller, Lyons, & Constantini-Ferrando, 1999). Alcohol lowers people's inhibitions to engage in impulsive acts, even self-destructive acts like suicide attempts.

There have been many theories of suicide risk. Much of the most recent research focuses on biological causes. There is some evidence that suicide runs in families (Tsuang, 1983), although this may not represent a specific genetic risk for suicide but rather a genetic risk for depression and other psychological problems. One twin study found a concordance rate for serious suicide attempts of 23% among identical twins and 0% among nonidentical twins (Statham et al., 1998), providing stronger evidence of a genetic risk.

Several studies have linked suicide to low serotonin levels (Mann, Brent & Arango, 2001). For example, postmortem studies of the brains of people who committed suicide find low levels of serotonin (Gross-Isseroff, Biegon, Voet, & Weizman, 1998). Suicide attempters with low serotonin levels are 10 times more likely to make another suicide attempt than those with higher serotonin levels (Roy, 1992). Low serotonin levels are linked with suicide even among people who are not depressed, suggesting that the connection between serotonin and suicidality is not due entirely to a common connection to depression. Serotonin may generally be linked to impulsive and aggressive behavior (Linnoila & Virkkunen, 1992). Low serotonin levels are most strongly associated with impulsive and violent suicides.

Controversial research suggests that there might be a link between low cholesterol levels and suicide (Brunner, Parhofer, Schwandt, & Bronisch, 2002). Studies of medical and death statistics show that people with low cholesterol levels, because they were on low-cholesterol diets, taking cholesterol-lowering medications, exercising more, or just naturally had low levels, have higher rates of suicide than people with higher cholesterol levels (Ellison & Morrison, 2001; Jamison, 1999; Kaplan & Kaufmann, 1993). Initially, researchers thought the link between low cholesterol and suicide might be false and due to both factors being tied to depression. Depressed people eat less and thus may have lower cholesterol levels, and they are more likely to commit suicide. When studies controlled for the link between depression and suicide, however, the link between low cholesterol and suicide remained (Fawcett, Busch, Jacobs, Kravitz, & Fogg, 1997).

How could low cholesterol contribute to suicidality? Speculations focus on a possible link between cholesterol and serotonin. Studies of monkeys show that feeding them a low-fat diet leads to increases in physical violence (Kaplan, Muldoon, Manuck, & Mann, 1997). Researchers speculate that lowering cholesterol lowers serotonin, which in turn increases impulsive, violent behavior, perhaps including suicide. Although there is a great deal more research to be done on this and other theories of suicidality, understanding the sources of self-destructive behavior is clearly an important goal for the future.

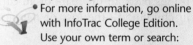 For more information, go online with InfoTrac College Edition. Use your own term or search:

- Psychology and suicide
- Diet and suicide

● **Table 15-4**
Cognitive Distortions in Depression

According to Beck's theory, these are the principal errors in thinking that characterize depressed individuals.

Overgeneralization	Drawing a sweeping conclusion on the basis of a single event. For example, a student concludes from his poor performance in one class on a particular day that he is inept and stupid.
Selective Abstraction	Focusing on an insignificant detail while ignoring the more important features of a situation. For example, from a conversation in which her boss praises her overall job performance, a secretary remembers the only comment that could be construed as mildly critical.
Magnification and Minimization	Magnifying small bad events and minimizing major good events in evaluating performance. For example, a woman gets a small dent in her car fender and views it as a catastrophe (magnification), while the fact that she gave an excellent presentation in class does nothing to raise her self-esteem (minimization).
Personalization	Incorrectly assuming responsibility for bad events in the world. For example, when rain dampens spirits at an outdoor buffet, the host blames himself rather than the weather.
Arbitrary Inference	Drawing a conclusion when there is little evidence to support it. For example, a man concludes from his wife's sad expression that she is disappointed in him; if he had checked out the situation, he would have discovered that she was distressed by a friend's illness.

cede and cause depressive episodes (Haaga, Dyck, & Ernst, 1991). Also, there is some evidence that depressed people may actually perceive reality more accurately than normal people: When asked to make judgments about how much control they have over situations that are actually uncontrollable, depressed people are quite accurate. In contrast, nondepressed people greatly overestimate the amount of control they have, especially over positive events (Alloy & Abramson, 1979).

A recent study that followed students through their college careers provides strong evidence that negative cognitive styles do precede and predict depression. Researchers measured the students' tendencies toward negative thinking patterns early in their first year of college and followed them for the next few years. Students who evidenced a negative cognitive triad or a pessimistic attributional style were much more likely to experience episodes of depression during their college years than those who did not, even if they had never been depressed before going to college (Abramson et al., 1999; Alloy, Abramson, Safford, & Gibb (in press); Alloy et al., 1999).

THE PSYCHOANALYTIC PERSPECTIVE Psychoanalytic theories interpret depression as a reaction to loss (Figure 15-11). Whatever the nature of the loss (rejection by a loved one, being fired from a job), the depressed person reacts to it intensely because the current situation brings back all the fears of an earlier loss that occurred in childhood—the loss of parental affection. The indi-

vidual's needs for affection and care were not satisfied in childhood. A loss in later life causes him or her to regress to the helpless, dependent state of childhood, when the original loss occurred. Part of the depressed person's behavior, therefore, represents a cry for love—a display of helplessness and an appeal for affection and security (Bibring, 1953; Blatt, 1974).

Reaction to loss is complicated by angry feelings toward the deserting person. An underlying assumption of psychoanalytic theories is that people who are prone to depression have learned to repress their hostile feelings because they are afraid of alienating those on whom they depend for support. When things go wrong, they turn their anger inward and blame themselves. For example, a woman may feel extremely hostile toward an employer who fired her, but because her anger arouses anxiety, she internalizes her feelings: She is not angry; rather, others are angry at her. She assumes that the employer had a reason for rejecting her: She is incompetent and worthless.

Psychoanalytic theories suggest that the depressed person's low self-esteem and feelings of worthlessness stem from a childlike need for parental approval. A small child's self-esteem depends on the approval and affection of the parents. But as a person matures, feelings of worth should also be derived from the individual's sense of his or her own accomplishments and effectiveness. The self-esteem of a person prone to depression depends primarily on external sources: the approval and support of others. When these supports fail, the individual may be thrown into a state of depression.

Psychoanalytic theories of depression thus focus on loss, overdependence on external approval, and internalization of anger. They seem to provide a reasonable explanation for some of the behaviors exhibited by depressed individuals, but they are difficult to prove or to refute.

▌ Figure 15-11
Psychodynamic Theories of Depression
Psychodynamic theories suggest that depressed people did not receive enough parental affection in childhood and that subsequent losses in adulthood trigger feelings of dejection and worthlessness.

◆ **Interim Summary**

- The mood disorders are divided into depressive disorders, in which individuals experience only depressed mood, and bipolar disorder (or manic-depression), in which individuals experience both depression and mania.

- Biological theories attribute mood disorders to genetic factors and to problems in regulation of the neurotransmitters serotonin and norepinephrine.

- Cognitive theories attribute depression to pessimistic views of the self, the world, and the future and to maladaptive attributional styles.

- Psychodynamic theories view depression as a reactivation of loss of parental affection in a person who is dependent on external approval and tends to turn anger inward.

SCHIZOPHRENIA

What then does schizophrenia mean to me? It means fatigue and confusion, it means trying to separate every experience into the real and the unreal and not sometimes being aware of where the edges overlap. It means trying to think straight when there is a maze of experiences getting in the way, and when the thoughts are continually being sucked out of your head so that you become embarrassed to speak at meetings. It means feeling sometimes that you are inside your head and visualizing yourself walking over your brain, or watching another girl wearing your clothes and carrying out actions as you think them. It means knowing that you are continually "watched," that you can never succeed in life because the laws are all against you and knowing that your ultimate destruction is never far away. (quoted in Rollin, 1980, p. 162)

Some of the feelings and experiences this woman is describing may sound familiar—difficulty in thinking straight, feeling as though you are watching yourself act, not being sure how to interpret events that happen. People with **schizophrenia**, however, have such difficulty in sorting out the real from the unreal, in keeping track of their thoughts, in responding to the everyday events of life, that they often become immobilized. Schizophrenia occurs in all cultures, even those that are remote from the stresses of industrialized civilization, and appears to have plagued humanity for at least 200 years. The disorder affects about 1% of the population and occurs equally in men and women. Schizophrenia exacts heavy costs both on the individual and on his or her family and community. People with schizophrenia must seek psychiatric and medical help frequently, and the direct medical costs amount to more than $20 billion per year in the United States alone (Torrey, 1995). The disorder usually begins in late adolescence or early adulthood, just when an individual is beginning a career and starting a family.

Unfortunately, schizophrenia is one of the most stigmatized disorders, so individuals with this disorder and their families often carry tremendous shame.

CHARACTERISTICS OF SCHIZOPHRENIA

Sometimes schizophrenia develops slowly as a gradual process of increasing seclusiveness and inappropriate behavior. Sometimes the onset is sudden, marked by intense confusion and emotional turmoil. Such acute cases are usually precipitated by a period of stress in individuals whose lives have tended toward isolation, preoccupation with self, and feelings of insecurity. Whether schizophrenia develops slowly or suddenly, the symptoms are many and varied. The primary characteristics of schizophrenia can be summarized under the following headings, although not every person diagnosed as having the disorder will exhibit all of these symptoms.

DISTURBANCES OF THOUGHT AND ATTENTION In schizophrenia, both the process of thinking and the content of thought may be disordered. The following excerpt from the writings of a person with schizophrenia illustrates how difficult it is to understand schizophrenic thinking.

If things turn by rotation of agriculture or levels in regards and timed to everything; I am referring to a previous document when I made some remarks that were facts also tested and there is another that concerns my daughter she has a lobed bottom right ear, her name being Mary Lou. Much of abstraction has been left unsaid and undone in these products milk syrup, and others, due to economics, differentials, subsidies, bankruptcy, tools, buildings, bonds, national stocks, foundation craps, weather, trades, government in levels of breakages and fuses in electronics too all formerly states not necessarily factuated. (Maher, 1966, p. 395)

By themselves, the words and phrases make sense, but they are meaningless in relation to each other. The juxtaposition of unrelated words and phrases and the idiosyncratic word associations (sometimes called **word salad**) are characteristic of schizophrenic writing and speech. They reflect a **loosening of associations** in which the individual's ideas shift from one topic to another in ways that appear unrelated. Moreover, the train of thought often seems to be influenced by the sound of words rather than by their meaning. The following account by a woman with schizophrenia of her thoughts in response to her doctor's questions illustrates this tendency to form associations by rhyming words, referred to as clang associations:

Doctor: How about the medication? Are you still taking the Haldol? [an antipsychotic drug]

Patient Thinks: Foul Wall. (She nods but does not reply.)

Doctor: What about the vitamins?

Patient Thinks: Seven sins. Has-beens. (She nods.)

Doctor: I don't think you're taking all your meds.

Patient Thinks: Pencil leads. (North, 1987, p. 261)

The confused thought processes that are the hallmark of schizophrenia seem to stem from a general difficulty in focusing attention and filtering out irrelevant stimuli. Most of us are able to focus our attention selectively. From a mass of incoming sensory information, we are able to select the stimuli that are relevant to the task at hand and ignore the rest. A person who suffers from schizophrenia is receptive to many stimuli at the same time and has trouble making sense of the profusion of inputs, as the following statement by a schizophrenic patient illustrates:

> I can't concentrate. It's diversions of attention that trouble me. I am picking up different conversations. It's like being a transmitter. The sounds are coming through to me, but I feel my mind cannot cope with everything. It's difficult to concentrate on any one sound. (McGhie & Chapman, 1961, p. 104)

A sense of being unable to control one's attention and focus one's thoughts is central to the experience of schizophrenia.

In addition to disorganized thought processes, people with schizophrenia experience disturbances in the content of thought. Most individuals suffering from schizophrenia show a lack of insight. When asked what is wrong or why they are hospitalized, they seem to have no appreciation of their condition and little realization that their behavior is unusual. They are also subject to **delusions,** beliefs that most people would view as misinterpretations of reality. The most common delusions are beliefs that external forces are trying to control one's thoughts and actions. These delusions of influence include the belief that one's thoughts are being broadcast to the world so that others can hear them, that strange thoughts (not one's own) are being inserted into one's mind, or that feelings and actions are being imposed on one by some external force. Also frequent are beliefs that certain people or certain groups are threatening or plotting against one (delusions of persecution). Less common are beliefs that one is powerful and important (delusions of grandeur).

The term **paranoid** is used to refer to an individual who has delusions of persecution. Such a person may become suspicious of friends and relatives, fear being poisoned, or complain of being watched, followed, and talked about. So-called motiveless crimes, in which an

The German psychiatrist Hans Privizhorn has assembled an extensive collection of artwork by mental patients. This painting, by August Neter, illustrates the hallucinations and paranoid fantasies experienced by many schizophrenic patients.

individual attacks or kills someone for no apparent cause, are sometimes committed by people who are later diagnosed as having paranoid schizophrenia. These incidents are quite rare, however. Most people with schizophrenia are not a danger to others, although their confusion may make them a danger to themselves.

The specific content of delusions in schizophrenia may vary across cultures (Tateyama, Asai, Hashimoto, Bartels, & Kasper, 1998). For example, delusions of persecution often focus on persons of authority in the culture. Thus, Americans with persecutory delusions may fear that the Central Intelligence Agency is out to get them, whereas Afro Caribbeans may believe that people are trying to kill them with curses (Westermeyer, 1993). Among the Japanese, people with schizophrenia might have delusions of being slandered, whereas Western Europeans with schizophrenia are more likely to have religious delusions of having committed a sin. These differences in the content of delusions probably reflect differences in a culture's belief systems as well as structures of authority.

DISTURBANCES OF PERCEPTION People experiencing acute schizophrenic episodes often report that the world appears different (noises seem louder, colors more intense). Their own bodies may no longer appear the same (their hands may seem too large or too small, their legs overly extended, their eyes dislocated in the face). Some people fail to recognize themselves in a mirror, or see their reflection as a triple image. The most dramatic disturbances of perception are **hallucinations,** sensory experi-

Privizhorn Collection, Ruprecht-KarlspUniversitat Heidelberg Klinikum ences in the absence of relevant or adequate external stimulation. Auditory hallucinations (usually voices telling one what to do or commenting on one's actions) are the most common. Visual hallucinations (such as seeing strange creatures or heavenly beings) are somewhat less frequent. Other sensory hallucinations (a bad odor emanating from one's body, the taste of poison in food, the feeling of being pricked by needles) occur infrequently.

Hallucinations are often frightening, even terrifying, as the following example illustrates:

> At one point, I would look at my co-workers and their faces would become distorted. Their teeth looked like fangs ready to devour me. Most of the time I couldn't trust myself to look at anyone for fear of being swallowed. I had no respite from the illness. Even when I tried to sleep, the demons would keep me awake, and at times I would roam the house searching for them. I was being consumed on all sides whether I was awake or asleep. I felt I was being consumed by demons. (Long, 1996)

In one sense, hallucinations are not far removed from ordinary experiences. We all know what visual hallucinations are like because we have them in dreams. But for most people dreams occur only during sleep. It is possible that some sort of neurotransmitter-mediated process inhibits dreams during the waking state and that this process has failed in schizophrenics who hallucinate (Assad & Shapiro, 1986).

Auditory hallucinations may have their origin in ordinary thought. We often carry on internal dialogues—for example, commenting on our actions or having an imaginary conversation with another person. We may even occasionally talk to ourselves aloud. The voices that people with schizophrenia hear, calling them names or telling them what to do, are similar to internal dialogues. But a person experiencing an auditory hallucination does not believe that the voices originate within the self or that they can be controlled. The inability to distinguish between external and internal, real and imagined, is central to the schizophrenic experience.

DISTURBANCES OF EMOTIONAL EXPRESSION People suffering from schizophrenia usually fail to exhibit normal emotional responses. They often are withdrawn and unresponsive in situations that should make them sad or happy. For example, a man may show no emotional response when informed that his daughter has cancer. However, this blunting of emotional expression can conceal inner turmoil, and the person may erupt with angry outbursts.

Sometimes individuals with schizophrenia express emotions that are inappropriately linked to the situation or to the thought being expressed, such as smiling while speaking of tragic events. Because our emotions are influenced by cognitive processes, it is not surprising that disorganized thoughts and perceptions are accompanied by changes in emotional responses. This point is illustrated in the following comments:

> Half the time I am talking about one thing and thinking about half a dozen other things at the same time. It must look queer to people when I laugh about something that has got nothing to do with what I am talking about, but they don't know what's going on inside and how much of it is running around in my head. You see I might be talking about something quite serious to you and other things come into my head at the same time that are funny and this makes me laugh. If I could only concentrate on one thing at the one time I wouldn't look half so silly. (McGhie & Chapman, 1961, p. 104)

MOTOR SYMPTOMS AND WITHDRAWAL FROM REALITY

People with schizophrenia often exhibit bizarre motor activity. They may grimace, adopt strange facial expressions, or gesture repeatedly using peculiar sequences of finger, hand, and arm movements. Some may become very agitated and move about in continual activity, as in a manic state. Some, at the other extreme, may become totally unresponsive and immobile, adopting an unusual posture and maintaining it for long periods of time. For example, a person may stand like a statue with one foot extended and one arm raised toward the ceiling, maintaining this state of catatonic immobility for hours. Such an individual, who appears to have completely withdrawn from reality, may be responding to inner thoughts and fantasies.

DECREASED ABILITY TO FUNCTION Besides the specific symptoms we have described, people with schizophrenia are impaired in their ability to carry out the daily routines of living. If the disorder occurs in adolescence, the individual shows a decreasing ability to cope with school and has limited social skills and few friends. Adults suffering from schizophrenia are often unsuccessful in obtaining or holding a job. Personal hygiene and grooming deteriorate, and the individual avoids the company of other people. The signs of schizophrenia are many and varied. Trying to make sense of the variety of symptoms is complicated by the fact that some may result directly from the disorder, whereas others may be a reaction to life in a mental hospital or to the effects of medication.

CULTURE AND THE PROGRESSION OF SCHIZOPHRENIA

Generally, schizophrenia is more chronic and debilitating than other psychological disorders. Between 50% and 80% of people who are hospitalized with one episode of schizophrenia are eventually rehospitalized for another episode at some time in their lives (Eaton et al., 1992). Not everyone with schizophrenia shows progressive deterioration in functioning, however. Between 20% and 30% of people treated for schizophrenia recover substantially from the illness within 10 to 20 years of its onset (Eaton et al., 1998; Jablensky, 2000).

Culture seems to play a strong role in the course of schizophrenia. People who have schizophrenia in developing countries, such as India, Nigeria, and Colombia, are less likely to remain incapacitated by the disorder for the long term than people who have schizophrenia in developed countries such as the United States, Great Britain, or Denmark (see Figure 15-12; Jablensky, 1989). Why might this be? It may be due partially to variations in the genes for schizophrenia across cultural groups (Jablensky, 2000). Differences in how cultures treat their schizophrenic members probably play a strong role also. In developing countries, people with schizophrenia are more likely cared for at home by a broad network of family members who share responsibility for the individual (Karno & Jenkins, 1993). In contrast, in developed countries, it is less likely that the person with schizophrenia lives with family or that his or her immediate family has other family members nearby who share in the care. Caring for a family member with schizophrenia can be a huge burden. When this burden is shouldered by only a few people, there can be tremendous conflict in the family, which may exacerbate the symptoms of the person with schizophrenia.

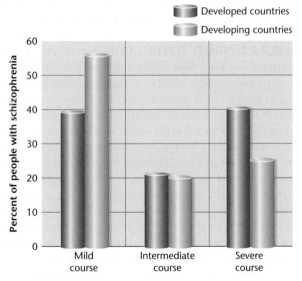

Figure 15-12
Cultural Differences in the Course of Schizophrenia
People with schizophrenia in developing countries are more likely to have a mild course of the disorder than are people in developed countries, whereas people in developed countries are more likely to have a severe course of the disorder than are people in developing countries. (A. Jablensky (1989). "Epidemiology and cross-cultural aspects of schizophrenia," in *Psychiatric Annals*, 19, 516–524. Reprinted by permission of SLACK, Inc.)

Laboratory of Psychology and Psychopathology, National Institute of Mental Health

The odds of all four of a set of identical quadruplets being diagnosed as schizophrenic are 1 in 2 billion—yet these quadruplets, the Genain sisters, all suffer from schizophrenia and have been hospitalized at various times since high school.

UNDERSTANDING SCHIZOPHRENIA

Schizophrenia probably has strong biological roots, but environmental stress may push people who are vulnerable to schizophrenia into more severe forms of the disorder or new episodes of psychosis.

The Neural Basis of Behavior

THE BIOLOGICAL PERSPECTIVE
Family studies show that there is a hereditary predisposition for schizophrenia. Relatives of people with schizophrenia are more likely to develop the disorder than people from families that are free of schizophrenia (Cardno, O'Donovan, & Owen, 2000; Lichtermann, Karbe, & Maier, 2000). Figure 15-13 shows the lifetime risk of developing schizophrenia as a function of how closely an individual is genetically related to a person diagnosed as schizophrenic. Note that an identical twin of a schizophrenic is 3 times more likely than a fraternal twin to develop schizophrenia and 46 times more likely than an unrelated person to develop the disorder. However, fewer than half of identical twins of people with schizophrenia develop schizophrenia themselves, even though they share the same genes. This fact demonstrates the importance of nongenetic variables.

How do the genetic abnormalities that predispose an individual to schizophrenia affect the brain? Current research focuses on two areas: brain structure and biochemistry. Two types of structural deficits have been found in the brains of people with schizophrenia. First, the prefrontal cortex is smaller and shows less activity

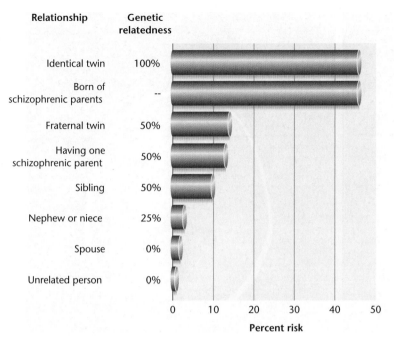

Relationship	Genetic relatedness
Identical twin	100%
Born of schizophrenic parents	--
Fraternal twin	50%
Having one schizophrenic parent	50%
Sibling	50%
Nephew or niece	25%
Spouse	0%
Unrelated person	0%

Percent risk

▌ Figure 15-13
Genetic Relationships and Schizophrenia
The lifetime risk of developing schizophrenia is largely a function of how closely an individual is genetically related to a schizophrenic person and not a function of how much their environment is shared. In the case of an individual with two schizophrenic parents, genetic relatedness cannot be expressed in terms of percentages, but the regression of the individual's "genetic value" on that of the parents is 100%, the same as it is for identical twins.
(*Schizophrenia: The Epigenetic Puzzle,* by I. I. Gottesman & J. Shields. Copyright © 1992 Cambridge University Press. Reprinted by permission of the publisher.)

▌ Figure 15-14
A Normal Brain Versus a Schizophrenic Brain
This PET scan shows the metabolic differences between the prefrontal cortex of a schizophrenic individual and the same areas in the brain of a normal individual.

in some people with schizophrenia than in people without the disorder (Andreasen, 2001; Buchsbaum, Haier, Potkin, & Nuechterlein, 1992; Vance et al., 2000; see Figure 15-14). The prefrontal cortex is the largest re-

gion of the brain in human beings, nearly 30% of the total cortex, and it has connections to all the other cortical regions, as well as to the limbic system, which is involved in emotion and cognition, and the basal ganglia, which is involved in motor movement. The prefrontal cortex plays important roles in language, emotional expression, planning and producing new ideas, and mediating social interactions. Thus, it seems logical that people whose prefrontal cortex is unusually small or inactive would show a wide range of deficits in cognition, emotion, and social interaction, as people with schizophrenia do.

Second, people with schizophrenia have enlarged ventricles and fluid-filled spaces in the brain (see Figure 15-15; Eyler Zorrilla et al., 1997; Galderisi et al., 2000). The presence of enlarged ventricles suggests atrophy or deterioration in other brain tissue. The specific areas of the brain that have deteriorated, resulting in ventricular enlargement, could lead to different manifestations of schizophrenia (Breier, Schreiber, Dyer, & Pickar, 1992).

Although neurochemical theories of mood disorders center on norepinephrine and serotonin, the culprit in schizophrenia is believed to be dopamine. Early dopamine theories of schizophrenia held that the disorder was the result of the presence of too much dopamine in key areas of the brain. This view is now considered too simple. The most recent theories suggest that there is a complicated imbalance in levels of dopamine in different areas of the brain (Conklin & Iacono, 2002). First, there may be excess dopamine activity in the mesolimbic system, a subcortical part of the brain involved in cognition and emotion, which leads to the "positive" symptoms of schizophrenia—hallucinations, delusions, disordered thought. On the other hand, there may be unusually low dopamine activity in the prefrontal area of the brain, which is involved in attention, motivation, and organization of behavior (see Figure 15-16; Taber, Lewis, & Hurley, 2001). Low dopamine activity in the prefrontal area may lead to the "negative" symptoms of schizophrenia—lack of motivation, inability to care for oneself, inappropriate emotional expression.

As we mentioned, these abnormalities in brain structure and neurochemical functioning could be due to genetics, but they also could be the result of insults to the brain of a fetus or young child. Studies have found that people who have schizophrenia are more likely to have a history of birth complications, perinatal brain damage, infections in the central nervous system (such as meningitis) in infancy, and maternal pregnancy complications or influenza in pregnancy (Jablensky,

Figure 15-15
Brain Functioning in Schizophrenia
The MRI on the left shows evidence of ventricular enlargement in the brain of a schizo-phrenic person compared with that of a nonschizophrenic person in the image on the right. (Courtesy of Silvana Galderisi, from Galderisi, Vita, Rossi, Stratta, Leonardi and Invernizzi, (2000) "Quali-tative MRI findings in patients with schizophrenia," *Psychiatry Research: Neuroimaging Section* 98:117–126, reprinted by permission.)

Figure 15-16
Dopamine Axons in Prefrontal Cortex and Schizophrenia
The photomicrograph on the left is from a nonschizophrenic person and shows a much denser network of dopamine axons in the prefrontal cortex than the photomicrograph on the right, which is from a person with schizophrenia (bar = 200 microns).

2000). Each of these might cause permanent damage to the central nervous system of the fetus or young child, perhaps contributing to risk for schizophrenia.

THE SOCIAL AND PSYCHOLOGICAL PERSPECTIVE

Although it is clear that stressful events cannot cause a person to develop the full syndrome of schizophrenia, psychosocial factors may play an important role in determining the eventual severity of the disorder in people with a biological predisposition, as well as in triggering new episodes of psychosis. The type of stress that has received the most attention in recent studies is family-related stress. Members of families that are high in expressed emotion are overinvolved with one another, overprotective of the disturbed family member, and, at the same time, critical, hostile, and resentful toward the disturbed member (Brown, Birley, & Wing, 1972; Vaughn & Leff, 1976). People with schizophrenia whose families are high in expressed emotion are three to four times more likely to suffer a new psychotic episode than those whose families are low in expressed emotion (Brown, Birley, & Wing, 1972; Leff & Vaughn, 1981; Mintz, Lieberman, Miklowitz, & Mintz, 1987). Being in a family with high levels of expressed emotion may create stresses that trigger new episodes of psychosis by overwhelming the schizophrenic person's ability to cope.

The link between expressed emotion and relapse in schizophrenia may help to explain the cross-cultural differences in the prognosis of this disorder. One study found that families of people with schizophrenia in Mexico and India scored lower on measures of expressed emotions than did families of people with schizophrenia in Europe and the United States (see Figure 15-17; Karno et al., 1987; Karno & Jenkins, 1993).

Critics of the research on expressed emotion argue that the hostility and intrusiveness observed in some families of people with schizophrenia might be the result of the symptoms exhibited by the disturbed member, rather than a factor contributing to the disorder (Parker, Johnston, & Hayward, 1988). Although families are often forgiving of positive symptoms like hallucinations, viewing them as uncontrollable, they can be unforgiving of the negative symptoms like lack of motivation (Brewin, MacCarthy, Duda, & Vaughn, 1991; Hooley, Richters, Weintraub, & Neale, 1987; Lopez & Guarnaccia, 2000). People with these symptoms may elicit more negative expressed emotion and may be especially prone to relapse.

Another alternative explanation for the link between expressed emotion and relapse comes from evidence that family members who are especially high in expressed emotion are themselves more likely to exhibit some form of psychopathology (Goldstein, Talovic, Nuechterlein, & Fogelson, 1992). In such families, people with schizophrenia may have high rates of relapse

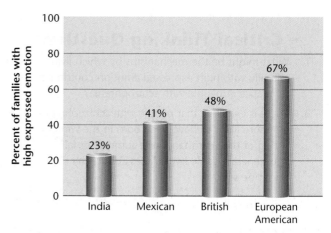

■ Figure 15-17
Cultural Differences in the Prevalence of Expressed Emotion in Families of Schizophrenics
Families of schizophrenics from developing countries tend to show lower levels of expressed emotion than do families of schizophrenics from developed countries. This may be one reason that schizophrenics from developing countries have fewer relapses than do schizophrenics from developed countries. (M. Karno & J. H. Jenkins (1993). "Cross-Cultural Issues in the Course and Treatment of Schizophrenia." *Psychiatric Clinics of North America,* 16, 339–350. Reprinted by permission of W. B. Saunders Co.)

because they have a greater genetic predisposition toward psychopathology, as evidenced by the presence of psychopathology in their families, rather than because their families are high in expressed emotion. Perhaps the best evidence that expressed emotion actually influences relapse is that treatments that reduce expressed emotion tend to reduce the relapse rate in schizophrenic family members. ■

◆ Interim Summary

- Schizophrenia is characterized by disturbances in thought, including disorganized thought processes, delusions, and lack of insight.

- Other symptoms include perceptual disturbances (such as hallucinations), inappropriate emotional expression, bizarre motor activity, withdrawal, and impaired functioning.

- Schizophrenia clearly is transmitted genetically.

- People with schizophrenia also have problems in dopamine regulation.

- Two types of brain abnormalities are consistently seen in schizophrenia: The prefrontal cortex is smaller and less active, and the ventricles are enlarged.

- Difficult environments probably cannot cause schizophrenia, but they may worsen the disorder and contribute to relapses.

1. What might be the mechanisms by which living in a family with high expressed emotion contributes to relapse in people with schizophrenia?

2. There is evidence that people with schizophrenia are more likely to have been born in the winter or spring of the year than in the summer or fall. Can you generate some hypotheses about why this might be so?

PERSONALITY DISORDERS

Personality disorders are long-standing patterns of maladaptive behavior. In Chapter 13, we described personality traits as enduring ways of perceiving or relating to the environment and thinking about oneself. When personality traits become so inflexible and maladaptive that they significantly impair the individual's ability to function, they are referred to as personality disorders. People with personality disorders experience themselves and the world in ways that are highly distressing to them and/or impair their ability to function in daily life. These experiences begin in childhood or adolescence and persist over time and across situations, affecting most areas of the person's life. The particular emotions, thoughts, and behaviors that an individual experiences vary according to the specific disorder.

Personality disorders are immature and inappropriate ways of coping with stress or solving problems. They are usually evident by early adolescence and may continue throughout the life span. Unlike people with mood or anxiety disorders, which also involve maladaptive behavior, people who have personality disorders often do not feel upset or anxious and may not be motivated to change their behavior. They do not lose contact with reality or display marked disorganization of behavior.

DSM-IV lists several personality disorders (see the Concept Review Table). The characteristics of these disorders tend to overlap, making it difficult to agree on how to classify some individuals. Moreover, it is difficult to say when a person's behavior is simply different from other people's behaviors and when the behavior is so severe that it warrants a diagnosis. The personality disorder that has been studied the most and is the most reliably diagnosed is the antisocial personality (formerly termed psychopathic personality and sometimes referred to as sociopathy). We discuss it in this section, along with borderline personality disorder, a controversial personality disorder that has received much attention in recent years.

CONCEPT REVIEW TABLE
Types of Personality Disorders

The DSM-IV recognizes several different personality disorders.

Diagnosis	Description
Antisocial Personality Disorder	Impulsive, callous behavior based on disregard for others and lack of respect for social norms.
Borderline Personality Disorder	Chronic instability of mood, relationships, and self-concept; self-destructive impulsiveness.
Histrionic Personality Disorder	Chronic intense need for attention and approval sought by dramatic behavior, seductiveness, and dependence.
Narcissistic Personality Disorder	Frequent grandiosity and obliviousness to others' needs; exploitative behavior; arrogance.
Paranoid Personality Disorder	Chronic and pervasive mistrust of others that is unwarranted.
Schizoid Personality Disorder	Chronic lack of interest in interpersonal relationships; emotional coldness.
Schizotypal Personality Disorder	Chronically inhibited or inappropriate emotional and social behavior; aberrant cognitions; disorganized speech.
Avoidant Personality Disorder	Avoidance of social interactions and restrictiveness in interactions due to chronic worry over being criticized.
Dependent Personality Disorder	Pervasive selflessness, need to be cared for, and fear of rejection.
Obsessive-Compulsive Personality Disorder	Pervasive rigidity in activities and relationships; extreme perfectionism.

ANTISOCIAL PERSONALITY

People who have **antisocial personality disorder** have little sense of responsibility, morality, or concern for others. Their behavior is determined almost entirely by their own needs. In other words, they lack a conscience. Whereas the average person realizes at an early age that some restrictions are placed on behavior and that pleasures must sometimes be postponed in consideration of the needs of others, individuals who have antisocial personalities seldom consider any desires except their own. They behave impulsively, seek immediate gratification of their needs, and cannot tolerate frustration. Extreme versions of this disorder were depicted by Woody Harrelson in the movie *Natural Born Killers* and by Anthony Hopkins in *The Silence of the Lambs*.

Antisocial behavior results from a number of causes, including membership in a delinquent gang or a criminal subculture, the need for attention and status, loss of contact with reality, and inability to control impulses. However, most juvenile delinquents and adult criminals show some concern for others (for example, family or gang members) and adhere to some code of moral conduct (never betray a friend). In contrast, people with antisocial personalities have little feeling for anyone except themselves and seem to experience little guilt or remorse, regardless of how much suffering their behavior may cause. Other characteristics of the antisocial personality (or sociopath) include a great facility for lying, a need for thrills and excitement with little concern for possible injury, and inability to alter behavior as a consequence of punishment. Such individuals are often attractive, intelligent, charming people who are adept at manipulating others—in other words, good con artists. Their façade of competence and sincerity wins them promising jobs, but they have little staying power. Their restlessness and impulsiveness soon lead them into an escapade that reveals their true nature; they accumulate debts, desert their families, squander company money, or commit crimes. When they are caught, their declarations of repentance are so convincing that they often escape punishment and are given another chance. But antisocial personalities seldom live up to these declarations; what they say has little relation to what they feel or do. Deceitfulness is one of the defining characteristics of antisocial personality (Kraus & Reynolds, 2001).

Fortunately, the full syndrome of antisocial personality disorder is relatively rare. It is much more common in men than in women, with about 3% of men and 1% of women having this disorder at some time in their lives (Kraus & Reynolds, 2001).

UNDERSTANDING ANTISOCIAL PERSONALITY DISORDER

What factors contribute to the development of an antisocial personality? Current research focuses on biological determinants, the quality of the parent-child relationship, and ways of thinking that promote antisocial behaviors.

 The Neural Basis of Behavior

BIOLOGICAL FACTORS Genetic factors appear to play a role in the development of antisocial personality. Twin studies show that if one identical twin has antisocial personality characteristics, the other twin also has these characteristics about 50% of the time. In contrast, among fraternal twins the concordance rate for antisocial personality is only about 20% (Carey & Goldman, 1997; Rutter et al., 1990). Adoption studies find that the criminal records of adopted sons are more similar to the records of their biological fathers than to those of their adoptive fathers (Cloninger & Gottesman, 1987; Mednick, Reznick, Hocevar, & Baker, 1987).

One of the cardinal features of antisocial personality is impulsivity (Rutter, 1997). Many animal studies and some human studies suggest that impulsive and aggressive behaviors are linked to low levels of the neurotransmitter serotonin (Berman, Kavoussi, & Coccaro, 1997; Ferris & de Vries, 1997; Moffitt et al., 1998). Could low serotonin levels be a cause of antisocial personality? We do not yet know.

People with antisocial personalities also show deficits in the ability to sustain concentration, in abstract reasoning and concept formation, in formulating and implementing goals, in self-monitoring and self-awareness, and in shifting from maladaptive patterns of behavior to more adaptive ones (Henry & Moffitt, 1997). Collectively, these are known as executive functions, and their control resides largely in the temporal and frontal lobes of the brain. In turn, some studies have found differences between antisocial adults (usually prison inmates) and the general population in the structure or functioning of these areas of the brain (Blake, Pincus & Buckner, 1995). These brain anomalies could be the result of medical illnesses and exposure to toxins during infancy and childhood, which are both more common in antisocial people than in controls, or to genetic abnormalities. Whatever their causes, deficits in executive functions could contribute to poor impulse control and difficulty in anticipating the consequences of one's actions.

Many studies have argued that people with antisocial personality disorder have low levels of arousability, which may lead them to seek stimulation and sensation through impulsive and dangerous acts (Raine, 1997). For example, one study compared two groups of adolescent male delinquents selected from the detention unit of a juvenile court. One group had been diagnosed as having antisocial personality disorder; the other group was diagnosed as exhibiting adjustment reactions to negative life events. The experimenters measured galvanic skin response (GSR) under stress (see Chapter 11). Dummy electrodes were attached to each participant's leg, and he was told that in 10 minutes he would be given a very strong but not harmful shock. A large clock was visible so that the participant knew precisely when the shock was supposed to occur. No shock was actually administered. The two groups showed no difference in GSR measures during periods of rest or in response to auditory or visual stimulation. However, during the 10 minutes of shock anticipation, the group with adjustment reactions showed significantly more tension than the antisocial group. At the moment when the clock indicated the shock was due, most members of the group with adjustment reactions showed GSR responses indicating a sharp increase in anxiety. None of the antisocial participants showed this reaction (Lippert & Senter, 1966). Low arousability to anxiety-provoking stimuli may also make it more difficult for people with antisocial personality disorder to learn from punishment because punishment is less aversive for them than for most people, and they will not be anxious in anticipation of the punishment.

SOCIAL FACTORS Although children who develop antisocial personalities may have a biological predisposition for the disorder, studies suggest that they are unlikely to develop the disorder unless they are also exposed to environments that promote antisocial behavior (Dishion & Patterson, 1997; Kraus & Reynolds, 2001). The parents of children with antisocial personalities often appear to be simultaneously neglectful and hostile toward their children. The children are frequently unsupervised for long periods. The parents often are not involved in the children's everyday lives, not knowing where they are or who their friends are. But when these parents do interact with their children, the interactions are often characterized by hostility, physical violence, and ridicule (Patterson, DeBaryshe, & Ramsey, 1989). This description does not fit all parents of such children, but parental noninvolvement and hostility are good predictors of children's vulnerability to antisocial personality disorder.

The biological and family factors that contribute to antisocial personality often coincide. Children who behave in antisocial ways often suffer from neuropsychological problems that are the result of maternal drug use, poor prenatal nutrition, prenatal and postnatal exposure to toxic agents, child abuse, birth complications, and low birth weight (Moffitt, 1993). Children with these neuropsychological problems are more irritable, impulsive, awkward, overreactive, and inattentive, and they learn more slowly than their peers. This makes them difficult to care for, and they are therefore at increased risk for maltreatment and neglect. In turn, the parents of these children are more likely to be teenagers or to have psychological problems of their own that contribute to ineffective, harsh, or inconsistent parenting. Thus, for these children a biological predisposition to disruptive, antisocial behaviors may be combined with a style of parenting that contributes to these behaviors. In a study of 536 boys, Moffitt (1990) found that those who had both neuropsychological deficits and adverse home environments scored four times higher on an aggression scale than those with neither neuropsychological deficits nor adverse home environments.

PERSONALITY FACTORS Children with antisocial personalities tend to process information about social interactions in ways that promote aggressive reactions to these interactions (Crick & Dodge, 1994). They assume that other children will be aggressive toward them, and they interpret other children's actions in line with these assumptions rather than using cues from the specific situations they actually face. In addition, they tend to believe that any negative action by a peer—such as taking their favorite pencil—are intentional rather than accidental. When deciding what action to take in response to a perceived provocation by a peer, children with antisocial personalities tend to think of a narrow range of responses, usually including aggression. When pressed to consider responses other than aggression, they make ineffective or vague responses and often consider responses other than aggression to be useless or unattractive.

Children who think about their social interactions in this way are likely to engage in aggressive behaviors toward others and may therefore suffer retaliation. Other children will hit them, parents and teachers will punish them, and they will be perceived more negatively by others. These actions may feed their assumptions that the world is against them, causing them to misinterpret future actions by others. In this way, a cycle of interactions can be established that maintains and encourages aggressive, antisocial behaviors.

BORDERLINE PERSONALITY DISORDER

Borderline personality disorder is a lifelong disorder characterized by extreme variability in mood, relationships, and self-perceptions. It has been the focus of considerable attention in the popular press and in clinical and research writings in psychology in the last couple of decades. The diagnosis of borderline personality disorder was added to the DSM in 1980, but clinicians have long used the label "borderline" to refer to people who seem to teeter between severe neurotic traits (such as emotional instability) and bouts of psychosis (see Millon, 1981).

Instability is a key feature of borderline personality disorder. The mood of individuals with this disorder is unstable, with bouts of severe depression, anxiety, or anger seeming to arise frequently, often without good reason. The self-concept is unstable, with periods of extreme self-doubt and grandiose self-importance. Interpersonal relationships are extremely unstable, and the person can switch from idealizing other people to despising them without provocation. A classic movie depiction of borderline personality disorder was given by Glenn Close in *Fatal Attraction*. People with borderline personality disorder often feel desperately empty and will initially cling to a new acquaintance or therapist in the hope that he or she will fill the tremendous void they feel in themselves. At the same time, they may misinterpret other people's innocent actions as signs of abandonment or rejection. For example, if a therapist has to cancel an appointment because she is ill, a person with borderline personality disorder might interpret this as a rejection and become extremely depressed or angry. Along with instability of mood, self-concept, and interpersonal relationships comes a tendency toward impulsive self-damaging behaviors, including self-mutilation and suicidal behavior. Self-mutilation often takes the form of burning or cutting. Finally, people with borderline personality disorder are prone to transient episodes in which they feel unreal, lose track of time, and may even forget who they are. The following case describes a person with borderline personality disorder (McGlashan, 1983, pp. 87–88).

Ms. Q was a 28-year-old, white single woman when admitted voluntarily [to a psychiatric hospital]. . . . In late adolescence, Ms. Q became romantically and sexually involved with a young artist. When he informed her that she was "just another woman" in his life, she became morose and moody. She began hallucinating his face on movie screens and newspapers. Shortly after the accidental drowning of a young boy from her neighborhood, Ms. Q started feeling guilty for his death and feared imminent apprehension by the police. In an act later described as a "manipulative gesture," she took an overdose of sleeping medication and was hospitalized briefly.

Over the next five years, Ms. Q attended college sporadically. She moved often between a variety of living situations: alone in hotels or dormitories or with one or the other of her divorced parents. Changes of domicile were often precipitated by quarrels. Although seldom alone, she developed relatively superficial social relationships. The few women whom she befriended tended to be older. She would frequently become attached to their parents and call them "mama and papa." Sexually she had three or four intense affairs, each lasting less than six months and each terminating painfully with one or the other partner refusing to marry. In all of her relationships, Ms. Q was described as manipulative, dependent, masochistic, hostile, and derogatory.

Mood swings between anger and despondency occurred weekly and sometimes daily. She frequently abused alcohol and barbiturates and made numerous manipulative suicidal threats. For the latter she was hospitalized briefly on two more occasions (one month or less in duration). . . .

In her mid-20s, Ms. Q joined the armed services. After an initial honeymoon period, she performed miserably. She cried "for hours over her typewriter and stayed in her room not eating." After ten months, she received a "neuropsychiatric" medical discharge. She began moving around again, trying various jobs, which she was unable to hold for more than a few days. She became more seclusive, even with fellow employees.

At age 26 Ms. Q began two years of intensive psychotherapy (up to four times per week). Her therapist recorded that Ms. Q tried "very hard to be sick" and was intent on causing "trouble with everyone she did not like" by "upsetting everyone during her bad spells."

Her hospitalization at [the psychiatric hospital] arose out of a visit home to her mother. She felt slighted in several ways. First, her mother's welcome was less than "gushing." Second, she felt insulted when her mother's boyfriend showed her a brochure describing a psychiatric residential treatment facility. Third, she discovered that a certain choice piece of family real estate was being willed to her least favorite sibling. Feeling rejected, she took an overdose of aspirin and was hospitalized at]the psychiatric hospital] shortly thereafter.

People with borderline personality disorder also tend to receive diagnoses of one of the acute disorders, including substance abuse, depression, generalized anxiety disorder, simple phobias, agoraphobia, post-traumatic stress disorder, and panic disorder (Kraus & Reynolds, 2001). Longitudinal studies of people with this disorder indicate that about 10% die by suicide, and perhaps 75% have attempted suicide (Kraus & Reynolds, 2001; Perry, 1993). The greatest risk of suicide appears to be in the first year or two after receiving a diagnosis of borderline personality disorder. This may be due to the fact that a person is often not diagnosed with this disorder until a crisis brings him or her into therapy.

The lifetime prevalence of borderline personality disorder is between 1% and 2% (Weissman, 1993). The disorder is diagnosed much more often in women than in men (Fabrega, Ulrich, Pilkonis, & Mezzich, 1991; Swartz, Blazer, George, & Winfield, 1990). People with this disorder tend to have stormy marital relationships, more job difficulties, and a higher rate of physical disability than average.

UNDERSTANDING BORDERLINE PERSONALITY DISORDER

Psychoanalytic theorists have provided the most comprehensive explanation of borderline personality disorder. They suggest that individuals with borderline personalities retain a foothold in the real world but rely on primitive defenses such as denial rather than more advanced defenses against their conflicts (Kernberg, 1979). In addition, such individuals have very poorly developed views of self and others, stemming from poor early relationships with caregivers. The caregivers of people with borderline personality disorder are characterized as deriving much gratification from the child's dependence on them early in life. They do not encourage the child to develop a separate sense of self and may punish attempts at individuation and separation. As a result, people with borderline personality disorder never learn to fully differentiate between their views of self and others. This makes them extremely sensitive to others' opinions of them and to the possibility of being abandoned. When others are perceived as rejecting them, they reject themselves and may engage in self-punishment or self-mutilation.

Individuals with borderline personalities also have never been able to integrate the positive and negative qualities of either their self-concept or their concept of others, because their early caregivers were comforting and rewarding when they remained dependent and compliant toward them but hostile and rejecting when they tried to separate from them. People with borderline personalities therefore tend to see themselves and others as either "all good" or "all bad" and vacillate between these two views. This process is referred to as splitting. The changeability of borderline individuals' emotions and interpersonal relationships is caused by splitting—their emotions and their perspectives on their relationships reflect their vacillation between the "all good" and the "all bad" self or other.

Other research suggests that many people with borderline personality disorder have a history of physical and sexual abuse during childhood (Perry, 1993). This abuse could lead to the problems in self-concept that most theorists believe to be at the core of this disorder. In addition, a child whose parent alternates between being abusive and being loving could develop a fundamental mistrust of others and a tendency to see others as all good or all bad.

◆ Interim Summary

- Personality disorders are lifelong patterns of maladaptive behavior that constitute immature and inappropriate ways of coping with stress or solving problems.
- Individuals with antisocial personality disorder are impulsive, show little guilt, are concerned only with their own needs, and are frequently in trouble with the law.
- Antisocial personality disorder probably has genetic and biological roots, but neglectful and hostile parenting may also contribute to the disorder.
- People with borderline personality disorder show instability in mood, self-concept, and interpersonal relationships.
- Psychodynamic theories suggest that the caregivers of people with this disorder required their children to be highly dependent and alternated between extreme expressions of love and hostility.

◆ Critical Thinking Questions

1. Do personality disorders seem to be just the extremes of normal personality traits or distinct entities that are qualitatively different from normal personality traits?

2. What similarities do you see between antisocial personality disorder and borderline personality disorder?

DISSOCIATIVE IDENTITY DISORDER

Dissociative identity disorder, also called *multiple personality disorder,* is the existence in a single individual of two or more distinct identities or personalities that alternate in controlling behavior. Usually, each personality has its own name and age and a specific set of memories and characteristic behaviors. In most cases, there is a primary identity that carries the individual's given name and is passive, dependent, and depressed. The alternate identities typically have characteristics that contrast with the primary identity—for example, hostile, controlling, and self-destructive (American Psychiatric Association, 2000). In some cases the personalities may even differ in such characteristics as handwriting, artistic or athletic abilities, and knowledge of a foreign language. The primary identity often has no awareness of the experiences of the other identities. Periods of unexplained amnesia—loss of memory for hours or days each week—can be a clue to the presence of dissociative identity disorder.

We should make clear that dissociative identity disorder is not classified as a personality disorder, like antisocial personality disorder or borderline personality disorder. Instead, it is classified as a dissociative disorder, because at the core of this disorder is the chronic tendency to dissociate—to split off different facets of one's sense of self, memories, or consciousness.

One of the most famous cases of multiple personality is that of Chris Sizemore, whose alternative personalities—Eve White, Eve Black, and Jane—were portrayed in the movie *The Three Faces of Eve* (Thigpen & Cleckley, 1957) and later described extensively in her autobiography, *I'm Eve* (Sizemore & Pittillo, 1977). Another well-studied case is that of Jonah, a 17-year-old who was admitted to a hospital complaining of severe headaches that were often followed by memory loss. Hospital attendants noticed striking changes in his personality on different days, and the psychiatrist in charge detected three distinct secondary identities. The relatively stable personality structures that emerged are diagrammed in Figure 15-18 and can be characterized as follows:

> *Jonah.* The primary personality. Shy, retiring, polite, and highly conventional, he is designated "the square." Sometimes frightened and confused during interviews, Jonah is unaware of the other personalities.
>
> *Sammy.* He has the most intact memories. Sammy can coexist with Jonah or set Jonah aside and take over. He claims to be ready when Jonah needs legal advice or is in trouble; he is designated "the mediator." Sammy remembers emerging at age 6, when Jonah's mother stabbed his stepfather and Sammy persuaded the parents never to fight again in front of the children.
>
> *King Young.* He emerged when Jonah was 6 or 7 years old to straighten out Jonah's sexual identity after his mother occasionally dressed him in girls' clothing at home and Jonah became confused about boys' and girls' names at school. King Young has looked after Jonah's sexual interests ever since; hence, he is designated "the lover." He is only dimly aware of the other personalities.
>
> *Usoffa.* A cold, belligerent, and angry person, Usoffa is capable of ignoring pain. It is his sworn duty to watch over and protect Jonah; thus, he is designated "the warrior." He emerged at age 9 or 10, when a gang of boys beat up Jonah without provocation. Jonah was helpless, but Usoffa emerged and fought viciously against the attackers. He, too, is only dimly aware of the other personalities.

The four personalities tested very differently on all measures having to do with emotionally laden topics but scored essentially alike on tests relatively free of emotion or personal conflict, such as intelligence or vocabulary tests.

Dissociative identity disorder reflects a failure to integrate various aspects of identity, memory, and consciousness. The dissociation is so complete that several different personalities seem to be living in the same body.

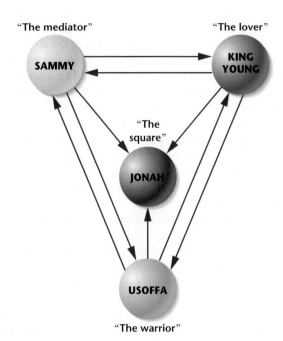

■ **Figure 15-18**
Jonah's Four Component Identities
The three personalities on the periphery have superficial knowledge of each other but are intimately familiar with Jonah, who in turn is totally unaware of them. (A. M. Ludwig, J. M. Brandsma, C. B. Wilbur, F. Benfeldt & D. H. Jameson (1972), "The Objective Study of a Multiple Personality," in *Archives of General Psychiatry*, 26:298–310. Copyright © 1972 by the American Medical Association.)

Observers note that the switch from one personality to another is often accompanied by subtle changes in posture and tone of voice. The new personality talks, walks, and gestures differently. There may even be changes in physiological processes such as blood pressure and brain activity (Putnam, 1991).

Individuals with dissociative identity disorder frequently report having experienced physical and sexual abuse during childhood (Ellason et al., 1996). The accuracy of such reports is controversial, because childhood memories may be subject to distortion, and individuals with this disorder tend to be very vulnerable to suggestion. Nevertheless, many theorists believe that this disorder develops as a defense against traumatic childhood experiences. The child copes with a painful problem by creating another personality to bear the brunt of the difficulty (Ross, 1997). In Jonah's case, Sammy (the mediator) emerged when Jonah had to deal with his mother's attack on his stepfather.

The child presumably learns to defend himself from the pain of abuse by dissociating the memory from consciousness. If the child is severely and repeatedly abused, this method of defense leads over time to dissociative identities in which only one or two subpersonalities are conscious of the abuse and the others have no memory of the pain. It is adaptive for the child to keep the personalities separate in order to keep awareness of the abuse from his or her other selves. That way the feeling and memories of abuse do not continually flood the child's consciousness when he or she cannot handle it—for instance, while at school or playing with friends (Braun, 1986).

Another factor in the development of dissociative identity disorder appears to be an enhanced susceptibility to self-hypnosis, a process by which one is able at will to put oneself into the kind of trance state characteristic of hypnosis. Patients with dissociative identity disorder often make excellent hypnotic subjects, and they report that the trance experience is identical to experiences they have had, dating back to childhood (Kihlstrom, Glisky, & Angiulo, 1994). One of the personalities of a patient said, "She creates personalities by blocking everything from her head, mentally relaxes, concentrates very hard, and wishes" (Bliss, 1980, p. 1392).

Once individuals discover that creating another identity relieves them of emotional pain, they are likely to create other personalities when confronted by emotional problems. Thus, when Jonah was beaten by a gang of boys at age 10, he created another personality, Usoffa Abdulla, to handle the problem. Some dissociative identity patients become so accustomed to defending against problems by means of alternate personalities that they continue the process throughout adulthood, creating new personalities in response to new problems, and they may end up with a dozen or more different personalities (Putnam, 1991).

Cases of dissociative identity disorder have always been fascinating but rare. However, recent years have seen a sharp rise in the number of cases reported in the United States. Some believe that this increase reflects increased awareness of the disorder among mental health professionals and, hence, identification of cases that previously were undiagnosed. Others believe that the disorder has been overdiagnosed in individuals who are highly suggestible (American Psychiatric Association, 2000). Dissociative identity disorder is much more frequently diagnosed in the United States than in Europe, India, or Japan (Ross, 1989). Within the United States, dissociative identity disorder is rarely diagnosed in Latinos (Martinez-Taboas, 1989). Some theorists believe that Latinos confronted by traumatic stressors are more likely to develop *ataque de nervios*, which we described earlier, rather than dissociative identity disorder.

◆ Interim Summary

- In dissociative identity disorder, two or more well-developed personalities alternate within the same individual.

- Many theorists attribute this disorder to child abuse.
- The ability to hypnotize oneself may also be key to the development of dissociative identity disorder.
- This is a rare disorder, although the frequency with which it is diagnosed has increased in recent decades, particularly in the United States.

◆ Critical Thinking Questions

1. Childhood abuse is more likely to contribute to dissociative identity disorder if it occurs chronically over a long period of time. Can you think of other traumas in the lives of modern children that might contribute to the development of dissociative identity disorder?

2. Most people experience mild dissociative experiences, such as finding themselves someplace but not knowing how they got there, or becoming so involved in a fantasy that it seems real, particularly when they are very tired, stressed, or have been drinking or taking drugs. Can you identify other common dissociative experiences and their possible sources?

INSANITY AS A LEGAL DEFENSE

Before leaving the subject of mental disorders, we should look briefly at the controversial issue of insanity. How should the law treat a mentally disturbed person who commits a criminal offense? Should individuals whose mental faculties are impaired be held responsible for their actions? These questions are of concern to behavioral and social scientists, members of the legal profession, and others who work with criminal offenders.

Over the centuries, an important part of Western law has been the concept that a civilized society should not punish a person who is mentally incapable of controlling his or her conduct. In 1724 an English court maintained that a man was not responsible for an act if "he doth not know what he is doing, no more than . . . a wild beast." Modern standards of legal responsibility, however, have been based on the M'Naghten decision of 1843. The **M'Naghten Rule** states that a defendant may be found not guilty by reason of insanity only if he was so severely disturbed at the time of his act that he did not know what he was doing, or if he did know what he was doing, did not know that it was wrong.

The M'Naghten Rule was adopted in the United States, and the distinction of knowing right from wrong remained the basis for most decisions of legal insanity for over a century. Some states added to their statutes the doctrine of "irresistible impulse," which recognizes that some mentally ill individuals may respond correctly when asked if a particular act is morally right or wrong but may be unable to control their behavior.

During the 1970s, a number of state and federal courts adopted the **American Law Institute Rule,** a broader legal definition of insanity proposed by the American Law Institute, which states: "A person is not responsible for criminal conduct if at the time of such conduct, as a result of mental disease or defect, he lacks substantial capacity either to appreciate the wrongfulness of his conduct or to conform his conduct to the requirements of the law." The word *substantial* suggests that any incapacity is not enough to avoid criminal responsibility but that total incapacity is not required either. The use of the word *appreciate* rather than *know* implies that intellectual awareness of right or wrong is not enough; individuals must have some understanding of the moral or legal consequences of their behavior before they can be held criminally responsible.

The problem of legal responsibility in the case of mentally disordered individuals became a topic of increased debate in the wake of John Hinckley Jr.'s acquittal, by reason of insanity, for the attempted assassination of President Reagan in 1981. Many Americans were outraged by the verdict and felt that the insanity defense was a legal loophole that allowed too many guilty people to go free. In response, Congress enacted the Insanity Defense Reform Act (1984), which contains a number of provisions designed to make it more difficult to absolve a defendant of legal responsibility. For example, the act changes the American Law Institute's "lacks substantial capacity . . . to appreciate" to "unable to appreciate"; it stipulates that the mental disease or defect be "severe" (the intent being to exclude nonpsychotic disorders such as antisocial personality); and it shifts the burden of proof from the prosecution to the defense (instead of the prosecution having to prove that the person was sane beyond a reasonable doubt at the time of the crime, the defense must prove he or she was not sane, and must do so with "clear and convincing evidence"). This law applies to all cases tried in federal courts and about half the state courts.

Another attempt to clarify the legal defense of insanity is the verdict "guilty but mentally ill." Initially proposed by Michigan, it has been adopted by 11 states. (In some of these states, this verdict replaces the not guilty by reason of insanity verdict; in others, it is an additional option.) Generally, the laws permit a finding of **guilty but mentally ill** when a defendant is found to have a sub-stantial disorder of thought or mood that afflicted him at the time of the crime and significantly impaired his judgment, behavior, capacity to recognize reality, or ability to cope with the ordinary demands of life. The effect of this mental illness, however, falls short of legal insanity. The verdict of guilty but mentally ill allows jurors to convict a person whom they perceive as dangerous while attempting also to ensure that he or she receives treatment for the disorder. The individual could be given treatment in prison or be treated in a mental hospital and returned to prison when deemed fit to complete the sentence.

Public concern that the insanity defense may be a major loophole in the criminal law is largely groundless. The defense is rarely used, and actual cases of acquittal by reason of insanity are even rarer. Jurors seem reluctant to believe that people are not morally responsible for their acts, and lawyers, knowing that an insanity plea is likely to fail, tend to use it only as a last resort. Fewer than 1% of defendants charged with serious crimes are found not guilty by reason of insanity.

◆ Interim Summary

- Although the use of insanity as a legal defense is a subject of considerable controversy, in reality the defense is rarely used and even more rarely successful.

- The M'Naghten Rule states that a defendant may be found not guilty by reason of insanity only if he was so severely disturbed at the time of his act that he did not know what he was doing, or if he did know what he was doing, did not know that it was wrong.

- The American Law Institute Rule states: "A person is not responsible for criminal conduct if at the time of such conduct, as a result of mental disease or defect, he lacks substantial capacity either to appreciate the wrongfulness of his conduct or to conform his conduct to the requirements of the law."

- Courts now allow a finding of guilty but mentally ill when a defendant is found to have a substantial disorder of thought or mood that afflicted him at the time of the crime and significantly impaired his judgment, behavior, capacity to recognize reality, or ability to cope with the ordinary demands of life.

◆ Critical Thinking Questions

1. Most of the people judged guilty but mentally ill never receive adequate psychiatric treatment in prison. Do you think this invalidates this verdict as an alternative to the insanity defense? Why or why not?

2. Why do you think most people believe that many criminals "get off" on the insanity defense?

Is Attention Deficit/Hyperactivity Disorder (ADHD) Overdiagnosed?

ADHD IS OVERDIAGNOSED

Caryn L. Carlson, The University of Texas at Austin

The growing public attention to ADHD over the past decade has increased the detection of legitimate cases and led to much-needed research. We must be cautious, however, that we do not allow the diagnostic pendulum to swing too far, since finding answers about ADHD depends on the rigor and integrity of our classification system.

There is reason to believe that ADHD is currently being overdiagnosed in some areas of the United States. Prescriptions of stimulant medications, which are almost exclusively for ADHD, provide a "proxy" for diagnostic rates and afford an examination of trends over time and place. Use of methylphenidate in the United States, already high by worldwide standards (International Narcotics Control Board, 1998), skyrocketed in the early 1990s, more than doubling from 1990 through 1995 (Safer, Zito, & Fine, 1996) and has continued to increase since then. While rates are up for all age groups, the largest increase is for teenagers and adults; among school-age children in one region, the proportion of high school students using stimulant medication tripled from 1991 through 1995 (Safer, Zito, & Fine, 1996). Certainly the true prevalence of ADHD has not increased at this rate, although part of the increase no doubt reflects the detection of previously unrecognized ADHD. While some reports suggest that even now many ADHD children may not be recognized or treated (Wolraich, Hannah, Baumgaertel, & Feurer, 1998), the average rates are now quite high (Safer, Zito, & Fine, 1996).

Part of the dramatic increase probably reflects overdiagnosis, particularly when considered in light of the vast disparities across geographical locales in the United States. The rate of methylphenidate consumption per capita in 1995 was 2.4 times higher in Virginia than in neighboring West Virginia, and nearly 4 times higher than in California (Spanos, 1996). Even more troubling are the high discrepancies across counties within states. For example, although the per capita rate for males of ages 6–12 in 1991 in New York was 4.1% statewide, rates varied by a factor of 10 among counties, ranging up to 14% (Kaufman, 1995).

What factors might lead to overdiagnosis of ADHD? We know from epidemiological research that unreasonable prevalence rates (e.g., up to nearly 23% of school-age boys [Wolraich, Hannah, Baumgaertel, & Feurer, 1998]) are obtained when ADHD is identified based merely on simple ratings from one source, but become much lower when full diagnostic criteria—including age of onset by 7, presence across settings, and confirmation of impairment—are imposed. The wide variability in diagnostic rates across locations suggests that clinicians are applying diagnostic criteria inconsistently. Some clinicians diagnose without assessing all criteria, and often they rely only on parent reports. While underdiagnosis may be occurring in some places, overdiagnosis is occurring in others.

When is overdiagnosis most likely? It seems that the diagnosis of ADHD has become fashionable for those who experience some negative life event—such as school failure or job loss—and desire to attribute such problems to a disorder rather than accept personal responsibility. This tendency is apparent even in more mundane arenas, such as feeling bored or unmotivated—"What a relief: the fact that I find it difficult to pay attention in my 'history of Swedish cartographers' class isn't my fault. I have ADHD."

One safeguard against misdiagnosis is the current criteria that symptoms must appear by age 7. But how early and by what means can we detect ADHD if we agree that it is present from an early age? Since objective measures that can reliably identify ADHD are currently unavailable, we must rely on symptom reports from others. Setting the age of onset at 7 years recognizes that normal behavior patterns may be similar to symptoms of ADHD up to about age 5, when normally activity decreases and attention increases (but not in children with ADHD). Also, impairment may not occur outside the demands of a classroom environment. But if individuals do not have symptoms early but develop them later for a variety of reasons, including life situations or stress, then diagnosis does not seem warranted. Should such problems be recognized? By all means. Should they be treated? Of course, by teaching people organizational and behavior management strategies, and possibly even with medication. But significant problems in living are not the

Caryn Carlson

equivalent of disorders, and to call them that will deter us in the search for etiologies of ADHD.

Is Attention Deficit/Hyperactivity Disorder (ADHD) Overdiagnosed?

ADHD IS NEITHER OVERDIAGNOSED NOR OVERTREATED
William Pelham, SUNY Buffalo

Because ADHD is the most widely diagnosed mental health disorder of childhood and because its frequency of treatment with medication has been increasing exponentially through the 1990s, it has become fashionable in many quarters—particularly among educators—to argue that it is overdiagnosed and consequently overtreated. Histrionic diatribes aside, there is no solid empirical evidence that ADHD is overdiagnosed or overtreated.

First, consider the accusation that ADHD is only a relatively recent phenomenon. To the contrary, the diagnosis was often widely used in the past but played second fiddle to other diagnoses. For example, one of the more important early studies in treatment of conduct disordered children (Patterson, 1974) noted, almost as an aside that more than two-thirds of the boys had hyperkinesis, an early label for ADHD. Thus while ADHD may well be *diagnosed* more often than in the past 30 years, it is simply being diagnosed more appropriately and given the prominence it deserves.

It is important to note that the major reason for the increasing rate of ADHD identification in the 1990s is a result of the 1991 change in the status of ADHD in the Individuals with Disabilities Education Act (IDEA), the federal law that governs special education throughout the United States. This change included ADHD as a handicapping condition. Further, the U. S. Office of Education sent a memorandum to all state officers of education directing them to consider ADHD as a condition eligible for special education. As a result of this directive, school districts throughout the country for the

first time were required to establish screening and diagnostic procedures for ADHD. The increase in diagnosis for ADHD is thus not a conspiracy or a fatal flaw in education or an indictment of current parenting practices, but is instead a natural by-product of a change in federal regulations governing education in the United States.

What about the criticism that ADHD is a disorder with diagnostic rates that vary widely both within North America and across the world? The explanation is that local school districts and states vary dramatically in the degree to which they have implemented the mandated changes in the IDEA. Furthermore, ADHD when similar diagnostic criteria are applied, comparable rates to those in North America exist in a diverse collection of countries that include Italy, Spain, South Africa, Israel, Argentina, and Vietnam.

The most important factor in deciding whether a mental health disorder is overdiagnosed is whether the diagnosed individuals have impairments in daily life functioning sufficient to justify the label. ADHD is a particularly compelling example of this issue because the children suffer from dramatic impairment in relationships with peers, parents, teachers, and siblings, as well as in classroom behavior and academic performance. To take a single example, in one classic study of consecutive referrals to a clinic, 96% of ADHD children were rejected by their peers on sociometric nominations at a rate higher than their class averages (Pelham & Bender, 1982). In the field of child psychopathology, the number of negative nominations received on a classroom peer nomination inventory in

elementary school is widely thought to be the best indicator of severe impairment in childhood and poor outcome in adulthood, so this elevated rate of negative nominations highlights the impairment that ADHD children suffer in the peer domain.

A corollary of the argument that many children are inappropriately diagnosed with ADHD is the complaint that these children are being inappropriately treated—usually with medication. In fact, the literature shows that only a small minority of diagnosed ADHD children (or all children with mental health disorders for that matter) receive treatment—medication or otherwise. We should be happy that treatment rates for the disorder are increasing. The dramatic rise in the treatment of ADHD—pharmacological or otherwise—clearly results from the increase in the rates of diagnosis, which are secondary to the change in the IDEA noted above. Notably, one of the studies that supports these arguments regarding impairment and treatment was conducted with children identified using only teacher ratings, which have been the main target for complaints of overdiagnosis (Wolraich et al, 1998).

In summary, ADHD is the most common mental health disorder of childhood, and it is one of the most impairing and refractory, and one with poor long-term prognosis. Current diagnostic rates are in line with scientific views of the nature of the disorder. If anything, we need to accurately identify *more* children with ADHD and provide the evidence-based treatments—both behavioral and pharmacological—that they need.

CHAPTER SUMMARY

1. The diagnosis of abnormal behavior is based on social norms, statistical frequency, adaptiveness of behavior, and personal distress. Characteristics of good mental health include efficient perception of reality, control of behavior, self-esteem, ability to form affectionate relationships, and productivity.

2. DSM-IV classifies mental disorders according to specific behavioral symptoms. Such a classification system helps communicate information and provides a basis for research. However, each case is unique, and diagnostic labels should not be used to pigeonhole individuals.

3. Theories about the causes of mental disorders and proposals for treating them can be grouped according to those that focus on the brain and other biological factors, those that focus on the mind, including psychoanalytic, behavioral, and cognitive perspectives, and those that focus on sociocultural and environmental factors. The vulnerability-stress model emphasizes the interaction between a predisposition (biological and/or psychological) that makes a person vulnerable to a particular disorder, and stressful environmental conditions encountered by the individual.

4. Anxiety disorders include generalized anxiety (constant worry and tension), panic disorders (sudden attacks of overwhelming apprehension), phobias (irrational fears of specific objects or situations), and obsessive-compulsive disorders (persistent unwanted thoughts, or obsessions, combined with urges, or compulsions, to perform certain acts).

5. Biological theories of anxiety disorders attribute them to genetic predispositions or to biochemical or neurological abnormalities. Most anxiety disorders run in families, and twin studies strongly suggest that panic disorder and obsessive-compulsive disorder have an inherited component. People who suffer panic attacks have an overreactive fight-or-flight response, perhaps because of serotonin deficiencies in the limbic system. People with obsessive-compulsive disorder may have serotonin deficiencies in areas of the brain that regulate primitive impulses.

6. Cognitive and behavioral theorists suggest that people with anxiety disorders are prone to catastrophizing cognitions and to rigid, moralistic thinking. Maladaptive behaviors such as avoidant behaviors and compulsions arise through operant conditioning when the individual discovers that the behaviors reduce anxiety. Phobias may emerge through classical conditioning. Psychodynamic theories attribute anxiety disorders to unconscious conflicts that are disguised as phobias, obsessions, or compulsions.

7. Mood disorders are divided into depressive disorders (in which the individual has one or more periods of depression) and bipolar disorders (in which the individual alternates between periods of depression and periods of elation, or mania). Sadness, loss of gratification in life, negative thoughts, and lack of motivation are the main symptoms of depression.

8. Biological theories attribute mood disorders to genetic factors and to problems in regulation of the neurotransmitters serotonin and norepinephrine. Cognitive theories attribute depression to pessimistic views of the self, the world, and the future and to maladaptive attributional styles. Psychodynamic theories view depression as a reactivation of loss of parental affection in a person who is dependent on external approval and tends to turn anger inward.

9. Schizophrenia is characterized by disturbances in thought, including disorganized thought processes, delusions, and lack of insight. Other symptoms include perceptual disturbances (such as hallucinations), inappropriate emotional expression, bizarre motor activity, withdrawal, and impaired functioning.

10. Schizophrenia clearly is transmitted genetically. People with schizophrenia also have problems in dopamine regulation, as well as two types of brain abnormalities: The prefrontal cortex is smaller and less active, and the ventricles are enlarged. Difficult environments probably cannot cause schizophrenia, but they may worsen the disorder and contribute to relapses.

11. Personality disorders are lifelong patterns of maladaptive behavior that are immature and inappropriate ways of coping with stress or solving problems. Individuals with antisocial personalities are impulsive, show little guilt, are concerned only with their own needs, and are frequently in trouble with the law. Antisocial personality disorder probably has genetic and biological roots, but neglectful and hostile parenting may also contribute to the disorder.

12. People with borderline personality disorder show instability in mood, self-concept, and interpersonal relationships. Psychodynamic theories suggest that the caregivers of people with this disorder required their children to be highly dependent and alternated between extreme expressions of love and hostility.

13. In dissociative identity disorder, two or more well-developed personalities alternate within the same individual. Many theorists attribute this disorder to child abuse.

14. Although the use of insanity as a legal defense is a subject of considerable controversy, in reality the defense is rarely used and even more rarely successful.

CORE CONCEPTS

cultural relativist perspective
abnormal
maladaptive
distress
normality
Diagnostic and Statistical Manual of Mental Disorders, 4th edition (DSM-IV)
neuroses
psychoses
biological perspective
psychological perspective
psychoanalytic perspective
behavioral perspective
cognitive perspective
cultural or sociological perspective

vulnerability-stress model
anxiety disorders
generalized anxiety disorder
panic attack
panic disorder
ataque de nervios
agoraphobia
phobia
simple phobia
social phobia
obsessive-compulsive disorder
obsession
compulsion
mood disorders
depressive disorders
bipolar disorders

anhedonia
manic episode
schizophrenia
word salad
loosening of associations
delusion
paranoid
hallucination
personality disorder
antisocial personality disorder
borderline personality disorder
dissociative identity disorder
M'Naghten Rule
American Law Institute Rule
guilty but mentally ill

 # WEB RESOURCES

http://psychology.wadsworth.com/atkinson14e

Take a quiz, try the activities and exercises, and explore web links.

http://bama.ua.edu/~jhooper/tableofc.html

This forensic psychiatry resource page by James Hooper offers a discussion of insanity and the law, as well as a listing of landmark cases that involve the insanity defense.

http://www.chovil.com/

This personal site by schizophrenic patient Ian Chovil includes a marvelous life story that helps give a "face" to schizophrenia. Chovil also explains the biology of schizophrenia and therapy for people with the disease.

http://www2.health-center.com/mentalhealth/therapy/

This site outlines a variety of different psychological disorders, discusses the major kinds of therapy, and provides links to related articles.

 InfoTrac Online Library
http://www.infotrac-college.com/wadsworth

Use InfoTrac College Edition to find popular and scientific articles by using the search terms below or your own relevant terms.

- Antisocial personality disorder
- Bipolar disorder
- Dissociative identity disorder
- Schizophrenia

CD-ROM LINKS

 Psych Odyssey

Check out CD Chapter 16, Abnormal Psychology
A. Classifying and Diagnosing Abnormal Behavior
B. Mood Disorders
C. Schizophrenic Disorders

 Psyk.trek 2.0

Check out CD Unit 11, Abnormal Behavior and Therapy
11a Anxiety Disorders
11b Mood Disorders
11c Schizophrenic Disorders

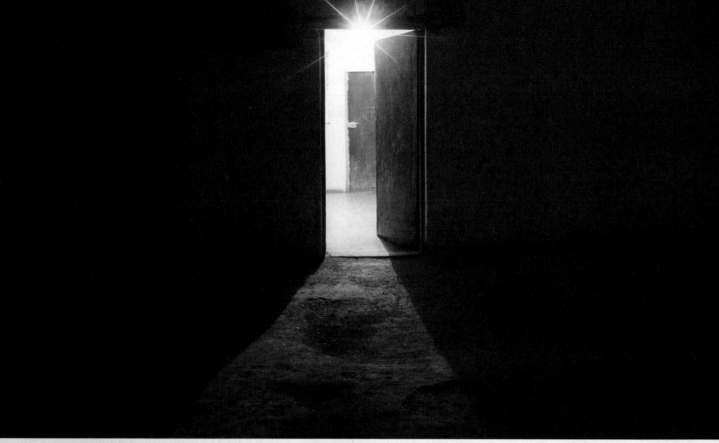

TREATMENT OF PSYCHOLOGICAL DISORDERS

16

Steve M. has paranoid schizophrenia. He frequently hears voices berating him and accusing him of having done something wrong. He was convinced that a transmitter had been implanted in his head, through which he was receiving these messages. When he takes his medications, the voices are quieted and the paranoid beliefs begin to recede.

Over the last 5 years, Steve has been hospitalized three times. Each time he had stopped his medication, twice believing himself well and once, just tired of the whole thing. In between hospitalizations, he has spent some time in a day treatment program and some time taking classes at college. He still struggles with determining what is real and what is not, but he has learned through ther-

apy that he can check this out with the people he trusts, principally his stepmother, brother, and father. Steve has developed a long-term relationship with a psychologist from the clinic whom he sees once a week (in addition to his medication checks with the psychiatrist). Together they confront the very real challenges that his illness and the stigma attached to it poses. His parents, through the parent-support group they have joined, are learning to do the same. (Adapted from Bernheim, 1997, pp. 126–130).

Steve and his family are making use of a variety of types of treatment to control his paranoid schizophrenia. The medications he is taking are one form

of biological treatment for psychological disorders. He is also seeing a psychotherapist to learn new ways of coping with his disorder. His parents are making use of community-based resources to understand Steve's problems.

In this chapter we look at methods for treating abnormal behavior. The most frequently used methods are listed in the Concept Review Table. Each of these treatments is linked to a particular theory of the causes of mental disorders. As we discuss in the next section, our theories of mental disorders, and therefore our treatment of these disorders, has changed a great deal over history.

CONCEPT REVIEW TABLE
Methods of Therapy

Type of Therapy	Example	Description
Psychodynamic Therapies	Traditional psychoanalysis	Through free association, dream analysis, and transference, attempts to discover the unconscious basis of the client's current problems so as to deal with them in a more rational way.
	Contemporary psychodynamic therapies (e.g., interpersonal therapy)	More structured and short-term than traditional psychoanalysis; emphasize the way the client is currently interacting with others.
Behavior Therapies	Systematic desensitization	The client is trained to relax and then presented with a hierarchy of anxiety-producing situations and asked to relax while imagining each one.
	In vivo exposure	Similar to systematic desensitization except that the client actually experiences each situation.
	Flooding	A form of in vivo exposure in which a phobic individual is exposed to the most feared object or situation for an extended period without an opportunity to escape.
	Selective reinforcement	Reinforcement of specific behaviors, often through the use of tokens that can be exchanged for rewards.
	Modeling	A process in which the client learns behaviors by observing and imitating others; often combined with behavioral rehearsal (e.g., in assertiveness training).
Cognitive-Behavior Therapies		Treatment methods that use behavior modification techniques but also incorporate procedures designed to change maladaptive beliefs.
Humanistic Therapies (e.g., client-centered therapy)		In an atmosphere of empathy, warmth, and genuineness, the therapist attempts to facilitate the process through which the client works out solutions to his or her own problems.
Biological Therapies	Psychotherapeutic drugs	Use of drugs to modify mood and behavior.
	Electroconvulsive therapy (ECT)	A mild electric current is applied to the brain to produce a seizure.

HISTORICAL BACKGROUND

Among the earliest beliefs about mental disorders, dating back to the Stone Age, was that a person who behaved in unusual ways was possessed by evil spirits. These demons were removed or exorcised through such techniques as prayer, incantation, and magic. If these techniques were unsuccessful, more extreme measures were taken to ensure that the body would be an unpleasant dwelling place for the evil spirit. Flogging, starving, burning, and causing the person to bleed profusely were frequent forms of "treatment."

Some of the earliest written texts on mental disorders are from the Chinese, who viewed the human body as containing both a positive and negative force. If the two forces were not in balance, illness, including insan-

ity, could result. The ancient Chinese also believed that emotions could be caused when "vital air" flows on specific internal organs. For example, sorrow was caused when air flowed on the lungs, anger was caused when air flowed on the liver, and worry was caused when air flowed on the spleen.

In the Western world, the Greek physician Hippocrates (circa 460–377 B.C.) is credited with bringing a medical perspective to the study of mental disorders. He believed that unusual behaviors were the result of a disturbance in the balance of bodily fluids. Hippocrates, and the Greek and Roman physicians who followed him, argued for more humane treatment of the mentally ill. They stressed the importance of pleasant surroundings, exercise, proper diet, massage, and soothing baths, as well as some less desirable treatments, such as purging and mechanical restraints. Although there were no institutions for the mentally ill, many individuals were

© Stock Montage

Philippe Pinel in the courtyard of the hospital of Salpetriere.

cared for with great kindness in temples dedicated to the gods of healing.

This progressive view of mental illness did not continue, however. Primitive superstitions and belief in demon possession were revived during the Middle Ages. The mentally ill were considered to be in league with Satan and to possess supernatural powers with which they could cause floods, pestilence, and injuries to others. Seriously disturbed individuals were treated cruelly: It was believed that beating, starving, and torturing the mentally ill served to punish the devil. This type of cruelty culminated in the witchcraft trials of the 15th, 16th, and 17th centuries, in which thousands of people, many of whom may have been mentally ill, were sentenced to death.

EARLY ASYLUMS

In the late Middle Ages, cities created asylums to cope with the mentally ill. These asylums were simply prisons; the inmates were chained in dark, filthy cells and treated more as animals than as human beings. It was not until 1792, when Philippe Pinel was placed in charge of an asylum in Paris, that some improvements were made. As an experiment, Pinel removed the chains that restrained the inmates. Much to the amazement of skeptics who thought Pinel was mad to unchain such "animals," the experiment was a success. When released from their restraints, placed in clean, sunny rooms, and treated kindly, many people who for years had been considered hopelessly insane improved enough to leave the asylum.

By the beginning of the 20th century, the fields of medicine and psychology were making great advances. In 1905, a mental disorder known as general paresis was shown to have a physical cause: a syphilis infection acquired many years before the symptoms of the disorder appeared. The syphilis spirochete remains in the body after the initial genital infection disappears, and it gradually destroys the nervous system. The results include the syndrome known as **general paresis**—a gradual decline in mental and physical functioning, marked changes in personality, and delusions and hallucinations. If the disorder is not treated, death occurs within a few years. At one time, general paresis accounted for more than 10% of all admissions to mental hospitals, but today few cases are reported, owing to the effectiveness of penicillin in treating syphilis (Dale, 1975).

The discovery that general paresis was the result of a disease encouraged those who believed that mental illness has biological causes. Nevertheless, in the early 1900s the public still did not understand mental illness and viewed mental hospitals and their inmates with fear and horror. Clifford Beers undertook the task of educating the public about mental health. As a young man, Beers had developed a bipolar disorder and been confined for 3 years in several private and state hospitals. At the time, lack of funds made the average state mental hospital—with its overcrowded wards, poor food, and badly trained attendants—a highly unpleasant place to live. After his recovery, Beers described his experiences in a book titled *A Mind That Found Itself* (1908), which attracted considerable public attention. Beers worked ceaselessly to educate the public about mental illness and helped organize the National Committee for Mental Hygiene. The mental hygiene movement played an invaluable role in stimulating the organization of child-guidance clinics and community mental health centers to aid in the prevention and treatment of mental disorders.

© Corbis/Bettmann

The crib, a restraining device used in a New York mental institution in 1882.

Modern Treatment Facilities

Mental hospitals have been upgraded markedly since Beers's day, but there is still much room for improvement. The best mental hospitals are comfortable and well-kept places that provide therapeutic activities: individual and group psychotherapy, recreation, occupational therapy (designed to teach skills as well as provide relaxation), and educational courses to help patients prepare for jobs upon release from the hospital. The worst are primarily custodial institutions where patients lead a boring existence in run-down, overcrowded wards and receive little treatment beyond medication. Most mental hospitals fall somewhere between these extremes.

Beginning in the early 1960s, emphasis shifted from treating mentally disturbed individuals in hospitals to treating them in their own communities. This movement toward deinstitutionalization was motivated partly by the recognition that hospitalization has some inherent disadvantages, regardless of how good the facilities may be. Hospitals remove people from the social support of family and friends and the familiar patterns of daily life, and they encourage dependence. They are also very expensive.

During the 1950s, psychotherapeutic drugs (discussed later in the chapter) were discovered that could relieve depression and anxiety and reduce psychotic behavior. When these drugs became widely available in the 1960s, many hospitalized patients could be discharged and returned home to be treated as outpatients. The Community Mental Health Centers Act of 1963 made federal funds available for the establishment of community treatment centers designed to provide outpatient treatment and other services, including short-term and partial hospitalization. In partial hospitalization, individuals may receive treatment at the center during the day and return home in the evening, or they can work during the day and spend nights at the center. The movement toward discharge of institutionalized mental patients to community-based services became known as **deinstitutionalization**.

As Figure 16-1 shows, the number of patients treated in state and county mental hospitals has decreased dramatically. For some patients, deinstitutionalization has been successful. The services of mental health centers and private clinicians, along with help from their families and the use of psychotherapeutic drugs, have enabled them to resume satisfactory lives. For others, however, deinstitutionalization has had unfortunate consequences, largely because the facilities in most communities are far from adequate.

Many individuals who improve with hospitalization and could manage on their own with assistance do not receive adequate follow-up care in terms of outpatient therapy, monitoring of medication, or help in finding friends, housing, and jobs. As a consequence, they lead a "revolving-door" existence, going in and out of institutions between unsuccessful attempts to cope on their own. About half of all patients discharged from state hospitals are readmitted within a year.

Some discharged patients are too incapacitated to even attempt to support themselves or function without custodial care. They often live in dirty, overcrowded housing or on the streets. The disheveled man standing on the corner talking to himself and shouting gibberish may be one victim of deinstitutionalization. The woman with all her possessions in a shopping bag who spends one night in the doorway of an office building and the next in a subway station may be another. At least a third of street people suffer from some sort of mental disorder (Rossi, 1990).

The increasing visibility of homeless mentally ill individuals, particularly in large cities, has aroused public concern and prompted a move toward reinstitutionalization. However, this raises an important ethical issue. If such people are not readjusting to society, should they be involuntarily committed to a mental hospital? One of the most cherished civil rights in a democratic society is the right to liberty.

Some experts believe that legal action is warranted only if a person is potentially dangerous to others. The rare, but highly publicized, occasions when a mentally ill person experiencing a psychotic episode attacks an innocent bystander have generated fears for public safety. But dangerousness is difficult to predict (Monahan, 2001). Recent studies suggest that people who have both serious mental disorders and a substance abuse problem (such as alcoholism) do appear to commit violent crimes more often than mentally healthy people (Steadman et

▮ Figure 16-1
Patients in Mental Hospitals
The number of patients cared for in U.S. state and county mental hospitals has decreased dramatically since 1955. (After Lamb, 2001)

▌ Figure 16-2
Likelihood of Violence

The percent of patients with or without a substance abuse problem, and community comparisons with or without a substance abuse problem, who committed a violent act in the previous 10 weeks. Note that the community comparison group was assessed only at one time—at the end of the day. SA refers to substance abuse. (H. J. Steadman, E. P. Mulvey, J. Monahan, P. C. Robbins, P. S. Applebaum, T. Grisso, L. Roth, & E. Silver (1998). Violence by people discharged from acute psychiatric inpatient facilities and by others in the same neighborhoods. *Archives of General Psychiatry, 55,* 393–401. © 1998 American Medical Association.)

al., 1998). Figure 16-2 provides data from a large study in which patients with mental disorders were compared with mentally healthy people in the community. Those with mental disorders and a substance abuse problem were more likely to commit a serious violent act than the community comparison group or than the patients with mental disorders but no substance abuse problem. In addition, patients with mental disorders but no substance abuse problem were slightly more likely to commit violent acts than mentally healthy people with no substance abuse problem. Note, however, that the presence of a substance abuse problem was as strong a predictor of violence as the presence of a mental disorder in this study. In general, experts' opinions regarding whether a given individual with a mental disorder will commit violent crimes are often incorrect, particularly for the long term (Gardner, Lidz, Mulvey, & Shaw, 1996).

Moreover, our legal system is designed to protect people from preventive detention. A person is assumed to be innocent until proven guilty by the courts, and prisoners are released from penitentiaries even though statistics show that most will commit additional crimes. Should mentally ill individuals not have the same rights? And what about people who appear more dangerous to themselves than to others? Should they be committed? These complex issues have yet to be resolved.

Aside from the legal issues, the problem of providing care for the mentally ill remains. Many people with mental disorders might voluntarily seek treatment but cannot because they do not have the means to pay for good treatment. About 40% of people with a serious mental disorder receive little or no regular care (Torrey, 1997).

PROFESSIONALS WHO PROVIDE PSYCHOTHERAPY

Whether a person receives therapy in a hospital, a community mental health center, or a private office, several different types of professionals may be involved.

A psychiatrist has an M.D. degree and has completed a three-year residency (after medical school) in a mental health facility, during which he or she received supervision in the diagnosis of abnormal behavior, drug therapy, and psychotherapy. As a physician, the psychiatrist can prescribe medication and, in most states, hospitalization.

The term *psychoanalyst* is reserved for individuals who have received specialized training at a psychoanalytic institute learning the methods and theories derived from Freud. The program usually takes several years, during which the trainees must undergo their own psychoanalyses as well as treat several clients psychoanalytically while under supervision.

Psychologists who work as therapists have obtained graduate training in clinical, counseling, or school psychology. Usually, they hold a Ph.D. (Doctor of Philosophy) or Psy.D. (Doctor of Psychology) degree. The Ph.D. emphasizes training in research as well as diagnosis and therapy. The Psy.D. is a more applied degree, focusing mainly on diagnosis and therapy. Both degrees require 4 to 5 years of postgraduate study, plus a year or more of internship. In addition, most states require psychologists to pass a licensing or certification examination.

Clinical psychologists work with people suffering from a broad range of mental disorders. Counseling psychologists focus more on problems of adjustment and often concentrate on specific areas such as student, marriage, or family counseling. School psychologists are concerned with young people who have academic difficulties.

Psychiatric social workers have completed a 2-year master's degree program (M.S.W.), which includes training in interviewing, therapy, and in extending treatment procedures to the home and community. Some psychiatric social workers also go on to complete a doctorate in social work. A psychiatric social worker often is called on to collect information about a patient's home situation and to assist the patient in getting help from community resources (such as hospitals, clinics, and social agencies).

Sometimes these professionals work as a team. The psychiatrist prescribes psychotherapeutic medications and monitors their effectiveness; the psychologist sees the same client in individual or group psychotherapy; the social worker monitors the home environment and acts as a liaison with community agencies for the client. In mental hospitals, a fourth professional is available: the psychiatric nurse. Psychiatric nursing is a field within the nursing profession that requires special training in the understanding and treatment of mental disorders. In our discussion of psychotherapeutic techniques, we will not specify the profession of the psychotherapists. Instead, we will assume that they are trained and competent members of any one of these professions.

◆ Interim Summary

- Treatment of the mentally ill has progressed from the ancient notion that abnormal behavior resulted from possession by evil spirits that needed to be punished, to custodial care in asylums, to modern mental hospitals and community mental health centers.

- The policy of deinstitutionalization was intended to move hospitalized mental patients into the community, where they would receive outpatient services.

- The deinstitutionalization movement was never adequately funded and, despite its good intentions, has added to the number of homeless mentally ill individuals, causing concern about civil rights and adequate care.

- Several different mental health professionals provide service to people with mental disorders, including psychiatrists, psychologists, psychiatric social workers, and psychiatric nurses.

◆ Critical Thinking Questions

1. What do you think society's obligations are to people with serious mental disorders? What laws should be enacted to protect the rights of these people?

2. Does society have any right or obligation to see to it that children with serious mental disorders receive treatment, even if their parents do not agree to the treatment?

TECHNIQUES OF PSYCHOTHERAPY

Psychotherapy refers to the variety of psychological interventions that share the goal of alleviating human problems and facilitating effective functioning in society. Some psychotherapists (such as psychoanalysts) believe that modification of behavior is dependent on the indi-

vidual's understanding of his or her unconscious motives and conflicts. Others (such as behavior therapists and cognitive-behavior therapists) focus on changing habitual patterns of thinking and behavior rather than on unconscious conflicts. Despite differences in techniques, most methods of psychotherapy have certain basic features in common. They involve a helping relationship between two people: the client (patient) and the therapist. The client is encouraged to discuss intimate concerns, emotions, and experiences freely without fear of being judged by the therapist or having confidences betrayed. The therapist, in turn, offers empathy and understanding, engenders trust, and tries to help the client develop more effective ways of handling problems.

PSYCHODYNAMIC THERAPIES

A key assumption of **psychodynamic therapies** is that a person's current problems cannot be resolved successfully without a thorough understanding of their unconscious basis in early relationships with parents and siblings. The goal of these therapies is to bring conflicts (repressed emotions and motives) into awareness so that they can be dealt with in a more rational and realistic way. The psychodynamic therapies include traditional Freudian psychoanalysis and more recent therapies based on it (see Vakoch & Strupp, 2000).

One of the main techniques that psychodynamic therapists use to recover unconscious conflicts is **free association,** in which the client is encouraged to give free rein to thoughts and feelings and to say whatever comes to mind without editing or censoring it. This is not easy to do, however. In conversation, we usually try to keep a connecting thread running through our remarks and exclude irrelevant ideas. With practice, free association becomes easier. But even individuals who conscientiously try to give free rein to their thoughts will occasionally find themselves blocked, unable to recall the details of an event or finish a thought. Freud believed that blocking, or resistance, results from the individual's unconscious control over sensitive areas and that these are precisely the areas that need to be explored.

Another technique often used in traditional psychoanalytic therapy is **dream analysis,** which consists of talking about the content of one's dreams and then free associating to that content. Freud believed that dreams are "the royal road to the unconscious"; they represent an unconscious wish or fear in disguised form. He distinguished between dreams' manifest content (the obvious, conscious content) and their latent content (the hidden, unconscious content). By talking about the manifest content of a dream and then free associating to that content, the analyst and client attempt to discover the dream's unconscious meaning.

© 2002 Sidney Harris

"HAVE A COUPLE OF DREAMS, AND
CALL ME IN THE MORNING."

As the therapist and client interact during therapy, the client will often react to the therapist in ways that seem exaggerated or inappropriate. The client may become enraged when the therapist must reschedule an appointment, or may be excessively deferential to the therapist. The term **transference** refers to the tendency for the client to make the therapist the object of thoughts and emotions: The client expresses attitudes toward the analyst that are actually felt toward other people who are, or were, important in his or her life. By pointing out how their clients are reacting to them, therapists help their clients achieve a better understanding of how they react to others. The following passage illustrates an analyst's use of transference, followed by the use of free association:

> Client: I don't understand why you're holding back on telling me if this step is the right one for me at this time in my life.
>
> Therapist: This has come up before. You want my approval before taking some action. What seems to be happening here is that one of the conflicts you have with your wife is trying to get her approval of what you have decided you want to do, and that conflict is occurring now between us.
>
> Client: I suppose so. Other people's approval has always been very important to me.
>
> Therapist: Let's stay with that for a few minutes. Would you free associate to that idea of getting approval from others. Just let the associations come spontaneously—don't force them. (Adapted from Woody & Robertson, 1988, p. 129)

Traditional psychoanalysis is a lengthy, intensive, and expensive process. Client and analyst usually meet for 50-minute sessions several times a week for at least a year and often for several years. Many people find self-exploration under traditional psychoanalysis to be of value; however, for some people it is unaffordable. In addition, people suffering from acute depression, anxiety, or psychosis typically cannot tolerate the lack of structure in traditional psychoanalysis and need more immediate relief from their symptoms.

In response to these needs, as well as to changes in psychoanalytic theory since Freud's time, newer psychodynamic therapies tend to be more structured and short-term than traditional psychoanalysis. One such therapy is called **interpersonal therapy** (Klerman, Weissman, Rounsaville, & Chevron, 1984). Sessions are scheduled less frequently, usually once a week. There is less emphasis on complete reconstruction of childhood experiences and more attention to problems arising from the way the individual is currently interacting with others. Free association is often replaced with direct discussion of critical issues, and the therapist may be more direct, raising pertinent topics when appropriate rather than waiting for the client to bring them up. Although transference is still considered an important part of the therapeutic process, the therapist may try to limit the intensity of the transference process. Research has found interpersonal therapy to be helpful in the treatment of depression, anxiety, drug addiction, and eating disorders (Markowitz & Weissman, 1995).

Still central, however, is the psychoanalytic therapist's conviction that unconscious motives and fears are at the core of most emotional problems and that insight is essential to a cure (Auld & Hyman, 1991). As we will see in the next section, behavior therapists do not agree with these views.

BEHAVIOR THERAPIES

The term **behavior therapy** includes a number of therapeutic methods based on the principles of learning and conditioning (see Chapter 7). Behavior therapists assume that maladaptive behaviors are learned ways of coping with stress and that some of the techniques developed in experimental research on learning can be used to substitute more appropriate responses for maladaptive ones (Follette & Hayes, 2000). Whereas psychoanalysis is concerned with understanding how the individual's past conflicts influence behavior, behavior therapy focuses more directly on the behavior itself.

Behavior therapists point out that although the achievement of insight is a worthwhile goal, it does not ensure behavioral change. Often we understand why we behave the way we do in a certain situation but are unable to change our behavior. If you are unusually timid about speaking in class, you may be able to trace this fear to past events (your father criticized your opinions whenever you expressed them, your mother made a point of correcting your grammar, you had little experience in public speaking during high school because you were afraid to compete with your older brother, who was captain of the debate team). Understanding the reasons behind your fear does not necessarily make it easier for you to contribute to class discussions.

In contrast to psychodynamic therapy, which attempts to change certain aspects of the personality, behavior therapies attempt to modify behaviors that are maladaptive in specific situations. In the initial session, the therapist listens carefully to the client's statement of the problem. What exactly does the client want to change? Is it a fear of flying or of speaking in public? Difficulty in controlling eating or drinking? Feelings of inadequacy and helplessness? Inability to concentrate and get work done? The first step is to define the problem clearly and break it down into a set of specific therapeutic goals. If, for example, the client complains of general feelings of inadequacy, the therapist will try to get the client to describe these feelings more specifically: to pinpoint the kinds of situations in which they occur and the kinds of behaviors associated with them. Inadequate to do what? To speak up in class or in social situations? To get assignments completed on time? To control eating? Once the behaviors that need to be changed have been specified, the therapist and client work out a treatment program, choosing the treatment method that is most appropriate for the particular problem.

SYSTEMATIC DESENSITIZATION AND IN VIVO EXPOSURE Systematic desensitization is a method of eliminating fears by substituting a response that is incompatible with anxiety—namely, relaxation. (It is difficult to be both relaxed and anxious at the same time.) The client is first trained to relax deeply. One way is to progressively relax various muscles, starting, for example, with the feet and ankles and proceeding up the body to the neck and face. The person learns what muscles feel like when they are truly relaxed and how to discriminate among various degrees of tension. Sometimes drugs and hypnosis are used to help people who cannot relax otherwise.

The next step is to make up a hierarchy of the anxiety-producing situations. The situations are ranked in order from the one that produces the least anxiety to the one that produces the most. In systematic desensitization, the client is then asked to relax and imagine each situation in the hierarchy, starting with the one that is least anxiety-producing. In vivo exposure is a method highly similar to systematic desensitization that requires the client to actually experience the anxiety-producing situations. In vivo exposure is more effective than simply imagining anxiety-producing situations, but some clients need to begin with

imagination and eventually move to actually experiencing feared situations.

An example will make these procedures clearer. Suppose that the client is a woman who suffers from a phobia of snakes. The phobia is so strong that she is afraid to walk in her own back yard, let alone go for a walk in the countryside or on a vacation in a wooded area. Her anxiety hierarchy might begin with a picture of a snake in a book. Somewhere around the middle of the hierarchy might be viewing a snake in a glass cage at the zoo. At the top of the hierarchy would be actually handling a snake. After this woman has learned to relax and has constructed the hierarchy, the therapist begins taking her through her list. In systematic desensitization, she sits with her eyes closed in a comfortable chair while the therapist describes the least anxiety-provoking situation. If she can imagine herself in the situation without any increase in muscle tension, the therapist proceeds to the next item on the list. If the woman reports any anxiety while visualizing a scene, she concentrates on relaxing, and the same scene is visualized until all anxiety has been neutralized. This process continues through a series of sessions until the situation that originally provoked the most anxiety now elicits only relaxation. At this point, the woman has been systematically desensitized to anxiety-provoking situations through the strengthening of an incompatible response—relaxation.

During in vivo exposure, the woman would actually experience each of the situations on her list, beginning with the least feared one, with the coaching of the therapist. Before she actually handled a snake herself, the therapist might model handling the snake without being fearful—the therapist would hold the snake in the client's presence, displaying confidence and no anxiety. Eventually the client would handle the snake herself, allowing it to crawl on her while using relaxation to control her anxiety. In vivo exposure therapy of this sort has proven extremely effective in the treatment of phobias (Bandura, Blanchard, & Ritter, 1969).

The specific learning process operating in in vivo exposure may be extinction. Exposing oneself to a fear-arousing stimulus and discovering that nothing bad happens extinguishes the conditioned fear response. Relaxation may be merely a useful way to encourage a person to confront the feared object or situation. Indeed, if phobic individuals can force themselves to stay in the feared situation for a long period (for example, a claustrophobic person sits in a closet for hours or someone who fears contamination goes for days without washing), the initial terror gradually subsides. The term *flooding* is used to refer to this procedure, a type of in vivo therapy in which a phobic individual is exposed to the most feared object or situation for an extended period without an opportunity to escape. This approach has proved to be

Behavioral treatments for phobias require people to actually confront the object of their phobia.

particularly effective in the treatment of agoraphobia and obsessive-compulsive disorders (Thorpe & Olson, 1997).

SELECTIVE REINFORCEMENT Systematic desensitization and in vivo exposure are based on principles of classical conditioning. **Selective reinforcement,** or strengthening of specific desired behaviors, is based on the principles of operant conditioning and has also proved to be an effective method of modifying behavior, especially with children.

The procedure can be illustrated by the case of a third-grade student who was inattentive in school, refused to complete assignments or participate in class, and spent most of her time daydreaming. In addition, her social skills were poor and she had few friends. The behavior to be reinforced was defined as "on-task" behavior, which included paying attention to schoolwork or instructions from the teacher, completing reading assignments, and taking part in class discussions. The reinforcement consisted of beans that were used as tokens to be exchanged for special privileges that the girl valued, such as standing first in line (three beans) or being allowed to stay after school to help the teacher with special projects (nine beans). Whenever the teacher observed the student performing on-task behaviors, she placed one bean in a jar.

During the first 3 months of treatment, the girl completed 12 units of work, compared with none during the previous 3 months. In the final 3 months, she completed 36 units and was performing at the same level as the rest of the class. A follow-up the next year showed that the girl was maintaining her academic performance. She also showed marked improvement in social skills and was accepted more by the other children (Walker, Hedberg, Clement, & Wright, 1981). This is a common finding: Improving behavior in one area of life often produces benefits in other areas (Kazdin, 1982).

Reinforcement of desirable responses can be accompanied by extinction of undesirable ones. For example, a boy who habitually shouts to get his mother's attention could be ignored whenever he does so and reinforced by her attention only when he comes to her and speaks in a conversational tone.

Operant conditioning procedures involving rewards for desirable responses and no rewards for undesirable ones have been used successfully in dealing with a broad range of childhood problems, including bed-wetting, aggression, tantrums, disruptive classroom behavior, poor school performance, and social withdrawal. Similar procedures have been used with autistic children, retarded adults, and severely disordered mental patients.

MODELING Another effective means of changing behavior is modeling. Modeling is the process by which person learns behaviors by observing and imitating others. Because observing others is a major way in which humans learn, watching people who are displaying adaptive behavior should teach people with maladaptive responses better coping strategies. Observing the behavior of a model (either live or videotaped) has proved effective in reducing fears and teaching new skills. For example, observing a therapist handle a snake can reduce the fears of a person with a snake phobia, making it possible for him or her to eventually handle the snake also.

Modeling is effective in overcoming fears and anxieties because it provides an opportunity to observe someone else go through the anxiety-provoking situation without getting hurt. Watching videotapes of models enjoying a visit to the dentist or going through various hospital procedures has proved successful in helping both children and adults overcome their fears of such experiences (Melamed & Siegel, 1975; Shaw & Thoresen, 1974).

BEHAVIORAL REHEARSAL In a therapy session, modeling is often combined with **behavioral rehearsal,** or role playing. The therapist helps the client rehearse or practice more adaptive behaviors. In the following excerpt, a therapist helps a young man overcome his anxieties about asking women for dates. The young man has been pretending to talk to a woman over the phone and finishes by asking for a date.

> Client: Um, I was wondering, you wouldn't want to go out on a date Saturday night, or anything, would you?
>
> Therapist: Okay, that's a start. Can you think of another way of asking her out that sounds a bit more positive and confident? For example, "There's a concert I'd like to see on Saturday night and I'd like very much to take you, if you are free."

Client: That's great!

Therapist: Okay, you try it.

Client: Um, I've got two tickets to the concert Saturday night. If you don't have anything to do, you might want to come along.

Therapist: That's better. Try it one more time, but this time try to convey to her that you'd really like her to go.

Client: I've got two tickets for Saturday's concert. It would be great if you'd go with me, if you're not busy.

Therapist: Great! Just practice it a couple of more times, and you're ready to pick up the phone.

This example illustrates the use of behavioral rehearsal in a type of behavior therapy known as assertiveness training. Like the young man in the example, many people have trouble asking for what they want or refusing to allow others to take advantage of them. By practicing assertive responses (first in role-playing with the therapist and then in real-life situations), the individual not only reduces anxiety but also develops more effective coping techniques. The therapist determines the kinds of situations in which the person is passive and then helps him or her think of and practice some assertive responses that might be effective. The following are examples of situations that might be worked through during a sequence of therapy sessions:

Someone steps in front of you in line.

A friend asks you to do something that you do not want to do.

Your boss criticizes you unjustly.

You return defective merchandise to a store.

You are annoyed by the conversation of people behind you in a movie theater.

The mechanic did an unsatisfactory job of repairing your car.

Most people do not enjoy dealing with such situations, but some are so fearful of asserting themselves that they say nothing and instead build up feelings of resentment and inadequacy. In assertiveness training, the client rehearses with the therapist effective responses that could be made in such situations and then gradually tries them out in real life. The therapist tries to teach the client to express his or her needs in a way that is straightforward and forceful but is not seen by others as hostile or threatening (see Table 16-1).

SELF-REGULATION Because the client and therapist seldom meet more than once per week, the client must learn to control or regulate his or her own behavior so

● **Table 16-1**
Some Elements of an Assertive Response

Decide what you want to say and stick with it rather than giving in to others the minute they disagree with you. For example, when a clerk says you cannot return a defective product, say, "This is defective and I want to return it" repeatedly until the clerk allows you to return it or at least calls the manager, whom you tell, "This is defective and I want to return it" until you get your money back.

Ask for small, specific changes in a situation or another person's behavior rather than requesting global changes. For example, rather than saying, "I want you to be more loving," say, "I want you to listen to me when I talk."

Use "I" phrases instead of accusatory phrases when discussing a difficult situation with another person. Four pieces to an "I" statement are:
I feel . . .
when you . . .
because . . .
what I want . . .
For example, "*I feel* angry *when you* don't show up for an appointment *because* it wastes my time. *What I want* is for you to call me and cancel our appointment when you think you won't be able to make it."

that progress can be made outside the therapy hour. Moreover, if people feel that they are responsible for their own improvement, they are more likely to maintain whatever gains they make. **Self-regulation** involves monitoring, or observing, one's own behavior and using various techniques—self-reinforcement, self-punishment, control of stimulus conditions, development of incompatible responses—to change maladaptive behavior. An individual monitors his or her behavior by keeping a careful record of the kinds of situations that elicit the maladaptive behavior and the kinds of responses that are incompatible with it. For example, a person who is concerned with alcohol abuse would note the kinds of situations in which he or she is most tempted to drink and would try to control such situations or devise a response that is incompatible with drinking (see Marlatt's Seeing Both Sides essay for an application of these techniques). A man who finds it hard not to join his coworkers in a noontime cocktail might plan to eat lunch at his desk, thereby controlling his drinking behavior by controlling his environment. If he is tempted to relax with a drink upon arriving home from work, he might substitute a game of tennis or a jog around the block as a means of relieving tension. Both of these activities would be incompatible with drinking.

Self-reinforcement is rewarding yourself immediately for achieving a specific goal. The reward could be praising yourself, watching a favorite television program, telephoning a friend, or eating a favorite food. Self-punishment is arranging for an aversive consequence for failing to

● Table 16-2
Self-Regulation of Eating

This program illustrates the use of learning principles to help control food intake. (After Stuart & Davis, 1972; O'Leary & Wilson, 1975)

Self-Monitoring

Daily Log
Keep a detailed record of everything you eat. Note the amount eaten, the type of food and its caloric value, the time of day, and the circumstances of eating. This record will establish the caloric intake that is maintaining your present weight. It will also help identify the stimuli that elicit and reinforce your eating behavior.

Weight Chart
Decide how much weight you want to lose, and set a weekly weight loss goal. Your weekly goal should be realistic (between 1 and 2 pounds). Record your weight each day on graph paper. In addition to showing how your weight varies with food intake, this visual record will reinforce your dieting efforts as you observe progress toward your goal.

Controlling Stimulus Conditions

Use these procedures to narrow the range of stimuli associated with eating:

1. Eat only at predetermined times, at a specific table, using a special place mat, napkin, dishes, and so forth. Do *not* eat at other times or in other places (for example, while standing in the kitchen).
2. Do *not* combine eating with other activities, such as reading or watching television.
3. Keep in the house only the foods that are permitted on your diet.
4. Shop for food only after having had a full meal; buy only items that are on a previously prepared list.

Modifying Actual Eating Behavior

Use these procedures to break the chain of responses that makes eating automatic.

1. Eat very slowly, paying close attention to the food.
2. Finish chewing and swallowing before putting more food on the fork.
3. Put your utensils down for periodic short breaks before continuing to eat.

Developing Incompatible Responses

When tempted to eat at times other than those specified, find a substitute activity that is incompatible with eating. For example, exercise to music, go for a walk, talk with a friend (preferably one who knows that you are dieting), or study your diet plan and weight graph, noting how much weight you have lost.

Self-Reinforcement

Arrange to reward yourself with an activity that you enjoy (watching television, reading, planning a new wardrobe, visiting a friend) when you have maintained appropriate eating behavior for a day. Plan larger rewards (for example, buying something you want) for a specified amount of weight loss. Self-punishment (other than forgoing a reward) is probably less effective because dieting is a fairly depressing business anyway. But you might decrease the frequency of binge eating by immediately reciting to yourself the aversive consequences or by looking at an unattractive picture of yourself in a bathing suit.

achieve a goal, such as depriving yourself of something you enjoy (not watching a favorite television program, for instance) or making yourself do an unpleasant task (such as cleaning your room). Depending on the kind of be-

havior you want to change, various combinations of self-reinforcement, self-punishment, or control of stimuli and responses may be used. Table 16-2 outlines a program for self-regulation of eating.

Often, many of the techniques of behavior therapy are used in combination to treat people with serious mental disorders. Behavior therapy has proven effective for several of the anxiety disorders, including panic disorder, phobias, and obsessive-compulsive disorders (Fals-Stewart & Allen, 1993; Lindsay, Crino, & Andrews, 1997; Ollendick & King, 1998, 2000), for depression (Jacobson & Hollon, 1996), for problems in sexual functioning (Rosen & Leiblum, 1995), and for several childhood disorders (Thorpe & Olson, 1997).

COGNITIVE-BEHAVIOR THERAPIES

The behavior therapy procedures discussed so far have focused on modifying behavior directly. They devote little attention to the individual's thinking and reasoning processes. Initially, behavior therapists discounted the importance of cognition, preferring a strict stimulus-response approach. However, in response to evidence that cognitive factors—thoughts, expectations, and interpretations of events—are important determinants of behavior, many behavior therapists now incorporate cognitions in their approaches to therapy (Bandura, 1986).

Cognitive-behavior therapy is a general term for treatment methods that use behavior modification techniques but also incorporate procedures designed to change maladaptive beliefs (A. T. Beck, Rush, Shaw, & Emery, 1979; J. S. Beck, 1995). The therapist helps the client control disturbing emotional reactions, such as anxiety and depression, by teaching more effective ways of interpreting and thinking about experiences. For example, as we noted in discussing Beck's cognitive theory of depression (see Chapter 15), depressed individuals tend to appraise events from a negative and self-critical viewpoint. They expect to fail rather than succeed, and they tend to magnify failures and minimize successes in evaluating their performance. In treating depression, cognitive-behavior therapists help clients recognize the distortions in their thinking and make changes that are more in line with reality. The following dialogue illustrates how a therapist, through carefully directed questioning, makes a client aware of the unrealistic nature of her beliefs.

Therapist: Why do you want to end your life?

Client: Without Raymond, I am nothing. . . . I can't be happy without Raymond. . . . But I can't save our marriage.

Therapist: What has your marriage been like?

Client: It has been miserable from the very beginning. . . . Raymond has always been unfaithful. . . . I have hardly seen him in the past five years.

Therapist: You say that you can't be happy without Raymond. . . . Have you found yourself happy when you are with Raymond?

Client: No, we fight all the time and I feel worse.

Therapist: You say you are nothing without Raymond. Before you met Raymond, did you feel you were nothing?

Client: No, I felt I was somebody.

Therapist: If you were somebody before you knew Raymond, why do you need him [in order] to be somebody now?

Client: (puzzled) Hmmm. . . .

Therapist: If you were free of the marriage, do you think that men might be interested in you—knowing that you were available?

Client: I guess that maybe they would be.

Therapist: Is it possible that you might find a man who would be more constant than Raymond?

Client: I don't know. . . . I guess it's possible. . . .

Therapist: Then what have you actually lost if you break up the marriage?

Client: I don't know.

Therapist: Is it possible that you'll get along better if you end the marriage?

Client: There is no guarantee of that.

Therapist: Do you have a real marriage?

Client: I guess not.

Therapist: If you don't have a real marriage, what do you actually lose if you decide to end the marriage?

Client: (long pause) Nothing, I guess. (Beck, 1976, pp. 280–291)

The behavioral component of the treatment comes into play when the therapist encourages the client to formulate alternative ways of viewing her situation and then test the implications of those alternatives. For example, the woman client in the preceding dialogue might be asked to record her moods at regular intervals and then note how her depression and feelings of self-esteem fluctuate as a function of what she is doing. If she finds that she feels worse after interacting with her husband than when she is alone or is interacting with someone else, this information could serve to challenge her belief that she "can't be happy without Raymond."

A cognitive-behavioral program to help someone overcome agoraphobia might include training in more adaptive thinking, along with in vivo exposure (accompanied excursions that take the individual progressively farther from home). The therapist teaches the client to replace self-defeating internal dialogues ("I'm so nervous, I know I'll faint as soon as I leave the house") with positive self-instructions ("Be calm; I'm not alone; even if I have a panic attack, I can cope"). Table 16-3 de-

Instruction in Self-Change Skills

Pinpointing the target behavior and recording its baseline rate of occurrence; discovering the events or situations that precede the target behavior and the consequences (either positive or negative) that follow it; setting goals for change and choosing reinforcers.

Relaxation Training

Learning progressive muscle relaxation to handle the anxiety that often accompanies depression; monitoring tension in daily situations; and applying relaxation techniques.

Increasing Pleasant Activities

Monitoring the frequency of enjoyable activities and planning weekly schedules so that each day contains a balance between negative/neutral activities and pleasant ones.

Cognitive Strategies

Learning methods for increasing positive thoughts and decreasing negative ones; for identifying irrational thoughts and challenging them; and for using self-instructions to help handle problem situations.

Assertiveness Training

Identifying situations in which being nonassertive adds to feelings of depression; learning to handle social interactions more assertively via modeling and role playing.

Increasing Social Interaction

Identifying the factors that are contributing to low social interaction (such as getting into the habit of doing things alone, feeling uncomfortable due to few social skills); deciding on activities that need to be increased (such as calling friends to suggest getting together) or decreased (such as watching television) in order to increase the level of pleasant social interaction.

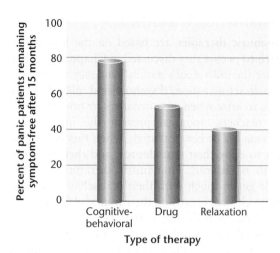

▌Figure 16-3
Percentage of Panic Patients Remaining Symptom-Free After 15 Months
People receiving cognitive-behavioral therapy for panic disorder were more likely to remain symptom-free over 15 months than people receiving only drug therapy or relaxation training. (After Clark et al., 1994)

scribes a program for the treatment of depression that includes techniques for modifying behavior and changing attitudes.

Cognitive-behavior therapists agree that it is important to alter a person's beliefs in order to bring about an enduring change in behavior. Most maintain that behavioral procedures are more powerful than strictly verbal ones in affecting cognitive processes. For example, to overcome anxiety about giving a speech in class, it is helpful to think positively: "I know the material well, and I'm sure I can present my ideas effectively" and "The topic is interesting, and the other students will enjoy what I have to say." But first presenting the speech to a roommate and again before a group of friends will probably do more to reduce anxiety. Successful performance increases our feeling of mastery. In fact, it has been suggested that all therapeutic procedures that are effective give the client a sense of mastery or self-efficacy. Observing others cope and succeed, being verbally persuaded that we can handle a difficult situation, and judging from internal cues that we are relaxed and in control contribute to feelings of self-efficacy. But the greatest sense of efficacy comes from actual performance, from the experience of mastery. In essence, nothing succeeds like success (Bandura, 1995).

Cognitive-behavioral therapies have proven highly effective in treating an array of nonpsychotic conditions, including depression, anxiety disorders, eating disorders, drug and alcohol dependence, and sexual dysfunctions (Chambless & Ollendick, 2001; Fairburn et al., 1995; Jacobson & Hollon, 1996; Margraf, Barlow, Clark, & Telch, 1993; Marlatt, Larimer, Baer, & Quigley, 1993; Rosen & Lieblum, 1995; see Figure 16-3). These therapies tend not only to help people overcome troubling thoughts, feelings, and behaviors but also to prevent relapses after therapy has ended.

Humanistic Therapies

Humanistic therapies are based on the humanistic approach to personality discussed in Chapter 13. They emphasize the individual's natural tendency toward growth and self-actualization. Psychological disorders are assumed to arise when circumstances or other people (parents, teachers, spouses) prevent the individual from achieving his or her potential. When this occurs, people begin to deny their true desires, and their potential for growth is reduced. Humanistic therapies seek to help people get in touch with their real selves and make deliberate choices regarding their lives and behavior rather than being controlled by external events.

Like the psychoanalyst, the humanistic therapist attempts to increase the client's awareness of underlying emotions and motives. But the emphasis is on what the individual is experiencing in the here and now, rather than in the past. The humanistic therapist does not interpret the client's behavior (as a psychoanalyst might) or try to modify it (as a behavior therapist would), because this would amount to imposing the therapist's views on the patient. The goal of the humanistic therapist is to facilitate exploration of the individual's own thoughts and feelings and to assist the individual in arriving at his or her own solutions. This approach will become clearer as we look at client-centered therapy (also called *nondirective therapy*), one of the first humanistic therapies.

Client-centered therapy, developed in the 1940s by the late Carl Rogers, is based on the assumption that each individual is the best expert on himself or herself and that people are capable of working out solutions to their own problems. The task of the therapist is to facilitate this process—not to ask probing questions, make interpretations, or suggest courses of action. In fact, Rogers preferred the term *facilitator* to *therapist*, and he called the people he worked with *clients* rather than *patients* because he did not view emotional difficulties as indications of an illness to be cured.

The therapist facilitates the client's progress toward self-insight by restating what the client says about his or her needs and emotions. Rogers believed that the most important qualities for a therapist are empathy, warmth, and genuineness. Empathy refers to the ability to understand the feelings the client is trying to express and the ability to communicate this understanding to the client. The therapist must adopt the client's frame of reference and strive to see the problems as the client sees them. By warmth, Rogers meant acceptance of individuals the way they are, including the conviction that they have the capacity to deal constructively with their problems. A therapist who is genuine is open and honest and does not play a role or operate behind a professional façade. People are reluctant to reveal themselves to those whom

they perceive as phony. Rogers believed that a therapist who possesses these three attributes will facilitate the client's growth and self-exploration (Rogers, 1970).

Rogers was the first therapist to make tape recordings of therapy sessions and permit them to be studied and analyzed. He and his colleagues have contributed much to psychotherapy research. Client-centered therapy has some limitations, however. Like psychoanalysis, it appears to be successful only with individuals who are fairly verbal and are motivated to discuss their problems. For people who do not voluntarily seek help or are seriously disturbed and unable to discuss their feelings, more directive methods are usually necessary. In addition, by using the client's self-reports as the only measure of psychotherapeutic effectiveness, the client-centered therapist ignores behavior outside the therapy session. Individuals who feel insecure and ineffective in their interpersonal relationships often need more structured help in modifying their behavior.

Sociocultural Approaches to Therapy

Sociocultural approaches to treatment view the individual as part of a larger system of relationships, influenced by social forces and culture, and believe that this larger system must be addressed in therapy.

GROUP THERAPY Many emotional problems involve difficulties in relating to others, including feelings of isolation, rejection, and loneliness and an inability to form meaningful relationships. Although the therapist can help the client work out some of these problems, the final test lies in how well the person can apply the attitudes and responses learned in therapy to relationships in everyday life. **Group therapy** permits clients to work out their problems in the presence of others, observe how other people react to their behavior, and try out new ways of responding when old ones prove unsatisfactory (Forsyth & Corazzini, 2000). It is often used as a supplement to individual psychotherapy.

Psychoanalytic, humanistic, and cognitive-behaviorist therapists have modified their techniques so that they can be used with groups. Group therapy has been used in a variety of settings: in hospital wards and outpatient psychiatric clinics, with parents of disturbed children, and with teenagers in correctional institutions, to name a few. Typically, a group consists of a small number of individuals (six to eight is considered optimal) who have similar problems. The therapist usually remains in the background, allowing group members to exchange experiences, comment on one another's behavior, and discuss their own problems as well as those of the other members. However, in some groups the therapist is quite active. For example, in a group desensitization session, people who share the same phobias (such as fear of flying or anxiety about tests) may be led through a systematic desensitization hierarchy. Or in a session for training social skills, a group of shy and unassertive individuals may be coached in a series of role-playing scenes.

Group therapy has several advantages over individual therapy. It uses the therapist's resources more efficiently because one therapist can help several people at once. An individual can derive comfort and support from observing that others have similar, perhaps more severe problems. A person can learn vicariously by watching how others behave and can explore attitudes and reactions by interacting with a variety of people, not just with the therapist. Groups are particularly effective when they give participants opportunities to acquire new social skills through modeling and to practice these skills in the group.

Most groups are led by a trained therapist. However, the number and variety of self-help groups—groups that are conducted without a professional therapist—are increasing. **Self-help groups** are voluntary organizations of people who meet regularly to exchange information and support one another's efforts to overcome a common problem. Alcoholics Anonymous is the best known of these groups (see Humphreys's Seeing Both Sides essay for a discussion of AA). Other groups help people cope with specific stressful situations, such as bereavement, divorce, and single parenthood. Table 16-4 lists a variety of self-help groups.

MARITAL AND FAMILY THERAPY Problems in communicating feelings, satisfying one's needs, and responding appropriately to the needs and demands of others become intensified in the intimate context of marriage and family life. To the extent that they involve more than one client and focus on interpersonal relationships, **marital therapy**—in which a married or partnered couple undergoes therapy—and **family therapy**—in which the entire family undergoes therapy together—can be considered specialized forms of group therapy.

The high divorce rate and the number of couples seeking help for difficulties in their relationships have made marital or couples therapy a growing field. Studies show that joint therapy for both partners is more effective in solving marital problems than individual therapy for only one partner (Baucom, Epstein, & Gordon, 2000). Marital therapy can also be very helpful when one partner has a psychological disorder whose symptoms or consequences are disrupting the marriage.

There are many approaches to marital therapy, but most focus on helping the partners communicate their feelings, develop greater understanding and sensitivity to each other's needs, and work on more effective ways of

● Table 16-4
Examples of Self-Help Groups

Listed here are some of the self-help groups available in one large community. *(After San Diego Mental Health Association, 1989)*

AIDS Counseling Program

AIRS (teenage chemical dependency)

Adult Children of Alcoholics

Adults Molested as Children

Affective Disorders Group (mood disorders)

Al-Anon (families of alcoholics)

Ala-Teen (teenage alcohol abuse)

Alcoholics Anonymous

Alzheimer's Disease Family Support Group

Arthritis Support Group

Battered Women's Support Group

Bi-Polar Support Group (manic-depression)

CREATE (college students recovering from mental illness)

Emotional Health Anonymous

Epilepsy Support Group

Gay Men's Coming-Out Group

Grandmothers' Support Group (mothers of teenage mothers)

Lesbian Support Group

Loss Support (grief recovery)

Make Today Count (breast cancer support)

PMS Association (premenstrual syndrome)

Parent Aid (parents at risk for child abuse)

Parents United (sexual abuse)

Parkinson's Disease Support Group

Pre Ala-Teen (child alcohol dependency)

Project Return (recovering mental patients)

Recovery, Inc.

Phobia Foundation

Single Parent Support Group

Survivors of Suicide

Teen Mothers Support Group

Victims of Homicide (family and loved ones)

Voices (schizophrenic support group)

handling their conflicts. Some couples enter marriage with very different and often unrealistic expectations about the roles of husband and wife. The therapist can help them clarify their expectations and work out a mutually agreeable compromise. Sometimes the couple negotiates behavioral contracts, agreeing on the behavior changes each person is willing to make in order to create a more satisfying relationship, and specifying rewards and penalties for making, or not making, the desired changes.

Family therapy overlaps with marital therapy but has a somewhat different origin. It developed in response to the discovery that many people who improved in individual therapy away from their families—often in institutional settings—relapsed when they returned home. It became apparent that many of these people came from disturbed family settings that must be modified if the individual's gains were to be maintained. In the case of children with psychological problems, it is particularly important that the family be treated. The basic premise of family therapy is that the problem shown by the identified patient is a sign that something is wrong with the entire family; the family system is not operating properly. The difficulty may lie in poor communication among family members or in an alliance between some family members that excludes others. For example, a mother whose relationship with her husband is unsatisfactory may focus all her attention on her son. As a result, the husband and daughter feel neglected, and the son, upset by his mother's excessive attention and the resentment directed toward him by his father and sister, develops problems in school. Although the boy's school difficulties may be the reason for seeking treatment, it is clear that they are only a symptom of a more basic family problem.

In family therapy, the family meets regularly with one or two therapists (usually a male and a female). The therapist observes the interactions among family members and tries to help each member become aware of the way he or she relates to the others and how his or her actions may be contributing to the family's problems. Sometimes videotape recordings are played back to make the family members aware of how they interact. At other times, the therapist may visit the family at home to observe conflicts and verbal exchanges as they occur in their natural setting. It often becomes apparent that problem behaviors are being reinforced by the responses of family members. For example, a child's temper tantrums or a teenager's eating problems may be inadvertently reinforced by the attention they elicit from the parents. The therapist can teach the parents to monitor their own and their children's behavior, determine how their reactions may be reinforcing the problem behavior, and then alter the reinforcement contingencies.

An important application of family therapy is in teaching families of people with schizophrenia to communicate more positively and clearly (Goldstein, 1987). People with schizophrenia in families in which conflict and hostility are expressed in hurtful ways and in which family members are overinvolved in each other's lives tend to have more frequent relapses than those in families in which conflict and hostility are expressed more calmly and family members respect each other's independence. Training programs that enhance family members' skills in expressing negative emotion and interacting in positive ways can reduce relapse rates for people with schizophrenia.

Family therapies seek to treat the family as a whole.

COMMUNITY-BASED PROGRAMS A variety of community resources have been developed to serve the psychological needs of different groups. One such resource is the **halfway house,** where patients who have been hospitalized can live while making the transition back to independent living in the community. Residential centers are also available for people who are recovering from alcohol and drug problems, for delinquent or runaway youths, and for battered wives. Rap centers, where troubled teenagers can discuss their problems with other teenagers and with sympathetic counselors, play an important role in many communities, and youth centers provide job counseling, remedial education, and help with family and personal problems.

Crisis intervention provides immediate help for individuals and families undergoing intense stress. During periods of acute emotional turmoil, people often feel overwhelmed and incapable of dealing with the situation. They may not be able to wait for a therapy appointment, or they may not know where to turn. One form of crisis intervention is provided by 24-hour walk-in services, often in a community mental health center, where a person can receive immediate attention. A therapist helps clarify the problem, provides reassurance, suggests a plan of action, and mobilizes the support of other agencies or family members. This kind of therapy is usually short-term (five or six sessions) and provides the support the person requires to handle the crisis at hand. Such short-term intervention often makes hospitalization unnecessary.

Another form of crisis intervention is the telephone hot line. Telephone crisis centers are usually staffed by volunteers under the direction of mental health professionals. Some focus specifically on suicide prevention; others help distressed callers find the particular kind of assistance they need. The volunteers usually receive training that emphasizes listening with care, evaluating the potential for suicide, conveying empathy and understanding, providing information about community resources, offering hope and reassurance, and recording the caller's name and phone number before he or she hangs up so that a professional can follow up on the problem. Most major cities in the United States have developed some form of telephone hot line to help people who are undergoing periods of severe stress, as well as specialized hot lines to deal with child abuse, rape victims, battered wives, and runaways. The phone numbers are widely publicized in the hope of reaching those who need help.

Most of the community programs we have discussed could not function without the help of paraprofessionals. Because the need for psychological services outstrips the supply of available therapists, concerned citizens can play a valuable role. People of all ages and backgrounds have been trained to work in the field of community mental health. College students have served as companions for hospitalized patients. Older individuals who have raised families have been trained to work with adolescents in community clinics, to counsel parents of youngsters with behavior problems, and to work with schizophrenic children. Former mental patients, recovered drug addicts, and ex-convicts have been trained to help individuals faced with problems similar to the ones they have experienced.

Many residential mental health programs are run by nonprofessionals in consultation with trained therapists. An outstanding example is Achievement Place, a home-style facility in Kansas where couples act as surrogate parents for a group of youngsters who have been referred by the courts because of delinquent behavior. Behavior therapy methods are used to extinguish aggressive behavior and reward social skills. Follow-up data show that youths who graduate from Achievement Place have fewer contacts with courts and police and achieve slightly higher grades than youths who are placed on probation or in a traditional institution for delinquents (Fixsen, Phillips, Phillips, & Wolf, 1976). There are numerous other Achievement Places throughout the United States modeled after the original Kansas facility.

CULTURALLY SPECIFIC THERAPIES Many cultural groups, both within modern industrialized countries and in developing countries, have their own forms of therapy for distressed people. Native American treatments focus on the religious practices, psychological well-being, and physical health of the individual (LaFromboise, Trimble, & Mohatt, 1998). Distressed persons are encouraged to view themselves as embedded in their community and as an expression of the community. Their family and friends participate with them in ceremonies involving prayers, songs, and dances that emphasize their cultural heritage and the reintegration of the individual into the cultural network. In addition, the individual may be pre-

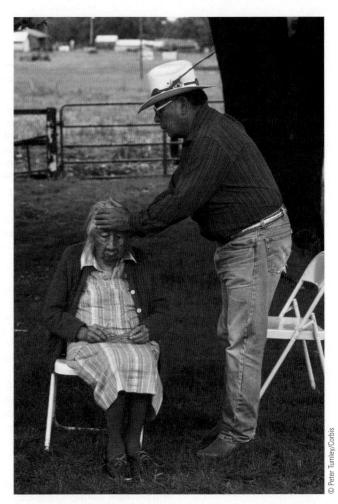

Some Native American groups have their own healing rituals for people with psychological distress.

scribed herbal medicines that have been used for hundreds of years.

Latinos in the southwestern United States and Mexico may consult folk healers, known as *curanderos* or *curanderas* (Koss-Chioino, 1995; Martinez, 1993). *Curanderos* use religiously based rituals to overcome the folk illnesses believed to cause psychological and physical problems. These illnesses may be the result of curses placed on the individuals. Healing rituals include prayers, the use of holy palm, and incantations. *Curanderos* may also apply healing ointments or oils and prescribe herbal medicines.

AN ECLECTIC APPROACH

There are many variations of psychotherapy besides the ones described here. Several are listed in Table 16-5. Most psychotherapists do not adhere strictly to any single method. Instead, they take an eclectic approach, selecting from the different techniques the ones that they

● Table 16-5
Other Approaches to Psychotherapy

Listed here are several psychotherapies that are not discussed in the text.

Name	Focus of Therapy	Principal Methods
Gestalt therapy	To become aware of the whole personality by working through unresolved conflicts and discovering aspects of the individual's being that are blocked from awareness. Emphasis is on becoming intensely aware of how one is feeling and behaving at the moment.	Therapy in a group setting, but therapist works with one individual at a time. Acting out fantasies, dreams, or the two sides to a conflict are methods used to increase awareness. Combines psychoanalytic emphasis on resolving internal conflicts with behaviorist emphasis on awareness of one's behavior and humanistic concern for self-actualization.
Reality therapy	To clarify the individual's values and evaluate current behavior and future plans in relation to these values. To force the individual to accept responsibility.	Therapist helps the individual perceive the consequences of possible courses of action and decide on a realistic solution or goal. Once a plan of action has been chosen, a contract may be signed in which the client agrees to follow through.
Rational-emotive therapy	To replace irrational ideas (It is essential to be loved and admired by everyone all the time; I should be competent in all respects; people have little control over their sorrow and unhappiness) with more realistic ones. Assumes that cognitive change will produce emotional changes.	Therapist attacks and contradicts the individual's ideas (sometime subtly, sometimes directly) in an attempt to persuade her or him to take a more rational view of the situation. Similar to Beck's cognitive therapy, but the therapist is more direct and confrontive.
Transactional analysis	To become aware of the intent behind the individual's communications; to eliminate subterfuge and deceit so that the individual can interpret his or her behavior accurately.	Therapy in a group setting. Communications between married couples or group members are analyzed in terms of the part of the personality that is speaking—"parent," "child," or "adult" (similar to Freud's super-ego, id, and ego)—and the intent of the message. Destructive social interactions or "games" are exposed for what they are.
Hypnotherapy	To relieve the symptoms and strengthen ego processes by helping the individual set reality aside and make constructive use of imagery.	Therapist uses various hypnotic procedures in an attempt to reduce conflict and doubt by focusing the individual's attention, to modify symptoms through direct suggestion or displacement, and to strengthen the individual's ability to cope.

feel are most appropriate, given the client's personality and specific symptoms. Although their theoretical orientation may be toward a particular method or school (for example, more psychoanalytic than behaviorist), eclectic psychotherapists feel free to discard concepts that they view as not especially helpful and to select techniques from other schools. In addition, many psychotherapists use both psychotherapeutic techniques and drug therapies in treating clients with more severe problems. (Psychotherapists who are not physicians will work with a psychiatrist who will prescribe drugs for their patients.)

In dealing with a highly anxious individual, for instance, an eclectic psychotherapist might first prescribe tranquilizers or relaxation training to help reduce the client's level of anxiety. (Most psychoanalysts would not take this approach, however, because they believe that anxiety is necessary to motivate the client to explore his

or her conflicts.) To help the client understand the origins of his or her problems, the therapist might discuss certain aspects of the patient's history but might consider it unnecessary to explore childhood experiences to the extent that a psychoanalyst would. The therapist might use educational techniques, such as providing information about sex and reproduction to help relieve the anxieties of an adolescent boy who feels guilty about his sexual impulses, or explaining the functioning of the autonomic nervous system to reassure an anxious woman that some of her symptoms, such as heart palpitations and hand tremors, are not indications of a disease.

Recognizing that often no single therapeutic approach deals successfully with all aspects of a problem, more and more therapists are specializing in specific problems. For example, some clinicians specialize in sexual dysfunction. They learn all they can about the

© 2002 Sidney Harris

"I UTILIZE THE BEST FROM FREUD, THE BEST FROM JUNG AND THE BEST FROM MY UNCLE MARTY, A VERY SMART FELLOW."

physiological processes that lead to orgasm; the effects of drugs such as alcohol, tranquilizers, and other medications on sexual performance; and how such factors as anxiety, sexual traumas, and poor communication between partners contribute to sexual dysfunction. Once they have learned all they can about the variables involved in normal and abnormal sexual functioning, they examine the various therapeutic systems to see what techniques can be applied to specific problems. Although sex therapists may draw upon all of the approaches we have discussed, biological and cognitive-behavioral methods are most often used in treating sexual dysfunctions.

Other therapists specialize in anxiety, depression, alcoholism, and marital problems. Some concentrate on certain age groups, seeking to learn all they can about the problems of children, adolescents, or the aged. Within their area of specialization, therapists generally use an eclectic approach.

SPECIAL ISSUES IN TREATING CHILDREN

Every therapy we have described has probably been used at one time or another to treat children and adolescents with psychological disorders. Studies of the effectiveness of psychological and biological therapies generally show that children and adolescents who receive therapy have better outcomes than those who receive no therapy (Roberts, Vernberg, & Jackson, 2000). The effectiveness of any specific type of therapy may depend largely on the type of disorder the child or adolescent has.

Designing and applying effective therapies for children and adolescents is made difficult by a number of factors. First, the therapy must be matched to the child's developmental level. Children must be able to under-

stand what the therapist is saying and participate in the therapy to benefit from it. Therapies that are over their heads do them little good. Second, children are embedded in families, and often the family as well as the child must be treated. Yet, sometimes the family refuses to be treated or to recognize how they may be contributing to the child's problems. Finally, children and adolescents seldom refer themselves for treatment but instead are most often brought to treatment by their parents or other adults. This can substantially reduce their motivation to engage in therapy.

Unfortunately, most children who could benefit from therapy do not receive it. Treatment facilities specializing in children's problems are not available in many parts of the United States. Perhaps 50% of psychologically disturbed children receive advice or medications only from their family physicians, who are not trained in the assessment and treatment of psychological disorders (Tuma, 1989). The child welfare system sees many troubled children, often the victims of abuse and neglect. Increasingly, such children are placed in long-term foster care rather than given specialized psychological treatment. Many children in the juvenile justice system suffer from psychological disorders, but few receive long-term intensive treatment (Tuma, 1989). There is considerable room for the expansion of services to psychologically disturbed children.

THE EFFECTIVENESS OF PSYCHOTHERAPY

How effective is psychotherapy? Which methods work best? One survey of the American public found that most people who have had psychotherapy think it helped them (Figure 16-4; Seligman, 1995). In describing each of the psychotherapies, we mentioned some studies of their effectiveness. In this section, we look briefly at how research on the effectiveness of therapy is done (see Haaga & Stiles, 2000).

EVALUATING PSYCHOTHERAPY It is difficult to objectively evaluate the effectiveness of psychotherapy because so many variables must be considered. For instance, some people with psychological problems get better without any professional treatment. This phenomenon is called *spontaneous remission*. People with some types of mental disorders do improve simply with the passage of time. More often, however, improvement that occurs in the absence of treatment is not spontaneous. Rather, it is the result of external events such as the help of another person or changes in the individual's life situation.

Many emotionally disturbed people who do not seek professional assistance improve with the help of a non-professional, such as a friend, teacher, or religious ad-

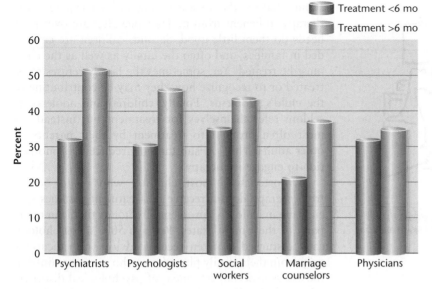

■ Figure 16-4
Percentage of People Who Reported That Treatment "Made Things a Lot Better" in a Study by *Consumer Reports* (1995)
A novel study by the magazine *Consumer Reports* simply asked people who had received some treatment for psychological symptoms whether it had been helpful or not. (M. E. P. Seligman (1995). The effectiveness of psychotherapy: The Consumer Reports study. *American Psychologist, 50,* 965–974. Copyright © 1995 by the American Psychological Association. Reprinted with permission.)

viser. We cannot consider these recoveries to be spontaneous, but because they are not due to psychotherapy, they are included in the rate of spontaneous remission, which ranges from about 30% to 60%, depending on the particular disorder being studied (Haaga & Stiles, 2000). To allow for those who would have improved without treatment, any evaluation of psychotherapy must compare a treated group with an untreated control group. Psychotherapy is judged to be effective if the client's improvement after therapy is greater than any improvement that occurs without therapy over the same period. The ethical problem of allowing someone to go without treatment is usually resolved by composing the control group of individuals on a waiting list. Members of the waiting-list control group are interviewed at the beginning of the study to gather baseline information, but they receive no treatment until after the study. Unfortunately, the longer the study (and time is needed to measure improvement, especially with insight therapies), the harder it is to keep people on a waiting list.

A second major problem in evaluating psychotherapy is measuring the outcome. How do we decide whether a person has been helped by therapy? We cannot always rely on the individual's own assessment. Some people report that they are feeling better simply to

please the therapist or to convince themselves that their money was well spent. The therapist's evaluation of the treatment as successful cannot always be considered an objective criterion, either. The therapist has a vested interest in proclaiming that the client is better. And sometimes the changes that the therapist observes during the therapy session do not carry over into real-life situations. Assessment of improvement, therefore, should include at least three independent measures: the client's evaluation of progress, the therapist's evaluation, and the judgment of third parties such as family members and friends or a clinician not involved in the treatment.

Despite these problems, researchers have been able to conduct many psychotherapy evaluation studies. In 1952, the well-known British psychologist Hans Eysenck stunned the field when he reviewed studies evaluating the effectiveness of psychotherapy and concluded that psychotherapy did not work. People who had received psychotherapy apparently fared no better than people who were not treated or were placed on a waiting list. The number and quality of studies evaluating psychotherapies prior to 1952 was limited, however. Not surprisingly, Eysenck's review prompted a great deal of new research.

Several reviews of this research over the last five decades have concluded that psychotherapy does indeed have positive effects and is better than no treatment at all or various placebos (Lambert & Bergin, 1994; Luborsky, Singer, & Luborsky, 1975; Smith, Glass, & Miller, 1980; Wampold et al., 1997). In 1980, for example, a group of investigators located 475 published studies that compared at least one therapy group with an untreated control group. Using the statistical procedure known as meta-analysis (see Chapter 6), they determined the magnitude of effect for each study by comparing the average change produced in treatment (on measures such as self-esteem, anxiety, and achievement in work and school) with that experienced by the control group. They concluded that individuals receiving therapy were better off than those who had received no treatment. The average psychotherapy patient showed greater improvement than 80% of the untreated patients (Smith, Glass, & Miller, 1980). A subsequent review that analyzed a new sample of studies yielded comparable results (Shapiro & Shapiro, 1982).

COMPARING PSYCHOTHERAPIES Psychotherapy produces greater improvement than no treatment, but are the different therapeutic approaches equally effective? A number of reviews have analyzed studies in which the results of different psychotherapies (usually including behavioral, cognitive-behavioral, and sometimes client-centered therapies) were compared (Bergin & Lambert, 1979; Rachman & Wilson, 1980; Smith, Glass, & Miller, 1980). The conclusion of most of these reviews is that there is little difference in effectiveness between therapies. How can therapies that espouse such different methods produce such similar results? Numerous possible explanations have been suggested (Stiles, Shapiro, & Elliott, 1986). We will discuss two of them here.

Perhaps certain therapies are effective for certain problems or disorders but relatively ineffective for others. When specific therapies are used to treat a wide range of disorders, they may help in some cases but not in others. Thus, averaging results over cases may conceal the special strengths of a particular therapy. We need to know which treatment is effective for which problem (Chambless & Hollon, 1998). In several controlled studies, different types of psychotherapy were compared with drug therapy or with controls in which people received no therapy for a specific disorder. These studies clearly suggest that certain forms of psychotherapy can be highly effective in the treatment of depression, anxiety disorders, eating disorders, substance abuse disorders, and several childhood disorders (De Rubeis & Crits-Cristoph, 1998; Kazdin & Weisz, 1998; Roth et al., 1996). Psychotherapy can also help reduce symptoms of autism and schizophrenia and lower the risk of relapse in schizophrenia (Hogarty, 1986; Kazdin & Weisz, 1998).

Not all forms of psychotherapy have undergone rigorous empirical tests for effectiveness, however. In general, proponents of behavioral and cognitive approaches have been interested in testing the efficacy of their therapies, so many studies have focused on these types of therapies. In contrast, proponents of psychodynamic and humanistic therapies have been less concerned with empirical tests of their therapies (De Rubeis & Crits-Cristoph, 1998).

Another reason why different psychotherapies may be equally effective in helping clients is because they all share certain factors. It may be these common factors, rather than the specific therapeutic techniques employed, that promote positive change.

Common Factors in Psychotherapies

One school of therapy emphasizes insight; another, modeling and reinforcement; yet another, rational cognitions. But perhaps these variables are not the crucial ones. Other factors that are common to most psychotherapies may be more important (Garfield, 1994; Orlinsky & Howard, 1987; Snyder, Ilardi, Michael, & Cheavens,

2000). They include a strong alliance between the therapist and client, reassurance and support, desensitization, reinforcement of adaptive responses, and insight.

AN INTERPERSONAL RELATIONSHIP OF WARMTH AND TRUST Regardless of the type of therapy, in a good therapeutic relationship the client and the therapist have mutual respect and regard. The client must believe that the therapist understands and is concerned with his or her problems. A therapist who understands our problems and believes we can solve them earns our trust, which increases our sense of competence and our confidence that we can succeed.

Our problems often seem insurmountable and unique to us. Discussing them with an expert who accepts our difficulties as not unusual and indicates that they can be resolved is reassuring. Having someone help us with problems that we have not been able to solve alone also provides a sense of support and a feeling of hope, and hope may be critical to recovery from psychological problems (Snyder et al., 2000). In fact, the most successful therapists, regardless of method, are those who form a helpful, supportive relationship with their clients (Luborsky, McLellan, Woody, O'Brien, & Auerbach, 1985).

DESENSITIZATION We have already talked about systematic desensitization, the specific techniques of behavior therapy aimed at helping individuals lose their fear of certain objects or situations. But many types of psychotherapy can encourage a broader kind of desensitization. When we discuss troubling events and emotions in the accepting atmosphere of a therapy session, they gradually lose their threatening quality. Problems that we brood about alone can become magnified beyond proportion, and sharing those problems with someone else often makes them seem less serious. Several other hypotheses can also explain how desensitization occurs in psychotherapy. For example, putting disturbing events into words may help us reappraise the situation in a more realistic manner. From the viewpoint of learning theory, repeatedly discussing distressing experiences in the security of a therapeutic setting may gradually extinguish the anxiety associated with them. Whatever the process, desensitization does appear to be common to many kinds of psychotherapy.

REINFORCEMENT OF ADAPTIVE RESPONSES Behavior therapists use reinforcement as a technique to increase positive attitudes and actions. But any therapist who wins the trust of a patient serves as a reinforcing agent because the therapist tends to express approval of behaviors or attitudes that are conducive to better adjustment, while ignoring or expressing disapproval of maladaptive attitudes or responses. Which responses are re-inforced depends on the therapist's orientation and therapeutic goals. The use of reinforcement may be intentional or unintentional; in some instances, the therapist may be unaware that he or she is reinforcing or failing to reinforce a particular behavior. For example, client-centered therapists believe in letting the client determine what is discussed during the therapy sessions, and they do not wish to influence the trend of the client's conversation. However, reinforcement can be subtle; a smile, a nod, or a simple "um hmm" in response to certain statements may increase the likelihood of their recurrence.

Because the goal of all psychotherapies is to bring about a change in the client's attitudes and behaviors, some type of learning must take place in therapy. The therapist needs to be aware of his or her role in influencing the client by means of reinforcement and should use this knowledge to facilitate desired changes.

UNDERSTANDING OR INSIGHT All of the psychotherapies we have been discussing provide an explanation of the client's difficulties—how they arose, why they persist, and how they can be changed (Frank & Frank, 1991). For a patient in psychoanalysis, this explanation may take the form of gradual understanding of repressed childhood fears and the ways in which these unconscious feelings have contributed to current problems. A behavior therapist might inform the client that current fears are the result of previous conditioning and can be conquered by learning responses that are incompatible with the current ones. A client in a cognitive-behavior treatment program might be told that his or her difficulties stem from the irrational belief that one must be perfect or must be loved by everyone.

How can such different explanations all produce positive results? Perhaps the precise nature of the insights and understanding provided by the therapist is relatively unimportant. It may be more important to provide the client with an explanation for the behavior or feelings that are so distressing and to present a set of activities (such as free association or relaxation training) that both the therapist and the client believe will alleviate the distress. A person who is experiencing disturbing symptoms and is unsure of their cause or how serious they might be will feel reassured by a professional who seems to know what the problem is and offers ways of relieving it. The knowledge that change is possible gives rise to hope, and hope is an important variable in facilitating change.

Our discussion of the factors shared by all forms of psychotherapy is not intended to deny the value of some specific treatment methods. Perhaps the most effective therapist is one who recognizes the importance of these common factors and utilizes them in a planned manner

for all patients but also selects the specific procedures that are most appropriate for each individual.

◆ Interim Summary

- Psychotherapy is the treatment of mental disorders by psychological means. One type of psychotherapy is psychoanalysis, which was developed by Freud. Free association, dream analysis, and transference are used to help the patient gain insight into problems. Contemporary psychodynamic therapies are briefer than traditional psychoanalysis and place more emphasis on the client's current interpersonal problems.

- Behavior therapies apply methods based on learning principles to modify the client's behavior, including systematic desensitization, in vivo exposure, reinforcement of adaptive behaviors, modeling and rehearsal of appropriate behavior, and techniques for self-regulation of behavior.

- Cognitive-behavior therapies use behavior modification techniques but also incorporate procedures for changing maladaptive beliefs. The therapist helps the client replace irrational interpretations of events with more realistic ones.

- Humanistic therapies help clients become aware of their real selves and solve their problems with a minimum of intervention by the therapist. Carl Rogers, who developed client-centered psychotherapy, believed that the therapist must have three characteristics in order to promote the client's growth and self-exploration: empathy, warmth, and genuineness.

- Sociocultural approaches view individuals as embedded in larger social systems, including families and societies. Community-based programs seek to integrate people with mental disorders back into the community while providing treatment. Several cultures have treatments specific to that culture and based on their own religious and cultural beliefs.

- The effectiveness of psychotherapy is hard to evaluate because of the difficulty of defining a successful outcome and controlling for spontaneous remission. Factors common to the various psychotherapies—a warm and trustful interpersonal relationship, reassurance and support, desensitization, insight, and reinforcement of adaptive responses—may be more important in producing positive change than the specific therapeutic methods used.

◆ Critical Thinking Questions

1. How might a psychotherapist adapt the therapeutic methods described in this section to help a person

with schizophrenia? Which methods do you think would be helpful for a person with schizophrenia? Which methods would not be helpful?

2. A major controversy these days is whether medical insurance should cover the cost of psychotherapy. Do you think it should or should not? What is your judgment based upon?

The Neural Basis of Behavior

BIOLOGICAL THERAPIES

The biological approach to abnormal behavior assumes that mental disorders, like physical illnesses, are caused by biochemical or physiological dysfunctions of the brain. Biological therapies include the use of drugs and electroconvulsive shock.

PSYCHOTHERAPEUTIC DRUGS

By far the most successful biological therapy is the use of drugs to modify mood and behavior (see the Concept Review Table for a review). The discovery in the early 1950s of drugs that relieved some of the symptoms of schizophrenia represented a major breakthrough in the treatment of severely disturbed individuals. Intensely agitated patients no longer had to be physically restrained by straitjackets, and patients who had been spending

most of their time hallucinating and exhibiting bizarre behavior became more responsive and functional. As a result, psychiatric wards became more manageable, and patients could be discharged more quickly. A few years later, the discovery of drugs that could relieve severe depression had a similar beneficial effect on hospital management and population. We saw in Figure 16-1 the reduction in the number of mental hospital residents after the introduction of antipsychotic and antidepressant drugs. At about the same time, drugs were being developed to relieve anxiety.

ANTIPSYCHOTIC DRUGS The first drugs that were found to relieve the symptoms of schizophrenia belonged to the family called **phenothiazines.** Examples are Thorazine (chlorpromazine) and Prolixin (fluphenazine). These drugs have been called *major tranquilizers,* but this term is not really appropriate because they do not act on the nervous system in the same way as barbiturates or antianxiety drugs. They may cause some drowsiness and lethargy, but they do not induce deep sleep, even in massive doses. They also seldom create the pleasant, slightly euphoric feeling associated with low doses of antianxiety drugs. In fact, the psychological effects of the antipsychotic drugs when administered to normal individuals are usually unpleasant. These drugs are seldom abused.

In Chapter 15, we discussed the theory that schizophrenia is caused by excessive activity of the neurotransmitter dopamine. Antipsychotic drugs block dopamine receptors. Because the drugs' molecules are structurally similar to dopamine molecules, they bind to the postsynaptic receptors of dopamine neurons,

CONCEPT REVIEW TABLE
Drug Treatments for Mental Disorders

These are the major types of drugs used to treat several kinds of mental disorders.

Type of Drug	Purpose	Mode of Action
Antipsychotic drugs (e.g., Thorazine, Haldol, Clozaril)	Reduce symptoms of psychosis (loss of reality testing, hallucinations, delusions)	Block dopamine receptors
Antidepressant drugs (e.g., Elavil, Prozac)	Reduce symptoms of depression	Increase functional levels of serotonin and norepinephrine
Lithium	Reduce symptoms of bipolar disorder (mania and depression)	Regulates levels of serotonin, norepinephrine, and other neurotransmitters
Antianxiety drugs (e.g., Valium, Xanax)	Reduce symptoms of anxiety	Depresses central nervous system
Stimulants (e.g., Ritalin, Dexedrine)	Increase attention and concentration	Possibly by increasing levels of dopamine

thereby blocking the access of dopamine to its receptors. (The drug itself does not activate the receptors.) A single synapse has many receptor molecules. If all of them are blocked, transmission across the synapse will fail. If only some of them are blocked, transmission will be weakened. The clinical potency of an antipsychotic drug is directly related to its ability to compete for dopamine receptors.

Antipsychotic drugs are effective in alleviating hallucinations and confusion and restoring rational thought processes. These drugs do not cure schizophrenia, and most patients must continue to use the drugs to function outside of a hospital. Many of the characteristic symptoms of schizophrenia—emotional blunting, seclusiveness, difficulties in sustaining attention—remain. Nevertheless, antipsychotic drugs shorten the length of time patients must be hospitalized, and they prevent relapse. Studies of people with schizophrenia living in the community find that the relapse rate for those taking one of the phenothiazines is typically half the relapse rate for those receiving a placebo (Hogarty et al., 1979).

Unfortunately, antipsychotic drugs do not help all people with schizophrenia. In addition, the drugs have unpleasant side effects—dryness of the mouth, blurred vision, difficulty in concentrating—that prompt many patients to discontinue their medication. One of the most serious side effects is a neurological disorder known as **tardive dyskinesia,** which involves involuntary movements of the tongue, face, mouth, or jaw. Patients with this disorder may involuntarily smack their lips, make sucking sounds, stick out their tongue, puff their cheeks, or make other bizarre movements, over and over again. Tardive dyskinesia is often irreversible and may occur in more than 20% of people who use antipsychotic drugs for long periods (Morgenstern & Glazer, 1993).

In recent years, new drugs called **atypical antipsychotics** have been found to reduce symptoms of schizophrenia without causing so many side effects (Wilson & Clausen, 1995). These drugs include clozapine and risperidone. They appear to work by binding to a different type of dopamine receptor than the other drugs, although they also influence several other neurotransmitters, including serotonin.

ANTIDEPRESSANT DRUGS **Antidepressant drugs** help elevate the mood of depressed individuals. These drugs energize, apparently by increasing the availability of two neurotransmitters (norepinephrine and serotonin) whose levels are deficient in some cases of depression (see Chapter 15). Antidepressant drugs act in different ways to increase neurotransmitter levels. **Monoamine oxidase (MAO) inhibitors** block the activity of an enzyme that can destroy both norepinephrine and serotonin, thereby increasing the concentration of these two neurotransmitters in the brain. **Tricyclic antidepressants** prevent the reuptake of serotonin and norepinephrine, thereby prolonging the action of the neurotransmitter. (Recall that reuptake is the process by which neurotransmitters are drawn back into the nerve terminals that released them.) Both classes of drugs have proved effective in relieving depression.

Like the antipsychotic drugs, the antidepressants can produce some undesirable side effects. The most common of these are dry mouth, blurred vision, constipation, and urinary retention. They can also cause a severe drop in blood pressure when a person stands up, as well as changes in heart rate and rhythm. An overdose of tricyclic antidepressants can be fatal, a serious concern when a depressed patient may be suicidal. The MAO inhibitors can interact with certain foods, including cheese, chocolate, and red wine, to create severe cardiac problems.

The search for drugs that are more effective, have fewer side effects, and act more quickly has intensified in the past 20 years. As a result, new drugs appear on the market almost daily. The **serotonin reuptake inhibitors** selectively increase serotonin levels by blocking its reuptake. Examples are Prozac (fluoxetine), Paxil (paroxetine), and Zoloft (sertraline). Even more recent drugs increase the availability of both serotonin and norepinephrine (such as Remeron). In addition to relieving depression, these drugs have proved helpful in treating the anxiety disorders, including obsessive-compulsive disorder and panic disorder (Schatzberg, 2000). They tend to produce fewer side effects than the other antidepressants, although they can cause inhibited orgasm, nausea and diarrhea, dizziness, and nervousness.

People with bipolar disorder often take an antidepressant medication to control their depression but must take other drugs to control their mania. **Lithium** reduces extreme mood swings and returns the individual to a more normal emotional state. It appears to do so by stabilizing a number of neurotransmitter systems, including serotonin and dopamine, and may also stabilize levels of the neurotransmitter glutamate (Thase et al., 2002). People with bipolar disorder who take lithium must take it even when they are not suffering from acute mania. Otherwise, about 80% will lapse into new episodes of mania or depression (Maj, Pirozzi, Magliano, & Bartoli, 1998).

Unfortunately, only about 30% to 50% of people with bipolar disorder respond to lithium (Bowden, 2000; Thase et al., 2002). In addition, it has severe side effects, including abdominal pain, nausea, vomiting, diarrhea, tremors, and twitches (Jamison, 1995). Patients complain of blurred vision and problems in concentration and attention that interfere with their ability to work. Lithium can cause kidney dysfunction, birth defects, and a form of diabetes if taken by women during the first trimester of pregnancy.

Anticonvulsant medications (such as Tegretol, Valproate and Depakote) are now commonly used to treat bipolar disorder. These drugs can be highly effective in reducing the symptoms of severe and acute mania but do not seem to be as effective as lithium for long-term treatment of bipolar disorder (Post et al., 1998). The side effects of the anticonvulsants include dizziness, rash, nausea, and drowsiness. Antipsychotic medications may also be prescribed for people who suffer severe mania (Post et al., 1998).

ANTIANXIETY DRUGS Several drugs traditionally used to treat anxiety belong to the family known as **benzodiazepines.** They are commonly known as tranquilizers and are marketed under such trade names as Valium (diazepam), Librium (chlordiazepoxide), and Xanax (alprazolam). Antianxiety drugs reduce tension and cause drowsiness. Like alcohol and the barbiturates, they depress the action of the central nervous system. Family physicians often prescribe tranquilizers to help people cope during difficult periods in their lives. The drugs are also used to treat anxiety disorders, withdrawal from alcohol, and physical disorders related to stress. For example, in the treatment of a phobia, antianxiety drugs may be combined with systematic desensitization to help the individual relax when confronting the feared situation.

Although tranquilizers may be useful on a short-term basis, their overall benefits are debatable and they clearly are overprescribed and misused. Until quite recently (before some of the dangers became apparent), Valium and Librium were the two most widely prescribed drugs in this country (Julien, 1992). Long-term use of tranquilizers can lead to physical dependence (see Chapter 6). Although tranquilizers are not as addictive as barbiturates, tolerance does develop with repeated use, and the individual experiences severe withdrawal symptoms if use of the drug is discontinued. In addition, tranquilizers impair concentration, including driving performance, and can cause death if combined with alcohol.

In recent years, researchers have discovered that certain antidepressant drugs also reduce symptoms of anxiety. This is particularly true of the serotonin reuptake inhibitors discussed previously. These drugs may relieve anxiety as well as depression because they affect biochemical disturbances that are common to both conditions.

STIMULANTS **Stimulant drugs** are used to treat the attentional problems of children with attention deficit hyperactivity disorder (ADHD). One of the most commonly used stimulants has the trade name Ritalin.

Although it may seem odd to give a stimulant to a hyperactive child, between 60% and 90% of children with ADHD respond to these drugs with decreases in disruptive behavior and increases in attention (Gadow, 1992). Stimulant drugs may work by increasing levels of dopamine in the synapses of the brain.

The use of Ritalin is a subject of controversy because some schools and physicians have been too quick to diagnose ADHD in schoolchildren and to prescribe Ritalin for them (Hinshaw, 1994). Stimulant drugs have significant side effects, including insomnia, headaches, tics, and nausea (Gadow, 1991, 1992). Children must be accurately diagnosed with ADHD before stimulant drugs are prescribed.

In sum, drug therapy has reduced the severity of some types of mental disorders. Many individuals who would require hospitalization otherwise can function within the community with the help of these drugs. On the other hand, there are limitations to the application of drug therapy. All therapeutic drugs can produce undesirable side effects. Many people with medical problems, as well as women who are pregnant or nursing, often cannot take psychoactive drugs. In addition, many psychologists feel that these drugs alleviate symptoms without requiring the patient to face the personal problems that may be contributing to the disorder or may have been caused by the disorder (such as marital problems caused by the behaviors of a manic person).

ELECTROCONVULSIVE THERAPY

In **electroconvulsive therapy (ECT),** also known as electroshock therapy, a mild electric current is applied to the brain to produce a seizure similar to an epileptic convulsion. ECT was a popular treatment from about 1940 to 1960, before antipsychotic and antidepressant drugs became readily available. Today it is used primarily in cases of severe depression when the patient has failed to respond to drug therapy.

ECT has been the subject of much controversy. At one time it was used indiscriminately in mental hospitals to treat such disorders as alcoholism and schizophrenia, for which it produced no beneficial results. Before more refined procedures were developed, ECT was a frightening experience for the patient, who was often awake until the electric current triggered the seizure and produced momentary unconsciousness. The patient frequently suffered confusion and memory loss afterward. Occasionally, the intensity of the muscle spasms accompanying the brain seizure resulted in physical injuries.

Today, ECT is much safer. The patient is given a short-acting anesthesia and injected with a muscle

CUTTING-EDGE RESEARCH
Can Common Herbs Treat Mental Disorders?

You've heard of them—St. John's wort, kava, valerian, gingko biloba—herbal medicines once used only by counterculture folks. These herbals are now a $4 billion industry, and it is estimated that one of every three Americans has used herbal medicines (Brevoort, 1998). One of the most common uses for herbals is in the treatment for psychological symptoms such as depression and anxiety. But do they work, and are they safe?

Herbal medicines have actually been part of mainstream treatment for psychological problems in Europe and Asia for centuries. St. John's wort, an aromatic perennial that is native to Europe but also grows wild in parts of Asia, North America, and South America, is used more often to treat depression in Germany than standard antidepressant medications manufactured by pharmaceutical companies (Beaubrun & Gray, 2000). Dozens of studies, most conducted in Germany, suggested that St. John's wort is effective in the treatment of mild to moderate depression, although it may not be potent enough to relieve more serious depression (Linde et al., 1996). Criticisms were raised of the methods of these studies, however, so the National Institute of Health initiated a large study in America comparing St. John's wort to placebo in treating serious depression (Shelton et al., 2001). St. John's wort did not fare well in this study—it proved no more effective than placebo on several measures of depression.

One reason people had hoped that St. John's wort would prove helpful for depression is that its side effects tend to be less severe than the side effects of antidepressant drugs. One study found that less than 3% of people taking St. John's wort experienced any side effects (Woelk, Burkard, & Grunwald, 1994). The most common side effects are gastrointestinal irritation, allergic reactions, dry mouth, sedation, headache, and increased sensitivity to light.

In the last few years, however, the safety of St. John's wort has been seriously questioned by evidence that it can interact with medications people take for medical ailments. For example, there are several reports that St. John's wort interferes with the efficacy of drugs used to treat patients who have recently received organ transplants, resulting in the rejection of the new organs. It may also interfere with drugs used to treat heart disease, seizures, and certain cancers (see http://www.nimh.nih.gov/events/stjohnwort.cfm). Thus, there are increasing concerns about the widespread use of St. John's wort, because people may be exposing themselves to potential drug-drug interactions with little reason for hope that they will gain relief from depressive symptoms.

Two products used to treat anxiety, valerian and kava, have also received some scientific scrutiny. Kava is the psychoactive member of the pepper family, widely used in Polynesia, Micronesia, and Melanesia as a ceremonial, tranquilizing beverage, and in Europe and the United States for anxiety and insomnia (Beaubrun & Gray, 2000; Fugh-Berman & Cott, 1999). Kava appears to have few side effects in moderate dosages, although some people experience gastrointestinal distress or allergic reactions. Valerian is a perennial native to Europe and Asia. Some studies suggest it can relieve insomnia, although not all studies show it is better than placebo (Beaubrun & Gray, 2000). Again, side effects from valerian are rare but can include gastrointestinal upset, allergies, headache, and restless sleep. Both kava and valerian can enhance the effects of other sedatives, leading to severe side effects, and thus should not be taken in combination with benzodiazepines, other prescription antianxiety drugs, or alcohol.

Particularly with the aging of the baby-boomer generation, claims that gingko biloba can improve memory have gotten a lot of media attention (see Chapter 8 for more information). Gingko biloba is an antioxidant that has been used for more than 2,000 years in China as a treatment for asthma. A widely publicized study in the United States showed that gingko biloba can enhance cognitive functioning in people with Alzheimer's disease and other forms of dementia (Le Bars et al., 1997). Although side effects of gingko biloba are unusual (and include gastrointestinal upset, allergic reactions, and headaches), it does have anticoagulant effects and in rare cases has been associated with serious bleeding problems, usually in people who are already taking anticoagulant drugs.

One of the greatest dangers of the tremendous increase in popularity of the herbal medicines is that many people are taking them without medical supervision. They are widely available in supermarkets and drug stores, and many people who take these substances are also taking prescription medications that may interact with the herbal remedies. The emerging evidence that St. John's wort is not as safe, nor as effective, as was thought even 5 years ago raises concerns that, as millions more people try herbal medicines, we will discover additional dangers associated with these medicines.

In addition, the herbals are not as tightly regulated in the United States as in Germany. Products can vary greatly in their potency, depending on variations in the raw plant material and in the methods of preparing the final product (Beaubrun & Gray, 2000). An analysis of 10 different brands of St. John's wort showed that the amount of hypericin, a component of St. John's wort often used for standardization purposes, varied from 20% to 140% of the amount claimed on the label, with half of the brands containing less than 80% of the labeled amount and two brands containing more than 120% of the labeled amount (Monmaney, 1998).

Although people think of herbal medicines as natural and therefore safe, they must be considered and treated like a drug.

 For more information, go online with InfoTrac College Edition. Use your own term or search:

- St. John's wort
- Kava
- Valerian
- Gingko

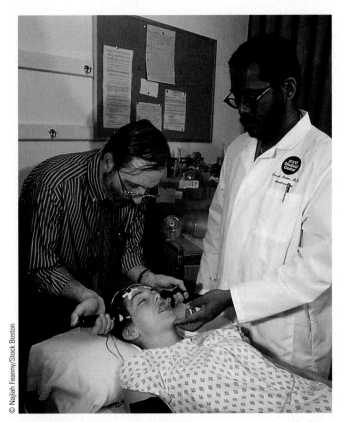
Electroconvulsive therapy is relatively effective in the treatment of depression.

relaxant. A brief, very weak electric current is applied to the brain, typically to the temple on the side of the nondominant cerebral hemisphere. The minimum current required to produce a brain seizure is administered, because the seizure itself—not the electricity—is therapeutic. The muscle relaxant prevents convulsive muscle spasms. The individual awakens within a few minutes and remembers nothing about the treatment. Four to six treatments are usually administered over a period of several weeks.

The most troublesome side effect of ECT is memory loss. Some patients report a gap in memory for events that occurred up to 6 months before ECT, as well as impaired ability to retain new information for a month or two after the treatment. However, if very low dosages of electricity are used (the amount is carefully calibrated for each patient to be just sufficient to produce a seizure) and administered only to the nondominant side of the brain, memory problems are minimal (Schwartz, 1995).

No one knows how the electrically induced seizures relieve depression. Brain seizures cause massive release of norepinephrine and serotonin, and, as noted in Chapter 15, deficiencies of these neurotransmitters may be an important factor in some cases of depression.

Currently, researchers are trying to determine the similarities and dissimilarities between ECT and antidepressant drugs in terms of the way each affects neurotransmitters. However it works, ECT is effective in bringing some people out of severe, immobilizing depression, and it does so faster than drug therapy.

COMBINING BIOLOGICAL AND PSYCHOLOGICAL THERAPIES

Although in this chapter we divided therapies into psychological and biological therapies, today there is a movement toward combined biological and psychological treatments. In depression and the anxiety disorders, often both the patient's biochemistry and his or her functioning in social and occupational settings are affected by the disorder, and it can be helpful to provide treatment at both the biological and psychosocial levels. Even in disorders like schizophrenia, whose primary cause is biological, the patient often experiences severe losses in social skills and ability to function on a job. Supplementing antipsychotic drugs with psychotherapy designed to help the person cope with the consequences of schizophrenia can be very useful.

The fact that a wide range of both psychotherapies and drugs are effective in the treatment of some disorders (especially depression) suggests that intervening at one level of a person's bio-psycho-social system can affect all levels of the system. For example, intervening at the psychological level may cause changes in the patient's biochemistry and social behaviors. When this occurs, it is because our biochemistry, our personalities and thought processes, and our social behaviors are so thoroughly intertwined that each can affect the other in both positive and negative ways. ▌

◆ Interim Summary

- Biological therapies include electroconvulsive therapy (ECT) and the use of psychotherapeutic drugs. Of the two, drug therapy is by far the more widely used.

- Antipsychotic drugs, which alter levels of the neurotransmitter dopamine, have proved effective in the treatment of schizophrenia.

- Antidepressants help to elevate the mood of depressed patients by affecting levels of the neurotransmitters serotonin and norepinephrine. Lithium has been effective in treating bipolar disorders.

- Antianxiety drugs depress the action of the central nervous system and are used to reduce severe anxiety and help clients cope with life crises.

- Stimulant drugs are used to treat attention deficit hyperactivity disorder in children.

EFFECTS OF CULTURE AND GENDER ON THERAPY

Culture and gender can influence the process of psychotherapy at many stages (Gray-Little & Kaplan, 2000). A person's cultural background and gender can affect the type of diagnosis they are given for their symptoms. They can affect their willingness to seek psychotherapy and to remain in psychotherapy. And they can affect the type of therapy an individual feels is appropriate.

For example, studies using standardized criteria to make psychiatric diagnoses find that the rates of severe mood disorders and schizophrenia are very similar among African Americans, whites, and Hispanics (Robins et al., 1984). (Rates of these disorders among Native Americans and Asian Americans are not available.) African Americans may be more frequently misdiagnosed as suffering from schizophrenia than whites, however (Mukherjee, Shukla, Woodle, Rosen, & Olarte, 1983). Because this diagnosis often leads to hospitalization, it may explain the overrepresentation of African Americans among hospitalized mental patients.

Men and women are hospitalized at about the same rate for mental disorders (Narrow, Regier, Rae, Manderscheid, & Locke, 1993), but the types of disorders for which they are hospitalized differ considerably. Men are more often hospitalized for substance abuse than women, but women are more often hospitalized for a mood disorder than men. There are no gender differences in the rate of hospitalization for schizophrenia.

Most people who seek treatment for a psychological disorder are not hospitalized. They are more likely to receive treatment from private-practice psychologists, psychiatrists, or general-practice physicians. In fact, one

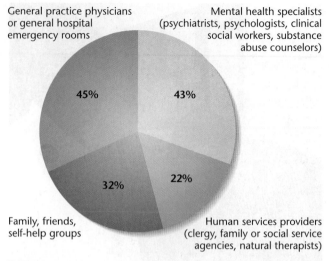

I Figure 16-5
Sources of Mental Health Care for People with Mental Disorders
People receive mental health care from several sources in addition to mental health specialists. (After Narrow, Regier, Rae, Maunderscheid, & Locke, 1993)

large study found that people in the United States are twice as likely to seek help for emotional or mental problems from their general-practice physicians than from a mental health professional (Figure 16-5; Narrow et al., 1993). Women are much more likely than men to talk to their general-practice physicians about mental and emotional problems and somewhat more likely to seek help from a mental health professional for these problems.

Hispanics and Asian Americans appear to be more likely to care for a family member who is suffering from a major mental disorder in the home than non-Hispanic whites (Gaw, 1993; Gray-Little & Kaplan, 2000). These trends may be due both to emphasis on the family as the center of problem solving and to the stigma associated with seeking mental health care. In contrast, African Americans tend to seek mental health treatment more quickly after the onset of symptoms than members of other groups.

Several cross-cultural theorists have made recommendations about the type of psychotherapy that might prove most acceptable to members of specific ethnic groups (see Sue & Sue, 1999, for a review). For example, some studies suggest that people from Latino, Asian, and Native American cultures are more comfortable with structured and action-oriented therapies, such as behavior or cognitive-behavior therapies, than with unstructured therapies (Apointe, Rivers, & Wohl,

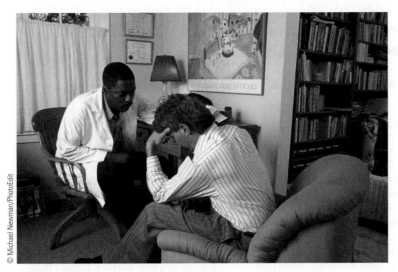
Therapists and clients from different backgrounds sometimes must struggle to understand each other.

1995; Atkinson & Hackett, 1998). Although some clinicians have suggested that women find therapies that focus on interpersonal relations and expression of feelings more appealing and helpful than other types of therapies, there is little evidence for this assertion (Garfield, 1994). For example, in the largest study of the treatment of depression, clients who were matched with a therapist of their gender did not recover more quickly or fully than clients who were matched with a therapist of the other gender (Zlotnick, Elkin & Shea, 1998).

The specific form of therapy may not matter as much as the cultural and gender sensitivity exhibited by the therapist. Members of minority groups are much more likely than whites to drop out of therapy (Atkinson & Hackett, 1998). Although there has been much effort put into recruiting persons from ethnic minority groups to become psychotherapists, the majority of therapists are still white. Minority clients may find the suggestions of white therapists strange and unhelpful.

Therapists and clients who are members of the same ethnic or racial group do not necessarily share the same value system, however. For example, a fourth-generation Japanese American who has fully adopted the competitive and individualistic values of U.S. society may clash with a recent immigrant from Japan who adheres to the self-sacrificing, community-oriented values of Japanese culture. Similarly, a woman therapist who has strong feminist values may clash with a woman client who holds traditional sex-role expectations. These value differences among people of the same ethnic-racial group or the same gender may explain why studies show that

matching the ethnicity or race or gender of therapist and client does not necessarily lead to a better outcome (Sue & Sue, 1999).

Some clients care deeply about having a therapist of the same ethnic group or gender, but others may trust only a therapist who corresponds to their stereotype of a "doctor," and still others have no preferences regarding the ethnicity or gender of their therapist. For clients who wish to be matched with a therapist of the same ethnic or gender group, this matching may be necessary if the client is to trust the therapist and have faith in the therapy. As noted earlier, the relationship between client and therapist and the client's beliefs about the likely effectiveness of therapy contribute strongly to the effectiveness of the therapy.

◆ Interim Summary

- Ethnic differences in treatment-seeking may be caused by differences in attitudes toward hospitalization and in the availability of nonprofessional sources of care. In addition, African Americans may be over-diagnosed with schizophrenia, which leads to their higher hospitalization rates.

- Men and women are equally likely to be hospitalized or to seek a mental health professional for psychological problems, but men more frequently seek care for substance abuse than women, and women more frequently seek care for a mood disorder than men. Women are also more likely than men to talk with their general-practice physician about mental health problems.

- Some clients may wish to work with a therapist of the same culture or gender, but it is unclear whether matching the therapist and the client is necessary for therapy to be effective.

- It is important for therapists to be sensitive to the influences of culture and gender on a client's attitudes toward therapy and on the acceptability of different types of solutions to their problems.

◆ Critical Thinking Questions

1. Should society fund more research on alternative therapies, such as those based on the beliefs of specific cultures? Why or why not?

2. Why might African Americans be more frequently misdiagnosed with schizophrenia than European Americans?

SEEING BOTH SIDES

Is Alcoholics Anonymous (AA) an Effective Intervention for Alcohol Abuse?

AA HELPS PROBLEM DRINKERS

Keith Humphreys, Stanford University and Veterans Affairs Palo Alto Health Care System

Alcoholics Anonymous (AA) is a worldwide fellowship of approximately 2 million alcohol-dependent individuals who are committed to helping each other permanently abstain from alcohol, as well as become more honest, humble, compassionate, and spiritually serene. In over 50 nations, AA members meet in mutual help groups on a regular basis, where they use AA principles (e.g., the "Twelve Steps") and their personal "experience, strength, and hope" to promote sobriety. In the United States, AA is the most commonly sought source of help for alcohol problems (Weisner, Greenfield, & Room, 1995), far outstripping all professional interventions combined. AA also enjoys an excellent reputation among most treatment professionals. At the same time, some clinicians and researchers doubt AA's effectiveness (Ogborne, 1993), noting that the organization offers a loosely monitored and unstandardized program based primarily on the experience and spiritual outlook of its members rather than a standardized professional treatment derived from objective, scientific research. AA attempts to change many aspects of members' lives, and hence the question of whether AA "works" can be framed in many different ways. Here, I focus on one of AA's intended benefits—abstinence from alcohol—and describe how recent studies provide credible evidence that AA helps problem drinkers stop consuming alcohol.

For example, Cross and colleagues (Cross, Morgan, Martin, & Rafter, 1990) followed up a sample of 158 alcohol de-

pendent patients 10 years after treatment to determine what factors (e.g., problem severity, age, sex) predicted long-term abstinence from alcohol. Of all the variables examined, only AA involvement increased the likelihood of abstinence. These findings supporting AA's effectiveness were essentially replicated in an 8-year follow-up of a sample of 628 alcohol-abusing individuals conducted by a different research group (Humphreys, Moos, & Cohen, 1997). Although not a study of AA per se, the randomized clinical trial known as Project Match (Project Match Research Group, 1997) demonstrated that counseling facilitating AA involvement is as effective at reducing alcohol consumption as are other established psychotherapies for alcohol-dependent clients.

Because AA attendance is free of charge, the organization is probably the most cost-effective way for alcohol-dependent individuals to become abstinent. One study of 201 alcohol abusers illustrating this point compared 135 individuals who initially chose to attend AA with 66 individuals who initially chose to seek professional outpatient treatment (Humphreys & Moos, 1996). Despite the fact that individuals were not randomly assigned to each condition, at baseline, there were no significant differences between groups on demographic variables, alcohol problems, or psychopathology. By the three-year follow-up, the AA attenders had reduced their daily alcohol intake an average of 75% and had decreased their alcohol dependence symptoms (e.g., blackouts) an average of

71%. Individuals receiving professional treatment improved comparably. However, alcohol-related health care costs over the three-year study were 45% ($1,826 per person) lower in the AA group than in the treated group. Hence, AA not only promotes abstinence, but does so in a cost-effective fashion that probably takes a substantial burden off of the formal health care system.

Research on the effects of AA participation has improved substantially in recent years, but still has considerable room for growth. Confidence in AA's effectiveness would be increased if more studies employed longitudinal designs, included comparison groups, and used biological tests or collateral data sources to confirm self-reports of abstinence. Further, even well-designed studies do not show that AA works for every participant or that its benefits are always substantial. However, the same could be said for virtually every professional psychosocial treatment for alcohol dependence. Therefore, particularly in light of AA's availability and minimal financial cost, it

Keith Humphreys

clearly is one of society's more important resources for helping alcohol-dependent individuals recover.

SEEING BOTH SIDES

Is Alcoholics Anonymous (AA) an Effective Intervention for Alcohol Abuse?

AA IS NOT THE ONLY WAY
G. Alan Marlatt, University of Washington

Although Alcoholics Anonymous (AA) is the most well-known self-help group for many people who are recovering from alcoholism, it is not the only way to help many individuals to stop drinking, and for some problem drinkers, AA may be a barrier to successful treatment. Studies show that of every two people who attend their first meeting of AA, only one returns for a second or subsequent meeting.

Why does AA appeal to some and not to others? Although AA is described as a "spiritual fellowship" and is not explicitly identified with any specific religious group, many first-timers are put off by the requirement to admit that one is powerless over one's drinking and that only by turning over personal control to a "higher power," recovery is possible. Others are discouraged by the AA doctrine that alcoholism is basically a physical disease that cannot be cured, only "arrested" by total lifelong abstinence from any alcoholic beverages. For those adherents of the disease model, including almost all AA members, there is no possibility of future moderate or controlled drinking. Once an alcoholic, always an alcoholic, according to AA beliefs.

Research has yet to reveal whether it is the specific teachings (theory) associated with AA, or the group support that the meetings provide that is most effective in helping people change their personal habits. Recent evidence indicates the latter is primarily responsible for AA success, which suggests other groups with different theories or beliefs about alcoholism and recovery can also be effective. In recent years, several new self-help groups for alcoholics have become available, including (1) Rational Recovery, based on rational principles of behavioral change without the need for a "higher power" in order to maintain abstinence; (2) Self Management and Recovery Training (SMART), based on the principles of cognitive-behavioral therapy such as relapse prevention and social skills training; and (3) Women for Sobriety, for women who have problems relating to the mainly masculine flavor of many AA meetings and who could benefit from addressing alcohol problems shared by many women drinkers.

Another alternative to AA is "Moderation Management" self-help groups. After several failed attempts at making AA work for her, Audrey Kishline (1994) developed "Moderation Management," a program of drinking moderation that has been used in many self-help groups in recent years (including some groups that meet on the Internet rather than in person).

Moderate or controlled drinking programs are also known in the addictions treatment field as examples of a "harm-reduction" approach. The goal of harm-reduction programs (such as moderation for heavy drinkers, nicotine replacement therapy for smokers who can't fully kick the habit, etc.) is to reduce the harmful consequences to oneself, one's family, and one's community caused by the drug problem. Although abstinence is accepted as an ideal goal for recovery, any steps toward this goal that reduce harm are considered steps in the right direction toward enhanced health and the prevention of disease.

Harm-reduction programs have been successful in teaching high-risk college students to drink more safely. Alcohol harm-reduction programs are designed to teach the novice drinker skills about drinking behavior and corresponding levels of intoxication. A recent study of high-risk, first-year college students found those who attended the program showed a significant drop in binge drinking, black-outs, severe hangovers, and acts of vandalism, etc. compared with students in a control group who did not receive this training program. Thus for students who choose to drink and are at risk for experiencing serious drinking problems, harm reduction offers a viable alternative to abstinence (see my article in the August 1998 issue of the *Journal of Consulting and Clinical Psychology*).

In AA, if someone does not accept the requirement of total abstinence, he or she is likely to be told to go away and not to come back until having "hit bottom"—in other words, until the person has experienced such profound negative consequences from drinking that he or she sees no other choice but to go back to AA and pursue total abstinence. But what do we do with those drinkers who have not yet "hit bottom," even though they may be experiencing serious harmful consequences? Harm reduction offers a variety of helpful strategies for this group to get them started on the road to recovery.

ENHANCING MENTAL HEALTH

Aside from seeking professional help, there are many ways in which we can positively influence our own psychological well-being. By monitoring our feelings and behavior, we can determine the kinds of actions and situations that cause us pain or get us into difficulty and, conversely, the kinds that benefit us the most. By trying to analyze our motives and abilities, we can enhance our capacity to make active choices in our lives instead of passively accepting whatever happens. The problems that people face vary greatly, and there are no universal guidelines for staying psychologically healthy. However, a few general suggestions have emerged from the experiences of therapists.

ACCEPT YOUR FEELINGS Anger, sorrow, fear, and a feeling of having fallen short of ideals or goals are all unpleasant emotions, and we may try to escape anxiety by denying these feelings. Sometimes we try to avoid anxiety by facing situations unemotionally, which leads to a false kind of detachment or "cool" that may be destructive. We may try to suppress all emotions, thereby losing the ability to accept as normal the joys and sorrows that are part of our involvement with other people.

Unpleasant emotions are a normal reaction to many situations. There is no reason to be ashamed of feeling homesick, being afraid when learning to ski, or becoming angry at someone who has disappointed us. These emotions are natural, and it is better to recognize them than to deny them. When emotions cannot be expressed directly (for example, it may not be wise to yell at your boss), it helps to find another outlet for releasing tension. Taking a long walk, pounding a tennis ball, or discussing the situation with a friend can dissipate anger. As long as you accept your right to feel emotion, you can express it in indirect or alternative ways when direct channels of expression are blocked.

KNOW YOUR VULNERABILITIES Discovering the kinds of situations that upset you or cause you to overreact may help you guard against stress. Perhaps certain people annoy you. You could avoid them, or you could try to understand just what it is about them that disturbs you. Maybe they seem so poised and confident that they make you feel insecure. Trying to pinpoint the cause of your discomfort may help you see the situation in a new light. Perhaps you become very anxious when you have to speak in class or present a pa-

per. Again, you could try to avoid such situations, or you could gain confidence by taking a course in public speaking. (Many colleges offer courses on controlling speech anxiety.) You could also reinterpret the situation. Instead of thinking, "Everyone is waiting to criticize me as soon as I open my mouth," you could tell yourself, "The class will be interested in what I have to say, and I'm not going to let it worry me if I make a few mistakes."

Many people feel especially anxious when they are under pressure. Careful planning and spacing of work can help you avoid feeling overwhelmed at the last minute. The strategy of purposely allowing more time than you think you need to get to classes or appointments can eliminate one source of stress.

DEVELOP YOUR TALENTS AND INTERESTS People who are bored and unhappy seldom have many interests. Today's college and community programs offer almost unlimited opportunities for people of all ages to explore their talents in many areas, including sports, academic interests, music, art, drama, and crafts. Often, the more you know about a subject, the more interesting it (and life) becomes. In addition, the feeling of competence gained from developing skills can do a great deal to bolster self-esteem.

BECOME INVOLVED WITH OTHER PEOPLE Feelings of isolation and loneliness are at the core of most emotional disorders. We are social beings, and we need the support, comfort, and reassurance provided by other people. Focusing all your attention on your own problems can lead to an unhealthy preoccupation with yourself. Sharing your concerns with others often helps you view your troubles in a clearer perspective. Also, being concerned for the welfare of other people can reinforce your feelings of self-worth.

KNOW WHEN TO SEEK HELP Although these suggestions can help promote emotional well-being, there are limits to self-understanding and self-help. Some problems are difficult to solve alone. Our tendency toward self-deception makes it hard to view problems objectively, and we may not be aware of all the possible solutions. When you feel that you are making little headway toward gaining control over a problem, it is time to seek professional help from a counseling or clinical psychologist, a psychiatrist, or some other trained therapist. Willingness to seek help is a sign of emotional maturity, not weakness; do not wait until you feel overwhelmed. Obtaining psychological help when it is needed should be as accepted a practice as going to a physician for medical problems.

◆ Interim Summary

- Accepting your feelings is the first step to responding effectively to them.

- Knowing your vulnerabilities allows you to avoid triggers for distress and seek help in overcoming certain vulnerabilities.

- Developing your talents gives you multiple sources of self-esteem and joy.

- Seeking out others is a good strategy for distress. Helping others can increase your self-esteem.

- Not all problems can be handled alone; it's important to seek help when you need it.

◆ Critical Thinking Questions

1. In what circumstances do you think self-help books are helpful, and when might they not be helpful?

2. Some people seem never to be overwhelmed by stress and appear able to handle almost anything. What do you think makes such people super-resilient?

CHAPTER SUMMARY

1. Treatment of the mentally ill has progressed from the ancient notion that abnormal behavior resulted from possession by evil spirits that needed to be punished, through custodial care in asylums, to modern mental hospitals and community mental health centers. The policy of deinstitutionalization, despite its good intentions, has added to the number of homeless mentally ill individuals, causing concern about civil rights and adequate care.

2. Psychotherapy is the treatment of mental disorders by psychological means. One type of psychotherapy is psychoanalysis, which was developed by Freud. Through the methods of free association and dream analysis, repressed thoughts and feelings are brought to the patient's awareness. By interpreting these dreams and associations, the analyst helps the patient gain insight into his or her problems. Transference, the tendency to express feelings toward the analyst that the client has for important people in his or her life, provides another source of interpretation.

3. Contemporary psychodynamic therapies are briefer than traditional psychoanalysis and place more emphasis on the client's current interpersonal problems (as opposed to a complete reconstruction of childhood experiences).

4. Behavior therapies apply methods based on learning principles to modify the client's behavior. These methods include systematic desensitization (the individual learns to relax in situations that previously produced anxiety), reinforcement of adaptive behaviors, modeling and rehearsal of appropriate behavior, and techniques for self-regulation of behavior.

5. Cognitive-behavior therapies use behavior modification techniques but also incorporate procedures for changing maladaptive beliefs. The therapist helps the client replace irrational interpretations of events with more realistic ones.

6. Humanistic therapies help clients become aware of their real selves and solve their problems with a minimum of intervention by the therapist. Carl Rogers, who developed client-centered psychotherapy, believed that the therapist must have three characteristics in order to promote the client's growth and self-exploration: empathy, warmth, and genuineness.

7. Sociocultural approaches view individuals as embedded in larger social systems, including families and societies. Group therapy provides an opportunity for clients to explore their attitudes and behavior in interaction with others who have similar problems. Marital therapy and family therapy are specialized forms of group therapy that help couples, or parents and children, learn more effective ways of relating to one another and handling their problems. Community-based programs seek to integrate people with mental disorders back into the community while providing treatment. Several cultures have treatments specific to that culture and based on their own religious and cultural beliefs.

8. Rather than adhering strictly to any single method, many therapists take an eclectic approach, selecting from the different techniques those that are most appropriate for a given client. Some therapists specialize in treating specific problems, such as alcoholism, sexual dysfunction, or depression.

9. The effectiveness of psychotherapy is hard to evaluate because of the difficulty of defining a successful outcome and controlling for spontaneous remission.

Research results indicate that psychotherapy does help but that different approaches do not differ greatly in effectiveness. Factors common to the various psychotherapies—a warm and trustful interpersonal relationship, reassurance and support, desensitization, insight, and reinforcement of adaptive responses—may be more important in producing positive change than the specific therapeutic methods used.

10. Biological therapies include electroconvulsive therapy (ECT) and psychotherapeutic drugs. Of the two, drug therapy is by far the most widely used. Antipsychotic drugs have proved effective in the treatment of schizophrenia, antidepressants help to elevate the mood of depressed patients, and lithium has been effective in treating bipolar disorders. Antianxiety drugs are used to reduce severe anxiety and help clients cope with life crises.

11. African Americans and Native Americans are more likely than members of other ethnic groups to be hospitalized for a psychological disorder or to seek outpatient mental health services for a psychological problem. Hispanics and whites have similar hospitalization rates, but Asian Americans are much less likely than members of other ethnic groups to be hospitalized for psychological problems. These ethnic differences may be caused by differences in attitudes toward hospitalization and in the availability of nonprofessional sources of care. In addition, African Americans may be overdiagnosed with schizophrenia, which leads to their more frequent hospitalization compared with other groups.

Men and women are equally likely to be hospitalized or to seek a mental health professional for psychological problems, but men more frequently seek care for substance abuse and women more frequently seek care for a mood disorder. Women are also more likely than men to talk with their general-practice physician about mental health problems.

12. Some clients may wish to work with a therapist of the same culture or gender, but it is unclear whether matching the therapist and the client is necessary for therapy to be effective. It is important for therapists to be sensitive to the influences of culture and gender on a client's attitudes toward therapy and on the acceptability of different types of solutions to their problems.

CORE CONCEPTS

general paresis
deinstitutionalization
psychotherapy
psychodynamic therapies
free association
dream analysis
transference
interpersonal therapy
behavior therapy
systematic desensitization
in vivo exposure
selective reinforcement

behavioral rehearsal
self-regulation
cognitive-behavior therapy
humanistic therapy
client-centered therapy
group therapy
self-help groups
marital therapy
family therapy
halfway house
phenothiazines
tardive dyskinesia

atypical antipsychotics
antidepressant drugs
monoamine oxidase (MAO)
    inhibitors
tricyclic antidepressants
serotonin reuptake inhibitors
lithium
benzodiazepines
stimulant drugs
electroconvulsive therapy (ECT)

WEB RESOURCES

http://psychology.wadsworth.com/ atkinson14e

Take a quiz, try the activities and exercises, and explore web links.

http://www.uea.ac.uk/~wp276/what.htm

Learn more about the antipsychiatry movement on this site.

http://neurosurgery.mgh.harvard.edu/psysurg.htm

Explore the historical background of surgery as a treatment for psychological disorders, and then read about the anatomy and physiology of these controversial procedures.

http://www.npap.org/

This detailed site from the National Psychological Association for Psychoanalysis discusses psychotherapy with an emphasis on psychoanalysis.

 InfoTrac Online Library

http://www.infotrac-college.com/ wadsworth

Use InfoTrac College Edition to find popular and scientific articles by using the search terms below or your own relevant terms.

- Behavior therapy
- Cognitive therapy
- Psychoanalysis
- Psychotherapy

CD-ROM LINKS

 Psych Odyssey

Check out CD Chapter 17, Psychotherapy
A. Psychotherapies
B. Drug Therapies

 Psyk.trek 2.0

Check out CD Unit 11, Abnormal Behavior and Therapy
11d Insight Therapies
11e Behavioral and Biomedical Therapies

AP/Wide World Photos

SOCIAL INFLUENCE

17

People sometimes do the inexplicable—or what seems inexplicable. Our newspapers and history books provide plenty of examples.

From 1933 to 1945, millions of innocent people—mostly Jews—were forced to live in concentration camps in Nazi Germany. Only after World War II did the world community realize that these camps were in fact high-efficiency death "factories" that systematically slaughtered more than 8 million people. How could this genocide happen? What kind of people could design and operate these death factories? The actions of the Nazi regime seem inexplicable.

On November 18th, 1978, U.S. Congressman Leo Ryan was concluding his visit to Jonestown, a settlement of the People's Temple (formerly of San Francisco) in Guyana, South America. Ryan was investigating Jonestown because reports had come back to the United States that people were being held there against their will. As Ryan boarded his plane to leave Guyana, he and four others were shot and killed by Temple gunmen. Meanwhile, Jim Jones, the leader of the People's Temple,

gathered the nearly 1,000 r[...] Jonestown and asked them to kill themselves by drinking strawberry-flavored poison. They complied. How could this happen? What kind of people would kill themselves at another person's request? The actions of the members of the People's Temple seem inexplicable.

On September 11, 2001, four U.S. planes were hijacked. Two crashed into New York City's twin World Trade Center towers, one crashed into U.S. military headquarters at the Pentagon, outside Washington, D.C., and the fourth crashed in Pennsylvania, missing its intended target. In addition to the hundreds of people killed on board the airplanes and in the Pentagon, nearly 3,000 people remained in the World Trade Center towers when they collapsed from the impact. How could this happen? What kind of people could take so many innocent lives, as well as their own? The actions of these suicide hijackers seem inexplicable.

THOSE WHO DO NOT REMEMBER THE PAST ARE CONDEMNED TO REPEAT IT.

Horrific world events often seem completely inexplicable. How could people do these things to themselves and to others? Social psychologists argue that answers that appeal only to personality or character traits overlook the powerful influence that social situations can have in shaping human behavior.

In trying to make sense of these seemingly inexplicable horrors of humanity, our first reaction is often to pin evil (or crazy) actions on evil (or crazy) individuals. "The suicide hijackers were evil terrorists." "Jim Jones's followers were crazy." "The Nazis were evil racists." These sorts of explanations provide some comfort. They distance us "good" and "normal" people, from those "bad" and "crazy" people. To be sure, there is a grain of truth within explanations that attribute evil actions to evil characters. Osama bin Laden, Jim Jones, and Adolf Hitler, for instance, might well be classified as evil leaders. Even so, social psychologists have argued that explanations that attribute the full cause of an action to someone's personality are often wrong—so often wrong that social psychologists identify these explanations as instances of the fundamental attribution error. The **fundamental attribution error** refers to the tendency to explain other people's actions by overestimating the influence of personality or character and underestimating the influence of situations or circumstances. Moreover, we make this fundamental error not only when trying to make sense of unfathomable horrors but also when making sense of the ordinary, everyday actions of our roommates, classmates, and others.

Social psychology is the scientific study of the ways that people's behavior and mental processes are shaped by the real or imagined presence of others. Social psychologists begin with the basic observation that human behavior is a function of both the person and the situation. Each individual brings a unique set of personal attributes to a situation, leading different people to act in different ways in the same situation. But each situation also brings a unique set of forces to bear on an individual, leading him or her to act in different ways in different situations. Research has repeatedly shown that situations are more powerful determinants of behavior than our intuitions lead us to believe. Thus, one of the foremost contributions of social psychology is an understanding of how powerful situations shape people's behavior and mental processes. Our two-chapter discussion of social psychology begins with this focus on the power of situations.

Yet people do not simply react to the objective features of situations but rather to their subjective interpretations of them. As we learned in Chapter 11 on emotions, the person who interprets an offensive act as the product of hostility reacts differently than the person who construes the same act as the product of mental illness. Accordingly, Chapter 18 examines the power that subjective interpretations and people's modes of thinking have in shaping their thoughts, feelings, and social behavior, a topic known as social cognition. We begin, however, with a focus on social influence and the power of situations themselves.

THE PRESENCE OF OTHERS

SOCIAL FACILITATION AND SOCIAL INHIBITION

In 1898, while examining the speed records of bicycle racers, psychologist Norman Triplett noticed that many cyclists achieved better times when they raced against each other than when they raced against the clock. This led him to perform one of social psychology's earliest laboratory experiments. He instructed children to turn a fishing reel as fast as possible for a fixed period. Sometimes two children worked at the same time in the same room, each with his or her own reel. At other times they worked alone. Triplett reported that many children worked faster when someone else doing the same task was present (a situation termed **coaction**) than when they worked alone.

In the more than 100 years since Triplett conducted his experiment, many other studies have demonstrated the facilitating effects of coaction with both human and animal subjects. For example, worker ants in groups dig more than three times as much sand per ant than when alone (Chen, 1937), many animals eat more food if other members of their species are present (Platt, Yaksh, & Darby, 1967), and college students complete more multiplication problems in coaction than when alone (F. H. Allport, 1920, 1924).

Soon after Triplett's experiment on coaction, psychologists discovered that the presence of a passive spectator—an audience rather than a coactor—also facilitates performance. For example, the presence of an

In 1898 psychologist Norman Triplett noticed that cyclists achieved better times when they raced against other cyclists than when they raced against the clock. This led him to study the phenomenon of social facilitation.

audience had the same facilitating effect on students' multiplication performance as the presence of coactors in the earlier study (Dashiell, 1930). The term **social facilitation** is used to refer to the boosting effects of coactors and audiences on performance.

But this simple case of social influence turned out to be more complicated than social psychologists first thought. For example, researchers found that people made more errors on the multiplication problems when in coaction or in the presence of an audience than when they performed alone (Dashiell, 1930). In other words, accuracy decreased even though speed increased. In many other studies, both the speed and accuracy of performance decreased when others were present. The term **social inhibition** was introduced to refer to the sometimes derailing effects of coactors and audiences on performance.

How can we predict whether the presence of others—either coacting or observing—will improve our performance or impair it? The answer to this question first emerged in the mid-1960s (Zajonc, 1965) and was solidified two decades later in a meta-analysis of 241 studies (Bond & Titus, 1983). The basic finding is that the presence of coactors and audiences improves the speed and accuracy of performance on simple or well-learned tasks but impairs the speed and accuracy of performance on complex or poorly learned tasks.

So social facilitation holds for simple tasks, and social inhibition holds for complex tasks. Despite this useful generalization, this pattern of results still requires explanation. Why does it occur? Social psychologists have offered two competing explanations.

The first explanation, offered by Robert Zajonc (1965), appeals to drive theories of motivation (see Chapter 10). These suggest that high levels of drive or arousal tend to energize the dominant responses of an organism. If the mere presence of another member of the species raises the general arousal or drive level of an organism, the dominant response will be facilitated. For simple or well-learned behaviors, the dominant response is most likely to be the correct response, and performance should be facilitated. For complex behaviors or behaviors that are just being learned, the dominant or most probable response is likely to be incorrect. Consider the multiplication problems discussed earlier. There are many wrong responses but only one correct one. Accurate performance on this complex task should therefore be inhibited.

A number of experiments have confirmed these predictions. For example, people learn simple mazes or easy word lists more quickly but learn complex mazes or difficult word lists more slowly when an audience is present than when it is not (Cottrell, Rittle, & Wack, 1967; Hunt & Hillery, 1973). A study using cockroaches found that, when attempting to escape light, roaches run an easy route more quickly but a difficult route more slowly if other roaches watch from the sidelines (or run with them) than if they run without other roaches present (Zajonc, Heingartner, & Herman, 1969).

The second explanation for social facilitation and social inhibition appeals to attention factors (Baron, 1986; Huguet, Galvaing, Monteil, & Dumas, 1999). The core idea is that the presence of others is often distracting, which can produce a mental overload that results in a narrowed focus of attention. This view can also explain the different effects for simple and complex tasks: Social facilitation should occur when tasks are simple and require that we focus on only a small number of central cues, and social inhibition should occur when tasks are complex and require our attention to a wide range of cues.

Which explanation is correct? In most circumstances, the two explanations make the same predictions and so cannot be tested against one another. A recent study solved this problem, however, by locating a task for which the two views offer different predictions (Huguet et al., 1999). The Stroop task (MacLeod, 1991; Stroop, 1935) is a complex, poorly learned task that involves only a few key stimuli. In this task, a person is asked to identify the ink color in which words or symbols (like "+++") are printed. See Figure 17-1 for an example. People perform this task relatively quickly for symbols but are particularly slowed for words that are incongruent (like the word *red* printed in yellow ink). This phenomenon, called **Stroop interference**, results because word reading is such a dominant and automatic response among skilled readers that it is difficult to follow the instruction to ignore the printed word and name the word's ink color. Because the Stroop task is complex and the automatic response is to name the word (not the ink color),

▮ Figure 17-1
Items From a Stroop Task
Say aloud the color of the inks you see in the top row. Now do the same for the bottom row. Notice how much slower you were to name the ink colors for words versus symbols. This is called *Stroop interference*. Studies show that people perform better on the Stroop task when in the presence of others, a finding that supports the attention explanation for social facilitation.

the dominant-response view predicts that social presence should derail performance, producing social inhibition. At the same time, because the Stroop task involves only two key stimuli—the word and the ink color—and a narrowed focus of attention can reduce attention to the irrelevant information (the word), the attention view, by contrast, predicts that social presence should improve performance, producing social facilitation.

The data from several experiments that have manipulated the presence or absence of an audience or coactors during Stroop performance provide clear support for the attention view and fail to support the dominant-response view: People perform *better* on the Stroop task when in the presence of others (Huguet et al., 1999). These and other studies also identify two key limits to social facilitation effects. First, the mere presence of another person does not produce much social facilitation. If the audience member is reading or blindfolded, for example, social facilitation is greatly reduced (Cottrell, Wack, Sekerak, & Rittle, 1968; Huguet et al., 1999). Second, competition and social comparison with coactors seem to be critical. If coactors perform much worse than participants themselves—that is, if they are no competition—social facilitation is also greatly reduced (Dashiell, 1930; Huguet et al., 1999).

The lineage of studies on social facilitation and social inhibition begins to convey the power of situations. You might have thought that your physical performance (like throwing free throws in basketball) or academic performance (like taking a calculus exam) merely reflected your ability. But the studies described here suggest that whether the performance situation includes others, and what those others are doing (evaluating or providing competition), also critically determines your level of performance. Yet whether the presence of others helps or hurts your performance depends on whether the task at hand is simple or complex for you. A pro basketball player and a student who has mastered the basics of calculus are likely to do better when the situation involves others. For them, the task becomes simple because it is well learned. For a novice basketball player and a student who neglects studying, the situation pulls for much worse.

DEINDIVIDUATION

At about the same time that Triplett was performing his experiment on social facilitation, another observer of human behavior, Gustave LeBon, was also studying the effects of coaction. In *The Crowd* (1895), LeBon complained that "the crowd is always intellectually inferior to the isolated individual." He believed that the aggressive and immoral behaviors shown by lynch mobs (and, in his view, French revolutionaries) spread through a

Audience effects on performance vary depending on whether the task is easy or difficult for them and on how much the person feels that he or she is being evaluated.

mob or crowd by contagion, like a disease, breaking down an individual's moral sense and self-control. Such breakdowns, he argued, caused crowds to commit destructive acts that few individuals would commit when acting alone.

LeBon's early observations of crowd behavior fueled the development of a concept that social psychologists have called *deindividuation*, first introduced in the 1950s (Festinger, Pepitone, & Newcomb, 1952) but revisited and revised in each subsequent decade (in the 1960s by Zimbardo [1969], in the 1970s by Diener [1977, 1980], in the 1980s by Prentice-Dunn & Rogers [1982, 1989], and in the 1990s by Postmes & Spears [1998]). Although the explanations for the phenomenon have shifted over the decades, the core idea within **deindividuation** is that certain group situations can minimize the salience of people's personal identities, reduce their sense of public accountability, and in doing so produce aggressive or unusual behavior (for a meta-analysis of 60 studies, see Postmes & Spears, 1998). Two key characteristics of group situations that contribute to deindivid-

People often behave differently in a crowd than when alone. Some researchers believe that in a situation like a riot, individuals experience deindividuation—a feeling that they have lost their personal identities and merged anonymously into the group.

uation are group size and anonymity. Early explanations for the effects of deindividuation suggested that a reduced sense of public accountability weakened the normal restraints against impulsive and unruly behavior (Diener, 1980; Festinger et al., 1952; Zimbardo, 1969).

In one famous study of deindividuation, groups of four college women were required to deliver electric shocks to another woman who was supposedly participating in a learning experiment. Half of the groups were deindividuated by making them feel anonymous. They were dressed in bulky laboratory coats and hoods that hid their faces, and the experimenter spoke to them only as a group, never referring to any of them by name (see Figure 17-2). The remaining groups were individuated by having them remain in their own clothes and wear large identification tags. In addition, the women in the latter groups were introduced to one another by name. During the experiment, each woman had a shock button in front of her, which she was to push when the learner made an error. Pushing the button appeared to deliver a shock to the learner (in reality, it did not). The results showed that the deindividuated women delivered twice as much shock to the learner as the individuated women (Zimbardo, 1969).

Another study was conducted at several homes on Halloween night. Children out trick-or-treating were greeted at the door by a woman who asked that each child take only one piece of candy. The woman then disappeared into the house briefly, giving the children the opportunity to take more candy. Some

of the children had been asked their names, and others remained anonymous. Children who came in groups or who remained anonymous stole more candy than children who came alone or had given their names to the adult (Diener, Fraser, Beaman, & Kelem, 1976).

These experiments are not definitive, however. For instance, you can see in Figure 17-2 that the laboratory coats and hoods in the first study resembled Ku Klux Klan outfits. Similarly, Halloween costumes often represent witches, monsters, or ghosts. These all carry aggressive or negative connotations. It may be that these costumes did not simply provide anonymity but that they also activated social norms that encouraged aggression. **Social norms** are implicit or explicit rules for acceptable behavior and beliefs. To test whether social norms rather than anonymity produced aggressive behavior, the shock experiment was repeated, but this time each participant wore one of three outfits: a Ku Klux Klan-type costume, a nurse's uniform, or the participant's own clothes. Compared with the group who wore their own clothes, participants wearing Ku Klux Klan-type costumes delivered somewhat more shocks to the learner (but not reliably so). More significantly, participants wearing nurses' uniforms actually gave fewer shocks than participants who wore their own clothes. This study shows that anonymity does not inevitably lead to increased aggression (Johnson & Downing, 1979).

The finding that cues that are specific to the situation (like a nurse's uniform) evoke social norms that

▌**Figure 17-2**
Anonymity Can Increase Aggression
When women were disguised so that they felt anonymous, they delivered more shock to another person than did nondisguised women.

guide behavior within anonymous groups led to a later reformulation of the mental processes involved in deindividuation. This view holds that situations that reduce public accountability—like group size and anonymity—do not simply reduce the salience of people's personal identities but also simultaneously enhance the salience of people's group identities (like being a nurse, or a member of the People's Temple). Plus, situations that make group identities salient promote behavior that is normative for the salient group (like being less aggressive if you are role-playing a nurse). So whereas earlier explanations of deindividuation suggested that groups and anonymity produce a breakdown of the normal restraints against unruly behavior, this more recent explanation suggests that these same features of group situations promote greater conformity to situation-specific social norms (Lea, Spears, & de Groot, 2001; Postmes & Spears, 1998).

Again, the research on deindividuation conveys the power of situations in determining people's behavior. So the next time you find yourself in a large group situation in which you feel anonymous (not uncommon on a college campus), you may notice yourself getting caught up with the group's behavior. If the group is focused on peaceful activities (like a candlelight vigil for victims of terrorist attacks), you may act more patriotic and reverent than you might on your own. Yet if the group is focused on more raucous activities (like looting or harassing others), watch out!

BYSTANDER EFFECTS

Earlier we noted that people do not react simply to the objective features of a situation but also respond to their subjective interpretations of it. We have seen that even social facilitation, a primitive kind of social influence, depends in part on the individual's interpretation of what other people are doing or thinking. But as we will now see, defining or interpreting the situation is often the very mechanism through which individuals influence one another.

In 1964 a young woman named Kitty Genovese was attacked outside her New York apartment late at night. She fought back for more than half an hour, but in the end she was murdered. At least 38 neighbors heard her screams for help, but nobody came to her aid. No one even called the police.

The American public was horrified by this incident, and social psychologists began to investigate the causes of what came to be called the **bystander effect,** referring to the finding that people are less likely to help when others are present. You might suppose that if you needed help in an emergency, you'd be more likely to receive it if many people witnessed the event. Simple odds should

Although many passers-by have noticed the man lying on the sidewalk, no one has stopped to help—to see if he is asleep, sick, drunk, or dead. Research shows that people are more likely to help if no other bystanders are present.

increase the chances that helpful souls are in the crowd, right? Unfortunately not. Research on bystander effects shows just the reverse: Often it is the very presence of other people that prevents us from taking action. In fact, by 1980 more than 50 studies of bystander effects had been conducted, and most of them showed that people reduced helping when others were present (Latané, Nida, & Wilson, 1981). Latané and Darley (1970) suggest that the presence of others deters an individual from taking action by (1) defining the situation as a nonemergency through the process of pluralistic ignorance and (2) diffusing the responsibility for acting.

DEFINING THE SITUATION Many emergencies begin ambiguously. Is that staggering man ill or simply drunk? Is the woman being threatened by a stranger, or is she arguing with her husband? Is that smoke from a fire or just steam pouring out the window? A common way of dealing with such uncertainties is to postpone action, act as if nothing is wrong, and discreetly glance to see how other people are reacting. What you are likely to see, of course, are other people who, for the same reasons, are also acting as if nothing is wrong. Because people often show blank expressions when confronted with ambiguity, especially if trying to maintain their cool, a state of **pluralistic ignorance** develops—that is, everybody in the group misleads everybody else by defining the situation as a nonemergency. We have all heard about crowds panicking because each person causes everybody else to overreact. The reverse situation–in which a crowd lulls its members into inaction—may be even more common. Several experiments demonstrate this effect.

In one experiment, male college students were invited to an interview. As they sat in a small waiting room completing a questionnaire, what appeared to be smoke began to stream through a wall vent. Some participants were alone in the waiting room when this occurred; others were in groups of three. The experimenters observed them through a one-way window and waited 6 minutes to see if anyone would take action or report the situation. Of the participants who were tested alone, 75% left the room and reported the potential fire. In contrast, less than 13% of the participants who were tested in groups reported the smoke, even though the room was so filled with smoke they had to wave it away to complete their questionnaires. Those who did not report the smoke subsequently reported that they had decided that it must have been steam, air conditioning vapors, or smog—practically anything but a real fire or an emergency. This experiment thus showed that bystanders can define situations as nonemergencies for one another (Latané & Darley, 1968).

But perhaps these participants were simply afraid to appear cowardly. To check on this possibility, a similar study was designed in which the "emergency" did not involve personal danger. Participants waiting in the testing room heard a female experimenter in the next office climb up on a chair to reach a bookcase, fall to the floor, and yell, "Oh my God—my foot. . . . I can't move it. Oh . . . my ankle. . . . I can't get this thing off me." She continued to moan for about a minute longer. The entire incident lasted about 2 minutes. Only a curtain separated the woman's office from the testing room, in which participants waited either alone or in pairs. The results confirmed the findings of the smoke study. Of the participants who were alone, 70% came to the woman's aid, but only 40% of those in two-person groups offered help. Again, those who had not intervened claimed later that they were unsure of what had happened but had decided that it was not serious (Latané & Rodin, 1969). In these experiments, the presence of others produced pluralistic ignorance; each person, observing the calmness of the others, resolved the ambiguity of the situation by deciding that no emergency existed.

Pluralistic ignorance appeared to govern a more recent and disturbing example of the bystander effect. In 1993, near Liverpool, England, two 10-year-old boys kidnapped 2-year-old James Bulger at a local shopping mall. They led the toddler away on a meandering walk, cruelly tortured him along the way, and eventually beat him to death. Over the course of the day, at least 38 adults came across the three boys. Later testimony of these bystanders revealed that they had assumed—or were told—that the three boys were brothers (Levine, 1999). Interpreting aggressive actions as "family squabbles" seemed to define the situation as a nonemergency.

A shopping mall surveillance video shows 2-year-old James Bulger being led away by one of his two 10-year-old kidnappers, who tortured and eventually murdered the toddler. Many adults saw the boys together that day. Yet even though the toddler's head was cut and bruised and his face was tear-streaked, nobody intervened on James Bulger's behalf. Another devastating outcome of pluralistic ignorance.

This is especially troublesome. If the boys were in fact related, would the frightened and injured toddler be in less need of adult intervention? Similarly, is a woman threatened by her boyfriend or husband in less trouble than one threatened by a stranger? Crime statistics suggest not.

DIFFUSION OF RESPONSIBILITY Pluralistic ignorance can lead individuals to define a situation as a nonemergency, but this process does not explain incidents like the Genovese murder, in which the emergency is abundantly clear. Moreover, Kitty Genovese's neighbors could not observe one another behind their curtained windows and could not tell whether others were calm or panicked. The crucial process here was **diffusion of responsibility.** When each individual knows that many others are present, the burden of responsibility does not fall solely on him or her. Each can think, "Someone else must have done something by now; someone else will intervene."

To test this hypothesis, experimenters placed participants in separate booths and told them that they would take part in a group discussion about personal problems faced by college students. To avoid embarrassment, the discussion would be held through an intercom system. Each person would speak for 2 minutes. The microphone would be turned on only in the booth of the person speaking, and the experimenter would not be listening. In reality, all the voices except the participant's were tape recordings. On the first round, one person mentioned that he had problems with seizures. On the second round, this individual sounded as if he were actually starting to have a seizure and begged for help. The experimenters waited to see if the participant would leave the booth to report the emergency and how long it would take. Note that (1) the emergency is not at all ambiguous, (2) the participant could not tell how the bystanders in the other booths were reacting, and (3) the participant knew that the experimenter could not hear the emergency. Some participants were led to believe that the discussion group consisted only of themselves and the seizure victim. Others were told that they were part of a three-person group, and still others that they were part of a six-person group.

Of the participants who thought that they alone knew of the victim's seizure, 85% reported it; of those who thought they were in a three-person group, 62% reported the seizure; and of those who thought they were part of a six-person group, only 31% reported it (see Figure 17-3). Later interviews confirmed that all the participants perceived the situation to be a real emergency. Most were very upset by the conflict between letting the victim suffer and rushing for help. In fact, the participants who did not report the seizure appeared more upset than those who did. Clearly, we cannot interpret their nonintervention as apathy or indifference. Instead, the presence of others diffused the responsibility for acting (Darley & Latané, 1968; Latané & Darley, 1968).

If pluralistic ignorance and diffusion of responsibility are minimized, will people help one another? To find out, three psychologists used the New York City subway system as their laboratory (Piliavin, Rodin, & Piliavin, 1969). Two male and two female experimenters boarded a subway train separately. The female experimenters took seats

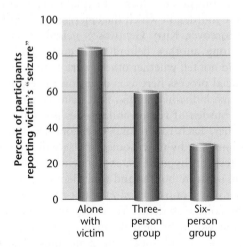

▮ Figure 17-3
Diffusion of Responsibility
The percentage of individuals who reported a victim's apparent seizure declined as the number of other people the individual believed were in his or her discussion group increased. (Adapted from M. M. Darley & B. Latané (1968), "Bystander Intervention in Emergencies: Diffusion of Responsibility," in *Journal of Personality and Social Psychology,* 8:377–383. Copyright © 1968 by the American Psychological Association. Adapted with permission.)

and recorded the results, while the two men remained standing. As the train moved along, one of the men staggered forward and collapsed, remaining prone and staring at the ceiling until he received help. If no help came, the other man finally helped him to his feet. Several variations of the study were tried: The victim either carried a cane (so he would appear disabled) or smelled of alcohol (so he would appear drunk). Sometimes the victim was white, sometimes black. There was no ambiguity when the person with a cane fell. Clearly the victim needed help, so pluralistic ignorance was minimized in that case. Diffusion of responsibility was also minimized because each bystander could not continue to assume that someone else was intervening. So if pluralistic ignorance and diffusion of responsibility are the main obstacles to helping, people should help the victim with a cane in this situation.

The results supported this optimistic expectation. The victim with the cane received spontaneous help on more than 95% of the trials, within an average of 5 seconds. The "drunk" victim received help on half of the trials, within an average of 2 minutes. Both black and white cane victims were aided by black and white bystanders. Plus, there was no relationship between the number of bystanders and the speed of help, suggesting that diffusion of responsibility had indeed been minimized.

THE ROLE OF HELPING MODELS In the subway study, as soon as one person moved to help, many others followed. This suggests that just as individuals use other people as models to define a situation as a nonemergency (as in pluralistic ignorance), they also use other people as models to indicate when to be helpful. This possibility was tested by counting the number of drivers who would stop to help a woman who was parked at the side of a road with a flat tire. It was found that significantly more drivers would stop to help if they had seen another woman with car trouble receiving help about a quarter of a mile earlier. Similarly, people are more likely to donate to a person soliciting for charity if they observe others doing so (Bryan & Test, 1967; Macaulay, 1970). These experiments indicate that others not only help us decide when not to act in an emergency but also serve as models to show us how and when to be good Samaritans.

Even role models on television can promote helping. In one study, 6-year-old children were shown an episode of *Lassie* in which a child rescues one of Lassie's pups from a mine shaft. Children in two control groups saw either a scene from *Lassie* that did not show a rescue or a scene from *The Brady Bunch*. Later, while the children were playing a game in which the winner would be given a prize, they were exposed to some whining puppies. Even though helping the puppies would diminish their chances of winning the prize, children who had watched the rescue episode spent more time comforting the puppies than children who had seen the control episodes (Sprafkin, Liebert, & Poulous, 1975). Another study found that children exposed to programs such as *Mister Rogers' Neighborhood* or *Sesame Street* were more likely to behave in giving ways than children who were not exposed to the shows (Forge & Phemister, 1987). These findings reiterate the powerful role that television has in shaping young people's behavior. (Revisit Chapter 11 for a discussion of media violence and aggression.)

THE ROLE OF INFORMATION Now that you have read about the factors that deter bystanders from intervening in an emergency, will you be more likely to act in such a situation? An experiment at the University of Montana suggests that you would. Undergraduates were either given a lecture or shown a film based on the material discussed in this section. Two weeks later, each undergraduate was confronted with a simulated emergency while walking with one other person (a confederate of the experimenters). A person needing aid was sprawled on the floor of a hallway. The confederate was trained to react as if the situation was not an emergency. Those who had heard the lecture or seen the film were significantly more likely than others to offer help (Beaman, Barnes, Klentz, & McQuirk, 1978). This study provides hope: Simply learning about social psychological phenomena—as you are doing now—can begin to lessen the power that situations have to produce unwelcome behavior—at least in this case of intervening in emergencies.

◆ Interim Summary

- Situational forces have tremendous power to shape human behavior, and yet these powerful situational forces are often invisible. People often mistakenly make sense of others' behavior by referring to their personality or character, called the *fundamental attribution error.*

- People perform simple tasks better—and complex tasks worse—when in the presence of coactors or an audience. These social facilitation and social inhibition effects occur because the presence of others narrows people's attention.

- The aggressive behavior sometimes shown by mobs and crowds may be the result of a state of deindividuation, in which individuals feel that they have lost their personal identities and merged into the group. Both anonymity and group size contribute to deindividuation. Deindividuation creates increased sensitivity to situation-specific social norms linked with the group. This can increase aggression when the group's norms are aggressive and reduce aggression when the group norms are benign.

- A bystander to an emergency is less likely to intervene or help if in a group than if alone. Two factors that deter intervention are pluralistic ignorance and diffusion of responsibility. By attempting to appear calm, bystanders may define the situation for one another as a nonemergency, thereby producing a state of pluralistic ignorance. The presence of other people also diffuses responsibility so that no one person feels the necessity to act.

◆ Critical Thinking Questions

1. The presence of others not only alters people's behavior but also alters their mental processes or patterns of thinking. Drawing from studies of (1) social facilitation, (2) deindividuation, and (3) bystander effects, describe three distinct mental processes that are altered by the presence of others in each context.

2. Reconsider the case of the mass suicides at Jonestown described at the opening of this chapter. One thing to know about the members of the People's Temple is that they were devoted to "the Cause," a utopian vision of social equality and racial harmony painted by Jim Jones. They moved to the jungle of Guyana for "the Cause." They signed over their worldly possession, gave up legal custody of their children, and lived separately from their spouses, all for "the Cause." Imagine being in this crowd of followers when Jim Jones asked them to drink the poison. Describe how deindividuation might have played a role in people's compliance to Jim Jones's request.

COMPLIANCE AND OBEDIENCE

CONFORMITY TO A MAJORITY

When we are in a group, we may find ourselves in the minority on some issue. This is a fact of life to which most of us have become accustomed. If we decide that the majority is a more valid source of information than our own experience, we may change our minds and conform to the majority opinion. But imagine yourself in a situation in which you are absolutely sure that your own opinion is correct and that the group is wrong. Would you yield to social pressure and conform under those circumstances? This is the kind of conformity that social psychologist Solomon Asch decided to investigate in a series of classic studies (1952, 1955, 1958).

▌ Figure 17-4
A Representative Stimulus in Asch's Study
After viewing display (a), participants were told to pick the matching line from display (b). The displays shown here are typical in that the correct decision is obvious. (After Asch, 1958)

swer that produces the strong forces toward conformity (Ross, Bierbrauer, & Hoffman, 1976). Disagreements in real life typically involve difficult or subjective judgments, such as which economic policy will best prevent recession or which of two paintings is more aesthetically pleasing. In these cases, we expect to disagree with others occasionally. We even know that being a minority of one in an otherwise unanimous group is a plausible, if uncomfortable, possibility.

The situation in Asch's experiments is much more extreme. Here the participant is confronted with unanimous disagreement about a simple physical fact, a bizarre and unprecedented occurrence that appears to have no rational explanation. Participants are clearly puzzled and tense. They rub their eyes in disbelief and jump up to look more closely at the lines. They squirm, mumble, giggle in embarrassment, and look searchingly at other members of the group for some clue to the mystery. After the experiment, they offer halfhearted hypotheses about optical illusions or suggest that perhaps the first person occasionally made a mistake and each

In Asch's standard procedure, a participant was seated at a table with a group of seven to nine others (all confederates of the experimenter). The group was shown a display of three vertical lines of different lengths and asked to judge which line was the same length as a line in another display (see Figure 17-4). Each individual announced his or her decision in turn, and the participant sat in the next-to-last seat. The correct judgments were obvious, and on most trials everyone gave the same response. But on several predetermined trials the confederates had been instructed to each give the wrong answer. Asch then observed the amount of conformity this procedure would elicit from participants.

The results were striking. Even though the correct answer was always obvious, the average participant conformed to the incorrect group consensus about a third of the time; about 75% of the participants conformed at least once. Moreover, the group did not have to be large to produce such conformity. When Asch varied the size of the group from 2 to 16, he found that a group of 3 or 4 confederates was just as effective at producing conformity as larger groups (Asch, 1958).

Why didn't the obviousness of the correct answer provide support for the participant's independence from the majority? Why isn't a person's confidence in his or her ability to make simple sensory judgments a strong force against conformity? According to one line of argument, it is precisely the obviousness of the correct an-

In a study of conformity to majority opinion, (*top*) all of the group members except the man sixth from the left are confederates who have been instructed to give uniformly wrong answers on 12 of the 18 trials. Number 6, who has been told that he is participating in an experiment on visual judgment, therefore finds that he is a lone dissenter when he gives the correct answers. (*bottom left*) The participant, showing the strain of repeated disagreement with the majority, leans forward anxiously to look at the exhibit in question. (*bottom right*) This particular participant persists in his opinion, saying that "he has to call them as he sees them." (The Asch Study of the Resistance of Majority Opinion, from *Scientific American*, November 1995, Vol. 193, No. 5, by Solomon E. Asch)

successive person followed suit because of pressure to conform (Asch, 1952).

Consider what it means to dissent from the majority under these circumstances. Just as the judgments of the group seem incomprehensible to the participant, so the participant believes that his or her dissent will be incomprehensible to the group. Group members will surely judge the dissenter to be incompetent, even out of touch with reality. Similarly, if the participant dissents repeatedly, this would seem to constitute a direct challenge to the group's competence, a challenge that requires enormous courage when one's own perceptual abilities are suddenly and inexplicably called into question. Such a challenge violates a strong social norm against insulting others. This fear of "What will they think of me?" and "What will they think I think of them?" inhibits dissent and generates the strong pressure to conform in Asch's experiments.

If Asch's conformity situation is unlike most situations in real life, why did he use a task in which the correct answer was obvious? The reason is that he wanted to study **compliance, pure public conformity, uncontaminated by the possibility that participants were actually changing their minds about the correct answers.** Several variations of Asch's study have used more difficult or subjective judgments, and although they may reflect conformity in real life more faithfully, they do not permit us to assess the effects of pure pressure to conform to a majority when we are certain that our own minority judgment is correct (Ross et al., 1976).

One of the most important findings from Asch's and later experiments on conformity is that the pressure to conform is far less strong when the group is not unanimous. If even one confederate breaks with the majority, the amount of conformity drops from 32% of the trials to about 6%. In fact, a group of eight containing only one dissenter produces less conformity than a unanimous majority of three (Allen & Levine, 1969; Asch, 1958). Surprisingly, the dissenter does not even have to give the correct answer. Even when the dissenter's answers are more inaccurate than the majority's, the majority influence is broken, and participants are more inclined to give their own correct judgments (Asch, 1955). Nor does it matter who the dissenter is. In a variation that approaches the absurd, conformity was significantly reduced even though the participants thought the dissenter was so visually handicapped that he could not see the stimuli (Allen & Levine, 1971). It seems clear that the presence of just one other dissenter to share the potential disapproval or ridicule of the group permits the participant to dissent without feeling totally isolated.

Here we see the power of situations to shape behavior yet again. A situation in which we face a unanimous majority creates a strong pull for conformity. By contrast, a seemingly minor change in that situation—a simple break in the unanimity—allows us to "be ourselves." Yet whether or not a situation includes a unanimous majority is a central feature of the situation, so perhaps it is not surprising that rates of conformity depend on it. What about subtler background features of situations? Like what newspaper article you just read, or what's playing on the television in the corner of the room? Recent variations on Asch's experiment have explored the influence of such seemingly trivial situational factors by examining how simple exposure to words and pictures can push us conform. The key is whether these words and pictures prime—or activate—ideas about conformity or ideas about nonconformity. In one experiment, some participants were exposed to words like *adhere, comply,* and *conform,* whereas others were exposed to words like *challenge, confront,* and *deviate* (Epley & Gilovich, 1999). In another study, the experimenters primed conformity in some participants by showing them a photo of "Norman, an accountant," whereas they primed nonconformity in others with a photo of "Norman, a punk rocker" (Pendry & Carrick, 2001). In both experiments, participants with prior exposure to the mere idea of conformity actually behaved in more conforming ways when later faced with a unanimous majority. This evidence shows how exquisitely

Simple images can activate the concepts of conformity or nonconformity. Once activated, these concepts can influence people's behavior. Researchers found more conformity among those who saw a picture of "Norman, an accountant" than among those who saw a picture of "Norman, a punk rocker." (After Pendry & Carrick, 2001)

CUTTING-EDGE RESEARCH
Pluralistic Ignorance and College Drinking

A little knowledge can be a powerful thing. Sometimes, it can even stand up to the power of situational forces and lessen their impact on our behavior. We saw this triumph of knowledge earlier when we discussed the role of information in bystander effects. The study from the University of Montana demonstrated that simply learning about the social psychological factors that deter bystanders from intervening produced more offers to help.

One of the key insights about social influence illustrated in studies of bystander effects is the concept of pluralistic ignorance (Schanck, 1932). When we don't know exactly what to do in a complex or confusing situation, we delay action while we gather information from others around us. Yet rarely do we seek out information directly by going up to others and asking them what they think or feel. Instead, we maintain a calm, cool demeanor—basically pretending that we know what we're doing—and

then slyly check out what others are doing. Suppose everyone does the same? What you get is a group of people who *look* like they know what they're doing, but inside they are each in turmoil, confused and uncertain. This is pluralistic ignorance. Everybody—the plurality—is ignorant of everyone else's true feelings.

This group-level phenomenon characterizes many situations beyond bystanders' reactions to emergencies. You and your classmates have probably experienced it countless times in large lecture courses. Your professor, after presenting some new and complex material, asks the class if they have any questions. Do you raise your hand? Probably not. Why would you want to acknowledge your confusion? You don't want to be known as the one who asks stupid questions. Do your classmates raise their hands? No. They obviously understand the material, which is all the more reason to keep your questions to yourself. Do you see the pluralistic ignorance at work? You and all your classmates are behaving identically—you are all sitting quietly, asking no questions. Even faced with this identical behavior, it's common to interpret your own private feelings as different from those of

others: You alone are confused, whereas others are confident. In this case, pluralistic ignorance can make students feel alienated from their classmates. Imagine how much more at ease you'd feel if the person next to you leaned over and whispered, "I have no idea what she's been saying!" Perhaps you'd even find the courage to raise your hand with your own question!

What does all this have to do with college drinking? As you are no doubt already aware, students' alcohol use is a major concern of parents and college administrators across the United States. Alcohol-related accidents are the number one cause of death among college students, and alcohol use is linked to lower academic performance and higher rates of destructive behavior. Ninety percent of college students, when surveyed, indicate that they've tried alcohol, and about 25% show problems like binge drinking. We know already that peers exert a big influence on students' drinking. The question is how? Do peers cajole each other into drinking and drinking more? Well, sometimes. Other times, pluralistic ignorance is at work. If 90% of students are drinking, it looks like everyone is comfortable with it. Despite this,

responsive to situational factors our behavior can be. Even features of the situation that are in the background—outside our conscious awareness—can exert their power and pull us to conform.

To be sure, we conform to the behavior of others for a number of reasons. Sometimes we find ourselves in ambiguous situations and don't know how to behave. What do you do, for instance, if you don't know which of several forks to use first at a fancy restaurant? You look to see what others do, and conform. This type of conformity is called **informational social influence.** In these cases, we conform because we believe that other people's interpretations of an ambiguous situation are more correct than our own. At other times we find ourselves simply wanting to fit in and be accepted by a group. Perhaps you felt this way when you started college or joined a new high school. This type of conformity is called **nor-**

mative social influence. In these cases, we conform to a group's social norms or typical behaviors to become liked and accepted. We go along to get along. Because the correct line length was not ambiguous in Asch's famous study, we know that normative social influence is what pulled Asch's participants to conform. Luckily, it turns out that age plays an important role in conformity. Although informational social influence continues to produce conformity in old age—suggesting that we still value others' expertise in late life—the pressures to fit in and be liked that fuel normative social influence appear to lessen as people grow older (Pasupathi, 1999).

Sometimes it's easy to tell what the group's norms are because it's evident in the group's behavior. Again, this was true in the Asch study. In real life, however, group norms may be more difficult to identify. In these cases, pluralistic ignorance may promote conformity to imag-surveys show that many students have clear misgivings about drinking. Perhaps you've nursed a sick roommate, heard about a recent death from binge drinking, or seen that your own hangovers have harmed your academic performance. Even though you have a drink or two at a party, you may not be completely comfortable with the amount of drinking on your campus.

Here again is a pattern of pluralistic ignorance: Everyone's behavior looks basically the same—they all look comfortable as they drink. And yet, even while holding that plastic cup full of beer, many students harbor private misgivings about drinking, while assuming that the group norm is to be unconcerned about drinking. What are the consequences for misperceiving this group norm? Conformity with it—an increase in drinking over time! A series of studies at Princeton University documented this problematic outcome (Prentice & Miller, 1993).

Yet as we've seen, knowledge of social psychology can be a powerful tool. Princeton University also developed and tested a new kind of alcohol education program. First-year students attended a dorm-based discussion about alcohol use that was either peer-oriented, including

information about pluralistic ignorance, or individual-oriented, focusing on decision making in drinking situations. Four to 6 months later, those who learned about the concept of pluralistic ignorance reported drinking less. A little knowledge can be a powerful thing! Moreover, the study's evidence suggested that knowledge of this social psychological principle did not so much change students' perceptions of the group norm but rather lessened the norm's power to induce conformity (Schroeder & Prentice, 1998).

So the next time you find yourself at a party deciding whether you should have a drink (or another drink) and surrounded by nonchalant drinkers, consider basing your choice on your own hunches rather than the apparent beliefs of your companions. Social situations exert powerful pressures toward conformity. But you can fight back with the power of knowledge!

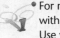 For more information, go online with InfoTrac College Edition. Use your own term or search:

- Pluralistic ignorance
- College drinking

© Chuck Savage/CORBIS

When everybody assumes that their peers are comfortable with the amount of drinking on their campus, pluralistic ignorance can, over time, increase alcohol consumption. Fortunately, knowledge of how pluralistic ignorance pulls for conformity can curtail alcohol consumption.

ined social norms rather than actual social norms. Recall that pluralistic ignorance occurs when group members mistakenly believe they know what others think. In the case of bystander effects, people mistakenly believe that other bystanders know that the situation is a nonemergency. Understanding how the concept of pluralistic ignorance fuels conformity can also be used to reduce pressures to conform. See the Cutting-Edge Research box to learn how Princeton University used this social psychological concept to reduce campus alcohol consumption.

MINORITY INFLUENCE

A number of European scholars have been critical of social psychological research in North America because of its preoccupation with conformity and the influence of the majority on the minority. As they correctly point out,

intellectual innovation, social change, and political revolution often occur because an informed and articulate minority begins to convert others to its point of view (Moscovici, 1976). Why not study innovation and the influence that minorities can have on the majority?

To make their point, these European investigators deliberately began their experimental work by setting up a laboratory situation virtually identical to Asch's conformity situation. Participants were asked to make a series of simple perceptual judgments in the face of confederates who consistently gave the incorrect answer. But instead of placing a single participant in the midst of several confederates, these investigators planted two confederates, who consistently gave incorrect responses, in the midst of four real participants. The experimenters found that the minority was able to influence about 32% of the participants to make at least one incorrect judgment. For this to occur, however, the minority had to remain consistent throughout the experiment. If they wavered or showed any inconsistency in their judgments, they were unable to influence the majority (Moscovici, Lage, & Naffrechoux, 1969).

Since this initial demonstration of minority influence, more than 90 related studies have been conducted in both Europe and North America, including several that required groups to debate social and political issues rather than make simple perceptual judgments (Wood, Lundgren, Ouellette, Busceme, & Blackstone, 1994). The general finding of **minority influence** is that minorities can move majorities toward their point of view if they present a consistent position without appearing rigid, dogmatic, or arrogant. Such minorities are perceived to be more confident and, occasionally, more competent than the majority (Maass & Clark, 1984). Minorities are also more effective if they argue a position that is consistent with the developing social norms of the larger society. For example, in two experiments in which feminist issues were discussed, participants were moved significantly more by a minority position that was in line with feminist social norms than by one opposed to feminist norms (Paicheler, 1977).

But the most interesting finding of this research is that the majority members in these studies show a change of private attitude—that is, internalization—not just the public conformity that was found in the Asch experiments. In fact, minorities sometimes cause private attitude change in majority members even when they fail to obtain public conformity.

One investigator has suggested that minorities are able to produce attitude change because they lead majority individuals to rethink the issues. Even when they fail to convince the majority, they broaden the range of acceptable opinions. In contrast, unanimous majorities are rarely prompted to think carefully about their position (Nemeth, 1986).

Another view suggests that minority influence occurs in part because majority members believe that they won't be influenced by the minority but simply extend them the courtesy of hearing them out. That is, simply to show their open-mindedness, those in the majority may thoughtfully consider the minority opinion but don't expect this deliberation to change their own views. Ironically, however, it does change people's minds, because thoughtful deliberation unsettles whole sets of related beliefs, which become more likely to change down the road. This process reflects what psychologists have called an **implicit leniency contract** in the treatment of minority group members, meaning that simply to appear fair, majority members let minority members have their say, but by doing so they unwittingly open the door to minority influence (Crano & Chen, 1998).

These findings remind us that majorities typically have the social power to approve and disapprove, to accept or reject, and it is this power that can produce public compliance or conformity. In contrast, minorities rarely have such social power. But if they have credibility, they have the power to produce genuine attitude change and, hence, innovation, social change, and even revolution.

OBEDIENCE TO AUTHORITY

We opened this chapter with some of the most chilling horrors of humanity—perhaps none is more sobering in sheer magnitude than the systematic genocide undertaken by Nazi Germany during World War II. Think back to all the lives lost (and tears shed) on September 11, 2001, in the terrorist attacks on the United States. Now multiply that by 2,500! You're still below the death count amassed within the Nazi concentration camps. The mastermind of that horror, Adolf Hitler, may well have been a psychopathic monster. But he could not have done it alone. What about the people who ran the day-to-day operations, who built the ovens and gas chambers, filled them with human beings, counted bodies, and did the necessary paperwork? Were they all monsters, too?

Not according to social philosopher Hannah Arendt (1963), who observed the trial of Adolf Eichmann, a Nazi

© Jon Jones/Corbis Sygma

Social change—such as the end of apartheid in South Africa—is sometimes brought about because a few people manage to persuade the majority in power to change its attitudes.

war criminal who was found guilty and executed for causing the murder of millions of Jews. She described him as a dull, ordinary bureaucrat, who saw himself as a little cog in a big machine. The publication of a partial transcript of Eichmann's pretrial interrogation supports Arendt's view. Several psychiatrists found Eichmann to be quite sane, and his personal relationships were quite normal. In fact, he believed that the Jews should have been allowed to emigrate to a separate territory. Moreover, he had a Jewish mistress in secret—a crime for an SS officer—and a Jewish half-cousin whom he arranged to have protected during the war (Von Lang & Sibyll, 1983).

In her book about Eichmann, subtitled *A Report on the Banality of Evil,* Arendt concluded that most of the "evil men" of the Third Reich were just ordinary people following orders from superiors. This suggests that all of us might be capable of such evil and that Nazi Germany was less wildly alien from the normal human condition than we might like to think. As Arendt put it, "In certain circumstances the most ordinary decent person can become a criminal." This is not an easy conclusion to accept because it is more comforting to believe that monstrous evil is done only by monstrous individuals. In fact, our emotional attachment to this explanation of evil was vividly demonstrated by the intensity of the attacks on Arendt and her conclusions.

The problem of obedience to authority arose again in Vietnam in 1968, when a group of American soldiers, claiming that they were simply following orders, killed civilians in the community of My Lai. Again the public was forced to ponder the possibility that ordinary citizens are willing to obey authority, even in violation of their own moral consciences.

This unsettling issue was explored empirically in some of the most important studies in all of social psychology, conducted by Stanley Milgram (1963, 1974) at Yale University. Ordinary men and women were recruited through a newspaper ad that offered $4 for 1 hour's participation in a "study of memory." When they arrived at the laboratory, each participant met another participant (in actuality, a confederate of the experimenter) and was told that one of them would play the role of teacher in the study, and the other would play the learner. The two participants then drew slips of paper out of a hat, and the real participant discovered that he or she would be the teacher. In that role, the participant was to read a list of word pairs to the learner and then test his memory by reading the first word of each pair and asking him to select the correct second word from four alternatives. Each time the learner made an error, the participant was to press a lever that delivered an electric shock to him.

The participant watched while the learner was strapped into a chair and an electrode was attached to his wrist. The participant was then seated in an adjoining room in front of a shock generator whose front panel contained 30 lever switches in a horizontal line (see photos). Each switch was labeled with a voltage rating, ranging in sequence from 15 to 450 volts, and groups of adjacent switches were labeled descriptively, ranging from "Slight Shock" through "Danger: Severe

The "shock generator" used in Milgram's experiment on obedience (*top left*). The "learner" is strapped into the "electric chair" (*top right*). A participant receives a sample shock before starting the "teaching session" (*bottom left*). Participant refuses to go on with the experiment (*bottom right*). Most participants became deeply disturbed by the role they were asked to play, whether they remained in the experiment to the end or refused at some point to go on. (From the film *Obedience,* distributed by New York University Film Library, copyright © 1965 by Stanley Milgram, Reprinted by permission of Alexandra Milgram)

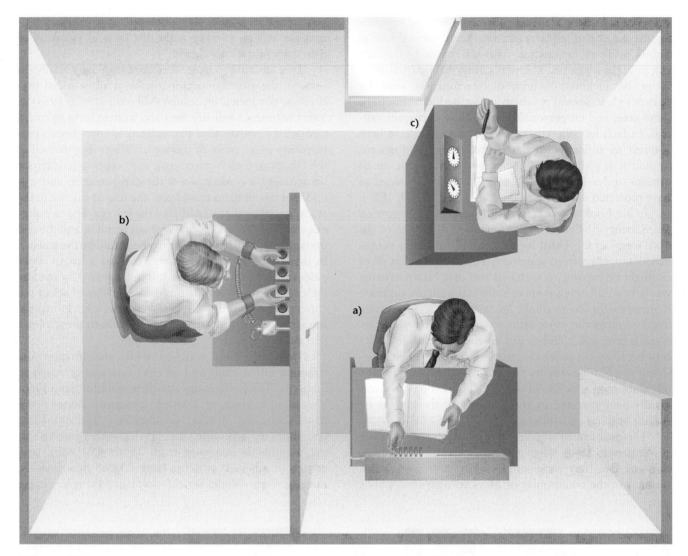

▌Figure 17-5
Milgram's Experiment on Obedience
The "teacher" (a) was told to give the "learner" (b) a more intense shock after each error. If
the "teacher" objected, the experimenter (c) insisted that it was necessary to go on. (From
Obedience to Authority: An Experimental View by Stanley Milgram. Copyright © 1974 by Stanley Milgram.
Reprinted by permission of Alexandra Milgram.)

Shock" up to the extreme, labeled simply "XXX." When a switch was depressed, an electric buzzer sounded, lights flashed, and the needle on a voltage meter deflected to the right. To illustrate how it worked, the participant was given a sample shock of 45 volts from the generator. As the procedure began, the experimenter instructed the participant to move one level higher on the shock generator after each successive error by the learner (see Figure 17-5).

The learner did not actually receive any shocks. He was a mild-mannered 47-year-old man who had been specially trained for his role. As he began to make errors and the shock levels escalated, he could be heard protest-

ing through the adjoining wall. As the shocks became stronger, he began to shout and curse. At 300 volts, he began to kick the wall, and at the next shock level (marked "Extreme Intensity Shock"), he no longer answered the questions or made any noise. As you might expect, many participants began to object to this excruciating procedure, pleading with the experimenter to call a halt. But the experimenter responded with a sequence of calm prods, using as many as necessary to get the participant to go on: "Please continue," "The experiment requires that you continue," "It is absolutely essential that you continue," and "You have no other choice— you must go on." Obedience to authority was measured by the maximum amount of shock the participant would administer before refusing to continue.

When college students first learn the details of Milgram's procedure and are asked whether they themselves would continue to administer the shocks after the learner begins to pound on the wall, about 99% say that they would not (Aronson, 1995). Milgram himself surveyed psychiatrists at a leading medical school. They predicted that most participants would refuse to go on after reaching 150 volts, that only about 4% would go beyond 300 volts, and that less than 1% would go all the way to 450 volts.

What did Milgram find? That 65% of the participants continued to obey throughout, going all the way to the end of the shock series (450 volts, labeled "XXX"). Not one participant stopped before administering 300 volts, the point at which the learner began to kick the wall (see Figure 17-6).

What makes us so unable to fathom the degree of obedience evident in Milgram's work? The answer ties back to the fundamental attribution error, introduced at the start of the chapter. We assume that people's behavior reflects their inner qualities—their wishes and their personalities. We underestimate—even overlook altogether—the power that situations hold over us. So we put Milgram's procedures together with the knowledge that most people would not wish to inflict severe bodily harm to another innocent person and conclude that few would obey.

▌ Figure 17-6
Obedience to Authority
The percentage of participants who were willing to administer a punishing shock did not begin to decline until the intensity level of the shock reached 300 volts (the danger level). (Graph based on "Table 2 Distribution of Breakoff Points" in S. Milgram (1963), "Behavioral Study of Obedience," from *Journal of Abnormal and Social Psychology*, 67, p. 376. Used by permission of Alexandra Milgram.)

It is true that few *wanted* to obey. Most voiced considerable distress and reservations about delivering the shocks. And yet they continued. Somehow their intentions to "do no harm"—although voiced—failed to govern their behavior. In assuming that people's intentions guide their behavior, we've failed to see how subtle features of the situation powerfully pulled for obedience.

How do we know that it's the situation at work here? Maybe these were particularly aggressive or spineless people? Maybe Milgram had unleashed the unconscious aggressive drive that Freud discussed?

We know it's the situation because Milgram conducted many variations on the standard procedure and assigned participants at random to different situations. And each variation in the situation led to drastic changes in the rates of obedience. Four important features of the situation include (1) surveillance, (2) buffers, (3) the presence of role models, and (4) its emerging nature.

SURVEILLANCE One situational comparison varied the degree to which the experimenter supervised the participant. When the experimenter left the room and issued his orders by telephone, the rate of obedience dropped from 65% to 21% (Milgram, 1974). Moreover, several of the participants who continued under these conditions cheated by administering shocks of lower intensity than they were supposed to. So the constant presence or surveillance of the experimenter is one situational factor that pulls for obedience.

BUFFERS Another set of situational comparisons varied the proximity of the teacher and learner. In the standard procedure, the learner was in the next room, out of sight and only heard through the wall. When the learner was in the same room as the participant, the rate of obedience dropped from 65% to 40%. When the participant had to personally ensure that the learner held his hand on a shock plate, obedience declined to 30%. By contrast, when the psychological distance was increased and the learner offered no verbal feedback from the next room, the rate of obedience shot up to 100%. So a second situational factor that pulls for obedience is buffers. Milgram's participants believed that they were committing acts of violence, but there were several buffers that obscured this fact or diluted the immediacy of the experience. The more direct the participants' experience with the victim—the fewer buffers between the person and the consequences of his or her act—the less the participant will obey.

The most common buffer found in warlike situations is the remoteness of the person from the final act of violence. Thus, Eichmann argued that he was not directly responsible for killing Jews; he merely arranged for their deaths. Milgram conducted an analog to this

Modern warfare allows individuals to distance themselves from the actual killing, giving them the feeling that they are not responsible for enemy deaths.

"link-in-the-chain" role by requiring participants only to pull a switch that enabled another teacher (a confederate) to deliver the shocks to the learner. Under these conditions, the rate of obedience soared: A full 93% of the participants continued to the end of the shock series. In this situation, the participant can shift responsibility to the person who actually delivers the shock.

The shock generator itself served as a buffer—an impersonal mechanical agent that actually delivered the shock. Imagine how obedience would have declined if participants were required to hit the learner with their fists. In real life, we have analogous technologies that permit us to destroy distant fellow humans by remote control, thereby removing us from the sight of their suffering. Although we probably would all agree that it is worse to kill thousands of people by pushing a button that releases a guided missile than it is to beat one individual to death with a rock, it is still psychologically easier to push the button. Such are the effects of buffers.

ROLE MODELS One reason Milgram's experiment obtained such high levels of obedience is that the social pressures were directed toward a lone individual. If the participant was not alone, would he or she be less obedient? We have already seen some data to support this possibility: A participant in the Asch conformity situation is less likely to go along with the group's incorrect judgments if there is at least one other dissenter.

A similar thing happens in Milgram's obedience situation. In one variation of the procedure, two additional confederates were employed. They were introduced as participants who would also play teacher roles. Teacher 1 would read the list of word pairs, Teacher 2 would tell the learner if he was right or wrong, and Teacher 3 (the participant) would deliver the shocks. The confederates complied with the instructions through the 150-volt shock, at which point Teacher 1 informed the experimenter that he was quitting. Despite the experimenter's insistence that he continue, Teacher 1 got up from his chair and sat in another part of the room. After the 210-volt shock, Teacher 2 also quit. The experimenter then turned to the participant and ordered him to continue alone. Only 10% of the participants were willing to complete the series in this situation. In a second variation, there were two experimenters rather than two additional teachers. After a few shocks, they began to argue. One of them said that they should stop the experiment; the other said that they should continue. Under these circumstances, not a single participant would continue, despite the orders to do so by the second experimenter (Milgram, 1974).

So role models who disobeyed allow participants to follow their own conscience. But before we congratulate these participants on their autonomy in the face of social pressure, we should consider the implication of these findings more closely. They suggest participants were not choosing between obedience and autonomy but between obedience and conformity: Obey the commanding experimenter or conform to the emerging norm to disobey.

Obeying or conforming may not strike you as a very heroic choice. But these are among the processes that provide the social glue for the human species. One social historian has noted that "disobedience when it is not criminally but morally, religiously, or politically motivated is always a collective act and it is justified by the values of the collectivity and the mutual engagements of its members" (Walzer, 1970, p. 4).

EMERGING SITUATIONS So far, when we've discussed the power of situations, we've painted situations in fairly broad brushstrokes. For instance, we've considered how a group with a unanimous opinion exerts more social pressure than a group that includes a single dissenter. These broad brush strokes obscure the fact that the meaning of any given situation unfolds and changes over time. What begins benignly may insidiously evolve into something horrifying. Yet the emerging nature of situations—just like the power of situations more generally—often eludes us.

For instance, many people who hear about the Milgram study wonder why anyone would ever agree to administer the first shock. Most everyone claims that they themselves wouldn't do it. But that's because people tend to focus on the end of the story—how outrageous the situation ends up, with participants delivering shocks so intense they are beyond description ("XXX") to a man who has presumably lost consciousness. What we need to do is focus on the how the situation started and, more importantly, how it evolved.

The situation began innocuously enough. Participants replied to an advertisement and agreed to participate in a study at Yale University. By doing so they implicitly agreed to cooperate with the experimenter, follow the directions of the person in charge, and see the job through to completion. This is a very strong social norm, and we tend to underestimate how difficult it is to break such an agreement and go back on our implied word to cooperate. And when participants arrived, they found themselves in a fairly straightforward learning experiment. They might have been thinking, "How hard could it be to learn these simple word pairs?" "I bet the threat of shock will speed up the learning process."

Plus, the first shock was just 15 volts—perhaps not even noticeable. And the shock level increased by a mere 15 volts at a time. Although it's abundantly clear that administering 450 volts is not a good thing, the change from innocuous to unfathomable is not so clear. Once participants gave the first shock, there was no longer a natural stopping point. By the time they wanted to quit, they were trapped. The true character of the situation had emerged only slowly over time.

Making matters worse, in order to break off, participants had to suffer the guilt and embarrassment of acknowledging that they were wrong to begin at all. And the longer they put off quitting, the harder it became to admit their misjudgment in going as far as they had. It is often easier to continue with bad behavior than to admit our mistakes.

Perhaps most significantly, Milgram's participants had no time to reflect. They had no time to think about the strange situation they now found themselves in, and what their own conscience would dictate. This effectively prevented them from accessing their own definition of the situation (as "horrifying"). Instead, participants were torn apart by two conflicting definitions of the situations: the authority's definition—"The experiment requires that you continue"—and the victim's definition—"Let me out of here! My heart is starting to bother me!" Most often, in this fast-paced and evolving situation, the participants' behavior reflected other people's definitions of the situation: either the definition offered by the experimenter, which pulled for obedience, or the definitions offered by peers who themselves broke off, which produced disobedience. Participants' own wishes and desires—although voiced—did not steer their behavior. Imagine how much less obedience there would have been if there had been a 15-minute break after 300 volts.

CONCEPT REVIEW TABLE
Situational Features of Obedience to Authority

Feature	Experimental Evidence Within Milgram's Studies
Surveillance	Obedience rate drops when experimenter is not physically present.
Buffers	Obedience rates drop when "victim" is moved closer to the participant and increase when the "victim" is never heard.
Role Models	Obedience rates drop when a fellow "teacher" or a second experimenter stops cooperating.
Emerging Situations	Obedience rates seem to depend on the innocuous start to the study, the small rate of change in shock intensity, and the lack of time for the participant to reflect.

IDEOLOGICAL JUSTIFICATION On top of all the situational factors that pull for obedience (see the Concept Review Table for a review) are societal factors. Milgram suggested that the potential for obedience to authority is such a necessary requirement for communal life that it has probably been built into our species by evolution. The division of labor in a society requires that individuals be willing at times to subordinate their own independent actions to serve the goals of the larger social organization. Parents, school systems, and businesses nurture this willingness by reminding the individual of the importance of following the directives of others who "know the larger picture." To understand obedience in a particular situation, then, we need to understand the individual's acceptance of an **ideology**—a set of beliefs and attitudes—that legitimates the authority of the person in charge and justifies following his or her directives. As an example of ideological justification, the Islamic extremists who became suicide hijackers on September 11, 2001, believed that, as martyrs, they would enter infinite paradise if they followed the directives of Osama bin Laden. With eerie similarity, the members of the People's Temple believed that, in drinking the poison, they were "crossing over" into paradise for the sake of "the Cause" that Jim Jones illuminated. Ideologies not only guide the bizarre behaviors of religious extremists but also guide the day-to-day activities of military organizations. Nazi officers believed in the primacy of the German state and hence in the legitimacy of orders issued in its name. Similarly, the American soldiers who followed orders to kill enemy civilians in Vietnam had already

Soldiers follow orders because they believe that national security requires that they do so. This provides an ideological justification for their obedience.

committed themselves to the premise that national security requires strict obedience to military commands.

In the Milgram experiments, "the importance of science" is the ideology that legitimated even extraordinary demands. Some critics have argued that the Milgram experiments were artificial, that the prestige of a scientific experiment led participants to obey without questioning the dubious procedures in which they participated, and that in real life people would never do such a thing (Baumrind, 1964). Indeed, when Milgram repeated his experiment in a rundown set of offices and removed any association with Yale University from the setting, the rate of obedience dropped somewhat from 65% to 48% (Milgram, 1974).

But this criticism misses the major point. The prestige of science is not an irrelevant artificiality but an integral part of Milgram's demonstration. Science serves the same legitimating role in the experiment that the German state served in Nazi Germany and that national security serves in wartime killing. It is precisely their belief in the importance of scientific research that prompts individuals to subordinate their moral autonomy and independence to those who claim to act on behalf of science.

ETHICAL ISSUES Milgram's experiments have been criticized on several grounds. First, critics argue that Milgram's procedures created an unacceptable level of stress in the participants during the experiment itself. In support of this claim, they quote Milgram's own description:

> [Participants] were observed to sweat, tremble, stutter, bite their lips, groan, and dig their fingernails into their flesh. These were characteristic rather than exceptional responses to the experiment. . . . One sign of tension was the regular occurrence of nervous laughing fits. . . . On one occasion we observed a seizure so violently convulsive that it was necessary to call a halt to the experiment. (Milgram, 1963, p. 375)

Second, critics express concern about the long-term psychological effects on participants of having learned that they would be willing to give potentially lethal shocks to a fellow human being. Third, critics argue that participants are likely to feel foolish and "used" when told the true nature of the experiment, thereby making them less trusting of psychologists in particular and of authority in general.

In response to these and other criticisms, Milgram pointed out that after his experiments he conducted a careful **debriefing;** that is, he explained the reasons for the procedures and reestablished positive rapport with the participant. This included a reassuring chat with the "victim" who the participant had thought was receiving the shocks. After the completion of an experimental series, participants were sent a detailed report of the purposes and results of the experiment. Milgram then conducted a survey, which revealed that 84% of the participants were glad to have taken part in the study; 15% reported neutral feelings; and 1% stated that they were sorry to have participated. These percentages were about the same for those who had obeyed and those who had defied the experimenter. In addition, 74% indicated that they had learned something of personal importance as a result of being in the study.

Milgram also hired a psychiatrist to interview 40 of the participants to determine whether the study had any injurious effects. This follow-up revealed no indications of long-term distress or traumatic reactions (Milgram, 1964).

In Chapter 1 we noted that research guidelines set forth by the U.S. government and the American Psychological Association emphasize two major principles: minimal risk and informed consent. Milgram's studies were conducted in the early 1960s, before these guidelines were in effect. Despite the importance of the research and the precautions that Milgram took, it seems likely that most of the review boards that must now approve federally funded research projects would not permit these experiments to be conducted today.

OBEDIENCE IN EVERYDAY LIFE Because the Milgram experiments have been criticized for being artificial (Orne & Holland, 1968), it is instructive to look at an example of obedience to authority under more ordinary conditions. Researchers investigated whether nurses in public and private hospitals would obey an order that violated hospital rules and professional practice (Hofling, Brotzman, Dalrymple, Graves, & Pierce, 1966). While on regular duty, the participant (a nurse) received a phone call from a doctor whom she knew to be on the staff but had not met: "This is Dr. Smith from Psychiatry calling. I was asked to see Mr. Jones this morning, and I'm going to have to see him again tonight. I'd like him to have had some medication by the time I get to the ward. Will you please check your medicine cabinet and see if you have some Astroten? That's A-S-T-R-O-T-E-N." When the nurse checked the medicine cabinet, she saw a pillbox labeled:

ASTROTEN
5 mg capsules
Usual dose: 5 mg
Maximum daily dose: 10 mg

After she reported that she had found it, the doctor continued, "Now will you please give Mr. Jones a dose of 20 milligrams of Astroten. I'll be up within 10 minutes; I'll sign the order then, but I'd like the drug to have started taking effect." A staff psychiatrist, posted unobtrusively nearby, terminated each trial by disclosing its true nature when the nurse either dispensed the medication (actually a harmless placebo), refused to accept the order, or tried to contact another professional.

This order violated several rules: The dose was clearly excessive. Medication orders may not be given by telephone. The medication was unauthorized—that is, it was not on the ward stock list clearing it for use. Finally, the order was given by an unfamiliar person. Despite all this, 95% of the nurses started to give the medication. Moreover, the telephone calls were all brief, and the nurses put up little or no resistance. None of them insisted on a written order, although several sought reassurance that the doctor would arrive promptly. In interviews after the experiment, all the nurses stated that such orders had been received in the past and that doctors became annoyed if the nurses balked.

Again, these results surprise us. And they surprise professionals as well. When nurses who had not been participants in the study were given a complete description of the situation and asked how they themselves would respond, 83% reported that they would not have given the medication, and most of them thought that a majority of nurses would also refuse. Twenty-one nursing students who were asked the same question all asserted that they would not have given the medication as ordered.

This again portrays the immense power of situational forces, as well as our reluctance to see that power. We make the mistake of assuming that people's behavior reflects their character and their intentions. We make this fundamental attribution error time and again.

◆ Interim Summary

- Asch's classic experiments on conformity found that a unanimous group exerts strong pressure on an individual to conform to the group's judgments—even when those judgments are clearly wrong. Much less conformity was observed if even one person dissented from the group.

- A minority within a larger group can move the majority toward its point of view if it maintains a consistent dissenting position without appearing to be rigid, dogmatic, or arrogant, a process called *minority influence*. Minorities sometimes even obtain private attitude change from majority members, not just public conformity. This is thought to occur through an implicit leniency contract in which majority members agree to let minority members have their say but don't expect to be influenced by them.

- Milgram's classic experiments on obedience to authority demonstrated that ordinary people would obey an experimenter's order to deliver strong electric shocks to an innocent victim. Situational factors conspiring to produce the high obedience rates include (1) surveillance by the experimenter, (2) buffers that distance the person from the consequences of his or her acts, (3) role models, and (4) the emerging properties of situations. An ideology about the importance of science also helped to justify obedience to the experimenter.

- Although Milgram's research is unquestionably important, the ethics of his experiments have generated considerable controversy. It is unclear whether similar research could be conducted today.

◆ Critical Thinking Questions

1. One account of how ordinary individuals are recruited to become suicide terrorists suggests that a charismatic leader indoctrinates a group of people at once, asking them to "please step forward" if they have any doubts about becoming martyrs for the cause. How does this account exploit the concept of pluralistic ignorance?

2. Consider the unsettling message of Milgram's studies: That if a situation is arranged properly and supported by ideological beliefs, ordinary people—like you—can be pulled to act in ways that you find morally reprehensible. How will you fight against the power of such situations in your own life? Can certain other situations pull you to follow your own conscience?

INTERNALIZATION

Most studies of conformity and obedience focus on whether individuals overtly comply with the social influence wielded within the situation. In everyday life, however, those who attempt to influence us usually seek **internalization**; that is, they want to change our private attitudes, not just our public behaviors, and to obtain changes that will be sustained even after they are no longer on the scene. Certainly the major goal of parents, educators, clergy, politicians, and advertisers is internalization, not just compliance. In this section we begin to examine social influence that persuades rather than coerces.

Self-Justification

When discussing the emerging situational predicament that Milgram's participants found themselves in, we concluded that sometimes it's easier to continue with bad behavior than to admit our mistakes. Why is that? Why is it so difficult for us to come clean and say, "I changed my mind. I no longer think that doing this is right"? Part of the answer is that (at least in Western culture) people hate being inconsistent. The pressure to be consistent can be so strong that often people will justify—or rationalize—past behavior by forming or adjusting their private beliefs to support it.

A classic study of social influence tested the power of this pull to be consistent. To get a sense of the study, imagine that you were to knock on the doors of homeowners in your community, identify yourself as belonging to the Community Committee on Public Safety, and ask those who answered: "Could we install a public service billboard on your front lawn?" Naturally, you'd want to give folks a sense of what the billboard would look like, so you'd show them a photo of an attractive home nearly obscured by a huge, poorly lettered sign that reads "Drive Carefully." Would people agree? Not many. In the early 1960s, a research team found that only 17% said yes (Freedman & Fraser, 1966). Although few could argue with the mission of promoting safe driving, the request was simply too large. There is probably no way that people would hand over the use of their front lawn for this or any other cause. Or is there?

Suppose an associate of yours had approached these homeowners a few weeks earlier with a relatively minor request: "Would you place this sign in your living room window?" Your associate would then show them a small, 3-inch-square sign that reads "Be a Safe Driver." The cause is good and the request so small that nearly everyone says yes. And although the actions taken by the homeowner are relatively minor, their effects are powerful and lasting. For the next few weeks, every time these people look at their window, they face a salient reminder that they care about public safety, so much so that they took action. When guests ask about the sign, they will find themselves explaining how important the matter of safe driving is to them and why they had to do something about it. Now, 2 weeks later, you drop by with your large request about the billboard. What happens under these circumstances? The study done in the 1960s found that a full 76% said yes (Freedman & Fraser, 1966). Consider how hard it was for these poor homeowners to say no! After all, they're already known to the community and to themselves as the sort of people who care enough about safe driving to take action on the matter, so be it if that action involves a sacrifice.

This study illustrates the social influence tool called the **foot-in-the-door technique:** To get people to say yes to requests that would ordinarily lead to no, one approach is to start with a small request that few would refuse. Ideally, the small request is a miniature version of the larger request that you already have in mind. Once people have publicly complied with this easy request, they'll start reexamining who they are and what they stand for. The result is that their private attitudes will swing more strongly in line with their public behavior, making it harder for them to say no to the larger request.

COGNITIVE DISSONANCE THEORY The foot-in-the-door technique also illustrates that one way to influence people's attitudes is through their behavior. If you can induce people to act in a way that is consistent with the attitude you'd like them to adopt, then they will eventually justify their behavior by adopting the sought-after attitude. The most influential explanation of this sequence of events is Leon Festinger's **cognitive dissonance theory.** This theory assumes that there is a drive toward cognitive consistency, meaning that two cognitions—or thoughts—that are inconsistent will produce discomfort, which will in turn motivate the person to remove the inconsistency and bring the cognitions into harmony. The term *cognitive dissonance* refers to the discomfort produced by inconsistent cognitions (Festinger, 1957).

Although cognitive dissonance theory addresses several kinds of inconsistency, it has been most provocative in predicting the aftermath of behaving in ways that run counter to one's attitudes. One label we have for attitude-behavior discrepancies is hypocrisy. For instance, we call the fundamentalist preacher who frequents strip bars a hypocrite. The sheer negativity of this label offers insight into the discomfort caused by any discrepancies between what we do and what we believe. A core idea within cognitive dissonance theory is that when attitudes and behavior are at odds, we take the easiest route to ridding ourselves of the unpleasant state of dissonance. That is, we create consonance or consistency by changing our attitudes. Past behavior, after all, cannot be changed. And changing a line of action already undertaken—like stopping the shocks in the Milgram experiment or quitting smoking—can produce even more dissonance because it introduces the idea that your initial judgment was poor, a thought that is inconsistent with your generally favorable view of yourself. So, the behavior is maintained or justified by changing or adding new consonant cognitions. **Rationalization** is another term for this process of self-justification. In the case of the Milgram experiment, some participants were likely to tell themselves, "At least I'm following orders, unlike that unruly guy who won't learn these word pairs." If you smoke cigarettes, you may reduce dissonance by telling yourself and others something like, "I know they say smoking is bad for your health, but it relaxes me so much, and that's more important to me."

One of the earliest and most famous studies of cognitive dissonance examined the effects of induced compliance. College students participated one at a time in an experiment in which they worked on a dull, repetitive task: They were asked to turn wooden pegs on a pegboard, over and over again. After completing the boring task, the experimenter asked participants a favor. They were told that the study was really about how people's expectations influence their performance, and that the guy who normally plays the confederate role and tells people what to expect wasn't available. Under this guise, some participants were offered $1 to tell the next participant that the tasks had been fun and interesting. Others were offered $20 to do this. All of the participants complied with the request. Later they were asked how much they had enjoyed the tasks. As shown in Figure 17-7, participants who had been paid only $1 stated that they had in fact enjoyed the tasks. But participants who had been paid $20 did not find them significantly more enjoyable than did members of a control group who never spoke to another participant (Festinger & Carlsmith, 1959). The small incentive for complying with the experimenter's request—but not the large incentive—led participants to believe what they had heard themselves say. Why should this be so?

According to cognitive dissonance theory, being paid $20 provides a very clear and consonant reason for complying with the experimenter's request to talk

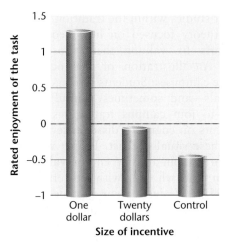

Figure 17-7
An Induced-Compliance Experiment
The smaller incentive for agreeing to say that the tasks were interesting led participants to infer that they had actually enjoyed the tasks. The larger incentive did not. (After Festinger & Carlsmith, 1959)

to the waiting participant, and so the person experiences little or no dissonance. The inconsistency between the person's behavior (telling the next person that the task was interesting) and his or her attitude toward the task (the task was boring) is outweighed by the far greater consistency between the compliance and the huge monetary incentive for complying. (Recall that this study was done in the 1950s, and $20 then was likely to feel more like $100 today!) Accordingly, the participants who were paid $20 did not change their attitudes. Those who were paid $1, however, had no clear or consonant reason for complying. Accordingly, they experienced dissonance, which they reduced by coming to believe that they really did enjoy the tasks. The general conclusion is that dissonance-causing behavior will lead to attitude change in induced-compliance situations when the behavior can be induced with a minimum amount of pressure, whether in the form of reward or punishment.

Experiments with children have confirmed the prediction about minimal punishment. If children obey a very mild request not to play with an attractive toy, they come to believe that the toy is not as attractive as they first thought—a belief that is consistent with their observation that they are not playing with it. But if the children refrain from playing with the toy under a strong threat of punishment, they do not change their liking for the toy (Aronson & Carlsmith, 1963; Freedman, 1965).

Other studies within the tradition of cognitive dissonance theory focused on how people justify their past efforts by valuing their chosen paths more strongly. An illustration of this occurs each year on college campuses: Students often go through elaborate rituals—and sometimes painful and dangerous hazings—to join campus fraternities and sororities. Experiments on cognitive dissonance provide clues as to why these rituals persist. People who go through more effort to join a group end up valuing that group more than those who join with little effort (Aronson & Mills, 1959). We justify our past decisions similarly (Brehm, 1956). Before a decision is made, a number of alternatives may seem equally attractive. Perhaps you had to decide which of several universities to attend. No doubt they each had their good features, but of course, you could only attend one. After you made your decision, cognitive dissonance theory predicts that the simple act of choosing one alternative would create dissonance in you, because it is inconsistent with the good features of the alternatives not chosen. To reduce this unpleasant state, the theory predicts that you will justify your choice by downplaying the good features of the paths not taken and exaggerating the good features of the path you took. Does this prediction fit with your own experience?

SELF-PERCEPTION THEORY Over the years, alternative explanations have been offered for some of the findings of cognitive dissonance theory. For instance, social psychologist Daryl Bem argued that a simpler theory, which he called *self-perception theory*, could explain all results of the classic dissonance experiments without reference to any inner turmoil or dissonance. In brief, self-perception theory proposes that individuals come to know their own attitudes, emotions, and other internal states partially by inferring them from observations of their own behavior and the circumstances in which the behavior occurs. To the extent that internal cues are weak, ambiguous, or uninterpretable, **self-perception theory** states that the individual is like any outside observer who must rely on external cues to infer the individual's inner states (Bem, 1972). Self-perception theory is illustrated by the common remark, "This is my second sandwich; I guess I was hungrier than I thought." Here the speaker has inferred an internal state by observing his or her own behavior. Similarly, the self-observation "I've been biting my nails all day; something must be bugging me" is based on the same external evidence that might lead a friend to remark, "You've been biting your nails all day; something must be bugging you."

With this alternative theory in mind, reconsider the classic peg-turning study (Festinger & Carlsmith,

1959). Recall that participants were induced to tell a waiting participant that a dull peg-turning task had in fact been fun and interesting. Participants who had been paid $20 to do this did not change their attitudes, whereas participants who had been paid only $1 came to believe that the tasks had in fact been enjoyable. Self-perception theory proposes that, just as an observer tries to understand the cause of someone else's behavior, so, too, participants in this experiment looked at their own behavior (telling another participant that the tasks were interesting) and implicitly asked themselves, "Why did I do this?" Self-perception theory further proposes that they sought an answer the same way an outside observer would, by trying to decide whether to explain the behavior with reference to the person (he did it because he really did enjoy the task) or with reference to the situation (he did it for the money). When the individual is paid only $1, the observer is more likely to credit the person: "He wouldn't be willing to say it for only $1, so he must have actually enjoyed the tasks." But if the individual is paid $20, the observer is more likely to credit the situation: "Anyone would have done it for $20, so I can't judge his attitude toward the tasks on the basis of his statement." If the individual follows the same inferential process as this hypothetical outside observer, participants who are paid $1 infer their attitude from their own behavior: "I must think the tasks were enjoyable. Otherwise I would not have said so." But participants who are paid $20 attribute their behavior to the money and therefore express the same attitudes toward the tasks as the control participants who made no statements to another participant.

Importantly, all the participants in the peg-turning study were willing to tell the next participant that the task was enjoyable—even if they were offered only $1 to do so. But the participants themselves did not know this. Thus, when participants who were paid $1 inferred that they must think the tasks are enjoyable because otherwise they would not have said so, they were wrong. They should have inferred that they talked to the next participant because they were paid $1 to do so. In other words, they committed the fundamental attribution error: They overestimated causes due to the person and underestimated causes due to the situation.

The opposite can also happen: People sometimes overestimate causes due to the situation and underestimate causes due to the person. We saw this back in Chapter 1, when we discussed the unexpected effects of rewarding kids with free pizza for meeting monthly reading goals. Kids do read more if reading earns them pizza. But do they enjoy reading? And do they continue reading once the pizza program ends? Dozens of studies, based on the principles of self-perception theory, suggest that rewards can undermine intrinsic interest and motivation. This happens because when people see that their behavior is caused by some external, situational factor—like a free pizza—they discount the input of any internal, personal factors—like their own enjoyment of the activity. So when kids ask themselves why they read, they'll say it's for the pizza. And when there's no more pizza to be had, they'll see no other compelling reason to read. Even though they might have enjoyed reading, the rewards loomed larger. Recall that this undermining effect of rewards is called the **overjustification effect,** whereby people go overboard and explain their own behavior with too much emphasis on salient situational causes and not enough emphasis on personal causes.

So which theory wins? Does cognitive dissonance theory or self-perception theory best explain our tendencies to justify our actions by changing our attitudes? In general, each of the alternative theories has generated data that the other theory cannot explain. Some studies find evidence that participants do experience arousal and discomfort when arguing for positions that are contrary to their true beliefs, a finding that is consistent with cognitive dissonance theory but not with self-perception theory (Elliot & Devine, 1994; Elkin & Leippe, 1986). Others have concluded that each theory may be correct—under slightly different circumstances—and that the focus of research should be on specifying when and where each theory applies (Baumeister & Tice, 1984; Fazio, Zanna, & Cooper, 1977; Paulhus, 1982). Recent experiments actually pose a challenge to both theories. A replication of classic self-justification paradigms used participants who were either amnesiac or under cognitive load (that is, multitasking and therefore having impaired attention and working memory). The results showed just as much attitude change, even when participants couldn't even remember the recent behavior that their newly adopted attitude justified! (Lieberman, Ochsner, Gilbert, & Schacter, 2001). These findings suggest that behavior-induced attitude change can happen automatically, without much conscious thought. So although both cognitive dissonance theory and self-perception theory hold that people "rationalize" their past actions by changing their attitudes, the process may not actually involve the deliberate consonance-seeking or sense-making that either theory has presumed.

These various perspectives on self-justification describe the psychological aftermath of potent social influence techniques. Throughout this chapter, we've seen one core lesson within social psychology illustrated time and again: Situational forces are powerful. A related core lesson within social psychology is that these powerful situational forces are often invisible. When some form of social influence pressures us to behave in a certain way, we often fail to recognize it; and when left to make sense of our actions, we wittingly or unwittingly change our inner attitudes to be in line with our outward behavior. From this perspective, the classic experiments on self-justification can be viewed as social influence techniques in action.

SELF-JUSTIFICATION IN JONESTOWN Knowing how self-justification processes lead people to rationalize their actions by changing their attitudes, think back to the Jonestown case mentioned at the start of the chapter. When the public first learned of the mass suicide, the fundamental attribution error reigned: Jim Jones's followers must have been crazy or weak-willed. Who else would take their own lives at another's request? Later news reports challenged this view by highlighting the diversity of the People's Temple membership. Although some were poor, uneducated, and perhaps more gullible than most, many were educated professionals. Recall that the lesson within the fundamental attribution error is that we underestimate the power of situations. Taking this to heart, a social psychological analysis of the Jonestown tragedy examines followers' paths to Jonestown and the social influence tactics used by Jim Jones (Osherow, 1984).

Oddly enough, we have a window into daily practices within Jonestown because Jim Jones insisted that most events be audiotaped, including the final act of suicide. Reports from former members of the People's Temple also help complete the picture. From this evidence, it becomes clear that Jim Jones was artfully exploiting the foot-in-the-door technique. Jones did not start off by asking would-be members: "Give me your life savings and your children and move with me to the jungle." Rather, he first got prospective members to comply with small requests and then gradually stepped up the level of commitment. Recall that Jim Jones had painted a utopian vision of social equality and racial harmony that became known simply as "the Cause." At first, members were just asked to donate their time to the Cause, later their money, and still later their possessions, legal custody of their children, and so on. Little by little, followers' options became more limited. Step by step, they become motivated to explain or to justify their past behavior in support of the Cause. The easiest way to do that was to become even more committed to the Cause.

Jeanne Mills managed to defect from the People's Temple before the move to Guyana. She became a vocal critic of the group (and was later murdered). In her book, *Six Years With God* (1979), Mills describes the forces of self-justification at work:

> We had to face painful reality. Our life savings were gone. Jim [Jones] had demanded that we sell the life insurance policy and turn the equity over to the church, so that was gone. Our property had all been taken from us. . . . We thought that we had alienated our parents when we told them we were leaving the country. Even the children whom we had left in the care of [others in the church] were openly hostile toward us. Jim had accomplished all this in such a short time! All we had left now was Jim and the Cause, so we decided to buckle under and give our energies to these two. (Mills, 1979, cited in Osherow, 1984).

So, wittingly or unwittingly, Jim Jones used virtually invisible social influence techniques to extract behavioral compliance from his followers. This strategy takes advantage of people's tendencies to self-justify and results in members intensifying their beliefs in Jim Jones and the Cause, while minimizing their assessments of the noxiousness of the costs of membership.

Once in Guyana, Jim Jones continued to escalate the level of commitment he required of members by introducing the idea of the "final ritual" or "revolutionary suicide." He staged events called "White Nights," which were essentially suicide drills. Jones would pass out wine and then announce later that the wine had been poisoned and that they would all soon die. To test his followers' faith, Jones asked them whether they were ready to die for the Cause. One time, the membership was even asked to vote on its own fate. Later in the evening, Jones would announce, "Well, it was a good lesson, I see you're not dead." One ex-member re-counted how these White Nights affected him and other followers:

> [Jones] made it sound like we needed the 30 minutes to do very strong, introspective type of thinking. We all felt strongly dedicated, proud of ourselves . . . [Jones] taught that it was a privilege to die for what you believed in. (Winfrey, 1979, cited in Osherow, 1984)

This brief social psychological analysis of the events leading up to the Jonestown mass suicides illustrates social influence in action. It gives a window onto the power that situational forces had to alter the internalized ideologies of Jim Jones's followers.

REFERENCE GROUPS AND IDENTIFICATION

Nearly every group to which we belong has an implicit or explicit set of beliefs, attitudes, and behaviors that it considers correct. Any member of the group who strays from these social norms risks isolation and social disapproval. Through social rewards and punishments, the groups to which we belong obtain compliance from us. Groups may also pull for **identification.** If we respect or admire other individuals or groups, we may obey their norms and adopt their beliefs, attitudes, and behaviors in order to be like them or to identify with them.

Reference groups are groups with which we identify; we refer to them in order to evaluate and regulate our opinions and actions. Reference groups can also serve as a frame of reference by providing us not only with specific beliefs and attitudes but also with a general perspective from which we view the world—an ideology or set of ready-made interpretations of social issues and events. If we eventually adopt these views and integrate the group's ideology into our own value system, the reference group will have produced internalization. The process of identification, then, can provide a bridge between compliance and internalization.

An individual does not necessarily have to be a member of a reference group to be influenced by its values. For example, lower-middle-class individuals often use the middle class as a reference group. An aspiring athlete may use professional athletes as a reference group.

Life would be simple if each of us identified with only one reference group. But most of us identify with several reference groups, which often leads to conflicting pressures. Perhaps the most enduring example of competing reference groups is the conflict that many young people experience between their family reference group

© Bettmann/Corbis

Jim Jones artfully exploited people's tendencies to self-justify.

and their college or peer reference group. The most extensive study of this conflict is Theodore Newcomb's classic Bennington Study—an examination of the political attitudes of the entire population of Bennington College, a small, politically liberal college in Vermont. The dates of the study (1935–1939) are a useful reminder that this is not a new phenomenon.

Today Bennington College tends to attract liberal students, but in 1935 most students came from wealthy conservative families. (It is also coed today, but in 1935 it was a women's college.) More than two-thirds of the parents of Bennington students were affiliated with the Republican Party. Most people at Bennington College were liberal during the 1930s, but this was not the reason that most of the women selected the college.

Newcomb's main finding was that with each year at Bennington, students moved further away from their parents' attitudes and closer to the attitudes of the college community. For example, in the 1936 presidential campaign, about 66% of parents favored the Republican candidate, Alf Landon, over the Democratic candidate, Franklin Roosevelt. Landon was supported by 62% of the Bennington freshmen and 43% of the sophomores, but only 15% of the juniors and seniors.

For most of the women, increasing liberalism reflected a deliberate choice between the two competing reference groups. Two women discussed how they made this choice:

All my life I've resented the protection of governesses and parents. At college I got away from that, or rather, I guess I should say, I changed it to wanting the intellectual approval of teachers and more advanced students. Then I found that you can't be reactionary and be intellectually respectable.

Becoming radical meant thinking for myself and, figuratively, thumbing my nose at my family. It also meant intellectual identification with the faculty and students that I most wanted to be like. (Newcomb, 1943, pp. 134, 131)

Note that the second woman uses the term *identification* in the sense that we have been using it. Note, too, how the women describe a mixture of change produced by social rewards and punishments (compliance) and change produced by attraction to an admired group that they strive to emulate (identification).

FROM IDENTIFICATION TO INTERNALIZATION As mentioned earlier, reference groups also serve as frames of reference by providing their members with new perspectives on the world. The Bennington community, particularly the faculty, gave students a perspective on the Depression of the 1930s and the threat of World War II that their home environments had not, and this began to move them from identification to internalization: Listen to how two other Bennington women described the process:

It didn't take me long to see that liberal attitudes had prestige value. . . . I became liberal at first because of its prestige value; I remain so because the problems around which my liberalism centers are important. What I want now is to be effective in solving problems.

Prestige and recognition have always meant everything to me. . . . But I've sweat[ed] blood in trying to be honest with myself, and the result is that I really know what I want my attitudes to be, and I see what their consequences will be in my own life. (Newcomb, 1943, pp. 136–137)

Many of our most important beliefs and attitudes are probably based initially on identification. Whenever we start to identify with a new reference group, we engage in a process of "trying on" a new set of beliefs and attitudes. What we "really believe" may change from day to day. The first year of college often has this effect on students, because many of the views they bring from the family reference group are challenged by students and faculty from very different backgrounds. Students often try on the new beliefs with great intensity and strong conviction, only to discard them for still newer beliefs when the first set does not quite fit. This is a natural process of growth. Although the process never really ends for people who remain open to new experiences, it is greatly accelerated during the college years, before the individual has formed a nucleus of permanent beliefs on which to build more slowly and less radically. The real work of college is to evolve an ideological identity from the numerous beliefs and attitudes that are tested in order to move from identification to internalization.

As noted earlier, one advantage of internalization over compliance is that the changes are self-sustaining. The original source of influence does not have to monitor the individual to maintain the induced changes. The test of internalization, therefore, is the long-term stability of the induced beliefs, attitudes, and behaviors. Was the identification-induced liberalism of Bennington women maintained when the students returned to the "real world"? The answer is yes. Two follow-up studies conducted 25 and 50 years later found the women had remained liberal. For example, in the 1984 presidential election, 73% of Bennington alumnae preferred the Democratic candidate, Walter Mondale, over the Republican candidate, Ronald Reagan, compared with less than 26% of women of the same age and educational level. Moreover, about 60% of Bennington alumnae were politically active, most (66%) within the Democratic Party (Alwin, Cohen, & Newcomb, 1991; Newcomb et al., 1967).

We never outgrow our need for identification with supporting reference groups. The political attitudes of Bennington women remained stable partly because after college they selected new reference groups that supported the attitudes they had developed in college. Those who married more conservative men were more likely to be politically conservative in later life. As Newcomb noted, we often select our reference groups because they share our attitudes, and our reference groups, in turn, help develop and sustain our attitudes. The relationship is circular. The distinction between identification and internalization is a useful one for understanding social influence, but in practice it is not always possible to disentangle them.

◆ Interim Summary

- Cognitive dissonance theory suggests that when people's behavior conflicts with their attitudes it creates an uncomfortable tension that motivates them to change their attitudes to be more in line with their actions. This is one explanation for the process of rationalization, or self-justification.

- Self-perception theory challenged cognitive dissonance theory by stating that inner turmoil does not necessarily occur. To the extent that internal cues are weak, ambiguous, or uninterpretable, people may simply infer their attitudes from their past behavior.

- In the process of identification, we obey the norms and adopt the beliefs, attitudes, and behaviors of groups that we respect and admire. We use such reference groups to evaluate and regulate our opinions and actions. A reference group can regulate our attitudes and behavior by administering social rewards and punishments or providing a frame of reference, a ready-made interpretation of events and social issues.

- Most people identify with more than one reference group, which can lead to conflicting pressures on beliefs, attitudes, and behaviors. College students frequently move away from the views of their family reference group toward the college reference group. These new views are usually sustained in later life because (1) they become internalized and (2) after college we tend to select new reference groups that share our views.

◆ Critical Thinking Questions

1. Rites of passage or initiation rituals are common in young adulthood across many cultures. Explain how these rituals capitalize on people's tendencies to self-justify. What are the outcomes of the self-justification process? How would cognitive dissonance theory and self-perception theory differ in their explanations of the process?

2. Can you identify any changes in your beliefs and attitudes that have come about by being exposed to a new reference group?

GROUP INTERACTIONS

So far in our discussions of social influence and the power of situations we have emphasized the effects of these forces on lone individuals. Among the questions we've addressed are: How and why is an individual's performance affected by the presence of others? How and why is an individual's public behavior shaped by a group's unanimity? How and why do an individual's private attitudes change following social influence? In this section, our focus changes from lone individuals to groups of people. We will look at group interactions more generally to understand the dynamics and outcomes of group processes.

INSTITUTIONAL NORMS

Group interactions are often governed by institutional norms. **Institutional norms** are like social norms—implicit or explicit rules for acceptable behavior and beliefs—except they are applied to entire institutions, or organizations of the same type, like schools, prisons, governments, or commercial businesses. Group interaction patterns within these settings can often become "institutionalized," meaning that behavioral expectations are prescribed for people who occupy particular roles—roles like employee or boss, politician or military officer. Under these circumstances, behavior depends more on particular role expectations than on the individual character of the person who occupies the role. In other words, institutional settings are another potent situation that influences human behavior.

A famous study showing just how potent institutional norms can be is the Stanford Prison Experiment, directed by Philip Zimbardo. Zimbardo and his colleagues were interested in the psychological processes involved in taking the roles of prisoner and prison guard. They created a simulated prison in the basement of the Psychology Department at Stanford University and placed an ad in a local newspaper for participants to take part in a psychological experiment for pay. From the people who responded to the ad, they selected 24 "mature, emotionally stable, normal, intelligent white

(all) © Philip Zimbardo

These photos were taken of participants in the now-famous Stanford Prison Experiment. The results demonstrated that group interactions are often shaped by powerful institutional norms. Here we see that prison norms pulled for dehumanizing and violent behavior from guards, and servile and despondent behavior from prisoners.

male college students from middle-class homes throughout the United States and Canada." None had a prison record, and all seemed very similar in their values. By the flip of a coin, half were assigned to be prison guards and half to be prisoners.

The "guards" were instructed about their responsibilities and made aware of the potential danger of the situation and their need to protect themselves. The "prisoners" were unexpectedly picked up at their homes by a mock police car, handcuffed, and taken blindfolded to the improvised jail, where they were searched, deloused, fingerprinted, given numbers, and placed in "cells" with two other prisoners.

The participants had signed up for the sake of the money, and all expected to be in the experiment for about 2 weeks. But by the end of the sixth day the researchers had to abort the experiment because the results were too frightening to allow them to continue. As Zimbardo explained:

> It was no longer apparent to most of the [participants] (or to us) where reality ended and their roles began. The majority had indeed become prisoners or guards, no longer able to clearly differentiate between role playing and self. There were dramatic changes in virtually every aspect of their behavior, thinking, and feeling. In less than a week the experience of imprisonment undid (temporarily) a lifetime of learning; human values were suspended, self-concepts were challenged, and the ugliest, most base, pathological side of human nature surfaced. We were horrified because we saw some boys (guards) treat others as if they were despicable animals, taking pleasure in cruelty, while other boys (prisoners) became servile, dehumanized robots who thought only of escape, of their own individ-

ual survival, and of their mounting hatred for the guards. (1972, p. 243)

Far faster and more thoroughly than the researchers thought possible, "the experiment had become a reality."

The Stanford Prison Experiment is a demonstration of the extraordinary power of situations. It also illustrates the power of institutional norms within prison-like settings. Keep in mind that the participants were randomly assigned to the roles of prisoner and guard. Nothing in their character or backgrounds, then, could explain their behavior. Even though those playing the roles of guard and prisoner were essentially free to interact in any way they wished, the group's interactions tended be negative, hostile, and dehumanizing, a pattern remarkably similar to interactions in actual prisons. These findings suggest that the situation itself—the very institution of prison—is so pathological that it can distort and rechannel the behavior of normal individuals.

It's been more than 30 years since the Stanford Prison Experiment was conducted. Has U.S. prison policy benefited from it? Have institutional norms and practices within U.S. prisons improved? Unfortunately not. Indeed, Zimbardo and one of his original collaborators have argued that U.S. criminal justice policies have turned a blind eye to the lessons of their well-known experiment about the power of situations within prisons (Haney & Zimbardo, 1998). As just one example, they cite the national trend toward "Supermax" prisons, super-maximum security prisons in which the most violent and disruptive prisoners are completely segregated from other prisoners and subjected to extreme social isolation, very limited environmental stimulation, and ex-

GROUP INTERACTIONS   633

traordinary control over their every move. The use of Supermax prisons for so-called problem prisoners ignores the situational roots of prisoners' problematic behavior. Lessons from the Stanford Prison Experiment warn that as "problem prisoners" are removed from the typical prison environment, the continuing pathological prison situation will generate new replacements to assume the roles of those prisoners who have been taken away. Such is the power of institutional norms.

GROUP DECISION MAKING

Many decisions are made not by individuals but by groups. Members of a family jointly decide where to spend their vacation; a jury judges a defendant to be guilty; a city council votes to raise property taxes. How do such decisions compare with those that might have been made by individual decision makers? Are group decisions better or worse, riskier or more cautious? These are the kinds of questions that concern us in this section.

GROUP POLARIZATION In the 1950s, it was widely believed that decisions made by groups were typically cautious and conservative. For example, it was argued that because business decisions were increasingly being made by committees, the bold, innovative risk taking of entrepreneurs like Andrew Carnegie was a thing of the past (Whyte, 1956). James Stoner, then a graduate business student at MIT, decided to test this assumption (1961).

In Stoner's study, participants were asked to consider a number of hypothetical dilemmas. In one, an electrical engineer must decide whether to stick with his present job at a modest but adequate salary or take a job with a new firm offering more money, a possible partnership in the venture if it succeeds, but no long-term security. In another, a man with a severe heart ailment must seriously curtail his customary way of life or else undergo a medical operation that would either cure him completely or prove fatal. Participants were asked to decide how good the odds of success would have to be before they would advise the person to try the riskier course of action. For example, they could recommend that the engineer take the riskier job if the chances that the new venture would succeed were 5 in 10, 3 in 10, or only 1 in 10. By using numerical odds like these, Stoner was able to compare the riskiness of different decisions quantitatively.

Participants first made their decisions alone, as individuals. They then met in groups and arrived at a group decision for each dilemma. After the group discussion, they again considered the dilemmas privately as individuals. When Stoner compared the group's decisions with the average of the individuals' pregroup

Group polarization often occurs in juries, especially when they are required to reach unanimous decisions.

decisions, he found that the group's decisions were riskier than the individuals' initial decisions. Moreover, this shift reflected genuine opinion change on the part of group members, not just public conformity to the group decision: The private individual decisions made after the group discussion were significantly riskier than the initial decisions.

These findings were replicated by other researchers, even in situations that presented real rather than hypothetical risks (Bem, Wallach, & Kogan, 1965; Wallach, Kogan, & Bem, 1962, 1964,). The phenomenon was initially called the *risky shift effect*. This turned out not to be an accurate characterization, however. Even in the early studies, group decisions tended to shift slightly but consistently in the cautious direction on one or two of the hypothetical dilemmas (Wallach, Kogan, & Bem, 1962). The phenomenon is now called the **group polarization effect** because after many more studies it became clear that group discussion leads to decisions that are not necessarily riskier but are more extreme than the individual decisions. If group members are initially inclined to take risks on a particular dilemma, the group's decisions will become riskier; if group members are initially inclined to be cautious, the group will be even more cautious (Myers & Lamm, 1976).

More than 300 studies of the group polarization effect have been conducted, with a dazzling array of variations. For example, in one study, active burglars actually cased houses and then provided individual and group estimates of how easy each would be to burglarize. Compared with the individual estimates, the group estimates were more conservative; that is, they rated the homes to be more difficult to break into successfully (Cromwell, Marks, Olson, & Avary, 1991).

Group polarization extends beyond issues of risk and caution. For example, group discussion caused French students' initially positive attitudes toward the country's premier to become even more positive and their initially negative attitudes toward Americans to become even more negative (Moscovici & Zavalloni, 1969). Jury decisions can be similarly affected, leading to more extreme verdicts (Isozaki, 1984). Polarization in juries is more likely to occur on judgments concerning values and opinions (such as deciding on an appropriate punishment for a guilty defendant) than on judgments concerning matters of fact (such as the defendant's guilt), and they are most likely to show polarization when they are required to reach unanimous decisions (Kaplan & Miller, 1987).

Many explanations for the group polarization effect have been offered over the years, but the two that have stood up best to intensive testing refer to the concepts of informational social influence and normative social influence that we considered earlier in our discussion of conformity to a majority (Isenberg, 1986). Recall that informational social influence occurs when people see others as valid sources of information. During group discussions, members learn new information and hear novel arguments relevant to the decision under discussion. For example, in discussing whether the electrical engineer should go with the new venture—a decision that almost always shifts in the risky direction—it is quite common for someone in the group to argue that riskiness is warranted because electrical engineers can always find good jobs. A shift in the conservative direction occurred in the burglar study after one member of the group noted that it was nearly 3 P.M. and children would soon be returning from school and playing nearby.

The more arguments are raised in support of a position, the more likely it is that the group will move toward that position. And this is where the bias enters: Members of a group are most likely to present points in support of the position they initially favor and to discuss information they already share (Stasser, Taylor, & Hanna, 1989; Stasser & Titus, 1985). Accordingly, the discussion will be biased in favor of the group's initial position, and the group will move toward that position as more of the group members become convinced. Interestingly, the polarization effect still occurs, even when all participants are given an extensive list of arguments before the experiment begins—a finding that casts doubt on explanations based solely on informational social influence (Zuber, Crott, & Werner, 1992).

Normative social influence, you will recall, occurs when people want to be liked and accepted by a group.

Under this type of social influence, people compare their own views with the norms of the group. During the discussion, they may learn that others have similar attitudes or even more extreme views than they themselves do. If they are motivated to be seen positively by the group, they may conform to the group's position or even express a position that is more extreme than the group's. As one researcher noted, "To be virtuous . . . is to be different from the mean—in the right direction and to the right degree" (Brown, 1974, p. 469).

But normative social influence is not simply pressure to conform. Often the group provides a frame of reference for its members, a context within which they can reevaluate their initial positions. This is illustrated by a common and amusing event that frequently occurs in group polarization experiments. For example, in one group a participant began the discussion of the dilemma facing the electrical engineer by confidently announcing, "I feel this guy should really be willing to take a risk here. He should go with the new job even if it has only a 5 in 10 chance of succeeding." Other group members were incredulous: "You think that 5 in 10 is being risky? If he has any guts, he should give it a shot even if there is only 1 chance in 100 of success. I mean, what has he really got to lose?" Eager to reestablish his reputation as a risk taker, the original individual quickly shifted his position further in the risky direction. By redefining "risky," the group moved both its own decision and its members' postdiscussion attitudes further toward the risky extreme of the scale (Wallach, Kogan, & Bem, 1962; from the authors' notes).

As this example illustrates, both informational and normative social influence occur simultaneously in group discussions, and several studies have attempted to untangle them. Some studies have shown that the group polarization effect occurs if participants simply hear the arguments of the group, without knowing the actual positions of other members of the group (Burnstein & Vinokur, 1973, 1977). This demonstrates that informational social influence by itself is sufficient to produce polarization. Other studies have shown that the polarization effect also occurs when people learn others' positions but do not hear any supporting arguments, demonstrating that normative social influence by itself is sufficient (Goethals & Zanna, 1979; Sanders & Baron, 1977). Typically, however, the effect of informational social influence is greater than the effect of normative social influence (Isenberg, 1986).

GROUPTHINK "How could we have been so stupid?" This was President John Kennedy's reaction to the disastrous failure of his administration's attempt to invade Cuba at the Bay of Pigs in 1961 and overthrow the government of Fidel Castro. The plan was badly conceived at many levels. For example, if the initial landing was unsuccessful, the invaders were supposed to retreat into the mountains. But no one in the planning group had studied the map closely enough to realize that no army could have gotten through the 80 miles of swamp that separated the mountains from the landing area. As it turned out, this didn't matter, because other miscalculations caused the invading force to be wiped out long before the retreat would have taken place.

The invasion had been conceived and planned by the president and a small group of advisers. Writing 4 years later, one of these advisers, the historian Arthur Schlesinger Jr., blamed himself

> for having kept so silent during those crucial discussions in the Cabinet Room, though my feelings of guilt were tempered by the knowledge that a course of objection would have accomplished little save to gain me a name as a nuisance. I can only explain my failure to do more than raise a few timid questions by reporting that one's impulse to blow the whistle on this nonsense was simply undone by the circumstances of the discussion. (1965, p. 255)

What were the "circumstances of the discussion" that led the group to pursue such a disastrous course of action? After reading Schlesinger's account, social psychologist Irving Janis introduced the term **groupthink** to describe the phenomenon in which members of a group are led to suppress their own dissent in the interests of group consensus (Janis, 1982). After analyzing several other foreign policy decisions, Janis set forth a broad theory to describe the causes and consequences of groupthink.

Groupthink, according to Janis's theory, is caused by (1) a cohesive group of decision makers, (2) isolation of the group from outside influences, (3) no systematic procedures for considering both the pros and cons of different courses of action, (4) a directive leader who explicitly favors a particular course of action, and (5) high stress, often due to an external threat, recent failures, moral dilemmas, and an apparent lack of viable alternatives. The theory suggests that these conditions foster a strong desire to achieve and maintain group consensus and avoid rocking the boat by dissenting.

Janis argued that the consequences or symptoms of groupthink include (1) shared illusions of invulnerability, morality, and unanimity, (2) direct pressure on dissenters, (3) self-censorship (as Schlesinger's account notes), (4) collective rationalization of a decision rather than realistically examination of its strengths and weaknesses, and (5) self-appointed mindguards, group members who actively attempt to prevent the group from considering information that would challenge the effectiveness or morality of its decisions. For example, the attorney general (President Kennedy's brother Robert) privately warned Schlesinger, "The President has made his mind up. Don't push it any further." The secretary of state also withheld information that had been provided by intelligence experts who warned against an invasion of Cuba (Janis, 1982). Janis proposed that these symptoms of groupthink combine to produce damaging flaws in the decision-making process—like incomplete information search and failure to develop contingency plans—which in turn lead to bad decisions.

Janis's theory of groupthink has been extremely influential within social psychology, across the social sciences, and within the culture at large (Turner & Pratkanis, 1998b). Yet it has also received sharp criticism (such as Fuller & Aldag, 1998). First, it is based more on historical analysis of select cases than on laboratory experimentation. Plus, the few dozen experiments that have tested the theory have produced only mixed and limited support (Callaway, Marriott, & Esser, 1985; Courtright, 1978; Flowers, 1977; Longley & Pruitt, 1980; McCauley, 1989; Turner, Pratkanis, Probasco, & Lever, 1992). As just one example, Janis's claim that cohesive groups are most likely to succumb to groupthink has not stood up to empirical test. Cohesive groups may, in fact, provide a sense of psychological safety, which has been shown to improve group learning and performance (Edmondson, 1999). One later reformulation of the theory, supported by experimental data, argues that group cohesion yields poor decisions only when combined with threats to the group's positive image of itself. Faced with such threats, group members narrow their focus of attention to the goal of protecting and maintaining their positive group identity, a focus that often comes at the cost of effective decision making (Turner & Pratkanis, 1998a).

Another reformulation of the theory states that the presence or absence of groupthink depends on the specific content of a group's social norms. Recall that social norms are implicit or explicit rules for acceptable behavior and beliefs. In some cases, group norms favor maintaining consensus, and in these cases, the adverse effects of groupthink should take hold, resulting in poor-quality decisions. In other cases, group norms favor critical thinking, and in these cases, group discussion should actually improve decision quality. A recent experiment tested these ideas (Postmes, Spears, &

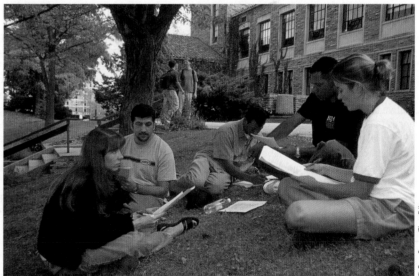

Figure 17-8
Group Norms and the Effectiveness of Group Decisions
Group norms can influence the quality of group decisions. In this experiment, the decisions made by groups with norms for consensus seeking did not benefit from group discussion, whereas those with norms for critical thinking did. (Adapted from Figure 1 on p. 923 in T. Postmes, R. Spears, & S. Cihangir (2001), "Quality of decision making and group norms," in *Journal of Personality and Social Psychology,* 80, 918–930. Copyright © 2001 by the American Psychological Association. Adapted with permission.)

Cihangir, 2001). In it, the researchers manipulated group norms by randomly assigning several groups (of four college students each) to engage either in a task that fostered a norm of consensus seeking (making a poster together) or in a task that fostered a norm of critical thinking (discussing an unpopular policy proposal). Next, all groups participated in an unrelated group decision task. The researchers assessed the quality of decisions both before and after the group discussion. Figure 17-8 portrays the results. Inspection of Figure 17-8 shows that when the group norm favored consensus, group discussion did little to improve decision quality, yet when the group norm favored critical thinking, group discussion improved decision quality dramatically. You might notice that this reformulation of groupthink echoes the reformulation of deindividuation described earlier: In both cases, situation-specific social norms guide behavior more than more general features of the group, like group cohesion or personal anonymity.

This study on group norms spotlights one way to minimize the damaging effects of groupthink: Fostering norms for critical thinking—as a college education intends—should produce better group decisions. Other ways to improve group decisions include providing groups with trained facilitators who encourage a full sharing of ideas and alternating private idea-generating sessions with group sessions. Another beneficial strategy is to make the group a heterogeneous mix of people. A diverse group is more likely than a homogeneous group to generate a wide range of ideas (Paulus, 1998). Diversity within groups has other benefits as well. Surveys of college students across the United States have found that students of all ethnic backgrounds—European American, African American, Asian American and Hispanic American—reach higher levels of intellectual engagement and ability when their college classrooms reflect ethnic diversity and when they interact informally with diverse peers outside of class. In addition, ethnic diversity on campus fosters perspective-taking and other skills that aid democracy (Gurin, Dey, Hurtado, & Gurin, in press). Yet despite the evidence that ethnic diversity produces better individual and group outcomes, the value of affirmative action policies continues to be hotly debated. Two social psychological sides of this debate are featured in the Seeing Both Sides section at the end of this chapter. Many of the ideas raised within these essays—like how we decide what caused our own or someone else's success and the self-fulfilling nature of prejudicial stereotypes—will be addressed further in Chapter 18, our second in this two-chapter series on social psychology.

Evidence shows that diversity on college campuses predicts intellectual attainment and skills that foster democracy.

Are the Effects of Affirmative Action Positive or Negative?

NEGATIVE ASPECTS OF AFFIRMATIVE ACTION
Madeline E. Heilman, New York University

Most people would say that rewards should be given according to merit. What happens, then, when people get rewarded not because of their accomplishments but because of who they are or what group they belong to? Many people, perhaps including yourself, react negatively.

This is the heart of the affirmative action dilemma. While created to ensure nondiscriminatory treatment of women and minorities, affirmative action has come to be seen as little more than preferential selection and treatment without regard to merit (Kravitz & Platania, 1993). This, of course, may not depict reality, but it is this *perception* of affirmative action that is so problematic. There are a number of detrimental consequences.

First, affirmative action can stigmatize its intended beneficiaries, causing inferences of incompetence. If you believe that someone has been the beneficiary of preferential selection based on non-merit criteria, then you are likely to "discount" that individual's qualifications. In fact, you are likely to make the assumption that this person would not have been selected without the help of affirmative action.

There has been research linking affirmative action with incompetence inferences (Garcia, Erskine, Hawn, & Casmay, 1981; Heilman, Block, & Lucas, 1992). It has been conducted in the laboratory, where people review employee records, and in the field, where people are asked to evaluate co-workers in their work units. Inferences of incompetence have been found whether the target beneficiary is a woman or a member of a racial minority, and whether the research par-

ticipants are male or female, or students or working people (Heilman, Block, & Stathatos, 1997).

A second negative consequence of affirmative action concerns nonbeneficiaries. When women and minorities are believed to be preferentially selected, those who traditionally would have been selected for jobs often feel they are really the more deserving, and consequently, they feel unfairly bypassed (Nacoste, 1987). This has been suggested as a major reason for the "backlash" against affirmative action.

Evidence indicates that there are indeed unfortunate by-products of feeling unfairly bypassed by affirmative action. In one study, male participants were paired with a female who subsequently was preferentially selected for the more desirable task role on the basis of her gender (Heilman, McCullough, & Gilbert, 1996). Those who believed themselves to be more (or even equally) skilled than the female reported being less motivated, more angry, and less satisfied than those who were told the female was the more skilled and therefore the more deserving of the two.

The third negative consequence of affirmative action concerns its potential effect on the intended beneficiary. When people believe that they have been preferentially selected on the basis of irrelevant criteria there can be a chilling effect on self-view. Ironically, then, affirmative action may sometimes hurt those it was intended to help.

A series of laboratory experiments in which participants were selected for a desired task role (leader) either on the basis of merit or preferentially on the basis of their gender found strong support

for the idea that preferential selection can trigger negative self-regard. In repeated studies, women, but not men, who were preferentially selected were found to rate their performance more negatively, view themselves as more deficient in leadership ability, be more eager to relinquish their desirable leadership role, and shy away from demanding and challenging tasks (see Heilman, 1994, for a review of these studies).

Given these consequences, it appears that affirmative action, as it currently is understood, can undermine its own objectives. The stigma associated with affirmative action is apt to fuel rather than discredit stereotypic thinking and prejudiced attitudes. Depriving individuals of the satisfaction and pride that comes from knowing that they have achieved something on their own merits can be corrosive, decreasing self-efficacy and fostering self-views of inferiority. And the frustration resulting from feeling unfairly bypassed for employment opportunities because one does not fit into the correct demographic niche can aggravate workplace tensions and intergroup hostilities. So, paradoxically, despite its success in expanding employment opportunities for women and minorities, affirmative action may contribute to the very conditions that gave rise to the problems it was designed to remedy.

Madeline E. Heilman

Are the Effects of Affirmative Action Positive or Negative?

THE BENEFITS OF AFFIRMATIVE ACTION
Faye J. Crosby, University of California, Santa Cruz

To assess the effects of affirmative action, you must first know what affirmative action is and what it *is not*. According to the American Psychological Association (APA): "Affirmative action occurs when an organization expends energy to make sure there is no discrimination in employment or education and, instead, equal opportunity exists" (APA, 1995, p. 5). Affirmative action goes beyond reactive policies that passively endorse justice, but waiting until a problem has erupted before enacting measures. Affirmative action requires resources and vigilance. It does not require or endorse quotas, sacrifice standards to diversity, or substitute preference for merit (Turner & Pratkanis, 1994).

For employment, affirmative action law began in earnest in 1965 (Holloway, 1989). Today it applies to all government agencies and most organizations that contract work with the federal government. Chances are that you or someone you know works for an affirmative action employer; one in four employed

Faye Crosby

Americans does (Crosby & Cordova, 1996)! Affirmative action employers monitor themselves to make sure they employ qualified people from the "targeted classes" in proportion to their availability. With the help of the Office of Federal Contract Compliance Programs, any organization can get easy access to well-established methods for calculating availability.

How does the system work? Think about your professors as employees of your school. Imagine that 10% of the social science professors in your school are women (utilization 10%). Availability is calculated mostly from the proportion of social science PhDs who are female. If 30% of PhDs in the social sciences are women, while only 10% of the professors are, something is wrong! Detected problems should be corrected. Corrective measures can include flexible goals (not rigid quotas) and realistic timetables.

What are the effects of affirmative action in employment? Economists show that white women and people of color who work for affirmative action employers benefit in terms of hiring, retention, pay, and promotions (Kravitz et al., 1997). Do men of color and women feel stigmatized by affirmative action? Generally not. Do white men feel resentment or fear? Some do, especially if they are racist or sexist or if they equate affirmative action with quotas (Golden, Hinkle, & Crosby, 1998); but, in fact, most do not. Actually, three quarters of Americans endorse affirmative action (Tomasson, Crosby, & Herzberger, 1996).

Many white men—including heads of some huge corporations—endorse affirmative action out of economic realism. When the game is opened to white women and ethnic minorities, it is also opened to talented white men who previously had no inside track. Affirmative action firms appear to be more profitable than other firms (Reskin, 1998). Like effective fire-fighting units where small people squiggle into small spaces while big people maneuver big equipment, diverse business teams seem to enjoy a competitive edge (Leonard, 1986).

In education, affirmative action also entails the two steps of monitoring and correcting. If monitoring reveals, for example, that Hispanics comprise less of the undergraduate student body than expected from high-school graduation rates, corrective steps (e.g., outreach programs) may be undertaken. Affirmative action in education need not entail lowering standards; but it must result in close, sometimes painful, examination of three provocative questions: (1) What traits do we value in individuals? (2) How can we accurately assess these traits? and (3) What kinds of teams of individuals do we want to construct?

One misconception is that white women and students of color feel undermined by affirmative action. Nobody likes to be told that he or she is advancing through unjustified preferential treatment, including quotas, rather than merit (Heilman, 1994). Fortunately, most of the direct beneficiaries do not confuse affirmative action with quotas (Truax, Wood, Wright, Cordova & Crosby, 1998), especially if they feel secure in their ethnic identity (Schmermund, Sellers, Mueller, & Crosby, 1998).

A recent landmark study by the former presidents of Harvard and Princeton has fastidiously documented the positive consequences of considering race in college and university admissions. Bowen and Bok (1998) looked at long-term outcomes for hundreds of black students who had been admitted through affirmative action to 24 elite colleges in 1951, 1976, and 1989. The black students graduated from school and obtained advanced degrees at rates comparable to white students. And even more than white alumni/ae, black graduates became civic leaders—giving back to the society that had nurtured them!

What, then, are the overall effects of well-applied affirmative action in education? They are great. Everyone benefits.

◆ Interim Summary

- Institutions have norms that strongly govern the behavior of people who occupy critical roles within the institution. An example of how institutional norms shape group interactions is provided by the Stanford Prison Experiment, in which ordinary young men were randomly assigned roles of "prisoner" and "guard" in a simulated prison.

- When groups make decisions, they often display group polarization: The group decision is in the same direction but is more extreme than the average of the group members' initial positions. This is not just public conformity; group members' private attitudes typically shift in response to the group discussion as well.

- The group polarization effect is due in part to informational social influence, in which group members learn new information and hear novel arguments that are relevant to the decision under discussion. Group polarization is also produced by normative social influence, in which people compare their own initial views with the norms of the group. They may then adjust their position to conform to that of the majority.

- An analysis of disastrous foreign policy decisions led to a proposal that cohesive groups of decision makers can fall into the trap of groupthink, in which members of the group suppress their own dissenting opinions in the interest of group consensus. Later research suggests that group cohesion is not so much the problem, but rather threats to the group's positive identity and group norms of consensus seeking. Evidence suggests that group outcomes can be improved by fostering norms of critical thinking and promoting group diversity.

◆ Critical Thinking Questions

1. How are institutional norms, like those that operated in the Stanford Prison Experiment, communicated to new institutional members? What roles might informational and normative social influence and pluralistic ignorance play in the process of getting new members to conform to institutional norms?

2. Discuss how informational and normative social influence might produce group polarization in a jury's deliberations. How might groupthink operate to affect such deliberations? Can you think of a specific trial in which some of these phenomena appear to have been present?

RECAP: SOCIAL PSYCHOLOGICAL VIEWS OF THE SEEMINGLY INEXPLICABLE

We opened this chapter with several chilling examples—drawn both from recent world events and from history—that portray seemingly inexplicable and horrifying human behavior. How does a hijacker fly a plane into a world-famous skyscraper, killing himself, his passengers, and the thousands of people working in and visiting that building? How does a religious follower decide to drink lethal poison for "the Cause"? How does a military official orchestrate and oversee the deaths of millions of innocent people?

Although we may uncover some clues about the origins of these puzzling actions by looking to the character or personality traits of the people involved, one of the foremost lessons of social psychology is that stopping our inquiry at this level is a mistake, one that goes by the name of the fundamental attribution error. To build a more complete understanding of any form of human social behavior—from the extraordinary to the everyday—we need to also search for clues within situational forces.

In the days, months, and years after September 11, 2001, the world—including many social psychologists—struggles to understand more fully the origins and consequences of that day's tragic events. Knowing that social psychologists have had much to say in the years since the Jonestown massacre and the holocaust of World War II, you can expect social psychologists' analyses of the events on and after September 11 to soon emerge.

These social psychological perspectives will no doubt refer to the power of situations and social influence in shaping people's behavior. As you have seen, social psychologists dissect situations to uncover the particular tools of social influence at work. These tools include, among others, situation-specific social norms, pluralistic ignorance, informational and normative social influence, salient role models, internalized ideologies, and group polarization. Knowing how these and other social psychological concepts operate can help explain behavior that at first seems inexplicable. Many human actions may in fact be inexplicable from the exclusive perspective of personality psychology, but social psychology illuminates a different vantage point altogether.

In Chapter 18, our second in this two-chapter series on social psychology, we take a closer look at the subjective inner workings of people as they make sense of the social world around them. There you will be introduced to the topics and concepts of social cognition.

◆ Critical Thinking Questions

1. Now that you are acquainted with several types of social influence that have been used to explain people's behavior from a social psychological perspective, what sorts of clues about particular situations would you look for to explain the behavior of those who hijacked U.S. planes on September 11, 2001?

2. Think of an example from your own experience when, while trying to explain what caused someone's behavior, you may have committed the fundamental attribution error. What was your initial explanation based on personality or character? What is a possible explanation that makes reference to situational influences?

CHAPTER SUMMARY

1. One of the foremost lessons within social psychology is that situational forces have tremendous power to shape human behavior. A related lesson within social psychology is that these powerful situational forces are often invisible, and we mistakenly make sense of people's behavior by referring to their personality or character. This mistake is so common that social psychologists call it the fundamental attribution error.

2. Both humans and animals respond more quickly when in the presence of other members of their species. This social facilitation occurs whether the others are performing the same task (coactors) or simply watching (an audience). The presence of others appears to narrow people's attention. This facilitates the correct performance of simple responses but hinders the performance of complex ones. For humans, cognitive factors such as concern with evaluation also play a role.

3. The uninhibited aggressive behavior sometimes shown by mobs and crowds may be the result of a state of deindividuation, in which individuals feel that they have lost their personal identities and merged into the group. Both anonymity and group size contribute to deindividuation. A consequence of deindividuation is an increased sensitivity to situation-specific social norms linked with the group. This can increase aggression when the group's norms are aggressive but reduce aggression when the group norms are benign.

4. A bystander to an emergency is less likely to intervene or help if in a group than if alone. Two major factors that deter intervention are defining the situation and diffusion of responsibility. By attempting to appear calm, bystanders may define the situation for one another as a nonemergency, thereby producing a state of pluralistic ignorance. The presence of other people also

diffuses responsibility so that no one person feels the necessity to act. Bystanders are more likely to intervene when these factors are minimized, particularly if at least one person begins to help.

5. In a series of classic studies on conformity, Solomon Asch found that a unanimous group exerts strong pressure on an individual to conform to the group's judgments—even when those judgments are clearly wrong. Much less conformity is observed if even one person dissents from the group.

6. A minority within a larger group can move the majority toward its point of view if it maintains a consistent dissenting position without appearing to be rigid, dogmatic, or arrogant. Minorities sometimes obtain private attitude change from majority members even when they fail to obtain public conformity.

7. In a series of classic studies on obedience, Stanley Milgram demonstrated that ordinary people would obey an experimenter's order to deliver strong electric shocks to an innocent victim. Factors conspiring to produce the high obedience rates include surveillance by the experimenter, buffers that distance the person from the consequences of his or her acts, the emerging properties of situations, and the legitimating role of science, which leads people to abandon their autonomy to the experimenter. There has been considerable controversy about the ethics of the experiments themselves.

8. One way that people come to internalize attitudes and beliefs that are consistent with their actions is through the processes of self-justification. Cognitive dissonance theory suggests that when people's behavior conflicts with their attitudes, it creates an uncomfortable tension that motivates them to change their attitudes to be more in line with their actions. Self-perception theory

challenged this view by stating that inner turmoil does not necessarily occur. To the extent that internal cues are weak, ambiguous, or uninterpretable, people may simply infer their attitudes from their past behavior.

9. In the process of identification, we obey the norms and adopt the beliefs, attitudes, and behaviors of groups that we respect and admire. We use such reference groups to evaluate and regulate our opinions and actions. A reference group can regulate our attitudes and behavior by administering social rewards and punishments or providing a frame of reference, a ready-made interpretation of events and social issues.

10. Most people identify with more than one reference group, which can lead to conflicting pressures on beliefs, attitudes, and behaviors. College students frequently move away from the views of their family reference group toward the college reference group. These new views are usually sustained in later life because (1) they become internalized and (2) after college we tend to select new reference groups that share our views.

11. When groups make decisions, they often display group polarization: The group decision is in the same direction but is more extreme than the average of the group members' initial positions. This is not just public conformity; group members' private attitudes typically shift in response to the group discussion as well. The effect is due in part to informational social influence, in which group members learn new information and hear novel arguments that are relevant to the decision under discussion. Group polarization is also produced by normative social influence, in which people compare their own initial views with the norms of the group. They may then adjust their position to conform to that of the majority.

12. An analysis of disastrous foreign policy decisions led to a proposal that cohesive groups of decision makers can fall into the trap of groupthink, in which members of the group suppress their own dissenting opinions in the interest of group consensus. Later research suggests that group cohesion is not so much the problem but rather threats to the group's positive identity and group norms of consensus seeking. Evidence suggests that group outcomes can be improved by fostering norms of critical thinking and promoting group diversity.

CORE CONCEPTS

fundamental attribution error	diffusion of responsibility	cognitive dissonance theory
social psychology	compliance	rationalization
coaction	informational social influence	self-perception theory
social facilitation	normative social influence	overjustification effect
social inhibition	minority influence	identification
Stroop interference	implicit leniency contract	reference groups
deindividuation	ideology	institutional norms
social norms	debriefing	group polarization effect
bystander effect	internalization	groupthink
pluralistic ignorance	foot-in-the-door technique	

WEB RESOURCES

http://psychology.wadsworth.com/
atkinson14e

Take a quiz, try the activities and exercises, and explore web links.

http://www.kassiber.de/cults.htm

This site includes a plethora of links to information about different cults. You can research everything from the Freemasons and Hare Krishna to killer cults like the People's Temple and Heaven's Gate.

http://choo.fis.utoronto.ca/FIS/Courses/LIS2149/
Groupthink.html

This online model highlights some of the pitfalls associated with groupthink.

 InfoTrac Online Library

http://www.infotrac-college.com/
wadsworth

Use InfoTrac College Edition to find popular and scientific articles by using the search terms below or your own relevant terms.

- Groupthink
- Social influence
- Social psychology

CD-ROM LINKS

 Psych Odyssey

Check out CD Chapter 14, Social Psychology: Interpersonal and Group Perspectives

A. Conformity
B. Compliance
C. Prosocial Behavior

Taxi/Getty Images

SOCIAL COGNITION

18

People think about—and judge—other people all the time. For instance, when engaged in casual people-watching on campus, you might surmise that one cluster of people are football players, another are sorority members, and still another a group of library nerds. Another person reminds you of your best friend from grade school, and you smile. And many people—male and female alike—believe that women are, by nature, more emotional than men. More chilling examples of social cognition can be drawn from recent history: Osama bin Laden said in a 2001 televi-

sion interview that all Americans were enemies of Islam—or infidels—and so all Americans should be targeted for attack. And after the terrorist attacks on the United States of September 2001, people around the world became more aware of their Arab-born neighbors, wondering if they, too, held the anti-American attitudes of bin Laden and his followers.

Our thoughts and judgments about others don't simply help us pass the time. They have consequences. How you categorize your college classmates, for instance, determines whether and

how you interact with them and whether they become friends or rivals. As we saw in Chapter 11, endorsing the stereotype that women are more emotional than men can shape people's perceptions of their own and others' emotions. And the generalization made by bin Laden and his followers that all Americans are the enemy led to the deaths of thousands of innocent civilians on September 11, 2001, and the subsequent suspicions about Arab-born neighbors has, in some instances, fueled additional prejudice and racially motivated hate crimes.

Recall that social psychology concerns the ways that people's behavior and mental processes are shaped by the real or imagined presence of others. In Chapter 17, we saw one of the foremost lessons of social psychology: that social situations—like the presence of others, unanimous majorities, requests from authorities, social norms, and group interactions—have enormous power to influence people's behavior, thoughts, and feelings, power that often goes unrecognized. In this chapter, we will encounter another core lesson of social psychology: that to more fully understand people's social behavior, we need to "get inside their heads." The study of **social cognition** does just that. It examines people's subjective interpretations of their social experiences, as well as their modes of thinking about the social world.

As social psychologists have peered inside people's heads, looking for clues that might illuminate social behavior, they have found evidence for two different modes of thinking, one more automatic and unintentional, often outside conscious awareness, and another more controlled and deliberate, of which we are fully aware. This idea that there are two different modes of thinking should be familiar to you. In Chapter 11, we saw that people's cognitive appraisals—their interpretations of their current circumstances that trigger emotions—can occur at both conscious and unconscious levels. When appraisals are unconscious, people may feel emotions without knowing why. The same can happen for social cognition more generally. Sometimes thinking is automatic and unintended, and other times it is under our conscious control. This is an important discovery because whether thinking is automatic or controlled turns out to influence how and when the contents of mind influence social behavior and social reactions (Chaiken & Trope, 1999). We will see how these two different modes of thinking work as we consider the processes of impression formation, attitudes, and interpersonal attraction.

IMPRESSION FORMATION

When you come across someone new, how do you come to know him or her? How do you form impressions of others? Does the color or apparent age of their skin matter? Their body size and shape? In other words, do your impressions of new people depend on their ethnicity, age, and gender? Do your ulterior motives matter? That is, does it matter whether you simply pass them in the street or whether you are looking for a roommate? Or whether you expect to collaborate with them on an important project? These and other questions guide our discussion of impression formation.

STEREOTYPES

Like many others, social psychologists are invested in social justice—fair treatment for all people. This is why considerable energy within the study of social cognition is devoted to the study of stereotypes. If we can understand why, when, and how stereotypes operate, social psychologists argue, we can be better prepared to limit their adverse effects and treat people more fairly.

Several decades of research on stereotypes tells us that, whether we like it or not, our initial impressions of others are biased by our preexisting expectations. As we saw in previous chapters, this is true of perception more generally. Whenever we perceive any object or event, we implicitly categorize it, comparing the incoming information with our memories of previous encounters with similar objects and events. In earlier chapters, we saw that memories are not usually photograph-like reproductions of the original stimuli but simplified reconstructions of our original perceptions. As noted in Chapter 8, such representations or memory structures are called **schemas;** they are organized beliefs and knowledge about people, objects, events, and situations. The process of searching in memory for the schema that is most consistent with the incoming data is called **schematic processing,** or top-down thinking. Schemas and schematic processing permit us to organize and process enormous and potentially overwhelming amounts of information very efficiently. Instead of having to perceive and remember all the details of each new object or event, we can simply note that it is like one of our preexisting schemas and encode or remember only its most prominent features. For instance, schematic processing is what allows us to readily categorize consumables as either food or drink and then put one on a plate and the other in a glass.

As with objects and events, we also use schemas and schematic processing in our encounters with people. For example, we categorize people into groups based on salient physical attributes—like race, gender, or age—or by their relation to our own social identity—as in "us versus them." Schemas can also be more narrowly defined: When someone tells you that you are about to meet someone who is outgoing, you retrieve your "extravert" schema in anticipation of the coming encounter. The extravert schema is a set of interrelated traits such as sociability, warmth, and possibly loudness and impulsiveness. As mentioned in Chapter 8, **stereotypes** are schemas for classes or subtypes of people. The stereotype of an extravert, a student at a rival school, or an African American is a mini-theory about what particular traits or behaviors go with certain other traits or behaviors. We focus on stereotypes in this section because they are a kind of person schema that has far-reaching consequences for impression formation. You should keep in mind, though, that in addition to schemas for classes of people, we also have schemas for particular individuals, such as the president of the United States or our parents. And as discussed in Chapter 13, we also have a **self-schema** or schema about ourselves—a set of organized self-concepts stored in memory (Markus, 1977). When you see a job advertisement for a peer counselor, for instance, you can evaluate the match between your counselor schema and your self-schema to decide whether you should apply for the job.

AUTOMATIC STEREOTYPE ACTIVATION The associations conveyed within stereotypes—for example, that African Americans are hostile, that women are passive, or that old people are slow—can become overlearned and automatic. We saw in Chapter 6 that through repeated practice driving a car becomes so habitual and automatic that we scarcely need to devote any conscious attention to it. A similar process happens with repeated exposure to stereotypes about people: They, too, can become habitual and automatic, operating outside conscious awareness.

Experiments that demonstrate the automaticity of stereotypes rely on priming techniques. You will recall from Chapter 8 that **priming** refers to the incidental activation of schemas by situational contexts. Beyond effects on memory, we saw in Chapter 17 that priming can also influence social behavior: Simply exposing people to words like *adhere, comply,* and *conform* increased the likelihood that they would later conform to a unanimous majority.

Priming can also activate stereotypes automatically, outside conscious awareness. In one experiment, participants were given a purported test of language ability called the "Scrambled Sentence Test." Each of 30 items on the test consisted of five words. Participants were told to use any four of the five words to construct a grammatically correct sentence as quickly as possible. There were actually two versions of the Scrambled Sentence Test. The critical version primed the elderly stereotype by including words like *old, gray, Florida, retired,* and *bingo.* The other version contained words unrelated to the elderly stereotype (such as *thirsty, clean, private*). Participants took part in the study one at a time. When they finished the Scrambled Sentence Test, the experimenter excused them and directed them toward the elevator. Only after participants left the laboratory did the researchers assess the impact of the elderly stereotype: Those primed with the elderly stereotype actually walked more slowly down the hall to the elevator! Priming the elderly stereotype—which includes the idea that old people are slow—influenced the behavior of young people at a nonconscious level. We know that it's the

Many types of advertising can activate stereotypes of women and trigger sexist behavior.

stereotype at work here because none of the critical words made reference to speed or time directly. We also know that the effect occurred at a nonconscious level because completing the Scrambled Sentence Test does not produce conscious awareness of any theme or stereotype. It is viewed simply as a test of language ability (Bargh, Chen, & Burrows, 1996).

One major source of primed stereotypes is the visual media—television, movies, billboards, and the like. In Chapter 11, we saw that exposure to media violence clearly increases children's aggressive behavior. The same holds for exposure to media stereotypes. By now you've come to recognize that the people you see in the visual mass media are hardly representative of people in the real world. People on television, for instance, are younger, slimmer, and more attractive than people you come across in your hometown. Portrayals of women are especially stereotyped. Many times women are portrayed simply as sex objects valued only for their physical appearance. Although exposure to media stereotypes of women may seem harmless, it does damage. In Chapter 10, we saw how such media promote eating disorders in girls and women. More generally, people who watch a lot of television endorse more sexist attitudes toward women (Gerbner, Gross, Morgan, & Signorielli, 1986). But that's simply a correlation. Maybe television does not cause sexism. An experiment that manipulated television exposure provides the necessary causal evidence. The researchers used television advertisements (drawn from regular U.S. prime-time broadcasts) to prime the stereotype of women as sex objects in one group of men. A separate control group watched other, nonsexist TV ads. All the men were later asked to interview a woman for a job as a research assistant. Compared with men in the control group, those primed by TV ads to think of women in stereotypical terms chose more sexist questions when interviewing the female job candidate and behaved in a more sexualized manner toward her (Rudman & Borgida, 1995).

Stereotypes can also be activated through nonconscious priming. We saw in Chapter 11 that very brief, subliminal exposure to pictures of spiders and snakes (less than 30 milliseconds) can produce physiological arousal and aversive feelings in phobics, even though the phobics could not report having seen anything frightening. The same holds for stereotypes. In one experiment, participants (who were not African American) were shown photographs of young, male faces that were either European American or African American for less than 30 milliseconds, too fast for conscious awareness. These nonconscious, subliminal primes were embedded within a tedious computer task. The computer was rigged so that after participants had spent considerable time on the task, it produced an error message: "F11 error: failure

saving data." It then informed participants that they would need to do the entire computer task over again. Hidden video cameras recorded participants' facial reactions to this news. Those primed with African American faces reacted to the computer error with more hostility. Here, priming the African American stereotype—which includes the idea that African Americans are hostile—automatically generated hostile behavior in unsuspecting participants (Bargh et al., 1996). In fact, people don't even have to personally endorse the stereotype to be affected by it: Stereotypic behavior was activated equally so for those who scored high and low on questionnaire measures of racist attitudes (see also Devine, 1989; Fazio, Jackson, Dunton, & Williams, 1995).

So simply encountering a person can activate a stereotype as we categorize that person by ethnicity, age, or gender, or as "us versus them." But when we categorize others, do we also evaluate them? Experiments suggest that we do. Evidence that automatically activated racial categories carry emotional evaluations comes from a series of studies in which African American and European Americans viewed faces of many ethnic backgrounds, including African American and European American faces. For African Americans, European American faces represent an out-group, whereas the reverse is true for European Americans. The faces were embedded within a word evaluation task in which participants were asked to indicate whether a given adjective (such as *attractive, likeable, annoying,* or *offensive*) was either "good" or "bad" and to make this judgment as quickly and as accurately as possible. Participants made these judgments for dozens of words while the experimenters recorded their reaction times. The results of this study are shown in Figure 18-1. For European American participants, viewing African American faces sped responses to negative words. The opposite was true for African American participants: Viewing European American faces sped responses to negative words (Fazio et al., 1995). These findings suggest that when we categorize others as members of an out-group ("them" as opposed to "us"), we simultaneously and automatically activate negative associations, which facilitates negative responses.

Corroborating evidence comes from a study that used brain imaging (see Chapter 2). Both African American and European American participants viewed photographs of unfamiliar African American and European American faces several times. Imaging data showed that initial exposure to all faces produced activation in the amygdala, an area of the brain that is involved in monitoring

Nonconscious exposure to photographs like these is sufficient to activate stereotypes and influence social behavior.

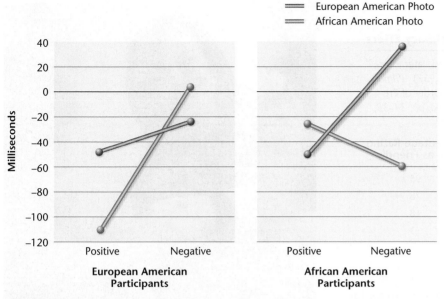

Figure 18-1
Automatic Stereotype Activation

These two graphs plot the mean response times for classifying positive and negative adjectives as good or bad when preceded by photos of African American and European American faces. Higher scores indicate faster responses. Notice that for European American participants, the difference in response times for the positive and negative words is greater when preceded by African American faces, with negative judgments made faster. The reverse pattern emerged for African American participants—their negative judgments were facilitated by viewing European American faces. These data indicate that classifying another person as in a racial "out-group" automatically carries with it negative evaluations. (Adaptation of Figure 1 on p. 1018 from R. H. Fazio, J. R. Jackson, B. C. Dunton, & C. J. Williams (1995), "Variability in automatic activation as an unobtrusive measure of racial attitudes: A bona fide pipeline?" in *Journal of Personality and Social Psychology, 69*, 1013–1027. Copyright © 1995 by the American Psychological Association. Adapted with permission.)

emotion-eliciting stimuli at a nonconscious level (see Chapter 11). On reexposure to these same faces, amygdala activation lessened for in-group faces, whereas it remained high for out-group faces (Hart et al., 2000). These data suggest that unfamiliar faces in general, regardless of racial category, are initially perceived as threatening. Over time, however, this threat response abates for those who are "like us" but not for those who are "not like us."

STEREOTYPES AND INFORMATION PROCESSING Research confirms that stereotypes, like schemas more generally, help us process information. For example, if people are explicitly instructed to remember as much information as they can about a person, they actually remember less than if they are simply told to try to form an impression (Hamilton, 1979). This is because the instruction to

form an impression induces them to search for relevant schemas or stereotypes that help them organize and recall material better.

Without stereotypes, then, we would be overwhelmed by the information that inundates us. If you had no way to organize or access your expectations about different types of people, you would be extraordinarily slow to form impressions of them. But the price we pay for the efficiency that stereotypes bring are biases in our perceptions and our memories of the information given and in the inferences we make. Consider, for example, the impression you form of Jim from the following observations of his behavior:

Jim left the house to get some stationery. He walked out into the sun-filled street with two of his friends, basking in the sun as he walked. Jim entered the stationery store, which was full of people. Jim talked with an acquaintance while he waited to catch the clerk's eye. On his way out, he stopped to chat with a school friend who was just coming into the store. Leaving the store, he walked toward the school. On his way he met the girl to whom he had been introduced the night before. They talked for a short while, and then Jim left for school. After school, Jim left the classroom alone. Leaving the school, he started on his long walk home. The street was brilliantly filled with sunshine. Jim walked down the street on the shady side. Coming down the street toward him, he saw the pretty girl whom he had met on the previous evening. Jim crossed the street and entered a candy store. The store was crowded with students, and he noticed a few familiar faces. Jim waited quietly until he caught the counterman's eye and then gave his order. Taking his drink, he sat down at a side table. When he had finished his drink, he went home. (Luchins, 1957, pp. 34–35)

What impression do you have of Jim? Do you think of him as friendly and outgoing or as shy and introverted? If you think of him as friendly, you agree with 78% of people who read this description. But examine the description closely; it is actually composed of two very different portraits. Up to the sentence that begins "After school, Jim left," Jim is portrayed in several situations as fairly friendly. After that point, however, a nearly identical set of situations shows him to be much more of a loner. Whereas 95% of the people who are shown only the first half of the description rate Jim as friendly, just 3% of the people who are shown only the second half do so. Thus, in the combined description, Jim's friendliness dominates the overall impression. But when people read the same description with the un-

● **Table 18-1**
Schematic Processing and the Primacy Effect

Once a schema of Jim has been established, later information is assimilated into it. *(A. Luchens (1957) "Primary Recovery in Impression Formation," in* The Order of Presentation Persuasion, *edited by C. I. Hovland, pp. 34–35. Yale University Press.)*

Conditions	Percentage Rating Jim as Friendly
Friendly description only	95
Friendly first—unfriendly last	78
Unfriendly first—friendly last	18
Unfriendly description only	3

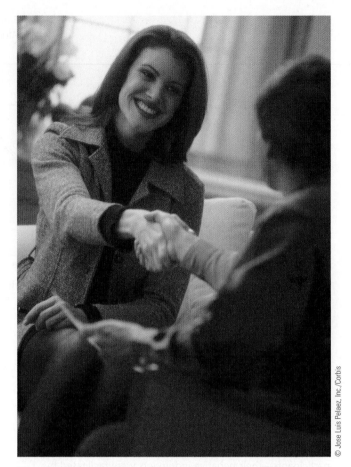

The first information we receive has a greater impact on our overall impressions than later information. This is why people usually wear business suits to interview for a job.

friendly half of the paragraph appearing first, only 18% rate Jim as friendly; his unfriendly behavior leaves the major impression (see Table 18-1). This study illustrates the **primacy effect:** In general, the first information we receive has the greater impact on our overall impressions.

The primacy effect has been found repeatedly in several kinds of studies of impression formation, including studies using real rather than hypothetical individuals (Jones, 1990). For example, people who watched a male student attempt to solve a series of difficult multiple-choice problems were asked to assess his general ability (Jones, Rock, Shaver, Goethals, & Ward, 1968). Although the student always solved exactly 15 of the 30 problems correctly, he was judged more capable if the successes came mostly at the beginning of the series than if they came near the end. Moreover, when asked to recall how many problems the student had solved, participants who had seen the 15 successes bunched at the beginning estimated an average of 21, but participants who had seen the successes at the end estimated an average of 13.

Although several factors contribute to the primacy effect, it appears to be primarily a consequence of schematic processing or top-down thinking. When we are first attempting to form our impressions of a person, we actively search in memory for the schemas or stereotypes that best match the incoming data. At some point we make a preliminary decision: This person is extraverted, or this person is smart (or some such judgment). We then assimilate any further information to that judgment and dismiss discrepant information as not representative of the person we have come to know. For example, when asked to reconcile the apparent contradictions in Jim's behavior, participants sometimes say that Jim is really friendly but was probably tired by the end of the day (Luchins, 1957). Our stereotype of extraverts, activated by Jim's initial behaviors, shapes our perception of all subsequent data about Jim. More generally, our subsequent perceptions become

schema-driven and therefore relatively impervious to new data. There is thus a great deal of truth in the conventional warning that first impressions are important.

Stereotypes also help us make **inferences,** which means to make judgments that go beyond the information given. A classic study by Solomon Asch in 1946 illustrates this effect. To get a sense of the study, form an impression in your mind of Sam, someone described as "intelligent, skillful, industrious, cold, determined, practical, and cautious." Based on the impression you have now formed, do you think that Sam is generous? Could you ask him to lend you his car for the day? If you think not, you agree with the participants in Asch's original study: Only 9% inferred that a person was generous, given these traits. But what if Sam was described as "intelligent, skillful, industrious, warm, determined, practical, and cautious?" Only one trait differs: *Cold* is replaced by *warm*. Now would you think that Sam is generous? Probably so. A full 91% of those in Asch's original study inferred generosity from the same trait constellation that included *warm* instead of *cold*. So although no information is given about Sam's likely generosity, we can use our expectations or stereotypes about warm or cold people to go beyond what's given and make an inference. Studies like Asch's have also been done with real rather than hypothetical individuals. For instance, students told that an upcoming guest lecturer was "rather cold" came to evaluate him quite negatively, whereas other students told that this same guest lecturer was "rather warm" came to evaluate him quite favorably, even though they observed the same lecturer behaving in the same way (Kelley, 1950). The bottom line here is that advance reputations are hard to shake!

Stereotypes about race and gender have also been found to shape our interpretations of other people's behavior. Suppose you learn that someone performed exceptionally well on a math test. Studies show that if that someone is male, most people think he's smart, whereas if she's female, they think she got lucky by studying the right material (Deaux, 1984; Swim & Sanna, 1996). Likewise, when European Americans hear that an African American man punched someone, they tend to conclude that he's aggressive, but if they learn that a European American man punched someone, they tend to wonder what provoked him (Hewstone, 1990; Pettigrew, 1979). In these examples, we see that information consistent with a stereotype is taken as diagnostic of that person's underlying ability or personality, whereas information inconsistent with a stereotype is dismissed as not characteristic of them.

Similar evidence comes from the experiment, described earlier, in which one group of men was primed by viewing TV ads with stereotypic images of women. In a later word-recognition task (disguised as a separate study), primed men, compared with men who were not primed, were faster to recognize sexist words (like *babe* and *bimbo*) and slower to recognize nonsexist words (like *mother* and *sister*) (Rudman & Borgida, 1995). Simply through media exposure, these men were primed to see the world through the lens of the activated gender stereotype.

To sum, stereotypes (like top-down, schematic processing more generally) determine how we perceive, recall, and interpret information about people. So, as we form impressions of others, we don't simply take in the available information about them and process it in an unbiased manner. Instead, we filter incoming information through our preexisting stereotypes and actively construct our perceptions, memories, and inferences. Making matters worse, the effects of stereotypes on perception and thinking often remain invisible to us: We often take our constructions to be direct and unbiased representations of reality! In other words, we rarely see the role of stereotypes in shaping our interpretations but instead believe that we simply "call it like it is." You can begin to see how entrenched and persistent stereotypes

can be: Even if initially incorrect, people can come to believe that a stereotype is "true" because they construct—and see—a world in which it is.

SELF-FULFILLING STEREOTYPES Stereotypes can also be like omens—they can predict the future. But this is not because stereotypes are necessarily true. Rather, once activated, stereotypes can set in motion a chain of behavioral processes that serve to draw out from others behavior that confirms the initial stereotype, an effect called the **self-fulfilling prophecy** (Jussim, 1991; Rosenthal & Jacobson, 1968; Snyder, Tanke, & Berscheid, 1977). This works because stereotypes don't just reside in our heads. They leak out in our actions. To get feel for this, suppose that women who attend your rival university have the reputation for being snobs. In actuality, most are quite friendly, but your sources tell you differently. How will you act toward a student from that university when you cross paths with her before a football game? Most likely you'll look away. Why should you bother to smile and say hello to a snob? And how will she act? Now that you've given her the cold shoulder, she'll probably do the same. And now that you see her cold, aloof manner, you'll take that as proof positive that she *is* a snob and fail to see your own role in producing this evidence! So your stereotype of women from the rival school, although initially wrongly applied to the woman you met, shaped your own behavior, which in turn shaped her behavior, which in turn provided behavioral confirmation for your initially erroneous stereotype. Beliefs have a way of becoming reality.

In a classic study illustrating this process, investigators first noted that European American job interviewers displayed a less friendly manner when interviewing African American applicants than when interviewing European American applicants. They hypothesized that this could cause African American applicants to come off less well in the interviews. To test this hypothesis, they trained interviewers to reproduce both the less friendly and the more friendly interviewing styles. Applicants (all European Americans) were then videotaped while being interviewed by an interviewer using one of these two styles. Judges who viewed the videotapes rated applicants who had been interviewed in a less friendly manner much lower on their interview performance compared with those who had been interviewed in the friendlier manner (Word, Zanna, & Cooper, 1974). The study thus confirmed the hypothesis that people who hold stereotypes can interact in ways that actually evoke the stereotyped behaviors that sustain their biased beliefs.

Self-fulfilling prophecies can occur completely outside conscious awareness. Earlier we saw that when people's stereotypes about African Americans were primed through brief, subliminal exposure to young African

American male faces, they were more likely to act in a hostile manner. Is this hostile behavior potent enough to draw out hostility from others? Another experiment tested this possibility. The same priming procedure was used for one person in a pair before the two played a potentially frustrating game with each other. Replicating the first study, those who had been primed with African American faces showed greater hostility than those primed with European American faces. Plus, as the self-fulfilling prophecy predicts, the partners of those primed with African American faces (who were *not* themselves primed) also showed greater hostility than those whose partners were primed with European American faces. Moreover, the primed participants saw their partners as hostile but did not see their own role in drawing that hostility out (Chen & Bargh, 1997). These data suggest that the mere presence of a stereotyped person can activate stereotypes that soon become self-fulfilling.

Stereotypes that we hold about our own group can also be self-fulfilling. When college students are primed with racial stereotypes—which include the idea that African Americans are intellectually inferior—African Americans perform worse than European Americans on difficult academic tests. But when no racial stereotype is activated, African Americans perform equal to European Americans (Steele & Aronson, 1995). The same holds for the stereotype that women are bad at math: When the stereotype is activated, women perform worse than men on difficult math tests. When it is not activated, women perform equal to men (Spencer, Steele, & Quinn, 1999). Stereotypes about the elderly can be similarly self-fulfilling. When a negative stereotype is activated by brief, subliminal exposure to words like *senile*, elderly participants perform worse on a later memory test. By contrast, elderly participants who are subliminally primed with positive stereotypes about their group (such as *wise*) perform better on the same memory task (Levy, 1996).

The dominant explanation for the self-fulfilling nature of self-stereotypes appeals to a concept called **stereotype threat**, which suggests that the mere threat of being identified with a stereotype can raise an individual's anxiety level, which in turn degrades his or her performance (Steele, 1997). Other explanations downplay the role of experienced threat and appeal more to simple mental representations of the behaviors associated with the activated stereotypes. Through a principle called **ideomotor action**, mentally activating these behavioral representations—simply thinking about them—can make actual corresponding behaviors more likely. For example, if the stereotype of African Americans—which includes the trait of "laziness"—is activated in a testing situation, it can automatically yield "lazy" behavior, like guessing or failing to read test items carefully (Dijksterhuis & Bargh, 2001;

Wheeler & Petty, 2001). The ideomotor perspective predicts that stereotypes don't have to target one's own group to harm performance in testing situations, and some experiments have shown this to be the case (Wheeler, Jarvis, & Petty, 2001; for a review, see Wheeler & Petty, 2001).

INDIVIDUATION

As we've seen, stereotypes can be activated automatically, simply by seeing someone's face. Plus, once activated, stereotypes can influence our thinking and behavior in ways that actually draw out stereotype-confirming behaviors from ourselves and from others. (For a review of the various cognitive and behavioral effects of stereotypes, see the Concept Review Table.) If the effects of stereotypes are so automatic and far-reaching, can we ever truly come to know another person accurately? In the 1960s, Martin Luther King Jr. expressed a similar yearning to be free from the pernicious effects of stereotypes. In his famous speech entitled "I Have a Dream," King voiced his hope that African American children might "one day live in a nation where they will not be judged by the color of their skin, but by the content of their character." Dr. King was actually describing a process that social psychologists call **individuation**, which means assessing an individual's personal qualities on a person-by-person basis. Fortunately, Martin Luther King Jr.'s dream can come true: We can sometimes override the effects of stereotypes and form more accurate and personalized impressions of others through individuation. But typically, this more accurate impression formation requires a more thoughtful and controlled mode of thinking.

CONCEPT REVIEW TABLE
Summary of the Effects of Stereotypes

Cognitive Effects

1. Automatic evaluation
2. Biased perceptions of incoming information
3. Biased memories
4. Biased inferences and interpretations

Behavioral Effects

1. Automatic emotion expression
2. Automatic behavioral tendencies
3. Self-fulfilling prophecies

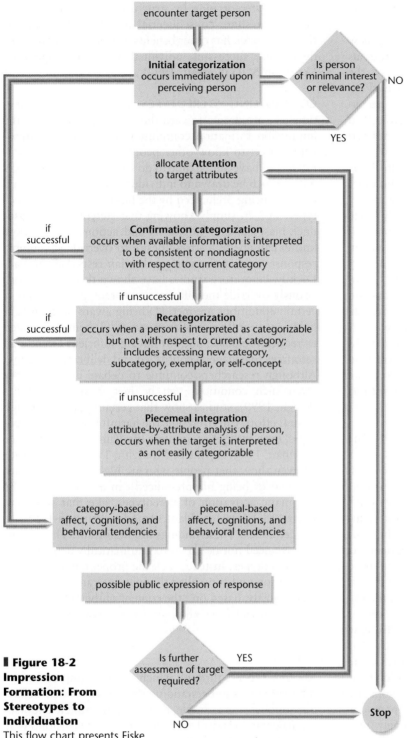

| Figure 18-2
Impression Formation: From Stereotypes to Individuation

This flow chart presents Fiske and Neuberg's continuum model of impression formation. It shows the continuum of impression formation processes ranging from stereotyping to individuation as a function of attention and interpretation. Here the most individuating stage is called "piecemeal integration." The information available about the person perceived and the perceivers' motivational goals determine how attention and interpretations combine to shape the process of impression formation. (From S. T. Friske, M. Lin, & S. L. Neuberg (1999). "The continuum model: Ten years later," in S. Chaiken & Y. Trope (eds.), *Dual-process Theories in Social Psychology*, pp. 231–254. New York: Guilford Press.)

TRIGGERS OF INDIVIDUATION When and how do we move beyond stereotyping to individuation? One influential model of impression formation, called the **continuum model,** describes the full continuum of processes from stereotyping to individuation (Fiske, Lin, & Neuberg, 1999). The model is described by the flow chart shown in Figure 18-2. You can see in this flow chart that the automatic stereotyping that we've discussed so far is the first psychological process set in motion when we first encounter a person (called "initial categorization" in Figure 18-2). Within milliseconds of an initial encounter, we have already automatically and nonconsciously categorized the person in terms of gender, ethnicity, and age. These categories are used first because they (1) apply to most people, (2) are available immediately and physically (in face-to-face encounters), and (3) often have important cultural meanings relevant to our interaction goals. Whether we move beyond simple stereotyping depends on whether the person we've encountered has any personal relevance to us. If, for instance, you are deciding whether to share an apartment with this new person, you most certainly will devote more attention to forming your impression.

As Figure 18-2 shows, the first thing that we do once we move into this more thoughtful process of impression formation is try to confirm our initial categorization. Return to that potential roommate. You might want to know whether the young man you've just met is a "typical 20-year-old guy." Will he be interested in loud parties, fast cars, and frequent dates? Or is he more of a loner, truly engaged with his studies? You notice that his backpack is overflowing with texts for the most advanced courses, and he tells you that he spends most evenings at the library. So the available information suggests that the initial categorization won't do. Now you find another, narrower category for him: A studious nerd. This is called "recategorization" in Figure 18-2. Because you are also engaged with your studies most evenings, you suspect that you'd be compatible roommates. You decide to share the apartment.

Over time, and as you learn more about your new roommate, you come to recognize that being a studious nerd is just one facet of his character. He also plays the saxophone, competes in triathlons, and has traveled extensively across South America. Only now do you recognize that he doesn't fit any one category fully, so instead you form an impression of him by piecing together and integrating all the different things you know about him, a process called "piecemeal integration" in Figure 18-2. So, when ample information about someone becomes available, and when we are motivated and able to pay close attention to that information, we eventually judge people "by the content of their character." And that's individuation. The most important thing to note, however, is how slowly we move away from stereotyping and categorization toward individuation. In fact, many social psychologists would argue that we never fully abandon categorizing people, however well intentioned we are, because doing so provides a wealth of information with little mental effort. Even so, when others become personally relevant to us—that is, if our future outcomes depend on them in some way—we become motivated to make more thoughtful, accurate, and individuated impressions of them.

STRUCTURES THAT PROMOTE INDIVIDUATION The importance of personal relevance carries a lesson for those who aim to reduce stereotyping in their schools, businesses, or other organizations. Studies show that structured cooperative contact between members of different social groups reduces stereotyping and fosters individuation. In one study, participants met another student who was identified as a former mental patient. At first, participants expected this new acquaintance to be somewhat depressed, fearful, and insecure, traits that fit the stereotype of a former mental patient. Next, the experimenters randomly assigned participants to either cooperate with this new acquaintance to jointly learn new material on an assigned topic or to simply study that new material independently but in the same room as the new acquaintance. Compared with those who didn't cooperate on the learning task, those who did cooperate moved away from their initial stereotyped impressions and judged the new acquaintance more positively, presumably because the cooperative structure of the task provided the opportunity to individuate. Perhaps more importantly, participants extended their favorable impressions of their learning partner to former mental patients in general (Desforges et al., 1991). So if you find yourself teaching or leading a group of others who seem to be divided by their stereotyped impressions of one another, remember that you can greatly reduce the harmful

effects of stereotyping by structuring in the need to cooperate or share consequential information. Cooperation, of course, has other benefits as well. It can also produce more successful individual and group outcomes (Aronson & Thibodeau, 1992).

CONTROLLING STEREOTYPES As we've seen, sometimes we are drawn toward the individuation end of the impression formation continuum because we are motivated to get to know other people personally and accurately and have ample time to do so. Other times, we may not so much be drawn to individuate as we are motivated to avoid being prejudiced by the biasing effects of stereotypes. In fact, simply knowing that stereotypes can produce biases in our judgments and actions (as you now know) can create a strong desire to override stereotypic responses and apply more egalitarian responses instead. Luckily, laboratory studies have shown that we can consciously override the influence of stereotypes, but only if certain conditions are met: (1) being aware of the potential negative influence of stereotypes, (2) being motivated to reduce prejudice, and (3) having sufficient attentional resources to engage in controlled and deliberate thinking. Although researchers continue to debate how and how often such conditions can be met in day-to-day life (Bargh, 1999), studies show that certain people, through mental effort, can overcome the harmful effects of stereotypes, even in brief encounters (Bodenhausen, Macrea & Sherman, 1999; Devine & Monteith, 1999). Recent studies even show that people who are highly identified with the goal of being nonprejudiced can also overcome the automatic activation of stereotypes, like that shown in Figure 18-1 (Devine, Plant, Amodio, Harmon-Jones, & Vance, 2002). These findings are important. They tell us that we need not be slaves to automatically activated social stereotypes. Instead, with the proper combination of motivation and controlled thought, we can learn to treat people justly, based on "the content of their character," a manner in which we all deserve to be treated.

ATTRIBUTIONS

Another process through which we form impressions of others involves understanding the causes of their behavior. Suppose, for example, that a famous athlete endorses a particular brand of athletic shoes on television. Why does he do it? Does he really like those shoes, or is he doing it for the money? You see a woman give a $5 donation to Planned Parenthood. Why? Is she altruistic? Was she being pressured? Did she need a tax write-off? Does she believe in the work of the organization?

Each of these cases creates an attribution problem. We witness some behavior and must decide to which of many possible causes the action should be attributed.

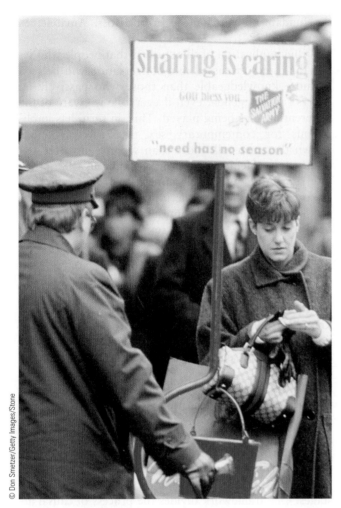

Is this woman giving money to the Salvation Army because she supports its work, because she feels pressured, or because she is generally altruistic?

Attribution refers to our intuitive attempts to infer the causes of behavior. It has long been a central topic in social psychology and continues to be today (Heider, 1958; Kelley, 1967; Malle, 1999; Trope & Gaunt, 1999).

THE FUNDAMENTAL ATTRIBUTION ERROR REVISITED

As the two preceding examples illustrate, one of the major attribution tasks we face is deciding whether an observed behavior reflects something about the person or something about the situation in which we observed the person. The former option is called an internal or **dispositional attribution.** We infer that something about the person is primarily responsible for the behavior (for instance, the athlete really loves those shoes). Here, *disposition* here refers to a person's beliefs, attitudes, and personality characteristics. The alternative choice is called an external or **situational attribution.** We infer that some external cause is primarily

responsible for the behavior (for instance, money, social norms, threats).

Fritz Heider, the founder of attribution theory, noted that an individual's behavior is so compelling to us that we take it as a face value representation of a person and give insufficient weight to the circumstances surrounding it (1958). Research has confirmed Heider's observation. We underestimate the situational causes of behavior, jumping too easily to conclusions about the person's disposition. If we observe someone behaving aggressively, we too readily assume that he or she has an aggressive personality, rather than concluding that the situation might have provoked similar aggression in anyone. To put it another way, we have a schema of cause and effect for human behavior that gives too much weight to the person and too little to the situation. In Chapter 17, you learned one of the foremost lessons of social psychology: that situations are, in fact, powerful causes of people's social behavior. You also learned a corollary lesson: that in our everyday reasoning, we often overlook the causal power of situations. And you will recall that this corollary lesson has a name of its own: the fundamental attribution error. Formally stated, the **fundamental attribution error** occurs when we underestimate the situational influences on behavior and assume that some personal characteristic of the individual is responsible (Ross, 1977).

In the classic early studies that revealed this bias, participants read a debater's speech that either supported or attacked Cuban leader Fidel Castro. The participants were explicitly told that the debate coach had assigned each debater one side of the issue or the other; the debater had no choice as to which side to argue. Despite this knowledge, when asked to estimate the debater's actual attitude toward Castro, participants inferred a position close to the one argued in the debate. In other words, the participants made a dispositional attribution, even though situational forces were fully sufficient to account for the behavior (Jones & Harris, 1967). This effect is quite powerful. Even when the participants themselves designate which side of the issue a speaker is to argue, they still tend to see him or her as actually holding that opinion (Gilbert & Jones, 1986). The effect occurs even if the presentations are deliberately designed to be drab and unenthusiastic and the speaker simply reads a transcribed version of the speech in a monotone and uses no gestures (Schneider & Miller, 1975).

An experiment designed as a quiz game illustrates how both participants and observers make the same fundamental attribution error in the same setting. Pairs of male or female participants were recruited to take part in a question-and-answer game testing general knowledge. One member of the pair was randomly assigned to be the questioner and to make up 10 difficult questions to which he or she knew the answers (such as "What is the world's largest glacier?"). The other participant acted as the contestant and attempted to answer the questions. When the contestant was unable to answer a question, the questioner gave the answer. In a reenactment of the study, observers watched the contest. After the game, both participants and observers were asked to rate the level of general knowledge possessed by the questioner and the contestant, relative to that possessed by the "average student." Note that participants and observers all knew that the roles of questioner and contestant had been assigned randomly.

As Figure 18-3 shows, questioners judged both themselves and the contestant to be about average in level of general knowledge. But contestants rated the questioner as superior and themselves as inferior to the average student. They attributed the outcome of the game to their (and the questioner's) level of knowledge rather than taking into account the overwhelming situational advantage enjoyed by the questioner, who was able to decide which questions to ask and to omit any questions to which he or she did not know the answer. Observers, aware that the questioner could ask questions that neither they nor the contestant could answer, rated the questioner's level of knowledge even higher. In other words, both contestants and observers gave too much weight to disposition and too little to the situation—the fundamental attribution error (Ross, Amabile, & Steinmetz, 1977).

One implication of this study is that people who select the topics discussed in a conversation will be seen as more knowledgeable than those who passively let others set the agenda, even if everyone is aware of the differential roles being played. This, in turn, has implications for contemporary sex roles. Research has shown that men talk more than women in mixed-sex interactions (Henley, Hamilton, & Thorne, 1985), they interrupt more (West & Zimmerman, 1983), and they are more likely to raise the topics discussed (Fishman, 1983). The questioner-contestant study implies that one consequence of these sex-role patterns is that women leave most mixed-sex interactions thinking themselves less knowledgeable than the men, with bystanders of both sexes sharing this illusion. The take-home message is clear: The fundamental attribution error can work for or against you. If you want to appear knowledgeable both to yourself and to others, learn how to structure the situation so that you control the choice of topics discussed. Be the questioner, not the contestant!

Causal attributions, like other aspects of impression formation, have also been found to be governed by two different modes of thinking, one more automatic and unintentional, and another more controlled and deliberate. This turns out to influence how frequently the fundamental attribution error occurs. To understand why, it's helpful to break the attribution process down into stages. One framework divides the process of causal attribution into at least two parts. The first step is a dispositional inference (what trait does this action imply?), and the second is situational correction (what situational constraints might have caused that action?). Experiments suggest that the first step of dispositional inference is more automatic than the second step of situational correction (Gilbert & Malone, 1995; Gilbert, Pelham, & Krull, 1988) This suggests that we make the fundamental attribution error so often because it is an overlearned, automatic process that frequently occurs outside conscious awareness. Only when we have the cognitive resources to think deliberately and carefully can we correct our initial, automatic dispositional attributions with reference to plausible situational causes. Although it may seem encouraging that effortful thinking can override the fundamental attribution error, we need to recognize that most often, as we're forming our impressions of others, we are cognitively busy, thinking about many things at once, like planning our next move, anticipating the other's reaction, and managing the impression that others form of us. All this "cognitive busyness" means that we will continue to commit the fundamental attribution error time and again (Gilbert & Malone, 1995).

Questioner rated

Contestant rated

▋ Figure 18-3
The Fundamental Attribution Error
Ratings of questioners and contestants after they had participated in a quiz game. The questioner is rated as superior by both the contestant and observers even though the questioner had an overwhelming situational advantage. Both contestants and observers gave too much weight to dispositional causes and too little to situational causes. (After Ross, Amabile, & Steinmetz, 1977)

Culture and Cognition

For centuries, Western philosophers and psychologists have discussed cognitive processes—or modes of thinking—as if they were the same for all normal adults. In fact, much of the research and thinking on social cognition conveyed within this very chapter has made a similar assumption: that the cognitive processes described are universal, characteristic of humans everywhere. Although it's obvious that different cultures practice different social customs, these were thought to be irrelevant to "basic" cognitive processes like categorization and causal reasoning. Cutting-edge research in social cognition shatters this assumption and argues that divergent social systems in fact create and reinforce distinct systems of thought (Nisbett, Peng, Choi, & Norenzayan, 2001).

The first evidence that aspects of social cognition might not be universal after all took aim at the fundamental attribution error itself. Early studies showed that whereas Americans have long been shown to explain other people's behavior in terms of dispositional attributions, Hindu Indians and Chinese people preferred to explain similar behavior in terms of situational attributions (Miller, 1984, Morris & Peng, 1994; Norenzayan & Nisbett, 2000).

In addition, the classic study in which participants read a speech that another person had been assigned to produce (such as supporting or denouncing Cuban leader Fidel Castro) was replicated with both Korean and American students (Choi, Nisbett, & Norenzayan, 1999). Here the speechwriter had no choice of topics, so it is a mistake to conclude that his or her attitude corresponds to the arguments within the speech. Even so, like Americans, Koreans inferred that the speechwriter held the position he or she was advocating, a dispositional inference that reflects the fundamental attribution error. Yet Americans and Koreans responded quite differently if they had the opportunity to "walk in the shoes" of the speechwriter before making their judgments. In a variation of the classic study,

they were each first assigned to prepare a speech themselves using a set of arguments given by the experimenter, an experience that should highlight the strong situational constraints on attitude expression. With this personal experience salient, Koreans no longer made dispositional inferences, whereas Americans continued to do so just the same. From this and other studies, the authors conclude that East-West differences in the commission of the fundamental attribution error do not so much reflect cultural differences in the propensity to make dispositional attributions. Indeed, both Koreans and Americans made the dispositional error in the standard condition. Instead, cultural differences in attribution reflect a greater sensitivity to contexts and situational constraints among East Asians when those situational constraints are salient (Choi et al., 1999).

Evidence continues to mount that East Asians, more than Westerners, pay more attention to contexts and situations (Masuda & Nisbett, 2001) and are more influenced by them (Ji, Peng, & Nisbett, 2000). These and countless other East-West differences in styles of thinking are now taken as evidence that East Asians engage in more holistic thinking, whereas Westerners engage in more analytic thinking (Nisbett et al., 2001). **Holistic thought** is defined as an orientation toward the entire context or field and assigning causality to it, making relatively little use of categories and formal logic, and relying instead on dialectical reasoning, which involves recognizing and transcending apparent contradictions. By contrast, **analytic thought** is defined as an orientation toward objects, detached from their contexts, with much use of categories and formal logic and the avoidance of contradiction.

How did such wide-scale differences in thinking styles emerge? From long-standing different social practices, leading researchers say. In Chapter 1, we introduced the distinction between collectivist and individualist cultures. Collectivist cultures, you will recall, emphasize the fundamental connectedness and interdependence among people, whereas individualist cultures emphasize the fundamental separateness and independence of indi-

viduals. Indeed, we saw in Chapter 11 that the very emotions people experience and express reflect their cultural upbringing.

Collectivist tendencies can be traced back to the ancient Chinese focus on social harmony and collective agency, whereas individualist tendencies can be traced back to the ancient Greek focus on personal agency. These quite divergent views of human agency not only infused East-West differences in social practices but also shaped their respective advances in science, mathematics, and philosophy. The legacy of these distinct ancient orientations toward the locus of causality includes the cultural differences in cognition that we find evidence of today: that contemporary East Asians are more holistic in their thinking, whereas contemporary Westerners are more analytical (Nisbett et al., 2001). The ways we use our brains, then, are not universal or dictated by biology. Rather, our styles of thinking are malleable, shaped by those in our culture who came millennia before us, and reinforced by contemporary social practices.

These recent advances in the understanding of culture and cognition undermine all prior claims of universality made within the study of cognition and social cognition. Indeed, one of the most influential texts on social cognition in the 1980s was written by one of the scholars who now leads the foray into culture and cognition. Listen to what he says about his past work:

Two decades ago, [I] wrote a book with Lee Ross entitled, modestly, *Human Inference* (Nisbett & Ross, 1980). Roy D'Andrade, a distinguished cognitive anthropologist, read the book and told [me] he thought it was a "good ethnography." [I] was shocked and dismayed. But [I] now wholeheartedly agree with D'Andrade's contention about the limits of research conducted in a single culture. Psychologists who choose not to do cross-cultural psychology may have chosen to be ethnographers instead. (Nisbett et al., 2001, p. 306)

For more information, go online with InfoTrac College Edition. Use your own term or search:

- Attribution error
- Situational constraints

◆ Interim Summary

- Through schematic processing, we perceive and interpret incoming information in terms of simplified memory structures called *schemas*. Schemas are mini-theories about everyday objects and events that allow us to process information efficiently. Stereotypes are schemas about groups of people.

- Through repeated exposure, stereotypes can become habitual and automatic, operating outside conscious awareness.

- Because schemas and stereotypes simplify reality, schematic processing produces biases and errors in our processing of social information. In forming impressions of other people, for example, we are prone to the primacy effect: The first information we receive evokes an initial schema and, hence, becomes more powerful in determining our impression than does later information. Schemas and stereotypes also govern our inferences.

- Once activated, stereotypes can set in motion a chain of behavioral processes that serve to draw out from ourselves and others behavior that confirms the initial stereotype, an effect called the *self-fulfilling prophecy*. This behavioral sequence can occur completely outside conscious awareness.

- Individuation is the process of forming impressions of others by assessing their personal qualities on a person-by-person basis. The continuum model of impression formation, presented in Figure 18-2, details when and how people come to individuate others. Cooperative activities can promote individuation.

- Although stereotypes are activated automatically, under the right conditions they can also be controlled through effortful thinking.

- Attribution is the process by which we interpret and explain the behavior of other people. One major attribution task is to decide whether someone's action should be attributed to dispositional causes (the person's personality or attitudes) or to situational causes (social forces or other external circumstances). We tend to give too much weight to dispositional factors and too little to situational factors, a bias called the *fundamental attribution error*.

◆ Critical Thinking Questions

1. Suppose you perform badly on an exam. You know it's because you hardly studied at all, but your professor has made the fundamental attribution error and comes to conclude that you're not too bright. Some social psychologists have claimed that the fundamental attribution error is self-erasing—that, over time, it ceases to be an error. Building on the example of your bad test performance, use the concepts of the self-fulfilling prophecy and stereotype threat to explain the logic of this claim.

2. Think of someone you have come to know well over the past few months or years. Did your initial impressions of this person match your current impressions? If not, can you see how stereotypes and categorizations might have influenced your initial impressions? Can you trace your increasing individuation of this person through the continuum model, presented in Figure 18-2?

ATTITUDES

So far our discussion of social cognition has focused on the processes of perceiving, thinking, and impression formation. With the concept of attitude, we take a broader look at how feelings and opinions influence social cognition and social behavior.

Attitudes are likes and dislikes—favorable or unfavorable evaluations of and reactions to objects, people, situations, or other aspects of the world, including abstract ideas and social policies. We often express our attitudes in statements of opinion: "I love grapefruit" or "I can't stand liberals." But even though attitudes express feelings, they are often linked to cognitions—specifically, to beliefs about the attitude objects ("Grapefruit contain lots of vitamins" or "Liberals just want to tax and spend"). Moreover, attitudes are sometimes linked to the actions we take with respect to the attitude objects ("I eat a grapefruit every morning" or "I never vote for liberal candidates").

Accordingly, social psychologists usually conceive of attitudes as comprising a cognitive component, an affective component, and a behavioral component. For example, in studying negative attitudes toward groups, social psychologists often distinguish between negative stereotypes (negative beliefs and perceptions about a group—the cognitive component), prejudice (negative feelings toward the group—the affective component), and discrimination (negative actions against members of the group—the behavioral component). Some theorists prefer to define an attitude as only the cognitive and affective components; others include only the affective component. But despite differing definitions, all share a concern with the interrelationships among the pertinent beliefs, feelings, and behaviors.

Research on attitudes has kept social psychologists busy for decades. As early as the 1950s, attitudes were dubbed "the primary building stone in the edifice of social psychology" (Allport, 1954). But why exactly are attitudes so important? Two reasons are most critical. The first reason is that, at least in democratic societies, people talk about their attitudes a lot. They also ask about others' attitudes a lot. When we leave the movie theater, for instance, the first thing we ask our companion is "Did you like it?" After we've introduced our new heart-throb to our friends, we ask, "What do you think?" Facing a critical election, we ask respected others, "Who will you vote for?" Marketing and scientific polls turn such queries into formal assessments of public opinion, predicting everything from the box office success of Hollywood movies to the outcomes of presidential elections, and describing everything from month-by-month ratings of public support for a country's elected officials to the public's attitude toward teaching evolutionary theory in elementary schools.

The second reason attitudes have been so central to social psychology and cause for so much talk and polling is a key underlying assumption: that people's attitudes predict their behavior. This assumption is so widely accepted that it has served as the base for psychology's neighboring behavioral science of economics and underlies other rational views of human nature. This assumption can be decomposed into three parts: First, human behavior is intentional and reflects individual preferences. This is the heart of utility theory within economics and the notion of free will within philosophy. Second, attitudes represent preferences. And third, to predict behavior, we can simply look at attitudes. A corollary to this logic is that if we wish to change people's behaviors, we should start by changing their attitudes.

A long-standing agenda among social psychologists, then, has been to find ways to change people's attitudes. You will recall from Chapter 17 that one way this agenda has been pursued is through social influence techniques. In particular, research on self-justification shows that we can sometimes change people's attitudes by slyly inducing them to engage in some hypocritical (counterattitudinal) action, like telling another person that a boring task was fun. Reference groups can also play a role in changing people's attitudes, as was illustrated in the study of Bennington College students. Here we take up more direct approaches to attitude change, those undertaken through persuasive communication, like political speeches, advertisements, sermons, and other forms of formal or informal lobbying.

PERSUASIVE COMMUNICATION

Just as the practices of Nazi Germany under Hitler created interest in obedience to authority (see Chapter 17), so did wartime propaganda efforts prompt the study of persuasive communication. Intensive research began in the late 1940s at Yale University, where investigators sought to determine the characteristics of successful persuasive communicators, successful communications, and the kinds of people who are most easily persuaded (Hovland, Janis, & Kelley, 1953). As research on these topics continued over the years, a number of interesting phenomena were discovered, but few general principles emerged. The results became increasingly complex and difficult to summarize, and every conclusion seemed to require several "it depends" qualifications. Beginning in the 1980s, however, interest in the two modes of cogni-

Priests and politicians are among those who seek to present persuasive messages that will change the attitudes and behavior of their audiences.

tive processing that we've been discussing—one more automatic and effortless and the other more controlled and effortful—gave rise to new theories of persuasion that provided a more unified framework for analyzing persuasive communication (Chaiken, 1987; Chen & Chaiken, 1999; Petty & Cacioppo, 1981; 1986; Petty & Wegener, 1999).

THE ELABORATION LIKELIHOOD MODEL The elaboration likelihood model is one of the more prominent dual-process theories of persuasion (Petty & Cacioppo, 1981, 1986; Petty & Wegener, 1999). It aims to predict when certain aspects of a persuasive communication—like argument strength and source credibility—will matter and when they won't. A key idea within this model is that people experience a continuum of elaboration likelihood. In simple terms, this means that sometimes we are motivated and able to pay attention, think, and elaborate on the persuasive message, and other times we are not. Which end of this continuum we're on at any given moment determines the cognitive processes that govern persuasion. So, according to the **elaboration likelihood model,** if we're at the high end of the continuum—willing and able to think deeply— then persuasion is said to follow a central route, relying on controlled and effortful thinking; if we're at the low end of the continuum—for whatever reasons, not willing or able to think deeply—then persuasion is said to follow a peripheral route, relying on automatic and effortless thinking.

THE CENTRAL ROUTE TO PERSUASION Persuasion is said to follow the **central route** when an individual mentally responds to—and elaborates on—the persuasive communication. The central route to persuasion is taken only when the individual is motivated to generate thoughts in response to the substantive content of a communication and has the ability and opportunity to do so. These thoughts can be about the content of the communication itself or about other aspects of the situation, such as the credibility of the communicator. If the communication evokes thoughts that support the position being advocated, the individual will move toward that position; if the communication evokes unsupportive thoughts (such as counterarguments or disparaging thoughts about the communicator), the individual will remain unconvinced or even shift away from the position being advocated (Greenwald, 1968; Petty, Ostrom, & Brock, 1981).

A number of studies provide evidence that effortful thought accounts for the central route to persuasion. In one, each participant read a communication containing arguments about a controversial issue and wrote a one-sentence reaction to each argument. One week later, the participants were unexpectedly given a memory test ask-ing them to recall both the arguments in the communication and their written reactions to those arguments. Participants' opinions on the issue were assessed before receiving the communication and again at the time of the memory test. The results showed that the amount of opinion change produced by the communication was significantly correlated with both the supportiveness of participants' reactions to the communication and with their later recall of those reactions, but it was not significantly correlated with their recall of the arguments themselves (Love & Greenwald, 1978). This experiment not only supports the central route to persuasion but also explains what had previously been a puzzling observation: that the persistence of opinion change is often unrelated to an individual's memory of the arguments that produced that change.

In a sense, then, the central route to persuasion can be considered self-persuasion produced by the thoughts that the person generates while reading, listening to, or even just anticipating the communication. Those thoughts turn out to be more influential than the communication itself.

THE PERIPHERAL ROUTE TO PERSUASION Persuasion is said to follow the **peripheral route** when the individual responds to non-content cues in a communication (such as the sheer number of arguments it contains) or to the context of the communication (such as the credibility of the communicator or the pleasantness of the surroundings). The peripheral route is taken when the individual is—for whatever reason—unable or unwilling to do the cognitive work required to carefully evaluate the content of the communication.

Classical conditioning (which you learned about in Chapter 7) is one of the most primitive means of changing attitudes through the peripheral route. Advertisers use classical conditioning quite a lot, by repeatedly pairing their initially neutral or unknown product with images or ideas that are known to produce positive feelings, like attractive people or beautiful scenery. Through classical conditioning—a peripheral route to persuasion— viewers should come to hold positive attitudes toward the new product as well.

Another peripheral route to persuasion relies on heuristics, or rules of thumb (discussed in Chapter 9) to infer the validity of persuasive messages. Examples of such rules might include "Messages with many arguments are more likely to be valid than messages with few arguments," "Politicians always lie," and "College professors know what they are talking about" (Chaiken, 1980, 1987; Eagly & Chaiken, 1984). Communications that follow these rules of thumb can be persuasive—even if their substantive content is unconvincing—to the extent that listeners are unlikely to elaborate on the information given.

CENTRAL OR PERIPHERAL? Several factors can influence which route—central or peripheral—will be taken. One such factor is personal involvement. If a communication addresses an issue in which the individual has a personal stake, he or she is more likely to attend carefully to the arguments. In such a case, the individual is also likely to have a rich store of prior information and opinions on the issue. On the other hand, if an issue has no personal relevance for the individual, he or she is not likely to make much of an effort either to support or refute arguments about it. What happens then?

The elaboration likelihood model has been tested in several studies. In one rather complex study, college undergraduates read an essay allegedly written by the chairperson of a university committee charged with advising the chancellor on changes in academic policy. The essay proposed that the university institute a comprehensive examination that every undergraduate would have to pass before being permitted to graduate. To manipulate the students' involvement in the issue, half of them were told that any policy changes adopted by the chancellor would be instituted the next year (high involvement), and the other half were told that any changes would take effect in 10 years (low involvement). Different forms of the essay were also used. Some contained strong arguments, others weak ones. Some contained only three arguments, others nine.

The post-communication attitudes of students in the high-involvement conditions are shown in Figure 18-4a. It can be seen that strong arguments produced more favorable attitudes overall than did weak arguments. But more important, nine strong arguments produced greater agreement with the essay than did three strong arguments, whereas nine weak arguments produced less agreement than did three weak arguments. How can we make sense of these patterns?

The elaboration likelihood model predicts that students in the high-involvement conditions will be motivated to process the essay's substantive arguments and thus generate topic-relevant cognitive responses. This is the central route of persuasion, which holds that strong arguments will evoke more supportive cognitive responses and fewer counterarguments than will weak arguments and hence will produce more agreement with the essay—as, indeed, they did. Moreover, nine strong arguments should be more persuasive than three strong arguments because the more strong arguments the individual encounters, the more supportive cognitive responses he or she will generate. In contrast, nine weak arguments should be less persuasive than three weak arguments because the more weak arguments the individual encounters, the more counterarguments he or she will generate. These predictions are in accordance with the findings displayed in Figure 18-4a.

As shown in Figure 18-4b, a different pattern emerges for students in the low-involvement conditions. Here the elaboration likelihood model predicts that students in the low-involvement conditions will not be motivated to scrutinize the essay's arguments closely and will instead rely on simple heuristics to evaluate its merits and form their attitudes. This is the peripheral route, which holds that an individual in this setting will not even bother to determine whether the arguments are strong or weak but will simply invoke the

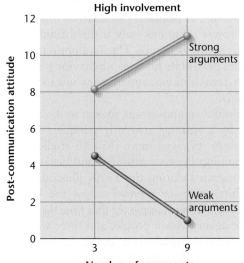

a) **Post-communication attitudes through the central route.** When individuals have high involvement in the issue, nine strong arguments produce more agreement than three strong arguments, but nine weak arguments produce less agreement than three weak arguments.

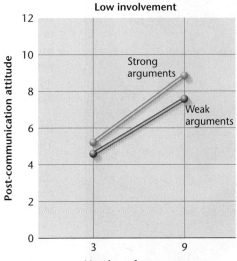

b) **Post-communication attitudes through the peripheral route.** When individuals have low involvement in the issue, nine arguments produce more agreement than three arguments, regardless of whether the arguments are strong or weak.

▌ Figure 18-4
A Test of the Elaboration Likelihood Model
(R. E. Petty & J. T. Cacioppo (1984), "The effects of involvement on responses to arguments quantity and quality, central and peripheral routes to persuasion," in *Journal of Personality & Social Psychology,* 46:6–81. Copyright © 1984 by the American Psychological Association. Adapted with permission.)

heuristic rule "Messages with many arguments are more likely to be valid than messages with few arguments." Thus, strong arguments will be no more effective than weak arguments, and nine arguments will be more persuasive than three arguments—regardless of whether they are strong or weak. This is precisely the pattern shown in Figure 18-4b: Overall, there were no significant differences between strong and weak arguments, but nine arguments were more effective than three arguments in both conditions (Petty & Cacioppo, 1984).

An experiment that varied the expertise of the communicator rather than the number of arguments found similar results: Participants in the high-involvement conditions were more influenced by the strength of the arguments, but participants in the low-involvement conditions relied more on the heuristic "Arguments made by an expert are more valid than arguments made by a nonexpert" (Petty, Cacioppo, & Goldman, 1981).

Although much research on persuasion has been conducted in laboratories, there has always been an interest

Whether an ad like this coaxes a girl to smoke Newport cigarettes depends on the thoughts that the ad prompts in her. If she thinks the woman is attractive, she is more likely to begin smoking. But if she thinks the ad exploits women, she is less likely to begin smoking.

in the practical applications of the findings. An example is an educational program designed to inoculate junior high school students against peer pressure to smoke. High school students conducted sessions in which they taught seventh-graders how to generate counterarguments. For example, in role-playing sessions they were taught to respond to being called "chicken" for not taking a cigarette by saying things like "I'd be a real chicken if I smoked just to impress you." They were also taught to respond to advertisements implying that liberated women smoke by saying, "She's not really liberated if she is hooked on tobacco." Several inoculation sessions were held during seventh and eighth grades, and records were kept of how many of the students smoked from the beginning of the study through the ninth grade. The results showed that inoculated students were half as likely to smoke as students at a matched junior high school that used a more typical smoking education program (McAlister, Perry, Killen, Slinkard, & Maccoby, 1980). Similar programs have been designed to inoculate elementary school children against being taken in by deceptive television commercials (Cohen, 1980; Feshbach, 1980).

ATTITUDES AND BEHAVIOR

As we've said, a major reason for studying attitudes is the expectation that they will enable us to predict a person's future behavior. A political candidate is interested in a survey of voters' opinions only if the attitudes expressed relate to voting behavior. The assumption that a person's attitudes determine his or her behavior is deeply ingrained in Western thinking, and in many instances the assumption holds.

But this central assumption was shaken to the core in the late 1960s by a scathing scholarly critique (Wicker, 1969). The critique reviewed more than 40 studies that tested the relationship between attitudes and behavior. A classic study conducted during the 1930s illustrated the problem. A white professor traveled across the United States with a young Chinese couple. At that time there was strong prejudice against Asian people, and there were no laws against racial discrimination in public accommodations. The three travelers stopped at more than 200 hotels, motels, and restaurants and were served at all the restaurants and all but one of the hotels and motels without a problem. Later, a letter was sent to all of the restaurants and hotels asking them whether they would accept a Chinese couple as guests. Of the 128 replies received, 92% said that they would not. In other words, these proprietors expressed attitudes that were much more prejudiced than their actual behavior (LaPiere, 1934). Drawing on this and many other studies, critics argued that attitudes did not predict behavior at all. Some even recommended that social psychologists abandon the attitude concept altogether and focus instead on the situational determinants of behavior. The logic of this recommendation, you will see, parallels the fundamental attribution error: that even social psychologists had overestimated the causal force of dispositional factors—like attitudes—on determining behavior and underestimated the causal force of situations.

Certainly people's behavior is determined by many factors other than their attitudes. One obvious factor is the degree of constraint in the situation: We must often act in ways that are not consistent with what we feel or believe. As children, we ate vegetables that we detested, and as adults we attend lectures and dinner parties that we consider boring. In Chapter 17, we saw the power of situations time and again. In the Asch study, participants conformed to the majority, even when they knew the majority was wrong. In the Milgram study, participants delivered shocks even when doing so went against their consciences. And in the racial discrimination study just described, the prejudiced proprietors may have found it difficult to act on their prejudices when actually faced with the Chinese couple seeking service.

Peer pressure can exert similar influences on behavior. For example, a teenager's attitude toward marijuana is moderately correlated with his or her actual use of marijuana, but the number of marijuana-using friends the teenager has is an even better predictor of his or her marijuana use (Andrews & Kandel, 1979). Can you see a similarity here to the classic Asch study?

Far from ending research on attitudes, this critical challenge to the assumption that attitudes predict behavior served to kindle a new generation of research on attitudes that aimed to specify the special conditions under which attitudes do in fact predict behavior. In general, attitudes have been found to predict behavior best when (1) they are strong and consistent, (2) they are specifically related to the behavior being predicted, (3) they are based on the person's direct experience, and (4) the individual is aware of his or her attitudes. We will look briefly at each of these factors.

STRONG AND CONSISTENT ATTITUDES

Strong and consistent attitudes predict behavior better than weak or ambivalent ones. Many voters experience ambivalence because they are under pressure from friends and associates who do not agree with one another. For example, a Jewish businessperson belongs to an ethnic group that generally holds liberal political positions, but she also belongs to a business community that frequently holds conservative political positions, particularly on economic issues. When it comes time to vote, she is subjected to conflicting pressures.

Ambivalence and conflict can arise from within the person as well. When the affective and cognitive components of an attitude are not consistent—for example, when we like something that we know is bad for us—it is often difficult to predict behavior (Norman, 1975). In general, when the components of an attitude are clear and consistent, they better predict behavior (Millar & Tesser, 1989).

ATTITUDES SPECIFICALLY RELATED TO BEHAVIOR

Another finding is that attitudes that are specifically related to the behavior being assessed predict the behavior better than attitudes that are only generally related to it. For example, in one study students in the United States, Britain, and Sweden were asked both about their general attitudes toward nuclear war and about their specific attitudes toward nuclear war, nuclear weapons, and nuclear power plants. Specific attitudes were much better predictors of activist behaviors (such as writing a letter to a newspaper or signing a petition) than more general attitudes (Newcomb, Rabow, & Hernandez, 1992).

ATTITUDES BASED ON DIRECT EXPERIENCE

Attitudes based on direct experience predict behavior better than attitudes formed from reading or hearing about an issue (Fazio, 1990). For example, during a housing shortage at a university, many freshmen had to spend the first few weeks of the term in crowded temporary housing. Researchers measured students' attitudes toward the housing crisis and their willingness to sign and distribute petitions or join committees to study it. For students who actually had to live in the temporary housing, there was a high correlation between their attitude toward the crisis and their willingness to take action to solve it. But for students who had not directly experienced the temporary housing, no such correlation existed (Regan & Fazio, 1977).

AWARENESS

Finally, there is evidence that people who are more aware of their attitudes are more likely to behave in ways that are consistent with those attitudes. This is true of people who are generally more focused on their thoughts and feelings as part of their personalities (Scheier, Buss, & Buss, 1978), as well as of people who are placed in situations designed to make them more aware, such as in front of a mirror or video camera (Carver & Scheier, 1981; Hutton & Baumeister, 1992; Pryor et al., 1977).

◆ Interim Summary

- Attitudes are likes and dislikes—favorable or unfavorable evaluations of and reactions to objects, people, events, or ideas. Attitudes have a cognitive component, an affective component, and a behavioral component.

- The elaboration likelihood model states that persuasion can take two routes in producing belief and attitude change: the central route, in which the individual responds to the substantive arguments of a communication, and the peripheral route, in which the individual responds to non-content cues in a communication (such as the number of arguments) or to context cues (such as the credibility of the communicator or the pleasantness of the surroundings).

- A communication about an issue of personal relevance is more likely to generate thoughts in response to the communication's substantive arguments. When an issue is of little personal relevance or people are unwilling or unable to respond to the substantive content of a communication, they tend to use simple heuristics—rules of thumb—to judge the merits of the communication.

- Attitudes tend to predict behavior best when they are (1) strong and consistent, (2) specifically related to the behavior being predicted, and (3) based on the person's direct experience, as well as (4) when the individual is aware of his or her attitudes.

◆ Critical Thinking Questions

1. Suppose you are running for political office. What sort of television ad should you design if you suspect that your audience will be distracted? What sort of ad should you design if you suspect that your audience will be motivated to think deeply? Can you appeal to both audiences in the same ad?

2. Many young people are addicted to shopping at the expense of other interests. Based on what you now know about attitude change and the links between attitudes and behavior, identify at least two ways that you could prevent your younger sister from spending all of her time and money shopping for the latest advertised fashions.

INTERPERSONAL ATTRACTION

In our discussion of attitudes, we distinguished between the cognitive and affective components—thinking and feeling. There is, however, no area of human behavior in which cognitions and affects are intertwined in a more complex way than in interpersonal attraction: liking, loving, and sexual desire. Research in these areas has often confirmed common knowledge, but it has also produced a number of surprises and contradictions. We begin with liking—namely, friendship and the early stages of more intimate relationships.

LIKING AND ATTRACTION

We cannot all be beautiful film stars, but when two such people become a couple, they do illustrate several of the determinants of interpersonal attraction that apply even to us ordinary mortals: physical attractiveness, proximity, familiarity, and similarity. As the high divorce rate among contemporary couples also illustrates, however, these factors are not always sufficient to sustain a long-term relationship.

PHYSICAL ATTRACTIVENESS To most of us, there is something mildly undemocratic about the possibility that a person's physical appearance is a determinant of how well others like him or her. Unlike character and personality, physical appearance is a factor over which we seemingly have little control, and so it seems unfair to use it as a criterion for liking someone. In fact, surveys conducted over a span of several decades have shown that people do not rank physical attractiveness as very important in their liking of other people (Buss & Barnes, 1986; Hudson & Hoyt, 1981; Perrin, 1921; Tesser & Brodie, 1971).

But research on actual behavior shows otherwise (Brehm, 1992). One group of psychologists set up a "computer dance" in which college men and women were randomly paired. At intermission, everyone filled out an anonymous questionnaire evaluating his or her date. In addition, the experimenters obtained several personality test scores for each person, as well as an independent estimate of his or her physical attractiveness. The results showed that only physical attractiveness played a role in how much the person was liked by his or her partner. None of the measures of intelligence, social skills, or personality was related to the partners' liking for each other (Walster, Aronson, Abrahams, & Rottman, 1966). This experiment has been replicated many times, and in each case the results have been similar to those just described. Moreover, the importance of physical attractiveness has been found to operate not only on first dates but on subsequent dates (Mathes, 1975) and in marriages (Margolin & White, 1987) as well.

Why is physical attractiveness so important? Part of the reason is that our social standing and self-esteem are enhanced when we are seen with physically attractive companions. Both men and women are rated more favorably when they are with an attractive romantic partner or friend than when they are with an unattractive companion (Sheposh, Deming, & Young, 1977; Sigall & Landy, 1973). But there is an interesting twist to this: Both men and women are rated less favorably when they are seen with a stranger who is physically more attractive than they are (Kernis & Wheeler, 1981). Apparently they suffer by comparison with the other person. This effect has been found in other studies. For example, male college students who had just watched a television show starring beautiful young women gave lower attractiveness ratings to a photograph of a more typical-looking woman (Kendrick & Gutierres, 1980).

Fortunately, there is hope for the unbeautiful among us. First of all, physical attractiveness appears to decline in importance when a permanent partner is being chosen (Stroebe, Insko, Thompson, & Layton, 1971). And, as we will see, several other factors can work in our favor.

PROXIMITY An examination of 5,000 marriage license applications in Philadelphia in the 1930s found that one-third of the couples lived within five blocks of each other (Rubin, 1973). Research shows that the best single predictor of whether two people are friends is **proximity,** or how far apart they live. In a study of friendship patterns in apartment houses, residents were asked to name the three people they saw socially most often. Residents mentioned 41% of neighbors who lived in the apartment next door, 22% of those who lived two doors away (about 30 feet), and only 10% of those who lived at the other end of the hall (Festinger, Schachter, & Back, 1950). Studies of college dormitories show the same effect. After a full academic year, roommates were twice as likely as floormates to be friends, and floormates were more than twice as likely as dormitory residents in general to be friends (Priest & Sawyer, 1967).

There are cases, of course, in which neighbors and roommates hate one another, and the major exception to the friendship-promoting effect of proximity seems to occur when there are initial antagonisms. In a test of this, a participant waited in a laboratory with a female confederate who treated the participant pleasantly or unpleasantly. When she was pleasant, the closer she sat to the participant, the better she was liked; when she was unpleasant, the closer she sat to the participant, the less she was liked. Proximity simply increased the intensity of the initial reaction (Schiffenbauer & Schiavo, 1976). But because most initial encounters probably range from neutral to pleasant, the most frequent result of sustained proximity is friendship.

Those who believe in miracles when it comes to matters of the heart may believe that there is a perfect mate chosen for each of us waiting to be discovered somewhere in the world. But if this is true, the far greater miracle is the frequency with which fate conspires to place this person within walking distance.

FAMILIARITY One of the major reasons that proximity creates liking is that it increases familiarity, and there is now abundant evidence for what is called the **mere exposure effect,** the finding that familiarity all by itself increases

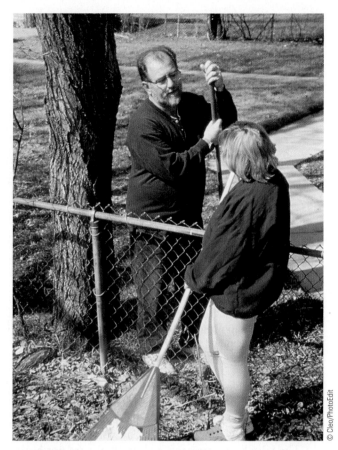

These neighbors are likely to form a friendship simply because of proximity.

liking (Zajonc, 1968). This familiarity-breeds-liking effect is a very general phenomenon. For example, rats repeatedly exposed to the music of either Mozart or Schoenberg enhance their liking for the composer they have heard, and humans repeatedly exposed to selected nonsense syllables or Chinese characters come to prefer those they have seen most often. The effect occurs even when individuals are unaware that they have been previously exposed to the stimuli (Bornstein, 1992; Bornstein & D'Agostino, 1992; Moreland & Zajonc, 1979; Wilson, 1979). More germane to the present discussion is a study in which participants were exposed to pictures of faces and then asked how much they thought they would like the person shown. The more frequently they had seen a particular face, the more they said they liked it and thought they would like the person (Zajonc, 1968) (see Figure 18-5). Similar results are obtained when individuals are exposed to one another in real life (Moreland & Beach, 1992).

In one clever demonstration of the mere exposure effect, the investigators took photographs of college women and then prepared prints of both the original face and its mirror image. These prints were then shown to the women themselves, their female friends, and their lovers. The

© Cleo/PhotoEdit

▌Figure 18-5
Familiarity Breeds Liking
People were asked to rate photographs of unknown faces according to how much they thought they would like the person. The lowest ratings of liking were made by those who had never seen the photograph before; the highest ratings of liking were made by those who had seen the photograph most often. This illustrates the mere exposure effect. (After Zajonc, 1968)

women themselves preferred the mirror-image prints by a margin of 68% to 32%, but the friends and lovers preferred the nonreversed prints by a margin of 61% to 39% (Mita, Dermer, & Knight, 1977). Can you guess why?

The take-home message is clear. If you are not beautiful or you find your admiration of someone unreciprocated, be persistent and hang around. Proximity and familiarity are your most powerful weapons.

SIMILARITY An old saying declares that opposites attract, and lovers are fond of recounting how different they are from each other: "I love boating, but she prefers mountain climbing." "I'm in engineering, but he's a history major." What such lovers overlook is that they both like outdoor activities; they are both preprofessionals; they are both Democrats; they are both the same nationality, the same religion, the same social class, and the same educational level; and they are within 3 years of each other in age and within 5 IQ points of each other in intelligence. In short, the old saying is mostly false.

Research dating all the way back to 1870 supports this conclusion. More than 95% of the married couples in the United States are of the same race, and most are of the same religion. Moreover, statistical surveys show that husbands and wives are significantly similar to each other not only in sociological characteristics—such as age, race, religion, education, and socioeconomic class—but also with respect to psychological characteristics like intelligence and physical characteristics such as height and eye color (Rubin, 1973). A study of dating couples finds the same patterns, in addition to finding that cou-

ples were also similar in their attitudes about sexual behavior and sex roles. Moreover, couples who were most similar in background at the beginning of the study were most likely to be together a year later (Hill, Rubin, & Peplau, 1976). Of particular pertinence to our earlier discussion is the finding that couples are closely matched on physical attractiveness as well (Feingold, 1988).

For example, in one study, judges rated photographs of each partner of 99 couples for physical attractiveness without knowing who was paired with whom. The physical attractiveness ratings of the couples matched each other significantly more closely than did the ratings of photographs that were randomly paired into couples (Murstein, 1972). Similar results were obtained in a real-life field study in which separate observers rated the physical attractiveness of members of couples in bars and theater lobbies and at social events (Silverman, 1971).

This matching of couples on physical attractiveness appears to come about because we weigh a potential partner's attractiveness against the probability that the person would be willing to pair up with us. Put bluntly, less attractive people seek less attractive partners because they expect to be rejected by someone more attractive than themselves. A study of a video dating service found that both men and women were most likely to pursue a relationship with someone who matched them in physical attractiveness. Only the most attractive people sought dates with the most attractive partners (Folkes, 1982). The overall result of this process is attractiveness similarity: Most of us end up with partners who are about as attractive as we are.

But similarities on dimensions other than physical attractiveness are probably even more important over the long-term course of a relationship. A longitudinal study of 135 married couples found that spouses who were more similar to each other in personality also resembled each other more in terms of how much they enjoyed similar daily activities like visiting friends, going out for dinner, and participating in community activities and professional meetings. These couples also reported less marital conflict and greater closeness, friendliness, and marital satisfaction than less similar spouses (Caspi & Herbener, 1990).

In an ambitious study of similarity and friendship, male students received free room for the year in a large house at the University of Michigan in exchange for their participation. On the basis of information from tests and questionnaires, some men were assigned roommates who were quite similar to them, and others were assigned roommates who were quite dissimilar. The investigator observed the friendship patterns that developed over the course of the year and obtained more questionnaire and attitude data from the participants at regular intervals. In all other respects, the men lived as they would in any dormitory.

Partners in successful long-term relationships tend to be similar to each other in characteristics such as age, race, and education, as well as in their interests, personality traits, and even physical attractiveness.

Roommates who were initially similar generally liked each other and ended up as better friends than those who were dissimilar. When the study was repeated with a new group of men the next year, however, the familiarity-breeds-liking effect turned out to be even more powerful than similarity. Regardless of whether low or high similarity had been the basis for room assignments, roommates came to like each other (Newcomb, 1961).

One possible reason that similarity produces liking is that people value their own opinions and preferences and enjoy being with others who validate their choices, boosting their self-esteem in the process. But perhaps the major reason that similarity produces liking is that both social norms and situational circumstances throw us together with people who are like us. Most religious groups prefer (or insist) that their members date and mate within the religion, and cultural norms regulate what is considered acceptable in terms of race and age matches—a couple comprising an older woman and a younger man is still viewed as inappropriate. Situational circumstances also play an important role. Many couples meet in college or graduate school, thus ensuring that they will be similar in educational level, general intelligence, and professional aspirations, and probably in age and socioeconomic status. Moreover, tennis players will have met on the tennis courts, political liberals at a pro-choice rally, and gay people at a gay pride parade or a meeting of the Lesbian, Gay, and Bisexual Task Force.

Despite all this, it is often suggested that the saying that opposites attract may still apply to certain comple-mentary personality traits (Winch, Ktsanes, & Ktsanes, 1954). To take the most obvious example, one partner may be quite dominant and therefore require someone who is relatively more submissive. A person with strong preferences may do best with someone who is very flexible or even wishy-washy. But despite the plausibility of this complementarity hypothesis, there is not much evidence for it (Levinger, Senn, & Jorgensen, 1970). In one study, marital adjustment among couples who had been married for up to 5 years was found to depend more on similarity than on complementarity (Meyer & Pepper, 1977). Attempts to identify the pairs of personality traits that bring about complementarity have not been very successful (Strong et al., 1988).

TRANSFERENCE In Chapter 16, you learned about transference, or the tendency for clients to transfer their feelings and assumptions about a particular significant other—like their parent or spouse—onto their therapist. Recent work from a social cognitive perspective applies the concept of **transference** more generally, arguing that any time we encounter someone new who reminds us of someone who has been important to us in our past, that sense of recognition influences our perceptions—and indeed our liking—of the new person (Chen & Andersen, 1999). The approach follows the tradition of social cognition because it holds that simply being reminded of someone who has been significant to us in the past automatically activates stored knowledge—or schemas—about that significant other. This, in turn, leads us to process information about the newly encountered person in ways consistent with the activated schema.

Laboratory experiments have tested the influence of transference on interpersonal liking. In one study, participants were tested twice. In a pretest session, they identified two of their significant others—one whom they felt good about and one they disliked—and provided several short descriptions of them ("Terry is sincere" or "Pat likes to go dancing"). More than 2 weeks later, these same participants were tested again. This time, they learned about a new person—supposedly seated next door—with whom they would soon interact. The descriptions of this new person were rigged to resemble participants' significant others by mirroring some of the descriptions gathered in the pretest phase. For one experimental group, the new person resembled a liked significant other. For another experimental group, the new person resembled a disliked significant other. To control for the valence of the descriptions used, each was given to another participant as well. For these control groups, the description of the new person resembled somebody else's significant other, not their own. The results are shown in Figure 18-6. When a new person resembled a significant other, he or she is liked or disliked, depending on the participant's attitude toward the significant other—participants even smiled more when the new

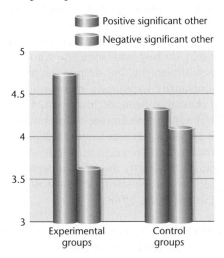

▌ Figure 18-6
Transference in Interpersonal Attraction
How much participants liked a new acquaintance depended on whether that new person shared characteristics with the participants' significant others and whether they held positive or negative attitudes about those significant others. Notice that evaluations were more extreme when new acquaintances resembled a participant's own significant other (the experimental groups) than when they resembled someone else's significant other (the control groups). (From S. Chen & S. M. Andersen (1999), "Relationships from the past in the present: significant-other representations and transference in interpersonal life," in *Advances in Experimental Social Psychology, 31,* 123–190. Copyright © 1999, Elsevier Science (USA), reproduced by permission of the publisher.)

person resembled their significant other! Additional experiments using this same procedure confirm that this effect of transference on liking is carried by activated schemas. As we learned at the start of this chapter (and in Chapter 8), schemas can be activated (or primed) automatically and, once activated, they influence various aspects of information processing, including memory and inferences. Our schemas for significant others, when triggered by new acquaintances who in some way resemble them, produce all the cognitive and behavioral effects that social psychologists have come to expect (Chen & Andersen, 1999).

The take-home message here is that if you want to forge a new friendship or relationship, and not merely recycle an old one, you need to start with a new acquaintance who is like no other. And you should be cautious when someone approaches you and says, "You remind me of someone."

LOVING AND MATING

Love is more than just strong liking. Most of us know people we like very much but do not love, and some of us have felt passionate attraction for someone we did not particularly like. Research confirms these everyday observations. One of the first researchers to study romantic love compiled a number of statements that people thought reflected liking and loving and then constructed separate scales to measure each (Rubin, 1973). Items on the liking scale tap the degree to which the other person is regarded as likable, respected, admired, and having maturity and good judgment. Items on the love scale tap three main themes: a sense of attachment ("It would be hard for me to get along without _____"), a sense of caring for the other person ("I would do almost anything for _____"), and a sense of trust ("I feel that I can confide in _____ about virtually everything"). The two scales are only moderately correlated: .56 for men and .36 for women.

LOVE AND MARRIAGE The concept of romantic love is an old one, but the belief that it has much to do with marriage is more recent and far from universal. In some non-Western cultures, marriage is still considered to be a contractual or financial arrangement that has nothing to do with love. In the United States, the link between love and marriage has actually become stronger over the past 30 years. In 1967, U.S. college students were asked, "If a man (woman) had all the other qualities you desired, would you marry this person if you were not in love with him (her)?" About 65% of the men said no, but only 24% of the women said no (only 4% actually said yes; the majority of the women were undecided) (Kephart, 1967). The women's movement had just begun at that time, and it may be that women were more likely than they are now to consider marriage necessary for financial security.

When the survey was repeated in 1984, 85% of both men and women said that they would refuse to marry without being in love (Simpson, Campbell, & Berscheid, 1986).

LOVE AND SELF-EXPANSION Why do people fall in love? Why do they forge close, loving relationships? At one level, the answer is obvious—because love feels good! But then you could ask, why does love feel good? Some social psychologists have suggested that a primary motivation for falling in love lies in the urge to expand the self (Aron, Norman, & Aron, 1998). Close relationships are said to produce **self-expansion**—or increase our potential abilities and resources—in multiple ways. As we become close to another person, we gain access to that person's resources, perspectives, and identities—this might include someone's circle of friends, cooking skills, views on politics or religion, or popularity more generally—each of which can help us to achieve our own goals. People are motivated to expand the self, the reasoning continues, not only to become more able themselves but also because self-expansion, particularly rapid expanding, is exhilarating. So falling in love feels good, this logic suggests, because it produces rapid self-expansion.

The researchers tested the association between falling in love and self-expansion by targeting a large group of first-year college students over the fall semester. Every 2 weeks for 10 weeks, these students answered the question, "Who are you today?" by listing as many self-descriptive words or phrases as came to mind in a 3-minute period. They also answered a number of other questions, including whether they had fallen in love since the last testing session. First-year college students, it so happens, have a very high chance of falling in love in their first semester—a full one-third of them do! (Aron, 2002). This large sample of those "lucky in love" enabled the researchers to compare self-descriptions made just prior to falling in love to those made just after. The comparisons provided clear evidence of self-expansion: The diversity of self-descriptions increased significantly after falling in love, an effect that could not be attributed to positive mood. (The self-descriptions of those unlucky in love provided an additional comparison for the degree of change that might be expected in the absence of love; Aron, Norman, & Aron, 1998.)

A corollary to the notion that love produces self-expansion is the claim that within close relationships, people tend to think about their beloved in the same manner in which they think of the self. That is, the close other becomes fused—even confused—with the self. One study tested the idea that we "include the other in the self" by asking married participants to choose as quickly and accurately as possible whether each of a large set of personality traits was "me" or "not me." Based on prior testing, the researchers knew that some of those traits were true of the participant's self but not true of their spouse, or true of the spouse but not true of the self. As expected, participants were slower to respond—and made more errors—for traits on which they and their spouse differed (Aron, Aron, Tudor, & Nelson, 1991). So, for instance, if you are not particularly gracious, but your beloved is, when faced with deciding whether the term *gracious* describes you, you get confused. It takes you a moment to sort out that even though you benefit from your beloved's graciousness, you are not actually gracious yourself! But this confusion is a good thing. Other research has shown that the extent to which couples "include the other in the self" on a simple pictorial measure (see Figure 18-7) predicts how long they will stay together (Aron, Aron, & Smollen, 1992).

PASSIONATE AND COMPANIONATE LOVE Several social scientists have attempted to distinguish among different kinds of love. One of the most widely accepted distinctions is between passionate and companionate love (Hatfield, 1988; Peele, 1988).

Passionate love is defined as an intensely emotional state in which "tender and sexual feelings, elation and pain, anxiety and relief, altruism and jealousy coexist in a confusion of feelings" (Berscheid & Walster, 1974, p. 177). It has been suggested that the experience of passionate love combines physiological arousal with the perception that the arousal is evoked by the beloved (Berscheid & Walster, 1974).

In contrast, **companionate love** is defined as "the affection we feel for those with whom our lives are deeply

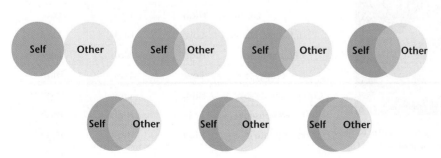

❚ Figure 18-7
Including the Other in the Self
People are asked to circle the picture that best describes their relationship. Research has found that the degree to which people include the other in the self predicts how long a relationship will last. (Fig. 1, p. 597, from A. Aron, E. N. Aron, & D. Smollan (1992), "Inclusion of other in the self scale and the structure of interpersonal closeness," in *Journal of Personality and Social Psychology*, 63, 596–612. Copyright © 1992 by the American Psychological Association. Reprinted with permission.)

intertwined" (Hatfield, 1988, p. 205). The characteristics of companionate love are trust, caring, tolerance of the partner's flaws and idiosyncrasies, and an emotional tone of warmth and affection rather than high-pitched emotional passion. As a relationship continues over time, interdependence grows, and the potential for strong emotion actually increases. This can be seen when long-time partners experience intense feelings of loneliness and desire when temporarily separated or in the emotional devastation typically experienced by someone who loses a long-time partner. But, paradoxically, because companionate couples become so compatible and coordinated in their daily routines, the actual frequency of strong emotions is usually fairly low (Berscheid, 1983).

Many of the young men and women in the survey cited earlier stated that if love disappears from a marriage, that is sufficient reason to end it. Those who equate love with passionate love, however, are likely to be disappointed. Most successful long-term couples emphasize the companionate elements of their relationship, and both theory and research suggest that the intense feelings that characterize passionate love are unlikely to persist over time (Berscheid, 1983; Solomon & Corbit, 1974). As the 16th-century writer Giraldi put it, "The history of a love affair is in some sense the drama of its fight against time."

This point is illustrated in a study that compared long-term marriages in the United States—where couples claim to marry for love—with marriages in Japan that had been arranged by the couples' parents. As expected, the American marriages started out with a higher level of expressed love and sexual interest than the Japanese marriages. But the amount of love expressed decreased in both groups until after 10 years there were no differences between the two groups. Nevertheless, many couples in this study reported quite gratifying marriages, marriages that had evolved into a deep companionate love characterized by communication between the partners, an equitable division of labor, and equality of decision-making power (Blood, 1967).

In later life the passionate component of romantic love tends to become less important than the companionate component.

The take-home message is that passionate love might be terrific for starters, but the sustaining forces of a good long-term relationship are less exciting, require more work, and have more to do with equality than with passion. In fact, as we will see shortly, there may even be a built-in incompatibility between passionate and companionate love.

THE TRIANGULAR THEORY OF LOVE Other researchers find the strategy of dichotomizing love into two kinds—passionate and companionate—to be too simplistic. One of the more differentiated classifications offered is the **triangular theory of love**. It divides love into three components: intimacy, passion, and commitment (Sternberg, 1986). **Intimacy** is the emotional component and involves closeness and sharing of feelings. **Passion**, the motivational component, consists of sexual attraction and the romantic feeling of being "in love." **Commitment** is the cognitive component; it reflects the intention to remain in the relationship. Combining these three components in different ways yields the eight kinds of relationships shown in Table 18-2. As can be seen, in this scheme passionate love is split into two types: infatuated love and romantic love. Both are characterized by high passion and low commitment, but infatuated love is low in intimacy whereas romantic love is high in intimacy. Companionate love is characterized by high intimacy and commitment but low passion.

PAIR BONDING AND MATING STRATEGIES One of the newest approaches to romantic and sexual attraction is also one of the oldest: Darwin's theory of evolution. As noted in Chapter 1, evolutionary psychology is concerned with the origins of psychological mechanisms. The key idea is that, just like biological mechanisms, psy-

● **Table 18-2**
The Triangular Theory of Love

The three dimensions of love combine to produce eight types of love relationships. *(R. Sternberg (1986), "Triangular Theory of Love," in* Psychological Review, *93:119–135. Copyright © 1986 by the American Psychological Association. Adapted by permission.)*

	Intimacy	Passion	Commitment
Nonlove	Low	Low	Low
Liking	High	Low	Low
Infatuated love	Low	High	Low
Romantic love	High	High	Low
Empty love	Low	Low	High
Companionate love	High	Low	High
Fatuous love	Low	High	High
Consummate love	High	High	High

chological mechanisms must have evolved over millions of years through a process of natural selection. They therefore have a genetic basis and have proved useful to the human species in the past for solving some problems of survival or increasing the chances of reproducing.

The renewed interest in evolution among social psychologists has led to a (sometimes controversial) reexamination of several behavioral phenomena. Among these are pair bonding in humans and differences between men and women in sexual behavior and mating strategies.

From an evolutionary perspective, men and women mate to produce offspring who will pass their genes along to future generations. To do this, individuals must solve several problems, including (1) winning out over competitors in gaining access to fertile members of the other sex, (2) selecting mates with the greatest reproductive potential, (3) engaging in the necessary social and sexual behavior to achieve conception, (4) preventing the mate from defecting or deserting, and (5) ensuring the survival and reproductive success of one's offspring (Buss, 1994). According to evolutionary psychologists, humans have evolved to form intense, long-term bonds with a partner to ensure that human offspring survive to reproductive age. As noted in Chapter 3, the more complex an organism's nervous system, the longer the time required to reach maturity. A chimpanzee will be a functioning adult member of its species years before a human of the same age is ready to fend for itself. Accordingly, in the history of our species it has been important to have both parents stick around to defend, provide for, and help rear the young. In contrast to humans, both male and female chimpanzees are quite promiscuous, and males have little or no involvement in rearing the young.

Evolutionary psychology further argues that because men and women play different roles in reproduction, the mating tactics and strategies used by the two sexes might also have evolved to be different as well. Because it is theoretically possible for a man to father hundreds of children, it is to his evolutionary advantage to impregnate as many women as possible in order to pass along the greatest number of his own genes. The woman, however, must invest a great deal of time and energy in each birth and can have only a limited number of offspring. It is to her advantage to select a mate who is most willing and best able to assist in protecting and raising her children, thereby maximizing the likelihood of passing her genes along to future generations. This reasoning suggests that evolution would have made men more promiscuous and less discriminating in their choice of sexual partners than women. In fact, it has been documented repeatedly that in most societies men are more promiscuous than women, and societies that permit one man to mate with more than one woman far outnumber those in which one woman may mate with many different men (Wilson, 1978).

Evolutionary psychology also predicts that a man should prefer to mate with the most fertile young women available because they are most likely to bear his children. A woman should prefer to mate with a man of high social status and solid material resources, one who can give the children the best chance of surviving to adulthood and reproducing in their turn. As a result, evolutionary psychologists predict that men will prefer younger women (with many more fertile years ahead of them), whereas women will prefer older men (who have more resources). This sex difference in mate preference was strongly confirmed in a study of 37 different cultures (Buss, 1989), and is summarized one of the Seeing Both Sides essays at the end of this chapter.

Evolutionary psychology has not gone unchallenged. (See the other Seeing Both Sides essay!) Some critics argue that even if a behavioral pattern appears across many or all cultures, it does not necessarily follow that it is programmed into the genes. For example, some universal cross-cultural sex differences may have arisen simply because women had less upper body strength than men and—until very recently in technological societies—were pregnant or nursing during most of their adult lives. This created sex-based divisions of labor in virtually all societies, which placed political power and decision making in the hands of men and confined women to the domestic sphere (Bem, 1993). Greater sexual freedom for men could easily emerge from such power differences.

It is often instructive to ask whether evolutionary reasoning could also have predicted a different or opposite outcome. For example, we have seen the argument that a male's ability to produce many hundreds of offspring would create an evolutionary push toward male promiscuity. But the need to ensure that one's offspring survive to reproductive age—the same need that presumably gave rise to human pair bonding in the first place—would provide an opposing evolutionary push toward monogamy. In other words, evolutionary theory could be invoked to explain either male promiscuity or male sexual fidelity.

Despite these criticisms, there is no doubt that evolutionary thinking has reinvigorated both personality and social psychology. There is probably no other single principle in the behavioral sciences with as much potential explanatory power as the principle of evolution. Moreover, the emergence of evolutionary psychology shows once again the important role of biological evidence in contemporary psychology. Even social psychologists who study the processes of social cognition now theorize about how and why our strategies for processing social information might have evolved (Nisbett & Ross, 1980; see also Buss & Kenrick, 1998).

Are the Origins of Gender Differences in Mate Selection Primarily Due to Evolution or Social Learning?

EVOLUTIONARY ORIGINS OF SEX DIFFERENCES IN MATE PREFERENCES

David M. Buss, University of Texas at Austin

Evolutionary psychology provides a powerful theoretical guide to identifying both commonalities and differences between men and women. The logic stems from understanding the *adaptive problems* the sexes have faced over the long course of human evolutionary history—problems of survival and reproduction. Both sexes have faced many similar survival problems—the need to select food, combat diseases, and fend off predators. Where men and women have confronted similar adaptive problems, evolutionary psychologists predict the sexes will be similar. Both sexes, for example, have similar taste preferences (e.g., sugar, protein, and fat) and similar fears (e.g., snakes).

In reproduction, however, the sexes have faced fundamentally different adaptive problems, and here we expect sex differences in adaptive solutions. Women, for example, bear the burdens and joys of a nine-month minimum obligatory investment (pregnancy) to produce a single child; men's minimum investment is as low as a few hours, a few minutes, or a few seconds.

Much evidence, emerging from varied data sources—self-reports, behavioral studies, and laboratory studies—confirms several sex differences predicted in advance by evolutionary psychologists. One pertains to choosiness. When approached by an opposite-sex stranger, 50% of women agreed to a date, 6% agreed to go back to his apartment, and 0% agreed to sex. In contrast, of the men approached by women, 50% agreed to a date, 69% agreed to go back to her apartment, and 75% agreed to sex (Clarke & Hatfield, 1989). This is one among hundreds of studies that document that women are more selective and discriminating in short-term mating contexts (Buss, 2003). This psychological sex difference stems from a long evolutionary history of an asymmetry between the sexes in parental investment.

Humans, unlike most other primates, also pursue long-term mating. Because of women's heavy parental investment, they are predicted to value mates who are able and willing to invest resources in them and their children. In my study of 10,047 individuals in 37 cultures located on six continents and five islands, from coastal Australia to the Zulu tribe in South Africa, this prediction was soundly supported. Women placed a greater premium on a mate's financial resources, ambition, and industriousness. Women also desired spouses who were roughly three years older.

Sometimes an alternative explanation is proposed—women do not have an evolved desire for resourceful men, but rather are forced to prefer such men because they have been excluded from other means to economic resources (Buss & Barnes, 1986). Although reasonable, the available evidence fails to support it. Women living in more economically equal cultures, such as Sweden and Norway, show just as strong a desire for mates with resources as women in more economically unequal cultures such as Japan or Iran (Buss, 1989). Furthermore, women in the United States who are economically successful place even more emphasis on a man's resources. Although more tests are needed, the available evidence supports the hypothesis that women have an evolved desire for resourceful mates.

Another key sex difference stems from ovulation. Unlike most other primate females, who experience estrus cycles with large red genital swellings, women's ovulation evolved to be cryptic or concealed. This posed a unique adaptive problem for ancestral men—how to identify fertile women in the absence of obvious estrus cues. According to one evolutionary hypothesis, men evolved to value certain features of physical appearance because appearance provides a wealth of cues to a woman's age and health, and hence to her fertility. The 37-culture study supports this explanation. Men worldwide, from Zambia to Austria, value women who are young and physically attractive, precisely as predicted.

Although these findings and their evolutionary explanations are upsetting to some people, there are three important qualifications. First, discoveries that men and women have evolved psychological differences does not justify discrimination based on sex, nor does it excuse behavior some consider immoral, such as sexual infidelity. Second, neither men nor women can be considered superior or inferior; each sex has evolved adaptations to solve its own unique problems. Third, in most psychological domains, the sexes are similar since both sexes have faced similar adaptive problems, such as identifying who will be a good long-term cooperator. Both sexes equally value a potential mate's intelligence, kindness, dependability, creativity, and adaptability. And both sexes in all 37 cultures place a premium on love and mutual attraction, which may be evolution's way of bringing the sexes together over the long term to transcend whatever differences they display.

Are the Origins of Gender Differences in Mate Selection Primarily Due to Evolution or Social Learning?

THE INFLUENCE OF SOCIAL LEARNING AND SOCIAL ROLES ON MATE SELECTION

Janet S. Hyde, University of Wisconsin, Madison

A man's attraction to a woman is, on average, powerfully determined by her physical appearance. Women, too, are attracted to good-looking men but, on average, physical appearance is less important to women (Feingold, 1990). Women are more likely to take other characteristics of men such as success—into account in their attractions. Furthermore, men prefer women who are younger than themselves, and women prefer men who are slightly older than they are. Why do these differences occur?

The answer lies in social roles and social learning. Let's first consider social roles, specifically gender roles (Eagly & Wood, 1999). One key feature of gender roles in American society, as in most other societies around the world, is that women have less power and status than men. In the United States, women earn only 75 cents for every dollar that men earn. Women are sparsely represented in the seats of power such as the U.S. Senate and House of Representatives. In a study of *Fortune 500* companies, only 12 percent of corporate officers and fewer than 1 percent of CEOs were women (Wellington & Giscombe, 2001). A second key feature of gender roles in American society is the gendered division of labor, both in paid work and in home work. Most occupations are highly gender segregated. For example, only 3.4 percent of airline pilots are women, as are 1.2 percent of carpenters.

Janet Hyde

Only 2.9 percent of childcare workers are men, as are only 1.9 percent of dental assistants (Costello & Stone, 2001). Women and men, even today, occupy quite different roles. Given the wage gap and women's lesser access to high-paid, high-status occupations, is it any wonder that women, on average, are attracted to men who are successful and earn more? They literally can't afford to do otherwise. Or is it any wonder that men do not take into account women's occupational success or earnings?

A key aspect of the female role is beauty and heterosexual attractiveness. Women's beauty is highly visible in American society and is used to sell everything from mattresses to sportscars. Girls quickly learn that they should be beautiful, and boys learn that they should be associated with beautiful girls. Gender roles also specify that certain age pairings are acceptable. When ads or TV programs show silver-haired men, they are often paired with romantic partners who are much younger than they are. Have you ever seen the reverse pairing?

How and why does each new generation of children generally adopt behaviors that are consistent with gender roles? The answer lies in social learning, particularly reinforcement, punishment, and modeling (Bussey & Bandura, 1999). Gender-role violations typically receive severe punishments, particularly in adolescent culture. Suppose that Ernie, a high school sophomore, invites Ellen, who is pleasant and friendly, to the class dance. Because she is not good looking, Ernie's friends tease him mercilessly for dating a "dog." Ernie won't make that mistake again. Justin, one of Ernie's friends, observed what happened and Justin will be careful to invite only good-looking girls to dances in the fu-

ture. According to cognitive social learning theory, Justin only needed to observe Ernie's punishment to learn that boys shouldn't date unattractive girls.

Any good psychological theory should be able to specify the processes or mechanisms that produce the behaviors it seeks to explain. One of the problems with evolutionary psychology is that it does not specify mechanisms. The theory simply says there was evolutionary selection for a predisposition to this behavior and that is why it is present in modern culture. But evolution affects behavior only if genetic factors influence the behavior. Evolution acts through genes. Genes, in turn, have their effect by directing the synthesis of various biochemicals in the body, such as hormones and neurotransmitters. None of this is specified in evolutionary psychology. In contrast, social learning theory tells us exactly the processes that produce human behavior that conforms to gender roles.

A problem with the evidence from evolutionary psychologists is that, although they may have data from many different cultures, all of those cultures have a gender-based division of labor, and the division of labor is generally quite similar to the one in the United States (Eagly & Wood, 1999)—that is, women have more responsibility for caring for the home and children, and men occupy positions of power. Therefore, in regard to gender roles, the other cultures may not be as different from ours as they at first appear.

Gender differences in attraction to romantic partners are quite clearly shaped by gender roles through the process of social learning by reinforcements, punishments, and modeling.

◆ Interim Summary

- Many factors influence whether we will be attracted to a particular individual. The most important are physical attractiveness, proximity, familiarity, similarity, and transference.

- Theorists have suggested that one reason people fall in love is that doing so expands the self.

- There have been several attempts to classify types of love. Passionate love is characterized by intense and often conflicting emotions, whereas companionate love is characterized by trust, caring, tolerance of the partner's flaws, and an emotional tone of warmth and affection. Another classification of love divides it into the components of intimacy, passion, and commitment.

- Evolutionary psychology suggests that humans have evolved to form long-term bonds with a partner because historically such pair bonds operated to ensure the survival of offspring to reproductive age. A more controversial hypothesis from evolutionary psychology is that men and women have evolved to pursue different mating strategies, with men evolving to be more promiscuous and seek out younger women.

◆ Critical Thinking Questions

1. Proximity most often leads to liking because proximity creates familiarity. But why does familiarity—or mere exposure—lead to liking? Provide some possible explanations.

2. Which of the three components of love featured in Sternberg's triangular theory of love is most likely to be associated with self-expansion? Justify your choice.

RECAP: A TALE OF TWO MODES OF SOCIAL COGNITION

The major lesson of this chapter is that, in addition to understanding the power of social situations (the major lesson of Chapter 17), to more fully understand people's social behavior we also need to "get inside their heads" and examine how they think about others. The field of social cognition takes this task on. It examines the processes by which stereotypes and other social schemas become activated and affect people's thinking and behavior. It also examines the processes by which people can get beyond stereotypes to more accurately know one another. And it examines the processes by which people are persuaded to change their minds and even fall in love.

Across these many domains of study, social psychologists have repeatedly found that social cognition—or thinking about others—happens in two modes: One mode is more automatic and outside of conscious awareness, and the other is more effortful and deliberate. This recognition has produced a range of "dual-process theories" within social psychology. Two theories that received the spotlight in this chapter—the continuum model of impression formation (see Figure 18-2) and the elaboration likelihood model of persuasion (see pages 660–662)—illustrate dual-process perspectives, but there are many other renditions (see Chaiken & Trope, 1999). Recognizing these two modes of thinking helps us better understand and even alter social outcomes. To the extent that we are able and willing to engage in effortful thinking, we can curb stereotyping, avert peripheral routes to persuasion, and minimize transference. But when, for whatever reasons, we are unable engage in effortful thought—perhaps because we're busy carrying on a conversation, conducting an interview, or trying to manage the impression others form of us—we are more susceptible to various forms of automatic social cognition and behavior.

◆ Critical Thinking Questions

1. We all succumb to stereotyping others at times. Identify a time when you stereotyped someone. Now examine the circumstances. Were there situational forces that pulled for automatic thinking? What conditions would have been required for you to engage in effortful thinking?

2. Think of a time when someone tried to persuade you to her or his opinion, but you resisted. Considering the persuasion attempt, was that person expecting you to be in an automatic or deliberate mode of thinking? In actuality, was your thinking automatic or deliberate?

1. Social cognition is the study of people's subjective interpretations of their social experiences, as well as their modes of thinking about the social world. Two different modes of thinking have been found to be critical within social cognition: one more automatic and unintentional, often outside conscious awareness, and another more controlled and deliberate, of which we are fully aware.

2. Schematic processing is the perceiving and interpreting of incoming information in terms of simplified memory structures called *schemas*. Schemas are mini-theories about everyday objects and events. They allow us to process social information efficiently by permitting us to encode and remember only the unique or most prominent features of a new object or event. Stereotypes are schemas about groups of people.

3. Through repeated exposure, stereotypes can become habitual and automatic, operating outside conscious awareness.

4. Because schemas and stereotypes simplify reality, schematic processing produces biases and errors in our processing of social information. In forming impressions of other people, for example, we are prone to the primacy effect: The first information we receive evokes an initial schema and, hence, becomes more powerful in determining our impression than does later information. Schemas and stereotypes also govern our inferences.

5. Once activated, stereotypes can set in motion a chain of behavioral processes that serve to draw out from others behavior that confirms the initial stereotype, an effect called the *self-fulfilling prophecy*. This behavioral sequence can occur completely outside conscious awareness.

6. Stereotypes about the self can be self-fulfilling as well. Two explanations for the phenomenon have been offered: One refers to stereotype threat, the other to the principle of ideomotor action.

7. Individuation is the process of forming impressions of others by assessing their personal qualities on a person-by-person basis. The continuum model of impression formation details when and how people come to individuate others. Cooperative activities can promote individuation.

8. Although stereotypes are activated automatically, under the right conditions they can also be controlled through effortful thinking.

9. Attribution is the process by which we attempt to interpret and explain the behavior of other people—that is, to discern the causes of their actions. One major attribution task is to decide whether someone's action should be attributed to dispositional causes (the person's personality or attitudes) or to situational causes (social forces or other external circumstances). We tend to give too much weight to dispositional factors and too little to situational factors. This bias has been called the *fundamental attribution error*.

10. Ancient cultural practices and beliefs about the locus of causality are believed to have shaped contemporary cultural differences in styles of thinking. Research has shown repeatedly that East Asians think more holistically, whereas Westerners think analytically. This work challenges all claims to universality made about human cognition, both basic and social.

11. Attitudes are likes and dislikes—favorable or unfavorable evaluations of and reactions to objects, people, events, or ideas. Attitudes have a cognitive component, an affective component, and a behavioral component.

12. The elaboration likelihood model states that persuasion can take two routes in producing belief and attitude change: the central route, in which the individual responds to the substantive arguments of a communication, and the peripheral route, in which the individual responds to non-content cues in a communication (such as the number of arguments) or to context cues (such as the credibility of the communicator or the pleasantness of the surroundings). A communication about an issue of personal relevance is more likely to generate thoughts in response to the communication's substantive arguments. When an issue is of little personal relevance or people are unwilling or unable to respond to the substantive content of a communication, they tend to use simple heuristics—rules of thumb—to judge the merits of the communication.

13. Attitudes tend to predict behavior best when they are (1) strong and consistent, (2) specifically related to the behavior being predicted, and (3) based on the per-

son's direct experience, as well as (4) when the individual is aware of his or her attitudes.

14. Many factors influence whether we will be attracted to a particular individual. The most important are physical attractiveness, proximity, familiarity, similarity, and transference.

15. Theorists have suggested that one reason people fall in love is that doing so expands the self.

16. There have been several attempts to classify types of love. Passionate love is characterized by intense and often conflicting emotions, whereas companionate love is characterized by trust, caring, tolerance of the partner's flaws, and an emotional tone of warmth and affection. Even though passionate love decreases over time in long-term relationships, the potential for strong emotion actually increases. But because companionate couples become so compatible in their daily routines, the actual frequency of strong emotions is fairly low. Another classification of love divides it into the components of intimacy, passion, and commitment.

17. Evolutionary psychology suggests that humans have evolved to form long-term bonds with a partner because historically such pair bonds operated to ensure the survival of offspring to reproductive age. A more controversial hypothesis from evolutionary psychology is that men and women have evolved to pursue different mating strategies, with men evolving to be more promiscuous and seek out younger women.

CORE CONCEPTS

social cognition
schemas
schematic processing
stereotypes
self-schema
priming
primacy effect
inferences
self-fulfilling prophecy
stereotype threat
ideomotor action

individuation
continuum model
attribution
dispositional attribution
situational attribution
fundamental attribution error
holistic thought
analytic thought
attitudes
elaboration likelihood model
central route

peripheral route
proximity
mere exposure effect
transference
self-expansion
passionate love
companionate love
triangular theory of love
intimacy
passion
commitment

WEB RESOURCES

Take a quiz, try the activities and exercises, and explore web links.

http://www.socialpsychology.org/

Everything you ever wanted to know about social psychology and more! This huge warehouse of information offers a wide array of direct links, as well as a search engine to help you find exactly what you are looking for.

http://www.apa.org/pi/oema/racism/contents.html

This site from the American Psychological Association offers a frank discussion of racism and stereotypes.

 InfoTrac Online Library
**http://www.infotrac-college.com/
wadsworth**

Use InfoTrac College Edition to find popular and scientific articles by using the search terms below or your own relevant terms.

- Attribution
- Stereotype
- Transference

CD-ROM LINKS

  Psych Odyssey
Check out CD Chapter 13, Social Psychology: Personal Perspectives
A. Attribution Theory
B. Attraction, Liking, and Loving
C. Sternberg's Triangular Theory of Love

Psyk.trek 2.0
Check out CD Unit 12, Social Psychology
12a Attribution Processes
12b Theories of Love
12c Attitude Change
12d Prejudice

APPENDIX

STATISTICAL METHODS AND MEASUREMENT

DESCRIPTIVE STATISTICS

Frequency Distributions
Measures of Central Tendency
Measures of Variation

STATISTICAL INFERENCE

Populations and Samples
The Normal Distribution
Scaling of Data
How Representative Is a Mean?
The Significance of a Difference

THE COEFFICIENT OF CORRELATION

Product-Moment Correlation
Interpreting a Correlation Coefficient

Much of the work of psychologists calls for making measurements—either in the laboratory or under field conditions. This work may involve measuring the eye movements of infants when first exposed to a novel stimulus, recording the galvanic skin response of people under stress, counting the number of trials required to condition a monkey that has a prefrontal lobotomy, determining achievement test scores for students using computer-assisted learning, or counting the number of patients who show improvement following a particular type of psychotherapy. In all these examples, the *measurement operation* yields numbers; the psychologist's problem is to interpret them and to arrive at some general conclusions. Basic to this task is statistics—the discipline that deals with collecting numerical data and with making inferences from such data. The purpose of this appendix is to review certain statistical methods that play an important role in psychology.

This appendix is written on the assumption that the problems students have with statistics are essentially problems of clear thinking about data. An introductory acquaintance with statistics is not beyond the scope of anyone who understands enough algebra to use plus and minus signs and to substitute numbers for letters in equations.

DESCRIPTIVE STATISTICS

Statistics serves, first of all, to provide a shorthand description of large amounts of data. Suppose that we want to study the college entrance examination scores of 5,000 students recorded on cards in the registrar's office. These scores are the raw data. Thumbing through the cards will give us some impressions of the students' scores, but it will be impossible for us to keep all of them in mind. So we make some kind of summary of the data, possibly averaging all the scores or finding the highest and lowest scores. These statistical summaries make it easier to remember and to think about the data. Such summarizing statements are called *descriptive statistics*.

FREQUENCY DISTRIBUTIONS

Items of raw data become comprehensible when they are grouped in a *frequency distribution*. To group data, we must first divide the scale along which they are measured into intervals and then count the number of items that fall into each interval. An interval in which scores are grouped is called a *class interval*. The decision of how many class intervals the data are to be grouped into is not fixed by any rules but is based on the judgment of the investigator.

Table 1 provides a sample of raw data representing college entrance examination scores for 15 students. The scores are listed in the order in which the students were tested (the first student tested had a score of 84; the second, 61; and so on). Table 2 shows these data arranged in a frequency distribution for which the class interval has been set at 10. One score falls in the interval from 50 to 59, three scores fall in the interval from 60 to 69, and so on. Note that most scores fall in the interval from 70 to 79 and that no scores fall below the 50 to 59 interval or above the 90 to 99 interval.

A frequency distribution is often easier to understand if it is presented graphically. The most widely used graph form is the *frequency histogram*; an example is

● Table 1
Raw Scores

College entrance examination scores for 15 students, listed in the order in which they were tested.

84	75	91
61	75	67
72	87	79
75	79	83
77	51	69

● Table 2
A Frequency Distribution

Scores from Table 1, accumulated by class intervals.

Class Interval	Number of Persons in Class
50–59	1
60–69	3
70–79	7
80–89	3
90–99	1

shown in the top panel of Figure 1. Histograms are constructed by drawing bars, the bases of which are given by the class intervals and the heights of which are determined by the corresponding class frequencies. An alternative way of presenting frequency distributions in graph form is to use a *frequency polygon*, an example of which is shown in the bottom panel of Figure 1. Frequency polygons are constructed by plotting the class frequencies at the center of the class interval and connecting the points obtained by straight lines. To complete the picture, one extra class is added at each end of the distribution; since these classes have zero frequencies, both ends of the figure will touch the horizontal axis. The frequency polygon gives the same information as the frequency histogram but by means of a set of connected lines rather than bars.

In practice, we would obtain a much greater number of items than those plotted in Figure 1, but a minimum amount of data is shown in all of the illustrations in this appendix so that you can easily check the steps in tabulating and plotting.

MEASURES OF CENTRAL TENDENCY

A *measure of central tendency* is simply a representative point on our scale—a central point that summarizes important information about the data. Three such measures are commonly used: the *mean*, the *median*, and the *mode*.

The mean is the familiar arithmetic average obtained by adding the scores and dividing by the number of scores. The sum of the raw scores in Table 1 is 1,125. If we divide this by 15 (the number of students' scores), the mean turns out to be 75.

The median is the score of the middle item, which is obtained by arranging the scores in order and then counting into the middle from either end. When the 15 scores in Table 1 are placed in order from highest to lowest, the eighth score from either end turns out to be 75.

Histogram

Polygon

▌Figure 1
Frequency Diagrams
The data from Table 2 are plotted here. A frequency histogram is on the left, a frequency polygon on the right.

If the number of cases is even, we simply average the two cases on each side of the middle.

The mode is the most frequent score in a given distribution. In Table 1, the most frequent score is 75; hence, the mode of the distribution is 75.

In a *normal distribution*, in which the scores are distributed evenly on either side of the middle (as in Figure 1), the mean, median, and mode all fall together. This is not true for distributions that are *skewed*, or unbalanced. Suppose we want to analyze the departure times of a morning train. The train usually leaves on time; occasionally it leaves late, but it never leaves early. For a train with a scheduled departure time of 8:00 AM, one week's record might be as follows:

M	8:00	Mean = 8:07
Tu	8:04	Median = 8:02
W	8:02	Mode = 8:00
Th	8:19	
F	8:22	
Sat	8:00	
Sun	8:00	

The distribution of departure times in this example is skewed because of the two late departures; they raise the mean departure time but do not have much effect on the median or the mode.

Skewness is important because, unless it is understood, the differences between the median and the mean may sometimes be misleading (see Figure 2). If, for example, company executives and the company's union are arguing about the prosperity of the company's workforce, it is possible for the mean and median incomes to move in opposite directions. Suppose that a company raises the

▌Figure 2
Skewed Distribution Curves
Note that skewed distributions are designated by the direction in which the tail falls. Also note that the mean, median, and mode are not identical for a skewed distribution; the median commonly falls between the mode and the mean.

wages of most of its employees, but cuts the wages of its top executives, who were at the extremely high end of the pay scale. The median income of the company might have gone up while the mean went down. The party wanting to show that incomes were getting higher would choose the median, and the party wanting to show that incomes were getting lower would choose the mean.

The mean is the most widely used measure of central tendency, but there are times when the mode or the median is a more meaningful measure.

MEASURES OF VARIATION

Usually more information is needed about a distribution than can be obtained from a measure of central tendency. For example, we need a measure to tell us whether scores cluster closely around their average or whether they scatter widely. A measure of the spread of scores around the average is called a *measure of variation.*

Measures of variation are useful in at least two ways. First, they tell us how representative the average is. If the variation is small, we know that individual scores are close to it. If the variation is large, we cannot use the mean as a representative value with as much assurance. Suppose that clothing is being designed for a group of people without the benefit of precise measurements. Knowing their average size would be helpful, but it also would be important to know the spread of sizes. The second measure provides a yardstick that we can use to measure the amount of variability among the sizes.

To illustrate, consider the data in Figure 3, which show frequency distributions of entrance examination scores for two classes of 30 students. Both classes have the same mean of 75, but they exhibit clearly different degrees of variation. The scores of all the students in Class I are clustered close to the mean, whereas the scores of the students in Class II are spread over a wide range. Some measure is required to specify more exactly how these two distributions differ. Three measures of variation frequently used by psychologists are the *range,* the *variance,* and the *standard deviation.*

To simplify arithmetic computation, we will suppose that five students from each class seek entrance to college and that their entrance examination scores are as follows:

Student scores from Class I:
73, 74, 75, 76, 77 (mean = 75)

Student scores from Class II:
60, 65, 75, 85, 90 (mean = 75)

We will now compute the measures of variation for these two samples. The range is the spread between the highest score and the lowest score. The range of scores

Class 1
Class 2

▌Figure 3
Distributions Differing in Variation

It is easy to see that the scores for Class I cluster closer to the mean than the scores for Class II, even though the means of the two classes are identical (75). For Class I, all the scores fall between 60 and 89, with most of the scores falling in the interval from 70 through 79. For Class II, the scores are distributed fairly uniformly over a wide range from 40 through 109. This difference in variability between the two distributions can be measured using the standard deviation, which is smaller for Class I than for Class II.

for the five students from Class I is 4 (from 73 to 77); the range of scores from Class II is 30 (from 60 to 90).

The range is easy to compute, but the variance and standard deviation are more frequently used. They are more sensitive measures of variation because they account for every score, not just extreme values as the range does. The variance measures how far the scores making up a distribution depart from that distribution's mean. To compute the variance, first compute the deviation d of each score from the mean of the distribution by subtracting each score from the mean (see Table 3). Then, each of the deviations is squared to get rid of negative numbers. Finally, the deviations are added together and divided by the total number of deviations to obtain the average deviation. This average deviation is the variance. When this is done for the data in Figure 3, we find that the variance for Class I is 2.0 and the variance for Class II is 130. Obviously, Class II has much more variability in its scores than Class I.

One disadvantage of the variance is that it is expressed in squared units of measurement. Thus, to say that Class I has a variance of 2 does not indicate that, on average, scores varied an average of 2 points from the mean. Instead, it indicates that 2 is the average of the squared number of points that scores varied from the

Class I Scores (Mean = 75)		
	d	*d²*
77 − 75 =	2	4
76 − 75 =	1	1
75 − 75 =	0	0
74 − 75 =	−1	1
73 − 75 =	−2	4
		10

Sum of *d²* = 10
Variance = mean of *d²* = 10/5 = 2.0
Standard Deviation (σ) = $\sqrt{2.0}$ = 1.4

Class II Scores (Mean = 75)		
	d	*d²*
90−75 =	15	225
85−75 =	10	100
75−75 =	0	0
65−75 =	−10	100
60−75 =	−15	225
		650

Sum of *d²* = 650
Variance = mean of *d²* = 650/5 = 130
Standard Deviation (σ) = $\sqrt{130}$ = 11.4

mean. In order to obtain a measure of variability that is expressed in the original units of measurement (in this case, points on an exam), simply take the square root of the variance. This is known as the standard deviation. The standard deviation is denoted by the lowercase Greek letter *sigma*, σ, which also is used in several other statistical calculations, as we will discuss shortly. The formula for the standard deviation is:

$$\sigma = \sqrt{\frac{\text{sum of } d^2}{N}}$$

The scores for the samples from the two classes are arranged in Table 3 for easy computation of the standard deviation. The first step involves subtracting the mean from each score (the mean is 75 for both classes). This operation yields positive *d* values for scores above the mean and negative *d* values for scores below the mean. The minus signs disappear when the *d* values are squared in the next column. The squared deviations are

added and then divided by *N*, the number of cases in the sample; in our example, *N* = 5. Taking the square root yields the standard deviation.*

STATISTICAL INFERENCE

Now that we have become familiar with statistics as a way of describing data, we are ready to turn to the processes of interpretation—to the making of inferences from data.

POPULATIONS AND SAMPLES

First, it is necessary to distinguish between a *population* and a *sample* drawn from that population. The United States Census Bureau attempts to describe the whole population by obtaining descriptive material on age, marital status, and so on from everyone in the country. The word *population* is appropriate to the census because it represents *all* the people living in the United States.

In statistics, the word "population" is not limited to people or animals or things. The population may be all of the temperatures registered on a thermometer during the last decade, all of the words in the English language, or all of any other specified supply of data. Often we do not have access to the total population, and so we try to represent it by a sample drawn in a *random* (unbiased) fashion. We may ask some questions of a random fraction of the people, as the Census Bureau has done as part of recent censuses; we may derive average temperatures by reading the thermometer at specified times, without taking a continuous record; we may estimate the number of words in the encyclopedia by counting the words on random pages. These illustrations all involve the selection of a sample from the population. If any of these processes are repeated, we will obtain slightly different results due to the fact that a sample does not fully represent the whole population and therefore contains *errors of sampling*. This is where statistical inference enters.

A sample of data is collected from a population in order to make inferences about that population. A sam-

---

* For this introductory treatment, we will use sigma (σ) throughout. However, in the scientific literature, the lowercase letter s is used to denote the standard deviation of a sample and s is used to denote the standard deviation of the population. Moreover, in computing the standard deviation of a sample s, the sum of *d²* is divided by *N* − 1 rather than by *N*. For reasonably large samples, however, the actual value of the standard deviation is only slightly affected whether we divide by *N* − 1 or *N*. To simplify this presentation, we will not distinguish between the standard deviation of a sample and that of a population; instead, we will use the same formula to compute both. For a discussion of this point, see Phillips (1992).

ple of census data may be examined to see whether the population is getting older, for example, or whether there is a trend of migration to the suburbs. Similarly, experimental results are studied to determine what effects experimental manipulations have had on behavior—whether the threshold for pitch is affected by loudness, whether child-rearing practices have detectable effects later in life. To make *statistical inferences*, we have to evaluate the relationships revealed by the sample data. These inferences are always made under some degree of uncertainty due to sampling errors. If the statistical tests indicate that the magnitude of the effect found in the sample is fairly large (relative to the estimate of the sampling error), then we can be confident that the effect observed in the sample holds for the population at large.

Thus, statistical inference deals with the problem of making an inference or judgment about a feature of a population based solely on information obtained from a sample of that population. As an introduction to statistical inference, we will consider the normal distribution and its use in interpreting standard deviations.

THE NORMAL DISTRIBUTION

When large amounts of data are collected, tabulated, and plotted as a histogram or polygon, they often fall into a roughly bell-shaped symmetrical distribution known as the *normal distribution*. Most items fall near the mean (the high point of the bell), and the bell tapers off sharply at very high and very low scores. This form of curve is of special interest because it also arises when the outcome of a process is based on a large number of *chance* events all occurring independently. The demonstration device displayed in Figure 4 illustrates how a sequence of chance events gives rise to a normal distribution. The chance factor of whether a steel ball will fall to the left or right each time it encounters a point where the channel branches results in a symmetrical distribution: More balls fall straight down the middle, but occasionally one reaches one of the end compartments. This is a useful way of visualizing what is meant by a chance distribution closely approximating the normal distribution.

The normal distribution (Figure 5) is the mathematical representation of the idealized distribution approximated by the device shown in Figure 4. The normal distribution represents the likelihood that items within a normally distributed population will depart from the mean by any stated amount. The percentages shown in Figure 5 represent the *percentage of the area* lying under the curve between the indicated scale values; the total area under the curve represents the whole population. Roughly two thirds of the cases (68%) will fall between plus and minus one standard deviation from

▌Figure 4
A Device to Demonstrate a Chance Distribution
The board is held upside down until all the steel balls fall into the reservoir. Then the board is turned over and held vertically until the balls fall into the nine columns. The precise number of balls falling into each column will vary from one demonstration to the next. On average, however, the heights of the columns of balls will approximate a normal distribution, with the greatest height in the center column and gradually decreasing heights in the outer columns.

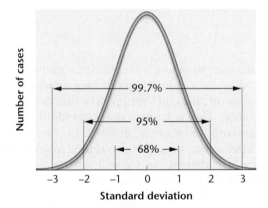

▌Figure 5
The Normal Distribution
The normal distribution curve can be constructed using the mean and the standard deviation. The area under the curve below -3σ and above $+3\sigma$ is negligible.

the mean ($\pm 1\sigma$); 95% of the cases within $\pm 2\sigma$ and virtually all cases (99.7%) within $\pm 3\sigma$. A more detailed listing of areas under portions of the normal curve is given in Table 4.

● Table 4
The Area of the Normal Distribution as a Proportion of Total Area

Standard Deviation	(1) Area to the Left of This Value	(2) Area to the Right of This Value	(3) Area Between This Value and Mean
-3.0σ	.001	.999	.499
-2.5σ	.006	.994	.494
-2.0σ	.023	.977	.477
-1.5σ	.067	.933	.433
-1.0σ	.159	.841	.341
-0.5σ	.309	.691	.191
0.0σ	.500	.500	.000
$+0.5\sigma$	.691	.309	.191
$+1.0\sigma$	.841	.159	.341
$+1.5\sigma$	.933	.067	.433
$+2.0\sigma$	.977	.023	.477
$+2.5\sigma$	.994	.006	.494
$+3.0\sigma$	.999	.001	.499

Using Table 4, let us trace how the 68% and 95% values in Figure 5 are derived. We find from Column 3 of Table 4 that between -1σ and the mean lies .341 of the total area and between $+1\sigma$ and the mean also lies .341 of the area. Adding these values gives us .682, which is expressed in Figure 5 as 68%. Similarly, the area between -2σ and $+2\sigma$ is $2 \times 477 = .954$, which is expressed as 95%.

These percentages have several uses. One is in connection with the interpretation of standard scores, to which we turn next. Another is in connection with tests of significance.

SCALING OF DATA

In order to interpret a score, we often need to know whether it is high or low in relation to other scores. If a person taking a driver's test requires .500 seconds to brake after a danger signal, how can we tell whether the performance is fast or slow? Does a student who scores 60 on a physics examination pass the course? To answer questions of this kind, we have to derive a scale against which the scores can be compared.

RANKED DATA By placing scores in rank order from high to low, we derive one kind of scale. An individual score is interpreted on the basis of where it ranks among the group of scores. For example, the graduates of West Point know where they stand in their class—perhaps 35th or 125th in a class of 400.

STANDARD SCORES The standard deviation is a convenient unit to use in scaling because we can interpret how far away 1σ or 2σ is from the mean (see Table 4). A score based on a multiple of the standard deviation is known as a *standard score*. Many scales used in psychological measurement are based on the principle of standard scores.

Table 1 presented college entrance scores for 15 students. Without more information, we do not know whether these scores are representative of the population of all college applicants. On this examination, however, we will assume that the population mean is 75 and the standard deviation is 10.

What, then, is the standard score for a student who had 90 on the examination? We must express how far this score lies above the mean in multiples of the standard deviation.

Standard score for grade of 90:

$$\frac{90 - 75}{10} = \frac{15}{10} = 1.5\sigma$$

As a second example, consider a student with a score of 53.

Standard score for grade of 53:

$$\frac{53 - 75}{10} = \frac{-22}{10} = -2.2\sigma$$

In this case, the minus sign tells us that the student's score is below the mean by 2.2 standard deviations. Thus, the sign of the standard score (+ or −) indicates whether the score is above or below the mean, and its value indicates how far from the mean the score lies in standard deviations.

HOW REPRESENTATIVE IS A MEAN?

How useful is the mean of a sample in estimating the population mean? If we measure the height of a random sample of 100 college students, how well does the sample mean predict the true population mean (that is, the mean height of *all* college students)? These questions raise the issue of making an *inference* about a population based on information from a sample.

The accuracy of such inferences depends on *errors of sampling*. Suppose we were to select two random samples from the same population and compute the mean for each sample. What differences between the first and the second mean could be expected to occur by chance?

Successive random samples drawn from the same population will have different means, forming a distribution of *sample means* around the *true mean* of the population. These sample means are themselves numbers for which the standard deviation can be computed. We call this standard deviation the standard error of the mean, or σ_M, and can estimate it on the basis of the following formula:

$$\sigma_M = \frac{\sigma}{\sqrt{N}}$$

where σ is the standard deviation of the sample and N is the number of cases from which each sample mean is computed.

According to the formula, the size of the standard error of the mean decreases as the sample size increases; thus, a mean based on a large sample is more trustworthy (more likely to be close to the actual population mean) than a mean based on a smaller sample. Common sense would lead us to expect this. Computations of the standard error of the mean permit us to make clear assertions about the degree of uncertainty in our computed mean. The more cases in the sample, the more uncertainty has been reduced.

THE SIGNIFICANCE OF A DIFFERENCE

In many psychological experiments, data are collected on two groups of subjects; one group is exposed to certain specified experimental conditions, and the other serves as a control group. The question is whether there is a difference in the mean performance of the two groups, and if such a difference is observed, whether it holds for the population from which these groups of subjects have been sampled. Basically, we are asking whether a difference between two sample means reflects a true difference or whether this difference is simply the result of sampling error.

As an example, we will compare the scores on a reading test for a sample of first-grade boys with the scores for a sample of first-grade girls. The boys score lower than the girls as far as mean performances are concerned, but there is a great deal of overlap; some boys do extremely well, and some girls do very poorly. Thus, we cannot accept the obtained difference in means without making a test of its *statistical significance*. Only then can we decide whether the observed differences in sample means reflect true differences in the population or are due to sampling error. If some of the brighter girls and some of the duller boys are sampled by sheer luck, the difference could be due to sampling error.

As another example, suppose that we have set up an experiment to compare the grip strength of right-handed and left-handed men. The top panel of Table 5 presents hypothetical data from such an experiment. A sample of five right-handed men averaged 8 kilograms stronger than a sample of five left-handed men. In general, what can we infer from these data about left-handed and right-handed men? Can we argue that right-handed men are stronger than left-handed men? Obviously not, because the averages derived from most of the right-handed men would not differ from those from the left-handed men; the one markedly deviant score of 100 tells us we are dealing with an uncertain situation.

Now suppose that the results of the experiment were those shown in the bottom panel of Table 5. Again, we find the same mean difference of 8 kilograms, but we are now inclined to have greater confidence in the results, because the left-handed men scored consistently lower than the right-handed men. Statistics provides a precise way of taking into account the reliability of the mean differences so that we do not have to depend solely on intuition to determine that one difference is more reliable than another.

These examples suggest that the significance of a difference will depend on both the size of the obtained difference and the variability of the means being compared. From the standard error of the means, we can compute the *standard error of the difference between two means*, $\sigma\Delta_M$. We can then evaluate the obtained difference by using a *critical ratio*—the ratio of the obtained difference between the means D_M to the standard error of the difference:

$$\text{Critical Ratio} = \frac{D_M}{\sigma D_M}$$

This ratio helps us evaluate the significance of the difference between the two means. As a rule of thumb, a critical ratio should be 2.0 or larger for the difference between means to be accepted as significant. Throughout

Two examples that compare the difference between means are shown. The difference between means is the same (8 kilograms) in both the top and bottom panel. However, the data in the bottom panel indicate a more reliable difference between means than do the data in the top panel.

Strength of Grip in Kilograms, Right-Handed Men	Strength of Grip in Kilograms, Left-Handed Men
40	40
45	45
50	50
55	55
100	60
Sum 290	Sum 250
Mean 58	Mean 50

Strength of Grip in Kilograms, Right-Handed Men	Strength of Grip in Kilograms, Left-Handed Men
56	48
57	49
58	50
59	51
60	52
Sum 290	Sum 250
Mean 58	Mean 50

this book, statements that the difference between means is "statistically significant" indicate that the critical ratio is at least that large.

Why is a critical ratio of 2.0 selected as statistically significant? Simply because a value this large or larger can occur by chance only 5 out of 100 times. Where do we get the 5 out of 100? We can treat the critical ratio as a standard score because it is merely the difference between two means, expressed as a multiple of its standard error. Referring to Column 2 in Table 4, we note that the likelihood is .023 that a standard deviation as high as or higher than +2.0 will occur by chance. Because the chance of deviating in the opposite direction is also .023, the total probability is .046. This means that 46 times out of 1,000, or about 5 times out of 100, a critical ratio as large as 2.0 would be found by chance if the population means were identical.

The rule of thumb that says a critical ratio should be at least 2.0 is just that—an arbitrary but convenient rule that defines the "5% level of significance." Following

this rule, we will make fewer than 5 errors in 100 decisions by concluding on the basis of sample data that a difference in means exists when in fact there is none. The 5% level need not always be used; a higher level of significance may be appropriate in certain experiments, depending on how willing we are to make an occasional error in inference.

The computation of the critical ratio calls for finding the *standard error of the difference between two means*, which is given by the following formula:

$$\sigma_{\Delta_M} = \sqrt{(\sigma M_1)^2 + (\sigma M_2)^2}$$

In this formula, σM_1, and σM_2 are the standard errors of the two means being compared.

As an illustration, suppose we wanted to compare reading achievement test scores for first-grade boys and girls in the United States. A random sample of boys and girls would be identified and given the test. We will assume that the mean score for the boys was 70 with a standard error of .40 and that the mean score for the girls was 72 with a standard error of .30. On the basis of these samples, we want to decide whether there is a real difference between the reading achievement of boys and girls in the population as a whole. The sample data suggest that girls do achieve better reading scores than boys, but can we infer that this would have been the case if we had tested all the girls and all the boys in the United States? The critical ratio helps us make this decision.

$$\sigma D_M = \sqrt{(\sigma M_1)^2 + (\sigma M_2)^2}$$
$$= \sqrt{.16 + .09} = \sqrt{.25}$$
$$= .5$$

$$\text{Critical Ratio} = \frac{D_M}{\sigma D_M} = \frac{72 - 70}{.5} = \frac{2.0}{.5} = 4.0$$

Because the critical ratio is well above 2.0, we may assert that the observed mean difference is statistically significant at the 5% level. Thus, we can conclude that there is a reliable difference in performance on the reading test between boys and girls. Note that the sign of the critical ratio could be positive or negative, depending on which mean is subtracted from which; when the critical ratio is interpreted, only its magnitude (not its sign) is considered.

THE COEFFICIENT OF CORRELATION

Correlation refers to the parallel variation of two measures. Suppose that a test is designed to predict success in college. If it is a good test, high scores on it will be related to high performance in college and low scores will be re-lated to poor performance. The *coefficient of correlation* gives us a way of stating the degree of relationship more precisely.

PRODUCT-MOMENT CORRELATION

The most frequently used method of determining the co-efficient of correlation is the *product-moment method*, which yields the index conventionally designated by the lowercase letter *r*. The product-moment coefficient *r* varies between perfect positive correlation ($r = +1.00$) and perfect negative correlation ($r = -1.00$). Lack of any relationship yields $r = .00$.

The formula for computing the product-moment correlation is:

$$r = \frac{\text{Sum }(dx)(dy)}{N\sigma_x\sigma_y}$$

Here, one of the paired measures has been labeled the *x*-score; the other, the *y*-score. The *dx* and *dy* refer to the deviations of each score from its mean, *N* is the num-ber of paired measures, and σ_x and σ_y are the standard deviations of the *x*-scores and the *y*-scores.

The computation of the coefficient of correlation re-quires the determination of the sum of the $(dx)(dy)$ prod-ucts. This sum, in addition to the computed standard de-viations for the *x*-scores and *y*-scores, can then be entered into the formula.

Suppose that we have collected the data shown in Table 6. For each subject, we have obtained two scores—the first being a score on a college entrance test

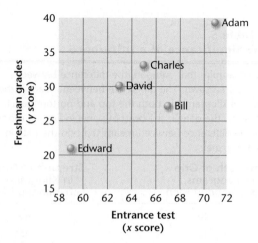

Figure 6
A Scatter Design
Each point represents the *x*- and *y*-scores for a particular stu-dent. The letters next to the points identify the students in the data table (A = Adam, B = Bill, and so on).

(to be labeled arbitrarily the *x*-score) and the second be-ing freshman grades (the *y*-score).

Figure 6 is a *scatter diagram* of these data. Each point represents the *x*-score and *y*-score for a given sub-ject; for example, the uppermost right-hand point is for Adam (labeled A). Looking at these data, we can easily detect that there is some positive correlation between the *x*-scores and the *y*-scores. Adam attained the highest score on the entrance test and also earned the highest freshman grades; Edward received the lowest scores on both. The other students' test scores and grades are a lit-

Table 6
Computation of a Product-Moment Correlation

Student	Entrance Test (x-score)	Freshman Grades (y-score)	(dx)	(dy)	(dx)(dy)
Adam	71	39	6	9	+54
Bill	67	27	2	−3	−6
Charles	65	33	0	3	0
David	63	30	−2	0	0
Edward	59	21	−6	−9	+54
Sum	325	150	0	0	+102
Mean	65	30			

$$\sigma_x = 4$$
$$\sigma_y = 6$$

$$r = \frac{\text{Sum }(dx)(dy)}{N\sigma_x\sigma_y} = \frac{+102}{5 \times 4 \times 6} = +.85$$

tle irregular, so we know that the correlation is not perfect; hence, *r* is less than 1.00.

We will compute the correlation to illustrate the method, although no researcher would consent, in practice, to determining a correlation for so few cases. The details are given in Table 6. Following the procedure outlined in Table 3, we compute the standard deviation of the *x*-scores and then the standard deviation of the *y*-scores. Next, we compute the $(dx)(dy)$ products for each subject and total the five cases. Entering these results in our equation yields an *r* of +.85.

INTERPRETING A CORRELATION COEFFICIENT

We can use correlations in making predictions. For example, if we know from experience that a certain entrance test correlates with freshman grades, we can predict the freshman grades for beginning college students who have taken the test. If the correlation were perfect, we could predict their grades without error. But *r* is usually less than 1.00, and some errors in prediction will be made; the closer *r* is to 0, the greater the sizes of the errors in prediction.

Although we cannot go into the technical problems of predicting freshman grades from entrance examinations or of making other similar predictions, we can consider the meanings of correlation coefficients of different sizes. It is evident that with a correlation of 0 between *x* and *y*, knowledge of *x* will not help to predict *y*. If weight is unrelated to intelligence, it does us no good to know a subject's weight when we are trying to predict his or her intelligence. At the other extreme, a perfect correlation would mean 100% predictive efficiency—knowing *x*, we can predict *y* perfectly. What about intermediate values of *r*? Some appreciation of the meaning of correlations of intermediate sizes can be gained by examining the scatter diagrams in Figure 7.

In the preceding discussion, we did not emphasize the sign of the correlation coefficient, since this has no bearing on the strength of a relationship. The only distinction between a correlation of $r = +.70$ and $r = -.70$ is that increases in *x* are accompanied by increases in *y* for the former, and increases in *x* are accompanied by decreases in *y* for the latter.

Although the correlation coefficient is one of the most widely used statistics in psychology, it is also one of the most widely misused procedures. Those who use it sometimes overlook the fact that *r* does not imply a

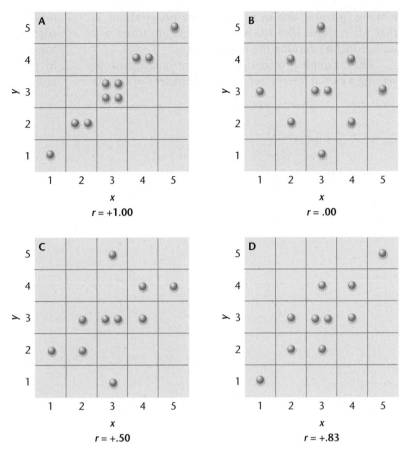

❚ Figure 7
Scatter Diagrams Illustrating Correlations of Various Sizes
Each dot represents one individual's score on two tests, *x* and *y*. In A, all cases fall on the diagonal and the correlation is perfect ($r = +1.00$); if we know a subject's score on *x*, we know that it will be the same on *y*. In B, the correlation is 0; knowing a subject's score on *x*, we cannot predict whether it will be at, above, or below the mean on *y*. In both C and D, there is a diagonal trend to the scores, so that a high score on *x* is associated with a high score on *y* and a low score on *x* with a low score on *y*, but the relationship is imperfect.

cause-and-effect relationship between *x* and *y*. When two sets of scores are correlated, we may suspect that they have some causal factors in common, but we cannot conclude that one of them causes the other.

Correlations sometimes appear paradoxical. For example, the correlation between study time and college grades has been found to be slightly negative (about −.10). If a causal interpretation were assumed, we might conclude that the best way to raise grades would be to stop studying. The negative correlation arises because some students have advantages over others in grade making (possibly due to better college preparation), so that often those who study the hardest are those who have difficulty earning the best grades.

This example provides sufficient warning against assigning a causal interpretation to a coefficient of correlation. It is possible, however, that when two variables are correlated, one may be the cause of the other. The search for causes is a logical one, and correlations can help us by providing leads to experiments that can verify cause-and-effect relationships.

GLOSSARY

The glossary defines the technical words that appear in the text and some common words that have special meanings when used in psychology. No attempt is made to give the range of meanings beyond those used in the text. For fuller definitions and other shades of meaning, consult any standard dictionary of psychology.

A

abnormal. Away from the norm.

absolute threshold. The minimum magnitude of a stimulus that can be reliably discriminated from no stimulus at all.

abstractions. Properties that characterize sets of instances rather than just single instances.

accommodation. (1) The process by which the lens of the eye varies its focus. (2) In Piaget's theory of cognitive development, the process by which an infant modifies a pre-existing schema in order to include a novel object or event.

action potential. An electrochemical impulse that travels from the dendritic area down to the end of the axon.

activation model. In memory, the proposal that retrieval of an item depends on the activation of that item reaching a critical level.

actualizing tendency. A tendency toward fulfillment or actualization of all the capacities of the organism.

addiction. A pattern of compulsive and destructive drug-taking behavior.

adolescence. The period of transition from childhood to adulthood.

adolescent growth spurt. A period of rapid physical growth that accompanies the onset of puberty.

affect. Emotions and feelings.

affective neuroscience. The study of how emotional phenomena are executed in the brain.

aggression. Behavior that is intended to injure another person (physically or verbally) or to destroy property.

agnosia. The general term for breakdowns or disorders in recognition.

agonists. A drug that binds to receptors and activates them in much the same way that another drug does.

agoraphobia. Fear of places where one might be trapped or unable to receive help in an emergency.

alliesthesia. An interaction between incentive and drive theories of motivation which states that any external stimulus that corrects an internal trouble is experienced as pleasurable.

altered states of consciousness. A change from an ordinary pattern of mental functioning to a state that seems different to the person experiencing the change.

alternative form reliability. The consistency between two or more versions of the same test when given to the same person.

American College Test (ACT). An example of a group-administered general-ability test.

American Law Institute. "A person is not responsible for criminal conduct if at the time of such conduct, as a result of mental disease or defect, he lacks substantial capacity either to appreciate the wrongfulness of his conduct or to conform his conduct to the requirements of the law."

amnesia. Partial loss of memory.

amphetamines. Central nervous system stimulants that produce restlessness, irritability, anxiety, and rapid heart rate. Dexedrine sulfate ("speed") and methamphetamine ("meth") are two types of amphetamines.

amplitude (of a tone). The difference in pressure between the peak and the trough.

amygdala. A brain structure located below the cerebral cortex that is involved in consolidation of emotional memories.

anal stage. The second stage in Freud's psychoanalytic theory of psychosexual development, following the oral stage. The sources of gratification and conflict have to do with the expulsion and retention of feces.

analytic thought. An orientation toward objects, detached from their contexts, with much use of categories and formal logic and the avoidance of contradiction.

Anderson's theory of intelligence. The theory that differences in intelligence result from differences in the "basic processing mechanism" that implements thinking, which in turn yields knowledge. Individuals vary in the speed at which basic processing occurs.

androgenization. Influence of androgen on anatomy and brain development.

anhedonia. The loss of the ability to experience joy, even in response to the most joyous occasions.

anomic aphasic. Patients who primarily have problems in retrieving and recognizing words (as a result of some brain damage).

anorexia nervosa. Self-imposed weight loss—at least 15 percent of the individual's minimum normal weight.

antagonists. A drug that locks onto receptors but in a way that does not activate them; the drug serves to "block" the receptors so that another drug cannot gain access to them.

anterior system (for attention). Designed to control when and how the perceptual features of an object (location in space, shape, color) will be used for selection. See also posterior system (for attention).

anterograde amnesia. Loss of memory for events and experiences occurring subsequent to an amnesia-causing trauma; the patient is unable to acquire new information, although recall of information learned prior to the onset may be largely unaffected.

antidepressant. Drug used to elevate the mood of depressed individuals, presumably by increasing the availability of the neurotransmitters norepinephrine and/or serotonin. Examples are imipramine (Tofranil), isocarboxazid (Marplan), and fluoxetine (Prozac).

antisocial personality. A type of personality disorder marked by impulsivity, inability to abide by the customs and laws of society, and lack of anxiety or guilt regarding behavior (syn. sociopathic personality, psychopathic personality).

antisocial personality disorder. A disorder characterized by deficits in normal emotional responding—especially for shame, guilt, and fear—as well as deficits in empathy for the emotions of others.

anxiety. A state of apprehension, tension, and worry. Synonymous with fear for some theorists, although others view the object of anxiety (such as a vague danger or foreboding) as less specific than the object of a fear (such as a vicious animal).

anxiety disorders. A group of mental disorders characterized by intense anxiety or by maladaptive behavior designed to relieve anxiety. Includes generalized anxiety and panic disorders, phobic and obsessive-compulsive disorders. Major category of DSM-IV covering most of the disorders formerly called neuroses.

aphasia. Language deficits caused by brain damage.

apnea. The individual stops breathing while asleep.

assimilation. In Piaget's theory of cognitive development, the process by which an infant comprehends a novel object or event in terms of a pre-existing schema.

associationist psychology. The view that the mind is filled with ideas that enter by way of the senses and then become associated through principles such as similarity and contrast.

associative learning. Learning that certain contingencies (or relations) exist between events; learning that one event is associated with another.

ataque de nervios. Trembling, feelings of out of control, sudden crying, screaming uncontrollably, verbal and physical aggression, and sometimes seizure-like or fainting episodes and suicidal gestures.

Atkinson-Shiffrin theory (of memory). The basis for the distinction between different memories corresponding to different time intervals.

attachment. An infant's tendency to seek closeness to particular people and to feel more secure in their presence.

attention. The ability to select some information for more detailed inspection, while ignoring other information.

attitudes. Favorable or unfavorable evaluations of and reactions to objects, people, situations, or other aspects of the world.

attribution. The process by which we attempt to explain the behavior of other people. Attribution theory deals with the rules people use to infer the causes of observed behavior.

attributional styles. Styles of making attributions for the events in one's life.

atypical antipsychotics. Reduce symptoms of schizophrenia without causing so many side effects.

auditory cue. A sound cue that is presented immediately after the array.

auditory system. The ears, parts of the brain, and the various connecting neural pathways.

augmented network. A network that includes inhibitory as well as excitatory connections.

autism. A mental disorder, first evident during early childhood, in which the child shows significant deficits in communication, social interaction, and bonding and play activities, and engages in repetitive stereotyped behaviors and self-damaging acts.

automaticity. The habituation of responses that initially requires conscious attention.

autonomic nervous system. The division of the peripheral nervous system that regulates smooth muscle (organ and glandular) activities. It is divided into the sympathetic and parasympathetic divisions.

autonomic system. Connects with the internal organs and glands.

autonomy. A child's independence from caretakers.

available wavelengths. The wavelengths of the light that is reflected off the paper reaching your eyes.

axon. That portion of a neuron that transmits impulses to other neurons.

B

back projections. Activities that modify the way sensory input is processed.

backward masking. A method used in psychological testing. The participant is shown a picture for only 30 milliseconds, which is then masked by a neutral picture so that participants are unaware of the picture's content.

basic level. In a hierarchy of concepts, the level at which one first categorizes an object.

basilar membrane. A membrane of the ear within the coils of the cochlea supporting the organ of Corti. Movements of the basilar membrane stimulate the hair cells of the organ of Corti, producing the neural effects of auditory stimulation.

behavior genetics. Combines the methods of genetics and psychology to study the inheritance of behavioral characteristics.

behavior therapy. A method of psychotherapy based on learning principles. It uses such techniques as counterconditioning, reinforcement, and shaping to modify behavior (syn. behavior modification).

behavioral medicine. The study of how social, psychological, and biological factors interact to contribute to physical illness (syn. health psychology).

behavioral perspective. An approach to psychology that focuses only on observable behavior, and tries to explain it in terms of its relation to environmental events.

behavioral rehearsal. Role-playing.

behaviorism. A school or system of psychology associated with the name of John B. Watson; it defined psychology as the study of behavior and limited the data of psychology to observable activities. In its classical form it was more restrictive than the contemporary behavioral viewpoint in psychology.

behaviorist approach (to personality). Emphasizes the importance of environmental, or situational, determinants of behavior.

benzodiazepines. A class of drugs with similar chemical structures that are effective in reducing anxiety. Examples are diazepam (Valium) and alprazolam (Xanax).

bias. A criterion, set by the observer, for making a particular response.

"Big Five." Five trait dimensions capture most of what we mean by personality. They are Openness to experience, Conscientiousness, Extraversion, Agreeableness, and Neuroticism.

binding problem. How activity in different parts of the brain, corresponding to different primitives such as color and shape, are combined into a coherent perception of an object.

binocular disparity (as a depth cue). The difference in the views seen by each eye.

biofeedback. Receiving information (feedback) about an aspect of one's physiological state and then attempting to alter that state.

biological perspective. An approach to psychology that tries to explain behavior in terms of electrical and chemical events taking place inside the body, particularly within the brain and nervous system.

biological psychologist. A psychologist concerned with the relationship between biological processes and behavior.

bipolar disorders. Alternating between periods of depression and periods of mania. (syn. manic-depression).

blocking. A phenomenon in classical conditioning: if one conditioned stimulus reliably predicts an unconditioned stimulus, and another conditioned stimulus is added, the relation between the added conditioned stimulus and the unconditioned stimulus will not be learned.

borderline personality disorder. A mental disorder in which the individual has manifested unstable moods, relationships with others, and self-perceptions chronically since adolescence or childhood.

bottom-up processes. Processes in perception, learning, memory, and comprehension that are driven solely by the information input, and that do not involve the organism's prior knowledge and expectations.

brain imaging. Techniques such as event-related potentials (ERPs), positron emission tomography (PET), and functional magnetic resonance imaging (fMRI).

brain's dopamine system. The neurons of this system lie in the upper brain stem and send their axons through the nucleus accumbens and up to the prefrontal cortex. As their name implies, these neurons use the neurotransmitter dopamine to convey their message.

brightness. How much light appears to be reflected from a colored surface.

broaden-and-build theory. The theory that positive emotions broaden our typical ways of thinking and acting and, in turn, build our lasting personal resources.

Broca's aphasia. Disrupted language caused by damage to Broca's area, that portion of the left cerebral hemisphere involved in the control of speech. Individuals with damage in this area have difficulty enunciating words correctly and speak in a slow and labored way; their speech often makes sense, but it includes only key words.

bulimia. Recurrent episodes of binge eating (rapid consumption of a large amount of food in a discrete period of time), followed by attempts to purge the excess by means of vomiting or laxatives.

bystander effect. The rule that people are less likely to help when others are present.

C

cannabis. The hemp plant from which marijuana is obtained.

case histories. Biographies designed for scientific use.

categorization. The process of assigning an object to a concept.

catharsis. Purging an emotion by experiencing it intensely.

cathartic effect. The hypothesized reduction of aggression that follows the vicarious expression of it.

causality heuristic. The use of the strength of the causal connections between the events in a claim to estimate the probability of that claim.

Ceci's bioecological theory. This theory proposes "multiple cognitive potentials," rather than a single underlying general intelligence. These multiple abilities are biologically based and place limits on mental processes and their emergence is shaped by the challenges and opportunities in the individual's environment, or context.

central core. The most central portion of the brain, including structures that regulate basic life processes.

central nervous system. All the neurons in the brain and spinal cord.

central route. When an individual mentally responds to and elaborates on the persuasive communication.

cerebellum. Lobed structure attached to the rear of the brain stem that regulates muscle tone and coordination of intricate movements.

cerebral cortex. The surface layer of the cerebral hemispheres in higher animals, including humans, commonly called gray matter.

cerebrum. The brain's two cerebral hemispheres.

childhood amnesia. The inability to recall events from the first years of one's life.

chromosomes. Structures found in the nucleus of each cell in the body.

chunking. Recoding new material into larger, more meaningful units and storing those units in working memory.

circadian rhythm. Rhythms of the body that occur approximately every 24 hours.

classical conditioning. A learning process in which a previously neutral stimulus becomes associated with another stimulus through repeated pairing with that stimulus.

client-centered therapy. A method of psychotherapy developed by Carl Rogers in which the therapist is nondirective and reflective and does not interpret or advise. The operating assumption is that the client is the best expert on his or her problems and can work them out in a nonjudgmental, accepting atmosphere (syn. nondirective counseling).

clinical psychologist. A psychologist, usually with a Ph.D. or Psy.D. degree, trained in the diagnosis and treatment of emotional or behavioral problems and mental disorders.

clock-dependent alerting process. The process in the brain that arouses us at a particular time each day.

coaction. The interaction between individuals performing the same task.

cocaine. A central nervous system stimulant derived from leaves of the coca plant. Increases energy, produces euphoria, and in large doses causes paranoia.

cochlea. The portion of the inner ear containing the receptors for hearing.

cognitive appraisal. The interpretation of an event or situation with respect to one's goals and well-being. The cognitive appraisal of an event influences both the quality and intensity of the emotion experienced and the degree of perceived threat.

cognitive approach (to personality). A general empirical approach and a set of topics related to how people process information about themselves and the world.

cognitive behavior therapy. A therapy that attempts to help people identify the kinds of stressful situations that produce their physiological or emotional symptoms and alter the way they cope with these situations.

cognitive dissonance theory. This theory assumes that there is a drive toward cognitive consistency, meaning that two cognitions—or thoughts—that are inconsistent will produce discomfort, which will in turn motivate the person to remove the inconsistency and bring the cognitions into harmony.

cognitive map. A hypothetical structure in memory that preserves and organizes information about the various events that occur in a learning situation; a mental picture of the learning situation.

cognitive neuroscience. An interdisciplinary approach that combines aspects of cognitive psychology and neuroscience to study how mental activities are executed in the brain.

cognitive perspective. An approach to psychology that focuses on mental processes such as perceiving, remembering, reasoning, deciding, and problem solving, and tries to explain behavior in terms of these mental processes.

collective unconscious. A part of the mind that is common to all humans and consisting of primordial images or archetypes inherited from our ancestors.

collectivism. Refers to cultures that emphasize the fundamental connectedness and interdependence among people.

color constancy. The tendency to see a familiar object as of the same color, regardless of changes in illumination on it that alter its stimulus properties.

color-matching experiment. An experiment that measures an observer's inclination to see two physically different lights as having the same color.

commitment. The cognitive component of love that reflects the intention to remain in the relationship.

companionate love. Contrasted with passionate love. The affection we feel for those with whom our lives are deeply intertwined.

complex cell. A cell in the visual cortex that responds to a bar of light or straight edge of a particular orientation located anywhere in the visual field.

compliance. We comply with the wishes of the influencer but do not necessarily change our beliefs or attitudes.

comprehension of language. Understanding language by hearing sounds, attaching meanings to the sounds in the form of words, combining the words to create a sentence, and then somehow extracting meaning from it.

compulsion. Irresistible urges to carry out certain acts or rituals that reduce anxiety.

concept. The set of properties that we associate with a particular class.

concrete operational stage. Piaget's third stage of cognitive development (ages 7 to 11 years) during which children become capable of logical thought and conservation.

conditioned aversion. Learning that occurs when negative associative memories cause something (often food) to subsequently be experienced as unpleasant.

conditioned reinforcer. A stimulus that has become reinforcing through prior association with a reinforcing stimulus (syn. secondary reinforcer).

conditioned response (CR). The learned or acquired response to a stimulus that did not evoke the response originally (i.e., a conditioned stimulus).

conditioned satiety. The idea that the fullness we feel after a meal is at least in part a product of learning.

conditioned stimulus (CS). A previously neutral stimulus that comes to elicit a conditioned response through association with an unconditioned stimulus.

cone. In the eye, a specialized cell of the retina found predominantly in the fovea and more sparsely throughout the retina. The cones mediate both chromatic and achromatic sensations.

connectionist models. Models of cognitive processes (like perception) that incorporate a network of nodes, with excitatory and inhibitory connections between them.

conscious. Our current awareness.

consciousness. (a) Monitoring ourselves and our environment so that percepts, memories, and thoughts are represented in awareness. (b) Controlling ourselves and our environment so that we are able to initiate and terminate behavioral and cognitive activities.

conservation. The understanding that the amount of a substance remains the same even when its form is changed.

constancy. The brain's ability to maintain a perception of the underlying physical characteristics of an object, such as shape, size or color, even when the sensory manifestations of these objects change drastically.

construct validity. The ability of a test or assessment instrument to confirm predictions of the theory underlying some theoretical concept or construct. Confirming results validate both the concept and the assessment instrument simultaneously.

constructive perception. What is perceived forms the basis for the initial memory; therefore, if what is originally perceived differs systematically from the objective world, the perceiver's initial memory of what happened will likewise be distorted.

constructive processes. The processes by which perception is based on prior knowledge and inference in addition to the objective data from the environment.

continuum model. This model describes the full continuum of processes from stereotyping to individuation.

contrast acuity. The ability to see differences in brightness.

control group. In an experiment, the group in which the condition under study is absent.

controllability. The degree to which we can stop an event or bring it about.

controlled stimulation. Conditions in which the perceptual experiences of an organism are systematically varied in order to determine the effect on subsequent performance. For example, rearing kittens in an environment where they see only vertical stripes for the first few months of life.

conventional level of moral development. Level of moral development in which children evaluate actions in terms of other people's opinions.

coping. The process by which a person attempts to manage stressful demands.

core. The part of a concept that contains the properties that are more essential for determining membership in the concept.

core relational theme. The personal meaning that results from a particular pattern of appraisals about a specific person-environment relationship.

coronary heart disease. The narrowing or closing of the blood vessels that supply the heart muscles by the gradual buildup of a hard, fatty substance called plaque, blocking the flow of oxygen and nutrients to the heart.

correlation coefficient. An estimate of the degree to which two variables are related.

counseling psychologist. A trained psychologist, usually with a Ph.D. or Psy.D. degree, who deals with personal problems not classified as illness, such as academic, social, or vocational problems of students. He or she has skills similar to those of the clinical psychologist but usually works in a nonmedical setting.

criterion problem in assessment. The difficulty that arises in validating a test or assessment instrument when there is no criterion behavior the investigator is willing to accept as the "true" measure of the concept being evaluated.

criterion validity. The ability of a test or assessment instrument to predict the behavior it is designed to predict (syn. empirical validity).

critical periods. Crucial time periods in a person's life during which specific events occur if development is to proceed normally.

cue. A directing stimulus such as a small arrow that directs the subject to attend either to the left or to the right.

cultural perspective (of abnormality). The view that mental disorders are not situated in the brain or mind of the individual but in the social context in which the individual lives.

cultural psychology. An interdisciplinary approach involving psychologists, anthropologists, sociologists, and other social scientists that is concerned with how an individual's culture influences his or her mental representations and psychological processes.

cultural relativist perspective (for acceptable behavior). This perspective follows that people should respect each culture's definitions of abnormality for the members of that culture.

D

dark adaptation. The increased sensitivity to light when the subject has been continuously in the dark or under conditions of reduced illumination.

dark-adaptation curve. The absolute threshold decreases with the length of time the person is in darkness.

data-driven learning. A kind of associative learning in which people have no prior beliefs about the relation that has to be learned; learning is driven only by the input or data.

debriefing. The meeting between researcher and participant following a study in which the researcher tells the participant the reasons for keeping them in ignorance—or deceiving them—about the procedures or hypotheses. The researcher also deals with any of the participants' residual emotional reactions so that participants leave with their dignity intact and their appreciation for the research enhanced.

decibel scale. A logarithmic scale of loudness. A change of 10 decibels corresponds to a change in sound power of 10 times; 20 decibels, a change of 100 times; and so forth.

deductive validity. It is impossible for the conclusion of the argument to be false if its premises are true.

deductive validity (of an argument). According to logicians, an argument in which it is impossible for the conclusion of the argument to be false if its premises are true.

defense mechanisms. Strategies that people use to deal with anxiety, which are largely unconscious.

degradation. The process in which enzymes in the membrane of a receiving neuron react with a neurotransmitter to break it up chemically and make it inactive; one method (in addition to reuptake) of terminating a neurotransmitter's action.

deindividuation. A feeling that one has lost his or her personal identity and merged anonymously into a group.

deinstitutionalization. The movement toward discharge of institutionalized mental patients to community-based services.

delusions. Beliefs that most people would view as misinterpretations of reality.

dendrite. The specialized portion of the neuron that (together with the cell body) receives impulses from other neurons.

denial. A defense mechanism by which unacceptable impulses or ideas are not perceived or allowed into full awareness.

dependent variable. A variable that is hypothesized to depend on the value of the independent variable.

depressants. Drugs that depress the central nervous system.

depressive disorders. Having one or more periods of depression without a history of manic episodes.

depth cues. Different kinds of visual information that, logically or mathematically, provide information about some object's depth.

developmental psychologist. A psychologist whose research interest lies in studying the changes that occur as a function of the growth and development of the organism, in particular the relationship between early and later behavior.

***Diagnostic and Statistical Manual of Mental Disorders*, 4th edition.** The classification of mental disorders used by most mental health professionals in the United States.

dichromatism. Color blindness in which either the red-green or the blue-yellow system is lacking. The red-green form is relatively common; the blue-yellow form is the rarest of all forms of color blindness.

difference reduction. A problem-solving strategy in which one sets up subgoals that, when obtained, put one in a state closer to the goal.

difficult temperament. Term used to describe a child who is irritable, has irregular sleeping and eating patterns, and responds intensely and negatively to new situations.

diffusion of responsibility. The tendency for persons in a group situation to fail to take action (as in an emergency) because others are present, thus diffusing the responsibility for acting. A major factor in inhibiting bystanders from intervening in emergencies.

digit-span task. An experiment in which the observer is shown various sequences of unrelated items (digits, letters, or words) and is then asked to recall the items in order.

dimensional appraisal theories. A group of appraisal theories that identify a range of appraisal dimensions thought to be sufficient to account for differences among emotions.

direct observation. The observation of a particular phenomenon under study as it occurs naturally.

discrimination. A reaction to differences.

disorganized. Term used to describe a child who exhibits contradictory behaviors related to attachment to his or her caretaker.

displacement. (a) A defense mechanism whereby a motive that may not be directly expressed (such as sex or aggression) appears in a more acceptable form. (b) The principle of loss of items from short-term memory as too many new items are added.

display rules. A culture's rules for the types of emotions people should experience in certain situations, and the behaviors (including facial expressions) appropriate for each emotion.

dispositional attribution. Attributing a person's actions to internal dispositions (attitudes, traits, motives), as opposed to situational factors.

dissociation. Under certain conditions some thoughts and actions become split off, or dissociated, from the rest of consciousness and function outside of awareness.

dissociative identity disorder. The existence in a single individual of two or more distinct identities or personalities that alternate in controlling behavior. Formerly called multiple personality disorder.

distress. Feelings of anxiety, depression, or agitation, or experiences such as insomnia, loss of appetite, or numerous aches and pains.

dream analysis. Talking about the content of one's dreams and then free associating to that content.

dreaming. An altered state of consciousness in which remembered images and fantasies are temporarily confused with external reality.

drive theories. Theories of motivation that emphasize the role of internal factors.

drug abuse. Continued use of a drug by a person who is not dependent on it (that is, shows no signs of tolerance, withdrawal, or compulsive craving), despite serious consequences.

drug dependence. A pattern of compulsive drug use usually characterized by tolerance (the need to take more and more of the drug to achieve the same effect), withdrawal (unpleasant physical and psychological reactions if the drug is discontinued), and compulsive use (taking more of the drug than intended, being unable to control drug use, or spending a great deal of time trying to obtain the drug).

dynamic control theory. Instead of an early, hard-wired system sensitive to a small number of visual primitives, there is a malleable system whose components can be quickly reconfigured to perform different tasks at different times.

E

eardrum. The membrane at the inner end of the auditory canal, leading to the middle ear.

easy temperament. Term used to describe a child who is playful, regular in his or her sleeping and eating patterns, and adapts readily to new situations.

eclectic approach. An approach to looking at topics within psychology using multiple psychological perspectives.

educational psychologist. A psychologist whose research interest lies in the application of psychological principles to the education of children and adults in schools.

ego. The executive of the personality.

egocentrism. The condition of being unaware of perspectives other than one's own and believing that everyone perceives the environment in the same way.

elaboration. A memory process wherein one expands verbal material so as to increase the number of ways to retrieve the material.

elaboration likelihood model. According to this model, if a person is at the high end of the continuum—willing and able to think deeply—then persuasion is said to follow a central route, relying on controlled and effortful thinking; if a person is at the low end of the continuum—for whatever reasons not willing or able to think deeply—then persuasion is said to follow a peripheral route, relying on automatic and effortless thinking.

electroconvulsive therapy (ECT). A mild electric current is applied to the brain to produce a seizure similar to an epileptic convulsion. Also known as electroshock therapy.

emergent features. Features that owe their existence to the configuration of other features.

emotion. A complex condition that arises in response to certain affectively toned experiences.

emotion-focused coping. Ways of reducing anxiety or stress that do not deal directly with the emotion-producing situation; defense mechanisms are a form of emotion-focused coping.

emotion regulation. People's responses to their own emotions.

encoding stage. Occurs when environmental information is translated into and stored as a meaningful entity.

engineering psychologist. A psychologist who specializes in the relationship between people and machines, seeking, for example, to design machines that minimize human error.

episodic memory. A type of memory that stores facts about personal episodes. The fact or episode is encoded with respect to the memorizer, and often with respect to the specific time and place as well.

evocative interaction. The interaction between individuals and their environments that arises because the behavior of different individuals evokes different responses from others.

evolutionary psychology. An area of research that studies how psychological processes have evolved by means of natural selection; those behaviors that aided survival or increased the chance of reproduction have tended to persist through the course of evolutionary history.

excitatory conditioning. The ability of a CS to increase the probability or magnitude of a given behavior.

excitatory connections. Connections between two nodes in a connectionist network that are positive: An increase in one leads to an increase in the other.

exotic-becomes-erotic. A theory about the determinants of sexual orientation that integrates nature and nurture views.

experiment. The strongest test of hypotheses about cause and effect in which an investigator carefully controls conditions and takes measurements to discover the causal relationships among variables.

experimental group. In an experiment, the group of subjects given the treatment whose effect is under investigation.

experimental psychologist. A psychologist who uses experimental methods to study how people (and other animals) react to sensory stimuli, perceive the world, learn and remember, reason and respond emotionally.

explicit memory. The kind of memory that underlies a conscious recollection of something in the past.

exponent (of a power function). A unique number that characterizes the function of each sensory modality.

extinction. (a) The experimental procedure, following classical or operant conditioning, of presenting the conditioned stimulus without the usual reinforcement. (b) The reduction in response that results from this procedure.

extracellular thirst. The psychological manifestation of the need for water that occurs when our bodies lose water because we have gone without drinking or have exercised intensively.

F

facial expressions. The muscle actions that move facial landmarks in particular ways.

facial feedback hypothesis. The hypothesis that people's subjective experience of an emotion is determined by feedback from the physiological arousal caused by engaging in specific facial expressions.

facial preference. In infants, an inborn, unlearned preference for faces.

factor analysis. A statistical method used in test construction and in interpreting scores from batteries of tests. The method enables the investigator to compute the minimum number of determiners (factors) required to account for the intercorrelations among the scores on the tests making up the battery.

false-alarm rate. The proportion of false alarms over all the trials in an experiment.

false alarms. The response of incorrectly responding yes when only noise is present.

family therapy. Psychotherapy with the family members as a group rather than treatment of the patient alone.

feature-integration theory. A cornerstone of understanding object perception that was initially proposed by Anne Treisman.

fetal alcohol syndrome. Mental retardation and multiple deformities of the infant's face and mouth due to exposure to alcohol in the womb.

fight-or-flight response. A pattern of bodily responses that prepares the organism for an emergency. Includes increases in pupil size, heart rate, blood pressure, respiration, muscle tension, and the secretion of epinephrine, norepinephrine, ACTH and other hormones; decreases in saliva, mucous, digestive activity, and the size of blood vessels.

figure. The objects of interest, which appear more solid than the ground and appear in front of it. The figure and ground regions are the two most elementary forms of perceptual organization.

fixation. In Freud's psychoanalytic theory, arrested development through failure to pass beyond one of the earlier stages of psychosexual development or to change the objects of attachment (such as fixation at the oral stage or fixation on the mother).

fixed interval schedule. The organism is reinforced for its first response after a certain amount of time has passed since its last reinforcement.

fixed ratio schedule (FR). The number of responses that has to be made before reinforcement is fixed at a particular value.

flashbulb memory. A vivid and relatively permanent record of the circumstances in which one learned of an emotionally charged, significant event.

foot-in-the-door technique. To get people to say "yes" to requests that would ordinarily lead to "no," this technique suggests beginning with a small request that few would refuse.

forebrain. The structures located in the front, or anterior, part of the brain.

formal operational stage. Piaget's fourth stage of cognitive development in which the child becomes able to use abstract rules.

fovea. In the eye, a small area in the central part of the retina, packed with cones; the most sensitive part of the retina for detail vision and color vision in daylight.

free association. A patient is instructed to say everything that comes to mind, regardless of how trivial or embarrassing it may seem.

frequency. The number of cycles per second.

Freudian slip. In psychoanalytic theory, a mistake or substitution of words in speaking or writing that is contrary to the speaker's conscious intention and presumably expresses wishes or thoughts repressed to the unconscious.

frustration-aggression hypothesis. The hypothesis that frustration (thwarting a person's goal-directed efforts) induces an aggressive drive, which, in turn, motivates aggressive behavior.

functional fixedness. When a person has difficulty with a problem, presumably because they represent components of the problem as having a different function than that needed to solve the problem.

functional magnetic imaging (fMRI). A brain imaging technique that measures and records brain activity while participants are engaged in tasks.

functionalism. Studying how the mind works so that an organism can adapt to and function in its environment.

fundamental attribution error. The tendency to underestimate situational influences on behavior and assume that some personal characteristic of the individual is responsible.

G

g. General intelligence factor.

ganglia (sing. ganglion). A group of neuronal cell bodies found outside the brain and spinal cord.

ganzfeld procedure. Tests for telepathic communication between a participant who serves as the "receiver" and another participant who serves as the "sender."

Gardner's theory of multiple intelligences. The theory that there are seven distinct kinds of intelligence that are independent of one another, each operating as a separate system (or module) in the brain according to its own rules. These are (1) linguistic, (2) musical, (3) logical-mathematical, (4) spatial, (5) bodily-kinesthetic, (6) intrapersonal, and (7) interpersonal.

gate control theory of pain. According to this theory, the sensation of pain requires not only that pain receptors be activated, but also that a neural gate in the spinal cord allow these signals to continue to the brain. Pressure stimulation tends to close the gate; this is why rubbing a hurt area can relieve pain. Attitudes, suggestions, and drugs may act to close the gate.

gender identity. A firm sense of oneself as either male or female.

gender schema. A mental structure that organizes the person's perceptual and conceptual world into gender categories (male-female, masculine-feminine).

gene. A segment of a deoxyribonucleic acid molecule.

general adaptation syndrome. A set of responses that is displayed by all organisms in response to stress.

general paresis. A gradual decline in mental and physical functioning, marked changes in personality, and delusions and hallucinations.

generalization. (a) In learning, the detection of a characteristic or principle common to a class of objects or events. (b) In conditioning, the principle that once a conditioned response has been established to a given stimulus, similar stimuli will also evoke that response.

generalized anxiety disorder. A constant sense of tension and dread.

genital stage. In Freud's psychoanalytic theory, the final stage of psychosexual development, beginning at puberty and culminating in mature adult sexuality.

geon. In perception, geometric forms (such as cylinders, cones, blocks, and wedges) that comprise the features of objects. Recognition of an object is good to the extent that the geons of the object can be recovered.

Gestalt. A German word meaning "form" or "configuration." Gestalt psychologists are interested primarily in perception and believe that perceptual experiences depend on the patterns formed by stimuli and on the organization of experience.

glia cells. Supporting cells (not neurons) composing a substantial portion of brain tissue; recent speculation suggests that they may play a role in neural conduction.

grain size. A limiting feature in both imaginal and perceptual processing. It can be thought of as our images are occurring in a mental medium whose grain limits the amount of detail we can detect in an image.

grammatical morpheme. A morpheme that is not a word, including what are commonly referred to as articles and prepositions.

ground. The region that appears to be behind the figure. The figure and ground regions are the two most elementary forms of perceptual organization.

group polarization effect. The tendency of groups to arrive at decisions that are in the same direction but are more extreme than the mean of the pre-discussion decisions of the individuals in the group.

group therapy. A group discussion or other group activity with a therapeutic purpose participated in by more than one client or patient at a time.

grouping by proximity. If the vertical distance between dots is reduced columns will most likely be seen.

grouping by similarity. Grouping like with like.

groupthink. A phenomenon in which members of a group are led to suppress their own dissent in the interests of group consensus.

guilty but mentally ill. A defendant is found to have a substantial disorder of thought or mood that afflicted him at the time of the crime and significantly impaired his judgment, behavior, capacity to recognize reality, or ability to cope with the ordinary demands of life.

H

habit. A learned stimulus-response sequence.

habituation. The reduction in the strength of a response to a repeated stimulus.

habituation method. A technique used to study perception in infants. It is based on the fact that while infants look directly at novel objects they soon tire of doing so (habituation). Hence one can determine the degree to which an infant perceives an object as novel by measuring the time spent looking at it.

hair cells. In audition, hairlike receptors in the cochlea that bend due to vibration of the basilar membrane and then send electrical impulses to the brain.

halfway house. A place where patients who have been hospitalized can live while making the transition back to independent living in the community.

hallucinations. Sensory experiences in the absence of relevant or adequate external stimulation.

hallucinogens. Drugs whose main effect is to change perceptual experience (syn. psychedelic drugs).

hardiness. Resistance to becoming physically or emotionally impaired even in the face of major stressful events.

hashish. A form of cannabis commonly used in the Middle East.

hemispheres. Structures on the left and right sides of the brain that are connected by the corpus callosum.

heritability. The percentage of the variance in any trait that is accounted for by genetic differences among the individuals in a population.

heroin. An extremely addictive central nervous system depressant derived from opium.

hertz (Hz). The unit used to measure the frequency of a sound wave, specifically the number of cycles per second.

heuristic. A short-cut procedure that is relatively easy to apply and can often yield the correct answer, but not inevitably so.

hidden observer. A part of the mind that is not within awareness seems to be watching the person's experience as a whole.

hierarchy of needs. Maslow's way of classifying needs and motives, from the basic biological needs to the more complex psychological motivations that become important only after the basic needs have been satisfied.

hindbrain. All the structures located in the hind, or posterior, part of the brain, closest to the spinal cord.

hippocampus. A brain structure located below the cerebral cortex that is involved in the consolidation of new memories; its role seems to be that of a cross-referencing system, linking together aspects of a particular memory that are stored in separate parts of the brain.

hit rate. The proportion of hits over all the trials in an experiment.

hits. The response of correctly responding "yes" when a signal is present.

holistic thought. An orientation toward the entire context or field and assigning causality to it, making relatively little use of categories and formal logic, and relying instead on dialectical reasoning, which involves recognizing and transcending apparent contradictions.

homeostasis. The normal level of functioning that is characteristic of the healthy organism (Chapter 2); a constant internal state (Chapter 10).

homeostatic sleep drive. A physiological process that strives to obtain the amount of sleep required for a stable level of daytime alertness.

hormones. Chemicals secreted by the endocrine glands into the bloodstream and transported to other parts of the body, where they have specific effects on cells that recognize their message.

hue. The quality best described by the color's name.

humanistic therapies. A general term for approaches to psychotherapy that emphasize the individual's subjective experiences, free will, and ability to solve his or her own problems. Client-centered therapy and Gestalt therapy are examples.

hypercomplex cell. A cell in the visual cortex that responds to a particular orientation and length.

hypnosis. A willing and cooperative individual relinquishes some control over his or her behavior to the hypnotist and accepts some distortion of reality.

hypothalamus. A small but very important structure located just above the brain stem and just below the thalamus. Considered a part of the central core of the brain, it includes centers that govern motivated behavior such as eating, drinking, sex, and emotions; it also regulates endocrine activity and maintains body homeostasis.

hypothesis. A statement that can be tested.

I

id. The most primitive part of the personality and the part from which the ego and the superego later develop.

identification. Respecting or admiring other individuals or groups and obeying their norms and adopting their beliefs, attitudes, and behaviors in order to be like them and identify with them.

identity confusion. Occurs when a person has no consistent sense of self or set of internal standards for evaluating his or her self-worth in major areas of life.

identity crisis. In Erikson's theory of psychosocial development, a period of self-doubt and active questioning about one's definition of self ("Who am I?" "Where am I going?") which typically takes place during adolescence.

ideology. A set of beliefs and attitudes.

ideomotor action. Mentally activating (thinking about) behavioral representations can make actual corresponding behaviors more likely.

illusion. A percept that is false or distorted.

illusory conjunction. An incorrect combination of two separate attributes of an object.

imaginal thought. Images, particularly visual ones, that we can "see" in our mind.

implicit leniency contract. To appear fair, majority members let minority members have their say, but by doing so they unwittingly open the door to minority influence.

implicit memory. The kind of memory that underlies perceptual and cognitive skills. It is often expressed as an improvement on some perceptual or cognitive task without any conscious recollection of the experiences that led to the improvement.

imprinting. A type of early learning in which a newborn forms an attachment with some kind of model (normally, a parent).

in vivo exposure. A method of therapy highly similar to systematic desensitization that requires the client to actually experience the anxiety-producing situations.

incentive motivation. Wanting something.

incentive salience. Objects and events that have become linked with anticipated affect, which serves to grab attention and steer seeking behavior.

incentive theory. A theory of motivation that emphasizes the importance of negative and positive incentives in determining behavior; internal drives are not the sole instigators of activity.

incus. One of three small bones located in the middle ear.

independent variable. A variable that is independent of what the participant does.

individualism. Refers to cultures that emphasize the fundamental separateness and independence of individuals.

individuation. Assessing an individual's personal qualities on a person-by-person basis.

inductive reasoning. Reasoning about arguments in which it is improbable that the conclusion is false if the premises are true.

inductive strength. It is improbable that the conclusion is false if the premises are true.

inferences. (a) A perceptual or memorial process based on what is believed to be true rather than what necessarily is true. (b) Judgments that go beyond the information given.

information-processing model. In general, a model based on assumptions regarding the flow of information through a system; usually best realized in the form of a computer program. In cognitive psychology, theories of how the mind functions are often represented in the form of an information-processing model. By simulating the model on a computer, one can study the properties and implications of the theory.

information-processing skills. Skills that help one gather and analyze information from the environment.

informational social influence. We conform because we believe that other people's interpretations of an ambiguous situation are more correct than our own.

informed consent. The participants must enter a study voluntarily and be permitted to withdraw from it at any time without penalty if they so desire.

inhibitory conditioning. The ability of a CS to decrease the probability or magnitude of a behavioral response.

inhibitory connections. Connections between two nodes in a connectionist network that are negative: An increase in one leads to a decrease in the other.

insecurely attached. Term used to describe a child who is ambivalent and/or shows resistance to his or her caretaker during a reunion episode.

insomnia. Dissatisfaction with the amount or quality of one's sleep.

institutional norms. Like social norms—implicit or explicit rules for acceptable behavior and beliefs—except they are applied to entire institutions, or organizations of the same type.

instrumental conditioning. Certain responses that are learned because they operate on, or affect, the environment.

intellectualization. A defense mechanism whereby a person tries to gain detachment from an emotionally threatening situation by dealing with it in abstract, intellectual terms.

intelligence. (a) That which a properly standardized intelligence test measures. (b) The ability to learn from experience, think in abstract terms, and deal effectively with one's environment.

intelligence quotient (IQ). A ratio of mental age to chronological age.

intensity. How strong a particular stimulus is.

interference. A factor that can impair retrieval from long-term memory. It arises when different items are associated with the same retrieval cue; attempted retrieval of one of these items can be blocked by the inadvertent retrieval of the other item.

interjudge reliability. The consistency achieved by two or more observers when assessing or rating some behavior (for example, in rating the aggressiveness of nursery-school children). Also called interrater agreement.

internal conflicts. Unresolved issues that may be either conscious or unconscious.

internal consistency. A form of test reliability. Specifically, the homogeneity of a set of items on a test, the degree to which they are all measuring the same variable.

internalization. We are convinced that the influencer is correct and change our beliefs and attitudes.

interpersonal therapy. A style of therapy that tends to be more structured and short-term than traditional psychoanalysis.

interposition (as a depth cue). If one object is positioned so that it obstructs the view of the other, the viewer perceives the overlapping object as being nearer.

interrater agreement. See interjudge reliability.

interval schedules. Reinforcement is available only after a certain time interval has elapsed.

intimacy. The emotional component of love which involves closeness and sharing of feelings.

intracellular thirst. The psychological manifestation of the need for water that is caused by osmosis—the tendency of water to move from zones where it is plentiful to zones where it is relatively rare.

introspection. The observation and recording of one's own perceptions, thoughts, and feelings.

introversion–extraversion. The personality dimension first identified by Carl Jung that refers to the degree to which a person's basic orientation is turned inward toward the self or outward toward the external world. At the introversion end are shy individuals who tend to withdraw into themselves; at the extraversion end are sociable individuals who prefer to be with others.

ion channel. A specialized protein molecule that permits specific ions to enter or leave cells. Some ion channels open or close in response to appropriate neurotransmitter molecules; others open or close in response to voltage changes across the cell membrane. This process regulates depolarization and the firing of nerve impulses.

J

James, William. The author of the very first psychology textbook, published in 1890.

James–Lange theory. A classical theory of emotion, named for the two men who independently proposed it. The theory states that the stimulus first leads to bodily responses, and then the awareness of these responses constitutes the experience of emotion.

just noticeable difference (jnd). The minimum difference in stimulus magnitude necessary to tell two stimuli apart.

K

knowledge. According to knowledge acquisition approaches to development, the child's understanding of how facts in a particular domain are organized.

L

language. A multilevel system for relating thoughts to speech by means of word and sentence units.

latency period. In Freud's psychoanalytic theory, a period in middle childhood, roughly the years 6–12, when both sexual and aggressive impulses are said to be in a quiescent state.

lateral hypothalamic syndrome. An apparent total lack of hunger caused by the destruction of the lateral hypothalamus.

law of effect. The principle that any behavior that is followed by reinforcement is strengthened; from the infinite pool of possible responses, those that lead to reinforcement are repeated, whereas those that do not are extinguished.

learned helplessness. A condition of apathy or helplessness created experimentally by subjecting an organism to unavoidable trauma (such as shock, heat, or cold). Being unable to avoid or escape an aversive situation produces a feeling of helplessness that generalizes to subsequent situations.

learning. A relatively permanent change in behavior that occurs as the result of practice.

libido. (Latin for "lust.") In Freud's psychoanalytic theory, the psychic energy of the id.

liking. Friendship and the early stages of more intimate relationships.

limbic system. A set of structures that are closely interconnected with the hypothalamus and appear to impose additional controls over some of the instinctive behaviors regulated by the hypothalamus and the brain stem.

literature review. A scholarly summary of the existing body of research on a given topic.

lobes. Large regions of the cerebral cortex that perform diverse functions.

long-term depression. A long-lasting decrease in synaptic transmission at synapses in the cerebellar cortex.

long-term potentiation. A phenomenon concerning the neural bases of learning. Once stimulated, neurons will show an increase in their rate of activity when subsequently stimulated (at least up to a period of months).

long-term store. The large repository of information where we maintain all information that is generally available to us.

loosening of associations. Occurs when the individual's ideas shift from one topic to another in ways that appear unrelated.

loudness. An intensity dimension of hearing correlated with the amplitude of the sound waves that constitute the stimulus. Greater amplitudes yield greater loudnesses.

LSD. A potent drug that produces hallucinations at very low doses. See also hallucinogen.

lucid dream. A dream in which events seem so normal (lacking the bizarre and illogical character of most dreams) that the dreamer believes he or she is awake and conscious.

M

magnetic resonance imaging (MRI). A computer-based scanning procedure that uses strong magnetic fields and radio-frequency pulses to generate a picture of a cross section of the brain or body. Provides greater precision than the CT scanner.

maladaptive. Having adverse effects on the individual or on society.

malleus. One of three small bones located in the middle ear.

manic episodes. An episode in which an individual is energetic, enthusiastic, full of self-confidence, talks continually, rushes from one activity to another with little need for sleep, and makes grandiose plans, paying little attention to their practicality.

marijuana. The dried leaves of the hemp plant (cannabis); also known as hashish, "pot," or "grass." Hashish is actually an extract of the plant material and, hence, is usually stronger than marijuana. Intake may enhance sensory experiences and produce a state of euphoria.

marital therapy. Psychotherapy with both members of a couple aimed at resolving problems in their relationship (syn. couples therapy).

maturation. An innately determined sequence of growth and change that is relatively independent of external events.

McGurk effect. Results from conflicting auditory and visual information.

mean. The technical term for an arithmetic average.

meaning. The concept named by a word.

means-ends analysis. A problem-solving strategy in which one compares one's current state to the goal state in order to find the most important difference between them; eliminating this difference then becomes the main subgoal.

measurement. A system for assigning numbers to variables.

meditation. Achieving an altered state of consciousness by performing certain rituals and exercises.

medulla. The lowest section of the brainstem, a slight enlargement of the spinal cord as it enters the skull; the point at which the major nerve tracts cross over so that the right cerebral hemisphere controls the left side of the body, and the left cerebral hemisphere controls the right side.

melatonin. A hormone that induces sleep.

menarche. The first menstrual period.

mental imagery. Mental representations that are picture-like. Not the same as eidetic imagery.

mental model. A concrete mental representation of a problem situation that may be useful in solving the problem.

mental rotation. The notion that a mental image of an object can be rotated in the mind in fashion analogous to rotating the real object.

mere exposure effect. The finding that familiarity all by itself increases liking.

meta-analysis. A form of literature review in which authors use statistical techniques to combine and draw conclusions about studies previously conducted.

metacognition. Thinking about thinking.

metamers. A pair of such matching lights—that is, two lights with different physical makeups that appear identical.

methadone. An agonist drug used in treating heroin-dependent individuals.

method of loci. An aid to serial memory. Verbal material is transformed into mental images, which are then located at successive positions along a visualized route, such as an imaged walk through the house or down a familiar street.

midbrain. The middle of the brain.

middle ear. The part of the ear that transmits sound waves from the eardrum to the oval window of the inner ear by means of three tiny connecting bones (malleus, incus, and stapes).

minimal risk. The principle that risks anticipated in the research should be no greater than those ordinarily encountered in daily life.

minimalist appraisal theories. A group of appraisal theories that are based on reducing the number of appraisal dimensions to minimum, often based on fundamental themes.

Minnesota Multiphasic Personality Inventory (MMPI). A pencil-and-paper version of a psychiatric interview that consists of more than 550 statements concerning attitudes, emotional reactions, physical and psychological symptoms, and experiences. Test takers respond to each statement by answering, "True," "False," or "Cannot say."

minority influence. Minorities can move majorities toward their point of view if they present a consistent position without appearing rigid, dogmatic, or arrogant.

misattribution of arousal. Lingering physiological arousal can be mistakenly attributed to subsequent circumstances and intensify our emotional reactions to those circumstances.

M'Naghten Rule. A defendant may be found not guilty by reason of insanity only if he was so severely disturbed at the time of his act that he did not know what he was doing, or if he did know what he was doing, did not know that it was wrong.

model of the environment. A representation of the world within our brains that we use to consciously perceive, make decisions, and behave.

monoamine oxidase (MAO). One of the enzymes responsible for the breakdown of a group of neurotransmitters called biogenic amines (norepinephrine, dopamine, and serotonin are examples); believed to be important in the regulation of emotion. Drugs that inhibit the action of this enzyme (MAO inhibitors) are used in treating depression.

monoamine oxidase inhibitor (MAOI). A class of drugs used to treat depression; the drug inhibits the action of an enzyme (monoamine oxidase) that breaks down certain neurotransmitters (such as dopamine, norepinephrine, and serotonin), thereby prolonging the action of these neurotransmitters.

monochromatism. Total color blindness, the visual system being achromatic. A rare disorder.

mood disorder. A mental disorder characterized by disturbances of mood. Depression, mania (exaggerated excitement), and bipolar disorders in which the individual experiences both extremes of mood are examples.

moods. Free-floating and diffuse affective states.

moral judgment. Children's understanding of moral rules and social conventions.

morpheme. Any small linguistic unit that carries meaning.

motivation. A condition that energizes behavior and gives it direction.

multimodal attention. Attention can move within a modality, such as from one visual stimulus to another, or between modalities.

multivariate experiment. A type of experiment that involves the simultaneous manipulation of several independent variables.

Munsell system. A scheme for specifying colored surfaces by assigning them one of 10 hue names and two numbers, one indicating saturation and the other brightness.

N

naïve realism. People's tendency to take their constructed, subjective realities to be faithful renderings of an objective world.

naltrexone. An antagonist drug that blocks the action of heroin because it has a greater affinity for the opioid receptors than does heroin itself.

narcolepsy. Recurring, irresistible attacks of drowsiness with the likelihood of falling asleep at any time.

narrative review. A form of literature review in which authors use words to describe studies previously conducted and to discuss the strength of the available psychological evidence.

nature view. The view that human beings enter the world with an inborn store of knowledge and understanding of reality.

nature-nurture issue. The problem of determining the relative importance of heredity (nature) and the result of upbringing in a particular environment (nurture) on behavior.

negative hallucinations. In a hypnotic state, when a person does not perceive something that normally would be perceived.

negative reinforcement. Reinforcing a response by the removal of an aversive stimulus.

negatively correlated. As the value of one variable increases, the value of another decreases.

nerve. A bundle of elongated axons belonging to hundreds or thousands of neurons.

neural sensitization. Potentially permanent changes in the brain that follow drug addition whereby dopamine neurons are activated more highly by drugs and drug-related stimuli.

neuron. A specialized cell that transmits neural impulses or messages to other neurons, glands, and muscles.

neurosis (pl. neuroses). A mental disorder in which the individual is unable to cope with anxieties and conflicts and develops symptoms that he or she finds distressing, such as obsessions, compulsions, phobias, or anxiety attacks. In Freud's psychoanalytic theory, neurosis results from the use of defense mechanisms to ward off anxiety caused by unconscious conflicts. No longer a diagnostic category of DSM-IV.

neurotic anxiety. Fear that is out of proportion to the actual danger posed (such as stage fright).

neuroticism. The name of the emotional instability–stability dimension in Eysenck's factor-analytic theory of personality. Moody, anxious, and maladjusted individuals are at the neurotic or unstable end; calm, well-adjusted individuals are at the other.

neurotransmitter. A chemical that diffuses across the synaptic gap and stimulates the next neuron.

noise. Anything in the environment irrelevant to what the observer is trying to detect.

nonassociative learning. Learning about a single stimulus.

non-REM sleep (or NREM sleep). Refers to the other four sleep stages (besides REM) in which eye movements are virtually absent, heart and breathing rates decrease markedly, the muscles are relaxed, and the brain's metabolic rate decreases 25 to 30 percent compared to wakefulness.

normality. Appropriate perception of reality, ability to exercise voluntary control over behavior, self-esteem and acceptance, ability to form affectionate relationships, and productivity.

normative social influence. We conform to a group's social norms or typical behaviors to become liked and accepted.

noun phrase. A phrase that centers on a noun and specifies the subject of an underlying proposition.

nuclei (sing. nucleus). A collection of nerve cell bodies grouped in the brain or spinal cord.

nurture view. The view that human knowledge is acquired through experiences and interactions with the world.

O

obese. Being 30% or more above the weight level that would be appropriate for a person's body structure and height.

object permanence. The awareness that an object continues to exist even when it is not present.

object relations theory. An outgrowth of psychoanalytic theory that deals with the person's attachments to others over the course of development. Emphasizes ego functioning more than did classical psychoanalytic theory.

objectification theory. A sociocultural account of how being raised in a culture that sexually objectifies the female body fundamentally alters girls' and women's self-views and well-being.

objective anxiety. Fear that is proportionate to the danger posed.

observational learning. People can learn by observing the actions of others and noting the consequences of those actions.

obsessions. Persistent intrusions of unwelcome thoughts, images, or impulses that elicit anxiety.

obsessive-compulsive disorder. An anxiety disorder taking one of three forms: (a) persistent intrusions of unwelcome thoughts, images, or impulses that elicit anxiety (obsessions); (b) irresistible urges to carry out certain acts or rituals that reduce anxiety (compulsions); (c) both of these in combination.

Oedipal conflict. In Freud's psychoanalytic theory, the conflict that arises during the phallic stage of psychosexual development in which the individual is sexually attracted to the parent of the opposite sex and perceives the same-sex parent as a rival.

olfactory bulb. A region of the brain involved in olfaction (smell); it is a way station between the receptors in the nasal passage and the olfactory cortex.

olfactory cortex. The area in the brain responsible for the sense of smell. Located on the inside of the temporal lobes.

olfactory system. The receptors in the nasal passage, certain regions of the brain, and interconnecting neural pathways.

omission training. Behavior that prevents an appetitive stimulus.

operant conditioning. Certain responses are learned because they operate on, or affect, the environment.

operation. A mental routine for separating, combining, and otherwise transforming information in a logical manner.

opiates. Drugs that diminish physical sensation and the capacity to respond to stimuli by depressing the central nervous system.

opponent-color theory. A theory of color perception that postulates two types of color-sensitive units that respond in opposite ways to the two colors of an opponent pair. One type of unit responds to red or green, the other to blue or yellow. Since a unit cannot respond in two ways at once, reddish-greens and yellowish-blues cannot occur.

opponent-process model of sleep and wakefulness. A theory that states that the brain possesses two opponent processes that govern the tendency to fall asleep or remain awake: the homeostatic sleep drive and the clock-dependent alerting process.

oral stage. In Freud's psychoanalytic theory, the first stage of psychosexual development; pleasure derives from the lips and mouth, as in sucking at the mother's breast.

organizational psychologist. A psychologist concerned with selecting people who are most suitable for particular jobs or designing structures that facilitate collaboration and teamwork.

outer ear. The external ear and auditory canal, whose purpose is to funnel sound waves towards the inner ear.

oval window. A membrane on the cochlea of the inner ear that receives vibrations from the ear drum via three connecting bones (malleus, incus, and stapes). Vibrations at the oval window set up similar vibrations in the internal fluid of the cochlea, ultimately activating the hair cells that serve as auditory receptors.

overextension. Tendency to apply a new word too widely.

overjustification effect. Explaining one's own behavior with too much emphasis on salient situational causes and not enough emphasis on personal causes, like intrinsic interest.

P

panic attack. An episode of acute and overwhelming apprehension or terror.

panic disorder. An anxiety disorder in which the individual has sudden and inexplicable episodes of terror and feelings of impending doom accompanied by physiological symptoms of fear (such as heart palpitations, shortness of breath, muscle tremors, faintness).

paranoid. An individual who has delusions of persecution.

parapsychology. Phenomena that are "beside psychology," including telepathy, clairvoyance, precognition, psychokinesis.

parasympathetic nervous system. A division of the automatic nervous system, the nerve fibers of which originate in the cranial and sacral portions of the spinal cord. Active in relaxed or quiescent states of the body and to some extent antagonistic to the sympathetic division, or system.

partial-report condition. After viewing an array of letters in Sperling's partial-report procedure an observer is asked to report only one, randomly chosen row of letters.

partial-report procedure. An experiment devised by George Sperling in which a varied array of letters is flashed to observers for a brief period.

passion. The motivational component of love which consists of sexual attraction and the romantic feeling of being "in love."

passionate love. Contrasted with companionate love. An intensely emotional state in which tender and sexual feelings, elation and pain, anxiety and relief, altruism and jealousy coexist in a confusion of feelings.

PCP. Sold as a hallucinogen (under such street names as "angel dust," "Shermans," and "superacid"), this drug is technically a dissociative anesthetic.

peak experiences. Transient moments of self-actualization.

perceptual interference. The finding that objects had to eventually be more focused for the observers to recognize them in the very-out-of-focus condition than in the moderately-out-of-focus condition.

periaqueductal gray. A section of the brain in which neurons are connected to other neurons that inhibit cells that would normally carry the pain signals arising in the pain receptors. This area appears to be the main place where strong painkillers such as morphine affect neural processing.

peripheral nervous system. The nerves connecting the brain and spinal cord to other parts of the body.

peripheral route. When an individual responds to noncontent cues in a communication or to the context of a communication.

personal construct. The dimensions that individuals themselves use to interpret themselves and their social worlds.

personality. The distinctive and characteristic patterns of thought, emotion, and behavior that define an individual's personal style of interacting with the physical and social environment.

personality disorders. Ingrained habitual, and rigid patterns of behavior or character that severely limit the individual's adaptive potential; often society sees the behavior as maladaptive whereas the individual does not.

personality inventory. An inventory for self-appraisal, consisting of many statements or questions about personal characteristics and behavior that the person judges to apply or not to apply to him or her.

personality psychologist. A psychologist whose area of interest focuses on classifying individuals and studying the differences between them. This specialty overlaps both developmental and social psychologists to some extent.

person-environment relationship. The objective situation in which a person finds herself.

perspective (as a depth cue). When parallel lines in a scene appear to converge in the im-age, they are perceived as vanishing in the distance.

phallic stage. In Freud's psychoanalytic theory, the third stage of psychosexual development in which gratification is associated with stimulation of the sex organs and sexual attachment is to the parent of the opposite sex.

phasic pain. The kind of sharp pain experienced immediately upon suffering an injury; usually brief with a rapid increase in intensity followed by a decrease.

phenothiazines. A group of antipsychotic drugs that relieve the symptoms of schizophrenia by blocking the access of the neurotransmitter dopamine to its receptors. Chlorpromazine (Thorazine) and fluphenazine (Prolixin) are examples.

pheromones. Chemicals that float through the air to be sniffed by other members of the species.

phobia. Intense fear of a stimulus or situation that most people do not consider particularly dangerous.

phoneme. Discrete speech categories.

phonological buffer. One of the two distinct stores of working memory that briefly stores information in an acoustic code.

phonological code. Memory encoding that is based on the sounds of the names of the digits.

photon. The smallest unit of light energy.

physical description (of an object). A listing of all the information necessary to completely reproduce the object.

physiology. The study of the functions of the living organism and its parts.

pitch. A sensation based on the frequency of sound.

place theory of pitch perception. A theory of hearing that associates pitch with the place on the basilar membrane where activation occurs.

pluralistic ignorance. The phenomenon in which everybody in a group misleads everybody else by defining an ambiguous situation as a nonemergency.

positive hallucinations. In a hypnotic state, when a person sees objects or hears voices that are not actually present.

positive psychology. The study of how positive experiences, emotions, and personality traits promote human flourishing.

positive reinforcement. Reinforcing a response by the presentation of a positive stimulus.

positively correlated. The values of two variables either increase together or decrease together.

positron emission tomography (PET). A computer-based scanning procedure that measures regional changes in blood flow to map the neural activities of the brain.

postconventional level of moral development. Level of moral development in which children evaluate actions in terms of higher-order ethical principles.

posterior system (for attention). Represents the perceptual features of an object, such as its location in space, shape, and color, responsible for selecting one object among many on the basis of the features associated with that object.

post-event memory construction. During memory formation, we may add new information that is suggested to us by others.

posthypnotic amnesia. A particular form of posthypnotic suggestion in which the hypnotized person forgets what has happened during the hypnosis until signaled to remember.

posthypnotic response. A response that occurs when a subject who has been roused from hypnosis responds with movement to a prearranged signal by the hypnotist.

post-traumatic stress disorder. An anxiety disorder in which a stressful event that is outside the range of usual human experience, such as military combat or a natural disaster, brings in its aftermath such symptoms as a re-experiencing of the trauma and avoidance of stimuli associated with it, a feeling of estrangement, a tendency to be easily startled, nightmares, recurrent dreams, and disturbed sleep.

power function. The relation between Ψ and Φ, which is (basically) $\Psi = \phi^r$.

pragmatic rules. Rules used in deductive reasoning that are less abstract than logical rules, but still applicable to many different domains of life. An example is the permission rule.

precognitive emotions. Emotions that are not based on appraisal.

preconscious. All the information that is not currently "on our mind" but that we could bring into consciousness if called upon to do so.

preconscious memories. Memories that are accessible to consciousness.

preconventional level of moral development. Level of moral development in which children evaluate actions are as right or wrong on the basis of anticipated punishment.

predictability. The degree to which we know if and when an event will occur.

preferential looking method. A method of examining infants' perceptual preferences by presenting them two stimuli simultaneously and noting the amount of time the infants gaze at each object.

prefrontal lobes. The lobes just behind the forehead.

preoperational stage. Piaget's second stage of cognitive development. The children think in terms of symbols, but does not yet comprehend certain rules or operations.

primacy effect. The tendency for first information we receive to have a greater impact on our overall impressions.

primary reinforcer. A reinforcer that is able to act as a reward independently of prior learning.

priming. The increased accessibility or retrievability of information stored in memory produced by the prior presentation of relevant cues.

primitive features. Qualities such as shape and color.

proactive interaction. The interaction between individuals and their environments that arises because different individuals choose to enter different situations and to shape those situations differently after entering them.

problem-focused coping. Reducing anxiety or stress by dealing in some way with the anxiety-producing situation. Escaping the situation or finding a way to alter it are examples.

production of language. Producing language by starting with a thought that translates into a sentence and ends up with sounds that express the sentence.

projection. Repressing one's own unacceptable impulses and expressing hostile attitudes toward others who are perceived to possess those impulses.

projective test. Presents an ambiguous stimulus to which the person may respond as he or she wishes.

proposition. A statement that expresses a factual claim.

propositional thought. Expresses a proposition or claim.

prosopagnosia. A loss in the ability to recognize faces that results from brain damage.

prototype. The properties that describe the best examples of the concept.

proximity. How far apart they live.

psi. Processes of information and/or energy exchange that are not currently explicable in terms of known science.

psychoactive drugs. Drugs that affect behavior, consciousness, and/or mood.

psychoanalysis. (a) The method developed by Freud and extended by his followers for treating mental disorders. (b) The theory of personality which grew out of experiences with the psychoanalytic method of treatment. The theory emphasizes the role of unconscious processes in personality development and in motivation.

psychoanalytic perspective. An approach to psychology that tries to explain certain kinds of behaviors in terms of unconscious beliefs, fears, and desires.

psychoanalytic theory. The premise that much of what we think and do is driven by unconscious processes.

psychodynamic therapies. A style of therapy based on the idea that a person's current problems cannot be resolved successfully without a thorough understanding of their unconscious basis in early relationships with parents and siblings.

psychological determinism. The doctrine that all thoughts, emotions, and actions have causes.

psychological perspective. A distinct approach or way of looking at topics within psychology.

psychological perspectives (of abnormality). A group of theories that see mental disorders as problems in the functioning of the mind.

psychology. The scientific study of behavior and mental processes.

psychoneuroimmunology. The study of how the body's immune system is affected by stress and other psychological variables.

psychophysical function. Performance as a function of stimulus intensity.

psychophysical procedures. Procedures used to determine thresholds of sensory modalities.

psychophysiological disorder. Physical disorders in which emotions are believed to play a central role.

psychosexual stages. Freud's term for the stages (oral, anal, phallic) during the first 5 years of life in which the individual progresses through developmental periods that affect his or her personality.

psychosis (pl. psychoses). A severe mental disorder in which thinking and emotion are so impaired that the individual is seriously out of contact with reality. No longer a major diagnostic category in DSM-IV.

psychotherapy. The treatment of mental disorders by psychological (rather than physical or biological) means.

puberty. The period of sexual maturation that transforms a child into a biologically mature adult capable of sexual reproduction.

punishment. A procedure used to decrease the strength of a response by presenting an aversive stimulus whenever the response occurs.

pupil. In the eye, a circular opening in the iris (the colored part of the eye) that expands and contracts, varying according to the intensity of light present.

Q

Q-sort. An assessment technique by which a rater provides a systematic description of an individual's personality by sorting a set of personality statements (for example, "Has a wide range of interests") into groups, ranging from those that are least descriptive to those that are most descriptive of the individual.

quality. A sensory description of what a particular stimulus is like.

R

random assignment. A system for assigning participants to experimental and control groups so that each participant has an equal chance of being assigned to any group.

ratio schedules. Reinforcement schedules where reinforcement depends on the number of responses the organism makes.

rationalization. A defense mechanism in which self-esteem is maintained by assigning plausible and acceptable reasons for conduct entered on impulsively or for less acceptable reasons.

reaction formation. A defense mechanism in which a person denies a disapproved motive through giving strong expressions to its opposite.

reactive interaction. The interaction between individuals and their environments that arises because different individuals interpret, experience, and react to situations in different ways.

recall test. When a person is asked to produce a memorized item using minimal retrieval cues.

receptor. A specialized cell sensitive to particular kinds of stimuli and connected to nerves composed of afferent neurons (such as the retina of the eye). Used more loosely, the organ containing these sensitive portions (such as the eye or the ear).

recognition test. When a person must decide whether he or she has seen a particular item before.

reconstructive processes. The processes by which memory, once formed, is systematically altered based on inference and post-event information.

reductionism. Reducing psychological notions to biological ones.

reference groups. Groups with which we identify; we refer to them in order to evaluate and regulate our opinions and actions.

reflectance characteristic. Determines how the paper reflects some wavelengths more than others.

rehearsal. The conscious repetition of information in short-term memory, usually involving speech. The process facilitates the short-term recall of information and its transfer to long-term memory.

reinforcement. (a) In classical conditioning, the experimental procedure of following the conditioned stimulus by the unconditioned stimulus. (b) In operant conditioning, the analogous procedure of following the occurrence of the operant response by the reinforcing stimulus. (c) The process that increases the strength of conditioning as a result of these arrangements.

relative height (as a depth cue). In perception, a monocular cue for depth. Among identical objects, those that are higher in an image are perceived as being farther away.

relative motion (as a depth cue). The different speeds of two objects can be a depth cue.

relative size (as a depth cue). In perception, a monocular cue for depth. If an image contains an array of objects of similar shape, the smaller objects are perceived as being farther away.

relaxation training. Training in various techniques for relaxing muscle tension. The procedure is based on Jacobson's progressive relaxation method, in which the person learns how to relax muscle groups one at a time, the assumption being that muscular relaxation is effective in bringing about emotional relaxation.

reliability. Yielding reproducible and consistent results.

REM sleep. The period of sleep during which rapid eye movements occur.

repression. The ego pushes a threatening thought or forbidden impulse out of awareness into the unconscious.

resonance. The degree to which a sound of a particular frequency reverberates over a mathematically matched distance.

responses to emotion. How people cope with or react to their own emotion or the situation that elicited it.

resting membrane potential. The electrical potential across the nerve cell membrane when it is in its resting state (in other words, not responding to other neurons); the inside of the cell membrane is slightly more negative than the outside.

reticular formation. A system of ill-defined nerve paths and connections within the brain stem, lying outside the well-defined nerve pathways, and important as an arousal mechanism.

retina. The portion of the eye sensitive to light, containing the rods and the cones.

retrieval stage. Occurs when one attempts to pull from one's memory information that was previously encoded and stored there.

retrograde amnesia. Loss of memory for events and experiences occurring in a period of time prior to the amnesia-causing trauma.

reuptake. The process by which a neurotransmitter is "taken up" again (reabsorbed) by the synaptic terminals from which it had been released.

right to privacy. Information about a person acquired during a study must be kept confidential and not made available to others without his or her consent.

rod. In the eye, an element of the retina mediating achromatic sensation only; particularly important in peripheral vision and night vision.

Rorschach Test. A projective test developed by the Swiss psychiatrist Hermann Rorschach, consisting of a series of 10 cards, each of which displays a rather complex inkblot.

S

saccade. The quick movement of the eyes between eye fixations.

saltatory conduction. Occurs when the nerve impulse jumps from one node of Ranvier to the next.

saturation. The purity of the color.

schema (pl. schemas). Theory about how the physical and social worlds operate (Chapter 3); a mental representation of a class of people, objects, events, or situations (Chapter 8); a cognitive structure that helps us perceive, organize, process, and utilize in-

formation (Chapter 13); organized beliefs and knowledge about people, objects, events, and situations.

schematic processing. The cognitive process of searching for the schema in memory that is most consistent with the incoming information.

schizophrenia. A group of disorders characterized by severe personality disorganization, distortion of reality, and inability to function in daily life.

Scholastic Assessment Test (SAT). An example of a group-administered general-ability test.

school psychologist. A professional psychologist employed by a school or school system, with responsibility for testing, guidance, research, and so on.

scientific. Research methods used to collect data are scientific when they are (1) unbiased (do not favor one hypothesis over another) and (2) reliable (other qualified people can repeat the observations and obtain the same results).

second-order conditioning. Conditioning in which the UCS is not biologically significant (such as food, water, or shock) but gains power as a UCS by being consistently paired with a biologically significant UCS.

secondary reinforcer. A reinforcer that gains its status as a reward at least partly through learning about its relationship with other events.

securely attached. Term used to describe a child who seeks to interact with his or her caretaker during a reunion episode.

selective adaptation. In perception, a loss of sensitivity to motion that occurs when we view motion. The adaptation is selective because we lose sensitivity to the motion viewed, and to similar motions, but not to motion that differs significantly in direction or speed. Presumably the result of fatigued neurons in the cerebral cortex.

selective breeding. A method of studying genetic influences by mating animals that display certain traits and selecting for breeding from among their offspring those that express the trait. If the trait is primarily determined by heredity, continued selection for a number of generations will produce a strain that breeds true for that trait.

selective reinforcement. Strengthening of specific desired behaviors.

self. All the ideas, perceptions, and values that characterize "I" or "me."

self-expansion. Increase our potential abilities and resources.

self-fulfilling prophecy. Once activated, stereotypes can set in motion a chain of behavioral processes that serve to draw out from others behavior that confirms the initial stereotype.

self-help groups. Groups that are conducted without a professional therapist.

self-objectification. When a person thinks about and values her own body more from a third-person perspective, focusing on observ-

able body attributes ("How do I look?"), rather than from a first-person perspective, focusing on privileged, or unobservable body attributes ("How do I feel?").

self-perception theory. The theory that attitudes and beliefs are influenced by observations of one's own behavior; sometimes we judge how we feel by observing how we act.

self-regulation. Monitoring, or observing, one's own behavior.

self-schema (pl. self-schemas). Cognitive generalizations about the self, derived from past experience, that organize and guide the processing of self-related information.

semantic code. Memory encoding that is based on some meaningful association that the digits have.

semantic memory. A type of memory that stores general knowledge, such as the meanings of words. Knowledge is encoded in relation to other knowledge rather than in relation to the memorizer.

sensations. Experiences associated with simple stimuli.

sensitive periods. Periods that are optimal for a particular kind of development.

sensitive responsiveness. A characteristic of a caretaker who responds promptly when the baby cries and behaves affectionately when they pick up the baby. The caregiver also tailors their response to the baby's needs.

sensitization. The process by which an organism learns to strengthen its reaction to a stimulus if a threatening or painful stimulus follows.

sensorimotor stage. A period in which infants are busy discovering the relationships between their actions and the consequences of those actions.

sensory coding. How stimuli are transmitted from the sensory receptors to the brain.

sensory response. The magnitude of nervous activity, which rises and then falls.

sensory store. The place in the memory where information arriving from the environment is first placed.

sentence unit. Grammatical units that can be either a sentence or a phrase.

separation anxiety. Distress when a caretaker is not nearby.

serial search (of memory). Comparing a test stimulus in sequence to each item in short-term memory.

serotonin reuptake inhibitors. A class of antidepressant drugs that work by increasing levels of the neurotransmitter serotonin in the synapse.

set point. The point at which body weight is set and that the body strives to maintain.

sex typing. The acquisition of behaviors and characteristics that a culture considers appropriate to one's sex.

sexual orientation. The degree to which an individual is sexually attracted to members of the opposite sex and/or to members of the same sex.

sexual selection. A special case of natural selection that yields traits that promote reproductive success in the sex with the greater potential reproductive rate.

shading and shadows (as a depth cue). The configuration of shading and shadows provides information about an object's depth.

shadowing. Repeating back one auditory message.

sham feeding. A result of a surgical procedure so that whenever something is eaten, it will fall out of the body rather than be digested.

shaping. Reinforcing only variations in response that deviate in the direction desired by the experimenter.

short-term store. The second repository of information (after the sensory store), into which attended information from sensory store is placed.

signal. What the observer is trying to detect in an experiment.

signal detection theory. A theory of the sensory and decision processes involved in psychophysical judgments, with special reference to the problem of detecting weak signals in noise.

similarity heuristic. The use of similarity—to a specific case or to a prototype—to estimate the probability of an event.

simple cell. A cell in the visual cortex that responds to a bar of light or straight edge of a particular orientation and location in the visual field.

simple phobia. Excessive fear of a specific object, animal, or situation in the absence of real danger.

situational attribution. Attributing a person's actions to factors in the situation or environment, as opposed to internal attitudes and motives.

sleep disorder. When inability to sleep well produces impaired daytime functioning or excessive sleepiness.

slow to warm up temperament. Term used to describe a child who is relatively inactive, tends to withdraw from new situations in a mild way, and requires more time than easy infants to adapt to new situations.

Snellen acuity. Acuity measured relative to a viewer who does not need to wear glasses.

social cognition. The examination of people's subjective interpretations of their social experiences, as well as their modes of thinking about the social world.

social cognitive neuroscience. The study of how stereotyping, attitudes, person perception, and self-knowledge are executed in the brain.

social desirability effects. A particular form of bias that can occur during a survey when some people try to present themselves in a favorable light.

social facilitation. The effects of coaction and the presence of an audience.

social inhibition. The sometimes derailing effects of coactors and audiences on performance.

social norms. Implicit rules and expectations that dictate what we ought to think and how we ought to behave.

social phobia. Extreme insecurity in social situations accompanied by an exaggerated fear of embarrassing oneself.

social psychologist. A psychologist who studies social interaction and the ways in which individuals influence one another.

social psychology. The study of how people think and feel about their social world and how they interact and influence one another.

social stereotype. Personality traits or physical attributes given to a whole class of people.

social-cognitive theory (to personality). Reciprocal determinism, in which external determinants of behavior (such as rewards and punishments) and internal determinants (such as beliefs, thoughts, and expectations) are part of a system of interacting influences that affect both behavior and other parts of the system.

social-learning theory. The application of learning theory to the problems of personal and social behavior (syn. social behavior theory).

sociocultural approach to development. An approach that characterizes the child not as a physical scientist seeking "true" knowledge but as a newcomer to a culture who seeks to become a native by learning how to look at social reality through the lens of that culture.

somatic system. Carries messages to and from the sense receptors, muscles, and the surface of the body.

sound wave. A wave defined by periodically varying air pressure over time.

source wavelengths. Wavelengths coming from some light source.

span of apprehension. The number of immediately recallable items.

spontaneous recovery. A phenomenon in classical conditioning discovered by Pavlov. When an organism undergoes execution of a conditioned response and is then moved to a new context, the conditioned response may reappear.

stages of development. Developmental periods, usually following a progressive sequence, that appear to represent qualitative changes in either the structure or the function of the organism (such as Freud's psychosexual stages, Piaget's cognitive stages).

standard. An arbitrary level of stimulus intensity against which other intensities are judged.

Stanford-Binet Intelligence Scale. Stanford revision of the Binet test which measures the kinds of changes in intelligence ordinarily associated with growing older.

stapes. One of three small bones located in the middle ear.

statistical significance. The trustworthiness of an obtained statistical measure as a state-

ment about reality; for example, the probability that the population mean falls within the limits determined from a sample. The expression refers to the reliability of the statistical finding and not to its importance.

statistics. The discipline that deals with sampling data from a population of individuals and then drawing inferences about the population from those data.

stereotype. A set of inferences about the personality traits or physical attributes of a whole class of people; schemas of classes of people.

stereotype threat. The mere threat of being identified with a stereotype can raise an individual's anxiety level, which in turn degrades his or her performance.

Sternberg memory-scanning task. Type of experiment introduced by Sternberg in which during each trial a participant is shown a set of digits that he or she must temporarily maintain in the working memory.

Sternberg's triarchic theory. This theory has three parts or subtheories. The componential subtheory, which deals with thought processes; the experiential subtheory, which deals with the effects of experience on intelligence; and the contextual subtheory, which considers the effects of the individual's environment and culture.

stimulants. Drugs that increase alertness and general arousal.

storage stage. The maintenance of stored information over time.

stress. Experiencing events that are perceived as endangering one's physical or psychological well-being.

stress responses. Reactions to events an individual perceives as endangering his or her well-being. These may include bodily changes that prepare for emergency (the fight-or-flight response) as well as such psychological reactions as anxiety, anger and aggression, apathy and depression, and cognitive impairment.

stressors. Events that an individual perceives as endangering his or her physical or psychological well-being.

stroboscopic motion. An illusion of motion resulting from the successive presentation of discrete stimulus patterns arranged in a progression corresponding to movement, such as motion pictures.

Stroop interference. Results because word reading is such a dominant and automatic response among skilled readers it is difficult for them to ignore a printed word and name the word's ink color when the word is a color that is different from the color of the ink.

structuralism. The analysis of mental structures.

subjective experience. The affective state or feeling tone.

subjectivist perspective. An orientation toward understanding behavior and mental processes in terms of the subjective realities people actively construct.

superego. The part of personality that judges whether actions are right or wrong.

suprathreshold conditions. Conditions in which stimulus intensity is above threshold.

survey method. A method of obtaining information by questioning a large sample of people.

symbol. Anything that stands for or refers to something other than itself.

sympathetic nervous system. A division of the autonomic nervous system, characterized by a chain of ganglia on either side of the spinal cord, with nerve fibers originating in the thoracic and lumbar portions of the spinal cord. Active in emotional excitement and to some extent antagonistic to the parasympathetic division.

synapse. The close functional connection between the axon of one neuron and the dendrites or cell body of another neuron.

synaptic plasticity. Changes in the morphology and/or physiology of synapses involved in learning and memory.

syntax. A specification of the relationships between words in phrases and sentences.

systematic desensitization. A behavior therapy technique in which hierarchies of anxiety-producing situations are imagined (or sometimes confronted in reality) while the person is in a state of deep relaxation. Gradually the situations become dissociated from the anxiety response.

T

tabula rasa. Latin, meaning "blank slate." The term refers to the view that human beings are born without any innate knowledge or ideas; all knowledge is acquired through learning and experience. Proposed by the 17th- and 18th-century British empiricists (Locke, Hume, Berkeley, Hartley).

tardive dyskinesia. Involuntary movements of the tongue, face, mouth, or jaw.

taste receptors. Receptors for taste located in clusters on the tongue and around the mouth. Also called taste buds.

temperament. Mood-related personality characteristics.

temporal-integration paradigm. An experiment in which 24 dots are presented in 24 of the 25 squares of an imaginary 55 array, and the observer's task is to report the location of the missing dot.

temporal pattern. The spacing sequence of electrical impulses.

temporal theory of sound. A theory of pitch perception which assumes that the frequency of neural impulses traveling up the auditory nerve correspond to the frequency of a tone.

test. Presents a uniform situation to a group of people who vary in a particular trait.

thalamus. Two groups of nerve cell nuclei located just above the brain stem and inside the cerebral hemispheres. Considered a part of the central core of the brain. One area acts as a sensory relay station, the other plays a role in sleep and waking; this portion is considered part of the limbic system.

Thematic Apperception Test (TAT). A participant is shown up to 20 ambiguous pictures of persons and scenes and asked to make up a story about each picture.

theory. An interrelated set of propositions about a particular phenomenon.

theory of ecological optics. The information from the environment—or more specifically, its two-dimensional representation on our retina—is all that is really necessary to live a normal life.

theory of mind. The child's understanding of basic mental states, such as desires, percepts, beliefs, knowledge, thoughts, intentions, and feelings.

thirst. The psychological manifestation of the need for water.

thought and action tendencies. Urges to think and act in certain ways.

timbre. Our experience of the complexity of a sound.

tolerance. The need for a greater amount of a drug to achieve the same euphoria.

tonic pain. The kind of steady, long-lasting pain experienced after an injury has occurred; usually produced by swelling and tissue damage. In contrast to phasic pain.

top-down feedback connections. Connections that go from the higher levels to the lower levels.

top-down processes. Processes in perception, learning, memory, and comprehension that are driven by the organism's prior knowledge and expectations, rather than by the input.

transduction. Translate physical energy into electrical signals that can make their way to the brain.

transference. The tendency for the client to make the therapist the object of emotional responses.

traumatic events. Situations of extreme danger that are outside the range of usual human experience.

triangular theory of love. This theory divides love into three components: intimacy, passion, and commitment.

trichromatic theory. A theory of color perception that postulates three basic color receptors (cones), a "red" receptor, a "green" receptor, and a "blue" receptor. The theory explains color blindness by the absence of one or more receptor types (syn. Young-Helmholtz theory).

tricyclic antidepressant. A class of antidepressants that relieve the symptoms of depression by preventing the reuptake of the neurotransmitters serotonin and norepinephrine, thereby prolonging their action. Imipramine (brand names, Tofranil and Elavil) is one drug commonly prescribed.

two-factor theory. The theory that emotions result from the combination of two factors—an initial state of unexplained arousal plus a cognitive explanation (or appraisal) for that arousal.

type A pattern. A behavior pattern discovered in studies of coronary heart disease. Type As are people who have a sense of time urgency, find it difficult to relax, and become impatient and angry when confronted with delays or with people whom they view as incompetent. Type As are at risk for heart disease.

U

unconditional positive regard. Feeling that oneself is valued by parents and others even when their feelings, attitudes, and behaviors are less than ideal.

unconditioned response (UCR). In classical conditioning, the response given originally to the unconditioned stimulus used as the basis for establishing a conditioned response to a previously neutral stimulus.

unconditioned stimulus (UCS). In classical conditioning, a stimulus that automatically elicits a response, typically via a reflex, without prior conditioning.

unconscious. The thoughts, attitudes, impulses, wishes, motivations, and emotions of which we are unaware (Chapter 1); contains some memories, impulses, and desires that are not accessible to consciousness (Chapter 6); impulses, wishes, and inaccessible memories that affect our thoughts and behavior (Chapter 13).

undoing effect of positive emotions. Positive emotions may be particularly suited for helping people recover from any lingering arousal that follows negative emotions.

V

validity. Measuring what is intended to be measured.

variable. Something that can occur with different values.

variable interval schedule. Reinforcement still depends on a certain interval having elapsed, but the interval's duration varies unpredictably.

variable ratio schedule. The organism is reinforced only after making a certain number of responses, but that number varies unpredictably.

ventromedial hypothalamic syndrome. Extreme appetites caused by lesions of the ventromedial hypothalamus.

verb phrase. The section of a sentence that gives the predicate of the proposition.

vicarious learning. Learning by observing the behavior of others and noting the consequences of that behavior (syn. observational learning).

visceral perception. Our perception of our own arousal.

visual acuity. The eye's ability to resolve details.

visual code. A mental picture of digits.

visual cortex. The part of the brain that is concerned with vision.

visual field. The total visual array acting on the eye when it is directed toward a fixation point.

visual neglect. A patient who, although not blind, ignores everything on one side of their visual field (usually the left side).

visual search task. A task in which the observer is asked to determine whether some target object is present in a cluttered display.

visual-spatial sketchpad. One of the two distinct stores of working memory that briefly stores information in a visual or spatial code.

vulnerability-stress model. An interactive model of physical or mental disorders that proposes that an individual will develop a disorder only when he or she has both some constitutional vulnerability (predisposition) and experiences stressful circumstances. Same as diathesis-stress model.

W

wanting. The anticipation of pleasure, as in cravings.

weapon focus. Rapt attention on a weapon in the scene.

Weber fraction. The constant of proportionality.

Wechsler Adult Intelligence Scale. A verbal scale and a performance scale that yield separate scores as well as a full-scale IQ.

Wernicke's aphasia. A language defect caused by damage to Wernicke's area, that portion of the left cerebral hemisphere involved in language understanding. Individuals with damage in this area are not able to comprehend words; they can hear words, but they do not know their meanings.

whole-report condition. After viewing an array of letters for a brief period of time, the observer is asked to report as many letters as possible.

withdrawal. The intensely aversive reaction to the cessation of drug use.

withdrawal symptoms. Unpleasant physiological and psychological reactions that occur when a person suddenly stops taking an addictive drug; these range from nausea, anxiety, mild tremors, and difficulty sleeping at low levels of dependence to vomiting, cramps, hallucinations, agitation, and severe tremors or seizures at higher levels.

word salad. Unrelated words and phrases and idiosyncratic word associations.

working backwards. A problem-solving strategy in which one works backwards from the goal towards the current state.

working memory. Memories that are stored for only a few seconds.

REFERENCES

ABBOTT, B. B., SCHOEN, L. S., & BADIA, P. (1984). Predictable and unpredictable shock: Behavioral measures of aversion and physiological measures of stress. *Psychological Bulletin, 96,* 45–71.

ABELSON, R. P. (1968). Computers, polls, and public opinion—Some puzzles and paradoxes. *Transaction, 5,* 20–27.

ABRAMSON, L. Y., ALLOY, L. B., HOGAN, M. E., WHITEHOUSE, W. G., DONOVAN, P., ROSE, D., PANZARELLA, C., & RANIERE, D. (1999). Cognitive vulnerability to depression: Theory and evidence. *Journal of Cognitive Psychotherapy: An International Quarterly, 13,* 5–20.

ABRAMSON, L. Y., METALSKY, G. I., & ALLOY, L. B. (1989). Hopelessness depression: A theory-based subtype of depression. *Psychological Review, 96,* 358–372.

ABRAMSON, L. Y., SELIGMAN, M. E. P., & TEASDALE, J. (1978). Learned helplessness in humans: Critique and reformulation. *Journal of Abnormal Psychology, 87,* 49–74.

ADAMS, J. L. (1974). *Conceptual blockbusting.* Stanford, CA: Stanford Alumni Association.

ADAMS, M., & COLLINS, A. (1979). A schema-theoretic view of reading. In R. O. Freedle (Ed.), *New Directions Discourse Processing,* Vol. 12. Norwood, NJ: Ablex.

ADER, R. (2001). Psychoneuroimmunology. *Current Directions in Psychological Science, 10,* 94–98.

ADKINS-REGAN, E. (1988). Sex hormones and sexual orientation in animals. *Psychobiology, 16,* 335–347.

ADORNO, T. W., FRENKEL-BRUNSWIK, E., LEVINSON, D. J., & SANFORD, R. N. (1950). *The authoritarian personality.* New York: Harper.

AFFLECK, G., & TENNEN, H. (1996). Construing benefits from adversity: Adaptational significance and dispositional underpinnings. *Journal of Personality, 64,* 899–922.

AFFLECK, G., TENNEN, H., CROOG, S., & LEVINE, S. (1987a). Causal attribution, perceived benefits and morbidity after a heart attack: An eight-year study. *Journal of Consulting and Clinical Psychology, 55,* 29–55.

AFFLECK, G., TENNEN, H., CROOG, S., & LEVINE, S. (1987b). Causal attribution, perceived control, and recovery from a heart attack. *Journal of Social and Clinical Psychology, 5,* 339–355.

AGRAS, W. S. (1993). Short term psychological treatments for binge eating. In C. G. Fairburn & G. T. Wilson (Eds.), *Binge eating: Nature, assessment, and treatment.* New York: Guilford.

AINSWORTH, M. D. S., BLEHAR, M. C., WALTERS, E., & WALL, S. (1978). *Patterns of attachment: A psychological study of the strange situation.* Hillsdale, NJ: Erlbaum.

AKERS, C. (1984). Methodological criticisms of parapsychology. In S. Krippner (Ed.), *Advances in parapsychological research* (Vol. 4). Jefferson, NC: McFarland.

AKHTAR, S., WIG, N. N., VARMA, V. K., PERSHARD, D., & VERMA, S. K. (1975). A phenomenological analysis of symptoms in the obsessive-compulsive neurosis. *British Journal of Psychiatry, 127,* 342–348.

ALBERTS, B., BRAY, D., LEWIS, J., RAFF, M., ROBERTS, K., & WATSON, J. D. (1994). *Molecular biology of the cell* (3rd ed.). New York: Garland.

ALDAG, R. J., & FULLER, S. R. (1993). Beyond fiasco: A reappraisal of the groupthink phenomenon and a new model of group decision processes. *Psychological Bulletin, 113,* 533–552.

ALLEN, J. B., KENRICK, D. T., LINDER, D. E., & MCCALL, A. M. (1989). Arousal and attraction: A response-facilitation alternative to misattribution and negative-reinforcement models. *Journal of Personality and Social Psychology, 57,* 261–270.

ALLEN, V. L., & LEVINE, J. M. (1969). Consensus and conformity. *Journal of Experimental Social Psychology, 5,* 389–399.

ALLEN, V. L., & LEVINE, J. M. (1971). Social support and conformity: The role of independent assessment of reality. *Journal of Experimental Social Psychology, 7,* 48–58.

ALLOY, L., & ABRAMSON, L. Y. (1997, May). *The cognitive vulnerability to depression project.* Paper presented to the Midwestern Psychological Association, Chicago.

ALLOY, L. B., & ABRAMSON, L. Y. (1979). Judgment of contingency in depressed and nondepressed students: Sadder but wiser? *Journal of Experimental Psychology: General, 108,* 441–485.

ALLOY, L. B., ABRAMSON, L. Y., SAFFORD, S. M., & GIBB, B. E. (in press). The Cognitive Vulnerability to Depression (CVD) Project: Current findings and future directions. In L. B. Alloy & J. H. Riskind (Eds.), *Cognitive vulnerability to emotional disorders.* Hillsdale, NJ: Erlbaum.

ALLOY, L. B., ABRAMSON, L. Y., WHITEHOUSE, W. G., HOGAN, M. E., PANZARELLA, C., ROBINSON, M. S., ROSE, D. T., & DONOVAN, P. (2001). *Prospective incidence of Axis I disorders in individuals at high and low cognitive risk for depression.* Manuscript in preparation, Temple University.

ALLOY, L. B., ABRAMSON, L. Y., WHITEHOUSE, W. G., HOGAN, M. E., TASHMAN, N., STEINBERG, D., ROSE, D. T., & DONOVAN, P. (1999). Depressogenic cognitive styles: Predictive validity, information processing and personality characteristics, and developmental origins. *Behaviour Research and Therapy, 37,* 503–531.

ALLOY, L. B., & TABACHNIK, N. (1984). Assessment of covariation by animals and humans: Influence of prior expectations and current situational information. *Psychological Review, 91,* 112–149.

ALLPORT, F. H. (1920). The influence of the group upon association and thought. *Journal of Experimental Psychology, 3,* 159–182.

ALLPORT, F. H. (1924). *Social psychology.* Boston: Houghton Mifflin.

ALLPORT, G. H. (1954). *The nature of prejudice.* Reading, MA: Addison-Wesley.

ALLPORT, G. W., & ODBERT, H. S. (1936). Trait-names: A psycholexical study. *Psychological Monographs, 47* (1, Whole No. 211).

ALTEMEYER, B. (1988). Enemies of freedom: Understanding right-wing authoritarianism. San Francisco: Jossey-Bass.

ALWIN, D. F., COHEN, R. L., & NEWCOMB, T. M. (1991). *Personality and social change: Attitude persistence and changes over the lifespan.* Madison: University of Wisconsin Press.

AMERICAN ACADEMY OF PAIN MEDICINE AND AMERICAN PAIN SOCIETY CONSENSUS STATEMENT. (1997). The use of opioids for the treatment of chronic pain. *Pain Forum, 6,* 77–79.

AMERICAN ACADEMY OF PEDIATRICS. (2001). Clinical practice guideline: Treatment of school-aged children with attention-deficit/hyperactivity disorder. *Pediatrics, 108,* 1033–1045.

AMERICAN PSYCHIATRIC ASSOCIATION. (1994). *Diagnostic and statistical manual of mental disorders* (4th ed.). Washington, DC: American Psychiatric Association.

AMERICAN PSYCHOLOGICAL ASSOCIATION. (1996). *Affirmative action: Who benefits?* Washington, DC: Author.

AMERICAN PSYCHIATRIC ASSOCIATION. (2000). *Diagnostic and Statistical Manual of Mental Disorders* (4th ed., text revision). Washington, DC: American Psychiatric Association Press.

AMERICAN PSYCHOLOGICAL ASSOCIATION. (1990). Ethical principles of psychologists. *American Psychologist, 45,* 390–395.

ANCH, M. A., BROWMAN, C. P., MITLER, M. M., & WALSH, J. K. (1988). Sleep: A scientific perspective. Englewood Cliffs, NJ: Prentice-Hall.

ANCOLI-ISRAEL, S., KRIPKE, D. F., & MASON, W. (1987). Characteristics of obstructive and central sleep apnea in the elderly: An interim report. *Biological Psychiatry, 22,* 741–750.

ANDERSEN, S. M., & GLASSMAN, N. S. (1996). Responding to significant others when they are not there: Effects on interpersonal inference, motivation, and affect. In R. M. Sorrentino & E. T. Higgins (Eds.), *Handbook of motivation and cognition* (Vol. 3, pp. 262–321). New York: Guilford.

ANDERSON, C. A., & BUSHMAN, B. J. (2001). Effects of violent video games on aggressive behavior, aggressive cognition, aggressive affect, physiological arousal, and prosocial behavior: A meta-analytic review of the scientific literature. *Psychological Science, 12,* 353–359.

ANDERSON, J. R. (1983). *The architecture of cognition.* Cambridge, MA: Harvard University Press.

ANDERSON, J. R. (1987). Skill acquisition: Compilation of weak-method problem solutions. *Psychological Review, 94,* 192–210.

ANDERSON, J. R. (1990). *Cognitive psychology and its implications* (3rd ed.). New York: Freeman.

ANDERSON, J. R. (1991). The adaptive nature of human categorization. *Psychological Review, 98,* 409–429.

ANDERSON, M. (1992). *Intelligence and development: A cognitive theory.* Oxford: Blackwell.

ANDERSSON, B. E. (1992). Effects of day-care on cognitive and socioemotional competence of thirteen-year-old Swedish schoolchildren. *Child Development, 63,* 20–36.

ANDREASEN, N. C. (1988). Brain imaging: Applications in psychiatry. *Science, 239,* 1381–1388.

ANDREASEN, N. C., FLAUM, M., SCHULTZ, S., DUZYUREK, S., & MILLER, D. (1997). Diagnosis, methodology, and subtypes of schizophrenia. *Neuropsychobiology, 35,* 61–63.

ANDREASEN, N. C., FLAUM, M., SWAYZE, V. W., TYRRELL, G., & ARNDT, S. (1990). Positive and negative symptoms in schizophrenia: A critical reappraisal. *Archives of General Psychiatry, 47,* 615–621.

ANDREWS, K. H., & KANDEL, D. B. (1979). Attitude and behavior. *American Sociological Review, 44,* 298–310.

ANGHOFF, W. H., & JOHNSON, E. G. (1988). *A study of the differential impact of curriculum on aptitude test scores. Research report 88-46.* Princeton, NJ: Educational Testing Service.

ANGOFF, W. H. (1988). The nature-nurture debate, aptitudes, and group differences. *American Psychologist, 43,* 713–720.

ANTROBUS, J. (1983). REM and NREM sleep reports: Comparisons of word frequencies by cognitive classes. *Psychophysiology, 20,* 562–568.

ANTROBUS, J. (1991). Dreaming: Cognitive processes during cortical activation and high afferent thresholds. *Psychological Review, 98,* 96–121.

ANTROBUS, J. (1993). Dreaming: Could we do without it? In A. Moffitt, M. Kramer, & R. Hoffman (Eds.), *The functions of dreaming.* Albany: State University of New York Press.

APOINTE, J. F., RIVERS, R. Y., & WOHL, J. (1995). *Psychological interventions and cultural diversity.* Boston: Allyn & Bacon.

ARCHER, D., & MCDANIEL, P. (1995). Violence and gender: Differences and similarities across societies. In R. B. Ruback & N. A. Weiner (Eds.), *Interpersonal violent behaviors: Social and cultural aspects* (pp. 63–87). New York: Springer.

ARDREY, R. (1966). *The territorial imperative.* New York: Dell.

ARENDT, H. (1963). *Eichmann in Jerusalem: A report on the banality of evil.* New York: Viking Press.

ARMOR, D. A., & TAYLOR, S. E. (1998). Situated optimism: Specific outcome expectancies and self-regulation. In M. P. Zanna (Ed.), *Advances in experimental social psychology* (vol. 30, pp. 309–379). New York: Academic Press.

ARMSTRONG, S. L., GLEITMAN, L. R., & GLEITMAN, H. (1983). What some concepts might not be. *Cognition, 13,* 263–308.

ARNOLD, M. (1949). A demonstrational analysis of the TAT in a clinical setting. *Journal of Abnormal and Social Psychology, 44,* 97–111.

ARNTZ, A., DRESSON, L., & DE JONG, P. (1994). The influence of anxiety on pain: Attentional and attributional mediators. *Pain, 56,* 307–314.

ARON, A. (2002, January). Self-expansion as a motivational basis for positive psychology. In M. Green & T. McLaughlin-Volpe (Chairs), *Positive Relationships,* Symposium presented at the first annual pre-conference on Positive Psychology, Savannah, GA: Society for Personality and Social Psychology.

ARON, A., ARON, E. N., & SMOLLAN, D. (1992). Inclusion of other in the self scale and the structure of interpersonal closeness. *Journal of Personality and Social Psychology, 63,* 596–612.

ARON, A., ARON, E. N., TUDOR, M., & NELSON, G. (1991). Close relationships as including other in the self. *Journal of Personality and Social Psychology, 60,* 241–253.

ARON, A., NORMAN, C. C., & ARON, E. N. (1998). The self-expansion model and motivation. *Representative Research in Social Psychology, 22,* 1–13.

ARONSON, E. (1995). *The social animal* (7th ed.). San Francisco: Freeman.

ARONSON, E., & CARLSMITH, J. M. (1963). The effect of the severity of threat on the devaluation of forbidden behavior. *Journal of Abnormal and Social Psychology, 66,* 584–588.

ARONSON, E., & MILLS, J. (1959). The effect of severity of initiation on liking for a group. *Journal of Abnormal and Social Psychology, 59,* 177–181.

ARONSON, E., & THIBODEAU, R. (1992). The jigsaw classroom: A cooperative strategy for reducing prejudice. In J. Lynch, C. Modgil, & S. Modgil (Eds.), *Cultural diversity in the schools.* London: Falmer Press.

ARRIGO, J. M., & PEZDEK, K. (1997). Lessons from the study of psychogenic amnesia. *Current Directions in Psychological Science, 6,* 148–152.

ARTMAN, L., & CAHAN, S. (1993). Schooling and the development of transitive inference. *Developmental Psychology, 29,* 753–759.

ASCH, S. E. (1946). Forming impressions of personality. *Journal of Abnormal and Social Psychology, 41,* 258–290.

ASCH, S. E. (1952). *Social psychology.* Englewood Cliffs, NJ: Prentice-Hall.

ASCH, S. E. (1955). Opinions and social pressures. *Scientific American, 193,* 31–35.

ASCH, S. E. (1958). Effects of group pressure upon modification and distortion of judgments. In E. E. Maccoby, T. M. Newcomb, & E. L. Hartley (Eds.), *Readings in social psychology* (3rd ed.). New York: Holt, Rinehart & Winston.

ASHMEAD, D. H., DAVIS, D. L., WHALEN, T., & ODOM, R. D. (1991). Sound localization and sensitivity to interaural time differences in human infants. *Child Development, 62,* 1211–1226.

ASLIN, R. N. (1987). Visual and auditory development in infancy. In J. D. Osofsky (Ed.), *Handbook of infant development* (2nd ed.). New York: Wiley.

ASLIN, R. N., & BANKS, M. S. (1978). Early visual experience in humans: Evidence for a critical period in the development of binocular vision. In S. Schneider, H. Liebowitz, H. Pick, & H. Stevenson (Eds.), *Psychology: From basic research to practice.* New York: Plenum.

ASLIN, R. N., PISONI, D. V., & JUSCZYK, P. W. (1983). Auditory development and speech perception in infancy. In P. H. Mussen (Ed.), *Handbook of child psychology* (Vol. 2). New York: Wiley.

ASPINWALL, L. G., & BRUNHART, S. M. (1996). Distinguishing optimism from denial: Optimistic beliefs predict attention to health threats. *Personality and Social Psychology Bulletin, 22,* 993–1003.

ASSAD, G., & SHAPIRO, B. (1986). Hallucinations: Theoretical and clinical overview. *American Journal of Psychiatry, 143,* 1088–1097.

ATKINSON, D. (1983). Ethnic similarity in counseling psychology: A review of the research. *Counseling Psychologist, 11,* 79–92.

ATKINSON, D., MARUYAMA, M., & MATSUI, S. (1978). The effects of counselor race and counseling approach on Asian Americans' perceptions of counselor credibility and utility. *Journal of Counseling Psychology, 25,* 76–83.

ATKINSON, D. R., & HACKETT, G. (1998). *Counseling diverse populations.* Boston: McGraw-Hill.

ATKINSON, R. C. (1975). Mnemotechnics in second-language learning. *American Psychologist, 30,* 821–828.

ATKINSON, R. C., HERRNSTEIN, R. J., LINDZEY, G., & LUCE, R. D. (Eds.). (1988). *Stevens' handbook of experimental psychology* (Vols. 1 and 2). New York: Wiley.

ATKINSON, R. C., & SHIFFRIN, R. M. (1971a). The control of short-term memory. *Scientific American, 225,* 82–90.

ATKINSON, R. C., & SHIFFRIN, R. M. (1971b). Human memory: A proposed system and its control processes. In K. W. Spence (Ed.), *The psychology of learning and motivation: Advances in research and theory* (pp. 89–195). New York: Academic Press.

AULD, F., & HYMAN, M. (1991). *Resolution of inner conflict: An introduction to psychoanalytic therapy.* Washington, DC: American Psychological Association.

AVERILL, J. R. (1983). Studies on anger and aggression: Implications for theories of emotion. *American Psychologist, 38,* 1145–1160.

AWAYA, S., MIYAKE, Y., IMAYUMI, Y., SHIOSE, Y., KNADA, T., & KOMURO, K. (1973). Amblyopia. *Japanese Journal of Ophthalmology, 17,* 69–82.

AX, A. (1953). The physiological differentiation between fear and anger in humans. *Psychosomatic Medicine, 15,* 433–442.

BAARS, B. J. (1988). *A cognitive theory of consciousness.* New York: Cambridge University Press.

BACHMAN, J. G., JOHNSTON, L. D., & O'MALLEY, M. (1998). Explaining recent increase in students' marijuana use: Impacts of perceived risks and disapproval, 1976 through 1996. *American Journal of Public Health, 88,* 887–892.

BADDELEY, A. D. (1986). *Working memory.* Oxford: Clarendon.

BADDELEY, A. D. (1990). *Human memory: Theory and practice.* Boston: Allyn and Bacon.

BADDELEY, A. D., & HITCH, G. J. (1974). Working memory. In G. H. Bower (Ed.), *The psychology of learning and motivation* (Vol. 8). New York: Academic Press.

BADDELEY, A. D., THOMPSON, N., & BUCHANAN, M. (1975). Word length and the structure of short-term memory. *Journal of Verbal Learning and Verbal Behavior, 14,* 575–589.

BAER, P. E., & FUHRER, M. J. (1968). Cognitive processes during differential trace and delayed conditioning of the G. S. R. *Journal of Experimental Psychology, 78,* 81–88.

BAHRICK, H. P., & PHELPHS, E. (1987). Retention of Spanish vocabulary over eight years. *Journal of Experimental Psychology: Learning, Memory and Cognition, 13,* 344–349.

BAILEY, J. M., & MARTIN, N. G. (1995, September). *A twin registry study of sexual orientation.* Paper presented at the twenty-first annual meeting of the International Academy of Sex Research, Provincetown, MA.

BAILEY, J. M., & PILLARD, R. C. (1991). A genetic study of male sexual orientation. *Archives of General Psychiatry, 48,* 1089–1096.

BAILEY, J. M., & PILLARD, R. C. (1995). Genetics of human sexual orientation. *Annual Review of Sex Research, 6,* 126–150.

BAILEY, J. M., PILLARD, R. C., NEALE, M. C., & AGYEI, Y. (1993). Heritable factors influence sexual orientation in women. *Archives of General Psychiatry, 50,* 217–223.

BAILEY, J. M., & ZUCKER, K. J. (1995). Childhood sex-typed behavior and sexual orientation: A conceptual analysis and quantitative review. *Developmental Psychology, 31,* 43–45.

BAILLARGEON, R. (1987). Object permanence in 3½- and 4½-month-old infants. *Developmental Psychology, 23,* 655–664.

BAILLARGEON, R., & DEVOS, J. (1991). Object permanence in young infants: Further evidence. *Child Development, 62,* 1227–1246.

BAILLARGEON, R., SPELKE, E. S., & WASSERMAN, S. (1985). Object permanence in five month old infants. *Cognition, 20,* 191–208.

BANDURA, A. (1969). *Principles of behavior modification.* New York: Holt, Rinehart and Winston.

BANDURA, A. (1973). *Aggression: A social learning analysis.* Englewood Cliffs, NJ: Prentice-Hall.

BANDURA, A. (1977). *Social learning theory.* Englewood Cliffs, NJ: Prentice-Hall.

BANDURA, A. (1986). *Social foundations of thought and action: A social cognitive theory.* Englewood Cliffs, NJ: Prentice-Hall.

BANDURA, A. (1995). *Self-efficacy in changing societies.* New York: Cambridge University Press.

BANDURA, A. (2001). Social cognitive theory: An agentic perspective. *Annual Review of Psychology, 52,* 1–26.

BANDURA, A., BLANCHARD, E. B., & RITTER, B. (1969). The relative efficacy of desensitization and modeling approaches for inducing behavioral, affective, and attitudinal changes. *Journal of Personality and Social Psychology, 13,* 173–199.

BANKS, W. P., & PRINTZMETAL, W. (1976). Configurational effects in visual information processing. *Perception and Psychophysics, 19,* 361–367.

BANKS, W. P., & SALAPATEK, P. (1983). Infant visual perception. In P. H. Mussen (Ed.), *Handbook of child psychology* (Vol. 2). New York: Wiley.

BANYAI, E. I., & HILGARD, E. R. (1976). A comparison of active-alert hypnotic induction with traditional relaxation induction. *Journal of Abnormal Psychology, 85,* 218–224.

BAREFOOT, J. C., DODGE, K. A., PETERSON, B. L., DAHLSTROM, W. G., WILLIAMS, R. B., Jr. (1989). The Cook-Medley Hostility scale: Item content and ability to predict survival. *Psychosomatic Medicine, 51,* 46–57.

BAREFOOT, J. C., WILLIAMS, R. B., & DAHLSTROM, W. G. (1983). Hostility, CHD incidence and total mortality: A 25-year follow-up study of 255 physicians. *Psychosomatic Medicine, 45,* 59–63.

BARGH, J. A. (1997). The automaticity of everyday life. In R. S. Wyer Jr. (Ed.), *Advances in social cognition* (Vol. 10). Mahway, NJ: Erlbaum.

BARGH, J. A. (1999). The cognitive monster: The case against the controllability of automatic stereotype effects. In S. Chaiken & Y. Trope (Eds.), *Dual-process theories in social psychology* (pp. 361–382). New York: Guilford.

BARGH, J. A., CHEN, M., & BURROWS, L. (1996). Automaticity of social behavior: Direct effects of trait construct and stereotype activation on action. *Journal of Personality and Social Psychology, 71,* 230–244.

BARKOW, J., COSMIDES, L., & TOOKY, J. (1990). *The adapted mind: Evolutionary psychology and the generation of culture.* New York: Oxford University Press.

BARLOW, D. H. (1988). *Anxiety and its disorders: The nature and treatment of anxiety and panic.* New York: Guilford.

BARLOW, H. B., & MOLLON, J. D. (1982). *The senses.* Cambridge, England: Cambridge University Press.

BARON, R. S. (1986). Distraction-conflict theory: Progress and problems. In L. Berkowitz (Ed.), *Advances in experimental social psychology* (Vol. 19). New York: Academic Press.

BARRERA, M. E., & MAURER, D. (1981). Recognition of mother's photographed face by the three-month-old infant. *Child Development, 52,* 714–716.

BARRERA, M. E., & MAURER, D. (1981). Discrimination of strangers by the three-month-old. *Child Development, 52,* 558–563.

BARSALOU, L. W. (1985). Ideals, central tendency, and frequency of instantiation as determinants of graded structure in categories. *Journal of Experimental Psychology: Learning, Memory, and Cognition, 11,* 629–654.

BARSALOU, L. W. (1992). *Cognitive psychology: An overview for cognitive scientists.* Hillsdale, NJ: Erlbaum.

BARTLETT, F. C. (1932). *Remembering: A study in experimental and social psychology.* Cambridge, England: Cambridge University Press.

BARTOSHUK, L. M. (1979). Bitter taste of saccharin: Related to the genetic ability to taste the bitter substance propylthiourial (PROP). *Science, 205,* 934–935.

BARTOSHUK, L. M. (1993). Genetic and pathological taste variation: What can we learn from animal models and human disease? *Ciba Foundation Symposium (D7X), 179,* 251–262.

BARTOSHUK, L. M. (2000). Psychophysical advances aid the study of genetic variation in taste. *Appetite, 34,* 105.

BARTSCH, K., & WELLMAN, H. M. (1995). *Children talk about the mind.* New York: Oxford University Press.

BASOGLU, M. (Ed.). (1992). *Torture and its consequences: Current treatment approaches.* Cambridge, England: Cambridge University Press.

BASOGLU, M., & MINECKA, S. (1992). The role of uncontrollable and unpredictable stress in posttraumatic stress responses in torture survivors. In M. Basoglu (Ed.), *Torture and its consequences: Current treatment approaches.* (pp. 182–225). New York: Cambridge University Press.

BASOGLU, M., MINEKA, S., PAKER, M., AKER, T., LIVANOU, M., & GOEK, S. (1997). Psychological preparedness for trauma as a protective factor in survivors of torture. *Psychological Medicine, 27,* 1421–1433.

BATESON, P. (1978). Sexual imprinting and optimal outbreeding. *Nature, 273,* 659–660.

BATSON, C. D. (1991). *The altruism question: Toward a social-psychological answer.* Hillsdale, NJ: Erlbaum.

BAUCOM, D. H., EPSTEIN, N., & GORDON, K. C. (2000). Marital therapy: Theory, practice, and empirical status. In C. R. Snyder & R. Ingram (Eds.), *Handbook of Psychological Change* (pp. 280–308). New York: Wiley.

BAUCOM, D. H., SHOHAM, V., MUESSER, K. T., DAIUTO, A. D., & STICKLE, T. R. (1998). Empirically supported couple and family interventions for marital distress and adult mental health problems. *Journal of Consulting and Clinical Psychology, 66,* 53–88.

BAUM, A., & POSLUSZNY, D. M. (1999). Health psychology: Mapping biobehavioral contributions to health and illness. *Annual Reviews of Psychology, 50,* 147–163.

BAUMEISTER, R. F., & TICE, D. M. (1984). Role of self-presentation and choice in cognitive dissonance under forced compliance: Necessary or sufficient causes? *Journal of Personality and Social Psychology, 43,* 838–852.

BAUMRIND, D. (1964). Some thoughts on ethics of research: After reading Milgram's "Behavioral study of obedience." *American Psychologist, 19,* 421–423.

BAUMRIND, D. (1971). Current patterns of parental authority. *Developmental Psychology Monographs, 1,* 1–103.

BAUMRIND, D. (1980). New directions in socialization research. *American Psychologist, 35,* 639–652.

BAXTER, L., SCHWARTZ, J., BERGMAN, K., & SZUBA, M. (1992). Caudate glucose metabolic rate changes with both drug and behavior therapy for obsessive-compulsive disorder. *Archives of General Psychiatry, 49,* 681–689.

BAXTER, L. R., SCHWARTZ, J. M., GUZE, B. H., & BERGMAN, K. (1990). PET imaging in obsessive compulsive disorder with and without depression. *Journal of Clinical Psychiatry, 51(suppl.),* 61–69.

BAYLEY, J. (1999). *Elegy for Iris.* New York: St. Martin's Press.

BEAMAN, A. L., BARNES, P. J., KLENTZ, B., & MCQUIRK, B. (1978). Increasing helping rates through information dissemination: Teaching pays. *Personality and Social Psychology Bulletin, 4,* 406–411.

BEAUBRUN, G., & GRAY, G. E. (2000). A review of herbal medicines for psychiatric disorders. *Psychiatric Services, 51,* 11301–134.

BECHARA, A., TRANEL, D., DAMASIO, H., ADOLPHS, R., ROCKLAND, C., & DAMASIO, A. R. (1995). Double dissociation of conditioning and declarative knowledge relative to the amygdala and hippocampus in humans. *Science, 269,* 1115–1118.

BECHARA, A., TRANEL, D., DAMASIO, H., & DAMASIO, A. R. (1996). Failure to respond autonomically to anticipated future outcomes following damage to prefrontal cortex. *Cerebral Cortex, 6,* 215–225.

BECK, A. T. (1976). *Cognitive therapy and the emotional disorder.* New York: International Universities Press.

BECK, A. T., RUSH, A. J., SHAW, B. F., & EMERY, G. (1979). *Cognitive therapy of depression.* New York: Guilford.

BECK, J. G. (1995). Hypoactive sexual desire: An overview. *Journal of Consulting and Clinical Psychology, 42,* 861–865.

BEECHER, H. K. (1961). Surgery as placebo. *Journal of the American Medical Association, 176,* 1102–1107.

BEHRMANN, M., & HAIMSON, C. (1999). The cognitive neuroscience of visual attention. *Current Opinion in Neurobiology, 9,* 158–163.

BÉKÉSY, G. VON (1960). *Experiments in hearing* (E. G. Weaver, Trans). New York: McGraw-Hill.

BELL, A. P. (1982). Sexual preference: A postscript. *Siecus Report, 11,* 1–3.

BELL, A. P., & WEINBERG, M. S. (1978). *Homosexualities: A study of diversity among men and women.* New York: Simon & Schuster.

BELL, A. P., WEINBERG, M. S., & HAMMER-SMITH, S. K. (1981a). *Sexual preference: Its development in men and women*. Bloomington: Indiana University Press.

BELL, A. P., WEINBERG, M. S., & HAMMER-SMITH, S. K. (1981b). *Sexual preference: Its development in men and women. Statistical appendix*. Bloomington: Indiana University Press.

BELL, C. J., & NUTT, D. J. (1998). Serotonin and panic. *British Journal of Psychiatry, 172,* 465–471.

BELL, S. M., & AINSWORTH, M. D. (1972). Infant crying and maternal responsiveness. *Child Development, 43,* 1171–1190.

BELOFF, H. (1957). The structure and origin of the anal character. *Genetic Psychology Monographs, 55,* 141–172.

BELSKY, J. (1986). Infant day care: A cause for concern? *Zero to Three, 7,* 1–7.

BELSKY, J., FISH, M., & ISABELLA, R. A. (1991). Continuity and discontinuity in infant negative and positive emotionality: Family antecedents and attachment consequences. *Developmental Psychology, 27,* 421–431.

BELSKY, J., & ROVINE, M. J. (1987). Temperament and attachment security in the strange situation: An empirical rapprochement. *Child Development, 58,* 787–795.

BELSKY, J., & ROVINE, M. J. (1988). Nonmaternal care in the first year of life and the security of infant-parent attachment. *Child Development, 59,* 157–167.

BELSKY, J., WOODWORTH, S., & CRNIC, K. (1996). Trouble in the second year: Three questions about family interactions. *Child Development, 60,* 649–662.

BEM, D. J. (1972). Self-perception theory. In L. Berkowitz (Ed.), *Advances in experimental social psychology* (Vol. 6). New York: Academic Press.

BEM, D. J. (1995). *Exotic becomes erotic: A developmental theory of sexual orientation.* Unpublished manuscript, Cornell University, Ithaca, New York.

BEM, D. J. (1996). Exotic becomes erotic: A developmental theory of sexual orientation. *Psychological Review, 103,* 320–335.

BEM, D. J. (2000). Exotic becomes erotic: Interpreting the biological correlates of sexual orientation. *Archives of Sexual Behavior, 29,* 531–548.

BEM, D. J., & HONORTON, C. (1994). Does psi exist? Replicable evidence for an anomalous process if information transfer. *Psychological Bulletin, 115,* 4–18.

BEM, D. J., PLAMER, J., & BROUGHTON, R. S. (2001). Updating the ganzfeld database: A victim of its own success? *Journal of Parapsychology, 65,* 207–218.

BEM, D. J., WALLACH, M. A., & KOGAN, N. (1965). Group decision-making under risk of aversive consequences. *Journal of Personality and Social Psychology, 1,* 453–460.

BEM, S. L. (1975). Sex role adaptability: One consequence of psychological androgyny. *Journal of Personality and Social Psychology, 31,* 634–643.

BEM, S. L. (1981). Gender schema theory: A cognitive account of sex typing. *Psychological Review, 88,* 354–364.

BEM, S. L. (1985). Androgyny and gender schema theory: A conceptual and empirical integration. In T. B. Sonderegger (Ed.), *Nebraska symposium on motivation 1984: Psychology and gender* (pp. 179–226). Lincoln: University of Nebraska Press.

BEM, S. L. (1987). Gender schema theory and the romantic tradition. In P. Shaver & C. Hendrick (Eds.), *Review of personality and social psychology* (Vol. 7, pp. 251–271). Newbury Park, CA: Sage.

BEM, S. L. (1989). Genital knowledge and gender constancy in preschool children. *Child Development, 60,* 649–662.

BEM, S. L. (1993). *The lenses of gender: Transforming the debate on sexual inequality.* New Haven, CT: Yale University Press.

BENJAMIN, J., LI, L., PATTERSON, C., GREENBERG, B. D., MURPHY, D. L., & HAMER, D. H. Population and familial association between the D4 dopamine receptor gene and measures of novelty seeking. *Nature Genetics, 12,* 81–84.

BENOTSCH, E. G., CHRISTENSEN, A. J., & MCKELVEY, L. (1997). Hostility, social support, and ambulatory cardiovascular activity. *Journal of Behavioral Medicine, 20,* 163–176.

BENSON, D. F. (1985). Aphasia. In K. M. Heilman & E. Valenstein (Eds.), *Clinical neuropsychology* (2nd ed., pp. 17–47). New York: Oxford University Press.

BERENT, I. (2001). Can connectionist models of phonology assembly account for phonology? *Psychonomic Bulletin and Review, 8,* 661–676.

BERGER, T. W. (1984). Long-term potentiation of hippocampal synaptic transmission affects rate of behavioral learning. *Science, 224,* 627–630.

BERGIN, A. E., & LAMBERT, M. J. (1978). The evaluation of therapeutic outcomes. In S. L. Garfield & A. E. Bergin (Eds.), *Handbook of psychotherapy and behavior change* (2nd ed.). New York: Wiley.

BERGIN, A. E., & LAMBERT, M. J. (1979). Counseling the researcher. *Counseling Psychologist, 8,* 53–56.

BERK, L. E. (1997). *Child development* (4th ed.). Needham Heights, MA: Allyn and Bacon.

BERKOWITZ, L. (1965). The concept of aggressive drive. In L. Berkowitz (Ed.), *Advances in experimental social psychology* (Vol. 2). New York: Academic Press.

BERKOWITZ, L. (1981). On the difference between internal and external reactions to legitimate and illegitimate frustration: A demonstration. *Aggressive Behavior, 7,* 83–96.

BERLIN, B., & KAY, P. (1969). *Basic color terms: Their universality and evolution.* Los Angeles: University of California Press.

BERMAN, A. L., & JOBES, D. A. (1991). *Adolescent suicide assessment and intervention.* Washington, DC: American Psychological Association.

BERMAN, K. F., TORREY, E. F., DANIEL, D. G., & WEINBERGER, D. R. (1992). Regional cerebral blood flow in monozygotic twins discordant and concordant for schizophrenia. *Archives of General Psychiatry, 49,* 927–934.

BERMAN, M. E., KAVOUSSI, R. J., & COCCARO, E. F. (1997). Neurotransmitter correlates of human aggression. In D. M. Stoff, J. Breiling, & J. D. Maser (Eds.), *Handbook of antisocial personality disorder* (pp. 305–314). New York: Wiley.

BERNHEIM, K. F. (1997). *The Lanahan cases and readings in abnormal behavior.* Baltimore: Lanahan.

BERNSTEIN, I. L. (1978). Learned taste aversions in children receiving chemotherapy. *Science, 200,* 1302–1303.

BERRIDGE, K. C., & VALENSTEIN, E. S. (1991). What psychological process mediates feeding evoked by electrical stimulation of the lateral hypothalamus? *Behavioral Neuroscience, 105,* 3–14.

BERSCHEID, E. (1983). Emotion. In H. H. Kelley, E. Berscheid, A. Christensen, J. H. Harvey, T. L. Huston, G. Levinger, E. McClintock, L. A. Peplau, & D. R. Peterson (Eds.), *Close relationships* (pp. 110–168). New York: Freeman.

BERSCHEID, E., & WALSTER, E. H. (1974). A little bit about love. In T. Huston (Ed.), *Foundation of interpersonal attraction.* New York: Academic Press.

BEST, J. B. (1992). *Cognitive psychology.* New York: West.

BIBRING, E. (1953). The mechanism of depression. In P. Greenacre (Ed.), *Affective disorders* (pp. 13–48). New York: International Universities Press.

BIEDERMAN, I. (1987). Recognition by components: A theory of human image understanding. *Psychological Review, 94,* 115–1947.

BIEDERMAN, I. (1990). Higher-level vision. In D. N. Osherson, S. M. Kossyln, & J. M. Hollerbach (Eds.). *An invitation to cognitive science: Visual cognition and action* (Vol. 2). Cambridge, MA: MIT Press.

BIEDERMAN, I., & JU, G. (1988). Surface versus edge-based determinants of visual recognition. *Cognitive Psychology, 20,* 38–64.

BIERBRAUER, G. (1973). *Attribution and perspective: Effects of time, set, and role on interpersonal inference.* Unpublished Ph.D. dissertation, Stanford University.

BILLINGS, A. G., & MOOS, R. H. (1984). Coping, stress, and social resources among adults with unipolar depression. *Journal of Personality and Social Psychology, 46,* 887–891.

BINET, A., & SIMON, T. (1905). New methods for the diagnosis of the intellectual level of subnormals. *Annals of Psychology, 11,* 191.

BINNS, K. E., & SALT, T. E. (1997). Post eye-opening maturation of visual receptive field diameters in the superior colliculus of normal- and dark-reared rats. *Brain Research: Developmental Brain Research, 99,* 263–266.

BISIACH, E., & LUZZATI, C. (1978). Unilateral neglect of representational space. *Cortex, 14,* 129–133.

BLAGROVE, M. (1992). Dreams as a reflection of our waking concerns and abilities: A critique of the problem-solving paradigm in dream research. *Dreaming, 2,* 205–220.

BLAGROVE, M. (1996). Problems with the cognitive psychological modeling of dreaming. *Journal of Mind and Behavior, 17,* 99–134.

BLAGROVE, M., & AKEURST, L. (2000). *In search of the light: The adventures of a parapsychologist.* Amherst, NY: Prometheus Books.

BLAKE, P., PINCUS, J., & BUCKNER, C. (1995). Neurologic abnormalities in murderers. *Neurology, 45,* 1641–1657.

BLAKE, R. (1981). Strategies for assessing visual deficits in animals with selective neural deficits. In R. N. Aslin, J. R. Alberts, & M. R. Petersen (Eds.), *Development of perception: Vol. 2. The visual system* (pp. 95–110). New York: Academic Press.

BLAKESLEE, S. (1998, October 13). Placebos prove so powerful even experts are surprised. *New York Times,* pp. F1, F4.

BLAMEY, P. J., DOWELL, R. C., BROWN, A. M., CLARK, G. M., & SELIGMAN, P. M. (1987). Vowel and consonant recognition of cochlear implant patients using formant-estimating speech processors. *Journal of the Acoustical Society of America, 82,* 48–57.

BLANCK, G. (1990). Vygotsky: The man and his cause. In L. C. Moll (Ed.), *Vygotsky and education.* New York: Cambridge University Press.

BLATT, S. J. (1974). Levels of object representation in anaclitic and introjective depression. *Psychoanalytic Study of the Child, 29,* 107–159.

BLAZER, D. G., GEORGE, L., & HUGHES, D. (1991). The epidemiology of anxiety disorders. In C. Salzman & B. Liebowitz (Eds.), *Anxiety disor-*

ders in the elderly (pp. 17–30). New York: Springer-Verlag.

BLISS, E. L. (1980). Multiple personalities: Report of fourteen cases with implications for schizophrenia and hysteria. *Archives of General Psychiatry, 37,* 1388–1397.

BLISS, T. V. P., & LMO, T. (1973). Long-lasting potentiation of synaptic transmission in the dentate area of the anesthetized rabbit following stimulation of the preforant path. *Journal of Physiology, 232,* 331–356.

BLOCK, J. (1961/1978). *The Q-sort method in personality assessment and psychiatric research.* Palo Alto: Consulting Psychologists Press.

BLOOD, R. O. (1967). *Love match and arranged marriage.* New York: Free Press.

Bloom, P. (2000). *How children learn the meaning of words.* Cambridge, MA: MIT Press.

BLUM, G. S. (1953). *Psychoanalytic theories of personality.* New York: McGraw-Hill.

BLUM, K., CULL, J. G., BRAVERMAN, E. R., & COMINGS, D. E. (1996). Reward deficiency syndrome. *American Scientist, 84,* 132–145.

BLUMENTHAL, J. A., EMERY, C. F., MADDEN, D. J., SCHNIEBOLK, S., WALSH-RIDDLE, M., GEORGE, L. K., MCKEE, D. C., HIGGIN-BOTHAM, M. B., COBB, F. R., & COLEMAN, R. E. (1991). Long term effects of exercise on psychological functioning in older men and women. *Journal of Gerontology, 46,* 352–361.

BODENHAUSEN, G. V., MACRAE, C. N., & SHERMAN, J. W. (1999). On the dialectics of discrimination: Dual processes in social stereotyping. In S. Chaiken & Y. Trope (Eds.), *Dual-process theories in social psychology* (pp. 271–290). New York: Guilford.

BOFF, K. R., KAUFMAN, L., & THOMAS, J. P. (Eds.). (1986). *Handbook of perception and human performance* (Vol. 1). New York: Wiley.

BOLLES, R. C. (1970). Species-specific defense reactions and avoidance learning. *Psychological Review, 77,* 32–48.

BONANNO, G. A., & SINGER, J. L. (1990). Repressive personality style: Theoretical and methodological implications for health and pathology. In J. L. Singer (Ed.), *Repression and dissociation* (pp. 435–465). Chicago: University of Chicago Press.

BOND, C. F. (1982). Social facilitation: A self-presentational view. *Journal of Personality and Social Psychology, 42,* 1042–1050.

BOND, C. F., & TITUS, L. J. (1983). Social facilitation: A meta-analysis of 241 studies. *Psychological Bulletin, 94,* 265–292.

BOON, S., & DRAIJER, N. (1993). Multiple personality disorder in The Netherlands: A clinical investigation of 71 patients. *American Journal of Psychiatry, 150,* 489–494.

BOOTH, A., SHELLEY, G., MAZUR, A., THARP, G., & KITTOK, R. (1989). Testosterone and winning and losing in human competition. *Hormones and Behavior, 23,* 556–571.

BOOTH, D. (1990). Learned role of tastes in eating motivation. In E. D. Capaldi et al. (Eds.), *Taste, experience, and feeding* (pp. 179–194). Washington, DC: American Psychological Association.

BOOTH, D. A. (1987). Cognitive experimental psychology of appetite. In R. A. Boakes (Ed.), *Eating habits: Food, physiology, and learned behavior* (pp. 175–209). New York: Wiley.

BOOTH, D. A. (1991). Learned ingestive motivation and the pleasures of the palate. In R. C. Bolles (Ed.), *The hedonics of taste* (pp. 29–58). Hillsdale, NJ: Erlbaum.

BOOTH-KEWLEY, S., & FRIEDMAN, H. S. (1987). Psychological predictors of heart disease: A quantitative review. *Psychological Bulletin, 101,* 343–362.

BOOTZIN, R. R., KIHLSTROM, J. F., & SCHACTER, D. L. (Eds.). (1990). *Sleep and cognition.* Washington, DC: American Psychological Association.

BORGIDA, E., & NISBETT, R. E. (1977). The differential impact of abstract vs. concrete information on decisions. *Journal of Applied Social Psychology, 7,* 258–271.

BORING, E. G. (1930). A new ambiguous figure. *American Journal of Psychology, 42,* 444–445.

BORNSTEIN, R. F. (1992). Subliminal mere exposure effects. In R. F. Bornstein & T. S. Pittman (Eds.), *Perception without awareness: Cognitive, clinical and social perspectives* (pp. 191–210). New York: Guilford.

BORNSTEIN, R. F., & D'AGOSTINO, P. R. (1992). Stimulus recognition and the mere exposure effect. *Journal of Personality and Social Psychology, 63,* 545–552.

BOTMAN, H., & CROVITZ, H. (1992). Dream reports and autobiographical memory. *Imagination, Cognition and Personality, 9,* 213–214.

BOUCHARD, C., TREMBLAY, A., DESPRES, J. P., NADEAU, A., LUPIEN, P. J., THERIAULT, G., DUSSAULT, J., MOORJANI, S., PINAULT, S., & FOURNIER, G. (1990). The response to long-term overeating in identical twins. *New England Journal of Medicine, 322,* 1477–1482.

BOUCHARD, T. J., & MCGUE, M. (1981). Familial studies of intelligence: A review. *Science, 212,* 1055–1059.

BOUCHARD, T. J., JR. (1984). Twins reared apart and together: What they tell us about human diversity. In S. Fox (Ed.), *The chemical and biological bases of individuality.* New York: Plenum.

BOUCHARD, T. J., JR. (1995). *Nature's twice-told tale: Identical twins reared apart—What they tell us about human individuality.* Paper presented at the annual meeting of the Western Psychological Association, Los Angeles.

BOUCHARD, T. J., JR., LYKKEN, D. T., MCGUE, M., SEGAL, N. L., & TELLEGEN, A. (1990). Sources of human psychological differences: The Minnesota study of twins reared apart. *Science, 250,* 223–228.

BOURIN, M., BAKER, G. B., & BRADWEJN, J. (1998). Neurobiology of panic disorder. *Journal of Psychosomatic Research, 44,* 163–180.

BOURNE, L. E. (1966). *Human conceptual behavior.* Boston: Allyn and Bacon.

BOUTON, M. E., MINEKA, S., & BARLOW, D. H. (2001). A modern learning theory perspective on the etiology of panic disorder. *Psychological Review, 108,* 4–32.

BOWDEN, C. L. (2000). Efficacy of lithium in mania and maintenance therapy of bipolar disorder. *Journal of Clinical Psychiatry, 61,* 35–40.

BOWEN, W. G., & BOK, D. (1998). *The shape of the river: Long-term consequences of considering race in college and university admissions.* Princeton, NJ: Princeton University Press.

BOWER, G. H. (1981). Mood and memory. *American Psychologist, 6,* 129–148.

BOWER, G. H., BLACK, J. B., & TURNER, T. R. (1979). Scripts in memory for text. *Cognitive Psychology, 11,* 177–220.

BOWER, G. H., & CLARK, M. C. (1969). Narrative stories as mediators for serial learning. *Psychonomic Science, 14,* 181–182.

BOWER, G. H., CLARK, M. C., WINZENZ, D., & LESGOLD, A. (1969). Hierarchical retrieval schemes in recall of categorized word lists. *Journal of Verbal Learning and Verbal Behavior, 8,* 323–343.

BOWER, G. H., & SPRINGSTON, F. (1970). Pauses as recoding points in letter series. *Journal of Experimental Psychology, 83,* 421–430.

BOWER, J. E., KEMENY, M. E., TAYLOR, S. E., & FAHEY, J. L. (1998). Cognitive processing, discovery of meaning, CD 4 decline, and AIDS-related mortality among bereaved HIV-seropositive men. *Journal of Consulting and Clinical Psychology, 66,* 979–986.

BOWER, J. E., TAYLOR, S. E., & FAHEY, J. L. (1998). Cognitive processing, discovery of meaning, CD4 decline, and AIDS-related mortality among HIV-seropositive men. *Journal of Consulting and Clinical Psychology, 66,* 979–986.

BOWLBY, J. (1969). *Attachment and loss,* Vol. 1: *Attachment.* New York: Basic Books.

BOWLBY, J. (1973). *Attachment and loss: Separation, anxiety and anger* (Vol. 2). London: Hogarth Press.

BOYNTON, R. M. (1979). *Human color vision.* New York: Holt, Rinehart & Winston.

BOZZA, T. C., & MOMBAERTS, P. (2001). Olfactory coding: Revealing intrinsic representations of odors. *Current Biology, 11,* R687–R690.

BRADLEY, S. J., OLIVER, G. D., CHERNICK, A. B., & Zucker, K. J. (1998). Experiment of nurture: ablatio penis at 2 months, sex reassignment at 7 months, and a psychosexual follow-up in young adulthood. *Pediatrics, 102,* 9.

BRADSHAW, G. L., & ANDERSON, J. R. (1982). Elaborative encoding as an explanation of levels of processing. *Journal of Verbal Learning and Verbal Behavior, 21,* 165–174.

BRAINARD, D. H. (1999). Color Vision. In R. Wilson & F. Keil (Eds.), *MIT Encyclopedia of the Cognitive Sciences.* Cambridge, MA: MIT Press.

BRANSFORD, J. D., & JOHNSON, M. K. (1973). Considerations of some problems of comprehension. In W. G. Chase (Ed.), *Visual information processing.* New York: Academic Press.

BRAUN, B. G. (1986). *Treatment of multiple personality disorder.* Washington, DC: American Psychiatric Press.

BRAZELTON, T. B. (1978). The remarkable talents of the newborn. *Birth and Family Journal, 5,* 4–10.

BREEDLOVE, S. M. (1994). Sexual differentiation of the human nervous system. *Annual Review of Psychology, 45,* 389–418.

BREGGIN, P. R. (1994). *Talking back to Prozac.* New York: St. Martin's Press.

BREGMAN, A. S. (1990). *Auditory scene analysis.* Cambridge, MA: MIT Press.

BREHM, J. W. (1956). Postdecision changes in the desirability of alternatives. *Journal of Abnormal and Social Psychology, 52,* 384–389.

BREHM, S. S. (1992). *Intimate relationships* (2nd ed.). New York: McGraw-Hill.

BREIER, A., SCHREIBER, J. L., DYER, J., & PICKAR, D. (1992). Course of illness and predictors of outcome in chronic schizophrenia: Implications for pathophysiology. *British Journal of Psychiatry, 161,* 38–43.

BRELAND, K., & BRELAND, M. (1966). *Animal behavior.* New York: Macmillan.

BREMNER, J. D. (1998). Neuroimaging of posttraumatic stress disorder. *Psychiatric Annals, 28,* 445–455.

BRENNER, C. (1980). A psychoanalytic theory of affects. In R. Plutchik & H. Kellerman (Eds.), *Emotion: Theory, research, and experience* (Vol. 1). New York: Academic Press.

BREVOORT, P. (1998). The booming U.S. botanical market: A new overview. *HerbalGram, 44,* 33–46.

BREWIN, C. R., MACCARTHY, B., DUDA, K., & VAUGHN, C. E. (1991). Attribution and expressed emotion in the relatives of patients with schizophrenia. *Journal of Abnormal Psychology, 100,* 546–554.

BRIDGER, W. H. (1961). Sensory habituation and discrimination in the human neonate. *American Journal of Psychiatry, 117,* 991–996.

BRITT, T. W., ADLER, A. B., & BARTONE, P. T. (2001). Deriving benefits from stressful events: The role of engagement in meaningful work and hardiness. *Journal of Occupational Health Psychology, 6,* 53–63.

BROADBENT, D. E. (1958). *Perception and communication.* London: Pergamon.

BROMAN, C. L. (1987). Race differences in professional help seeking. *American Journal of Community Psychology, 15,* 473–489.

BROOKS-GUNN, J., & RUBLE, D. N. (1983). The experience of menarche from a developmental perspective. In J. Brooks-Gunn & A. C. Petersen (Eds.), *Girls at puberty: Biological and psychological perspectives.* New York: Plenum.

BROWN, A. E. (1936). Dreams in which the dreamer knows he is asleep. *Journal of Abnormal Psychology, 31,* 59–66.

BROWN, D. P. (1977). A model for the levels of concentrative mediation. *International Journal of Clinical and Experimental Hypnosis, 25,* 236–273.

BROWN, E. L., & DEFFENBACHER, K. (1979). *Perception and the senses.* Oxford: Oxford University Press.

BROWN, G. W., BIRLEY, J. L., & WING, J. K. (1972). Influence of family life on the course of schizophrenic disorders: A replication. *British Journal of Psychiatry, 121,* 241–258.

BROWN, J. (1991). Staying fit and staying well: Physical fitness as a moderator of life stress. *Journal of Personality and Social Psychology, 60,* 555–561.

BROWN, J. D. (1986). Evaluations of self and others: Self-enhancement biases in social judgments. *Social Cognition, 4,* 353–376.

BROWN, L. L., TOMKARKEN, A. J., ORTH, D. N., LOOSEN, P. T., KALIN, N. H., & DAVIDSON, R. J. (1996). Individual differences in repressive-defensiveness predict basal salivary cortisol levels. *Journal of Personality and Social Psychology, 70,* 362–371.

BROWN, R. (1973). *A first language: The early stages.* Cambridge, MA: Harvard University Press.

BROWN, R. (1974). Further comment on the risky shift. *American Psychologist, 29,* 468–470.

BROWN, R. (1986). *Social psychology: The second edition.* New York: Free Press.

BROWN, R., & KULIK, J. (1977). Flashbulb memories. *Cognition, 5,* 73–99.

BROWN, R., CAZDEN, C. B., & BELLUGI, U. (1969). The child's grammar from 1 to 3. In J. P. Hill (Ed.), *Minnesota symposium on child psychology* (Vol. 2). Minneapolis: University of Minnesota Press.

BROWN, R. W., & MCNEILL, D. (1966). The "tip-of-the-tongue" phenomenon. *Journal of Verbal Learning and Verbal Behavior, 5,* 325–337.

BROWNELL, K. (1988, January). Yo-yo dieting. *Psychology Today, 22,* 20–23.

BROWNELL, K. D., & RODIN, J. (1994). The dieting maelstrom: Is it possible and advisable to lose weight? *American Psychologist, 49,* 781–791.

BRUCH, H. (1973). *Eating disorders: Obesity, anorexia nervosa, and the person within.* New York: Basic Books.

BRUNER, J., PARHOFER, K. G., SCHWANDT, P., & BRONISCH, T. (2002). Cholesterol, essential fatty acids, and suicide. *Pharmacopsychiatry, 35,* 1–5.

BRUNER, J. S. (1957). Going beyond the information given. In *Contemporary approaches to cognition: A symposium held at the University of Colorado.* Cambridge, MA: Harvard University Press.

BRUNER, J. S., GOODNOW, J. J., & AUSTIN, G. A. (1956). *A study of thinking.* New York: Wiley.

BRUNER, J. S., OLVER, R. R., GREENFIELD, P. M., & Collaborators. (1966). *Studies in cognitive growth.* New York: Wiley.

BRUNER, J. S., & POTTER, M. C. (1964). Interference in visual search. *Science, 144,* 424–425.

BRUYER, R., LATERRE, C., SERON, X., & Collaborators. (1983). A case of prosopagnosia with some preserved covert remembrance of familiar faces. *Brain and Cognition, 2,* 257–284.

BRYAN, J. H., & TEST, M. A. (1967). Models and helping: Naturalistic studies in aiding behavior. *Journal of Personality and Social Psychology, 6,* 400–407.

BUB, D., BLACKS, S., & HOWELL, J. (1989). Word recognition and orthographic context effects in a letter-by-letter reader. *Brain and Language, 36,* 357–376.

BUCHANAN, C. M., ECCLES, J. S., & BECKER, J. B. (1992). Are adolescents the victims of raging hormones? Evidence for activational effects of hormones on moods and behavior at adolescence. *Psychological Bulletin, 111,* 62–107.

BUCHSBAUM, M. S., HAIER, R. J., POTKIN, S. G., & NUECHTERLEIN, K. (1992). Fronostriatal disorder of cerebral metabolism in never-medicated schizophrenics. *Archives of General Psychiatry, 49,* 935–942.

BUCHSBAUM, M. S., SOMEYA, T., WU, J. C., TANG, C. Y., & BUNNEY, W. E. (1997). Neuroimaging bipolar illness with positron emission tomography and magnetic resonance imaging. *Psychiatric Annals, 27,* 489–495.

BUCK, L., & AXEL, R. (1991). A novel multigene family may encode odorant receptors: A molecular basis for odor recognition. *Cell, 65,* 175–187.

BURNAM, M. A., STEIN, J. A., GOLDING, J. M., SIEGEL, J. M., SORENSON, S. B., FORSYTHE, A. B., & TELLES, C. A. (1988). Sexual assault and mental disorders in a community population. *Journal of Consulting and Clinical Psychology, 56,* 843–850.

BURNSTEIN, E., & VINOKUR, A. (1973). Testing two classes of theories about group-induced shifts in individual choice. *Journal of Experimental Social Psychology, 9,* 123–137.

BURNSTEIN, E., & VINOKUR, A. (1977). Persuasive arguments and social comparison as determinants of attitude polarization. *Journal of Experimental Social Psychology, 13,* 315–332.

BUSBY, P. A., TONG, Y. C., & CLARK, G. M. (1993). Electrode position, repetition rate, and speech perception by early- and late-deafened cochlear implant patients. *Journal of the Acoustical Society of America, 93,* 1058–1067.

BUSEY, T. A., TUNNICLIFF, J., LOFTUS, G. R., & LOFTUS, E. F. (2000). Accounts of the confidence-accuracy relation in recognition memory. *Psychonomic Bulletin and Review, 7,* 26–48.

BUSS, A. H., & PLOMIN, R. (1975). *A temperament theory of personality development.* New York: Wiley.

BUSS, D. (1999). *Evolutionary psychology: The new science of the mind.* Needham Heights, MA: Allyn & Bacon.

BUSS, D. (2000). *The dangerous passion: Why jealousy is as necessary as love and sex.* New York: Free Press.

BUSS, D., SHACKELFORD, T. K., KIRKPATRICK, L. A., CHOE, J. C., LIM, H. K., HASEGAWA, M., HASEGAWA, T., & BENNETT, K. (1999). Jealousy and the nature of beliefs about infidelity: Tests of competing hypotheses about sex differences in the United States, Korea, and Japan. *Personal Relationships, 61,* 125–150.

BUSS, D. M. (1988). The evolution of human intrasexual competition: Tactics of mate attraction. *Journal of Personality and Social Psychology, 54,* 616–628.

BUSS, D. M. (1989). Sex differences in human mate preferences: Evolutionary hypotheses testing in 37 cultures. *Behavioral and Brain Sciences, 12,* 1–49.

BUSS, D. M. (1991). Evolutionary personality psychology. *Annual Review of Psychology, 42,* 459–491.

BUSS, D. M. (1994a). *The evolution of desire: Strategies of human mating.* New York: Basic Books.

BUSS, D. M. (1994b). Personality evoked: The evolutionary psychology of stability and change. In T. F. Heatherton & J. Weinberger (Eds.), *Can personality change?* Washington DC: APA Press.

BUSS, D. M. (2003). *The evolution of desire: Strategies of human mating* (rev. ed.). New York: Basic Books.

BUSS, D. M., & BARNES, M. (1986). Preferences in human mate selection. *Journal of Personality and Social Psychology, 50,* 559–570.

BUSS, D. M., & KENRICK, D. T. (1998). Evolutionary social psychology. In D. T. Gilbert, S. T. Fiske, & G. Lindzey (Eds.), *Handbook of social psychology,* Vol 2 (4th ed., pp. 982–1026). Boston: McGraw-Hill.

BUSS, D. M., LARSEN, R. J., WESTERN, D., & SEMMELROTH, J. (1992). Sex differences in jealousy: Evolution, physiology, and psychology. *Psychological Science, 3,* 251–255.

BUSS, D. M., & SCHMIDT, D. P. (1993). Sexual strategies theory: An evolutionary perspective on human mating. *Psychological Review, 100,* 204–232.

BUSS, D. M., & SHACKELFORD, T. K. (1997). Human aggression in evolutionary psychological perspective. *Clinical Psychology Reviews, 17,* 605–619.

BUTLER, J. M., & HAIGH, G. V. (1954). Changes in the relation between self-concepts and ideal concepts consequent upon client centered counseling. In C. R. Rogers & R. F. Dymond (Eds.), *Psychotherapy and personality change: Coordinated studies in the client-centered approach* (pp. 55–76). Chicago: University of Chicago Press.

BUTTERFIELD, E. L., & SIPERSTEIN, G. N. (1972). Influence of contingent auditory stimulation on nonnutritional sucking. In J. Bosma (Ed.), *Oral sensation and perception: The mouth of the infant.* Springfield, IL: Charles B. Thomas.

CABANAC, M. (1979). Sensory pleasure. *Quarterly Review of Biology, 54,* 1–29.

CABANAC, M. (1992). Pleasure: The common currency. *Journal of Theoretical Biology, 155,* 173–200.

CACIOPPO, J. T., BERNTSON, G. G., LARSEN, J. T., POEHLMANN, K. M., & ITO, T. A. (2000). The psychophysiology of emotion. In M. Lewis & J. M. Haviland-Jones (Eds.), *Handbook of emotions* (2nd ed., pp. 173–191). New York: Guilford.

CACIOPPO, J. T., KLEIN, D. J., BEMSTON, G. G., & HATFIELD, E. (1993). The psychophysiology of emotion. In M. Lewis & J. M. Haviland (Eds.), *The handbook of emotions.* New York: Guilford.

CADORET, R. J., & CAIN, C. A. (1980). Sex differences in predictors of antisocial behavior in adoptees. *Archives of General Psychiatry, 37,* 1171–1175.

CAHILL, L., BABINSKY, R., MARKOWITSCH, H. J., & MCGAUGH, J. L. (1996). The amygdala and emotional memory. *Nature, 377*, 295–296.

CAHILL, L., PRINS, B., WEBER, M., & MCGAUGH, J. L. (1994). Adrenergic activation and memory for emotional events. *Nature, 371*, 702–704.

CAIN, W. S. (1988). Olfaction. In R. C. Atkinson, R. J. Hernstein, G. Lindzey, & R. D. Luce (Eds.), *Stevens' handbook of experimental psychology* (Vol. 1, pp. 409–459). New York: Wiley.

CALLAWAY, M. R., MARRIOTT, R. G., & ESSER, J. K. (1985). Effects of dominance on group decision making: Toward a stress-reduction explanation of group-think. *Journal of Personality and Social Psychology, 49*, 949–952.

CAMPOS, J. J., BARRETT, K. C., LAMB, M. E., GOLDSMITH, H. H., & STENBERG, C. (1983). Socioemotional development. In P. Mussen (Ed.), *Handbook of child psychology* (Vol. 1, pp. 1–101). New York: Wiley.

CANINO G. J., BURNAM, A., & CAETANO, R. (1992). The prevalence of alcohol abuse and/or dependence in two Hispanic Communities. In J. E. Helzer & G. J. Canino (Eds.), *Alcoholism in North America, Europe & Asia* (pp. 131–155). New York: Oxford University Press.

CANNON, W. B. (1927). The James-Lange theory of emotions: A critical examination and an alternative theory. *American Journal of Psychology, 39*, 106–124.

CAPLAN, D., & WATERS, G. (2002). Working memory and connectionist models of parsing: A reply to MacDonald and Christiansen. *Psychological-Review, 109*, 66–74.

CARAMAZZA, A. (2000). The organization of conceptual knowledge in the brain. In M. S. Gazzaniga (Ed.), *The new cognitive neurosciences*. Cambridge: MIT Press.

CARAMAZZA, A., & ZURIF, E. B. (1976). Dissociation of algorithmic and heuristic processes in language comprehension: Evidence from aphasia. *Brain and Language, 3*, 572–582.

CARDNO, A. G., O'DONOVAN, M. C., & OWEN, M. J. (2000). Genetic risk factors for depression. *International Journal of Mental Health, 29*, 13–38.

CARDON, L. R., FULKER, D. W., DEFRIES, J. C., & PLOMIN, R. (1992). Continuity and change in general cognitive ability from 1 to 7 years of age. *Developmental Psychology, 28*, 64–73.

CARDOZO, B. L., VERGARA, A., AGAIN, F., & COTWAY, C. A. (2000). Mental health, social functioning, and attitudes of Kosovar Albanians following the war in Kosovo. *Journal of the American Medical Association, 284*, 569–577.

CAREY, G. & GOLDMAN, D. (1997). The genetics of antisocial behavior. In D. M. Stoff, J. Breiling, & J. D. Maser (Eds.), *Handbook of Antisocial Personality Disorder* (pp. 243–254). New York: Wiley.

CARLSON, N. R. (1994). *Physiology of behavior* (5th ed.). Boston: Allyn and Bacon.

CARLSON, N. R. (1998). *Foundations of physiological psychology* (4th ed.). Boston: Allyn and Bacon.

CARLSON, N. R. (2001). *Physiology of behavior* (7th ed.). Boston: Allyn and Bacon.

CARLSON, R. (1971). Where is the person in personality research? *Psychological Bulletin, 75*, 203–219.

CARLSON, W. R. (1986). *Physiology of behavior* (3rd ed.). Boston: Allyn and Bacon.

CARMICHAEL, L., HOGAN, H. P., & WALTER, A. A (1932). An experimental study of the effect of language on the reproduction of visually perceived form. *Journal of Experimental Psychology, 15*, 73–86.

CARPENTER, P. A., JUST, M. A., & SHELL, P. (1990). What one intelligence test measures: A theoretical account of the processing in the Raven Progressive Matrices Test. *Psychological Review, 97*, 404–431.

CARROLL, D. W. (1985). *Psychology of language.* Monterey, CA: Brooks/Cole.

CARROLL, J. B. (1988). Individual differences in cognitive functioning. In R. C. Atkinson, R. J. Herrnstein, G. Lindzey, & R. D. Luce (Eds.), *Stevens' handbook of experimental psychology* (Vol. 2). New York: Wiley.

CARROLL, J. B. (1993). *Human cognitive abilities: A survey of factor-analytic studies.* New York: Cambridge University Press.

CARSKADON, M. A., MITLER, M. M., & DEMENT, W. C. (1974). A comparison of insomniacs and normals: Total sleep time and sleep latency. *Sleep Research, 3*, 130.

CARTER, M. M., HOLLON, S. D., CARON, R. S., & SHELTON, R. C. (1995). Effects of a safe person on induced distress following a biological challenge in panic disorder with agoraphobia. *Journal of Abnormal Psychology, 104*, 156–163.

CARTERETTE, E. C., & FRIEDMAN, M. P. (Eds.). (1974–1978). *Handbook of perception* (Vols. 1–11). New York: Academic Press.

CARTWRIGHT, R. (1978, December). Happy endings for our dreams. *Psychology Today*, pp. 66–67.

CARTWRIGHT, R. (1992). Masochism in dreaming and its relation to depression. *Dreaming, 2*, 79–84.

CARTWRIGHT, R. (1996). Dreams and adaptation to divorce. In D. Barrett (Ed.), *Trauma and dreams.* Cambridge, MA: Harvard University Press.

CARTWRIGHT, R. D. (1974). The influence of a conscious wish on dreams. A methodological study of dream meaning and function. *Journal of Abnormal Psychology, 83*, 387–393.

CARVER, C. S., & SCHEIER, M. F. (1981). *Attention and self-regulation: A control-theory approach to human behavior.* New York: Springer-Verlag.

CARVER, C. S., & SCHEIER, M. F. (2000). *Perspectives on personality.* Boston: Allyn & Bacon.

CASE, R. (1985). *Intellectual development: A systematic reinterpretation.* New York: Academic Press.

CASE, R., & OKAMOTO, Y. (1996). The role of central conceptual structures in the development of children's thoughts. *Nomographs of the Society for Research in Child Development, 61*, 1–265.

CASE, R. B., HELLER, S. S., CASE, N. B., & MOSS, A. J. (1985). Type A behavior and survival after acute myocardial infarction. *New England Journal of Medicine, 312*, 737.

CASPI, A., & HERBENER, E. S. (1990). Continuity and change: Assortative marriage and the consistency of personality in adulthood. *Journal of Personality and Social Psychology, 58*, 250–258.

CASPI, A., & MOFFIT, T. E. (1991). Individual differences are accentuated during periods of social change: The sample case of girls at puberty. *Journal of Personality and Social Psychology, 61*, 157–168.

CATTELL, R. B. (1957). *Personality and motivation structure and measurement.* Yonkers-on-Hudson, NY: World.

CATTELL, R. B. (1966). *The scientific analysis of personality.* Chicago: Aldine.

CATTERALL, W. A. (2000). From ionic currents to molecular mechanisms: the structure and function of voltage-gated sodium channels. *Neuron, 26*, 13–25.

CAVALLERO, C., CICOGNA, P., NATALE, V., & OCCIONERO, M. (1992). Slow wave sleep dreaming. *Sleep, 15*, 562–566.

CECI, S. J. (1990). *On intelligence . . . more or less: A bio-ecological treatise on intellectual development.* Englewood Cliffs, NJ: Prentice-Hall.

CECI, S. J. (1996). *On intelligence: A bioecological treatise.* Cambridge, MA: Harvard University Press.

CECI, S. J., & BRUCK, M. (1993). The suggestibility of the child witness: A historical review and synthesis. *Psychological Bulletin, 113*, 403–409.

CECI, S. J., & ROAZZI, A. (1994). The effect of context on cognition: Postcards from Brazil. In R. J. Sternberg & R. K. Wagner (Eds.), *Mind in context: Interactionist perspectives on human intelligence.* Cambridge, England: Cambridge University Press.

CENTERS FOR DISEASE CONTROL. (1988). Health status of Vietnam veterans: Psychosocial characteristics. *Journal of the American Medical Association, 259*, 2701–2707.

CERNOCH, J. M., & PORTER, R. H. (1985). Recognition of maternal axillary odors by infants. *Child Development, 56*, 1593–1598.

CHAIKEN, S. (1980). Heuristic versus systematic information processing and the use of source versus message cues in persuasion. *Journal of Personality and Social Psychology, 39*, 752–766.

CHAIKEN, S. (1987). The heuristic model of persuasion. In M. P. Zanna, J. N. Olson, & C. P. Herman (Eds.), *Social influence: The Ontario symposium* (Vol. 5, pp. 3–39). Hillsdale, NJ: Erlbaum.

CHAIKEN, S., & TROPE, Y. (1999). *Dual-process theories in social psychology.* New York: Guilford.

CHAMBLESS, D. L., & HOLLON, S. D. (1998). Defining empirically supported therapies. *Journal of Consulting and Clinical Psychology, 66*, 7–18.

CHAMBLESS, D. L., & OLLENDECK, T. H. (2001). Empirically supported psychological interventions. *Annual Reviews of Psychology, 52*, 685–716.

CHAPMAN, L. J., & CHAPMAN, J. P. (1969). Illusory correlation as an obstacle to the use of valid psychodiagnostic signs. *Journal of Abnormal Psychology, 74*, 271–280.

CHARNEY, D. S., SOUTHWICK, S. M., KRYSTAL, J. H., DEUTCH, A. Y., MURBURG, M. M., & DAVIS, M. (1994). Neurobiological mechanisms of PTSD. In M. M. Murburg (Ed.), *Catecholamine function in posttraumatic stress disorder: Emerging concepts* (pp. 131–158). Washington DC: American Psychiatric Press.

CHASE, W. G., & SIMON, H. A. (1973a). The mind's eye in chess. In W. G. Chase (Ed.), *Visual information processing.* New York: Academic Press.

CHASE, W. G., & SIMON, H. A. (1973b). Perception in chess. *Cognitive Psychology, 4*, 55–81.

CHAUDURI, H. (1965). *Philosophy of meditation.* New York: Philosophical Library.

CHELAZZI, L., DUNCAN, J., MILLER, E. K., & DESIMONE, R. (1998). Responses of neurons in inferior temporal cortex during memory guided visual search. *Journal of Neurophysiology, 80*, 2818–2940.

CHEN, M., & BARGH, J. A. (1997). Nonconscious behavioral confirmation processes: The self-fulfilling consequences of automatic stereotype activation. *Journal of Experimental Social Psychology, 33*, 541–560.

CHEN, S., & ANDERSEN, S. M. (1999). Relationships from the past in the present: Significant-other representations and transference in interpersonal life. *Advances in Experimental Social Psychology, 31*, 123–190.

CHEN, S., & CHAIKEN, S. (1999). The heuristic-systematic model in its broader context. In S. Chaiken & Y. Trope (Eds.), *Dual-process theories in social psychology* (pp. 73–96). New York: Guilford.

CHEN, S. C. (1937). Social modification of the activity of ants in nest-building. *Physiological Zoology, 10*, 420–436.

CHEN, X. H., GELLER, E. B., & ADLER, M. W. (1996). Electrical stimulation at traditional acupuncture sites in periphery produces brain opioid-receptor-mediated antinociception in rats. *Journal of Pharmacology and Experimental Therapy, 277,* 654–660.

CHENG, P. W., HOLYOAK, K. J., NISBETT, R. E., & OLIVER, L. (1986). Pragmatic versus syntactic approaches to training deductive reasoning. *Cognitive Psychology, 18,* 293–328.

CHERNISS, C. (2000). Social and emotional competence in the workplace. In R. Bar-On & J. D. A. Parker (Eds.), *The handbook of emotional intelligence.* San Francisco: Jossey-Bass.

CHERRY, E. C. (1953). Some experiments on the recognition of speech with one and with two ears. *Journal of the Acoustical Society, 25,* 975–979.

CHESS, S., & THOMAS, A. (1984). *Origins and evolution of behavior disorders: Infancy to early adult life.* New York: Brunner/Mazel.

CHI, M. (1978). Knowledge structures and memory development. In R. S. Siegler (Ed.), *Children's thinking: What develops?* Hillsdale, NJ: Erlbaum.

CHI, M., GLASER, R., & REES, E. (1982). Expertise in problem solving. In R. Sternberg (Ed.), *Advances in the psychology of human intelligence* (Vol. 1). Hillsdale, NJ: Erlbaum.

CHOCOLLE, R. (1940). Variations des temps de réaction auditifs en fonction de l'intensité à diverses fréquences. *Année Psychologique, 41,* 65–124.

CHOI, I., NISBETT, R. E., & NORENZAYAN, A. (1999). Causal attribution across cultures: Variation and universality. *Psychological Bulletin, 125,* 47–63.

CHOMSKY, N. (1957). *Syntactic structures.* Hague: Mouton.

CHOMSKY, N. (1965). *Aspects of the theory of syntax.* Cambridge, MA: MIT Press.

CHOMSKY, N. (1972). *Language and mind* (2nd ed.). New York: Harcourt Brace Jovanovich.

CHOMSKY, N. (1980). *Rules and representations.* New York: Columbia University Press.

CHOMSKY, N. (1991, March). Quoted in Discover.

CHORNEY, M. J., CHORNEY, K., SEESE, N., OWEN, M. J., DANIELS, J., MCGUFFIN, P., THOMPSON, L. A., DETTERMAN, D. K., BENBOW, C., LUBINSKI, D., ELEY, T., & PLOMIN, R. (1998). A quantitative trait locus associated with cognitive ability in children. *Psychological Science, 13,* 159–166.

CHRISTIE, R., & JOHODA, M. (Eds.). (1954). *Studies in the scope and method of "the authoritarian personality."* New York: Free Press.

CHURCHLAND, P. M. (1995) *The engine of reason, the seat of the soul.* Cambridge, MA: MIT Press.

CHURCHLAND, P. S., & SEJNOWSKI, T. J. (1988). Perspectives on cognitive neuroscience. *Science, 242,* 741–745.

CLARK, D. A., & DESILVA, P. (1985). The nature of depressive and anxious, intrusive thoughts: Distinct or uniform phenomena? *Behaviour Research and Therapy, 23,* 383–393.

CLARK, D. A., & PURDON, C. (1993). New perspectives for a cognitive theory of obsessions. *Australian Psychologist, 28,* 161–167.

CLARK, D. M. (1988). A cognitive model of panic attacks. In S. Rachman & J. D. Maser (Eds.), *Panic: Psychological perspectives.* Hillsdale, NJ: Erlbaum.

CLARK, D. M., SALKOVSKIS, P. M., HACKMANN, A., MIDDLETON, H., & collaborators. (1994). A comparison of cognitive therapy, applied relaxation, and imipramine in the treatment of panic disorder. *British Journal of Psychiatry, 164,* 759–769.

CLARK, E. V. (1983). Meanings and concepts. In P. H. Mussen (Ed.), *Handbook of child psychology* (Vol. 3). New York: Wiley.

CLARK, H. H. (1984). Language use and language users. In G. Lindzey & E. Aronson (Eds.), *The handbook of social psychology* (Vol. 2, 3rd ed.). New York: Harper & Row.

CLARK, H. H., & CLARK, E. V. (1977). *Psychology and language: An introduction to psycholinguistics.* New York: Harcourt Brace Jovanovich.

CLARK, R. D., & HATFIELD, E. (1989). Gender differences in receptivity to sexual offers. *Journal of Psychology and Human Sexuality, 2,* 39–55.

CLARKE-STEWART, K. A. (1973). Interactions between mothers and their young children: Characteristics and consequences. *Monographs of the Society for Research in Child Development, 38* (6 & 7, Serial No. 153).

CLARKE-STEWART, K. A. (1989). Infant day care: Maligned or malignant? *American Psychologist, 44,* 266–273.

CLONINGER, C. R., & GOTTESMAN, I. I. (1987). Genetic and environmental factors in antisocial behavior disorders. In S. A. Mednick, T. E. Moffitt, & S. A. Stack (Eds.), *The causes of crime: New biological approaches* (pp. 92–109). New York: Cambridge University Press.

CLONINGER, C. R., SYRAKIC, D. M., & PRZYBECK, T. R. (1993). A psychobiological model of temperament and character. *Archives of General Psychiatry, 50,* 975–990.

CLORE, G. L, GASPER, K., & GARVIN, E. (2001). Affect as information. In J. P. Forgas (Ed.), *Handbook of affect and social cognition* (pp. 121–144). Mahwah, NJ: Erlbaum.

COHEN, C. E. (1981). Person categories and social perception: Testing some boundaries of the processing effects of prior knowledge. *Journal of Personality and Social Psychology, 40,* 441–452.

COHEN, D., & NISBETT, R. E. (1994). Self-protection and culture of honor: Explaining Southern violence. *Personality and Social Psychology Bulletin, 20,* 551–567.

COHEN, J. D., AARCH, D. M., CARTER, C., & SERVAN SCHREIBER, D. (1999). Context processing deficits in schizophrenia: Converging evidence from three theoretically motivated cognitive tasks. *Journal of Abnormal Psychology, 108,* 120–133.

COHEN, N. J., & SQUIRE, L. R. (1980). Preserved learning and retention of pattern analyzing skill in amnesia: Dissociation of knowing how and knowing that. *Science, 210,* 207–209.

COHEN, S. (1980, September). *Training to understand TV advertising: Effects and some policy implications.* Paper presented at the American Psychological Association convention, Montreal.

COHEN, S. (1996). Psychological stress, immunity, and upper respiratory infections. *Current Directions in Psychological Science, 5,* 86–90.

COHEN, S., & EDWARDS, J. R. (1989). Personality characteristics as moderators of the relationship between stress and disorder. In R. J. Neufeld (Ed.), *Advances in the investigation of psychological stress* (pp. 235–283). New York: Wiley.

COHEN, S., TYRRELL, D. A. J., & SMITH, A. P. (1991). Psychological stress and susceptibility to the common cold. *New England Journal of Medicine, 325,* 606–612.

COLAS, E. (1998). *Just checking: Scenes from the life of an obsessive-compulsive.* New York: Pocket Books.

COLBY, A., KOHLBERG, L., GIBBS, J., & LIEBERMAN, M. A. (1983). A longitudinal study of moral judgment. *Monographs of the Society for Research in Child Development, 48,* 1–2.

COLBY, C. L., & GOLDBERG, M. E. (1999). Space and attention in parietal cortex. *Annual Review of Neuroscience, 22,* 319–349.

COLE, M., & COLE, S. R. (1993). *The development of children* (2nd ed.) New York: Scientific American Books.

COLE, M., & COLE, S. R. (2001). *The development of children.* New York: Worth.

COLE, P. M., ZAHN-WAXLER, C., & SMITH, K. D. (1994). Expressive control during a disappointment: Variations related to preschoolers' behavior problems. *Developmental Psychology, 30,* 835–846.

COLE, S. W., KEMENY, M. E., TAYLOR, S. E., VISSCHER, B. R., & FAHEY, J. L. (1995). Accelerated course of human immunodeficiency virus infection in gay men who conceal their homosexual identity. *Psychosomatic Medicine, 58,* 219–238.

COLE, S. W., KEMENY, M. E., TAYLOR, S. E., & VISSCHER, B. R. (1996). Elevated physical health risk among gay men who conceal their homosexual identity. *Health Psychology, 15,* 243–251.

COLEGROVE, F. W. (1899). Individual memories. *American Journal of Psychology, 10,* 228–255.

COLLINS, A. M., & LOFTUS, E. G. (1975). A spreading-activation theory of semantic processing. *Psychological Review, 82,* 407–428.

COLTHEART, M. (1980). Iconic memory and visible persistence. *Perception and Psychophysics, 27,* 183–228.

COMREY, A. L., & LEE, H. B. (1992). *A first course in factor analysis* (2nd ed.). Hillsdale, NJ: Erlbaum.

CONKLIN, H. M. & IACONO, W. G. (2002). Schizophrenia: A neurodevelopmental perspective. *Current directions in Psychological Science, 11,* 33–37.

CONRAD, R. (1964). Acoustic confusions in immediate memory. *British Journal of Psychology, 55,* 75–84.

COOPER, L. A., & SHEPARD, R. N. (1973). Chronometric studies of the rotation of mental images. In W. G. Chase (Ed.), *Visual information processing.* New York: Academic Press.

COOPER, L. M. (1979). Hypnotic amnesia. In E. Fromm & R. E. Shor (Eds.), *Hypnosis: Developments in research and new perspectives* (Rev. Ed.). New York: Aldine.

CORBETTA, M., MIEZIN, F. M., DOBMEYER, S., SCHULMAN, G. L., & PETERSON, S. E. (1990). Attentional modulation of neural processing of shape, color, and velocity in humans. *Science, 248,* 1556–1559.

CORBETTA, M., MIEZIN, F. M., SHULMAN, G. L., & PETERSEN, S. E. (1991). Selective attention modulates extrastriate visual regions in humans during visual feature discrimination and recognition. In D. J. Chadwick & J. Whelan (Eds.), *Ciba Foundation symposium 163: Exploring brain functional anatomy with positron tomography* (pp. 165–180). Chichester, England: Wiley.

CORBETTA, M., MIEZIN, F. M., SHULMAN, G. L., & PETERSEN, S. E. (1993). A PET study of visuospatial attention. *Journal of Neuroscience, 13,* 1202–1226.

COREN, S. (1992). The moon illusion: A different view through the legs. *Perceptual and Motor Skills, 75,* 827–831.

COREN, S., & GIRGUS, J. S. (1980). Principles of perceptual organization and spatial distortion: The gestalt illusions. *Journal of Experimental Psychology: Human Perception and Performance, 6,* 404–412.

COREN, S., WARD, L. M., & ENNS, J. T. *Sensation and perception* (5th ed.). Fort Worth: Harcourt Brace.

COSCINA, D. V., & DIXON, L. M. (1983). Body weight regulation in anorexia nervosa: Insights from an animal model. In F. L. Darby, P. E. Garfinkel, D. M. Garner, & D. V. COSCINA (Eds.),

Anorexia nervosa: Recent developments. New York: Allan R. Liss.

COSMIDES, L. (1989). The logic of social exchange: Has natural selection shaped how we reason? *Cognition, 31,* 187–276.

COSMIDES, L., & TOOBY, J. (1989). Evolutionary psychology and the generation of culture, part II. *Ethology and Sociobiology, 10,* 51–97.

COSTELLO, C., & STONE, A. (Eds.). (2001). *The American Woman, 2001–02.* New York: Norton.

COTT, J. M., & FUGH-BERMAN, A. (1998). Is St. John's wort (*Hypericum perforatum*) an effective antidepressant? *Journal of Nervous and Mental Disease, 186,* 500–501.

COTTRELL, N. B. (1972). Social facilitation. In C. G. McClintock (Ed.), *Experimental social psychology.* New York: Holt, Rinehart & Winston.

COTTRELL, N. B., RITTLE, R. H., & WACK, D. L. (1967). Presence of an audience and list type (competitional or noncompetitional) as joint determinants of performance in paired-associates learning. *Journal of Personality, 25,* 425–434.

COTTRELL, N. B., WACK, D. L., SEKERAK, G. J., & RITTLE, R. H. (1968). Social facilitation of dominant responses by the presence of an audience and the mere presence of others. *Journal of Personality and Social Psychology, 9,* 245–250.

COURAGE, M. L., & ADAMS, R. J. (1990a). Visual acuity assessment from birth to three years using the acuity card procedures: Cross-sectional and longitudinal samples. *Optometry and Vision Science, 67,* 713–718.

COURAGE, M. L., & ADAMS, R. J. (1990b). The early development of visual acuity in the binocular and monocular peripheral fields. *Infant Behavioral Development, 13,* 123–128.

COURTRIGHT, J. A. (1978). A laboratory investigation of groupthink. *Communications Monographs, 43,* 229–246.

COUSINS, S. D. (1989). Culture and self-perception in Japan and the U.S. *Journal of Personality and Social Psychology, 56,* 124–131.

CRAIGHEAD, L. W., STUNKARD, A. J., & O'BRIEN, R. M. (1981). Behavior therapy and pharmacotherapy for obesity. *Archives of General Psychiatry, 38,* 763–768.

CRAIK, F. I. M., & TULVING, E. (1975). Depth of processing and the retention of words in episodic memory. *Journal of Experimental Psychology: General, 104,* 268–294.

CRANO, W. D., & CHEN, X. (1998). The leniency contract and persistence of majority and minority influence. *Journal of Personality and Social Psychology, 74,* 1437–1450.

CRARY, W. G. (1966). Reactions to incongruent self-experiences. *Journal of Consulting Psychology, 30,* 246–252.

CRASILNECK, H. B., & HALL, J. A. (1985). *Clinical hypnosis: Principles and applications* (2nd ed.). Orlando, FL: Grune & Stratton.

CRASKE, M. G., & BARLOW, D. H. (2001). Panic disorder and agoraphobia. *Clinical handbook of psychological disorders: a step-by-step treatment manual* (3rd ed., pp. 1–59). New York: Guilford.

CREWS, F. C. (Ed.). (1998). *Unauthorized Freud: Doubters confront a legend.* New York: Viking.

CRICK, F. (1994). *The astonishing hypothesis: The scientific search for the soul.* New York: Macmillan.

CRICK, F., & MITCHINSON, G. (1983). The function of dream sleep. *Nature, 304,* 111–114.

CRICK, N. R., & DODGE, K. A. (1994). A review and reformulation of social information-processing mechanisms in children's social adjustment. *Psychological Bulletin, 115,* 74–101.

CRITS-CHRISTOPH, P., COOPER, A., & LUBORSKY, L. (1990). The measurement of accuracy of interpretations. In L. Luborsky & P. Crits-Christoph (Eds.), *Understanding transference: The CCRT method* (pp. 173–188). New York: Basic Books.

CROMWELL, P. F., MARKS, A., OLSON, J. N., & AVARY, D. W. (1991). Group effects on decision-making by burglars. *Psychological Reports, 69,* 579–588.

CROSBY, A. E., CHELTENHAM, M. P., & SACKS, J. J. (1999). Incidence of suicidal ideation and behavior in the United States, 1994. *Suicide and Life-Threatening Behavior, 29,* 131–140.

CROSBY, F., & CORDOVA, D. I. (1996). Words worth of wisdom. *Journal of Social Issues, 52,* 33–49.

CROSS, S. E., & MARKUS, H. R. (1999). The cultural constitution of personality. In L. A. Pervin & O. P. John (Eds.), *Handbook of personality: theory and research* (pp. 378–398). New York: Guilford Press.

CROYLE, R. T., SUN, Y., & HART, M. (1997). Processing risk factor information: Defensive biases in health-related cognitions. In J. A. Petrie & J. A. Weinman (Eds.), *Perceptions of health and illness: Current research and applications* (pp. 267–290). Singapore: Harwood Academic.

CURCI, A., LUMINET, O., FINKENAUER, C., & GISLE, L. (2001). Flashbulb memories in social groups: A comparative test-retest study of the memory of French President Mitterrand's death in a French and a Belgian group. *Memory, 9,* 81–101.

CURTISS, S. (1977). *Genie: A psycholinguistic study of a modern-day "wild child."* New York: Academic Press.

CURTISS, S. (1989). The independence and task-specificity of language. In M. H. Bornstein & J. S. Bruner (Eds.), *Interaction in human development.* Hillsdale, NJ: Erlbaum.

CUTLER, W. B., PRETI, G., KRIEGER, A., HUGGINS, G. R., GARCIA, C. R., & LAWLEY, H. J. (1986). Human axillary secretions influence women's menstrual cycles: The role of donor extract from men. *Hormones and Behavior, 20,* 463–473.

CUTTING, J. E. (1986). *Perception with an eye for motion.* Cambridge, MA: MIT Press.

CYANDER, M., TIMNEY, B. N., & MITCHELL, D. E. (1980). Period of susceptibility of kitten visual cortex to the effects of monocular deprivation extends beyond 6 months of age. *Brain Research, 191,* 545–550.

DABBS, J. M., & MORRIS, R., JR. (1990). Testosterone, social class, and antisocial behavior in a sample of 4,462 men. *Psychological Science, 1,* 209–211.

DALE, A. J. D. (1975). Organic brain syndromes associated with infections. In A. M., Freeman, H. I. Kaplan, & B. J. Sadock (Eds.), *Comprehensive textbook of psychiatry* (Vol. 2, pp. 1121–1130). Baltimore, MD: Williams & Wilkins.

DALY, M., & WILSON, M. I. (1990). Killing the competition: Female/female and male/male homicide. *Human Nature, 1,* 81–107.

DAMASIO, A. R. (1985). Disorders of complex visual processing: Agnosia, achromatopsia, Balint's syndrome, and related difficulties of orientation and construction. In M. M. Mesulam (Ed.), *Principles of behavioral neurology* (pp. 259–288). Philadelphia: F. A. Davis.

DAMASIO, A. R. (1990). Category-related recognition defects as a clue to the neural substrates of knowledge. *Trends in Neurosciences, 13,* 95–98.

DAMASIO, A. R. (1994). *Descartes' error.* New York: Putnam.

DAMASIO, H., GRABOWSKI, T., FRANK, R., GALABURDA, A. M., & DAMASIO, A. R. (1994). The return of Phineas Gage: Clues about the brain from the skull of a famous patient. *Science, 264,* 1102–1105.

DAMON, W. (1977). *The social world of the child.* San Francisco: Jossey-Bass.

DAMON, W. (1983). *Social and personality development.* New York: Norton.

DANEMAN, M., & CARPENTER, P. A. (1980). Individual differences in working memory and reading. *Journal of Verbal Learning and Verbal Behavior, 19,* 450–466.

DANNER, D. D., SNOWDON, D. A., & FRIESEN, W. V. (2001). Positive emotions in early life and longevity: Findings from the nun study. *Journal of Personality and Social Psychology, 80,* 804–813.

DARIAN-SMITH, I. (Ed.). (1984). *Handbook of physiology: The nervous system: Section 1, Vol. 3. Sensory processes.* Bethesda, MD: American Physiological Society.

DARLEY, C. F., TINKLENBERG, J. R., ROTH, W. T., HOLLISTER, L. E., & ATKINSON, R. C. (1973a). Influence of marijuana on storage and retrieval processes in memory. *Memory and Cognition, 1,* 196–200.

DARLEY, C. F., TINKLENBERG, J. R., ROTH, W. T., HOLLISTER, L. E., & ATKINSON, R. C. (1973b). Marijuana and retrieval from short-term memory. *Psychopharmacologia, 29,* 231–238.

DARLEY, C. F., TINKLENBERG, J. R., ROTH, W. T., VERNON, S., & KOPELL, B. S. (1977). Marijuana effects on long-term memory assessment and retrieval. *Psychopharmacology, 52,* 239–241.

DARLEY, J. M., & LATANÉ, B. (1968). Bystander intervention in emergencies: Diffusion of responsibility. *Journal of Personality and Social Psychology, 8,* 377–383.

DARWIN, C. (1872/1998). *The expression of the emotions in man and animals.* New York: Oxford University Press.

DARWIN, C. (1859). *On the origin of the species.* London: Murray.

DARWIN, C. (1872). *The expression of emotion in man and animals.* New York: Philosophical Library.

DASHIELL, J. F. (1930). An experimental analysis of some group effects. *Journal of Abnormal and Social Psychology, 25,* 190–199.

DASHIELL, J. F. (1935). Experimental studies of the influence of social situations on the behavior of individual human adults. In C. Murchison (Ed.), *Handbook of social psychology.* Worcester, MA: Clark University.

DAVIDSON, J. (1989). Sexual emotions, hormones, and behavior. *Advances, 6,* 56–58.

DAVIDSON, K., & PRKACHIN, K. (1997). Optimism and unrealistic optimism have an interacting effort on health-promoting behavior and knowledge changes. *Personality and Social Psychology Bulletin, 23,* 617–625.

DAVIDSON, R. J., PUTNAM, K. M., & LARSON, C. L. (2000). Dysfunction in the neural circuitry of emotion regulation—A possible prelude to violence. *Science, 289,* 591–594.

DAVIS, C. G., NOLEN-HOEKSEMA, S., & LARSON, J. (1998). Making sense of loss and benefiting from the experience: Two construals of meaning. *Journal of Personality and Social Psychology, 75,* 561–574.

DAVIS, K. L., KAHN, R. S., KO, G., & DAVIDSON, M. (1991). Dopamine in schizophrenia: A review and conceptualization. *American Journal of Psychiatry, 148,* 1474–1486.

DE WAAL, F. B. M. (1996). *Good natured: The origins of right and wrong in humans and other animals.* Cambridge, MA: Harvard University Press.

DE WIT, H., KIRK, J. M., & JUSTICE, A. (1998). Behavioral pharmacology of cannabinoids. In R. E. Tarter (Ed.), *Handbook of substance abuse: Neurobehavioral pharmacology.* (pp. 131–146). New York: Plenum.

DEAKIN, J. W., & GRAEFF, F. G. (1991). 5-HT and mechanisms of defense. *Journal of Psychopharmacology, 5,* 305–315.

DEARY, I. (1992). Multiple minds. *Science, 259,* 28.

DEARY, I. J., WHALLEY, L. J., LEMMON, H., CRAWFORD, J. R., & STARR, J. M. (2000). The stability of individual differences in mental ability from childhood to old age: Follow-up of the 1932 Scottish Mental Survey. *Intelligence, 28,* 49–55.

DEAUX, K. (1984). From individual differences to social categories: Analysis of a decade's research on gender. *American Psychologist, 39,* 105–116.

DECASPER, A. J., & FIFER, W. P. (1980). Of human bonding: Newborns prefer their mothers' voices. *Science, 208,* 1174–1176.

DECASPER, A. J., & PRESCOTT, P. A. (1984). Human newborns' perception of male voices: Preference, discrimination and reinforcing value. *Developmental Psychobiology, 17,* 481–491.

DECASPER, A. J., & SPENCE, M. J. (1986). Prenatal maternal speech influences newborns' perception of speech sounds. *Infant Behavior and Development, 9,* 133–150.

DEFFENBACHER, K. (1980). Eyewitness accuracy and confidence: Can we infer anything about their relationship? *Law and Human Behavior, 4,* 243–260.

DEHART, G. B., SROUFE, L. A., & COOPER, R. G. (2000). *Child Development: Its Nature and Course.* Boston: McGraw Hill.

DEIKMAN, A. J. (1963). Experimental meditation. *Journal of Nervous and Mental Disease, 136,* 329–373.

DEMBROSKI, T. M., MACDOUGALL, J. M., WILLIAMS, B., & HANEY, T. L. (1985). Components of type A hostility and anger: Relationship to angiographic findings. *Psychosomatic Medicine, 47,* 219–233.

DEMENT, W. C., & KLEITMAN, N. (1957). The relation of eye movements during sleep to dream activity: An objective method for the study of dreaming. *Journal of Experimental Psychology, 53,* 339–346.

DEMENT, W. C., & WOLPERT, E. (1958). The relation of eye movements, bodily mobility, and external stimuli to dream content. *Journal of Experimental Psychology, 55,* 543–553.

DENNIS, W., & DENNIS, M. (1940). The effects of cradling practices upon the onset of walking in Hopi children. *Journal of Genetic Psychology, 56,* 77–86.

DEPUE, R. A., & COLLINS, P. F. (1999). Neurobiology of the structure of personality: Dopamine, facilitation of incentive motivation and extraversion. *Behavioral and Brain Sciences, 22,* 491–569.

DERRYBERRY, D., & TUCKER, D. M. (1994). Motivating the focus of attention. In P. M. Neidenthal & S. Kitayama (Eds.), *The heart's eye: Emotional influences in perception and attention* (pp. 167–196). San Diego: Academic Press.

DERUBEIS, R. J., & CRITS-CHRISTOPH, P. (1998). Empirically supported individual and group psychological treatments for adult mental disorders. *Journal of Abnormal Psychology, 101,* 371–382.

DESFORGES, D. M., LORD, C. G., RAMSEY, S. L., MASON, J. A., VAN LEEUWEN, M. D., WEST, S. C., & LEPPER, M. R. (1991). Effects of structured cooperative contact on changing negative attitudes toward stigmatized social groups. *Journal of Personality and Social Psychology, 60,* 531–544.

DEVALOIS, R. L., & DEVALOIS, K. K. (1980). Spatial vision. *Annual Review of Psychology, 31,* 309–341.

DEVALOIS, R. L., & JACOBS, G. H. (1984). Neural mechanisms of color vision. In I. Darian-Smith (Ed.), *Handbook of physiology* (Vol. 3). Bethesda, MD: American Physiological Society.

DEVINE, P. G. (1989). Stereotypes and prejudice: Their automatic and controlled components. *Journal of Personality and Social Psychology, 56,* 5–18.

DEVINE, P. G., & MONTEITH, M. J. (1999). Automaticity and control in stereotyping. In S. Chaiken & Y. Trope (Eds.), *Dual-process theories in social psychology* (pp. 339–360). New York: Guilford.

DEVINE, P. G., PLANT, E. A., AMODIO, D. M., HARMON-JONES, E., & VANCE, S. L. (2002). The regulation of explicit and implicit race bias: The role of motivations to respond without prejudice. *Journal of Personality and Social Psychology, 82,* 835–848.

DIJKSTERHUIS, A., & BARGH, J. A. (2002). The perception-behavior expressway: Automatic effects of social perception on social behavior. In M. Zanna (Ed.), *Advances in Experimental Social Psychology, 33,* 1–40.

DI LOLLO, V. (1980). Temporal Integration in Visual Memory. *Journal of Experimental Psychology: General, 109,* 75–97.

DI LOLLO, V., KAWAHARA J., ZUVIC, S. M., & VISSER, T. A. W. (2001) The preattentive emperor has no clothes: A dynamic redressing. *Journal of Experimental Psychology: General, 130,* 479–492.

DIAMOND, M. (1982). Sexual identity, monozygotic twins reared in discordant sex roles and a BBC follow-up. *Archives of Sexual Behavior, 11,* 181–186.

DIAMOND, M., (1996). Prenatal predisposition and the clinical management of some pediatric conditions. *Journal of Sex and Marital Therapy, 22,* 139–147.

DIAMOND, M., & SIGMUNDSON, K. (1997). Sex reassignment at birth: Long-term review and clinical implications. *Archives of Pediatric Medicine, 151,* 298.

DIENER, E. (1977). Deindividuation: Causes and consequences. *Social Behavior and Personality, 5,* 143–155.

DIENER, E. (1979). Deindividuation, self-awareness, and disinhibition. *Journal of Personality and Social Psychology, 37,* 1160–1171.

DIENER, E. (1980). Deindividuation: The absence of self-awareness and self-regulation in group members. In P. B. Paulus (Ed.), *The psychology of group influence.* Hillsdale, NJ: Erlbaum.

DIENER, E., FRASER, S. C., BEAMAN, A. L., & KELEM, R. T. (1976). Effects of deindividuation variables on stealing among Halloween trick-or-treaters. *Journal of Personality and Social Psychology, 33,* 178–183.

DIENSTBIER, R. A. (1989). Arousal and physiological toughness: Implications for mental and physical health. *Psychological Review, 96,* 84–100.

DIGMAN, J. M., & INOUYE, J. (1986). Further specification of the five robust factors of personality. *Journal of Personality and Social Psychology, 50,* 116–123.

DILLBECK, M. C., & ORME-JOHNSON, D. W. (1987). Physiological differences between transcendental meditation and rest. *American Psychologist, 42,* 879–881.

DINGES, D. F., & BROUGHTON, R. J. (Eds.). (1989). *Sleep and alertness: Chronobiological, behavioral, and medical aspects of napping.* New York: Raven.

DIPIETRO, J. A. (2001). Fetal neurobehavioral assessment. In L. T. Singer (Ed.), *Biobehavioral assessment of the infant.* (pp. 43–80). New York: Guilford.

DISHION, T. J., & PATTERSON, G. R. (1997). The timing and severity of antisocial behavior: Three hypotheses within an ecological framework. In D. M. Stoff, J. Breiling, & J. D. Maser (Eds.), *Handbook of antisocial personality disorder* (pp. 205–217). New York: Wiley.

DIXON, J. F., & HOKIN, L. E. (1998). Lithium acutely inhibits and chronically up-regulates and stabilizes glutamate uptake by presynaptic nerve endings in mouse cerebral cortex. *Neurobiology, 95,* 8363–8368.

DOBB, E. (1989, November–December). The scents around us. *The Sciences, 29,* 46–53.

DOBELLE, W. H., MEADEJOVSKY, M. G., & GIRVIN, J. P. (1974). Artificial vision for the blind: Electrical stimulation of visual cortex offers hope for a functional prosthesis. *Science, 183,* 440–444.

DOLLARD, J., DOOB, L. W., MILLER, N. E., MOWRER, O. H., & SEARS, R. R. (1939). *Frustration and aggression.* New Haven, CT: Yale University Press.

DOMHOFF, G. W. (1985). *The mystique of dreams.* Berkeley: University of California Press.

DOMHOFF, G. W. (1996). *Finding meaning in dreams: A quantitative approach.* New York: Plenum.

DOMHOFF, G. W., & SCHNEIDER, A. (1998). *The quantitative study of dreams.* http://zzyx.ucsc.edu?~dreams/.

DOMJAN, M., & BURKHARD, B. (1986). *The principles of learning and behavior.* Monterey, CA: Brooks/Cole.

DOWLING, J. E., & BOYCOTT, B. B. (1966). Organization of the primate retina. *Proceedings of the Royal Society of London, Series b, 166,* 80–111.

DOYLE, A. C. (1892/1981). *The original illustrated Sherlock Holmes.* Secaucus, NJ: Castle Books. (Originally published in America by Harper & Bros. in McClure's Magazine, 1893).

DUCLAUX, R., & KENSHALO, D. R. (1980). Response characteristics of cutaneous warm fibers in the monkey. *Journal of Neurophysiology, 43,* 1–15.

DREVETS, W. C. (2000). Neuroimaging studies of mood disorders. *Biological Psychiatry, 48,* 813–829.

DREVETS, W. C., BURTON, H., VIDEEN, T. O., SNYDER, A. Z., SIMPSON, J. R., & RAICHLE, M. E. (1995). Blood flow changes in human somatosensory cortex during anticipated stimulation. *Nature, 373,* 249–252.

DREVETS, W. C., VIDEEN, T. O., PRICE, J. L., PRESKORN, S. H., CARMICHAEL, S. T., & RAICHLE, M. E. (1992). A functional anatomical study of unipolar depression. *Journal of Neuroscience, 12,* 3628–3641.

DRONKERS, N. F., REDFERN, B. B., & KNIGHT, R. T. (2000). The neural architecture of language disorders. In: M. S. Gazzaniga (Ed.), *The new cognitive neuroscience* (2nd ed., pp. 949–958). Cambridge, MA: MIT Press.

DUBOIS, D. L., BULL, C. A., SHERMAN, M. D., & ROBERTS, M. (1998). Self-esteem and adjustment in early adolescence: A social-contextual perspective. *Journal of Youth and Adolescence, 27,* 557–583.

DUJARDIN, K., GUERRIEN, A., & LECONTE, P. (1990). Sleep, brain activation and cognition. *Physiology and Behavior, 47,* 1271–1278.

DUNCAN, J., & HUMPHREYS, G. W. (1989). Visual search and stimulus similarity. *Psychological Review, 96,* 433–458.

DUNCAN, P. D., and collaborators. (1985). The effects of pubertal timing on body image, school behavior, and deviance. *Journal of Youth and Adolescence, 14,* 227–235.

DUNCAN, R. D., SAUNDERS, B. E., KILPATRICK, D. G., HANSON, R. F., & RESNICK, H. S. (1996). Childhood physical assault as a risk factor for PTSD, depression, and substance abuse: Findings from a national survey. *American Journal of Orthopsychiatry, 66,* 437–448.

DUTTON, D. G., & ARON, A. P. (1974). Some evidence for heightened sexual attraction under conditions of high anxiety. *Journal of Personality and Social Psychology, 30,* 510–517.

EAGLY, A. H., & CHAIKEN, S. (1984). Cognitive theories of persuasion. In L. Berkowitz (Ed.), *Advances in experimental social psychology* (Vol. 17, pp. 267–359). New York: Academic Press.

EAGLY, A. H., & WOOD, W. (1999). The origins of sex differences in human behavior: Evolved dispositions versus social roles. *American Psychologist, 54,* 408–423.

EATON, W. W., MOORTENSENK, P. B., HERRMAN, H., & FREEMAN, H. (1992). Long-term course of hospitalization for schizophrenia: risk for rehospitalization. *Schizophrenia Bulletin, 18,* 217–228.

EATON, W. W., THARA, R., FEDERMAN, E., & THIEN, A. (1998). Remission and relapse in schizophrenia: the Madras longitudinal study. *The Journal of Nervous and Mental Disease, 186,* 357–363.

EBBESEN, E., DUNCAN, B., & KONECNI, V. (1975). Effects of content of verbal aggression on future verbal aggression: A field experiment. *Journal of Experimental Psychology, 11,* 192–204.

EBBINGHAUS, H. (1885). *Uber das gedachthis.* Leipzig: Dunckes and Humbolt.

EDGAR, D. M., & DEMENT, W. C. (1992). Evidence for opponent processes in sleep/wake regulation. *Sleep Research, 20A,* 2.

EDMONDSON, A. (1999). Psychological safety and learning behavior in work teams. *Administrative Science Quarterly, 44,* 350–383.

EHLERS, A. (1995). A 1-year prospective study of panic attacks: Clinical course and factors associated with maintenance. *Journal of Abnormal Psychology, 104,* 164–172.

EHLERS, A., & BREUER, P. (1992). Increased cardiac awareness in panic disorder. *Journal of Abnormal Psychology, 101,* 371–382.

EHRHARDT, A. A., MEYER-BAHLBURG, H. F., ROSEN, L. R., FELDMAN, J. F., VERIDIANO, N. P., ELKIN, E. J., & MCEWEN, B. S. (1989). The development of gender-related behavior in females following prenatal exposure to diethylstilbestrol (DES). *Hormones and Behavior, 23,* 526–541.

EIBL-EIBESFELDT, I. (1970). *Ethology: The biology of behavior* (E. Klinghammer, Trans.). New York: Holt, Rinehart & Winston.

EICH, J. E. (1980). The cue-dependent nature of state-dependent retrieval. *Memory and Cognition, 8,* 157–173.

EICHENBAUM, H. (2000). A cortical-hippocampal system for declarative memory. *Nature Reviews Neuroscience, 1,* 41–50.

EIMAS, P. D. (1975). Speech perception in early infancy. In L. B. Cohen & P. Salapatek (Eds.), *Infant perception: From sensation to cognition* (Vol. 2). New York: Academic Press.

EIMAS, P. D. (1985). The perception of speech in early infancy. *Scientific American, 252,* 46–52.

EISENBERG, N., CUMBERLAND, A., & SPINRAD, T. L. (1998). Parental socialization of emotion. *Psychological Inquiry, 9,* 241–273.

EKMAN, P. (1972). Universals and cultural differences in facial expressions of emotion. In J. Cole (Ed.), *Nebraska symposium on motivation, 1971* (pp. 207–283). Lincoln: University of Nebraska Press.

EKMAN, P. (1982). *Emotion in the human face* (2nd ed.). New York: Cambridge University Press.

EKSTROM, R. B., FRENCH, J. W., & HARMAN, H. H. (1979). *Cognitive factors: Their identification and replication. Multivariate behavioral research monographs.* Fort Worth: Society for Multivariate Experimental Psychology.

EKSTROM, R. B., FRENCH, J. W., HARMAN, H. H., & DERMAN, D. (1976). *Manual for kit of factor-referenced cognitive tests, 1976.* Princeton, NJ: Educational Testing Service.

ELKIN, I. SHEA, T., WATKINS, J. T., IMBER, S. D., SOTSKY, S. M., COLLINS, J. F., GLASS, D. R., PILKONIS, P. A., LEBER, W. R., DOCHERTY, J. P., FIESTER, S. J., & PARLOFF, M. B. (1989). National Institute of Mental Health treatment of depression collaborative research program: General effectiveness of treatments. *Archives of General Psychiatry, 46,* 971–982.

ELKIN, R. A., & LEIPPE, M. R. (1986). Physiological arousal, dissonance, and attitude change: Evidence of a dissonance-arousal link and a "don't remind me" effect. *Journal of Personality and Social Psychology, 51,* 55–65.

ELLASON, J. W., ROSS, C. A., FUCHS, D. L. (1996). Lifetime Axis I and II comorbidity and childhood trauma history in dissociative identity disorder. *Psychiatry: Interpersonal & Biological Processes, 59,* 255–266.

ELLIOT, A. J., & DEVINE, P. G. (1994). On the motivational nature of cognitive dissonance: Dissonance as psychological discomfort. *Journal of Personality and Social Psychology, 67,* 382–394.

ELLIS, L., & AMES, M. A. (1987). Neurohormonal functioning and sexual orientation: A theory of homosexuality-heterosexuality. *Psychological Bulletin, 2,* 233–258.

ELLISON, C. G., & LEVIN, J. S. (1998). The religion-health connection: Evidence, theory, and future directions. *Health Education and Behavior, 25,* 700–720.

ELLISON, L. F., & MORRISON, H. I. (2001). Low serum cholesterol concentration and risk of suicide. *Epidemiology, 12,* 168–172.

ELLSWORTH, P. (1991). Some implications of cognitive appraisals on theories of emotion. In K. T. Strongman (Ed.), *International review of studies on emotion* (Vol. 1). New York: Wiley.

ELMES, D. G., KANTOWITZ, B. H., & ROEDIGER, H. L. (1989). *Research methods in psychology* (3rd ed.). St. Paul, MN: West.

EMMELKAMP, P. M. G. (1994). Behavior therapy with adults. In A. E. Bergin & S. L. Garfield (Eds.), *Handbook of psychotherapy and behavior change* (4th ed., pp. 379–427). New York: Wiley.

EMMELKAMP, P., & KUIPERS, A. (1979). Agoraphobia: A follow-up study four years after treatment. *British Journal of Psychiatry, 134,* 352–355.

ENGEN, T. (1982). *The perception of odors.* New York: Academic Press.

ENNS, J. T., & GIRGUS, J. S. (1985). Perceptual grouping and spatial distortion: A developmental study. *Developmental Psychology, 21,* 241–246.

ENNS, J. T., & PRINZMETAL, W. (1984). The role of redundancy in the object-line effect. *Perception and Psychophysics, 35,* 22–32.

ENNS, J. T., & RENSINK, R. A. (1990). Sensitivity to three-dimensional orientation in visual search. *Psychological Science, 1,* 323–326.

EPLEY, N., & GILOVICH, T. (1999). Just going along: Nonconscious priming and conformity to social pressure. *Journal of Experimental Social Psychology, 35,* 578–589.

EPSTEIN, S., & MEIER, P. (1989). Constructive thinking: A broad coping variable with specific components. *Journal of Personality and Social Psychology, 57,* 332–350.

ERDELYI, M. H. (1985). *Psychoanalysis: Freud's cognitive psychology.* New York: Freeman.

ERICSSON, K. A., CHASE, W. G., & FALOON, S. (1980). Acquisition of a memory skill. *Science, 208,* 1181–1182.

ERICSSON, K. A., & SIMON, H. A. (1993). *Protocol analysis: Verbal reports as data* (Rev. Ed.). Cambridge, MA: MIT Press.

ERIKSEN, C. W., & COLLINS, J. F. (1967). Some temporal characteristics of visual pattern perception. *Journal of Experimental Psychology, 74,* 476–484.

ERIKSON, E. H. (1963). *Childhood and society* (2nd ed.). New York: Norton.

ERIKSON, E. H. (1968). *Identity: Youth and crisis.* New York: Norton.

ERON, L. D. (1987). The development of aggressive behavior from the perspective of a developing behaviorism. *American Psychologist, 42,* 435–442.

ERON, L. D., HUESMANN, L. R., LEFKOWITZ, M. M., & WALDER, L. O. (1972). Does television violence cause aggression? *American Psychologist, 27,* 253–263.

ERVIN-TRIPP, S. (1964). Imitation and structural change in children's language. In E. H. Lenneberg (Ed.), *New directions in the study of language.* Cambridge, MA: MIT Press.

ESCOBAR, J. I. (1993). Psychiatric epidemiology. In A. C. Gaw (Ed.), *Culture, ethnicity and mental illness* (pp. 43–73). Washington, DC: American Psychiatric Press.

ESTERSON, A. (1993). *Seductive mirage: An exploration of the work of Sigmund Freud.* Chicago: Open Court.

ESTES, W. K. (1972). An associative basis for coding and organization in memory. In A. W. Melton & E. Martin (Eds.), *Coding processes in human memory.* Washington, DC: Winston.

ESTES, W. K. (Ed.). (1975–1979). *Handbook of learning and cognitive processes* (Vols. 1–6). Hillsdale, NJ: Erlbaum.

ESTES, W. K. (1994). *Classification and cognition.* New York: Oxford University Press.

ETCOFF, N. L. (1985). The neuropsychology of emotional expression. In G. Goldstein & R. E. Tarter (Eds.), *Advances in clinical neuropsychology* (Vol. 3). New York: Plenum.

EVANS, C. (1984). *Landscapes of the night: How and why we dream.* New York: Viking.

EXNER, J. (1986). *The Rorschach: A comprehensive system* (2nd ed., Vol. 1). New York: Wiley.

EXNER, J. E., & WEINER, I. B. (1995). *The Rorschach: A comprehensive system.* Volume 3: Assessment of children and adolescents (2nd ed.). New York: Wiley.

EYLER ZORRILLA, L. T., CANNON, T. D., KRONENBERG, S., MEDNICK, S. A., SCHULSINGER, F., PARNAS, J., PRAESTHOLM, J., BESTERGAARD, A. (1997). Structural brain abnormalities in schizophrenia: a family study. *Biological Psychiatry, 42,* 1080–1086.

EYSENCK, H. J. (1953). *The structure of human personality.* New York: Wiley.

EYSENCK, H. J., & KAMIN, L. (1981). *The intelligence controversy.* New York: Wiley.

EYSENCK, J. H., & RACHMAN, S. (1973). The future of clinical psychology. *Bulletin of the British Psychological Society, 26,* 113–116.

FABREGA, H., ULRICH, R., PILKONIS, P., & MEZZICH, J. (1991). On the homogeneity of personality disorder clusters. *Comprehensive Psychiatry, 32,* 373–386.

FAGOT, B. I. (1978). The influence of sex of child on parental reactions to toddler children. *Child Development, 49,* 459–465.

FAIKKONEN, K., MATTHEWS, K. A., FLORY, J. D., OWENS, J. F., & GUMP, B. B. (1999). Effects of optimism, pessimism, and trait anxiety on ambulatory blood pressure and mood during everyday life. *Journal of Personality and Social Psychology, 76,* 104—113.

FAIRBURN, C. G., & HAY, P. J. (1992). Treatment of bulimia nervosa. *Annals of Medicine, 24,* 297–302.

FAIRBURN, C. G., NORMAN, P. A., WELCH, S. L., O'CONNOR, M. E., DOLL, H. A., & PEVELER, R. C. (1995). A prospective study of outcome in bulimia nervosa and the long-term effects of three psychological treatments. *Archives of General Psychiatry, 52,* 304–312.

FAIRBURN, C. G., WELCH, S. L., & HAY, P. J. (1993). The classification of recurrent overeating: The "binge eating disorder" proposal. Fifth International Conference on Eating Disorders (1992, New York). *International Journal of Eating Disorders, 13,* 155–159.

FALS-STEWART, W. M., & ALLEN, P. J. (1993). A comparison of behavioral group therapy and individual behavior therapy in treating obsessive-compulsive disorder. *Journal of Nervous and Mental Disease, 18,* 189–193.

FANSELOW, M. S. (1997). Species-specific defense reactions: Retrospect and prospect. In M. E. Bouton & M. S. Fanselow (Eds.), *Learning, motivation, and cognition: The functional behaviorism of Robert C. Bolles* (pp. 321–341). Washington, DC: American Psychological Association.

FANTZ, R. L. (1961). The origin of form perception. *Science, 204,* 66–72.

FANTZ, R. L. (1970). Visual perception and experience in infancy: Issues and approaches. In National Academy of Science, *Early experience and visual information processing in perceptual and reading disorders* (pp. 351–381). New York: National Academy of Science.

FARAH, M., HAMMOND, K. M., & LEVINE, D. N. (1988). Visual and spatial mental imagery: Dissociable systems of representation. *Cognitive Psychology, 20,* 439–462.

FARAH, M. J. (1990). *Visual agnosia: Disorders of object recognition and what they tell us about normal vision.* Cambridge, MA: MIT Press.

FARAH, M. J. (2000). *The cognitive neuroscience of vision.* Malden, MA: Blackwell.

FARAH, M. J., & MCCLELLAND, J. L. (1991). A computational model of semantic memory impairment. *Journal of Experimental Psychology: General, 120,* 339–357.

FARAONE, S. V., and collaborators. (1990). Genetic transmission of major affective disorders: Quantitative models and linkage analyses. *Psychological Bulletin, 108,* 109–127.

FARBER, E. W., SCHWARTZ, J. A. J., SCHAPER, P. E., MOONEN, D. J., & MCDANIEL, J. S. (2000). Resilience factors associated with adaptation to HIV disease. *Psychosomatics, 41,* 140–146.

FARRINGTON, D. P. (1995). The challenge of teenager antisocial behavior. In M. Rutter (Ed.), *Psychosocial disturbances in young people: Challenges for prevention.* (pp. 83–130). New York: Cambridge University Press.

FARTHING, G. W. (1992). *The psychology of consciousness.* Englewood Cliffs, NJ: Prentice Hall.

FAUST, I. M. (1984). Role of the fat cell in energy balance physiology. In A. T. Stunkard & E. Stellar (Eds.), *Eating and its disorders.* New York: Raven Press.

FAVA, M., COPELAND, P. M., SCHWEIGER, U., & HERZOG, D. B. (1989). Neurochemical abnormalities of anorexia nervosa and bulimia nervosa. *American Journal of Psychiatry, 146,* 963–971.

FAWCETT, J., BUSCH, K. A., JACOBS, D., KRAVITZ, H. M., & FOGG, L. (1997). Suicide: A four-pathway clinical-biochemical model. *Annals of the New York Academy of Sciences, 836,* 288–301.

FAZIO, R., ZANNA, M. P., & COOPER, J. (1977). Dissonance and self-perception: An integrative view of each theory's proper domain of application. *Journal of Experimental Social Psychology, 13,* 464–479.

FAZIO, R. H. (1990). Multiple processes by which attitudes guide behavior: The MODE model as an integrative framework. In M. P. Zanna (Ed.), *Advances in experimental social psychology* (Vol. 23). San Diego: Academic Press.

FAZIO, R. H., JACKSON, J. R., DUNTON, B. C., & WILLIAMS, C. J. (1995). Variability in automatic activation as an unobtrusive measure of racial attitudes: A bona fide pipeline? *Journal of Personality and Social Psychology, 69,* 1013–1027.

FECHNER, G. T. (1860/1966). *Elements of psychophysics* (H. E. Adler, Trans.). New York: Holt, Rinehart & Winston.

FEINGOLD, A. (1988). Cognitive gender differences are disappearing. *American Psychologist, 43,* 95–103.

FELDMAN, H., GOLDIN-MEADOW, S., & GLEITMAN, L. R. (1978). Beyond Herodotus: The creation of language by linguistically deprived children. In A. Lock (Ed.), *Action, gesture, and symbol: The emergence of language.* London: Academic Press.

FELDMAN, H., MEYER, J.S. & QUENZER, L. S. (1997). *Principles of neuropsychopharmacology.* New York: Sinauer.

FELDMAN BARRETT, L., ROBIN, L., PIETROMONACO, P. R., & EYSSELL, K. M. (1998). Are women the "more emotional" sex? Evidence from emotional experiences in social context. *Cognition and Emotion, 12,* 555–578.

FENWICK, P. (1987). Meditation and the EEG. In M. A. West (Ed.), *The psychology of meditation.* Oxford, England: Oxford University Press.

FERGUSON, M. L., & KATKIN, E. S. (1996). Visceral perception, anhedonia, and emotion. *Biological Psychology, 42,* 131–145.

FERRIS, C. F., & DE VRIES, G. J. (1997). Ethological models for examining the neurobiology of aggressive and affiliative behaviors. In D. M. Stoff, J. Breiling, & J. D. Maser (Eds.) *Handbook of antisocial personality disorder* (pp. 255–268). New York: Wiley.

FESHBACH, N. D. (1980, September). *The child as psychologist and economist: Two curricula.* Paper presented at the American Psychological Association convention. Montreal.

FESTINGER, L. (1957). *A theory of cognitive dissonance.* Stanford: Stanford University Press.

FESTINGER, L., & CARLSMITH, J. M. (1959). Cognitive consequences of forced compliance. *Journal of Abnormal and Social Psychology, 58,* 203–210.

FESTINGER, L., PEPITONE, A., & NEWCOMB, T. M. (1952). Some consequences of deindividuation in a group. *Journal of Abnormal and Social Psychology, 47,* 383–389.

FESTINGER, L., SCHACHTER, S., & BACK, K. (1950). *Social pressures in informal groups: A study of human factors in housing.* New York: Harper & Row.

FIELD, J. (1987). The development of auditory-visual localization in infancy. In B. E. McKenzie & R. H. Day (Eds.), *Perceptual development in early infancy.* Hillsdale, NJ: Erlbaum.

FIELD, T. (1991). Quality infant day care and grade school behavior and performance. *Child Development, 62,* 863–870.

FIELD, T. (1998). Massage therapy effects. *American Psychologist, 53,* 1270–1281.

FIELD, T. (2001). Massage therapy facilitates weight gain in preterm infants. *Current Directions in Psychological Science, 10,* 51–53.

FIELD, T., GRIZZLE, N., SCAFIDI, F., ABRAMS, S., & RICHARDSON, S. (1996). Massage therapy for infants of depressed mothers. *Infant Behavior and Development, 19,* 109–114.

FIELD, T., HENTELEFF, T., HERNANDEZ-REIF, M., MARTINEZ, E., MAVUNDA, K., KUHN, C., & SCHANBERG, S. (1998). Children with asthma have improved pulmonary function after massage therapy. *Journal of Pediatrics, 132,* 854–858.

FIELD, T., HERNANDEZ-REIF, M., SELIGMAN, S., KRASNEGOR, J., SUNSHINE, W., RIVAS-CHACON, R., SCHANBERG, S., & KUHN, C. (1997). Juvenile rheumatoid arthritis: Benefits from massage therapy. *Journal of Pediatric Psychology, 22,* 607–617.

FIELD, T., HERNANDEZ-REIF, M., SHAW, K. H., LA GRECA, A., SCHANBERG, S., & KUHN, C. (1997). Glucose levels decreased after giving massage therapy to children with diabetes mellitus. *Diabetes Spectrum, 10,* 23–25.

FIELD, T., SCHANBERG, S. M., SCAFIDI, F., BAUER, C. R., VEGA-LAHR, N., GARCIA, R., NYSTROM, J., & KUHN, C. (1986). Tactile/kinesthetic stimulation effects on preterm neonates. *Pediatrics, 77,* 654–658.

FINCK, H. T. (1887). *Romantic love and personal beauty: Their development, causal relations, historic and national pecularities.* London: Macmillan.

FINKE, R. A. (1985). Theories relating mental imagery to perception. *Psychological Bulletin, 98,* 236–259.

FISCHER, A. H. (2000). *Gender and emotion: Social psychological perspectives.* New York: Cambridge University Press.

FISCHER, A. H., MANSTEAD, A. S. R., & MOSQUERA, P. M. R. (1999). The role of honour-related vs. individualistic values in conceptualizing pride, shame, and anger: Spanish and Dutch cultural prototypes. *Cognition and Emotion, 13,* 149–179.

FISHBEIN, M., TRIANDIS, H. C., KANFER, F. H., BECKER, M., MIDDLESTADT, S. E., & EICHLER, A. (1998). Factors influencing behavior and behavior change. *Handbook of Health Psychology.* In press.

FISHER, G. H. (1967). Preparation of ambiguous stimulus materials. *Perception and Psychophysics, 2,* 421–422.

FISHER, P. J., TURIC, D., WILLIAMS, N. M., MCGUFFIN, P., ASHERSON, P., BALL, D., CRAIG, I., ELEY, T., HILL, L., CHURNEY, K., CHURNEY, M. J., BENBOW, C. P., LUBINSKI, D., PLUMIN, R., OWEN, M. J. (1999). DNA pooling identifies QTLs on chromosome 4 for general cognitive ability in children. *Human Molecular Genetics, 8,* 915–922.

FISHER, R. A. (1958). *The cancer controversy.* London: Oliver & Boyd.

FISHER, S., & GREENBERG, R. (1977). *The scientific credibility of Freud's theories and therapy.* New York: Basic Books.

FISHER, S., & GREENBERG, R. (1996). *Freud scientifically appraised.* New York: Wiley.

FISHMAN, P. (1983). Interaction: The work women do. In B. Thorne, C. Kramarae, & N. Henley

(Eds.), *Language, gender, and society*. Rowley, MA: Newbury House.

FISKE, S. T. (1993). Social cognition and social perception. *Annual Review of Psychology, 44*, 155–194.

FISKE, S. T., & TAYLOR, S. E. (1991). *Social cognition* (2nd ed.). New York: McGraw-Hill.

FISKE, S. T., LIN, M., & NEUBERG, S. L. (1999). The continuum model: Ten years later. In S. Chaiken & Y. Trope (Eds.), *Dual-process theories in social psychology* (pp. 231–254). New York: Guilford.

FITZSIMONS, J. T. (1969). The role of a renal thirst factor in drinking induced by extra cellular stimuli. *Journal of Physiology, London, 201*, 349–368.

FITZSIMONS, J. T. (1990). Thirst and sodium appetite. In E. M. Stricker (Ed.), *Neurobiology of food and fluid intake* (pp. 23–44). New York: Plenum.

FIVUSH, R., & BUCKNER, J. P. (2000). Gender, sadness, and depression: The development of emotional focus through gendered discourse. In A. H. Fischer (Ed.), *Gender and emotion: Social psychological perspectives* (pp. 232–253). New York: Cambridge University Press.

FIVUSH, R., & HAMOND, N. R. (1991). Autobiographical memory across the preschool years: Toward reconceptualizing childhood memory. In R. Fivush & N. R. Hamond (Eds.), *Knowing and remembering in young children*. New York: Cambridge University Press.

FIXSEN, D. L., PHILLIPS, E. L., PHILLIPS, E. A., & WOLF, M. M. (1976). The teaching-family model of group home treatment. In W. E. Craighead, A. E. Kazdin, & M. J. Mahoney (Eds.), *Behavior modification: Principles, issues, and applications*. Boston: Houghton Mifflin.

FLAVELL, J. H. (1992). *Cognitive development* (3rd ed.). Englewood Cliffs, NJ: Prentice Hall.

FLAVELL, J. H. (1999). Cognitive development: Children's knowledge about the mind. *Annual Review of Psychology, 50*, 21–45.

FLEMING, J., & DARLEY, J. M. (1986). *Perceiving intention in constrained behavior: The role of purposeful and constrained action cues in correspondence bias effects*. Unpublished manuscript, Princeton University.

FLODERUS-MYRED, B., PETERSEN, N., & RASMUSON, I. (1980). Assessment of heritability for personality based on a short form of the Eysenck Personality Inventory. *Behavior Genetics, 10*, 153–161.

FLOR, H., FYDRICH, T., & TURK, D. C. (1992). Efficacy of multidisciplinary pain treatment: A meta-analytic review. *Pain, 49*, 221–230.

FLOWERS, M. L. (1977). A laboratory test of some implications of Janis's groupthink hypothesis. *Journal of Personality and Social Psychology, 35*, 888–896.

FLUOXETINE BULIMIA NERVOSA STUDY GROUP (1992). Fluoxetine in the treatment of bulimia nervosa: A multi-center, placebo-controlled, double-blind trial. *Archives of General Psychiatry, 49*, 156–162.

FLYNN, J. R. (1987). Massive IQ gains in 14 nations: What IQ tests really measure. *Psychological Bulletin, 101*, 171–191.

FOA, E., & STEKETEE, G. (1989). Obsessive-compulsive disorder. In C. Lindemann (Ed.), *Handbook of phobia therapy*. Northvale, NJ: Jason Aronson.

FOA, E. B., & FRANKLIN, M. E. (2001). Obsessive-compulsive disorder. *Clinical handbook of psychological disorders: a step-by-step treatment manual* (3rd ed., pp. 209–263). New York: Guilford.

FOA, E. D., & RIGGS, D. S. (1995). Posttraumatic stress disorder following assault: Theoretical considerations and empirical findings. *Current Directions in Psychological Science, 4*, 61–65.

FODOR, J. A., BEVER, T. G., & GARRETT, M. F. (1974). *The psychology of language: An introduction to psycholinguistics and generative grammar*. New York: McGraw-Hill.

FOLEY, D. L., PICKLES, A., MAES, H. H., SILBERG, J. L., HEWITT, J. K., & EAVES, L. J. (2001). Parental concordance and comorbidity for psychiatric disorder and associate risks for current psychiatric symptoms and disorders in a community sample of juvenile twins. *Journal of Child Psychology and Psychiatry & Allied Disciplines, 42*, 381–394.

FOLKES, V. S. (1982). Forming relationships and the matching hypothesis. *Personality and Social Psychology Bulletin, 8*, 631–636.

FOLLETTE, W. C., & HAYES, S. C. (2000). Contemporary behavior therapy. In C. R. Snyder & R. Ingram (Eds.), *Handbook of psychological change* (pp. 381–408). New York: Wiley.

FORDYCE, W. E. (1976). *Behavioral methods for chronic pain and illness*. St. Louis, MO: C. V. Mosby.

FORGE, K. L., & PHEMISTER, S. (1987). The effect of prosocial cartoons on preschool children. *Child Development Journal, 17*, 83–88.

FORSYTH, D. R., & CORAZZINI, J. G. (2000). Groups as change agents. In C. R. Snyder & R. Ingram (Eds.), *Handbook of psychological change* (pp. 309–336). New York: Wiley.

FOSS, D. J., & HAKES, D. T. (1978). *Psycholinguistics: An introduction to the psychology of language*. Englewood Cliffs, NJ: Prentice-Hall.

FOULKES, D. (1985). *Dreaming: A cognitive-psychological analysis*. Hillsdale, NJ: Erlbaum.

FOULKES, D. (1993). Data constraints on theorizing about dream function. In A. Moffitt, M. Kramer, & R. Hoffman (Eds.), *The functions of dreaming*. Albany: State University of New York Press.

FOULKES, D (1999). *Children's dreaming and the development of consciousness*. Cambridge, MA: Harvard University Press.

FOULKES, D., & SCHMIDT, M. (1983). Temporal sequence and unit comparison composition in dream reports from different stages of sleep. *Sleep, 6*, 265–280.

FRABLE, D. E. (1989). Sex typing and gender ideology: Two facets of the individual's gender psychology that go together. *Journal of Personality and Social Psychology, 56*, 95–108.

FRANK, J. D., & FRANK, J. B. (1991). *Persuasion and healing: A comparative study of psychotherapy* (3rd edition). Baltimore: Johns Hopkins University Press.

FRANKENHAEUSER, M. (1983). The sympathetic-adrenal and pituitary-adrenal response to challenge: Comparison between the sexes. In T. M. Dembroski, T. H. Schmidt, & G. Blumchen (Eds.), *Biobehavioral bases of coronary heart disease*. Basel: Karger.

FRANKLIN, J. (1987). *Molecules of the mind*. New York: Atheneum.

FRANTZ, R. L. (1966). Pattern discrimination and selective attention as determinants of perceptual development from birth. In A. H. Kikk & J. F. Rivoire (Eds.), *Development of perception: Vol. 2, The visual system* (pp. 143–173). New York: International University Press.

FRAZIER, K. (1987). Psychic's imagined year fizzles (again). *Skeptical Inquirer, 11*, 335–336.

FREDRICKSON, B. L. (1998). What good are positive emotions? *Review of General Psychology, 2*, 300–319.

FREDRICKSON, B. L. (2000). Cultivating positive emotions to optimize health and well-being. *Prevention and Treatment*. Available on the World Wide Web: http://journals.apa.org/prevention.

FREDRICKSON, B. L. (2001). The role of positive emotions in positive psychology: The broaden-and-build theory of positive emotions. *American Psychologist, 56*, 218–226.

FREDRICKSON, B. L. (2002). Positive emotions. In C. R. Snyder & S. J. Lopez (Eds.), *Handbook of positive psychology* (pp. 120–134). New York: Oxford University Press.

FREDRICKSON, B. L., & BRANIGAN, C. (2001). Positive emotions. In T. J. Mayne & G. A. Bonnano (Eds.), *Emotion: Current issues and future developments* (pp. 123–151). New York: Guilford.

FREDRICKSON, B. L., & BRANIGAN, C. (2002). *Positive emotions broaden the scope of attention and thought-action repertoires*. Manuscript under review.

FREDRICKSON, B. L., & JOINER, T. (2002). Positive emotions trigger upward spirals toward emotional well-being. *Psychological Science, 13*, 172–175.

FREDRICKSON, B. L., & LEVENSON, R. W. (1998). Positive emotions speed recovery from the cardiovascular sequelae of negative emotions. *Cognition and Emotion, 12*, 191–220.

FREDRICKSON, B. L., MANCUSO, R. A., BRANIGAN, C., & TUGADE, M. M. (2000). The undoing effect of positive emotions. *Motivation and Emotion, 24*, 237–258.

FREE, L. A., & CANTRIL, H. (1967). *The political beliefs of Americans*. New Brunswick, NJ: Rutgers University Press.

FREEDMAN, J. L. (1965). Long-term behavioral effects of cognitive dissonance. *Journal of Experimental Social Psychology, 1*, 145–155.

FREEDMAN, J. L., & FRASER, S. C. (1966). Compliance without pressure: The foot-in-the-door technique. *Journal of Personality and Social Psychology, 4*, 195–203.

FREESTON, M. H., LADOUCEUR, R., THIBODEAU, N., & GAGNON, F. (1992). Cognitive intrusions in a non-clinical population: II. Associations with depressive, anxious, and compulsive symptoms. *Behaviour Research and Therapy, 30*, 263–271.

FREUD, A. (1946/1967). *The ego and the mechanisms of defense* (Rev. Ed.). New York: International Universities Press.

FREUD, A. (1958). Adolescence. *The Psychoanalytic Study of the Child, 13*, 255–278.

FREUD, S. (1885). *Ueber coca*. Vienna: Mortiz Perles. (Translated in Freud, 1974)

FREUD, S. (1885/1974). *Cocaine papers* (edited and introduction by R. Byck; notes by A. Freud). New York: Stonehill.

FREUD, S. (1900/1953). *The interpretation of dreams* (Reprint ed., Vols. 4, 5). London: Hogarth Press.

FREUD, S. (1901/1960). *Psychopathology of everyday life* (Standard ed., Vol. 6). London: Hogarth Press.

FREUD, S. (1905/1962). *Three contributions to theory of sex* (4th ed.; A. A. Brill, Trans.). New York: Nervous and Mental Disease Monograph.

FREUD, S. (1915/1976). Repression. In J. Strachey (Ed. and Trans.), *The complete psychological works: Standard edition* (Vol. 14). London: Hogarth Press.

FREUD, S. (1920/1975). *Beyond the pleasure principle*. New York: Norton.

FREUD, S. (1925/1961). Some psychical consequences of the anatomical distinctions between the sexes. In J. Strachey (Ed. and Trans.), *The complete psychological works: Standard edition* (Vol. 18). London: Hogarth Press.

FREUD, S. (1933/1964). *New introductory lectures on psychoanalysis* (J. Strachey, Ed. and Trans.). New York: Norton.

FREUD, S. (1933/1965). Revision of the theory of dreams. In J. Strachey (Ed. and Trans.), *New introductory lectures on psychoanalysis* (Vol. 22, Lect. 29). New York: Norton.

FREUD, S. (1940). An outline of psychoanalysis. *International Journal of Psychoanalysis, 21,* 27–84.

FRIEDMAN, M., & ROSENMAN, R. H. (1974). *Type A behavior.* New York: Knopf.

FRIEDMAN, M., THORESEN, C. E., GILL, J. J., ULMER, D., POWELL, L. H., PRICE, V., BROWN, B., THOMPSON, L., RABIN, D. D., and collaborators. (1994). Alteration of Type A behavior and its effect on cardiac recurrences in post myocardial infarction patients: Summary results of the recurrent coronary prevention project. In A. Steptoe (Ed.), *Psychosocial processes and health: A reader.* Cambridge, England: Cambridge University Press.

FRIEDMAN, M. I. (1990). Making sense out of calories. In E. M. Stricker (Ed.), *Neurobiology of food and fluid intake* (pp. 513–528). New York: Plenum.

FRIJDA, N. H. (1986). *The emotions.* Cambridge, England: Cambridge University Press.

FRISCHHOLZ, E. J. (1985). The relationship among dissociation, hypnosis, and child abuse in the development of multiple personality disorder. In R. P. Kluft (Ed.), *Childhood antecedents of multiple personality.* Washington, DC: American Psychiatric Press.

FRODI, A., & THOMPSON, R. (1985). Infants' affective responses in the strange situation: Effects of prematurity and of quality of attachment. *Child Development, 56,* 1280–1290.

FUGH-BERMAN, A., & COTT, J. M. (1999). Dietary supplements and natural products as psychotherapeutic agents. *Psychosomatic Medicine, 61,* 712–728.

FULLER, S. R., & ALDAG, R. J. (1998). Organizational Tonypandy: Lessons from a quarter century of groupthink phenomenon. *Organizational Behavior and Human Decision Processes, 73,* 163–184.

FUNDER, D. C. (2001). Personality. *Annual Reviews of Psychology, 52,* 197–221.

FUNKENSTEIN, D. (1955). The physiology of fear and anger. *Scientific American, 192,* 74–80.

FYER, A. J., MANNUZZA, S., CHAPMAN, T. F., & LIEBOWITZ, M. R. (1993). A direct interview family study of social phobia. *Archives of General Psychiatry, 50,* 286–293.

FYER, A. J., MANNUZZA, S., GALLOPS, M. S., & MARTIN, L. Y. (1990). Familial transmission of simple phobias and fears: A preliminary report. *Archives of General Psychiatry, 47,* 252–256.

GADOW, K. D. (1991). Clinical issues in child and adolescent psychopharmacology. *Journal of Consulting and Clinical Psychology, 59,* 842–852.

GADOW, K. D. (1992). Pediatric psychopharmacotherapy: A review of recent research. *Journal of Child Psychology and Psychiatry, 33,* 153–195.

GALANTER, E. (1962). Contemporary psychophysics. In R. Brown & collaborators (Eds.), *New directions in psychology* (Vol. 1). New York: Holt, Rinehart & Winston.

GALDERISI, S., VITA, A., ROSSI, A., STRATTA, P., LEONARDI, A., & INVERNIZZI, G. (2000). Qualitative MRI findings in patients with schizophrenia: A controlled study. *Psychiatry Research, 98,* 117–126.

GALINSKY, E., HOWES, C., KONTOS, S., & SHINN, M. (1994). The study of children in family child care and relative care: Highlights of findings. New York: Families and Work Institute.

GALLANT, J. L., SHUOP, R. E., & MAZER, J. A. (2000) A human extrastriate area functionally homologous to macaque V4. *Neuron, 27,* 227–235.

GALLUP ORGANIZATION (1995). *Sleep in America: A national survey of U.S. adults.* Poll conducted for the National Sleep Foundation. Princeton, NJ: National Sleep Foundation.

GALOTTI, K. M. (1989). Approaches to studying formal and everyday reasoning. *Psychological Bulletin, 105,* 331–351.

GAMSON, W. B., FIREMAN, B., & RYTINA, S. (1982). *Encounters with unjust authority.* Homewood, IL: Dorsey Press.

GANELLEN, R. J., & CARVER, C. S. (1985). Why does self-reference promote incidental encoding? *Journal of Personality and Social Psychology, 21,* 284–300.

GARCIA, J., & KOELLING, R. A. (1966). The relation of cue to consequence in avoiding learning. *Psychonomic Science, 4,* 123–124.

GARCIA, L. T., ERSKINE, N., HAWN, K., & CASMAY, S. R. (1981). The effect of affirmative action on attributions about minority group members. *Journal of Personality, 49,* 427–437.

GARDNER, B. T., & GARDNER, R. A. (1972). Two-way communication with an infant chimpanzee. In A. M. Schrier & F. Stollnitz (Eds.), *Behavior of nonhuman primates* (Vol. 4). New York: Academic Press.

GARDNER, E. L. (1992). Brain reward mechanisms. In J. H. Lowinson, P. Ruiz, & R. B. Millman (Eds.), *Substance abuse: A comprehensive textbook* (2nd ed.). Baltimore, MD: Williams & Wilkins.

GARDNER, H. (1975). *The shattered mind.* New York: Knopf.

GARDNER, H. (1985). *The mind's new science: A history of the cognitive revolution.* New York: Basic Books.

GARDNER, H. (1993a). *Frames of mind: The theory of multiple intelligences.* New York: Basic Books.

GARDNER, H. (1993b). *Multiple intelligences: The theory in practice.* New York: Basic Books.

Gardner, H. (1999) *Intelligence reframed: Multiple intelligences for the 21st century.* New York: Basic Books.

GARDNER, H., KORNHABER, M. L., & WAKE, W. K. (1996). *Intelligence: Multiple perspectives.* Fort Worth: Harcourt Brace.

GARDNER, M. (1981). *Science: Good, bad, and bogus.* New York: Prometheus.

GARDNER, W., LIDZ, C. W., MULVEY, E. P., & SHAW, E. C. (1996). Clinical versus actuarial predictions of violence in patients with mental illnesses. *Journal of Consulting and Clinical Psychology, 64,* 602–609.

GARFIELD, S. L. (1994a). Research on client variables in psychotherapy. In S. L. Garfield & A. E. Bergen (Eds.), *Handbook of psychotherapy and behavior change* (pp. 190–228). New York: Wiley.

GARFIELD, S. L. (1994b). Research on client variables in psychotherapy. In A. E. Bergin (Ed.), *Handbook of psychotherapy integration* (pp. 190–228), New York: Wiley.

GARNER, D. M., & GARFINKEL, P. E. (1980). Socio-cultural factors in the development of anorexia nervosa. *Psychological Medicine, 10,* 647–656.

GARRETT, M. (1997). The effects of infant child care on infant-mother attachment security: Results of the NICHD Study of Early Child Care. *Child Development, 68,* 860–879.

GARRETT, M. F. (1990). Sentence processing. In D. N. Osherson & H. Lasnik (Eds.), *An invitation to cognitive science: Language* (Vol. 1). Cambridge, MA: MIT Press.

GARRISON, C. Z., BRYANT, E. S., ADDY, C. L., SPURRIER, P. G., FREEDY, J. R., & KILPATRICK, D. G. (1995). Posttraumatic stress disorder in adolescents after Hurricane Andrew. *Journal of the American Academy of Child and Adolescent Psychiatry, 34,* 1193–1201.

GARROD, S. C., & PICKERING, M. J. (1999). *Language processing of words.* Hove, UK: Psychology Press.

GARRY, M., MANNING, C., LOFTUS, E. F., & SHERMAN, S. J. (1996) Imagination inflation. *Psychonomic Bulletin & Review, 3,* 208–214.

GATES, A. I. (1917). Recitation as a factor in memorizing. *Archives of Psychology, 40.*

GAW, A. (1993). *Culture, ethnicity, and mental illness.* Washington, DC: American Psychiatric Press.

GAZZANIGA, M. S. (1985). *The social brain: Discovering the networks of mind.* New York: Basic Books.

GE, X., CONGER, R. D., & ELDER, G. H., Jr. (1996). Coming of age too early: Pubertal influences on girls' vulnerability to psychological distress. *Child Development, 67,* 3386–3400.

GEEN, R. G. (1990). *Human aggression.* Pacific Grove, CA: Brooks/Cole.

GEER, J. H., & MAISEL, E. (1972). Evaluating the effects of the prediction-control confound. *Journal of Personality & Social Psychology, 23,* 314–319.

GELLATLY, A. R. H. (1987). Acquisition of a concept of logical necessity. *Human Development, 30,* 32–47.

GENTER, D., & STEVENS, A. L. (1983). *Mental models.* Hillsdale, NJ: Erlbaum.

GERBNER, G., GROSS, L., MORGAN, M., & SIGNORIELLI, N. (1986). Living with television: The dynamics of the cultivation process. In J. Bryant & D. Zillmann (Eds.), *Perspectives on media effects.* Hillsdale, NJ: Erlbaum.

GERSHON, E. S. (1990). Genetics. In F. K. Goodwin & K. R. Jamison (Eds.), *Manic-depressive illness* (pp. 373–401). New York: Oxford University Press.

GESCHWIND, N. (1972). Language and the brain. *Scientific American, 226,* 76–83.

GESCHWIND, N. (1979). Specializations of the human brain. *Scientific American, 241,* 180–199.

GESELL, A., & THOMPSON, H. (1929). Learning and growth in identical twins: An experimental study by the method of co-twin control. *Genetic Psychology Monographs, 6,* 1–123.

GHEORGHIU, V. A., NETTER, P., EYSENCK, H. J., & ROSENTHAL, R. (Eds.). (1989). *Suggestion and suggestibility: Theory and research.* New York: Springer-Verlag.

GIANOULAKIS, C., KRISHNAN, B., & THAVUNDAYIL, J. (1996). Enhanced sensitivity of pituitary β-endorphin to ethanol in subjects at high risk of alcoholism. *Archives of General Psychiatry, 53,* 250–257.

GIBSON, E. J., & WALK, R. D. (1960). The "visual cliff." *Scientific American, 202,* 64–71.

GIGERENZER, G., & GOLDSTEIN, D. G. (1996). Reasoning the fast and frugal way: Models of bounded rationality. *Psychological Review, 103,* 650–669.

GILBERT, D. T., & JONES, E. E. (1986). Perceiver-induced constraint: Interpretations of self-generated reality. *Journal of Personality and Social Psychology, 50,* 269–280.

GILBERT, D. T., & MALONE, P. S. (1995). The correspondence bias. *Psychological Bulletin, 117,* 21–38.

GILBERT, D. T., PELHAM, B. W., & KRULL, D. S. (1988). On cognitive busyness: When person perceivers meet persons perceived. *Journal of Personality and Social Psychology, 54,* 733–740.

GILCHRIST, A. L. (1988). Lightness contrast and failures of constancy: A common explanation. *Perception and Psychophysics, 43,* 415–424.

GILLIGAN, C. (1982). *In a different voice.* Cambridge, MA: Harvard University Press.

GILLIN, J. C. (1985). Sleep and dreams. In G. L. Klerman, M. M. Weissman, P. S. Applebaum, & L. H. Roth (Eds.), *Psychiatry* (Vol. 3). Philadelphia: Lippincott.

GINSBERG, A. (1983). *Contrast perception in the human infant.* Unpublished manuscript.

GLANZER, M. (1972). Storage mechanisms in recall. In G. H. Bower & J. T. Spence (Eds.), *The psychology of learning and motivation* (Vol. 5). New York: Academic Press.

GLASER, R., RICE, J., SPEICHER, C. E., STOUT, J. C., & KIECOLT-GLASER, J. K. (1986). Stress depresses interferon production by leukocytes concomitant with a decrease in natural killer cell activity. *Behavioral Neuroscience, 100,* 675–678.

GLASS, D. C., & SINGER, J. E. (1972). *Urban stress: Experiments on noise and social stressors.* New York: Academic Press.

GLASS, G. V., MCGAW, B., & SMITH, M. L. (1981). *Meta-analysis in social research.* Beverly Hills, CA: Sage.

GLEITMAN, H. (1986). *Psychology* (2nd ed.). New York: Norton.

GLEITMAN, L. R. (1986). Biological predispositions to learn language. In P. Marler & H. S. Terrace (Eds.), *The biology of learning.* New York: Springer-Verlag.

GODDEN, D., & BADDELEY, A. D. (1975). Context-dependent memory in two natural environments: On land and under water. *British Journal of Psychology, 66,* 325–331.

GOEL, V., GOLD, B., KAPUR, S., & HOULE, S. (1998). Neuroanatomical correlates of human reasoning. *Journal of Cognitive Neuroscience, 10,* 293–302.

GOETHALS, G. P., & ZANNA, M. P. (1979). The role of social comparison in choice shifts. *Journal of Personality and Social Psychology, 37,* 1469–1476.

GOLDEN, H., HINKLE, S., & CROSBY, F. J. (1998). *Affirmative action: Semantics and substance.* Ann Arbor: University of Michigan.

GOLDIN-MEADOW, S. (1982). The resilience of recursion: A structure within a conventional model. In E. Wanner & L. R. Gleitman (Eds.), *Language acquisition: The state of the art.* Cambridge, England: Cambridge University Press.

GOLDMAN-RAKIC, P. S. (1987). Circuitry of primate prefrontal cortex and regulation of behavior by representational memory. In F. Plum (Ed.), *Handbook of physiology: The nervous system.* Bethesda, MD: American Physiology Society.

GOLDMAN-RAKIC, P. S. (1996). Regional and cellular fractionation of working memory. *Proceedings of the National Academy of Science of the United States of America, 93,* 13473–13480.

GOLDSTEIN, A. (1994). *Addiction: From biology to drug policy.* New York: Freeman.

GOLDSTEIN, E. B. (1989). *Sensation and perception* (3rd ed.). Belmont, CA: Wadsworth.

GOLDSTEIN, M. (1987). Family interaction patterns that antedate the onset of schizophrenia and related disorders: A further analysis of data from a longitudinal prospective study. In K. Hahlweg & M. Goldstein (Eds.), *Understanding major mental disorders: The contribution of family interaction research* (pp. 11–32). New York: Family Process Press.

GOLDSTEIN, M. J., TALOVIC, S. A., NUECHTERLEIN, K. H., & FOGELSON, D. L. (1992). Family interaction versus individual psychopathology: Do they indicate the same processes in the families of schizophrenia? *British Journal of Psychiatry, 161,* 97–102.

GOLEMAN, D. (1995, May 2). Biologists find the site of working memory. *New York Times.*

GOLEMAN, D. J. (1988, October 18). Chemistry of sexual desire yields its elusive secret. *New York Times.*

GOODALL, J. (1978). Chimp killings: Is it the man in them? *Science News, 113,* 276.

GOODGLASS, H., & BUTTERS, N. (1988). Psychobiology of cognitive processes. In R. C. Atkinson, R. J. Hernstein, G. Lindzey, & R. D. Luce (Eds.), *Stevens' handbook of experimental psychology* (Vol. 2). New York: Wiley.

GOODWIN, F. K., & JAMISON, K. R. (1990). *Manic-depressive illness.* New York: Oxford University Press.

GORDON, W. (1989). *Learning & memory.* Pacific Grove, CA: Brooks/Cole.

GOTTESMAN, I. I. (1991). *Schizophrenia genesis: The origins of madness.* New York: W. H. Freeman.

GOTTESMAN, I. I., & SHIELDS, J. (1982). *Schizophrenia, the epigenetic puzzle.* New York: Cambridge University Press.

GOTTFRIED, A. E., FLEMING, J. S., & GOTTFRIED, A. W. (1998). The role of cognitively stimulating home environment on children's academic intrinsic motivation. *Child Development, 69,* 1448–1460.

GOTTLIEB, G. (2000). Environmental and behavioral influences on gene activity. *Current Directions in Psychological Science, 9,* 93–97.

GOULD, E., BEYLIN, A., TANAPAT, P., REEVES, A., & SHORS, T. J. (1999). Learning enhances adult neurogenesis in the hippocampal formation. *Nature Neuroscience, 2,* 260–265.

GOY, R. W. (1968). Organizing effect of androgen on the behavior of rhesus monkeys. In R. F. Michael (Ed.), *Endocrinology of human behaviour.* London: Oxford University Press.

GRACZYK, P. A., WEISSBERG, R. P., PAYTON, J. W., ELIAS, M. J., GREENBERG, M. T., & ZINS, J. E. (2000). Criteria for evaluating the quality of school-based social and emotional learning programs. In R. Bar-On & J. D. A. Parker (Eds.), *The handbook of emotional intelligence,* San Francisco: Jossey-Bass.

GRADY, C. L., HAXBY, J. V., HORWITZ, B., SCHAPIRO, M. B., RAPOPORT, S. I., UNGERLEIDER, L. G., MISHKIN, M., CARSON, R. E., & HERSCOVITCH, P. (1992). Dissociation of object and spatial vision in human extrastriate cortex: Age-related changes in activation of regional cerebral blood flow measured with [^{15}O] water and positron emission tomography. *Journal of Cognitive Neuroscience, 4,* 23–34.

GRAF, P., & MANDLER, G. (1984). Activation makes words more accessible, but not necessarily more retrievable. *Journal of Verbal Learning and Verbal Behavior, 23,* 553–568.

GRAF, P., & MASSON, M. E. J. (Eds.). (1993). *Implicit memory: New directions in cognition, development, and neuropsychology.* Hillsdale, NJ: Erlbaum.

GRAHAM, J. R. (1990). *The MIMPI-2: Assessing personality and psychopathology.* New York: Oxford University Press.

GRANDIN, T. (1995). *Thinking in pictures and other reports from my life with autism.* New York: Vintage Books.

GRANRUD, C. E. (1986). Binocular vision and spatial perception in 4- and 5-month-old infants. *Journal of Experimental Psychology: Human Perception and Performance, 12,* 36–49.

GRAY, E., & COSGROVE, J. (1985). Ethnocentric perception of childbearing practices in protective services. *Child Abuse and Neglect, 9,* 389–396.

GRAY, J. (1982). Precis of the neuropsychology of anxiety: An enquiry into the functions of the septohippocampal system. *Behavioural and Brain Sciences, 5,* 469–534.

GRAY, J. (1992). *Men are from Mars, women are from Venus: A practical guide for improving communication and getting what you want in your relationships.* New York: HarperCollins.

GRAY, J. A. (1987). *The psychology of fear and stress* (2nd ed.). Cambridge, England: Cambridge University Press.

GRAY, J. A. (1994) Personality dimensions and emotion systems. In P. Ekman & R. J. Davidson (Eds.), *The nature of emotion: Fundamental questions* (pp. 329–331). New York: Oxford University Press.

GRAY-LITTLE, B., & HAFDAHL, A. R. (2000). Factors influencing racial comparisons of self-esteem: A quantitative review. *Psychological Bulletin, 126,* 26–54.

GRAY-LITTLE, B. & KAPLAN, D. (2000). Race and ethnicity in psychotherapy research. In C. R. Snyder & R. E. Ingram (Eds.), *Handbook of psychological change: Psychotherapy processes and practices for the 21st century* (pp. 592–613). New York: Wiley.

GRAZZANI-GAVAZZI, I., & OATLEY, K. (1999). The experience of emotions of interdependence and independence following interpersonal errors in Italy and Anglophone Canada. *Cognition and Emotion, 13,* 49–63.

GREEN, B. L., LINDY, J. D., GRACE, M. C., & LEONARD, A. C. (1992). Chronic post-traumatic stress disorder and diagnostic comorbidity in a disaster sample. *Journal of Nervous and Mental Disease, 180,* 760–766.

GREEN, D. M., & WIER, C. C. (1984). Auditory perception. In I. Darian-Smith (Ed.), *Handbook of physiology* (Vol. 3). Bethesda, MD: American Physiological Society.

GREEN, J. G., FOX, N. A., & LEWIS, M. (1983). The relationship between neonatal characteristics and three-month mother-infant interaction in high-risk infants. *Child Development, 54,* 1286–1296.

GREEN, R. (1987). *The "sissy boy syndrome" and the development of homosexuality.* New Haven, CT: Yale University Press.

GREENFIELD, P. M., & SAVAGE-RUMBAUGH, S. (1990). Grammatical combination in *Pan Paniscus:* Processes of learning and invention in the evolution and development of language. In S. Parker & K. Gibson (Eds.), *"Language" and intelligence in monkeys and apes: Comparative developmental perspectives.* New York: Cambridge University Press.

GREENWALD, A. G. (1968). Cognitive learning, cognitive response to persuasion, and attitude change. In A. G. Greenwald, T. C. Brock, & T. M. Ostrom (Eds.), *Psychological foundations of attitudes.* New York: Academic Press.

GREENWALD, A. G. (1992). Unconscious cognition reclaimed. *American Psychologist, 47,* 766–779.

GRICE, H. P. (1975). Logic and conversation. In G. Harman & D. Davidson (Eds.), *The logic of grammar.* Encino, CA: Dickinson.

GRIGGS, R. A., & COX, J. R. (1982). The elusive thematic-materials effect in Watson's selection task. *British Journal of Psychology, 73,* 407–420.

GRILL, H. J., & KAPLAN, J. M. (1990). Caudal brainstem participates in the distributed neural control of feeding. In E. M. Stricker (Eds.), *Neurobiology of food and fluid intake* (pp. 125–149). New York: Plenum Press.

GRODZINSKY, Y. (1984). The syntactic characterization of agrammatism. *Cognition, 16,* 99–120.

GROSS, J. J. (2001). Emotion regulation in adulthood: Timing is everything. *Current Directions in Psychological Science, 10,* 214–219.

GROSS, J. J., & LEVENSON, R. W. (1997). Hiding feelings: The acute effects of inhibiting positive and negative emotions. *Journal of Abnormal Psychology, 106,* 95–103.

GROSS-ISSEROFF, R., BIEGON, A., VOET, H., & WEIZMAN, A. (1998) The suicide brain: A review of postmortem receptor/transporter binding studies. *Neuroscience and Biobehavioral Reviews, 22,* 653–661.

GROSSMAN, M., & WOOD, W. (1993). Sex differences in intensity of emotional experience: A social role interpretation. *Journal of Personality and Social Psychology, 65,* 1010–1022.

GROVES, P. M., & REBEC, G. V. (1992). *Introduction to biological psychology* (4th ed.). Dubuque, IA: Brown.

GRÜNBAUM, A. (1984). *The foundations of psychoanalysis.* Berkeley, CA: University of California Press.

GUARNACCIA, P. J., CANINO, G., RUBIO-STIPEC, M., & BRAVO, M. (1993). The prevalence of ataques de nervios in the Puerto Rico Disaster Study: The role of culture in psychiatric epidemiology. *Journal of Nervous and Mental Disease, 181,* 157–165.

GUARNACCIA, P. J., GUEVARA-RAMOS, L. M., GONZALES, G., CANINO, G. J., & BIRD, H. (1992). Cross-cultural aspects of psychiatric symptoms in Puerto Rico. *Community and Mental Health, 7,* 99–110.

GUARNACCIA, P. J., RIVERA, M., FRANCO, F., NEIGHBORS, C., & ALLENDE-RAMOS, C. (1996). The experiences of ataques de nervios: Toward an anthropology of emotions in Puerto Rico. *Culture, Medicine and Psychiatry, 15,* 139–165.

GUILFORD, J. P. (1982). Cognitive psychology's ambiguities: Some suggested remedies. *Psychological Review, 89,* 48–49.

GUMPERZ, J. J., & LEVINSON, S. C. (Eds.). (1996). *Rethinking linguistic relativity.* Cambridge: Cambridge University Press.

GURIN, P., DEY, E. L., HURTADO, S., & GURIN, G. (in press). Diversity and higher education: Theory and impact on educational outcomes. *Harvard Educational Review.*

GURNEY, R. (1936). The hereditary factor in obesity. *Archives of Internal Medicine, 57,* 557–561.

HAAGA, D. A. F., DYCK, M. J., & ERNST, D. (1991). Empirical status of cognitive theory of depression. *Psychological Bulletin, 110,* 215–236.

HAAGA, D. F., & STILES, W. B. (2000). Randomized clinical trials in psychotherapy research: Methodology, design and evaluation. In C. R. Snyder & R. Ingram (Eds.), *Handbook of psychological change* (pp. 14–39) New York: Wiley.

HABER, R. N. (1969). Eidetic images. *Scientific American, 220,* 36–55.

HABER, R. N. (1979). Twenty years of haunting edetic imagery: Where's the ghost? *Behavioral and Brain Sciences, 24,* 583–629.

HABERLANDT, K. (1993). *Cognitive psychology.* Boston, MA: Allyn and Bacon.

HAITH, M. M. (1998). Who put the cog in infant cognition: Is the rich interpretation too costly? *Infant Behaviour and Development, 21,* 167–180.

HAITH, M. M., BERGMAN, T., & MOORE, M. J. (1977). Eye contact and face scanning in early infancy. *Science, 198,* 853–855.

HALL, C., & VAN DE CASTLE, R. (1966). *The content analysis of dreams.* New York: Appleton-Century-Crofts.

HALL, C. S. (1947). Diagnosing personality by the analysis of dreams. *Journal of Abnormal and Social Psychology, 42,* 68–79.

HALL, C. S. (1953). A cognitive theory of dreams. *Journal of General Psychology, 48,* 169–186.

HAMER, D., & COPELAND, P. (1994). *The science of desire: The search for the gay gene and the biology of behavior.* New York: Simon & Schuster.

HAMER, D. H., HU, S., MAGNUSON, V. L., HU, N., & PATTATUCCI, A. M. L. (1993). A linkage between DNA markers on the X chromosome and male sexual orientation. *Science, 261,* 321–327.

HAMILTON, D. L. (1979). A cognitive-attributional analysis of stereotyping. In L. Berkowitz (Ed.), *Advances in experimental social psychology* (Vol. 12). New York: Academic Press.

HAMILTON, D. L., & GIFFORD, R. K. (1976). Illusory correlation in interpersonal perception: A cognitive basis of stereotypic judgments. *Journal of Experimental Social Psychology, 12,* 392–407.

HAMILTON, D. L., & SHERMAN, S. J. (1989). Illusory correlations: Implications for stereotype theory and research. In D. Bar-Tal, C. F. Gravmann, A. W. Kruglanski, & W. Stroebe (Eds.), *Stereotypes and prejudice: Changing conceptions.* New York: Springer-Verlag.

HANEY, C., & ZIMBARDO, P. (1998). The past and the future of U.S. prison policy: Twenty-five years after the Stanford Prison Experiment. *American Psychologist, 53,* 709–727.

HANNIGAN, S. L., & REINITZ, M. T. (2001). A demonstration and comparison of two types of inference-based memory errors. *Journal of Experimental Psychology: Learning, Memory, and Cognition, 37,* 931–940.

HARDIN, C. L., & MAFFI, L. (Eds.). (1997). Color categories in thought and language. *Contemporary Psychology, 3,* 684.

HARE, R. D. (1980). A research scale for the assessment of psychopathy in criminal populations. *Personality and Individual Differences, 1,* 111–119.

HARE, R. D. (1999). *Without conscience: The disturbing world of the psychopaths among us.* New York: Guilford.

HARLOW, H. F. (1971). *Learning to love.* San Francisco: Albion.

HARLOW, H. F., & HARLOW, M. K. (1969). Effects of various mother-infant relationships on rhesus monkey behaviors. In B. M. Foss (Ed.), *Determinants of infant behavior* (Vol. 4). London: Methuen.

HARLOW, J. M. (1868). Recovery from passage of an iron bar through the head. *Boston Medical and Surgical Journal, 39,* 389–393.

HARRIS, J. R. (1995). Where is the child's environment? A group socialization theory of development. *Psychological Review, 102,* 458–489.

HARRIS, M. J., & ROSENTHAL, R. (1988). *Interpersonal expectancy effects and human performance research.* Washington, DC: National Academy Press.

HARRIS, P. R. (1996). Sufficient grounds for optimism? The relationship between perceived controllability and optimistic bias. *Journal of Social and Clinical Psychology, 15,* 9–52.

HART, A. J., WHALEN, P. J., SHIN, L. M., MCINERNEY, S. C., FISCHER, H., & RAUCH, S. L. (2000). Differential response in the human amygdala to racial outgroup vs. ingroup face stimuli. *Neuroreport, 11,* 2351–2355.

HARTER, S. (1998). The development of self-representation. In N. Eisenberg (Ed.), *Handbook of child psychology* (5th ed.), Vol 3: Social, emotional, and personality development (pp. 553–617). New York: Wiley.

HARTMANN, E. (1968). The day residue: Time distribution of waking events. *Psychophysiology, 5,* 222.

HATFIELD, E. (1988). Passionate and companionate love. In R. J. Sternberg & M. L. Barnes (Eds.), *The psychology of love* (pp. 191–217). New Haven, CT: Yale University Press.

HATHAWAY, S. R., & MCKINLEY, J. C. (1943). *Manual for the Minnesota Multiphasic Personality Inventory.* New York: Psychological Corporation.

HAWKINS, R. D., & KANDEL, E. R. (1984). Is there a cell-biological alphabet for simple forms of learning? *Psychological Review, 91,* 375–391.

HAXBY, J. V., GRADY, C. L., HORWIZ, B., UNGERLEIDER, L. G., MISHKIN, M., CARSON, R. E., HERSCOVITCH, P., SCHAPIRO, M. B., & RAPOPORT, S. I. (1990). Dissociation of object and spatial visual processing pathways in human extrastriate cortex. *Neurobiology, 88,* 1621–1625.

HAYDON, P. G. (2001). GLIA: listening and talking to the synapse. *Nature Reviews Neuroscience, 2,* 185–193.

HAYES, J. R. (1989). *The complete problem solver* (2nd ed.). Hillsdale, NJ: Erlbaum.

HAYES, L. A., & WATSON, J. S. (1981). Neonatal imitation: Fact or artifact. *Developmental Psychology, 17,* 655–660.

HAYNE, H., ROVEE-COLLIER, C., & BORZA, M. A. (1991). Infant memory for place information. *Memory and Cognition, 19,* 378–386.

HAYNES, S. G., & FEINLEIB, M. (1980). Women, work, and coronary heart disease: Prospective findings from the Framingham heart study. *American Journal of Public Health, 70,* 133–141.

HAYNES, S. G., FEINLEIB, M., & KANNEL, W. B. (1980). The relationship of psychosocial factors to coronary heart disease in the Framingham study: Pt. 3. Eight-year incidence of coronary heart disease. *American Journal of Epidemiology, 111,* 37–58.

HE, Z. J., & NAKAYAMA, K. (1992). Surfaces versus features in visual search. *Nature, 359,* 231–233.

HEATH, R. G. (1972). Pleasure and brain activity in man. Deep and surface electroencephalograms during orgasm. *Journal of Nervous and Mental Disease, 154,* 3–18.

HEBB, D. O. (1982). Understanding psychological man: A state-of-the-science report. *Psychology Today, 16,* 52–53.

HECHT, S., SHALER, S., & PIREENE, M. H. (1942). Energy, quanta, and vision. *Journal of General Physiology, 25,* 819–840.

HEIDER, F. (1958). *The psychology of interpersonal relations.* New York: Wiley.

HEILBRUN, K. S. (1982). Silverman's subliminal psychodynamic activation: A failure to replicate. *Journal of Abnormal Psychology, 89,* 560–566.

HEILMAN, M. E. (1994). Affirmative action: Some unintended consequences for working women. In B. Staw & L. L. Cummings (Eds.), *Research in organizational behavior* (vol. 16, pp. 125–169). Greenwich, CT: JAI Press.

HEILMAN, M. E., BLOCK, C. J., & LUCAS, J. A. (1992). Presumed incompetent? Stigmatization and affirmative action efforts. *Journal of Applied Psychology, 77,* 536–544.

HEILMAN, M. E., BLOCK, C. J., & STATHATOS, P. (1987). The affirmative action stigma of incompetence: Effects of performance information ambiguity. *Academy of Management Journal, 40,* 603–625.

HEILMAN, M. E., MCCULLOUGH, S. F., & GILBERT, D. (1996). The other side of affirmative action. Reactions of non-beneficiaries to sex-based preferential selection. *Journal of Applied Psychology, 81,* 346–357.

HELBURN, S. W. (Ed.). (1995). *Cost, quality and child outcomes in child care centers.* Denver: University of Colorado.

HELD, R. (1965). Plasticity in sensory motor systems. *Scientific American, 21,* 84–94.

HELD, R., & HEIN, A. (1963). Movement produced stimulation in the development of visually guided behavior. *Journal of Comparative and Physiological Psychology, 56,* 872–876.

HELLIGE, J. B. (1990). Hemispheric asymmetry. *Annual Review of Psychology, 41,* 55–80.

HELLIGE, J. B. (1993). Unity of thought and action: Varieties of interaction between left and right hemispheres. *Current Directions in Psychological Science, 2,* 21–25.

HELZER, J. E., & CANINO, G. J. (1992). *Alcoholism in North America, Europe, and Asia.* New York: Oxford University Press.

HELZER, J. E., BUCHOLZ, K., & ROBINS, L. N. (1992). Five communities in the United States: Results of the Epidemiologic Catchment Area Survey. In J. E. Helzer & G. J. Canino (Eds.). *Alcoholism in North America, Europe & Asia.* New York: Oxford University Press.

HEMMI, T. (1969). How we have handled the problem of drug abuse in Japan. In F. Sjoqvist & M. Tottie (Eds.), *Abuse of central stimulants.* New York: Raven Press.

HENCHY, T., & GLASS, D. C. (1968). Evaluation apprehension and social facilitation of dominant and subordinate responses. *Journal of Personality and Social Psychology, 10,* 445–454.

HENDERSON, J. M., WEEKS, P. A. JR., & HOLLINGWORTH, A. (1999). The effects of semantic consistency on eye movements during complex scene viewing. *Journal of Experimental Psychology: Human Perception and Performance, 25,* 210–228.

HENLEY, N., HAMILTON, M., & THORNE, B. (1985). Womanspeak and manspeak: Sex differences and sexism in communication, verbal and nonverbal. In A. G. Sargent (Ed.), *Beyond sex roles.* St. Paul, MN: West.

HENRY, B., & MOFFITT, T. E. (1997). Neuropsychological and neuroimaging studies of juvenile delinquency and adult criminal behavior. In D. M. Stoff, J. Breiling, & J. D. Maser (Eds.) *Handbook of antisocial personality disorder* (pp. 280–288). New York: Wiley.

HENSEL, H. (1973). Cutaneous thermoreceptors. In A. Iggo (Ed.), *Handbook of sensory physiology* (Vol. 2). Berlin: Springer-Verlag.

HERDT, G. H. (Ed.) (1984). *Ritualized homosexuality in Melanesia.* Berkeley: University of California Press.

HEREK, G. M. (1986). The instrumentality of attitudes: Toward a neofunctional theory. *Journal of Social Issues, 42,* 99–114.

HEREK, G. M. (1987). Can functions be measured? A new perspective on the functional approach to attitudes. *Social Psychology Quarterly, 50,* 285–303.

HERING, E. (1878). *Outlines of a theory of the light sense* (L. M. Hurvich & D. Jameson, Trans.). Cambridge, MA: Harvard University Press.

HERING, E. (1920). Memory as a universal function of organized matter. In S. Butler (Ed.), *Unconscious memory.* London: Jonathon Cape.

HERMAN, C. P., & MACK, D. (1975). Restrained and unrestrained eating. *Journal of Personality, 43,* 647–660.

HERMAN, C. P., & POLIVY, J. (1980). Retrained eating. In A. J. Stunkard (Ed.), *Obesity.* Philadelphia: Saunders.

HERRNSTEIN, R. J., & MURRAY, C. (1994). *The bell curve: Intelligence and class structure in American life.* New York: Free Press.

HESS, E. H. (1972). "Imprinting" in a natural laboratory. *Scientific American, 227,* 24–31.

HETHERINGON, E. M., & BRACKBILL, Y. (1963). Etiology and covariation of obstinacy, orderliness, and parsimony in young children. *Child Development, 34,* 919–943.

HETTEMA, J. M., NEALE, M. C., & KENDLER, K. S. (2001). A review and meta-analysis of the genetic epidemiology of anxiety disorders. *American Journal of Psychiatry, 158,* 1568–1578.

HEWLETT, W. A. (2000). Benzodiazepines in the treatment of obsessive-compulsive disorder. *Obsessive-compulsive disorder: contemporary issues in treatment* (pp. 405–429). Mahwah, NJ: Lawrence Erlbaum Associates, Inc.

HEWSTONE, M. (1990). The "ultimate attribution error"? A review of the literature on intergroup causal attribution. *European Journal of Social Psychology, 20,* 311–335.

HIGGINS, E. T. (1987). Self-discrepancy: A theory relating self and affect. *Psychological Review, 94,* 319–340.

HILGARD, E. R. (1965). *Hypnotic susceptibility.* New York: Harcourt Brace Jovanovich.

HILGARD, E. R. (1968). *The experience of hypnosis.* New York: Harcourt Brace Jovanovich.

HILGARD, E. R. (1986). *Divided consciousness: Multiple controls in human thought and action.* New York: Wiley-Interscience.

HILGARD, E. R. (1987). *Psychology in America: A historical survey.* San Diego: Harcourt Brace Javanovich.

HILGARD, E. R., & HILGARD, J. R. (1975). *Hypnosis in the relief of pain.* Los Altos, CA: Kaufmann.

HILGARD, E. R., HILGARD, J. R., MACDONALD, H., MORGAN, A. H., & JOHNSON, L. S. (1978). Covert pain in hypnotic analgesia: Its reality as tested by the real-simulator design. *Journal of Abnormal Psychology, 87,* 655–663.

HILL, C., RUBIN, Z., & PEPLAU, L. A. (1976). Breakups before marriage: The end of 103 affairs. *Journal of Social Issues, 32,* 147–168.

HILLIER, L., HEWITT, K. L., & MORRON-GIELTO, B. A. (1992). Infants' perception of illusions in sound localization: Reaching to sounds in the dark. *Journal of Experimental Child Psychology, 53,* 159–179.

HILLYARD, S. A. (1985). Electrophysiology of human selective attention. *Trends in Neuroscience, 8,* 400–406.

HILLYARD, S. A., VOGEL, E. K., & LUCK, S. J. (1998). Sensory gain control (amplification) as a mechanism of selective attention: Electrophysiological and neuroimaging evidence. *Philosophical Transactions of the Royal Society: Biological Science, 353,* 1257–1270.

HINDE, R. (1982). *Ethology: Its nature and relations with other sciences.* New York: Oxford University Press.

HINSHAW, S. P. (1994). *Attention deficits and hyperactivity in children.* Thousand Oaks, CA: Sage.

HIRSCH, J., & BATCHELOR, B. R. (1976). Adipose tissue cellularity and human obesity. *Clinical Endocrinology and Metabolism, 5,* 299–311.

HIRSCH, S. M., & BOLLES, R. C. (1980). On the ability of prey to recognize predators. *Zeitschrift für Tierpscholiogie, 54,* 71–84.

HOBSON, J. A. (1988). *The dreaming brain.* New York: Basic Books.

HOBSON, J. A. (1989). *Sleep.* New York: Freeman.

HOBSON, J. A. (1994). *The chemistry of conscious states, how the brain changes its mind.* New York: Little, Brown.

HOBSON, J. A. (1997). Dreaming as delirium: A mental status analysis of our nightly madness. *Seminars in Neurology, 1,* 121–128.

HOEBEL, B. G., & TEITELBAUM, P. (1966). Effects of force-feeding and starvation on food intake and body weight on a rat with ventromedial hypothalamic lesions. *Journal of Comparative and Physiological Psychology, 61,* 189–193.

HOFFMAN, H. G., DOCTOR, J. N., PATTERSON, D. R., CARROUGHER, G. J., & FURNESS, T. A. III. (2000). Use of virtual reality for adjunctive treatment of adolescent burn pain during wound care: A case report. *Pain, 85,* 305–309.

HOFFMAN, H. G, PATTERSON, D. R., & CARROUGHER, G. J. (2000). Use of virtual reality for adjunctive treatment of adult burn pain during physical therapy: A controlled study. *Clinical Journal of Pain, 16,* 244–250.

HOFLING, C. K., BROTZMAN, E., DALRYMPLE, S., GRAVES, N., & PIERCE, C. M. (1966). An experimental study in nurse-physician relationships. *Journal of Nervous and Mental Disease, 143,* 171–180.

HOGARTY, G. E. (1986). Family psychoeducation, social skills training, and maintenance chemotherapy in the aftercare treatment of schizophrenia: I. One-year effects of a controlled study on relapse and expressed emotion. *Archives of General Psychiatry, 43,* 633–642.

HOGARTY, G. E., SCHOOLER, N. R., ULRICH, R., MUSSARE, F., FERRO, P., & HERRON, E. (1979). Fluphenazine and social therapy in the after care of schizophrenic patients. *Archives of General Psychiatry, 36,* 1283–1294.

HOGBEN, J. H., & DI LOLLO, V. (1974). Perceptual integration and perceptual segregation of brief visual stimuli. *Vision Research, 14,* 1059–1069.

HOHMANN, G. W. (1962). Some effects of spinal cord lesions on experienced emotional feelings. *Psychophysiology, 3,* 143–156.

HOLLAND, J. H., HOLYOAK, K. J., NISBETT, R. E., & THAGARD, P. R. (1986). *Induction: Processes of inference, learning, and discovery.* Cambridge, MA: MIT Press.

HOLLINGWORTH, A., & HENDERSON, J. M. (2000). Semantic informativeness mediates the detection of changes in natural scenes. *Visual Cognition, 7,* 213–235.

HOLLOWAY, F. A. (1989). What is affirmative action? In F. A. Blanchard & F. J. Crosby (Eds.), *Affirmative action in perspective* (pp. 9–19). New York: Springer Verlag.

HOLMES, D. S. (1974). Investigations of repression: Differential recall of material experimentally or naturally associated with ego threat. *Psychological Bulletin, 81,* 632–653.

HOLMES, D. S. (1984). Meditation and somatic arousal reduction: A review of the experimental evidence. *American Psychologist, 39,* 1–10.

HOLMES, D. S. (1985a). To meditate or rest? The answer is rest. *American Psychologist, 40,* 728–731.

HOLMES, D. S. (1985b). Self-control of somatic arousal: An examination of the effects of meditation and feedback. *American Behavioral Scientist, 28,* 486–496.

HOLMES, T. H., & RAHE, R. H. (1967). The social readjustment rating scale. *Journal of Psychosomatic Research, 11*, 213–218.

HOLROYD, K. A., APPEL, M. A., & ANDRASIK, F. (1983). A cognitive behavioral approach to psychophysiological disorders. In D. Meichenbaum & M. E. Jaremko (Eds.), *Stress reduction and prevention.* New York: Plenum.

HONIG, W. K., & STADDON, J. E. R. (Eds.). (1977). *Handbook of operant behavior.* Englewood Cliffs, NJ: Prentice-Hall.

HONORTON, C. (1985). Meta-analysis of psi ganzfeld research: A response to Hyman. *Journal of Parapsychology, 49*, 51–91.

HOOLEY, J. M., RICHTERS, J. E., WEINTRAUB, S., & NEALE, J. M. (1987). Psychopathology and marital distress: The positive side of positive symptoms. *Journal of Abnormal Psychology, 96*, 27–33.

HOON, P. W., WINCZE, J. P., & HOON, E. F. (1977). A test of reciprocal inhibition: Are anxiety and sexual arousal in women mutually inhibitory? *Journal of Abnormal Psychology, 86*, 65–74.

HOPKINS, J. R. (1977). Sexual behavior in adolescence. *Journal of Social Issues, 33*, 67–85.

HORM, J., & ANDERSON, K. (1993). Who in America is trying to lose weight? *Annals of Internal Medicine, 119*, 672–676.

HORNE, J. A., & MCGRATH, M. J. (1984). The consolidation hypothesis for REM sleep function: Stress and other confounding factors—A review. *Biological Psychology, 18*, 165–184.

HOROWITZ, F. D. (1974). Visual attention, auditory stimulation, and language stimulation in young infants. *Monographs of the Society for Research in Child Development, 31*, Serial No. 158.

HOROWITZ, M. (1986). Stress-response syndromes: A review of postraumatic and adjustment disorders. *Hospital and Community Psychiatry, 37*, 241–249.

HOVLAND, C., JANIS, I., & KELLEY, H. H. (1953). *Communication and persuasion.* New Haven, CT: Yale University Press.

HOWES, C. (1990). Can the age of entry into child care and the quality of child care predict adjustment in kindergarten? *Developmental Psychology, 26*, 292–303.

HOWES, C., PHILLIPS, D. A., & WHITEBOOK, M. (1992). Thresholds of quality: Implications for the social development of children in center-based child care. *Child Development, 63*, 449–460.

HSER, Y. I., ANGLIN, D., & POWERS, K. (1993). A 24-year follow-up of California narcotics addicts. *Archives of General Psychiatry, 50*, 577–584.

HU, S., PATTATUCCI, A. M., PATTERSON, C., LI, L., FULKER, D. W., CHERNY, S. S., KRUGLYAK, L., HAMER, D. H. (1995). Linkage between sexual orientation and chromosome Xq28 in males but not in females. *Nature Genetics, 11*, 248–256.

HUBEL, D. H., & WIESEL, T. N. (1963). Receptive fields of cells in striate cortex of very young visually inexperienced kittens. *Journal of Neurophysiology, 26*, 994–1002.

HUBEL, D. H., & WIESEL, T. N. (1968). Receptive fields and functional architecture of monkey striate cortex. *Journal of Physiology, 195*, 215–243.

HUDSON, J. L., & RAPEE, R. M. (2000). The origins of social phobia. *Behavior Modification, 24*, 102–129.

HUDSON, J. W., & HOYT, L. L. (1981). Personal characteristics important in mate preference among college students. *Social Behavior and Personality, 9*, 93–96.

HUESMANN, L. R., ERON, L. D., LEFKOWITZ, M. M., & WALDER, L. O. (1984). The stability of aggression over time and generations. *Developmental Psychology, 20*, 1120–1134.

HUGHES, J. R. (1986). Genetics of smoking: A review. *Behavior Therapy, 17*, 335–345.

HUGUET, P., GALVAING, M. P., MONTEIL, J. M., & DUMAS, F. (1999). Social presence effects in the Stroop task: Further evidence for an attentional view of social facilitation. *Journal of Personality and Social Psychology, 77*, 1011–1025.

HUMMEL, J. E., & BIEDERMAN, I. (1992). Dynamic binding in a neutral network for shape recognition. *Psychological Review, 99*, 480–517.

HUNT, E. (1990). A modern arsenal for mental assessment. *Educational Psychologist, 25*, 223–241.

HUNT, E. (1996). *Will we be smart enough?* New York: Russell Sage.

HUNT, M. (1974). *Sexual behavior in the 1970's.* Chicago: Playboy Press.

HUNT, P. J., & HILLERY, J. M. (1973). *Social facilitation at different stages in learning.* Paper presented at the Midwestern Psychological Association Meetings, Cleveland.

HUNTER, I. M. L. (1974). *Memory.* Baltimore: Penguin.

HURVICH, L. M., & JAMESON, D. (1974). Opponent processes as a model of neural organizations. *American Psychologist, 29*, 88–102.

HUSELID, R. F., & COOPER, M. L. (1992). Gender roles as mediators of sex difference in adolescent alcohol use and abuse. *Journal of Health and Social Behavior, 33*, 348–362.

HUTTON, D. C., & BAUMEISTER, R. F. (1992). Self-awareness and attitude change: Seeing oneself on the central route to persuasion. *Personality and Social Psychology Bulletin, 18*, 68–75.

HYMAN, I. E., HUSBAND, T. H., & BILLINGS, F. G. (1995). False memories of childhood experiences. *Applied Cognitive Psychology, 9*, 181–197.

HYMAN, R. (1985). The ganzfeld psi experiment: A critical appraisal. *Journal of Parapsychology, 49*, 3–49.

HYMAN, R. (1994). Anomaly or Artifact? Comments on Bem and Honorton. *Psychological Bulletin, 115*, 19–24.

HYMAN, R., & HONORTON, C. (1986). A joint communiqué: The psi ganzfeld controversy. *Journal of Parapsychology, 50*, 351–364.

IMPERATO-MCGINLEY, J., PETERSON, R. E., GAUTIER, T., & STURLA, E. (1979). Androgens and the evolution of male gender identity among male pseudohermaphrodites with 5 alpha reductase deficiency. *New England Journal of Medicine, 300*, 1233–1237.

INGRAM, R. E., HAYES, A., & SCOTT, W. (2000). Empirically supported treatments: A critical analysis. In C. R. Snyder & R. Ingram (Eds.), *Handbook of psychological change* (pp. 40–60). New York: Wiley.

INSEL, T. R. (Ed.). (1984) *New findings in obsessive-compulsive disorder.* Washington, DC: American Psychiatric Press.

INSTITUTE OF MEDICINE. (1982). *Marijuana and health.* Washington, DC: National Academy Press.

INTERNATIONAL NARCOTICS CONTROL BOARD (1998). *Psychotropic substances: Statistics for 1996.* New York: United Nations.

INTRAUB, H, & RICHARDSON, M. (1989) Wide-angle memories of close-up scenes. *Journal of Experimental Psychology: Learning, Memory, and Cognition, 15*, 179–187.

IRONSON, G., WYNINGS, C., SCHNEIDERMAN, N., BAUM, A., RODRIGUEZ, M. GREENWOOD, D., BENIGHT, C., ANTONI, M., LAPERRIER, A., HUANG, H. S., KLIMAS, N., & FLETCHER, M. A. (1997). Posttraumatic stress symptoms, intrusive thoughts, loss and immune function after Hurricane Andrew. *Psychosomatic Medicine, 59*, 128–141.

ISABELLA, R. A., & BELSKY, J. (1991). Interactional synchrony and the origins of infant-mother attachment: A replication study. *Child Development, 62*, 373–384.

ISEN, A. M. (2002). A role for neuropsychology in understanding the facilitating effects of positive affect on social behavior and cognitive processes. In C. R. Snyder & S. J. Lopez (Eds.), *Handbook of positive psychology* (pp. 528–540). Oxford: Oxford University Press.

ISEN, P. M. (1985). The asymmetry of happiness and sadness in effects on memory in normal college students. *Journal of Experimental Psychology: General, 114*, 388–391.

ISEN, P. M., SHALKER, T. E., CLARK, M., & KARP, L. (1978). Affect, accessibility of material in memory, and behavior: A cognitive loop? *Journal of Personality and Social Psychology, 36*, 1–12.

ISENBERG, D. J. (1986). Group polarization: A critical review and meta-analysis. *Journal of Personality and Social Psychology, 50*, 1141–1151.

ISOZAKI, M. (1984). The effect of discussion on polarization of judgments. *Japanese Psychological Research, 26*, 187–193.

JABLENSKY, A. (1989). Epidemiology and cross-cultural aspects of schizophrenia. *Psychiatric Annals, 19*, 516–524.

JABLENSKY, A. (2000). Epidemiology of schizophrenia: The global burden of disease and disability. *European Archives of Clinical Psychiatry and Neuroscience, 250*, 274–285.

JACKENDOFF, R. (1990). *Consciousness and the computational mind.* Cambridge, MA: MIT Press.

JACOBS, D., BLACKBURN, H., HIGGINS, M., REED, D., ISO, H., MCMILLAN, G., NEATON, J., NELSON, J., POTTER, J., RIFKIND, B., ROSSOUW, J., SHEKELLE, R., & YUSUF, S. (1992). Report of the conference on low blood cholesterol: Mortality associations. *Circulation, 86*, 1046–1060.

JACOBS, W. J., & NADEL, W. (1985). Stress-induced recovery of fears and phobias. *Psychological Review, 92*, 512–531.

JACOBSON, A. L., FRIED, C., & HOROWITZ, S. D. (1967). Classical conditioning, pseudoconditioning, or sensitization in the planarian. *Journal of Comparative and Physiological Psychology, 64*, 73–79.

JACOBSON, N. S., DOBSON, K. S., TRUAX, P. A., ADDIS, M. E., KOERNER, K., GOLLAN, J. K., GORTNER, E., & PRINCE, S. E. (1996). A component analysis of cognitive-behavioral treatment for depression. *Journal of Consulting and Clinical Psychology, 64*, 295–304.

JACOBSON, N. S., & HOLLON, S. D. (1996). Cognitive-behavior therapy versus pharmacotherapy: Now that the jury's returned its verdict, it's time to present the rest of the evidence. *Journal of Consulting and Clinical Psychology, 64*, 74–80.

JAMES, W. (1884). What is an emotion? *Mind, 9*, 188–205.

JAMES, W. (1890/1950). *Principles of psychology,* Vol. 2. New York: Dover.

JAMISON, K. R. (1995, February). Manic-depressive illness and creativity. *Scientific American* 46–51.

JAMISON, K. R. (1995). *An unquiet mind.* New York: Knopf.

JAMISON, K. R. (1999). *Night falls fast: understanding suicide.* New York: Knopf.

JAMISON, R. N. (1976). *Mastering chronic pain: A professional's guide to behavioral treatment.* Sarasota, FL: Professional Resource Press.

JAMISON, R. N., RAYMOND, S. A., SLAWSBY, E. A. NEDELJKOVIC, S. S., & KATZ, N. P. (1998). Opioid therapy for noncancer back pain: A randomized prospective study. *Spine, 23*, 2591–2600.

JANET, P. (1889). *L'automisme psychologigue*. Paris: Félix Alcan.

JANIS, I. L. (1982). *Groupthink: Psychological studies of policy decisions and fiascoes* (2nd ed.). Boston: Houghton Mifflin.

JANIS, I. L. (1985). Sources of error in strategic decision making. In J. M. Pennings (Ed.), *Organizational strategy and change*. San Francisco: Jossey-Bass.

JANOFF-BULMAN, R. (1992). *Shattered assumptions: Toward a new psychology of trauma*. New York: Maxwell Macmillan International.

JANOF-BULMAN, R., & MCPHERSON FRANTZ, C. (1997). The impact of trauma on meaning: From meaningless world to meaningful life. In M. Power & C. R. Brewin (Eds.), *The transformation of meaning in psychological therapies: Integrating theory and practice* (pp. 245–266). New York: Wiley.

JASMOS, T. M., & HAKMILLER, K. L. (1975). Some effects of lesion level and emotional cues on affective expression in spinal cord patients. *Psychological Reports, 37*, 859–870.

JEMMOTT, J. B., III, BORYSENKO, M., MCCELLAND, D. C., CHAPMAN, R., MEYER, D., & BENSON, H. (1985). Academic stress, power motivation, and decrease in salivary secretory immunoglobulin: A secretion rate. *Lancet, 1*, 1400–1402.

JENNINGS, D., AMABILE, T. M., & ROSS, L. (1982). Informal covariation assessment: Database vs. theory-based judgments. In A. Tversky, D. Kahneman, & P. Slovic (Eds.), *Judgment under uncertainty: Heuristics and biases*. New York: Cambridge University Press.

JI, L., PENG, K., & NISBETT, R. E. (2000). Culture, control, and perception of relationship in the environment. *Journal of Personality and Social Psychology, 78*, 943–955.

JOHANSSON, G., & FRANKENHAEUSER, J. (1973). Temporal factors in sympatho-adrenomedullary activity following acute behavioral activation. *Biological Psychology, 1*, 63–73.

JOHANSSON, G., VON HOFSTEN, C., & JANSON, G. (1980). Event perception. *Annual Review of Psychology, 31*, 27–63.

JOHN, O. P. (1990). The "Big Five" factor taxonomy: Dimension of personality in the natural language and in questionnaires. In L. A. Pervin (Ed.), *Handbook of personality: Theory and research* (pp. 66–100). New York: Guilford.

JOHNSON, E. J., & TVERSKY, A. (1983). Affect, generalization, and the perception of risk. *Journal of Personality and Social Psychology, 45*, 20–31.

JOHNSON, M. H. (1997). *Developmental cognitive neuroscience: An introduction*. Oxford, England: Blackwell.

JOHNSON, R. D., & DOWNING, L. L. (1979). Deindividuation and valence of cues: Effect on prosocial and antisocial behavior. *Journal of Personality and Social Psychology, 37*, 1532–1538.

JOHNSON-LAIRD, P. N. (1985). The deductive reasoning ability. In R. J. Sternberg (Ed.), *Human abilities: An information processing approach*. New York: Freeman.

JOHNSON-LAIRD, P. (1988a). A computational analysis of consciousness. In A. J. Marcel & E. Bisiach (Eds.), *Consciousness in contemporary science*. New York: Oxford University Press.

JOHNSON-LAIRD, P. N. (1988b). *The computer and the mind: An introduction to cognitive science*. Cambridge, MA: Harvard University Press.

JOHNSON-LAIRD, P. N. (1989). Mental models. In M. I. Posner (Ed.), *Foundations of cognitive science*. Cambridge, MA: MIT Press.

JOHNSON-LAIRD, P. N., & BYRNE, R. M. J. (1991). *Deduction*. Hillsdale, NJ: Erlbaum.

JOHNSON-LAIRD, P. N., LEGRENZI, P., GIROTTO, V., LEGRENZI, M. S., & CAVERNI, J. P. (1999). Naïve probability: A mental model theory of extensional reasoning. *Psychological Review, 106*, 62–88.

JOHNSTON, L. D., O'MALLEY, P. M., & BACHMAN, J. G. (1995). *National survey results on drug use*. Rockville, MD: National Institute on Drug Abuse.

JONES, E. E. (1978). Effects of race on psychotherapy process and outcome: An exploratory investigation. *Psychotherapy: Theory, Research, and Practice, 15*, 226–236.

JONES, E. E. (1990). *Interpersonal perception*. New York: Freeman.

JONES, E. E., & HARRIS, V. A. (1967). The attribution of attitudes. *Journal of Experimental Social Psychology, 3*, 1–24.

JONES, E. E., ROCK, L., SHAVER, K. G., GOETHALS, G. R., & WARD, L. M. (1968). Pattern of performance and ability attribution: An unexpected primacy effect. *Journal of Personality and Social Psychology, 9*, 317–340.

JONES, H. C., & LOVINGER, P. W. (1985). *The marijuana question and science's search for an answer*. New York: Dodd, Mead.

JUDD, L., AKISKAL, H., MASER, J., ZELLER, P. J., ENDICOTT, J., CORYELL, W., PAULUS, M., KUNOVAC, J., LEON, A., MUELLER, T., RICE, J., & KELLER, M. (1998). A prospective 12-year study of subsyndromal and syndromal depressive symptoms in unipolar major depressive disorders. *Archives of General Psychiatry, 55*, 694–700.

JULIEN, R. M. (1988). *Drugs and the body*. New York: Freeman.

JULIEN, R. M. (1992). *A primer of drug action: A concise, nontechnical guide to the actions, uses, and side effects of psychoactive drugs* (6th ed.). New York: Freeman.

JUSSIM, L. (1991). Social perception and social reality: A reflection-construction model. *Psychological Review, 98*, 54–73.

JUST, M. A., & CARPENTER, P. A. (1980). A theory of reading: From eye fixations to comprehension. *Psychological Review, 87*, 329–354.

JUST, M. A., & CARPENTER, P. A. (1992). A capacity theory of comprehension: Individual differences in working memory. *Psychological Review, 99*, 122.

KAGAN, J. (1979). Overview: Perspectives on human infancy. In J. D. Osofsky (Ed.), *Handbook of infant development*. New York: Wiley-Interscience.

KAGAN, J. (1998). *Three seductive ideas*. Cambridge, MA: Harvard University Press.

KAGAN, J., KEARSLEY, R. B., & ZELAZO, P. (1978). *Infancy: Its place in human development*. Cambridge, MA: Harvard University Press.

KAGAN, J., & SNIDMAN, N. (1991). Temperamental factors in human development. *American Psychologist, 46*, 856–862.

KAGAN, N. (1984). *The nature of the child*. New York: Basic Books.

KAGAN, N., & MOSS, H. A. (1962). *Birth to maturity*. New York: Wiley.

KAHNEMAN, D., SLOVIC, P., & TVERSKY, A. (Eds.). (1982). *Judgment under uncertainty: Heuristics and biases*. New York: Cambridge University Press.

KAHNEMAN, D., & TVERSKY, A. (1996). On the reality of cognitive illusions. *Psychological Review, 103*, 582–591.

KAIL, R. (1989). *The development of memory in children* (3rd ed.). New York: Freeman.

KALAT, P. W. (2001). *Biological psychology* (7th ed.). Belmont, CA: Wadsworth/Thomson Learning.

KAMEN-SIEGEL, L., RODIN, J., SELIGMAN, M. E., & DWYER, J. (1991). Explanatory style and cell-mediated immunity in elderly men and women. *Health Psychology, 10*, 229–235.

KAMIN, L. J. (1974). *The science and politics of IQ*. Hillsdale, NJ: Erlbaum.

KANDEL, E. R., SCHWARTZ, J. H., & JESSELL, T. M. (Eds.) (1991). *Principles of neural science* (3rd ed.). New York: Elsevier.

KAPLAN, J. R., & KAUFMANN, P. (1993). Low or lowered cholesterol and risk of death from suicide and trauma. *Metabolism, 42* (supp. 1), 45–56.

KAPLAN, J. R., MULDOON, M. F., MANUCK, S. B., & MANN, J. J. (1997). Assessing the observed relationship between low cholesterol and violence-related mortality: Implications for suicide risk. In Stoff, D. M. (Ed.), *The neurobiology of suicide: From the bench to the clinic* (pp. 57–85), New York: New York Academy of Sciences.

KAPLAN, M. R., & MILLER, C. E. (1987). Group decision making and normative versus informational influence: Effects of type of issue and assigned decision rule. *Journal of Personality and Social Psychology, 53*, 306–313.

KARASEK, R., BAKER, D., MARXER, F., AHLBOM, A., & THEORELL, T. (1981). Job decision latitude, job demands, and cardiovascular disease: A prospective study of Swedish men. *American Journal of Public Health, 71*, 694–705.

KARASEK, R. A., THEORELL, T. G., SCHWARTZ, J., PIEPER, C., & ALFREDSSON, L. (1982). Job, psychological factors and coronary heart disease: Swedish prospective findings and U.S. prevalence findings using a new occupation inference method. *Advances in Cardiology, 29*, 62–67.

KARNI, A., TANNE, D., RUBENSTEIN, B. S., ASKENASY, J. J. M., & SAGI, D. (1994). Dependence on REM sleep of overnight improvement of a perceptual skill. *Science, 265*, 679–682.

KARNO, M., & GOLDING, J. M. (1991). Obsessive compulsive disorder. In L. R. Robins & D. A. Regier (Eds.), *Psychiatric disorders in America: The epidemiologic catchment area study*. New York: Maxwell Macmillan International.

KARNO, M., HOUGH, R., BURNAM, A., ESCOBAR, J. I., TIMBERS, D. M., SANTANA, F., & BOYD, J. H. (1987). Lifetime prevalence of specific psychiatric disorders among Mexican-Americans and non-Hispanic whites in Los Angeles. *Archives of General Psychiatry, 44*, 695–701.

KARNO, M., & JENKINS, J. H. (1993). Cross-cultural issues in the course and treatment of schizophrenia. *Psychiatric Clinics of North America, 16*, 339–350.

KARYLOWSKI, J. J. (1990). Social reference points and accessibility of trait-related information in self-other similarity judgments. *Journal of Personality and Social Psychology, 58*, 975–983.

KASSIN, S.M. (1997). The psychology of confession evidence. *American Psychologist, 52*, 221–233.

KASTNER, S., DE WEERD, P., DESIMONE, R., & UNGERLEIDER, L. G. (1998). Mechanisms of directed attention in the human extrastriate cortex as revealed by functional MRI. *Science, 282*, 108–111.

KASTNER, S., & UNGERLEIDER, L. G. (2000). Mechanisms of visual attention in the human cortex. *Annual Review of Neuroscience, 23*, 315–341.

KATZ, D. (1960). The functional approach to the study of attitudes. *Public Opinion Quarterly, 24*, 163–204.

KATZ, L. C., & SHATZ, C. J. (1996). Synaptic activity and the construction of cortical circuits. *Science, 274*, 1133.

KATZ, R., & WYKES, T. (1985). The psychological difference between temporally predictable and unpredictable stressful events: Evidence for information control theories. *Journal of Personality and Social Psychology, 48,* 781–790.

KAUFMAN, G. (1995, November). *Methylphenidate findings from New York's triplicate prescription data.* Presented at the annual conference of the National Association of State Controlled Substances Authorities.

KAUFMAN, L., & ROCK, I. (1989). The moon illusion thirty years later. In M. Hershenson (Ed.), *The moon illusion* (pp. 193–234). Hillsdale, NJ: Erlbaum.

KAZDIN, A. E. (1982). Symptom substitution, generalization, and response covariation: Implications for psychotherapy outcome. *Psychological Bulletin, 91,* 349–365.

KAZDIN, A. E., & WEISZ, J. R. (1998). Identifying and developing empirically supported child and adolescent treatments. *Journal of Consulting and Clinical Psychology, 66,* 19–36.

KEIL, F. C. (1989). *Concepts, kinds, and cognitive development.* Cambridge, MA: MIT Press.

KEIL, F. C., & BATTERMAN, N. A. (1984). Characteristic-to-defining shift in the development of word meaning. *Journal of Verbal Learning and Verbal Behavior, 23,* 221–236.

KELLER, M. B., & BAKER, L. A. (1991). Bipolar disorder: Epidemiology, course, diagnosis, and treatment. *Bulletin of the Menninger Clinic, 55,* 172–181.

KELLEY, H. H. (1950). The warm-cold variable in first impressions of persons. *Journal of Personality, 18,* 431–439.

KELLEY, H. H. (1967). Attribution theory in social psychology. In D. Levine (Ed.), *Nebraska symposium on motivation* (Vol. 15). Lincoln: University of Nebraska Press.

KELLMAN, P. J. (1984). Perception of three-dimensional form by human infants. *Perception and Psychophysics, 36,* 353–358.

KELLY, G. A. (1955). *The psychology of personal constructs.* New York: Norton.

KELTNER, D., ELLSWORTH, P. C., & EDWARDS, K. (1993). Beyond simple pessimism: Effects of sadness and anger on social perception. *Journal of Personality and Social Psychology, 64,* 740–752.

KENDLER, K. S., NEALE, M. C., KESSLER, R. C., & HEATH, A. C. (1992). Major depression and generalized anxiety disorder: Same genes, (partly) different environments? *Archives of General Psychiatry, 49,* 716–722.

KENDLER, K. S., NEALE, M. C., KESSLER, R. C., & HEATH, A. C. (1993). Panic disorder in women: A population-based twin study. *Psychological Medicine, 23,* 397–406.

KENDLER, K. S., NEALE, M. C., KESSLER, R. C., HEATH, A. C., & EAVES, L. J. (1992). The genetic epidemiology of phobias in women. *Archives of General Psychiatry, 49,* 273–281.

KENRICK, D. T. (2001). Evolutionary psychology, cognitive science, and dynamical systems: Building an integrative paradigm. *Current Directions in Psychological Science, 10,* 13–17.

KENDRICK, D. T., & GUTIERRES, S. E. (1980). Contrast effects and judgments of physical attractiveness: When beauty becomes a social problem. *Journal of Personality and Social Psychology, 38,* 131–140.

KENRICK, D. T., & KEEFE, R. C. (1992). Age preferences in mates reflect sex differences in human reproductive strategies. *Behavioral and Brain Sciences, 15,* 75–91.

KENRICK, D. T., SADALLA, E. K., GROTCH, G., & TROST, M. R. (1990). Evolution, traits and the stages of human courtship: Qualifying the parental

investment model. *Journal of Personality, 58,* 97–116.

KENSHALO, D. R., NAFE, J. P., & BROOKS, B. (1961). Variations in thermal sensitivity. *Science, 134,* 104–105.

KEPHART, W. M. (1967). Some correlates of romantic love. *Journal of Marriage and the Family, 29,* 470–474.

KERNBERG, P. F. (1979). Psychoanalytic profile of the borderline adolescent. *Adolescent Psychiatry, 7,* 234–256.

KERNIS, M. H., & WHEELER, L. (1981). Beautiful friends and ugly strangers: Radiation and contrast effects in perception of same-sex pairs. *Journal of Personality and Social Psychology, 7,* 617–620.

KESSLER, R. C., BROWN, R. L., & BROMAN, C. L. (1981). Sex differences in psychiatric help-seeking: Evidence from four large-scale surveys. *Journal of Health and Social Behavior, 22,* 49–64.

KESSLER, R. C., DAVIS, C. G., & KENDLER, K. S. (1997). Childhood adversity and adult psychiatric disorder in the US National Comorbidity Survey. *Psychological Medicine, 27,* 1101–1119.

KESSLER, R. C., MCGONAGLE, K. A., ZHAO, S., NELSON, C., HUGHES, M., ESHLEMAN, S., WITTCHEN, H., & KENDLER, K. (1994). Lifetime and 12-month prevalence of DSM-III-R psychiatric disorders in the United States. *Archives of General Psychiatry, 51,* 8–19.

KESSLER, R. C., STEIN, M. B., & BERGLUND, P. (1998). Social phobia subtypes in the National Comorbidity Survey. *American Journal of Psychiatry, 155,* 613–619.

KIECOLT-GLASER, J. K., and collaborators. (1985). Psychosocial enhancement of immunocompetence in a geriatric population. *Health Psychology, 4,* 25–41.

KIECOLT-GLASER, J. K., GLASER, R., CACIOPPO, J. T., & MALARKEY, W. B. (1998). Marital stress: Immunologic, neuroendocrine, and autonomic correlates. *Annals of the New York Academy of Sciences, 840,* 656–663.

KIECOLT-GLASER, J. K., KENNEDY, S., MALKOFF, S., FISHER, L., SPEICHER, C. E., & GLASER, R. (1988). Marital discord and immunity in males. *Psychosomatic Medicine, 50,* 213–229.

KIECOLT-GLASER, J. K., MCGUIRE, L., ROBLES, T. F., & GLASER, R. (2002). Emotions, morbidity, and mortality: New perspectives from psychoneuroimmunology. *Annual Review of Psychology, 53,* 83–107.

KIECOLT-GLASER, J. K., PAGE, G. G., MARUCHA, P. T., MACCALLUM, R. C., & GLASER, R. (1998). Psychological influences on surgical recovery. *American Psychologist, 53,* 1209–1218.

KIEHL, K. A., SMITH, A. M., HARE, R. D., MENDREK, A., FORSTER, B. B., BRINK, J., & LIDDLE, P. F. (2001). Limbic abnormalities in affective processing by criminal psychopaths as revealed by functional magnetic resonance imaging. *Biological Psychiatry, 50,* 677–684.

KIESLER, C. A., & SIBULKIN, A. E. (1987). *Mental hospitalization: Myths and facts about a national crisis.* Newbury Park, CA: Sage.

KIHLSTROM, J. F. (1984). Conscious, subconscious, unconscious: A cognitive view. In K. S. Bowers & D. Meichenbaum (Eds.), *The unconscious: Reconsidered.* New York: Wiley.

KIHLSTROM, J. F. (1985). Hypnosis. *Annual Review of Psychology, 36,* 385–235.

KIHLSTROM, J. F. (1987). The cognitive unconscious. *Science, 237,* 1445–1452.

KIHLSTROM, J. F. (1994). Psychodynamics and social cognition: Notes on the fusion of psychoanalysis and psychology. *Journal of Personality, 62,* 681–696.

KIHLSTROM, J. F. (1999). The psychological unconscious. In L. R. Pervin & O. John (Eds.), *Handbook of personality* (2nd ed., pp. 424–442). New York: Guilford.

KIHLSTROM, J. F., GLISKY, M. L., & ANGIULO, M. J. (1994). Dissociative tendencies and dissociative disorders. *Journal of Abnormal Psychology, 103,* 117–124.

KIM, L. I. C. (1993). Psychiatric care of Korean-Americans. In A. C. Gaw (Ed.). *Culture, ethnicity and mental illness* (pp. 347–345). Washington, DC: Government Printing Office.

KIMMEL, D. C., & WEINER, I. B. (1985). *Adolescence: A developmental transition.* Hillsdale, NJ: Erlbaum.

KINDER, D. R., & SEARS, D. O. (1985). Public opinion and political action. In G. Lindzey & E. Aronson, (Eds.), *The handbook of social psychology* (3rd ed., Vol. 2). New York: Random House.

KING, N. J., GULLONE, E, TONGE, B. J., & OLLENDICK, T. H. (1993). Self-reports of panic attacks and manifest anxiety in adolescents. *Behavior Research and Therapy, 31,* 111–116.

KINSEY, A. C., POMEROY, W. B., & MARTIN, C. E. (1948). *Sexual behavior in the human male.* Philadelphia: Saunders.

KINSEY, A. C., POMEROY, W. B., MARTIN, C. E., & GEBHARD, P. H. (1953). *Sexual behavior in the human female.* Philadelphia: Saunders.

KIRSCH, I., & LYNN, S. J. (1998). Dissociation theories of hypnosis. *Psychological Bulletin, 123,* 100–115.

KISHLINE, A. (1994). *Moderate drinking.* New York: Three Rivers Press.

KITAYAMA, S., MARKUS, H. R., & KUROKAWA, M. (2000). Culture, emotion, and well-being: Good feelings in Japan and the United States. *Cognition and Emotion, 14,* 93–124.

KLAHR, D. (1982). Nonmonotone assessment of monotone development: An information processing analysis. In S. Strauss (Ed.), *U-shaped behavioral growth.* New York: Academic Press.

KLATZKY, R. L., LEDERMAN, S. J., & METZGER, V. A. (1985). Identifying objects by touch: An expert system. *Perception and Psychophysics, 37,* 299–302.

KLEIN, S. B., & LOFTUS, J. (1988). The nature of self-referent encoding: The contributions of elaborative and organizational processes. *Journal of Personality and Social Psychology, 55,* 5–11.

KLEIN, S. B., LOFTUS, J., & BURTON, H. A. (1989). Two self-reference effects: The importance of distinguishing between self-descriptiveness judgments and autobiographical retrieval in self-referent encoding. *Journal of Personality and Social Psychology, 56,* 853–865.

KLERMAN, G. L., WEISSMAN, M. M., ROUNSAVILLE, B., & CHEVRON, E. (1984). *Interpersonal psychotherapy of depression.* New York: Basic Books.

KLINE, P. (1972). *Fact and fancy in Freudian theory.* London: Methuen.

KLINEBERG, O. (1938). Emotional expression in Chinese literature. *Journal of Abnormal and Social Psychology, 33,* 517–520.

KLING, K. C., HYDE, J. S., SHOWERS, C. J., & BUSWELL, B. N. (1999). Gender differences in self-esteem: A meta-analysis. *Psychological Bulletin, 125,* 70–500.

KLÜVER, H., & BUCY, P. C. (1937). "Psychic blindness" and other symptoms following temporal lobectomy in rhesus monkeys. *American Journal of Physiology, 119,* 352–353.

KNITTLE, J. L., & HIRSCH, J. (1968). Effect of early nutrition on the development of rat epididymal fat pads: Cellularity and metabolism. *Journal of Clinical Investigation, 47,* 2091.

KNOBLICH, G., & KING, R. (1992). Biological correlates of criminal behavior. In J. McCord (Ed.), *Advances in criminological theory: Facts, frameworks, and forecasts* (pp. 1–21). New Brunswick, NJ: Transaction.

KNUTSON, B., WOLKOWITZ, O. M., COLE, S. W., CHAN, T., MOORE, E. A., JOHSON, R. C., TERPSTRA, J., TURNER, R. A., & REUS, V. I. (1998). Selective alteration of personality and social behavior by serotonergic intervention. *American Journal of Psychiatry, 155,* 373–379.

KOBASA, S. C. (1979). Stressful life events, personality, and health: An inquiry into hardiness. *Journal of Personality and Social Psychology, 37,* 1–11.

KOBASA, S. C., MADDI, S. R., & KAHN, S. (1982). Hardiness and health: A prospective study. *Journal of Personality and Social Psychology, 42,* 168–177.

KOENIG, H. G., HAYS, J. C., GEORGE, L. K., BLAZER, D. G., LARSON, D. B., & LANDERMAN, L. R. (1997). Modeling the cross-sectional relationships between religion, physical health, social support and depressive symptoms. *American Journal of Geriatric Psychology, 5,* 131–144.

KOHLBERG, L. (1966). A cognitive-developmental analysis of children's sex role concepts and attitudes. In E. E. Maccoby (Ed.), *The development of sex differences* (pp. 82–173). Stanford, CA: Stanford University Press.

KOHLBERG, L. (1969). Stage and sequence: The cognitive-developmental approach to socialization. In D. A. Goslin (Ed.), *Handbook of socialization theory and research.* Chicago: Rand McNally.

KOHLBERG, L. (1976). Moral stages and moralization: The cognitive-developmental approach. In T. Lickong (Ed.), *Moral development and behavior.* New York: Holt, Rinehart & Winston.

KOHLER, W. (1925). *The mentality of apes.* New York: Harcourt Brace. (Reprint ed., 1976. New York: Liveright.)

KOHNSTAMM, G. A., BATES, J. E., & ROTHBART, M. K. (Eds.) (1989). *Temperament in childhood.* Chichester: Wiley.

Kolata, G. (2002, May). Runner's High? Endorphins? Fiction, Some Scientists Say. *New York Times.*

KOLB, B., & WHISHAW, I. Q. (1985). *Fundamentals of human neuropsychology* (2nd ed.). San Francisco: Freeman.

KOLODNY, J. A., (1994). Memory processes in classification learning. *Psychological Science, 5,* 164–169.

KOOB, G. F., & BLOOM, F. E. (1988). Cellular and molecular mechanisms of drug dependence. *Science, 242,* 715–723.

KORNER, A. F. (1973). Individual differences at birth: Implications for early experience and later development. In J. C. Westman (Ed.), *Individual differences in children.* New York: Wiley.

KORNHABER, M., & GARDNER, H. (1991). Critical thinking across multiple intelligences. In S. Maclure & P. Davies (Eds.), *Learning to think: Thinking to learn.* Oxford, England: Pergamon.

KORNHABER, M., KRECHEVSKY, M., & GARDNER, H. (1990). Engaging intelligence. *Educational Psychologist, 25,* 177–199.

KORNITZER, M., MAGOTTEAU, V., DEGRE, C., KITTEL, F., STRUYVEN, J., & VAN THIEL, E. (1982). Angiographic findings and the type A pattern assessed by means of the Bortner Scale. *Journal of Behavioral Medicine, 5,* 313–320.

KOSAMBI, D. D. (1967). Living prehistory in India. *Scientific American, 215,* 105.

KOSS, M., & BOESCHEN, L. (1998). Rape. In *Encyclopedia of Mental Health,* (Vol. 3). New York: Academic Press.

KOSS-CHIONO, J. D. (1995). Traditional and folk approaches among ethnic minorities. In J. F. Aponte (Ed.), *Psychological interventions and cultural diversity* (pp. 145–163). Boston: Allyn & Bacon.

KOSSLYN, S. M. (1980). *Image and mind.* Cambridge, MA: Harvard University Press.

KOSSLYN, S. M. (1983). *Ghosts in the mind's machine.* New York: Norton.

KOSSLYN, S. M. (1988). Aspects of a cognitive neuroscience of mental imagery. *Science, 240,* 1621–1626.

KOSSLYN, S. M. (1994). *The resolution of the imagery debate.* Cambridge, MA: MIT Press.

KOSSLYN, S. M., ALPERT, N. M., THOMPSON, W. L., MALJKOVIC, V., WEISE, S. B., CHABRIS, C. F., HAMILTON, S. E., RAUCH, S. L., & BUONANNO, F. S. (1993). Visual mental imagery activates topographically organized visual cortex. *Journal of Cognitive Neuroscience, 5,* 263–287.

KOSSLYN, S. M., BALL, T. M., & REISER, B. J. (1978). Visual images preserve metric spatial information: Evidence from studies of image scanning. *Journal of Experimental Psychology: Human Perception and Performance, 4,* 47–60.

KOSSLYN, S. M., & KOENIG, O. (1992). *Wet mind: The new cognitive neuroscience.* New York: Free Press.

KOULACK, D., & GOODENOUGH, D. R. (1976). Dream recall and dream recall failure: An arousal-retrieval model. *Psychological Bulletin, 83,* 975–984.

KRAMER, P. D. (1993). *Listening to Prozac.* New York: Viking.

KRAUS, G., & REYNOLDS, D. J. (2001). The "A-B-C's" of the cluster B's: Identifying, understanding and treating cluster B personality disorders. *Clinical Psychology Review, 21,* 345–373.

KRAUT, R. E. (1982). Social presence, facial feedback, and emotion. *Journal of Personality and Social Psychology, 42,* 853–863.

KRAVITZ, D., & PLATANIA, J. (1993). Attitudes and beliefs about affirmative action: Effects of target and/or respondent sex and ethnicity. *Journal of Applied Psychology, 78,* 928–938.

KRAVITZ, D. A., HARRISON, D. A., TURNER, M. E., LEVINE, E. L., CHAVES, W., BRANNICK, M. T., DENNING, D. L., RUSSELL, C. J., & CONARD, M. A. (1997). *Affirmative action: A review of psychological and behavioral research.* Bowling Green, OH: Society for Industrial and Organizational Psychology.

KRING, A. (2000). Gender and anger. In A. H. Fischer (Ed.), *Gender and emotion: Social psychological perspectives* (pp. 211–231). New York: Cambridge University Press.

KRIPKE, D. F. (1985). Biological rhythms. In G. L. Klerman, M. M. Weissman, P. S. Applebaum, & L. H. Roth (Eds.), *Psychiatry* (Vol. 3). Philadelphia: Lippincott.

KRIPKE, D. F., & GILLIN, J. C. (1985). Sleep disorders. In G. L. Klerman, M. M. Weissman, P. S. Applebaum, & L. N. Roth (Eds.), *Psychiatry* (Vol. 3). Philadelphia: Lippincott.

KRYGER, M. H., ROTH, T., & DEMENT, W. C. (Eds.). (1994). *Principles and practice of sleep medicine.* Philadelphia: Saunders.

KUCH, K., & COX, B. J. (1992). Symptoms of PTSD in 124 survivors of the Holocaust. *American Journal of Psychiatry, 149,* 337–340.

KUHL, P. K., WILLIAMS, K. A., LACERDA, F., STEVENS, K. N., & LINDBLOM, B. (1992). Linguistic experience alters phonetic perception in infants by 6 months of age. *Science, 255,* 606–608.

KUHN, C., SWARTZWELDER, S., & WILSON, W. (1998). *Buzzed: The straight facts about the most used and abused drugs.* New York: Norton.

KUIPER, N. A., MACDONALD, M. R., & DERRY, P. A. (1983). Parameters of a depressive self-schema. In J. Suls & A. G. Greenwald (Eds.), *Psychological perspectives on the self* (Vol. 2). Hillsdale, NJ: Erlbaum.

KUIPER, N. A., OLINGER, L. J., MACDONALD, M. R., & SHAW, B. F. (1985). Self-schema processing of depressed and nondepressed content: The effects of vulnerability on depression. *Social Cognition, 3,* 77–93.

KUIPER, N. A., & ROGERS, T. B. (1979). Encoding of personal information: Self-other differences. *Journal of Personality and Social Psychology, 37,* 499–514.

KUJAWA, M. J., & NEMEROFF, C. B. (2000). The biology of bipolar disorder. In A. Marneros & J. Angst (Eds.), *Bipolar disorders: 100 years after manic-depressive insanity* (pp. 281–314). Great Britain: Kluwer Academic Publishers.

KUMAN, I. G., FEDROV, C. N., & NOVIKOVA, L. A. (1983). Investigation of the sensitive period in the development of the human visual system. *Journal of Higher Nervous Activity, 33,* 434–441.

KURTINES, W., & GREIF, E. B. (1974). The development of moral thought: Review and evaluation of Kohlberg's approach. *Psychological Bulletin, 81,* 453–470.

LA BERGE, D. (1995). *Attentional processing: The brain's art of mindfulness.* Cambridge, MA: Harvard University Press.

LAFROMBOISE, T. D., TRIMBLE, J. E., & MOHATT, G. V. (1998). Counseling intervention and American Indian tradition: An integrative approach. In D. R. Atkinson (Ed.), *Counseling American minorities* (5th Ed.) Boston: McGraw-Hill.

LAGERSPETZ, K., VIEMERO, V., & AKADEMI, A. (1986). Television and aggressive behavior among Finnish children. In L. R. Huesmann & L. D. Eron (Eds.), *Television and the aggressive child.* New York: Erlbaum.

LAGRECA, A. M., SLIVERMAN, W. K., VERNBERG, E. M., & PRINSTEIN, M. J. (1996). Symptoms of posttraumatic stress in children after Hurricane Andrew: A prospective study. *Journal of the American Academy of the Child and Adolescent Psychiatry, 27,* 330–335.

LAKOFF, G. (1987). *Women, fire, and dangerous things.* Chicago: University of Chicago Press.

LAMB, M. E., & BORNSTEIN, M. H. (1987). *Development in infancy: An introduction* (2nd ed.). New York: Random House.

LAMBERT, M. J., & BERGIN, A. E. (1994). The effectiveness of psychotherapy. In A. Bergin (Ed.), *Handbook of psychotherapy and behavior change* (4th ed., pp. 143–189). New York: Wiley.

LAND, E. H. (1977). The retinex theory of color vision. *Scientific American, 237,* 108–128.

LAND, E. H. (1986). Recent advances in retinex theory. *Vision Research, 26,* 7–21.

LANGLOIS, J. H., & DOWNS, A. C. (1980). Mothers, fathers, and peers as socialization agents of sex-typed play behaviors in young children. *Child Development, 51,* 1237–1247.

LAPIERE, R. (1934). Attitudes versus actions. *Social Forces, 13,* 230–237.

LARKIN, J. H., MCDERMOTT, J., SIMON, D. P., & SIMON, H. A. (1980). Expert and novice performance in solving physics problems. *Science, 208,* 1335–1342.

LARSEN, R. J., & SEIDMAN, E. (1986). Gender schema theory and sex role inventories: Some conceptual and psychometric considerations. *Journal of Personality and Social Psychology, 50,* 205–211.

LARSON, R., & RICHARDS, M. H. (1991). Daily companionship in late childhood and early adolescence: Changing developmental contexts. *Child Development, 62*, 284–300.

LATANÉ, B., & DARLEY, J. M. (1968). Group inhibition of bystander intervention in emergencies. *Journal of Personality and Social Psychology, 10*, 215–221.

LATANÉ, B., & DARLEY, J. M. (1970). *The unresponsive bystander: Why doesn't he help?* New York: Appleton-Century-Crofts.

LATANÉ, B., NIDA, S. A., & WILSON, D. W. (1981). The effects of group size on helping behavior. In J. P. Rushton & R. M. Sorrentino (Eds.), *Altruism and helping behavior: Social personality, and developmental perspectives*. Hillsdale, NJ: Erlbaum.

LATANÉ, B., & RODIN, J. (1969). A lady in distress: Inhibiting effects of friends and strangers on bystander intervention. *Journal of Experimental and Social Psychology, 5*, 189–202.

LAUDENSLAGER, M. L., RYAN, S. M., DRUGAN, R. C., HYSON, R. L., & MAIER, S. F. (1983). Coping and immunosuppression: Inescapable but not escapable shock suppresses lymphocyte proliferation. *Science, 221*, 568–570.

LAUMANN, E. O., GAGNON, J. H. MICHAEL, R. T., & MICHAELS, S. (1994). *The social organization of sexuality: Sexual practices in the United States*. Chicago: University of Chicago Press.

LAZARUS, R. S. (1991a). Cognition and motivation in emotion. *American Psychologist, 46*, 352–367.

LAZARUS, R. S. (1991b). *Emotion and adaptation*. New York: Oxford University Press.

LAZARUS, R. S., & FOLKMAN, S. (1984). *Stress, appraisal, and coping*. New York: Springer.

LAZARUS, R. S., KANNER, A. D., & FOLKMAN, S. (1980). Emotions: A cognitive-phenomenological analysis. In R. Plutchik & H. Kellerman (Eds.), *Emotion: Theory, research, and experience* (Vol. 1). New York: Academic Press.

LE BARS, P. L., KATZ, M. M., BERMAN, N., ITIL, T. M., FREEDMAN, A. M., & SCHATZBERG, A. F. (1997a). *A placebo-controlled, double-blind, randomized trial of an extract of ginkgo biloba for dementia*. Tarrytown: New York Institute for Medical Research.

LE BARS, P. L., KATZ, M. M., BERMAN, N., ITIL, T. M., FREEDMAN, A. M., & SCHATZBERG, A. F. (1997b). A placebo-controlled, double-blind randomized trial of an extract of ginkgo biloba for dementia. *Journal of the American Medical Association, 278*, 1327–1332.

LE BON, G. (1895). *The crowd*. London: Ernest Benn.

LE DEOX, J. E. (1989). Cognitive-emotional interactions in the brain. *Cognition and Emotion, 3*, 267–289.

LE DOUX, J. E., & PHELPS, E. A. (2000). Emotional networks in the brain. In M. Lewis & J. M. Haviland-Jones (Eds.), *Handbook of emotions* (2nd ed., pp. 157–172). New York: Guilford.

LEA, M., SPEARS, R., & DE GROOT, D. (2001). Knowing me knowing you: Anonymity effects on social identity processes within groups. *Personality and Social Psychology Bulletin, 27*, 526–537.

LEEDHAM, B., MEYEROWITZ, B. E., MUIRHEAD, J., & FRIST, M. H. (1995). Positive expectations predict health after heart transplantation. *Health Psychology, 14*, 74–79.

LEFF, J. P., & VAUGHN, C. E. (1981). The role of maintenance therapy and relatives' expressed emotion in relapse of schizophrenia: A two-year follow-up. *British Journal of Psychiatry, 139*, 102–104.

LEIPPE, M. R. (1980). Effects of integrative memorial and cognitive processes on the correspondence of eyewitness accuracy and confidence. *Law and Human Behavior, 4*, 261–274.

LENNEBERG, E. H. (1967). *Biological foundations of language*. New York: Wiley.

LENNON, M. C., & ROSENFIELD, S. (1992). Women and mental health: The interaction of job and family conditions. *Journal of Health and Social Behavior, 33*, 316–327.

LEO, R. (1996). Miranda's revenge: Police interrogation as a confidence game. *Law and Society Review, 30*, 259–288.

LEONARD, J. S. (1986). The effectiveness of equal employment law and affirmative action regulation. In R. G. Ehrenberg (Ed.), *Research in labor economics* (vol. 8, pp. 319–350). Greenwich, CT: JAI Press.

LERMAN, C., CAPORASO, N. E., AUDRAIN, J., MAIN, D., BOWMAN, E. D., LOCKSHIN, B., BOYD, N. R., & SHIELDS, P. G. (1999). Evidence suggesting the role of specific genetic factors in cigarette smoking. *Health Psychology, 18*, 14–20.

LERNER, B. (1972). *Therapy in the ghetto: Political impotence and personal disintegration*. Baltimore: Johns Hopkins University Press.

LERNER, J. S., & KELTNER, D. (2001). Fear, anger, and risk. *Journal of Personality and Social Psychology, 81*, 146–159.

LESHNER, A. I. (1997). Addiction is a brain disease, and it matters. *Science, 278*, 45–47.

LEVAV, I., FRIEDLANDER, Y., KARK, J. D., & PERITZ, E. (1988). An epidemiologic study of mortality among bereaved parents. *New England Journal of Medicine, 319*, 457–461.

LEVAY, S. (1991). A difference in hypothalamic structure between heterosexual and homosexual men. *Science, 253*, 1034–1037.

LEVAY, S. (1996). *Queer science: The use and abuse of research into homosexuality*. Cambridge, MA: MIT Press.

LEVENSON, R. W. (1992). Autonomic nervous system differences among emotions. *Psychological Science, 3*, 23–27.

LEVENSON, R. W. (1994). Human emotions: A functional view. In P. Ekman & R. Davidson, (Eds.). *The nature of emotion: Fundamental questions* (pp. 123–126). New York: Oxford University Press.

LEVENSON, R. W., EKMAN, P., & FRIESEN, W. V. (1990). Voluntary facial action generates emotion-specific nervous system activity. *Psychophysiology, 27*, 363–384.

LEVENSON, R. W., EKMAN, P., HEIDER, K., & FRIESEN, W. V. (1992). Emotion and autonomic nervous system activity in an Indonesian culture. *Journal of Personality and Social Psychology, 62*, 927–988.

LEVINE, M. (1999). Rethinking bystander nonintervention. Social categorization and the evidence of witnesses at the James Bulger murder trial. *Human Relations, 52*, 1133–1155.

LEVINE, S. (1960). Stimulation in infancy. *Scientific American, 202*, 80–86.

LEVINGER, G., SENN, D. J., & JORGENSEN, B. W. (1970). Progress toward permanence in courtship: A test of the Kerckhoff-Davis hypotheses. *Sociometry, 33*, 427–443.

LEVY, B. (1996). Improving memory in old age through implicit stereotyping. *Journal of Personality and Social Psychology, 71*, 1092–1107.

LEVY, J. (1985). Right brain, left brain: Facts and fiction. *Psychology Today, 19*, 38–44.

LEVY, S. M., & HEIDEN, I., (1991). Depression, distress and immunity: Risk factors for infectious disease. *Stress Medicine, 7*, 45–51.

LEVY, S., HERBERMAN, R., WHITESIDE, T., SANZO, K., LEE, J., & KIRKWOOD, J. (1990). Perceived social support and tumor estrogen/progesterone receptor status as predictors of natural killer cell activity in breast cancer patients. *Psychosomatic Medicine, 52*, 73–85.

LEWINSOHN, P. M., MISCHEL, W., CHAPLIN, W., & BARTON, R. (1980). Social competence and depression: The role of illusory self-perceptions. *Journal of Abnormal Psychology, 89*, 203–212.

LEWINSOHN, P. M., ROHDE, P., & SEELEY, J. R. (1996). Alcohol consumption in high school adolescents: Frequency of use and dimensional structure of associated problems. *Addiction, 91*, 375–390.

LEY, R. G., & BRYDEN, M. P. (1982). A dissociation of right and left hemispheric effects for recognizing emotional tone and verbal content. *Brain and Cognition, 1*, 3–9.

LIBERMAN, A. M., COOPER, F., SHANKWEILER, D., & STUDERT-KENNEDY, M. (1967). Perception of the speech code. *Psychological Review, 74*, 431–459.

LICHTERMAN, D., KARBE, E., & MAIER, W. (2000). The genetic epidemiology of schizophrenia and of schizophrenia spectrum disorders. *European Archives of Clinical Psychiatry and Neuroscience, 250*, 304–310.

LICKEY, M. E., & GORDON, B. (1991). *Medicine and mental illness*. New York: Freeman.

LIDZ, C. W., MULVEY, E. P., & GARDNER, W. (1993). The accuracy of predictions of violence to others. *Journal of the American Medical Association, 269*, 1007–1011.

LIEBERMAN, L. R., & DUNLAP, J. T. (1979). O'Leary and Borkovec's conceptualization of placebo: The placebo paradox. *American Psychologist, 34*, 553–554.

LIEBERMAN, M. D., OCHSNER, K. N., GILBERT, D. T., & SCHACTER, D. L. (2001). Attitude change in amnesia and under cognitive load. *Psychological Science, 12*, 135–140.

LIGHT, P., & PERRETT-CLERMONT, A. (1989). Social context effects in learning and testing. In A. R. H. Gellatly, D. Rogers, & J. Sloboda (Eds.), *Cognition and social worlds*. Oxford: Clarendon Press.

LILIENFELD, S. O., WOOD, J. W., & GARB, H. N. (2000). The scientific status of projective techniques. *Psychological science in the public interest, 1*, 27–66.

LINDE, K., RAMIREZ, G., MULROW, C. D., PAULS, A., WEIDENHAMMER, W., & MELCHART, D. (1996). St. John's wort for depression: An overview and meta-analysis of randomized clinical trials. *British Medical Journal, 313*, 253–258.

LINDSAY, M., CRINO, R., & ANDREWS, G. (1997) Controlled trial of exposure and response prevention in obsessive-compulsive disorder. *British Journal of Psychiatry, 171*, 135–139.

LINE, L. (1998, August–September). Leader of the flock. *National Wildlife*, pp. 20–27.

LINN, R. L. (1982). Ability testing: Individual differences, prediction, and differential prediction. In A. Wigdor & W. Gardner (Eds.), *Ability testing: Uses, consequences, and controversies*. Washington, DC: National Academy Press.

LINNOILA, N., VIRKUNNEN, M., SCHEININ, M., NUTTILA, A., RIMON, R., & GOODWIN, F. (1983). Low cerebrospinal fluid 5-hydroxyindoleacetic acid concentration differentiates impulsive from nonimpulsive violent behavior. *Life Sciences, 33*, 2609–2624.

LINNOILA, V. M., & VIRKKUNEN, M. (1992). Aggression, suicidality, and serotonin. *Journal of Clinical Psychiatry, 53*, 46–51.

LIOTTI, M., & MAYBERG, H. S. (2001). The role of functional neuroimaging in the neuropsychology of depression. *Journal of Clinical and Experimental Neuropsychology, 23,* 121–136.

LIPPERT, W. W., & SENTER, R. J. (1966). Electrodermal responses in the sociopath. *Psychonomic Science, 4,* 25–26.

LIVINGSTONE, M., & HUBEL, D. (1988). Segregation of form, color, movement, and depth: Anatomy, physiology, and perception. *Science, 240,* 740–750.

LOFTUS, E., & KETCHAM, K. (1994). *The myth of repressed memory.* New York: St. Martin's Press.

LOFTUS, E. F. (1997). Creating false memories. *Scientific American, 277,* 70–75.

LOFTUS, E. F., COAN, J. A., & PICKRELL, J. E. (1996). Manufacturing false memories using bits of reality. In L. Reder (Ed.) *Implicit memory and metacognition* (pp. 195–220). Mahwah, NJ: Erlbaum.

LOFTUS, E. F., & LOFTUS, G. R. (1980). On the permanence of stored information in the human brain. *American Psychologist, 35,* 409–420.

LOFTUS, E. F., LOFTUS, G. R., & MESSO, J. (1987). Some facts about "weapon focus." *Law and Human Behavior, 11,* 55–62.

LOFTUS, E. F., & PALMER, J. C. (1974). Reconstruction of automobile destruction. *Journal of Verbal Learning and Verbal Behavior, 13,* 585–589.

LOFTUS, E. F., & PICKRELL, J. E. (1995). The formation of false memories. *Psychiatric Annals, 25,* 720–725.

LOFTUS, E. F., SCHOOLER, J. W., & WAGENAAR, W. A. (1985). The fate of memory: Comment on McCloskey and Zaragoza. *Journal of Experimental Psychology: General, 114,* 375–380.

LOFTUS, G. R. (1972). Eye fixations and recognition memory for pictures. *Cognitive Psychology, 3,* 525–551.

LOFTUS, G. R., & IRWIN, D. E. (1998). On the relations among different measures of visible and informational persistence. *Cognitive Psychology, 35,* 135–199.

LOFTUS, G. R., & MACKWORTH, N. H. (1978). Cognitive determinants of fixation location during picture viewing. *Journal of Experimental Psychology: Human Perception and Performance, 4,* 565–572.

LOGUE, A. W. (1991). *The psychology of eating and drinking: An introduction* (2nd ed.). New York: Freeman.

LONG, P. W. (1996). *Internet mental health.* http://www.mentalhealth.com/

LONGLEY, J., & PRUITT, D. G. (1980). Groupthink: A critique of Janis's theory. In L. Wheeler (Ed.), *Review of personality and social psychology* (Vol. 1). Beverly Hills, CA: Sage.

LOOMIS, A. L., HARVEY, E. N., & HOBART, G. A. (1937). Cerebral states during sleep as studied by human potentials. *Journal of Experimental Psychology, 21,* 127–144.

LOPEZ, A., ATRAN, S., MEDIN, D. L., COOLEY, J., & SMITH, E. E. (1997). The tree of life: Universals of folk biological taxonomies and inductions. *Cognitive Psychology, 32,* 251–295.

LOPEZ, S. R., & GUARNACCIA, P. J. (2000). Cultural psychopathology: Uncovering the social world of mental illness. *Annual Review of Psychology, 51,* 571–598.

LORD, C. G. (1980). Schemas and images as memory aids: Two modes of processing social information. *Journal of Personality and Social Psychology, 38,* 257–269.

LORD, C. G., ROSS, L., & LEPPER, M. R. (1979). Biased assimilation and attitude polarization: The effects of prior theories on subsequently considered evidence. *Journal of Personality and Social Psychology, 37,* 2098–2109.

LORENZ, K. (1966). *On aggression.* New York: Harcourt Brace Jovanovich.

LOVE, R. E., & GREENWALD, A. C. (1978). Cognitive responses to persuasion as mediators of opinion change. *Journal of Social Psychology, 104,* 231–241.

LOVIBOND, P. F., SIDDLE, D. A. T., & BOND, N. W. (1993). Resistance to extinction of fear-relevant stimuli: Preparedness or selective sensitization? *Journal of Experimental Psychology: General, 122,* 449–461.

LUBINSKI, D. (2000). Scientific and social significance of assessing individual differences: "Sinking shafts at a few critical points." *Annual Reviews of Psychology, 51,* 405–444.

LUBORSKY, L. L., MCLELLAN, A. T., WOODY, G. E., O'BRIEN, E. P., & AUERBACH, A. (1985). Therapist success and its determinants. *Archives of General Psychiatry, 42,* 602–611.

LUBORSKY, L. L., SINGER, B., & LUBORSKY, L. (1975). Comparative studies of psychotherapies: Is it true that "everyone has won and all must have prizes"? *Archives of General Psychiatry, 32,* 995–1008.

LUCHINS, A. (1957). Primacy-recency in impression formation. In C. L. Hovland (Ed.), *The order of presentation in persuasion.* New Haven: Yale University Press.

LUNDIN, R. W. (1985). *Theories and systems of psychology* (3rd ed.). Lexington, MA: Heath.

LURIA, Z., & RUBIN, J. Z. (1974). The eye of the beholder: Parents' views on sex of newborns. *American Journal of Orthopsychiatry, 44,* 512–519.

LYKKEN, D. T. (1980). *Tremor in the blood: Uses and abuses of the lie detector.* New York: McGraw-Hill.

LYKKEN, D. T. (1982). Research with twins: The concept of emergenesis. *The Society for Psychophysiological Research, 19,* 361–373.

LYKKEN, D. T. (1984). Polygraphic interrogation. *Nature, 307,* 681–684.

LYKKEN, D. T., MCGUE, M., TELLEGEN, A., & BOUCHARD, T. J., JR. (1992). Emergenesis: Genetic traits that may not run in families. *American Psychologist, 47,* 1565–1577.

LYNN, S. J., KIRSCH, I., BARABASZ, A., CARDENA, E., & PATTERSON, D. (1999). Hypnosis as an empirically supported clinical intervention: The state of the evidence and a look to the future. *International Journal of Clinical and Experimental Hypnosis, 48,* 239–259.

LYNN, S. J., KIRSCH, I., BARABASZ, A., CARDENA, E., & PATTERSON, D. (1999). Hypnosis as an empirically supported clinical intervention: The state of the evidence and a look to the future. *International Journal of Clinical and Experimental Hypnosis, 48,* 239–259.

LYUBOMIRSKY, S., & NOLEN HOEKSEMA, S. (1995). Effects of self-focused rumination on negative thinking and interpersonal problem solving. *Journal of Personality and Social Psychology, 69,* 176–190.

MAAS, J. B. (1998). *Power sleep: The revolutionary program that prepares your mind for peak performance.* New York: HarperCollins.

MAASS, A., & CLARK, R. D., III (1984). Hidden impact of minorities: Fifteen years of minority influence research. *Psychological Bulletin, 95,* 428–450.

MACAULAY, J. (1970). A shill for charity. In J. Macaulay & L. Berkowitz (Eds.), *Altruism and helping behavior* (pp. 43–59). New York: Academic Press.

MACCOBY, E. (1998). *The two sexes.* Cambridge, MA: Harvard University Press.

MACCOBY, E. E. (1980). *Social development: Psychological growth and the parent-child relationship.* New York: Harcourt Brace Jovanovich.

MACCOBY, E. E., & JACKLIN, C. N. (1974). *The psychology of sex differences.* Stanford, CA: Stanford University Press.

MACKINNON, D., JAMISON, R., & DEPAULO, J. R. (1997). Genetics of manic depressive illness. *Annual Review of Neuroscience, 20,* 355–373.

MACLEAN, P. D. (1973). *A triune concept of the brain and behavior.* Toronto: Toronto University Press.

MACLEOD, C. M. (1991). Half a century of research on the Stroop effect: An integrative review. *Psychological Bulletin, 109,* 163–203.

MACMILLAN, M. B. (1996). *Freud evaluated: The completed arc.* Cambridge, MA: MIT Press.

MADDEN, D. R. (2002). The structure and function of glutamate receptor ion channels. *Nature Reviews Neuroscience, 3,* 91–101.

MAHER, B. A. (1966). *Principles of psychotherapy: An experimental approach.* New York: McGraw-Hill.

MAIER, S. F., & SELIGMAN, M. E. P. (1976). Learned helplessness: Theory and evidence. *Journal of Experimental Psychology: General, 105,* 3–46.

MAIN, M., & CASSIDY, J. (1988). Categories of response to reunion with parents at age 6: Predictable from infant attachment classifications and stable over a 1-month period. *Developmental Psychology, 24,* 415–426.

MAIN, M., & SOLOMON, J. (1986). Discovery of an insecure-disorganized/disoriented attachment pattern: Procedures, findings and implications for the classification of behavior. In T. B. Brazelton, & M. Yogman (Eds.), *Affective development in infancy* (pp. 95–124). Norwood, NJ: Ablex.

MAJ, M., PIROZZI, R., MAGLIANO, L., & BARTOLI, L. (1998). Long-term outcome of lithium prophylaxis in bipolar disorder: A 5-year prospective study of 402 patients at a lithium clinic. *American Journal of Psychiatry, 155,* 30–35.

MALINOW, R., OTMAKHOV, N., BLUM, K. I., & LISMAN, J. (1994). Visualizing hippocampal synaptic function by optical detection of $Ca2+$ entry through the N-methyl-D-aspartate channel. *Proceedings of the National Academy of Sciences of the United States of America, 91,* 8170–8174.

MALLE, B. F. (1999). How people explain behavior: A new theoretical framework. *Personality and Social Psychology Review, 3,* 23–48.

MALOF, M., & LOTT, A. J. (1962). Ethnocentrism and the acceptance of Negro support in a group pressure situation. *Journal of Abnormal and Social Psychology, 65,* 254–258.

MALONE, K., & MANN, J. J. (1993). Serotonin and major depression. In J. J. Mann & D. J. Kupfer (Eds.), *Biology of depressive disorders: Part A. A systems perspective* (pp. 29–49). New York: Plenum Press.

MALONEY, L. T., & WANDELL, B. A. (1986). Color constancy: A method for recovering surface spectral reflectance. *Journal of the Optical Society of America, 3,* 29–33.

MANDLER, J. (1983). Representation. In P. H. Mussen (Ed.), *Handbook of child psychology* (Vol. 3). New York: Wiley.

MANN, J. J., & ARANGO, V. (1999). The neurobiology of suicidal behavior. In D. G. Jacobs (Ed.), *The Harvard Medical School guide to suicide assessment and intervention.* San Francisco: Jossey-Bass.

MANN, J. J., BRENT, D. A., & ARANGO, V. (2001). The neurobiology and genetics of suicide and attempted suicide: a focus on the serotonergic system. *Neuropsychopharmacology, 24,* 467–477.

MANSON, S., BEALS, J., O'NELL, T., PIASECKI, J., BECHTOLD, D., KEANE, E., & JONES, M. (1996). Wounded spirits, ailing hearts: PTSD and related disorders among American Indians. In A. J. Marsella, M. J. Friedman, E. T. Gerrity, & R. M. Scurfield (Eds.), *Ethnocultural aspects of posttraumatic stress disorder* (pp. 255–283). Washington, DC: American Psychiatric Press.

MANSON, S. M., SHORE, J. H., BARON, A. E., ACKERSON, L., & NELIGH, G. (1992). Alcohol abuse and dependence among American Indians. In J. E. Helzer & G. J. Canino (Eds.), *Alcoholism in North America, Europe, and Asia* (pp. 113–127). New York: Oxford University Press.

MANUCK, S. B., KAPLAN, J. R., & MATTHEWS, K. A. (1986). Behavioral antecedents of coronary heart disease and atherosclerosis. *Arteriosclerosis, 6,* 1–14.

MAO, J., PRICE, D. D., & MAYER, D. J. (1995). Mechanism of hyperalgesia and morphine tolerance. Current review of their possible interactions. *Pain, 62,* 259–274.

MARBLY, N. (1987). But you weren't there. In T. Williams (Ed.), *Posttraumatic stress disorders: A handbook for clinicians.* Cincinnati, OH: Disabled American Veterans.

MARCIA, J. E. (1966). Development and validation of ego identify status. *Journal of Personality and Social Psychology, 3,* 551–558.

MARCIA, J. E. (1980). Identity in adolescence. In J. Adelson (Ed.), *Handbook of adolescent psychology.* New York: Wiley.

MARCUS, G. F. (1996). Why do children say "breaked"? *Current Directions in Psychological Science, 5,* 81–85.

MAREN, S. (2001). Neurobiology of Pavlovian fear conditioning, *Annual Review of Neuroscience, 24,* 897–931.

MAREN, S., & FANSELOW, M. S. (1996). The amygdala and fear conditioning: Has the nut been cracked? *Neuron, 16,* 237–240.

MARGOLIN, L., & WHITE, L. (1987). The continuing role of physical attractiveness in marriage. *Journal of Marriage and the Family, 49,* 21–27.

MARGRAF, J., BARLOW, D. H., CLARK, D. M., & TELCH, M. J. (1993). Psychological treatment of panic: Work in progress on outcome, active ingredients, and follow-up. *Behaviour Research & Therapy, 31,* 1–8.

MARKMAN, E. M. (1979). Classes and collections: Conceptual organization and numerical abilities. *Cognitive Psychology, 11,* 395–411.

MARKMAN, E. M. (1987). How children constrain the possible meanings of words. In U. Neisser (Ed.), *Concepts and conceptual development: Ecological and intellectual factors in categorizations.* New York: Cambridge University Press.

MARKOWITZ, J. C., & WEISSMAN, M. M. (1995). Interpersonal psychotherapy. In E. E. Beckham & W. R. Leber (Eds.), *Handbook of depression* (2nd ed.). New York: Guilford.

MARKUS, H. (1977). Self-schemata and processing information about the self. *Journal of Personality and Social Psychology, 35,* 63–78.

MARKUS, H., & NURIUS, P. (1986). Possible selves. *American Psychologist, 41,* 954–969.

MARKUS, H., & SENTIS, K. (1982). The self in social information processing. In J. Suls (Ed.), *Psychological perspectives on the self* (Vol. 1). Hillsdale, NJ: Erlbaum.

MARKUS, H., & SMITH, J. (1981). The influence of self-schema on the perception of others. In N. Cantor & J. F. Kihlstrom (Eds.), *Personality, cognition, and social interaction.* Hillsdale, NJ: Erlbaum.

MARKUS, H. R., & KITAYAMA, S. (1991). Culture and the self: Implication for cognition, emotion, and motivation. *Psychological Review, 98,* 224–253.

MARLATT, G. A., LARIMER, M. E., BAER, J. S., & QUIGLEY, L. A. (1993). Harm reduction for alcohol problems: Moving beyond the controlled drinking economy. *Behavior Therapy, 24,* 461–503.

MARR, D. (1982). *Vision.* San Francisco: Freeman.

MARSHALL, D. A., BLUMER, L., & MOULTON, D. G. (1981). Odor detection curves for n-pentanoic acid in dogs and humans. *Chemical Senses, 6,* 445–453.

MARSHALL, G., & ZIMBARDO, P. G. (1979). Affective consequences of inadequately explained physiological arousal. *Journal of Personality and Social Psychology, 37,* 970–988.

MARTIN, A., UNGERLEIDER, L., & HAXBY, J. V. (2000). Category specificity and the brain: The sensory/motor model of semantic representations of objects. In M. S. Gazzaniga (Ed.), *The new cognitive neurosciences* (pp. 1023–1036). Cambridge, MA: MIT Press.

MARTIN, N., BOOMSMA, D., & MACHIN, G. (1997). A twin-pronged attack on complex traits. *Nature Genetics, 17,* 387–392.

MARTINEZ, C. (1993). Psychiatric care of Mexican-Americans. In A. C. Gaw (Ed.), *Culture, ethnicity, and mental illness* (pp. 431–466). Washington, DC: American Psychiatric Association Press.

MARTINEZ-TABOAS, A. (1989). Preliminary observations on MPD in Puerto Rico. *Dissociation: Progress in the Dissociative Disorders, 2,* 128–131.

MARUCHA, P. T., KICOLT-GLASER, J. K., & FAV-AGEHI, M. (1998). Mucosal wound healing is impaired by examination stress. *Psychosomatic Medicine, 60,* 362–365.

MASLACH, C. (1979). The emotional consequences of arousal without reason. In Izard, C. E. (Ed.), *Emotion in personality and psychopathology.* New York: Plenum.

MASLACH, C., SCHAUFELI, W. B., & LEITER, M. P. (2001). Job burnout. *Annual Reviews of Psychology, 52,* 397–422.

MASLOW, A. H. (1970). *Motivation and personality* (2nd ed.). New York: Harper and Row.

MASSARO, D., & LOFTUS, G. R. (1996). Sensory storage: Icons and echoes. In E. L. Bjork & R. A. Bjork (Eds.), *Handbook of perception and cognition* (Vol. 10, pp. 68–101). New York: Academic Press.

MASSON, J. M. (1984). *The assault on truth.* New York: Farrar, Straus & Giroux.

MASTERS, W. H., & JOHNSON, V. E. (1966). *Human sexual response.* Boston: Little, Brown.

MASUDA, M., & HOLMES, T. H. (1978). Life events: Perceptions and frequencies. *Psychosomatic Medicine, 40,* 236–261.

MASUDA, T., & NISBETT, R. E. (2001). Attending holistically versus analytically: Comparing the context sensitivity of Japanese and Americans. *Journal of Personality and Social Psychology, 81,* 922–934.

MATAS, L., AREND, R. A., & SROUFE, L. A. (1978). Continuity of adaption in the second year: The relationship between quality of attachment and later competence. *Child Development, 49,* 547–556.

MATHES, E. W. (1975). The effects of physical attractiveness and anxiety on heterosexual attraction over a series of five encounters. *Journal of Marriage and the Family, 37,* 769–773.

MATTHEWS, D. F. (1972). Response patterns of single neurons in the tortoise olfactory epithelium and olfactory bulb. *Journal of General Physiology, 60,* 166–180.

MAYER, J. D., & SALOVEY, P. (1997). What is emotional? In P. Savoley & D. Sluyter (Eds.), *Emotional development and emotional intelligence: Implications for educators* (pp. 3–31.) New York: Basic Books.

MAYER, J. D., SALOVEY, P., & CARUSO, D. (2000). Models of emotional intelligence. In *Handbook of intelligence,* (pp. 396–420). Cambridge: Cambridge University Press.

MAYER, R. E. (1983). *Thinking, problem solving and cognition.* New York: Freeman.

MAZZONI, G., & LOFTUS, E. (1998). Dreaming, believing, and remembering. In J. de Rivera & T. R. Sarbin (Eds.), *Believed-in imaginings: The narrative construction of reality* (pp. 145–156). American Psychological Association. Washington, DC: American Psychological Association Press.

MCALISTER, A., PERRY, C., KILLEN, J., SLINKARD, L. A., & MACCOBY, N. (1980). Pilot study of smoking, alcohol and drug abuse prevention. *American Journal of Public Health, 70,* 719–721.

MCBRIDE, P., BROWN, R. P., DEMEO, M., & KEILP, J. (1994). The relationship of platelet 5-HT-sub-2 receptor indices to major depressive disorder, personality traits, and suicidal behavior. *Biological Psychiatry, 35,* 295–308.

MCBURNEY, D. H. (1978). Psychological dimensions and the perceptual analysis of taste. In E. C. Carterette & M. P. Friedman (Eds.), *Handbook of perception* (Vol. 6). New York: Academic Press.

MCCARTHY, R. A., & WARRINGTON, E. K. (1990). *Cognitive neuropsychology: A clinical introduction.* New York: Academic Press.

MCCAULEY, C. (1989). The nature of social influence in groupthink: Compliance and internalization. *Journal of Personality and Social Psychology, 57,* 250–260.

MCCLANAHAN, K. K., GOLD, J. A., LENNEY, E., RYCKMAN, R. M., & KULBERG, G. E. (1990). Infatuation and attraction to a dissimilar other: Why is love blind? *Journal of Social Psychology, 130,* 433–445.

MCCLELLAND, D. C. (1987). *Human motivation.* New York: Cambridge University Press.

MCCLELLAND, J. L., & RUMELHART, D. E. (1981). An interactive model of context effects in letter perception: Pt. 1. An account of basic findings. *Psychological Review, 88,* 375–407.

MCCLINTOCK, M. K. (1971). Menstrual synchrony and suppression. *Nature, 229,* 244–245.

MCCOLSKEY, M., WIBLE, C. G., & COHEN, N. J. (1988). Is there a flashbulb-memory system? *Journal of Experimental Psychology, 117,* 171–181.

MCCONAGHY, M. J. (1979). Gender permanence and the genital basis of gender. Stages in the development of constancy of gender identity. *Child Development, 50,* 1223–1226.

MCCRAE, R. R., & COSTA, P. T., JR. (1987). Validation of the five-factor model of personality across instruments and observers. *Journal of Personality and Social Psychology, 52,* 81–90.

MCCRAE, R. R., & COSTA, P. T., Jr. (1999). A five-factor theory of personality. In L. A. Pervin (Ed.), *Handbook of Personality: Theory and Research.* New York: Guilford.

MCDOUGALL, W. (1908). *Social psychology.* New York: Putnam.

MCELREE, B. DOSHER, B. A. (1989). Serial position and set size in short-term memory. The time course of recognition. *Journal of Experimental Psychology: General, 118,* 346–373.

MCEWEN, B. S. (1999). Allostasis and allostatic load: Implications for neuropsychopharmacology. *Neuropsychopharmacology, 22,* 108–124.

MCFARLAND, S. G., AGEYEV, V. S., & ABALAKINA-PAAP, M. A. (1992). Authoritarianism in the former Soviet Union. *Journal of Personality and Social Psychology, 63,* 1004–1010.

MCGHIE, A., & CHAPMAN, J. (1961). Disorders of attention and perception in early schizophrenia. *British Journal of Medical Psychology, 34,* 103–116.

MCGLASHAN, T. H. Omnipotence, helplessness, and control with the borderline patient. *American Journal of Psychotherapy, 37,* 49–61.

MCGRATH, E., KEITA, G. P., STRICKLAND, B. R., & RUSSO, N. F. (1990). *Women and depression: Risk factors and treatment issues.* Washington, DC: American Psychological Association.

MCGRAW, M. B. (1975). *Growth: A study of Johnny and Jimmy.* New York: Acno Press. (Originally published 1935).

MCGUFFIN, P. (2001). Toward behavioral genomics. *Science, 291,* 1232–1249.

MCGUFFIN, P., KATZ, R., & RUTHERFORD, J. (1991). Nature, nurture and depression: A twin study. *Psychological Medicine, 21,* 329–335.

MCGURK, H., & MACDONALD, J. (1976). Hearing lips and seeing voices. *Nature, 264,* 746–748.

MCHUGH, P. R. (1990). Clinical issues in food ingestion and body weight maintenance. In E. M. Stricker (Ed.), *Neurobiology of food and fluid intake* (pp. 531–547). New York: Plenum.

MCINTOSH, D. N., SILVER, R. C., & WORTMAN, C. B. (1993). Religion's role in adjustment to a negative life event: Coping with the loss of a child. *Journal of Personality and Social Psychology, 65,* 812–821.

MCINTOSH, J. L. (1991). Epidemiology of suicide in the United States. In A. A. Leenaars (Ed.), *Life span perspectives of suicide: Time-lines in the suicide process.* New York: Plenum.

MCKENNA, R. J. (1972). Some effects of anxiety level and food cues on the eating behavior of obese and normal subjects. *Journal of Personality and Social Psychology, 22,* 311–319.

MCNALLY, R. J. (1994). Choking phobia: A review of the literature. *Comprehensive Psychiatry, 35,* 83–89.

MCNALLY, R. J. (2001). The cognitive psychology of repressed and recovered memories of childhood sexual abuse: clinical implications. *Psychiatric Annals, 31,* 509–514.

MCNALLY, R. J. (2001). Vulnerability to anxiety disorders in adulthood. In *Vulnerability to psychopathology: Risk across the lifespan* (pp. 304–321). New York: Guilford.

MCNALLY, R. J., & REISS, S. (1984). The preparedness theory of phobias: The effects of initial fear level on safety signal conditioning to fear-relevant stimuli. *Psychophysiology, 21,* 647–652.

MCNEILL, D. (1966). Developmental psycholinguistics. In F. Smith & G. A. Miller (Eds.), *The genesis of language: A psycholinguistic approach.* Cambridge, MA: MIT Press.

MEANEY, M. J., AITKENS, D. H., BERKEL, C., BHATNAGAR, S., SARRIEAU, A., & SAPOLSKY, R. M. (1987). *Post-natal handling attenuates age-related changes in the adrenocortical stress response and spatial memory deficits in the rat.* Paper presented at the 17th Annual Meeting of the Society of Neuroscience, New Orleans.

MECHANIC, D. (1962). *Students under stress.* New York: Free Press.

MEDCOF, J., & ROTH, J. (Eds.). (1988). *Approaches to psychology.* Philadelphia: Open University Press, Milton Keynes.

MEDIN, D. L., & ROSS, B. H. (1992). *Cognitive psychology.* Fort Worth: Harcourt Brace.

MEDNICK, B., REZNICK, C., HOCEVAR, D., & BAKER, R. (1987). Long-term effects of parental divorce on young adult male crime. *Journal of Youth and Adolescence, 16,* 31–45.

MEDNICK, S. A., GABRIELLI, W. F., & HUTCHINGS, B. (1984). Genetic influences in criminal convictions: Evidence from an adoption cohort. *Science, 224,* 891–894.

MEEHL, P. E., & DAHLSTROM, W. G. (1960). Objective configural rules for discriminating psychotic from neurotic MMPI profiles. *Journal of Consulting Psychology, 24,* 375–387.

MEGARGEE, E. I. (1972). *The California psychological inventory handbook.* San Francisco: Jossey-Bass.

MEIER, R. P. (1991). Language acquisition by deaf children. *American Scientist, 79,* 60–76.

MELAMED, B. G., & SIEGEL, L. J. (1975). Reduction of anxiety in children facing hospitalization and surgery by use of filmed modeling. *Journal of Consulting and Clinical Psychiatry, 43,* 511–521.

MELTON, A. W. (1963). Implications of short-term memory for a general theory of memory. *Journal of Verbal Learning and Verbal Behavior, 1,* 1 21.

MELZAK, R. (1973). *The puzzle of pain.* New York: Basic Books.

MELZAK, R. (1990). The tragedy of needless pain. *Scientific American, 262,* 27–33.

MELZAK, R., & WALL, P. D. (1982, 1988). *The challenge of pain.* New York: Basic Books.

MENDOLA, R., TENNEN, H., AFFLECK, G., MCCANN, L., & FITZGERALD, R. (1990). Appraisal and adaptation among women with impaired fertility. *Cognitive Therapy and Research, 14,* 79–93.

MERVIS, C. B., & PANI, J. R. (1981). Acquisition of basic object categories. *Cognitive Psychology, 12,* 496–522.

MERVIS, C. B., & ROSCH, E. (1981). Categorization of natural objects. In M. R. Rosenz & L. W. Porter (Eds.), *Annual review of psychology* (Vol. 21). Palo Alto, CA: Annual Reviews.

MESQUITA, B. (2001). Emotions in collectivist and individualist contexts. *Journal of Personality and Social Psychology, 80,* 68–74.

MESQUITA, B., & FRIJDA, N. H. (1992). Cultural variations in emotions: A review. *Psychological Bulletin, 112,* 179–204.

MESSICK, S. (1992). Multiple intelligences or multilevel intelligence? Selective emphasis on distinctive properties of hierarchy: On Gardner's Frames of mind and Sternberg's Beyond IQ in the context of theory and research on the structure of human abilities. *Journal of Psychological Inquiry, 1,* 305–384.

METALSKY, G. I., HALBERSTADT, L. J., & ABRAMSON, L. Y. (1987). Vulnerability to depressive mood reactions: Toward a more powerful test of the diathesis-stress and causal meditation components of the reformulated theory of depression. *Journal of Personality and Social Psychology, 52,* 386–393.

METZNER, R. J. (1994, March 14). Prozac is medicine, not a miracle. *Los Angeles Times,* p. B7.

MEYER, J. P., & PEPPER, S. (1977). Need compatibility and marital adjustment in young married couples. *Journal of Personality and Social Psychology, 8,* 331–342.

MEZZACAPPA, E. S., KATKIN, E. S., & PALMER, S. N. (1999). Epinephrine, arousal, and emotion: A new look at two-factor theory. *Cognition and Emotion, 13,* 181–199.

MIDDLETON, F. A., & STRICK, P. L. (1994). Anatomic evidence for cerebellar and basal ganglia involvement in higher cognitive function. *Science, 266,* 458–463.

MIGNAULT, A (2001). Connectionist models of the perception of facial expressions of emotion. *Dissertation Abstracts International: Section B: The Sciences and Engineering.* 61, 6743.

MIGNOT, E. (1998). Genetic and familial aspects of narcolepsy. *Neurology, 50,* 16–22.

MILGRAM, S. (1963). Behavioral study of obedience. *Journal of Abnormal and Social Psychology, 67,* 371–378.

MILGRAM, S. (1974). *Obedience to authority: An experimental view.* New York: Harper & Row.

MILLAR, M. G., & TESSER, A. (1989). The effects of affective-cognitive consistency and thought on the attitude-behavior relation. *Journal of Experimental Social Psychology, 25,* 189–202.

MILLER, D. T., & ROSS, M. (1975). Self-serving biases in attribution of causality: Fact or fiction? *Psychological Bulletin, 82,* 213–225.

MILLER, E. K., & COHEN, J. D. (2001) An integrative theory of prefrontal cortex function. *Annual Review of Neuroscience, 24,* 167–202.

MILLER, G. A. (1956). The magical number seven plus or minus two: Some limits on our capacity for processing information. *Psychological Review, 63,* 81–97.

MILLER, G. A., & GILDEA, P. M. (1987). How children learn words. *Scientific American, 257,* 94–99.

MILLER, J. G. (1984). Culture and the development of everyday social explanation. *Journal of Personality and Social Psychology, 46,* 961–978.

MILLER, J. M., & SPELMAN, F. A. (1990). *Cochlear implants: Models of the electrically stimulated ear.* New York: Springer-Verlag.

MILLER, N. E., & KESSEN, M. L. (1952). Reward effects of food via stomach fistula compared with those of food via mouth. *Journal of Comparative and Physiological Psychology, 45,* 555–564.

MILLER, P. A., & EISENBERG, N. (1988). The relation of empathy to aggressive and externalizing/antisocial behavior. *Psychological Bulletin, 103,* 324–344.

MILLER, P. H. (1993). *Theories of developmental psychology* (3rd ed.). New York: Freeman.

MILLON, T. (1981). *Disorders of personality: DSM-III.* New York: Wiley.

MILLS, J. (1979). *Six years with God.* New York: A & W Publishers.

MILNER, B. (1970). Memory and the medial temporal regions of the brain. In K. H. Pribram & D. E. Broadbent (Eds.), *Biology of memory.* New York: Academic Press.

MILNER, B., CORKIN, S., & TEUBER, H. L. (1968). Further analysis of the hippocampal amnesic syndrome: 14-year follow-up study of H. M. *Neuropsychologia, 6,* 215–234.

MINARD, R. D. (1952). Race relations in the Pocahontas coal field. *Journal of Social Issues, 8,* 29–44.

MINEKA, S. (1987). A primate model of phobic fears. In H. Eysenck & I. Martin (Eds.), *Theoretical foundation of behavior therapy* (pp. 81–111). New York: Plenum.

MINEKA, S., DAVIDSON, M., COOK, M., & KEIR, R. (1984). Observational conditioning of snake fear in rhesus monkeys. *Journal of Abnormal Psychology, 93,* 355–372.

MINTZ, L. I., LIEBERMAN, R. P., MIKLOWITZ, D. J., & MINTZ, J. (1987). Expressed emotion: A call for partnership among relatives, patients, and professionals. *Schizophrenia Bulletin, 13,* 227–235.

MINUCHIN, S., ROSMAN, B. L., & BAKER, L. (1978). *Psychosomatic families: Anorexia nervosa in context.* Cambridge, MA: Harvard University Press.

MISCHEL, W. (1966). A social learning view of sex differences in behavior. In E. E. Maccoby (Ed.), *The development of sex differences*. Stanford, CA: Stanford University Press.

MISCHEL, W. (1973). Toward a cognitive social learning reconceptualization of personality. *Psychological Review, 80*, 272–283.

MISCHEL, W. (1993). *Introduction to personality* (5th ed.). Fort Worth: Harcourt Brace Jovanovich.

MISCHEL, W. (1999). Personality coherence and dispositions in a cognitive-affective personality (CAPS) approach. In *The coherence of personality: Social-cognitive bases of consistency, variability, and organization* (pp. 37–60). New York: Guilford.

MISCHEL, W., & SHODA, Y. (1999). Integrating dispositions and processing dynamics within a unified theory of personality: The cognitive-affective personality system. In *Handbook of personality: Theory and research* (2nd ed.; pp. 197–218.). New York: Guilford.

MISHKIN, M., UNGERLEIDER, L. G., & MACKO, K. A. (1983). Object vision and spatial vision: Two cortical pathways. *Trends in Neuroscience, 6*, 414–417.

MITA, T. H., DERMER, M., & KNIGHT, J. (1977). Reversed facial images and the mere-exposure hypotheses. *Journal of Personality and Social Psychology, 35*, 597–601.

MITCHELL, J. E., & DEZWAAN, M. (1993). Pharmacological treatments of binge eating. In C. E. Fairburn & G. T. Wilson (Eds.), *Binge eating: Nature, assessment, and treatment*. New York: Guilford.

MIYAHARA, E., POKORNY, J., & SMITH, V. C. (1996). Increment threshold and purity discrimination spectral sensitivities of x chromosome linked color defective observers culprit. *Vision Research, 36*, 1597–1613.

MOFFITT, T. E. (1990). Juvenile delinquency and attention deficit disorder: Boys' development trajectories from age 3 to age 15. *Child Development, 61*, 893–910.

MOFFITT, T. E. (1993). The neuropsychology of conduct disorder. *Development and Psychopathology, 5*, 135–151.

MOFFITT, T. E., BRAMMER, G. L., CASPI, A., FAWCET, J. P., RALEIGH, M., YUWILER, A, & SILVA, P. A. (1998). Whole blood serotonin relates to violence in an epidemiological study. *Biological Psychiatry, 43*, 446–457.

MONAHAN, J. (1992). Mental disorder and violent behavior: Perceptions and evidence. *American Psychologist, 47*, 511–521.

MONAHAN, J. (2001). Major mental disorder and violence: Epidemiology and risk assessment. In G. Pinard & L. Pagani (Eds.) *Clinical assessment of dangerousness*. New York: Cambridge University Press.

MONAHAN, J., & WALKER, L. (1990). *Social science in law: Cases and materials*. Westbury, NY: Foundation Press.

MONEY, J. (1980). Endocrine influences and psychosexual status spanning the life cycle. In H. M. Van Praag (Ed.), *Handbook of biological psychiatry* (Part 3). New York: Marcel Dekker.

MONEY, J. (1987). Sin, sickness, or status? Homosexual gender identity and psychoneuroendocrinology. *American Psychologist, 42*, 384–400.

MONEY, J. (1988). *Gay, straight, and in-between: The sexology of erotic orientation*. New York: Oxford University Press.

MONEY, J., & EHRHARDT, A. A. (1972). *Man and woman, boy and girl: The differentiation and dimorphism of gender identity from conception to maturity*. Baltimore: Johns Hopkins University Press.

MONEY, J., SCHWARTZ, M., & LEWIS, V. G. (1984). Adult heterosexual status and fetal hormonal masculinization and demasculinization: 46, XX congenital virilizing adrenal hyperplasia and 46, XY androgen-insensitivity syndrome compared. *Psychoneuroendocrinology, 9*, 405–414.

MONEY, J., WEIDEKING, C., WALKER, P. A., & GAIN, D. (1976). Combined antiandrogenic and counseling programs for treatment for 46 XY and 47 XXY sex offenders. In E. Sacher (Ed.), *Hormones, behavior and psychopathology*. New York: Raven Press.

MONMANEY, T. (1998, August 31). Labels' potency claims often inaccurate, analysis finds. *Los Angeles Times*, p. A10.

MONSELL, S. (1979). Recency, immediate recognition memory, and reaction time. *Cognitive Psychology, 10*, 465–501.

MOORE, B. C. J. (1982). *An introduction to the psychology of hearing* (2nd ed.). New York: Academic Press.

MOOS, R. H. (1988). *Coping responses inventory manual*. Palo Alto, CA: Social Ecology Laboratory, Department of Psychiatry, Stanford University and Veterans Administration Medical Centers.

MORAN, J., & DESIMONE, R. (1985). Selective attention gates visual processing in the extrastriate cortex. *Science, 229*, 782–784.

MORAY, N. (1969a). Attention in dichotic listening: Affective cues and the influence of attention. *Quarterly Journal of Experimental Psychology, 11*, 56–60.

MORAY, N. (1969b). *Attention: Selective processes in vision and hearing*. London: Hutchinson.

MORELAND, R. L., & BEACH, S. R. (1992). Exposure effects in the classroom: The development of affinity among students. *Journal of Experimental Social Psychology, 28*, 255–276.

MORELAND, R. L., & ZAJONC, R. B. (1979). Exposure effects may not depend on stimulus recognition. *Journal of Personality and Social Psychology, 37*, 1085–1089.

MOREY, L. C. (1993). Psychological correlates of personality disorder. *Journal of Personality Disorders (suppl.)*, 149–166.

MORGENSTERN, H., & GLAZER, W. M. (1993). Identifying risk factors for tardive dyskinesia among long-term outpatients maintained with neuroleptic medications: Results of the Yale tardive dyskinesia study. *Archives of General Psychiatry, 50*, 723–733.

MORRIS, M. W., & PENG, K. (1994). Culture and cause: American and Chinese attributions for social and physical events. *Journal of Personality and Social Psychology, 67*, 949–971.

MOSCOVICI, S. (1976). *Social influence and social change*. London: Academic Press.

MOSCOVICI, S., LAGE, E., & NAFFRECHOUX, M. (1969). Influence of a consistent minority on the responses of a majority in a color perception task. *Sociometry, 32*, 365–379.

MOSCOVICI, S., & ZAVALLONI, M. (1969). The group as a polarizer of attitudes. *Journal of Personality and Social Psychology, 12*, 125–135.

MOSKOWITZ, H. R., KUMRAICH, V., SHARMA, H., JACOBS, L., & SHARMA, S. D. (1975). Cross-cultural difference in simple taste preference. *Science, 190*, 1217–1218.

MOVSHON, J. A., & VAN SLUYTERS, R. C. (1981). Visual neural development. *Annual Review of Psychology, 32*, 477–522.

MOWRER, O. H. (1947). On the dual nature of learning: A reinterpretation of "conditioning" and "problem-solving." *Harvard Educational Review, 17*, 102–148.

MOYER, K. E. (1976). *The psychobiology of aggression*. New York: Harper & Row.

MUKHERJEE, S., SHUKLA, S., WOODLE, J., ROSEN, A. M., & OLARTE, S. (1983). Misdiagnosis of schizophrenia in bipolar patients: A multi-ethnic comparison. *American Journal of Psychiatry, 140*, 1571–1574.

MUKHOPADHYAY, P., & TURNER, R. M. (1997). Biofeedback treatment of essential hypertension. *Social Science International, 13*, 1–9.

MURAVEN, M., TICE, D. M., & BAUMEISTER, R. F. (1998). Self-control as a limited resource: Regulatory depletion patterns. *Journal of Personality and Social Psychology, 74*, 774–789.

MURDOCK, B. B., JR. (1962). The serial position effect in free recall. *Journal of Experimental Psychology, 64*, 482–488.

MURPHY, G. L., & BROWNELL, H. H. (1985). Category differentiation in object recognition: Typicality constraints on the basic category advantage. *Journal of Experimental Psychology, 11*, 70.

MURSTEIN, B. I. (1972). Physical attractiveness and marital choice. *Journal of Personality and Social Psychology, 22*, 8–12.

MUSSEN, P. H. (Ed.) (1983). *Handbook of child psychology* (4th ed.). New York: Wiley.

MYERS, D. G. (1993). *Social psychology* (4th ed.). New York: McGraw-Hill.

MYERS, D. G., & LAMM, H. (1976). The group polarization phenomenon. *Psychological Bulletin, 83*, 602–627.

NACOSTE, R. W. (1987). But do they care about fairness? The dynamics of preferential treatment and minority interest. *Basic and Applied Social Psychology, 8*, 117–191.

NARROW, W. E., REGIER, D. A., RAE, D., MANDERSCHEID, R. W., & LOCKE, B. Z. (1993). Use of services by persons with mental and addictive disorders. *Archives of General Psychiatry, 50*, 95–107.

NASAR, S. (1998). *A beautiful mind*. New York: Simon & Schuster.

NATHANS, J. (1987). Molecular biology of visual pigments. *Annual Review of Neuroscience, 10*, 163–164.

NATIONAL INSTITUTE OF MENTAL HEALTH. (2000). *Suicide facts*. Washington DC: Author. Retrieved January 26, 2000 from the World Wide Web: http://www.nimh.nih.gov/genpop/su_fact.htm.

NATIONAL INSTITUTE ON DRUG ABUSE. (2002). 2001 *Monitoring the future survey released*. www.nida.nih.gov/MedAQdv/00/HHS12-14.html.

NEISSER, U. (Ed.). (1982). *Memory observed: Remembering in natural contexts*. New York: Freeman.

NEISSER, U., & HARSCH, N. (1993). Phantom flashbulbs: False recollections of hearing the news about *Challenger*. In E. Winograd & U. Neisser (Eds.), *Affect and accuracy in recall: Studies of "flashbulb" memories* (pp. 9–31). Cambridge: Cambridge University Press.

NELSON, C. B., & WITTCHEN, H. (1998). DSM-IV alcohol disorders in a general population sample of adolescents and young adults. *Addiction, 93*, 1065–1077.

NELSON, R. J., & CHIAVEGATTO, S. (2001). Molecular basis of aggression. *Trends in Neurosciences, 24*, 713–719.

NEMETH, C. (1986). Differential contributions of majority and minority influence. *Psychological Review, 93*, 23–32.

NESTADT, G., SAMUELS, J., RIDDLE, M., BIENVENU, J., LABUDA, M., GRADOS, M., &

HOEHN-SARIC, R. (2000). A family study of obsessive-compulsive disorder. *Archives of General Psychiatry, 57,* 358–363.

NEW YORK TIMES/CBS NEWS POLL. (1999, October 20). Teen-ager's concerns. *New York Times,* A1.

NEUMANN, R. (2000). The causal influence of attributions on emotions. A procedural priming approach. *Psychological Science, 11,* 179–182.

NEWCOMB, M. D., RABOW, J., & HERNANDEZ, A. C. R. (1992). A cross-national study of nuclear attitudes, normative support, and activist behavior: Additive and interactive effects. *Journal of Applied Social Psychology, 22,* 780–200.

NEWCOMB, T. M. (1943). *Personality and social change.* New York: Dryden Press.

NEWCOMB, T. M. (1961). *The acquaintance process.* New York: Holt, Rinehart & Winston.

NEWCOMB, T. M., KOENING, K. E., FLACKS, R., & WARWICK, D. P. (1967). *Persistence and change: Bennington College and its students after twenty-five years.* New York: Wiley.

NEWELL, A., & SIMON, H. A. (1972). *Human problem solving.* Englewood Cliffs, NJ: Prentice-Hall.

NEWMAN, D. L., TELLEGEN, A., & BOUCHARD, T. J., Jr. (1998). Individual differences in adult ego development: Sources of influence in twins reared apart. *Journal of Personality and Social Psychology, 74,* 985–995.

NEWPORT, E. L. (1990). Maturational constraints on language learning. *Cognitive Science, 14,* 11–28.

NEZU, A. M., NEZU, C. M., & PERRI, M. G. (1989). *Problem-solving therapy for depression: Theory, research, and clinical guidelines.* New York: Wiley.

NICHD Early Child Care Research Network. (1996). Characteristics of infant child care: Factors contributing to positive caregiving. *Early Childhood Research Quarterly, 11,* 296–307.

NICHD Early Child Care Research Network (1997). Familial factors associated with the characteristics of nonmaternal care for infants. *Journal of Marriage and the Family, 59,* 389–408.

NICHD Early Child Care Research Network. (1998). Early child-parent self-control, compliance, and problem behavior at 24 to 36 months. *Child Development, 69,* 1145–1170.

NIELSON, T., & POWELL, R. (1992). The day-residue and dream-lag effect. *Dreaming, 2,* 67–77.

NILSON, D. C., NILSON, L. B., OLSON, R. S., & MCALLISTER, B. H. (1981). *The planning environment report for the Southern California Earthquake Safety Advisory Board.* Redlands, CA: Social Research Advisory & Policy Research Center.

NISAN, M., & KOHLBERG, L. (1982). Universality and variation in moral judgment: A longitudinal and cross-sectional study in Turkey. *Child Development, 53,* 865–876.

NISBETT, R. E., & ROSS, L. (1980). *Human inference: Strategies and shortcomings of social judgment.* Englewood Cliffs, NJ: Prentice-Hall.

NISBETT, R. E., & WILSON, T. D. (1977). Telling more than we can know: Verbal reports on mental processes. *Psychological Review, 84,* 231–259.

NISBETT, R. E., KRANZ, D. H., JEPSON, D., & KUNDA, Z. (1983). The use of statistical heuristics in everyday inductive reasoning. *Psychological Review, 90,* 339–363.

NISBETT, R. E., PENG, K., CHOI, I., & NORENZAYAN, A. (2001). Culture and systems of thought: Holistic versus analytic cognition. *Psychology Review, 108,* 291–310.

NOLEN-HOEKSEMA, S. (1991). Responses to depression and their effects on the duration of depressive episodes. *Journal of Abnormal Psychology, 100,* 569–582.

NOLEN-HOEKSEMA, S. (2002). Gender differences in depression. In I. H. Gotlib & C. L. Hammen (Eds.), *Handbook of depression.* New York: Guilford.

NOLEN-HOEKSEMA, S., & LARSON, J. (1999). *Coping with loss.* Mahwah, NJ: Erlbaum.

NOLEN-HOEKSEMA, S., & MORROW, J. (1991). A prospective study of depression and distress following a natural disaster: The 1989 Loma Prieta earthquake. *Journal of Personality and Social Psychology, 61,* 105–121.

NORENZAYAN, A., & NISBETT, R. E. (2000). Culture and causal cognition. *Current Directions in Psychological Science, 9,* 132–135.

NORMAN, R. (1975). Affective-cognitive consistency, attitudes, conformity, and behavior. *Journal of Personality and Social Psychology, 32,* 83–91.

NORTH, C. (1987). *Welcome silence.* New York: Simon and Schuster.

NOSOFSKY, R. M., & JOHANSEN, M. K. (2000). Exemplar-based accounts of "multiple-system" phenomena in perceptual categorization. *Psychonomic Bulletin and Review, 7,* 375–402.

NUCCLI, L. (1981). The development of personal concepts: A domain distinct from moral or societal concepts. *Child Development, 52,* 114–121.

OATLEY, K., & JENKINS, J. M. (1996). *Understanding emotions.* Cambridge, MA: Blackwell.

OFFIR, C. (1982). *Human sexuality.* San Diego: Harcourt Brace Jovanovich.

OFSHE, R. (1992). Inadvertent hypnosis during interrogation: False confessions to dissociative state; misidentified multiple personality and the satanic cult hypothesis. *International Journal of Clinical and Experimental Hypnosis, 40,* 125–156.

OFSHE, R., & WATTERS, E. (1994). *Making monsters: false memories, psychotherapy, and sexual hysteria.* New York: Charles Scribner's Sons.

OHMAN, A. (1986). Face the beast and fear the face: Animal and social fears as prototypes for evolutionary analyses of emotion. *Psychophysiology, 23,* 123–145.

OHMAN, A. (2000). Fear and anxiety: Evolutionary, cognitive, and clinical perspectives. In M. Lewis & J. M. Haviland-Jones (Eds.), *Handbook of emotions* (2nd ed., pp. 573–593). New York: Guilford.

OJEMANN, G. (1983). Brain organization for language from the perspective of electrical stimulation mapping. *Behavioral and Brain Sciences, 6,* 189–230.

OLLENDICK, T. H., & KING, N. J. (1998). Empirically validated treatments in clinical psychology. *Australian Psychologist, 33,* 89–95.

OLLENDICK, T. H., & KING, N. J. (2000). Empirically supported treatments for children and adolescents. In *Child & adolescent therapy: Cognitive-behavioral procedures* (2nd ed.), New York: Guilford.

OLSEN, G., & SHERMAN, T. (1983). Attention, learning and memory in infants. In P. H. Mussen (Series Ed.), M. M. Haith & J. J. Campos (Eds.), *Handbook of child psychology: Vol. 2. Infancy and developmental psychobiology* (4th ed., pp. 1001–1080). New York: Wiley.

OLSHO, L. W. et al. (1982). Auditory frequency discrimination in infancy. *Developmental Psychology, 18,* 721–726.

OLTON, D. S. (1978). Characteristics of spatial memory. In S. H. Hulse, H. F. Fowler, & W. K. Honig (Eds.), *Cognitive processes in animal behavior.* Hillsdale, NJ: Erlbaum.

OLTON, D. S. (1979). Mazes, maps, and memory. *American Psychologist, 34,* 583–596.

OLWEUS, D. (1969). *Prediction of aggression.* Stockholm: Scandinavian Test Corporation.

OLWEUS, D., MATTSSON, A., SCHALLING, D., & LOW, H. (1988). Circulating testosterone levels and aggression in adolescent males: A causal analysis. *Psychosomatic Medicine, 50,* 261–272.

OMAN, D., & REED, D. (1998). Religion and mortality among the community dwelling elderly. *American Journal of Public Health, 88,* 1469–1475.

ORLINSKY, D. E., & HOWARD, K. I. (1987). A generic model of psychotherapy. *Journal of Integrative and Eclectic Psychotherapy, 6,* 6–27.

ORNE, M. T., & HOLLAND, C. C. (1968). On the ecological validity of laboratory deceptions. *International Journal of Psychiatry, 6,* 282–293.

OSHEROW, N. (1984). Making sense of the nonsensical: An analysis of Jonestown. In E. Aronson (Ed.), *Readings about the social animal* (4th ed., pp. 68–86). New York: Freeman.

OSHERSON, D., PERANI, D., CAPPA, S., SCHNUR, T., GRASSI, F., & FAZIO, F. (1998). Distinct brain loci in deductive versus probabilistic reasoning. *Neuropsychologia, 36,* 369–376.

OSHERSON, D. N., KOSLYN, S. M., & HOLLERBACH, J. M. (1990). *An invitation to cognitive science* (Vol. 2). Cambridge, MA: MIT Press.

OSHERSON, D. N., & LASNIK, H. (1990). *An invitation to cognitive science* (Vol. 1). Cambridge, MA: MIT Press.

OSHERSON, D. N., & SMITH, E. E. (1990). *An invitation to cognitive science* (Vol. 3). Cambridge, MA: MIT Press.

OSHERSON, D. N., SMITH, E. E., WILKIE, O., LOPEZ, A., & SHAFIR, E. B. (1990). Category based induction. *Psychological Review, 97,* 185–200.

OSOFSKY, J. D. (Ed.) (1987). *Handbook of infant development* (2nd ed.). New York: Wiley.

OVERMEIER, J. B., & SELIGMAN, M. E. P. (1967). Effects of inescapable shock upon subsequent escape and avoidance responding. *Journal of Comparative and Physiological Psychology, 63,* 28.

OVERMIER, J. B., & MURRISON, R. (1998). Animal models reveal the "psych" in the psychosomatics of peptic ulcers. *Current Directions I Psychological Science, 6,* 180–184.

OZER, D. J., & REISE, S. P. (1994). Personality assessment. *Annual Review of Psychology, 45,* 357–388.

PAFFENBERGER, R. S., HYDE, R. T., WING, A. L., & HSIEH, C. (1986). Physical activity, all-cause mortality, and longevity of college alumni. *New England Journal of Medicine, 314,* 605–613.

PAICHELER, G. (1977). Norms and attitude change: Pt. 1. Polarization and styles of behavior. *European Journal of Social Psychology, 7,* 5–14.

PALLIS, C. A. (1955). Impaired identification of faces and places with agnosia for colors. *Journal of Neurology, Neurosurgery, and Psychiatry, 18,* 218–224.

PALMER, J., VERGHESE, P., & PAVEL, M. (2000). The psychophysics of visual search. *Vision Research, 40,* 1227–1268.

PALMER, S. E. (1975). The effect of contextual scenes on the identification of objects. *Memory and Cognition, 3,* 519–526.

PANKSEPP, J. (1998). *Affective neuroscience: The foundations of human and animal emotions.* New York: Oxford University Press.

PARKER, G., & HADZZI-PAVLOVIC, D. (1990). Expressed emotion as a predictor for schizophrenic relapse: An analysis of aggregated data. *Psychological Medicine, 20,* 961–965.

PARKER, G., JOHNSTON, P., & HAYWARD, L. (1988). Parental "expressed emotion" as a predictor of schizophrenic relapse. *Archives of General Psychiatry, 45,* 806–813.

PARKINSON, B., & MANSTEAD, A. S. R. (1992). Appraisal as the cause of emotion. In M. S. Clark (Ed.), *Review of personality and social psychology* (Vol. 13, pp. 122–149). Newbury Park, CA: Sage.

PARKINSON, B., & TOTTERDELL, P. (1999). Classifying affect-regulation strategies. *Cognition and Emotion, 13,* 277–303.

PASHLER, H. (2001). *Semantic oddities draw early saccades.* Talk presented at the meetings of the Psychonomics Society, Orlando.

PASUPATHI, M. (1999). Age differences in responses to conformity pressure for emotional and nonemotional material. *Psychology and Aging, 14,* 170–174.

PASZTOR, A. (1996, July 1). An air-safety battle brews over the issue of pilots' rest time. *Wall Street Journal.*

PATALANO, A. L., SMITH, E. E., JONIDES, J., & KOEPPE, R. A. (2002). PET evidence for multiple strategies of categorization. *Cognitive, Affective, and Behavioral Neuroscience, 1,* 360–370.

PATEL, V. L., & GROEN, G. J. (1986). Knowledge based solution strategies in medical reasoning. *Cognitive Science, 10,* 91.

PATTERSON, F. G. (1978). The gestures of a gorilla: Language acquisition in another pongid. *Brain and Language, 5,* 72–97.

PATTERSON, F. G., & LINDEN, E. (1981). *The education of Koko.* New York: Holt, Rinehart & Winston.

PATTERSON, G. (1974). Intervention for boys with conduct problems: Multiple settings, treatment, and criteria. *Journal of Consulting and Clinical Psychology, 42,* 471–483.

PATTERSON, G. R., DEBARSHYE, B. D., & RAMSEY, E. (1989). A developmental perspective on antisocial behavior. *American Psychologist, 44,* 329–335.

PATTERSON, G. R., LITTMAN, R. A., & BRICKER, W. A. (1967). Assertive behavior in children: A step toward a theory of aggression. *Monographs of the Society for Research in Child Development* (Serial No. 113), 5.

PATTERSON, G. R., REID, J. B., & DISHION, T. J. (1992). *Antisocial boys.* Eugene, OR: Castalia Press.

PAUL, G. L. (1967). Insight versus desensitization in psychotherapy two years after termination. *Journal of Consulting Psychology, 31,* 333–348.

PAUL, G. L., & LENTZ, R. J. (1977). *Psycho-social treatment of chronic mental patients: milieu versus social learning programs.* Cambridge, MA: Harvard University Press.

PAULHUS, D. (1982). Individual differences, self-presentation, and cognitive dissonance: Their concurrent operation in forced compliance. *Journal of Personality and Social Psychology, 43,* 838–852.

PAULUS, P. B. (1998). Developing consensus about groupthink after all these years. *Organizational Behavior and Human Decision Processes, 73,* 362–374.

PAULUS, P. B., & MURDOCK, P. (1971). Anticipated evaluation and audience presence in the enhancement of dominant responses. *Journal of Experimental Social Psychology, 7,* 280–291.

PAVLOV, I. P. (1927). *Conditioned reflexes.* New York: Oxford University Press.

PECHURA, C. M., & MARTIN, J. B. (Eds.). (1991). *Mapping the brain and its functions.* Washington, DC: National Academy Press.

PEDERSEN, N. L., PLOMIN, R., MCCLEARN, G. E., & FRIBERG, L. (1988). Neuroticism, extraversion and related traits in adult twins reared apart and reared together. *Journal of Personality and Social Psychology, 55,* 905–957.

PEELE, S. (1988). Fools for love: The romantic ideal, psychological theory, and addictive love. In R. J. Sternberg & M. L. Barnes (Eds.), *The psychology of love* (pp. 159–188). New Haven, CT: Yale University Press.

PELHAM, W. E., & BENDER, M. E. (1982). Peer relationships in hyperactive children. In K. Gadow & I. Bialer (Eds.), *Advances in learning and behavioral disabilities* (vol. 1, pp. 365–436). Greenwich, CT: JAI Press.

PELLEGRINO, J. W. (1985). Inductive reasoning ability. In R. J. Sternberg (Ed.), *Human abilities: An information-processing approach.* New York: Freeman.

PENDRY, L., & CARRICK, R. (2001). Doing what the mob do: Priming effects on conformity. *European Journal of Social Psychology, 31,* 83–92.

PENG, K., & NISBETT, R. E. (1999). Naive dialecticism and its effects on reasoning and judgment about contradiction. *American Psychologist, 54,* 741–754.

PENNEBAKER, J. W. (1990). *Opening up: The healing power of confiding in others.* New York: William Morrow.

PENNEBAKER, J. W. (1997a). *Opening up: The healing power of expressing emotions* (rev. ed.). New York: Guilford.

PENNEBAKER, J. W. (1997b). Writing about emotional experiences as a therapeutic process. *Psychological Science, 8,* 162–167.

PENNEBAKER, J. W., KIECOLT-GLASER, J. K., & GLASER, R. (1988). Disclosure of traumas and immune function: Health implications for psychotherapy. *Journal of Consulting and Clinical Psychology, 56,* 239–245.

PENNEBAKER, J. W., & O'HEERON, R. C. (1984). Confiding in others and illness rates among spouses of suicide and accidental-death victims. *Journal of Abnormal Psychology, 93,* 473–476.

PENROD, S., & CUTLER, B. (1995). Witness confidence and witness accuracy: Assessing their forensic relation. Special Issue: Witness memory and law. *Psychology, Public Policy, & Law, 1,* 817–845.

PEPLAU, L. A., RUBIN, Z., & HILL, C. T. (1977). Sexual intimacy in dating relationships. *Journal of Social Issues, 33,* 86–109.

PERKINS, K. A., & STITZER, M. (1998). Behavioral pharmacology of nicotine. In R. E. Tarter (Ed.), *Handbook of substance abuse: Neurobehavioral pharmacology.* (pp. 299–317). New York: Plenum.

PERRIN, F. A. C. (1921). Physical attractiveness and repulsiveness. *Journal of Experimental Psychology, 4,* 203–217.

PERRY, D. G., & BUSSEY, K. (1984). *Social development.* Englewood Cliffs, NJ: Prentice-Hall.

PERRY, D. G., PERRY, L. C., & BOLDIZAR, J. P. (1990). Learning of aggression. In M. Lewis & S. Miller (Eds.), *Handbook of developmental psychopathology* (pp. 135–146). New York: Plenum.

PERRY, J. C. (1993). Longitudinal studies of personality disorders. *Journal of Personality Disorders, 1* (Suppl.), 63–85.

PETERSEN, A. C. (1989). Adolescent development. In M. R. Rosenzweig & L. W. Porter (Eds.), *Annual review of psychology* (Vol. 39). Palo Alto, CA: Annual Reviews.

PETERSON, C. (1995). *Explanatory style.* Hillsdale, NJ: Erlbaum.

PETERSON, C., & BOSSIO, L. M. (2001). Optimism and physical well-being. In *Optimism and pessimism: Implications for theory, research and practice.* Washington, DC: American Psychological Association.

PETERSON, C., & SELIGMAN, M. E. P. (1984). Causal explanations as a risk factor for depression: Theory and evidence. *Psychological Review, 91,* 347–374.

PETERSON, C., SELIGMAN, M. E., VAILLANT, G. E. (1988). Pessimistic explanatory style is a risk factor for physical illness: A thirty-five-year longitudinal study. *Journal of Personality & Social Psychology, 55,* 23–27.

PETRIE, K. J., BOOTH, R. J., & PENNEBAKER, J. W. (1998). The immunological effects of thought suppression. *Journal of Personality and Social Psychology, 75,* 1264–1272.

PETTIGREW, T. F. (1959). Regional differences in anti-Negro prejudice. *Journal of Abnormal and Social Psychology, 59,* 28–36.

PETTIGREW, T. F. (1979). The ultimate attribution error: Extending Allport's cognitive analysis of prejudice. *Personality and Social Psychology Bulletin, 5,* 461–476.

PETTY, R. E., & CACIOPPO, J. T. (1981). *Attitudes and persuasion: Classic and contemporary approaches.* Dubuque, IA: Wm. C. Brown.

PETTY, R. E., & CACIOPPO, J. T. (1984). The effects of involvement on responses to argument quantity and quality: Central and peripheral routes to persuasion. *Journal of Personality and Social Psychology, 46,* 69–81.

PETTY, R. E., & CACIOPPO, J. T. (1986). Elaboration likelihood model of persuasion. In L. Berkowitz (Ed.), *Advances in experimental social psychology* (Vol. 19, pp. 123–205). New York: Academic Press.

PETTY, R. E., CACIOPPO, J. T., & GOLDMAN, R. (1981). Personal involvement as a determinant of argument-based persuasion. *Journal of Personality and Social Psychology, 41,* 847–855.

PETTY, R. E., OSTROM, T. M., & BROCK, T. C. (1981). Historical foundations of the cognitive response approach to attitudes and persuasion. In R. E. Petty, T. M. Ostrom, & T. C. Brock (Eds.), *Cognitive responses in persuasion.* Hillsdale, NJ: Erlbaum.

PETTY, R. E., & WEGENER, D. T. (1999). The elaboration likelihood model: Current status and controversies. In S. Chaiken & Y. Trope (Eds.), *Dual-process theories in social psychology* (pp. 41–72). New York: Guilford.

PEZDEK, K., FINGER, K., & HODGE, D. (1997). Planting false childhood memories: The role of event plausibility. *Psychological Science, 8,* 437–441.

PHILLIPS, D. A., MCCARTNEY, K., & SCARR, S. (1987). Child-care quality and children's social development. *Developmental Psychology, 23,* 537–543.

PHILLIPS, D. A., VORAN, M., KISKER, E., HOWES, C., & WHITEBROOK, M. (1994). Child care for children in poverty: Opportunity or inequity? *Child Development, 65,* 472–492.

PHILLIPS, J. L., JR. (1981). *Piaget's theory: A primer.* San Francisco: Freeman.

PHILLIPS, J. L., JR. (1992). *How to think about statistics* (rev. ed.). New York: Freeman.

PHINNEY, J. S., & ALIPURIA, L. L. (1990). Ethnic identity in college students form four ethnic groups. *Journal of Adolescence, 13,* 171–183.

PHOENIX, C. H., GOY, R. H., & RESKO, J. A. (1968). Psychosexual differentiation as a function of androgenic stimulation. In M. Diamond (Ed.), *Reproduction and sexual behavior.* Bloomington: Indiana University Press.

PIAGET, J. (1932/1965). *The moral judgment of the child.* New York: Free Press.

PIAGET, J. (1950a). *The origins of intelligence in children.* New York: International Universities Press.

PIAGET, J. (1950b). *The psychology of intelligence.* New York: International Universities Press.

PIAGET, J., & INHELDER, B. (1956). *The child's conception of space.* London: Routledge & Kegan Paul. (originally published 1948)

PIAGET, J., & INHELDER, B. (1969). *The psychology of the child.* New York: Basic Books.

PICCIONE, C., HILGARD, E. R., & ZIMBARDO, P. G. (1989). On the degree of stability of measured hypnotizability over a 25-year period. *Journal of Personality and Social Psychology, 56,* 289–295.

PICCIOTTO, M. R., ZOLI, M., RIMONDI, R., LENA, C., MARUBIO, L. M., PICH, E. M., FUXE, K., & CHAGENEUX, J. P. (1998). Acetylcholine receptors containing the B2 subunit are involved in the reinforcing properties of nicotine. *Nature, 391,* 173–177.

PICKEL, K. L. (1998). Unusualness and threat as possible causes of "weapon focus." *Memory, 6,* 277–295.

PICKERING, T. G., DEVEREUX, R. B., JAMES, G. D., GERIN, W., LANDSBERGIS, P., SCHNALL, P. L., & SCHWARTZ, J. E. (1996). Environmental influences on blood pressure and the role of job strain. *Journal of Hypertension, 14* (Suppl.), S179–S185.

PILIAVIN, I. M., RODIN, J., & PILIAVIN, J. A. (1969). Good Samaritanism: An underground phenomenon: *Journal of Personality and Social Psychology, 13,* 289–299.

PINKER, S. (1984). *Language learnability and language development.* Cambridge, MA: Harvard University Press.

PINKER, S. (1991). Rules of language. *Science, 253,* 530–555.

PINKER, S. (1994). *The language instinct.* New York: Morrow.

PINKER, S. (1997). *How the mind works.* New York: Norton

PINKER, S., & PRINCE, A. (1988). On language and connectionism: Analysis of a parallel distributed processing model of language acquisition. *Cognition, 28,* 71–193.

PINNELL, C. M., & COVINO, N. A. (2000). Empirical findings on the use of hypnosis in medicine: A critical review. *International Journal of Clinical and Experimental Hypnosis, 48,* 170–194.

PION, G. M. (1991). Psychologists wanted: Employment trends over the past decade. In R. R. Kilburg (Ed.), *How to manage your career in psychology.* Washington, DC: American Psychological Association.

PLANT, A. E., HYDE, J. S., KELTNER, D., & DEVINE, P. G. (2000). The gender stereotyping of emotions. *Psychology of Women Quarterly, 24,* 81–92.

PLATT, J. J., YAKSH, T., & DARBY, C. L. (1967). Social facilitation of eating behavior in armadillos. *Psychological Reports, 20,* 1136.

PLOMIN, R. (1989). Environment and genes: Determinants of behavior. *American Psychologist, 44,* 105–111.

PLOMIN, R. (1994). *Genetics and experience.* Thousand Oaks, CA: Sage.

PLOMIN, R., & DANLIES, D. (1987). Why are children in the same family so different from one another? *Behavioral and Brain Sciences, 10,* 1–60.

PLOMIN, R., DEFRIES, J. C., & LOEHLIN, J. C. (1977). Genotype-environment interaction and correlation in the analysis of human behavior. *Psychological Bulletin, 84,* 309–322.

PLOMIN, R., FULKER, D. W., CORLEY, R., & DEFRIES, J. C. (1997). Nature, nurture, and cognitive development from 1 to 16 years: A parent-offspring adoption study. *Psychological Science, 8,* 442–447.

PLOMIN, R., & KOSSLYN, S. M. (2001). Genes, brain and cognition. *Nature Neuroscience, 4,* 1153–1154.

PLOMIN, R., OWEN, M. J., & MCGUFFIN, P. (1994). The genetic basis of complex human behaviors. *Science, 264,* 1733–1739.

POLIVY, J., & HERMAN, C. P. (1985). Dieting and bingeing: A causal analysis. *American Psychologist, 40,* 193–201.

POLIVY, J., & HERMAN, C. P. (1993). Etiology of binge eating: Psychological mechanisms. In C. E. Fairburn & G. T. Wilson (Eds.), *Binge eating: Nature, assessment, and treatment.* New York: Guilford.

POMERLEAU, O., & KARDIA, S. (1999). Introduction to the featured section: research on smoking. *Health Psychology, 18,* 3–6.

PORTENOY, R. K. (1990). Chronic opioid therapy in nonmalignant pain. *Journal of Pain and Symptom Management, 5,* S46–S62.

PORTENOY, R. K., & FOLEY, K. M. (1986). Chronic use of opioid analgesics in non-malignant pain: Report of 38 cases. *Pain, 25,* 171–186.

PORTER, R. H., MAKIN, J. W., DAVIS, L. B., & CHRISTENSEN, K. M. (1992). An assessment of the salient olfactory environment of formula-fed infants. *Physiology and Behavior, 50,* 907–911.

PORTER, S., YUILLE, J. C., & LEHMAN, D. R. (1999). The nature of real, implanted, and fabricated memories for emotional childhood events: Implications for the recovered memory debate. *Law and Human Behavior, 23,* 517–537.

POSNER, M. I. (1988). Structures and functions of selective attention. In T. Boll & B. K. Bryant (Eds.), *Clinical neuropsychology and brain function: Research, measurement, and practice.* Washington, DC: American Psychological Association.

POSNER, M. I. (1993). Seeing the mind. *Science, 262,* 673–674.

POSNER, M. I., & DEHAENE, S. (1994). Attentional networks. *Trends in Neuroscience, 17,* 75–79.

POSNER, M. I., & RAICHLE, M. E. (1994). *Images of mind.* New York: Scientific American Library.

POST, R. FRYE, M., DENICOFF, K., LEVERICH, G., KIMBRELL, T., & DUNN, R. (1998). Beyond lithium in the treatment of mental illness. *Neuropsychopharmacology, 19,* 206–219.

POSTMES, T., & SPEARS, R. (1998). Deindividuation and antinormative behavior: A meta-analysis. *Psychological Bulletin, 123,* 238–259.

POSTMES, T., SPEARS, R., & CIHANGIR, S. (2001). Quality of decision making and group norms. *Journal of Personality and Social Psychology, 80,* 918–930.

POWELL, R. A., & BOER, D. P. (1994). Did Freud mislead patients to confabulate memories of abuse? *Psychological Reports, 74,* 1283–1298.

PREMACK, D. (1971). Language in chimpanzees? *Science, 172,* 808–822.

PREMACK, D. (1985). "Gavagi!" Or the future history of the animal language controversy. *Cognition, 19,* 207–296.

PREMACK, D., & PREMACK, A. J. (1983). *The mind of an ape.* New York: Norton.

PRENTICE, D. A., & MILLER, D. T. (1993). Pluralistic ignorance and alcohol use on campus: Some consequences of misperceiving the social norm. *Journal of Personality and Social Psychology, 64,* 243–256.

PRENTICE-DUNN, S., & ROGERS, R. W. (1982). Effect of public and private self-awareness on deindividuation and aggression. *Journal of Personality and Social Psychology, 43,* 503–513.

PRENTICE-DUNN, S., & ROGERS, R. W. (1989). Deindividuation and the self-regulation of behavior. In P. B. Paulus (Ed.), *The psychology of group influence* (2nd ed., pp. 86–109). Hillsdale, NJ: Erlbaum.

PRESSLEY, M., LEVIN, J. R., & DELANEY, _H. D. (1982). The mnemonic keyword method. *Review of Educational Research, 52,* 61–91.

PRETI, G., CUTLER, W. B., GARCIA, C. R., HUGGINS, G. R., and collaborators. (1986). Human axillary secretions influence women's menstrual cycles: The role of donor extract of females. *Hormones and Behavior, 20,* 474–482.

PRICE, D. D. (2000). Psychological and neural mechanisms of the affective dimensions of pain. *Science, 288,* 1769–1772.

PRIEST, R. F., & SAWYER, J. (1967). Proximity and peership: Bases of balance in interpersonal attraction. *American Journal of Sociology, 72,* 633–649.

PRINZMETAL, W. (1981). Principles of feature integration in visual perception. *Perception and Psychophysics, 30,* 330–340.

PROTHRO, E. T. (1952). Ethnocentrism and anti-Negro attitudes in the deep South. *Journal of Abnormal and Social Pathology, 47,* 105–108.

PRYOR, J. B. (1977). Self-focused attention and self-report validity. *Journal of Personality, 45,* 513–527.

PUTNAM, F. W. (1991). Recent research on multiple personality disorder. *Psychiatric Clinics of North America, 14,* 489–502.

QUIRK, G. J., REPA, C., & LEDOUX, J. E. (1995). *Neuron, 15,* 1029–1039.

RAAIJMAKERS, J. G., & SHIFFRIN, R. M. (1981). Search of associative memory. *Psychological Review, 88,* 93–134.

RAAIJMAKERS, J. G., & SHIFFRIN, R. M. (1992). Models for recall and recognition. *Annual Review of Psychology, 43,* 205–234.

RACHMAN, S. (1993). Obsessions, responsibility and guilt. *Behaviour Research and Therapy, 31,* 149–154.

RACHMAN, S. J., & HODGSON, R. J. (1980). *Obsessions and compulsions.* Englewood Cliffs, NJ: Prentice-Hall.

RACHMAN, S. J., & WILSON, G. T. (1980). *The effects of psychological therapy* (2nd ed.). Elmsford, NY: Pergamon Press.

RAEIKKOENEN, K., MATTHEWS, K. A., FLORY, J. D., & OWENS, J. F. (1999). Effects of hostility on ambulatory blood pressure and mood during daily living in healthy adults. *Health Psychology, 18,* 44–53.

RAGSDALE, D. S., MCPHEE, J. C., SCHEUER, T., & CATTERALL, W. A. (1994). Molecular determinants of state-dependent block of Na channels by local anesthetics. *Science, 265,* 1724–1728.

RAICHLE, M. E. (1994). Images of the mind: Studies with modern imaging techniques. *Annual Review of Psychology, 45,* 333–356.

RAINE, A. (1997). Antisocial behavior and psychophysiology: A biological perspective. In D. M. Stoff, J. Breiling, & J. D. Maser (Eds.) *Handbook of antisocial personality disorder* (pp. 289–304). New York: Wiley.

RAMACHANDRAN, V. S., & BLAKESLEE, S. (1998). *Phantoms in the brain.* New York: William Morrow.

RAMACHANDRAN, V. S., & GREGORY, R. L. (1991). Perceptual filling in of artificially induced scotomas in human vision. *Nature, 350,* 699–702.

RAMACHANDRAN, V. S., LEVI, L., STONE, L., ROGERS-RAMACHANDRAN, D., and collaborators. (1996). Illusions of body image: What they reveal about human nature. In R. R. Llinas & P. S. Churchland (Eds.), *The mind-brain continuum: Sensory processes* (pp. 29–60). Cambridge, MA: MIT Press.

RANDI, J. (1982). *Flim-flam! Psychics, ESP, unicorns and other delusions.* Buffalo: Prometheus Books.

RAPAPORT, D. (1942). *Emotions and memory*. Baltimore: Williams & Wilkins.

RAPAPORT, J. L. (1989). The biology of obsessions and compulsions. *Scientific American, March*, 83–89.

RAPAPORT, J. L. (1990). *The boy who couldn't stop washing*. New York: Plume.

RAPAPORT, J. L. (1991). Recent advances in obsessive-compulsive disorder. *Neuropsychopharmacology, 5*, 1–10.

RAPEE, R. M., BROWN, T. A., ANTONY, M. M., & BARLOW, D. H. (1992). Response to hyperventilation and inhalation of 5.5% carbon dioxide-enriched air across the DSM III-R anxiety disorders. *Journal of Abnormal Psychology, 101*, 538–552.

RASMUSSEN, S. A., & EISEN, J. L. (1990). Epidemiology of obsessive compulsive disorder. *Journal of Clinical Psychiatry, 51* (suppl.), 10–13.

RATHBUN, C., DI VIRGILIO, L., & WALDFOGEL, S. (1958). A restitutive process in children following radical separation from family and culture. *American Journal of Orthopsychiatry, 28*, 408–415.

RAVENS, J. C. (1965). *Advanced progressive matrices, sets II and II*. London: H. K. Lewis.

RAVUSSIN, E., and collaborators. (1988). Reduced rate of energy expenditure as a risk factor for bodyweight gain. *New England Journal of Medicine, 318*, 467–472.

RAY, O., & KSIR, C. (1993). *Drugs, society, and human behavior*. St. Louis: Mosby.

RAY, W. J., & RAVIZZA, R. (1988). *Methods toward a science of behavior and experience* (3rd ed.). Belmont, CA: Wadsworth.

RAYNER, K. (1978). Eye movements, reading and information processing. *Psychological Bulletin, 6*, 618–660.

REDER, L. M., & ANDERSON, J. R. (1980). A comparison of texts and their summaries: Memorial consequences. *Journal of Verbal Learning and Verbal Behavior, 19*, 121–134.

REED, G. M., KEMENY, M. E., TAYLOR, S. E., WANG, H.-Y. J., & VISSCHER, B. R. (1994). "Realistic acceptance" as a predictor of decreased survival time in gay men with AIDS. *Health Psychology, 13*, 299–307.

REGAN, D., BEVERLEY, K. I., & CYNADER, M. (1979). The visual perception of motion depth. *Scientific American, 241*, 136–151.

REGAN, D. T., & FAZIO, R. (1977). On the consistency between attitudes and behavior: Look to the method of attitude information. *Journal of Experimental Social Psychology, 13*, 28–45.

REICHER, G. M. (1969). Perceptual recognition as a function of the meaningfulness of the material. *Journal of Experimental Psychology, 81*, 275–280.

REIMAN, E. M., LANE, R. D., AHERN, G. L., SCHWARTZ, G. E., & DAVIDSON, R. J. (2000). Positron emission tomography in the study of emotion, anxiety, and anxiety disorders. In *Cognitive neuroscience of emotion*. New York: Oxford University Press.

REINISCH, J. M. (1981). Prenatal exposure to synthetic progestins increases potential for aggression in humans. *Science, 211*, 1171–1173.

REISENZEIN, R. (1983). The Schachter theory of emotion: Two decades later. *Psychological Bulletin, 94*, 239–264.

RESCORLA, R. A. (1967). Pavlovian conditioning and its proper control procedures. *Psychological Review, 74*, 71–80.

RESCORLA, R. A. (1972). Informational variables in Pavlovian conditioning. In G. H. Bower (Ed.), *Psychology of learning and motivation* (Vol. 6). New York: Academic Press.

RESCORLA, R. A. (1980). Overextension in early language development. *Journal of Child Language, 7*, 321–335.

RESCORLA, R. A. (1987). A Pavlovian analysis of goal-directed behavior. *American Psychologist, 42*, 119–129.

RESCORLA, R. A., & SOLOMON, R. L. (1967). Two-process learning theory: Relations between Pavlovian conditioning and instrumental learning. *Psychological Review, 74*, 151–182.

RESKIN, B. (1998). *The realities of affirmative action in employment*. Washington, DC: American Sociological Association.

RESNICK, H. S., KILPATRICK, D. G., DANSKY, B. S., & SAUNDERS, B. E. (1993). Prevalence of civilian trauma and posttraumatic stress disorder in a representative national sample of women. *Journal of Consulting and Clinical Psychology, 61*, 984–991.

RESNICK, H. S., YEHUDA, R., PITMAN, R. K., & FOY, D. W. (1995). Effect of previous trauma on acute plasma cortisol level following rape. *American Journal of Psychiatry, 152*, 1675–1677.

REUBENS, A. B., & BENSON, D. F. (1971). Associative visual agnosia. *Archives of Neurology, 24*, 305–316.

REYNOLDS, D. V. (1969). Surgery in the rat during electrical analgesia induced by focal brain stimulation. *Science, 164*, 444–445.

RHEINGOLD, H. F., & COOK, K. V. (1975). The content of boys' and girls' rooms as an index of parent behavior. *Child Development, 46*, 459–463.

RICE, B. (1978). The new truth machine. *Psychology Today, 12*, 61–78.

RICHARDS, J. M., & GROSS, J. J. (2000). Emotion regulation and memory: The cognitive costs of keeping one's cool. *Journal of Personality and Social Psychology, 79*, 410–424.

RICHARDSON, J. L., SHELTON, D. R., KRAILO, M., & LEVINE, A. M. (1990). The effect of compliance with treatment in survival among patients with hematologic malignancies. *Journal of Clinical Oncology, 8*, 356.

RICHARDSON, K. (1986). Theory? Or tools for social selection? *Behavioral and Brain Sciences, 9*, 579–581.

RIESEN, A. H. (1947). The development of visual perception in man and chimpanzee. *Science, 106*, 107–108.

RIMM-KAUFMAN, S., & KAGAN, J. (1996). The psychological significance of changes in skin temperature. *Motivation and Emotion, 20*, 63–78.

RIPS, L. J. (1983). Cognitive processes in propositional reasoning. *Psychological Review, 90*, 38–71.

RIPS, L. J. (1994). *The psychology of proof*. Cambridge, MA: MIT Press.

ROBERT, M. (1989). Reduction of demand characteristics in the measurement of certainty during modeled conservation. *Journal of Experimental Child Psychology, 47*, 451–466.

ROBERTS, M. C., VERNBERG, E., & JACKSON, Y. (2000). Psychotherapy with children and families. In C. R. Snyder,., & R. Ingram (Eds.) *Handbook of psychological change* (pp. 500–519). New York: Wiley.

ROBINS, L. N., HELZER, J. E., WEISSMAN, M. M., ORVASCHEL, H., GRUENBERG. E., BURKE, J. D., & REIGIER, D. A. (1984). Lifetime prevalence of specific psychiatric disorders in three sites. *Archives of General Psychiatry, 41*, 949–958.

ROBINSON, M. D. (1998). Running from William James' bear: A review of preattentive mechanisms and their contributions to emotional experience. *Cognition and Emotion, 12*, 667–696.

ROBINSON, T. E., & BERRIDGE, K. C. (1993). The neural basis of drug craving: An incentive-sensitization theory of addiction. *Brain Research Review, 18*, 247–291.

RODIN, J. (1981). Current status of the internal-external hypothesis of obesity: What went wrong? *American Psychologist, 36*, 361–372.

ROFFWARG, H. P., HERMAN, J. H., BOWER-ANDERS, C., & TAUBER, E. S. (1978). The effects of sustained alterations of waking visual input on dream content. In A. M. Arkin, J. S. Antrobus, & S. J. Ellman (Eds.), *The mind in sleep*. Hillsdale, NJ: Erlbaum.

ROGERS, C. R. (1951). *Client-centered therapy*. Boston: Houghton Mifflin.

ROGERS, C. R. (1959). A theory of therapy, personality, and interpersonal relationships as developed in the client-centered framework. In S. Koch (Ed.), *Psychology: A study of a science*: Vol. 3. *Formulations of the person and the social context*. New York: McGraw-Hill.

ROGERS, C. R. (1963). The actualizing tendency in relation to motives and to consciousness. In M. Jones (Ed.), *Nebraska symposium on motivation* (pp. 1–24). Lincoln: University of Nebraska Press.

ROGERS, C. R. (1970). *On becoming a person: A therapist's view of psychotherapy*. Boston: Houghton Mifflin.

ROGERS, T. B., KUIPER, N. A., & KIRKER, W. S. (1977). Self-reference and the encoding of personal information. *Journal of Personality and Social Psychology, 35*, 677–688.

ROGOFF, B. (1990). *Apprenticeship in thinking*. New York: Oxford University Press.

ROGOFF, B. (2000). *Culture and development*. New York: Oxford University Press.

ROITBLAT, H. L. (1986). *Introduction to comparative cognition*. New York: Freeman.

ROLAND, P. E., & FRIBERG, L. (1985). Localization of cortical areas activated by thinking. *Journal of Neurophysiology, 53*, 1219–1243.

ROLLIN, H. R. (1980). *Coping with schizophrenia*. London: Burnnet Books.

ROLLS, E. T. (2000) Hippocampo cortical and cortico cortical back-projections. *Hippocampus, 10*, 380–388.

ROOK, K. (1984). The negative side of social interaction: Impact on psychological well-being. *Journal of Personality and Social Psychology, 46*, 1097–1108.

ROSCH, E. (1974). Linguistic relativity. In A. Silverstein (Ed.), *Human communication: Theoretical perspectives*. New York: Halsted Press.

ROSCH, E. (1978). Principles of categorization. In E. Rosch & B. L. Lloyd (Eds.), *Cognition and categorization*. Hillsdale, NJ: Erlbaum.

ROSCH, E. (1997). Transformation of the wolf man. In J Pickering (Ed.), *The authority of experience*. London: Curzon.

ROSE, J. E., BRUGGE, J. F., ANDERSON, D. J., & HIND, J. E. (1967). Phase-locked response to lower frequency tones in single auditory nerve fibers of the squirrel monkey. *Journal of Neurophysiology, 390*, 769–793.

ROSEMAN, I. J. (1984). Cognitive determinants of emotion: A structural theory. *Review of Personality and Social Psychology, 5*, 11–36.

ROSEN, R. C., & LEIBLUM, S. R. (1995). Treatment of sexual disorders in the 1990s: An integrated approach. *Journal of Consulting and Clinical Psychology, 63*, 877–890.

ROSENBERG, E. L. (1998). Levels of analysis and the organization of affect. *Review of General Psychology, 2*, 247–270.

ROSENBLITH, J. F. (1992). *In the beginning: Development from conception to age two years* (2nd ed.). Newbury Park, CA: Sage.

ROSENBLOOM, P. S., LAIRD, J. E., NEWELL, A., & MCCARL, R. (1991). A preliminary analysis of the foundations of Soar. *Artificial Intelligence, 47,* 289–325.

ROSENMAN, R. H., BRAND, R. J., JENKINS, C. D., FRIEDMAN, M., STRAUS, R., & WRUM, M. (1976). Coronary heart disease in the Western Collaborative Group Study: Final follow-up experience of 8½ years. *Journal of the American Medical Association, 233,* 878–877.

ROSENTHAL, R. (1984). *Meta-analytic procedures for social research.* Beverly Hills, CA: Sage.

ROSENTHAL, R., & JACOBSON, L. (1968). *Pygmalion in the classroom: Teacher expectation and student intellectual development.* New York: Holt, Rinehart, & Winston.

ROSENZWEIG, M. R., BREEDLOVE, S. M., & LEIMAN, A. L. (2001). *Biological psychology* (3rd ed.). Sunderland, MA: Sinauer Press.

ROSENZWEIG, M. R., & LEIMAN, A. L. (1989). *Physiological psychology* (2nd ed.). Lexington, MA: Heath.

ROSS, B. H. (1984). Reminders and their effects in learning a cognitive skill. *Cognitive Psychology, 16,* 371–416.

ROSS, C. A. (1989). *Multiple personality disorder: diagnosis, clinical features, and treatment.* New York: Wiley.

ROSS, C. A. (1997). *Dissociative identity disorder: diagnosis, clinical features, and treatment of multiple personality.* Toronto: Wiley.

ROSS, L. (1977). The intuitive psychologist and his shortcomings: Distortions in the attribution process. In L. Berkowitz, (Ed.), *Advances in experimental social psychology* (Vol. 10). New York: Academic Press.

ROSS, L., AMABILE, T. M., & STEINMETZ, J. L. (1977). Social roles, social control, and biases in social-perception processes. *Journal of Personality and Social Psychology, 35,* 485–494.

ROSS, L., BIERBRAUER, G., & HOFFMAN, S. (1976). The role of attribution processes in conformity and dissent. Revisiting the Asch situation. *American Psychologist, 31,* 148–157.

ROSS, L., LEPPER, M. R., & HUBBARD, M. (1975). Perseverance in self perception and social perception: Biased attributional processes in the debriefing paradigm. *Journal of Personality and Social Psychology, 32,* 880–892.

ROSS, L., LEPPER, M. R., STRACK, F., & STEINMETZ, J. L. (1977). Social explanation and social expectation: The effects of real and hypothetical explanations upon subjective likelihood. *Journal of Personality and Social Psychology, 35,* 817–829.

ROSS, L., & NISBETT, R. E. (1991). *The person and the situation: Perspectives of social psychology.* New York: McGraw-Hill.

ROSSI, P. (1990). The old homelessness and the new homelessness in historical perspective. *American Psychologist, 45,* 954–959.

ROTH, A., FONAGY, P., PARRY, G., TARGET, M., and collaborators. (1996). *What works for whom? A critical review of psychotherapy research.* New York: Guilford.

ROTH, M. (1998). *Freud: Conflict and culture.* New York: Knopf.

ROTHBART, M., & BATES, J. (1998). Temperament. In W. Damon (Series Ed.) and N. Eisenberg (Vol. Ed.), Handbook of child psychology: Vol. 3. *Social, emotional and personality development* (5th ed., pp. 105–176.). New York: Wiley.

ROTTER, J. B. (1954). *Social learning and clinical psychology.* Englewood Cliffs, NJ: Prentice-Hall.

ROTTER, J. B. (1982). *The development and applications of social learning theory: Selected papers.* New York: Praeger.

ROVEE-COLLIER, C. (1999). The development of infant memory. *Current Directions in Psychological Science, 8,* 80–85.

ROVEE-COLLIER, C., & HAYNE, H. (1987). Reactivation of infant memory: Implications for cognitive development. In H. W. Reese (Ed.), *Advances in child development and behavior* (Vol. 20). New York: Academic Press.

ROWLAND, N. E., & ANTELMAN, S. M. (1976). Stress-induced hyperphagia and obesity in rats: A possible model for understanding human obesity. *Science, 191,* 310–312.

ROY, A. (1992). Genetics, biology, and suicide in the family. In R. W. Maris, A. L. Berman, J. T. Maltsberger, & R. I. Yufit (Eds.), *Assessment and prediction of suicide* (pp. 574–588). New York: Guilford.

ROYCE, J. R., & MOS, L. P. (Eds.). (1981). *Humanistic psychology: Concepts and criticisms.* New York: Plenum.

ROZIN, P. N., & SCHULKIN, J. (1990). Food selection. In E. M. Stricker (Ed.), *Neurobiology of food and fluid intake* (pp. 297–328). New York: Plenum.

RUBIN, Z. (1973). *Liking and loving.* New York: Holt, Rinehart & Winston.

RUCH, J. C. (1975). Self-hypnosis: The result of heterohypnosis or vice versa? *International Journal of Clinical and Experimental Hypnosis, 23,* 282–304.

RUCH, J. C., MORGAN, A. H., & HILGARD, E. R. (1973). Behavioral predictions from hypnotic responsiveness scores when obtained with and without prior induction procedures. *Journal of Abnormal Psychology, 82,* 543–546.

RUDERMAN, A. J. (1986). Dietary restraint: A theoretical and empirical review. *Psychological Bulletin, 99,* 247–262.

RUDMAN, L. A., & BORGIDA, E. (1995). The afterglow of construct accessibility: The behavioral consequences of priming men to view women as sexual objects. *Journal of Experimental Social Psychology, 31,* 493–517.

RUMELHART, D. E., & MCCLELLAND, J. L. (1987). Learning the past tenses of English verbs: Implicit rules or parallel distributed processing? In B. MacWhinney (Ed.), *Mechanisms of language acquisition.* Hillsdale, NJ: Erlbaum.

RUMELHART, D. E., MCCLELLAND, J. L., & THE PDP RESEARCH GROUP. (1986). *Parallel distributed processing: Explorations in the microstructure of cognition.* Volume 1: *Foundations.* Cambridge, MA: Bradford Books/MIT Press.

RUSSELL, J. A., & FELDMAN BARRETT, L. (1999). Core affect, prototypical emotional episodes, and other things called emotion: Dissecting the elephant. *Journal of Personality and Social Psychology, 76,* 805–819.

RUSSELL, M. J. (1976). Human olfactory communication. *Nature, 260,* 520–522.

RUSSELL, M. J., SWITZ, G. M., & THOMPSON, K. (1980). Olfactory influence on the human menstrual cycle. *Pharmacology, Biochemistry and Behavior, 13,* 737–738.

RUSSO, N. F., & SOBEL, S. B. (1981). Sex differences in the utilization of mental health facilities. *Professional Psychology, 12,* 7–19.

RUTTER, M. (1997). Antisocial behavior: Developmental psychopathology perspectives. In D. M. Stoff, J. Breiling, & J. D. Maser (Eds.), *Handbook of antisocial personality disorder* (pp. 115–124). New York: Wiley.

RUTTER, M., MACDONALD, H., CONTEUR, A. L., HARRINGTON, R., BOLTON, P., & BAILEY, A. (1990). Genetic factors in child psychiatric disorders: II. Empirical findings. *Journal of Child Psychology and Psychiatry, 31,* 39–83.

RUTTER, M., QUINTON, D., & HILL, J. (1990). Adult outcome of institution-reared children: Males and females compared. In L. Robins (Ed.), *Straight and devious pathways from childhood to adulthood* (pp. 135–157). Cambridge, England: Cambridge University Press.

RYMER, R. (1992a, April 13). A silent childhood. *New Yorker,* pp. 41–53.

RYMER, R. (1992b, April 20). A silent childhood, pt. II. *New Yorker,* pp. 43–47.

SABOL, S. Z., NELSON, M. L., FISHER, C., GUNZERATH, L., BRODY, C. L., HU, S., SIROTA, L. A., MARCUS, S. E., GREENBERG, B. D., LUCAS, F. R., BENJAMIN, J., MURPHY, D. L., & HAMER, D. H. (1999). A genetic association for cigarette smoking behavior. *Health Psychology, 18,* 7–13.

SACHS, J. D. S. (1967). Recognition memory for syntactic and semantic aspects of connected discourse. *Perception and Psychophysics, 2,* 437–442.

SACKS, O. (1985). *The man who mistook his wife for a hat and other clinical tales.* New York: Harper Perennial.

SACKS, O. W. (1983). *Awakenings.* New York: Dutton.

SAFER, D. J., ZITO, J. M., & FINE, E. M. (1996). Increased methylphenidate usage for attention deficit disorder in the 1990s. *Pediatrics, 98,* 1084–1088.

SALAMY, J. (1970). Instrumental responding to internal cues associated with REM sleep. *Psychonomic Science, 18,* 342–343.

SALAPATEK, P. (1975). Pattern perception in early infancy. In L. B. Cohen & P. Salapatek (Eds.), *Infant perception: From sensation to cognition* (Vol. 1). New York: Academic Press.

SALKOVSKIS, P. M. (1989). Cognitive-behavioral factors and the persistence of intrusive thoughts in obsessional problems. *Behaviour Research & Therapy, 27,* 677–682.

SANDERS, G. S. (1984). Self-presentation and drive in social facilitation. *Journal of Experimental Social Psychology, 20,* 312–322.

SANDERS, G. S., & BARON, R. S. (1975). The motivating effects of distraction on task performance. *Journal of Personality and Social Psychology, 32,* 956–963.

SANDERS, G. S., & BARON, R. S. (1977). Is social comparison irrelevant for producing choice shifts? *Journal of Experimental Social Psychology, 13,* 303–314.

SANDERSON, W. C., RAPEE, R. M., & BARLOW, D. H. (1989). The influence of illusion of control on panic attacks induced via inhalation of 5.5% carbon dioxide-enriched air. *Archives of General Psychology, 46,* 157–162.

SAPOLSKY, R. M. (1990). Stress in the wild. *Scientific American, 262,* 116–123.

SATINOFF, E. (1964). Behavioral thermoregulation in response to local cooling of the rat brain. *American Journal of Physiology, 206,* 1389–1394.

SATINOFF, E. (1983). A reevaluation of the concept of the homeostatic organization of temperature regulation. In E. Satinoff & P. Teitelbaum (Eds.), *Motivation* (pp. 443–474). New York: Plenum Press.

SAUNDERS, D. R. (1985). On Hyman's factor analyses. *Journal of Parapsychology, 49,* 86–88.

SAXE, L., DOUGHERTY, D., & CROSS, T. (1985). The validity of polygraph testing. *American Psychologist, 40,* 355–366.

SAXENA, S., BRODY, A. L., SCHWARTZ, J. M., & BAXTER, L. R. (1998). Neuroimaging and frontal-subcortical circuitry in obsessive-compulsive disorder. *British Journal of Psychiatry, 173,* 26–37.

SCAFIDI, F., & FIELD, T. (1986). Massage therapy improves behavior in neonates born to HIV positive mothers. *Journal of Pediatric Psychology, 21,* 889–898.

SCAFIDI, F., FIELD, T., SCHANBERG, S., BAUER, C., TUCCI, K., ROBERTS, J., MORROW, C., & KUHN, C. M. (1990). Massage stimulates growth in preterm infants: A replication. *Infant Behavior and Development, 13,* 167–168.

SCARR, S. (1985). An author's frame of mind: Review of Frames of mind, by Howard Gardner. *New Ideas in Psychology, 3,* 95–100.

SCARR, S. (1988). How genotypes and environments combine: Development and individual differences. In N. Bolger, A. Caspi, G. Downey, & M. Moorehouse (Eds.), *Persons in context: Developmental processes* (pp. 217–244). New York: Cambridge University Press.

SCARR, S. (1992). Developmental theories for the 1990s: Development and individual differences. *Child Development, 63,* 1–19.

SCARR, S. (1996). How people make their own environments: Implications for parents and policy makers. *Psychology, Public Policy, and Law, 2,* 204–228.

SCARR, S., & EISENBERG, M. (1993). Child care research: Issues, perspectives, and results. *Annual Review of Psychology, 44,* 613–644.

SCARR, S., & McCARTNEY, K. (1983). How people make their own environments: A theory of genotype-environment effects. *Child Development, 54,* 424–435.

SCARR, S., PHILLIPS, D., McCARTNEY, K., & ABBOTT-SHIM, M. (1993). Quality of child care as an aspect of family and child care policy in the United States. *Pediatrics, 91,* 182–188.

SCARR, S., WEINBERG, R. A., & LEVINE, A. (1986). *Understanding development.* San Diego: Harcourt Brace Jovanovich.

SCHACHTEL, E. G. (1982). On memory and childhood amnesia. In U. Neisser (Ed.), *Memory observed: Remembering in natural contexts.* San Francisco: Freeman.

SCHACHTER, S. (1964). The interaction of cognitive and physiological determinants of emotional state. In L. Berkowitz (Ed.), *Advances in experimental social psychology* (pp. 49–80). New York: Academic Press.

SCHACHTER, S., & SINGER, J. E. (1962). Cognitive, social and physiological determinants of emotional state. *Psychological Review, 69,* 379–399.

SCHACTER, D. L. (1989). Memory. In M. Posner (Ed.), *Foundations of cognitive science.* Cambridge, MA: MIT Press.

SCHAFER, R. (1976). *A new language for psychoanalysis.* New Haven, CT: Yale University Press.

SCHANCK, R. L. (1932). A study of a community and its groups and institutions conceived of as behaviors of individuals. *Psychological Monographs, 43,* 1–133.

SCHARNBERG, M. (1993). *The nonauthentic nature of Freud's observations: Vol. 1. The seduction theory.* Philadelphia: Coronet.

SCHATZBERG, A. F. (2000). New indications for antidepressants. *Journal of Clinical Psychiatry, 61,* 9–17.

SCHEIER, M. F., BUSS, A. H., & BUSS, D. M. (1978). Self-consciousness, self-reports of aggressiveness, and aggressions. *Journal of Research in Personality, 12,* 133–140.

SCHEIER, M. F., & CARVER, C. S. (1992). Effects of optimism on psychological and physical well-being: Theoretical overview and empirical update. *Cognitive Therapy and Research, 16,* 201–228.

SCHEIER, M. F., MATTHEWS, K. A., OWENS, J. F., MAGOVERN, G. J., LEFEBYRE, R. C., ABBOTT, R. A., & CARVER, C. S. (1989). Dispositional optimism and recovery from coronary artery bypass surgery: The beneficial effects on physical and psychological well-being. *Journal of Personality and Social Psychology, 57,* 1024–1040.

SCHERRER, J. F., XIAN, H., LYONS, M. J., EISEN, S. A., GOLDBERG, J., LIN, N., & TSUANG, M. T. (2000). Evidence for genetic influences common and specific to symptoms of generalized anxiety and panic. *Journal of Affective Disorders, 57,* 25–35.

SCHIFF, W., & FOULKE, E. (Eds.). (1982). *Tactual perception: A sourcebook.* Cambridge, England: Cambridge University Press.

SCHIFFENBAUER, A., & SCHIAVO, R. S. (1976). Physical distance and attraction: An intensification effect. *Journal of Experimental Social Psychology, 12,* 274–282.

SCHINDLER, R. A., & MERZENICH, M. M. (Eds.). (1985). *Cochlear implants.* New York: Raven Press.

SCHLEIDT, M., HOLD, B., & ATTILI, G. (1981). A cross-cultural study on the attitude toward personal odors. *Journal of Chemical Ecology, 7,* 19–31.

SCHLEIFER, S. J., KELLER, S. E., MCKEGNEY, F. P., & STEIN, M. (1979, March). *The influence of stress and other psychosocial factors on human immunity.* Paper presented at the 36th Annual Meeting of the Psychosomatic Society, Dallas.

SCHLENGER, W. E., KULKA, R. A., FAIRBANK, J. A., & HOUGH, R. L. (1992). The prevalence of post-traumatic stress disorder in the Vietnam generation: A multi-method multi-source assessment of psychiatric disorders. *Journal of Traumatic Stress, 5,* 333–363.

SCHLESINGER, A. M., JR. (1965). *A thousand days.* Boston: Houghton Mifflin.

SCHMERMUND, A., SELLERS, R., MUELLER, B., & CROSBY, F. (2001). Attitudes toward affirmative action as a function of racial identity among black college students. *Political Psychology 22,* 759–774.

SCHMIDT, D. P., & BUSS, D. M. (1996). Strategic self-promotion and competitor derogation: Sex and context effects on the perceived effectiveness of mate attraction tactics. *Journal of Personality and Social Psychology, 70,* 1185–1204.

SCHMITT, B. H., GILOVICH, T., GOORE, N., & JOSEPH, L. (1986). Mere presence and social facilitation: One more time. *Journal of Experimental Social Psychology, 22,* 242–248.

SCHMOLCK, H., BUFFALO, E. A., & SQUIRE, L. (2000). Memory distortions develop over time: Recollections of the O. J. Simpson trial verdict after 15 and 32 months. *Psychological Science, 11,* 39–45.

SCHNEIDER, A. M., & TARSHIS, B. (1986). *An introduction to physiological psychology* (3rd ed.). New York: Random House.

SCHNEIDER, D. J., & MILLER, R. S. (1975). The effects of enthusiasm and quality of arguments on attitude attribution. *Journal of Personality, 43,* 693–708.

SCHNEIDER, F., R., JOHNSON, J., HORNIG, C. D., & LIEBOWITZ, M. R. (1992). Social phobia: Comorbity in an epidemiologic sample. *Archives of General Psychiatry, 49,* 282–288.

SCHNEIDERMAN, N., ANTONI, M. H., SAAB, P. G., & IRONSON, G. (2001). Health psychology: Psychosocial and biobehavioral aspects of chronic disease management. *Annual Reviews of Psychology, 52,* 555–580.

SCHNEIER, F. R., JOHNSON, J., HORNIG, C. D., & LIEBOWITZ, M. R. (1992). Social phobia: Comorbidity and morbidity in an epidemiologic sample. *Archives of General Psychiatry, 49,* 282–288.

SCHROEDER, C. M., & PRENTICE, D. A. (1998). Exposing pluralistic ignorance to reduce alcohol use among college students. *Journal of Applied Social Psychology, 28,* 2150–2180.

SCHULTZ, D. (2000). *A history of modern psychology* (7th ed.). Fort Worth: Harcourt.

SCHULZ, R., BOOKWALA, J., KNAPP, J. E., SCHEIER, M., & WILLIAMSON, G. (1996). Pessimism, age, and cancer mortality. *Psychology and Aging, 11,* 304–309.

SCHULTZ, S. K., O'LEARY, D. S., BOLES PONTO, L. L., ARNDT, S., MAGNOTTA, V., WATKINS, G. L., HICHWA, R. D., & ANDREASEN, N. C. (2002). Age and regional cerebral blood flow in schizophrenia: Age effects in anterior cingulate, frontal, and parietal cortex. *Journal of Neuropsychiatry and Clinical Neuroscience, 14,* 19–24.

SCHUR, E. M. (1971). *Labeling deviant behavior: Its sociological implications.* New York: Harper & Row.

SCHWARTZ, B. (1989). *Psychology of learning and behavior* (3rd ed.). New York: Norton.

SCHWARTZ, B., & REISBERG, D. (1991). *Learning and memory.* New York: Norton.

SCHWARTZ, B., SNIDMAN, N., & KAGAN, J. (1996). Early childhood temperament as a determinant of externalizing behavior in adolescence. *Development and Psychopathology, 8,* 527–537.

SCHWARTZ, J., STOESSEL, P. W., BAXTER, L. R., MARTIN, K. M., & PHELPS, M. C. (1996). Systemic changes in cerebral glucose metabolic rate after successful behavior modification treatment of obsessive compulsive disorder. *Archives of General Psychiatry, 53,* 109–113.

SCHWARTZBERG, S. S. (1993). Struggling for meaning: How HIV-positive gay men make sense of AIDS. *Professional Psychology: Research and Practice, 24,* 483–490.

SCOTT, T. R., & MARK, G. P. (1986). Feeding and taste. *Progress in Neurobiology, 27,* 293–317.

SEARS, R. R. (1943). *Survey of objective studies of psychoanalytic concepts.* Social Science Research Council Bulletin, No. 51.

SEARS, R. R. (1944). Experimental analyses of psychoanalytic phenomena. In J. Hunt (Ed.), *Personality and the behavior disorders* (Vol. 1, pp. 306–332). New York: Ronald.

SEARS, R. R., MACCOBY, E. E., & LEVIN, H. (1957) *Patterns of child rearing.* New York: Harper & Row.

SEGERSTROM, S. C., SOLOMON, G. F., KEMENY, M. E., & FAHEY, J. L. (1998). Relationship of worry to immune sequelae of the Northridge earthquake. *Journal of Behavioral Medicine, 21,* 433–450.

SEGERSTROM, S. C., TAYLOR, S. E., KEMENY, M. E., & FAHEY, J. L. (1998). Optimism is associated with mood, coping, and immune change in response to stress. *Journal of Personality and Social Psychology, 74,* 1646–1655.

SEGERSTROM, S. C., TAYLOR, S. E., KEMENY, M. E., REED, G. M., & VISSCHER, B. R. (1996). Causal attributions predict rate of immune decline in HIV-seropositive gay men. *Health Psychology, 15,* 485–493.

SEIFERT, C. M., ROBERTSON, S. P., & BLACK, J. B. (1985). Types of inferences generated during reading. *Journal of Memory and Language, 24,* 405–422.

SEKULER, R. (1975). Visual motion perception. In E. C. Carterette & M. Friedman (Eds.), *Handbook of perception* (Vol. 5, pp. 387–433). New York: Academic Press.

SEKULER, R., & BLAKE, R. (1985). *Perception.* New York: Knopf.

SELIGMAN, M. E. P. (1975). *Helplessness.* San Francisco: Freeman.

SELIGMAN, M. E. P. (1996). The effectiveness of psychotherapy: The *Consumer Reports* study. *American Psychologist, 50,* 965–974.

SELIGMAN, M. E. P., & BINIK, Y. M. (1977). The safety signal hypothesis. In H. Davis & H. Hurwitz (Eds.), *Pavlovian operant interactions.* Hillsdale, NJ: Erlbaum.

SELLERS, R. M., SMITH, J. A., SHELTON, J. N., ROWLEY, S. A. J., & CHAVOUS, T. M. (1998). Multidimensional model of racial identity: A reconceptualization of African American racial identity. *Personality and Social Psychology Review, 2,* 18–39.

SELYE, H. (1978). *The stress of life.* New York: McGraw-Hill.

SEWELL, W. H., & MUSSEN, P. H. (1952). The effects of feeding, weaning, and scheduling procedures on childhood adjustment and the formation of oral symptoms. *Child Development, 23,* 185–191.

SHALLICE, T. (1988). *From neuropsychology to mental structure.* Cambridge, England: Cambridge University Press.

SHALLICE, T., FLETCHER, P., FRITH, C. D., GRASBY, P., FRACKOWIAK, R. S. J., & DOLAN, R. J. (1994). Brain regions associated with acquisition and retrieval of verbal episodic memory. *Nature, 368,* 633–635.

SHANKS, D. R., & DICKINSON, A., (1987). Associative accounts of causality judgment. *Psychology of Learning and Motivation, 21,* 229–261.

SHANNON, R. V., & OTTO, S. R. (1990). Psychophysical measures from electrical stimulation of the human cochlear nucleus. *Hearing Research, 47,* 159–168.

SHAPIRO, A. K., & MORRIS, L. A. (1978). The placebo effect in medical and psychological therapies. In S. L. Garfield & A. E. Bergin (Eds.), *Handbook of psychotherapy and behavior change* (2nd ed.). New York: Wiley.

SHAPIRO, D. A., & SHAPIRO, D. (1982). Meta-analysis of comparative therapy outcome studies: A replication and refinement. *Psychological Bulletin, 92,* 581–604.

SHAPLEY, R., & LENNIE, P. (1985). Spatial frequency analysis in the visual system. *Annual Review of Neurosciences, 8,* 547–583.

SHAW, D. W., & THORESEN, C. E. (1974). Effects of modeling and desensitization in reducing dentist phobia. *Journal of Counseling Psychology, 21,* 415–420.

SHEDLER, J., MAYMAN, M., & MANIS, M. (1993). The illusion of mental health. *American Psychologist, 48,* 1117–1131.

SHEINGOLD, K., & TENNEY, Y. J. (1982). Memory for a salient childhood event. In U. Neisser (Ed.), *Memory observed: Remembering in natural contexts.* San Francisco: Freeman.

SHEKELLE, R., NEATON, J. D., JACOBS, D., HULLEY, S., & BLACKBURN, H. (1983). *Type A be-*havior pattern in MRFIT. A paper presented to the American Heart Association Council on Epidemiology Meetings, San Diego.

SHELTON, R. C., KELLER, M. B., GELENBERG, A., DUNNER, D. L., HIRSCHFIELD, R., THASE, M. E., RUSSEL, J., LYDIARD, L., CRITS-CRISTOPH, P., GALLOP, R., TODD, L., HELLERSTEIN, D., GOODNICK, P., KEITNER, G., STAHL, S. M., & HALBRIECH, U. (2001)., Effectiveness of St. John's wort in major depression: A randomized controlled-trial. *JAMA, 285,* 1978–1993.

SHEPARD, R. N., & COOPER, L. A. (1982). *Mental images and their transformations.* Cambridge, MA: MIT Press, Bradford Books.

SHEPHER, J. (1971). Mate selection among second generation kibbutz adolescents and adults: Incest avoidance and negative imprinting. *Archives of Sexual Behavior, 1,* 293–307.

SHEPOSH, J. P., DEMING, M., & YOUNG, L. E. (1977, April). *The radiating effects of status and attractiveness of a male upon evaluating his female partner.* Paper presented at the annual meeting of the Western Psychological Association, Seattle.

SHERWIN, B. (1988). A comparative analysis of the role of androgen in human male and female sexual behavior: Behavioral specificity, critical thresholds, and sensitivity. *Psychobiology, 16,* 416–425.

SHIN, L. M., KOSSLYN, S. M., MCNALLY, R. J., ALPERT, N. M., THOMPSON, W. L., RAUCH, S. L., MACKLIN, M. L., & PITMAN, R. K. (1997). Visual imagery and perception in posttraumatic stress disorder: A positron emission tomographic investigation. *Archives of General Psychiatry, 54,* 233–241.

SHORS, T. J., MIESEGAES, G., BEYLIN, A., ZHAO, M., RYDEL, T., & GOULD, E. (2001). Neurogenesis in the adult is involved in the formation of trace memories. *Nature, 410,* 372–376.

SHRESTHA, N. M., SHARMA, B., VAN OMMEREN, M., REGMI, S., MAKAJU, R., KOMPROE, I., SHRESTHA, G. B., & DE JONG, J. T. V. M. (1998). Impact of torture on refugees displaced within the developing world. *Journal of the American Medical Association, 280,* 443–448.

SHWEDER, R. A. (1984). Anthropology's romantic rebellion against the enlightenment, or there's more to thinking than reason and evidence. In R. A. Shweder & R. A. LeVine (Eds.), *Culture theory: Essays on mind, self, and emotion* (pp. 27–66). Cambridge, England: Cambridge University Press.

SIEGEL, P., & WEINBERGER, J. (1998). Capturing the "MOMMY AND I ARE ONE" merger fantasy: The oneness motive. In R. F. Bornstein & J. M. Masling (Eds.), *Empirical perspectives on the psychoanalytic unconscious* (pp. 71–98). Washington, DC: APA Press.

SIEGLER, R. S. (1991). *Children's thinking* (2nd ed.). Englewood Cliffs: NJ: Prentice-Hall.

SIEMER, M. (2001). Mood-specific effects on appraisal and emotion judgments. *Cognition and Emotion, 15,* 453–485.

SIERRA, M., & BERRIOS, G. (2000). Flashbulb and flashback memories. In G. Berrios & J. R. Hodges (Ed.), *Memory disorders in psychiatric practice* (pp. 369–383). Cambridge: Cambridge University Press.

SIGALL, H., & LANDY, D. (1973). Radiating beauty: The effects of having a physically attractive partner on person perception. *Journal of Personality and Social Psychology, 31,* 410–414.

SILVERBERG, S. B., & STEINBERG, L. (1990). Psychological well-being of parents with early adoles-cent children. *Developmental Psychology, 26,* 658–666.

SILVERMAN, I. (1964). Self-esteem and differential responsiveness to success and failure. *Journal of Abnormal and Social Psychology, 69,* 115–119.

SILVERMAN, I. (1971). Physical attractiveness and courtship. *Sexual Behavior, 1,* 22–25.

SIMMONS, J. V. (1981). *Project sea hunt: A report on prototype development and tests.* Technical Report 746, Naval Ocean Systems Center, San Diego.

SIMMONS, R. G., & BLYTH, D. A. (1988). *Moving into adolescence: The impact of pubertal change and school context.* Hawthorne, NY: Aldine.

SIMON, H. A. (1985, June). Using cognitive science to solve human problems. Paper presented at Science and Public Policy Seminar, Federation of Behavioral, Psychological, and Cognitive Sciences.

SIMON, H. A., & GILMARTIN, K. (1973). A simulation of memory for chess positions. *Cognitive Psychology, 5,* 29–46.

SIMPSON, J. A., CAMPBELL, B., & BERSCHEID, E. (1986). The association between romantic love and marriage: Kephart (1967) twice revisited. *Personality and Social Psychology Bulletin, 12,* 363–372.

SINGER, J. L., & SINGER, D. G. (1981). *Television, imagination and aggression.* Hillsdale, NJ: Erlbaum.

SINGH, M., & HOFFMAN, D. M. (2001). Part-based representations of visual shape and implications for visual cognition. In B. K. Shipley, F. Thomas, & P. J. Kellman (Eds.), *From fragments to objects: Segmentation and grouping in vision. Advances in Psychology* (pp. 401–459). New York: Elsevier Science.

SIQUELAND, E. R., & LIPSITT, J. P. (1966). Conditioned head-turning in human newborns. *Journal of Experimental Child Psychology, 3,* 356–376.

SIZEMORE, C. C., & PITTILLO, E. S. (1977). *I'm Eve.* Garden City, NY: Doubleday.

SKINNER, B. F. (1938). *The behavior of organisms.* New York: Appleton-Century-Crofts.

SKINNER, B. F. (1948). "Superstition" in the pigeon. *Journal of Experimental Psychology, 38,* 168–172.

SKINNER, B. F. (1971). *Beyond freedom and dignity.* New York: Knopf.

SKINNER, B. F. (1981). Selection by consequences. *Science, 213,* 501–504.

SKYRMS, B. (1986). *Choice and chance: An introduction to inductive logic.* Belmont, CA: Dickenson.

SLOBIN, D. I. (1971). Cognitive prerequisites for the acquisition of grammar. In C. A. Ferguson & D. I. Slobin (Eds.), *Studies of child language development.* New York: Holt, Rinehart & Winston.

SLOBIN, D. I. (1979). *Psycholinguistics* (2nd. ed.). Glenville, IL: Scott, Foresman.

SLOBIN, D. I. (Ed.). (1985). *The cross-linguistic study of language acquisition.* Hillsdale, NJ: Erlbaum.

SLOBIN, D. I. (1996). From "thought and language" to "thinking to speaking." In J. J. Gumperz & S. C. Levinson (Eds.), *Rethinking linguistic relativity* (pp. 70–96). Cambridge, England: Cambridge University Press.

SMITH, A. (1937). *A theory of moral sentiments.* New York: Modern Library. (Originally published 1759).

SMITH, C. A., & ELLSWORTH, P. C. (1985). Patterns of cognitive appraisal in emotion. *Journal of Personality and Social Psychology, 48,* 813–848.

SMITH, C. A., & ELLSWORTH, P. C. (1987). Patterns of appraisal and emotion related to taking an exam. *Journal of Personality and Social Psychology, 52,* 475–488.

SMITH, D., KING, M., & HOEBEL, B. G. (1970). Lateral hypothalamic control of killing: Evidence for a cholinoceptive mechanism. *Science, 167,* 900–901.

SMITH, E. E. (1989). Concepts and induction. In M. I. Posner (Ed.), *Foundations of cognitive science.* Cambridge, MA: MIT Press.

SMITH, E. E. (1995). Concepts and categorization. In E. E. Smith & D. Osherson (Eds.), *Invitation to cognitive science,* Vol. 3, *Thinking* (2nd ed.). Cambridge, MA: MIT Press.

SMITH, E. E., & JONIDES, J. (1994). Neuropsychological studies of working memory. In M. Gazzaniga (Ed.), *The cognitive neurosciences.* Cambridge, MA: MIT Press. SMITH, E. E., JONIDES, J., & KOEPPE, R. A. (1996). Dissociating verbal and spatial working memory using PET. *Cerebral Cortex, 6,* 11–20.

SMITH, E. E., & MEDIN, D. L. (1981). *Categories and concepts.* Cambridge, MA: Harvard University Press.

SMITH, E. E., PATALANO, A. L., & JONIDES, J. (1998). Alternative strategies of categorization. *Cognition, 65,* 167–196.

SMITH, G. P., & GIBBS, J. (1994). Satiating effect of cholecystokinin. *Annals of the New York Academy of Sciences, 713,* 236–241.

SMITH, M. B., BRUNER, J. S., & WHITE, R. W. (1956). *Opinions and personality.* New York: Wiley.

SMITH, M. L., GLASS, G. V., & MILLER, T. I. (1980). *The benefits of psychotherapy.* Baltimore: Johns Hopkins University Press.

SMITH, V. C., & POKORNY, J. (1975). Spectral sensitivity of the foveal cones between 400 and 500 nm. *Vision Research, 15,* 161.

SMUTS, B. B. (1986). Gender, aggression, and influence. In B. Smuts, D. Cheney, R. Seyfarth, R. Wrangham, & T. Struhsaker (Eds.), *Primate societies.* Chicago: University of Chicago Press.

SNAITH, P. (1998). Meditation and psychotherapy. *British Journal of Psychiatry, 173,* 193–195.

SNODGRASS, J. G., LEVY-BERGER, G., & HAYDON, M. (1985). *Human experimental psychology.* New York: Oxford University Press.

SNOW, C. (1987). Relevance of the notion of a critical period to language acquisition. In M. H. Bornstein (Ed.), *Sensitive periods in development: Interdisciplinary perspectives.* Hillsdale, NJ: Erlbaum.

SNOWDEN, L. R. (1988). Ethnicity and utilization of mental health services: An overview of current findings. In *Oklahoma Mental Health Research Institute, 1988 professional symposium* (pp. 227–238). Oklahoma City: Oklahoma Mental Health Research Institute.

SNOWDEN, L., & CHEUNG, F. (1990, March). Use of inpatient mental health services by members of ethnic minority groups. *American Psychologist, 45,* 347–355.

SNYDER, C. R., ILARDI, S., MICHAEL, S. T., & CHEAVENS, J. (2000). Hope theory: Updating a common process for psychological change. In C. R. Snyder & R. E. Ingram (Eds.), *Handbook of psychological change: Psychotherapy processes and practices for the 21st Century.* New York: Wiley.

SNYDER, C. R., & INGRAM, R. E.(2000). *Handbook of psychological change: Psychotherapy processes and practices for the 21st century.* New York: Wiley.

SNYDER, M., TANKE, E. D., & BERSCHEID, E. (1977). Social perception and interpersonal behavior: On the self-fulfilling nature of stereotypes.

Journal of Personality and Social Psychology, 35, 656–666.

SOLMS, M. (1997). The neuropsychology of dreams: A clinico-anatomical study. Mahwah, NJ: Erlbaum.

SOLOMON, G. F., SEGERSTROM, S. C., GROHR, P., KEMENY, M., & FAHEY, J., (1997). Shaking up immunity: Psychological and immunologic changes following a natural disaster. *Psychosomatic Medicine, 59,* 114–127.

SOLOMON, R. L., & CORBIT, J. D. (1974). An opponent-process theory of motivation: I. Temporal dynamics of affect. *Psychological Review, 81,* 119–145.

SONTHEIMER, H. (1995). Glial neuronal interactions: A physiological perspective. *The Neuroscientist, 1,* 328–337.

SORCE, J. F., EMDE, R. N., CAMPOS, J., & KLINNERT, M. D. (1985). Maternal emotional signaling: Its effect on the visual cliff behavior of 1-year-olds. *Developmental Psychiatry, 21,* 195–200.

SOUTHWICK, S. M., YEHUDA, R., & WANG, S. (1998). Neuroendocrine alterations in posttraumatic stress disorder. *Psychiatric Annals, 28,* 436–442.

SPANOS, B. (1996, December). Quotas, ARCOs, UN report, and statistics. In G. Feussner (Moderator), *Prevalence of ADHD and psychostimulant utilization for treatment.* Symposium conducted at Drug Enforcement Administration meeting on stimulant use in the treatment of ADHD.

SPANOS, N. P. (1986). Hypnotic behavior: A socialpsychological interpretation of amnesia, analgesia, and "trance logic." *Behavioral and Brain Sciences, 9,* 449–502.

SPANOS, N. P., & HEWITT, E. C. (1980). The hidden observer in hypnotic analgesia: Discovery or experimental creation? *Journal of Personality and Social Psychology, 39,* 1201–1214.

SPEARMAN, C. (1904). "General intelligence" objectively determined and measured. *American Journal of Psychology, 15,* 201–293.

SPECA, M., CARLSON, L. E., GOODEY, E., & ANGEN, M. (2000). A randomized wait-list controlled clinical trial: The effect of a mindfulness meditation-based stress reduction program on mood and symptoms of stress in cancer patients. *Psychosomatic Medicine, 62,* 613–622.

SPEIGEL, J. M., & BRAINARD, D. H. (1999). Predicting color from gray: The relationship between achromatic adjustment and asymmetric matching, *Journal of the Optical Society of America, 16,* 2370–2376.

SPELKE, E. S. (1998). Nativism, empiricism, and the origins of knowledge. *Infant Behaviour and Development, 21,* 181–200.

SPENCER, S., STEELE, C. M., & QUINN, D. (1997). *Under suspicion of inability: Stereotype threat and women's math performance.* Unpublished manuscript, Stanford University.

SPENCER, S., STEELE, C. M., & QUINN, D. M. (1999). Stereotype threat and women's math performance. *Journal of Experimental Social Psychology, 35,* 4–28.

SPERLING, G. (1960). The information available in brief visual presentations. *Psychological Monographs, 74,* 329.

SPERLING, G. (1967). Successive approximations to a model for short term memory. *Acta Psychologica, 27,* 285–292.

SPERRY, R. W. (1968). Perception in the absence of neocortical commissures. In Association for Research in Nervous and Mental Disease, *Perception and its disorders.* New York: Williams & Wilkins.

SPERRY, R. W. (1970). Perception in the absence of the neocortical commissures. *Research Publications—Association for Research in Nervous and Mental Disease, 48,* 123–128.

SPIEGEL, D. (1991). Mind matters: Effects of group support on cancer patients. *Journal of NIH Research, 3,* 61–63.

SPIEGEL, D., BLOOM, J. R., KRAEMER, H. C., & GOTTHEIL, E. (1989). Psychological support for cancer patients. *Lancet, 2,* 1447.

SPIELBERGER, C. D., JOHNSON, E. H., RUSSELL, S. F., CRANE, R. S., JACOBS, G. A., & WORDEN, T. J. (1985). The experience and expression of anger: Construction and validation of an anger expression scale. In M. A. Chesney & R. H. Rosenman (Eds.), *Anger and hostility in cardiovascular and behavioral disorders.* New York: Hemisphere/McGraw-Hill.

SPIVEY, C. B., & PRENTICE-DUNN, S. (1990). Assessing the directionality of deindividuated behavior: Effects of deindividuation, modeling, and private self-consciousness on aggressive and prosocial responses. *Basic and Applied Social Psychology, 11,* 387–403.

SPRAFKIN, J. N., LIEBERT, R. M., & POULOUS, R. W. (1975). Effects of a prosocial televised example on children's helping. *Journal of Personality and Social Psychology, 48,* 35–46.

SPRINGER, S. P., & DEUTSCH, G. (1989). *Left brain, right brain* (3rd ed.). San Francisco: Freeman.

SQUIER, L. H., & DOMHOFF, G. W. (1998). *The presentation of dreaming and dreams in introductory psychology textbooks: A critical examination.* Unpublished paper.

SQUIRE, L. R. (1987). *Memory and brain.* New York: Oxford University Press.

SQUIRE, L. R. (1992). Memory and the hippocampus: A synthesis from findings with rats, monkeys, and humans. *Psychological Review, 99,* 195–231.

SQUIRE, L. R., & BUTTERS, N. (Eds.). (1984). *The neuropsychology of memory.* New York: Guilford.

SQUIRE, L. R., & FOX, M. M. (1980). Assessment of remote memory: Validation of the television test by repeated testing during a seven-day period. *Behavioral Research Methods and Instrumentation, 12,* 583–586.

SQUIRE, L. R., & KANDEL, E. R. (2000). *Memory: From mind to molecules.* New York: Scientific American Library.

SQUIRE, L. R., & KNOWLTON, B. J. (1995). Learning about categories in the absence of memory. *Proceedings of the National Academy of Sciences, USA, 92,* 12470–12474.

SQUIRE, L. R., KNOWLTON, B., & MUSEN, G. (1993). The structure and organization of memory. *Annual Review of Psychology, 44,* 453–495.

SQUIRE, L. R., OJEMANN, J. G., MIEZIN, F. M., PETERSEN, S. E., VIDEEN, T. O., & RAICHLE, M. E. (1992). Activation of the hippocampus in normal humans: A functional anatomical study of memory. *Proceedings of the National Academy of Science, 89,* 1837–1841.

SQUIRE, L. R., & ZOLA, S. M. (1996). Ischemic brain damage and memory impairment: A commentary. *Hippocampus, 6,* 546–552.

SQUIRE, L. R., ZOLA-MORGAN, S., CAVE, C. B., HAIST, F., MUSEN, G., & SUZUKI, W. A. (1990). Memory: Organization of brain systems and cognition. In *Symposium on quantitative biology, the brain* (Vol. 55). Cold Spring Harbor, NY: Cold Spring Harbor Laboratory.

STAATS, A. W. (1968). *Language, learning, and cognition.* New York: Holt, Rinehart & Winston.

STANGOR, C., & MCMILLAN, D. (1992). Memory for expectancy-congruent and expectancy-incongruent information: A review of the social and social developmental literature. *Psychological Bulletin, 111,* 42–61.

STASSER, G., & TITUS, W. (1985). Pooling of unshared information in group decision making: Biased information sampling during discussion. *Journal of Personality and Social Psychology, 48,* 1467–1478.

STATHAM, D. J., HEATCH, A. C., MADDEN, P., BUCHOLZ, K., BIERUT, L., DINWIDDIE, S. H., SLUTSKE, W. S., DUNNE, M. P., & MARTIN, N. G. (1998). Suicidal behavior: An epidemiological study. *Psychological Medicine, 28,* 839–855.

STATTIN, H., & MAGNUSSON, D. (1990). *Pubertal maturation in female development.* Hillsdale, NJ: Erlbaum.

STAYTON, D. J. (1973, March). *Infant responses to brief everyday separations: Distress, following, and greeting.* Paper presented at the meeting of the Society for Research in Child Development.

STEADMAN, H. J., MULVEY, E. P., MONAHAN, J., ROBBINS, P. C., APPLEBAUM, P. S., GRISSO, T., ROTH, L., & SILVER, E. (1998). Violence by people discharged from acute psychiatric inpatient facilities and by others in the same neighborhoods. *Archives of General Psychiatry, 55,* 393–401.

STEBLAY, N. M (1992). A meta-analytic review of the weapon focus effect. *Law and Human Behavior, 16,* 413–424.

STEELE, C. M. (1997). A threat in the air: How stereotypes shape intellectual identify and performance. *American Psychologist, 52,* 613–629.

STEELE, C. M., & ARONSON, J. (1995). Stereotype threat and the intellectual test performance of African Americans. *Journal of Personality and Social Psychology, 69,* 797–811.

STEIN, D. J. (Ed.). (1997). *Cognitive science and the unconscious.* Washington, DC: American Psychiatric Press.

STEINBERG, L. (1996). *Adolescence* (4th ed.). New York: Knopf.

STEINBERG, L., & MORRIS, A. S. (2001). Adolescent development. *Annual Reviews of Psychology, 52,* 83–110.

STEINER, J. E. (1979). Human facial expressions in response to taste and smell stimulation. *Advances in Child Development and Behavior, 13,* 257–295.

STEKETEE, G., & WHITE, K. (1990). *When once is not enough.* Oakland, CA: New Harbinger.

STELLAR, J. R., & STELLAR, E. (1985). *The neurobiology of motivation and reward.* New York: Springer-Verlag.

STERN, R. S., & COBB, J. P. (1978). Phenomenology of obsessive-compulsive neurosis. *British Journal of Psychiatry, 132,* 233–239.

STERNBERG, R. (2000). *Handbook of intelligence.* New York: Cambridge University Press.

STERNBERG, R., & GRIGORENKO, E. (2001). *Environmental effects on cognitive abilities.* Mahwah, NJ: Erlbaum.

STERNBERG, R., GRIGORENKO, E., & BUNDY, D. (2001) The predictive value of IQ. *Merrill-Palmer Quarterly, 47,* 1–41.

STERNBERG, R., GRIGORENKO, E., CASTEJON, J. L., PRIETO, M. D., & HAUTAMEKI, J. (2001). Confirmatory factor analysis of the Sternberg Triarchic Abilities Test in three international samples: An empirical test of the triarchic theory of intelligence. *European Journal of Psychological Assessment, 17,* 1–16.

STERNBERG, R. J. (1985). *Beyond IQ: A triarchic theory of human intelligence.* Cambridge, England: Cambridge University Press.

STERNBERG, R. J. (1986). *Intelligence applied: Understanding and increasing your intellectual skills.* San Diego: Harcourt Brace Jovanovich.

STERNBERG, R. J. (1988). *The triarchic mind: A new theory of human intelligence.* New York: Viking.

STERNBERG, R. J. (2000). The concept of intelligence. In *Handbook of intelligence* (pp. 3–16). Cambridge, England: Cambridge University Press.

STERNBERG, R. J., & KAUFMAN, J. C. (1998). Human abilities. *Annual Reviews of Psychology, 49,* 479–502.

STERNBERG, R. J., & WILLIAMS, W. M. (1997). Does the Graduate Record Examination predict meaningful success in the graduate training of psychologists? A case study. *American Psychologist, 52,* 630–651.

STERNBERG, S. (1966). Highspeed scanning in human memory. *Science, 153,* 652–654.

STERNBERG, S. (1975). Memory scanning: New findings and current controversies. *Quarterly Journal of Experimental Psychology, 27,* 1–32.

STEUER, F. B., APPLEFIELD, J. M., & SMITH, R. (1971). Televised aggression and the interpersonal aggression of preschool children. *Journal of Experimental Child Psychology, 11,* 422–447.

STEVENSON, H. W., LEE, S., & GRAHAM, T. (1993). Chinese and Japanese kindergartens: Case study in comparative research. In B. Spodek (Ed.), *Handbook of research on the education of young children.* New York: Macmillan.

STILES, W. B., SHAPIRO, D. A., & ELLIOTT, R. (1986). Are all psychotherapies equivalent? *American Psychologist, 41,* 165–180.

STOLL, A. L., RENSHAW, P. F., YURGELUN-TODD, D., & COHEN, B. M. (2000). Neuroimaging in bipolar disorder: What have we learned? *Biological Psychiatry, 48,* 505–517.

STONER, J. A. F. (1961). *A comparison of individual and group decisions involving risk.* Unpublished master's thesis, Massachusetts Institute of Technology.

STOWERS, L., HOLY, T. E., MEISTER, M., DULAC, C., & KOENTEGES, G. (2002). Loss of sex discrimination and male-male aggression in mice deficient for TRP2. *Science, 295,* 1493–1500.

STRACK, F., MARTIN, L. L., & STEPPER, S. (1988). Inhibiting and facilitating conditions of the human smile: A non-obtrusive test of the facial feedback hypothesis. *Journal of Personality and Social Psychology, 54,* 768–777.

STREISSGUTH, A. P., BARR, H. M., BOOKSTEIN, F. L., SAMPSON, P. D., & OLSON, H. C. (1999). The long-term neurocognitive consequences of prenatal alcohol exposure: A 14-year study. *Psychological Science, 10,* 186–190.

STREISSGUTH, A. P., CLARREN, S. K., & JONES, K. L. (1985). Natural history of the fetal alcohol syndrome: A 10-year follow-up of eleven patients. *Lancet, 2,* 85–91.

STROEBE, W., INSKO, C. A., THOMPSON, V. D., & LAYTON, B. D. (1971). Effects of physical attractiveness, attitude similarity and sex on various aspects of interpersonal attraction. *Journal of Personality and Social Psychology, 18,* 79–91.

STRONG, S. R., HILLS, H. J., KILMARTIN, C. T., DEVRIES, H., LANIER, A. K., NELSON, B. N., STRICKLAND, D., & MEYER, C. W., III (1988). The dynamic relations among interpersonal behaviors: A test of complementarity and anti-comple-

mentarity. *Journal of Personality and Social Psychology, 54,* 798–810.

STROOP, J. R. (1935). Studies of interference in serial-verbal reaction. *Journal of Experimental Psychology, 18,* 643–662.

STUNKARD, A. J. (1982). Obesity. In M. Hersen, A. Bellack, & A. Kazdin (Eds.), *International handbook of behavior modification and therapy.* New York: Plenum.

STUNKARD, A. J. (1996). *The origins and consequences of obesity.* Chichester, England: Wiley.

STUNKARD, A. J., HARRIS, J. R., PEDERSEN, N. L., & MCCLEARN, G. E. (1990). A separated twin study of the body mass index. *New England Journal of Medicine, 322,* 1483–1487.

STYRON, W. (1990). *Darkness visible.* New York: Vintage Books.

SUAREZ, E. C., KUHN, C. M., SCHANBERG, S. M., WILLIAMS, R. B., JR., & ZIMMERMAN, E. A. (1998). Neuroendocrine, cardiovascular, and emotional responses of hostile men: The role of interpersonal challenge. *Psychosomatic Medicine, 60,* 78–88.

SUE, D. W. & SUE, D. (1999). Counseling the culturally different: Theory and practice (3rd ed.). New York: Wiley.

SUE, S., ALLEN, D., & CONAWAY, L. (1978). The responsiveness and equality of mental health care to Chicanos and Native Americans. *American Journal of Community Psychology, 6,* 137–146.

SUE, S., & ZANE, N. (1987). The role of culture and cultural techniques in psychotherapy: A critique and reformulation. *American Psychologist, 42,* 37–51.

SULLIVAN, H. S. (1953). *The interpersonal theory of psychiatry.* New York: Norton.

SULLIVAN, P. F., NEALE, M. C., & KENDLER, K. S. (2000). Genetic epidemiology of major depression: Review and meta-analysis. *American Journal of Psychiatry, 157,* 1552–1562.

SUTKER, P. B., DAVIS, J. M., UDDO, M., & DITTA, S. R. (1995). Assessment of psychological distress in Persian Gulf troops: Ethnicity and gender comparisons. *Journal of Personality Assessment, 64,* 415–427.

SVENSON, O. (1981). Are we all less risky and more skillful than our fellow drivers? *Acta Psychologica, 47,* 143–148.

SWARTZ, C. (1995). Setting the ECT stimulus. *Psychiatric times, 12,* 6 (Reprint addition).

SWARTZ, M., BLAZER, D., GEORGE, L., & WINFIELD, I. (1990). Estimating the prevalence of borderline personality disorder in the community. *Journal of Personality Disorders, 4,* 257–272.

SWEDO, S, PIETRINI, P., & LEONARD, H. (1992). Cerebral glucose metabolism in childhood-onset obsessive-compulsive disorder. *Archives of General Psychiatry, 49,* 690–694.

SWETS, J. A., & BJORK, R. A. (1990). Enhancing human performance: An evaluation of "new age" techniques considered by the U.S. Army. *Psychological Science, 1,* 85–96.

SWIM, J. K., & SANNA, L. J. (1996). He's skilled, she's lucky: A meta-analysis of observer's attributions for women's and men's successes and failures. *Personality and Social Psychology Bulletin, 22,* 507–519.

SWINNEY, D. A. (1979). Lexical access during sentence comprehension: Consideration of context effects. *Journal of Verbal Learning and Verbal Behavior, 18,* 645–659.

SYMONS, D. (1992). On the use and misuse of Darwinism in the study of human behavior. In J. H. Barkow & L. Cosmides (Eds.), *The adapted mind: Evolutionary psychology and the generation of cul-*

ture (pp. 137–159). New York: Oxford University Press.

SZASZ, T. S. (1971). The sane slave: An historical note on the use of medical diagnosis as justificatory rhetoric. American Journal of Psychotherapy, 25, 228–239.

SZKRYBALO, J., & RUBLE, D. N. (1999). "God made me a girl": Sex-category constancy and judgments and explanations revisited. Developmental Psychology, 35, 392–402.

TABER, K. H., LEWIS, D. A., & HURLEY, R. A. (2001). Schizophrenia: What's under the microscope. Journal of Clinical Neuropsychiatry, 13, 1–4.

TANENHAUS, M. G., LEIMAN, J., & SEIDENBERG, M. (1979). Evidence for multiple stages in the processing of ambiguous words in syntactic contexts. Journal of Verbal Learning and Verbal Behavior, 18, 427–441.

TANNEN, D. (1990). You just don't understand: Women and men in conversation. New York: Ballantine Books.

TANNEN, D. (1998). The argument culture. New York: Random House.

TARTTER, V. C. (1986). Language processes. New York: Holt, Rinehart & Winston.

TATEYAMA, M, & KASPER, S. (1998). Transcultural study of schizophrenic delusions: Tokyo versus Vienna versus Tuebingen (Germany). Psychopathology, 31, 59–68.

TAVRIS, C., & SADD, S. (1977). The Redbook report on female sexuality. New York: Dell.

TAYLOR, S. (1999). Health psychology (4th ed.). Boston: McGraw-Hill.

TAYLOR, S., KEMENY, M., ASPINWALL, L., SCHNEIDER, S., RODRIGUEZ, R., & HERBERT, M. (1992). Optimism, coping, psychological distress, and high-risk sexual behavior among men at risk for acquired immunodeficiency syndrome (AIDS). Journal of Personality and Social Psychology, 63, 460–473.

TAYLOR, S., KEMENY, M. E., REED, G. M., BOWER, J. E., & GRUENWALD, T. L. (2000). Psychological resources, positive illusions, and health. American Psychologist, 55, 99–109.

TAYLOR, S. E., & BROWN, J. D. (1988). Illusion and well-being: A social psychological perspective on mental health. Psychological Bulletin, 103, 193–210.

TAYLOR, S. E., KEMENY, M., ASPINWALL, L. G., SCHNEIDER, S. G., RODRIGUEZ, R., & HERBERT, M. (1992). Optimism, coping, psychological distress, and high-risk sexual behavior among men at risk for AIDS. Journal of Personality and Social Psychology, 63, 460–473.

TAYLOR, S. E., & THOMPSON, S. C. (1982). Stalking the elusive "vividness" effect. Psychological Review, 89, 155–181.

TEASDALE, J. D., SEGAL, Z. V., WILLIAMS, J. M. G., RIDGEWAY, V. A., SOULSBY, J. M., & LAU, M. A. (2000). Prevention of relapse/recurrence in major depression by mindfulness-based cognitive therapy. Journal of Consulting and Clinical Psychology, 68, 615–523.

TEITELBAUM, P., & EPSTEIN, A. N. (1962). The lateral hypothalamic syndrome: Recovery of feeding and drinking after lateral hypothalamic lesions. Psychological Review, 69, 74–90.

TELLEGEN, A., BOUCHARD, T. J., WILCOX, K. J., SEGAL, N. L., LYKKEN, D. T., & RICH, S. (1988). Journal of Personality and Social Psychology, 54, 1031–1039.

TELLEGEN, A., LYKKEN, D. T., BOUCHARD, T. J., JR., WILCOX, K. J., SEGAL, N. L., & RICH, S. (1988). Personality similarity in twins reared apart and together. Journal of Personality and Social Psychology, 54, 1031–1039.

TELLER, D. Y. (1979). The forced-choice preferential looking procedure: A psychophysical technique for use with human infants. Infant Behavior and Development, 2, 135–153.

TELLER, D. Y., & MOVSHON, J. A. (1986). Visual development. Vision Research, 26, 1483–1506.

TEMPLIN, M. C. (1957). Certain language skills in children: Their development and interrelationships. Minneapolis: University of Minnesota Press.

TENNEN, H., & AFFLECK, G. (1999). Finding benefits in adversity. In C. R. Snyder (Ed), Coping: The psychology of what works (pp. 279–304). New York: Oxford University Press.

TERMAN, L. M., & ODEN, M. H. (1959). Genetic studies of genius, Vol. IV: The gifted group at midlife. Stanford, CA: Stanford University Press.

TERRACE, H. S., PETITTO, L. A., SANDERS, D. J., & BEVER, T. G. (1979). Can an ape create a sentence? Science, 206, 891–902.

TESSER, A., & BRODIE, M. (1971). A note on the evaluation of a "computer date." Psychonomic Science, 23, 300.

THASE, M., JINDAL, & HOWLAND. (2002). Biological aspects of depression. In I. H. Gotlib & C. L. Hammen (Eds.), Handbook of depression. New York: Guilford.

THIGPEN, C. H., & CLECKLEY, H. (1957). The three faces of Eve. New York: McGraw-Hill.

THOMAS, A., & CHESS, S. (1977). Temperament and development. New York: Brunner/Mazel.

THOMAS, A., & CHESS, S. (1986). The New York longitudinal study: From infancy to early adult life. In R. Plomin & J. Dunn (Eds.), The study of temperament: Changes, continuities and challenges (pp. 39–52). Hillsdale, NJ: Erlbaum.

THOMAS, A., CHESS, S., BIRCH, H., HERTZIG, M., & KORN, S. (1963). Behavioral individuality in early childhood. New York: New York University Press.

THOMAS, F. L., & ROBINSON, H. A. (1982). Improving reading in every class. Boston: Allyn and Bacon.

THOMPSON, P. M., CANNON, T. D., NARR, K. L., VAN ERP, T., POUTANEN, V. P., HUTTUNEN, M., LONNQVIST, J., STANDERTSKJOLD-NORDENSTAM, C. G., KAPRIO, J., KHALEDY, M., DAIL, R., ZOUMALAN, C. I., & TOGA, A. W. (2001). Genetic influences on brain structure. Nature Neuroscience, 4, 1253–1258.

THOMPSON, R. A., LAMB, M., & ESTES, D. (1982). Stability of infant-mother attachment and its relationship to changing life circumstances in an unselected middle-class sample. Child Development, 53, 144–148.

THOMPSON, S. C. (1991). The search for meaning following a stroke. Basic and Applied Social Psychology, 12, 81–96.

THOMPSON, S. K. (1975). Gender labels and early sex role development. Child Development, 46, 339–347.

THOMPSON, W. R. (1954). The inheritance and development of intelligence. Proceedings of the Association for Research on Nervous and Mental Disease, 33, 209–231.

THORESEN, C. E., TELCH, M. J., & EAGLESTON, J. R. (1981). Altering type A behavior. Psychosomatics, 8, 472–482.

THORNDIKE, E. L. (1898). Animal intelligence: An experimental study of the associative processes in animals. Psychological Monographs, 2, 8.

THORPE, G. L., & OLSON, S. L. (1997). Behavior therapy: Concepts, procedures, and applications (2nd ed.). Boston: Allyn and Bacon.

THURSTONE, L. L. (1938). Primary mental abilities. Psychometric Monographs, No. 1. Chicago: University of Chicago Press.

TIMMERS, M., FISCHER, A. H., & MANSTEAD, A. S. R. (1998). Gender differences in motives for regulating emotions. Personality and Social Psychology Bulletin, 24, 974–985.

TIZARD, B., & REES, J. (1975). The effect of early institutional rearing on the behavioural problems and affectional relationships of four-year-old children. Journal of Child Psychology and Psychiatry, 16, 61–73.

TOATES, F. (1986). Motivational systems. Cambridge, England: Cambridge University Press.

TOLMAN, E. C. (1932). Purpose behavior in animals and men. New York: Appleton-Century-Crofts. (Reprinted 1967. New York: Irvington)

TOMASSON, R. F., CROSBY, F. J., & HERZBERGER, S. D. (1996). Affirmative action: the pros and cons of policy and practice. Washington, DC: American University Press.

TOMPKINS, S. S. (1962). Affect, imagery, consciousness: Vol. 1. The positive affects. New York: Springer.

TOMPKINS, S. S. (1980). Affect as amplification: Some modifications in theory. In R. Plutchik & H. Kellerman (Eds.), Emotion: Theory, research and experience (Vol. 1). New York: Academic Press.

TONAY, V. (1993). Personality correlates of dreams. Dreaming, 3, 1–8.

TONG, F., & ENGEL, S. A. (2001). Interocular rivalry revealed in the human cortical blind spot representation. Nature, 411, 195–199.

TOOBY, J., & COSMIDES, L. (1990). The past explains the present: Emotional adaptations and the structure of ancestral environments. Ethology and Sociobiology, 11, 375–424.

TOPPING, K., HOLMES, E. A., & BREMNER, W. (2000). The effectiveness of school-based programs for the promotion of social competence. In R. Bar-On & J. D. A. Parker (Eds.), The Handbook of Emotional Intelligence, San Francisco: Jossey-Bass.

TORGERSEN, S. (1986). Genetic factors in moderately severe and mild affective disorders. Archives of General Psychiatry, 49, 690–694.

TORREY, E. F. (1995). Surviving schizophrenia: A manual for families, consumers and providers (3rd ed.). New York: Harper Perennial.

TORREY, E. F. (1997). Out of the shadows: Confronting America's mental illness crisis. New York: Wiley.

TOWNSHEND, B., COTTER, N., VAN COMPERNOLLE, D., & WHITE, R. L. (1987). Pitch perception by cochlear implant subjects. Journal of the Acoustical Society of America, 82, 106–115.

TRAFIMOW, D., TRIANDIS, H. C., & GOTO, S. G. (1991). Some tests of the distinction between the private self and the collective self. Journal of Personality and Social Psychology, 60, 649–655.

TRANEL, D., BECHARA, A., & DAMASIO, A. R. (2000). Decision making and the somatic marker hypothesis. In: M. S. Gazzaniga (Ed.), The new cognitive neurosciences (pp. 1047–1061). Cambridge, MA: MIT Press.

TREISMAN, A. (1969). Strategies and models of selective attention. Psychological Review, 76, 282–299.

TREISMAN, A. (1986). Features and objects in visual processing, Scientific American, 254, 114–125.

TREISMAN, A., & GELADE, G. (1980). A feature integration theory of attention. Cognitive Psychology, 12, 97–136.

TREISMAN, A. M. (1986). Features and objects in visual processing. *Scientific American, 255*, 114B–125.

TRIANDIS, H. C. (1989). The self and social behavior in different cultures. *Psychological Review, 96*, 506–520.

TRINDER, J. (1988). Subjective insomnia without objective findings: A pseudodiagnostic classification. *Psychological Bulletin, 103*, 87–94.

TRIPP, C. A. (1987). *The homosexual matrix* (2nd ed.). New York: New American Library.

TRIVERS, R. L. (1972). Parental investment and sexual selection. In B. Campbell (Ed.), *Sexual selection and the descent of man: 1871–1971* (pp. 136–179). Chicago: Aldine.

TROPE, T., & GAUNT, R. (1999). A dual-process model of overconfident attributional inferences. In S. Chaiken & Y. Trope (Eds.), *Dual-process theories in social psychology* (pp. 161–178). New York: Guilford.

TRUAX, K., WOOD, A., WRIGHT, E., CORDOVA, D. I., & CROSBY, F. J. (1998). Undermined: Affirmative action from the targets' point of view. In J. K. Swim & C. Stagnor (Eds.), *Prejudice: The target's perspective* (pp. 171–188). New York: Academic Press.

TSIEN J. Z. (2000). Building a brainier mouse. *Scientific American, 282*, 62–68.

TSUANG, M. T. (1983). Suicide in the relatives of schizophrenics, manics, depressives and controls. *Journal of Clinical Psychiatry, 44*, 396–400.

TULVING, E. (1974). Cue-dependent forgetting. *American Scientist, 62*, 74–82.

TULVING, E. (1983). *The elements of episodic memory.* New York: Oxford University Press.

TULVING, E. (1985). How many memory systems are there? *American Psychologist, 40*, 385–398.

TULVING, E., KAPUR, S., CRAIK, F. I. M., MOSCOVITCH, M., & HOULE, S. (1994). Hemispheric encoding/retrieval asymmetry in episodic memory: Positron emission tomography findings. *Proceedings of the National Academy of Science of the United States of America, 91*, 2016–2020.

TULVING, E., KAPUR, S., MARKOWITSCH, H. J., CRAIK, F. I. M., HABIB, R., & HOULE, S. (1994). Neuroanatomical correlates of retrieval in episodic memory: Auditory sentence recognition. *Proceedings of the National Academy of Science of the United States of America, 91*, 2012–2015.

TULVING, E., & PEARLSTONE, Z. (1966). Availability versus accessibility of information in memory for words. *Journal of Verbal Learning and Verbal Behavior, 5*, 381–391.

TUMA, J. M. (1989). Mental health services for children: The state of the art. *American Psychologist, 44*, 188–199.

TUNNELL, G. (1981). Sex role and cognitive schemata: Person perception in feminine and androgynous women. *Journal of Personality and Social Psychology, 40*, 1126–1136.

TURIEL, E. (1983). The development of social knowledge: Morality and convention. Cambridge, England: Cambridge University Press.

TURK, D. C. (1996). Clinician attitudes about prolonged use of opioids and the issue of patient heterogeneity. *Journal of Pain and Symptom Management, 11*, 218–230.

TURK, D. C., & OKIFUJI, A. (1997). What factors affect physicians' decisions to prescribe opioids for chronic non-cancer pain patients? *Clinical Journal of Pain, 13*, 330–336.

TURKHEIMER, E. (1998). Heritability and biological explanation. *Psychological Review, 105*, 782–791.

TURNER, M. E., & PRATKANIS, A. R. (1998a). A social identity model of groupthink. *Organizational Behavior and Human Decision Processes, 73*, 210–235.

TURNER, M. E., & PRATKANIS, A. R. (1998b). Twenty-five years of groupthink theory and research: Lessons from the evaluation of a theory. *Organizational Behavior and Human Decision Processes, 73*, 105–115.

TURNER, M. E., & PRATKANIS, A. R. (1994). Affirmative action as help: A review of recipient reactions to preferential selection and affirmative action. *Basic and Applied Social Psychology, 15*, 43–69.

TURNER, M. E., PRATKANIS, A. R., PROBASCO, P., & LEVER, C. (1992). Threat, cohesion, and group effectiveness: Testing a social identity maintenance perspective in groupthink. *Journal of Personality and Social Psychology, 63*, 781–796.

TVERSKY, A., & KAHNEMAN, D. (1973). On the psychology of prediction. *Psychological Review, 80*, 237–251.

TVERSKY, A., & KAHNEMAN, D. (1983). Extensional versus intuitive reasoning: The conjunction fallacy in probability judgment. *Psychological Review, 90*, 293–315.

TYE-MURRAY, N., SPENCER, L., & WOODWORTH, G. G. (1995). Acquisition of speech by children who have prolonged cochlear implant experience. *Journal of Speech and Hearing Research, 38*, 327–337.

TYLER, H. (1977). The unsinkable Jeane Dixon. *Humanist, 37*, 6–9.

UCHINO, B. N., UNO, D., & HOLT-LUNSTAD, J. (1999). Social support, physiological processes, and health. *Current Directions in Psychological Science, 8*, 145–148.

ULLMAN, M. T., CORKIN, S., COPPOLA, M., HICKOK, G., GROWDON, J. H., KOROSHETZ, W. J., & PINKER, S. (1997). A neural dissociation within language: Evidence that the mental dictionary is part of declarative memory, and that grammatical rules are processed by the procedural system. *Journal of Cognitive Neuroscience, 9*, 266–276.

URSIN, H. (1978). Activation, coping, and psychosomatics. In H. Ursin, E. Baade, & S. Levine (Eds.), *Psychobiology of stress: A study of coping men.* New York: Academic Press.

UTTS, J. (1986). The gansfeld debate: A statistician's perspective. *Journal of Parapsychology, 50*, 393–402.

VAKOCH, D. A., & STRUPP, H. H. (2000). Psychodynamic approaches to psychotherapy: Philosophical and theoretical foundations of effective practice. In C. R. Snyder & R. Ingram (Eds.), *Handbook of psychological change* (pp. 200 216) New York: Wiley.

VAN DEN HEUVEL, O. A., VAN DE WETERING, B. J. M., VELTMAN, D. J., & PAULS, D. L. (2000). Genetic studies of panic disorder: A review. *Journal of Clinical Psychiatry, 61*, 756–766.

VAN PRAAG, H., KEMPERMANN, G., & GAGE, F. H. (1999). Running increases cell proliferation and neurogenesis in the adult mouse dentate gyrus. *Nature Neuroscience, 2*, 266–270.

VAN PRAAG, H., SCHINDER, A. F., CHRISTIE, B. R., TONI, N., PALMER, T. D., & GAGE, F. H. (2002). Functional neurogenesis in the adult hippocampus. *Nature, 415*, 1030–1034.

VAN VORT, W., & SMITH, G. P. (1987). Sham feeding experience produces a conditioned increase of meal size. *Appetite, 9*, 21–29.

VANCE, A. L., VELAKOULIS, D., MARUFF, P., WOOD, S. J., DESMOND, P., & PANTELIS, C.

(2000). Magnetic resonance spectroscopy and schizophrenia: What have we learnt? *Australian and New Zealand Journal of Psychiatry, 34*, 14–25.

VAUGHN, B. E., LEFEVER, G. B., SEIFER, R., & BARGLOW, P. (1989). Attachment behavior, attachment security, and temperament during infancy. *Child Development, 60*, 728–737.

VAUGHN, C. E., & LEFF, J. P. (1976). The influence of family and social factors on the course of psychiatric illness: A comparison of schizophrenic and depressed neurotic patients. *British Journal of Psychiatry, 129*, 125–137.

VELMANS, M. (1991). Is human information processing conscious? *Behavioral and Brain Sciences, 14*, 651–726.

VISINTAINER, M. A., VOLPICELLI, J. R., & SELIGMAN, M. E. P. (1982). Tumor rejection in rats after inescapable or escapable shock. *Science, 216*, 437–439.

VOGT, T., & BELLUSCIO, D. (1987). Controversies in plastic surgery: Suction-assisted lipectomy (SAL) and the HCG (human chorionic gonadotropin) protocol for obesity treatment. *Aesthetic Plastic Surgery, 11*, 131–156.

VON LANG, J., & SIBYLL, C. (Eds.). (1983). *Eichmann interrogated* (R. Manheim, Trans.). New York: Farrar, Straus & Giroux.

VYGOTSKY, L. S. (1986). *Thought and language* (A. Kozulin, Trans.). Cambridge, MA: MIT Press. (originally published 1934)

WADDEN, T. A., BERKOWITZ, R. I., VOGT, R. A., STEEN, S. N., STUNKARD, A. J., & FOSTER, G. D. (1997). Lifestyle modification in the pharmacological treatment of obesity: A pilot investigation of a potential primary care approach. *Obesity Research, 5*, 218–226.

WAGNER, W. M., & MONNET, M. (1979). Attitudes of college professors toward extrasensory perception. *Zetetic Scholar, 5*, 7–17.

WAHLBERG, D. (1999, October 21). Binge drinking remains problem. *Ann Arbor News*, A1.

WALKER, C. E., HEDBERG, A., CLEMENT, P. W., & WRIGHT, L. (1981). *Clinical procedures for behavior therapy.* Englewood Cliffs, NJ: Prentice-Hall.

WALKER, E. (1978). *Explorations in the biology of language.* Montgomery, VT: Bradford.

WALLACE, SCHNEIDER, MCGRIFFIN (2002). Genetics of depression. In I. H. Gotlib & C. L. Hammen (Eds.), *Handbook of depression.* New York: Guilford.

WALLACH, M. A., KOGAN, N., & BEM, D. J. (1962). Group influence on individual risk taking. *Journal of Abnormal and Social Psychology, 65*, 75–86.

WALLACH, M. A., KOGAN, N., & BEM, D. J. (1964). Diffusion of responsibility and level of risk taking in groups. *Journal of Abnormal and Social Psychology, 68*, 263–274. WALLACH, M. A., & WALLACH, L. (1983). *Psychology's sanction for selfishness.* San Francisco: Freeman.

WALLER, S. J., LYONS, J. S., & CONSTANTINI-FERRANDO, M. F. (1999). Impact of comorbid affective and alcohol use disorders on suicide ideation and attempts. *Journal of Clinical Psychology, 55*, 585–595.

WALSTER, E., ARONSON, E., ABRAHAMS, D., & ROTTMAN, L. (1966). Importance of physical attractiveness in dating behavior. *Journal of Personality and Social Psychology, 4*, 508–516.

WALTERS, J., & GARDNER, H. (1985). The development and education of intelligences. In F. Link (Ed.), *Essays on the intellect.* Washington, DC:

Curriculum Development Associates/Association for Supervision and Curriculum Development.

WALZER, M. (1970). *Obligations*. Cambridge, MA: Harvard University Press.

WAMPOLD, B. E., MONDIN, G. W., MOODY, M., STICH, F., BENSON, K., & AHN, H. (1997). A meta-analysis of outcome studies comparing bona fide psychotherapies: Empirically, "all must have prizes." *Psychological Bulletin, 122*, 203–215.

WANDELL, B. A. (1995). *Foundations of Vision*. Sunderland, MA: Sindaur Associates.

WANDELL, B. A., & Maloney, L. T. (1986). Color constancy: A method for recovering surface spectral reflectance. *Journal of the Optical Society of America, 3*, 29–33.

WARD, I. L. (1992). Sexual behavior: The products of perinatal hormonal and prepubertal social factors. In A. A. Gerall, H. Motz, & I. L. Ward (Eds.), *Sexual differentiation* (pp. 157–179). New York: Plenum.

WARRINGTON, E. K., & SHALLICE, T. (1984). Category specific semantic impairments. *Brain, 107*, 829–853.

WARRINGTON, E. K., & WEISKRANTZ, L. (1978). Further analysis of the prior learning effect in amnesic patients. *Neuropsychologica, 16*, 169–177.

WASON, P. C., & JOHNSON-LAIRD, P. N. (1972). *Psychology of reasoning: Structure and content*. London: Batsford.

WASSERMAN, E. A. (1990). Detecting response-outcome relations: Toward an understanding of the causal texture of the environment. *Psychology of Learning and Motivation, 26*, 27–82.

WATERMAN, A. S. (1985). Identity in the context of adolescent psychology. In A. S. Waterman (Ed.), *Identity in adolescence: Progress and contents*. San Francisco: Jossey-Bass.

WATSON, J. B. (1930). *Behaviorism* (rev. ed.). New York: Norton.

WATSON, J. B., & RAYNER, R. (1920). Conditioned emotional reactions. *Journal of Experimental Psychology, 3*, 1–14.

WATSON, M., HAYILAND, J. S., GREER, S., DAVIDSON, J., & BLISS, J. M. (1999). Influence of psychological response on survival in breast cancer: A population-based cohort study. *Lancet, 354*, 1331–1336.

WEAVER, E. G. (1949). *Theory of hearing*. New York: Wiley.

WECHSLER, D. (1958). *The measurement and appraisal of adult intelligence*. Baltimore: Williams.

WECHSLER, H., DAVENPORT, A., DOWDALL, G., MOEYKENS, B., & CASTILLO, S. (1994). Health and behavioral consequences of binge drinking in college, a national survey of students at 140 campuses. *Journal of the American Medical Association, 272*, 1672–1677.

WECHSLER, H., DOWDALL, G. W., MAENNER, G., GLEDHILL-HOYT, J., & LEE, H. (1998). Changes in binge drinking and related problems among American college students between 1993 and 1997. *Journal of American College Health, 47*, 57–68.

WEGNER, D. M., SCHNEIDER, D. J., CARTER, S., III, & WHITE, L. (1987). Paradoxical consequences of thought suppression. *Journal of Personality and Social Psychology, 53*, 1–9.

WEIGLE, D. S. (1994). Appetite and the regulation of body composition. *FASEB Journal, 8*, 302–310.

WEINBERG, M. S., SCHWARTZ, G. E., & DAVIDSON, R. E. (1979). Low-anxious, high-anxious, and repressive coping styles: Psychometric patterns and behavioral and physiological responses to stress. *Journal of Abnormal Psychology, 88*, 369–380.

WEINBERGER, D. (1990). The construct validity of the repressive coping style. In J. L. Singer (Ed.), *Repression and dissociation: Implications for personality theory, psychopathology, and health* (pp. 337–385). Chicago: University of Chicago Press.

WEINBERGER, J. (1996). Common factors aren't so common: The common factors dilemma. *Clinical Psychology: Science and Practice, 2*, 45–69.

WEINBERGER, J., & MCCLELLAND, D. C. (1990). Cognitive vs. traditional motivational models: Irreconcilable or complementary? In R. Sorrentino & E. T. Higgins (Eds.), *Handbook of motivation and cognition* (pp. 562–597). New York: Guilford.

WEINE, S. M., BECKER, D. F., MCGLASHAN, T. H., LAUB, D., LAZROVE, S., VOJVODA, D., & HYMAN, L. (1995). Psychiatric consequences of "ethnic cleansing": Clinical assessments and trauma testimonies of newly resettled Bosnian refugees. *American Journal of Psychiatry, 152*, 536–542.

WEINE, S. M., VOJVODA, D., BECKER, D. F., MC-GLASHAN, T. H., HODZIC, E., LAUB, D., HY-MAN, L., SAWYER, M., & LAZROVE, S. (1998). PTSD symptoms in Bosnian refugees 1 year after resettlement in the United States. *American Journal of Psychiatry, 155*, 562–564.

WEINSTEIN, N. D. (1980). Unrealistic optimism about future events. *Journal of Personality and Social Psychology, 39*, 806–820.

WEINSTEIN, N. D. (1987). Unrealistic optimism about susceptibility to health problems. Conclusions from a community-wide sample. *Journal of Behavioral Medicine, 10*, 481–500.

WEINSTEIN, N. D. (1989). Optimistic biases about personal risks. *Science, 246*, 1232–1233.

WEINSTEIN, N. D. (1998). Accuracy of smokers' risk perceptions. *Annals of Behavioral Medicine, 20*, 135–140.

WEIR, C., & SEACREST, M. (2000). Developmental differences in understanding of balance scales in the United States and Zimbabwe. *Journal of Genetic Psychology*. 2000, 161, 5–22.

WEISS, D. D., & LAST, C. G. (2001). *The developmental psychopathology of anxiety*. New York: Oxford University Press.

WEISS, J. M., GLAZER, H. I., POHORECKY, L. A., BRICK, J., & MILLER, N. E. (1975). Effects of chronic exposure to stressors on avoidance-escape behavior and on brain norepinephrine. *Psychosomatic Medicine, 37*, 522–534.

WEISS, R. D., MIRIN, S. M., & BARTEL, R. L. (1994). *Cocaine* (2nd ed.). Washington, DC: American Psychiatric Press.

WEISSMAN, M. M. (1993). Family genetic studies of panic disorder. Conference on panic and anxiety: A decade of progress. *Journal of Psychiatric Research, 27* (suppl.), 69–78.

WEISSTEIN, N. A., & WONG, E. (1986). Figure-ground organization and the spatial and temporal responses of the visual system. In E. C. Schwab & H. C. Nusbaum (Eds.), *Pattern recognition by humans and machines*. Vol. 2. *Visual perception* (pp. 31–64). Orlando, FL: Academic Press.

WEISZ, J. R., DONENBERG, G., HAN, S., & KAUNECKIS, D. (1995). Child and adolescent psychotherapy outcomes in experiments versus clinics: Why the disparity? *Journal of Abnormal Child Psychology, 23*, 83–106.

WELLER, L., & WELLER, A. (1993). Human menstrual synchrony: A critical assessment. *Neuroscience and Behavioral Reviews, 17*, 427–439.

WELLINGTON, S., & GISCOMBE, K. (2001). Women and leadership in corporate America. In C. Costello & A. Stone (Eds.), *The American woman, 2001–02* (pp. 87–106). New York: Norton.

WELLMAN, H. M. (1994). Early understanding of the mind: The normal case. In S. Baron-Cohen (Ed.), *Understanding other minds: Perspectives from autism.* (pp. 10–39). New York: Oxford University Press.

WELLS, G. L., FERGUSON, T. J., & LINDSAY, R. C. L. (1981). The tractability of eyewitness confidence and its implication for triers of fact. *Journal of Applied Psychology, 66*, 688–696.

WERTHEIMER, M. (1912/1932). Experimentelle studien uber das sehen von beugung. *Zeitschrift Für Psychologie, 61*, 161–265.

WERTHEIMER, M. (2000). *A brief history of psychology* (6th ed.). Fort Worth: Harcourt.

WEST, C., & ZIMMERMAN, D. H. (1983). Small insults: A study of interruptions in cross-sex conversations between unacquainted persons. In B. Thorne, C. Kramarae, & N. Henley (Eds.), *Language, gender, and society*. Rowley, MA: Newbury House.

WESTBROOK, G. L. (1994). Glutamate receptor update. *Current Opinion in Neurobiology, 4*, 337–346.

WESTEN, D. (1998). The scientific legacy of Sigmund Freud: Toward a psychodynamically informed psychological science. *Psychological Bulletin, 124*, 333–371.

WESTERMEYER, J. (1993). Cross-cultural psychiatric assessment. In A. C. Gaw (Ed.), *Culture, ethnicity, and mental illness* (pp. 125–144). Washington, DC: American Psychiatric Press.

WHALEN, P. J., RAUCH, S. L., ETCOFF, N. L., MCINERNEY, S. C., LEE, M. B., & JENIKE, M. A. (1998). Masked presentation of emotional facial expressions modulate amygdala activity without explicit knowledge. *Journal of Neuroscience, 18*, 411–418.

WHEEDEN, A., SCAFIDI, F. A., FIELD, T., IRONSON, G., BANDSTRA, E., SCHANBERG, S., & VALDEON, C. (1993). Massage effects on cocaine-exposed preterm neonates. *Journal of Developmental and Behavioral Pediatrics, 14*, 318–322.

WHEELER, S. C., & PETTY, R. E. (2001). The effects of stereotype activation on behavior: A review of possible mechanisms. *Psychological Bulletin, 127*, 797–826.

WHEELER, S. C., JARVIS, W. B. G., & PETTY, R. E. (2001). Think unto others: The self-destructive impact of negative racial stereotypes. *Journal of Experimental Social Psychology, 37*, 173–180.

WHITAM, F. L., & MATHY, R. M. (1986). *Male Homosexuality in Four Societies: Brazil, Guatemala, the Philippines, and the United States. Vol. Special Studies*. New York: Praeger.

WHITAM, F. L., & MATHY, R. M. (1991). Childhood cross-gender behavior of homosexual females in Brazil, Peru, the Philippines, and the United States. *Archives of Sexual Behavior, 20*, 151–170.

WHITE, C. (1977). Unpublished Ph.D. dissertation, Catholic University, Washington, DC.

WHITE, G. L., FISHBEIN, S., & RUTSTEIN, J. (1981). Passionate love and the misattribution of arousal. *Journal of Personality and Social Psychology, 41*, 56–62.

WHITE, G. L., & KIGHT, T. D. (1984). Misattribution of arousal and attraction: Effects of salience of explanations for arousal. *Journal of Experimental Social Psychology, 20*, 55–64.

WHORF, B. L. (1956). *Language, thought, and reality: Selected writings of Benjamin Lee Whorf* (edited by T. B. Carroll). Cambridge, MA: MIT Press; New York: Wiley

WHYTE, W. H. (1956). *The organization man.* New York: Simon & Schuster.

WICKER, A. W. (1969). Attitudes versus actions: The relationship between verbal and overt behavioral responses to attitude objects. *Journal of Social Issues, 25,* 41–78.

WIEBE, D. J., & MCCALLUM, D. M. (1986). Health practices and hardiness as mediators in the stress-illness relationship. *Health Psychology, 5,* 425–438.

WIENS, S., MEZZACAPPA, E. S., & KATKIN, E. S. (2000). Heartbeat detection and the experience of emotions. *Cognition and Emotion, 14,* 417–427.

WILCOXIN, H. C., DRAGOIN, W. B., & KRAL, P. A. (1971). Illness-induced aversions in rat and quail: Relative salience of visual and gustatory cues. *Science, 171,* 823–828.

WILKES, A. L., & KENNEDY, R. A. (1969). Relationship between pausing and retrieval latency in sentences of varying grammatical form. *Journal of Experimental Psychology, 79,* 241–245.

WILKINS, W. (1984). Psychotherapy: The powerful placebo. *Journal of Consulting and Clinical Psychology, 52,* 570–573.

WILLIAMS, D. C. (1959). The elimination of tantrum behavior by extinction procedures. *Journal of Abnormal and Social Psychology, 59,* 269.

WILLIAMS, G. C. (1996). *Plan and purpose in nature.* London: Weidenfeld and Nicholson.

WILLIAMS, J. M., & DUNLOP, L. C. (1999). Pubertal timing and self-reported delinquency among male adolescents. *Journal of Adolescence, 22,* 157–171.

WILLIAMS, M. D., & HOLLAN, J. D. (1981). The process of retrieval from very long-term memory. *Cognitive Science, 5,* 87–119.

WILLIAMS, R. B. (1995). Somatic consequences of stress. In M. J. Friedman (Ed.), *Neurobiological and clinical consequences of stress: From normal adaptation to post-traumatic stress disorder.* Philadelphia: Lippincott-Raven.

WILLIAMS, R. B., JR., BAREFOOT, J. C., HANEY, T. L., HARRELL, F. E., BLUMENTHAL, J. A., PRYOR, D. B., & PETERSON, B. (1988). Type A behavior and angiographically documented coronary atherosclerosis in a sample of 2,289 patients. *Psychosomatic Medicine, 50,* 139–152.

WILSON, E. O. (1963). Pheromones. *Scientific American, 208,* 100–114.

WILSON, E. O. (1975). *Sociobiology: The new synthesis.* Cambridge, MA: Harvard University Press.

WILSON, E. O. (1978). *On human nature.* Cambridge, MA: Harvard University Press.

WILSON, M. A., & MCNAUGHTON, B. L. (1994). Reactivation of hippocampal ensemble memories during sleep. *Science, 265,* 676–679.

WILSON, M. I., & DALY, M. (1985). Competitiveness, risk-taking and violence: The young male syndrome. *Ethology and Sociobiology, 6,* 59–73.

WILSON, P. (1995). *Instant calm.* New York: Plume.

WILSON, T. D., DUNN, D. S., KRAFT, D., & LISLE, D. J. (1989). Introspection, attitude change, and attitude-behavior consistency: The disruptive effects of explaining why we feel the way we do. In L. Berkowitz (Ed.), *Advances in experimental social psychology* (Vol. 22). San Diego: Academic Press.

WILSON, T. D., LASER, P. S., & STONE, J. I. (1982). Judging the predictors of one's mood: Accuracy and the use of shared theories. *Journal of Experimental Social Psychology, 18,* 537–556.

WILSON, W. H., & CLAUSEN, A. M. (1995). 18-month outcome of clozapine treatment for 100 patients in a state psychiatric hospital. *Psychiatric Services, 46,* 386–389.

WILSON, W. R. (1979). Feeling more than we can know: Exposure effects without learning. *Journal of Personality and Social Psychology, 37,* 811–821.

WINCH, R. F., KTSANES, T., & KTSANES, V. (1954). The theory of complementary needs in mate selection: An analytic and descriptive study. *American Sociological Review, 29,* 241–249.

WINDHOLZ, M. J., MARMAR, C. R., & HOROWITZ, M. J. (1985). A review of the research on conjugal bereavement: Impact on health and efficacy of intervention. *Comprehensive Psychiatry, 26,* 433–447.

WINGER, G., HOFFMAN, F. G., & WOODS, J. H. (1992). *A handbook on drug and alcohol abuse* (3rd ed.). New York: Oxford University Press.

WINSON, J. (1990). The meaning of dreams. *Scientific American, 262,* 86–96.

WINTER, D. G. (1973). *The power motive.* New York: Free Press.

WINTER, D. G., STEWART, A. J., JOHN, O. P., KLOHNEN, E. C., & DUNCAN, L. E. (1998). Traits and motives: Toward an integration of two traditions in personality research. *Psychological Review, 105,* 230–250.

WISE, R. A. (1982). Neuroleptics and operant behavior: The anhedonia hypothesis. *Behavioral and Brain Sciences, 5,* 39–87.

WISNIEWSKI, E. J., & MEDIN, D. L. (1991). Harpoons and longsticks: The interaction of theory and similarity in rule induction. In D. Fisher, M. Pazzani, & P. Langley (Eds.), *Concept formation: Knowledge and experience in unsupervised learning.* San Mateo, CA: Morgan-Kaufman.

WOELK, H., BURKARD, G., & GRUNWALD, J. (1994). Benefits and risks of the hypericum extract LI 160: Drug monitoring study with 3,250 patients. *Journal of Geriatric Psychiatry and Neurology, 7* (suppl. 1), 34–38.

WOLCHIK, S. A., BEGGS, V. E., WINCZE, P. P., SAKHEIM, D. K., BARLOW, D. H., & MAVISSAKALIAN, M. (1980). The effect of emotional arousal on subsequent sexual arousal in men. *Journal of Abnormal Psychology, 89,* 595–598.

WOLMAN, B. B., DALE, L. A., SCHMEIDLER, G. R., & ULLMAN, M. (Eds.). (1986). *Handbook of parapsychology.* New York: Van Nostrand & Reinhold.

WOLPE, J. (1958). *Psychotherapy by reciprocal inhibition.* Stanford, CA: Stanford University Press.

WOLRAICH, M., HANNAH, J., BAUMGAERTEL, A., & FEUER, I. (1998). Examination of DSM-IV criteria for attention deficit hyperactivity in a county-wide sample. *Journal of Developmental and Behavioral Pediatrics, 19,* 162–168.

WOOD, G. (1986). *Fundamentals of psychological research* (3rd ed.). Boston: Little, Brown.

WOOD, W., LUNDGREN, S., OUELLETTE, J. A., BUSCEME, S., & BLACKSTONE, T. (1994). Minority influence: A meta-analytic review of social influence processes. *Psychological Bulletin, 115,* 323–345.

WOOD, W., WONG, F. Y., & CHACHERE, J. G. (1991). Effects of media violence on viewers' aggression in unconstrained social situations. *Psychological Bulletin, 109,* 371–383.

WOODY, R. H., & ROBERTSON, M. (1988). *Becoming a clinical psychologist.* Madison, CT: International Universities Press.

WORD, C. O., ZANNA, M. P., & COOPER, J. (1974). The nonverbal mediation of self-fulfilling prophecies in interracial interaction. *Journal of Experimental Social Psychology, 10,* 109–120.

WORTMAN, C. B., & BREHM, J. W. (1975). Responses to uncontrollable outcomes: An integration of reactance theory and the learned helplessness model. *Advances in Experimental and Social Psychology, 8,* 277–236.

WRIGHT, L. (1988). The type A behavior pattern and coronary artery disease, quest for the active ingredients and the elusive mechanism. *American Psychologist, 43,* 2–14.

WURTZ, R. H., GOLDBERG, M. E., & ROBINSON, D. L. (1980). Behavioral modulation of visual responses in monkeys. *Progress in Psychobiology and Physiological Psychology, 9,* 42–83.

WURTZEL, E. (1995). *Prozac nation.* New York: Berkley.

YAGER, T., LAUFER, R., & GALLOPS, M. (1984). Some problems associated with war experience in men of the Vietnam generation. *Archives of General Psychiatry, 41,* 327–333.

YARBUS, D. L. (1967). *Eye movements and vision.* New York: Plenum.

YEHUDA, R. (2000). Biology of posttraumatic stress disorder. *Journal of Clinical Psychiatry, 61,* 14–21.

YEHUDA, R., MCFARLANE, A. C., & SHALEY, A. Y. (1998). Predicting the development of posttraumatic stress disorder from the acute response to a traumatic event. *Biological Psychiatry, 44,* 1305–1313.

YESAVAGE, J. A., LEIER, V. O., DENARI, M., & HOLLISTER, L. E. (1985). Carry-over effect of marijuana intoxication on aircraft pilot performance: A preliminary report. *American Journal of Psychiatry, 142,* 1325–1330.

YOST, W. A., & NIELSON, D. W. (1985). *Fundamentals of hearing* (2nd ed.). New York: Holt, Rinehart & Winston.

YOUNGER, J., ADRIANCE, W., & BERGER, R. J. (1975). Sleep during transcendental meditation. *Perceptual and Motor Skills, 40,* 953–954.

YU, B., ZHANG, W., JING, Q., PENG, R., ZHANG, G., & SIMON, H. A. (1985). STM capacity for Chinese and English language materials. *Memory and Cognition, 13,* 202–207.

ZAHN-WAXLER, C., KLIMES-DOUGAN, B., & SLATTERY, M. J. (2000). Internalizing problems of childhood and adolescence: Prospects, pitfalls, and progress in understanding the development of anxiety and depression. *Development and Psychopathology, 12,* 443–466.

ZAJONC, R. B. (1965). Social facilitation. *Science, 149,* 269–274.

ZAJONC, R. B. (1968). Attitudinal effects of mere exposure. *Journal of Personality and Social Psychology, Monograph Supplement, 9,* 1–29.

ZAJONC, R. B. (1980). Compresence. In P. B. Paulus (Ed.), *Psychology of group influence.* Hillsdale, NJ: Erlbaum.

ZAJONC, R. B. (1984). On the primacy of affect. *American Psychologist, 39,* 117–123.

ZAJONC, R. B., HEINGARTNER, A., & HERMAN, E. M. (1969). Social enhancement and impairment of performance in the cockroach. *Journal of Personality and Social Psychology, 13,* 83–92.

ZAJONC, R. B., MURPHY, S. T., & INGLEHART, M. (1989). Feeling and facial efference: Implications of the vascular theory of emotion. *Psychological Review, 96,* 394–416.

ZALUTSKY, R. A., & NICOLL, R. A. (1990). Comparison of two forms of longterm potentiation in single hippocampal neurons. *Science, 248,* 1619–1624.

ZAMANSKY, H. S., & BARTIS, S. P. (1985). The dissociation of an experience: The hidden observer observed. *Journal of Abnormal Psychology, 94,* 243–248.

ZEKI, S. (1993). *A vision of the brain.* Boston: Blackwell Scientific Publications.

ZELAZO, P. R., ZELAZO, N. A., & KOLB, S. (1972). Walking in the newborn. *Science, 176,* 314–315.

ZHANG, Y., PROENCA, R., MAFFEI, M., BARONE, M., LEOPOLD, L., & FRIEDMAN, J. M. (1994). Positional cloning of the mouse obese gene and its human homologue. *Nature, 372,* 425–431.

ZILLMANN, D. (1984). *Connections between sex and aggression.* Hillsdale, NJ: Erlbaum.

ZILLMANN, D., & BRYANT, J. (1974). Effect of residual excitation on the emotional response to provocation and delayed aggressive behavior. *Journal of Personality and Social Psychology, 30,* 782–791.

ZIMBARDO, P. G. (1969). The human choice: Individuation, reason and order vs. deindividuation, impulse, and chaos. In W. J. Arnold & D. Levine (Eds.), *Nebraska symposium on motivation* (pp. 237–307). Lincoln: University of Nebraska Press.

ZIMBARDO, P. G. (1970). The human choice: Individuation, reason and order versus deindividuation, impulse and chaos. In W. J. Arnold & D. Levine (Eds.), *Nebraska symposium on motivation* (Vol. 16). Lincoln: University of Nebraska Press.

ZIMBARDO, P. G. (1972). Pathology of imprisonment. *Society, 9,* 4–8.

ZLOTNICK, C., ELKIN, I., & SHEA, M. T. (1998). Does the gender of a patient or the gender of a therapist affect the treatment of patients with major depression? *Journal of Consulting and Clinical Psychology, 66,* 655–659.

ZOLA-MORGAN, S., & SQUIRE, L. R. (1985). Medial-temporal lesions in monkeys impair memory on a variety of tasks sensitive to human amnesia. *Behavioral Neuroscience, 99,* 22–34.

ZOLA-MORGAN, S. M., & SQUIRE, L. R. (1990). The primate hippocampal formation: Evidence for a time-limited role in memory storage. *Science, 250,* 228–290.

ZOLA-MORGAN, S. M., SQUIRE, L. R., & AMARAL, D. G. (1989). Lesions of the hippocampal formation but not lesions of the fornix or the mamalary nuclei produce long-lasting memory impairments in monkeys. *Journal of Neuroscience, 9,* 898–913.

ZUBER, J. A., CROTT, H. W., & WERNER, J. (1992). Choice shift and group polarization: An analysis of the status of arguments and social decision schemes. *Journal of Personality and Social Psychology, 62,* 50–61.

ZUCKER, K. J. (1990). Gender identity disorders in children: Clinical description and natural history. In R. Blanchard (Ed.) *Clinical management of gender identity disorders in children and adults* (pp. 3–23). Washington DC: American Psychiatric Press.

ZUCKER, K. J., & BRADLEY, S. J. (1995). *Gender identity disorder and psychosexual problems in children and adolescents.* New York: Guilford.

ZUCKERMAN, M. (1979). *Sensation seeking: Beyond the optimal level of arousal.* Hillsdale, NJ: Erlbaum.

ZUCKERMAN, M. (1991). *Psychobiology of personality.* Cambridge, England: Cambridge University Press.

ZUCKERMAN, M. (1995). Good and bad humors: Biochemical bases of personality and its disorders. *Psychological Science, 6,* 325–332.

ZURIF, E. B. (1990). Language and the brain. In D. N. Osherson & H. Lasnik (Eds.), *An invitation to cognitive science: Language* (Vol. 1). Cambridge, MA: MIT Press.

ZURIF, E. B. (1995). Brain regions of relevance to syntactic processing. In: D. N. Osherson, L. R. Gleitman, & M. Liberman (Eds.) *An invitation to cognitive science, second edition: Language* (Vol. 1), pp. 381–397. Cambridge, MA: MIT Press.

ZURIF, E. B., CARAMAZZA, A., MYERSON, R., & GALVIN, J. (1974). Semantic feature representations for normal and aphasic language. *Brain and Language, 1,* 167–187.

CREDITS

This page constitutes an extension of the copyright page. We have made every effort to trace the ownership of all copyrighted material and to secure permission from copyright holders. In the event of any question arising as to the use of any material, we will be pleased to make the necessary corrections in future printings. Thanks are due to the following authors, publishers, and agents for permission to use the material indicated.

Photographs
Chapter 1
1: © Artville/Getty Images; 2: © Laura Dwight; 4: (left) © Jonathan Nourok/Photo Edit; 4: © Bill Aron/Photo Edit; 5: © Bettmann/CORBIS; 6: Archives of the History of American Psychology, the University of Akron; 7: (bottom left) © CORBIS; (bottom center, right) © Bettmann/CORBIS; 10: © Volker Steoer/Peter Arnold, Inc.; 11: (left) © Mary Kate Denny/Photo Edit; (right) © David Young-Wolff/Photo Edit; 12: Kactus Foto/SuperStock; 13: © John Eastcott/Yva Momatiuk/Stock Boston; 23: © Michael Newman/Photo Edit/PictureQuest

Chapter 2
30: © Digital Art/CORBIS; 36: © Omicron/Science Source/Photo Researchers; 43: F2-9: © Martin Rotker/Phototake; 47: (above) © Le Duc/Monkmeyer; (below) Courtesy of Marcus E. Raichle; 50: © Bertrand Rieger/Getty/Stone; 56: F2-18: © CNRI/SPL/Photo Researchers; 57: © The Everett Collection; 58: (left) © Laura Doss/CORBIS; (right) © Margaret Ross/Stock Boston

Chapter 3
64: © Marco Cauz/CORBIS; 66: (both) © Corbis/Bettmann; 68: (all) © Laura Dwight; 70: F3-2: © Creatas/PictureQuest; 71: © Michael Newman/Photo Edit; 72: F3-3 (above): Courtesy of Carolyn Rovee-Collier; F3-4 (below): © Rick Malkames; 75: © Laura Dwight; 76: F3-5 (both): © Laura Dwight; 77: (all) © Laura Dwight; 80: © Monika Graff/The Image Works; 81: F3-9 (top left): © Bios (Michael Gunther)/Peter Arnold, Inc.; (top right) © IFA/Peter Arnold, Inc.; (bottom left) © Hans Pfletschinger/Peter Arnold, Inc.; (bottom right) © Fred Bruemmer/Peter Arnold, Inc.; 83: © Michelle Bridwell/Photo Edit; 84: (left) © Lawrence Migdale/Stock Boston; (right) © David Young-Wolff/Photo Edit; 87: © Michael Newman/Photo Edit; 88: © Laura Dwight; 90: F3-11: © Martin Rogers/Stock Boston; 91: © Will & Deni McIntyre/Photo Researchers; 93: © Elizabeth Crews; 94: (left)

© Sylvie Villeger/Explorer/Photo Researchers; (right) © Kathy Sloane/Photo Researchers; 95: © Mark Richards/Photo Edit; 98: © Joel Gordon; 99: © Ariel Skelley/CORBIS

Chapter 4
106: © Jerry Tobias/CORBIS; 109: © Ake Lindau IBL, Rex Instock/Stock Connection/PictureQuest; 112: F4-5: Courtesy of Geoffrey Loftus; 121: © David Sutherland/Getty Images/Stone; 122: F4-18: Courtesy of Macbeth/Munsell Color, New Windsor, NY; 127: © Charles & Josette Lenars/CORBIS; 128: © Ralf-Finn Hestoft/Index Stock Imagery/PictureQuest; 134: Courtesy of Geoffrey Loftus; 135: © Porter Gifford/Stock Boston; 136: © Joel Gordon; 137: © Peter Vandermark/Stock Boston

Chapter 5
146: © Renee Lynn/CORBIS; 147: © The McNeil River State Game Sanctuary, photo by Jon C. Pascal; 150: F5-2: D. L. Yarbuss (1967) "Eye Movements and Vision," *Plenum Publishing Corporation*. Reproduced by permission of the publisher; 151: © Norbert vonder Groeben/The Image Works; 154: F5-4: Salvador Dali, *Slave Market with Disappearing Bust of Voltaire,* 1950, The Salvador Dali Museum, St. Petersburg, Florida; 157: F5-7: © Macduff Everton/CORBIS; 159: California Museum of Photography, University of California, Riverside; 160: © Tim Davis/Getty Images/Stone; 161: © Tim Davis/Getty Images/Stone; 170: © Najlah Feanny/Stock Boston; 174: © David Frazier/The Image Works; 177: © Hiroyuki Matsumoto/Getty Images/Stone; 178: © Baron Wolman/Woodfin Camp; 180: M. Corbetta, F.M. Miezen, S. Dobmeyer, D.L. Shulman, S.E. Persen, "Attentional modulation of neural processing of shape, color and velocity in humans, *Science* V. 248, p. 1558 1990, Reprinted by permission of the American Association for the Advancement of Science; 184: F5-34 (above): © Lawrence Migdale/Photo Researchers; F5-35 (below): From *Sensations and Perception* by E. Bruce Goldstein, © 1989, 1984, 1980 Wadsworth Publishing Co.; 185: F5-36: © Martin Rogers/Stock Boston

Chapter 6
194: © Peter Holst/The Image Bank/Getty Images; 196: © Bonnie Kamin/Photo Edit; 202: © Chuck Savage/Corbis Stock Market; 204: (both) © Louis Psihoyos/Matrix International; 205: © Christian Blackman/CORBIS; 207: © Joel Gordon; 209: © Oscar Burriel/Latin Stock/SPL/Photo

Researchers; 211: © H. Arneson; 212: © Paul A. Souders/CORBIS; 215: © James Shaffer/Photo Edit; 219: © Mark Antman/The Image Works; 225: (left) © Jeremy Walker/SPL/Photo Researchers; (right) Courtesy of Dr. Charles Honorton

Chapter 7
232: © Taxi/Getty Images; 235: © Corbis/Bettmann; 240: © Tom & Dee Ann McCarthy/CORBIS; 243: F7-6: © Richard Wood/Index Stock; (right) Nina Leen, © Life Magazine/TimePix; 245: F7-7: Courtesy of Naval Oceans System Center; 246: © Jose Luis Pelaez Inc./Corbisstockmarket.com; 248: © Jeff Greenberg/Peter Arnold, Inc.; 249: © William Johnston/Stock Boston; 250: © Jerry McCormick-Ray/Photo Researchers; 252: © R. Malmares, WNET/Thirteen; 253: F7-10: Yerkes Primate Research Center, Emory University; F7-11 (all): © SuperStock; 254: © Najlah Feanny/CORBIS SABA

Chapter 8
266: © Firefly Productions/CORBIS; 268: © Tom Stewart/CORBIS; 269: © Corbis/Hulton Deutsch Collection; 275: (right) © Jose Luis Pelaez Inc./Corbisstockmarket.com; F8-5 (left): © Michael Newman/Photo Edit; From *Alice in Wonderland,* Abridged by Josette Frank, Random House, 1955; 282: © Shackman/Monkmeyer Press; 287: © Patrick Durand/Corbis Sygma; 289: © Mary Kate Denny/Photo Edit; 296: © Jeff Greenberg/Photo Edit; 297: © David G. Curran/Rainbow; 299: © Gaitano/CORBIS

Chapter 9
312: © Mug Shots/CORBIS; 317: © Owen Franken/CORBIS; 320: © Laura Dwight; 323: © David Young-Wolff/Photo Edit; 325: (left) © Michael Nichols/Magnum Photos; (right) © Paul Fusco/Magnum Photos; 327: (left) © Russell Hansen/Peter Arnold, Inc.; (right) © Art Wolfe/Photo Researchers; 330: © James Shaffer/Photo Edit; 343: © Bob Daemmrich/The Image Works; 344: F9-13: © Susan Holtz; 345: © David Young-Wolff/Stone/Getty Images; 348: © Susan Holtz

Chapter 10
352: © R.W. Jones/CORBIS; 354: (left) © Amy C. Etra/Photo Edit; (right) © Topham/The Image Works; 356: Courtesy of K.C. Berridge; 358: © Joel Gordon; 360: © Michael Newman/Photo Edit; 361: © Bryce Flynn/Stock Boston; 364: © Richard Howard; 370: (left) © Corbis/Bettmann; (right): © AFP/CORBIS; 373: © Camera

M.D. Studios, 1973, all rights reserved;
377: © David C. Fritts/Animals, Animals

Chapter 11

388: © Eyewire/Getty Images; 396: F11-3: From Whalen, Rauch, Etcoff, McInerney, Lee & Jenike, Masked presentation of emotional facial expressions modulate amygdala activity without explicit knowledge; *Journal of Neuroscience* 1998, 18: 411-418; 399: (left) © D. Lowe/Stock Boston; (right) © Paula Lerner/Woodfin Camp; 404: © Syracuse Newspapers/The Image Works; 407: (top, all) New Guinea faces from *Face of Man*, New York, Garland, 1980, Paul Ekman/Pergamon; (bottom, all) © Paul Ekman; 412: Courtesy of Ashby Plant; 413: © Bob Daemmrich/Stock Boston; 415: © Catherine Ursillo/Photo Researchers; 416: F11-8 (both): Courtesy of Dr. Jose M.R. Delgado; 417: F11-10: © Albert Bandura; 422: (left) © Byron/Monkmeyer Press; (right) © Michael Newman/Photo Edit

Chapter 12

426: © Getty Images/Stone; 428: © Gary Wagner/Stock Boston; 430: © 1986, Reproduced with permission of The Riverside Publishing Company, Chicago, Illinois; 434: AP/Wide World Photos; 437: (top) © Bob Daemmrich/Stock Boston; (middle) © Jeff Greenberg/Rainbow; (bottom) © Jack Grove/Photo Edit; 441: © Ellen B. Senisis/The Image Works; 444: © Mary Kate Denny/Photo Edit; 448: (left) © Michael Newman/Photo Edit; (right) © Sidney/Monkmeyer Press

Chapter 13

452: © Jon Feingersh/CORBIS; 453: © Peter Byron; 455: © Arnold Gold/The Image Works; 462: © ER Productions/CORBIS; 463: © Bettmann/Corbis; 464: © Tony Freeman/Photo Edit; 465: © Laura Dwight; 466: F13-3: © Spencer Grant/Stock Boston; 467: AP/Wide World Photos; 470: © Cindy Roesinger/Photo Researchers; 472: © Albert Bandura; 473: © Laima Druskis/Stock Boston; 475: © Mary Steinbacher/Photo Edit; 477: Carl Rogers Memorial Library; 480: (left) AP/Wide World; (right) © Bettmann/Corbis; 481: © AFP/CORBIS; 485: © Myrleen Ferguson Cate/Photo Edit; 488: © Alison Wright/Stock Boston

Chapter 14

492: © PhotoDisc/Getty Images; 494: (left) © Laima Druskis/Stock Boston; (right) © David Young-Wolff/Photo Edit; 495: © Ilkkla Uimonen/Corbis Sygma; 497: © Larry L. Miller/Photo Researchers; 500: © Kindra Clineff/Getty Images/Stone; 501: © Vincent DeWitt/Stock Boston; 505: F14-05: Courtesy of Dr. Lisa Shin, from Shin, Kosslyn, Alpert, Rauch, Macklin, & Pittman (1997), "Visual imagery and Perception in Posttraumatic Stress Disorder: A Positron Emission Tomographic Investigation." *Archives of General Psychiatry* 54: 233-241; F14-06: Courtesy of J. Douglas Bremner, MD; 509: © Bob Daemmrich/Stock Boston; 511: AP/Wide World Photos; 513: © AFP/CORBIS; 515: © Gerard Vandystadt/Photo Researchers; 516: © Amy C. Etra/Photo Edit; 519: © Dan McCoy/Rainbow

Chapter 15

526: © Artville/Getty Images; 528: (left) © Bettmann/Corbis; (right) © Wartenberg/Picture Press/Corbis; 529: © Steven Peters/Getty Images/Stone; 537: © John Cancalosi/Peter Arnold; 540: F15-5 (left): © Dr. Lewis Baxter/Peter Arnold, Inc.; F15-6

(right): UCLA School of Medicine, from Schwartz, Stoessel, Baxter, Martin & Phelps (1996) Systematic change in cerebral glucose metabolic rate after successful behavior modification treatment of obsessive-compulsive disorder, *Archives of General Psychiatry* 53: 109-113; 543: AP Wide World Photos; 545: F15-9 (above): Courtesy of Monte S. Buchsbaum, MD; F15-10 (below): Courtesy of Dr. Wayne Drevets, NIMH, from Drevets, WC, Todd, RD, Depression, mania and related disorders, in: *Adult Psychiatry*, Guze, SB (ed), Mosby Year Book 1997: 99-141, St. Louis, MO; 550: Privizhorn Collection, Ruprecht-Karls-Universitat Heidelberg Klinikum; 552: Laboratory of Psychology and Psychopathology, National Institute of Mental Health; 553: F15-14: © Photo Researchers; 554: F15-15 (above): Courtesy of S. Galderisi, from Galderisi, Vita, Rossi, Stratta, Leonardi & Invernizzi. (2000) Qualitative MRI findings in patients with schizophrenia. *Psychiatry Research: Neuroimaging Section*, 98: 117-126; F15-16 (below): Courtesy of David A. Lewis, MD, University of Pittsburgh School of Medicine

Chapter 16

568: © CORBIS; 571: (above) © Stock Montage; (below) © Corbis/Bettmann; 577: © Michael Newman/Photo Researchers; 584: © Frank Pedrick/The Image Works; 585: © Peter Tumley/Corbis; 595: © Najlah Feanny/Stock Boston; 597: © Michael Newman/Photo Edit

Chapter 17

604: AP/Wide World Photos; 605: (all) AP/Wide World Photos; 606: © Getty Images/Stone; 608: © Mark E. Gibson; 609: (above) © Peter Tumley/CORBIS; F17-2 (below): Philip G. Zimbardo, Inc.; 610: © David M. Grossman/Photo Researchers; 611: www.crimelibrary.com; 614: (all) The Asch Study of the Resistance of Majority Opinion from *Scientific American*, November, 1995, Vol. 193, No. 5, by Solomon E. Asch; 615: (left) © Bill Lai/Rainbow; (right) © Sandy Felsenthal/CORBIS; 617: © Chuck Savage/CORBIS; 618: © Jon Jones/Corbis Sygma; 619: (all) From the film *Obedience*, distributed by the New York University Film Library; © 1965 by Stanley Milgram, Reprinted by permission of Alexandra Milgram; 622: © Steve Kaufman/CORBIS; 624: © Bossu Regis/Corbis Sygma; 630: © Bettmann/Corbis; 633: (all) © Philip Zimbardo; 634: © John Neubauer/Photo Edit; 637: © Gary Conner/Photo Edit

Chapter 18

644: © Taxi/Getty Images; 647: © Bonnie Kamin/Photo Edit; 648: (both) © Joel Gordon; 650: © Jose Luis Pelaez, Inc./CORBIS; 655: © Don Smetzer/Getty Images/Stone; 659: (left) © Michael Newman/Photo Edit; (right) © David Young-Wolff/Photo Edit; 662: © Susan Van Etten/Photo Edit; 665: © Cleo/Photo Edit; 667: (left) © Ronnie Kaufman/CORBIS; (right) © Zigy Kaluzny/Getty Images/Stone; 670: © Comstock

Tables, Boxes, Illustrations
Chapter 1

3: K. Sheingold and Y. J. Tenney (1982) "Recall of An Early Memory," adapted from "Memory for a Salient Childhood Event," from U. Neisser (ed.) Memory Observed: Remembering in Natural Context, copyright © 1982 by W. H. Freeman & Company. Adapted by permission of the publisher.

4: L. Eron, et al. (1972) "Does Television Violence Cause Aggression?" American Psychologist, 27:253-262. Copyright © 1972 by The American Psychological Association. Adapted by permission.

Chapter 2

32: Adapted from Human Anatomy by Anthony J. Gaudin and Kenneth C. Jones. Copyright © 1988 by Anthony J. Gaudin and Kenneth C. Jones. Reprinted by permission of the authors. 32: Adapted from Human Anatomy by Anthony J. Gaudin and Kenneth C. Jones. Copyright © 1988 by Anthony J. Gaudin and Kenneth C. Jones. Reprinted by permission of the authors. 36: Adapted from Search for the Human Mind by Robert Sternberg. Copyright © 1994 by Harcourt Brace & Company, reproduced by permission of the publisher. 43: Adapted from Human Anatomy by Anthony J. Gaudin and Kenneth C. Jones. Copyright © 1988 by Anthony J. Gaudin and Kenneth C. Jones. Reprinted by permission of the authors. 45: Adapted from Human Anatomy by Anthony J. Gaudin and Kenneth C. Jones. Copyright © 1988 by Anthony J. Gaudin and Kenneth C. Jones. Reprinted by permission of the authors. 48: Reprinted from Neuropsychologia, Volume 9, by R. D. Nebes and W. Sperry, p. 247. Copyright © 1971, with kind permission of Elsevier Science, Ltd., The Boulevard, Langford Lane, Kiddington, Oxford, OX5 1DX, UK. 58: Reprinted from Proceedings of the Association for Research in Nervous and Mental Diseases, Volume 33, by R. W. Thompson, p. 209-231. Copyright © 1954.

Chapter 3

73: T. Field, "Massage Therapy Facilitates Weight Gain in Preterm Infants," Current Directions in Psychological Science, 10, p. 51-53. © 1986 Blackwell Publishers. Reprinted by permission. 75: From Review of Child Development Research, Vol. 1, edited by M. L. Hoffman & L. W. Hoffman. Copyright © 1964 by the Russell Sage Foundation. Reprinted by permission of Russell Sage Foundation. 79: Adapted from Baillargeon, R., "Object Performance in $3\frac{1}{2}$ and $4\frac{1}{2}$ Month Old Infants," from Developmental Psychology, 23:655-664. Copyright © 1987. Reprinted with permission of the Academic Press. 85: Kohlberg, L. (1969) "Stages of Moral Reasoning," from "Stages and Sequence: The Cognitive Developmental Approach to Socialization" in Handbook of Socialization Theory and Research, D. A. Goslin (ed.) Reprinted by permission of Rand McNally. 89: Reprinted by permission of the publisher from Infancy: Its Place in Human Development by Jerome Kagan, R. B. Kearsley and P. R. Zelazo, p. 107, Cambridge, Mass.: Harvard University Press, Copyright © 1978 by the President and Fellows of Harvard College.

Chapter 4

108: Galanter, E. (1962) "Contemporary Psychophysics," from Roger Brown & collaborators (eds.), New Directions in Psychology, Vol. 1. Reprinted by permission of Roger Brown. 115: From Sensation and Perception by E. Bruce Goldstein. Copyright © 1989, 1984, 1980 by Wadsworth Publishing Company. Reprinted by permission of Wadsworth, a division of Thomson Learning. 116: Adapted from Human Color Vision by Robert M. Boynton, copyright © 1979 by Holt, Rinehart & Winston. Reprinted by permission of Harcourt Brace & Company. 117: Adapted from Human Color Vision by Robert M. Boynton, copyright © 1979 by

Holt, Rinehart & Winston. Reprinted by permission of Harcourt Brace & Company. **117:** J. E. Dowling and B. B. Boycott (1969) "Organization of the Primate Retina" from Proceedings of the Royal Society of London, Series B, Vol. 166, p. 80-111. Adapted by permission of the Royal Society of London. **124:** Reprinted from "Spectral Sensitivity of the Foveal Cone Photopigments Between 400 and 500 nm," in Vision Search, 15, p. 161-171. © 1975, with permission from Elsevier Science. **129:** From Sensation and Perception, 3/e, by S. Coren and L. Ward, © 1989. Used by permission of John Wiley & Sons, Inc. **136:** E. H. Erickson, "Sensory Neural Patterns in Gustation," from Zotterman (ed.), Olfaction and Taste, Vol. 2, p. 205-213. Copyright © 1963, with kind permission of Elsevier Science. **138:** D. D. Kosambi (1967) "Living Prehistory in India," from Scientific American 215:105. Copyright 1967 by D. D. Kosambi. Reprinted by permission of Dr. Meera Kosambi and Mr. Jijoy B. Surka.

Chapter 5

165: Based on G. M. Reicher (1969) "Perception of Letters & Words" from "Perceptual Recognition as a Function of the Meaningfulness of the Material," in Journal of Experimental Psychology, 81:275-280. **166:** From L. Biederman, Computer Vision, Graphics, and Image Processing, 32, p. 29-73, © 1985 Academic Press. Used with permission. **167:** From L. Biederman, Computer Vision, Graphics, and Image Processing, 32, p. 29-73, © 1985 Academic Press. Used with permission. **168:** From E. G. Boring (1930) "A New Ambiguous Figure," from American Journal of Psychology, 42:444-445. **168:** From G. H. Fisher (1967) "Perception of Ambiguous Stimulus Materials," from Perception & Psychophysics, 2:421-422. Reprinted by permission of the Psychonomic Society. **181:** After Mortimer Mishkin, Leslie G. Ungerleider, & Kathleen A. Macko (1983), "Object vision and spatial vision: two cortical pathways," Trends in Neuroscience, 6(10):414-417. **187:** R. Held and A. Held (1963) "Movement Produced in the Development of Visually Guided Behavior," from Journal of Comparative and Physiological Psychology, 56:872-876. Copyright © 1963 by the American Psychological Association. Adapted with permission.

Chapter 6

198: © The New Yorker Collection 1979, Dana Fradon from cartoonbank.com. All Rights Reserved. **203:** G. M. Pion (1991) "Psychologists Wanted: Employment Trends Over the Past Decade," in R. R. Kilbur (ed.) How to Manage Your Career in Psychology, copyright © 1991 by the American Psychological Association. Reprinted by permission. **213:** From L. A. Warner, R. C. Kessler, M. Hughes, J. C. Anthony, & C. B. Nelson (1995). Prevalence and correlates of drug use and dependence in the United States. Archives of General Psychiatry, 52, 219-229. **224:** © Bill Yates. Reprinted with special permission of King Features Syndicate.

Chapter 7

236: Adapted from Conditioned Reflexes by E. P. Pavlov. Copyright © 1927 by Oxford University Press. Reprinted by permission of Oxford University Press. **237:** "The Sensory Generalization of Conditioned Responses With Varying Frequencies of Tone," from Journal of General Psychology, Vol. 17, p. 125-148, 1937. Reprinted by permission of the Helen Dwight Reid Educational Foundation.

238: Adapted from "Differential Classical Conditioning: Verbalization of Stimulus Contingencies," by M. J. Fuhrer & P. E. Baer, reprinted by permission from Science, Vol. 150, December 10, 1965, p. 1479-1481. Copyright © 1965 by American Association for the Advancement of Science. **239:** R. A. Rescorla (1967) "Pavlovian Conditioning & Its Proper Control Procedures," from Psychological Review, Vol. 74:71-80. Copyright © 1967 by the American Psychological Association. **241:** J. Garcia and R. A. Koelling (1966) 'The Relation of Cue to Consequence in Avoidance Learning," from Psychonomic Science, 4:123-124. Reprinted by permission of the Psychonomic Society. **247:** Adapted from Barry Schwartz, Psychology of Learning and Behavior, 3/e, with permission of W. W. Norton & Co., Inc. **252:** From Brain, Mind and Behavior by Bloom and Lazerton. Copyright © 1988 by Educational Broadcasting Corporation. Used with permission of W. H. Freeman and Company.

Chapter 8

268: A. W. Melton (1963) "Implication of Short-Term Memory for a General Theory of Memory," from Journal of Verbal Learning and Verbal Behavior, 2:1-21. Adapted by permission of the Academic Press. **274:** DOONESBURY © Garry B. Trudeau. Reprinted with permission of UNIVERSAL PRESS SYNDICATE. All rights reserved. **277:** Adapted from "High Speed Scanning in Human Memory," reprinted with permission from Science, Vol. 153, August 5, 1966, p. 652-654 by S. Sternberg. Copyright © 1966 by the American Association for the Advancement of Science. **278:** © 1985, reprinted courtesy of Bill Hoest and Parade Magazine. **278:** P. A. Carpenter, M. A. Just, and P. Shell (1990), "What one intelligence test measures: A theoretical account of the Processing in the Raven Progressive Matrices Test," Psychological Review, 97(3): 404-431. Adapted by permission of the American Psychological Association. **279:** B. B. Murdock (1962) 'The Serial Position Effect in Free Recall," from Journal of Experimental Psychology, 64:482-488. Copyright © 1962 by the American Psychological Association. Adapted by permission. **283:** E. Tulving and Z. Pearlstone (1976) "Availability and Accessibility," from Journal of Memory and Language, 5:381-391. Reprinted by permission of Academic Press. **286:** D. Godden and A. D. Baddeley (1975) "Context-Dependent Memory in Two Natural Environments: On Land & Under Water," from British Journal of Psychology, 66:325-331. **290:** Reprinted from Neuropsychologia, Vol. 16, p. 169-172, by W. K. Warrington and L. Weiskrantz, "Further Analysis of the Proper Learning Effect in Amnesiac Patients." Copyright © 1978, with permission from Elsevier Science, Ltd. **302:** Adapted from "Acquisition of a Memory Skill," reprinted by permission from Science, Vol. 208, 1980, p. 1181-1182 by I. A. Ericsson, et al. Copyright © 1980 by American Association for the Advancement of Science.

Chapter 9

322: Dan I. Slobin (1971) from "Developmental Psycholinguistic," in A Survey of Linguistic Science, edited by W. O. Dingwall, p. 298-400. **331:** E. J. Wesniewski and D. L. Medin (1991) "Harpoons & Logisticks: The Interaction of Theory & Similarity in Rule Induction," in Concept Formation: Knowledge & Experience in Unsupervised Learning, ed. by D. Fisher, M. Pazzani, & P. Langley. Copyright © 1991 by Morgan Kaufman Publishers,

Inc. Reprinted by permission of the publisher. **340:** L. A. Cooper & R. N. Shepard (1973) "Chronometric Studies of the Rotation of Mental Images," in Visual Information Processing, ed. by W. G. Chase. Adapted by permission of Academic Press. **340:** L. A. Cooper & R. N. Shepard (1973) "Chronometric Studies of the Rotation of Mental Images," in Visual Information Processing, ed. by W. G. Chase. Adapted by permission of Academic Press. **340:** S. M. Kosslyn, et al. (1978) "Scanning Mental Images," from "Visual Images Preserve Metric Spatial Information: Evidence from Studies of Image Scanning," in Journal of Experimental Psychology, 4:47-60. Copyright © 1978 by the American Psychological Association. Adapted by permission of the American Psychological Association. **341:** From Robert J. Sternberg, Beyond IQ: A Triarchic Theory of Human Intelligence, © 1985 by Robert J. Sternberg. Reprinted by permission of Cambridge University Press.

Chapter 10

365: B. G. Hoeble and P. Teitelbaum (1970) "Effects of Force Feeding and Starvation, Food Intake and Body Weight of a Rat With Ventromedial Hypothalamic Lesions," in Journal of Comparative & Physiological Psychology, 61:189-193. Copyright © 1966 by the American Psychological Association. Adapted by permission. **369:** L. M. Craighead, A. J. Stunkard, & R. M. O'Brien (1981) "Behavior Therapy and Pharmacotherapy for Obesity," in Archives of General Psychiatry, 38:763-768. Copyright © 1981 by the American Medical Association. **378:** J. R. Hopkins (1977) "Sexual Behaviors in Adolescence," in Journal of Social Issues, Vol. 33(2):67-85. Adapted with permission of the Society for the Psychological Study of Social Issues. **380:** A. P. Bell, M. A. Weinberg, & S. K. Hammerstein, Sexual Preference: Its Development in Men & Women.

Chapter 11

398: From D. D. Daner, D. A. Snowden, W. V. Friesen (2001). Positive emotions in early life and longevity: Findings from the nun study. Journal of Personality and Social Psychology, 80, 804-813. Copyright © 2001 by the American Psychological Association. Reprinted by permission of the American Psychological Association. **400:** From J. S. Lerner and D. Keltner (2001). "Fear, anger, and risk" in Journal of Personality and Social Psychology, 81, 146-159. Copyright © 2001 by the American Psychological Association. Reprinted by permission of the American Psychological Association. **401:** From L. F. Shafer (1947), "Symptoms of Fear in Combat Flying," in Journal of Consulting Psychology, 11:137-143. **402:** Adapted with permission from B. L. Frederickson, R. A. Mancuso, C. Branigan, & M. M. Tugade (2000), "The Undoing Effect of Positive Emotions, in Motivation and Emotion, 24:237-258. © 2000 Kluwer Academic/Plenum Publishers. **403:** Adapted from G. W. Hohmann, "The effect of dysfunctions of the autonomic nervous system on experienced feelings and emotions," Paper read at the New School for Social Research, New York, October 1962. **405:** Adapted from article by P. Ekman, et al., "Autonomic Nervous System Activity Distinguishes Among Emotions," from Science, Vol. 221, p. 1208-1210, September 16, 1983. Copyright © 1983 American Association for the Advancement of Science. **418:** Adapted from A. Bandura, et al., "Imitation of Film-Mediated Aggressive

Models," in Journal of Abnormal Psychology, 66:8. Copyright © 1963 by the American Psychological Association. Adapted by permission. **419:** After Eron, Huesmann, Lefkowitz, & Walder, 1972.

Chapter 12

431: From A. Anastasia and S. Urbina, Psychological Testing, 7/e, © 1997 Prentice-Hall. **433:** Copyright © 1949, 1974, 1991 by the Psychological Corporation. **435:** From The dynamic assessment of retarded performers by Reuven Feuerstein, © 1979 University Park Press. Used with permission. **441:** Adapted from A. Sameroff, et al. (1993), "Stability of intelligence from preschool to adolescence: The influence of social and family risk factors," in Child Development, 64, p. 80-94. Adapted by permission of the Society for Research in Child Development. **445:** From "Familiar Studies of Intelligence: A Review," T. Bouchard, et al., Science, Vol. 212, #4498, p. 1055-1059, 29 May 1981. Copyright © 1981 American Association for the Advancement of Science. Used by permission of Thomas Bouchard.

Chapter 13

454: From H. J. Eysenck and S. Rachman (1965), The Causes and Cures of Neurosis, by H. J. Eysenck. Copyright © 1965 by H. J. Eysenck and S. Rachman. Reprinted by permission of EdiTS. **460:** © 2002 by Sidney Harris. **478:** After Abraham H. Maslow, "Hierarchy of Needs," from Motivation and Personality. Copyright © 1954 by Harper and Row Publishers, Inc. Reprinted by permission of Pearson Education, Inc., Upper Saddle River, NJ. **479:** A. H. Maslow (1967), "Self-actualization and beyond." In Challenges of Humanistic Psychology, J. F. T. Bugenthal (ed.). Copyright © 1967 by Abraham H. Maslow. Used with permission of McGraw-Hill Publishers.

Chapter 14

497: Reprinted with permission from T. H. Holmes & R. H. Rahe (1967) "The Social Readjustment Rating Scale," in the Journal of Psychosomatic Research, Vol. 11, No. 2, p. 213-218. Copyright © 1967 Elsevier Science. **500:** Adapted from W. E. Schlenger, R. A. Kolka, J. A. Fairbank, & R. L. Hough (1992), "The Prevalence of Post-Traumatic Stress Disorder in the Vietnam Generation: A Multi-Method, Multi-Source Assessment of Psychiatric Disorders," from Journal of Traumatic Stress, 5, 333-363. **507:** After S. Cohen, D. A. J. Tyrrell, and A. P. Smith (1991) "Psychological stress and susceptibility to the common cold," The New England Journal of Medicine, 325:606-612. Used with permission from S. Cohen. **514:** From Type A Behavior and Your Heart by Meyer Friedman and R. N. Rosenman, copyright © 1974 by Meyer Friedman. Used by permission of Alfred A. Knopf, a division of Random House, Inc. **517:** From S. W. Cole, M. E. Kemeny, S. E. Taylor, and B. R. Visscher (1996), "Elevated Physical Health Risk Among Gay Men Who Conceal Their Homosexual Identity," Health Psychology, 15, p. 243-251.

Copyright © 1996 by the American Psychological Association. Reprinted with permission. **520:** G. E. Schwartz (1975) "Biofeedback, Self-Regulation, & the Patterning of Physiological Processes," in American Scientist 63:316. Reprinted by permission of The Scientific Research Association.

Chapter 15

530: From Diagnostic and Statistical Manual of Mental Disorders, Fourth Edition, Washington, DC: American Psychiatric Association, 1994. **531:** From R. C. Kessler, K. A. McGonagle, S. Zhao, and C. B. Nelson (1994), "Lifetime and 12-month prevalence of DSM-III-R psychiatric disorders in the United States: Results from the National Comorbidity Study," Archives of General Psychiatry, 51(1):8-19. Copyright © 1994 by the American Medical Association. **534:** From Abnormal Psychology: The Problem of Maladaptive Behavior, 7/e, by I. G. Sarason and B. R. Sarason. Copyright © 1993 by I. G. Sarason and B. R. Sarason. Adapted by permission of Prentice-Hall, Upper Saddle River, NJ. **535:** Adapted from R. M. Rapee, T. A. Brown, M. M. Anthony, & D. H. Barlow (1992), "Response to hyperventilation and inhalation of 5.5% carbon dioxide–enriched air across the DSM-III-R anxiety disorders," Journal of Abnormal Psychology, 101, 538-552. Copyright © 1992 by the American Psychological Association. Adapted with permission. **552:** A. Jablensky (1989). "Epidemiology and cross-cultural aspects of schizophrenia," in Psychiatric Annals, 19, 516-524. Reprinted by permission of SLACK, Inc. **553:** Schizophrenia: The Epigenetic Puzzle, by I. I. Gottesman & J. Shields. Copyright © 1992 Cambridge University Press. Reprinted by permission of the publisher. **555:** M. Karno & J. H. Jenkins (1993). Cross-cultural issues in the course and treatment of schizophrenia. Psychiatric Clinics of North America, 16, 339-350. Reprinted by permission of W. B. Saunders. **561:** A. M. Ludwig, J. M. Brandsma, C. B. Wilbur, F. Benfeldt, & D. H. Jameson (1972), "The Objective Study of a Multiple Personality," in Archives of General Psychiatry, 26:298-310. Copyright © 1972 by the American Medical Association.

Chapter 16

573: H. J. Steadman, E. P. Mulvey, J. Monahan, P. C. Robbins, P. S. Applebaum, T. Grisso, L. Roth, & E. Silver (1998). Violence by people discharged from acute psychiatric inpatient facilities and by others in the same neighborhoods. Archives of General Psychiatry, 55, 393-401. © 1998 American Medical Association. **575:** © 2002 by Sidney Harris. **581:** Reprinted with permission from The Coping with Depression Course: Psychoeducational Intervention for Unipolar Depression, by P. M. Lewinsohn, D. O. Antonucio, J. L. Skinmetz, & L. Teri. Copyright © 1984 by Castalia Publishing Company. All rights reserved. **587:** © 2002 by Sidney Harris. **588:** M. E. P. Seligman (1995). The effectiveness of psychotherapy: The Consumer Reports study. American Psychologist, 50, 965-974. Copyright © 1995 by

the American Psychological Association. Reprinted with permission.

Chapter 17

612: Adapted from M. M. Darley & B. Latane (1968), "Bystander Intervention in Emergencies: Diffusion of Responsibility," in Journal of Personality and Social Psychology, 8:377-383. Copyright © 1968 by the American Psychological Association. Adapted with permission. **620:** From Obedience to Authority: An Experimental View by Stanley Milgram. Copyright © 1974 by Stanley Milgram. Reprinted by permission of Alexandra Milgram. **621:** From Obedience to Authority: An Experimental View by Stanley Milgram. Copyright © 1974 by Stanley Milgram. Reprinted by permission of Alexandra Milgram. **637:** Adapted from Fig. 1 on p. 923 in T. Postmes, R. Spears, & S. Cihangir (2001), "Quality of decision making and group norms," in Journal of Personality and Social Psychology, 80, 918-930. Copyright © 2001 by the American Psychological Association. Adapted with permission.

Chapter 18

649: Adaptation of Fig. 1 on p. 1018 from R. H. Fazio, J. R. Jackson, B. C. Dunton, & C. J. Williams (1995), "Variability in automatic activation as an unobtrusive measure of racial attitudes: A bona fide pipelines?" in Journal of Personality and Social Psychology, 69, 1313-1027. Copyright © 1995 by the American Psychological Association. Adapted with permission. **650:** A. Luchens (1957) "Primary Recovery in Impression Formation, in The Order of Presentation Persuasion, edited by C. I. Hovland, p. 34-35. Yale University Press. **653:** From S. T. Friske, M. Lin, & S. L. Neuberg (1999). "The continuum model: Ten years later," in S. Chaiken & Y. Trope (eds.), Dual-process Theories in Social Psychology, p.231-254. New York: Guilford Press. **661:** R. E. Petty & J. T. Cacioppo (1984), "The effects of involvement on response to arguments quantity and quality, central and peripheral routes to persuasion," in Journal of Personality & Social Psychology, 46:6-81. Copyright © 1984 by the American Psychological Association. Adapted with permission. **668:** From S. Chen & S. M. Andersen (1999), "Relationships from the past in the present: Significant-other representation and transference in interpersonal life," in Advances in Experimental Social Psychology, 31, 123-190. Copyright 1999, Elsevier Science (USA), reproduced by permission of the publisher. **669:** Fig. 1, p. 597 from A. Aron, E. N. Aron, & D. Smollan (1992), "Inclusion of other in the self scale and the structure of interpersonal closeness," in Journal of Personality and Social Psychology, 63, 596-612. Copyright © 1992 by the American Psychological Association. Reprinted with permission. **670:** R. Sternberg (1986), "Triangular Theory of Love," in Psychological Review, 93:119-135. Copyright © 1986 by the American Psychological Association. Adapted with permission.

NAME INDEX

Titchener, E.B., 6
Tolman, Edward, 251
Townshend, Pete, 130
Treisman, Anne, 162
Triplett, Norman, 606–607, 606f, 608
Turk, Dennis C., 141

Voltaire, 154f
von Békésy, Georg, 131

von Helmholtz, Hermann, 124, 130, 460–461
Vygotsky, Lev, 74, 82

Watson, John, 7, 7f, 66, 196, 258, 471
Weber, Ernst Heinrich, 109–110
Wechsler, David, 432
Weinstein, Nell, 522

Wernicke, Carl, 50–51
Wertheimer, Max, 8, 158
Western, Drew, 487
White, Eve, 561
Wiesel, Torstein, 163
Williams, George C., 24
Wilson, Joseph Ruggles, 427
Wilson, Thomas Woodrow, 427
Wood, Elijah, 178

Woodrow, Janet, 427
Wundt, Wilhelm, 6, 6f

Young, Thomas, 124
Yufe, Jack, 453, 483

Zajonc, 607
Zimbardo, Philip, 632–634

SUBJECT INDEX

Page numbers followed by f indicate figures; t, tables; b, boxes.

Anxiety, 240
  castration, 463
  eclectic psychotherapists and, 586
  neurotic, 510
  objective, 510
  personality dynamics and, 461
  as reaction to stress, 498–501,
    499f, 500f
  retrieval interference via, forgetting
    and, 287–288
  theory of, Freud's, 469
Anxiety disorders, 533–541, 534t
APA. See American Psychological
    Association (APA).
Apartheid, 618f
Apathy as reaction to stress, 501–502
Aphasia, 50
  anomic, 322
  Broca's, 318–319
  conduction, 319
  expressive, 50
  receptive, 50–51
  Wernicke's, 318–319
Aplysia californica, 257, 257f
Apnea, 204
Apperception, definition of, 466
Appetite, 364–365
Appetite suppressants, 369
Appraisal
  in brain, 395–396, 396f
  cognitive, 390, 392–396
  conscious, 395
  discovery of, 392–393, 392f
  themes and dimensions of,
    393–395, 394t
  unconscious, 395
Apprehension, span of, 270
Appropriate perception of reality,
    normality and, 529
Aptitude
  accurate reflection of, by intelligence
    tests, 446–447
  intelligence tests and, 446–447
Arbitrary inference, depression and,
    547t
Arguments, inductively strong, 335
Arousal
  effects of hormones on, 376–377
  emotions and, 405
  misattribution of, 393
  obesity and, 368
Artificial ears and eyes, 132
Artificial mother, monkey's response
    to, 90f
ASL. See American Sign Language
    (ASL).
Assertiveness training, behavioral
    rehearsal and, 578, 578t
Assessment, criterion problem in, 429
Assignment, random, 18–19
Assimilation, 75
Association
  clang, schizophrenia and, 549–550
  free. See Free association.
  of Humanistic Psychology, 476, 479
  idiosyncratic word, schizophrenia
    and, 549
  loosening of, schizophrenia and, 549
  spurious, 255
Association areas, 43, 45
Associational psychology, 6
Associative agnosia, 169
Associative learning, 234, 235
Assumption in organization of
    data, 149
Asylum, early, treatment of
    psychological disorders and, 571
Asymmetries in brain, 47–50
Ataque de nervios, 532t, 534, 561
Atkinson-Shiffrin theory, memory
    and, 269

At-risk babies, massage therapy for,
    73–74
Attached shadow, 157–158
Attachment, 89–91, 90f, 90t, 92
Attended objects, neural processing
    on, 180, 180f
Attention
  auditory, 151
  brain systems and, 179–180
  directed, without eye movements,
    151
  disturbances of, schizophrenia and,
    549–550
  feelings in modification of, 397–400
  hypnotic state and, 209
  memory and perception and,
    151–153
  neural basis of, 179–180
  perception and, 149, 150–153
  peripheral, 197
  selective, 150–151
Attention deficit/hyperactivity disorder
    (ADHD), 564–565, 593
Attentive processes, recognition and,
    161–162, 161f
Attentive stage, recognition and, 162
Attitudes
  based on direct experience, 663
  and behavior, 662–664
  consistent, 663
  social cognition and, 658–664
  specifically related to behavior, 663
  strong, 663
Attraction
  interpersonal, 664–668, 664–674
  transference and, 668, 668f
Attractiveness, physical, interpersonal
    attraction and, 664–665
Attribution
  causal, 656
  dispositional, 655
  external, 655
  information processing and,
    654–658
  situational, 655
  trait, 3, 3f, 13
Attribution error, fundamental, 3,
    655–658, 656f
Attributional styles, 511
Atypical antipsychotics, 592
Auditory area, primary, 45
Auditory attention, 151
Auditory cue, 270
Auditory hallucinations, schizophrenia
    and, 551
Auditory prostheses, 132
Auditory system, hearing and,
    128–129, 128f, 129f
Augmented network, 165, 165f
Authority, obedience to, 618–625,
    620f, 621f
Autism, 83
Automatic stereotype activation,
    647–649, 649f
Automaticity, consciousness and,
    198–199
Automobile accidents, alcohol-related,
    216
Autonomic nervous system, 51, 52f
  emotion and, 390
  motor fibers of, 52f
Autonomic system, 40
Autonomy, 89
Available wavelengths, color
    and brightness constancy
    and, 174
Aversion, conditioned, 361
Aversive conditioning, instrumental
    conditioning and, 248–249
Avoidance, escape and, aversive
    conditioning and, 248–249

Avoidance learning, 248–249
Avoidant insecure attachment, 91
Awareness, behavior and, 663
Axon, 32

B
Baby and Child Care, 459
BAC. See Blood alcohol concentration
    (BAC).
Back projections, 108
Back-end differences, emotions and,
    410–411, 413–414
Backward masking, 395
Bad trip, LSD and, 221
Bad-me personification, 464–465
Baseline level, learning curves and, 243
Basilar membrane, 129
Bear, mistaking tent for, 147,
    160–161
Behavior
  ability to exercise voluntary control
    over, normality and, 529
  abnormal, classification of,
    529–531, 531t, 532t
  aggressive. See Aggression.
  attitudes and, 662–664
  evolution and genes and.
    See Evolution, genes and
    behavior and.
  gender-appropriate, 411
  genetic studies of, 57–59
  health-related, stress and, 509–510
  human, behaviorist portrait of, 471
  maladaptiveness of, psychological
    disorders and, 528
  molecular genetics of, 59
  neural basis of. See Neural basis of
    behavior.
  on-task, selective reinforcement
    and, 577
  pain, 141
  social, 88–89, 89f
  type A, 513–515, 514t, 521–524
  type B, 513
Behavior genetics, 54–55
Behavior modification, weight control
    and, 369, 369t
Behavior potential, 472
Behavior therapies in treatment of
    psychological disorders,
    575–580
Behavioral blueprint, 240
Behavioral medicine, 493
Behavioral perspective, 11, 532
Behavioral rehearsal in treatment of
    psychological disorders,
    577–578, 578t
Behavioral techniques in management
    of stress, 519–521
Behavioral theory, stress and, 511
Behaviorism, 7, 196
Behaviorist approach
  to human behavior, 471
  to personality development,
    469–471
Beliefs, prior, insight learning and,
    254–255
Benevolence, selfishness and, 24
Bennies, 220
Bennington College study, 631, 659
Benzedrine, 220
Benzodiazepines in treatment of
    anxiety, 593
Bias, 112, 113
Biculturalism, 102
Big Five, personality traits and, 455
Binding problems, recognition
    and, 161
Binges
  drinking, 216
  eating, 367, 370

Binocular cues in perception of
    distance, 156, 156f
Binocular disparity, 156
Bioecological Theory, Ceci's, 440–441,
    441f, 442, 442t
Biofeedback in management of stress,
    519, 519f
Biological approach to schizophrenia,
    552–555, 553f, 554f
Biological bases of aggressive
    behavior, 60–61
Biological causes of anorexia and
    bulimia, 372
Biological clock, sleep and, 202
Biological constraints
  classical conditioning and,
    240–241
  instrumental conditioning and,
    250–251
Biological factors of personality
    disorders, 557–558
Biological foundations of psychology,
    15, 30–63
  CD-ROM links for, 63
  endocrine system, 53–54
  evolution, genes, and behavior,
    54–61
  neurons, 32–37
  neurotransmitters, 37–38
  organization of nervous system,
    38–53
  web resources for, 63
Biological perspective, 10
Biological perspectives
  mental disorders and, 532
  psychological disorders and,
    544–545, 544f, 545f
  relationships between psychological
    perspectives and, 14
Biological psychologists, 15
Biological therapies
  combining, with psychological
    therapies, 595–596
  in treatment of psychological
    disorders, 591–596
Biologically based aggressive behavior,
    60–61
Biology of suicide, 546–547
Bipolar disorder, 542, 543, 545, 545f,
    592–593
Bisexuals, 379–384
Bitmaps, 171, 172
Bitterness, hunger and, 361
Blind spot, 118, 118f
Blindness, color, 57, 124, 124f
Blocking, psychodynamic therapies
    and, 574
Blood alcohol concentration (BAC),
    215–216, 215f
Blood flow in brain, post-traumatic
    stress disorder and, 505f
Blood pressure, operant conditioning
    of, 520f
Blueprint, behavioral, 240
Bodily changes and emotion,
    401–405, 401t, 402f
Bodily-kinesthetic intelligence, 437t
Body weight, lateral hypothalamus
    and, 365, 365f
Bonding, pair, and mating strategies,
    670–674
Bong, cannabis and, 222
Borderline personality disorder, 556,
    558–560
Bosnian refugees, post-traumatic
    stress disorder and,
    500–501, 501f
Bottom-up processes, 167–169
Botulinum toxin, 37
Boundary extension and abstraction,
    173f

Brain, 256
  anterior system of, 179
  appraisals in, 395–396, 396f
  asymmetries in, 47–50
  blood flow in, post-traumatic stress
      disorder and, 505f
  decision making and, 338
  depression and, 545, 545f
  divisions of labor in
      perception and, 179–183
      between working memory and
          long-term memory, 280
  functional organization of, 40f–41f
  language and, 50–51
  living, pictures of, 45–47
  locational organization of, 40f–41f
  normal, versus schizophrenic brain,
      553, 553f
  obsessive-compulsive disorder and,
      540, 540f
  posterior system of, 179
  schizophrenia and, 554f
  smarter, building, research and, 256
  stimulation of, aggression and, 416f
  systems of, attention and,
      179–180
Brain damage, face recognition and, 3
Brain imaging, 179
Brainstem, 40
BRDU, neurogenesis and, 46
Breakdown of conscious restraints,
    obesity and, 367–368
Breast cancer, pessimism and, 508
Breathalyzer, 215
Breeding, selective, 57–58, 58f
Brightness, 121
Brightness constancy, 174–175
Broaden-and-build theory, 399
Broca's aphasia, 318–319
Broca's area, 48, 51, 318
Buffers
  acoustic, 276f
  obedience to authority and,
      621–622, 623t
  visual, 276f
Bugs, cocaine and, 220
Bulimia, 369–372
Burn patients, distraction via virtual
    reality in diminishment of
    severe pain in, 152–153
Busyness, cognitive, 656
Bystander effect, 610–613

C
Caenorhabditis elegans, 236
Caffeine, 136, 212, 213, 361
California Psychological Inventory
    (CPI), 457–458
Cancer, lung, correlation between
    smoking and, 21
Candle problem, 344, 344f, 348f
Cannabinoid receptors, 222
Cannabis, 213t, 222–223, 223t
Capacities of newborn, 69–74
Carbon dioxide, fight-or-flight
    response and, 535, 535f, 536
Caricatures, 171
Caring tendencies, selfishness and, 25
Carousel, kitten, 186, 187f
Case histories, 22
Cast shadow, 157–158
Castration, 376
Castration anxiety, 463
CAT. See Computerized axial
    tomography (CAT; CT).
Categorization, 326, 332, 333
  in amnesiac patients, dot patterns
      and, 332, 332f
  as building block of thought,
      326–333
  initial, stereotypes and, 653

neural basis of behavior and,
    331–333, 332f
  processes of, 329–330
Catharsis, 418–423, 419f
Cathartic effect of violence, 4
Caudate nucleus, obsessive-compulsive
    disorder and, 540
Causal attribution, 656
Causality heuristic, 336–337
Causation, correlation and, 20–21
CCK. See Cholecystokinin (CCK).
CD-ROM links, 29
  consciousness, 231
  emotion, 425
  evolution, genes, and behavior, 63
  intelligence, 451
  language and thought, 351
  learning and conditioning, 264
  memory, 311
  motivation, 387
  perception and, 193
  personality, 491
  psychological development, 105
  psychological disorders, 567
  psychology, 29
  sensory processes, 145
  social cognition, 677
  social influence, 643
  stress, health and coping and, 525
Cell membrane, semipermeable, 33
Cells
  complex, response of, 163
  glial, 33
  hypercomplex, response of, 163
  simple, response of, 163, 163f
Cellular basis of learning,
    261, 262f
Central nervous system, 38–39
Central route to persuasion, 660,
    661–662, 661f
Central sulcus, 44
Central tendency, measures of,
    A2–A4, A3f
Cerebellum, 39–42
Cerebral cortex, 41, 43
Cerebrum, 40, 43–45, 43f
Chance distribution, A6, A6f
Change, detection of, 110f
CHD. See Coronary heart disease
    (CHD).
Checking, obsessive-compulsive
    behavior and, 539
Chemicals, endogenous, 313
Chemotherapy, 236–237
Chess, 80f, 254f, 344–345, 345f
Chiasm, optic, 44
Child rearing, instrumental
    conditioning and, 244
Childhood
  cognitive development in, 74–84
  gender nonconformity in, 380, 380t
Childhood amnesia, 3–4, 10, 16–17,
    290–291, 291f
Childhood memory, Piaget's, 294
Childhood viewing of violent television,
    adult aggression and, 4, 4f
Children
  aggression in, effects of media
      violence on, 4
  development of, influence of parents
      on, 100–101
  imitation of adult aggression by,
      417, 417f, 418f
  memories of, constructive memory
      and legal system and, 299–300
  with psychological disorders, 587
  stress of, at mother's departure, 89f
Chimpanzees
  aggression and, 414–415
  language experiments and,
      324–325, 325f

Chlordiazepoxide, 593
Chlorpromazine, 37–38, 591
Cholecystokinin (CCK), 363
Chromosomes and genes, 55–57, 56f
Chronic pain, opioids in treatment of,
    140–141
Chronological age (CA), 430
Chunking
  knowledge acquisition and, 80–81
  and memory span, 301–302, 302f
  working memory and, 276
Cigarette smoking, 212, 212f, 509
  correlation between lung cancer
      and, 21
  gene for, 214
Circadian rhythm, 202
Clairvoyance, 224
Clang associations, schizophrenia and,
    549–550
Class interval, frequency distributions
    and, A2
Classical conditioning, 234, 235–241,
    260–261
  constraints on, 240–241, 241t
  diagram of, 236f
  personality development and, 470
  stimuli and responses in, 235t
Cleansing, ethnic, 500
Client-centered therapy, 582
Cliff, visual, 185, 185f, 406
Clinical psychologists, 15, 573–574
Clinical psychology, 17
Clock-dependent alerting process,
    sleep theory and, 202
Closure, grouping and, 155
Clozapine, 37–38, 592
Coaction, 606
Coca-Cola, 220
Cocaine, 219f, 220, 221f, 223t
Cocaine bugs, 220
Cochlea, 128–129, 129f
Cochlear implant, 132, 133
Codeine, 218
Coding
  of intensity and quality, 114–115,
      114f, 115f
  phonological, 273
  sensory, 113–115
  visual, 273–274, 275f
Coefficient, validity, 429
Coefficient correlation, 20, 430,
    A9–A12, A11f
Cognition
  culture and, 657
  social. See Social cognition.
Cognitive appraisal and emotion, 390,
    392–396
Cognitive approach to personality
    development, 471–476
Cognitive behavior therapy, 521
Cognitive busyness, 656
Cognitive development
  Anderson's Theory of Intelligence
      and, 437–439
  in childhood, 74–84
Cognitive dissonance theory, 626–628,
    627f, 629
Cognitive factors
  classical conditioning and, 238–240
  instrumental conditioning and,
      249–250
Cognitive impairment as reaction to
    stress, 502
Cognitive map, 251–252, 252f
Cognitive neuroscience, 16
Cognitive perspective, 11–12
  mental disorders and, 532
  psychological disorders and,
      545–548, 547t
Cognitive potentials, multiple, Ceci's
    biological theory and, 440

Cognitive social-learning person
    variables, 473
Cognitive techniques in management
    of stress, 521
Cognitive theory, stress and, 511–513
Cognitive triad, 545–546
Cognitive-behavior therapies in
    treatment of psychological
    disorders, 580–581, 581f, 581t
Cognitive-developmental theory,
    gender identity and sex typing
    and, 95–96
Coitus, premarital, 378, 378f
Coke, 220
Colds, stress and, 507f
Collective unconscious, 464
Collectivism, 412–414
College drinking, pluralistic ignorance
    and, 616–617
College students
  alcohol usage by, 216
  hazings and, 628
Color
  and brightness constancy,
      perception and, 174–175
  seeing, 121–126, 121f
Color appearance, 121–122, 122f
Color blindness, 57, 124, 124f
Color circle, 123, 123f
Color constancy, 121
Color mixture, 122–123
Color solid, 122, 122f
Color vision, 124–126, 124f, 125f, 126f
Color-matching experiment, 122
Combat fatigue, 499
Commitment, triangular theory of
    love and, 670, 670t
Common herbs in treatment of mental
    disorders, 594
Communication
  of emotion through facial
      expressions, 406–408
  language and, 314–319
  persuasive, 659–662
Community Mental Health Centers
    Act of 1963, 572
Community-based programs in
    treatment of psychological
    disorders, 583–584
Companionate love versus passionate
    love, 669–670
Competencies, social learning theory
    and, 473
Competition, cooperation versus, 498
Complementary afterimages, 125, 125f
Complex cell, response of, 163
Complex learning, 234, 251–256
Complex sentences, development of
    language and, 321
Compliance
  induced, 627, 627f
  social influence and, 613–625
Componential subtheory, 439, 442
Compound conditioned stimulus
    presentation, 238
Comprehension
  effects of context on, 316–317, 316f
  of language, 314
Compulsive behavior, 539
Compulsive use of drugs, 213
Computer dance, interpersonal
    attraction and, 664
Computerized axial tomography
    (CAT; CT), 45
Computers
  drawing program on, 171, 171f
  psychological processes and, 8–9
Con artists, antisocial personality
    and, 557
Concentration, 196f
Concentrative meditation, 208

Concentrative *samadhi*, 208
Concept(s), 313
  abstract, complex learning and,
    251–252, 252f
  acquiring, 330–331
  biases in learning, 331, 331f
  as building block of thought,
    326–333
  development of language and,
    320–321
  functions of, 326
  hierarchies of, 328–329, 329f
  neural basis of behavior and,
    331–333, 332f
Concrete operational stage, 78
Conditional positive regard, 477–478
Conditioned aversion, 361
Conditioned discrimination, 238, 238f
Conditioned reinforcers, instrumental
  conditioning and, 245–246
Conditioned response (CR), 235,
  258–259
Conditioned satiety, 362
Conditioned stimulus (CS), 235, 236
Conditioning
  aversive, 248–249
  classical. *See* Classical conditioning.
  development of language and, 321
  in different species, 236–237
  excitatory, 238, 238f
  eyeblink, 260
  fear, 260–261, 260f
  instrumental, 242–251
  learning and. *See* Learning and
    conditioning.
  operant, 469–470
  personality development and,
    469–471
  second-order, 237
Conduction, saltatory, 34
Conduction aphasia, 319
Cones, 117, 119f
Confessions, forced, constructive
  memory and legal system
  and, 300
Confidence, constructive memory and
  legal system and, 298–299
Conflict, Oedipal, 93
Conformity, 613–617, 614f, 615f
Confucian moral ethic, 216
Confusion, identity, 99
Congenital insensitivity to pain, 137
Conjunction, illusory, attention and,
  161, 161f
Connectionist models, 164
Connections
  excitatory, 165
  inhibitory, 165
  meaningful, adding, long-term
    memory and, 281–282
  top-down, 165–166, 166f
Conscientiousness, 455, 455t
Conscious, 459, 459f
Conscious appraisals, emotion and,
  395
Conscious restraints, breakdown of,
  obesity and, 367–368
Consciousness, 194–231
  altered state of, 195
  aspects of, 196–199
  CD-ROM links, 231
  controlling, 197
  definition of, 196–197
  dreams and, 199–207
  hypnosis and, 208–212
  meditation and, 207–208
  monitoring, 197
  psi phenomena and, 224–229
  psychoactive drugs and, 212–223
  stages of sleep and, 199–207
  web resources, 231

Consent, informed, 23, 624
Conservation, 76, 77f
  early testing of, 81
  of energy, personality dynamics and,
    460–461
  of number, 77f
Consistency, internal, 428
Consistent attitudes, behavior and, 663
Constancies
  in all sensory modalities, 178–179
  brightness, 174–175
  perceptual, 173–179, 174f, 185
  shape, 175, 175f
  size, 175–176, 176f, 185
Constraints
  biological. *See* Biological
    constraints.
  on classical conditioning,
    240–241, 241t
  experiment on, 241t
Construct validity, 429
Construct-contrast pair, 474
Constructive memory, 293–301
Constructive perception, 294–295
Constructive process
  memory as, 294
  at time of memory encoding,
    294–295
Constructs, personal, 473–474, 473f
Contemporary psychological
  perspectives, 9–13
Contemporary theories of intelligence,
  436–443
Content, effects of, deductive
  reasoning and, 334–335, 334f
Context
  Ceci's biological theory and, 440
  effects of, on comprehension and
    production, 316–317, 316f
  importance of, recognition and,
    167–169, 168f
  long-term memory and,
    285–287, 286f
  and retrieval, memory and,
    303–304
  temporal, effects of, 168f
Context effects, 169, 288
Contextual subtheory, 439, 442
Contiguity
  versus predictability, 238–239, 239f
  temporal, 249
Contingency, 249, 250
Contingency learning, instrumental
  conditioning and, 250
Continuity theory of dreaming, 207
Continuum model, stereotypes
  and, 653
Contract, implicit leniency, 618f
Contrast acuity, 120
Contrast sensitivity, visual acuity
  and, 184
Control
  versus contingency, instrumental
    conditioning and, 249
  inadequate, psi phenomena and, 226
  instrumental conditioning and,
    249–250
  of movement, hypnosis and, 210
  neural, 377
  of stimulus conditions, self-
    regulation and, 578
Control group, 18
Controllability, stress and, 495–496
Controlled stimulation, perceptual
  development and, 186–187
Controlling consciousness, 197
Controlling stereotypes, 654
Conventional morality, 85
Cooperation
  versus competition, 498
  selfishness and, 25

Coping
  definition of, 515
  with depression, 581, 581t
  emotion-focused, 515, 516–519,
    517f
  problem-focused, 515–516
  repressive, 516
  skills of, 515–519
  stress and health and. *See* Stress,
    health and coping and.
Core relational theme, 393–394
Cores, learning, 330
Coronary heart disease (CHD), stress
  and, 506
Corpus callosum, 41, 48
Correction, situational, 656
Correlation, 19–21
  and causation, 20–21
  coefficient of, A9–A12, A11f
  negative, 20, 21f
  positive, 20, 21f
  product-moment, A10–A11,
    A10f, A10t
Correlation coefficient, 20, 430
Cortex
  feature detectors in, recognition
    and, 163, 163f
  left, specialization of function in, 44f
  prefrontal, schizophrenia and, 554f
  visual, perception and, 180–182,
    181f
Cortical activity, PET images
  and, 180f
Corticotropin-releasing factor
  (CRF), 54
Counseling psychologists, 15,
  573–574
CPI. *See* California Psychological
  Inventory (CPI).
CR. *See* Conditioned response (CR).
Crack cocaine, 220
Crash, amphetamines and, 220
Creative Imagination Scale, 298
CRF. *See* Corticotropin-releasing
  factor (CRF).
Crib, mental institution and, 571f
Crimes, motiveless, schizophrenia
  and, 550
Crisis, identity, 99
Crisis intervention, 585
Criterion problem in assessment, 429
Criterion validity, 429
Criterion-keyed method of empirical
  construction, 456
Critical periods
  development of language and,
    323–324
  in development of visual system,
    186
  in human development, 68–69
Cross-cultural perspectives on
  intelligence, 442–443
Cross-modal illusions, perception
  and, 178
Crowd, The, 608
CS. *See* Conditioned stimulus (CS).
CT. *See* Computerized axial
  tomography (CAT; CT).
Cuckoldry, 24
Cuddliness in infants, 86
Cues, 151
  binocular, in perception of distance,
    156, 156f
  depth, 156
  hunger, physiological, 362–363
  monocular, in perception of
    distance, 157–158, 157f
  non-content, persuasion and, 660
Cultural norms, deviation from,
  psychological disorders
  and, 528

Cultural psychology, 17
Cultural relativist perspective, 528
Culturally specific therapies in
  treatment of psychological
  disorders, 584–585
Culture
  alcohol disorders and, 216–217,
    216t, 217t
  and cognition, 657
  effects of, on psychotherapy,
    596–599, 596f
  emotions and, 410–414
  intelligence and, 434–436, 435f
  mental disorders and, 532
  progression of schizophrenia and,
    551–552, 552f
  schizophrenia and, 552, 552f
  sexuality and, 378–379, 378f
Culture-bound syndromes, 532t
Culture-fair test, 435
Cuna of South America, 378
Curanderas; curanderos, 586
Cutting edge research. *See* Research.
Cycles per second, 127

D
Dance, computer, interpersonal
  attraction and, 664
Dani, language of, 328
Dark-adaptation curve, 119–120, 119f
Darwin's theory of evolution, 6–7,
  242, 670–671
Data
  psychophysical, from magnitude-
    estimation experiment, 111f
  ranked, statistical inference
    and, A7
  scaling of, statistical inference and,
    A7–A8
Day care, 92–93, 93f, 101
Death, smell of, in insects, 134
Debriefing, 23, 624
Debt, sleep, 203
Deceitfulness antisocial personality
  and, 557
Decibel scale, 127
Decision making
  and the brain, 338
  group, 634–640
Decreased ability to function,
  schizophrenia and, 551
Deductive reasoning, 334–335, 334f
Deductive validity, 334
Deep Blue, 254f
Defense
  mechanisms of, Freud's, 469
  personality dynamics and, 461
Defense mechanisms, 461, 461t, 462f
Degradation, 36
Dehydration, drop in blood pressure
  caused by, 360
Deindividuation, 608–610, 609f
Deinstitutionalization, psychological
  disorders and, 572
Delta waves, 200
Delusions, schizophrenia and, 550
Dendrites, 32
Denial, 461t, 462–463
Deoxyribonucleic acid (DNA),
  55–57, 56f
Depakote, bipolar disorder and, 593
Departure, mother's, children's stress
  at, 89f
Dependence versus independence,
  497–498
Dependent variable, 18
Depolarization, 34
Depressants, 213f, 214–218
Depression, 542–543, 542f
  cognitive distortions in, 547t
  coping with, 581, 581t

long-term, eyeblink conditioning and, 260
neurotransmitters in, 544, 544f
psychodynamic theories of, 548, 548f
as reaction to stress, 501–502
Depressive disorders, 542
Deprivation, sleep, 202–203, 202f, 203f
Depth, perception of, perceptual development and, 185, 185f
Depth cues, 156, 176, 176f
Description, physical, abstraction and, 170
Descriptive statistics, A2–A5
Desensitization
psychotherapy and, 589
systematic, 576–577
systemic, 589
Desire, effects of hormones on, 376–377
Determinants, internal, 472
Determination of what objects are, recognition and, 162–164
Determinism
psychological, 459
reciprocal, 472
Detterman, Douglas K., 446
Development
adolescent, 97–102
of children, influence of parents on, 100–101
critical periods in, 68–69
identity, in adolescents, 99–102
of language, 319–325
later, attachment and, 92
of moral judgment, 84–86
perceptual, 183–189
personality, 463–464
sensitive periods in, 69
social, personality and, 86–97
sociocultural approach to, 82
of speech, 68
stages of, 68–69
Developmental psychologists, 15, 65
Deviation
from cultural norms, psychological disorders and, 528
standard, A4, A5
from statistical norms, psychological disorders and, 528–529
Dexedrine, 220
Diabetes, 59
Diagnostic and Statistical Manual of Mental Disorders, 4th edition (DSM-IV), 529, 537, 556, 556t, 559
Diagrams
frequency, A3f
scatter, A10, A10f
Diazepam, 593
Dichromats, 124–125
Diethylstilbestrol, 374
Dieting
limitations of, 368
and set points, 367
and weight control, 368
Difference, significance of, A8–A9, A9t
Difference reduction, 342, 343
Different sexual orientation, frequency of, 379–380
Differentiation of emotions, 404–405, 405f
Difficult temperament of infants, 87
Diffusion of responsibility, bystander effects and, 611–612, 612f
Digit span task, 276
Dimensional appraisal theories, 393
Dimensional organization of emotion, 420
Direct experience, attitudes based on, behavior and, 663
Direct observation, 21–22

Direct reinforcement, 470
Directed attention without eye movements, 151
Discrete emotions, 421
Discrimination, 238
classical conditioning and, 237–238, 237f, 238f
conditioned, 238, 238f
by infants, perceptual development and, 183–185
instrumental conditioning and, 246
Discrimination stimulus, 246
Discrimination training, 246
Disease model, mental disorders and, 532
Diseases of adaptation, 504
Disorganized parenting style, 91
Disparity, binocular, 156
Displacement, 461t, 463
Display rules, emotional, 406
Dispositional attribution, 655
Dispositional inference, 656
Dissociation, consciousness and, 198–199
Dissociative identity disorder, 560–562, 561f
Distance, perception of, 156–157
Distillation, 215
Distraction
emotions and, 410
via virtual reality in diminishment of severe pain, 152–153
Distress, personal, 528–529
Distribution
chance, A6, A6f
differing in variation, A4
normal, A3, A6–A7, A6f, A7t
skewed, A3, A3f
unbalanced, A3
Disturbances
of emotional expression, 551
of perception, 550–551
of thought and attention, 549–550
Divisions of labor in brain
perception and, 179–183
between working memory and long-term memory, 280
Dizygotic twins, 58
DNA. *See* Deoxyribonucleic acid (DNA).
Dominant genes, 56–57
Dopamine, 37–38, 591–593
bipolar disorder and, 592–593
incentive motivation and, 355–356, 357f, 358f
novelty seeking and, 59
personality and, 484
schizophrenia and, 553, 554f
Dot patterns, categorization in amnesiac patients and, 332, 332f
Doubt, obsessive-compulsive behavior and, 539
Down syndrome, 437
Drawing program on computer, 171, 171f
Dream analysis, 574, 575f
Dream work, 206
Dreaming, continuity theory of, 207
Dreams, 202, 204–206
age and, 204–205
awareness of, 205
control of content of, 205–206
length of, 205
lucid, 205
and sleep, 199–207
theories of, 206–207
Drinking, college, pluralistic ignorance and, 616–617
Drive theory
aggression and, 416f
motivation and, 353

Drives, homeostasis and, 358–360
Drug abuse, 212–223
Drug addiction and reward, 357–358
Drug dependence, 213
Drug Free School and Campuses Act, 216
Drugs, definition of, 212-223. *See also* Medications.
DSM-IV. *See Diagnostic and Statistical Manual of Mental Disorders,* 4th edition (DSM-IV).
Dwarfism, 54
Dwyer, Jim, 267
Dynamic control theory, 162
Dynamic theory, Freud's, 469
Dyskinesia, tardive, 592

E
Ear
artificial, 132
cross-section of, 128, 128f, 129f
middle, 128–129, 129f
outer, 128–129, 129f
Eardrum, 129
Early asylum, treatment of psychological disorders and, 571
Early intelligence tests, 429–430
Early sexual development, 373–374
Early social behavior, 88–89, 89f
Easy temperament of infants, 87
Eating, self-regulation of, 579t
Eating binges, 367, 370
EBE theory of sexual orientation. *See* Exotic-Becomes-Erotic (EBE) theory of sexual orientation.
Eclectic approach
to psychological topics, 10
in treatment of psychological disorders, 585–586, 585t
Eclectic psychotherapists, 586
Ecological optics, theory of, 149
ECT. *See* Electroconvulsive therapy (ECT).
Educational psychologists, 15
EEG. *See* Electroencephalogram (EEG).
Effect
law of, 2, 242
overjustification, 2, 3f
Egg dumping, 24
Ego, personality structure and, 460
Ego ideal, 460
Egocentric speech, 82
Egocentrism, 77, 78
Eidetic images, 275f
Elaboration
and encoding, 303
memory and, 269
Elaboration likelihood model, 660
Elderly, alcohol abuse and, 217–218
Electric shock experiment, 619–624, 619f, 620f, 621f, 623t, 626, 627
Electroconvulsive therapy (ECT), 285, 593–596, 595f
Electroencephalogram (EEG), 199–200, 200f, 201f
Electroshock therapy, 593–596
Elixir of youth, 292
Emergent features, 164, 164f
Emerging situations, obedience to authority and, 622–623, 623t
Emotion(s), 388–425
aggression and, 414–423
arousal and, 405
bodily changes and, 401–405
CD-ROM links, 425
cognitive appraisal and, 392–396
cognitive causes of, 394, 394t
communication of, through facial expressions, 406–408
components of, 390–391, 390f, 390t

culture and, 410–414
definition of, 390
differentiation of, 404–405, 405f
dimensional organization of, 420
discrete, 421
effect of nature on, 420–421
emotion regulation and, 408–410
facial expression and, 406–408
forgetting and, 287–288
gender and, 410–414
intensity of, 403–404, 403f
motives and, 389
nature in shaping of, 420–421
positive, 398–399, 402
predictability, regulation, 239–240
regulation of, 408–410, 409t
responses to, 390, 408–410
schematic diagram of process of, 390f
subjective experiences and, 396–401
web resources, 424–425
Emotional arousal, obesity and, 368
Emotional expression, disturbances of, schizophrenia and, 551
Emotional instability-stability, 454
Emotional intelligence, 438
Emotionality, relationship between spinal cord lesions and, 403, 403f
Emotion-focused coping, 515, 516–519, 517f
Empathy
client-centered therapy and, 582
selfishness and, 25
Empirical validity, 429
Encoding
elaboration and, 303
imagery and, 302–303, 302f, 303f, 303t
interactions between retrieval and, 285–287
long-term memory and, 281–282
of meaning, 281
memory, constructive processes at time of, 294–295
social learning theory and, 473
working memory and, 273–277
Encoding stage, memory and, 268, 268f
End plates, 37
Endocrine system, 53–54, 53f
Endogenous chemicals, 313
Endogenous morphine, 313
Endorphins, 59, 138, 219, 313
Energy
conservation of, personality dynamics and, 460–461
psychic, 461
Energy concept, Freud's, 469
Engineering psychologists, 15
Environment
hormones versus, sexuality and, 374–375
impact of, on IQ, 441, 441f
interactions between personality and, 483–489
model of, 149
shared, versus nonshared, effect of, on personality, 488–489
Environmental bases of aggressive behavior, 60–61
Environmental influences on gene action, 59
Environmentally based aggressive behavior, 60–61
Environment-genotype correlation, 483–484
Envy, penis, 468
Epinephrine, 54, 503
Episodic memory, 292
Equilateral triangle, 8f

ERPs. *See* Event-related potentials (ERPs).
Error
  fundamental attribution, 655–658, 656f
  of sampling, A5, A8
Escape and avoidance, aversive conditioning and, 248–249
Escape learning, 248–249, 250–251
ESP. *See* Extrasensory perception (ESP).
Estrogen, 376
Estrous cycle, 376
Ethanol, 215
Ethics
  obedience to authority and, 624
  of psychological research, 23–26
Ethnic cleansing, 500
Ethological approach, classical conditioning and, 240
Evaluations, feelings in modification of, 400–401, 400f
Event-related potentials (ERPs), 179
Events, experiencing, 493
Everyday life, obedience in, 624–625
Evocative interaction, 485, 488
Evolution
  of behavior, 55
  Darwin's theory of, 6–7, 242, 670–671
  gender differences in mate selection and, 672–673
  genes and behavior and, 54–61
    aggressive behavior, 60–61
    biological base of aggressive behavior, 60–61
    chromosomes and genes, 55–57, 56f
    environmental base of aggressive behavior, 60–61
    evolution of behavior, 55
    genetic studies of behavior, 57–59
Evolutionary approach
  to human nature, 482
  to personality development, 481–483
Evolutionary psychology, 16, 481, 671
Evolutionary theory, 481–483, 481f
Excitatory conditioning, 238
Excitatory connections, 165
Excitatory effect, 36
Executive functions, antisocial personality and, 557–558
Exemplar strategy, 330
Exercise, 509
  compulsive, anorexia and, 370
  in management of stress, 520–521
  neurogenesis and, 46
Exhaustion, stress and, 504
Exner system, 465, 467
Exotic-Becomes-Erotic (EBE) theory of sexual orientation, 381, 383
Expectancies, social learning theory and, 473
Expectancy value, 472
Experience
  direct, attitudes based on, 663
  learning through, 330–331, 331f
  openness to, 455, 455t
  subjective, emotion and, 390
Experiencing events, 493
Experiential subtheory, 439, 442
Experimental evidence, psi phenomena and, 224
Experimental groups, 18
Experimental psychologists, 15
Experimental research, terminology of, 18
Experiments, 18–19
  color-matching, 122
  electric shock, 619–624, 619f, 620f, 621f, 623t, 626, 627

free recall, 279, 279f
magnitude-estimation, 111f
multivariate, 19
natural, 180
on obedience, 619–624, 619f, 620f, 621f, 623t, 626, 627
partial-report, 270–271, 271f, 272–273, 272f
Pavlov's, 235–236, 236f
Rescorla's, 239, 239f
Skinner's, 242–245
Sperling's, 270–271, 271f
temporal integration, 271, 272–273, 272f
Experts versus novices in problem solving, 344–348
Explicit memory, 269
Exponent, 111
Exposure effect, mere, familiarity and, 665–667, 665f, 666f
Expression(s)
  aggressive, and catharsis, 418–423, 419f
  of Emotion in Man and Animals, 406
  emotional, disturbances of, 551
  facial. *See* Facial expressions.
  of impulses versus moral standards, 498
Expressive aphasia, 50
External attribution, 655
Externally provided suggestions, constructive memory and, 297–298
Extinction
  of conditioned response, 236, 236f
  learning curves and
    classical conditioning and, 236, 236f
    instrumental conditioning and, 243–244, 243f
  systematic desensitization and in vivo exposure and, 576
Extracellular reservoir, 359–360
Extracellular thirst, 359–360
Extrasensory perception (ESP), 224
Extraversion, 455, 455t
Extravert schema, 646
Eye movements
  directed attention without, 151
  selective attention and, 150–151, 150f
  in viewing pictures, 150, 150f
Eyeblink conditioning, 260
Eyes
  artificial, 132
  image formation in, 117, 117f
  right, top view of, 116, 116f

F
Face recognition, 3, 182
Faces, bitmap of, 171
Facial expressions, 407f, 412f
  communication of emotion through, 406–408
  emotion and, 390, 406–408
Facial feedback hypothesis, 392f, 408
Facial preference in newborn, 70
Facilitator, client-centered therapy and, 582
Factor analysis, 433
Factorial approach to intelligence, 433–434
Factors, intelligence tests and, 434
Failure of recognition, 169–170
Falling in love versus self-expansion, 669, 669f
False alarms, 113
False memory debate, 306–307
Familiarity, interpersonal attraction and, 665–666, 666f

Familiarity-breeds-liking effect, 665–667, 665f, 666f
Family
  anorexia and bulimia and, 372
  schizophrenia and, 555, 555f
Family therapy, 582–583, 584
Fantasy, hypnotic state and, 209
Fat cells, obesity and, 367
Fatal Attraction, 559
Fatigue, combat, 499
Fear, 400, 400f, 401, 401t
Fear conditioning, 260–261, 260f
Feature detectors in cortex, recognition and, 163, 163f
Feature integration theory
  problems with, 162
  recognition and, 161–162, 162f
Features
  of natural objects, 166–167, 166f, 167f
  relationships between, 163–164, 164f
Feedback, networks with, 165–166, 165f, 166f
Feeding, sham, 362
Feelings
  acceptance of, mental health and, 600
  in modification of attention and learning, 397–400
  in modification of evaluations and judgments, 400–401, 400f
Feminization, 374
Fenfluramine, 367
Fertility cycle in women, 376
Fetal alcohol syndrome, 216
FI. *See* Fixed interval (FI).
Fight-or-flight response, 42, 502–504, 503f, 504f, 533, 535–536, 537
Figure-ground organization, 154–155, 154f
File-drawer problem, psi phenomena and, 226–227
Final ritual, Jim Jones and, 630, 630f
Finding meaning in life's events, stress and, 512–513
Fistula, 235
Fix, heroin usage and, 218
Fixations, 150
Fixed interval (FI), 247–248, 247f, 247t
Fixed ratio (FR), 247, 247f, 247t
Fixedness, functional, 344
Flashbulb memories, forgetting and, 287
Flashing of light, cocaine and, 220
Flavor, hunger and, 361
Flooding, systematic desensitization and in vivo exposure and, 576–577
Fluoxetine, 592
Fluphenazine, 591
fMRI. *See* Functional magnetic resonance imaging (fMRI).
Focus, weapon, selective attention and, 151
Folk healers, Latinos and, 586
Follicle-stimulating hormone (FSH), 376
Foot-in-the-door technique, 626
Forced confessions, constructive memory and legal system and, 300
Forced feeding, effects on, on rats with VMH lesions, 365, 365f
Forebrain, 40
Foreclosure, identity crisis and, 102
Foreign language, key-word method for learning words in, 303, 303f, 303t

Forgetting, 285
  emotional factors in, 287–288
  as function of time, 284
  working memory and, 276–277
Formal operational stage, 78
Forms, perception of, 184–185, 184f
Fovea, 117–118, 150, 181
FR. *See* Fixed ratio.
Fraternal twins, 58
Free association, 8, 459
  interpersonal therapy and, 575
  psychodynamic therapies and, 574
Free recall experiment, 279, 279f
Frequency, 127, 379–380
Frequency diagrams, A3f
Frequency distribution, A2, A2t
Frequency histogram, A2
Frequency polygon, A2
Freudian slip, 198, 198f, 459–460
Freud's influence on psychology, 464–465, 486–487
Frontal association areas, 45
Frontal cortex, obsessive-compulsive disorder and, 540
Front-end differences, emotions and, 410–411, 413–414
Frustration-aggression hypothesis, 414, 501
FSH. *See* Follicle-stimulating hormone (FSH).
Function, decreased ability to, schizophrenia and, 551
Functional fixedness, 344
Functional magnetic resonance imaging (fMRI), 179, 268
Functionalism, 6–7
Fundamental attribution error, 3, 606, 655–658, 656f
Fundamental bits of information, 161

G
g. *See* General intelligence factor (*g*).
GABA. *See* Gamma-aminobutyric acid (GABA).
Galvanic skin response (GSR), 237–238, 496, 558
Gamma-aminobutyric acid (GABA), 38
Ganglion, 33
Ganglion cells, 118, 119f
Ganzfeld procedure, 224, 225f, 226
Gardner's Theory of Multiple Intelligences, 436, 437t
Gate control theory of pain, 138
Gay liberation movement, 480
Gay male couples, 379
Geen, Russell, 61
Gender
  effects of, on psychotherapy, 596–599, 596f
  emotions and, 410–414
  and sexuality, 373–384
Gender constancy, 96
Gender differences
  in alcohol disorders, 217–218
  emotions and, 411–412
  in mate selection, 672–673
Gender hierarchy, 411
Gender identity, 93–97, 373, 374
Gender nonconformity in childhood, 380, 380t
Gender schema theory, 96
Gender-appropriate behavior, 411
General adaptation syndrome, 504, 504f
General intelligence, 433–434
General intelligence factor (*g*), 434
General paresis, 571
Generalization, 237–238, 237f
  classical conditioning and, 237–238, 237f, 238f
  instrumental conditioning and, 246

Moral standards, expression of impulses versus, 498
Morality, selfishness and, 25
Moratorium, identity crisis and, 102
Morphemes, grammatical, 315
Morphine, 218, 313
  endogenous, 313
  hunger and, 364
Mother
  artificial, monkey's response to, 90f
  departure of, children's stress at, 89f
Motion
  patterns of, 159f
  perception of, 158–160
  real, perception of motion and, 158–160, 159f
  relative, 158
  stroboscopic, perception of motion and, 158, 158f
Motion parallax, 158
Motivation, 352–387, 355f
  CD-ROM links and, 387
  definition of, 353
  gender and, 373–384
  homeostasis and drives, 358–360
  hunger and, 361–372
  incentive, 354–358, 357f
  reward and, 354–358, 357f
  sexuality and, 373–384
  web resources, 386–387
Motiveless crimes, schizophrenia and, 550
Motives
  basic, 355f
  emotions and, 389
Motor area, primary, 44, 44f
Motor development, 67f
Motor fibers of autonomic nervous system, 52f
Motor nerves, 40
Motor neurons, 33
Motor symptoms, schizophrenia and, 551
Movement, control of, hypnosis and, 210
Movies
  stroboscopic motion and, 158
  3-D, binocular disparity and, 156, 156f
Moving lights, cocaine and, 220
MRI. See Magnetic resonance imaging (MRI).
Multimodal attention, 151
Multiple cognitive potentials, 440
Multiple Intelligences, Gardner's Theory of, 436–437, 437t
Multiple personality disorder, 560
Multiple sclerosis, 34
Multiple stick problem, 253f
Multivariate experiments, 19
Munsell system, 122, 122f
Murphy's law, psi phenomena and, 229
Muscles, smooth, 51
Musical intelligence, 437f, 437t
Myelin sheath, 34
Mystical experiences, meditation and, 207–208

N
Naïve realism, 13
Naltrexone, 219–220
Nanometer, 116, 121f
Narcolepsy, 204
Narcotics, 140–141, 213t, 218
Narrative review, 23
National Bureau of Standards, 122
National Committee for Mental Hygiene, 571
National Vietnam Veterans Readjustment Study, 499, 500f

Native Americans
  alcohol abuse and, 217
  treatments for distressed people by, 584–585, 584f
Natural Born Killers, 557
Natural experiments, 180
Natural objects
  features of, 166–167, 166f, 167f
  recognition of, 166–169
Natural selection, 54
Nature
  effect of, on emotions, 420–421
  in shaping of emotions, 420–421
Nature-nurture debate, 5–6, 66–69, 67f, 183, 381
Needle sharing, heroin use and, 218
Needs, hierarchy of, Maslow's, 478–479, 478f
Negative correlation, 20, 21f
Negative hallucinations, 210–211
Negative reinforcement, learning curves and, 243, 244t
Neglect, visual, 341
Neo-Piagetians, 80
Nerves, 33
  motor, 40
  sensory, 40
Nervous system
  asymmetries in brain, 47–50, 48f, 49f
  autonomic, 50–51, 51, 52f
  brain, 39, 40f–41f
  central core, 39–42
  cerebrum, 43–45, 43f
  divisions of, 38–39, 39f
  language and the brain, 50–51
  limbic system, 42–43
  organization of, 38–53
  parasympathetic, 402
  sympathetic, 402
Networks
  augmented, 165, 165f
  with feedback, 165–166, 165f, 166f
  node in, 165
  recognition and, 164–166
  simple, 164–165, 164f, 165f
Neural basis
  of attention, 179–180
  of behavior, 10–13, 14–15, 331–333
    appraisals in brain, 395–396, 396f
    behavioral perspective, 11
    biological approach to schizophrenia, 552–555, 553f, 554f
    biological factors of personality disorders, 557–558
    biological perspective of psychological disorders, 10, 544–545, 544f, 545f
    biological therapies and, 591–596
    cognitive perspective, 11–12
    division of brain labor between working memory and long-term memory, 280
    divisions of labor in brain, 179–183
    feature detectors in cortex, 163, 163f
    forgetting, 285
    imagery, 341–342, 341f
    integration of hunger signals, 363–365, 364f
    language, 318–319
    learning and conditioning, 256–262
    loss of information from storage, 285
    major subfields of psychology, 14–15
    neural control, 377
    physiological reactions to stress, 502–510

psychoanalytic perspective, 12–13
reasoning, 337–339
relationships between psychological and biological perspectives, 14
stages of sleep, 199–207, 200f, 201f
subjectivist perspective, 13
Neural circuit for classical fear conditioning, 260, 260f
Neural connection, 256
Neural control, 377
Neural processing on attended objects, 180, 180f
Neural sensitization, 357–358
Neuroanatomy, 46
Neurogenesis, 46
Neurons, 32–37, 32f, 33f, 34f, 35f, 36f, 256
  birth of, 46
  motor, 33
  resting, 34
  schematic diagram of, 32f
  sensory, 32–33
  shapes and relative sizes of, 33f
  synapses and, 32f, 36f
Neuropeptide Y, hunger and, 364
Neuroscience
  affective, 16
  cognitive, 16
  social cognitive, 16
Neurosis, 529
Neurotic anxiety, 510
Neuroticism, 454, 455, 455t
Neurotransmitters, 32, 37–38
  bipolar disorder and, 592–593
  immune system and, 509
  mood disorders and, 544
  release of, into synaptic gap, 36f
Newborn, capacities of, 69–74
Newfeld, Peter, 267
Nicotine, 212, 212f, 213, 367
N-methyl-D-aspartate (NMDA), 38, 256, 261
Node(s)
  in network, 165
  of Ranvier, 34
Noise, 112–113
  signals embedded in, 112, 112f
  white, 224
Nonassociative learning, 233, 257
Nonconformity, 615, 615f
  gender, in childhood, 380, 380t
Non-content cues, persuasion and, 660
Nondirective therapy, 582
Nondistimulus determinants of pain, 138–139, 138f, 139f
Noradrenaline, 54
Norepinephrine, 37, 38, 54, 592
  mood disorders and, 544
  schizophrenia and, 553
  seizures and, 595
  stress and, 503
Normal distribution, A3, A6–A7, A6f, A7t
Normality, definition of, 529
Normative social influence, 616
Norms
  cultural, deviation from, psychological disorders and, 528
  institutional, group interactions and, 632–634
  social, 609, 632
  statistical, deviation from, psychological disorders and, 528–529
Not-me personification, 464–465

Noun phrase, 315–316, 316f
Novelty seeking, molecular genetics of behavior, 59
Novices versus experts in problem solving, 344–348
Novocain, 34
NREM sleep, 200–202, 204
Nuclear magnetic resonance, 46
Nucleus, 33
Number, conservation of, 77f
Nursing, psychiatric, 574
Nurture-nature debate, 5–6, 66–69, 67f

O
Obedience
  to authority, 618–625, 620f, 621f
  in everyday life, 624–625
  experiment on, 619–624, 619f, 620f, 621f, 623t, 626, 627
  social influence and, 613–625
Obese, definition of, 365
Obesity, 4, 59, 365–369
Obesity gene, 367
Object permanence, 76, 76f, 79
Object recognition and geon recovery, 167, 167f
Object relations theory, 465
Objectification theory, 370–371, 371t
Objective anxiety, 510
Observation, 21–22
  direct, 21–22
  learning by, 416
Observational learning, 470
Observer, hidden, hypnosis and, 211–212
Obsessive-compulsive disorder (OCD), 533–541, 540f
OCD. See Obsessive-compulsive disorder (OCD).
OCEAN, 455, 455t
Odors, discrimination among, in newborns, 71
Oedipal conflict, 93, 463, 464, 464f, 538
Olfactory bulb, 134–135
Olfactory cortex, 135
Olfactory receptors, 135f
Olfactory system, 134–135
Omission training, learning curves and, 243, 244t
On-task behavior, selective reinforcement and, 577
Opening-up meditation, 208
Openness to experience, 455, 455t
Operant chamber, 243, 243f
Operant conditioning, 470
  of blood pressure and heart rate, 520f
  personality development and, 469–470
Operation, 76
Operational stages, Piaget's, 78
Opiate receptors, 218
Opiates, 213t, 218–220, 364
Opioid analgesics, 140–141
Opioid receptors, 219–220, 219f
Opioids, 140–141
Opium, 218
Opponent-color theory, 125, 126, 126f
Opponent-process model of sleep and wakefulness, 202
Opposites attract, similarity and, 666–667
Optic chiasm, 44
Optics, ecological, theory of, 149
Optimism
  stressful events and, 513
  unrealistic, 522–523
Oral personality, 463–464

Oral stage of psychosexual development, 463–464
Organization
  dimensional, of emotion, 420
  long-term memory and, 285
  memory and, 304, 304f, 305f
Organizational psychologists, 15
Orientation, sexual. See Sexual orientation.
Osmotic thirst, 360, 360f
Outer ear, 128–129, 129f
Outline of Psychoanalysis, An, 460
Oval window, 129
Overdose, heroin, 218
Overeating, 4f, 367
Overextension of words, 320
Overgeneralization, depression and, 547t
Overjustification effect, 2, 3f, 629

P
Pain, 137–139
  chronic, opioids in treatment of, 140–141
  congenital insensitivity to, 137
  distraction via virtual reality in diminishment of, 152–153
  gate control theory of, 138
  nonstimulus determinants of, 138–139, 138f, 139f
  phasic, 138
  system of, 138
  tonic, 138
Pain behaviors, 141
Pair bonding and mating strategies, 670–674
Panic, vulnerability-stress model of, 537, 537f
Panic attack, 534
Panic disorders, 534–537, 535f, 536f, 537f, 581, 581f
Paradigm, temporal-integration, 271, 272f
Parallax, motion, 158
Parallel play, 84, 84f
Paranoid, definition of, 550
Paranoid schizophrenia, 569
Paraprofessionals, 585
Parapsychology, 224–229
Parasympathetic nervous system, 51, 402
Parenting styles, 91–92
Parents
  influence of, on development of children, 100–101
  influence of, on personality or intelligence of their children, 100–101
Paresis, general, 571
Paroxetine, 592
Partial genetic identity, 24
Partial reinforcement, 246–247
Partial-report experiment, 270–271, 270f, 271f, 272–273, 272f
Passion, triangular theory of love and, 670, 670t
Passionate love versus companionate love, 669–670
Patterns
  seeing, 120, 120f
  temporal, 115
Pavlov's experiments, 235–236, 236f
Paxil, 38, 484, 592
PCP, 222, 223t
Peak experiences, 479
Peg-turning study, 627–628
Penicillin, 571
Penis envy, 468
People's Temple, 623, 629–630

Perception, 146–193, 148f
  abstraction and, 170–173
  active, perceptual development and, 186–187, 187f
  attention and, 150–153
  categories of, 149
  CD-ROM links, 193
  constructive, 294–295
  of depth, perceptual development and, 185, 185f
  of distance, 156–157
  disturbances of, schizophrenia and, 550–551
  divisions of labor in brain and, 179–183
  of forms, perceptual development and, 184–185, 184f
  localization and, 154–160
  of motion, 158–160
  perceptual development, 183–189
  perceptual constancies and, 173–179
  pitch, theories of, 130–131
  recognition and, 160–170
  use of, 148–149
  visceral, 403
  web resources, 193
Perceptual constancies, 173–179, 174f, 185
Perceptual development, 183–189
Perceptual interference, 295
Performance components, 439
Performance scale, Wechsler Adult Intelligence Scale and, 432
Performance-contingent rewards, 3
Perfume, 134, 134f
Periaqueductal gray, 138–139
Peripheral attention, 197
Peripheral nervous system, 38–39, 51
Peripheral route to persuasion, 660, 661–662, 661f
Peripheral signals, physiological hunger cues and, 363
Persistence, visible, sensory memory and, 271, 272–273, 272f
Personal Construct Theory, 473–474, 474f
Personal constructs, 473–474, 473f
Personal distress, psychological disorders and, 528–529
Personal involvement, persuasion and, 661, 661f
Personality, 452–491
  antisocial, 557–558
  assessment of, 454–459
  behaviorist approach to, 469–471
  CD-ROM links, 491
  of children, influence of parents on, 100–101
  cognitive approach to, 471–476
  definition of, 454
  development of, 463–464
  effect of medications on, 484
  evolutionary approach to, 481–483
  genetics of, 483–489
  humanistic approach to, 476–481
  interactions between environment and, 483–489
  medication and, 484
  oral, 463–464
  personality inventories, 456–459
  psychoanalytic approach to, 459–469
  psychopathic, 556
  and social development, 86–97
  structure of, 460
  web resources, 491
Personality disorders, 556–560
  biological factors of, 557–558
  borderline, 558–560
  personality factors of, 558

social factors of, 558
  types of, 556t
Personality dynamics, 460–463
Personality factors of personality disorders, 558
Personality inventories, 456–459
Personality psychologists, 15
Personality traits, 454–459
Personalization, depression and, 547t
Person-environment relationship, 392
Perspective, perception of distance and, 157
Persuasion, central and peripheral route to, 660, 661–662, 661f
Persuasive communication, 659–662
Pessimism
  breast cancer and, 508
  illness and, 511–512, 511f
PET. See Positron emission tomography (PET).
Phallic stage of psychosexual development, 463
Phasic pain, 138
Ph.D degree, psychologists and, 573–574
Phenomena
  classical conditioning and, 236–238, 236f
  instrumental conditioning and, 245–248
Phenothiazines, 591
Phenylketonuria (PKU), 56–57
Pheromones, 134
Phobias, 537–538
  conditioned, 258–259
  innate, 258–259
  simple, 537–538
  snake, 537f
  social, 538
  systematic desensitization and in vivo exposure and, 576
Phobic disorders, 533–541
Phonemes, 314–315
  combinations of, development of language and, 320
  development of language and, 320
Phonological buffer, 275
Phonological coding, working memory and, 273
Photographic albums, long-term memory and, 282
Photon, 109
Physical attractiveness, interpersonal attraction and, 664–665
Physical characteristics, behavior genetics and, 54
Physical description, abstraction and, 170
Physiological hunger cues, 362–363
Physiological psychologists, 15
Physiological reactions to stress, 502–510
Physiology, 5
Piaget's childhood memory, 294
Piaget's stages of cognitive development, 74–79
Piaget's theory
  alternatives to, 79–82
  critique of, 78–79, 79f
Picrotoxin, 38
Piecemeal integration, 654
Pitch, 127, 130–131
Pitch perception, theories of, 130–131
Pituitary gland, 54, 364f
PK. See Psychokinesis (PK).
PKU. See Phenylketonuria (PKU).
Place theory of pitch perception, 130
Plaque, coronary heart disease and, 505
Plasticity, synaptic, 261
Platform, chimpanzee constructing, 253f
Play, parallel, 84, 84f

Pluralistic ignorance, 610, 611–612
  college drinking and, 616–617
Polarization, group, group decision making and, 634–635
Polygenic, 57
Polygon, frequency, A2
Populations, statistical inference and, A5–A6
Positive correlation, 20, 21f
Positive emotions, 398–399, 402
Positive hallucinations, hypnosis and, 210–211
Positive psychology, 17
Positive regard, unconditional, 477–478
Positive reinforcement, learning curves and, 243, 244t
Positron emission tomography (PET), 46–47, 47f, 179–180, 180f, 182, 268, 341, 504, 545, 545f
Postconventional morality, 85
Posterior association areas, 45
Posterior system of brain, 179
Post-event memory reconstruction, 295–298
Posthypnotic amnesia, 209, 210, 210f
Posthypnotic response, 210
Posthypnotic suggestion, 462
Post-traumatic stress disorder (PTSD), 498–501, 499f, 500f, 501f, 504–505, 505f
Potassium, 370
Potentiation, long-term, 260–261
Power function of physical magnitude, 111
Practical abilities, componential theory and, 439
Pragmatic rules, 335
Preattentive processes, recognition and, 161–162, 161f
Precognition, 224
Precognitive dreams, 227
Preconscious, 459, 459f
Preconscious memories, 197
Preconventional morality, 85
Predicate, 315, 316f
Predictability
  classical conditioning and, 238–240
  contiguity versus, 238–239, 239f
  and emotion, 239–240
  stress and, 496
Preferential looking method of studying infants, 183
Prefrontal cortex, schizophrenia and, 554f
Prefrontal lobes, memory and, 280
Pregnancy, alcohol use and, 216
Premarital coitus, 378, 378f
Preoperational stage
  of cognitive development, 76–77
  Piaget's, 76–78, 77f, 78f
Presence of others, social influence and, 606–613
Pressure, sense of, 137
Primacy effect, schematic processing and, 650, 650t
Primary appraisal dimensions, 394, 394t
Primary auditory area, 45
Primary conditioned reinforcers, 245–246
Primary motor area, 44, 44f
Primary reinforcers, 354
Primary somatosensory area, 44
Primary visual area, 44, 45f
Primary visual cortex (V1), 180–181, 181f
Priming, 290
  memory in amnesia and, 289–290, 290t
  stereotypes and, 647

Sensory processes—cont'd
taste, 136–137
temperature, 137
vision, 116–126
web resources, 144
Sensory response magnitude, 272, 272f
Sensory store, memory and, 269
Sentence units, language units and processes and, 315–316, 316f
Sentences
complex, development of language and, 321
primitive, development of language and, 321
production of, 316, 316f
Separation anxiety, 89
Separation of objects, localization and, 154–155
September 11th bombing, 135f, 640, 645
Serial search, 277
Serotonin, 38, 55, 536, 592
antisocial personality and, 557
bipolar disorder and, 592
eating disorders and, 372
mood disorders and, 544
obsessive-compulsive disorder and, 540
personality and, 484
schizophrenia and, 553
seizures and, 595
Serotonin reuptake inhibitors, 592, 593
Sertraline, 592
Set point, 359, 367
Severe pain, distraction via virtual reality in diminishment of, 152–153
Sex, hormonal system involved in, 375, 375f
Sex differences
in mate preferences, evolutionary origins of, 672
sexuality and, 379
Sex hormones, 375–376
Sex typing, 93–97
Sex-linked disorders, 57
Sex-linked genes, 57
Sex-linked traits, 57
Sexual abuse, 496
Sexual Behavior
in the Human Female, 22
in the Human Male, 22
Sexual development
in adolescents, 97
early, 373–374
Sexual dysfunction, 586–587
Sexual objectification, 370–371
Sexual orientation, 379–384
causes of, 380–384, 380t
different, frequency of, 379–380
innateness of, 382–383
social determination of, 382–383
Sexual selection, 55
Sexuality
adult, 375–379, 375f
gender and, 373–384
human, 22
Shading, perception of distance and, 157–158
Shadow(s)
attached, 157–158
cast, 157–158
perception of distance and, 157–158
Shadowing, 151–152
Sham feeding, 362
Shape constancy, perception and, 175, 175f
Shaping
contextual subtheory and, 440
instrumental conditioning and, 244–245, 245f

Shared environments versus nonshared environments, effect of, on personality, 488–489
Shell shock, 499
Shermans, 222
Shock, shell, 499
Shock generator, 619–624, 619f, 620f, 621f, 623t, 626, 627
Short-term store, memory and, 269
Signal-detection theory, 111–113, 112f
Signals, 112–113
embedded in noise, 112, 112f
hunger, integration of, 363–365, 364f, 365f
peripheral, physiological hunger cues and, 363
Significance
of difference, A8–A9, A9t
statistical, A8
Silence of the Lambs, The, 557
Similarity, 336
grouping and, 155
interpersonal attraction and, 666–667
Simple cell, 163, 163f
Simple networks, 164–165, 164f, 165f
Simple phobias, 537–538
Single-cell recording, 114, 114f
Situation, defining, bystander effects and, 610–611
Situational attribution, 655
Situational correction, 656
Six Years With God, 630
Size, relative, perception of distance and, 157
Size constancy, 175–176, 176f, 185
Size-distance principle, 177
Skeletal muscles, 51
Skepticism, psi phenomena and, 228–229
Skewed distribution, A3, A3f
Skewness, A3–A4
Skills, memory in amnesia and, 289–290, 290t
Skin popping, heroin and, 218
Skinner box, 243, 243f, 252
Skinner's experiments, instrumental conditioning and, 242–245
Sleep
avoidance of problems in, 203, 203t
and dreams, 199–207
electrophysiological activity during, 201f
non-REM (NREM), 200–202, 204
opponent-process model of, 202
REM versus NREM, 200–202, 204
stages of, 199–207, 200f, 201f
succession of stages of, 200, 201f
Sleep apnea, 204
Sleep debt, 203
Sleep deprivation, 202–203, 202f, 203f, 509–510
Sleep disorders, 202–204
Sleep drive, homeostatic, 202
Sleep theory, 202
Sleeping pills, 204
Slow to warm up temperament, 87
Smarter brain, building, research and, 256
Smell, 132–135
of death in insects, 134
minimum stimuli for, 108t
in newborn, 71
system of, 134–135, 135f
Smoking, 212, 212f, 509
correlation between lung cancer and, 21
gene for, 214
Smooth muscles, 51
Snake phobia, 537f
Snellen acuity, 120

Sniffing, heroin and, 218
Snorting cocaine, 220
Snow lights, cocaine and, 220
Social behavior, early, 88–89, 89f
Social change, 618f
Social cognition, 644–677
attitudes, 658–664
CD-ROM links, 677
definition of, 646
impression formation and, 646–658
interpersonal attraction, 664–674
modes of, 674
web resources, 676
Social cognitive neuroscience, 16
Social desirability effects, 22
Social development, personality and, 86–97
Social facilitation, 606–608, 606f, 607f
Social factors of personality disorders, 558
Social influence, 604–643
CD-ROM links, 643
compliance and obedience, 613–625
group interactions, 632–640
informational, 616
internalization, 626–632
normative, 616
presence of others and, 606–613
social psychological views of inexplicable happenings, 640–641
web resources, 643
Social inhibition, 606–608, 607f
Social learning
gender differences in mate selection and, 672–673
personality development and, 469–471
Social learning theory, 414, 415–417, 416f
gender identity and sex typing and, 94–95
personality development and, 472–473
Social norms, 609, 632
Social perspective to schizophrenia, 555, 555f
Social phobias, 538
Social psychology, 606
Social roles, influence of, on mate selection, 673
Social stereotype, 296
Social workers, psychiatric, 573–574
Social-cognitive theory, 472–473
Socially acquired process, perceptual development as, 188–189
Sociobiology, 481
Sociocultural approaches
to development as alternative to Piaget's theory, 82
to therapy in treatment of psychological disorders, 582–586
Sociocultural causes of anorexia and bulimia, 370–372
Sociological perspective, mental disorders and, 532
Sociopaths, 389, 557
Solar spectrum, 121, 121f
Somatic system, 38–39, 51
Somatosensory area, primary, 44
Sound
physics and psychology of, 122
timbre of, 127–128, 127f
Sound intensity, 129–130, 129f
Sound waves, 127–128, 127f
Sounds, preference for, in newborns, 72, 72f
Source wavelengths, color and brightness constancy and, 174

Span of apprehension, 270
Spatial intelligence, 437f, 437t
Special factors (s), intelligence tests and, 434
Specialization, hemispheric, 10, 50
Species
animal, ability of, to learn human language, 324–325
conditioning in varieties of, 236–237
Specific abilities, intelligence and, 439
Specific processors, intelligence and, 439
Specificity, coding and, 115
Spectrum, solar, 121, 121f
Speech
development of, 68
egocentric, 82
private, 82
Speech sounds, language units and processes and, 314–315
Speed, 220
Speed freak, 220
Sperling's experiments, sensory memory and, 270–271
Spinal cord, 40
Spinal cord lesions, relationship between emotionality and, 403, 403f
Spindles, sleep and, 200
Split-brain research, 48–50, 48f, 49f
Spoken words as symbols, 148–149
Spontaneous recovery, 236
Spontaneous remission, psychotherapy and, 587–588
Spurious associations, 255
St. John's wort, 594
Stage theory of development, Erikson's, 465
Standard, stimulus intensity and, 109
Standard deviation, A4, A5
Standard scores, statistical inference and, A7–A8
Stanford Prison Experiment, 632–634, 633f
Stanford-Binet Intelligence Scale, 430–431, 430f, 431f, 431t, 432
Stapes, 129
Starvation, effects on, on rats with VMH lesions, 365, 365f
Statistical inference, A5–A9
Statistical methods and measurement, A1–A12
coefficient of correlation, A9–A12
descriptive statistics, A2–A5
statistical inference, A5–A9
Statistical norms, deviation from, psychological disorders and, 528–529
Statistical significance, 19, A8
Statistics, 18, 19
definition of, A1
descriptive, A2–A5
Stepping reflex, 68
Stereoscope, Holmes-Bates, 159f
Stereotype activation, automatic, 648, 649f
Stereotype threat, 652
Stereotypes, 646–647
automatic, 647–649, 649f
behavioral effects of, 652t
cognitive effects of, 652t
controlling, 654
effects of, 652t
impression formation and, 646–652, 653, 653f
and information processing, 649–651, 650t
self-fulfilling, 651–652
social, 296
Sternberg memory-scanning task, 277

TO THE OWNER OF THIS BOOK:

I hope that you have found *Atkinson & Hilgard's Introduction to Psychology*, 14th edition, useful. So that this book can be improved in a future edition, would you take the time to complete this sheet and return it? Thank you.

School and address: _____

_____

Department: _____

Instructor's name: _____

1. What I like most about this book is:_____

_____

_____

2. What I like least about this book is: _____

_____

_____

3. My general reaction to this book is: _____

_____

_____

4. The name of the course in which I used this book is: _____

_____

5. Were all of the chapters of the book assigned for you to read? _____

   If not, which ones weren't? _____

6. In the space below, or on a separate sheet of paper, please write specific suggestions for improving this book and anything else you'd care to share about your experience in using this book.

_____

_____

_____

_____

_____

_____

OPTIONAL:

Your name: _____ Date: _____

May we quote you, either in promotion for *Smith, Atkinson & Hilgard's Introduction to Psychology*, 14th edition, or in future publishing ventures?

Yes: _____ No: _____

Sincerely yours,

Edward E. Smith

Susan Nolen-Hoeksema

Barbara Fredrickson

Geoffrey R. Loftus

FOLD HERE

BUSINESS REPLY MAIL

FIRST CLASS   PERMIT NO. 358   PACIFIC GROVE, CA

POSTAGE WILL BE PAID BY ADDRESSEE

ATTN: Marianne Taflinger, Psychology

BROOKS/COLE/THOMSON LEARNING
511 FOREST LODGE ROAD
PACIFIC GROVE, CA   93950-9968

FOLD HERE